Foundations of psychology

NICKY HAYES is a Fellow of the British Psychological Society, and was awarded the British Psychological Society's Award for Distinguished Contributions to the Teaching of Psychology in 1997. She has a first degree and a doctorate in psychology, having specialised in the study of social representations and organisations, and is an active researcher in these areas. She also has a PGCE, and a Master's degree in education, specialising in science education and curriculum studies.

Nicky Hayes is an Honorary Life Member of the Association for the Teaching of Psychology, and was Honorary Secretary of the Association for the Teaching of Psychology from 1982 to 1985. In that year, she became a founder member, and the first Secretary, of the British Psychological Society's Special Group for the Teaching of Psychology. She has been actively involved in several training and educational initiatives of the Society, including the development of the Diploma in the Applied Psychology of Teaching, the Working Party on the Future of A Level Psychology which she chaired, and the Society's first initiatives in co-ordinating Continuing Professional Development for Psychologists. She is currently Visiting Senior Fellow in the Department of Psychology, School of Human Sciences, at the University of Surrey.

11

Nicky Hayes

Foundations of
psychology

THIRD EDITION

THOMSON™

Australia • Canada • Mexico • Singapore • Spain • United Kingdom • United States

THOMSON

Foundations of Psychology: 3rd Edition

Copyright © 2000 Nicky Hayes

The Thomson logo is a registered trademark used herein under licence.

For more information, contact Thomson Learning, High Holborn House, 50-51 Bedford Row, London WC1R 4LR or visit us on the World Wide Web at: http://www.thomsonlearning.co.uk

British Library Cataloguing-in-Publication Data
A catalogue record for this book is available from the British Library

ISBN 13: 978-1-86152-589-5
ISBN 10: 1-86152-589-3

First edition published 1994 by Routledge
Second edition published 1998 by Thomas Nelson
Third edition published 2000 by Thomson Learning
Reprinted 2003 and 2005 by Thomson Learning

Typeset by J&L Composition Ltd, Filey
Printed in Italy by Canale
Cover design by Malcom Harvey Young
Text Design by Malcom Harvey Young

ACKNOWLEDGEMENTS

The author and publisher would like to acknowledge permission granted to reproduce material from the following sources: Arts: Figure 7.1 courtesy of the Wellcome Institute Library, London; and figures 19.5 and 19.6 and tables 19.3, 19.4 and 19.5 reproduced with the permission of Blackwell Publishers © Judy Dunn 1988. Photographs: Figure 2.18 reproduced with permission of Mirian Mednick Rothmall, Executrix of the Estate of Sol Mednick,, Philadelpia PA, USA, Sol Mednick, photographer (source: Gregory 1968); Figure 2.27 reproduced with permission of Philip Clark, University of Bristol (source: Gregory 1968); Figure 15.2 Telegraph Colour Library; and Figure 18.3 reproduced with permission of Colin Smith, Huddersfield University.

Dedicated to the memory of my good friend
WAXUM DASWANI
who would have enjoyed the joke

Contents in brief **Foundations of Psychology**

Contents

Illustrations

Tables

Preface to third edition

Welcome to the new-look third edition of *Foundations of Psychology*. As you can see, it has a new page design, with some colour, new icons and logos, and some added features designed to make the whole book much more attractive and easier to use.

The text retains all the strengths of the previous editions, of course. From the very start, *Foundations of Psychology* has been well received. For me, as the author, that was important feedback: people liked its accessibility, its clarity, and the way that it dealt with fundamental psychological ideas. That reception validated the ideas that I was also expressing about the psychology curriculum, and how it should be approached at introductory levels.

In the second edition, I had the opportunity to sort out and restructure quite a few chapters, polish up a section here and there, and add a lot of new material to bring the text up-to-date. This new edition of *Foundations of Psychology* has built on this, presenting and consolidating that material in a way that will help students to learn. There aren't many changes to the main text, because the massive updating of the second edition is still current. But the whole book, in my opinion, has benefited from the changes which its new publishers - Thomson Learning - have brought to it.

So what are those changes? Firstly, there is a topic 'map' at the beginning of each chapter which should help to make it clear how the main ideas and topics can be grouped together. Each chapter also includes a set of learning objectives, and there are key terms highlighted in orange throughout the text, listed at the end of each chapter, and included in the glossary. Each chapter also ends with a set of self-assessment questions and practice essay questions.

Why have we bothered with all of this? Well, the main reason is that we have been looking closely at what a textbook is used for. 'That's obvious', I hear you say 'it's for a course'. Yes, but then there's the question of how we actually use a book of this kind. *Foundations* needs to be more than just readable - it needs to be a positive aid to learning. So we need to begin by looking at what we actually do with textbooks.

One thing we do, of course, is prop doors open with them, and I am afraid that here, this new edition of *Foundations* is a bit of a failure. Certainly, it's nothing like as big and chunky as the first edition, even though it contains a lot more words. We've used the page layouts a bit more artistically, and that has had the side-effect of getting more words on each page. So, not so many pages, and not quite as good as a doorstop. Sorry. On the plus side, though, it isn't quite as heavy to carry around.

A different way of using a textbook is for learning about an area of psychology. So it's important that the text is readable, and helps you to learn. I've talked elsewhere about my aims in writing *Foundations* in the first place. So I won't go into too many details here, except to say that *Foundations of Psychology* had, and still has, three major educational aims: to show that a psychology textbook can explain even quite complex ideas using readable, clearly comprehensible language; to show something of the way that ideas in psychology have developed over the past century or so; and to produce a textbook which reflects what is happening in modern psychology, right now. You'll find more about those aims in the preface to the second edition, and even more in the article 'The Psychological Foundations of *Foundations of Psychology*', both of which can be found on the special *Foundations of Psychology* website, at http://www.psych.co.uk (more about that later).

Another way we use textbooks is when we're doing coursework assignments. We use them as a source of knowledge - for looking things up and finding things out. We use them for guidance in structuring knowledge - to bring out focus points and to show us the particularly significant ideas. And we use them to help us to see how different ideas interconnect. A textbook doesn't give you all the answers for your assignment, obviously. You'll still have to think for yourself! But if you use it well, it can be a tremendous help.

So, some of the new things we have introduced are designed to help you in doing just that. The topic maps we have introduced at the beginning of each chapter will help you to see some structure and principles of organisation in that area of knowledge. The key terms, which have been highlighted throughout, will help you to identify the important ideas in the topic, so that you can make sure that your assignment is clearly focused. You can check the list at the end of the chapter to make sure you have grasped them all, and look up any you're not clear about in the glossary at the end of the book.

The text itself is full of cross-references, showing you where ideas come up in other chapters as well, or where a topic has been discussed somewhere else. Do check these out - there are lots of bits of psychology which have relevance for more than one area, so those references to other chapters in the main text are a useful guide for you to use. Following them up will help you to make sure that your assignment does show a full understanding of the area.

The other time that textbooks really come into their own is when we are revising for exams. So, some of the new features we have introduced are designed exactly for that purpose. One of the most useful ones for this purpose is the set of learning objectives at the beginning of the chapter, which you can use as a kind of check after you have gone through a chapter, or a section of a chapter. Turn back to the learning objectives, and see if you would be able to achieve each of the objectives that relate to that bit of the chapter.

I've even designed it so that you can do it in small chunks! The learning objectives are all tied to the chapter summaries. There are three learning objectives for each chapter summary point, so that gives you an easy way of dividing it up. If you like, you can even do it backwards. Read the chapter summary point first, then read the part of the chapter which relates to it, and then turn to the learning objectives and work out how they connect with what you have just done. There are eight chapter summary points for each chapter, so that should keep the sections appropriately 'bite-sized'!

In addition, we've included self-assessment questions at the end of each chapter, which you can use to test your recall for what you've just read. We've also included practice essay questions, which are very useful indeed when your exam is coming up! There are two main ways you can use them for revision. One is as timed questions. Get hold of a copy of your exam paper and find out how much time you have for each question; and then practice writing one of these essays in the time available. You'll find that it's a skill that definitely improves with practice, and if you force yourself to stick rigidly to the time, you'll find

that your exam will benefit too. It may still be hard, but at least you'll know that you can get what you want to do done in the time available!

The second way of using practice essay questions is for structuring your ideas clearly. For this, you do essay plans, rather than writing the essay itself. Organise your plan on the basis of taking five minutes to write a paragraph, and remember that each paragraph should contain just one idea (and preferably some evidence to back it up). So if your forthcoming exam will give you about 45 minutes for each essay, that means your essay will have at most nine paragraphs – although actually, it's more likely to be eight, because you'll need five minutes planning and thinking time – and that's just eight or nine main ideas.

So you can take your practice essay title, and write down eight numbered points, each of which represents a main idea in your essay. The first one, of course, will be the introductory paragraph, but don't waffle – there isn't time in exams. Use it to say or show something about the topic. The next six points are the core of your essay, and the last one is the conclusion – again, use it sensibly to say something, because that will help you to get as many marks as possible. Like the timed essays, this gets easier with practice, but it's a revision exercise that is well worth doing, because it will help you to learn how to cut out the irrelevant stuff and get to the heart of a topic.

All of the changes we've introduced for this third edition are designed to help you to use the book more effectively. But that's not all. We've also given you a great new website! You can find it on http://www.psych.co.uk, and there you'll find quizzes and crosswords for each chapter, links to general resources, PowerPoint presentations for lecturers to use when they are teaching from the book (lecturers should ask their local Thomson Learning sales representative for information about how to get the appropriate password), and links to all sorts of other sites - including my own 'How to tackle exam stress' site if things are really getting on top of you.

All in all, then, this new edition is continuing to express and develop my personal aims in producing *Foundations of Psychology*. In my view, it has continued to build it into a friendly, helpful book that will give assistance and, I hope, pleasure, to anyone who uses it. I hope you find that, too.

Nicky Hayes
January 2000

Acknowledgements

I am deeply grateful to the many lecturers and teachers of psychology who have offered me constructive criticisms of this book; and their comments have informed this second edition. I am also grateful to the following, for their specific help in various fields: Ray Ball, Windy Dryden, Jessica Saddington and Judith Lask, Steve Newstead, Pieter de Vries, Jeanette Garwood, Margaret Mitchell, Bob Morris, Julie Milton and other members of the parapsychology unit at the University of Edinburgh; and, of course, all of those who helped me with the first edition: Ian Toone, Simon Green, Mansur Lalljee, Michael Argyle, Bob Sternberg, the late Donald Broadbent, Paul Harris, Peter Stratton, Nasim Hasnie, Bernard Horsford, John Richardson, Jim Wright, John Blundell, Douglas Bethlehem, Steve Newstead, Mick Millard, Sue Hirschler, Alison Wadeley, Phil Banyard, Ann Searle, Paula Topley, Bernadette Rowland, and Mike Stanley.

Perspectives in psychology

| The philosophical origins of psychology | Schools of thought in psychology | Areas of psychology | Psychological perspectives |

Learning objectives

1.1. Philosophical perspectives
a identify major philosophical concepts in psychology
b describe the theory of evolution
c relate philosophical approaches to psychological theories

1.2. Introspectionism and behaviourism
a name major early introspectionist psychologists
b identify major concepts in behaviourist thinking
c compare behaviourist and introspectionist approaches

1.3. European psychology
a identify the basic assumptions of the Gestalt school
b show how Piaget's approach links with evolutionary theories
c contrast the European approach with behaviourism

1.4. Clinical psychology
a identify sources of evidence in psychoanalytic theory
b describe the basic assumptions of humanistic psychology
c compare behaviouristic, psychoanalytic and humanistic approaches in psychology

1.5. The cognitive revolution
a give reasons for the emergence of cognitive psychology
b evaluate the computer metaphor in cognitive psychology
c identify the cognitive approach in other areas of psychology

1.6. Ethics and methodology
a describe assumptions underpinning ethical practices in psychology
b show how ethical considerations have influenced psychological methods
c relate ethical methodology to major areas in psychology

1.7. Areas of psychology
a list the major areas of psychology
b describe the major areas of psychology
c compare the major areas of psychology

1.8. Perspectives
a define terms relating to psychological perspectives
b identify the major nature-nurture debates in psychology
c apply major perspectives to psychological theories

Although it began as a separate subject of study in the nineteenth century, it was throughout the twentieth century that psychology developed and expanded into the discipline that it is today. During that century, psychology went through many changes, each of which reflected the interests and ideas of its own period in history. Psychology has been defined as the study of the mind, as the study of behaviour, as the study of human information processing, or just simply as the study of why human beings act as they do (although psychologists study animals, too). Modern psychology covers all of these, and a few more, and all these different viewpoints contribute to our knowledge of human beings. In order to understand this, we need to understand something of psychology's history, and of the scope of modern psychology.

The philosophical origins of psychology

Psychology as a formal branch of knowledge is usually considered to date from round about the 1880s, with the work of the pioneers of psychology: Wilhelm Wundt, William James and Herman Ebbinghaus. Before that, it did not really exist as a separate discipline, but had been regarded as a branch of philosophy. Nonetheless, there were several philosophers and scientists whose work strongly influenced the development of psychology because their work established the philosophical and scientific assumptions for the new discipline. The three most influential individuals in this respect were the philosophers Descartes and Locke, and the scientist Charles Darwin.

Descartes
One of the most influential of the early philosophers of the mind was René Descartes (1596–1650). Descartes was responsible for putting forward the idea now known as **Cartesian dualism**: the idea that the mind and the body are separate and independent of one another. The body, Descartes believed, is essentially a machine, although a very complex one. It functions mechanistically, and its workings are essentially automatic. The mind, though, is the seat of the soul. As such, it forms a kind of essence, interacting with the body through the brain, but not really being part of it. Because of its separate

nature, too, the mind is not affected by what happens to the physical body.

This dualistic approach formed the basis of Western medical thinking, and it is only recently that we have begun to take seriously the idea that the mind and the body may actually be far more closely interlinked than Descartes thought. Descartes performed several studies which supported his view of the body as a sophisticated piece of machinery. One of the most famous of these was the dissection of an ox's eye, by which he showed how an image was projected on to the retina of the eye through the pupil and lens. The finding was of interest in its own right; but it also established a framework of investigation, which emphasised the idea that the body works like a machine. This approach largely ignored the more holistic or interactive aspects of bodily functioning, and it became very popular in medicine and biology. In many ways this mode of thinking is still with us today.

Cartesian dualism, though, has been challenged as a way of understanding the human being. Partly, the challenges come from the influence of other forms of knowledge from different parts of the world, which have retained a holistic, or unified, approach to the person, like Chinese acupuncture or Indian yoga. (Descartes' theory reflected the traditions of European thought, and Cartesian dualism is a distinctively Western way of looking at things.) Partly, though, the challenges resulted from medical and psychological research which showed that the mind and body are not as independent as all that – such as the way that long-term stress can lower the body's resistance to illness. Partly, too, the immune deficiency disease AIDS brought home to many medical researchers the way that their emphasis on mechanical aspects of bodily functioning had meant that general systems, like the body's own ways of dealing with infection and healing, had been overlooked.

Another aspect of Cartesian dualism was concerned with the distinction between human beings and animals. Descartes believed that animals operated by instinct, blindly programmed to act in ways appropriate for their survival. Human beings, on the other hand, were able to reason; and it was this which made them special. Descartes's famous phrase: 'I think, therefore I am' (*Cogito ergo sum*) comes from this: he was emphasising that it was the power of reasoning, above all else, which characterised human beings. Animals were not individuals, because they did not have minds. They operated blindly, by mechanical instinct, like machines.

Nowadays, we think rather differently about animals and how they act, partly because of the influence of evolutionary theory, and partly because it is clear that animal cognition and problem-solving is much more sophisticated than the Cartesian view allows. But this form of Cartesian dualism has exerted a powerful influence in psychology as well as in Western society, as we will see when we look at psychological research into animal behaviour in the final chapters of this book.

Locke

Other philosophers, too, left their influence on psychology. John Locke (1632–1704) argued that all knowledge was obtained through the senses, and that human beings did not inherit any knowledge or instincts. This view is known as **empiricism**, and it was not unique to Locke – several other philosophers around that time also subscribed to it. Empiricism had far-reaching effects for psychology. One of these was that it led eventually to the view that only the external stimuli which an organism was receiving, and the behaviour which it showed as a result, counted as valid data for understanding the human being – or any other animal, for that matter. Empiricists argued that internal processes, such as thinking, were unobservable, and unimportant. They were only reactions to external stimulation, and if they mattered, they would show it by influencing behaviour. So observing behaviour in response to stimulation would be quite enough. This 'black-box' model was a fundamental principle in the school of psychological thought known as **behaviourism**.

Locke perceived that we do not respond to each individual stimulus as it occurs. Instead, we respond to whole events, or episodes. But this was only possible, Locke believed, because we have combined together a number of chains of **associations**. We begin by linking one stimulus with another, and then go on to form ever more complex chains of associations as we gain more experience in life. So although it might seem as though we are dealing with a single, complete unit of interaction, it is really composed of many simple learned associations, combined together. This is known as **associationism**, and it was also important in behaviourist theory.

Darwin

The theory of evolution put forward by Charles Darwin in 1859 exerted a powerful influence on psychology, as it did on the rest of the scientific world. Essentially, the theory of evolution proposes that environmental demands result in a continuous process of development of species, as animals gradually adapt to them. The **adaptation** happens through a process of gradual genetic change which is often referred to as the 'survival of the fittest'. This continuous process has resulted in a vast diversity of living organisms, which can be classified into many different groups.

The classification known as primates includes monkeys, lemurs, and apes, and human beings are part of the last category – apes. So human beings are part of an evolutionary continuum, and have some characteristics in common with their close animal relatives. As a result, some psychologists have looked at animal behaviour to see if it will help us to understand more about human behaviour. Some of the first comparisons of this kind were by Darwin himself. In 1872, he published a comparison of the ways that animals and human beings express emotion, showing that there were definite similarities between human expressions of fear, rage and pleasure, and the expressions of the same emotions by other mammals.

Evolutionary theory implied that particular individual characteristics in animals would be likely to evolve if they helped the animal (or organism) to adapt to its environment. Such adaptation would allow it to survive threats facing members of its species which were not as well adapted. Its survival would make it more likely to breed and pass on the helpful characteristic to its offspring, so over the generations, all members of that species would come to share that characteristic. This functionalist approach carried into psychology, too. The assumption that psychological characteristics shared by all human beings, like consciousness or social awareness, have evolved to serve some kind of evolutionary or adaptive function is very deeply rooted indeed in psychological thought.

Schools of thought in psychology

It was against the philosophical background provided by Descartes, Locke, and Darwin (as well as others) that psychology first developed as a scientific discipline in its own right. From the seventeenth century onwards, an increasing number of philosophers became interested in how the human mind worked, and began to investigate it experimentally. Their field of interest was first known as **experimental philosophy**, but as it became more highly developed as a field of knowledge in its own right, it gained its 'independence' as the discipline of psychology.

Introspectionist psychology

The definition of psychology held by the early psychologists was quite clear: psychology was the study of how the mind worked. Many of their investigations involved introspection – they would attempt to understand the workings of the mind by analysing and reporting their own experiences and those of highly trained assistants. Introspection is not considered an adequate method of investigation now, although it is beginning to regain a place in some forms of psychological research. But in the early years of psychology, the method provided many valuable insights, and several of the theories which were developed through introspection are still useful today.

Wundt, James and Ebbinghaus

The three most famous of the introspectionist psychologists were Wilhelm Wundt, William James and Herman Ebbinghaus. Each of them contributed to the new discipline in different ways. The first ever psychological laboratory was opened by Wilhelm Wundt in Leipzig in 1879, and students from all over the world came to study with him. Wundt investigated a range of problems, such as physiological psychology, reaction times and the study of attention; and he also began a systematic study of social psychology. Wundt's main interest was the nature of human consciousness, and the analysis of the different elements which went to make up conscious experience, including social awareness and social beliefs.

William James, an American psychologist, also investigated mental experience through introspection, but he was focused more on individual or personal experience, and not on social psychology. In 1890 he published *Principles of Psychology*, a textbook which discussed and developed theories about a wide range of personal experience, ranging from adult memory and emotion to the skills and experience of the newborn

infant. James's theories provided the basis for many later investigations, and some of his ideas are very similar to theories which psychologists use today.

In 1885, Herman Ebbinghaus produced a monograph which outlined the findings from his work on human memory and how it worked. Many of the findings in this monograph are still current, and we will be referring to them in more detail in the chapter on memory. The most important feature of Ebbinghaus's work, perhaps, was the extremely detailed, painstaking manner in which he carried out his research. Both Ebbinghaus and Wundt set a tradition of experimental rigour which left a permanent impression on the new discipline of psychology. Laboratory classes, which train students in the basic principles of psychological methodology laid down by Ebbinghaus, Wundt and others, have formed an important part of the study of psychology ever since.

Behaviourism

The introspectionist approach to psychology continued for several decades, before it was challenged by a new approach: behaviourism. In 1913, J.B. Watson published a paper entitled *Psychology from the standpoint of a behaviorist*, in which he outlined his ideas for the new direction which psychology should take. Watson believed that the most important thing for psychology was that it should be scientific: introspectionism was too vague, he thought, and suffered from a lack of objectivity. Studying the mind was impossible, according to Watson, because we could never see directly into it. Instead, all we could observe directly was behaviour – whether that was verbal behaviour, specific acts or even general mannerisms. By limiting itself to the study of behaviour, Watson thought, psychology would produce observations which could be verified by other people, and which were not open to subjective bias and distortion.

During the previous two centuries, almost all of the major sciences had had discoveries or theories which had helped to clarify and make sense out of their material. In physics this was the theory that all matter was composed of atoms which combined to form molecules; in chemistry it was the concept of elements; in biology it was the cell theory of matter, which showed how all living things were composed of cells, and therefore allowed researchers to perceive the links between plants and animals for the first time; and in genetics it was the idea that development was guided by simple units of heredity, known as genes. Watson believed that it was the identification of basic elements or 'building blocks', which made a subject into a science.

S-R associationism

Accordingly, Watson looked for the basic units which would go to make up behaviour; and he believed that they would be found in the form of simple associations between stimuli in the external environment, and responses made by the organism. He argued that eventually we would be able to explain all human behaviour in terms of learned stimulus-response (S-R) associations, and that the study of psychology should be the study of how such learning took place. We can see that this is very similar to the philosophical approach outlined by Locke in the seventeenth century.

Watson's approach rested on five fundamental assumptions. Firstly, that learning was the most important factor in an understanding of behaviour, so understanding learning would lead to the understanding of all behaviour. Secondly, that learning arose from the association between an external stimulus and a behavioural response. Thirdly, that only objective, measurable information counted as valid scientific data, and fourthly, that any apparently mental processes, or inferences about what was going on inside an organism, should be rejected, since the only thing which could be observed directly was that organism's behaviour. The behaviourists favoured the term 'organism' rather than animal or human, because that reflected the fifth assumption, which was that all behaviour, whether animal or human, was learned in the same way.

Part of the reason for the dominance of behaviourism in American and British psychology was because the simple, straightforward mechanisms proposed by behaviourists fitted in well with the 'modernist' thinking of the time. In conjunction with many people of the time, the behaviourists suggested, and believed, that science would provide the key to addressing all of the world's problems, including the apparent intractability of human nature. This key, it was believed, would take the form of scientists discovering and applying a few essential principles.

Watson himself believed this fervently. In 1928, he said:

'*Give me a dozen healthy infants, well-formed, and my own specified world to bring them up, and I will guarantee to take any one at random and train him to become any type of specialist I might select – doctor, lawyer, artist, merchant-chief, and yes, even beggar-man and thief, regardless of his talents, penchants, tendencies, abilities, vocations and race of his ancestors.*'

This extreme view argued that the whole of human experience, therefore, was purely a matter of learning, and that the human infant was perfectly malleable. But notice that Watson specifies that he would also need his own specified world to bring these infants up in – in his view, the associations between stimulus and response needed to be carefully controlled, and providing infants with an ordinary upbringing would provide far too much random stimulation to be sure of the outcome.

Classical conditioning

Watson's ideas fitted closely with the research into conditioned reflexes being conducted by the Russian psychologist Ivan Pavlov, which eventually became the theory of **classical conditioning**. Classical conditioning developed as Pavlov observed how animals would produce reflexes in response to stimuli that had to have been learned. In the classic example, he had observed how his experimental dogs salivated at the sight of the assistant coming with the bucket containing their food. Since salivation should only have been a response to the food itself, Pavlov reasoned that the dogs must have learned that association. By ringing a bell each time food was delivered to the dogs, he showed how new associations could be formed between stimuli and responses – even responses which were automatic reflexes.

Pavlov's research led to the identification of three factors influencing conditioning. The first is **contiguity**, which is the connection in time and space between two events. The second is **frequency**: how often a stimulus is followed by the response. And the third is **reinforcement**: how the learned association is strengthened. Both Pavlov and Watson believed that reinforcement occurred through repetition of the link between stimulus and reponse: the more often it was repeated, the stronger it became. As the behaviourist approach developed, the work of B.F. Skinner introduced another form of reinforcement, which was the way that positive consequences could also strengthen an association between stimulus and response.

Operant conditioning

Behaviourism developed even further through the work of B.F. Skinner. Skinner identified a different way that stimulus–response associations were formed: through the method of learning which he named **operant conditioning**. Watson had argued that learned associations were formed simply because two stimuli happened together, and that they were reinforced, as we have seen, by repetition of the occurrence of stimulus and response. But Skinner showed how learning could also take place as a result of the consequences of an action. If an organism was rewarded in some way for doing the action, it would be more likely to repeat it. The reward might be positive, for example, receiving food, shelter, sex, or some other such event; or it might be negative, removing some unpleasant stimulus or allowing an animal to avoid it. But either way, the organism would be likely to repeat an action which had produced pleasant consequences, and in that way, it would learn.

Moreover, Skinner argued, the same mechanism could be used to build up new actions. This happened gradually, through a process known as **behaviour shaping**. In behaviour shaping, an animal – or rather, organism – is rewarded for performing an action which is close to, or at least similar to, the action which the rewarder wants them to perform. Gradually, they do this more and more often, and when that happens, sometimes they will do it in a way that is even more similar to the goal. When only those very similar actions are rewarded, the animal produces those more and more often, until their behaviour has gradually been shaped into something entirely new. Some of the applications of this concept are discussed in Box 1.1.

Skinner's demonstration that even entirely novel behaviour could be understood within the behaviourist framework greatly enhanced its influence in psychology as a whole. He used operant conditioning to account for novelty and unexpectedness in human behaviour, and even asserted that human language was only acquired through stimulus–response learning – an assertion which led to a classic confrontation between himself and the linguist Noam Chomsky, who argued that the predisposition for language was innate.

European psychology

Chomsky was not the only person who argued against behaviourism, however. Behaviourism was essentially a **reductionist** approach to psychology, arguing that (a) human psychology was nothing but the behaviour which was shown, and (b) the behaviour could be understood purely in terms of combinations of small units. But many psychologists, particularly in Europe, felt that there were aspects of human experience and behaviour which could not be understood by reducing them down to their component parts: some human experiences were holistic, or complete in themselves. Where American psychology was largely dominated by behaviourism, European psychology tended to emphasise the development of more holistic theories about psychological functioning.

The Gestalt school

In Germany, a school of psychology developed which became known as **Gestalt psychology**, after the German word 'Gestalt' – a complete form, or entity. The Gestalt psychologists investigated those aspects of human experience which they felt were whole in themselves – they could not be reduced to constituent parts and still be the same. For example, they believed that gaining a sudden insight into the nature of a problem, or perceiving patterns and completeness from incomplete images, are fundamental experiences in human psychology which cannot be understood as stimulus–response associations. We will be looking at some of their work when we look at the study of perception, and of some forms of thinking and of learning.

When the Gestalt psychologists migrated to America before or during WWII, they found themselves face to face with behaviourism, and their opposition to it became much more clearly articulated. They began to emphasise the social dimensions of experience much more – partly as a result of the behaviourist insistence that social experience was no more important than any other kind of stimulus. Their insistence that the whole was much more than just the sum of its parts, whether in perception, in thinking, or in learning, became a focus for many psychologists who were not prepared to accept the reductionism of the

Box 1.1 Applying behaviourist principles

When Watson left the academic world, as a result of a scandal involving his secretary and the investigation of human sexual behaviour, he turned to advertising. He applied behaviourist principles to the construction, timing and placing of advertisements, and proved to be extremely successful. (Another possible explanation for why behaviourism came to dominate Western psychology as it did might have been because it was so successfully applied in the commercial world.) But S-R principles were also applied in many other areas. The most well-known of these were in treatments for phobias, classroom management, in programmed learning, and token economy systems.

Treatments for phobias, along with Watson's own work on advertising, relied very directly on associations between stimulus and response. The use of colours in advertisements, such as the way that blue is used to imply freshness and green to imply relaxation, are direct descendants of Watson's work. Some applications, though, use operant rather than classical conditioning, and these tend to involve the technique of behaviour shaping.

In behaviour shaping, a desired kind of behaviour is achieved gradually, by systematically rewarding behaviour which is a step closer to the ultimate goal. Using operant conditioning in classroom management, for example, a problem child who was systematically disruptive would first be rewarded for spending just a few minutes engaged quietly in some activity. As a result, this would happen more and more often, and when it had become regular, the criteria by which the child was reinforced would change.

Now, a longer period of quiet would be required – a few minutes would not be sufficient. By adjusting what Skinner referred to as the reinforcement contingencies, the child's behaviour would be gradually shaped towards something that was socially acceptable.

Another important part of the application of operant conditioning is the avoidance of punishment. The idea is to reward appropriate behaviour, and so guide the child as to what is desirable. Undesirable behaviour would simply be ignored, because giving it any attention often acts as an unintended reinforcement. In the case of a severely disruptive child, this would be achieved by 'time-out' sessions, in which the child was simply withdrawn from the classroom. Token economy systems, like treatments for phobias, are discussed in Chapter 9, but they too work in a similar manner.

Programmed learning systems were another educational development from Skinner's work. They operated on the principle that the learning task should be structured in such a way that it was easier to give the right answer than a wrong one – in order to maximise reinforcement. Programmed learning systems operated in small chunks, with ample opportunity for a learner to go back over steps and get things right. Skinner predicted that ultimately, teaching machines based on programmed learning would replace human beings in the classroom. This never took place, but the concept of programmed learning did have an enormous influence on curriculum development, and the way that educationalists thought about the school curriculum.

behaviourist approach. And the therapeutic applications of Gestalt psychology formed a backdrop for the later development of humanistic theories of psychology.

Genetic epistemology

Another influential European theory was concerned with the development and evolution of human knowledge. Jean Piaget, a Swiss biologist, became interested in how human thinking could have evolved. In particular, he aimed to trace an evolutionary progression which would eventually

lead to formal logic, which he regarded as the most highly developed form of thought. Working on the then popular biological principle that 'ontogeny recapitulates phylogeny' – the idea that the development of the individual (ontogeny) retraces the evolutionary development of the species (phylogeny) – Piaget began to study how children's thinking developed, and how different forms of thought might have evolved – a process which he referred to as **genetic epistemology**.

The study of how the child's mind works came to occupy Piaget for the rest of his working life.

He studied the way that children understand numbers and quantities, the objects in the world around them, and even moral dilemmas. Eventually, this research resulted in a major theory about how the child's mind develops, which dominated child psychology for many years. We will be examining the theory later in this book, and also looking at some of the recent criticisms of it. Those criticisms mainly result from the way that Piaget, as a biologist by training, tended to ignore the complexities of social understanding, and so his theory nowadays is regarded as rather limited. But many of Piaget's insights are still valid, and his theory enhanced psychological understanding of the child's mind considerably.

European social psychology

In more recent times, European psychology has continued to focus on theoretical development. European researchers in both cognitive and social psychology have aimed to develop wide-scale theories, which can direct and integrate psychological research in a way which allows the psychological processes that they are studying to be seen as part of a more complex context. By contrast, American social psychology has traditionally been much more focused on empirical studies and on the applications of specific research findings. Although there are, of course, theories in American social psychology, they are more commonly used to explain research findings after those findings have been made, rather than to direct and shape the research in the first place.

European social psychology, which is probably the best example to take of the modern European approach, was brought together when Henri Tajfel founded the *European Journal of Social Psychology* in 1972. There are two major theories which form the backbone of this approach: social identity theory, and social representation theory. Social identity theory is concerned with how our membership of social groups can colour and shape our reactions to other people, and to our own actions. Social representation theory explores the social beliefs which are generally accepted in society, and offered as explanations for why things are like they are. Both of these theories developed as a result of European experiences during WWII and afterwards; and much of the work of European social psychologists takes place within the theoretical context which they provide.

Psychoanalysis

While all this was happening within the field of academic psychology, a completely different side of psychology was developing from medicine. This side of psychology was concerned with how psychological problems could be understood. It began with the work of Freud, who developed a new way of understanding mental illness, based on the technique of psychoanalysis. His work opened up a new type of psychological understanding, in which the emphasis was on analysing the unconscious mind and how it affects a person's thinking and physical well-being.

Psychoanalysis, as the new approach was called, saw the human mind as being essentially like an iceberg, with four-fifths of it below the surface. The surface, in this case, was consciousness. Psychoanalysts proposed that we can only be aware of a small part of the human mind, and that most of the important psychological processes which motivated our behaviour and drove our emotions were unconscious in nature. If there was disturbance in the unconscious part of the mind, caused by unresolved early traumas or conflicts, it could influence how the person acted, producing apparently irrational behaviour and even mental illness. And even in normal people, the unconscious mind could sometimes produce irrational or inappropriate reactions.

When Freud put forward his theories, at the beginning of the century, it was a radical challenge to the accepted beliefs of the previous century. Before psychoanalysis, it was generally accepted that for the most part, the human mind was rational, and could be governed by ordered thought and mental discipline. This approach was known as **rationalism**, and it tended to dominate nineteenth-century beliefs and values. Freud's research challenged this, and also provided a way of understanding some of the more puzzling aspects of human nature which were becoming apparent, and were impossible to explain by rational means. The approach became even more widely accepted as a result of the carnage of WWI – an experience which could not be explained using rationalist models.

Psychoanalysis gave therapists a different way of understanding human problems. There were some people who suffered from acute symptoms, such as physical pain or paralysis of a particular limb, which did not seem to have a physical cause, and which did not respond well to conventional psychiatric treatment. Freud and the other psychoanalysts who trained with him explained these cases in terms of deeply buried inner conflicts and anxieties. The mind, Freud argued, consisted of three parts: the **ego**, which was fairly practical and acted as the interface between the mind and reality; the **id**, which consisted of buried impulses, emotions and desires, and which demanded instant gratification of all of its needs or wishes; and the **superego**, which was the social sense of duty and responsibility and conscience – a very powerful force in pre-consumerist society.

According to Freud, the superego and the id were each as demanding and unrealistic as the other, and they both battled to influence the ego. The ego maintained a dynamic balance between their conflicting demands, giving way a little to one and a little to the other, but making sure that neither got out of hand. Both the ego and the superego were unconscious, but it was possible to deduce their existence, and their concerns, when they broke through to consciousness in slips of the tongue, symbolic dreams, and psychological anxieties. The aim of a therapist was to strengthen the ego by making the person consciously aware of these powerful inner forces, and allowing them to resolve the early conflicts and traumas which gave them their energy.

Psychoanalysis, then, was very different from the approaches used in academic psychology – not just in its theories, but also in what counted as evidence. Where academic psychology adhered to a belief that psychological evidence should have been derived from scientific study and some kind of empirical evidence, psychoanalysis operated on the basis of a far more **phenomenological** approach – taking mental experience as the most important information. Psychoanalysts believed that 'psychological truth' was just as valid for understanding human beings as objective, material reality – and much more useful in psychotherapy.

Psychoanalytic theories exerted considerable influence in some areas of psychology, particularly in the understanding of child development. We will be looking at these ideas more closely when we look at psychological therapies, and also when we look at developmental psychology. Psychoanalytic theories dominated the understanding of abnormal behaviour for the first part of this century, and they also left their mark on society as a whole, as psychoanalytic concepts – or at least, popularised versions of them – became part of everyday social understanding. But they were very different from the theories which academic psychologists were developing, and more-or-less the entire opposite of behaviourism, which was the dominating approach in psychology during the 1930s.

Behaviour therapy

As psychology developed, however, psychologists began to look for new ways of understanding people with problems, and analysing abnormal behaviour. A few psychologists even tried to bridge the gap between psychoanalysis and behaviourism. Perhaps the most successful of these were a group of American psychologists (e.g. Dollard *et al.*, 1939), who took established psychoanalytic concepts and re-conceptualised them in terms of classical and operant conditioning. Their work gave clinical psychologists a basis for applying the learning theory principles developed by academic psychologists to the treatment of specific problems, like phobias. The new treatments were remarkably successful, by comparison with anything else available at the time; and **behaviour therapy** quickly became a significant part of clinical psychology.

Some behaviour therapy was firmly based on stimulus-response principles. Treatments for phobias, for example, were explicitly trying to break existing stimulus-response links, and to establish new ones (see Chapter 9). The approach took the view that, since all human behaviour was learned (a central behaviourist belief, as we saw earlier) the abnormal behaviour produced by phobias had also been learned. In which case, other, more normal behaviours could also be learned. So the essence of the treatment was to identify the link between stimulus and response, and to substitute alternative responses to the same stimulus.

Aversion therapy worked also using classical conditioning, but this time to condition people into avoidance behaviour. If someone received an electric shock every time they came into contact with a particular stimulus, pretty soon they would react to that stimulus with fear and avoidance. But aversion therapy, although widely used – and misused – in the 1960s, was not generally as successful with human beings as the treatments for phobias were.

Gradually, a third form of behaviour therapy emerged, which drew on the work of Albert Bandura. Bandura had conducted extensive studies into imitation and identification, showing how some forms of learning did not take place through trial-and-error conditioning processes, but were able to happen much more rapidly. Clinical psychologists began to apply this type of learning to training people with behavioural problems, by modelling appropriate behaviours and encouraging patients to imitate the model's behaviour. This approach became known as **behaviour modification**, and it added considerably to the range of treatments available to clinical psychologists wishing to practise behaviour therapy as an alternative to psychoanalysis.

Humanistic psychology

After WWII, a third school of thought began to emerge in clinical psychology. This school of thought became known as **humanistic psychology**, and it took a view of human beings which was completely different from either the behaviourist or the psychoanalytic approaches. Humanistic psychology was largely based on insights gained through psychotherapy, where patients – particularly ones who were getting better – persisted in referring to themselves as whole people with intentions, plans and ambitions, instead of seeing themselves as battling ids and superegos, or as collections of stimulus-response links and behavioural contingencies. Perhaps, suggested the humanists, this implied that looking at the person as a whole might be a good idea.

This radical proposal was extremely influential in post-war psychology, and its influence grew with the advent of consumer society. There were two key theoreticians in humanistic psychology: Abraham Maslow, who studied human motivation (among other things), and Carl Rogers, who developed a model of human personality and an approach to psychotherapy which emphasised the importance of the patient's own decisions, ideas and views. We will be looking at the work of each of these psychologists in the relevant chapters, but each of them was extremely influential in his time, and continues to be so today.

A central part of the humanistic approach is the human capacity for positive **personal growth** and change. Human beings are not just passive victims of circumstances, or of early experiences: instead, the humanists argued, human beings strive to develop themselves, and to fulfil their potential. The problems occur when that striving is frustrated, because human beings have a deep-seated need to learn new things, to make their own choices, and to be in control of their own behaviour. If they cannot do these things, they develop neuroses, personality conflicts, and even psychotic disorders. So the humanistic psychologists regarded the exercise of free will and choice as vitally important in psychologically healthy human behaviour.

The humanistic psychologists also emphasised the **holistic** nature of the personality, rejecting the fragmented picture of a mind in perpetual conflict with itself which was presented by psychoanalysis, and also rejecting the atomistic picture of human behaviour presented by the behaviourists. While various factors may have combined to influence someone, that someone was nonetheless a person, complete in him/herself, with his/her own ideas and plans.

Another fundamental concept in humanistic psychology is that of **self-actualisation**. Literally, the term refers to actualising, or making real, the self. For Maslow, this meant achieving a state where all needs were satisfied, and individuals were able to realise their full potential. We will be looking at Maslow's hierarchical model of needs in the chapter on motivation. For Rogers, as the chapter on therapies will show, self-actualisation was less of a goal than a process. He regarded the need for self-actualisation as a fundamental one in all human beings: we all seek to develop ourselves, and realise our potential, and that is one of two basic psychological needs which must be satisfied – the other being our need for positive regard from other people.

The humanistic school of thought, in many ways, had far more influence than its size would suggest. It provided a way that psychologists could look at some of the more positive, or at least personal, aspects of human motivation and personality. It encouraged psychologists to take account of intentionality in human behaviour – the idea that people might sometimes do things because they planned to do them. It set the basis for the later acknowledgement of ethical concerns which made so much difference to the way psychologists went about their work. It encouraged the development of qualitative methodologies in psychology: we will be looking at these later in this book. And, most of all, it re-introduced the concept of the whole person to a psychology, which had become so bogged down in discussions of mechanisms and processes that the idea of the whole person had completely disappeared. In doing so, it set the foundations for many of the radical changes which have occurred in psychology during the last third of the twentieth century.

The cognitive revolution

By the late 1950s and early 1960s, academic psychologists were increasingly coming to view the behaviourist approach as useful but limited. The new work on communications technology, and later on computers, led to a growing interest in how human beings process information. The rapid growth of defence technology during WWII had stimulated psychological research into human cognition, particularly vigilance and attention, since questions like how long an operator could remain staring at a radar screen without making mistakes had acquired crucial importance. The 1950s also saw developments in research into human memory; and it saw the opening rounds of the major debate between B.F. Skinner (in the behaviourist corner) and Noam Chomsky (in the psycholinguistic corner) concerning how children acquire language.

The information-processing approach offered an appealing alternative to the limitations of behaviourism, and it rapidly became very popular. The growth of cognitive psychology continued throughout the 1970s and 1980s. Cognitive research explored many different facets of mental life, such as the use of imagery in representation, processes of decision-making and problem-solving; and reasoning. It combined the insights into human perception and learning from the Gestalt school with the findings from academic research into memory, and the computer provided an attractive model suggesting how human beings might deal with information on a cognitive level.

These changes became known as the **cognitive revolution**. From being the 'study of the mind', to the 'study of behaviour', psychology had come full circle. It was again the study of the mind, but this time with the additional insights and stricter experimental methods acquired from other phases in the discipline's history – and, most importantly,

with a very strong emphasis on empirical, laboratory-based investigation.

Limitations of the cognitive revolution

There were, however, two limitations to the cognitive revolution which gradually became apparent. One of these was the way that its emphasis on laboratory investigation tended to exclude other methods of investigation. Gradually, psychologists became increasingly aware that laboratory methods could investigate only a limited range of human behaviour. Pressure began to mount for more 'ecologically valid' methods of investigating what human beings do and how they think – methods which could acknowledge the complexities of human behaviour in everyday life.

The second limitation was related to the first, though not exactly the same. This was the growing influence of the computer metaphor in cognitive psychology. In the early years of the cognitive revolution, researchers like Jerome Bruner had shown how personal and social factors also influence cognitive processes. But as cognitive psychology theories became more closely tied to the idea that the human brain is 'like a computer', these concepts became increasingly overlooked, or ignored.

Opening up the cognitive dimension

The change which the cognitive revolution had brought to psychology was widespread, however, and researchers in other branches of psychology also became interested in how people make sense of their experiences. Social psychology shifted towards the study of social cognition, exploring how social understanding influences interaction. Developmental psychologists became increasingly interested in the child's developing social awareness, and its understanding of other people. In the physiological field, research psychologists became interested in areas like sleep, stress management, and cognitive neuropsychology; and even comparative psychologists began to accept investigations into animal cognition and intelligence. When the cognitive revolution was combined with the holistic approach to the human being developed by the humanistic psychologists, these new movements forged a more complex psychological awareness, which spanned several different levels of psychological explanation, and emphasised the importance of understanding human beings in their own contexts.

The growth of ethical concerns

The complex history of psychology (this has been a rather simplified account!) did not just contribute to major interests and definitions. It also left its mark on the methods that psychologists use to investigate their subject matter. For example, introspectionist methodology, such as the rigorous techniques of experimental control developed by Ebbinghaus, remained in psychology long after instrospectionism as a movement had died away. Similarly, long after the heyday of behaviourism, many areas of psychology remained influenced by the behaviourist insistence that only observable behaviour counted as valid information. But the move towards more holistic approaches also produced changes in psychological methodology, and in particular, an acceptance of much greater diversity. Psychologists began to accept that no one single method of investigation would give all the answers, and that sometimes it was better to adopt the technique of **triangulation** – using several different methods to investigate the same area.

The growth of concern about ethical issues in psychology was a major contributor to this trend. The traditional behaviourist and experimental approaches were essentially manipulative, seeing the human being purely as providing the raw material from which data could be obtained, and attempting to 'control' any intrusion of personality or reasoned thought from that person. Moreover, Western thought in the first part of this century tended to reinforce the view that the scientist, as a seeker after truth, need not be concerned with moral values. As a result, deception and manipulation became almost normal in psychological experiments at that time, and many psychological studies involved practices which nowadays we would consider to be quite unacceptable.

But part of coming to regard the human being as a complete person in its own right also resulted in taking more seriously the beliefs, ideas and reactions of that human being. In the 1960s, a few psychologists were beginning to voice concern about ethical issues, although most did not concern themselves with such matters. In 1963, Milgram published an account of a study of obedience, which had involved asking people to administer simulated, but apparently lethal, electric shocks to an apparently innocent victim. The following year, Baumrind published a paper dis-cussing the ethical issues raised by Milgram's study. Gradually, concerns about ethical issues increased, until eventually strict ethical codes of conduct were developed for psychologists.

Ethics and methodology

This change in orientation reflected the increasing concern with responsibility and ethics in society as a whole, and it required quite an adjustment in psychological methodology. The core of the concern about ethical issues is respect for the individual. That involved a number of modifications to traditional methods. Deception, for example, became something which had to be explicitly justified, rather than something which was a normal procedure in psychological studies. Psychological researchers now have 'research participants' helping them, rather than 'subjects' doing what they are told, and this change in vocabulary expresses the different way that these people are perceived. Research participants are also recognised as having rights, which the experimenter must respect. In other words, people who take part in psychological studies are acknowledged as autonomous beings, who are able to make informed choices about their mode of action and who are entitled to receive full information about their experiences. They are not seen simply as experimental material to be manipulated.

The attempt to build a psychology which respects its participants also led to an increased recognition that non-experimental, non-laboratory methods of enquiry could also provide useful data, even if it was not possible to control every possible variable. This insight resulted in a significant paradigm shift within the discipline. For example, psychologists began to develop an increased use of interview data and self-report to augment research of all kinds, even laboratory-based psychophysiological research. For this reason, too, psychologists became more interested in qualitative approaches to psychological research, in direct contrast to 'traditional' psychological methodology, which only accepted quantitative methods. Although experimental and laboratory research is still an important part of psychology, non-experimental investigative techniques are increasingly accepted as part of psychology's methodological tool-kit.

Of course, the kind of evidence which counts in psychology also depends on the area of psychology that is being investigated. In some areas, such as physiological psychology, medical evidence, experimental evidence and clinical case studies are all accepted as being useful indicators. In other areas, such as in cognitive psychology, it is still mainly experimental evidence which counts. Some areas, such as social psychology, encompass a mixture of experiments, observational studies and theoretical development; while the area of personality theory does not rest on data from experimental investigations, but instead draws from psychometric data and from clinical experience. Comparative psychology draws from biology, from ethological studies of animals in their natural environments and from laboratory work; and developmental psychology includes just about all of these methods, and more of its own. But ethical concerns span all the areas of psychology. We will be looking at them in more detail in the final section of this book.

Areas of psychology

What has emerged from the past century or so is that there is no simple way of understanding human beings. People are complicated, and have many sides to them. One consequence of the cognitive revolution and its aftermath was that psychologists began to recognise that a single, unitary approach to psychology was no longer even a desirable goal, let alone a practical one. Each different phase of psychological history left its mark, not just on the subject matter, but also on psychological methodology. Psychologists try to look at human behaviour from a range of different angles, so that they can get as complete a picture as possible. As a result, there are many different branches of psychology and areas of interest.

For convenience, we categorise these into general areas, but these categories are not at all exclusive, and often one topic will bring together knowledge from many different areas of psychology. This is because any human experience can be studied from various angles. The experience of emotion, for instance, has a physiological dimension, a cognitive dimension, a social dimension, a personality dimension, and several more. Most modern psychologists deal with the diversity of psychological knowledge by using the concept of **levels of explanation** – the idea that putting together knowledge from different levels of understanding, and different areas of psychology,

will lead us to a richer awareness of the full picture. The idea of levels of explanation helps us to see how the different ideas can fit together.

Cognitive psychology

'Cognition' is the general term which we give to mental activities, such as remembering, forming concepts, using language or attending to things. In its early days, as we have seen, psychology was defined as the study of mental life, and early researchers like Wilhelm Wundt (1862) studied such mental characteristics as memory, attention and the process of thinking.

There are many facets of cognitive psychology, but some of the major areas are perception, representation, memory and language. The study of perception involves looking at how information that has been received through the senses is interpreted and understood. This involves finding out how the brain decodes and makes sense of the information that it is receiving, so that it can be used, and/or stored. Representation refers to how we code mental information. For instance, it is unlikely that you actually think of your next-door neighbour using the words 'next-door neighbour'. Instead, you will have some kind of mental image which represents her or him, and which is activated when you bring that person to mind.

We all know pretty well what memory is: how we store information and retrieve it at future times. Much psychological research on memory has quite clear and definite implications for such real-life situations as revising for examinations, or remembering what happened in an accident. Other cognitive functions such as thinking, decision-making and concept formation also contribute to how we make sense out of our lives, and are often not nearly as straightforward as people like to imagine. Language forms an important part of most human activities; and the study of language involves both cognitive psychology and social psychology. Language helps us to develop and communicate sophisticated concepts and ideas; and it plays a significant role in organising and structuring human thought. For example, memories are often coded by means of verbal symbolism (words or phrases). Cognitive psychologists have also shown how our mental processes can be quite dramatically influenced by the language that we use.

Together, these processes form the basis of

cognition. But cognition does not take
s a mechanical data-processing routine: it
es alongside and in with the other areas of
psychology. For example, if we ignore the
role of social factors in cognition, we are unlikely
to be able to understand much of what people are
doing when they are making decisions. If we are
aiming to develop an understanding of people and
how they work, we have to look at other areas of
psychology as well.

Individual processes and abnormality

A large part of psychology, particularly in the
applied areas, has been concerned with describing
how people are similar to, or different from, one
another. This is the area of psychology broadly
known as individual differences. A substantial part
of this study has been concerned with **psychometric testing** – devising ways of measuring differences between people in a reliable, standardised
way. How is it, for instance, that some people
seem to be highly creative while others do not?
What do we mean by intelligence, and is it something that we can teach people? And how can we
learn to identify people's different talents and
aptitudes, so that we can identify the kinds of jobs
that they would enjoy doing, and be best at?
These are the kinds of issues that psychometrics
has concerned itself with.

Psychologists have also been interested in
personality. There are psychometric personality
tests, but there are also other ways of looking at
the human personality. The psychoanalytic
theories of Freud, Skinner's behaviourist model of
personality and the humanistic approach put
forward by Carl Rogers all contribute to psychological understanding in the area of personality.
The whole area of clinical and abnormal psychology is also closely linked with personality
theory, because many personality theories were
developed by clinical psychologists working in
psychiatric clinics or hospitals. They were able to
develop their ideas about what constitutes human
personality by working directly with concepts of
normality and abnormality, and seeing for themselves what it means to say that somebody is psychiatrically or psychologically disturbed.

Physiological psychology

Physiological psychology involves looking at how
the brain and the nervous system operate, and
how our experience can be affected by physiological processes and mechanisms. For example,
much physiological research has been devoted to
investigating stress, and the mechanisms by which
we respond to threatening circumstances. By
gaining understanding of these responses, we find
ourselves better placed to be able to cope with
stress when it arises, and also to minimise it if we
get the chance.

Physiological psychology also includes the study
of the nervous system, and which parts of the
brain are involved in behaviour and cognition.
The human brain is an astoundingly complex
organ, and we are continually learning new information about how it operates. Different parts of
the brain are involved in different functions, and
clinical neuropsychologists use data from people
with brain damage or abnormalities to study how
these different parts of the brain interact. Another
part of physiological psychology is concerned
with how sensory information is processed and
analysed, on its way to the higher regions of the
brain.

However, studying the parts which go to make
up our nervous system does not tell us about the
whole experience; and there are aspects of
physiological psychology which are also
concerned with the wider aspects of experience,
such as sleep, dreaming, consciousness and
motivation. These may involve the co-ordinated
action of many different parts of the nervous
system; but they also involve many other levels
of experience too. Dreaming may involve
measurable physiological changes, but that does
not mean we can measure what we dream about:
that is dependent on our experiences and
motivation as well. Physiological psychology
does not have to be reductionist (explaining
everything by reducing it down to its
component parts); instead, modern physiological
psychologists tend to emphasise how our
physiology *interacts* with social, cognitive and
cultural dimensions to produce the overall
experience.

Social psychology

Social psychology is the study of how people interact with one another, and also how they come to make sense of what is going on in their social worlds. People interact with one another non-verbally, using signs like gestures, uniforms and facial expressions, as well as by using words. A large part of social psychology has been concerned with the study of social behaviour, particularly in terms of conformity to social norms, obedience to authority and how people behave in large groups, like crowds. Social psychology also concerns itself with aspects of interpersonal relationships: how we become attracted to other people, theories of loving and what factors seem to influence whether we will like someone or not.

In recent years, social psychology has come to be increasingly concerned with **social cognition**, and how people interpret what is going on around them. The assumptions that we make, and the reasons that we attribute as underlying people's actions, are important in determining how we will behave. So are the ways that social knowledge and group identifications are shaped, since they all affect the ways that we interpret information. Consequently, social psychologists regard a knowledge of the processes which people use to make social judgements as being important. This includes the study of attitudes and personal values, as well as of prejudice. In Europe, in particular, social psychology also includes the study of cultural beliefs and the ways that social representations and social identities develop.

Developmental psychology

This branch of psychology is concerned with how people develop, throughout their lives, from infancy to old age. A number of different theories of development have been put forward, often by very famous psychologists such as Freud or Piaget, to explain what is happening, psychologically, as a child grows into an adult. Each of the major theoretica approaches has very different implications.

Much developmental psychology has been concerned with language and cognitive development, but that is not the whole story. Developmental psychology is concerned with just about any aspect of psychological or social development, and so developmental psychology includes special branches of all the other fields of psychology, such as the development of intelligence, or the development of social understanding.

People do not stop developing once they reach adolescence – they continue to change throughout their lives. So developmental psychology is also concerned with whole-life development. People change a great deal as they grow older, and different phases of the lifespan make different psychological demands on people. Accordingly, a considerable amount of recent research has been investigating the nature of those psychological demands, and how people respond to them.

Comparative psychology

Comparative psychology involves studying animals, and it gets its name from the way psychologists sometimes go on to make comparisons between animals and human beings, or between different species of animals, in to find out more about underlying mechanisms. In many ways, this has been one of the most controversial areas of psychology, partly because of the use of laboratory animals, although nowadays much comparative psychology is **ethological**, concerned with how animals behave in their natural environments. The other reason for the controversy is the way that some theorists – usually biologists, such as Morris or Lorenz – have used selected comparative studies to develop deeply controversial theories about 'human nature'. These are controversial because they ignore other levels of human functioning and concentrate just on biological ones, so the picture they present of human beings is seriously over-simplified.

The main link between human beings and animals, of course, is evolution; the general idea being that since human beings have physical similarities with other animals through evolution, by studying how other animals react to different stimuli, or how they learn simple tasks, we can find out about basic processes which human beings and animals have in common. Studies of maternal and social behaviour in higher animals too have often contributed to theories about human nature; although this can frequently become highly controversial, particularly in respect to theories of aggression or sexual stereotyping.

In this book, we will be looking at these different areas of psychology, and at what each area has to offer us in our attempt to understand the human being. We will also be looking at some of the debates in psychology, and some of the ways that different perspectives have influenced psychological thinking.

Psychological perspectives

Any psychologist – or any scientist, for that matter – who develops a theory makes certain assumptions. The assumptions are not just about the nature of the subject matter of the theory. They are also about what counts as knowledge, and how that knowledge should be obtained. Those assumptions, in turn, direct and organise the kinds of research which the scientist will undertake, and the kinds of questions they will ask. But they are not always the same: different theorists sometimes make different assumptions, and what a society will accept as a valid form of knowledge changes over time. The study of psychological perspectives involves looking at the assumptions which have underpinned psychological research thoroughout the history of psychology, and at some of the social issues and debates which have arisen from them.

Free will and determinism

The question of free will has been the subject of human enquiry for thousands of years. Are we entirely free agents, making all our own choices, or is what we do somehow determined by factors that are out of our control? Most of us experience the subjective impression that our own decisions will determine our behaviour; but at the same time we recognise that we are influenced by more than just our own intentions and ideas. In societies which are dominated by religious explanations of human behaviour, the question of determinism takes the form of how far individual destiny or fate has been pre-ordained by supernatural forces. In more secular societies, determinism is to do with identifying more immediate causes of behaviour, such as exploring whether they are genetic, environmental, social, etc. But the central issue remains the same: are we free, autonomous agents, or is our behaviour determined by influences outside our personal control?

Determinism is the idea that every event – whether it be a physical world event, an item of animal behaviour or a human action or emotion – is directly caused by something, or by a combination of somethings. It is an important foundation to psychological thinking: psychologists have always been concerned with finding out why people act as they do, and how they come to do it. Determinism holds that in order to understand any event or phenomenon, we must learn what caused it to occur, or to exist. Psychologists believe that such causality, or at least most of it, can be identified through appropriate research.

Intentionality

The most common alternative approach to determinism in looking at human behaviour is the attempt to explain behaviour in terms of the intentions of the individual undertaking the actions. The problem with this type of argument, though, is that it can end up as a rather circular form of explanation. Many theorists would argue that it does not really provide a genuine explanation of the behaviour at all. Instead, what it actually does is describe the purpose which the action is intended to achieve. But this does not explain why the person wanted to achieve that purpose rather than any other; or why they performed that particular behaviour just then. Such explanations are fine if we are looking at behaviour after it has happened, but they do not really allow us to predict how people will act in a new situation.

Any approach to understanding of human behaviour will take some kind of stance on the question of determinism. But determinism can take a number of forms, depending on what sorts of things are identified as the causal factors. If you are examining a theory or a piece of research for determinism, there are some useful questions to ask, such as: does this research assume that the person is regarded as a free agent? Are they able to make genuine choices, and to direct their own lives? Or are their choices seen as pre-determined, by forces or agencies outside their control, or by their own unconscious minds? The answers to these questions will provide you with a key to the model of human nature which underpins the research at which you are looking.

Reductionism and interactionism

Reductionism is a special form of determinism. It involves the belief that any particular event or

phenomenon can be understood simply by looking at the basic elements, or parts, which make it
up. The whole, in this view, is nothing more than
the sum of the parts. So the reductionist view is
that if you want to understand something, all you
have to do is find out its constituent parts, and
then add them all together, just like assembling a
jigsaw.

Reductionism in psychology takes many forms:
genetic reductionism involves explaining psychological phenomena as caused by the actions of
genes; physiological reductionism may explain
them as caused by hormones, or the nervous
system; social reductionism involves explaining
social events or phenomena purely in terms of the
individuals who were involved; S-R reductionism
involves explaining them simply as learned associations between a stimulus and a response.

The important question for psychologists is
how far reductionism is an adequate form of
explanation. It can be useful for some kinds of
enquiry, but it does not often tell us everything
we need to know. One of the main problems is
that the final product is often more than the sum
of its parts. There are **emergent properties**, which
the complete thing has, but its elements do not.
Taking a clock apart and examining its components may tell us a great deal about precision
engineering, but it cannot tell us what the clock
did when it was complete, or what the symbols
on the clock face meant, or how it was used by
people to regulate their behaviour.

Levels of analysis

The alternative to reductionist argument is **interactionism**: exploring how different levels of
analysis interact with one another. Social and psychological phenomena can be explored using a
number of different levels of analysis (see Table
1.1), and none of these can give us the whole
picture on its own. As a rough example, the levels
of analysis which are relevant to psychological
events and phenomena include cultural and
societal levels, subcultural and group interaction
levels, personal and cognitive levels, and behavioural and physiological levels. Any single psychological event is likely to include several of these
levels.

For example, if you wanted to explain why
someone had given up on revision for the evening
and gone out with a friend, you could explain it
in terms of group interactions, using ideas like

Table 1.1 Levels of analysis

Cultural influences
Socio-political influences
Subcultural and social status
Social groups, family, etc.*
Social cognition*
Interpersonal interaction*
Intentions and motives*
cognitive processes*
Acquired skills*
Habits and learned associations*
Emotional and physical reactions*
Genetics and evolutionary adaptations*
Physiological systems*
Cellular biology
Organic chemistry

---

*Matters of psychological relevance can occur at
any of these levels, although the main areas of
psychological interest lie in the levels indicated
by asterisks.*

---

peer-group pressure. But other factors might also
be involved, such as habits, or fatigue from previous study, or a personal wish to escape from
anxiety for a while. Each of these involves a
different level of explanation, but each
contributes to our understanding of why that
person acted as they did. An interactionist explanation would take that into account: it might
focus on one level for research purposes, but the
behaviour would be seen as resulting from interactions between the different levels, not as just
being caused by one. A reductionist explanation,
though, would focus on just one level and dismiss
the others as unimportant.

Reductionist accounts of human behaviour
have occurred frequently in psychology's history.
Many of them have occurred in areas of study
which are politically contentious or which stem
directly from cultural norms or beliefs rather than
from factual information. For example, reductionist arguments have been put forward as explanations of the mental disorder of schizophrenia,
arguing that it is 'just' the result of a build-up of
chemicals in the brain; or for masculine aggression, that it is simply the result of the hormone
testosterone; or for lesser social achievement by
women as being the inevitable outcome of the

influence exerted by other hormones. Such explanations are often seized on by the popular media, because they confirm social stereotypes and appear to be 'scientific'. But in reality, these theories can only be maintained by ignoring all psychological research at other levels of analysis, and also by disregarding the more complex messages coming from research at that same level, as well.

Nature-nurture debates

The **nature-nurture debate** is another example of determinism in psychology. A nature-nurture debate is a pair of opposing viewpoints concerned with what causes something to develop. On one side, nativists see development as arising from innate factors – from inherited characteristics. On the other side, empiricists see development as occurring because of experience and learning. Nature-nurture debates have a long history. At the beginning of this chapter, we looked briefly at the nativist philosophy of René Descartes, and at the empiricist philosophy of John Locke. Their ideas summarise the two extremes of the nature-nurture debate, with Descartes believing that human faculties and behaviour were largely inherited, and Locke believing that they were learned.

Problems with nature-nurture debates

Nature-nurture debates have been very common in psychology, as is shown in Table 1.2. There are a number of problems with the concept of nature-nurture, as two opposing mechanisms for development. The first of these is that it produces an artificial **polarisation**, in that both the environment and genetics are required in any meaningful sense to produce an organism. They act together, not in opposition. As Hebb pointed out in 1949, an egg cannot survive without its environment – take it away and the egg dies. But it cannot survive without its genetic base either – take that away and the egg would not have existed in the first place.

Another problem with the nature-nurture debate is that it portrays the two influences – nature and nurture – as **fixed**. In recent years, scientists have discovered that the genetic base of an organism is not as fixed as all that. Recent studies show how genetic material is constantly being shifted around in the living organism, and even though most of our DNA sequences do still seem to be fixed at birth, we have no way of

Table 1.2 Some nature-nurture debates in psychology	
perception	the idea that perceptual organisation was fixed and innate vs the idea that it was learned through experience
personality	fixed inherited 'traits' vs personality as response to the social environment: Eysenck vs Mischel
intelligence	the idea of intelligence as innate vs the idea of intelligence as learned through experience: Burt vs Binet
schizophrenia	the idea of schizophrenia as a genetic disorder vs the idea of it as a response to intolerable social and familial stress: Kallman vs Laing
depression	Bipolar depression shown to run in families: explained as inherited vs transmitted through family patterns and early learning
language	the idea of an innate automatic language decoder vs the idea that language was simply behaviour shaping: Chomsky vs Skinner
cognitive development	a fixed unfolding of capacity vs everything the result of learning and experience. Piaget vs Skinner
memory	the idea of a fixed, finite memory capacity vs memory as a response to personal experience and training: Ebbinghaus vs Bartlett

knowing how much effect the genetic changes and adjustments which occur throughout life may have. Similarly, the nature-nurture debate portrays the environment as a purely external, fixed phenomenon. But organisms act on their environments, and change them to suit their own needs. Even an amoeba changes the chemical balance of the water it swims in, and human beings adjust their environments all the time. The idea of there being two rigid, fixed phenomena of nature and nurture competing for influence on the growing individual simply does not work out when we look at the underlying biological process more closely.

The third problem with the nature–nurture approach has to do with the way that it ignores adaptation and interaction during life. Living is a **reciprocal process**, in which things influence one another. This operates on many levels, from the microbiological levels to large-scale evolutionary processes. Our personal experiences, for instance, are coloured and shaped by brain chemicals – drugs which alter that chemical balance result in a different experience of the world. But certain experiences can also stimulate the production of brain chemicals, or adjust their balance. So it is not simply that brain chemicals cause experience; and nor is it simply that experience causes the production of brain chemicals: there is a continual interaction between the two. We will discover more of this in the physiological psychology chapters. And in the comparative psychology chapters, we will see how this interaction results in **coevolution**: individuals evolve within an evironment, but they also change their environment: horses and grasslands evolved together, not separately.

The fourth major problem with the nature–nurture debate is that it ignores wider **evolutionary perspectives**, and in particular how control of behaviour has developed through varying species, and to involve a wide range of mechanisms. As we will see in the comparative chapters, there are many intermediate stages between behaviour which is wholly inherited, and behaviour which is wholly learned. For example, chicks and ducklings learn to recognise their mothers, and to follow them around; but this learning is very carefully managed during a critical period, switched on by genetic mechanisms, which makes sure that the learning only happens at the right time and under the right circumstances. Genetics and learning are not in opposition – they work together, and it is simply unrealistic to present them as if they were mutually exclusive.

Extreme nativist or empiricist arguments are by definition **reductionist**. By saying that some aspect of development is caused by nothing but genes, or nothing but experience, any further explanation is precluded: there is nothing else to say. The explanation focuses on one level of explanation and simply ignores the rest. But few modern psychologists would take either extreme of a nature–nurture debate. Nowadays, we tend to see biological predispositions as guiding development in particular directions, while experience influences how that development manifests itself. The two sources of influence are seen as interconnected, not as opposing alternatives, and it is the way that they interact which is the modern focus of interest. Nonetheless, during psychology's history, there have been a great number of nature–nurture debates, and several of the most influential ones are discussed in this book.

Nomothetic, idiographic and hermeneutic research

Nomothetic, idiographic and hermeneutic perspectives represent three entirely different approaches to explanation and understanding in psychological research. The **nomothetic** approach emphasises general aspects of human nature, which can be considered to apply in broad terms to all human beings, with only occasional exceptions. The main orientation of nomothetic social research is directed towards the discovery of general laws about human behaviour. The idea is that such laws will allow researchers to make predictions about how the majority of people are likely to behave in a given circumstance.

Psychologists conducting nomothetic research, therefore, tend to use quantitative, statistical methods which can allow for ordinary human variation. They take group measurements, and look for general differences between groups. They ignore individual differences, and try to make sure that their research designs will control them as far as possible. What they are interested in are overall differences, or correlations, and not idiosyncratic or personal qualities.

Idiographic research, on the other hand, is concerned with exploring the nature of individuality and human differences. As a result, idiographic psychological research often involves the exploration of single cases in considerable depth. The underlying aims of such detailed investigation of individuals are twofold: first, it is possible that a thorough understanding of one person may lead to the discovery of general principles which can apply to all people, and second, adopting an idiographic approach may provide a detailed understanding of one person as a complete being. The important distinctive aspect of idiographic research is in its emphasis on the individual rather than on groups.

Psychologists conducting idiographic research, therefore, tend to focus on just one or two cases, but in doing so they tend to use a combination of different techniques for gathering data. They may conduct interviews, they may ask the person to complete psychological tests or to carry out specific tasks, or they may observe a person's reactions carefully in controlled conditions. There are several reasons for using more than one data-gathering method, but an important one is because the person conducting idiographic research does not have a large reference group, or control group, to compare their research findings with. But collecting different sorts of data will allow them to identify recurrent and important themes or patterns in the information. If something emerges recurrently from different types of data, it is likely that it will be useful in developing a psychological understanding of what is happening with that person.

Hermeneutic research has to do with the study of meanings in social behaviour and experience. It is concerned with meanings on a number of levels, ranging through conscious, unconscious, personal and social levels to cultural and socio-political levels. Rather than simply looking at generalities of behaviour, or at experience, it is concerned with the ways that people interpret their experience, and with how various forms of symbolism are used to convey meaning in human life.

Psychologists conducting hermeneutic research tend to use qualitative approaches to data collection. That might involve conducting interviews, or looking at written material or artwork; but the important things about the way that they approach this data is that they are looking for meanings in it. They are not usually interested in statistical similarities, or representativeness, since a great deal of social meaning can often be contained in one special event, or one significant remark, or one particularly powerful symbol. But there are many different ways of going about qualitative analysis (see Hayes, 1997); and each of them can offer a psychologist the opportunity to make a careful and rigorous examination of the meanings of the information that they have gathered.

These different approaches have different underlying assumptions about the nature of human beings, and how they can be understood. The nomothetic approach tends to emphasise the general similarities of human beings, and looks for cause-and-effect mechanisms in human behaviour. The idiographic approach emphasises the study of the whole person and the personal choices that the person makes. The hermeneutic approach examines the symbolic nature of much human experience, and attempts to understand human behaviour in those terms. Each of these approaches involves different ways of asking questions, and utilises different research techniques.

This book contains examples of each of these different perspectives. The study of psychology is a fascinating one, which includes many different dimensions, levels of explanation and philosophical assumptions. One of the distinctive features of the modern psychologist is the ability to look at issues and problems from a number of different angles, and this is reflected in the discipline itself. The chapters which follow each represent a different aspect of psychological research, and discuss some of the different ways that psychologists have explored what people, or animals, do. They begin with one of the most fundamental of mental processes: that of perception.

Key terms

adaption The process of becoming successfully adjusted to environmental demands.

aversion therapy A technique of behaviour therapy which involves associating unpleasant stimuli with things that are to be avoided.

behaviour shaping A process whereby novel behaviour can be produced through operant conditioning, by selecting naturally-occuring variations of learned responses.

behaviour therapy The process of treating abnormal behaviour by looking only at the symptoms, and using conditioning techniques to modify them.

behaviourism A reductionist school of thought which holds that the observation and description of overt behaviour is all that is needed to comprehend the human being, and that manipulation of stimulus-response contingencies is all that is needed to change human behaviour. Behaviourism denies the relevance or importance of cognitive, personal or other dimensions of human experience.

Cartesian dualism The idea that the mind and body are entirely separate, distinct entities, with neither influencing the other except in voluntary action.

classical conditioning A form of learning which involves direct links between stimulus and response, learned through association.

ego According to Freud, that part of the mind which is in touch with reality, and balancing its demands with those of the id and superego.

empiricism An approach to knowledge which assumes that all knowledge of the world is learned through the input of information from the five external senses.

ethology The study of behaviour in the natural environment.

Gestalt psychology A school of psychology which opposed the S-R reductionism of the behaviourists and instead emphasised a human tendency towards wholeness of experience and cognition.

hermeneutic Concerned with the nature of social meaning and interpretation.

id The primitive part of the unconscious personality, according to Freud.

idiographic Describing ('*graphic*') the individual ('*idio*'). The term idiographic is particularly used to describe those personality tests which are concerned with looking in detail at the characteristics of the single person, and not with comparing that person with other members of the population.

interactionism The approach to understanding human and animal behaviour which emphasises links between different levels of explanation, and is therefore the opposite of reductionism.

introspection Looking 'inwards' to analyse or explore one's own mental state, beliefs or ideas.

nature-nurture debate Fairly pointless theoretical debates, popular in the 1950s, concerning whether a given psychological ability was inherited or whether it was learned through experience.

nomothetic A term which is used to describe those psychometric tests which are designed to assess how normal or typical someone is, by comparing their scores with what would normally be expected of members of that population.

operant conditioning The process of learning identified by B. F. Skinner, in which learning occurs as a result of positive or negative reinforcement of an animal or human being's action.

psychometric tests Instruments which have been developed for measuring mental characteristics. Psychological tests have been developed to measure a wide range of things, including creativity, job attitudes and skills, brain damage, and, of course, 'intelligence'.

reinforcement The strengthening of learning in some way. The term is usually used of learned associations, acquired through operant or classical conditioning, but it may also be applied to other forms of learning.

self-actualisation The making real of one's abilities and talents: using them to the full.

social cognition The way that we think about and interpret social information and social experience. In developmental psychology, the term refers to a theory of cognitive development which states the social interaction is the most important factor in a young child's cognitive development.

superego In Freudian theory, the part of the unconscious mind which acts as an internalised, strict parent, incorporating ideas of duty, obligation and conscience.

Summary

1 The philosophers Descartes and Locke, and the biologist Charles Darwin, were highly influential in setting the conceptual groundwork for the emergence of psychology as a discipline.

2 The early introspectionist psychologists studied the workings of the mind, by attempting to analyse their own and others' subjective experiences. However, the behaviourists rejected the study of mental processes, arguing that behaviour should be analysed in terms of stimulus-response connections.

3 European psychologists, such as members of the Gestalt school and Jean Piaget, developed wide-ranging theories concerned with understanding mental experience and mental development.

4 The clinical origins of psychology included the psychoanalytic school of thought, based on the work of Freud, and later included behaviour therapy and humanistic psychology.

5 The cognitive revolution reintroduced the study of the mind to psychology, but this time from an empirical, experimentally based standpoint. Other areas of psychology also began to acknowledge the importance of cognitive processes.

6 The modern emphasis on ethical issues in psychology brought with it an increased respect for the participant in psychological research, and a growing acceptance of non-experimental and qualitative research techniques.

7 Areas of psychological knowledge can be arbitrarily categorised into cognitive psychology, individual processes, physiological psychology, social psychology, developmental psychology and comparative psychology. But these categories overlap in many areas.

8 Perspectives in psychology include the issues raised by determinism, reductionism, interactionism, the nature nurture debates, and nomothetic, idiographic and hermeneutic research.

Self-assessment questions

1 Briefly describe the theory of evolution.

2 Outline the major areas of psychology.

3 What is meant by the term nature-nurture debate?

Practice essay questions

1 Discuss the relationship between psychology's history and its methodology.

2 How has the modern concern with ethical issues influenced psychological methodology?

3 How does the concept of levels of explanation help us to understand psychological issues?

Test your knowledge of this chapter with our online quizzes and games at: http://www.psych.co.uk

Explore perspectives in psychology further at:

General

http://www.sccu.edu/programs/academic/psych/amoebaweb.html – Excellent links to pages on all aspects of psychology.

http://www.alleydog.com – A straight-forward student resource, easy to use and understand. Class notes, glossary, coverage of all schools of thought.

http://www.psychwww.com/ – A collection of psychological resources webpages with links to worldwide psychology departments and the courses they run.

http://www.yorku.ca/dept/psych/orgs/apa26/resource.htm – good links to webpages with details of the history of psychology.

http://studyweb.chemek.cc.or.us/ – Useful tips on time management for struggling students.

Biographies

http://www.treasure-troves.com/bios/bios0.html – Information on scientists with biographies and major publications listed.

History/schools of thought

http://www.geocities.com/Athens/Delphi/6061/en linha.htm – Timeline of events from 600 BC to the present day detailing all of the major advances, key figures and publications.

http://www.earlham.edu/~peters/philinks.htm – Lots of links to philosophers on the internet.

http://www.yorku.ca/dept/psych/classics/ – Good on the philosophical roots and debates involved in psychology. Important texts and events are detailed.

Topics/debates

http://www.tiac.net/biz/drmike/Current.html – A-Z of topics with good descriptions and the opportunity to send in your own opinions on the areas of debate.

Bibliography

http://www.slu.edu/colleges/AS/PSY/510Guide.html – Comprehensive guide to books and articles covering the history of psychology.

Cognitive psychology

Perception and attention

```
Perceptual organisations
    ├─ Perceiving objects and backgrounds
    ├─ Perceiving distance
    └─ Pattern recognition

Interpreting perceptions
    ├─ Perceptual set and perceptual inference
    └─ Face recognition

Attention
    ├─ Selective attention
    └─ Sustained attention
```

Learning objectives

2.1. Organising sensory experience
a identify basic features of perceptual organisation
b link perceptual organisation with perceptual processes
c outline Marr's computational theory of perception

2.2. Perceiving depth
a name the major cues used in perceiving depth
b outline Gibson's theory of depth perception
c define key concepts in Gibson's theory of perception

2.3. Explaining pattern recognition
a identify relevant applications of pattern-recognition
b evaluate major approaches to pattern-recognition
c describe the pandemonium model of pattern recognition

2.4. Perceptual inference
a describe studies illustrating perceptual set
b compare perceptual and scientific hypotheses
c relate visual illusions to cognitive mechanisms

2.5. Face recognition
a evaluate a study relating to face recognition
b distinguish between the processes involved in recognition of familiar and unfamiliar faces
c identify top-down and bottom-up elements in face recognition

2.6. Sustained attention
a define terms relating to sustained attention
b list the major factors influencing vigilance
c describe the arousal explanation for sustained attention

2.7. Selective attention
a define terms relating to selective attention
b outline major models of selective attention
c relate empirical evidence to theoretical models of selective attention

2.8. Neisser's perceptual cycle
a define terms relating to Neisser's perceptual cycle
b describe Neisser's theory of perception
c relate the perceptual cycle to everyday experience

Perception is all about how we interpret the information that we receive through the sense organs of the body. Information which is received directly from the sense organs is known as **sensation**. It is the actual sensory impressions that we experience. But if we are to make any sense out of our sensory experiences – if they are to be something more than a jumbled blur of colour, sound, or smells, then we need to interpret them. In visual perception (vision is the sense that psychologists have studied in most depth) we need to be able to distinguish objects from their backgrounds; we need to be able to tell whether one object is further away than another one; we need to be able to recognise familiar patterns and faces, and so on. The psychological study of perception consists of investigations of how we go about this, and theories which psychologists have developed to explain it.

Attention is not the same as perception, but it is very closely linked to it. In this chapter, we will also be looking at how psychologists have studied attention – how long we can pay attention to something before we become bored and begin to make mistakes; and how we choose what we should be attending to out of the mass of sensory information that we receive.

Perceiving objects and backgrounds

The first step in interpreting sensory information is to organise it. Perceptual organisation involves converting our impressions of light, dark and colour into meaningful units, which can represent the world around us. The first step in this process is to be able to distinguish objects and figures from backgrounds. The way that we do this has been studied by psychologists for many decades.

Distinguishing figures from backgrounds is very basic to perception. It is so basic, in fact, that we will try to do it even if the figures are not 'really' there. If we are faced with a mass of confusing sensory information, we try to group together different stimuli so that we can detect patterns. And if we are faced with a completely meaningless grey blur, which covers the whole of our perceptual field, then our minds begin to form shapes and figures of their own. In the first part of this century, there were many psychological studies with 'Ganzfeld' equipment, which could produce this type of featureless visual field; and what all of

those studies seemed to demonstrate was how strong our tendency to see figures against backgrounds is.

We can see this, too, when we look at dual-image figures, like the cross or the vase figures (Figure 2.1). When we are looking at one of the figures – say, the silhouettes – then the vase disappears. And if we look at the vase, the silhouettes disappear. We can see objects against backgrounds, but the perceptual system does not let us see objects against objects. Organising our perception into figures against backgrounds is a very powerful factor in our perceptual systems.

The Gestalt laws of perception

During the 1930s, the Gestalt psychologists investigated how we go about perceiving objects and figures. They identified a set of principles of perception, which they referred to as the **laws of Prägnanz**. Prägnanz has the same linguistic origin as our word 'pregnant', and it means 'loaded with meaning'. The Gestalt laws of Prägnanz show how we attribute meaning of some sort even to the most simple collections of visual stimuli. There are four of them altogether.

The first is the **principle of similarity**. According to this principle, if we look at a set of stimuli, and if none of the other Gestalt laws apply, then we will automatically group similar ones together (Figure 2.2). We see them as 'belonging' to one another. But this is easily overtaken by the second principle: the **principle of proximity**. According to this principle, stimuli which are close to each other will be seen as forming a group, even if they are not particularly similar (Figure 2.3).

The third, and perhaps the strongest of the Gestalt principles of perception, is known as the **principle of closure**. Broadly speaking, it is that

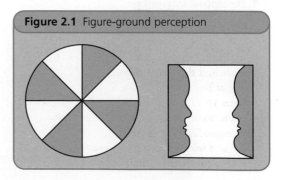

Figure 2.1 Figure-ground perception

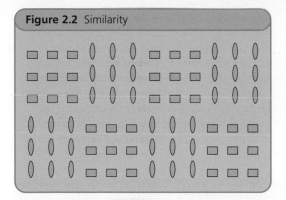

Figure 2.2 Similarity

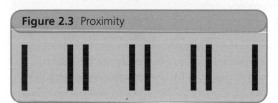

Figure 2.3 Proximity

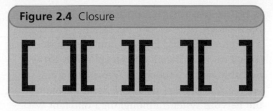

Figure 2.4 Closure

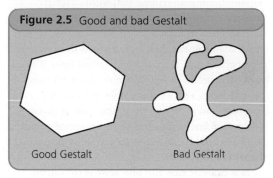

Figure 2.5 Good and bad Gestalt

Good Gestalt   Bad Gestalt

we have a strong tendency to prefer closed figures rather than fragmented or unconnected lines (Figure 2.4) This principle is so strong that it can override all of the others. And the fourth Gestalt law is the **principle of good Gestalt**. This affects our perception, in the form of a preference for figures which appear to be well rounded or symmetrical, rather than ones that seem fragmented or messy (Figure 2.5). Although we can learn to appreciate the latter, as in some forms of art, as a general rule people identify figures with 'good Gestalt' much more quickly than more complex or less structured forms.

Physiological factors in figure-ground perception

It seems, too, that the way that nerve fibres in the visual system are arranged may help figure-ground perception. In 1968, Hubel and Wiesel published a paper which gave the outcome of many years of research. They had recorded the actions of individual cells in the visual parts of the brain – specifically, the lateral geniculate nuclei of the thalamus, and the visual cortex (we will be looking at brain mechanisms more closely in Chapters 10 and 12). As they did this, they found that there were specialised cells in these areas which reponded very specifically to different visual stimuli, and seemed to represent an initial 'sorting out' of the information that the visual system was

receiving. They identified three types of cells altogether, which are organised in a hierarchical manner.

Simple, complex and hypercomplex cells

The lowest-level cell only seemed to respond to one, very simple, type of stimulus. **Simple cells** would respond to a dot in just one part of the visual field, or to a line at one particular angle and no other, in just one part of the visual field. They were very specific in their functions. But there were also large numbers of simple cells, so that between them they covered all of the visual field, collecting data about dots and lines.

Hubel and Wiesel found that the information obtained by simple cells is structured by **complex cells**. Each complex cell receives information from a number of simple cells, and links that information together. For example, a complex cell may receive information from lots of simple cells, about lines at a particular angle. That cell will then fire in response to a line at that particular angle anywhere in the visual field.

Complex cells in turn pass information on to **hypercomplex cells**, and these fire in response to simple figures or shapes. They combine the information that they receive from several complex cells, so that they could detect, say, a triangle, or a star shape. The implication of these findings is that the perception of basic shapes, at least, is hard-wired into our nervous system.

Is figure-ground perception innate?

Nearly forty years earlier, the Gestalt psychologists had considered that figure-ground perception was such a strong principle of perception that it was probably innate. Hubel and Wiesel's findings suggest that perhaps detecting figures is built in to the nervous system, although in a different way. Like most nature-nurture issues, however, the environment matters too. Blakemore (1984) reported a study in which kittens were brought up in a severely restricted visual environment, so that from the moment their eyes opened they were in a 'vertical world', seeing only vertical lines (Figure 2.6). Blakemore found that after about ten weeks, all but about 10% of the simple and complex cells had changed their functions, and now responded to vertical lines instead of to the range of angles which would be found in an animal with normal experience.

It is possible that this also applies to human beings, although probably not quite so drastically. Most people in Western cultures live in a highly carpentered environment, with many vertical and horizontal lines, and curved or diagonal lines are much less common. Annis and Frost (1973) investigated Canadian Cree Indians, whose traditional lives involve many straight lines, but at all sorts of angles (for example, they live in tepees). These were compared with people (also of the Cree population) who had grown up in an urban Western environment. Their task was to examine pairs of lines and to judge whether they were parallel or not. Those who had grown up in a carpentered environment were very good at judging vertical and horizontal lines, but much worse than the others at judging diagonals. It may be that the carpentered environment itself reflects a type of restricted experience which affects how visual cells develop. Blakemore also suggested that his findings might account for a common eye problem, astigmatism, in which people have difficulty seeing lines at certain angles, but not at others.

Marr's computational theory of perception

Marr (1982) was particularly concerned with how we come to identify objects or features from the mass of information in the retinal image. To understand this, Marr adopted a computational model, exploring how a perceptual system which is made up of simple and complex cells, and other such elements, could end up identifying complex figures like trees, people, or animals. Obviously we do not have hypercomplex cells for figures such as these, so they need a bit more explanation.

Marr argued that to be effective, a theory of vision would have to explain how it works on three levels: a computational level, an algorithmic level and an implementation level. The **computational level** concerns what the system is trying to do in the end. Since Marr's theory was about identifying how we recognise objects, then the immediate computational concern of the theory is to do with the detection of edges and boundaries. If we are to detect a figure against a background, we need to be able to tell where that figure begins and the background ends. So unless we can detect edges, we are unlikely to be able to make much sense of the information we receive.

The **algorithmic level** concerns how edges are worked out, or computed, by the system: what calculations have to be made in analysing the data, in order to achieve some kind of systematic way of detecting them, and of telling, for example, whether a darkened area is really an edge, or whether it is just a surface. And the **implementation level** is concerned with whether the relevant 'hardware', in the form of necessary nerve cells and connections, is actually present in the visual system, so the necessary algorithmic processes could actually take place. An elaborate theory which did not match up to the physiological structure of the visual system would not be much good.

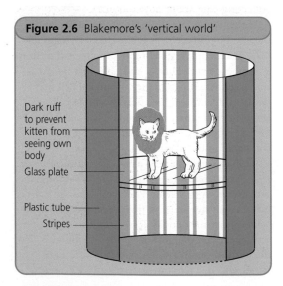

Figure 2.6 Blakemore's 'vertical world'

Dark ruff to prevent kitten from seeing own body

Glass plate

Plastic tube

Stripes

The optic array

Marr took as his starting point the idea that all the information that is needed is actually present in the light reaching the eyes – the optic array. The retinal image can be imagined as an array of points, with each point corresponding to a rod or cone cell (the light-detecting cells of the retina). Somehow or other, these points need to be organised: those which 'belong' together have to be identified as connected. Marr proposed that we do this by identifying two types of feature: **contours**, like the lines on a map which indicate the shape of the ground surface, and **regions of similarity**. We have to include contours as well as regions of similarity because in real life, objects are not all of one colour or intensity, and nor is the background, so just looking at similarity alone could be confusing.

Different kinds of contours can provide important clues to the shape of an object. Some contours represent convex surfaces, which curve outwards, like the surface of an apple or the outer corner of a building, other contours can be concave, forming an inward-facing edge, like the gap between cushions on a sofa. On their own and out of context, of course, these contours would not be very informative: several well-known visual illusions are based on a set of lines which can be seen as either a convex or a concave contour (Figure 2.7). But Marr was not really concerned with the perception of line drawings, but with real-life perception, in which the presence of all kinds of other information makes such ambiguity very much less likely to happen.

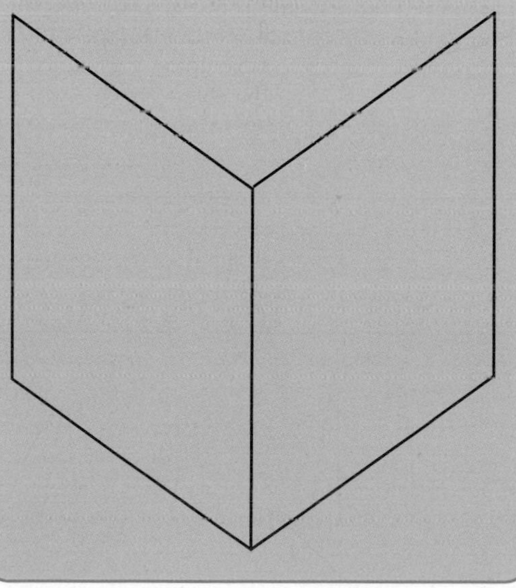

Marr suggested that it might be helpful to look at the retinal image by thinking of it as like a computer image. In a computer image, quite complicated pictures can be built up by dividing the picture into tiny regions known as pixels. Each pixel may be all one colour, or it may shade gradually from one side to another. By combining these pixels, we can get quite detailed pictures: the smaller the pixels, the more detail can be identified, and if they are small enough (as they are on a television screen), we do not even notice that the image is composed of dots (Figure 2.8).

Building up the image

In 1976, Marr showed how this basic image, called the raw primal sketch, can be built up just using dots, or pixels. By looking at the regions of the image where the optic array changes in intensity, he showed that areas of change in intensity could indicate some of the more important contours and regions – in a very fragmented form. Other information could be added to the raw primal sketch by adopting some of the basic Gestalt principles, like the principles of proximity and similarity which we looked at earlier. These would often produce an image which revealed the important basic structures of a scene – not in any detail, but giving something to go on. Marr called this adjusted image the **full primal sketch**.

Figure 2.7 The open book illusion

Figure 2.8 Images and pixels

Marr proposed that the visual processing system takes the full primal sketch, and then builds on it by adding information about depth and distance, obtained through binocular disparity and motion parallax (we will be looking at these in the next section). This can tell us a great deal more about the image: in particular, it can let us know whether one part lies in front of another. So it begins to give us a three-dimensional image, but not a complete one. For instance, it does not really allow us to compare distances between objects that lie in different parts of the visual field. Because it gives us part of the information that we need about depth, but not all of it, Marr described this as the $2\frac{1}{2}$**D sketch**. When we look at Gibson's theory later on in this chapter, we will see how adding in the influence of movement and action could perhaps account fully for 3D perception.

Marr and Nishihara (1978) showed that object perception could also be built up from the $2\frac{1}{2}$D sketch (Figure 2.9). They suggested that when we look at objects, an important feature of them is the volume that they represent: we do not see objects just as flat surfaces, we see them as complete things, taking up real space. Marr and Nishihara proposed that what the perceptual system deduces from the $2\frac{1}{2}$D sketch is a set of cone-like shapes. Any object, like a human being or tree, can be seen very roughly as a set of generalised cones, or tubes. This, they argued, would be the starting point that could be computed from the $2\frac{1}{2}$D sketch.

Different levels of detail in the image could be expressed in terms of progressively smaller cones, so the system would be hierarchical. If we look at a dog from a distance, for instance, the impression might simply be of generalised cones for head, body, legs and tail (as in Figure 2.9). But if we moved closer, we would come to distinguish ears and neck, and perhaps to subdivide each leg into segments. Each of these features could be deduced from the $2\frac{1}{2}$D sketch as a generalised cone, but Marr and Nishihara argued that the system would always tend to work from the more general levels first, and progress to more specific ones later. We would get the whole impression of the figure first, and sort out the details once that had been established.

Recognising objects

Another factor that would help us to identify objects quickly is the way that we can use the generalised cones to develop a kind of 'stick-figure' model (Figure 2.10). We do this by taking the axis running through each of the generalised cones in an image, and putting them together. These 'stick figures', Marr and Nisihara suggested, can then be matched up with a stored catalogue of models, used as reference images for comparisons. The images in the catalogue could have been learned, or, in the case of very important shapes like humans or animals, they might have been inherited. But either way, the catalogue would also be organised hierarchically, moving from general models, like 'humanoid', 'treelike', etc., down to more specific ones, like 'child', 'bush', etc.

Even with a very blurred or distant image, it is reasonably easy to tell a biped from a quadruped, but we need more detail to distinguish a dog from

Figure 2.9 The $2\frac{1}{2}$D sketch

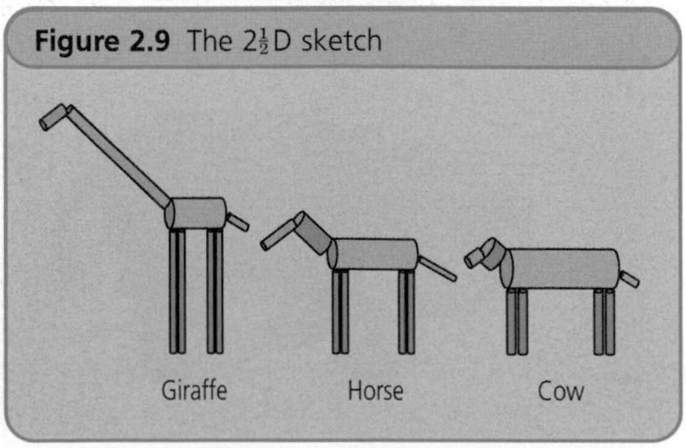

Giraffe   Horse   Cow

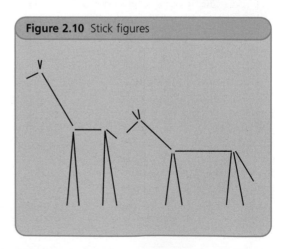

Figure 2.10 Stick figures

a cat, or a woman from a man. Matching up the stick-figure models with known ones from the basic catalogue would allow us to recognise familiar objects very easily. In fact, Marr argued that stick-figures and silhouettes might be particularly powerful images in drawing and art precisely because they capture the basic model which the brain uses for recognition.

The most important aspect of Marr's theory is that it shows how basic visual processes can combine to build up a picture of the outside world just by analysing the information that is actually present in the optic array, without any need for hypothesis-testing or guesswork from prior knowledge. Marr's computational metaphor can provide a possible explanation for human object-recognition, and it can also provide guidelines for researchers into robotics, who are trying to develop systems which can analyse visual information.

Perceiving distance

Another aspect of visual perception which has been studied extensively by psychologists is **depth perception**. This is concerned with how we can tell how far away something is. When we look at something, our eyes receive an image of it, and its surroundings, projected on to the retina. This is the optic array that Marr talked about – a kind of 'screen' of light-sensitive cells across the back of the eyeball, picking up an image of the outside world. But the retinal image is two-dimensional, so if we are going to know how far away something is, the brain must deduce it from the information in the image.

It does this by using **depth cues** – the features of the retinal image which give clues to the distance of an object or scene. There are two main types of depth cues: **monocular depth cues**, which operate equally well with one eye or two; and **binocular depth cues**, which involve matching up the images received from each eye, and deducing distances from the tiny differences between them. Some animals, like rabbits and most birds, have eyes on either side of the head. It gives them good all-round vision, because one eye gets a picture of everything to the rabbit's left, while the other sees what is to the right. But it means that the rabbit can only use monocular cues to depth. Other animals, though, such as monkeys, owls, and human beings, have frontally-mounted eyes. This allows them to use binocular depth cues as well as monocular ones, so they can be much more accurate in judgements of distance.

Monocular depth cues

Artists use monocular depth cues when they are trying to indicate distance in a painting. There are seven major ones altogether. One of them is the **relative size** of different objects: things seem smaller when they are further away (Figure 2.11). Another is **shadow**. Sign-writers often use shadow to make words appear to stand out from their background, giving the impression that the background is further away from the letters (Figure 2.12). A third monocular depth cue is **superposition**: a close object will cover up portions of the background, or parts of another object behind it. If we can see all of one object and only part of another one immediately next to it, we usually conclude that the partial one is further away (Figure 2.13).

When we look at a painting or picture, **height in plane** is an important cue. Distant objects appear to be higher up in the plane represented by the picture. The same cue applies when we are looking at a real scene: in general, things which are more distant appear higher and closer to the horizon (Figure 2.14). There is a **gradient of**

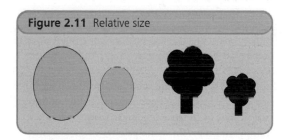

Figure 2.11 Relative size

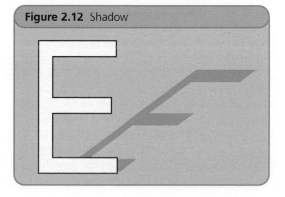

Figure 2.12 Shadow

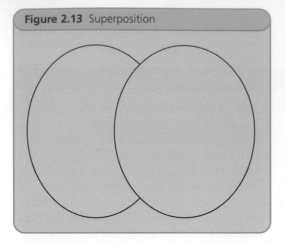

Figure 2.13 Superposition

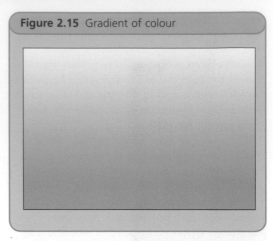

Figure 2.15 Gradient of colour

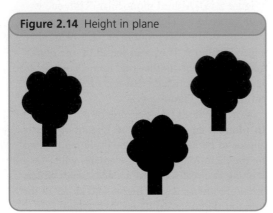

Figure 2.14 Height in plane

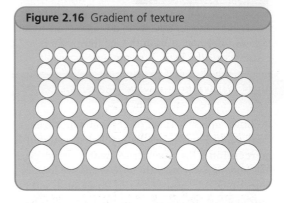

Figure 2.16 Gradient of texture

colour too, as objects approach the horizon. Close objects have clear, sharp colours but distant objects appear to be greyer (Figure 2.15). And details are less easily seen, so that there is a gradient of texture as well. As anyone who has ever been looking for a place to sit and have a picnic in the country will know, grass close by always seems to look lumpy and uneven, while patches of grass a little more distant appear smoother (Figure 2.16).

Movement provides information about depth, as well. If we move our heads – or ourselves – from side to side, different parts of the background are uncovered or covered up. This forms a seventh depth cue, known as **motion parallax**. One of the many fascinating things about holograms is how they can give an illusion of depth which includes parallax. If you look towards the 'side' of a holographic image, you can see more of the background behind it, exactly as if it were really a three-dimensional object. But a photograph, of course, looks the same from any angle.

Binocular depth cues

As we have seen, having frontally-mounted eyes gives us access to other depth cues, as well. For example, the amount of difference between the two images indicates how far away an object is. If you close one eye and line up a pencil with a distant object, you will find that if you then look at it with the other eye it seems to have 'jumped' relative to the object you lined it up with. Moreover, if you hold the pencil out at arm's length, it will seem to jump less then if you hold it fairly close to your eyes.

The difference between the images the two eyes receive is known as **binocular disparity**. It is an important depth cue, and it seems as though our visual system is structured to help it to happen. In 1977, Hubel and Wiesel showed how cells in the visual cortex of the brain respond to information using **ocular dominance columns**. What this means is that a simple or complex cell receiving information from the left eye will be

Figure 2.17 The Müller-Lyer illusion

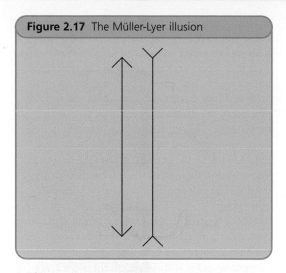

side-by-side with a cell receiving exactly the same type of information from the right eye. This suggests that the brain is matching up the two images, which allows it to calculate binocular disparity more effectively. We will be looking at this study in more detail in Chapter 10.

We gain additional information about depth by the amount of **convergence** shown by our eye muscles when we are focusing on near or far objects. If we are looking out to infinity, for example into the sky or out to sea, the direction of gaze from each eye is almost parallel. But if we

are looking at closer objects, our eyes are angled towards each other, so that both of them are focused on the object. The way that we use our eye muscles is different in the two cases. Near objects produce a higher degree of convergence than far objects, so these muscular cues also give us an indication of depth.

Combining these different cues allows us to develop a remarkably accurate ability to estimate how far away things are – knowledge which we put to use every day. Crossing a road, for instance, or driving a car, involves sophisticated mental calculations about distance, speed and time, which we perform quite unconsciously. Without a reasonably accurate system for estimating depth, we would be entirely unable to do this successfully.

Gregory (1963) argued that many **visual illusions** arise because depth cues in the stimulus mean that we interpret them as three-dimensional, when really they are not. One of the figures that he applied this argument to was the Müller-Lyer illusion – a powerful illusion based on two equal-length parallel lines (Figure 2.17). Gregory argued that the reason why this illusion works so strongly is because it brings in depth cues. For example, the arrow-head version of the Müller-Lyer reminds us of the outside or inside corners of buildings (Figure 2.18). And the dumb-bells version works because of superposition – the rings

Figure 2.18 A real-life version of the Müller-lyer illusion (Source: Gregory, 1968)

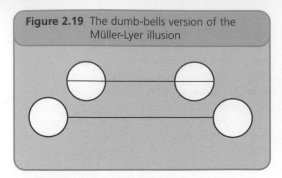

Figure 2.19 The dumb-bells version of the Müller-Lyer illusion

of the apparently longer one appear to be covering up the ends of the bar (Figure 2.19).

Gregory's arguments came from a more detailed theory of perception, which we will be looking at in this chapter, and which was based very firmly on the idea that a lot of our perception involves hypothesis-testing, or inference, on the part of the brain. The brain uses perceptual cues, such as depth cues or figure-ground cues, to develop hypotheses about what is probably there; and sometimes these hypotheses are wrong. But some psychologists have disagreed profoundly with the idea that perception works by inference, or hypothesis-testing, and one of the most influential of them was J.J. Gibson.

Gibson's theory of perception

Like Marr, Gibson (1950) was concerned with perception in everyday life, rather than the perception of laboratory diagrams or other out-of-context stimuli. He argued that perception is an active, direct process, which does not involve seeing things in a vacuum, but always in context. He referred to traditional theories of perception as 'air' theories, because they explored the perception of objects as if they took place suspended in mid-air, without any background. In real life, he argued, objects do not occur like that. They are always seen in a context, with a background, and this is a crucial feature which the brain uses in its perceptual analysis. To emphasise this, Gibson referred to his theory as a 'ground' theory.

The ecological model of perception

Gibson's theory is also referred to as an **ecological** model, because he thought that it was completely unrealistic to try to separate perceiving from movement and context. Perception, he argued, has a definite function for an organism. It has evolved

to help that organism in its day-to-day survival. In other words, perception has an ecological basis – it is about operating and surviving in the real world. And that means moving about in the world, not just staying in one place. The ability to move, to look at things from a different angle and to interpret visual information in terms of your own movement, is a crucial aspect of perception: it helps the individual to survive. And there is no need for inference, because if you take movement into account, then all of the information that you need for accurate perception is present in the optic array.

Gibson argued that the whole of the optic array consists of information about **surfaces**: they show different gradients of light and different gradients of texture, and it is these which form the main context for perception. We perceive them directly, he argued, not through inference. Moreover, objects, as features of the optic array, also consist of surfaces, which help them to be distinguished from backgrounds. The rest of their distinction is provided by how their boundaries intersect. For example, a nearby building will conceal some part of its background – its boundary, and its surfaces, will intersect with that of the background, and will be different from it. Gradient of texture also changes with movement, and provides a set of environmental cues which are always present in real-life perception (although not necessarily in laboratory-based perceptual experiments!)

Direct perception and the importance of motion

Gibson insisted that his theory was all about **direct perception**: he did not think that there was any need for us to use prior knowledge to make sense of things that we look at. He regarded theories of perception which argue that perception depends on prior knowledge, such as Gregory's hypothesis-testing theory, as only relevant for artificial laboratory situations where the available stimuli were very limited. Precisely because the stimuli were limited, people in those situations would have to use guesswork or prior information to work out what they were looking at. But in everyday life, Gibson argued, there is more than enough information available to us; and we add to it all the time because we move about in the world. Our nervous system is perfectly attuned to this information, and we automatically notice the possibilities and implications of relevant changes in the optic array. It is a direct process that does not require cognitive input.

Gibson did not believe that perception could be looked at in isolation. He argued that the perceptual system does not just consist of the eyes and the optic equipment, but includes the head and body too. Movement and action are fundamental to, and inseparable from, perception itself. For example, if you see something odd-looking about a building, you automatically move your head slightly and look at it from a slightly different angle. This clarifies what you are looking at, and can make all the difference between whether you understand what you see or not. Something which might have been a confusing illusion in a still photograph would not even be noticed in everyday living, just because of movement.

In 1979, Gibson clarified his ideas about the importance of motion. He argued that motion was so important for perception that without it, real perception simply would not be possible. If it was the perceiver who was moving, then there would be flow and change in the whole of the optic array; if the movement was concerned with 'events', or the movement of objects, there would be systematic changes in the boundaries and textures of the optic array as surfaces became temporarily covered by other surfaces. It is easy to tell whether it is the object or the perceiver which is moving, simply by the amount of the optic array that changes (see Table 2.1).

Affordances

We are linked to what we perceive because of our own activities. Because we are active creatures, moving around in the world, we also take into account the way that what is around us offers possibilities for action. Gibson argued that this is an important part of how we perceive objects. A sawn-off tree-trunk, for example, would not just be perceived as a flat surface, but would also afford the possibility of sitting down, or of putting things on, or of hopping on to, if you happen to be a frog or a particularly lively human. He called these possibilities for action **affordances**, and saw them as inseparable from the process of perceiving. We – and other animals too – look at the world in terms of the possibilities for action that it affords to us. But this is not a cognitive process: it is a part of perception itself, which incorporates affordances pretty well automatically. As far as Gibson was concerned, the object itself 'resonates' with

---

Table 2.1 Rules of flow in the optic array

Changes in the flow of the optic array gives important information about what type of movement is taking place. Gibson summarised this in four basic 'rules':

1 If there is a flow in the optic array, that means that the perceiver is moving. If there is no such flow, the perceiver is static.

2 The flow of the optic array will appear either to be coming out from a particular point; or moving towards one. The focus or centre of that movement indicates the direction in which the perceiver is moving.

3 If the flow in the optic array seems to be coming out from a particular point ('outflow'), that means that the perceiver is moving towards that point; but if the flow seems to be moving towards a point ('inflow'), then the perceiver is moving away.

4 If the focal point of the flow stays in the same place, that means that the perceiver is continuing to move in the same direction; if the centre of flow shifts, so that it seems to be coming from another place, it means that the perceiver has turned, and changed direction.

Source: Gibson, 1979

---

the possibility of action; and direct perception incorporates those possibilities as well as the factual information about objects.

Gibson maintained that perception is all about surviving, and surviving means being active. It is impractical, he argued, to attempt to study perceptual processes in isolation; or to try to build up models of perception just from analysing the retinal image. In that respect, many modern cognitive psychologists have come to agree with him, and his has been one of the most influential theories of perception in recent years. However, his view that perception involves a direct grasp of the 'affordances' of each object – a grasp which is acquired directly and without learning – has been rather more controversial, and not all of those who accept his theory accept that part of it without reservation.

Nonetheless, Gibson made the essential point that if we are to understand perception in real life, we have to look at the interaction between individual and environment – at what perception is for. His theory was also taken as a starting point by Neisser (1976), although Neisser considered the contribution made by the individual perceiver to the perceptual process to be important too. We will be looking at Neisser's model at the end of this chapter, as it incorporates several other aspects of perception, including research into perceptual set and selective attention.

Pattern recognition

It is one thing to identify simple figures or shapes, but quite another to see regularities and patterns. Think, for example, of what you do when you read. You recognise, pretty well instantly, the patterns made by particular words, and sometimes whole sets of words. If you did not do this, fluent reading would be impossible. We recognise pattern in all sorts of other aspects of life too. Indeed, some researchers see pattern recognition as forming the basis of all coherent perception. Naturally, this has led to a number of theories about how pattern recognition takes place.

The template-matching approach

One general explanation for pattern recognition is known as the **template-matching theory**. This approach maintains that we have internalised 'templates' stored in our memory for any given pattern or shape. When we look at a pattern we match it up to these templates, choosing the one that is most similar as the indicator of what the pattern is or represents. Experience gives us a wider library of templates, and so we learn to recognise more and different patterns as we become more sophisticated perceivers.

   The main drawback of this explanation, however, is that this type of system would be very inflexible: it could not explain how we can still recognise characters or shapes which are different from the template (Figure 2.20), but when we are reading handwriting, say, this happens all the time. We would have to store an infinite number of templates in order to take account of all the possible variations of a given shape. The rate at which people read is usually about two hundred words per minute and this suggests that such a search through all the possibilities does not happen. If it did, it would be very difficult for us to read at any reasonable speed.

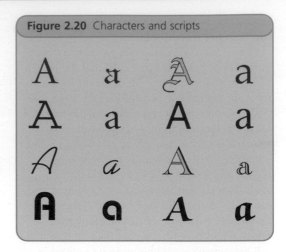

Figure 2.20 Characters and scripts

The distinctive-features approach

Another explanation for pattern recognition is the **distinctive-features** approach, sometimes referred to as the feature-detection approach. This involves the idea that we look for critical, special features, which will always occur in the target character even though several of its other features may vary. In this case, the whole form of the pattern is not so important. Instead, it is the distinctive features which matter, since pattern-recognition is entirely based on these. For example, we may look for a cross-bar on a handwritten letter 't' to identify the letter, and ignore all other aspects of the visual stimulus which are presented. Feature-detection approaches have formed the basis for a considerable amount of research into pattern perception, although to some extent they share many of the problems of template theory.

Prototype theories

The third major type of pattern recognition theory are **prototype** theories, in which patterns are still seen as being compared with mental representations, but this time with prototypes rather than templates. Prototypes are seen as being much more flexible than templates. They form idealised, abstract patterns which we use for comparison with any given stimulus – not looking for an exact match, but accepting something which resembles the prototype. We will be looking at this idea more closely in the chapter on representation, when we look at concept-formation; and we will find that it can sometimes provide a useful model to explain the recognition of letters and simple shapes.

The pandemonium model

One of the wide-scale theories which has been proposed to explain pattern recognition, and also some other aspects of perception, is the pandemonium model. It was first developed by Selfridge, in 1959, and it is a hierarchical model, based on feature-detection but also including some elements of prototype theories as well. It is based on the idea of the TOTE unit (see Box 2.1). The pandemonium model has been particularly applied to the problem of how we identify letters and numbers, given, as we saw before, how styles can be so very different yet still be perceived as the same letter.

The theory argues that on the very bottom level of the hierarchy is a layer of small **sub-demons**, each of which responds to a particular image or bit of sensory data. In the case of recognising a letter, this might be something like a line at a particular angle, or a special kind of curve. When a particular subdemon is stimulated, it 'shrieks'. But it can shriek loudly, or less loudly (it is unlikely that a demon would go so far as to shriek quietly!). If the triggering stimulus is very similar to the subdemon's particular feature, it will shriek very loudly, but if the stimulus is only slightly similar, then the shriek will be (relatively) quieter.

The second-to-bottom layer of the hierarchy consists of units of cognition which are responsible for specific tasks, such as recognising a particular letter. These units are known as **cognitive demons**. Each demon in sensitive to the shrieks of its own relevant set of subdemons. If their sub-demons shriek loudly enough, that will set the cognitive demons shrieking too, and the more subdemons who are shrieking at them, and the more loudly those subdemons are shrieking, the louder they will shriek. Since similar features could appear in more than one letter, it is likely that more than one cognitive demon will be set off by a stimulus letter, but only those cognitive demons responding to similar letters would be shrieking. Those responding to letters which are very different would not receive any, or enough, signals from their subdemons (Figure 2.21).

Box 2.1 The TOTE unit

The pandemonium model of cognition rests on the idea of the TOTE unit. This was proposed as a basic unit of behaviour by Miller *et al.*, in 1960, as an alternative to the mechanistic stimulus response links proposed by Watson (1913). TOTE stands for the four stages Test Operate Test Exit, which is shorthand for: (1) T Testing for a fit between the desired situation and the actual one; (2) initiating some kind of O Operation which is designed to bring the situation closer to what is wanted; (3) T Testing for fit again, and (4) if the fit is acceptable, E Exiting from that particular sequence. If the fit between what exists and what is desired still is not acceptable, the operating and testing stages would be repeated, as many times as were necessary.

Imagine a simple example: reaching out to take hold of a cup. First, you would test the situation by looking to see where your hand was and where the cup was, and whether they were in the same place. Then you would perform an operation to change the situation, by moving your arm muscles to bring your hand closer to the cup. Then you would test again, and perform another operation if the two still were not close enough. Finally, when your hand was round the cup, you would exit from that sequence of activity, and probably begin an entirely new TOTE unit to do with lifting the cup up and bringing it to your mouth.

Miller *et al.* suggested that this behavioural cycle is a more meaningful way of representing behaviour than a simple stimulus-response link, because it is self-correcting, and more appropriate for the complex kinds of behaviour which human beings and 'higher' animals show. Because smaller TOTE units can be nested inside the operation phase of the cycle, they argued that this model can also be used to analyse highly complex forms of behaviour, which are difficult to handle simply in terms of stimulus and response.

Figure 2.21 The pandemonium model

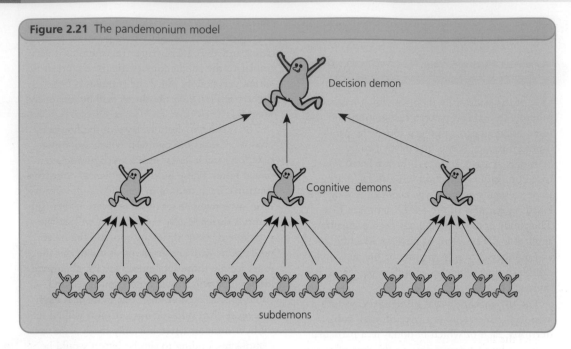

Decision demon

Cognitive demons

subdemons

The racket passes upwards in the hierarchy, to a **decision demon**. This demon has the task of deciding between all the different shrieking cognitive demons, and choosing which one seems to be the most appropriate. The cognitive demon which is shrieking loudest will be the one with the most features fitting the stimulus. As a result, it is most likely to be chosen by the decision demon. However, if there is some reason why that is not appropriate, the decision demon would listen to the other shrieking ones instead, and try out the next loudest. As you might imagine, all that shrieking would make things very noisy – hence the name of the theory!

The pandemonium theory provides one possible explanation for how feature-recognition systems can be involved to explain how we recognise complex patterns like words. In the same way that Marr's theory can tell us about how we perceive objects, and Gibson's theory can tell us how we go about perceiving in the real world, the pandemonium model can contribute to our understanding of how we perceive complex symbols.

There are other aspects to our perception, though. The theories of Marr, Gibson and Selfridge are all what we call bottom-up theories of perception. In other words, they explain perception by starting with the visual stimulus and its effects on the nerve cells of the visual system, and

piecing it together. But sometimes, we do not perceive what the stimulus material would imply. Human cognitive processes can be affected by many things, including personal factors and emotional states. Perception is no exception to this.

Perceptual set and perceptual inference

We are continually being bombarded with information from the world around us, which we have to make sense of somehow. But at any one moment there is far more information around us than we could take in: we need to select what we are going to notice, so that we can pay attention to what is relevant to us at any given moment.

One way that we achieve this is by 'focusing' our perception, so that we are more ready to perceive certain things than others. Cognitive processes can be put into a kind of state of readiness, which psychologists refer to as **set**. The word 'set' in this context is used in the same way as at the start of a race, where the athletes are told 'Get ready, get set, GO!': it means to be fully prepared and anticipating what is coming, so that we can act on it as effectively as possible. Memory, decision-making, reasoning, and learning can all be affected by set, and so can perception.

Perceptual set

In the 1950s, Jerome Bruner and his colleagues performed a number of intensive investigations of **perceptual set**. Their discoveries marked the very beginnings of what later became known as the cognitive revolution. They, and other psychologists who followed up this work, found that perception could be influenced by a variety of factors, ranging from simple expectation, to motivational states, personal attitudes, and even cultural values.

Expectation

In 1955, Bruner and Minturn showed how strongly expectations could influence perception. They began by showing people either letters or numbers, one at a time. Then they showed them an ambiguous figure, which could be read either as a B or as a 13 (see Figure 2.22). The research participants who had seen numbers unequivocally judged the figure to be a 13, while those who had seen letters previously saw it as a B. Moreover, when they were asked to reproduce what they had seen, their drawings showed no ambiguities: the gap in the figure was enlarged by those who believed it to be a 13, but those who believed it to be a B did not include any gap.

A similar study was done by Bugelski and Alampay in 1961, in which the participants in the research were shown either a series of animal pictures or a set of unrelated images – furniture, vehicles, and so on. When they were shown an ambiguous 'rat man' figure (Figure 2.23), people were significantly more likely to perceive it as a rat than as a man if they had experienced the prior exposure to animal pictures. Just seeing those figures had established an expectation that what

would follow would be more of the same thing, and that expectation had directed how they would perceive the stimulus.

Motivation

Sandford (1936) deprived research participants of food for various lengths of time up to four hours, and then showed them ambiguous pictures. Sandford found that the longer the participants had been food-deprived, the more likely they were to interpret the pictures as being something to do with food. A similar study by Gilchrist and Nesberg (1952) asked people to rate pictures for brightness, and found that the longer they had gone without food, the brighter the food pictures were rated, although the research participants' ratings of other pictures showed no change. These studies, and others of the same kind, implied that internal motivational states, in this case hunger, could directly affect perception.

Emotion

Reporting another study showing the effects of emotion on perception, Solley and Haigh (1958) described how children were asked to draw pictures of Santa Claus in the month leading up to Christmas and the month afterwards. The children's representations became larger and included more presents as Christmas approached, but shrank and included less detail after the season. This study implied that complex emotional states, such as anticipation and excitement, could also influence perceptual processes.

In 1951, Lazarus and McCleary performed a study which involved giving people minor electric

Figure 2.23 The rat-man

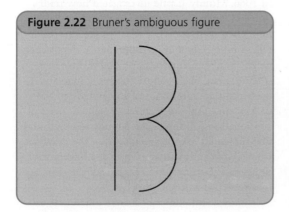

Figure 2.22 Bruner's ambiguous figure

shocks when they saw a particular nonsense syllable. This, naturally, produced an avoidance response to that syllable, which showed up in galvanic skin response measures (we will be looking more closely at these in the chapter on emotion). But Lazarus and McCleary showed that this response would also happen when those nonsense syllables were presented subliminally – so faintly that the research participants were not even aware that they had seen them. The implication was that the perceptual system could be affected by learning from previous experiences, even if the conscious mind was not involved.

Attitudes

Allport (1954) described a study which showed how prejudice could affect perception. The experimenters used a stereoscope, which is a device for presenting a separate picture to each eye at the same time. They showed their research participants mixed-race pairs of individuals, with one member of each pair shown to each eye. In general, people were most definite when they were picking out members of their own race, and more unsure when they were categorising people from other ethnic groups. But Afrikaaners, who were noted for their racial prejudices, differentiated far more sharply between the races. They perceived racial categories as very rigid, allowing for very few subcategories or uncertainties in classifying people. Allport interpreted this as showing how the strongly racist views held by these people had affected their perception.

Values and perceptual defence

In 1948, Postman, Bruner and McGinnies showed that sexual or other taboo words have higher **recognition thresholds** than ordinary words do. When their research participants were shown those words very quickly, they needed more microseconds to identify the taboo words than they did to identify the neutral ones. The researchers used a device known as a **tachisto-scope**, which presents stimuli for very brief, but measurable, periods of time.

Postman *et al.* argued that their findings were evidence for **perceptual defence** – the idea that our perceptual system tries to protect us against threatening or disturbing stimuli, by making them more difficult to identify. But Bitterman and Kniffin (1953) found that the time difference in recognition disappeared if people were allowed to

write down their responses instead of saying them out loud. They argued from this that the higher perceptual threshold was not really perceptual defence, but was simply a **response bias**. The research participants were simply unwilling to say rude words out loud.

The debate continued until a study by Worthington (1969) showed that perceptual defence did seem to be a real phenomenon. The research participants in this study were not asked to say any words at all. Instead, words were presented subliminally – so faintly that the research participants were entirely unaware of them. They were embedded in the centre of a dot of light projected on to a screen. Dots were presented in pairs, and all the research participants had to do was to say which dot was brighter or dimmer, or whether they were both the same. Worthington found that the dots with taboo words embedded in them were systematically rated as being dimmer than those with neutral words, even though the participants in the study were not aware of having seen any words at all.

Carpenter, Wiener and Carpenter (1956) asked people to complete sentences on sensitive topics, such as feelings of inadequacy, hostility or sex. From this, the participants in the study were categorised as being either 'sensitive' or 'repressed' in those areas. They found that participants showed differences in their reactions to stimuli: 'sensitive' people perceived taboo or disturbing words more easily than normal ones; while 'repressed' people perceived such words less readily. This study, too, suggests that personal differences in values and attitudes can influence perception strongly.

Culture and perception

In 1966, Mundy-Castle investigated how traditional Ghanaian children interpreted line drawings. They were shown a series of sketches, each of which used only a limited number of depth cues: height in plane, superposition and relative size (Figure 2.24). Each picture showed a man and a deer in the foreground, and an elephant in the background, and the pictures contained different combinations of these cues. Mundy-Castle found that the children's interpretations of the drawings were significantly different from the interpretations made by European children of the same ages (between five and ten years old).

Mundy-Castle described these differences as

Figure 2.24 Pictorial depth perception

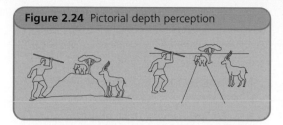

Figure 2.25 Perspectives of an elephant

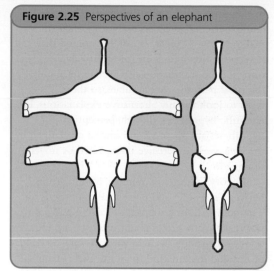

'errors' in interpreting the drawings, but it was noticeable that they were generally of the same kind. In particular, the children generally did not interpret cues which a Westerner would take as indicating depth, such as perspective lines intended to indicate a road going off into the distance. Some aspects of the drawings did seem to mean something, though. The children could tell that the deer was a kind of animal, and tended to name it after familiar ones, calling it, for example, a goat or a camel.

Perspective as a cultural artefact

Deregowski (1972) argued that perceiving perspective-based drawings is a specific cultural skill, which is learned rather than automatic. In fact, he argued, people from several cultures world-wide seem to prefer drawings which do not show perspective, but instead are split so as to show both sides of an object at the same time. In one study, children and adults from traditional African backgrounds were shown two pictures of an elephant: one as an elephant might look from above, and the other from the same viewpoint but with all four of the elephant's legs splayed out unrealistically. The participants in the study preferred the split drawing, even though to Western eyes it looked quite unrealistic (Figure 2.25).

Deregowski argued that this split-style representation is universal, and is even found in young European children, before they are taught not to draw that way. One possible explanation which Deregowski suggested was that such a style might allow for all the important characteristics of the object to be shown. The drawing would then be a way of representing someone's real experience of an object far more fully than a standard perspective drawing would.

Revisiting Gibson and Marr

If we look at other aspects of these findings, we can link some of them with the theories of perception which we looked at earlier in this chapter. It was noticeable, for instance, that the drawings did not include textural depth cues: when they did, as in photographs, the participants from traditional cultures had no trouble interpreting them. This could be seen as supporting Gibson's view of textural cues as all-important in real-life perceiving.

Another interesting point is the way that children could always recognise that a drawing was meant to be an animal, even though they were not familiar with line drawings. It may be that such a drawing is close enough to a basic stick-figure representation, as suggested by Marr, to be interpreted easily. If Marr is correct, that kind of representation would always be easy to interpret, because it is so close to the basic decoding system that we use anyway. But whatever the reasons for these findings, we can see that the culture we belong to can be a strong influence on our perception.

Gregory's inferential theory of perception

In 1973, Gregory argued that perception was more than simply the decoding of information received by the visual system. Instead, it is a process of making inferences about the data – developing reasonable guesses on the basis of what is most probable, or likely. As we have already seen, Gibson disagreed profoundly with this view; but the research into perceptual set, cultural influence and the like does imply that sometimes, higher mental processes do influence perception.

Gregory's is a **top-down theory** of perception,

in the sense that he considered prior knowledge and experience to be crucially important in making sense of what we see. He argued that perceptual hypotheses are 'most probable' explanations for the stimulation that we are receiving. For the most part, they are accurate, so there is no need to look for any alternative explanations. Like scientific hypotheses, though, perceptual hypotheses are tentative and can be challenged by the data: we can perceive unexpected or novel things too.

Gregory identified a number of similarities between scientific and perceptual hypothesising. The comparisons are given in Table 2.2. We do not make many errors about what we are looking at in ordinary life, because we have such a wealth of detailed information to go on. But perceptual hypotheses are based on the information available, so if we only have restricted information, then perception is more likely to go wrong. Table 2.2 also gives comparisons of inappropriate hypothesising, in scientific investigation and in perception.

The importance of visual illusions

It was by considering cases where the perceptual system's hypothesising is inappropriate that Gregory came to look so closely at **visual illusions**. He saw these illusions as giving us valuable clues to the mechanisms of normal perception. By looking at the types of errors which the brain makes under conditions of restricted stimulation, we would be able to discover important information about the way that the brain was operating the perceptual system. But not all illusions would be equally useful in that respect. Gregory made a distinction between illusions which depend on physiological mechanisms, and those which arise from cognitive strategies.

Mechanism illusions

Mechanism illusions occur as a direct consequence of the physical characteristics of the visual system. For example: continuous sensory stimulation produces **negative after-images**, in which the opposite sensation is experienced after the original stimulus has ceased. So looking at a patch of red for a long time produces a green after-image when you look away, and looking at a blue one produces a yellow after-image. These colours occur opposite one another in the colour spectrum, and the fact that they are also produced by

Table 2.2 Scientific and perceptual hypotheses

Appropriate scientific hypotheses may:	Appropriate perception may:
1 Allow signals to be used as data	Process sensory signals as data
2 Derive facts from data	Infer objects from sensory data
3 Generalise from data to wider instances	Generalise from data, allowing perceptual learning
4 Provide logical, deductive inferences	Allow perceptual inferences
5 Settle ambiguities in sets of data	Use sensory data to settle ambiguities
6 Resolve apparent paradoxes	Use sensory data to resolve paradoxes
7 Create novelty; i.e. discovery or invention	Generate appropriate novelty

Inappropriate scientific hypotheses may:	Inappropriate perception may:
1 Distort or ignore data from signals	Fail to process sensory signals as data
2 Distort or ignore facts from data	Fail to infer objects from sensory data
3 Derive misleading generalisations from data	Give misleading generalisations
4 Generate misleading inferences	Give fallacious perceptual inferences
5 Generate unnecessary ambiguity	Fail to settle ambiguities
6 Generate paradoxes	Fail to resolve paradoxes
7 Generate in-appropriate novelty	Create inappropriate novelty

Source: Gregory, 1973

the visual system as a result of over-stimulation has some interesting implications for our understanding of colour vision, which we will be looking at in Chapter 12.

Negative after-images also occur with movement. If we look at something which is continuously moving in one direction, we experience the **waterfall effect**, in which it seems as though stationary objects are moving in the opposite direction. You can get this from looking at a waterfall for a long time, of course; but you may also get it when a train stops at a station after you have been looking out of the window for a long time. Any continuous movement, as long as it only goes in one direction and carries on for long enough, will produce the waterfall effect. These illusions are not anything to do with hypotheses or inference. Instead, they arise from the way that sensory mechanisms adapt to the stimulation that they are receiving.

Similarly, another well-known illusion, the **autokinetic effect**, occurs as a side-effect of normal eye movement. This effect occurs if we look at a point of light in an otherwise totally dark room. The light appears to move around, and the effect has been used to good effect by social psychologists, to study conformity. The autokinetic effect happens because our eyes are continuously making small tremors and jerks. They help to make sure that our eyes do not become habituated to the stimulus that we are looking at, because if they did, the nerve cells would stop firing and we would not be able to see it after a while. When we are looking at things in normal light we do not notice these slight movements, but if we look at a point of light in a dark room, we do not have a background for reference, and the light appears to jerk about.

The **phi phenomenon** is an illusion in which two alternately flashing lights are seen as having continuous movement between them. It is used extensively in illuminated advertising signs and notices, to give an impression of movement. Gregory explained this as arising from normal perceptual mechanisms. If we are tracking a moving stimulus – that is, watching it continually – our perceptual system is designed to allow for brief interruptions of the stimulus. For example, if we were watching an animal moving in a wood, the visual image of the animal would appear and disappear as it passed behind the trees. So when we see lights flashing on and off, the visual system interprets the stimulus as continuous movement, passing behind obstacles.

Mechanism illusions, then, do not need to be explained in terms of perceptual inference. There are perfectly good explanations for them in what we know of how the visual system works. But there are other kinds of illusions which, according to Gregory, illustrate very clearly just how cognitive inference is involved in the perceptual system. These illusions happen as the cognitive system adopts inappropriate strategies for interpreting the stimulus.

Strategy illusions

There are several different types of strategy illusions, and one of the main types that Gregory identified occurs because of the perceptual process known as **perceptual constancy**. The retinal image that we receive of any given object can have a different shape, size or even colour depending on the circumstances in which we are viewing it. But we perceive it as constant, and do not notice these variations. A teacup seen from two different angles, for example, makes two very different shapes on the retina, but because we apply constancy scaling, we make allowances for the change in perspective (Figure 2.26). If we look at a car under an orange street light, our eyes receive light of a very different wavelength than the same car reflects in daylight, yet we see the car as being the same colour.

Perhaps the most well-known group of strategy illusions which Gregory identified are the illusions which seem to arise because of inappropriate constancy scaling. In our earlier discussion of depth perception and the Müller-Lyer illusion, we saw how depth cues can produce misleading interpretations of geometric figures. Gregory (1963) argued that many of these **geometric illusions** arise because depth cues in the stimulus mean that it is unconsciously interpreted as if it were three-dimensional. The Ponzo illusion is a classic example in this respect. The lines of the drawing conjure up an illusion of perspective, and the illusion becomes even stronger if it is superimposed on a photograph or real-life scene (Figure 2.27).

A second group of strategy illusions occurs with **ambiguous** figures. The most famous example of

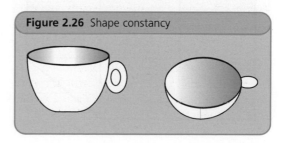

Figure 2.26 Shape constancy

Figure 2.27 The Ponzo illusion

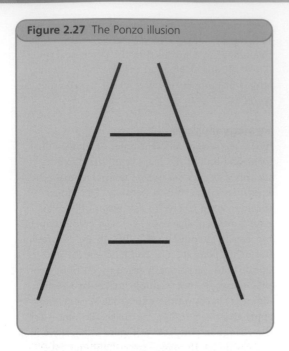

Photograph: © Philip Clark

these is the Necker cube, which is a line drawing of a cube-shape which appears to change its orientation as we look at it (Figure 2.28). The shaded side seems to flip backwards and forwards as we look steadily at it, and this flipping occurs even if we are trying not to let it happen. Gregory argued that the fact that the figure appears to change without any conscious decision on the part of the perceiver showed how perception is all about hypothesis-testing. In this case, both perceptual hypotheses are equally plausible, and the brain

is unable to decide between the two, so it switches backwards and forwards between them.

A third type of strategy illusion is the **paradoxical illusion**. These consist of figures which seem plausible when we look at them, but which are impossible to make in real-life. The 'impossible triangle' figure is a well-known example of this type of illusion (Figure 2.29). Gregory argues that these illusions happen because the brain uses cues to make assumptions about the information, but the assumptions that it makes contradict one other. In the case of the impossible triangle figure, the brain assumes that the figure represents a three-

Figure 2.28 The Necker cube

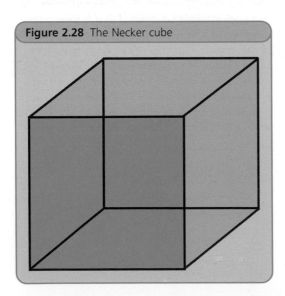

Figure 2.29 The impossible triangle

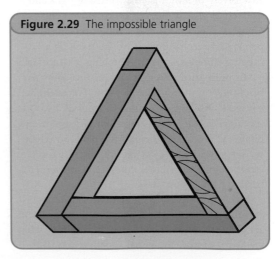

dimensional object. But it also assumes that the two ends of the triangle are at the same distance away and connected with one another. This creates a paradox, which results in the illusion. Paradoxical illusions were used to great effect by the artist M.C. Escher, in many famous paintings.

Another type of strategy illusion is produced creatively by our own perceptual processes. One clear example of this is the 'invisible triangle', where a triangle shape is suggested by surrounding stimuli, and it appears so clearly to the perceiver that the area of the triangle even seems to stand out from the paper or surface on which it is presented (Figure 2.30). Gregory argued that these **creative illusions** are additional evidence for the hypothesis-testing nature of perception.

Gregory gives several other examples of how cognitive strategies may be misapplied to produce illusions, although there is not space to go into them here. We can see, though, that his theory is very different from those put forward by Marr, Gibson and Selfridge. The main difference is the way that he sees perception as a top-down process, rather than a bottom-up one.

Gregory's theory is not the only top-down theory of perception. There are many more, including the important theory put forward by Ulrich Neisser. But since that theory brings together psychological findings about selective attention as well as perceptual set and objective forms of perception, we will be looking at it at the end of this chapter.

As we saw earlier, Gibson objected strenuously to the idea that perception involved hypothesis-testing. But Gibson was talking about the kind of perception which we use as we move about in the real world, while Gregory's theory deals with a very different type of perception. In 1964, Tulving, Mandler and Baumal performed a study which showed quite neatly how both top-down and bottom-up strategies can be involved in perception. In their study, research participants were asked to identify words that they were shown, and to do so as quickly and accurately as possible. The experimenters varied two things about the word: one was the exposure time – how long people were given to look at it. The other was its context – how much of a relevant sentence for the word had been shown to the research participants beforehand.

Not surprisingly, perhaps, both exposure time and context had an effect on how accurately the research participants perceived the words. They were more inclined to make use of the contextual information if the word was only presented very briefly. Increasing either the context or the duration of the stimulus improved their performance. What the study showed was that in conditions of uncertainty or ambiguity, top-down processing became important. But under clearer conditions, top-down processing was irrelevant, and did not matter.

The debate between Marr, Gibson and Gregory is about how much it matters in ordinary, everyday perception, but all perceptual stimuli are not the same. Some are much more ambiguous or puzzling than others, and it is with those that top-down processing comes into play.

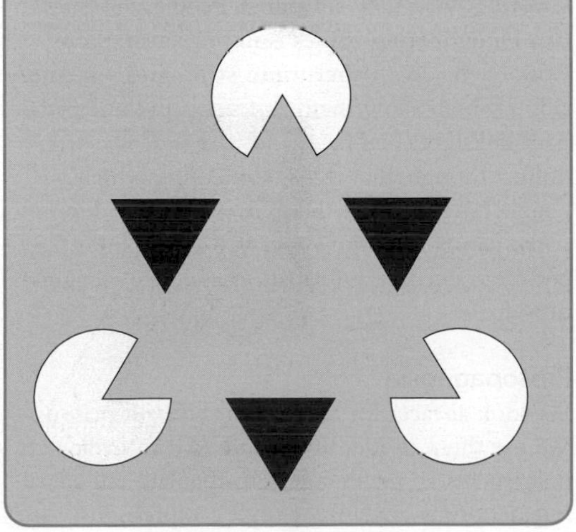

Face recognition

One area of research which forms an interesting link between top-down and bottom-up theories of perception is the study of how we go about recognising faces. Recognising people from their faces is something that we do quite automatically, yet when researchers analyse it, they find that it actually involves a number of very complex tasks. For instance, we can recognise the same person several years later, when their facial features have become changed with age; and we have no difficulty in recognising the same face even though it may be showing wildly different emotional expressions. This might seem straightforward, but

Figure 2.30 The invisible triangle

programming a computer to do that would be very difficult indeed, because human faces are so mobile and variable.

In general terms, it seems that we rely more on features from the upper part of the face, like hair or eyes; but Haig (1984) showed that the way that these features are combined is also important. By using a computer display which could be adjusted, Haig showed that it takes only a slight change in the spacing of features to affect whether we will recognise a face or not (Figure 2.31). When we are recognising faces that are familiar to us, we seem to use a combination of descriptive cues. Some of these are about the particular features of the face itself, such as the colour of the eyes or the shape of the mouth, while others are about the spacing between the different features.

Ellis, Shepherd and Davies (1979) found that when we are recognising familiar faces, we tend to concentrate more on the internal features of a face, like eyes, nose and mouth. When we are recognising unfamiliar faces, though, we concentrate more on external features like hair and chin. In fact, it seems as though we recognise familiar and unfamiliar faces in completely different ways, involving different cognitive mechanisms.

Face recognition units

Bruce and Young (1986) explored the implications of this, and other evidence, and suggested that we develop a **face recognition unit** for identifying people that we know. Faces of strangers do not have recognition units, and so when we are recognising those, we have to fall back on descriptive criteria, such as hair colour, to know whether we have seen that face (or a picture of it) before. This could also explain why we do not usually notice facial resemblances between our friends, although we often notice strangers who look like people

that we know. We have a special recognition unit for each friend, so their faces only stimulate their own unit. But the faces of strangers can trigger off other recognition units because they do not have one of their own.

Recognising faces and remembering names

A face recognition unit of this kind includes deeper knowledge about that person, and perhaps also our own feelings about them, such as whether we liked or disliked them. This is **semantic information** – in other words, it is meaningful information about how the stimulus actually affects us. It is different from remembering someone's name, which is only a descriptive label, and does not usually have any personal meaning.

Semantic information comes to us very quickly when we see someone we know, but remembering their name can take much longer! Bruce and Valentine (1985) showed that names are not very good for 'priming' recognition either. In one study, they showed how people would recognise a face quickly if they had seen another picture of it before, even if that picture was taken from a different angle. But reading the person's name, even just before seeing the picture, did not at all shorten the time they took to identify the face.

From this and many similar studies, Bruce and Young suggested that we do not have a direct, automatic link between a name and a face. Instead, putting names to faces has to be processed through other semantic information, like knowledge about where that person lives, or what they do. But we do have a link between recognising a face and knowing something about that person. We can know why they matter to us, without knowing what they are called. People who find that remembering names is important in their work often adopt **mnemonic strategies** – memory aids – which allow them to form rapid independent links between faces and names. It is worth noting, though, that this is something which people have to teach themselves to do. It does not come naturally, in the same way as the link between semantic information and face recognition does.

Prosopagnosia

We look at faces for all sorts of different reasons. We use them to identify friends and to make judgements about strangers; to regulate our social interaction by analysing people's expressions; and

Figure 2.31 Spacing of facial features

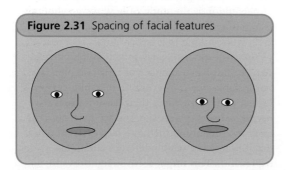

to help us to understand speech. Bruce and Young suggest that these are all separate functions. What we think of as face recognition actually involves a number of separate processes, which make independent connections with the general cognitive system. Part of the evidence for this idea comes from studying people with clinical disorders concerned with their facial recognition ability. This disorder is known as **prosopagnosia**.

One patient studied by Bruyer *et al.* (1983) could copy drawings of faces, identify whether a set of photographs taken from different angles were of the same person, and had no difficulty making sense out of, or copying, facial expressions. But he could not recognise the faces of people that he knew. By contrast, a patient studied by Malone *et al.* (1982) had no problems identifying familiar faces but could not match up photographs of unfamiliar ones, taken at different angles or with slightly different expressions. Shuttleworth, Syring and Allen (1982) studied a patient who was completely unable to identify familiar faces, but did not have any problem in identifying facial expressions.

The basic perceptual image

There seems to be something very basic about our tendency to respond to faces. As we will see when we look at child development, infants respond very powerfully to images which are arranged to look like human faces – even if the image is as simple as a couple of dots and lines in an oval shape. In fact, even very tiny babies will respond to face-like stimuli. Goren, Sarty and Wu (1975) showed that infants as young as nine minutes old would turn their head and eyes to follow a moving face-like pattern; but they were less likely to do it for one in which the features were scrambled. Such early programming implies that attending to faces is a very basic skill indeed.

Bruce (1988) suggested that a simple representation of a face, involving perhaps just two dots and a line arranged appropriately, could represent a 'primitive' sketch of a face in the same way as Marr suggested that stick figures do for objects. This would mean that such an image would be one of the most basic forms in decoding visual images, so perhaps it should not be surprising that infants are so prepared to respond to it. Moreover, there is a strong survival value for any social animal in being able to recognise faces of its own kind: if you are helpless and dependent, it is useful to be able to distinguish those parts of your environment which are likely to look after you!

All this clinical evidence does seem to suggest that face recognition involves several perceptual processing systems, rather than just one. Some of these perceptual units may be 'bottom-up', like the ability to know that what you are looking at is actually a face; and some of them may be 'top-down', involving our prior experience and knowledge. Recognising that something actually is a face may be hard-wired into our perceptual system, so we are attuned to it from birth. That would depend on bottom-up processing of the elements of the image.

Recognising people that we have met before, however, involves using a different kind of information: memories of our past experience, knowledge of how changes happen with age and also, sometimes, the social contexts in which we meet them. This is 'top-down' information: we do not just work out the information from the immediate stimulus available to us – we apply prior knowledge to interpret the sensory data. So our responses to faces in everyday life draw on both top-down and bottom-up processing mechanisms – and it is likely that this applies to most other forms of perception, as well.

Attention

From the very earliest years of psychology, psychologists have been interested in how we notice certain things rather than others, and what is happening when we 'pay attention' to something. James (1890) proposed that we can only really attend to one thing at a time: when we try to do two things at once, we are successful only if one of them has become so familiar that it is 'habitual', and we do not have to take much notice of it. We will be coming back to this idea later in this chapter.

William James and the other early psychologists who studied attention used the method of **introspection** – examining their own experience in detail. But this method is very open to subjective bias, which can be subtle and quite unconscious; and also, as we saw in Chapter 1, the behaviourists considered it to be unscientific. Consequently, when the behaviourist revolution occurred in the early years of this century, the study of attention was abandoned, and it was not until WWII that it was really taken up again.

As a result of the rapid technological changes that had occurred in the war, researchers began to be concerned with how people could make the most efficient use of technology. One major problem, for instance, was the way that operators of radar scanning devices needed to scan signals coming in, and to distinguish important information from the random 'noise' which is caused by atmospheric conditions. It was important for those in charge to know how long someone could keep up a task like this without making mistakes, since a mistake could be disastrous.

The new research was helped, too, by the development of technological advances like the development of the tape-recorder, which made it possible to control the stimuli to which research participants were exposed, allowing for a much more rigorous investigation of the factors involved. As a result of these new circumstances, the study of attention came back into psychology.

Vigilance

In 1950, Mackworth reported a series of studies which had investigated how long someone could keep up a boring task and still remain vigilant and alert. Mackworth set up a series of **signal detection tasks**, which involved the research participants pressing a small key when they noticed a particular signal. The signal might be a visual one, like an image on a radar screen; or it could be an auditory one, like a sustained tone. In a typical auditory signal detection task, the person might hear a series of tones of exactly the same length (usually about two seconds). But every now and then, a tone would be sounded which was about half a second longer than the others. That was the signal which the research participant had to indicate, by pressing the key.

By comparing the signals given with the participant's responses and counting errors, Mackworth could keep a record of whether they were managing to sustain their attention. If their attention wandered, they would be more likely to make mistakes. This might seem obvious, but the fact that this cognitive process could be inferred in this way was another factor which allowed the study of a mental process, like attention, to be accepted in spite of the behaviourist domination of the time. Mackworth showed that it was possible to make an **operational definition** of attention, using objective, observable data. Studying atten-

tion did not have to be a woolly, introspective process.

Mackworth's signal detection tasks revealed that there were a number of factors which affected how long someone could maintain vigilance. Typically, a research participant would start off accurately, but as time went on they would make increasing numbers of mistakes. Mackworth referred to this as their **performance decrement**. The longer the task continued, the greater this performance decrement would become.

Conditioning and performance decrement

Several different explanations of these findings were put forward. Mackworth himself explained performance decrement using the concept of inhibition. We will come across inhibition when we look in more detail at classical conditioning, and also when we look at how nerve cells function; but briefly, it is the idea that a response will die away if it occurs repeatedly without being explicitly strengthened. Mackworth argued that the research participants were producing a conditioned response to the key which they used to signal the errors, and that the response died away because it was not being reinforced by knowledge of results. Conditioning was a very popular type of explanation for human behaviour at that time.

But there are a number of weaknesses in this explanation, not least being the way that the person's accuracy would increase if the signal was presented more often. If what was happening really was extinction because of lack of reinforcement, then that should produce more errors, not fewer. Also, of course, although people became more inaccurate, the response never completely died out, which a conditioned response would have done (we will be looking at conditioning more closely in Chapter 18).

Vigilance and arousal

An alternative explanation is in terms of the level of **autonomic arousal** which was being experienced by the research participant. Mackworth, and later researchers too, had found that performance decrement could be reduced in a number of different ways, which are summarised in Table 2.3. Almost all of these factors are the kind of things which make the person more 'keyed-up' and alert, a state which is generally referred to as arousal (see Chapter 13). If people are alert in this way, they may be less likely to make mistakes. But if

Table 2.3 Reducing performance decrement

Influencing agent	Decrement reduced by:
Task factors	
Signal intensity	Brighter signals
Signal duration	Longer signals
Spatial probability	Signal near centre of display
Individual factors	
Feedback on performance	Any feedback, either true or false
Stimulant drugs (amphetamine)	Moderate doses
Eysenck personality scores	High introversion
Situational factors	
Environmental noise	Moderate disturbance (e.g. phones)
Social surroundings	Presence of others (esp. superiors

Source: Mackworth, 1950

they are less aroused – perhaps because they have become bored or sleepy – they can make mistakes very easily.

A study by Stroh (1971) involved measuring alpha rhythms in the EEG patterns which people showed while doing a vigilance task. Alpha rhythms are patterns of brain activity which occur when people are awake but relaxed, so a high level of alpha activity is quite a good indication that someone is calm and not experiencing physiological arousal. A simple version of the 'arousal' explanation would predict that people would be more accurate if they were aroused, so the presence of alpha rhythms would suggest that they were more likely to make mistakes.

In fact, Stroh found that people varied in their responses, although these variations were not random. Analysing the data, Stroh found that it was possible to sort responses to the task into three groups. One group of research participants had performed as predicted: if they showed high alpha activity, then they were likely to miss the next signal that they were shown. A second group showed no difference at all in their responses to signals preceded by alpha activity and their responses to those which were not; and a third group of participants showed the opposite. In this

group, a higher level of alpha activity seemed to mean that they became more accurate, not less!

When the results were examined more closely, Stroh found that the first group consisted mainly of older, calmer individuals, while the third group was mainly composed of young, highly neurotic people. Govier (1980) suggested that these findings could be explained in terms of the Yerkes-Dodson theory of arousal and performance, which suggests that arousal only improves performance up to a point. Too much arousal can interfere with performance, as we will see in Chapter 13. The older group of research participants were not particularly aroused in the first place, so when they became more alert, they performed more accurately. The younger group, however, were already experiencing a high level of arousal, and Govier suggested that they were on the other side of the inverted-U curve. Any increase in arousal level, therefore, meant that they did worse, not better, because they were becoming too agitated to be fully efficient.

The study of sustained attention, or vigilance, was one which had tremendous military significance. As a result, considerable resources were put into its study: Mackworth's reports summarised a great deal of research which had gone on during the war years, and subsequently. By showing that researchers could use operational definitions of attention, such as the ability to report a signal accurately, these researchers had opened the whole topic up to psychological study. Like Bruner's research into perceptual set, they showed how cognitive processes were not mystical, but could be studied objectively; and in so doing, helped to provide the groundwork for the cognitive revolution of the 1970s.

Selective attention

The other form of attention which attracted researchers as a result of the technological developments of WWII was that of selective attention. Where radar operators needed to be able to attend accurately to relatively monotonous displays for long periods of time, aeroplane pilots needed to be able to select the relevant information accurately from the mass of information presented on dials in the cockpit. Because they often needed to respond very quickly in situations where any mistake could be fatal, it was important to find out how people select and react to relevant information. So researchers began to investigate just how it is that we channel our attention, and can focus on just one stimulus amidst a plethora of other stimuli.

Selective attention, of course, is not limited to aeroplane pilots: it is something that we do every day. If you have ever made a tape-recording of someone speaking in a crowded place, you will probably have found that the background noise almost drowned out what the speaker was saying. But if you are actually in that sort of situation, you do not have any trouble: the conversation that you are listening to seems to stand out very clearly.

After the war, a series of studies commenced which investigated how people manage to pay attention to more than one stimulus at a time. In 1953, Cherry developed the **dichotic listening task**, in which research participants were simultaneously presented with two entirely different messages, using headphones which sent one message to one ear, and the other message to the other ear. The person receiving this information would be asked to repeat the message which was coming into one particular ear, out loud. This practice, which was called **shadowing**, allowed researchers to check which message they were attending to at any one time.

Another task designed to investigate selective attention was the **split-span task**, developed by Broadbent in 1958. These tasks also involved presenting research participants with two different types of information, using headphones. But in split-span tasks, the information concerned was pairs of digits, either letters or numbers, which were presented simultaneously. The right ear would receive one digit of the pair, while the left ear received the other; and the participants were

simply asked to say what they heard. But they were not asked to concentrate on one ear or the other.

Both methods of investigation seemed to indicate that people selected which message to attend to on the basis of the channel which was being used. Cherry found that people performing dichotic listening tasks were usually unaware of what had been in the unattended message, although they could sometimes identify its general physical characteristics, such as whether it was speech or noises, or whether the voice was male or female. Broadbent found that if people were asked to recall the digits they had heard in split-span studies, they would always recall the set that had been presented to one ear only. It seemed that the physical characteristics of the message, and in particular which channel it arrived on, determined whether it was attended to or not.

Broadbent's filter theory

Broadbent (1958) used these findings to create a model of selective attention. The model proposed that incoming information goes through a filter before being processed semantically (that is, for meaning) by the brain. This filter cuts out messages if they do not have the right physical characteristics (Figure 2.32). So, for example, if someone is listening to a message coming to their right ear, the information coming in through the left ear will be filtered out, and not analysed for meaning.

Broadbent's model, however, was rapidly shown to be inadequate. Gray and Wedderburn (1960) performed a set of split-span studies in which the units presented were combinations of words and numbers, Moreover, these combined units had

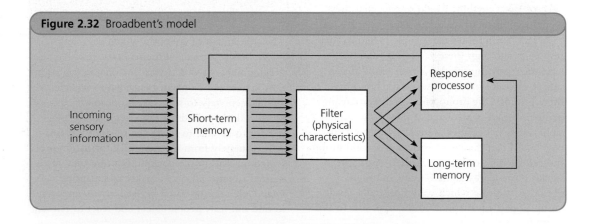

Figure 2.32 Broadbent's model

Incoming sensory information → Short-term memory → Filter (physical characteristics) → Response processor / Long-term memory

some meaning, although achieving that meaning required the person's attention to shift from one ear to another. So, for example, a participant in this study might hear 'dear four Jane' in one ear, and 'three aunt five' in the other.

Gray and Wedderburn found that their research participants would always report having heard a meaningful combination – in this case, either 'three four five' or, more usually, 'dear aunt Jane' – regardless of how it had changed its physical characteristics. The same thing happened when the different syllables of complete words were mixed with random digits. Even though the syllables were presented to different ears, the person would combine them and report hearing the whole word.

As research continued, it became apparent that people were not totally oblivious to the information in the unattended message, either. Moray (1959) discovered that they would pick up information from the unattended channel in a dichotic listening task, if it contained a stimulus which was personally important. About one-third of the time, for instance, people would detect their own name in the unattended channel. This became known as the **cocktail party phenomenon**, since cocktail parties, which were popular at that time, typically involved a number of conversations going on at the same time. Although any one person would only attend to the conversation that they were actually in, they would often hear their own name if someone else nearby said it. The rest of the conversation would be filtered out, but their own name would pass through the filtering.

Triesman's attenuation theory

If Broadbent's theory were correct, neither Gray and Wedderburn's findings, nor the cocktail party phenomenon would be possible. Broadbent's theory maintained that information was filtered on the basis of physical characteristics, before it was ever analysed for meaning. But these other researchers showed that meaningful information did sometimes get through. So clearly the filter was not screening out everything with the wrong physical characteristics.

Triesman (1964) proposed an alternative: that information with inappropriate physical characteristics was not actually filtered out, but that it was weakened, or **attenuated**, by the filter. Information would go through the physical filter first, which would weaken information with the wrong physical characteristics so that it was less likely to be noticed. Then it would pass through a second-stage analyser, which would process the information semantically. If an attentuated signal was special enough, it would be strengthened again. But most attenuated information would not be particularly significant to the listener, and so it would not get any further than the second-stage analyser (Figure 2.33).

Triesman proposed that the second-stage analyser worked by activating **dictionary units**, which analysed words or concepts. Some of these – the significant ones – would have a low **threshold of response**, which means that they would be triggered off very easily. But words which were less important would have a high threshold of response: they would need a very

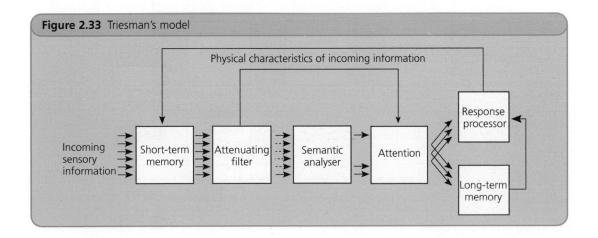

Figure 2.33 Triesman's model

strong signal to trigger off their dictionary unit. What would make the signal stronger would be if it had the powerful physical characteristics, like being louder or more distinctive than the information in the attended channel. The idea of dictionary units with changeable thresholds of response allowed Triesman to explain why it was that some information could still be noticed even if the person was not paying attention at the time.

There were a number of other studies which supported the idea that unattended information was processed semantically. In one study, Triesman asked her research participants to attend to a story being played to one ear, while a different message was played to the other ear. At some point, the messages changed over, so that the story was now continued in the other ear. Triesman found that the participants would automatically continue shadowing the story, but that they were often completely unaware that they had changed over (Triesman, 1960).

In another study, in 1964, Triesman used bilingual research participants who were equally fluent in French and English. She played a French message to one ear and an English message to the other. Sometimes, both of the messages had the same meaning. Although the participants were asked to shadow only one of these messages, she found that they usually knew if the other message had the same meaning. It was apparent that they were still processing both messages for meaning,

even if they were not consciously attending to one of them.

The pertinence model of selective attention

Although Triesman's attenuation model provided a reasonable explanation for these experimental findings, some researchers found it unnecessarily complex. An alternative model put forward by Deutsch and Deutsch, in 1963, and later revised by Norman (1976), proposed that there was no need for the existence of an initial attenuating filter, followed by a second-stage filter analysing information semantically. Instead, they proposed a model in which the filtering happened much later in the whole process. According to this model, all incoming information was analysed semantically, and assessed in terms of whether it was pertinent or not. Irrelevant information was filtered out later on (Figure 2.34).

The implication of this model is that all incoming information, regardless of its physical characteristics, is processed semantically. There was some experimental evidence supporting this idea. For example, Moray (1969) described a study in which research participants were shown a neutral word accompanied by a mild electric shock. Naturally, this produced stress, and this stress could be measured using a **galvanic skin response** (GSR) meter (see Chapter 13). After a few trials, the research participants would produce a strong galvanic skin response whenever they saw or heard the word. This was an example of straightforward classical conditioning.

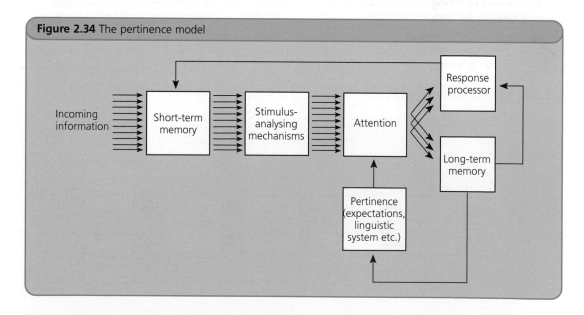

Figure 2.34 The pertinence model

Later, these research participants were asked to perform a set of dichotic listening tasks. In some of these tasks, the word to which they had been conditioned to respond was in the unattended message. Moray found that the participants would produce the GSR reaction if the word occurred in the unattended message, even though they were not consciously aware of having heard it. This was taken as evidence that the information was being processed semantically at an early stage.

Moray's study, however, does not really allow us to distinguish between the attenuation model and the pertinence model, since either could explain the results. The word would have acquired considerable personal significance for each research participant as a result of the electric shock, so it could be explained as passing through an attenuating filter. Moreover, the use of classical conditioning through electric shock means that the reaction might not have been a cognitive process at all, but could have been a much more basic pain-avoiding conditioned reflex. Even a flatworm, which does not have a brain at all, can learn to avoid things which give it an electric shock. So we do not need to talk about mental processing to explain why the research participants responded to the stimulus.

A later study, by Corteen and Wood (1972), however, showed that there could be semantic processing involved. Like Moray, they conditioned research participants to react to particular words by coupling the words with a mild electric shock. But then, instead of testing their participants by exposing them to the same words, they exposed them instead to **synonyms** of the words – words which had the same meaning – in the unattended part of a dichotic listening task. The research participants showed a GSR reaction to the synonyms, and this would not have been possible without semantic processing.

In terms of choosing between the two models, the Corteen and Wood study slightly favoured the pertinence model over the attenuation model, since it would seem a little clumsy to assume that the synonym of a word associated with an electric shock had also had its dictionary unit strengthened. But it is not impossible. In fact, either of these models can explain the experimental findings. As a general rule, we might favour the pertinence model because it is more **parsimonious** – in other words, it can explain things more simply and elegantly – but many researchers feel that

Triesman's idea of dictionary units is a useful concept, which can help us to understand word-recognition as well as selective attention.

Limited-capacity models of attention

An alternative to the filter models of selective attention was put forward by Norman and Bobrow, in 1975. They argued that the reason why we notice some things and not others is because we have only a limited capacity for our attention – there is a limit to how much we can take in at any one time. So rather than having a 'bottleneck', which channels the information through filters, they propose that the reason why we find it difficult to divide our attention is because we are spreading our limited resources too thinly.

Some tasks, according to Norman and Bobrow, are difficult for us to attend to because we are limited by the data available to us. No matter how hard we listen, for instance, we may find it hard to pick out one person's voice in a crowded room if they are a long way away and we have other, much louder voices near us. In this type of data-limited task, our selective attention fails us simply because the information available is not good enough for us to pick it out.

Other tasks, though, are what Norman and Bobrow referred to as **resource-limited**. Because they are reasonably complicated in themselves, we need to devote quite a lot of our resources to them in order to do them successfully, and if we are trying to pay attention to something else at the same time, then we are likely to make mistakes. Norman and Bobrow propose that we have a set upper limit to our capacities, and can do things successfully only if they stay within these limits. So, for instance, someone could hold a conversation while cooking a meal, as long as the tasks involved stayed within their upper limit. If they reached a part in the recipe which was new and complicated, then they would be likely to make mistakes in the recipe, unless they reduced the other demands on their attention, and stopped talking for a while.

Kahnemann (1973) also proposed that we have only a limited capacity for attention, and suggested that this is as a result of the amount of effort which we have to put into a given task. According to Kahnemann, the cognitive mechanisms which are involved in attention involve a **central processor** which allocates our mental resources to the task at hand. The number of demands being made on that processor will determine the resources which it can allocate to any given task, and the physiological state which we are in will affect how much 'mental energy' we have available in the first place. So if we are tired and emotionally stressed, we will have less 'mental energy' than if we are rested and alert.

Kahnemann suggested that the **allocation policy** of the central processor – in other words, what it decides to devote attention to – is influenced by three main sets of factors. One of these, as already described, is the capacity that we have available, and this is closely linked with an evaluation of how much mental effort the tasks under consideration will involve. The second set of factors consists of enduring dispositions, such as personality, habits or long-term goals. And the third set is to do with momentary intentions: the immediate relevance of the stimulus, our moods, the context, and so on. These three types of factors all combine to determine what our central processor will notice.

In a way, limited-capacity models of attention come back to William James's idea that we can pay attention to only one thing at a time – that we can only do two things at once if one of them is so habitual that we do not need to think about it. But several researchers have shown that people can learn to divide their attention between more than one task. The filter theories of attention operated on an implicit assumption that attention involves just one channel. But studies of divided attention have challenged that assumption.

Divided attention

Allport, Antonis and Reynolds (1972) suggested that we do not have a single general-purpose capacity for attention. Instead, we have several different mechanisms by which we process information. We encounter interference when we try to attend to more than one thing, they argued, because the two tasks are using the same sensory processing mechanisms. So if two tasks are very different, we do not experience those problems.

Shaffer (1975) studied the activities of a skilled audio-typist. The audio-typist typed material which was presented to one ear through a set of headphones, while at the same time performing a different task. In one condition, this different task involved shadowing a spoken message delivered to the other ear. In the other condition, the typist

was asked to read aloud information which was presented to her visually. Each of these conditions produced interference: although the typist could perform any of the tasks separately extremely well, combining them presented far more difficulty. Each task interfered with a different aspect of the audio-typing task: the first condition interfered with her ability to receive the auditory input, while the second interfered with her ability to produce the typed output. Shaffer suggested that it is the **similarity** of information which affects directly, how much we can attend to it.

In another study, Allport, Antonis and Reynolds (1972) asked research participants to learn a set of words which were presented to them through headphones, while at the same time shadowing a spoken message. They found that the participants were unable to learn the words. But when they asked the research participants to undertake a similar task, but this time being given pictures to learn, the participants remembered over 90% of the stimuli. Even when the material was words, but presented visually, the participants remembered far more than they had done when they were presented in auditory mode. The visual stimulus was different enough from the verbal shadowing task to make it possible to attend to both types of information.

Another factor which seems important in whether we can attend to more than one thing at the same time is how difficult the task is. Sullivan (1976) performed a dichotic listening study which involved asking research participants to shadow an auditory message, while at the same time identifying certain target words when they came up in the unattended message. The harder it was to shadow the main message, the fewer target words the participants spotted.

The effects of practice

There is some evidence, however, that we may be able to extend the 'upper limit' of our attentional capacity. Spelke, Hirst and Neisser (1976) found that, with practice, people could get better at paying attention to two tasks at once. They asked students to read stories while simultaneously writing down a list of words which was read out to them. The students practised this task at regular intervals for a college term. Once they could do it easily, the experimenters varied the task, so that this time they had to put down a word which related to the one that they were given – like writing 'dog' when they heard 'animal'. By the end of the term they could do this very successfully. From this, and other research, Spelke, Hirst and Neisser suggested that the skills of dividing our attention are ones which can be learned, through practice.

Shiffrin and Schneider (1977) challenged the idea that attention was being divided equally in this type of situation. Instead, they argued that the reason why practice improves people's ability to perform more than one task at the same time is because the skills involved in at least one of the tasks have become **automatised** – they become so well-learned that they are performed automatically, without requiring conscious attention. Shiffrin and Schneider argued that it is reasonably easy for people to divide their attention between several different types of input if they are using automatised processes. Processes become automatic, they argued, as a result of practice. In many respects, this argument comes back directly to William James's assertion that we can attend to two tasks at once only if one of them is habitual.

The role of practice

Norman and Shallice (1980) suggested that it is not just a simple question of whether a task is automatic or requires attention. Instead, they suggested that there are three distinct levels of attentional functioning, which are described in Table 2.4 (see page 46). Logan (1988) suggested that the process whereby a given task becomes automatised – or, in Norman and Shallice's terms, transfers from one level to another – is through practice. Practice, Logan argued, results in the different skills involved in performing tasks becoming welded together into a single unit. For example: changing gear comes to feel like a single action when you become an experienced driver, while to a novice it is several different actions, combined together. The more we practise a given skill, the more the various elements of the task are 'chunked' together into larger units. Since each unit can be retrieved directly from memory, in a single step, this means that the task needs less attention.

Cheng (1985), on the other hand, argued that practice produces automatisation because it

---

Table 2.4 Levels of attentional functioning

Level 1
Fully automatic processing — Information-processing is controlled by internalised plans, or schemata (see Chapter 5), and there is very little conscious awareness that the information is being monitored. You might easily fail to notice the colour of the bus which you travel on regularly; but the fact that you would notice if it suddenly changed colour shows that there was some automatic monitoring going on.

Level 2
Partially automatic processing — Information is still processed without conscious control, but there is more than one schema involved, and they compete for attention. If, for instance, you were chatting to a friend as you got on to a bus, you would find your attention divided between the demands of paying the bus driver and continuing your conversation. This conflict would be resolved by a process known as **contention scheduling**, in which your attention would be allocated alternately but rapidly to the two situations, so fluently that you would hardly be aware of it.

Level 3
Deliberate control — Conscious attention is devoted to the stimulus, to the exclusion of other conscious inputs. This, they proposed, involves a supervisory attentional system, involved in decision-making and resolving conflicts in unfamiliar and complex situations.

Source: Norman and Shallice, 1980

produces a complete cognitive restructuring of the task: the person comes to analyse what is involved quite differently, and to identify different units involved in undertaking the task. A skilled essay-writer, for example, might visualise writing an essay in terms of organising themes around a central argument, while a novice essay-writer might see it just in terms of collecting and writing down information. This means that the performance of someone who is skilled at a task is qualitatively different from that of someone who is just learning it – not just faster, or more chunked.

Challenges to limited-capacity models

There is some experimental evidence which does suggest that it may be possible for a skilled person to attend to two different, but quite challenging, tasks at once, in situations which a novice would find almost impossible. In Shaffer's case study of the audio-typist, she was asked to copy-type a passage in a language which she did not know: German. This task required attention, since the characteristic spellings and the form of words were unknown to her. Yet at the same time, she was able to shadow a prose passage which was presented to her through headphones. The typist performed these tasks almost as well together as separately. In another study, Allport, Antonis and Reynolds (1972) asked skilled pianists to shadow continuous speech presented to them through headphones, while at the same time sight-reading unfamiliar music. Again, the research participants were able to perform these tasks almost as well as they did when they were asked to do them singly.

In both of these examples, the tasks involved were very different, and the people concerned were highly skilled at the mechanics of the tasks which they were asked to do. Spelke, Hirst and Neisser (1976) argued that researchers into limited-capacity models of selective and divided attention had not taken our ability to develop specialised skills into account. When this learning ability is taken seriously, they argued, limited-capacity models of attention become pretty well redundant.

Allport (1980) not only challenged the idea of limited capacity, but also the whole idea that there is a single general-purpose 'attention' which we use for several different things. Instead, Allport argued, there are several different attention-processing mechanisms, and interference occurs

only when they are overlapping. This idea, however, was challenged by Eysenck (1984) on the grounds that some sort of central control is necessary, if only to co-ordinate behaviour and cognition. Eysenck proposed that the working memory model proposed by Baddeley and Hitch, which we will be looking at in the next chapter, might represent an appropriate model for how attention is co-ordinated. But an alternative way of looking at this was proposed by Neisser (1976), in a general theory of perception and cognition.

Neisser's theory of perception

The observation that people can learn to pay attention to several things at once is one which is not easily explained by either the filter models or the limited-capacity model. Neisser (1976) regarded attention as a skilled activity, without any fixed limit to how much we can attend to. As Spelke *et al.* showed, if we practise we can extend how much we can take in, yet still be attending to each task efficiently.

Neisser argued that there was no need to talk, either, of filtering information out of our awareness. We are continually surrounded with rich sources of information, from all of our senses; and we interpret that information in ways that are most useful to us. He argued that if we wanted to explain why someone picked only one apple from a laden apple tree, we would not need to propose a filter that stopped them from picking all the apples on the tree: they simply picked the one they wanted. In the same way, we choose what we are going to pay attention to, from the mass of possibilities. Our selection is based on the immediate situation and our anticipations about what is likely to be relevant to us. Human beings are not simply passive receivers of information, Neisser argued. They choose what they will notice, because they are active in the world and some items of information are more relevant to that activity than others.

Neisser regarded perception, including attention, as a skilled activity, that takes place over time, not a static, 'snapshot'-like process. He argued that traditional psychological studies of perception fail to take this into account: they take a stimulus out of context, keep it static and unchanging, and then expect research participants to react to that stimulus in the same way that they might react to something meaningful in their everyday lives. The essence of perception, Neisser argued, is an active cycle of cognitive activities which are directly concerned with making sense out of experience.

The perceptual cycle

The essence of the perceptual cycle is that the perceiver is actively involved in constructing a dynamic understanding of the world, and that this understanding is changing all the time. It is not a matter of creating a static representation, or model of the world: it is a matter of seeing cognition in its ecological context, as useful to the person, and continually being used. Because of this, perception changes all the time, and no two perceptual acts can ever really be exactly the same.

Neisser rested much of his approach on Gibson's theory of direct perception: there is little perceptual uncertainty in interpreting information, for the most part, because the optic array provides more than enough information for the perceiver. The perceiver samples the information available – not just visual information, but information from other sensory modalities, like touch and sound as well, and often combines them to make sense of what is going on. In cases of restricted stimulation, as in limited laboratory stimuli or visual illusions, the sample may be patchy and perceivers may need to draw heavily on assumptions and rules, as we saw with Gregory's model. In most cases, though, there will be far more information available than the perceiver could take in: they will notice those parts of it which are relevant to them.

In either case, the sampling process is not random: the perceiver actively explores the perceptual world, picking up relevant information and ignoring that which is unimportant. Our perceptual exploration is directed by what we expect to find as well as what we have already found: it is based on an active **schema**, which is itself continually being adjusted in the light of our experience. The schema directs our exploration of the perceptual world; our exploration leads us to sample part of the information available to us; and that information itself modifies the schema (Figure 2.35).

Neisser sees real-life perceptual events as involving several different anticipatory schemata at the same time. For example: if we see someone smile, we can interpret it on a number of levels. On the socio-cultural level, we know that it is a signal

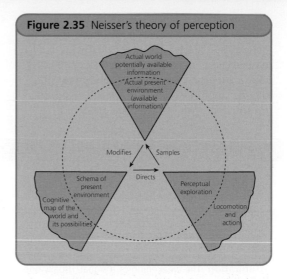

Figure 2.35 Neisser's theory of perception

with rules which constrain how we should react; on a personal level we may see the smile as kind, cynical or perhaps empty, depending on our anticipations about that person; on a communicative level we may take it as an indication that it is our turn to speak, and so on. These are all examples of different perceptual cycles, which we are engaged in simultaneously: the cycles extend over different amounts of time, and as we can see, past experience, present situation and future behaviour are inextricably linked.

This does not mean that we only perceive what we are expecting to see, because the information that we pick up from the environment is continually modifying and changing what we expect. But it does mean that we are more prepared to perceive certain things than others, at any given moment. Realistically, events in real life are not often totally unanticipated – even if a total stranger comes unexpectedly to the door, it is still the door that they appear at rather than coming in from a wall or window and there is some warning of their presence before the door is actually opened. If someone really did materialise with no warning we would be very disturbed by it. Laboratory experiments, though, take things out of context. As Neisser says:

'Most psychologists do not believe in ghosts, but they often experiment with stimuli that appear just as mysteriously. This may be a mistake; at the very least it creates an unusual situation.'

(Neisser, 1976: 41)

We can see, then, how Neisser's theory can provide a synthesis between top–down and bottom–up theories of perception. By his emphasis on perception as a cycle, rather than as a static information-processing system, both types of theorie can make sense – as can the supporting evidence for each of them. Perception is a complex process at all levels: physiological, cognitive, interpersonal and socio-cultural. We will be dealing with social perception later on in this book, as it is an area that merits a special chapter in its own right. In the next chapter, though, we will look at a different aspect of cognitive activity: memory.

Key terms

affordances In Gibson's theory of perception, the possibilities for action which are offered by an object (e.g. a tree affords possibilities for climbing, or hiding behind).

ambiguous Having more than one possible meaning.

attenuation The weakening of a signal, usually one which is being processed in terms of selective attention.

autokinetic effect A visual illusion in which a stationary dot of light in a dark room is perceived to be moving.

binocular disparity The difference in the retinal image received by the two eyes – used as a cue for judging distance.

bottom-up theory A theory which begins from the lowest level of observable data and shows how this may combine into higher-order forms.

cocktail party phenomenon The phenomenon in selective attention in which someone may be attending only to an immediate conversation yet may nonetheless catch their own name if it is mentioned elsewhere.

complex cells Nerve cells found in the thalamus which fire in response to lines at a particular orientation, anywhere in the visual field.

depth cue Something which gives an indication of how far away an object is.

dichotic listening task A way of studying selective attention by presenting different messages simultaneously to each ear, and asking people to report what they hear.

dictionary unit A word-recognition unit, or logogen, used in models of cognitive processing.

direct perception The idea that our nervous system is designed to allow us to pick up relevant information straight from the optic array, without the need for complex cognitive interpretation.

ecological Pertaining to 'real-life', or everyday situations, as opposed to artificially constructed laboratory simulation.

face recognition unit A hypothetical information-processing unit in the mind which is involved in identifying known people by their faces.

galvanic skin resistance (GSR) The electrical conductivity of the skin, which varies with degrees of stress and is therefore used in lie-detector tests and other methods of arousal.

geometric illusions Visual illusions which utilise geometric lines and figures to have their effect.

gradient of colour A monocular cue to depth which concerns how colours appear to fade with distance.

hypercomplex cells Cells in the thalamus which fire in response to simple shapes or sets of lines.

introspection Looking 'inwards' to analyse or explore one's own mental state, beliefs or ideas.

Laws of Prägnanz A set of perceptual principles identified by the Gestalt psychologists, through which visual information is given shape and form.

monocular depth cue An indication of how distant something is, which can be detected just as well with only one eye as it can with two.

motion parallax The way that the visual field changes with movement, such that objects further away appear to change position at a different rate than objects close up, when the viewer is in motion.

negative after-images The visual experience of 'seeing' the opposite form of colour or action after prolonged exposure to a single stimulus colour or movement.

ocular dominance columns Columns of nerve cells found in the visual cortex in which the cells at each level respond to the same stimulus, received by the same eye.

optic array The entire pattern of visual information falling on the retina of the eye.

perceptual constancy The process of perceiving an object or scene as consistent and unchanging despite variation in the physical light information reaching the eye.

perceptual defence A process whereby objects or events which are threatening or unconsciously unwelcome, are less easily perceived than more innocuous stimuli.

perceptual set A state of readiness to perceive certain kinds of stimuli rather than others.

performance decrement The decline in accuracy which occurs over time as an individual performs a task requiring sustained attention.

phi phenomenon The perceptual phenomenon in which discrete stimuli presented in rapid sequence are perceived as linked together.

prototypes Typical examples of a concept, containing all the relevant features.

raw primal sketch A first stage in the processing of visual information, according to Marr's computational theory.

response bias A tendency to answer questions or act in a way that is socially desirable.

schema A mental framework or structure which encompasses memories, ideas, concepts and programmes for action which are pertinent to a particular topic.

signal detection tasks Procedures used in studies of sustained attention in which the person is required to notice, or detect, a small signal whenever it occurs.

simple cells Cells in the thalamus which respond to basic units of visual information, such as a dot or line in a particular place on the retinal image.

split-span task A method of assessing selective attention in which the person is presented with two sets of stimuli simultaneously, one to each ear, and must divide their attention between them.

superposition A monocular depth cue in which images of objects which seem to obscure other images are perceived as being closer.

template theory The idea that patterns are identified by matching them up to a stored 'ideal type' or template.

threshold of response The point at which a stimulus becomes strong enough to trigger a response only 50% of the time.

top-down theory A theory which explains some aspect of cognition primarily in terms of the overall context and meaning of the information rather than in terms of its stimulus properties.

visual illusion A visual image which tricks the perceptual system, so that it is perceived as something other than it is.

waterfall effect A negative after-effect in which consistent visual experience of movement in one direction produces an after-image of movement in the opposite direction.

Summary

1 Perception is the process of interpreting sensory experience. We automatically tend to organise visual experience into figures against backgrounds. Marr's computational model of perception suggests how this organisation may take place in the visual system.

2 We use monocular and binocular depth cues to perceive distance. Gibson's theory of direct perception discusses how these cues, and physical movement, allow us to interpret the world around us.

3 Explanations for pattern-recognition include template-matching theories, prototype theories and distinctive-features theories. The pandemonium theory shows how a distinctive-features approach may be applied to word-recognition.

4 Perceptual set is a state of readiness to perceive certain things rather than others. It can result from knowledge, expectations and current circumstances. Gregory's theory of perception proposes that perception results from perceptual set and hypothesis-testing.

5 The process of recognising faces includes both top-down and bottom-up processing. Research suggests that several different cognitive mechanisms may be involved in face recognition.

6 Studies of sustained attention found that performance decrements over time are reduced by situational, task and personal variables, and might be influenced by the individual's habitual level of arousal.

7 Studies of selective attention resulted in filter theories and limited-capacity models, but research into divided attention showed that with practice it is possible to learn to attend to more than one thing at a time, which challenges single-channel and limited-capacity models.

8 Neisser proposed that perception is a skilled cyclic activity, which combines both top-down and bottom-up elements. Anticipatory schemata direct perceptual exploration of the environment. This results in a perceptual sampling of the information available, which in turn influences the anticipatory schemata.

Self-assessment questions

1 What depth cues can be used to explain the Ponzo illusion?

2 Briefly describe the template-matching approach to pattern recognition.

3 Outline the main stages involved in perceiving a tree, according to Marr.

Practice essay questions

1 What evidence do we have for the idea that figure-ground perception may be innate?

2 What can theories of pattern-recognition tell us about the process of reading?

3 Do bottom-up theories of perception really explain perception? Give specific examples.

Test your knowledge of this chapter with our online quizzes and games at: http://www.psych.co.uk

Explore perception and attention further at:

General
http://onesun.cc.geneseo.edu/~intd225/prcptn.html – Detaled information about the prceptual processes.
http://www.visionscience.com/ – Links to vision resource websites, including facial databases, illusion galleries, dictionaries of terms and a detailed bibliography.
http://www.yorku.ca/eye – A very good on-line textbook (*The Joy of Visual Perception*). Very well illustrated.

Visual illusions
http://www.illusionworks.com – A very detailed and fun to use guide to visual illusions.
http://dragon.uml.edu/psych/illusion.html – Not as exhaustive, but a decent gallery of visual illusions.

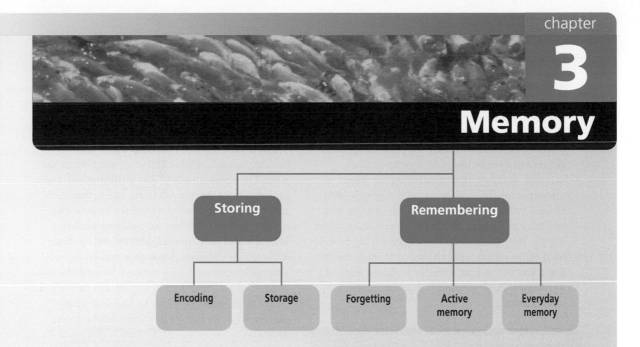

Memory

Storing

Remembering

Encoding | Storage | Forgetting | Active memory | Everyday memory

Learning objectives

3.1. Ebbinghaus and Bartlett
a distinguish between the methods used by Bartlett and Ebbinghaus to study memory
b state limitations of Ebbinghaus's methodology
c identify changes which occur with serial recall

3.2. Encoding memories
a define key terms in memory research
b describe a study of memory coding
c identify well-known mnemonic techniques

3.3. Memory storage
a distinguish between long-term and short-term memory
b evaluate the two-process theory of memory
c show how levels of processing may apply to everyday life

3.4. Working memory
a list the components of working memory
b define terms related to the theory of working memory
c describe a study of working memory

3.5. Forms of long-term memory
a define terms relating to long-term memory
b relate forms of long-term memory to everyday life
c distinguish between episodic and semantic memory

3.6. Retrieval
a describe a study of forgetting
b list theories of forgetting
c identify factors which can minimise forgetting

3.7. Memory as an active process
a define terms relating to memory as an active cognitive process
b outline the process of confabulation
c describe a study of active memory

3.8. Memory in everyday life
a define terms relating to everday memory
b describe significant concepts in the study of everyday memory
c evaluate different methodologies for studying memory

We use memory all the time, in everyday living as well as when we are studying. Think of the last time that you decided to play some recorded music at home: it will have involved several different kinds of memory, like remembering all the different steps involved in operating the record-player or tape-deck (switch the power on, place the record or tape the right way up in the machine, and so on), remembering the sound of the music, or the type of music that you wanted to hear, remembering what records or tapes are, and what they look like (not to mention recognising the relevant machinery), remembering how to hold on to things without dropping them on the floor; and on and on – the list is almost endless! Yet we use these memories almost completely unconsciously.

Two traditions in memory research

Memory research has a long and important history within psychology. One of the first researchers into memory was the introspectionist psychologist Herman Ebbinghaus (1885), who established a tradition of meticulous work in studying psychology as an experimental topic in the laboratory. His work established a methodology and approach which was highly influential in memory research right through to the 1970s. However, from 1932 onwards, a different tradition in memory research also emerged, originating with the work of Sir Frederick Bartlett. Bartlett studied how people make sense of the information that they receive, and how their personal values and ideas affect what they remember. This approach to 'real-life' memory also had its impact, eventually leading to a new emphasis on research into everyday memory in recent years.

Ebbinghaus's approach
Ebbinghaus published a book on memory based on his own research in 1885. In it, he detailed the extremely thorough methods which he used to investigate memory, in which he took great care to control as many different aspects of the experience as he could. He was particularly interested in how memories were formed, and so he decided to work with 'pure' material, uncontaminated by previous learning or associations. To do this, he used **trigrams** – nonsense syllables consisting of a consonant, then a vowel, then another consonant. These nonsense syllables resembled words, but did

not have any particular meaning, so that they would not be associated with anything already in the person's mind.

Using himself and his research assistant as the experimental material, Ebbinghaus developed systemati methods for learning the nonsense syllable, allowing a precise amount of time for looking at each syllable before moving on to the next. The testing method was **anticipation**: the trigrams were written on cards, and before each one was turned over he would try to anticipate what it would be. When he could remember a whole list of nonsense syllables by anticipation, Ebbinghaus considered that they had been successfully learned. This method formed the basic pattern of his experiments, but he also varied it in many different ways, to try to find out what factors might influence or inhibit learning (see Box 3.1).

Although Ebbinghaus's introspectionism was rejected as a result of the behaviourist revolution, many of his discoveries were still regarded as valid many decades later.

Bartlett's approach
The other great 'founding father' of memory research, Frederick Bartlett, highlighted how memory is an active process, and not just a factual record of events (Bartlett, 1932). We all have an impression that our memories are simply recordings of what went on. But Bartlett showed that really, they are rather different. Instead of simply 'tape-recording' factual information, we **organise** our memories, so that they fit with our expectations or our existing knowledge. Although all human beings do this, sometimes it is one of the hardest things to realise about ourselves, because it contradicts our subjective experience. Yet sometimes, no matter how accurate it might feel, what we remember simply is not what actually happened.

Bartlett developed a method of testing people's memories for events, which also allowed him to analyse the kinds of errors which they made. The method which he developed was known as **serial reproduction**, and consisted of the person reading or hearing a story, and then reproducing it – or as much of it as they could remember. You may have come across something similar to this in the old party game 'Chinese whispers', where someone whispers a message to someone, who then whispers it to someone else, and so on. By the

Box 3.1 Using nonsense syllables to study memory

The decision to use nonsense syllables in order to study 'pure' memory was one which lasted for over eighty years, and in the process shaped psychological research into an extremely artificial mould.

The idea that a 'pure' form of a cognitive process could be found has complex philosophical roots. Partly, these derive from Descartes, with his idea that the body functioned essentially as a machine, implying that therefore a process would operate in essentially the same way no matter what the basic material was. Partly, too, it derives from Aristotle, who argued that every knowable object has an 'ideal form'. And a third root lies in concepts of science – the idea that research can be 'scientific' only if there is no human involvement at all – or at least, as little as possible.

These assumptions, though commonplace in the history of psychology, are contentious. Research into the demand characteristics of psychological experiments shows that people do not stop being people just because they are acting as experimental participants. They continue to speculate, develop theories and think; and their ideas about the purpose of the experiment and how a co-operative subject should act exert a powerful influence over what they do (Silverman, 1977). A number of researchers have shown how human beings project meaning into meaningless material – even if these are simply triangles and circles moving around on a screen (Heider, 1944). There is no reason to believe that nonsense syllables are somehow exempt from this process – most of us can find

some meaning, or some resemblance to meaning, in trigrams like 'VOB' or 'ZID'.

A further question about the validity of conducting 'pure' cognitive research arises when we look at the functions of memory itself, and how we use it in everyday life. People seem to remember meaningful information quite differently from the way that they remember non-meaningful information. For example: one argument against the limited-capacity (7 +/− 2) model of short-term memory is that when we are having a real conversation with someone else, we retain far more than seven items of information in short-term memory. We can only recall a limited amount of meaningless information but once the information matters to us, as demonstrated in the study by Morris *et al.* (1981), we can remember far more than that.

Similarly, as we will see in Chapter 4, prior material, context and purpose are essential factors governing how we read; so studying what people remember of a single paragraph or sentence taken out of context in the laboratory is unlikely to be the same process as the one which is occurring when we read that paragraph or sentence in a book or magazine.

It seems likely, therefore, that the way we process meaningless information is entirely different from the way that we process information which matters to us. In which case, decontextualising material in order to control extraneous variables or study a 'pure' form of cognition is pointless.

time the message reaches the end of a line, so that everyone who is present has had a go at passing on the message, it has usually changed completely.

Using the serial reproduction method, Bartlett was able to identify a number of systematic types of changes which people make to story-like material as they pass it on. These changes are listed in Table 3.1. They show how we try to make sense out of our experiences – it is very difficult for us to recall things which do not make sense, so we adjust the information that we receive until it does. If a word is unclear, or does not fit, we think we must have heard a different word instead, and

we substitute it. If there are extraneous details which do not seem important to the story, we leave them out. And so on.

Both Ebbinghaus and Barlett contributed a great deal to our understanding of human memory, but in very different ways. Ebbinghaus, as we have seen, aimed to investigate 'pure' memory – memory that was not influenced by experiences, ideas, or thoughts – and he focused on the cognitive processes of how memory is coded, stored and retrieved. Bartlett, on the other hand, was concerned with the way that we use memory in everyday living, and how our experiences, ideas

Table 3.1 Changes occurring with serial recall

1	*Changes in significance*	The tendency to focus on one aspect of the story, and make that into the most important part, even if it was not in the original.
2	*Affective distortions*	Where people's own feelings and reactions to the story affected what they remembered.
3	*Drift*	The meaning of the passage would change gradually, from one reproduction to another.
4	*Shortening*	The story would become more and more truncated, as details were omitted in successive versions. Omitted details tended to be those which did not fit with the person's own understanding of the story.
5	*Coherence*	Changes made to the story to enable it to make sense to the person. This might include introducing new material, or changing the sequence of events.
6	*Conventionality*	Where well-known themes or clichés replaced the original phrasing, so that the story became increasingly conventional, fitting with the person's own culture and social context.
7	*Loss of names and numbers*	Numbers and proper names tended to become lost in the retelling, or changed into more familiar versions.

Source: Bartlett, 1932

and thoughts are involved in shaping those memories.

Modern memory research still reflects that distinction: some researchers, such as Baddeley and Atkinson, are purely concerned with the cognitive structures and processes of memory; while others, such as Loftus and Neisser, are concerned with how memories are used and adjusted in response to human experiences. We will begin this chapter by looking at some of the research reflecting the first of these traditions, in the form of studies of memory coding, storage, and retrieval, before going on to look at research stemming from the idea that memory is an active cognitive process, influenced by personal factors as well as specific events.

Encoding memories

Ebbinghaus proposed that there were three essential processes involved in memory: **encoding, storage**, and **retrieval**. Encoding is the first process: we need to receive the information that we are about to remember, and we need to convert it into a form in which it is memorable. When we have done that, we move into the second phase, which is that of storage. A memory is not considered to be a memory unless we have retained it for a period of time; but just how we store our memories, and how those stores are

structured is a question that several psychologists have investigated. The third stage of memory is retrieval – if we do not show that we remember information, it is questionable whether we are really able to say that it has been remembered. And, in fact, looking at failures of memory – that is, at how and why people forget things – may tell us quite a lot about the retrieval process.

Massed and spaced practice

The encoding process involves acquiring information, and then representing it in the mind. When we are wanting to learn new information, some ways of going about acquiring information have been shown to be more effective than others. For example, researchers from Ebbinghaus onwards have investigated the most effective way to use learning time, in order to maximise the amount that will be remembered. Their research shows that it is more effective to have a series of shorter learning sessions than to have one long period, even if both of them involve the same amount of time in the end. Moreover, this principle – that **spaced practice** is more effective than **massed practice** – applies both to physical skills and to the learning of factual or abstract information. It seems that, if we allow our memories time to 'settle', then we recall things more effectively.

Baddeley and Longman (1978) tried out different times for practice sessions for postmen who were learning to type postcodes (so that letters could be electronically sorted). They had four groups: the first group had two 2 hour practice sessions a day; the second group had one 2 hour session; the third group had two 1 hour sessions each day; and the fourth group just had one 1 hour session a day. They found that the postmen in the fourth group improved more quickly than the others, despite having less practising time. The second and third groups did not learn as quickly as the fourth, but they were better than the first group, despite the fact that the first group had more practice overall. The implication, then, is that it is not the amount of time spent learning a skill which is important, but the way in which that time is distributed.

Primacy and recency effects

Another aspect of coding memories concerns the way that the material is presented. Ebbinghaus is generally credited with having discovered primacy and recency effects; although this may not be strictly accurate. Scarborough and Furumoto (1987) describe how they had also been described by a woman psychologist, Mary Calkins, many years earlier. Whatever their origins, they are powerful phenomena in memory, and have been demonstrated in a number of contexts. Put simply, **primacy effects** concern the way that we tend to recall most clearly the first information of a kind that we come across and **recency effects** are the way that we also remember more clearly the last or latest items that we come across.

Murdock (1962) showed people a set of twenty words, one at a time, and gave them either one or two seconds to look at each one. Then they were asked to write down as many of the words as they could remember. Murdock found that most of the words that the research participants remembered had occupied the first or the last few places in the list, and not the middle places. Almost all the participant remembered the very last word! But the items in the middle of the list were easily forgotten.

Luchins, in 1959, showed how primacy effects can happen just as readily with social impressions as they do with lists of words. Research participants were given a description of a student, called 'Jim', and then asked whether they would describe 'Jim' as extroverted or introverted. The description was in two parts, but the order of the two parts

could be reversed. The two parts of the description were as follows:

'Jim left the house to get some stationery. He walked out into the sun-filled street with two of his friends, basking in the sun as he walked. Jim entered the stationery store, which was full of people. Jim talked with an acquaintance while he waited for the clerk to catch his eye. On his way out, he stopped to chat with a school friend who was just coming into the store. Leaving the store, he walked toward school. On his way out, he met the girl to whom he had been introduced the night before. They talked for a short while, and then Jim left for school.'

'After school, Jim left the classroom alone. Leaving the school, he started on his long walk home. The street was brilliantly filled with sunshine. Jim walked down the street on the shady side. Coming down the street toward him, he saw the pretty girl whom he had met on the previous evening. Jim crossed the street and entered a candy store. The store was crowded with students and he noticed a few familiar faces. Jim waited quietly until the counter man caught his eye and then gave his order. Taking a drink he sat down at a side table. When he had finished the drink he went home.'

One group of research participants were given the 'sociable' description first, as it appears here. The other group, though, was given the description the other way round. Luchins found that, although both groups of research participants had received the same information in the end, there were considerable differences in how they saw the character. Those who had the sociable description first judged 'Jim' to be an extroverted character, while those who had the 'unsociable' description first judged him to be an introvert. It seems primacy effects are important for more than lists of words: 'first impressions' of people count too.

Several explanations have been put forward to explain primacy and recency effects. One of them is the idea that we may pay more attention to the first few items in a list because they have novelty value – in other words, because they are new to us. Another explanation for recency effects comes from the idea that remembering some information can interfere with our memory for other material. This model proposes that we remember later items better because the information does not suffer from interference: nothing comes after it, so we do not confuse it with anything else.

There are other possible explanations. Glanzer

and Cunitz (1966) proposed that primacy and recency effects result from the words being retrieved from different memory stores. As we will see in the next section, many (though not all) psychologists believe that we have two different kinds of memory stores: a short-term memory which fades quickly, lasting for only a few seconds, and a long-term memory store which retains information for longer periods of time. Glanzer and Cunitz suggested that primacy effects come about because the words have been stored in long-term memory, whereas recency effects result from words being retrieved from short-term memory.

In one of their studies, Glanzer and Cunitz (1966) gave people lists of words to remember. Half of their research participants were asked to remember the words immediately after learning them, while the other half had a 30 second delay. The first group showed normal recency effects in their remembering of the words, but the second group had lost all recency effects completely (see Figure 3.1). Glanzer and Cunitz took this as evidence that recency effects did indeed result from short-term memory: the 30 second delay had been long enough for those memories to fade. However, there are also other explanations for this finding, like the possibility that other information, entering short-term memory during the 30 second delay, might have interfered with the most recent memories.

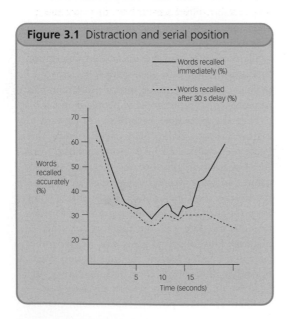

Figure 3.1 Distraction and serial position

Words recalled immediately (%)

Words recalled after 30 s delay (%)

Words recalled accurately (%)

70
60
50
40
30
20

5   10   15

Time (seconds)

Imagery and semantic coding

Once the information is acquired, it also needs to be represented in the mind, and this is part of the encoding stage as well. In Chapter 5, we will be looking at some other forms of representation, but one of the best-known methods of representing information is as sensory images, such as sounds or pictures. When we do this, it is as if we can 'hear' the sound or 'see' the picture when the memory comes back – your memory of your favourite record, for instance, is likely to be one which is stored in this way. Other memories might be coded in different kinds of sensory modes – the taste of lemon, for example, is one which people can often remember quite clearly. Or the feel of riding on a 'Waltzer' on the fairground, which is a kind of body-movement memory.

We can use imagery to develop memorising techniques, known as **mnemonics**. These can be very helpful when we have lots of things to remember. Raugh and Atkinson (1975) developed a 'key-word' system for remembering information using **mental imagery**. Using this technique, they showed that research participants who were asked to learn Spanish vocabulary were very much more successful than people who tried to learn the words using conventional repetition. In their study, the research participants were given a list of Spanish words, and asked to imagine an English word which had a similar sound. For instance, the Spanish word for tent, *carpa*, sounds like 'carp' in English. This was the key word. Once the participants had found this, they were asked to form an image which would link the key word with the English meaning of the Spanish word. So they might form a mental picture of, say, a carp in a tent at the bottom of its pool.

The research participants were given a list of 60 Spanish words to learn. One group of participants were asked to learn using the 'key-word' method, and the other group were not given any instructions about using a memory aid. Those using the 'key-word' method recalled, on average, 88% of the Spanish words correctly, whereas the control group only recalled an average of 28% accurately. The implication was that the use of imagery as mental representation can produce quite a dramatic improvement in memory.

One way that we can often tell which kind of imagery people are using is by the mistakes that they make. Conrad (1964) used this technique, by showing research participants a list of letters, and asking them to remember which letters they had seen. Although most of the research participants were able to get the lists right, when they did make errors these tended to come from substituting a letter which sounded similar – like a J instead of a K, or a T instead of a B. The conclusion was they they were using acoustic imagery rather than visual imagery. But if a participant had put a C instead of an O, this would have suggested they were using visual imagery instead. You may find it interesting to see which kinds of coding you prefer to use, by looking at the mistakes which you make when you are remembering telephone numbers or similar information.

Sensory images are not the only way that we store memories. Often, we will use symbols to stand for things that we want to remember – such as remembering by words or numbers. If I wanted to remember the length of my kitchen, in order to buy a new floor-covering, it would be rather pointless trying to remember what it looks like, and guessing how much to buy. Instead, I would measure it, and then remember the number of metres that I would need. That memory would have been stored using a symbol – a number – rather than as a sensory image. We can use symbols to store a huge amount of information. Most revision aids are all about developing more efficient symbols, so that a couple of words or a diagram helps the person to remember a great deal of information.

Such revision techniques rely on organising the information using **semantic coding** – in other words, using symbols to represent the meaning of the information. There is some evidence to suggest that symbolic representation can be even more useful than mental imagery when we are trying to learn things. Bower (1972) asked people to memorise lists of word-pairs. One group were asked to remember the word-pairs by forming mental images which would link the two, like imagining a shoe dropped in a pot of paint for the word-pair 'shoe – paint'. Another group were asked to use semantic coding (coding by meaning), forming a sentence which would link the pairs, like 'She put on her shoe and went to pick up the paint'. A third group were asked to imagine the objects separated in space, rather than connected, such as imagining a shoe in a shoe-shop and a pot of paint by a wall. Bower found that the group which used semantic coding

remembered the most word-pairs, closely followed by the group which had used connected imagery. Those who had used disconnected imagery did not recall very many of the word-pairs at all.

There are individual differences in the types of mental representation that people prefer to use, although each of us can use each kind to some extent. Kuhlman (1960) compared children who used mostly visual imagery for storing memories with children of the same age who used mostly symbolic memory. When it came to remembering unfamiliar shapes and images, the visual imagers showed themselves to be very much better than those who used symbolic representation. Their visual representations allowed them to recognise the shapes easily. But when it came to classifying different pictures into sets, it was the symbolic coders who had the advantage. Storing complex information, which can be connected in a variety of ways, seems to be much easier using symbolic representation, but the use of visual imagery has its place as well.

Memory storage

Once the information has been encoded, it needs to be stored. A number of different explanations have been put forward to explain how this happens, and how memory is structured. In this section, we will look at three of the most well-known current theories of how memory works. The first is the two-process theory of memory, which is also sometimes called the **structural model** of memory. The second was put forward as a challenge to the structural model, and is known as the **levels of processing** approach. And the third is the **working memory** model which provides an alternative to the idea of short-term memory storage.

The two-process theory of memory

The two-process theory of memory has a long history. In 1890, William James observed that we seem to possess more than one kind of memory. There is, he argued, the ordinary, lasting memory; but there is also a rapid, immediate memory, which seems to fade very quickly indeed, and just allows us to remember things for as long as we need them. James argued that these were two completely different processes of memory, and in doing so introduced a distinction which became widely accepted in memory research for the next 90 years.

The idea that there were two separate and distinct kinds of memory store was a convenient one which seemed to explain quite a number of experimental findings. The first type of memory store, researchers believed, lasted only for a few seconds, and was known as **short-term memory**, or **STM**. The other memory store carried information for much longer periods of time – days, months, or even years. So it was referred to as **long-term memory**, or **LTM**.

The two types of memory appeared to have entirely different characteristics. There was, for example, no observable limit to the amount of information that could be stored in long-term memory. But short-term memory could only hold a small amount of information. It was demonstrated using the **digit span test**, in which a list of digits – letters or numbers – would be read to research participants, and they would be asked to repeat the list. This test became known as the digit span test; and when it was found that the number of digits which someone could retain for just a few seconds in this way showed a moderate correlation with IQ, it became incorporated into many IQ tests.

Capacity and chunking

The two-process model stimulated a great deal of research into the way that STM and LTM worked. In 1956, Miller published a famous paper called *The Magical Number Seven, plus or minus Two: some limits on our capacity for processing information*. In this paper, he discussed just how much information short-term memory could hold. Drawing on research evidence, Miller demonstrated that the usual limit of the short-term memory store was seven units. In other words, most people could remember a string of up to seven numbers or letters, not more. This number varied, however, by up to two units either way: some people had a digit span of nine, some of five, but most would be somewhere in between these two. Only very exceptional people would have digit spans as high as ten or as low as four.

Miller proposed that there were only a finite number of available 'slots' in short-term memory. If additional information continued to enter short-term memory it would displace existing information, which would disappear on a first-in first-out basis. Only the seven most recent items of information would be in the short-term memory at any one time. But the important question was, what constitutes a unit of information? It was not always just a digit: Miller showed that we can increase the amount that we could remember in short-term memory by **chunking** the information into meaningful units. So, for instance, a string of letters such as:

M-P-I-B-M-S-T-D-B-T-B-B-C-I-T-V-C-H-4

might be far outside the limits of STM capacity, but if we chunked it, so that it read:

MP-IBM-STD-BT-BBC-ITV-CH4

then, at least to people in Britain, it would be much easier to retain. By chunking information into units that have meaning for us, we can extend its capacity dramatically. And this helps short-term memory to carry out its function: as an immediate store for information that we use in day-to-day living but do not really need to remember, like temporary instructions or numbers.

Coding and displacement

The study by Conrad (1964) that we looked at earlier was concerned with how we code short-term memories. By looking at the mistakes which people made when they were trying to remember items, Conrad was able to identify the kind of storage which they were using. For example, if someone made the mistake of saying 'eight' instead of 'three', that would imply that they were using visual coding. The sounds of the letters are very different, but the letters look fairly similar. But if they said 'five' instead of 'nine', it would indicate that they were using auditory coding, since the numbers look very different, but have similar kinds of sounds. Conrad found that when people are remembering items for short-term memory, they tend to code letters acoustically (as sounds). When they are remembering items for long-term memory, though, they are more likely to store information visually (as pictures).

The idea that STM involves acoustic coding fitted with the idea that it was a temporary, short-term store, with rapidly fading information which was quickly displaced by new information. If someone talks to you while you are trying to remember a telephone number that you've just looked up, you are quite likely to forget the number, and may even have to look it up again. The new information (the person's speech) has displaced the previous material (the phone number). In fact, if we want to keep information in STM, we try to prevent displacement from happening by repeating it over and over again. This is known as rehearsal.

Rehearsal, though, is a very vulnerable technique, and if we encounter any interference, we forget information in STM instantly. This was convincingly demonstrated in a series of studies reported by Brown, in 1958, and also by Peterson and Peterson, in 1959. The researchers had used the same method, which is now referred to as the **Brown–Peterson technique**. It involved asking participants to remember trigrams, like the ones that Ebbinghaus had used, for up to twenty seconds at a time. During that time, though, the participants were asked to count backwards, aloud, so they could not rehearse the trigrams.

The researchers showed that the amount of information which people could keep in short-term memory under these conditions depended directly on how long the delay was. They could manage it for a couple of seconds, but by the time 18 seconds had gone past, they only retained about a tenth of the information that they had been given in the first place. Peterson and Peterson believed that this happened because the memory trace decayed, but other researchers, notably Reitman (1974), argued that it had really happened because the new information had displaced the earlier trigrams. Since short-term memory had such a limited capacity, any new information coming in would push out the older stuff, and this was what had happened.

Waugh and Norman (1965) performed a different study of STM **displacement**. They read their research participants a list of eleven or twelve numbers, and then gave each of them a 'probe' number. The participants had to say whether the probe digit had been in the list that they had heard or not. Waugh and Norman found that the position of the word in the list was crucial: people were far more likely to remember numbers that had occurred towards the end of the list, and the nearer the end it was, the more likely it was to be remembered. Digits near the beginning were unlikely to be recalled at all.

Waugh and Norman interpreted these findings

as showing how information in STM is continually being replaced. Because of the limited capacity, new information coming in displaces older information. In another study investigating this idea further, Sternberg (1966) suggested that, during 'probe' studies, each of the items in STM is inspected in turn until the correct one is found. Sternberg measured the exact amount of time that people took to identify whether a particular probe digit was in a list that they had just heard, and found that the time would vary between 400 and 700 ms, depending on the number of items that the person had in STM. If someone was recalling several items, they took longer than when they were recalling fewer.

The Atkinson and Shiffrin model

Other researchers went on to find that STM seems to be mainly used in active thought, and that it depends a great deal on rehearsal. In 1968, Atkinson and Shiffrin proposed a formal version of the informal two-process theory that researchers had been using for most of the century. They argued that when information first arrives, it is picked up by a short-term sensory store, which usually lasts for less than a second. This store just echoes the information – leaving an impression of a sound, or of a visual image – but its information decays quickly, and only a small part of it passes on to short-term memory.

Once it is in short-term memory, the information has to be rehearsed if it is to be retained; and it can be easily displaced, as we have seen. But the important part of the Atkinson and Shiffrin model was that they argued that STM acts as the first stage for long-term memory storage. According to their model, incoming information goes through the STM store, and is transferred into long-term memory by rehearsal. This model managed to bring together quite a lot of different research findings, and to explain why rehearsal seems to be so important (Figure 3.2).

Atkinson and Shiffrin's model of memory has several names. Sometimes, it is known as the **two-process theory of memory** (the sensory store is not really a cognitive process, because it is completely passive). Sometimes it is described as the **modal model** of memory, because each of the stores involves a different mode for representing the information. And sometimes it is referred to as the **structural model** of memory, because it emphasises the idea of cognitive structures, in the

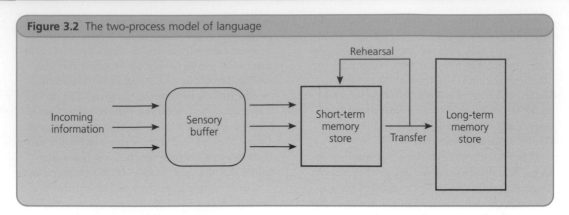

Figure 3.2 The two-process model of language

form of specific stores, as the basis for how memory works.

Problems with the two-process theory of memory

Morris (1982) argued that the main problem of the two-process approach to memory was that it did not really take into account the overall functions of memory for the individual. For example, the idea that STM only has a limited capacity is not a problem in laboratory studies, where people are mostly being asked to learn lists of words, or short sentences. In everyday life, though, we are dealing with much more relevant information, which would not happen as separate, intrinsically meaningless bits, but as part of a whole sequence of interaction. Taking part in a conversation and listening to what the other person says, for example, would involve the use of short-term memory, but at those times we need to retain far more than seven items of information simultaneously – and we do it quite successfully.

Understanding what speech means presents some other challenges to this model too. The generally accepted idea, as we have seen, has been that STM depends on simple acoustic coding. Decoding speech, however, requires both semantic analysis, as we work out what the words mean; and syntactic analysis, as we take into account the order and grammatical arrangements of the words which are being used. These are very much more complex forms of coding than can be explained by a limited-capacity storage model of short-term memory, operating on the basis of acoustic coding.

Other problems with the two-process theory of memory proposed by Atkinson and Shiffrin concern their presentation of STM as a first stage

for information before it is transferred to LTM. If this were the case, we would expect that the more complex, second-stage information – semantic information, to do with meanings and implications of the material – would take longer to be retrieved than phonemic information, concerned only with speech sounds. But Ball, Wood and Smith (1975) performed a **meta-analysis** (an analysis of many different studies of the same phenomenon) which showed how research data from many studies indicate that semantic information can be retrieved from memory just as quickly as phonemic information. Some clinical case studies, too, concern people with brain damage or injury who show very poor STM, but quite ordinary recall on LTM tasks, like remembering a short story. If STM were the first stage for LTM, then we would expect to find that LTM would also be affected.

According to the Atkinson and Shiffrin model, **rehearsal** (repeating information over and over again) is the way that information is transferred from STM to LTM. However, many researchers have challenged this idea, on the grounds that in practice rehearsal often turns out to be a very bad strategy for memorising, by comparison with other techniques. This was supported in a study by Bekerian and Baddeley (1980), which looked at how well people remembered the new radio frequencies which were introduced by the BBC in Britain in the late 1970s. Despite the BBC's policy of saturation advertising (most people heard the new information literally hundreds of times), they still did not retain the information; which suggested that passive rehearsal simply was not adequate to transfer information into LTM.

Yet another problem with the two-process theory of memory comes from studies of brain damage. Shallice and Warrington (1970) studied a man referred to as K.F., who had a serious motorbike accident when he was in his twenties. The accident had caused damage to the parietal-occipital area of the brain (we will be looking at brain areas more closely in Chapter 10), and he had to undergo brain surgery. When he was tested, eleven years later he had normal long-term memory storage; but his digit span was only two, and he found it extremely difficult to repeat things that were said to him. In other words, he appeared to have virtually no short-term memory, but ordinary long-term memory. If STM were the first stage for transferring information to LTM, as Atkinson and Shiffrin had argued, this should not have been possible.

The two-process theory of memory, then, has a number of weaknesses. It has been the framework within which memory research has proceeded for over 90 years, but in many ways it is possible to perceive the distinction as redundant. Morris (1982) pointed out that many of the research findings, like acoustic coding, serial search and displacement, which were thought to be indicators that STM was qualitatively different from LTM, could just as well be interpreted as examples of superficial, or passive, memory processing. They were valid findings, but they could be interpreted in more than one way, and so they could not be construed as incontrovertible evidence for the two-process theory of memory.

The levels of processing theory

As a result of these criticisms of the two-process theory of memory, many researchers began to wonder whether, in fact, it was necessary to make the distinction at all. Wickelgren (1974) suggested that, from the available evidence, it might make more sense to see memory as a single store, but with some items of information being stored more 'strongly' than others; and with some forgetting taking place because other information was producing interference. This idea connects directly with the model of memory which we will be looking at next: the idea that apparent differences in memory stores are really a by-product of how deeply the information has been processed in the first place.

In 1972, Craik and Lockhart argued that the reasons why we remember things for different periods of time is not because we put it in differ-

ent memory stores, but because we simply do not bother to process the information which we are given for short-term retention. Researchers have repeatedly shown that information which is received only passively is not retained as well as information that we work with, elaborate, and think about – in other words, that we process, cognitively. Information which matters to us in some way gets processed a great deal: we think about it, work out its significance in terms of other events in our lives, look at it from different angles, and so on. But who bothers doing all that with a string of digits? Things that are unimportant are forgotten almost immediately; things that are mildly important to us are remembered for a bit longer, and then they too are forgotten; while information which really matters a lot stays for a very long time.

Coding and processing

Craik and Lockhart performed a study in which they compared different techniques for coding memories. Research participants were shown words and then asked different types of questions about them, but they were not asked to learn or memorise the words that they saw. One group was asked questions which referred to the types of visual image that they had seen, such as 'Is it written in capital letters?'. The second group was asked questions which related to auditory coding, such as 'Does it rhyme with 'mouse'?', and the third group was asked questions which related to semantic coding, like 'Would it fit into the sentence "He dropped the …"?'.

You can see from this that each of these three conditions involved different amounts of mental 'work' which the research participants had to do. With the visual questions, they simply had to describe what they were looking at, but with the auditory questions they had to convert the visual information they were receiving into something like a sound image; and with the semantic condition they had to think about what the word actually meant. So each type of question involved a different amount of cognitive processing.

When they asked the participants to recall the words later on in the experiment, the researchers found dramatic differences between the conditions. The more cognitive processing that had been involved, the more the research participants remembered. The outcomes of the study are given in Figure 3.3. But what it shows is that even a

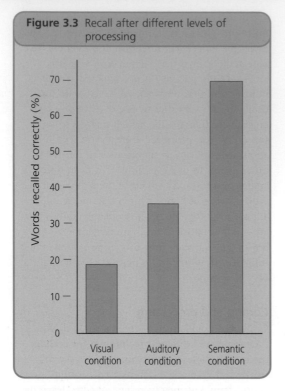

Figure 3.3 Recall after different levels of processing

simple thing like asking people to imagine what a word sounds like makes it more likely that they will remember that word later.

Craik and Lockhart explained their findings in terms of **levels of processing** – the degree, or amount, of cognitive processing that the person undertakes with the material. Information which you do not have to process much is easily forgotten: simply describing what a letter looks like while you look at it is a very passive way of dealing with the information, because nothing much needs to be done with it. Imagining what the word would sound like if it were spoken out loud at least involves you in processing the information from a visual input to an auditory image, whereas thinking about what the word means – in order to tell if it makes sense or not – involves processing the information even more.

So Craik and Lockhart's research participants in the auditory condition remembered more words simply because they had to process the information more deeply than people who were just asked what they looked like. And research participants who had to consider the meanings of words recalled even more, because meaning is an even deeper level of processing. It shows us how semantic coding of information may be a distinct

advantage when we need to recall that information later on – something that students who are revising for exams may find very helpful!

Craik and Lockhart distinguished between two types of cognitive processing. Type I is rote repetition, and they argued that this is really a very ineffectual way of attempting to memorise things. Effectively, it is a passive technique, which only requires superficial processing. Type II processing, on the other hand, is about analysing material for meaning, and identifying its implications. This, they argued, was a more effective form of learning, which led not only to a deeper understanding of the material, but also enabled people to remember the information for longer.

Processing and cognition

In a sense, according to the levels of processing theory, memory is almost a by-product: what really matters is how we process the information in the first place, and how long we remember it, or how well, stems from that. This model fits well with Neisser's (1976) model of the cognitive cycle, which we looked at in Chapter 2, and it allows us to make sense of a large number of different puzzles relating to memory, like the way that our emotions, motivation and ideas can affect our memory.

Morris *et al.* (1981) studied enthusiastic football supporters, and found that they could recall more real football scores than non-supporters could. According to the levels of processing theory, this happened because they were processing the information more fully. They were fitting the information in with what they already knew, and thinking about its implications for other teams. The ones who were not interested in football, on the other hand, were simply receiving the information passively, and not processing it much at all. We will be coming back to this study later in this chapter, when we consider memory as an active process.

Problems with the levels of processing approach

A number of researchers have criticised the levels of processing model of memory, on various grounds. Some have attempted to defend rehearsal as a memorising strategy. As we have already seen, it is not a very good technique for long-term recall of information. But Glenberg, Smith and Green (1977) showed that it could, in some cases, improve recognition of stimuli. In other words, rehearsing information makes you more likely to recognise it if you come across it again, but not to recall it for yourself. Glenberg *et al.* argued that this challenges the levels of processing theory, because it shows that the information is still remembered in some form. But other researchers have argued that it does not really, because the levels of processing model was really discussing memory in the form of recall, and recognition is a more superficial form of remembering.

Eysenck (1979) showed that the more distinctive or unusual information is, the better it is remembered. He argued from this that it is not the level of processing as such which matters, but whether the processing requires the person to deal with unusual information. This has sometimes been put forward as a direct challenge to the levels of processing theory; but Craik and Lockhart were never suggesting that all Type II processing was of equal value. Their concept of levels implied that there could be a wide range of deeper or more superficial ways of processing; and Eysenck's evidence supports that view.

Following on from this, though, Eysenck (1986) argued that simply thinking of memory in terms of levels of processing was too narrow. Levels of processing on their own, he argued, could not account for the variability in how information was remembered, although it might account for some. Eysenck argued that there are at least four factors involved in effective memory: the nature of the task, the type of material which is to be remembered, the person's own knowledge of the area concerned, and the way that memory performance is tested. Other psychologists might want to add to this list – he left out the social context of the information and the memorising situation, for example, and this can be a crucial factor too – but the point is reasonable enough.

How much weight we give it, however, depends on what we think the levels of processing model was trying to achieve. While an all-purpose theory of memory would need to address all of these matters, the general principle that levels of processing might be a more useful way of research findings than the concept of short-term and long-term memory stores is not particularly challenged by these criticisms.

Perhaps a more serious criticism was put forward by Baddeley, in 1978. Baddeley criticised the levels of processing model, on the grounds that the concept of levels was circular, and did not really lead anywhere. The theory states that material which has been strongly processed will be remembered better; but it also works backwards: if we find that material is well remembered, then we argue that it must have been processed deeply! This makes the theory very difficult to test, and Baddeley challenged it on those grounds.

Despite the problems with the concept of levels, though, many psychologists feel that the levels of processing approach has a great deal to offer. For one thing, it is a dynamic theory, which sees memory as a process rather than as a set of passive stores. For another, it has the ability to provide meaningful links between memory and other areas of cognitive psychology – for example, it can connect with Neisser's model of perception, and it can help us to understand when visual imagery is effective in learning and when it is less so.

The working memory model

Another dynamic model of memory was put forward by Baddeley and Hitch, in 1974. They proposed an alternative to the classical idea of the short-term memory store, as represented in Atkinson and Shiffrin's theory, arguing instead that it was more useful to think of immediate memory as a kind of **working memory**, used to deal with a particular problem or set of information, something along the lines of a computer's RAM. Such a model would need to explain the findings of previous research on short-term memory, but could be much more precise about exactly how those effects took place.

The central executive

Hitch (1980) suggested that the working memory consists of a general-purpose **central executive**, which can deal with most kinds of information, and several different subsystems (see Figure 3.4 overleaf). The central executive is used for cognitively demanding tasks, which require a lot of attention. This, like the older concept of the short-term memory store, is seen as having only a limited capacity, so that it cannot handle very much information at a time. Unlike STM, though, it is not a passive store, but an active cognitive mechanism.

A passive short-term memory store would simply hold information. But a true working memory, used to deal with and process information that the person is paying attention to at the

Figure 3.4 The working memory model

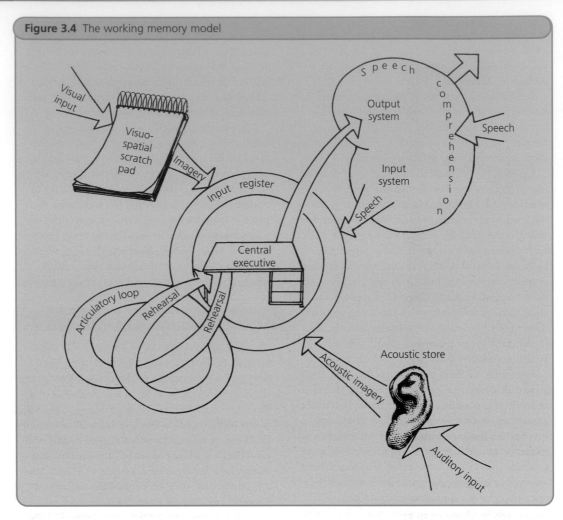

time would involve more than that – it would involve some way of monitoring information, and some selection of which information to pay most attention to. The central executive would be the part of the system making these decisions.

One study, described by Baddeley in 1986, looked at how successful people would be at doing a reasoning task and a digit span test simultaneously. The reasoning task consisted of being presented with two letters, A or B, in either order, and then judging statements about which order they had been in. Some tasks were simple, such as the person being shown B, then A, and then given the statement 'A follows B'. Others were more complex, such as the person being shown A, then B, and then given the statement 'B is not preceded by A'. Figure 3.5 shows how the more numbers the person had to remember, the longer it took them to work out the answer to the problem.

Even though the research participants took longer, though, their error rate stayed about the same throughout. Most importantly, they could still do both tasks, which implied that working memory was a dynamic system that could be adjusted to deal with different types of information, not a passive store.

Other components of working memory

The other components of the working memory system are seen as minor systems, used for particular purposes by the central executive. Rather than immediate memory being one store, as the STM model proposes, the concept of working memory is a kind of summary of all the different memory systems which are being used during a given task. So, for instance, to understand speech, we would use the central executive, but also a visual sub-system allowing us to deal with non-verbal infor-

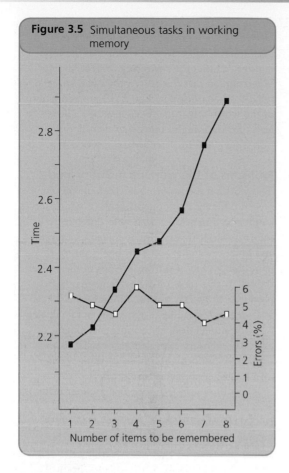

Figure 3.5 Simultaneous tasks in working memory

that although the visuo-spatial scratch pad does deal with both visual and spatial processing, the spatial processing is more important. You may find it interesting to connect this idea with Gibson's proposals about the importance of movement in vision, and the idea of the perceptual system as having evolved mainly to serve an animal which is actively moving around in the world. In that context, it would make sense if the working memory system, too, is primarily concerned with spatial processing.

A third component of the working memory system is the **articulatory loop**. This involves a kind of internal voice, as if words are being spoken sub-vocally; and which is seen as being very closely connected with the formation of normal speech. This articulatory loop is used to add to the amount that the central executive can store, by being used to rehearse verbal input. Baddeley, Thomson and Buchanan, in 1975, found that more short words could be held and rehearsed in working memory, than long words. They concluded from this that the articulatory loop operates on the basis of syllables, rather than whole words.

The idea of the articulatory loop can be used to make sense of the previous experimental evidence, which seemed to show how important rehearsal was to short-term memory. According to Eysenck (1984), suppressing the workings of the articulatory loop by asking research participants to repeat simple utterances like 'the' or 'hi-ya' produces a noticeable reduction in memory span (which is generally considered to depend on rehearsal of the information). The working memory model suggests that such rehearsal would be taking place in the articulatory loop, rather than in the central executive.

Hitch and Baddeley (1976) asked research participants to solve verbal reasoning tasks while at the same time repeating a well-known sequence of numbers: 'one-two-three-four-five-six'. The idea was that the repetition of the numbers would produce articulatory suppression, by engaging the articulatory loop; whereas the verbal reasoning task would involve the central executive. They found that research participants could manage both tasks relatively easily, but not when they substituted a random sequence of numbers instead of a familiar one. In that condition, participants performed noticeably worse on the verbal reasoning task, and it was suggested that this was because

mation, an input system allowing us to deal with the sounds of the spoken words, and perhaps a system which allows us to record the words that have already been, and match them up with what is still coming in.

One of the components of this working memory model is described as a **visuo-spatial scratch pad** – a kind of coding system which receives input and codes it into visual or spatial imagery. Of the two, spatial encoding seems to be more significant – or at least, Baddeley and Lieberman (1980) found that people tend to use it more than visual coding for their initial reception of information. In one study, they asked research participants to do a visual task – comparing the brightness of two lit areas at the same time as a spatial one – monitoring the swing of a pendulum by means of the sound that it made. They found that the spatial task seemed to be stronger, in that it interfered more with the visual task than the other way round.

From this, Baddeley and Lieberman concluded

remembering the random numbers involved the central executive, so it could not be purely devoted to the reasoning task and its capacity became overloaded.

In 1990, Baddeley proposed that the articulatory loop actually has two components: a phonological store, directly concerned with speech perception; and an articulatory control process, which is linked to speech production. Since it is the phonological store which is the main characteristic of this part of working memory, it became re-named the **phonological loop**. Eysenck (1995) discussed how this proposal helped researchers to make sense of a number of different experimental findings, such as that of a clinical patient, P.V., whose memory span was not affected by articulatory suppression. Eysenck proposed that this was possible because the stimuli went directly into the phonological store, bypassing the articulatory control process.

The acoustic store is another major component of the working memory system. This seems to involve coding acoustic information directly, independently of the articulatory loop. It was proposed when Baddeley *et al.* (1975) showed that information which is presented acoustically is not affected by suppressing the articulatory loop. Suppressing the articulatory loop only seemed to affect information which was shown to the person visually. This also explained a finding by Levy (1971), that if research participants experienced a simultaneous visual and auditory presentation (with the letters being read out aloud as they were shown to the person), articulatory suppression did not really make any difference to how well they performed.

Another study, performed by Baddeley and Lewis in 1981, involved research participants being shown a series of nonsense words. Some of these were homophones – that is, they sounded like real words even though they were spelt differently, like 'brane'. Others were simply nonsense words, like 'trenkle'. The research participants had to identify which of the words they had been shown were the homophones. Baddeley and Lewis found that they could still do this even if they were using the articulatory loop for another task, and they concluded that there must be a separate acoustic store, which coded how things sounded, as well as the articulatory loop.

The fifth component of the working memory model is an **input register**. Hitch (1980) suggest-ed that this operates as a kind of 'inner ear', which represents the most recent words which the person has heard – so the working of the input register can account for recency effect findings. Hitch argued that this is not just a passive 'echo' of what has been heard: rather, it is a representation of the words which has been analysed a little – at least into meaningful units – so that the information is prepared for later semantic processing.

Problems of the working memory model

The working memory model, then, involves several different components, each of which serves a different function or deals with different types of information. It is very closely linked to attention, and some researchers see it as being almost the same thing. One of the weaknesses of the model, though, is that most of the evidence has been produced from very abstract laboratory tasks, or well-defined ones like reading; it is not at all clear how the model deals with more meaningful, everyday memory experiences, or what form transferring information from working memory into longer-term stores would take.

Richardson (1984) argued that another major weakness of the model is that the idea of the central executive is vague, and not particularly helpful. Although it is used to explain anything which seems to have involved working memory and attention, nobody seems to have specified exactly what it does, or how it works. Allport (1980) questioned whether it was necessary at all, suggesting that it would be possible to explain all of the research findings by a model which simply involved specific processing components such as the visuo-spatial scratch pad, without any central executive at all. This view was challenged, however, by Eysenck (1986), who argued that such a system would be chaotic, and a central executive would be necessary for prioritising information, and deciding what should be attended to at any given time.

In addition, according to Richardson, research into working memory involves several circular arguments. For example, if people are given a task which involves suppressing the articulatory loop, and this affects their performance, working memory researchers assume that it means that the articulatory loop was involved. But if it is not, they assume that the central executive is active instead. There is no way that any results can prove the model to be wrong, because any component can be brought in to explain the findings.

Forms of long-term memory

As we have seen, Craik and Lockhart (1972), argued that it was false to propose that short-term memory and long-term memory were separate stores. One of the weaknesses of this idea is the problem presented by lumping all the different types of long-term memory together, as if they were all effectively the same. Remembering something for ten minutes is very different from remembering something for a few weeks, and that in turn is very different from remembering something for years. It does not seem to make much sense to talk about STM and LTM, when there are any number of middle-term types of memory, each of which presents its own distinguishing characteristics.

Tulving (1985) also argued that there are likely to be several different kinds of memory, on several grounds. The clinical evidence implies that there are several different types of memory, in that people who suffer from brain damage often lose some memory functions and not others. In addition, our evolution has provided us with several different types of of brain mechanism for visual perception, each of which serves different survival purposes, and it is not unreasonable to suppose that other cognitive functions may take several different forms, too. Moreover, Tulving argued, it is almost impossible to make generalisations about memory as a whole, although it is perfectly possible to make generalisations about particular kinds of memory.

Procedural and declarative memory

Squire (1992) suggested a different way of distinguishing between different forms of long-term memory. He described these as procedural memory and declarative memory. **Procedural memory**, he said, is concerned with the skills and underlying abilities and schemata which we have acquired during life, like the ability to understand language, or our general beliefs about right and wrong. It is concerned with knowing how to do things. **Declarative memory**, on the other hand, is concerned with knowing 'what' – with memory for specific items, facts, events or episodes. It is also sometimes referred to as **propositional memory**. And it uses entirely separate brain systems.

This way of understanding memory can help to explain why people who have lost their memory through brain damage or disease do not lose their underlying skills and abilities. For example, such people do not usually forget how to speak, or how to undress themselves, even though they may not retain any conscious memory of what job they do or where they live. Procedural memory can be seen as a kind of underlying, general manner of interpreting information, almost like a characteristic of personality; whereas declarative memories are very much more specific than that, and could perhaps be more easily dislodged in the event of brain damage of some kind.

Episodic and semantic memory

Declarative, or propositional memory, is not always of the same kind. In 1972, Tulving distinguished two different kinds of propositional memory, which he referred to as episodic and semantic memory. Some of the differences between them are listed in Table 3.2, drawn from a list which he published in a paper in 1983. **Episodic memory** stores information about events that happen, and how they relate to one another. It is concerned with the changing, temporary experiences that constitute our daily lives. Remembering that you had a dental appointment, or that you had been to visit an elderly aunt last Christmas, or that you had been asked to remember the word 'fugue' as part of a list in an experiment, would be episodic memory.

Semantic memory, on the other hand, is our organised knowledge of the world. It is our knowledge of rules, principles, ideas and properties. Knowing that velvet is soft is an example of semantic memory, and so is knowing

Table 3.2 Some differences between episodic and semantic memory	
Episodic memory	*Semantic memory*
Uses sensory experience as data.	Uses comprehension as data.
Units of information are episodes and events.	Units of information are concepts, ideas and facts.
Time-related organisation.	Conceptual organisation.
Emotional content very important.	Emotional content less important.
High likelihood of forgetting.	Low likelihood of forgetting.

Source: Tulving, 1983

that both a chair and a cupboard are examples of the category 'furniture'. Semantic memory includes our knowledge of the meanings of words, and how they connect with one another; but it also includes some information which we might not be able to put into words very clearly, like our knowledge that an action would be right or wrong, or of the feeling of carrying out a well-rehearsed action.

There was some experimental evidence to support the distinction between episodic and semantic memory. For example, Shoben, Wescourt and Smith (1978) found that semantic memory tasks could produce interference with other semantic memory tasks, but not with episodic memory tasks, and the other way round. If the two had not been different, Shoben et al. argued, they would be equally likely to produce interference with one another.

Underwood, Boruch and Malmi (1978) tested college students on episodic and semantic memory, and found that their scores on the two types of test did not really relate to one another. They used 28 different episodic memory tasks, and found that they correlated with one another, but not with the semantic memory tasks. Also, the five semantic memory tasks correlated with one another, but not with the episodic memory tasks. This, they concluded, was evidence that semantic and episodic memory really were different types of memory store.

Retrieval

The third stage of memory, according to the Ebbinghaus approach, is **retrieval**. The first stage, you will recall, was coding; the second, storage; and this is the third. In some senses, it is the most important – after all, we cannot know whether someone has really remembered something unless they show us that they have, by retrieving that information from memory in some way.

But there seem to be several different types of retrieval. Among many other findings, Ebbinghaus identified four different forms of retrieval, from the lists which he and his research assistant had memorised. The strongest of these was **recall**: when they could remember the word that would come next without any prompting. On other occasions, although a word could not be recalled, it could be recognised as having formed part of

the list, once it had been seen again. Ebbinghaus identified **recognition** as a second, though weaker, form of memory.

A third form of remembering was **reconstruction**: Ebbinghaus found that even if he was unable to recall or even recognise a set of trigrams, he still might be able to reconstruct the list in the order in which he had originally learned it, showing that there were still some traces of the original learning left. In the fourth, and weakest, form of remembering, recall, recognition and reconstruction of a list that had once been learned were impossible, but there were **re-learning savings** if the person tried to memorise the same list again. It took less time to learn than a completely un-familiar list would have taken.

Another way of looking at retrieval is to look at what happens when it fails. Psychological theories about why people forget often contain an implicit explanation for why people remember. And many of the theories of forgetting are actually about why we do not retrieve information when we want to do so.

Theories of forgetting

The past hundred years of memory research have seen several psychological explanations for forgetting. Some theories about forgetting have been very specific, concerning the decay of the memory trace; brain damage or disease; motivated forgetting; or interference from other material. In other cases, the reasons why we forget are to do with other characteristics of memory. There is a considerable amount of work, for instance, which shows how important context, cues and processing are for remembering; and so forgetting can some-times be seen as arising from inadequacy in this respect. We will look first at the specific theories of forgetting, and go on to examine some of the work on encoding memories.

Decay of the memory trace
One of the earliest ideas about memory storage was that each remembered item would leave a kind of physiological 'memory trace' in the brain, known as an **engram**. Unless this engram was strengthened by rehearsal, it would gradually become weaker until it eventually decayed altogether through lack of use. Recalling or recognising the item again would 'refresh' the engram. So memories which were not used would

die away, and those which were called to mind frequently would be strong.

This theory of forgetting is a plausible one, which fits with our subjective experience. But, in fact, it is almost impossible to test it out – we cannot possibly know if a memory exists unless we try to use it, and the act of doing that would presumably strengthen the engram. We also have the problem of constructive memory: as we will see, a person who is trying to remember something can unconsciously produce a plausible reconstruction, instead of a 'real' memory, and we would not be able to tell the difference.

Some cases of brain-damaged patients have produced evidence that memories may not decay completely, even though the person may not recall them for many years. Sacks (1985) described an 88-year-old woman who had lived in America since the age of five, after her mother's death. She had never been able to recall any of her early childhood in Ireland, although she had often tried to. But after a mild thrombosis in the temporal lobe of her brain, she suddenly began to hear Irish songs in her head. After neurological investigation, it emerged that these songs were a revived memory of her mother singing to her, in her early childhood. As she recovered from the stroke, the songs gradually faded away again. The implication here, and from similar neurological cases, would seem to be that memory traces do not actually decay completely, but seem to lie dormant instead. It is interesting, too, that brain damage can sometimes cause people to remember, as well as to forget!

Brain damage or disease

There are several different ways that amnesia can happen, ranging from brain damage or head injuries to problems arising through ageing. It is also difficult to be sure that a problem really is some form of amnesia: Talland (1968) showed how most people have failures of memory in normal life, so it is important not to confuse normal forgetting with a memory disorder. The usual standard is to assess whether a concentrated effort consistently fails to succeed in tasks which most people find relatively easy.

Post-traumatic amnesia is the kind of amnesia which follows a severe blow or wound to the head. This can often result in the loss of memory for the few minutes leading up to the accident. A study by Yarnell and Lynch (1973) involved inves-

tigating American football players who had just experienced concussion during play. As soon as they came round, the players were asked what strategy their team had been using just before the incident. Then they were asked again some twenty or so minutes later. Yarnell and Lynch found that the footballers could remember the name of the play immediately afterwards; but after twenty minutes that memory had gone, and never returned. This finding fits the belief of several researchers, that memories need to have some kind of consolidation period if they are to become fully absorbed into the person's memory.

According to Baddeley (1983), recovery from post-traumatic amnesia goes through a regular sequence, beginning with confusion about location and about the accident. Occasionally, people may even substitute a previous accident from some time in the past – thinking that is what has just happened to them. Often at first, the person cannot recall particular events and people from the past; but gradually these memories return – and usually the most distant memories return before the recent ones. Whitty and Zangwill (1966) showed that returning memories often cluster round 'islands of memory' – clear events which the person remembers – in quite a haphazard order. Interestingly, it is often quite trivial events which come back first, rather than deeply significant ones.

Being unable to remember things that have happened in the past is known as **retrograde amnesia**. Often, though, brain disease or injury can result in **anterograde amnesia**. This is where the individual is unable to store new memories, even though they may retain their memories from before the damage was done. Milner (1966) described a patient, H.M., who experienced **anterograde amnesia** as a result of brain surgery in which both sides of the hippocampus were removed. After the operation, H.M. found himself to be unable to retain new information, although he could still remember things that he knew before.

A later study by Warrington and Weiskrantz (1973) showed that, under special test conditions, H.M. could memorise some new information after all. Their findings suggested that his problems were more to do with actually retrieving information from memory than with learning it in the first place, which fits with other evidence from people with similar kinds of amnesia. Even with severely amnesiac people, anterograde amnesia is not always total. In particular, effective encoding of information can sometimes make a big difference. Jaffe and Katz (1975) reported a study with a patient suffering from Korsakoff's syndrome, who was unable to recall any of the names of staff in the hospital. When he was 'cued', by labelling each member of staff with their initials and then gradually fading them out, the patient finally managed to learn their names.

Korsakoff's syndrome is one of the most common sources of anterograde amnesia. It develops in long-term alcoholics, who have been drinking heavily and not eating well for many years. This produces a thiamine deficiency which eventually results in the person becoming unable to store new memories. People with Korsakoff's syndrome often become highly skilled at maintaining conversations by making general remarks; so it is often difficult to realise how badly their memory is damaged. But sometimes it is so severe that the person cannot recall someone that they have met only that morning, if they meet them later in the same day.

Typically, people with Korsakoff's syndrome do not show any impairment to short-term memory, or to basic skills like speech or driving, and often they are quite unaware that they have a problem. Those who do recognise it describe the experience as being like living in a dream, with no sense of continuity or ability to make plans for the future. In some cases, too, Korsakoff's syndrome can produce retrograde amnesia, in which the person cannot remember things that happened before the damage. Sacks (1985) described a patient with Korsakoff's syndrome who had had an active service career until 1965, with apparently fully functioning memory, but who now could only remember events up to 1945, and thought that it was still that date. When he met people that he used to know, like his brother, he was deeply disturbed at how much they had aged; and when he saw himself in a mirror in 1975, he became extremely upset at seeing an old man rather than the nineteen-year-old he thought he was.

Ageing

It is a common belief that your memory gets worse as you get older. But although there is some slight memory loss with ageing, it is not nearly as much as many people believe. In fact, there is some evidence to suggest that memories may even be better in older people. Harris and Sunderland (1981) compared everyday memory failures in younger people with older ones. In one part of their study, they compared people aged between 20 and 36 with retired people aged between 69 and 80, and found that the younger ones experienced significantly more memory failures than the older group.

Since the retired people in general had less active lives than the younger group, which might have given them less to remember in the first place, the researchers then performed a second study comparing another group of young participants with a pre-retirement group aged between 50 and 60. In this case, they found an even stronger difference: the younger group showed far more memory failures than the older people! The trouble is, of course, that because we expect our memories to get worse as we get older, we notice each little bit of forgetting more and more; whereas when we are younger we do not really bother much about it. In fact, despite society's stereotypes, most people go through old age in full possession of their faculties.

The same sort of problem comes up when we are looking at amnesia through brain damage. Williams (1969) pointed out that when someone has had an accident, or some other kind of brain damage, both they themselves and their relatives tend to attribute any forgetting to the accident itself, regardless of how much the person used to forget things before. So it is very difficult to distinguish just exactly what the effects of the injury are. At the moment psychology is a long way from understanding everyday lapses in memory, and until we understand those much better, we do not really have a basis for comparison.

When memory loss does happen, older people usually compensate for it by using memory aids and strategies, like diaries or other 'reminders'. But the 5% or so of old people who have brain damage through senile dementia or Alzheimer's disease, and also younger people with Huntington's chorea, do suffer real memory problems, and often can become quite confused. They also tend to make their memory impairment worse by not using any systematic strategies when they are trying to remember things. For example, Kral (1978) showed that when patients with senile dementia are trying to remember lists of words, they are unlikely to pay attention to what the material actually means or to how it is arranged. And if they are given extra time they do not use it to memorise more effectively – instead they wait passively for the next item.

The trouble is that passively receiving information is an exceptionally bad memorising technique at any age – as many students have found out to their cost when revising for exams! We should bear in mind, though, that the memory tasks themselves – which usually consisted of memorising lists of words – would probably have seemed thoroughly meaningless to the patients concerned, so they are unlikely to have wanted to try very hard. In view of this, it may be that these findings do not reflect their true capacity for remembering information.

Motivated forgetting

Freud (1901) considered that most, if not all, forgetting in everyday life happens because of **repression**. Repression is a defence mechanism which protects us from facing up to memories which would be emotionally disturbing or traumatic. According to Freud, such memories become buried by the unconscious mind – forgotten, because it would be too threatening to the conscious mind if they were remembered. Freud considered that repression was really the key to all forgetting. His idea was that even though something that we have forgotten might seem perfectly innocuous, it could, through a chain of associated ideas, lead to a traumatic memory. Because the unconscious mind is aware of the possible link, we forget the information, so it is protected from the threat.

Bower (1981) asked people to keep a diary for a week, taking particular note of all the things that happened which they experienced as either emotionally pleasant or emotionally unpleasant. At the end of the week, the research participants were hypnotised, and put into either a pleasant or an unpleasant mood. Then they were asked to remember what they had written in their diaries during the previous week. If they were in a pleasant mood, the research participants remembered mostly pleasant events, but those who were in an unpleasant mood tended to remember only the events which had been unpleasant. It is as if the mood we are in sets up a kind of mental set, so that we remember things that fit with it and forget things that do not.

Although Bower's study could be taken as partly supporting Freud, it is not really a psycho-analytic kind of repression. But that kind of repression is very difficult to study, and there is not much clear experimental evidence for it. Certainly, our emotions do seem to affect memory – emotional experiences 'stand out' in memory, whether they involve pleasant or unpleasant memories – but that is not really the same thing. It seems that we tend to spend more time thinking over emotional events anyway, and so the memories become 'practised'. Also, we probably pay more attention to emotional events as they happen than we do to neutral ones, which would help us to remember them.

Interference

Another reason why people may forget things is through **interference**. Interference occurs when one set of learned information interferes with another set. There are two types of interference: proactive interference and retroactive interference. **Proactive interference** is when something which you have already learned interferes with later learning. If you have already learned French, and you are now trying to learn German, you may find that, instead of a German word you are trying to remember, the equivalent French word comes to mind. That would be proactive interference.

Retroactive interference, on the other hand, involves new learning interfering with the recall of previously learned information. If, for instance, you learned French first, and then German later, you might find that when you think back and try to remember the French words which you used to know, only the more recent German ones come to mind instead. This would be an example of retroactive interference.

McGeoch (1942) showed that in general, interference is most likely to occur with information that is similar. Research participants were asked to learn lists of different items, like numbers, nouns or adjectives, and later asked to recall them. McGeoch found that there was very little interference between, say, a list of numbers and a list of adjectives; but that when participants had to learn two lists which were similar, such as two lists of adjectives, then interference was very strong. So one way that you might overcome interference if you are revising for examinations is to spend time emphasising all the differences between one set of material and another. This means that you would be more likely to categorise the information as being different, so interference is less likely to happen!

During the 1960s, interference was an extremely popular explanation for a number of memory phenomena. Hunter (1964) showed how the concept of interference could be applied as an explanation for primacy and recency effects, for the way that some information appears to transfer from short-term to long-term memory storage while other information does not, and, most importantly, for forgetting. Many psychologists of the time believed that new information either interfered with, or was interfered with by, existing information, and that this was the source of most forgetting.

The traditional view of interference, as we saw earlier, was that it mainly occurs with very similar material, and is unlikely therefore to affect information which is very different. But other researchers used the idea of interference more broadly. For example, Holmes (1974) argued that the reason why the emotions of worry and anxiety do not help people to remember work for exams is mainly because they bring in all sorts of extra thoughts, like 'I'm going to fail', or 'I'll never remember all this'. These thoughts, Holmes argued, produce interference, so all that the student actually remembers is the anxiety, rather than the material.

In the early 1960s several psychologists believed that interference occurred because there was only a finite capacity for human memory. New information would be bound to interfere with existing information because otherwise there would not be enough room to store it all. But there does not seem to be any real evidence for a limited-capacity model of memory: we seem to be able to remember any amount of meaningful information – although we are certainly limited in how much meaningless information we can take in. Even if one does accept a limited-capacity model, there are other explanations for forgetting, like the idea that information is displaced, or pushed out altogether. Nowadays interference, although it might occur, is not really regarded as the complete explanation for forgetting that many researchers considered it to be in the past.

There was empirical evidence too, which challenged the idea that forgetting mainly occurred as a result of interference. Tulving (1972) gave research participants a list of words to learn. Then they were given three different trials, in which they were asked to remember the words on the original list. If people forget because existing material interferes with recall or storage, then those words which survive the interference should be available for recall, and those which do not should be completely forgotten. But Tulving found that it was not as simple as that. When they were asked to remember what was on their list, the participants in the research tended to remember different words on each trial. They generally remembered roughly the same number of words on each occasion, but the words varied – only about half of the recalled words came up on all three trials. So it was clear that interference, in itself, was not an adequate explanation for forgetting.

Context

Anyone who has noticed how an old record or a particular smell can bring back a whole set of memories will know how important context is to remembering. Abernathy (1940) showed that if we are in the setting where our memories were first laid down, they are easier to recall. In this study, college students were given class tests in the room in which they were normally taught, and in unfamiliar rooms. Abernathy found that the students remembered more when they were in familiar surroundings and with their own tutor overseeing the work.

Williams and Hollan (1981) showed that mentally re-creating the context can be useful in retrieving information which has been forgotten. They asked research participants to recall the names of people that they used to know when they were at school. Despite the fact that the participants felt themselves to be completely unable to remember the names, if they were encouraged to think about the context as much as possible (like thinking about different classes and school activities that they had been in) they found that the names often came back to them. This process is known as **redintegration** – gradually retrieving whole memories from just one or two details by thinking about the overall context of the original events – and it shows just how powerful context can be in memory retrieval.

One of the most powerful examples of context in memory is that of **flashbulb memories,** where the memory of a particularly special event includes remembering exactly where you were at that time. We will be looking at flashbulb memory towards the end of this chapter. But context is important for less dramatic everyday memories as well. People who become temporarily bedridden often find that, after a week or so, they have difficulty in 'placing' their memories in time – remembering when and in what sequence things happened. It seems that being able to move around into different surroundings provides us with important reference points for remembering everyday life events.

Neisser (1976) argued that being active in the world, and forming cognitive maps within which events are perceived, is crucial to our cognitive processes. In Chapter 5 we will see how one of the most powerful memory aids is a system known as the method of loci, which involves locating items to be remembered in the context of a well-known walk or journey. This is just one example of how closely our memory is linked to our knowledge of the world, and its spatial relationships. Another that we have already come across is the discovery of how important spatial relationships are in working memory.

Godden and Baddeley (1975) asked deep-sea divers to memorise lists of words, either while they were on the beach, or while diving at a depth of fifteen feet. They found that it did not really matter where the divers learned the words – they learned them equally well in both environments. But it did matter where they were asked to recall them. If they had learned the words underwater, they remembered them best when they were underwater again. If they had learned them on dry land, they remembered them best when they were on dry land (Figure 3.6). The context exerted a powerful effect on how well they were able to retrieve the information from memory.

There is also an internal context which can affect remembering, in a form known as state-dependent memory. This occurs when the internal, physiological context – the state – of the body affects our memory. We are most likely to remember things when we know how information is recalled. So if someone is in a particular physiological state when they first learn something, then they are most likely to recall it when they are in that physiological state again. Goodwin et al. (1969) showed how alcoholics, when they were sober, were often unable to find money or alcohol that they had hidden when they were drunk. But once they were drunk again, they remembered the hiding-places.

Similarly, a study by Overton (1972) investigated the 'blackouts' that people sometimes experience

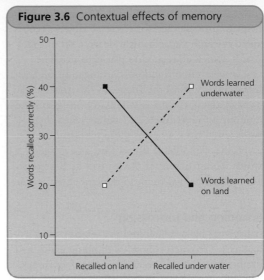

Figure 3.6 Contextual effects of memory

Source: Adapted from Baddeley, 1997

when they have been drinking very heavily. When they are sober again, they are unable to remember certain events or experiences that happened while they were drunk. But Overton showed that memory for the 'blackout' period often returned the next time that person got very drunk: the memory had not gone completely, but it needed the internal context of the person's intoxicated state before it could be retrieved.

Memory cues

In everyday memory, one thing often leads on to another, providing cues which in turn lead us to remember the next item. Many mnemonic techniques (memory aids) are based on developing memorable links between different bits of information, such that one item automatically leads on to the next. Alternatively, cues may be provided in the form of steps or categories: Tulving and Pearlstone (1966) asked research participants to remember lists of words, which were arranged in groups, each with a heading like 'animals', 'rocks', 'trees', or similar. The participants were not asked to learn the category names, just the list of words which fitted into each group. Later, half the participants were provided with the category names and asked to recall as many of the original words as possible. The other participants were also asked to recall the words, but they were not provided with any cues. Perhaps not surprisingly, those who had been given the cues recalled far more than those who were asked to 'free-recall'.

Organising information in a structured way also helps to provide cues for retrieval. Bower (1969) asked research participants to learn a set of 112 words, which all related to places to live. The words were either randomly arranged or organised hierarchically, from the largest to the smallest. On average, the participants who had been given the random list remembered 21 words when they were tested later, whereas those who had been given the hierarchical list recalled an average of 73 words. The structure of the list had itself provided cues which helped them to remember the words.

Encoding and processing

It has long been established that **elaborating** material – restructuring it, or thinking about its implications – helps people to remember things. But information which is just accepted passively is usually forgotten very quickly. As we saw earlier in this chapter, people who are football enthusiasts find it easier to remember real football scores than people who are not interested in the game; because the enthusiasts elaborate the material, making connections and drawing out its implications. The more thoroughly we process information which we receive, the more likely we are to recall it.

Bower and Karlin (1974) showed research participants a set of pictures of faces. They were asked questions about what they saw while they were looking at the pictures. Some of these questions were very straightforward and involved simple judgements, like assessing whether it was a male or female face. Other questions required the research participants to think about the faces more deeply. They might be asked, for instance, whether the face represented a likeable kind of person, or whether they would judge that person to be honest or not. The deeper the judgements that the participants had to make, the more likely they were to recognise the faces when they were shown them later.

The implied theory of forgetting here, then, is that we forget things simply because we have not processed them adequately when we were encoding them in the first place. This idea relates directly to the levels of processing theory put forward by Craik and Lockhart, which we looked at earlier in this chapter.

Explanations for forgetting, then, can tell us quite a lot about how we go about retrieving information from memory. In fact, it can also tell us quite a lot about the other two stages – coding and storage – as well. But that whole three-stage model of memory processes is very much based on the Ebbinghaus approach. Even though the material has become more realistic over time, and the explanations rather more complex, these theories still assume that what we are remembering is exactly what we have experienced. A lot of the time, though, our memory does not work like that at all.

Memory as an active process

As we saw at the beginning of this chapter, there are two distinct traditions in psychological research into memory. One of them is the one which was crystallised by Ebbinghaus – the idea that memory is a factual record of events, which is somehow coded in the brain, stored, and then retrieved when it is appropriate. The other tradition is that crystallised by Bartlett, who showed that memory can be very far from a factual record of events. Sometimes, in fact, we remember things that did not actually happen at all.

Have you ever been to the cinema to see a film that you used to enjoy years ago but have not seen for some time? If you have, you probably found that many of the details in the film were different from the way that you remembered them – even though, before seeing the film again, you may have been quite certain that your own memory was accurate in every respect. The way that our memories can adjust themselves to fit with our expectations and other things indicates that memory is not just like a tape-recording: it is an **active cognitive process** which interacts with our other mental processes and our experiences.

Serial reproduction studies

As we saw at the beginning of this chapter, Barlett used the method of serial reproduction to show how people adjust their memories to fit their own personal ideas about what is likely to have happened. The serial reproduction technique involves asking people to pass information that they have received on to another person, without allowing them the opportunity to go back to the original source and check their version of events. Because we always try to make sense of incoming information, the version that is passed on becomes adjusted until it seems to make sense to the person saying it. This is, of course, very much the way that social memories tend to happen – we see or experience something only once, and then we tell our friends about it. They in turn may tell other people, and the story can become extremely distorted in the process.

Rumour and serial reproduction

One of the most common real-life examples of serial reproduction is that of the transmission of rumours. People hear stories and bits of news, and they pass them on to one another. But the active nature of our memory processes means that if a message is at all ambiguous, it can become seriously distorted. If people do not have much information to go on, they will fill in the gaps, so that it makes a more consistent story. Allport and Postman (1947) investigated how rumours spread in wartime. Because information was very scarce during WWII, any little bit of it tended to be exaggerated and made more complex by the people who were passing it on, so that it made a more interesting story. Also, the information that was around was very unclear and ambiguous, and so it was interpreted in the light of existing 'knowledge'. This meant that there were all sorts of wild rumours flying around, which people would report with absolute certainty as if they were completely factual.

Allport and Postman's study showed how Bartlett's idea of 'effort after meaning' could be used to make sense out of the way that rumours occur. The people in Allport and Postman's study already had well-developed ideas about the war and the enemy – even though their ideas might not have been factually accurate. So each new bit of information was fitted into their existing mental frameworks – and adjusted if it did not quite fit with what was already there.

The same thing tends to happen with any alarming event which people do not actually know very much about. For example, the Yorkshire Ripper murders in the 1970s and 1980s produced a tremendous number of rumours in the district, which had little factual basis. Brunvand (1983) showed that often these were older stories which had been told in relation to earlier events, and had simply become adapted to the recent circumstance – like an often-repeated story of the hitchhiker who noticed a blood-stained hatchet in the back of a car. Interestingly, the people who recount these stories are usually completely convinced of their accuracy; but Brunvand pointed out that the person it is supposed to have happened to is always known to someone they know, but never known to them directly!

Schemata

Rumours develop as people integrate snippets of information with their existing **schemata** – the mental frameworks which we use to make sense out of everyday life. We will be looking at these more closely in Chapter 5. As Bartlett showed, we tend to adapt information until it fits into the relevant schema, and we may be reluctant to remember details which do not fit. There are plenty of examples of this in everyday life. For example, if a friend of yours does not like someone else, they will often be reluctant to admit that there is anything good about them – so much so that if they hear that the other person has done something kind and unselfish for someone else, say, they will often re-interpret that information by attributing some hidden selfish motive to their actions.

This does not mean that we are completely incapable of remembering unexpected or unwanted information, but it does mean that we are usually inclined to take the easier way. We are more likely to remember information that makes more sense to us, so if we can bend it to fit into our schemata, we often will – unconsciously, of course. Alternatively, we may forget the contradictory information altogether, and only remember the relevant information.

The idea of memory as being schema-based is an approach which links very well with Neisser's idea of the perceptual cycle, in which anticipatory schemata direct perceptual search, and the sample of the perceptual world which results in turn informs the schema (see Chapter 2). In a similar way, our existing schemata may direct our memories, in the sense of making us more prepared to remember some things than others, while the information which we do actually pick up and remember in turn influences the development of the schema.

Confabulation

Confabulation is another of the processes by which we adapt our memories to fit with our existing expectations or schemata. An example of confabulation was shown in a study by Loftus and Loftus (1975), who showed research participants a film of a traffic accident, and then asked them questions about it. There were two groups of participants, and each was asked slightly different questions. One of the groups was asked: 'How fast were the cars going when they hit each other?' The other group was asked: 'How fast were the cars going when they smashed into each other?'.

A week later, the research participants were asked about the film again, so that they had to think back and remember it. This time, they were all asked whether there had been any broken glass in the film, resulting from the accident. Although there had not been any, the group who had been asked with the words 'smashed into' distinctly remembered seeing broken glass scattered about the road after the accident. The words of the question had cued their expectations, and had meant that the research participants had produced active memories which fitted with their expectations: they remembered the accident as being far more serious than it actually had been.

Rigidity in confabulation

Often, people tend to stick to their own memories, even if they have been shown that they are inaccurate. Kay (1955) read people a passage and then asked them to write down as much of it as they could remember. After that, they heard the same passage read again. This was repeated once a week for seven weeks, with the same passage each time. Kay found that each week, the participants would produce the same version of the story that they had produced before, even though there were often quite large differences between their version and the original one. The fact that they were hearing the original version time and time again did not seem to make any difference.

It seems that once we have produced a set of memories which fits our existing ideas, we are inclined to stick with it, and we do not easily change our minds. This happens with social beliefs too: Kruglanski (1980) showed how people often 'freeze' on to a particular explanation, and will not change their minds even if they are shown incontrovertible evidence that it is inaccurate. We will be looking at this idea more closely in Chapter 13.

Eye-witness testimony

The question of human memory as an active mental process rather than a kind of mental tape-recording, is a serious problem for the law, especially when it comes to collecting eye-witness accounts of accidents, or other dramatic events. People will tend to interpret what they see in terms of what they expect to happen, and their memories tend to reflect that – so much so that it is a standing joke among police officers that if you have twenty witnesses to an accident you are likely to get accounts of twenty different accidents! Piecing together what really happened involves a careful process of comparison and analysis of the different accounts.

Another example of confabulation in memory comes up in the context of the use of **hypnotism** to help people remember events. Gibson (1982) discussed how hypnosis is sometimes used in police investigations, because many police officers believe that memory recall is a factual process, creating an accurate memory trace which can be 'played back' under hypnosis. But the reality is very different indeed.

People who have been hypnotised are in a very suggestible condition, where they try very hard to co-operate with the hypnotist or investigator as much as possible. It is this willingness to co-operate which makes the state of hypnosis special (see Chapter 11). Because of this, if people who have been hypnotised are asked about events, they will try very hard to answer with something plausible, putting together anything they can think of and sometimes unconsciously inventing details. They do this because they know that their questioner would like to hear something and they want to be helpful.

In this process of confabulation, people convince themselves that their memory is what 'really' happened. Confabulation has nothing to do with lying, because the person is often completely certain that what they are saying is true – they may be able to visualise the scene clearly, and remember small details (in the same way that the Loftus research participants could 'remember' the broken glass quite clearly). But human imaginations are vivid, and the slight cues given by the interrogator, which are often very subtle ones, together with the participants' own imagination and guesswork, can produce a memory which bears no relation to what actually happened.

Confabulation is not at all uncommon whenever people are asked to recall things under conditions of anxiety or of high motivation. Hypnotised people, being willing and co-operative, are very highly motivated indeed. And any police interrogation can provoke anxiety, even among people who know that they are not under suspicion. Which is why Gibson (1982) argued that using hypnosis in police investigations should be considered as equivalent to tampering with evidence, and should be forbidden by the courts.

John Dean's memory

In recent years there has been increasing interest in ecological approaches to memory: the study of how remembering happens in everyday life. As we have seen, many people see memory as if it were a kind of 'tape-recording' of events as they happen, but the research on eye-witness accuracy by Loftus and many others shows us that we are always actively processing our memories, and fitting them in with the schemata and beliefs that we hold about the situation.

One naturally occurring case study by Neisser (1981) involved examining testimony given in the Watergate hearings, as a result of which the then President of the United States, Richard Nixon, was deposed from office. In the early part of the hearings great interest centred on the testimony of John Dean, former counsel to the President. When examined, Dean showed a remarkably detailed memory for conversations and events which had taken place some time before. He said that he used a 'reconstructive' method, of looking into his collection of newspaper clippings from the time and thinking himself back into the situation.

Later on in the hearings, tapes of the same conversations were discovered and transcribed; and Neisser's study compared Dean's recall with the information on the tapes. He found that Dean's memory, although very clear to him, was often almost entirely inaccurate when it came to specific details. However, the gist of what had transpired tended to be recalled correctly: Dean was accurate in his memory for the social meanings of events, but not in his memory for the precise factual details. Neisser argued that it is only when we look at the overall meaning and context of a memory that we can really judge whether it is a truthful one: details are not always the most significant indicators of the real facts of the matter.

Emotion and motivation in memory

There have been several studies which have shown how other kinds of personal factors can influence how much we remember. In the study I mentioned earlier, Morris *et al.* (1981) asked research participants to memorise lists of word-digit pairs. Unlike most such lists used in memory experiments, however, these had some real meaning because they were the list of that day's football results, read out on the radio on Saturday afternoon. The researchers obtained two groups of participants, one of which consisted of enthusiastic football supporters, and the other of people who were not interested in football.

The research participants were asked to come along to the laboratory on a Saturday afternoon, and listen to that day's results. They had previously agreed not to follow any of the football reporting during the day. The participants then heard 64 sets of results once only – as they were reported on the radio – and afterwards were asked to write down as many as they could remember. By comparison with the control group, who were not particularly interested in football, the football supporters remembered significantly more of the scores they had heard. (We will be looking at the concept of statistical significance in Chapter 6.)

To test whether it was simply that these football enthusiasts were better at guessing the results anyway, the experimenters introduced another condition in the study, in which people were asked to predict what scores the teams would get on a particular day. The researchers found that the football supporters were not any better at this than the control group. Also, when they were asked to remember made-up scores, there was no difference either: it was their interest in football which meant that they were highly motivated to remember the scores, and so they did it better.

Another possibility was that the names of the teams might be unfamiliar to the non-supporters, but Morris *et al.* made sure that the non-supporters were familiar with these. That does not mean, of course, that they were equally familiar: obviously the football supporters would have been more accustomed to using those names; but that in itself is a manifestation of their higher level of motivation. The highly motivated football supporters were actively storing their memories, and connecting them with other information that they already knew; so for them each item of information had real meaning. For the non-supporters, one score was pretty much like any other, and so they did not find them particularly easy to remember.

Our emotions, too, can affect our memories: Bower, Minteiro and Gilligan (1978) asked research participants to memorise lists of words while they were in particular emotional states. The experimenters used light hypnosis to suggest either a 'happy' or a 'sad' mood in each partici-pant, and then gave each person a list to memorise. After that, each research participant was put into the other emotional state, again through light hypnosis, and given another list to learn. Then the participants were given distractor tasks to do, which, the researchers hoped, would take their minds off what they had just learned. Later, they were re-hypnotised, and, while in either a 'happy' or 'sad' emotional state, asked to recall the items from both of the lists. The experimenters found that people remembered most information when they were in the same emotional state as they had been when they had learned the lists.

All these studies tell us that human memory works in a very different way from a factual, objective, 'tape-recording' of what happens – even though it feels that way to us. Memory is an active process, which links closely with our per-ception and with the other systems of representa-tion, such as schemata and concepts, that we will be looking at more closely in Chapter 5.

Remembering in everyday life

Remembering in everyday life includes a number of different aspects of memory, many of which we have already looked at. Morris (1982) summarised the main areas in the field as including: eye-witness accuracy, the use of mnemonics and cog-nitive maps, the development of memory strate-gies, memory and ageing, absent-mindedness, remembering to do things, and the study of flash-bulb memories. We have already looked at some of these, so here we will look explicitly at research into flashbulb memory, remembering to do things, absent-mindedness, and an area which has come into prominence since Morris wrote his paper, which is that of autobiographical memory.

Flashbulb memory
Brown and Kulik (1977) found that dramatic events can often produce flashbulb memories, in which the whole context of the memory is remembered very clearly. They asked a number of people the question 'What were you doing when

you heard that President Kennedy had been assassinated?', and found that 79 out of the 80 people that they had asked remembered exactly where they were and what they had been doing at that moment. Their memories for that kind of contextual detail were remarkably clear – as if, the researchers said, they had been illuminated by a flashbulb.

Researchers into flashbulb memory have studied a number of different events. For example, Pillemer (1984) found comparable results for memories of an assassination attempt on President Reagan in 1981, and Conway et al. (1994) studied memories of the resignation of Margaret Thatcher. Other psychologists have studied the impact of the Space Shuttle Challenger disaster, and, more recently, the death of Princess Diana.

It is difficult, however, to explain what exactly is going on with flashbulb memories. Brown and Kulik drew on the work of Livingston (1967) for their explanation. Livingston had argued that sur-prising or emotional events activate lower brain centres, which trigger off general alert systems and a high level of brain activity. Because the brain is then working at a higher capacity, the events of the moment – including contextual information – become permanently fixed in the memory.

Other researchers, though, have challenged that idea. If it really were the case, then flashbulb memories would be a clear, factual record of what happened. But Neisser (1982) argued that when flashbulb memories are explored in more detail, they are often found to be inaccurate, containing details that simply did not happen. For example (although Neisser, of course, did not know about this one!) I personally have a strong flashbulb memory of hearing the news of President Kennedy's assassination, when I was about ten years old. I can remember exactly the room that I was in at the time, and have a vivid visual memory of seeing the event reported on the TV. Yet the fact is, that I could not have been in that particular room at that time, because I did not go to live in that house until a year later. And I certainly knew about the event before living in that house, because it was discussed at my other home, and at my other school. So my flashbulb memory has to be inaccurate, even though it is very strong, and feels as if it were true.

Neisser argued that there was no need to explain flashbulb memory by means of special brain activity. Instead, he suggested that what really produces flashbulb memories is the fact that we talk about these events so much after they happen. When we talk, we add the contextual details of where we were at the time, because they fit with the traditional schemata which we use when telling stories – which are known as **narrative conventions**. So it is the frequent rehearsal of these events which fixes them as flashbulb memories, and not neurological activation.

Not everyone agrees with Neisser, of course (psychologists, like other scientists, rarely come to total agreement about anything). Thompson and Cowan (1986) insisted that most flashbulb memories are pretty accurate, and that they only showed minor reconstruction errors. But although that does challenge Neisser's assertion that many flashbulb memories are inaccurate, it does not challenge his explanation, because reasonably accurate memories could happen whether the memory comes from narrative scripts, or from neurological activation. Most of our memory reconstruction is based on likelihood and probability, and so most examples drawn from narrative scripts would tend to correspond with reality. It is only the exceptions that could tell us anything about what is happening. But at present, we simply do not know enough about the process to be able to state definitively how it happens.

Prospective memory

Psychologists investigating memory have become concerned with everyday memory rather than with relatively abstract laboratory tasks, partly because the two often produce quite different results. Istomina (1975) compared children's memory for lists of words that they were asked to remember in laboratory conditions, with their memory for items that they were asked to remember as part of a shopping game. Although the two tasks were precisely equivalent, the children recalled significantly more words in the play condition than they did in the memory experiment.

Istomina's study was also investigating **prospective memory** – how we remember to do things, or remembering things for the future. The study involved children ranging from the age of three to seven, and there was a noticeable improvement as the children grew older. The very young children found it difficult to remember items on their shopping list, but the older children were more aware of the possibility that they might forget, and so made more careful attempts to remember.

Knowing about memory – for instance, knowing that you might forget something – is known as **metamemory**. Kreutzer et al. (1975) investigated metamemory in children by asking them to think of a way to make sure that they remembered to bring their skates to school the next morning. They found that the children tended to have quite a lot of insight into how their memory worked and whether they were likely to forget. Most of them suggested some kind of tactic like placing the skates where they could see them, or writing a note for the next morning. They asked children from four to seven years old, and found that the older children made more distinct plans, but that even the young ones had some insight into the way that they might forget.

Meacham and Leiman (1982) distinguished between **habitual remembering**, or remembering to do things which are more or less automatic, like brushing your teeth at night, and **episodic remembering**, which involves remembering to do unusual or infrequent things, like calling in at a neighbour's on the way home from work. The two types of prospective memory involve different types of memory aids: habitual remembering is helped if it is incorporated into other automatic routines; whereas episodic remembering is helped by things which are out of the ordinary, like something placed in an unusual position where it would be noticed.

Absent-mindedness

All of us experience errors of memory, or **absent-mindedness**, from time to time. Usually, mistakes caused by absent-mindedness are relatively trivial, but on some occasions they can be extremely serious – as in the case of a bus driver who destroyed the top deck of a double-decker bus by taking it under a bridge that was too low. He usually drove a single-decker bus on that route, and was simply acting out of habit. In many ways, the real difference between a major error or a minor error is not in the psychology underlying the mistake itself, but in its consequences. It does not matter much if you turn down a familiar road on the way home, instead of breaking the journey to make your intended call at the shops; but it did matter when that same error was committed by the bus driver on that particular route.

Reason (1984) distinguished between two major types of error: mistakes and slips. **Mistakes** are errors in the planned actions themselves, where things go wrong because of some kind of miscalculation; whereas **slips** are errors in which things do not go according to plan, usually because the person is not paying attention. Reason also describes particular kinds of slip, which he terms **lapses**, which are not usually apparent to an outside observer, but only to the person concerned – like forgetting someone's name. Although each of these types of errors has been studied, most research has concentrated on everyday slips.

Some researchers have investigated absent-mindedness by using **questionnaires**. Broadbent *et al.* (1982) found that when they asked people to report their own errors by means of questionnaires, and compared the results with ratings of the same person given by their spouse, the two measures correlated quite well; which suggests that questionnaires may be a useful way of measuring everyday errors. They also found that people who scored highly on one type of error, like failing to remember people's names, usually scored highly on other types of errors as well; and suggested that this implies that errors are to do with some kind of general overall cognitive control process rather than arising from the failure of a particular subsystem in memory.

Martin and Jones (1983) found that people who score highly on such questionnaires are often very poor at performing two tasks at once; although they have no difficulty doing each one separately. Similar results from other researchers resulted in the general idea that the 'central control' process involved is to do with how we allocate our attention to different things at once. This might also explain why people commonly report more of these types of errors when they are under stress: if more of their attention is taken up by the stressors which they are experiencing, then other everyday tasks will suffer.

Reason (1979) used a **diary method** of investigation, in which people were asked to note down any memory lapses or other errors that they made, as soon as they noticed that they had made them. From the data obtained from these diaries, Reason was able to draw several general conclusions about everyday errors, which are listed in Table 3.3. This study, and others like it, have allowed us to identify a number of different features about everyday memory and how it works. We can often learn most about a system if we study it when it fails – when everything is working smoothly it is not always easy to tell what is going on!

Autobiographical memory

Psychologists have also investigated people's memory for their own personal experiences, which is known as **autobiographical memory**. Linton (1975) kept a diary in which she noted

Table 3.3 The nature of everyday errors

1	*Habituality*	Slips of action are most likely to happen when people are carrying out automatic, habitual tasks in highly familiar surroundings.
2	*Inattention*	Errors usually happen when the person's atention is taken up by something else – either internally, for example if they are worrying about something, or externally, for example if they have been distracted by an arrival or sudden noise.
3	*Habit intrusions*	These account for about 40% of the action slips reported. They involve people slipping into a habitual routine at a time when they ought to be doing something different. They occur in familiar locations, and often involve similar movements to the actions that the person originally intended to make.
4	*Sequencing errors*	Errors in which people 'lose their place' in a sequence – forgetting where they have got to and starting again from the wrong place.
5	*Combination errors*	These are errors in which people 'blend' two different tasks together, or elements of the tasks – like, say, stirring a cup of coffee with a knife or spreading marmalade on the toast with the teaspoon!

Source: Reason, 1979

down two significant events a day, over a five-year period. Every month, she selected two items randomly, read the description, and tried to recall the date on which it had happened. If she had no recollection at all of the event, it was dropped from later samples.

Linton found a steady loss of memory for these items, of about 5% a year. But rehearsal also had a part to play. The random selection process meant that several items had come up more than once. And those items showed much less forgetting than those which had only been recalled on a single occasion. The more often they had been recalled, the less likely they were to be forgotten (see Figure 3.7).

There were other factors which Linton's study revealed. First events, for example, were particularly memorable. She used to attend meetings of a committee, which met some distance away, and she remembered the first meeting very clearly. Later meetings, though, were more easily forgotten. Another noteworthy finding was that events which seemed particularly emotional at the time that she noted them down, did not turn out to be more memorable than others, when she tried to recall them. Linton explained this as being because they no longer seemed to have emotional significance in retrospect – her feelings about them had changed over the intervening time.

Brown, Rips and Shevell (1985) asked research participants to date particular events, such as the Challenger disaster, or the eruption of Mount St

Helens. They found that their research participants tended to use landmarks in their own personal lives (for example, 'that was the year I got married …', or 'that was the year I graduated …') to locate the date. Over 70% of memories were dated in this way. But they also found that personal dating was more likely to be used for non-political events than for political ones. People mainly used other political events to date the political ones, rather than personal events.

Conway and Bekerian (1987) argued that auto-biographical memory is structured on three different levels. The highest, and apparently most important level, is that of **lifetime periods** – periods of time in which some aspect of personal life remained reasonably consistent, such as living with someone, or working for a particular company. The second level consists of **general events** – fairly major occurrences covering several days, or even months, such as a visit to Australia, or a period spent organising a conference. The third, and lowest level of autobiographical memory, according to Conway and Bekerian, is that of **event-specific knowledge**. This refers to the details and impressions associated with a particular event or happening in one's life.

Conway and Bekerian found that lifetime periods were much more powerful cues for helping people to retrieve particular memories than either of the other two levels. Each lifetime period seemed to have its own set of life-themes, goals, and emotions, and seemed to be the key to remembering a whole set of events. The other levels of autobiographical memory, it appeared, were organised hierarchically, so that they each depended on identifying the level above them, for retrieval. Conway and Rubin (1993) argued that this was supported by neurological evidence: nobody has yet been found who is unable to remember knowledge about life-themes and periods but can still remember event-specific knowledge, although often people cannot recall event-specific knowledge yet can still remember life-themes. We chart and organise our personal memories, it seems, through the various phases and periods we go through in our lives.

We can see, then, that psychologists have discovered a considerable amount about memory over the past hundred years. But despite this, we are still a very long way from understanding everything about human memory. It is a complex subject, which ties in very closely not just with

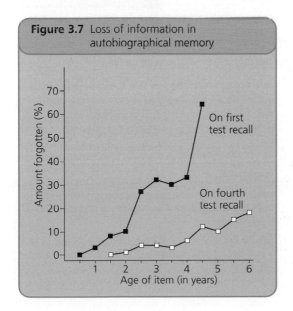

Figure 3.7 Loss of information in autobiographical memory

On first test recall

On fourth test recall

Amount forgotten (%)

Age of item (in years)

other areas of cognition, such as perception, language, and representation; but also with our social experiences. Social identifications, social representations, and social scripts can all affect what we remember, and shape how we understand it. As with all the areas of cognition, what we know so far is only the tip of the iceberg – but it can still be distinctly useful!

Key terms

acoustic store An element in Baddeley's working memory model, which stores mental representations of sounds.

anterograde amnesia The loss of memory for events taking place after the damage producing the amnesia.

articulatory loop A feature of Baddeley's working memory model to do with how information may be retained in working memory through constant rehearsal.

chunking Combining items of information into meaningful or semi-meaningful larger items, so permitting an extension of the amount which can be held in short-term memory.

confabulation Remembering events or information inaccurately as a result of applying pre-existing knowledge.

diary method A way of studying what human beings do in everyday life by asking them to note down specific items of information at regular intervals, or on appropriate occasions.

engram The name given to a theoretical 'memory trace' in the brain.

episodic memory A store of personal experiences and events, tied to specific contexts – memory for things which have happened.

flashbulb memories Fully complete contextual memories associated with dramatic happenings or events.

imagery Forms of mental representation which are based on, and seem to take the form of, physical sensations (e.g. mental pictures).

interference The distortion or disruption of memory which happens as a result of other information being learned or already stored in memory.

Korsakoff's syndrome A condition of severe memory loss and anterograde amnesia brought about by long-term alcohol abuse.

levels of processing theory The idea that what determines whether information is remembered, and for how long, is how deeply it is processed – i.e. thought about and linked with other information.

LTM The common abbreviation for long-term memory.

mental imagery See imagery.

meta-analysis A research method which analyses the outcomes of several studies investigating the same issues.

metamemory Awareness of how one's own memory works.

method of loci The mnemonic strategy which involves organising items to be remembered by visualising them in particular places.

mnemonics Strategies for helping people to remember information, usually involving cues such as rhyme or imagery.

post-traumatic amnesia Forgetting which occurs as a direct result of a brain injury or accident.

primacy effect The way that the first things you encounter make more of an impression than later ones do. So, for example, we are more likely to remember the first items in a list, or the first impression which someone made on us.

proactive interference A problem with memory storage in which information which has been learned interferes with the ability to learn new information.

prospective memory Memory for things which are yet to come, such as remembering an appointment.

recall Remembering information by retrieving it from memory.

recency effects The way that the last item of information on a list is usually remembered more clearly than earlier ones.

recognition A form of memory in which the person can identify previously learned information when it is presented, although they cannot recall it spontaneously.

redintegration The reconstructing of memories from relevant cues until an apparently complete record is achieved.

rehearsal Practice, e.g. the continuous repeating of information to be memorised.

retroactive interference The memory loss which occurs when new information displaces information which was learned previously.

retrograde amnesia A form of memory disorder in which the person becomes unable to recall events or information stored before the disorder occurred.

semantic coding Representing information in the brain by using the meaning of that information to determine how it should be stored.

semantic memory General world knowledge which does not particularly depend on individual experience.

serial reproduction A method of examining the accuracy of memory by asking people to reproduce what they recall of a story, on several successive occasions.

STM The abbreviation used for short-term memory, or memory which lasts for only a few seconds.

state-dependent memory A form of remembering which is dependent on its physiological context, e.g. the influence of drugs or emotion.

trigrams meaningless three-letter nonsense syllables, comprising a consonant, vowel and consonant (CVC) sequence.

two-process theory of memory The idea that short-term and long-term memory are actually two entirely different systems, as opposed to different levels of processing.

working memory Immediate memory, in use at a given time to perform a particular task.

Summary

1 There are two traditions in memory research: one initiated by Ebbinghaus, who established strict laboratory procedures and saw memory as a factual record; and the other by Barlett, who explored the importance of human meaning in memory, and saw it as an active cognitive process

2 Encoding memories includes research into practice, order effects, imagery, and semantic coding. Some mnemonic systems use imagery to facilitate remembering.

3 The two-process theory of memory suggests that short-term and long-term memory are entirely different stores, with different coding and storage processes. The levels of processing model challenges that distinction.

4 The working memory model has been suggested as a system linking attention and memory, and replacing short-term memory. It consists of a central executive, a visuo-spatial scratch pad, an articulatory loop, an acoustic store, and an input register.

5 There are different forms of long-term memory storage. Procedural memory concerns remembering how to do things, while declarative, or propositional memory concerns knowing information. Tulving distinguished between episodic and semantic forms of propositional memory.

6 Research into retrieval includes types of remembering, and reasons for forgetting. Forgetting may occur as a result of decay of the memory trace, brain damage or disease, motivation, interference from other material, inadequate cues and contexts, or inadequate processing.

7 The idea of memory as an active process includes research into the application of schemata, confabulation in eye-witness testimony, and the influence of emotion and motivation on memory.

8 Research into remembering in everyday life has included studies of flashbulb memory, prospective memory and metamemory, absent-mindedness, and autobiographical memory.

Self-assessment questions

1 What are the main changes which occur with serial recall?

2 Outline the main explanations for forgetting.

3 Describe the levels of processing theory of memory.

Practice essay questions

1 Memory is inseparable from the person who is doing the remembering. Discuss.

2 Evaluate clinical and laboratory evidence for the two-process model of memory.

3 How has everyday memory been studied by psychologists?

Test your knowledge of this chapter with our online quizzes and games at: http://www.psych.co.uk

Explore memory further at:

General

http://www.mindspring.com/~frudolph/lectures/Mem/memory.htm – Very detailed tutorial of all pertinent areas of memory, with summary slides.

Specific areas

http://www.valdosta.peachnet.edu/~whuitt/psy702/cogsys/infoproc.html – An in-depth guide to the act of processing information.

http://www.mtsu.edu/~schmidt/Cognitive/outline.html – Links to detailed lecture notes on encoding, retrieval, short and long term memories, etc.

Language and literacy

Using
language

Acquiring
language

Reading

Conversations

Language and
cognition

Theories

Stages

Theories
of reading

Reading
disorders

Learning objectives

4.1. Language and discourse
a define forms of communication
b identify the four basic components of
 conversation
c describe methods of discourse analysis

4.2. Linguistic relativity
a define linguistic relativity
b distinguish between the strong and weak forms
 of the linguistic relativity hypothesis
c describe a study of linguistic relativity

4.3. Verbal deprivation
a define terms relating to the verbal deprivation
 hypothesis
b distinguish between elaborated and restricted
 codes of language
c describe Labov's criticisms of the verbal
 deprivation hypothesis

4.4. Social aspects of language use
a define terms associated with social aspects of
 language use

b describe a study of accent or dialect
c discuss how sexist language can influence
 people's thinking

4.5. Theories of reading
a identify factors which can interfere with
 word-recognition
b list the major theories of reading
c outline the theory of reading as a selective search

4.6. Reading skills
a define terms relating to the study of fluent and
 novice reading
b outline the basic processes of reading
c distinguish between fluent and novice readers

4.7. Social influences on reading
a describe a study of scripts in reading
b show how social factors influence the process of
 reading
c identify the cognitive and social benefits of reading

4.8. Dyslexia
a distinguish between forms of dyslexia
b describe theories of dyslexia as a cognitive deficit
c evaluate the concept of dyslexia

Language is probably the most distinctive of all human attributes. Human communication takes place in a number of different ways. We can communicate by facial expressions, through signs, signals and gestures, and through actions. But these channels can also be used by other animals. Language, though, involves a highly sophisticated use of arbitrary conventional symbols (words) which are combined according to a culturally established system in order to convey specific meanings to other people. In Chapter 24 we will be looking at animal communication, and finding that, although some animals may have developed the ability to use basic forms of symbolism, none have really achieved anything like the human facility for language.

The psychological study of language draws from many different fields of expertise. A considerable amount of research has gone into the way that children acquire language, and many of the insights which have been gained from this have been directly applied in special education schemes. Psychologists have also studied how people make use of non-verbal communication to direct and regulate conversation and social interaction (see Chapter 15). Non-verbal communication is sometimes closely linked with the use of language, such as through tones of voice or intonation, which are used to clarify or amplify the verbal message.

Some of our understanding of the psychology of language has also come from direct investigations of the nature of language itself, through linguistics. **Linguistics**, like all other academic disciplines, has many different branches, and three of these branches have particularly concerned psychologists: psycholinguistics, sociolinguistics and ethnolinguistics. Of the three, **psycholinguistics** is perhaps the most important: it involves the study of the relationship between language and mind. Psycholinguistics is particularly concerned with the structure of language, and with features of language like syntax (rules governing the combining of words to produce meaningful communication) and semantics (the study of the meanings of words and word combinations).

The psychology of language, however, also includes understanding the way in which the language that people use, and the manner in which they use it, affects people's thinking and their social relationships. As such, the psychology of language draws from **sociolinguistics** – the study of language in relation to society. Language is a cultural institution too: indeed, it is often one of the main indicators of ethnic origin. Because culture is so important in the way that people interpret the world, ethnolinguistics – the study of language in relation to culture – also has relevance to the psychology of language. In the rest of this chapter, we will be drawing on studies from psycholinguistics, sociolinguistics and ethnolinguistics, as well as those from research psychologists, as we explore some of the major aspects of the psychology of language.

Conversations

Ellis and Beattie (1986) argue that if we want to study how human beings communicate with one another, then it is not very sensible to study language separately from non-verbal communication. They argue that human beings use more channels of communication than any other species, and that these work closely together to convey information, not independently. The same message can be communicated in several different ways: a shrug of the shoulders means the same as 'I don't know', or a shake of the head means 'no' (at least in Western culture). Instead of trying to separate out language from the whole range of human communication, Ellis and Beattie see it as preferable to look at how human beings use language in its social context. Because of this, their approach emphasises the analysis of conversations: they see the main ways that human beings use language as being through ordinary conversational give-and-take.

Conversations as co-operative interactions

Grice (1975) emphasised how conversations are co-operative ventures between participants. These co-operative ventures have four basic components: quantity, quality, relation, and manner. **Quantity** refers to the idea that the participants in a conversation should be as informative as necessary, but not over-elaborate, giving unnecessary details. The **quality** component covers things like how accurate or consistent the argument is, and whether, for example, there is evidence to back up what is being said. The **relation** component is to do with how relevant the information is to the matter being discussed – how well what is said relates to what is going on. And the fourth component of the co-operative principle – **manner** – is that what is said should be easy to understand. As a general rule, Grice argued, conversations tend to adhere to these principles for most of the time.

These principles emphasise the co-operative nature of conversation. Conversation is a social action, in which language is used as the medium of interaction. It operates on an interpersonal level, and that links closely with cognitive levels too. For example, Billig (1990) showed how the co-operative nature of conversation also leads to collective ideas or beliefs. Billig tape-recorded a series of conversations about the British Royal family, and showed how the conversation proceeded in such a way as to define and establish collective forms for remembering events, and to provide a generally accepted framework within which discussion about the Royal family took place.

Discourse and metaphor

A considerable amount of recent language research has focused on **discourse analysis**: looking at conversations which take place and investigating how patterns, speech styles and vocabulary can inform us about what is happening. Edwards (1997) argued that discourse is so central to human experience that if we are to achieve any kind of realistic understanding of human social interaction, we need to look at it in those terms. Analysing behaviour and cognitions, he argued, is both limited and impractical – it fails to take into account the reflexivity of social interactions, and the way that text and talk shape and re-shape our experiences.

Metaphorical frames

Lakoff and Johnson (1980) discussed the concept of **metaphorical frames**: how the choice of idioms which people use in conversation often fits an agreed pattern, which has the effect of defining how the topic is seen. For instance, arguments are usually described within an 'argument as war' type of metaphorical frame: people talk of 'attacking' someone else's argument, or 'demolishing' a set of ideas. This encourages the view of argument as a competitive venture, in which winning is paramount and losing can result in potential disaster. But a different metaphorical frame could present

an entirely different picture: if an argument were seen within a 'dance/performance' metaphorical frame, for instance, then the quality of arguments on both sides, and good techniques for presenting them, would become more of a focus of attention.

Beattie and Speakman (1983) showed that co-operation in conversation often involves developing agreement about the metaphorical frame. In analyses of interviews with politicians, they showed that a conversation would often need to settle on an agreed metaphor before explanations and questioning could proceed. For example, when talking about the economy of a country, a number of different metaphorical frames could be used, such as the 'illness/health' metaphor portraying the country as needing to be 'nursed' back to health, and involving terms like referring to the country as 'suffering'. An alternative might be the 'war/violence' metaphor, talking about 'fighting' inflation, and the 'battle' of the economy; or the 'gardening' metaphor, with participants in the conversation using terms like 'cultivating a growth economy' or 'pruning surplus expenditure'. What is interesting was that both participants in a typical political interview tend to spend some time at the beginning of the interview trying out different metaphors before settling on one which is acceptable to both participants.

Sherrard (1997) discussed how attitudes shift and alter during a conversation, and their functions also alter. By exploring inconsistencies in the discourse, and the forms of language which are used, Sherrard was able to show that attitudes are far from being fixed, consistent cognitive structures. Instead, they are flexible, and extremely responsive to the metaphors and rhetorical frames which are being applied during the course of the conversation. Sherrard's analysis focused on a discussion about aesthetic taste, and showed that there were specific conversational repertoires which arose at different points in the conversation, each of which had different implications for understanding what was going on, socially.

Social justifications

Lalljee and Widdicombe (1989) argued that discourse analysis is not only about looking at how and when language happens. It is also concerned with what language is being used for. For example, Van Dijk (1987) used discourse analysis to investigate the way that white Dutch racists expressed and transmitted their beliefs. Their discourse included several verbal strategies for making the speakers seem credible to listeners, while still expressing their prejudiced attitudes. The strategies were designed to make their nasty attitudes seem socially acceptable, and make it more difficult for the listener to accuse them of racism directly. The strategies are listed in Table 4.1.

In another study, Gilbert and Mulkay (1984) showed how scientists' discourse was very different when assertions in formal publications were compared with statements in interviews. The language in formal publications was tentative, and aimed only to suggest possibilities. When they were being interviewed, however, the scientists were much more definite about what they had found. This is not to say, of course, that the scientists were engaging in deliberate misrepresentation: the formal, tentative language of scientific journals is fairly difficult to process cognitively, and would be both socially and cognitively inappropriate in an interview.

Discourse analysis sometimes focuses on rhetoric: Potter and Wetherell (1987) showed that the way people construct their arguments is a revealing indicator of the social assumptions underpinning what they are saying. In 1988, Wetherell and Potter carried out a discourse analysis of interviews about the teaching of Maori culture in New Zealand schools – a practice described as cultural fostering. Their analysis involved identifying 'repertoires', or general themes, in the interviews, and they identified three of these (see Table 4.2). The three repertoires allowed the interviewees to pretend to support cultural fostering but also to assert that it was

Table 4.2 Repertoires in discourse

Culture fostering	The idea that Maori culture should be encouraged.
Pragmatic realism	The idea that it was necessary to keep up with the modern world (implying that therefore teaching Maori culture would not be appropriate).
Togetherness	The idea that everyone should 'work together' for the good of the country (which really meant that everyone else should conform to white New Zealander culture).

Source: Wetherell and Potter, 1988

really impractical or undesirable. Like Van Dijk's study, the use of discourse analysis revealed how racist talk often operates by apparently expressing a 'positive' viewpoint, and then apparently discrediting it by bringing in other arguments.

Explanations cannot really be understood without looking at the social context in which they happen. Lalljee (1981) identified four important aspects of that social context. The first is the **assumptions** which can be made in the context of that explanation – things which can be taken for granted, between the explainer and the receiver of the explanation. The second is to do with the **relationship** between the person making the excuse, and the person receiving it. The third is to do with the **social purpose** of the explanation: who we are explaining to, and why they should be the person to receive it; and the fourth is to do with the **interpersonal consequences** of the explanation – what may or may not happen as a result. Unless we look at these factors, Lalljee argued, we are not going to be able to develop a clear understanding of what an explanation or social justification is doing.

Antaki and Fielding (1981) discussed how everyday conversations, and in particular descriptions, contain much more social meaning than may appear on the surface. For example, if you turned up somewhere wearing shorts and received a quizzical look, you might respond by saying 'it's a hot day'. The statement itself would appear to be a simple description, but looking at the social context and purpose of why it was said would show that it was really offered as an explanation for your unusual attire. News broadcasts are partic-

Table 4.1 Verbal strategies used by racists

Credibility-enhancing moves	The person makes statements designed to show that they 'know' what they were talking about.
Positive self-presentation	The person disclaims being racist but provides reasons for disliking the minority group in question based on what they claim to be 'good' reasons, like unfair competition.
Negative other-presentation	The disliked group is described as engaging in negative or illegal behaviour.

Source: Van Dijk, 1987

ularly apt to contain this type of hidden explanation, but a great deal of other everyday description, too, is really offered as explanation or social justification.

Other researchers have looked at how people go about explaining things: for example, Stratton *et al.* (1986) developed a technique for analysing the attributions which people made in their conversation, during the course of family therapy. They found that the type of explanation which the person used was often very revealing about how they thought of stressful situations, and how they were likely to react to them. This analysis made it easier for the therapist to identify how that person might be able to develop more effective coping strategies. In 1997, Stratton discussed how attributional analysis could be applied in other types of contexts too – in this case, commercial research for an airline company which wanted to discover how their passengers saw air travel.

Language and cognition

Conversational and discourse analysis are all about the way that language is used socially. But psychologists have also been concerned with the relationship between language and cognitive processes. This includes studies of the way that language has affected the study of memory, and also of how closely language is related to thinking.

Language and memory

In a study by Carmichael, Hogan and Walter (1932), research participants were shown a set of fairly abstract figures. Each research participant was given a verbal label – a name – to go with each figure, which suggested what it might be; but there was a pair of different names for each image. For example, one figure was described to one group of research participants as 'curtains in a window', while being described to the other group as 'a diamond in a rectangle'. Carmichael found that when they were tested later, the research participants' visual memories had changed according to the verbal labels that they had been given. Moreover, when they were asked to draw the figures that they had seen, their drawings were much more similar to the verbal labels than to the original stimuli. Using the words to describe them

had shaped and adjusted the memory of the figures (Figure 4.1 overleaf).

When we are using language, we do not just de-code words or sentences in isolation: we apply the knowledge of the world that we already have, to make sense of the information. Bransford and Johnson (1972) showed how important our pre-existing knowledge of the world is, for understanding language. They asked research participants to read through short, unnamed passages, and then tested them to see how much they remembered of what they had read. The research participants who knew what the passage was about recalled 73% more of the information than those who did not.

One of the passages which Bransford and Johnson used was the following one. Try reading it through and then test yourself to see how much of it you remember:

The procedure is actually quite simple. First you arrange things into different groups depending on their makeup. Of course, one pile may be sufficient depending on how much there is to do. If you have to go somewhere else due to lack of facilities, that is the next step; otherwise you are pretty well set. It is important not to overdo any particular endeavour. That is, it is better to do too few things at once rather than too many. In the short run this may not seem important, but complications from doing too many can easily arise. A mistake can be expensive as well. The manipulation of the appropriate mechanisms should be self-explanatory, and we need not dwell on it here. At first the whole procedure will seem complicated. Soon, however, it will become just another facet of life. It is difficult to foresee any end to the necessity for this task in the immediate future, but then one can never tell. After the procedure is completed, one arranges the materials into different groups again. Then they can be put into their appropriate places. Eventually they will be used once more and the whole cycle will have to be repeated. However, that is part of life.

Once you have written down as much of the passage as you can remember, turn to page 130 to find out what the passage is about. Then try again to remember what the passage said. You will probably find, as Bransford and Johnson did with their research participants, that you can recall much more of it when you know what the author is talking about. Studies like this show us just how complex the relationship between thinking and language is, and how much our general assumptions and styles of thinking influence the messages that we receive through language.

Figure 4.1 Carmichael's figures

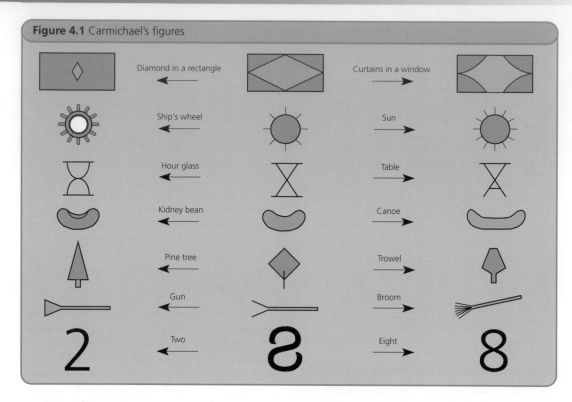

Inaccuracy in recall

As we saw in the last chapter, we tend to remember the sense of what has been said rather than what has literally been said to us, even though we may believe that our memory is precise and accurate. In one study, Bransford, Barclay and Franks (1972) gave people stimulus sentences to read, such as:

Three turtles rested on a floating log and a fish swam beneath them.

Later, they showed their research participants a number of sentences, and asked them which ones they had been shown before. The participants would often say that they recognised a sentence which was slightly different from the old one, but which effectively meant the same. For instance, if they had been shown the stimulus sentence above, they would be likely to say that they recognised the test sentence:

Three turtles rested on a floating log and a fish swam beneath it.

But if they were shown a stimulus sentence which described the turtles as resting beside the floating

log, they would not think that the test sentence was familiar.

The way that we adjust memories of what was said can help us to understand how misunderstandings occur in everyday life. Language can be used to convey misleading impressions, for example, and is often used that way in advertising. Because people tend to remember what they think they heard, or what they expected to hear, rather than what was actually said, they often remember the message as having been far more definite than it really was. Advertisers use this to their advantage. They give a tentative message (in a very positive voice) such as 'Brand X can help clear colds' (implication: but it might not), knowing that this is likely to result in the consumer remembering: 'Brand X helps clear colds' (implication: always).

The definite tone of voice is used to reinforce the certainty of the message, and this can be very powerful. Argyle, Alkema and Gilmour (1971) showed that when people are faced with conflicting verbal and non-verbal messages, they are four times more likely to believe the non-verbal one. This backs up Ellis and Beattie's argument that it is inadequate to try to study language in isolation, without considering the non-verbal dimension as well. In the case of advertising, the verbal and non-verbal messages are not actually in conflict: it is just that one is much more definite than the other. So although a strict analysis of what was said shows that there was nothing misleading, the psychological reality is that people seeing the advert are likely to have been misled.

Language and thinking

One of the most important areas for psychologists investigating language has been the way that language interlinks with other cognitive processes. In particular, the debate has centred around the precise relationship between language and thinking: are thinking and language one and the same thing, as the behaviourists asserted? Are they entirely different, at least in their origins? Or does speaking a particular language shape a person's thought, and if so, to what extent?

Thinking and language as the same thing

As we saw in Chapter 1, the behaviourists denied that cognitive processes existed as separate processes from human behaviour. Their view on thinking was that it was simply a form of sub-vocal speech. A small child talks aloud as it monitors its actions and works out problems, but as we grow older, we learn to suppress our speech movements. But according to the behaviourists, we do not suppress them entirely. They argued that what people generally refer to as thinking are really infinitesimal movements of the larynx and throat, which have become so habitual that the person no longer notices that they are happening. So for the behaviourists, at least, the processes of language and thinking were one and the same: thinking was nothing more than sub-vocal language.

The idea was tested by an ingenious study by Smith *et al.* in 1947. If thinking was merely sub-vocal speech, they reasoned, then preventing someone from making any speech movements at all, even minute ones, should mean that they are unable to think. The researchers used curare, a drug which paralyses the muscles, to investigate this. They gave research participants a dose of the drug, making sure that they were also receiving an artificial oxygen supply, to keep them alive and aware (curare paralyses breathing muscles too, which is why experiencing it normally results in death). While they were paralysed, they showed

them a series of cognitive puzzles. When the participants recovered, they not only remembered what had happened, but they had also been able to solve the puzzles, showing that they were able to think even though they could not make speech movements.

Other researchers showed that some forms of thinking do not need to involve language at all. In a study of concept-formation, Humphrey (1951) showed that if people were asked to identify the concept linking a series of cards which were turned over one at a time, they would generally find that they could select the right card long before they could articulate the rule that they were following. It was apparent, then, that some forms of cognitive representation could take place without language, and the behaviourist idea that language and thought were simply the same thing was largely discredited.

Language as dependent on thinking

The developmental psychologist Piaget, whose theory we will be exploring in Chapter 19, believed very firmly that knowledge was acquired through interaction with the environment, and represented internally as a result. Language, Piaget believed, is only one of several possible ways in which the child can represent its knowledge (Piaget, 1959). In other words, Piaget saw knowledge as being the precursor to language. First, the child has experiences, and then it uses language to represent that experience, both internally and socially. In this view, language is a symbolic system used to express thought, but the child might equally well use other forms of representation, such as symbolic play, imitation or even drawing.

Piaget's belief that knowledge precedes language also led to the idea that the language which the child uses will simply reflect its cognitive development. So, for example, the use of ego-centric language would indicate egocentric thought. As the child matures and acquires more subtle uses of language, Piaget believed, it does so because its underlying thought processes have become more subtle. The fact that children learn the word 'taller' after they have learned the word 'tall' indicated, to Piaget, that the child had a mental tendency to perceive in absolutes first, and relative concepts later. But as we will see in Chapter 19, the idea that what the child says is an accurate reflection of how the child thinks has been challenged by later researchers.

Language and thinking as independent processes

An alternative approach to the relationship comes from the theories of L.S. Vygotsky, a famous Russian psychologist who has been extremely influential among developmental psychologists in recent years. Vygotsky's ideas, although developed and published in the USSR in 1934, did not become available in English translation until 1962. When they were published, the theoretical perspective which Vygotsky applied to a number of different aspects of child development aroused a great deal of interest, and many modern researchers have adopted the Vygotskyan framework for understanding child development.

Vygotsky argued that although thinking and language do occur together, particularly in adults, they do not necessarily have the same origins. Thinking, he argued, is a cognitive activity which occurs as the infant learns about its world. It encounters experiences, and stores memories, and thinking originates in the need for the infant to use those stored memories and its awareness of what the world is like to make sense out of a situation, or to come to terms with discordant or contradictory bits of information. The kind of reasoning processes which most people recognise as thinking are forms of cognitive re-structuring, which allow us to interpret and make sense of our experiences.

Language, on the other hand, is an affiliative activity. Infants develop language because they hear it from other people. We will be looking at language acquisition later in this chapter; but what the research seems to show is that human contact is vital for children in acquiring language – hearing tapes or radio is simply not enough. Young infants often pick up the interactive aspects of language first: they may babble nonsense sounds, but they use the tones of voice, timing, and length of utterances that they hear from other people. Parent-infant interaction encourages the infant to develop these abilities further, and to use words to enhance its interaction with other people. But even in adults, a great deal of the language that we use is affiliative, rather than cognitive in nature. Language activities such as greeting rituals, or asking for a bus ticket, and what we refer to as 'small talk' often do not involve much mental processing at all!

At around two years of age, Vygotsky argued, the crucial moment occurs when the separate areas of pre-linguistic thought and pre-intellectual language join together. At this point, things change considerably: '*thought becomes verbal and speech rational*' (Vygotsky, 1962). From this time on, language has two different functions for the child. One is an internal function, to do with monitoring and directing internal thought. In this sense, language acts as a cognitive tool to help the child in its thinking. The second is an external social function, to do with engaging in social interaction, and communicating the results of thinking to other people. Vygotsky referred to these as separate modes, or **planes** of language.

Among adults, language has two different functions. For the most part, the cognitive functions of language are served by **inner speech**, which acts as a way of monitoring and structuring mental activity (see Box 4.1). The communicative functions of language are different, and come into play when the adult is speaking aloud or writing. But young children often produce **egocentric speech**, in which the child's speech reflects what is in its own mind without reference to any listener. Vygotsky argued that this happens because the child is unable to separate out the two functions of language. As it talks aloud about its plans and actions, it is using speech as a tool for cognition, not for communication.

As children become older, their egocentric speech becomes more condensed, and different from their social speech, until eventually they stop saying it out loud altogether. At this point, it has become a private form of language used for thinking. The external, social use of language, though, becomes clarified and more linguistically sophisticated, as the child gradually acquires a better idea of accepted meanings of words, and learns to communicate socially with other people.

Vygotsky's theory, then, portrays the two activities of language and thinking as having entirely independent roots. Language originates in our need to interact with other people, and to communicate socially; while thinking originates in our need to make sense of the world. According to Vygotsky, quite a lot of everyday thinking has no direct connection with language – the classic example being using tools. Language without thought can also occur, for instance in the process of repeating a poem learned by heart. So both thought and language can exist independently, but they overlap in the area of verbal thought.

But once a child has acquired language, then

Box 4.1 Inner speech

Inner speech has a different type of syntax and word-use than social speech. It tends to be telegraphic and abbreviated, and often involves words which are personally coded – certain words have a special, private meaning for the person who is using them, which is sometimes entirely different from their accepted social meaning.

Vygotsky described inner speech as dealing with 'sense' rather than 'meaning'. In this description, 'meaning' is what the word stands for – like a dictionary definition of a cat as 'a furry domestic quadruped'. 'Sense', on the other hand, refers to the whole complex of psychological events aroused by a word, such as the personal memories of your own pet cat and its mannerisms, the feel of its fur, and so on. It contains activities, impressions and personal meanings, not just accepted social definitions.

Inner speech is a kind of bridge between thought and the semantic aspects of language. If we are trying to solve difficult problems, we often engage in **cognitive monitoring** by saying things out loud. This is a kind of regression to egocentric speech – thinking out loud – which helps us to keep track of what we are thinking. This type of cognitive monitoring also happens sometimes in people who are deprived of social speech because they live alone. They often find themselves commenting on their own thoughts and actions. It has been suggested that this use of language occurs precisely because of the lack of opportunities for social speech, so the distinction between the two becomes blurred.

The different views of Piaget and Vygotsky on what constitutes egocentric speech generate different predictions. Piaget would expect egocentric speech to increase in cases of fewer social constraints; whereas Vygotsky would expect it to decrease. But studies of how children interact when they are communicating with deaf-mutes, strangers or foreigners show that the children decrease their egocentric speech significantly if they are unsure whether the person is fully understanding them. This finding not only supports Vygotsky's views, but also emphasises, again, the sophistication of the child's social understanding.

language acquires another useful function, which is that of monitoring thought processes, and acting as symbolic representation. As a result, we develop the ability to engage in verbal thought, and this ability allows us to extend our mental world considerably. So language eventually becomes a tool of thought, although it begins as an independent, social process.

Language as a tool of thought

The idea that language is a tool of thought is the most generally-accepted view of the relationship between language and thinking in psychology. Language is seen as facilitating some kinds of thinking, although not all kinds. In 1964, Bruner discussed the development of **mental representation**, looking at the way that the child uses enactive, iconic and symbolic forms of representation as it develops. We will be looking at this idea more closely in the next chapter, but according to Bruner, these forms of representation develop directly in response to environmental demands, and serve to accelerate or facilitate cognitive development. As part of this discussion, Bruner proposed that language is the most important system of cognitive representation that we possess.

Bruner argued that for the child, language provides the means of transforming experience as well as simply representing it in a number of ways. This means that it can directly augment and enhance the child's ability to think. One way in which it transforms experience is by allowing us to think about abstracts and possibilities. We can use language to speculate about things which have not happened – and may never happen at all. And language also focuses attention on salient features of the environment, which can have considerable implications for knowledge and problem-solving.

Using words as symbols to represent ideas allows us to develop classifications and general concepts. This means that we can structure our experience and understand connections between different experiences much more easily than we could with a more limited system of representation. We do not have to treat every animal which we hear about as if it were unique: we can use the linguistic concept 'animal', to group all our experiences with animals together, and so understand the world more subtly. Language also allows us to use information in a more flexible way: by permitting the hierarchical storage of concepts and terms, language can provide a structure for information which can be manipulated easily but which can also give us a framework to help problem-solving and thinking.

For Bruner, then, language is one of the most important tools of thought available to the child, mainly because of the way that it facilitates cognitive structuring and reorganisation. So unlike Piaget, Bruner saw language as taking a very active role in cognition: the flexible qualities of language directly affect what is possible in terms of cognitive organisation, and so are intimately linked with our thinking. According to Bruner, language does not just reflect thought, it also shapes it.

Linguistic relativity

The idea that language actually shapes thought leads directly to the question of whether different kinds of language facilitate different kinds of thinking. Some languages are more closely related than others: French, German and English, for example, are all moderately similar languages, in that most words in one language have equivalent forms in the other two. But even they have some words which do not translate exactly: we have already seen how psychologists had to import the word *Gestalt* to express the concept of wholeness and unity of shape or form. This idea could only be put rather clumsily in English, but it was expressed elegantly and simply by the German word.

Some languages, though, are very different. In Japanese, for example, the basic vocabulary of the language incorporates a whole world of social relationships and assumptions which do not have precise equivalents in English. And some languages do not include words for things which English speakers would consider basic: the Russian language, for example, has no word for 'hand' – only for fingers and arms. In Russian, too, male and female speakers use different word-endings to describe their past activities. These differences raise a number of questions about how far language shapes our thinking: what sort of an influence it actually has.

One of the best-known theories about the relationship between language and thinking is sometimes known as the **Sapir-Whorf hypothesis**, because it was developed by the American linguist and anthropologist Edward Sapir and his pupil Benjamin Lee Whorf. More usually, though, it is called the **linguistic relativity hypothesis**. It has two forms, the strong form, and the weak one. In the strong form, it is about linguistic determinism – the idea that language determines thinking. In other words, if there is no way to express a concept in a language, then that concept will not be available for people who speak that language. The weak form of the linguistic relativity hypothesis is less extreme, arguing simply that it would be more difficult for people who spoke that language to acquire the concept, though not impossible.

The strong form of the linguistic relativity hypothesis

The Sapir-Whorf hypothesis was stated in its strong form by Sapir, in 1947. Sapir argued that each individual is cognitively dependent on their language system, in the sense that the categories and distinctions which are encoded in that language will determine the kind of thinking of which someone is capable. In addition, each language system has its own unique set of such categories and distinctions, different from other languages. This is the 'linguistic relativity' part of the theory. Sapir believed that it would never really be possible to translate an idea perfectly from one language to another, because language determined thinking to such an extent.

In 1911 Boas had shown how different languages often involve distinctions which are special to the particular language. One of his most famous examples was that of an Eskimo or Inuit language which had 27 different words for snow – illustrating how the language, environment and culture of the people were interlinked. Pullum (1989) challenged this idea, arguing that the figure had become distorted with successive reportings, and that there were really only two words for snow in Inuit. These were *qanik*, referring to 'snow in the air' and *aput*, referring to 'snow on the ground'. There is some doubt, though, as to whether Pullum was referring to the same Inuit language, and also about the accuracy of the translation. In any case, the Lapp language does involve many different words for snow, the various meanings of which are listed in Table 4.3.

Table 4.3 Lapp words for snow

The Lapp language contains a special word for each of the following types of snow:

falling snow

recently fallen snow

snow on the ground

soft snow on the ground

wet falling snow

half-melted snow on the ground

drift of soft snow

drift of hard snow

re-frozen snow

snow rendered rough by rain and freezing

crystalline snow on the ground

fine coat of powdered snow

fine snow carried by the wind

thin coat of soft snow deposited on an object

snow whose surface is frozen

hard crust of snow giving way under footsteps

snow ready to melt, on the ground

snow for making water

melting snow used as cement for the snowhouse

snow which can be used for building a snowhouse

yellow or reddish falling snow

damp, compact snow

melting snow

light falling snow

very light falling snow, in still air

Source: Rovaniemi Science Centre, Lapland

However, these examples do not necessarily show that language determines thought, as Sapir believed, since they could equally well be taken to show that the environment causes language. Living in an environment where something like snow is so important, it is understandable that a community would develop an extensive vocabulary to describe it. Bruner's idea of language as the vehicle for categorisation and conceptualisation implies that people will tend to notice and remember things which are easily codable in their language. The English language, for example, has a large number of words for writing and drawing implements (such as pen, biro, pencil, crayon etc.), with the consequence that we can make subtle distinctions in these, which someone from a non-literate culture might regard as entirely unnecessary. After all, they all make marks on pieces of paper!

Even if a language does not have specialist words, though, languages can be adapted and developed when the need arises. The English language, for instance, has no single word for 'a-way-of-looking-at-the-world', but it imports the German word *Weltanschauung* for this purpose. English may not have 27 different words for snow, but skiers have developed several ways of describing different kinds of snow, despite the limitations of the language. Most groups with an occupational focus tend to develop specific vocabularies which allow them to refer to finer details of their occupation than might otherwise have been possible: this is the purpose of specialist 'jargon', for instance.

Another problem with the idea that language determines thought is its corollary: the idea that everyone who speaks that language will therefore tend to think in similar ways. Within a particular language speaking culture there are often many subcultures, which may be very different from one another, and sometimes people belonging to these subcultures have very different ways of seeing the world despite speaking the same language.

The weak form of linguistic relativity

In practice, neither Sapir nor Whorf subscribed completely to the strong form of the linguistic relativity hypothesis. Instead they adopted a weaker form, which simply stated that language could be influential in affecting the kind of thinking which people usually engaged in. There is a certain amount of supporting evidence for the weaker form of the linguistic relativity hypothesis. Farb (1974) studied Japanese women living in San Francisco who had married American servicemen. They spoke English to their husbands and children, but Japanese with each other. When they were interviewed in both languages, it was found that the attitudes that they expressed differed markedly depending on the language which they used. For instance, when they were asked to complete the statement: 'When my wishes conflict with my family's …', in Japanese they said '… it is a time of great unhappiness', but in English they said '… I do what I want'.

Farb explained this in terms of the 'language world' of cultural ideas and assumptions that was generated by using the language: the women expressed attitudes appropriate to the language world that they were inhabiting when they spoke. As we saw in Carmichael's study, changing the verbal labels of an image affected people's memories of that image. In a similar way, using Japanese would have brought back memories of their traditional upbringing for those women, which would have meant that those aspects of their personality became more salient to the question, while using English would have made their current lives, and modern assumptions, more salient.

That does not mean, though, that all of the examples raised in support of the linguistic relativity hypothesis have been equally convincing. One of the several examples given by Whorf, in 1956, for example, was that Hopi Indians use the same word for 'insect', 'air-pilot' and 'aeroplane'. He argued that this showed how underlying patterns of thought within that culture were different from those of Europeans, since European thinking could not perceive connections between these three different things. But in 1975, Greene pointed out that the same word, 'drive', is used in English to mean a number of different things: operating a motor vehicle, playing a golf stroke, a wide pathway leading to a house, an intense ambition, etc. But that does not mean that speakers of English see a connection between all the different meanings. Inferring cognitive patterns from linguistic data can be very misleading.

Colour terms

Some of the research into the linguistic relativity hypothesis has centred on how we name colours. This is for two main reasons. The first is that colour perception can be tested directly, by showing people different colours without having to use language at all. And the second is that different languages vary considerably in the number of words they have for colour. Some languages do not have words to distinguish colours at all, except for light and dark; others vary in how they classify colours. For example: there is no single word for 'blue' in the Russian language; it depends on whether the speaker is referring to light blue or dark blue; also, no single word in French means exactly what 'brown' does in English.

In 1969, Berlin and Kay put forward what became known as the **Berlin-Kay hypothesis.** They argued that there is a universal substructure in the vocabulary of colour: basic terms always describe the same colours and relate to the same wavelengths of light. Berlin and Kay saw this as happening as a result of the physiological characteristics of human perception (see Chapter 12).

Table 4.4 lists how colours are expressed in languages which have varying numbers of words for colour, ranging from two to eight. The eleven colours listed in the table represent the full set of basic colour terms identified by Berlin and Kay. Once these were established in a language, they argued, any number of graduations or different colour terms could be added.

The idea that colour terms are universal, and not dependent on language, challenged the linguistic relativity hypothesis and was investigated empirically by researchers. In 1974, Rosch showed that a tribe with only two basic colour terms in their language, the Dani, could perceive colour variations just as accurately and in the same way as people who had all eleven basic terms. Even though they did not have the vocabulary, they could distinguish colours. In this case at least, language does not seem to determine what people are capable of thinking about.

Research in other areas also questions whether language affects how capable people are of specific forms of thinking: Dixon (1980) performed an investigation of numeracy in speakers of an Australian Aboriginal language, which has no numerals higher than four. Those who learned English as a second language had no difficulty with numbers and could use them to perform calculations just as readily as native English speakers. Overall, the evidence seems to suggest that there is little evidence for underlying basic concepts being determined by language, although social

Table 4.4 Basic colour terms	
No. of colour terms in language	**Colours identified**
Two	Black and white
Three	Black, white, red
Four	Black, white, red, yellow
Five	Black, white, red, yellow, green
Six	Black, white, red, yellow, green, blue
Seven	Black, white, red, yellow, green, blue, brown
Eight	The colours already named, plus any one of purple, pink, orange or grey

Source: Berlin and Kay, 1969

concepts may be culturally specific, like 'individuality' in the Japanese/English example.

The verbal deprivation hypothesis

The **verbal deprivation hypothesis** is a theoretical approach which also arises from the view that thinking is dependent on language; or at least, that sophisticated forms of thinking like abstract reasoning and classification are. It implies that variations in language ability will produce variations in how capable language users are of thinking in sophisticated ways. The verbal deprivation hypothesis predicts that people who for one reason or another have only a limited command of a language will be less capable of sophisticated reasoning than people who have an extensive command of the same language.

One of the most well-known statements of the verbal deprivation hypothesis was made by Basil Bernstein, in 1973. Bernstein was a sociologist who was particularly interested in how different kinds of knowledge are distributed throughout society. In particular, he distinguished between universalistic and particularistic orders of meaning. **Universalistic meanings** in Bernstein's terms are to do with abstract, general principles: knowledge which can be looked at independently of specific contexts. **Particularistic meanings**, on the other hand, are to do with immediate, specific ideas or examples, which are often tightly dependent on the context in which they happen.

Bernstein argued that it is only by being able to perceive universalistic orders of meaning – general principles – that people can recognise the basis of their own experience, and so become able to change it. If their understanding of situations is particularistic – tied to the particular context – then they are much less able to change, because it becomes much more difficult to see alternatives. For example: if you interpret a long-term difficulty which you are having with a supervisor at work as being a matter of personal reactions to specific events, it is difficult to change that situation. But if you see it as a manifestation of racism, because you come from a different ethnic background, then it is possible (though not necessarily easy) to do something about it. In the first case, the particularistic understanding ties you to the specific situations and circumstances, so there is little you can do except try to avoid trouble. In the second case, the universalistic interpretation means that

you can see it as part of a more general pattern, and can register a formal complaint or bring other social controls into the situation.

Bernstein also argued that different forms of language use, which he initially referred to as **linguistic codes**, and later as **sociolinguistic codes**, serve to direct their users towards either universalistic or particularistic forms of meaning. Bernstein defined a 'code' as a set of principles of semantic organisation. He identified two main codes, which he called elaborated and restricted codes of language. Elaborated language codes, he said, allowed people access to universalistic forms of meaning, while restricted language codes were much more context-dependent, and so only allowed for particularistic meanings. Table 4.5 shows some of the differences which Bernstein identified between the two language codes.

Bernstein argued that the class system limits access to elaborated codes, through socialisation

Table 4.5 Elaborated and restricted codes of language

Elaborated codes	Restricted codes
Verbally explicit meaning	Verbally implicit meaning
High proportion of: subordinate clauses; the pronoun 'I'; passive verbs; uncommon adverbs, conjunctions and adjectives	*High proportion of:* personal pronouns, especially 'you' and 'they'; tag questions asking for agreement
Independent of extra-linguistic features (e.g. non-verbal signals shared experience)	Relies on extra-linguistic features for communication
Context-independent	Context-dependent
Readily used to handle abstract concepts	More appropriate for concrete concepts
Expresses speaker's individuality (e.g. personal values)	Stesses speaker's membership of group, with shared assumptions
Maintains social distance	Strengthens social relationships
More common among middle-class speakers	More common among working-class speakers
Used in formal settings (e.g. academic debate)	Used in informal settings (e.g. family, friends)

Source: Bernstein, 1973

into language use. Working-class children, he argued, tend to encounter restricted codes of language in their home and wider social context; whereas elaborated codes are the dominant form of language used in middle-class homes. Since school knowledge tends to require the explicit use of elaborated codes, middle-class children have an automatic advantage, because 'school language' is familiar to them; whereas working-class children encounter a different form of language at school than the one that they are familiar with from their home environment, and consequently begin school with a disadvantage.

Criticisms of the verbal deprivation hypothesis

Bernstein's work carried the implicit idea that working-class children were verbally deprived: that they grew up with less verbal stimulation than middle-class children, and that the verbal stimulation which they did receive was so highly context-dependent that it tied them to particularistic meanings and did not allow for abstract thinking. This concept of verbal deprivation was sharply challenged by Labov, in 1972, who argued that it is unrealistic as a representation of how working-class children actually learn language. Many such children, Labov argued, actually grow up in an environment with a very high level of linguistic stimulation, and participate fully in an actively verbal culture from a very young age. Although the language that they hear may be a dialect rather than a standard form, their environment is often linguistically enriched, and not deprived at all.

Labov performed a series of studies in which he showed that looking beyond the superficial forms of language use paints a very different picture. The reason why researchers often failed to grasp the abilities of restricted code users, he argued, is to do with the intimidating formal settings in which language use tends to be investigated. In a classic set of studies involving black children, Labov showed how a formal test setting – whether with a black or a white experimenter – resulted in very little verbal communication from the child. But in a situation where a black experimenter chatted informally to a child called Leon, using colloquial language and sitting on the floor sharing a packet of crisps, a very different picture emerged. Leon showed himself to be highly articulate and able to develop a complex abstract argument concerning

the existence of God – one which, in fact, was more conceptually sophisticated than the argument produced by a fluent elaborated code user on a similar question.

Labov argued that elaborated code use as described by Bernstein did not really have anything to do with conceptual ability, despite the superficial appearances given by the wide vocabulary and structure. Often, he argued, the use of elaborated language involved hesitations and obscurities which often covered up an underlying lack of ideas. Speakers of non-standard English were often very direct and conceptually inventive, saying exactly what they meant without 'dressing it up' in lots of words. Also, Labov argued that the verbal deprivation model does not really look at everyday speech, and the day-to-day rules of discourse and syntax. If these rules are borne in mind, and language use is investigated in reassuring, non-formal settings, speakers of non-standard English can be shown to be highly competent and sophisticated in their use of language.

Labov saw the verbal deprivation hypothesis as a dangerous myth, leading to stereotyping of children according to background and race; and to a denial of the validity of different kinds of language. Other researchers agreed with this idea. Cazden (1970) argued that communicative competence was more important than linguistic competence – if someone can communicate effectively with other people, then it is unimportant which code of language they use. Wells (1979) showed that much of the research in this area is very naïve, usually only looking at just one or two extreme kinds of variation which are easily measured, like social class, and completely ignoring more complex or individual factors affecting linguistic style, like the situations and context of speech.

Although Bernstein was obviously mistaken in arguing that language use correlated with conceptual ability, and in that respect his argument did produce a 'dangerous myth', it is nonetheless the case that variations in how we use language can have a dramatic effect on how people see us. The use of different forms of language can produce social stereotyping, and may end up limiting or enhancing people's social opportunities. In this respect, Bernstein's argument that the education system gave an advantage to children who used middle-class elaborated codes of language should not be dismissed too lightly.

Accent, dialect and idiolect

Lyons (1981) distinguished three major forms of everyday variation: accent, dialect and idiolect. An **accent** is a regional or social variation in the way that words are pronounced by the speaker – a special kind of inflection or emphasis. A **dialect**, on the other hand, is a variation of a language, which has its own distinctive grammatical constructions and vocabulary. Dialects can be either regional or social, but it is notable in Britain that social status tends to take precedence over geography. Upper-middle-class people living in Yorkshire or Northumberland, for instance, tend to speak standard English, or **received pronunciation**; while their working-class compatriots speak the regional dialect.

Dialects which are very different from the standard form are sometimes seen as another language altogether. But Haugen (1966) argued that distinguishing between a dialect and a language is really only a matter of size and prestige. If there are a large number of people who speak it, and they have reasonably high social status, it is likely to be considered a language; if not, it will be seen as a dialect. Flemish, for example, is now generally acknowledged as a language in its own right; but for many years the French-speaking sector of Belgian society insisted that it was merely a dialect of Dutch. The recognition is a result of improvements in the social status of Flemish speakers in Belgium: it has nothing to do with any change in the language.

The third form of language variation described by Lyons is **idiolect**. Each one of us has developed a personal style of language use, which includes individual speech patterns and habits, and sometimes characteristic grammatical constructions. But since each person has several alternative styles of language use available to them, and will adopt whichever seems appropriate in any given context, the notion of idiolect is not very much use in the general study of language – although it can be helpful in a detailed study of one person.

Accent and social judgements

Giles (1973) investigated whether the accent of someone presenting an argument for or against capital punishment would affect the attitudes of seventeen-year-olds towards that issue. The personal views of the research participants were obtained first, and then seven days later they were presented with an argument against capital punishment delivered in one of a number of accents, including standard pronunciation, South Welsh, Somerset and Birmingham accents. The research participants were then asked to rate the quality of the argument that was presented to them. Their ratings varied directly with the social status of the accent: the more prestigious the accent, the better people considered the argument to have been.

A study by Edwards, in 1979, involved playing student teachers a series of tapes of children reading the same passage, and asking them to rate the children on a variety of dimensions, such as 'intelligence', 'enthusiasm', 'happiness', etc. Half of the children had regional working-class accents, while the other half had middle-class accents. The student teachers rated the working-class children less positively on all the scales involved in the study. In view of research findings which show how teachers' expectations may become self-fulfilling prophecies, influencing how teachers treat those children, and the children's subsequent educational performance (Rosenthal and Jacobsen, 1968), this is quite a disturbing observation.

Findings like these show us how influential social judgements based on accent or dialect can be. Many forms of vernacular (everyday or working-class) speech are seen as carrying implications about social status: conveying a message of social inferiority. Almost every language has its 'high' and 'low' forms, associated with different aspects of social status; and while these have nothing to do with the person's ability to think, reason or act intelligently, they may call into play social restrictions which limit the person's opportunities. In modern society, these are less obvious than they used to be, since we claim that society's institutions are open to all; but social restrictions can be very subtle. Someone may not get promoted beyond a certain level in a company, for example, or a high-grade student might fail to gain access to the higher grades of professions like law or medicine because it is judged, on the basis of their accent, that they 'would not fit'.

Diglossia

When there are strong differences between standard and vernacular speech, speaking both kinds is sometimes seen as a special form of bilingualism, referred to as **diglossia**. As Labov showed, the ability to communicate with someone in a pattern of speech which they find familiar can lead to an insight into their abilities and ideas which is not granted to those who use a more formal speech pattern. Many people unconsciously 'pick up' accents from the people that they are talking to; and at times this may form a valuable aid to effective communication. Hudson (1980) argued that being able to handle linguistic variation like this permits people who can do it to engage in wider identification with different groups in society simultaneously.

Sexist language

Our choice of language can dramatically affect the actual message that we transmit, even when we are using words which seem to mean the same thing. Thouless (1974) showed how **emotive words** (words which imply value-judgements or strong emotions) can influence what is heard by a listener. For example: it makes a difference whether the ruling body of a country is referred to in the media as a 'regime' or as a 'government' – a subtly different message is being conveyed in each case. Similarly, people who actively and violently oppose a particular system may be called 'freedom fighters', by those who support their cause, or 'terrorists' by those involved in the system that they are opposing.

One of the clearest examples of the transmission of attitudes through language can be seen with sexist language, in which the impression of women as being 'inferior' or 'unimportant' is perpetuated through the use of language. This applies both to the way that language is used, and to the messages that the language is deemed to contain.

Sexism in language use

Lakoff (1975) argued that women are directly encouraged to use less assertive forms of language than men. For instance, tentative expressions such as 'I think' or 'perhaps' appear frequently in female speech, but are relatively uncommon in the speech of men. Differences in style of this kind result in women's speech being regarded as less important, because it sounds less definite, and transmits uncertainty. As a result, Lakoff argued, what women have to say is taken less seriously.

There have been several studies illustrating how conventional forms of language can have a direct effect on people's thinking. Eakins and Eakins (1978) showed how women are more often

referred to as the 'owned' than as the 'owner' in relationships ('John's daughter', 'Ed's widow', etc.), and found that this affected people's problem-solving abilities. In one study, their research participants were given the following passage:

'A man and his young son were apprehended in a robbery. The father was shot during the struggle and the son, in handcuffs, was rushed to the police station. As the police pulled the struggling boy into the station, the mayor, who had been called to the scene, looked up and said 'My God, it's my son!''

When they had read the passage, the participants were asked to answer the question: 'What relation was the mayor to the boy?'

They report that their research participants often made 'wild and ridiculous' guesses as to the answer, but very few of them thought of the right solution: that the mayor might be the boy's mother. Their sexist assumptions about who a mayor was likely to be had affected their ability to reason logically. It has been argued that mayor is a sex-specific term, since there is also the word 'mayoress' in the language, and so the example is misleading. This argument, however, shows how deeply rooted these sexist assumptions are, since the term 'mayoress' is not a female equivalent of 'mayor', but refers to a different social role. If a woman is appointed mayor, she appoints someone else to be her mayoress, since there are different duties attached to the position. And in any case, the example has been shown to be equally powerful if the word 'surgeon' is used instead of mayor.

Vocabulary and sexism

When we looked at the linguistic relativity hypothesis, we saw how the vocabulary of a language can draw attention to features of the environment or culture. This can also apply in reverse: Spender (1980) pointed out that the English language has no neutral terms to describe a strong woman; and Hage (1972) showed that there is no term for normal sexual power in women, such as the equivalent of 'virile' or 'potent' in men. On the other hand, when it came to pejorative terms, Stanley (1973) showed how the English language has 220 words for describing sexually promiscuous women, by comparison with only 20 for describing sexually promiscuous men. 'Word counts' like this often reveal common social assumptions. In this particular case, they make it more difficult for women to be judged by society on equal terms with men.

Vocabulary can be a powerful indicator of social assumptions, and this can apply even to apparently neutral scientific vocabulary, as well as everyday speech. Spender (1980) quoted an example of 'loaded' language when describing the finding that women tend to be more aware of the context in which a visual stimulus occurs, than men are (Witkin *et al.*, 1962). This phenomenon was labelled in such a way that it appeared that the women's perception was inferior: women were held to be 'field dependent', while men were described as 'field independent'. But other words could equally well have described the phenomenon: Spender suggested 'context-aware' and 'context-blind' as alternatives, which would mean that it was the men, rather than the women, whose perceptions were portrayed as being deficient or inferior.

'Man' as a generic term

The social assumptions hidden in conventional uses of language can have quite a dramatic effect on our cognition. There are some interesting examples of this from research into the use of the generic term 'man' to refer to the whole of the human race, including women. According to Spender (1980), this use of language was only introduced during the seventeenth century; previously people had simply used 'they' as either a singular or plural term when referring to both women and men. Spender argued that the use of 'man' as a generic term meant that women became linguistically invisible – and the result was that they were seen as irrelevant. Since this was also the period when modern knowledge was being shaped, the development had far-reaching effects on scientific knowledge, as well as on everyday living.

Morgan (1972) showed how influential the term had been in scientific discussions of human evolution, by re-evaluating the commonly accepted view, looking at the part played by women as well as men. Women, she argued, were generally ignored by writers on human evolution, which meant that the theories they developed did not really consider survival demands like the protection of the young. Morgan attributed this directly to the use of 'man' as a generic term, and the generic use of the pronoun 'he'. This, she argued, resulted in attention being focused only on male activities, and women's activities being ignored.

The under-acknowledgement of women as a result of this use of language applies in wider contexts too. A number of studies have shown that the generic use of 'man' in sentences results in the formation of masculine images, and that these images affect how people interpret what is being said to them. Nilsen (1973) showed that children thought that 'man' means males in sentences such as 'man needs food'. And a study by Schneider and Hacker (1973) showed that students thought of males when faced with phrases such as 'political man' or 'urban man'.

In another study, Martyna (1980) showed research participants pictures of either males or females, and asked them whether a stimulus sentence could apply to the person in the picture. Male pictures were always judged to apply to all sentences containing the generic use of 'he', but 40% of the participants in one study and 20% in another judged female pictures not to apply. In a further study, Mackay and Fulkerson (1979) showed that similar errors in the comprehension of sentences containing the generic 'he' occurred 87% of the time, when research participants were asked whether the sentence could apply to a woman.

Schultz (1975) showed how the use of 'man' as a general term for human being was often inconsistent. Although writers claimed to be using it generically, the content of what they wrote showed that really they were only thinking about males. Schultz found several examples of this, in sentences like: 'Man's basic needs are for food, shelter, and access to females'. And Martyna (1978) found from interviews that when men used the term, they thought of themselves, and of other men, although women tended to think of people in general. But women used the term less often than men did.

Semantic degeneration

Language is not static. It changes over time, as new words come into the language and existing words change their meanings. But these changes are not random. Schultz (1975) pointed out that comparable male and female terms do not remain equivalent during use: the female equivalent tends to acquire a derogatory or lesser status (for example master/mistress; governor/governess; sir/madam; etc.). This occurs with such frequency that some researchers see this as a basic semantic rule within the English language: the principle of **semantic degeneration**.

Miller and Swift (1976) showed that semantic degeneration also occurs with names. When boys' names are adopted for use by girls, they cease to be used for boys. Names like Hilary, Evelyn, and Shirley used to be boys' names, but now they are only seen as suitable for girls. The sequence in which words appear can also carry a social message: Smith (1985) pointed out that traditionally male terms almost always occur before female equivalents, which again reinforces the idea of the female as less important (brother and sister, man and woman, etc.).

It has become a general principle in many types of writing that using sexist language should be avoided. As a result, several new conventions of writing have been developed to replace the old ones. Some writers, for instance, have taken to using a generic 'she' rather than 'he', while others are careful to refer to both female and male forms – and to alternate the order in which they appear. In recent years, psychologists have become increasingly aware of how language can transmit sexist assumptions, and how we can avoid giving unintentional messages through language use; with the consequence that the British Psychological Society's Code of Conduct for psychologists also includes a set of guidelines on the use of non-sexist language (British Psychological Society, 1991).

We can see, then, that the links between language and other cognitive processes are many and deep. While few psychologists nowadays would consider that language actually determines thought, few would deny that it can have a powerful influence on it. But perhaps one of the most important messages which emerges from research into the psychology of language is that language is a social skill, as well as a cognitive one, and its social uses exert a direct influence on how language affects our cognition.

Language acquisition

Modern research into language acquisition opened up with a big bang, as a major controversy developed between the behaviourist school, led by B.F. Skinner, and the psycho-linguistic school of thought led by Noam Chomsky. Essentially, this was a **nature-nurture debate**: Skinner was arguing that children acquire language purely as a result of learning, whereas Chomsky was arguing that children acquire language as a result of an inherited capacity.

Skinner's theory of language acquisition

In 1957, Skinner published a book entitled Verbal Behavior, in which he argued that language was learned by the child through the process of **operant conditioning** (see Chapter 18). Skinner argued that young babies spend a large amount of time vocalising – they often babble to themselves while they are wakeful. During the course of their babbling, infants produce every known phoneme which occurs in any human language. (A **phoneme** is a basic unit of sound – it corresponds to a single sound, not a single word.) Although human beings are capable of producing a very large number of phonemes, any one human language uses only a restricted set – but that set is different for each language.

Skinner suggested that parents, particularly mothers, gradually narrow down the range of phonemes which their child produces. They do this by rewarding the ones which sound similar to the phonemes in their own language, and ignoring others. The reward consists of smiling or giving the child attention, which is a pleasant experience for the child. As a result, the child produces more and more of those phonemes, and fewer of the phonemes which are not part of that child's language.

The production of sounds becomes the production of words through behaviour-shaping. The child combines phonemes together as it babbles, and sometimes, these form **morphemes** (combinations of phonemes) which sound like words. For instance, it might combine a 'mmm' sound with an 'uh' sound, to make a sound like 'Muh-muh'. When this happens, the child's parents are pleased, because they feel that the child is beginning to talk. They reward the child with attention and approval, which makes the child more likely to make that sound again. Gradually, Skinner argued, the child's utterances are shaped from random noises into words, and this is how it acquires a vocabulary.

Once the child is producing words, it gains approval from adults by combining those words into sentences, and doing this in the right contexts also gains approval. This continual behaviour-shaping process ensures that inappropriate responses are gradually dropped from the child's repertoire, while appropriate ones are strengthened.

Eventually, Skinner argued, it results in the child being able to use language.

Skinner's theory represented an extreme behaviourist approach to language development. He denied any involvement of the mind in what the child was doing, seeing language entirely as 'verbal behaviour'. Perhaps not surprisingly, the theory caused a storm of outrage when it was first published, and one of the most outspoken critics of Skinner's ideas was the linguist Noam Chomsky. Chomsky produced a scathing review of Skinner's book, and in the process outlined an alternative theory of language acquisition.

Chomsky's theory of language acquisition

Chomsky (1959) challenged Skinner's approach to language on several grounds. He argued that Skinner's theory implied that children learn entirely through trial and error – that they try out possible utterances, and repeat them if they gain approval or abandon them if they do not. But, Chomsky argued, children acquire language very much more quickly than such a mechanism would allow. Within a relatively short period of about two years, they have acquired some complex grammatical rules and an extensive vocabulary. This would not be possible if they had to try out every possible combination by trial and error. This is not one of Chomsky's stronger arguments, though, since, as we will see in Chapter 18, conditioned responses can also be generalised to other stimuli.

Instead of learning by operant conditioning, Chomsky proposed that the child has an innate language acquisition device (LAD). This is an inherited mechanism which allows the child to decode the spoken language it hears around it so as to reveal the basic principles and rules of language. But since all human languages are different, obviously an inherited ability to decode underlying principles can work only if the underlying principles in all languages are the same.

Chomsky argued that they were, claiming that human languages differ only in what he referred to as their **surface structure** – the individual rules of grammar and vocabulary. Underneath those, though, was a **deep structure**, which the child's innate language acquisition device was geared to decode. The LAD would extract key distinctions and identify significant words, and then use these to work out how the language should be used. Deep language structures, Chomsky argued, are

concerned with fundamental meanings and actions, and are similar in all languages. He developed a complex grammatical system for extracting the deep structure from utterances, which he referred to as **transformational grammar** (Figure 4.2).

One of the problems with the Chomskyan approach, though, is that the idea of a deep structure came to be rather an article of faith in psycholinguistics, without a great deal of evidence being put forward to support it. Most of the examples which were cited to illustrate it were drawn from Indo-European languages, which have the same linguistic origins, and there was little systematic exploration of whether the same deep structure was really found in languages with different origins.

Another problem with Chomsky's model is the idea that the child has an innate ability to decode languages – that it is automatically able to perform transformational grammar, without needing to be taught. Chomsky believed that this would happen as long as the child was exposed to spoken language. But, as we shall see when we look at some more recent research, there is quite a lot of evidence to suggest that children do need to be taught; and moreover, that this teaching needs to be done by a human being. Exposure to spoken language is not enough on its own.

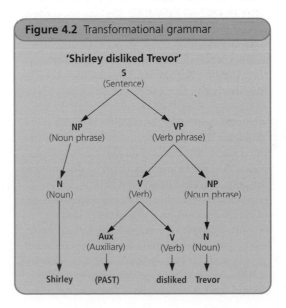

Figure 4.2 Transformational grammar

Lenneberg's theory of language acquisition

The idea that language acquisition might have an inherited, biological basis proved attractive to several researchers in the 1960s. Lenneberg (1967) argued that the ability to acquire language depended on whether the child experienced spoken language during a **critical period** in its development. A critical period is a time of genetic readiness for particular kinds of learning: we will be looking at them in more detail in Chapter 22. Lenneberg asserted that the critical period for children is before puberty. After that, he argued, biological changes result in the genetic prepared-ness being 'switched off', and the person will no longer be able to learn language.

Lenneberg's argument was based on the idea that it is harder for adults to learn other languages than it is for children. The theory formed the basis of a number of educational experiments in teach-ing children foreign languages while they were still in primary school. But as time went on, research evidence appeared to show that these children did not end up speaking French or Spanish any better than those who had learned after puberty. They did, however, show much more confidence, which was fairly important.

Perhaps the main criticisms of Lenneberg's model, however, came with the discovery of a child called Genie. Genie was well past puberty when she was discovered – she was nearly four-teen – but for all her life she had experienced very little human contact. She was an illegitimate child, who had been kept in an attic tied to a chair and fed on baby food. She was not spoken to, and punished if she made any noise herself.

Understandably, Genie showed no language abilities when she was discovered. If Lenneberg's theory were valid, she would never have been able to learn, but in fact, she picked up quite a few bits of language remarkably quickly during the period when she was being cared for by specialist psy-chologists. Her acquisition of language did show some slight differences from the usual observed stages, though. Fromkin *et al.* (1974) documented her language use, and showed that in many respects she seemed to condense the usual stages of language acquisition described in Box 4.2.

After a couple of years, though, Genie could use language to communicate clearly with other people, and she was obviously able to understand it. Although her language did not achieve the normal fluency for people of her own age, the level of competence which she showed was far above that which would have been possible if language acquisition had really been dependent on a biological critical period, as Lenneberg had suggested. Sadly, though, after two years her research programme funding was stopped, and she was placed in local authority care, where she degenerated rapidly.

Social interaction and language acquisition

As research progressed into how children acquire language, the importance of human interaction came to be more and more apparent. As we have seen, one of Chomsky's original criticisms of Skinner centred on the idea that children pick up language very quickly without being taught. Skinner had implied that language was simply verbal behaviour shaped by parents' responses; Chomsky, equally extreme, argued that parental interaction had more or less nothing to do with it. But the fact that children do not receive formal instruction in how to use language does not mean that they are not taught.

Jill and Peter de Villiers (1978) showed that the language which parents use to children, sometimes called **motherese**, is fundamentally different in structure from the language which adults use with each other, or the language which older children use with one another. Language directed towards very small children is made easier in a number of ways. Vowel sounds are made softer and difficult consonants are omitted – for instance, people often say 'wabbit' as opposed to 'rabbit' when they are talking to infants, because that is easier for a child to say. Also, rhythmic endings to words are often added, such as 'doggie-woggie'. These help the child to develop a sense of familiarity with the words and sounds which it is encountering. All these changes in language use, which mothers and other adults do almost automatically when dealing with small infants, help the child to pick up language.

De Villiers and de Villiers (1978) also showed how children's language games and rhymes can help the child to acquire language more readily. Parents often introduce the child to new words, or strengthen its existing knowledge, by placing them in a chant or sing-song framework. This means that the new word is highlighted. In a chant like: 'What's this? It's a fox. What's this? It's a cow. What's this? It's a rabbit' it is the animal name which is most important. Since the rest of the

Box 4.2 Stages of language acquisition

Psychologists have produced several accounts of infant language acquisition, which differ in their underlying theoretical perspectives. Fry was concerned with identifying the development of vocal behaviour. Braine was interested in the early development of syntax and grammar, while Brown was concerned with how language is used to communicate meaning.

Behavioural perspectives on language acquisition
Fry (1977) identified a behavioural sequence in language development:

0–2 months	The only vocalisations that the child makes tend to indicate discomfort, such as crying and whimpering.
2–4 months	The child begins to make noises indicating pleasure, e.g. burbling and cooing.
4–9 months	The child begins babbling – practising repetitive sounds, such as saying 'dadadada' repeatedly.
9–18 months	Babbling continues, but the child is now experimenting with similar sounds, e.g. 'mamamama' and 'bababab'. It is building up a phoneme system, which it will use later for making words. The first words start to appear.
18–30 months	The child begins to produce two-word phrases, like 'allgone milk'.
30 months–4 years	The child learns rules of grammar, expands its vocabulary, completes development of the phoneme system, and learns how to put together complex sentences.
4–6 years	The child has acquired all the basic adult grammar and syntax needed for communication. The main task from then on is extending and developing its vocabulary.

Structural perspectives on language acquisition
Chomsky's arguments (1959) led to an exploration of how children combined different words, and the rules which they observed when doing so. One example of this was the system of **pivot grammar** described by Braine, 1963, who looked at how children organise two- and three-word utterances. These, Braine argued, revealed that at this time, the child was using two significant classes of words: **pivot words** and **open words**. Pivot words (e.g. 'mine', or 'allgone' and 'gimme') could be used for several different utterances, and in conjunction with several different open words. They determined the ultimate meaning of the utterance. Open words (e.g. 'ball' and 'milk', 'play' or 'walk') indicated the target of the utterance.

Braine argued that pivot grammar was universal, and formed the earliest kind of syntax, reflecting the deep structure of the language. As such, it formed the basis of the child's later expansion of its linguistic skills, as it came to terms with the particular syntax and grammar of the parent language.

Semantic approaches to language acquisition
A third approach to the understanding of child language emphasised meaning and communicative intent, and reflected the increased emphasis on human social interaction in studies of child language. Brown's **semantic relations grammar** (Brown, 1970) described children's early speech as **telegraphic**, including only those words strictly necessary for communicating meaning. Function words like articles, prepositions, and conjunctions come later, as the child's use of language becomes more sophisticated.

Brown identified five stages in language acquisition:

Stage 1	The child utters only simple two-word sentences: 'want teddy' or 'mummy gone'.
Stage 2	The child starts to include endings of words, and some articles, e.g. 'that a doggy' or 'I goed'.
Stage 3	The child is beginning to ask the 'wh' questions, beginning with the relatively easy ones of 'what?', 'where?' and 'when?', and then later going on to 'how?' and 'why?'.
Stage 4	The child begins to introduce simple sentences with more than one clause, e.g. 'I had milk and teddy had milk'.

● ● ● ➤

Box 4.2 continued

Stage 5 The child is able to join sentences together with conjunctions, and to use sub-clauses: 'Mary who lives over there goes to our school'. This provides it with the material for most kinds of adult grammatical constructions: further development consists mainly of extending vocabulary.

The differences between these accounts of infant language acquisition reflect the wider debates in the study of language acquisition, and, to some extent, in the study of child development in general.

utterance is familiar, the child's attention is focused on the new word. De Villiers and de Villiers argued that the way adults use language with children is actually an intensive form of teaching. So Chomsky's argument that children acquire language without being taught does not hold up to close scrutiny.

A study by Bard and Sachs (1977) of a child born to deaf parents showed that children do not seem to decode language automatically as Chomsky had suggested. The child, Jim, was surrounded by spoken language in the form of radio and television, and his parents did not teach him sign language because they wanted him to grow up to speak normally. But Jim only succeeded in acquiring language once his case had been taken up by a speech therapist, when he was nearly four years old. When this happened, the child acquired language very quickly indeed, implying that there probably was some innate readiness. But without the human interaction with the speech therapist, there was no sign that Jim would have learned to speak. He needed the social interaction before his language ability could develop.

Skinner and Chomsky both took extreme positions, and few modern researchers would be prepared to be so dogmatic. Most researchers accept that there is some kind of inherited predisposition towards language: it is not entirely learned. For instance, attempts to teach animals language have been notoriously unsuccessful when dealing with the spoken word, as we will see in Chapter 24. But on the other hand, children do seem to need human contact and interaction to learn language, which implies that language acquisition is not entirely innate either.

A compromise position is the idea that the child may indeed have some kind of innate language acquisition system (LAS) but that this system is activated and brought into life only

through social interaction. As with many other cognitive processes, it seems to be our social interaction and the contact which we have with other members of our species which allows us to define and to develop our abilities.

Metalinguistic awareness

And children can become even more sophisticated at using that tool if they are aware of language itself. There is a certain amount of evidence to suggest that **metalinguistic** skills – to do with knowing about language and how it works – develop as early as two or three years old. De Villiers and de Villiers (1973) asked children of these ages to judge two types of sentences and to correct them. The first group of sentences violated rules of **syntax** – principles of word-order and grammar – in sentences such as 'Dog the walk'. The other group of sentences violated semantic rules – rules about meaning – in sentences like 'Drink the chair', which did not make any sense.

The researchers found that all the children they studied could detect and correct the semantic errors. But the two-year-olds were not able to judge and correct sentences which had syntactic errors, although the three-year-olds could. This suggests that the first aspect of language which a child acquires is semantic awareness, while syntactic awareness develops later. It also supports the idea that the child's primary involvement with language is not structural, as Chomsky suggested, but to do with meaning and social interaction.

One problem with the de Villiers study, however, is that it involved asking children to correct artificial sentences, and it may be that there is a difference when children are using language spontaneously themselves. Clark and Anderson (1979) recorded children's speech and searched through it for evidence of syntactical mistakes, and what they referred to as 'spontaneous repairs'. These were instances when the child would make a mistake, recognise it, and spontaneously correct it.

What they found was that children between the ages of two and three made both errors and repairs. For instance, a quotation from one child of two years and eight months which they gave was 'the kitty cat is – de spider's kissing the kitty cat's back'. And another, of two years eleven months, said: 'She – he didn't give her any food'. What is happening here is that the children begin to utter the sentence the wrong way round, recognise their error, and spontaneously correct it, which suggests that even two-year-olds are able to reflect on word order and use it appropriately.

Metaphor and riddles

The implication, then, is that metalinguistic skills begin to develop almost as quickly as the child's full use of language. However, there are many different aspects of metalinguistic awareness. A study by Winner, Rosensteil and Gardner (1976) looked at how children understand metaphors in speech, and showed how metalinguistic skills become increasingly sophisticated as children grow older. They asked children of different ages to explain what was meant by graphic metaphors, such as: 'My friend is a real tiger', and found distinct age differences (Table 4.6).

Ross and Killey (1977) argued that the process of questioning, reflection and distancing which takes place at school is necessary for a child to develop metacognitive awareness. Without formal education, they argued, children do not develop those skills. But evidence from non-technological societies shows that the use of riddles and highly sophisticated word-games is an intensive part of the traditional education process. Without metacognitive awareness, such games are meaningless. So although it may be true to say that schooling helps to articulate and develop some types of metacognitive skills, it does not seem to be the case that metacognitive awareness is completely dependent on formal schooling, as Ross and Killey implied.

Iona and Peter Opie (1959) investigated the types of games which children play in school playgrounds. These are passed, traditionally, from child to child, and not directly taught by adults, so they represent a good example of a 'children's culture', which sometimes forms an unbroken tradition lasting hundreds of years. The Opies travelled all

Table 4.6 Metalinguistic awareness in children

Children's responses to a metaphor such as: 'my friend is a real tiger':

5–6 years	Children are inclined to take the sentence literally, and may even become apprehensive about meeting this person, because they do not want to meet a real tiger.
7–8 years	These children understand that the statement is literally impossible, and so they try to make sense of it in some other way. Usually this takes the form of making some kind of story about it, like, 'my friend is friendly with the tiger,' or 'my friend has a stripey shirt like a tiger'.
9 years and older	These children understand the phrase as referring to characteristic styles of action or interaction. They have become aware that phrases can have multiple meanings, and they can understand that it meant that tigers and the friend might have some qualities in common.

Source: Winner, Rosensteil and Gardner, 1976

over the British Isles, asking children to give them examples of games, rhymes and riddles. As they collected examples, they found that many of these games involved sophisticated metalinguistic awareness, being based on rhymes, puns or on the use of language in ambiguous or deliberately misleading fashions. The Opies argued that this form of verbal play helps children to become aware of the different ways in which language can be used, and so helps them to develop their skills in using it.

Reading

When we read, we can experience language even if there is nobody else around, or directly talking to us. The process of interpreting the printed or displayed symbols which signify language has become an important skill in modern society, and a considerable amount of research has been devoted to studying it. Reading and writing are, by definition, metalinguistic skills. Without knowing about language, we could not learn how to use it in a more abstract or symbolic form, as we do when reading or writing.

Moreover, early metalinguistic experience seems

to be able to help language acquisition. Bradley and Bryant (1983) described a longitudinal study which examined the role of early language experience in reading and writing. One interesting finding was that experience with poems, nonsense jingles and nursery rhymes seems to exert a direct influence on how effectively children learn to read. Children who were exposed to rhymes in their pre-school years learned to read significantly more quickly than those who had not had such experiences.

One possible explanation for this might be the way that rhyming encourages children to focus their attention on language itself. By looking at words which have different meanings but which sound similar, the child is distancing itself, taking one step away from being absorbed in the meaning or use of language. So it becomes more able to explore the nature of the language that it is using. It may be that this early metalinguistic skill of focusing attention on the words themselves rather than on their meaning is the basis for the more complicated metalinguistic skill of being able to look at a word in written form and decode it as the equivalent of speech.

Theories of reading

The theories of reading put forward by psychologists have often reflected the approaches in psychology at the time that they were put forward. For instance, early research on reading looked mainly at connections between the stimulus and the response, following the S-R behaviourist tradition, and involved analysing the characteristics of the stimuli (written words and letters) in order to comprehend the reading process.

Reading as stimulus-response
During the behaviourist period, reading research concentrated on the written word as the stimulus. Nowadays, we are more likely to emphasise context and cognitive factors. But even though **stimulus characteristics** are not seen as the all-important factors that they were previously thought to be, they may still have some influence. Word-recognition, for the most part, can survive a number of handicaps, such as bad handwriting, gross misspellings or displacement of letters. But Rawlinson (1975) showed how some kinds of stimulus distortion can seriously interfere with our ability to recognise words. For example: a distortion like 'sivler' instead of silver, if it is seen in context, can easily be overlooked; but one like 'recahed' instead of 'reached' is likely to cause difficulty. Also, Rawlinson found, the more distortions there were in a piece of text, the more reading was disrupted.

In general, though, minor distortions of the stimulus seem to have little or no effect on reading. A major problem faced by proof-readers (people who check text for mistakes in printing) is the way that we read for meaning and do not notice minor distortions of the stimulus. So when reading proofs, the reader is easily distracted from inspecting the text into slipping into reading it for meaning, and this makes it easy to overlook errors in typesetting. Many proof-readers develop strategies which help them to avoid slipping into 'normal' reading, like reading the text backwards, but the tendency to read automatically is very strong.

A well-known effect in cognitive psychology, known as the **Stroop effect**, comes from this powerful tendency to read for meaning: if people are shown colour names written in non-matching coloured inks, they take longer to name the ink colour than if they are shown words with matching-coloured inks. The tendency to read for meaning is so strong and so automatic that they keep almost saying the word which is written instead of naming the colour of the ink (Stroop, 1935). We will be looking at this phenomenon more closely in the next chapter.

Reading as translation
The growth of linguistics during the 1960s produced a different emphasis for theories of reading, in which reading was seen as being essentially a process of **translation** from the written to the spoken word. There were two major variations within this approach: in Levin and Williams (1970), for example, Levin argued that reading occurred as written words were translated into the equivalent of 'heard' words, and processed in the same way as speech which has been heard. The alternative approach was put forward by Hochberg (1970), who saw reading as being the process of translating from the written word into the sub-vocal, 'inner' speech which people use when they are thinking to themselves (Vygotsky, 1962).

Although these approaches have sometimes been usefully applied to how children first learn to read, they do not really explain what happens with experienced, skilled readers or speed-readers. The main problem with the 'reading as translation' idea is how rapidly people read. A speed-reader can absorb information at the rate of 1,000 words per minute, without losing comprehension; and an ordinary skilled reader will absorb information far more rapidly than visual and auditory systems could process the spoken word. Skilled reading is in many respects completely different from decoding heard language, and the processes may not be identical at all, even though they may seem similar subjectively.

Reading as selective search

Many modern theories of reading see it as a **selective search** for information. A reader brings quite a lot of previously existing knowledge to the material, and will use this to direct and organise the search. Kennedy (1984) classifies this prior knowledge into conventions, competence and context. **Conventions** are accepted principles of language use, like grammar, syntax or the use of similes and metaphors. **Competence** is the knowledge of the subject which a reader already has – we always know something of what we are reading about, even if it is not very much, and sometimes we know far more than we realise. **Context** includes the overall purpose of the reading, like whether it is reading for pleasure, for an essay or exam, or just for interest; and it is also established by what has already been read: the previous text contributes directly to our understanding of what comes later.

It seems that we need to keep up a certain minimum speed in order to read fluently: if we have to fall back on word-by-word reading in order to understand a difficult passage, then we find the material more difficult to understand. Seeing reading as a search process implies that how quickly and efficiently we read will be influenced by how certain or uncertain we are of what is coming next. An unfamiliar content or style produces a slowing down in reading speed; and a high level of uncertainty can result in the loss of fluent reading altogether. Maintaining fluency is vitally important for skilled readers – if it cannot be regained, a skilled reader will usually lose interest and stop reading. Some psychologists believe that the need to keep up a certain reading speed to maintain fluency results from the rapid decay of the previous information in the working memory store (see Chapter 3).

Fluent and novice readers

Schemes for teaching children to read have tended to operate on the basis of a number of assumptions about the steps which are involved in reading, and how it can be made easier. One important aspect to developing such schemes is the need to identify just what the differences are between novices and skilled readers: in order to teach a skill effectively, we first need to know what the goals of our teaching are.

Spelling

Linguistic models of reading as the process of translation to speech led to a number of attempts to help reading in learners by emphasising the equivalence between spoken and written forms of language – between **graphemes**, the basic units of written language, and **phonemes**, the basic units of spoken language. So special reading schemes for young children were developed, such as the i.t.a. (initial teaching alphabet) scheme, which was adopted in many schools in Britain during the late 1960s and early 1970s. With this system, each phoneme had its equivalent grapheme, so that i.t.a. early-reading books allowed the child to know how something was pronounced just by looking at the word. It was thought that this would make learning to read easier, as it cut out peculiar and irregular spellings.

Gradually, however, it became apparent that reading involves more than a simple grapheme/phoneme equivalence. As we read, the words that we encounter convey images and connections, and spelling can be useful in helping us to grasp the language as a whole. Kennedy (1984) showed how such apparent 'simplifications' as removing the silent b from 'climb' actually made it more difficult for the child to grasp its relationship with the verb 'to clamber'. There are many other examples, like 'sign' and 'signal', or 'limb' and 'limber'.

Spelling in English is not nearly as random as many people believe. Similarities in the appearances of words often provide useful clues to their meanings, and the **lexical representation of a language** (its conventions of spelling and word combination) can be positively helpful in the development of reading skills. Expert readers tend to make full use of these cues, to the extent that they may gain an impression of the meaning of an unfamiliar word on the basis of its lexical aspects alone. Rather than being merely an inconvenience, the linguist Noam Chomsky stated in 1970 that the lexical representation of written English presented 'a near-optimal system for representing the spoken language' (Chomsky, 1970) – and its apparently peculiar spellings are an important part of that.

Phonics and meaning

Reading is a different experience for learners than it is for skilled readers in other respects too. For the skilled reader, sound equivalence is not really necessary: we can be familiar with a word in its written form, and yet not know how to pronounce it. Skilled readers seem to have developed a direct link between the word and its meaning, which bypasses the need to imagine the spoken word. This is the ultimate goal for the learner as well, but getting there is more difficult – particularly when some teaching methods introduce additional problems.

The process of teaching a child to read generally involves an intermediate stage, in which the child is expected to say the words out loud. Smith (1973) argued that teaching **phonics** – the correspondence between sound and letter – is not really helpful in teaching reading itself, because it means that the child is faced with two learning tasks rather than one. It would be more efficient and less difficult for the child if it were taught to recognise and understand the written word directly. This would also reduce the gap between novice and skilled reading. But other researchers have argued that it is unrealistic to expect a learner to be able to adopt expert strategies from the outset, since there are so many differences between novices and expert readers.

Visual cues

Another of these differences is the way that skilled readers use very few **visual cues**. They can identify large amounts of text very rapidly, because their previous experience allows them to recognise words simply by glancing at their shape or by guessing what they probably are from their context. But the learner does not have that experience to draw on, and so has to explore each word fully. As they practise reading, frequently occurring words become more familiar and need

less attention, until the reader gradually acquires the ability to identify words, phrases or whole sentences at a glance.

A striking feature of reading is how a reader needs to notice very small, almost insignificant, differences between stimuli. But a reader also needs to ignore quite major differences, such as different forms or size of script. When we are looking at everyday objects we tend to notice large differences relatively easily: the distinction between the two stimuli of a chair and a table is very noticeable. But the difference between two words with quite different meanings may be very small: the difference between 'ham' and 'hem' involves only a small change in the letters, but makes all the difference to the meaning. At more sophisticated levels of meaning too, very small stimulus changes can produce large semantic distinctions, like the difference between 'to affect' something (meaning to influence it), and 'to effect' something (meaning to cause it to happen).

Miles and Miles (1975) suggested that one source of reading difficulty might arise because some children have problems identifying the general features of words, so that they are confused by different typefaces or scripts, and see them as more important to the meaning of the passage than they are. This would also interfere with the process of familiarisation, since the reader would not recognise a word in a different typeface as being the one which they have become familiar with. We will be looking at reading difficulties later in this chapter.

Eye-movement and scanning

Another difference between fluent and novice readers concerns eye-movement and scanning. In reading, spatial organisation is essential for distinguishing information. The order of letters as well as words conveys meaning: the difference between 'saw' and 'was', for instance, is only in the sequence of the letters, but makes every difference to the meaning. Similarly, 'Mary wrote about John' means something entirely different from 'John wrote about Mary'. So in order to read skilfully, a reader must bear in mind the spatial organisation of the material as well as the particular words involved, and fluent reading involves scanning text in such a way as to absorb this information.

Fluent readers tend to scan text rapidly, making large eye-movements and sometimes skipping over familiar words or phrases. They sometimes re-inspect sections of the text, quickly, usually because of semantic demands like coming across a bit of obscure or ambiguous content. But learners tend to re-inspect text far more often than experienced readers, perhaps because words or combinations of words are less familiar to them. As learners become more fluent, they tend to make larger eye-movements and to move more quickly from one word to another.

Understanding meaningful units

During reading, we extract information which often goes far beyond what is actually on the page. Kennedy (1984) identified **metaphor** as one example. If we read something like 'Her reply staggered him', we do not take it as a literal description, but as an invitation to 'share' in the feeling that the person experienced. To understand metaphors, we need to infer meaning, rather than just receive it. If a metaphor is inappropriate, we do not make the necessary inference – a statement like 'Her reply walked him' would not produce much of a response (except perhaps puzzlement) on the part of the reader.

Scripts

Schank (1975) argued that the process of understanding reading is really all about **scripts**. Everyone has a large experience of situations and events, which provides them with ideas about what is likely to happen in any given situation. A sentence like 'As Jane was going to work, her bus was held up' elicits an unconscious 'script' from us – that Jane had to catch a bus in order to get to work, that the bus should have conformed to a particular timetable, etc. These scripts provide us with knowledge about likely events, in our own lives, and also in the world around us. We use them to go about our day to day lives, and we use them in reading all the time. By drawing on well-established scripts, the writer allows us to make inferences about what is happening, and to avoid being confused by gaps in the narrative.

Pichert and Anderson (1977) showed how powerful scripts are for understanding what we read. They asked research participants to read a piece of prose which gave an account of a schoolboy taking a friend to his parents' house. One group were asked to read the story as if they were potential house-buyers, while the other group

were asked to take the viewpoint of a potential burglar. When they were questioned later about the text, the two groups remembered different kinds of information. The 'house-buyers' remembered items of information like the fact that the house had a damp basement, while the 'burglars' remembered details like a side door which was habitually left unlocked.

Interestingly, too, some time later Pichert and Anderson asked the same research participants to recall the text from the other viewpoint. The 'house-buyers' now had to imagine that they were 'burglars', and vice versa. The research participants again remembered the relevant information for the role they were adopting – even though they had not re-read the passage. New information had become salient, because they were remembering their reading for a different purpose. Incidentally, this study helps us to understand why it is helpful for students to 'prime' themselves by reading past examination questions before reading through revision notes. It helps to bring out the salience of the information, and so makes it more memorable.

The concept of scripts also highlights how actively we process information. Whenever we read, we are using our existing knowledge to complete the gaps and to infer meaning. In fact, it is very difficult to write about anything in such a way that the reader does not have to infer anything. One reason why legal documents are so long and tortuous is because their writers try to avoid relying on implicit knowledge on the part of the reader, but even they are only partly successful

The importance of understanding

Kennedy (1984) emphasised the importance of recognising that understanding is the final goal of reading. Although this may seem obvious, it is not necessarily so to someone who is just learning to read. Many young children, for instance, think learning to read is all about the sounds of words, or the shapes of letters, and do not see any real purpose to it. In order for someone to learn to read fluently, they need to know that, in the end, they will be able to understand. Knowing that also helps to motivate children, so that they will be more likely to keep up an effort if they come across what seems like very obscure or difficult material.

Someone who has not realised the purpose of

reading will see little point in trying hard to develop what seems like a pretty pointless skill. And in reading, perseverance is essential: the first stages are extremely difficult, and it only becomes easier as fluency begins to develop – which only happens with practice. A child who can see that the result will be worthwhile is likely to put in the effort which is needed to get beyond the initial stages. But children who cannot see the purpose of reading are likely to give up, and do only as much as they are compelled to. They may get by with basic reading at school, but they will avoid reading anything additional – which can lead to functional illiteracy.

Expectations and understanding, then, are powerfully implicated in reading. In this respect, reading is like other cognitive processes: as we saw in Chapter 2, Neisser (1976) showed how our interpretation of situations produces anticipatory schemata, which influence what we select as relevant from the mass of information which we encounter. Reading too is an active process, with the individual selecting relevant information from the material by applying existing knowledge of the world and anticipations about what is likely to be there. In this way, the purpose of the reading and the prior knowledge which we bring to the material strongly influence what we understand and retain.

Word-recognition and automatisation

Smith (1973) even went so far as to argue that word-recognition skills are pretty well unimportant in the reading process. Expectancy and context, Smith argued, account for so much of how we read that the variables produced by stimulus characteristics or other features of reading are essentially trivial and unimportant. Certainly there are a great many instances where we read something which is rather different from the material which is actually in front of us – or we fail to read something, like not noticing the extra word in Figure 4.3. But Smith's argument seems a little over-stated, and may be best interpreted as a reaction to the excessive emphasis on stimulus characteristics in earlier theories, which led Smith to emphasise the point so very strongly.

Nonetheless, the process of activating scripts and understanding material in context does mean that fluent readers often fail to recognise significant parts of a written stimulus. One well-known example involves counting the number of 'F's in

Figure 4.3 Automisation (Paris in the spring)

PARIS

IN THE

THE SPRING

the example given in Figure 4.4. Although there are six of them altogether, fluent readers can often only count three – even knowing that there are really more. But interestingly, novice readers do not have that problem: they can count the six letter 'F's with no difficulty.

There are two factors working together in this. One of them is that fluent readers work so strongly with expectancy and context, as Smith argues, that they tend to read what they are expecting to read. The other is because fluent readers have come across familiar words so often that the skill of recognising them has become **automatised** – com-

Figure 4.4 The F factor

How many 'F's can you count in this sentence?

FINISHED FILES ARE THE

RESULT OF YEARS OF

SCIENTIFIC STUDY

COMBINED WITH THE

EXPERIENCE OF YEARS.

pletely automatic. So they do not actually look at those words – they just identify them fleetingly from their shape. As a result, they do not notice the letters in the word. Novice readers, on the other hand, have to look at, and notice, everything, because they are not so sure of what they are doing. As a result, they can solve this particular puzzle easily.

The importance of learning to read

Learning to read is an important part of an educational experience – and not just because of convention or convenience. Learning to read directly encourages cognitive growth. It opens up new areas of knowledge and meaning, and strengthens our use of symbolic representation. In addition, Donaldson (1978) argued that it helps for the child to develop **disembedded thinking** (thinking which is not dependent on the immediate context). Because written words are relatively permanent, and independent of the child's immediate surroundings, they allow the child to focus more on the language itself, and that makes it easier for the child to handle abstract logic and hypothetical reasoning.

Olson (1977) considers that literacy is special because it directly encourages the child to use **imagination** – particularly in writing, but also in reading. Reading, particularly certain types of fiction, encourages the development of imagination, and encourages the individual to speculate on possibilities and practicalities. In addition, through literacy we can move from the specific, concrete events around us to abstract ideas and logical arguments which deal not only with what has happened, but also with what could conceivably happen if things were different. Although it is possible to think like this without literacy, the process of reading and writing helps that ability to develop.

Reading disorders

Because reading is regarded as so important in our society, a considerable amount of research has gone into investigating **reading disorders**. Problems with learning to read can arise from factors other than disorders in reading itself. Conrad (1977) argued that deaf children rarely learn to read well, and suggested that this might be to do with methods of teaching children to read, which require the child to pronounce the words out loud. As we have already seen, this is

something which expert readers do not do, but which is usually considered necessary for learners. Since deaf children often have problems interpreting spoken words, this interferes with their learning, producing a reading deficit which increases as the child grows older. Recent projects involving teaching deaf children in different ways seem to support this argument.

In some cases, difficulties in learning to read can result from **verbal deprivation**. Although, as we saw earlier, Labov (1972) challenged the idea of verbal deprivation of whole classes or groups in society, some individual children do experience severe language deprivation which may later make it harder for them to learn to read. One such case would be that of the child Genie, who experienced no verbal contact until she was thirteen years old (Curtiss, 1977); or the severely deprived twins studied by Koluchova in 1976a, b (see Chapter 20).

More common instances of reading disorder arise from children growing up in homes in which nobody else reads. Because children usually take their models of behaviour from family members, such a child gets an implicit message that reading is a 'school' activity, and not really relevant for home. If there is also a conflict of values between home and school, the child can end up seeing school learning as irrelevant and tedious. Such children often make little effort to learn to read, seeing little or no purpose in it; and simply learn to conceal their non-reading from their teachers. Most of the adults who eventually join adult literacy schemes have been through this kind of process. Teachers who believe in verbal and cultural deprivation can sometimes make this worse, by labelling the child as 'verbally deprived' and seeing their efforts as pointless, because, they think, the child will not learn anyway.

Gunter (1983) showed how heavy television viewing at an early age could have a directly damaging effect on how well children learn to read. One reason for this seems to be the way that television provides 'instant' rewards. The child does not need to make any effort to understand what is on television, and the stimulus is rich and varying. Learning to read, on the other hand, is a slow and tedious process which requires considerable effort from the child in return for very little reward in the early stages. If the child is not convinced that the effort is worthwhile (for example if it sees television as a directly equivalent form of entertainment/instruction), then it is less likely to keep up the effort needed to get over the initial stages of learning to read, and progress into fluency.

People also vary in how rapidly they acquire reading skills. Despite the tendency for parents to become anxious about a child who appears to be learning more slowly than another child, as a genera rule, once the child does begin to learn, it makes up for any lost ground. Many children who are regarded by their parents as being slow readers and as possibly having reading disorders, are in fact showing nothing more than such normal individual differences.

Dyslexia

Reading disorder is known by the general term **dyslexia**. There are two main types of dyslexia: **acquired dyslexia**, which arises as a direct result of either accidental injury or brain disease, and developmental dyslexia, which becomes apparent during the time that a child is learning to read. Although most research has focused on **developmental dyslexia**, research into acquired dyslexia has also produced some interesting insights.

Acquired dyslexia

People who show reading disorders as a result of brain injury have what is known as acquired dyslexia. Marshall and Newcombe (1973) described a characteristic set of symptoms which involve the patient having problems with reading irregular words (ones with unusual spellings), and also tending to confuse words which sound the same – such as 'saw' and 'sore'. In addition, these patients tend to adopt strategies for spelling which mean that they spell things how they sound, such as 'lurn' for 'learn'. Marshall and Newcombe called this **surface dyslexia**. In this disorder, problems arise mainly with the forms of words, but not with understanding them.

A different kind of dyslexia, **deep dyslexia**, was described by Shallice and Warrington (1980). In deep dyslexia, the person's comprehension is affected, so they find it easier to read nouns and adjectives than harder words like verbs or function words. This seems to relate to how easy it is to form a mental image of a particular word – words like 'and' are difficult to imagine, while nouns are much easier. When people with this form of dyslexia were given different nouns to deal with, they found the nouns that were easiest

to picture much more manageable than more abstract ones. People with deep dyslexia also often have difficulty reading nonsense words, even ones which can be pronounced easily, like 'framble'; but this is not difficult for surface dyslexics.

Developmental dyslexia

In 1970, Critchley defined developmental dyslexia as: 'a disorder of children who, despite conventional classroom experience, fail to attain the language skills of reading, writing and spelling commensurate with their intellectual abilities'. Smith *et al.* (1983) suggested that some developmental dyslexias are genetic disorders. From an analysis of nine families, Smith *et al.* hypothesised that the disorder was carried as a dominant gene on chromosome 15, the chromosome known to be involved in the development of language areas in the left hemisphere of the brain.

However, other psychologists have criticised this form of research, on the grounds that the argument about specific genetic influence is only made by inference rather than by direct measurement. Also, of course, a trait which is passed on in families is not necessarily genetic, because families also provide environments in which children acquire values, motivations and priorities. As we have already seen, role models, the use of television and whether the child sees reading as worthwhile can all have an influence on whether a child learns to read or not.

Differences between forms of dyslexia

There has been considerable debate on the question of whether developmental and acquired dyslexia have common origins. Coltheart *et al.* (1983) argued that both surface and deep dyslexia can be identified in developmental dyslexia. They take this as evidence for the theory that developmental dyslexics have damage or lack of development in the language areas of the brain, similar to the damage which can be caused in later life by accidental injury and which results in acquired dyslexia. But this idea was strongly disputed by Baddeley *et al.* (1982). They studied dyslexic children in depth, and compared their findings with cases of acquired dyslexia. They came to the conclusion that although there seemed to be certain similarities, developmental and acquired dyslexia were different enough to justify thinking of them as having entirely different origins.

One study which they looked at involved comparing both kinds of dyslexics with 'normal' children, in tasks which involved picking out real words from pronounceable nonsense words. There were two kinds of nonsense words: some had no connection with any real words, such as 'trenkle', but the others were **homophones** of real words – they sounded the same, like 'frute'. All the children found it harder to distinguish real words from the homophonic nonsense words, but the adults – the acquired dyslexics – did not distinguish between homophones and ordinary nonsense words. The dyslexic children, though, were similar to normally reading children of a younger age-range. Baddeley *et al.* argued that this finding implies that developmental and acquired dyslexias have different origins.

Processing visual information

Other research on dyslexic children looked at how they process perceptual information. Vellutino (1979) showed that there were significant differences between dyslexics and normally reading children in figure-matching tasks. When it was a matter of matching two different visual forms, there was no difference, but when the task involved matching a visual and a verbal form, then it was clear that dyslexic children were much slower than children who were normal readers. If learning to read involves dealing with visual and auditory information simultaneously, as is the case in most teaching methods, then it is possible that some kinds of dyslexia come from problems in processing such information in the first place.

Farnham-Diggory (1978) showed that dyslexic children took noticeably longer than normal readers to tell the difference between two visual forms presented rapidly one after the other. If we are shown two shapes quickly enough we tend to 'merge' them – for instance, a cross immediately followed by a square might be seen as one figure: a square with a cross inside it. For ordinary children, the threshold for seeing two figures as separate is about 100 ms, while for dyslexic children it averages out at about 140 ms. This is not very different, but when the children were asked to say or draw what the two different figures actually were (as opposed to just recognising that there were two different ones), the ordinary children's threshold was 180 ms, while the dyslexics' was 320 ms.

Farnham-Diggory suggested that some dyslexia may come from the speed at which such children process information, resulting in the dyslexic child

getting a 'backlog' of information building up as it tries to process words. One suggestion that has been made from work of this kind is that the child should be taught reading by dealing with only one grapheme at a time, so that each unit can be fully processed before the child moves on to the next one. But some researchers would see this as making it more difficult for the child to grasp the reading process, as it would be far too slow to achieve a reasonable 'flow' of information.

Fatigue and memory scanning

Another study (Farnham-Diggory and Gregg, 1975) showed that dyslexic children might retain fatigue effects for a longer period of time than children who were normal readers. When they compared children doing either aural or visual tasks, they found that all the children did badly as they became more tired. But if they then changed the mode of the task, so that those who had previously been doing visual tasks were now doing aural ones, or vice versa, they found that the normal readers would recover from their fatigue, and regain their previous good performance. The dyslexic children, on the other hand, just showed a further decrement.

The same study showed that dyslexic children also differed from normally reading children when it came to memory-scanning tasks. The children either heard or were shown sequences of letters and then asked which letters came first, last or in the middle. For the normal readers, performance was much the same no matter how the information was presented. But the dyslexic children showed a strong decrement with the auditory task, although they were fine on the visual one. If this represents their ordinary behaviour in a natural setting (which may not be the case because these experiments are a bit artificial and abstract), then it suggests that dyslexic children may take longer to process things that they hear than things that they see. This would present increasing problems if the child was being taught with a 'look and say' reading task.

Does dyslexia exist?

The difficulty with these kinds of studies is that they tend to be very contrived, and many psychologists argue that they are not much like the real-life event of a child learning to read. They also argue that simply treating reading difficulties as if they are individual problems is not realistic because, as we have seen, social and motivational factors can be just as important.

Some psychologists even go so far as to argue that dyslexia does not really exist at all. They see it as a fiction which distracts attention from bad teaching and the 'labelling' of children in schools, by attributing the effects to the individual child. Whittaker, in 1982, described the concept of developmental dyslexia as 'a hoax in need of thorough exposure', on the grounds that the term was being used as a 'magical' concept to explain both individual differences in learning to read and inadequate educational experience. The term dyslexia has been widened so far since it was first developed, Whittaker argued, that it is now applied to any learning problems at all if they involve language. In fact, Miles (1978) showed that it was even applied in some cases to problems in arith-

metic. As a result, the definition has become so widely used that it has become effectively meaningless, at least in scientific terms.

Whittaker and other psychologists who take this view were not saying that specific reading difficulties do not occur. What they are saying is that to label them as 'dyslexia' does not help. The label presents the problem as if it were inevitable and fixed, whereas many apparently 'dyslexic' children do learn to read once they have more relevant teaching. In addition, over-anxiety on the part of parents or teachers, who are unwilling to accept the idea that the child might be slower at learning than others, often results in a child being labelled dyslexic. Despite the extensive research into dyslexia as a disorder, it remains a controversial idea, which is by no means as clear-cut as many researchers seem to imply.

Key terms

accent A distinctive pattern of pronunciation in a given language, shared by a regional or socio-economic group.

acquired dyslexia Dyslexia which occurs as a result of head injury or similar specific cause.

Berlin-Kay hypothesis The idea that the basic colour terms of a language form natural categories, intrinsic to all human thought, which do not vary from one culture to another except in number.

critical period A genetically-determined time during development when a particular form of learning must take place if it is ever to be learned at all.

deep dyslexia Dyslexia in which people find it particularly hard to comprehend words which cannot be concretely visualised.

deep structure The underlying organisation of a language, concerned with meanings and what the words of that language represent.

developmental dyslexia A form of dyslexia which does not seem to have any specific organic origin.

dialect A distinctive pattern of language use shared by a regional or socio-economic group, which has its own vocabulary and grammatical forms.

diglossia The ability to speak in more than one form of language, e.g. 'posh' English and colloquial English, as the situation demands.

discourse analysis A method of studying human experience by analysing the things people say to one another, and how they express them, both symbolically and behaviourally.

disembedded thought Thinking which is not applied in any meaningful context, but is just treated as a separate, distinct task with no relevance to the real world.

dyslexia A term given to disorders in the processing and interpretation of visual word information.

grapheme A basic unit of written language.

homophones Words which sound the same as one another.

idiolect The personal or idiosyncratic form of language used by a single individual.

lexical representation of a language The image of the world contained implicitly in the words of that language.

linguistic relativity hypothesis The idea that thinking depends on language, and so people who speak different languages also inhabit different conceptual worlds.

mental representation A theoretical model of how we hold information in the brain.

metaphorical frame The set of ideas invoked by the use of a particular metaphor, which then sets the context for further discussion.

morpheme The smallest meaningful units of language.

particularistic meanings Meanings of statements or utterances which only apply to their own specific contexts.

phoneme The basic unit of sound in spoken language.

psycholinguistics The study of language and language structure, particularly in terms of its inter-action with thinking.

script A well-known pattern of social action and interaction which has been socially established and accepted, and is implicitly and automatically followed by people in the relevant situation.

sociolinguistics The study of language as it relates to social and cultural phenomena.

Stroop effect A phenomenon demonstrating automaticity of information-processing, in which the identification of colour is interfered with by the name of a colour given in the stimulus material.

surface dyslexia A form of reading disorder in which the person has difficulty with the forms of words and letters, but not with their meanings.

surface structure The superficial characteristics of a language: its rules of formal grammar and habitual use of words.

syntax Rules governing which combinations of words and word-orders are acceptable within a specific language.

universalistic meanings Meanings of statements or utterances which apply generally in broad contexts, and to more than the immediate situation.

verbal deprivation hypothesis The idea that children who do not experience extended forms of language may suffer cognitive deficits as a consequence.

Summary

1 Language is a communication system which operates through combinations of arbitrary symbols. Research into language use in conversations has focused on the use of discourse and metaphor and on the social and co-operative aspects of conversational exchange.

2 Piaget saw language as entirely dependent on thought, whereas Bruner saw it as a tool which amplifies and augments thought. Vygotsky saw language and thought as having separate func-tions: language as a social skill, and thought as the child's way of making sense out of the world.

3 The strong form of the linguistic relativity hypothesis proposes that language determines thinking; its weaker form proposes that it provides a framework and channel which heavily influences thought.

4 Bernstein's verbal deprivation hypothesis suggested that the use of restricted codes limited access to certain forms of meaning. This argument was strongly challenged by Labov. Research into social aspects of language use such as accent, dialects and sexist language shows that language is an important factor in social cognition.

5 Theories of language acquisition include the nature-nurture debate between Chomsky and Skinner, and the more recent emphasis on human social contact in language learning. The child develops a sophisticated awareness of the appro-priate use of language from quite an early age.

6 Theories of reading skills have, at various times, portrayed reading as stimulus-response learning, as translation from visual to auditory stimuli, and as a selective search for meaning. Fluent and novice readers have been shown to differ in several respects.

7 Social knowledge in the form of scripts and assumptions are important in understanding and remembering language. Reading disorders can result from a number of social factors, including verbal deprivation, lack of role models and heavy television viewing.

8 Dyslexia is usually divided into acquired dyslexia, which has an identifiable organic origin, and developmental dyslexia, which concerns children failing to learn to read. Psychological explanations for developmental dyslexia include difficulties in processing visual information, fatigue and social labelling.

Self-assessment questions

1 What are the main concepts in the study of discourse and conversation?

2 Summarise the verbal deprivation debate.

3 Describe the major theories of reading.

Practice essay questions

1 'The English language is loaded to ensure that women cannot be perceived as equal to men'. Discuss.

2 How useful is the concept of verbal deprivation?

3 Outline and evaluate Vygotsky's theory of child language.

Test your knowledge of this chapter with our online quizzes and games at: http://www.psych.co.uk

Explore language and literacy further at:

General
http://www.psyc.memphis.edu/POL/POL.htm – Exhaustive links page to language researchers, journals, books and courses.

Linguistics
http://www.geneseo.edu/~intd225/linguist.html – Tutorial on the design features of linguistics.
http://www.emich.edu/~linguist/www-vl.html – Virtual library for linguistics resources, books and journals.

Disorders
http://www.dyslexia-inst.org.uk/faqs.htm – Information about dyslexia.

Note: the passage referred to earlier in the Chapter (on page 101) is about washing clothes.

Thinking and representation

- Goal-directed thinking
  - Problem-solving
  - Creativity
  - A I and computer simulation
- Human reasoning
  - Biases
  - Experience
  - Decision-making
- Representation
  - Develop-ment
  - Structures

Learning objectives

5.1. Types of thinking
a define terms relating to thinking and representation
b list the main types of thinking studied in psychology
c distinguish between goal-directed thinking and other forms

5.2. Problem-solving
a define terms relating to problem-solving
b describe aspects of mental set in problem-solving
c identify strategies for enhancing problem-solving

5.3. Creativity
a describe a study of cognitive styles
b outline stage models of creativity
c identify problems of creativity research

5.4. Computer simulation and artificial intelligence
a define terms relating to computer simulation and AI
b evaluate approaches to computer simulation
c describe types of research into artificial intelligence

5.5. Human reasoning
a identify distinctive aspects of human reasoning
b distinguish between human reasoning and formal logic
c describe a study of human reasoning

5.6. Decision-making
a define terms relating to the psychological study of decision-making
b analyse the heuristics involved in decision-making
c describe a study of decision-making

5.7. Concept-formation
a describe models of concept-formation
b define terms relating to concept-formation
c evaluate methods of studying concept-formation

5.8. Representation
a identify different models of representation
b describe a study of representation
c apply models of representation to everyday life examples

In this chapter, we will be looking at how we deal with information mentally. Thinking is concerned with the ways that we use information, and representation is the way that we model information in our minds. They have been studied by psychologists from many different angles, and in this chapter we will look at some of them. We will begin by looking at how psychologists have studied thinking and problem-solving, and what that might be able to tell us about human creativity. From there, we will look at research which has explored the potential of computers for problem-solving and reasoning. Then we will go on to look at human reasoning and expertise, and at the way that human beings make decisions. And finally, we will look at some of the different ways that people represent information mentally.

Thinking and problem-solving

Eysenck and Keane (1995) argue that there are three distinct features of thinking. Firstly, it has to involve some degree of **conscious awareness** – although that does not mean that we are aware of every aspect of our thinking. Usually, we are aware of the end product of our thinking, but not of all of the steps which we went through to get to that end product.

The second feature of thinking is that it can involve different amounts of **goal-orientation** – in other words, there is a lot of variation in how far thinking is directed towards a particular goal or end-point. Some of our thinking is very goal-oriented: that is the kind of thinking we do as we try to solve puzzles, or to find solutions to problems that are worrying us. But some of our thinking is not particularly goal-oriented at all. Gilhooly (1995) studied undirected thinking, where people just explore ideas or experience impressions, and found that this accounted for quite a significant proportion of our everyday thinking experience.

The third feature of thinking identified by Eysenck and Keane is that it can involve very different amounts of **knowledge**. Some thinking, such as that involved in thinking about social situations or making expert judgements, can draw on enormous amounts of knowledge, and they are sometimes referred to as 'knowledge-rich' situations. Other types, such as working out arithmetic problems or solving geometric puzzles, may only

involve a limited amount of knowledge, and psychologists tend to refer to these as 'knowledge-lean' problems.

Thinking takes all sorts of different forms, but most psychological research into thinking has tended to look at goal-directed thinking, like problem-solving, rather than the more nebulous kinds of thinking, like daydreaming, imagining, or speculating. In part, this is because such thinking is easier to study; but in part also it stems from the interest in similarities between human thinking and computer analysis which has developed since the advent of the computer.

Trial-and-error learning

One of the most important early studies of problem-solving was conducted by Thorndike, in 1911. Thorndike undertook a series of studies in animal problem-solving. One set of experiments involved putting a hungry cat into a 'puzzle box', with food outside the box. If the cat pulled a string which dangled from the roof of the box, the front of the box would open and the cat could escape and reach the food. Thorndike found that the more times a cat was placed in the box, the less time it would take to escape, and he was able to plot a **learning curve** which showed this relationship (Figure 5.1). The shape of the learning curve was similar for each animal, although the amount of time taken varied. Later studies showed that this type of learning curve holds true for most types of trial-and-error learning. Solving a Rubik's cube, for instance, takes a very long time the first time you do it, and quite a long time the second time, but as a rule the time becomes

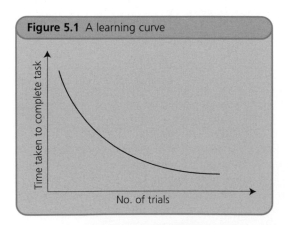

Figure 5.1 A learning curve

shorter on each occasion, in much the same fashion as the time the cat spent in the box.

Mental set

H.F. Harlow showed that rhesus monkeys could
develop generalised **learning sets** as a result of
repeated exposure to tasks which involved trial-
and-error learning (Harlow, 1949). Instead of
simply learning the solution to specific problems, a
rhesus monkey could learn how to solve particular
types of problems: it would develop a state of
readiness, or set, to solve a certain type of puzzle.
We will be coming back to Harlow's studies when
we look at animal learning, in Chapter 18, but the
idea of a learning set was one which researchers
investigated in human beings as well as in animals.

The Gestalt psychologists challenged the idea
that all problem-solving was a matter of trial-and-
error learning. They believed that effective
problem-solving developed mainly as a result of
people gaining insight into the problem, and
restructuring it productively to produce a solution. Although past experience could be important
in helping people to solve problems, the Gestalt
psychologists showed that it could also hinder it,
by establishing inappropriate mental sets.

Einstellung

Luchins, in 1942, demonstrated the power of set in
human problem-solving. Research participants
were given problems to solve which involved a
regular series of three steps. Each problem had to
be solved by using the same type of steps. Then
they were given a different problem, which could
be solved using the three-step method, but could
also be solved more quickly, in just two steps.
None of the research participants used the simpler
method. Moreover, when they were given a problem where only the two-step method would
work, very few of them solved it. But people who
had not been exposed to the early experience
with the three-step problems were much more
flexible in their approach, and could see alternative ways of solving the problem.

This study shows how previous experience can
make approaches more rigid. The subjects could
solve a familiar type of puzzle very easily, but their
previous experience had made them less able to
perceive a new solution. Luchins referred to this
fixed habit of mind as **Einstellung**, and described
how it prevented people from looking at problems

clearly and gaining insight into the nature of the
problem.

Functional fixedness

Glucksberg (1962) set research participants a
problem which involved using everyday items in
unfamiliar ways. Their task was to mount two
small candles on a wall, using only a box of
matches, the two candles and some drawing-pins.
Glucksberg found that people's ability to solve the
problem was seriously impaired by their tendency
to think of the objects only in terms of their usual
functions. This, Glucksberg argued, was another
form of mental set, which became known as
functional fixedness.

In a further version of the study, Glucksberg
found that the research participants' difficulties
were compounded by motivation: those who were
offered a $20 reward found more difficulty in
solving the problem than those who were not
receiving any financial incentive. Those without an
incentive were more ready to try alternatives than
those who stood to win money. It seems that high
motivation can make people unwilling to alter
their mental sets – which might account for why
so many students continue to use old, passive
revision techniques even when they know that
applying their knowledge of memory theory and
revising in a different way would be likely to
produce better results.

Gick and Holyoak (1980) presented research
participants with a problem to solve, which
involved working out how to dose a patient with
enough radiation to kill a malignant tumour,
when the same dose would damage the patient's
healthy tissues. The solution to the problem
entailed directing three different rays at the
tumour from different angles (see Figure 5.2), but
only 10% of their participants achieved this
solution.

The researchers then gave a different group of
research participants a set of three stories to learn.
One of the stories was similar to the tumour
problem, in that it involved an army advancing
along different roads to capture a fort. Later, when
the participants were given the tumour problem,
some of them were told that the stories they had
already heard might contain a hint. Of those who
knew that the stories might contain a hint, 92%
solved the problem successfully, but only 10% of
those who had not been told that the stories
might help, did so – in other words, they did not

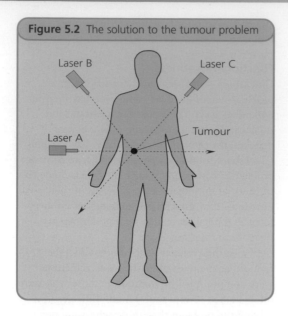

Figure 5.2 The solution to the tumour problem

Laser B

Laser C

Laser A

Tumour

do any better than the original group. Although they had been provided with information which could be useful in solving the problem, unless they recognised it as such they did not manage to apply it.

Social factors in problem-solving

Social processes can affect problem-solving too. In 1972, Janis analysed a number of American foreign-policy decisions which had been made between 1940 and 1970, and showed that very often decisions had been taken which were un-realistic and sometimes even disastrous when they were put into practice. This had occurred because of the process of **groupthink**, in which a group considers only a limited number of options, and does not really look at the wider context of its decisions.

One reason why groupthink occurs is because of the way that people in long-term real-life groups, like committees or action groups, often come to assume that everyone in the group thinks in the same way. This assumption puts pressure on the group members to conform to what seems to be the majority view, and so people are much less likely to disagree openly with one another (we will be looking at how powerful a force social conformity can be in Chapter 16). Since nobody disagrees openly, the group as a whole takes their view as being accurate, and makes no attempt to look for alternative viewpoints. After a while, even voicing an alternative view can be perceived as

disloyal, threatening the 'correctness' of the group – a process which can be observed in many politi-cal parties today.

Groupthink is a serious problem in decision-making situations, because it can produce such dramatic and serious results. Janis cited the un-successful American invasion of Cuba at the Bay of Pigs as an example. A search for outside informa-tion would have warned those making the decision as to the likely outcomes, but no such search was made, and the invasion was a military disaster.

There are a number of conditions which make groupthink more likely to happen: having a very cohesive group with a strong leader; insulating the group from information from the outside; failing to appraise all possible options systematically; and if the group feels under stress because it needs to act fast. Knowing how groupthink occurs, how-ever, does mean that we can do something about it. Janis (1972) described how, as a result of the Bay of Pigs fiasco, President Kennedy altered almost all these conditions when discussing decision-making strategy during the Cuban missile crisis. The committee was encouraged to debate and challenge decisions, and to criticise the underlying assumptions and ideas. Also, Kennedy absented himself from meetings from time to time, to limit his influence as leader. While it is difficult to evaluate political decisions, it certainly appeared as though the resulting action was rather more in touch with reality than the attempted invasion at the Bay of Pigs had been. Given the seriousness of the Cuban missile crisis, it was for-tunate that the dangers of groupthink had been recognised at the time.

The examples which Janis described were those of American political life in the 1950s and 1960s. But groupthink is an active psychological mechanism, which can be observed as having influenced many more recent political decisions. G. Moorhead, R. Ference and C. P. Neck (1991) discussed how it occurred in the 1980s, in the dis-astrous decision to launch the Space Shuttle Challenger. The shuttle exploded 73 seconds after launch, killing the seven people on board: six pro-fessional astronauts and a schoolteacher who would, if the mission had been successful, have been the first civilian in space. Moorhead, Ference and Neck examined the details of that decision, which were gathered by the ensuing Presidential Commission, and found that every single one of the conditions for groupthink was present.

The antecedent conditions Janis had identified were all present: the group had worked together for a long time and was very cohesive; two top-level managers actively promoted their opinions, as did other managers who pushed for launch; and they were insulated from the experts who insisted that the launch was not safe, since the engineers gave their warnings early in the evening and were not allowed to participate in any further discussion.

The eight symptoms listed in Table 5.1 were also present: the long history of freedom from accidents had produced an illusion of invulner-ability, and the group rationalised away the engineers' warnings by demanding absolute proof that the mission was unsafe – obviously impracti-cal, and in any case the normal procedure was to be certain that it was safe, not unsafe. The group also preserved its illusion of morality by refusing to acknowledge – and in some cases even notice – the strong ethical objections put forward by one high-level manager, and it dismissed the concerns of the engineers by stereotyping and dismissing them.

The top-level officials who supported the launch pressurised representatives of the major corporation involved in the launch, MTI. MTI originally recommended that the launch should not go ahead, but so much pressure was put on their personnel to prove that the launch was unsafe that it eventually produced self-censorship: a Vice-President of MTI objected strongly for a while, but met so much opposition that he bowed to this pressure after a while, and remained silent afterwards. This, as well as the silence from others taking his example, produced an illusion of unanimity which was taken as support for the decision by those in favour of it. Some members also engaged in mindguarding, by not revealing information which would have run counter to the group's expressed opinion.

The outcome, as might have been expected, was that the decision-making process showed all of the defects identified by Janis. The outcome was one of the worst disasters in space history, and one which crippled the American space programme. Another example was the decision by the Thatcher government in Britain to levy a poll tax – a decision which was politically disastrous, and acknowledged as such by many outside the cabi-net. Within it, however, the presence of the strong leader and the view that any challenge was 'dis-

Table 5.1 Symptoms of groupthink	
Invulnerability	The committee, board or task group operates under the illusion that it is largely invulnerable and that disasters are not possible.
Rationalisation	The committee tends to rationalise away unpopular solutions – to find excuses and justifications for the negative decisions it wishes to make
Stereotyping	A committee with a bad case of groupthink often falls back on stereotyping and deriding its opponents rather than arguing a case logically.
Conformity	The committee puts considerable pressure on doubters among its membership to conform, instead of investigating the source of their doubts.
Self-censorship	People on the committee, board or task group who have doubts about the wisdom of decision tend to keep quiet rather than speak up.
Illusion of unanimity	Some people see this as the most telling symptom of all: if every group member appears to agree with every decision, then either someone, somewhere, is hiding their true opinions, or the group needs some new members who will bring a fresh point of view!
Mindguarding	Some group members act as 'mindguards', by censoring undesirable information and opinions directly, or indirectly, by gentle hints that it is not really acceptable.
Illusion of morality	The group believes that all its actions or decisions are intrinsically right, and moral.

Source: Janis, 1983

loyal' meant that the political reality was not perceived. The phenomenon of groupthink is closely linked with the development of shared beliefs and **social representations**, which we will be looking at in Chapter 15.

Creative thinking

The ability to produce new ideas or approaches is one of the most important mainstays of a technological culture, and a considerable amount of effort has been put into understanding it. But creativity is an elusive thing to understand. One feature which seems apparent is that creativity involves escaping from conventional modes of thought or assumptions, and this has meant that much research into creativity has looked at novel styles of thought and originality in problem-solving.

Cognitive styles

In 1966, Hudson identified two different cognitive styles, based on an analysis of the approach which schoolboys took to their academic work. One of these styles was **convergent thinking**: convergent thinkers tended to focus tightly on particular problems, and to look for answers within well-established frameworks. The other style was referred to by Hudson as divergent thinking: divergent thinkers would range widely in their search for a solution to a problem, often moving far outside the usual accepted frameworks. Hudson believed that **divergent thinking** also had its spin-offs in terms of personality: that divergent thinkers were more likely to be perceived as witty or unusual by their friends, than were convergent thinkers.

One of the ways in which Hudson explored convergent and divergent thinking was to look at the kinds of original solutions which the schoolboys gave for problems. For example, one of the tests asked them to state how many uses they could think of for a brick. Convergent thinkers would tend to give conventional solutions, such as 'building a wall', or 'holding something up' – they showed quite a high level of functional fixedness. This also meant that they did not think of very many answers. Divergent thinkers, however, would think of many more uses, some of which would be quite unexpected. This was mainly because they would focus on the physical characteristics of the brick itself, and ignore its usual function. So a divergent thinker might describe a brick as a

possible tray for paper clips, because of the dip in the centre, or as a bookend or doorstop because of its weight and shape.

Real-life creativity

It is a questionable point, however, just how far Hudson's approach to creativity links with the type of creativity shown by a great artist or musician. Wood (1981) drew on a series of interviews and biographical writings compiled by Ghiselin, in 1952, which aimed to capture the creative experience of eminent artists, musicians, and scientists. Wood identified four consistent themes which emerged from this material.

The first theme was that highly creative people experienced their creativity as a kind of '**inner dialogue**' between the conscious mind and some other aspect of themselves. They were aware that some kind of idea or message was growing, but only partly conscious of it. This links with the second theme, which was that creators often spoke of producing their creations as if they, personally, were almost **spectators**. They described their ideas as having 'come to them' in their complete form relatively suddenly (although, as we have seen, they knew something was developing, so they were ready). Often, the idea surfaced suddenly as they woke up, as if it had crystallised during sleep. Once they had come to the surface, the artist/musician/scientist would wake and try to capture the essence of the idea.

In other words, Wood suggested, the creative process is experienced as though the idea is set up in the mind, mainly unconsciously, and then presented to the creator to be worked on. The creator is aware that there is a specific goal to be reached, even though it may not have been clearly articulated. Wood proposed that there may be a kind of continuum between explicitly goal-directed problem-solving, and full-scale creativity involving design and invention, to do with what types of solution or operations already exist, and are available. This is expressed in the flowchart in Figure 5.3.

A third theme which emerges from Ghiselin's collection is the way that, while the idea is incubating and beginning to take shape, the creator is very wary of trying to express it in words. There is a strong feeling of **distrust of words**, which, Wood suggests, may come from the fact that a creative act, by definition, is a novel one. Putting it into words means fitting it into an existing

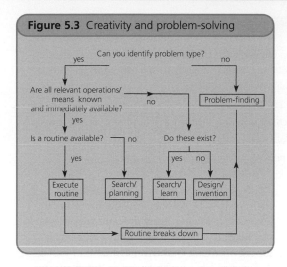

Figure 5.3 Creativity and problem-solving

structure, and this may constrain it so far that the essence of the idea vanishes.

The fourth theme identified by Wood, and in many ways the most important of all, is that of **practice**. All of the creative artists, scientists, and musicians involved had spent many years developing, practising, and working with their chosen media. Their abilities were finely tuned, and their knowledge of their particular tools was extensive. As a result, when the creative idea did develop, they were able to express it without having to pay any attention to the medium they were using to express it in. It came naturally to them, and so did not interfere with the expression of the idea.

This is an important idea, because it suggests that one of the most effective ways of encouraging creativity may not be to concentrate on the creativity itself, but instead to concentrate on the acquisition of expertise. Creativity may be actually inhibited if people are trying to express their ideas without having the means to express them in the way they want. But having lots of opportunity to develop a wide knowledge of the relevant tools – whether that be in art, music, literature or science – means that expertise can be used to help the creative process, and to allow ideas to come out and be expressed in the way that the unconscious, or conscious, mind intended.

Lateral thinking

Some forms of creativity may be less dramatic. Edward de Bono (1969) investigated the phenomenon of **lateral thinking**, which involved an individual's ability to escape from habitual modes and patterns of thought and to develop original

solutions to problems. This is similar to Hudson's concept of divergent thinking, and has similar implications in terms of personalities: some people seem to find it easier to engage in lateral thinking than others do. Lateral thinking involved finding solutions to problems which sidestep the conventional frame. For example, a conventional approach to a problem describing someone returning to an airport car park at night in midwinter and finding that their car locks were frozen up would be to look for ways of unfreezing the locks. But a lateral thinking approach might be to spend the night in the airport hotel instead, and drive the car away in the morning when the locks had unfrozen naturally.

In 1977, de Bono developed a training course designed to teach lateral thinking. This approach involved deliberately trying to identify the assumed or taken-for-granted limitations to problem-solving, and approaching the problem in a completely new way, as if nothing like it had ever been encountered before. An important part of this involved teaching people to become aware of the ways that mental set could limit their approaches to problems, and learn strategies to overcome it.

Brainstorming

Another technique which helps people to get away from the restrictions of mental sets and assumptions is known as **brainstorming**. This is a group-based technique, rather than an individual one, which has three stages, listed in Table 5.2. Brainstorming is a very useful technique for getting novel solutions to problems, and it is frequently used in marketing and advertising to develop new ideas.

The most important feature of brainstorming is that the first stage does not involve any selection or evaluation at all. This is crucial to the success of the technique, because it allows people to generate entirely novel ideas freely. People find it hard to develop new ideas if they feel that they might not be practical: there is a kind of **evaluation apprehension** which comes into play, which means that they do not want to say anything that others might think is stupid.

Often, though, an idea might seem silly at first, but the more it is explored the more it seems to work. If someone feels that all the ideas which they put forward have to be practical and realistic, they will self-censor the wilder ones, and not say

Table 5.2 Stages of brainstorming

1	*The idea-generating stage*	In this stage, a group of people get together to generate as many ideas as they possibly can. Nothing is rejected for any reason – it can be impractical, crazy or even just plain silly.
2	*The scrutiny stage*	In the second stage, the list of ideas which has been produced is scrutinised closely, and any which are obviously impractical or irrelevant are rejected.
3	*The evaluation stage*	The third stage involves going through the remaining possibilities, one by one, and discussing how each one might work in practice.

them. But by insisting that the first stage of a brainstorming programme is open and non-evaluative, these ideas can be collected much more freely.

Computer models of thinking

The advent of the computer in the late 1960s and early 1970s resulted in considerable interest in how information is processed in the brain, and, as we saw in Chapter 1, this formed a significant part of the cognitive revolution. The **computer metaphor** – seeing the brain as being like a computer – became extremely popular. Research in this field ultimately led to the growth of a new discipline of **cognitive science**, in which the computer-based aspects of cognitive psychology, information-processing aspects of linguistics and research into computers and human–computer interaction merged into a single discipline.

Research into computer models of thinking has tended to go along two paths: **computer simulation**, in which an attempt is made to replicate, or simulate, human thinking; and **artificial intelligence (AI)**, in which systems are developed to replace, enhance or aid human decision-making or problem-solving.

Computer simulation

If you think about it, you can see that life is full of different types of problem. Deciding what you should wear when you are going to a special event is a problem which needs solving. Working out which is the best way to get home is a problem. Organising your time so that you manage to get all your homework and revision done and still have some social life is another type of problem

that needs to be solved. Real-life problems are complex, involving many different factors which can make it difficult to see just exactly what problem-solving system is needed.

Since real-life problems are so complex, psychologists who are developing computer simulations of problem-solving tend to look at much less complex ones, in the hope that studying simple problems will throw light on the ways that more complex problems are solved as well. There is, of course, an implicit reductionism in this argument: as we saw in Chapter 1, psychological questions cannot necessarily be seen as nothing but the sum of their parts. Complex problems may be qualitatively different from simple ones. But the belief of those involved in this type of research is that developing computer programs which can solve simple problems may help to throw light on at least some of the mechanisms which underlie human problem-solving.

Means-end analysis

Research into computer problem-solving, at least at first, needed to work with relatively simple problems. These problems have tended to have three characteristics, which are listed in Table 5.3. One of the first models which was put forward from research using this approach was by Newell and Simon, in 1972. They developed the **general problem solver**, or **GPS**, a computer simulation system which used a technique known as means-end analysis.

Means-end analysis consists of comparing the state of affairs at the beginning of the problem – the initial state – with the state of affairs which will have been reached when the problem has been solved – the goal state. The difference between the initial state and the goal state is known as the **problem space**, or **problem**

Table 5.3 Characteristics of computer problem-solving tasks

1	*A well-defined initial state*	This makes it possible to know, exactly, where the starting point is, and what is involved from the outset.
2	*A well-defined goal state*	This makes it possible to know exactly what the final solution to the problem would be.
3	*Well-defined actions*	So that it is possible to find a sequence of actions which can be taken to try to solve the problem.

distance. The general problem-solver's task is to reduce the problem space.

There are two ways in which a given problem space can be reduced. One is to use an **algorithm**: a repetitive procedure which is guaranteed eventually to lead to a solution. However, even in the simplest problems the problem space may be quite large, and exploring all the possibilities is cumbersome. For example, deciding on each move in a chess game by trying out all the possibilities would eventually lead to a solution – but the number of possible moves is so great that it might take even a computer years!

Human beings, when they are solving problems, do not try out all the possibilities. Instead, we tend to plump for the strategy which looks as though it is most likely to produce a good result – a **heuristic**. Heuristics are strategies which will allow us to approach the problem one step at a time. Using a heuristical approach, the problem is broken down into a series of sub-goals, a step is taken, and then the problem distance is examined to see what the situation is. If the problem space has reduced, it looks as though the heuristic is helpful, and so it tends to be accepted.

The general problem-solver also used a heuristical strategy. By using means–end analysis, it would break down the problem into stages, or sub-goals. Then it would choose the strategy which looked most likely to reduce the problem space, by achieving that sub-goal. Once each sub-goal was reached, the GPS would recalculate the problem space, and identify the step which would allow the next sub-goal to be reached. By adopting a heuristical strategy, Newell and Simon showed that the computer was much more likely to solve the problem efficiently.

Heuristics can be very useful as 'short-cuts' to solving problems. But, of course, they can go wrong, because they can sometimes mean that we ignore alternative possibilities – in much the same

way as the development of a mental 'set' may mean that we do not consider fully what other options are available. However, the GPS proved to be appropriate for a number of simple problems. Ernst and Newell (1969) used it to solve eleven different puzzles, including finding the next letter for a given series, the Hobbits and Orcs problem, and the Tower of Hanoi problem (see Box 5.1 overleaf). The GPS solved all these problems successfully, although it did not seem to do so in quite the same way that human solvers did.

Protocol analysis

Another technique used in computer simulation is known as **protocol analysis**. Protocols are the steps which are taken in solving a problem. Identifying the protocols which human beings use in solving a given problem, therefore, could give useful information for the development of computer simulation systems. In early research into protocol analysis, it was thought that collecting verbal protocols – getting people to 'think out loud', describing what they were doing as they tackled a problem – would allow researchers to identify the steps that they were using. However, this research method quickly hit difficulties, for a number of reasons – the main one being that what people say is often quite different from what they do.

This can occur for a number of reasons, many of which concern aspects of cognitive psychology which we have discussed in the past few chapters. One of the biggest problems is the way that people often are not fully aware of what they are doing or why they are doing it. We all have well-developed habits and automatic routines, and these are not always amenable to consciousness. Writers, for instance, are notoriously bad at teaching people the basic mechanics of language: because they are so familiar with fluent language use, they find it difficult to break language down into its components.

Box 5.1 Problems used in computer simulation

Most early research into computer simulation involved the use of very explicit problems, with clearly defined ends. These are three of the most commonly used problems of this type.

1 *Finding the next letter in a given series*
The problem-solver (computer or human) would be provided with a series of letters, for example:

FHIL...?

They then had to state what the next letter should be. Typically, such problems involved mathematical relationships between numbers, and a clearly designated amount of baseline knowledge, like the accepted sequence of letters of the alphabet.

2 *Hobbits and Orcs*
This problem is stated as follows:

Three Hobbits have captured three Orcs on the borders of the Shire. They need to get their prisoners across the Brandywine river, so that they can be taken to the Rangers at Bree. They are on the river bank, and they have a boat. However, the boat can only carry two at a time, and they need to make sure that there are always at least as many Hobbits as there are Orcs in any one place. If there were more Orcs than Hobbits at any time, the Orcs would overpower the Hobbits and kill them. How should they go about getting across the river so that they can all arrive safely?

The problem has a clearly defined initial state, and a clearly defined end state. It also has a correct solution, which involves a number of definite steps, known as **protocols**. The task of the problem-solver is to identify those steps, and to describe them in their proper sequence.

3 *The Tower of Hanoi*
This is a spatial problem, which involves a board with three pegs, standing vertically. The peg at one end contains three rings: a large one, a middle-sized one and a small one, arranged in order, with the largest on the bottom. The task is to move the three rings to the peg at the other end, so that they are also arranged in size order, with the largest at the bottom. But only one ring can be moved at a time, and no ring may be placed on top of a ring which is smaller than itself.

Like the Hobbits and Orcs problem, this has a specified beginning state, a specified end state and a definite number of **protocols** involved in getting to the correct solution.

These kinds of problems, then, are highly specific ones, where it is possible to state exactly how the solution must be calculated. But it is questionable how useful such specific, tightly controlled problems are in telling us anything of how human beings go about problem-solving. Critics argue that real-life problem-solving has end-goals which are far less explicit, and stages in gaining the solution which are very much less apparent.

Nisbett and Wilson (1977) showed how, often, if you ask people to introspect as they perform a task, what they say is more commonly a justification for what they have done, than a reason for why they did it. So many tasks are done without conscious thought that people often just do not have genuine introspective insights into their actions.

That does not mean that the technique is useless, though. Ericsson and Simon (1980) argued that extracting verbal protocols from research participants could be useful under two circumstances: first, as long as the person was describing what they were doing at that moment, rather than what they had done before; and second, as long as what they were saying was reflected in their

behaviour, so that it was possible for observers to correlate the two measures. If both of these conditions were met, Ericsson and Simon argued, verbal protocol analysis could provide valuable information for researchers.

Production systems
Once protocols have been identified, it becomes necessary to find a way of making sense of them. The patterns of the protocols that a person has produced are known as **production systems**. Production systems involve a combination of conditions and actions: 'when conditions are like this, then you do that'. Some researchers have found it helpful to think of these in terms of stimuli and responses: whenever these conditions

hold (stimulus), that action is taken (response). Others, though, find little that is helpful in using this vocabulary.

Production systems are based on the protocols derived from just one person. Different production systems are derived from other people's protocols. But the different production systems which are identified also need to be compared. Some ways of going about problem-solving are more desirable than others, so developing a computer simulation system based on production systems also has to include a way of choosing the better option. This involves the development of **conflict resolution rules**, so that when a choice is available between two different production system it is possible to resolve that choice in a positive way. Using this system, a computer may be able to proceed through the steps of a well-defined problem – as long as that problem also has some kind of memory limitation built in, so that the total steps needed are within the computer's capacity.

As can be seen, then, research into computer simulation has achieved some success in programming computers to solve problems. However, the major difficulty with this research is that it can only deal with very specific, very well-defined problems. In 'real life', the problems that we have to deal with are much less well defined, and have wider parameters. If you have lost your house key but need to get into the house, you may be reluctant to take the obvious step of breaking a window for a number of reasons – not least of which might be how your parents or housemates would respond when they found out! In dealing with these types of problems, we need to apply a great deal of our knowledge of the world, of other people, and make probabilistic judgements about what the outcomes of certain actions are likely to be. Human beings are very good at this, but computers are not.

Connectionism

In recent years, research in computer simulation has attempted to address wider, less well-defined problems by using **parallel distributed processing (PDP)**. These systems are designed to tackle an issue from a number of different angles, making multiple connections between several different logical routes, rather than following a single channel of reasoning and tackling things one step at a time.

In fact, **connectionism**, as this approach is known, has very old theoretical roots. In psychology, it goes back to Thorndike's approach to problem-solving, which we looked at earlier in this chapter. The idea is that the existence of lots of possibilities means that the organism, or in this case the computer, can undertake several possible sets of actions (or calculations), but only some of them will prove fruitful. Those ones are reinforced, or rewarded, and that strengthens the connections between the incoming information and the resulting action.

Thorndike considered that connectionism was how animals 'learned', and the idea was taken up by W. O. Hebb, in 1949, who proposed that learning consisted of connections being forged between nerve cells. Each time a set of cells acted together to produce a result, the links between them were strengthened, and they would begin to act as complete units, which Hebb called **cell assemblies**.

This model has been taken up by a number of researchers into artificial intelligence, who have used it as a way of producing computer systems which can 'learn'. Dalenoort (1995) discussed how attempts to simulate the kinds of neural processes which are likely to occur in the human brain would require something very different from direct programming. Instead, Dalenoort proposed that it was more useful to approach the task using **neural networks**: sets of interlinked digital pathways which could be 'trained' to respond in preferred ways when faced with a particular stimulus.

These networks would involve the use of several parallel pathways at a time, and the 'neurones' concerned would 'fire' when they received a stimulus of a sufficient strength, in much the same way as those in the brain do. There would also need to be an inhibitory function, whereby a neurone which had just fired would be less likely to fire again. This too is a mechanism shared by brain neurones, as we will see in Chapter 12. Effectively, this type of computer system creates cell assemblies which are equivalent to memory traces, which are activated, or set off, when incoming information reaches a certain threshold, and cease functioning when they are no longer relevant.

Following on from this idea, Dalenoort (1997) discussed how it is impractical to expect to model complex information systems by means of pre-programmed computer systems. Instead, the important thing for those attempting to simulate such systems is to discover principles of self-organisation, so that those systems would be able to create their own knowledge structures. Dalenoort identified two different types of knowledge representation system which had been proposed to explain how human knowledge is stored: semantic networks, and conceptual networks. **Semantic networks** involve straightforward, linear connections between items of information, or 'nodes' (Figure 5.4). But in **conceptual networks**, the connections between nodes are also variable,

so the network operates by activating connections between different nodes.

The consequence of this is that more complex relationships between nodes can be produced, and the system can also begin to make wider associations, in the way that human systems do (Figure 5.5). It can be seen from this that the system is not simply coming up with a linear answer to the question. It is also activating related nodes, and associations, in a way that resembles the human associations which might be primed by the same type of question.

De Vries and Van Slochteren (1997) used this approach to develop a computer system which could undertake some of the complex (for a computer) task of text-processing, in a way which seems similar to the way that human beings do it. Their system was a simulation of a conceptual network, which required the application of a general spatial map, which would represent where objects were located in relation to other objects; and this map was used to generate rules about the linking of different cell assemblies. The piece of text being processed would trigger off a number of different cell assemblies; but only those which seemed to be close to one another, according to the map, were treated as if they were connected.

An essential characteristic of the network is that memory traces for the concepts of 'first', 'second' etc. can be linked, temporarily, with memory traces of the items in a list – such as the letters in a new word. In the network, a temporary binding

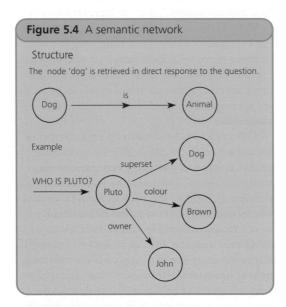

Figure 5.4 A semantic network

Structure

The node 'dog' is retrieved in direct response to the question.

Example

WHO IS PLUTO?

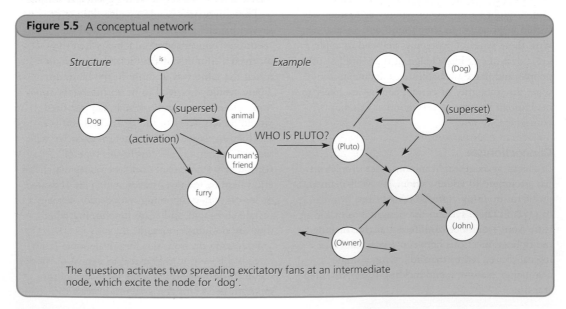

Figure 5.5 A conceptual network

The question activates two spreading excitatory fans at an intermediate node, which excite the node for 'dog'.

of this kind becomes active when the two memory traces are active at the same time, and in the same context. This is where the spatial map comes into play. If the memory traces are linked together for long enough, the trace can become permanent, which is how the system becomes able to 'learn' new words. Using this approach, the researchers showed that it was possible for the system to process, not just text it had been trained to recognise, but novel forms of text as well.

Computer simulation has had several critics. Many psychologists, myself included, have argued that attempts to simulate human cognitive processes are unlikely to be successful, on the grounds that the human brain is not a computer, and does not process information in the same way. This is still likely to be true for complex human reasoning, where we draw on our world-knowledge, social representations, and many other sources of information and bias. But the approach adopted by Dalenoort and his colleagues is a much more sophisticated form of computer simulation, which is closer to a human way of operating than earlier approaches. Modelling cognitive systems using a self-organising system of neural networks and cell assemblies seems to be a productive line of research, and it will be interesting to see how it develops in the future.

Artificial intelligence

A considerable amount of research has also been directed towards the question of **artificial intelligence**, known as **AI** for short. Most artificial intelligence systems involve the development of computer systems which can help human beings in their decision making, or in some cases can replace them. There are three major areas in artificial intelligence: interactive programs, expert systems, and robotics.

Interactive programs
One of the first areas of work in the AI field was the development of **interactive programs**. These are programs which engage in 'conversations' with people, through a computer keyboard. One of the first, and certainly the most famous, of these interactive programs was a therapeutic program known as **ELIZA**. When ELIZA was running, someone would sit at a keyboard and type in questions, and the computer was programmed to respond as if it were a therapist.

Although in reality the computer was simply responding to key words, people often reacted to ELIZA as if they were talking to a real person, and could become very angry if they were interrupted when they were 'discussing' their personal problems with the machine. In some cases, too, people who had wanted to see a therapist and were offered a session with ELIZA instead decided that talking with ELIZA had been quite sufficient, and refused to see a human therapist.

In a different study, Abelson and Carroll (1965) developed an interactive program based on the political views expressed by a right-wing American politician. By following a set of programmed 'rules', the program was able to draw inferences from information which it was given in a dialogue, and generated responses that were very similar to those expressed by the original politician.

Expert systems
A different area of artificial intelligence research is concerned with expert systems. These involve computer programs that provide an additional database of information which can be used to help human experts to make their professional decisions. The database does not make decisions itself, but provides easy access to extra information so that the expert can draw on a wider range of knowledge. The three components of an expert system are listed in Table 5.4 overleaf.

Although this may seem reasonably straightforward, it is not as easy as it might seem. Using computers as back-up systems for human experts also involves attempting to identify the components of expert skill in humans, and how it differs from the approaches taken by novices. We will be looking at this research later in this chapter, but it does show us that there are some powerful qualitative differences, both between experts and novices, and between human experts and computer experts. For one thing, human experts tend to have quite a lot of implicit knowledge, which is not easily verbalised or entered in a database. Human beings are also very good at recognising higher-order patterns or similarities, whereas computers can often only identify specific elements of a problem, and sometimes these may not be relevant.

Berry (1989) argued that explanations in AI are often inadequate in terms of what a human enquirer actually needs to know, because they

Table 5.4 Components of an expert system

1	*A knowledge base*	This provides lucid, task-specific information.
2	*An inference engine*	This allows the computer to select potentially relevant informaton from the vast range of data which is available in the knowledge base. It needs a matching system which will compare the details of the new problem with the stored information.
3	*A 'user-friendly' interface*	This allows the user to communicate requests clearly and simply, and to comprehend the responses which people make to it.

tend to concentrate on very specific aspects of information, while human enquirers generally want to know about much vaguer similarities or patterns. So it is unlikely that computer systems could actually replace a human expert; but they can, and do, provide valuable assistance by providing a back-up informational system.

Robotics

A third area of research into artificial intelligence is concerned with the development of **robotics**. Robots are independently moving systems which can undertake specific actions or do particular kinds of work – the word 'robot' derives from the Russian verb 'rabotat', meaning 'to work'. Early robots were only able to take on very specific tasks, such as rivetting pieces of metal together. But they were not simply automatic rivetters: they were able to work, to some extent, without human guidance. A robot combines a 'sensory' system, which it uses to detect its environment, with a navigational system, which it uses to move around, and an implementation system which it uses to perform operations on its environment. These are co-ordinated by the robot's **operating system**, to ensure that they work together and in the appropriate sequence.

Researchers developing robotic systems have developed complex operating systems, which are able to use varying types of input from the 'sensory' system in order to adjust their actions. They have developed mobile machines which are able to move around, detect and avoid obstacles, and even to pick up different items – something which human beings do without thinking, but which involve very complex calculations. If the machine grips something too tightly, it may break it; if it does not grip it hard enough it may drop it. Identifying the appropriate types of feedback needed to detect these factors, and then 'teaching'

the robot how to interpret them, was a challenge for the early robotics researchers. Effectively, the operating system needs to be an artificial intelligence system, capable of making deductions from inputs and developing plans for activity.

More recently, robotics research has been developing in more sophisticated directions. Sigaud (1997) looked at how a system might develop a conceptual basis for cognition. Sigaud began with Piagetian theory (see Chapter 19), which argues that we develop schemata through performing operations on the world. This led to three questions: firstly, what sort of structure would such operations form; secondly, whether the resulting structure would do something equivalent to concept-formation in human beings; and thirdly, whether it would be possible for concept-formation to begin from a tabula rasa, with no prior knowledge.

Sigaud went on to develop a system called 'Candide', which was a robot able to carry out a number of straightforward commands, such as 'turn left', 'turn right', 'go straight on', 'stop', etc. The system had sensory mechanisms to inform it of braking or steering, and these formed the input to its AI system. The AI's outputs were measures of what happened as a result of these actions, e.g. Candide's speed, its position, or its distance from its goal. Each of the inputs and outputs was assigned a numerical value, which indicated the extent of the movements that Candide had made.

Sigaud went on to measure the differences between these values, and then to examine those measurements for any systematic patterns. This was followed by a further analysis, looking for higher-order patterns, such as whether a characteristic pattern was often repeated, and if so, at what intervals. As a result of all this, Candide became able to move around by using general principles and concepts, rather than direct instructions. It could respond to different types of request: to go to a particular destination and stop; to move around in a particular area; to go from one region to another; or to find an appropriate route. Perhaps more importantly, Candide was able to 'learn' from its experiences: it could, for example, find routes using a system of trial, error and re-inforcement, and then use general 'concepts' from its previous experience when finding a different route.

The type of system developed by Sigaud may not look particularly impressive when compared with the ease with which human beings negotiate their way around the physical world. But that task is far more complex than we realise. The development of AI systems which can operate at general levels, and can develop 'concepts' based on their operations in the environment, rather than in response to very specific instructions, is a major development.

Twenty or thirty years ago, it was assumed that computers would eventually be able to out-perform humans. This assumption is no longer as common as it was. Nowadays we are much clearer about what computers do best and what human beings do better. For example, no computers can use language with anything like the flexibility of a human, although some can use it in very general ways. Computers are not able to apply the sophisticated social knowledge which human beings use in their reasoning. And as we have seen, the idea of an active cognitive cycle, in which anticipatory schemata direct a selective search for information, which in turn modifies the schema, is one which AI researchers are only just beginning to use.

Early research into computer simulation and artificial intelligence tended to assume that human thinking was essentially computer-like: based on logical chains, associations, and straightforward information inputs. However, this rather naïve model of human cognition does not really bear much resemblance to how human beings think. As AI specialists have become more aware of the complexities of human cognition, they have been able to develop more sophisticated computer systems, which can get closer to the way that human beings use plans, probabilities and experience. But researchers are still exploring human reasoning, and coming across new aspects of it all the time.

Reasoning and expertise

Studies of human reasoning have shown that, unlike computers, human beings do not always operate strictly logically. In 1966, Wason described some fundamental characteristics of the way that people reason, which show that human logic is not the same as formal logic, although it is extremely useful in everyday life. One of these characteristics is the way that people take longer to process negative statements than they do to process positive ones, even when the two state-ments are logically equivalent. It takes longer for someone to work out the meaning of: 'I'm not going to take the dog out if the sun does not shine' than: 'I'll only take the dog out if the sun shines'.

The confirming bias

Another characteristic of human reasoning which Wason identified is the way that we look for information which will confirm a hypothesis that we have formed, rather than looking for informa-tion which will disconfirm it – even if the latter would be the logical thing to do. In one of Wason's studies (Wason, 1968), people were pre-sented with four cards, each with its upwards face showing one of the letters and numbers E, K, 4 and 7 (see Figure 5.6). They were told that each card had a number on one side, and a letter on the other. Then they were asked which cards they would need to turn over, if they wanted to see whether the statement 'If a card has a vowel on one side then it has an even number on the other side' was true.

Most of the research participants in the study made one of two answers. Either they chose only the E card, or they chose the card which showed E and the one which showed the number 4. But really, the correct answer is E and 7. It does not matter what is on the other side of the 4 card, because the rule does not say that a 4 must have a vowel on the reverse of it – only that an E must have an even number. But it does matter what is

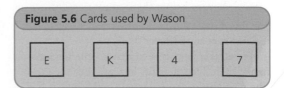

Figure 5.6 Cards used by Wason

| E | K | 4 | 7 |

on the other side of the 7 card, because if the 7 had an E on the other side of it, that would disprove the rule. And if the E had an odd number on the other side, that would disprove the rule too. The fact that people chose the 4 card was an example of how we tend to look for confirming instances, rather than disconfirming ones.

However, Wason and Shapiro (1971) suggested that these findings only apply if the problem is presented in an abstract form. When people were given the problem in a 'real-life' form, involving travelling to Manchester or Leeds, by car or by train, over 60% solved it correctly. Griggs and Cox (1982) showed that when American students (who did not know Manchester or Leeds) were given the same version, they performed just as badly as they did with the abstract version. But they had no problem finding the correct solution if the problem related to cities which they knew.

These findings imply that our human tendency to look for confirming instances is not inevitable. If we are dealing with real-life information, we can solve these puzzles well enough. But if we are dealing with information which is abstract or meaningless, the tendency to look for confirming instances comes into play, and means that we can end up reasoning inaccurately.

Applying social knowledge

Wason and Johnson-Laird (1972) showed that people apply their broader knowledge of what is likely when they are making deductions or inferences, and this can also mean that they do not reason according to strict formal logic. For example, if you heard someone say: 'I'll go for a walk on Sunday if the weather is fine' you would be likely also to conclude that they would not go for a walk if it was raining. To a human being, that just seems reasonable.

To a computer, though, operating by formal logic, there would be just as much chance of seeing your friend go for a walk in the rain as there would in the sunshine on that particular Sunday, because they had not said that they would not go out if it was raining, only that they *would* go if it was fine. According to formal logic, saying that 'I will do this if …' is not the same as saying 'I won't do this if not'. But in everyday life, it is generally taken to mean the same thing.

Henle (1962) suggested that people tend to make these logical errors because they focus on the meaning of the statement, and whether it is true or not, rather than on what has been logically implied. In Chapter 4 we saw how people read for meaning, and so often do not remember exactly what words were involved in what they read. It is the same when people talk to one another. Braine, Reiser and Rumain (1964) showed how social expectations produce this type of error. We expect people to tell us what we need to know, so we infer that (for example) fine weather is the only thing which will get the friend out for a walk. Moreover, our inference would usually be correct: if someone said that they would go out if it was fine, they would almost certainly mean that they would not go if it was raining. It may not be formal logic, but it is typically human reasoning.

Effectively, we rely on our shared social knowledge in this type of communication. We do not usually spell out everything that we mean, because we know that the other person will infer what we are trying to say. One of the major difficulties of applying criteria of strict logic to human speech is that it ignores the social dimension of communication, and the shared understandings and assumptions which people use when they talk to one another.

So in some respects, human reasoning can be seen as being quite different from formal logic. It is a matter for debate whether these features of human reasoning should be seen as 'errors', or as evidence that human reasoning is far more subtle and sophisticated than a logical system would be, since human reasoning includes the whole social context and the probable actions that people are likely to take as well as the 'pure' elements of the problem.

Johnson-Laird (1983) argued that the essence of the question is not which is right or wrong, but is to do with how human beings create mental models about the problems that they try to solve. If we have more world-knowledge to draw on, our existing mental models are likely to be appropriate, and so lead to effective social reasoning. If we only have limited knowledge, as we do in an abstract problem, then we can easily draw on inappropriate mental models, and encounter problems or difficulties as a result.

Expertise

Research into computer-based expert systems, as we have seen, led into a different area of research, exploring the nature of human expertise. Experts, in their own fields, are very different from ordinary people: they appear to use their expertise in ways that most people would find impossible. In particular, their approach to problem-solving and reasoning seems to be quite different from the more naïve approaches adopted by non-experts. So some psychologists have attempted to identify just what those differences are, and how human experts have come to acquire them.

The role of practice

One of the very first principles of acquiring expertise, it seems, is practice. Chase and Simon (1973) studied some of the distinctive characteristics of experts, and one of the most important things which emerged was the sheer amount of time they had spent acquiring their skills. Chase and Simon estimated that most chess grandmasters had studied for at least nine or ten years, to reach their current level. We have already seen how important practice is for fostering creativity – how highly creative people also tend to have a very high level of expertise – and when we look at skill learning, in Chapter 18, we will find that it is equally important for physical skills.

But practice does not lead to a smooth, gradual improvement. Lesgold (1984) showed that acquiring expertise is not a linear process – we do not just get better evenly all the time. Instead, if we are learning something, we quite often get worse before we get better. In radiographers interpreting X-ray photographs, a U-shaped curve of successful performance developed as they progressed through their training. Novices, Lesgold found, tended to make straightforward, simplistic 'rule-book' decisions, which were OK some of the time, although not all the time. Radiographers in the intermediate stages got worse as they tried to take more factors and subtleties into account in their interpretations, but this stage was only temporary, and formed the more sophisticated basis which they needed for the development of true expertise.

Chunking and strategies

The huge amount of practice which experts have undertaken produces some more specific differences between experts and novices. In 1973, Chase and Simon showed how, in chess-playing, experts see the game in terms of the relationships between the pieces, whereas novices tend only to see the individual pieces. The researchers also found that expert players 'chunked' information

better than novices and memorised more moves altogether. They argued that this occurred because expert players had better memory retention than novices do.

Holding, in 1985, challenged their explanation, arguing that improved skill led to better memory, not the other way round. Holding and Reynolds (1982) showed that chess skills can differ even when there are no memory differences between players. They argued that experts adopt entirely different strategies from novices – in particular, that they tend to work from the given state to the goal, whereas novices typically look first at the goal that they want to reach and then work backwards from there. If this is the case, then the kind of means-end analysis adopted in computer simulation studies bears more similarities to how novices go about solving problems than it does to the behaviour of human experts.

In research into how experts go about medical diagnosis, it appears that experts use a mixture of forwards and backwards strategies. Johnson (1984) showed that experts often adopt a hypothetico-deductive technique, reasoning from the evidence and then forming hypotheses on the basis of that reasoning. The researchers found that both experts and novices do this, but experts begin to make more specific hypotheses at an earlier stage.

Characteristics of expertise

Green and Gilhooly (1992) summed up research into expertise by identifying five aspects of human expertise, which are summarised in Table 5.5. The first three are to do with what experts are like, and the first of them is simply that human experts are better at remembering information. Perhaps because of their deeper understanding of the issues, they are able to store more information,

---

Table 5.5 Characteristics of experts

1 Experts remember better.

2 Experts use different problem-solving techniques.

3 Experts understand problems differently.

4 Experts know more.

5 Experts have practised their knowledge extensively.

Source: Green and Gilhooly, 1992

and to draw it up at relevant times. The second is that experts use different problem-solving techniques and strategies; and the third is that they also have better ways of representing the problem to themselves – in other words, their understanding of what the problem actually consists of is different, and clearer.

The last two aspects of human expertise identified by Green and Gilhooly (1992) concern how individuals come to be experts. The first of these (the fourth characteristic of the total list) is the point that expertise does not come from any basic capacity; it comes from the amount that people know about their particular area. And the final one is the way that human beings become expert, which is through extensive practice. In other words, people become experts by acquiring a lot of knowledge, and using that knowledge repeatedly, so that they become practised in applying it to different situations and circumstances. They do not become experts because they have some kind of special quality that other people do not have.

Decision-making

Problem-solving is just one example of goal-directed thinking. Sometimes, though, goal-directed thinking is not about finding definite answers – it is about making decisions. We make decisions all the time, ranging from trivial ones (What type of sandwich shall I have for lunch today?) to ones which can affect our whole lives (Should I go in for accountancy or science?).

Researchers into decision-making have identified a number of principles, or to be more precise, **heuristics**, of human decision-making. Heuristics, as we saw earlier, are rules of thumb, which work pretty well when they are applied in most situations. There are four main ones: representativeness, availability, anchoring, and decision frames. But as we saw in Chapter 2, it is sometimes easier to identify psychological mechanisms when things go wrong, so quite a lot of research into decision-making has been concerned with the times when applying these heuristics can lead to errors.

Representativeness

One of the heuristics which we apply when making decisions is concerned with **representativeness**.

We make judgements about whether a given example or instance is typical, or representative, of the population that it comes from, and base our decisions on these.

Bayes' theorem

In their well-known paper on decision-making, Kahnemann and Tversky (1973) argued that when we are working out judgements of probability, we should really go by **Bayes' theorem**, which states that probability is influenced by two factors: likelihood ratio and base rate. The **likelihood ratio** is how likely it is that a given instance will have come from a particular source, as opposed to other possible sources. In assessing this, we would really be looking at how typical that instance is of that particular group or source – if we were trying to decide whether somebody was an engineer or a musician, we might look at whether their personality (or what we knew of it) was more typical of engineers than it was of musicians in general, and this would be using the likelihood ratio.

But the other, equally important, factor in assessing how probable something is consists of **base-rate** information about how many of those instances occur in the population at large (by comparison with the other group). If we were looking at a population which contained very few musicians but lots of engineers, then the probability that the person was an engineer would be higher.

Kahnemann and Tversky discovered that people tend to ignore base-rate information when they are making judgements about probability. In one example, Kahnemann and Tversky (1973) set up a study in which research participants were asked to guess the occupations of people from a set of information which they were provided with. In each task, the participants were given a description of an individual and told that it had been chosen randomly from a set of 100 such descriptions. They were also given base-rate information about the original 100, such as, for example, that 70% of the descriptions had referred to engineers, while 30% had referred to lawyers.

The actual description which was given could apply equally well to either engineers or lawyers. For example, one typical description might be something like:

John is a 30-year-old married man with two children. He has high ability and motivation, and promises to be

quite successful in his field. He is well-liked by his
colleagues.

Since either choice of occupation is equally plausible, strict logic would assume that research participants would refer back to the base-rate information which they had been given, and conclude that there was a 70% probability of John being an engineer, and a 30% probability of him being a lawyer. But in fact, research participants did not do this. They looked at the descriptions and judged that there was an equal likelihood of either profession – in other words, they completely ignored the base-rate information which they had been given.

It seems that if we want people to take notice of base-rate information we have to emphasise it quite strongly. Manis *et al.* (1980) performed a study in which research participants were asked to judge how likely it was that people presented in a set of photographs favoured marijuana legalisation. During the study, the research participants were continuously provided with base-rate information, instead of its being provided just once. They took much more notice of it when they were making their judgements of probability than the research participants in Kahnemann and Tversky's original study had done. Nisbett and Ross (1980) proposed that making base-rate information clearer and more vivid also increases the likelihood that people will take notice of it.

In general, though, we pay more attention to likelihood than to base rates when we are making judgements. There appear to be several reasons involved in why we do this, and they mainly hinge on our readiness to regard a particular sample as representative of the population which it comes from. For example, although we know that a large sample is statistically more likely to represent the population than a small sample, we still treat small samples as if they were typical.

Random and patterned outcomes

In fact, our judgements of representativeness itself do not stick strictly to statistical probability. For example: we are much more likely to judge a sample as representative of its population if it looks random, than if it seems to have a pattern – even if a patterned outcome is just as likely. If you were tossing a coin six times, it is just as likely that you could get the outcome 'heads, heads, heads, tails, tails, tails', as that you would get the outcome

'heads, heads, tails, heads, tails, heads'. But if we were judging how likely these two outcomes were, we would tend to think that the second one was more likely to happen than the first – because the first looks patterned, and the second looks random.

Kahnemann and Tversky (1972) reported on how the random bombing of London during WWII had resulted in some areas being repeatedly hit, while others were not touched. They showed that this was perfectly likely to happen with random bombing – indeed, it would have been odd if it had not, since random bombing, by definition, would have been extremely unlikely to produce completely balanced effects. But people still believed that the bombing pattern was planned, and that these areas were being systematically targeted.

Availability

Another heuristic which we use when we are making decisions concerns the availability of information. Some items of information come more readily to mind than others, and so they are more likely to influence our decisions.

Vividness

The random bombing example given above demonstrates the influence of vivid examples and imagery. Dramatic, easily visualised examples make much more of an impact on our thinking than dry, abstract information. Statistics about, say, the number of cases of AIDS in African countries, show that the problem is far more widespread and acute than it is in Britain or America. But many people judge the problem to be more acute in the Western world, because of the specific and vivid examples of people dying of AIDS in the UK and America. These concrete and vivid images come to mind when we are thinking about the problem – they are more 'available' than the statistical information. Psychologically speaking, sheer numbers do not mean much to us, but individual cases do, which in turn leads to bias in our thinking.

Scripts

Another factor in the judgements and decisions that we make has to do with the everyday scripts which we can apply. If we can envisage a plausible situation in which something might happen, drawing on our existing social knowledge and what we know of alternatives and possibilities, then we use that script to base our decisions on. If we cannot envisage a plausible script, then we judge a given option as being unlikely. So, for example, someone may decide on a career as a doctor because they can conjure up a plausible script of studying to pass school exams, going to medical school, and through training, and so on. But they might reject an ambition to become, say, a pilot, because they could not envisage themselves going through the appropriate training and procedures – for them, the script simply would not be plausible, and so that career option would be counted out. And, of course, the judgement becomes self-fulfilling – somebody who has discounted the career option of becoming a pilot does not take the necessary actions, so after a while the discounted option could not happen anyway.

There are other instances in which scripts can influence decisions. For example, Abelson (1976) gave an example of a decision about whether to admit a student to a postgraduate course, because this particular student reminded the members of the committee about a similar case several years ago. The previous case presented a plausible script to the committee members making the decision, and that script formed the basis for the decision which the committee made about the more recent case – even though the two might have turned out completely differently.

Illusory correlation

One of the most fundamental tendencies in human thinking is to look for causes, or reasons why things happen. In social psychology, a considerable amount of modern research is concerned with investigating **causal attributions** – the reasons we give for why events or behaviours happened. But we have a general tendency to develop explanations, which concerns physical as well as social experience. Part of that tendency is the way that we are very likely to see events as connected in some way. In decision-making, this can lead to the error known as **illusory correlation**, in which two totally separate things are regarded as influencing one another in some way.

Chapman and Chapman (1969) investigated illusory correlation in the ways that clinicians use **projective tests**. These are tests which assume that patients project their unconscious conflicts or

impulses into the test material. One of the tests that they studied was the 'draw-a-person' test, in which people are asked to make a drawing of a human being, on the assumption that this will reveal hidden aspects of the personality. Many studies have shown that there is no real correlation between the two, but Chapman and Chapman found that many clinicians firmly believed that personality problems would be revealed in features of these drawings – for instance, that paranoid people would tend to draw figures with large staring eyes.

Chapman and Chapman (1969) asked psychiatric patients to take the draw-a-person test, and then paired those drawings entirely at random with descriptions of symptoms. When they then asked research participants to examine the drawings and the associated symptoms, and state which were connected with which, they found that they would still report the correlations between symptoms and features of the drawing, even though there was no evidence for them on the basis of the information that they had been given. In other words, they reported a correlation which was not really there – an illusory correlation.

Tversky and Kahnemann (1973) explained this particular illusory correlation in terms of the availability of information. Suspicion is generally seen as being associated with the eyes, so eyes would come to mind if one was judging paranoia. An alternative explanation is to look at how social representations – the shared beliefs prevalent in society – may lead us to accept social beliefs and assumptions about the nature of human beings and reality, even though these may at times contradict our own personal experience. We will be looking at this more closely in Chapter 15.

Anchoring

Anchoring is another powerful heuristic which we use in making decisions. If we are trying to make a guess about how common something is, we will often seize on the first figure we are given, and use this as the basis for our estimate. Tversky and Kahnemann (1974) asked research participants a number of questions requiring estimates of quantities – for example what percentage of African countries there are in the United Nations. They spun a wheel to generate a random number between 0 and 100, and asked research participants to tell them whether the answer was higher or lower than the number shown on the wheel. Interestingly, all the research participants used the number which had come up to anchor their answers. If a low number had come up then research participants made a low estimate, but if a high number had come up they made a high estimate. Even when the researchers paid their research participants for making accurate guesses, the anchoring effect was just as strong.

Northcraft and Neale (1987) asked estate agents and business school students to make estimates about the value of a particular house. These estimates included an appropriate advertising price, a reasonable price to pay if you were buying it and the lowest acceptable offer. Some research participants were given a high listing price to start off with, while others were given a lower one. They found that, in all cases, the estimates were heavily dependent on the listing price which the research participants had been given. Those who were given a high listing price made higher estimates than those given the low listing price. Moreover, this effect applied even in the case of estate agents who were used to making independent judgements of this kind. The anchoring effect appears to be a very powerful heuristic indeed for human decision-making.

Entrapment

Entrapment happens when someone feels unable to get out of a situation because they have already invested so much in it. Imagine, for example, that you have an old car which needs some fairly costly repairs. You get those done, but then immediately something else goes wrong. Do you pay for the next set of repairs on the grounds that otherwise you would have wasted the money you have already laid out? Or do you decide to give up and get rid of the car? The process of entrapment implies that you can easily end up spending far more than the car is worth, simply because you are trying to ensure that the money you have already spent was not wasted.

Entrapment can occur in a variety of situations, ranging from continuing with an unsatisfying relationship simply because of the amount of time that you have already spent together, to deciding to go ahead and finish a boring book just because it has been so much effort to get that far with it. Entrapment can be a powerful factor in political decision-making too: Teger (1979) described how entrapment meant that it became very nearly

impossible for politicians to decide to stop the American war in Vietnam. So many lives had been lost and so much money had been invested, that pulling out was a very difficult decision politically, despite the fact that they were obviously losing.

Hindsight bias

Another factor which affects decision-making is **hindsight bias**. There is a saying that 'hindsight is always 20/20' – that is, when we are judging a decision which has already been made, it is very easy to regard the outcome as obvious or predictable. In reality, though, the outcome of a decision is rarely so obvious at the time. Slovic and Fischoff (1977) asked research participants to make judgements about the likely outcome of an experiment. The experiment had already taken place, and one group of participants were told the result. The others were not.

The research participants were then told that the study was to be replicated, and were asked to estimate how likely certain outcomes were. Those who already knew what had happened in the first study rated the probability of the same thing happening very much more highly than members of the other group. Because they knew what had happened, they had developed a hindsight bias, which made the outcome seem much more probable. In reality, though, the research participants who did not already know the outcome were making more realistic judgements. It is worth remembering this, the next time you see the outcome of a psychological study as being 'obvious' – it might easily be your hindsight bias in operation!

Decision frames

In 1984, Kahnemann and Tversky argued that there are two further factors which exert a very large influence on decision-making. These are: the way in which the question is asked, or framed, and the background context in which it is placed. Both of these factors establish a **decision frame**, within which the decision must be made, and this decision frame can influence what is actually decided.

Asking the same question in two different ways can produce two different responses. In one study, Tversky and Kahnemann (1981) asked research participants to choose between two courses of action to combat a serious disease, which was expected to kill 600 people. One group of research participants were told that option A would result in 200 people being saved, while option B would result in a one-third chance of saving everyone, and a two-thirds chance of saving nobody. The second group of research participants were actually given exactly the same choices, but phrased differently. Instead of the question saying 200 people would be saved, they said that 400 people would die. The second option was phrased as a one-third probability that nobody would die and a two-thirds probability that all 600 people would die.

When they were asked to make their choice, 72% of the research participants in the first group chose the first option, of saving 200 people. But only 22% of research participants in the second group made the same choice. The problem, as we have seen, was the same in both cases, but the way that the question was framed affected how the research participants perceived it.

We can see, then, that it is possible to identify a number of different factors in human decision-making which influence the judgements that people make. But it is important to remember that, although these appear as errors in the artificial situations produced by psychology experiments, for the most part problem-solving heuristics work reasonably well in everyday living.

Representation

So far, we have been looking at goal-directed thinking: problem-solving, reasoning, and decision-making. But the study of thinking also involves looking at mental representation – the way that we store and organise our knowledge. Richardson (1989) discussed how early ideas of representation tended to be rather simple notions of a mental 'idea' or 'image', encapsulating the information. But the more researchers explored how the mind works, the more they realised that representation systems are often a lot more sophisticated than that.

Richardson went on to describe a number of different forms of representation that cognitive psychologists have studied. One of these is the study of **coding**: how information is changed so that it can be stored appropriately in the brain. We looked at this in Chapter 3. In that chapter, we also looked at larger forms of knowledge represen-

tation, such as the various **models of memory**. But there are other types of representation, too. Some of them involve knowledge frames, such as **schemata** and **scripts**; while others are episodic knowledge structures, like plans or **cognitive maps**, which allow us to deal with novel situations.

As Richardson pointed out, psychological research into representation is not separate: it links with other cognitive processes too. As we saw in the last chapter, ideas about knowledge frames have directly contributed to our understanding of reading, and to conceptual understanding in linguistics. Research into cognitive maps has shown itself to be useful in the work of environmental psychologists and geographers. There are many forms of representation, and each of these has some relevance for some aspect of understanding the human being. In this section, we will look at four forms of mental representation: concepts-, logogens, cognitive maps, and schemata. But we will begin by looking at one theory of how representation first develops.

The development of representation

Bruner (1964) developed a theory about how our use of representation develops. He argued that our use of different representational modes arises from the need to store more complicated types of information about the environment as we get older. As we learn more about the world, we have to develop ways to represent our knowledge and these ways become increasingly sophisticated as the demands of the knowledge we are representing become more complex.

Enactive, iconic and symbolic representation

A young baby does not need to store much about the wider world, but it does remember things which affect it directly, so most of its memories will be stored in 'muscle memories' – which Bruner called **enactive representation**. Enactive representation involves remembering things by the 'feel' of how it was to do them; for example, you may represent a fairground ride to yourself in terms of how it felt to ride in it. That is an example of enactive representation.

As it gets a little older, the child learns about other, more distant things, which may not involve many different actions. Reading books, for instance, or watching television, or playing different computer games, can involve much the same movements yet include a very different set of information. So as its experience develops, the young child develops an additional mode of representation, storing information as sensory images. Bruner referred to this mode as **iconic representation**. Iconic representation generally involves the use of visual imagery to represent objects in memory – information is stored by 'mental pictures'. We looked at imagery and its use as a form of representation in Chapter 3.

As the toddler begins to learn language and number, it starts to learn about more complex concepts, which cannot be sensed directly, like ownership or 'fairness'. Because of this, it begins to use another form of representation, perhaps using words to symbolise possession, like 'my ball', or 'mummy's chair', or using numbers to indicate amounts. Bruner referred to this as **symbolic representation**. Once the child is able to use this method of storing information it can store more or less anything which human beings know about, because it can use symbols to represent those things which cannot be pictured easily. Also, using symbols means that information can be categorised and organised more readily.

Most older people use a mixture of modes for storing their memories, but many children have vivid sensory imagery which they can use to remember most things. Some children even have **eidetic imagery** – visual images which are stored almost like a photograph, so that the person can look back at the memory as if it were a real picture, and identify details which they had not noticed before. Haber (1969) showed children a detailed picture on an easel for a brief period of time, and then asked them questions about it. The children who had eidetic imagery were able to answer questions in considerable detail – but if they looked away from the blank easel or blinked rapidly, the image seemed to disappear. Also, they seemed to retain the image for only a couple of minutes; but that is still longer than most people could manage. Some 5% of children seem to have this ability, but it usually disappears with adolescence – perhaps as symbolic representation becomes more important with the person's developing social understanding – so very few adults have it.

Concepts

A concept is a general term that we use to group, or classify, objects, events, or ideas. Concepts typically have a set of defining features, like 'hedgehogs have prickles', 'hedgehogs eat slugs', 'hedgehogs move slowly', etc. and a general set of rules about how these features can be combined, like 'if it has prickles and eats slugs, but is moving quite quickly, it is probably still a hedgehog'. **Classical concepts** are concepts in which every example of the concept has all the crucial defining features, with no exceptions. In everyday experience, though, classical concepts are rare. Instead we use **probabilistic concepts**, which define the concept in terms of the features which it is likely to have (but might not). For instance, the concept of 'chair' might include such features as having four legs and a back to lean on, but not every chair has all these features.

Associationist models of concept-formation

Early research into how we form concepts was performed within an associationist, stimulus-response framework. The features of an object were seen as the stimulus, and its classification as an example of that concept as the response. Hull (1920) argued that concepts were formed through the process of **stimulus generalisation**: people learn to produce a response to one stimulus, and then that response generalised to other, similar stimuli, so forming the concept.

Hull performed a series of experiments in which research participants were shown sets of Chinese characters. These had recurrent elements, known as radicals, embedded in them as part of the design. Each of the radicals was given a name, and research participants were then shown the characters one at a time and asked which of the six names applied to that figure. Hull's research participants improved with each trial: typically they would get less than 30% correct on the first test but about 60% correct by the fifth test. But when they were asked, most of his research participants were completely unable to say why they had chosen a correct answer. Hull took this as evidence that unconscious stimulus-response learning was taking place.

Hypothesis-testing models of concept-formation

In 1956, Bruner, Goodnow and Austin argued that concepts develop from active **cognitive search** strategies, rather than simply by association. They used sets of cards, which could be varied by colour, shape, or the number of images on them, to explore how people went about forming concepts (see Figure 5.7).

The experimenters would decide, privately, on a rule, such as 'three red shapes'. Then the research participants would be allowed to choose any of the cards one at a time, and to ask whether the card was an instance of the concept or not. They would receive a straightforward 'yes' or 'no' answer. From this feedback, the participants would gradually work out what the concept was. Bruner *et al.* found that people use a variety of scanning or focusing techniques in working out their answers, which are described in Box 5.2.

Bower and Trabasso (1964) suggested that when people are faced with a concept-formation problem they develop a whole set of different hypotheses. They then select one or more of these hypotheses and try them out. If they get a correct answer, they stay with that idea. But if the answer is incorrect, then the hypothesis is returned to the pool, and the person chooses a different one.

This idea implies that people will solve concept-formation problems in an 'all-or-none' manner, since either their hypothesis will be correct, or it will not. So studies of people solving concepts in this way are likely to show a sudden change from inaccuracy to accuracy, as they hit on the right hypothesis. By contrast, stimulus-response explanations for concept-learning predict that there will be a gradual learning curve, as the research participant develops the associations. Because of these different predictions, it is possible to compare the two approaches.

Bower and Trabasso tested their model by drawing up backward learning curves. Instead of looking at people's responses from the first trial onwards, they went backwards from the last error that the person had made. They found that the probability of the last-but-one response being correct was always round about 50%. This supported the idea that we develop concepts through mental hypothesis-testing, since the gradual increase predicted by the associationist model predicted that in the last-but-one trial research participants should be getting far more than half the responses correct.

How concepts are structured

Broadly speaking, there are two main views concerning how concepts are structured. **Feature-list theories** see the different items in a concept as being linked together because they share the same features; whereas **prototype theories** see concepts as being formed round a central, 'ideal' example of the concept, with other examples varying from the ideal to a greater or lesser degree.

Early associationist ideas about concepts used the feature-list model implicitly, and so did much of the research on strategies of concept-formation. In one well-known study, Collins and Quillian (1972) timed how long it took people to identify a given item as belonging within a concept or not. They found that research participants took less time to process statements where the item had most of the relevant features for the concept (for example 'a robin is a bird') than they did to process items which had fewer relevant features (for example 'an ostrich is a bird'). Collins and Quillian went on from there to propose that concepts are stored hierarchically, going from general features to specific ones. The amount of time taken to access a concept, they argued, depended on the number of decision or identification 'nodes' that were involved. So the more feature of the concept the item contained, the fewer decisions were needed and the faster it could be identified.

Rosch (1973) argued strongly against the feature-list approach to concept-formation. Much of the evidence for it, she claimed, occurred

Figure 5.7 Some concept-formation cards

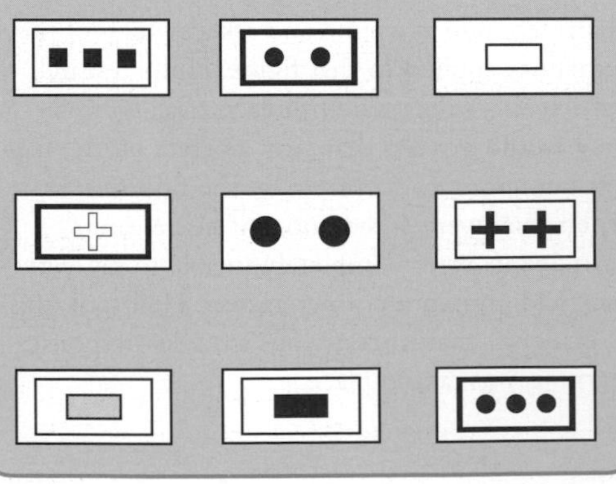

Bruner, Goodnow and Austin (1956) found that people adopt different approaches to concept formation problems. Some people use what Bruner called a **conservative focusing** strategy, taking all the possible attributes of a correct example, and then narrowing those attributes down until they reached the correct solution. So, for instance, if the first correct card showed three green triangles, their next choice would be a card which was only different in one attribute, such as two green triangles, or three green stars. By doing this systematically, they would gradually become able to home in on the correct answer.

Other people also used a focusing strategy, but in a slightly different way. They would make a second choice which differed in two features from the correct one. Bruner *et al.* called this **focus gambling**, because the person is taking a gamble that their choice will be correct: if it is incorrect they will not be able to tell which of the two features was the important one.

Some people would simply go through testing one hypothesis at a time. So if they were faced with one green circle, for instance, they might test out the idea that 'all green figures are positive'. If that did not work, they would go on to test another idea, such as 'all single figures are positive'. This is known as **scanning**, and although it does eventually lead to the correct answer, it can be very slow, as the person can try out only one idea at a time.

Some people used **simultaneous scanning**: keeping more than one idea in mind at a time, instead of trying each one singly. The important difference between scanning and focusing is that in scanning people start off with single features of the stimulus, whereas with focusing they start off with the whole figure and gradually narrow it down to the relevant features.

Bruner, Goodnow and Austin suggested that these different cognitive styles might represent preferred ways of approaching information, which could have implications for effective teaching and training.

mainly because researchers had used artificial concepts to study it. When natural concepts, occurring in real life, were studied, a different model emerged: the idea that concepts are represented by **prototypes**. In 1975, Rosch gave research participants a series of statements, which described items as belonging to a given concept ('a cable car is a vehicle', 'a peach is a fruit', etc.). The participants had to say, as quickly as possible, whether the statement was true or false. Rosch found that people took longer to judge items which were very different from the prototype than they did to judge ones which were similar. For example, it took more time to give the answer to 'a cable car is a vehicle' than it did to give the answer to 'a truck is a vehicle'.

The family resemblance idea also carries the implication that some features, though not all, will be shared by category members. The items in a concept which have most of the shared features will be the ones which are seen as 'typical' of that concept. They will also be most different from examples belonging to other concepts. So, for instance, a kitchen chair, which has many relevant features of the concept 'chair' and so would be

regarded as typical of it, is very different from a table. A stool, on the other hand, is less typical of the concept 'chair', since it does not have so many shared features, and it is not as different from a table. When we are judging whether something belongs to a particular concept or not, its closeness to the prototype is an important factor in our decision.

The idea that concepts involve matching items up to a central prototype was presented as being an alternative to feature-list theories of concept acquisition. However, Neumann (1974) argued that the feature-list approach was still viable, because of the way that items which contained a large number of the relevant features were judged as being the most typical ones. This means that it might perhaps be possible to combine the idea of the prototype with a feature-list approach. Bourne, Dominowsky and Loftus (1979) suggest that there may not really be much difference between them; but that each perspective is useful for different kinds of research.

Rosch's prototype model was also supported in an investigation of the Dani, a non-technological society in New Guinea. As we saw in the previous chapter, these people had only two words for colour, which simply expressed whether something was light or dark. But even though they did not have words for them, Dani people could distinguish and categorise many different colours. Rosch (1974) found that the categories which the Dani actually used corresponded quite closely to Western concepts of colour.

The cultural similarities in colour concepts, Rosch argued, were not accidental. They happened because the human nervous system automatically responded to a set of colour prototypes. So the same wavelength would be chosen as a perfect example of red – a 'quintessential red' – by most people, no matter what culture they came from. This wavelength represented the prototype for the colour red. Other wavelengths would then be classified as red on the basis of a 'family resemblance' to the prototype – they did not have to be identical, but they were more similar to the red prototype than they were to, say, a green colour. Deciding whether an item fitted into a concept was based on similarity, in much the same way as we recognise similarities between different members of the same family.

Natural categories

Rosch went on to argue that not all concepts are equally significant. Some are more general than others. She identified three levels of abstraction in concepts: the **superordinate** level, the **basic level** and the **subordinate** level. An example of a superordinate level concept might be 'animals'. This is a very general categorisation, containing a number of basic concepts. One example of a basic-level concept related to this would be 'cats'. This in turn could contain a number of subordinate concepts, such as 'Siamese cats'. Rosch argued that the main type of concept which we use in day to day living is the basic level.

Rosch et al. (1976) also found that basic-level concepts have most features associated with them. They asked people to list all the features which they associated with concepts on each of the three levels. The participants listed far more features for basic-level concepts than they did for either the superordinate or the subordinate concepts. This suggested that it is the basic level which gives us most information about a particular set of concepts. In a later part of the study, the research participants were asked to describe in detail the sequence of actions which they might use in

interacting with items at these three levels. They reported relatively few distinctive movements or actions associated with the superordinate or subordinate concepts, but several clearly distinctive ones when they were dealing with basic-level concepts.

Rosch et al. suggested that this observation provides the key to understanding concept-formation. Concepts, Rosch argued, are **natural categories**, formed around action. We group together things which we interact with in the same way. There are many specific kinds of chairs (subordinate level), and there are many different kinds of furniture (superordinate level). But the thing which distinguishes the basic-level concept of 'chair' from other items of furniture is what we do – we sit on it. We perform different actions with other items of furniture, so they belong to different basic-level concepts. And although we may sit on different chairs in different ways, we would not see something as a chair unless we could sit on it somehow.

Rosch's research, by emphasising actions and interactions as forming the basic level of concept, brings the idea of concepts very much closer to the idea of the schema. As we saw earlier in this chapter, the most important distinction between a concept and a schema has always been the way that the schema includes action and intentions as well as knowledge, and forms a basis for our interaction with the world. But Rosch's discovery that we also organise concepts around interactions suggests that perhaps the distinction between a concept and a schema is not as large as has previously been assumed.

One of the biggest problems of work on concepts and concept-formation, though, has been that it is almost exclusively laboratory research – it lacks **ecological validity**, in that it is not at all clear how the laboratory research actually relates to people's use of concepts in everyday life. Rosch's insistence on using natural concepts rather than artificial ones did make some improvement, but until researchers can look at the ordinary ways that people use concepts in everyday living we will not be able to see how relevant any of this research is. It is possible that people use entirely different criteria in the 'real world' than they do when they are undertaking an abstract, context-free laboratory task, whether it is based on a naturally occurring concept or not.

Word-recognition

A different aspect of the study of mental representations concerns how we store words. As we saw in Chapter 2, Triesman (1960) proposed that we have special word-recognition units as part of the cognitive system, which she referred to as **dictionary units**. These, she proposed, were units which were triggered off by a stimulus which reminded the person of the word, or if it was heard or read. Triesman used this concept to explain the finding that people could easily ignore a great deal of irrelevant verbal information, but that their attention would often be caught by the sound of a word which had special significance for them, like their own name.

Morton (1979) proposed that words are stored in special word-recognition units, much like Triesman's 'dictionary units', and quite similar to the facial-recognition units which have been proposed by researchers into face-recognition (see Chapter 2). Morton referred to these units as **logogens**, and suggested that there are discrete logogens for each word, which can be easily triggered off by associations or connected ideas. Each time a logogen is triggered, it makes the word more likely to come to mind next time. The process of learning to read, Morton argued, is one in which we develop a wider repertoire of logogens, which are triggered off when an individual looks at a familiar word. In this theory, logogens form the basic 'building blocks' of verbal thought, and so can be seen as one of the main units of mental representation.

Winnick and Daniel (1970) found that they could 'prime' research participants to recognise words more quickly if they had presented them with that same word sometime previously. It was important, though, that the participants should actually see the word in written form: if they were shown pictures and asked to speak the word for themselves, it did not help word-recognition later. Morton (1979) investigated this further, and found that the type of writing does not matter. The test words were always typed, but research participants were 'primed' just as easily if they saw the word in handwritten form beforehand as if they saw it in an identical typed form. Obviously, then, word-recognition was not just a matter of matching up an identical stimulus.

Morton argued that this implied that visual and auditory word-recognition mechanisms involve entirely separate cognitive systems. There is a visual lexicon of words that we recognise when we see them, and an auditory lexicon of words which we recognise when we hear them. But, as we have seen, the empirical evidence shows that there are differences between hearing or speaking the word, and seeing it written, so Morton suggested that the two lexicons involve different storage systems.

An idea like this might also explain how it is that human beings learn to understand spoken language from a very early age, and yet have to be taught how to read, which is a task which involves a certain amount of concentrated effort in the learning. If the visual lexicon and the auditory lexicon were the same, then it should be easy to transfer information from our highly sophisticated auditory lexicon to the reading task. But observations of children learning to read suggest that they do not do this. In the last chapter, we found that some researchers have suggested that teaching a child to say words out loud may actually interfere with the process of learning to read, by adding an additional task, and this also implies that the cognitive structures for written word-recognition are different from those by which we recognise spoken words.

The Stroop effect

Stroop, in 1935, noticed that a particularly interesting effect occurs with the naming of colour. This seems to be something to do with the cognitive conflicts produced when visual and semantic information contradict one another. In a task which has come to be known as the **Stroop task**, people were asked to read colour names aloud as soon as they saw them, or to name a patch of colour which was shown to them. Stroop found that research participants could name the patches of colour more quickly than they read the words, which suggested that colour identification is a faster and possibly more 'direct' cognitive process than colour naming – an observation that might fit with Gibson's theory of direct perception (see Chapter 2).

Following on from this work, Scheibe, Shaver and Carrier (1967) found that if the word to be identified was written in the same colour as its meaning (for example 'orange' written in orange-coloured ink), it would be identified more quickly than the same word written in a different colour (for example 'orange' written in green ink). The more closely linked the stimulus word and the colour of the stimulus, the more interference there was. So a word like 'cherry', which is already associated with the colour red, would produce more interference than the word 'window', although not as much as the word 'red' itself.

There have been a number of different investigations of the Stroop effect. Pritchatt (1968) showed that the amount of interference from a word could be reduced, although not completely eliminated, if people were asked to press coloured keys instead of actually naming the words concerned. It was suggested that the small amount of interference that was left might have come from the research participants naming the colours covertly, to themselves, instead of responding to the immediate colour stimulus of the key.

Preston and Lambert (1969) compared colour naming in both languages of bilingual research participants, and found that it was slowest – that is, there was most interference – when the colour names were similar in the two languages (for example brown – braun). They suggested that this might be because people were more likely to translate the words automatically in that situation. But Dyer (1973) proposed that it might happen just because the words sound similar, and so trigger each other off: there might be no translation at all. In order to test this out, Dyer tested English monolingual research participants on the same task, and found that similar-sounding words did produce interference even if the person did not speak the language.

In a further study with Spanish/English bilingual research participants, Dyer (1973) found results similar to those of Preston and Lambert, except that the amount of interference depended on whether or not the research participants were responding in the same language as the stimulus word. If they were responding in a different language, there was less interference. This again suggested that translation might not be as important a factor as Preston and Lambert had suggested.

A major debate about the Stroop effect concerns when the interference takes place – in other words, whereabouts in the cognitive system it is located. Some researchers argued that it occurs at the beginning of cognitive processing, when the person is first receiving the information. Murray, Mastronardi and Duncan (1972) asked people to name the colours in which words were printed, and found that they took longer to do this if the words that they were looking at were colour names, than they did if they were animal names. But when the same people were asked to sort cards according to whether the words and the colour of the printing were the same or different, they sorted colours faster than they sorted words. The researchers suggested that two distinct cognitive mechanisms were involved in the Stroop effect. Naming, they argued, was a different process from simply recognising the physical features of a stimulus.

Other researchers have argued that the interference comes later on, at the time that the person is actually producing their response. Egeth, Blecker and Kamlet (1969) asked research participants to decide whether or not items in a pair of stimuli were the same colour. The stimuli that they received were the same as in a conventional Stroop task, but they were not actually asked to name the colours. The researchers found that there was none of the usual interference on this task – although when their research participants were asked to identify words spelt 'SAME' or 'DIFF', there was considerable interference. Egeth *et al.* suggested that the effect might occur because there is a conflict between the semantic processing of the word and the participants' personal expectations of what their responses should be.

Cognitive maps

The idea of the cognitive map was first raised by Tolman, in 1948, following work on latent learning in which he showed that rats would perform significantly better in running a complex maze if they had been allowed to explore it beforehand. Tolman argued that this showed that the rats had developed an internal representation of the maze, which they could draw on when such knowledge became useful to them.

Tolman considered that much of human internal representation could be analysed in terms of the formation of **cognitive maps**. A cognitive map is a mental image which allows us to collect, store, organise and utilise information about the environment. We use cognitive maps every time we think in terms of the spatial organisation of objects or people. You may be using one when you consider the way home, or going around the supermarket, or when you think about which drawer contains your clean jumpers.

A number of researchers have looked at the

kinds of cognitive maps which people use. Lynch (1960) interviewed residents in three American towns about the cognitive maps which they held of their cities. The residents were asked to describe a journey from one part of town to another. From analysing the accounts which they gave, Lynch found that people tend to pay special attention to distinctive features, like open spaces, greenery and visual contrasts. Most people also had blank areas of their towns, which they were unable to describe. You might find it interesting to try drawing a cognitive map of your own town and comparing it with that drawn by a friend, to see whether you have the same areas as blanks.

Saarinen (1973) asked college students to draw maps of their university campuses, and found that there was a strong tendency for the students to enlarge those areas of the campus which contained buildings most important to them, and to expand the size and detail of the buildings themselves. Conversely, areas which were not known tended to shrink in size. By and large, the students' maps tended to be accurate for the areas which they used, but they were often wildly inaccurate for those areas with which they were unfamiliar.

Briggs (1971) found that familiarity is also a powerful influence on the judging of distance on a cognitive map. We tend to underestimate familiar distances, and to overestimate unfamiliar ones. In many cases, the underestimation caused by familiarity can mean that a cognitive map becomes distinctly inaccurate or disproportionate. In general, though, our main tendency is to overestimate distance: Canter and Tagg (1975) found that between neutral landmarks (that is, ones which are known but not necessarily very familiar) systematic overestimation was found.

Kozlowski and Bryant (1977) found that the accuracy of cognitive maps seems to link quite strongly with personal estimates about how good someone's sense of direction is. People who believed that they had a good sense of direction had more accurate cognitive maps than those who did not think they had a sense of direction that they could trust. Their estimate of their own sense of direction, however, did not correlate with how accurately they could point towards an out-of-sight building or road. They did, though, learn from their experience more efficiently than those people who judged themselves to have a poor sense of direction.

The method of loci

There is a very famous mnemonic known as the **method of loci** (the method of places); and this too involves cognitive mapping. It was first described by Simonides, an Ancient Greek, who had used it when he was trying to remember the guests who had been at a banquet when he was orating there. Simonides had been called outside after his oration, and so had escaped being crushed when the banqueting hall collapsed. The bodies of the other guests were unrecognisable after the accident, but Simonides found that he could remember who had been present by 'mentally' going round the table and recalling who had been sitting in each place. The location of each item in his mental image allowed him to retrieve the memory efficiently.

The use of the method of loci in more everyday circumstances involves mentally taking a familiar walk or journey with which the person is familiar, and forming a set of visual images which locate the items to be remembered at different points along that walk. (Some people revising for exams have found it useful to combine this with the 'key-word' method which we looked at earlier in this chapter, in forming the images.) Then, when the list is to be remembered, the person mentally visualises the stages of the walk or journey, and the images which come to mind at different stages form a reminder for the information which needs to be recalled. Neisser (1976) argued that the effectiveness of this method of training memory shows how very deeply cognitive maps are embedded in our cognitive systems.

Schemata, frames and scripts

A **schema** is a form of representation which we use to guide our actions. Rumelhart and Norman (1983) described schemata as varying considerably in the amount of information they contain – some are quite simple while others are extremely complex. You might, for instance, have a specific schema which is only to do with using radios; but you might also have more general schemata, about using any type of electrical equipment. They would be organised hierarchically, and the first schema would be likely to contain less information than the second (assuming that you were not a radio enthusiast, of course!)

One of the first people to use schemata in psychological explanation was Bartlett, in 1932. He described a schema as 'an active organisation of past reactions, or of past experiences, which must always be supposed to be operating in any well-adapted organismic response'. Bartlett's work on memory, which we looked at in Chapter 3, showed how people actively make sense of their memories, often at the expense of literal accuracy. Bartlett believed that these inaccuracies occurred because of the way that we use schemata to represent knowledge, and try to fit incoming information into them.

Assimilation and accommodation

The term 'schema' is also associated with the developmental theorist Jean Piaget. We will be looking at Piaget's work in more detail in Chapter 19; but his theory centred on the idea that cognitive development takes place through the formation and development of schemata. Schemata, Piaget argued, are formed by two important and fundamental processes: **assimilation**, in which new information is absorbed into the schema without particularly changing it, so that the schema's range simply extends itself a bit; and **accommodation**, in which the schema itself has to be developed and extended because it is not adequate to cope with the new information if it does not.

In its extreme form, accommodation can mean that the schema divides into two or more new schemata. For example: in Britain, a small child is likely to use the same schema for a bowl and a plate – something like 'things you eat out of '. But as it grows up, and comes to understand its world in a more sophisticated way, the general schema becomes divided into two, which have different functions: bowls are seen as appropriate for some foods, whereas plates are seen as appropriate for others.

The 'bowl' and 'plate' schemata would not just develop as a result of their social uses. They also have different physical actions associated with them. An important distinction between a schema and a concept is that the schema, like the cognitive map, is essentially about action – schemata act as a guide for planning and doing things. Concepts, on the other hand, are essentially to do with classifying objects and phenomena into groups or types (although, as we shall see, some recent work on concept-formation does suggest that action is important too). For Piaget, it is action that produces thinking: the child performs

operations – actions with consequences – on its environment, and so obtains the information which is assimilated or accommodated into the schema.

So the schema is simultaneously how the child uses its experience to guide its behaviour, and how it makes sense of the outcome when it has performed the behaviour. A schema includes the memories and the abstract associations that might be involved in a concept; but it is much richer than that. It is an internal representation system which includes sensory associations, skills and plans as well as actions and knowledge.

Anticipatory schemata

Neisser (1976) argued that the concept of the schema provides a means whereby the active aspects of cognition, and especially perception, can be meaningfully integrated. As we saw in Chapter 2, Neisser sees perception as being essentially a cyclic process, in which anticipatory schemata direct how we will explore our environment. For Neisser, life is not lived in a vacuum, and what happens to us is rarely completely unexpected. In day to day living, we are continually making unconscious predictions about what is likely to happen next, even if these are relatively trivial. As I type this, for instance, I am predicting that the keyboard will remain under my fingers: if it were to disappear I would be very surprised indeed! In that way, as I type I use an anticipatory schema which guides my actions.

Our actions, in turn, sample our environment. We are not in direct contact with everything around us; but we sample it through what we do. As I type, my fingers sample the keyboard part of my environment. These samples then modify the anticipatory schema, if it proves necessary. If I reach for the keyboard and hit an entirely different key from the one I was aiming for, then I revise my anticipatory schema. I might, for instance, conclude that the keyboard is slipping, and that I need to adjust my actions accordingly. With any action – even one as routine as typing – there is a continuous cycle going on, whereby what I anticipate (my schema) directs what I do (my actions), which sample what is around me (my environment) and feeds the information back to my schema again, modifying it if necessary.

For Neisser, it is how we use schemata in our interactions with the world that is the key to understanding cognition. We are active in our worlds, not passive; but we are also active in making sense of what is around us, and to do that we need internal representations to guide us. Gibson's theory of direct perception (see Chapter 2) showed that location and action are important factors in how we process perceptual information; and research into cognitive maps and absent-mindedness (see Chapter 3) shows that they are often quite important in memory too. The schema seems to represent a mechanism which allows us to come to terms with the importance of location and action in cognitive processing generally.

Defining schemata

One of the problems of schema theory has been that it is very difficult to define exactly what a schema is. Rumelhart (1980) identified four analogies of schema theory, which are listed in Table 5.6. Each of these analogies contains a slightly different model of the schema; and Rumelhart argued that all of them are relevant to understanding how the schema can make a contribution to our understanding of human cognition.

Some models portray schemata as very limited: Alba and Hasher (1987) argued that memory representation is much richer than schema theory would suggest; but they were adopting a rather limited model of the schema, which said that schemata first encoded only relevant information (nothing else), then extracted only relevant meaning – so that none of the original form of the information would be retained. When Alba and Hasher identified aspects of memory which were richer than that, and also included irrelevant details and sensory impressions, they concluded that schemata were not adequate to explain how representation works. But their approach used a far more limited definition of schema than Neisser's, or than that of many other theorists.

Frames and scripts

There are some other concepts that are very closely related to the idea of the schema – and indeed, are sometimes regarded as special types of schema. One of them is the idea of the **knowledge frame**, put forward by Minsky in 1975. Minsky proposed that a frame is a type of schema which contains information about familiar events – or at least, about their structures. So it provides a general description of the type of knowledge that is involved in familiar situations, and can be used accordingly. Minsky's idea of a frame focuses on stereotyped sequences of events as well as stereotyped events; so it would be possible to have a frame about, say, a typical day, as well as a frame about a particular type of event, like going to the cinema.

In 1977, Schank and Abelson put forward the idea of a **social script**, which is a similar kind of knowledge structure, that would again be applied to stereotypical or stereotyped events. They

Table 5.6 Analogies for schemata	
1 *Schemata as plays*	Schemata contain information about settings in which they would be appropriate; characters or roles that they concern themselves with; and scripts which prescribe how they would normally translate themselves into action.
2 *Schemata as theories*	By producing a meaningful construction of an event, object or situation, schemata allow us to form theories about the world, which we then test out by our actions.
3 *Schemata as computational procedures*	Schemata are active, information-processing structures, which form computational devices for assessing information, coding it and performing any necessary transformations on it.
4 *Schemata as parsers*	We can use schemata to decipher the components and elements of what is happening around us; similar to the process of deciphering a sentence by breaking it down into its grammatical and meaningful components.

Source: Rumelhart, 1980

suggested that scripts could be thought of as falling into three types: (1) **situational scripts**, involving typical social situations such as going to a restaurant; (2) **personal scripts**, like those involved in being a doctor, or a friend; and (3) **instrumental scripts**, which are concerned with stereotyped sequences of actions directed towards particular goals, like travelling home from work.

Scripts, according to Schank and Abelson, are built up through our experience, and applied in the relevant situations as seems appropriate. So they provide useful devices for integrating know-ledge into meaningful cognitive structures, which we can use in everyday living. Moreover, scripts tend to be triggered off quite automatically by appropriate stimuli. For the most part, we follow scripts unconsciously – in fact, we often only become aware of them when something happens which is outside the script. A waiter who brought

you coffee between the first and second courses would be breaking the script, and thus would be very noticeable. But if everything in a restaurant visit followed the conventional sequencing, we would not be likely to notice it at all. The habitual nature of scripts can sometimes present a problem, if we are trying to take a new angle on things.

In this chapter, we have looked at several different types of research into the ways that people think. But what we have covered is very far from being the whole story, or even a full account of the range of psychological research that already exists. It covers some of the main areas, but there is much more. In the next chapter, we will go on to look at some of the research which has been done into intelligence – and also at some of the fierce debates and discussions which the concept of intelligence has provoked.

Key terms

accommodation The process by which a schema adjusts to new information by extending or changing its form, or even by subdividing into two or more.

algorithm A problem-solving operation which, if repeated often enough, will eventually lead to a solution.

anchoring A feature of human problem-solving in which people use one item of information as a comparison for further judgements.

artificial intelligence (AI) Computer systems which are able to 'learn' and to produce the same kinds of outcomes as are produced by human thinking.

assimilation The process of incorporating new information without changing the original character of that which is doing the assimilating. For example, incorporating new information into a schema without changing that schema; or incorporating new cultural groups or ideas into a society without that society changing its character at all.

basic level concept In Rosch's categorisation, concepts which relate directly to action, and seem to link with natural categories.

causal attributions The reasons which people give for why things happen.

classical concepts Concepts in which each example of the concept possesses all of the distinguising features.

coding Converting information into a form in which it can be represented in the brain.

cognitive maps Mental images about where things are. People develop cognitive maps as they get to know a town or an institution; rats develop one as they explore experiential mazes.

cognitive science A multidisciplinary approach to studying artificial intelligence and similar phenomena, bringing together psychologists, linguists, information scientists and others.

computer metaphor The idea that the human brain works like a computer in the way that it processes information.

computer simulation The attempt to develop computer programmes which will replicate human processes such as skill learning or problem-solving.

convergent thinking Thinking which is directed towards getting a single 'right' answer to a problem, concentrating on strict logic, and ruling out creative or intuitive thinking.

decision frames The set of assumptions within which a particular decision is made.

divergent thinking Thinking which is intuitive or creative, often involving non-logical 'leaps' or sudden ideas.

ecological validity A way of assessing how valid a measure or test is (i.e. whether it really measures what it is supposed to measure) which is concerned with whether the measure or test is really like its counter-part in the real, everyday world. In other words, whether it is truly realistic or not.

eidetic memory 'Photographic' memory – visual or acoustic memory which is so accurate as to be almost like a factual record.

Einstellung A form of mental set in which the person becomes unable to solve problems because they are trying to do so within self-imposed constraints.

enactive representation Representing information in the mind by means of impressions of actions – 'muscle memories'.

entrapment The way that people, committees, etc. can become unable to withdraw from unwinnable situations because they feel that they have already invested too much in them to give up.

feature list theories Theories of concept formation which assume that an item is judged to belong in a category if it possesses the key features of that category.

functional fixedness The state of being unable to think of any other use for an object except the one that it is normally used for.

General Problem Solver An early computer simulation programme which used means-end analysis to solve simple problems.

groupthink The way that a committee, members of a club, or other group of people may become divorced from reality as a result of their own social consensus. Groupthink means that they may make decisions which are dangerous or stupid because the group fails to question their own assumptions or to take into account unwelcome aspects of reality which may have a bearing on the situation.

heuristics Strategies for solving problems which involve taking the step which looks most likely to lead towards a solution, even if this is uncertain.

hindsight bias The tendency to perceive a solution as obvious in retrospect, while it was nothing of the sort at the time.

iconic representation Coding information in the mind by means of sensory images, usually, though not always, visual ones.

illusory correlation The impression that two events or facts are related because they occur together, even though there may really be no connection between them.

interactive programmes Computer programmes which are designed to vary their responses depending on the input which they receive from the people using them.

knowledge frame The context and criteria of relevance within which a given problem is set.

lateral thinking An approach to problem-solving which deliberately steps outside conventional assumptions and frameworks in seeking solutions.

learning curve A distinctive graph pattern produced when mapping the time taken to learn a new behaviour.

learning sets A preparedness to undertake certain familiar types of learning.

logogen A hypothetical 'word-recognition unit' used in cognitive models of how verbal information is processed by the brain.

means-end analysis Solving problems by identifying strategies which look likely to bring the solver closer to the ultimate goal.

natural categories Concepts which seem to occur automatically, through inherited influences, as a fundamental part of the animal or human's adaptation to their world.

parallel distributed processing (PDP) A form of computer simulation in which several different logic pathways are at work simultaneously, with interconnections between them.

probabilistic concepts Concepts in which each item is likely to possess the important attributes, but may not necessarily (e.g. that birds can fly).

problem distance The term used in means-end analysis to describe the difference between the immediate situation and the desired goal, or end-state.

projective tests Psychometric tests which involve providing the person with ambiguous stimuli, and seeing what meanings they read into them. The idea is that this will illustrate the concerns of the unconscious mind.

protocol analysis The method of study which consists of analysing the steps or protocols involved in solving a problem. This might also include, for example, recording what people say they are doing as they undertake a creative process.

stimulus generalisation The phenomenon whereby an animal which has learned to respond to a particular stimulus will tend to extend its response to similar stimuli.

symbolic representation The coding of information in the brain by means of symbols as opposed to sensory images.

Summary

1 There are many different types of thinking, but most psychological research has focused on goal-directed thinking, such as problem-solving, reasoning, and decision-making.

2 Investigations of problem-solving identified a number of mechanisms which can limit cognitive flexibility, including learning sets, Einstellung, functional fixedness and groupthink. Divergent thinking, lateral thinking and brainstorming have been seen as ways of increasing creativity in thinking.

3 Studies of creativity have shown that people can have different cognitive styles, and also that high-level creativity often rests on a baseline of expertise, acquired through experience.

4 Research using computers has included computer simulations of human problem-solving, using production systems and more recently connectionist approaches; and also artificial intelligence, which includes the development of interactive programs, expert systems, and robotics.

5 Studies of human reasoning show that people apply social knowledge to problems, and may therefore appear to be making 'errors'. Studies of expertise show how there are qualitative differences between experts and novices.

6 Studies of decision-making have shown that judgements of representativeness, availability, anchoring and entrapment are heuristics which exert a powerful influence on the decisions which people make, as do the decision frames within which the problem is set.

7 Research into concept-formation includes associationist, hypothesis-testing and prototype models. Rosch showed how action and concepts were closely linked.

8 Other forms of representation include the study of concepts, word-recognition units, cognitive maps, and schemata, frames and scripts.

Self-assessment questions

1 Outline Rosch's theory of concept-formation.

2 What are the main factors which inhibit human problem-solving?

3 Describe an artificial intelligence expert system.

Practice essay questions

1 How are social and personal factors involved in knowledge representation?

2 'Human beings approach problem-solving in an illogical yet rational way'. Discuss.

3 Can computers simulate human thinking?

Test your knowledge of this chapter with our online quizzes and games at: http://www.psych.co.uk

Explore thinking and representation further at:

Problem solving
http://www.mindtools.com/page2.html – Links to explanations of methods of problem solving.

Decision making
http://penta.ufrgs.br/edu/telelab/2/lec10.htm – Models of processes of decision making.

Artificial intelligence
http://http.cs.berkeley.edu/~russell/ai.html#intro – Comprehensive site with links and resources on the subject of AI.

Individuality and abnormality

Intelligence

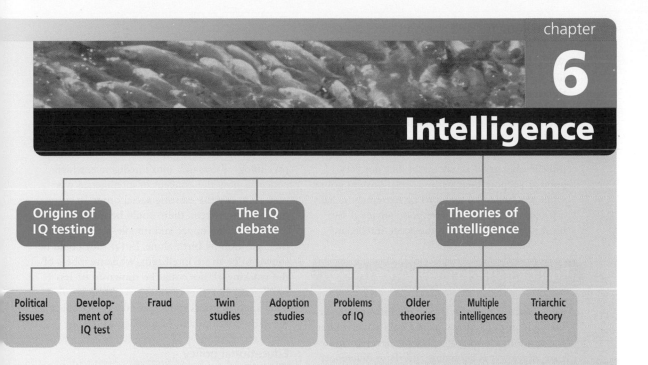

Origins of IQ testing
- Political issues
- Development of IQ test

The IQ debate
- Fraud
- Twin studies
- Adoption studies
- Problems of IQ

Theories of intelligence
- Older theories
- Multiple intelligences
- Triarchic theory

Learning objectives

6.1. The political context
a identify social and political influences on IQ research
b describe social and educational outcomes of IQ research
c evaluate the concept of eugenics

6.2. Political issues and Binet
a describe Binet's purpose in developing the IQ test
b calculate IQ using Binet's formula
c list Binet's three principles of intelligence testing

6.3. The early group IQ tests
a describe characteristics of the normal distribution
b evaluate the early IQ tests
c identify eugenic consequences of early IQ research

6.4. The concept of g
a define terms relating to the idea of general intelligence
b describe Spearman's model of intelligence
c evaluate the factor analytic approach to measuring intelligence

6.5. Nature-nurture studies
a evaluate Burt's evidence for the idea of heritability in intelligence
b outline the major twin studies of intelligence
c describe an adoption study of intelligence

6.6. Validity and bias in IQ testing
a define reliability, validity and standardisation in IQ testing
b distinguish between within-group and between-group variance
c identify sources of cultural bias in IQ testing

6.7. Multiple intelligences
a describe major theories of multiple intelligence
b list Gardner's seven types of intelligence
c evaluate evidence for Gardner's theory of intelligence

6.8. The triarchic theory of intelligence
a define terms relating to triarchic intelligence
b distinguish between subtheories of triarchic intelligence
c describe the features of componential intelligence

What do we mean by intelligence? In everyday life, we can mean a number of things: I might think of a speech given by a public figure as an intelligent speech, and mean something quite different from respecting the intelligence someone used while dealing with an emergency. Alternatively, you might know someone who is unbelievably good at, say, maths, but not very good at keeping their personal relationships going, while someone else seems to be extremely socially capable, and can always give good advice if you need it. Which of them is the more intelligent?

Political issues in intelligence theory

Intelligence is probably the single most controversial topic in psychology. People hold widely different opinions on what it is, how it develops and how relevant it is for living; and these differences have sometimes developed into highly acrimonious debates. One of the main reasons for this is that intelligence is not just an academic issue. There are deeply political implications in the question of whether intelligence depends on learning and experience, or whether it is fixed because it is inherited; and it is these underlying political implications which have kept the debate as active and as intense as it is today. The political implications of intelligence theory centre on three issues: social stratification, education, and eugenics.

Social stratification
The idea of intelligence as a 'thing' which some people had more or less of, only really emerged towards the end of the nineteenth century. Prior to that, while it was recognised that some people were more intellectual than others, or that some were gifted at invention or oratory, intelligence was seen more as a quality which imbued people's actions, not as an independent entity. It was an adjective or adverb, rather than a noun: you could act intelligently or perform an intelligent act; but there was little idea of 'intelligence' as something that you had. The process of converting a quality into a 'thing' as if it has an independent existence is known as **reification**, and the reification of the concept of intelligence occurred in tandem with the changes in the social order.

Towards the end of the nineteenth century, the Western world was moving towards a meritocratic system, in which it was believed that high-status positions should be occupied by those who were highly capable, regardless of their origins, and away from a belief that one's position in society should depend on family or inherited wealth. It was at this time and in this context that the concept of intelligence first emerged. And this raises one of the first political issues concerning psychological research into intelligence, which concerns how the concept of intelligence was used to justify the existing social order. In a meritocratic system, there could be no justification for those in the upper and middle-classes holding their position by birth alone. But if they could be shown to be more intelligent, while members of the working-classes could be shown to be less intelligent, then their position could be justified. This socio-political issue exerted a direct effect on the early development of intelligence testing.

Educational policy
The educational question is closely linked with the issue of social stratification, although it is not the same. The schooling and educational practices available within a society have dramatic effects on people's lives. In a technological society, in which social advancement is based on education, debates and assertions about who is or who is not intelligent are crucially important in determining the type of education which is offered to people within that society. These debates and assertions therefore also have implications for social programmes and social spending. Theories of intelligence have been directly influential in the development of school systems and of educational practices – and their influence remains in Britain today.

Eugenics
The final political issue in intelligence testing produced even more extreme political and social outcomes. This centres on the question of **eugenics**. Eugenics was both a theory and a political movement initiated by Francis Galton (1884). In his book *Hereditary Genius*, Galton argued from studies of the families of eminent Victorians that since intelligence clearly ran in families, it was therefore inherited. He went on to observe with alarm that the 'lower classes' in society were breeding prolifically, and argued that this would result in a lowering of the overall intelligence of the nation, or of the race, contaminating society with an excessively large number of wasters,

drunks and degenerates. Consequently, the eugenic argument – which called itself scientific – was that those who were genetically inferior should be prevented from breeding in order to keep society racially 'pure' and to prevent it from becoming 'mongrelised'.

Galton's ideas were so widely accepted, and became so ingrained into society, that laws which enforced compulsory sterilisation of those with low IQs were passed by several American states. Moreover, as Gould (1997) reported, these laws continued to be implemented – at least in the state of Virginia – right up until 1972. The eugenics movement was – and to some extent still is, although less overtly – influential in shaping immigration policies in both Britain and America, and has re-emerged in the concept of 'ethnic cleansing' in recent years.

Eugenic principles of weeding out 'undesirables' to encourage genetic 'progress' underlay the massive extermination programme of Jews and gypsies conducted by the Third Reich. This was linked with a spurious form of evolutionary theory, popular for some time, which held that human races had 'evolved' in a sequential order, with each later stage being more advanced than the last: so blacks were considered to be the most primitive, and the Aryan race the most advanced, with the others falling somewhere in between. For the Nazis, 'miscegenation', or racial mixing, was a serious crime, because, following Galton's eugenic principles, they saw it as weakening the genetic stock of the human being and hindering the evolution of the 'superman.' They were particularly hostile to Jewish people, and to gypsies, because they saw them as being genetically inferior, but close enough to Aryan stock to make 'miscegenation' a serious problem.

The political impact of psychological theorising about intelligence, therefore, has been extreme. To ignore these issues would be naïve, since they have been present in the views and attitudes of psychologists working in this field from the very beginning, and have directly shaped how psychological research in this area has proceeded. In this chapter, we will look first at the development of intelligence testing, and at some of the ways that political issues and psychological evidence have been linked. Later, we will look at some of the theories of intelligence which have been put forward, and at how modern researchers into intelligence are conceptualising the subject.

The development of intelligence testing

Intelligence tests fall into two groups. The first type to be developed were tests based on **age-correlation**: the idea that people can be expected to know different things and to have different skills at different ages. This type of test examines whether the individual matches up to the standards expected of somebody of their age, and calculates their intelligence accordingly. The second type of intelligence test emerged later, and these were tests based on the statistical principle of **factor analysis**. In factor analytic tests, common factors which seem to underlie the results to different questions in an intelligence test are identified statistically.

Age-correlation tests

The very first intelligence test was developed by Alfred Binet, in France in 1905 (Binet and Simon, 1905). The French education department had established special schools for the 'feeble-minded' or subnormal, and Binet was commissioned to develop an objective test which could identify such children.

Binet reasoned that intelligence in children was a developmental process, and so might reasonably be identified in terms of what could be expected of a child at a given age. For example, you would not expect a two-year-old to be able to recite the days of the week, but it would be reasonable to expect an eight-year-old to be able to do it. Together with his colleague, Theodore Simon, Binet collected a series of such developmental tasks and, by sampling large numbers of children, they were able to develop a test which matched these tasks to different ages. They also devised a technique for expressing how a child matched up to its peers in a single numerical figure (Binet and Simon, 1911). This became known as the **intelligence quotient**, or **IQ**, and was calculated by comparing the child's mental age (as assessed by the developmental tasks) with its real, or chronological age, according to the formula:

$$IQ = \frac{\text{mental age}}{\text{chronological age}} \times 100$$

As you can see from the formula, if a child's mental age is exactly the same as its chronological age, then its IQ will come out as exactly 100; a child with a mental age lower than would be expected for its chronological age will come out with an IQ of less than 100, and one which is mentally 'advanced' for its age will come out with an IQ over 100.

Unlike subsequent researchers, Binet did not regard IQ scores as fixed in any way. Instead, he viewed them as a simple snapshot of how the child was at that moment in time. Binet went on to argue that the value of assessing IQ in this way was that it showed where educational efforts should be directed – the child who scored below 100 should be put through a course of 'mental orthopaedics', designed to help it to catch up with others of its age. In response to the idea that intelligence might be a fixed quantity, and unchangeable, he argued: '*We must protest and react against this brutal pessimism*' (Binet, 1913: 140–1). This was very different from the views held by those who developed subsequent intelligence tests.

Binet's principles of intelligence testing

Binet insisted on three basic principles for using his tests. The first was that the scores which he had devised should be regarded purely as a practical device, and should not be taken as indicating anything innate or permanent. He insisted that they should not be taken as indicating intelligence, or as supporting any theory of what the intellect is. His second principle was that the scale was simply a rough guide for identifying children who were mildly retarded or learning-disabled, and who needed special help. He was insistent that it should not be used for ranking normal children. And the third principle was that the scores were not a label – they should be used to identify where special help could produce improvement, not to label children as being innately limited.

Ironically, most modern psychologists and others who use IQ tests have come back to an acceptance of these principles of Binet's – although often without realising that they were present from the very earliest days. Nowadays, most psychologists regard an IQ score as a useful indicator of someone's present condition, but not as a fixed limit. For the most part, intelligence tests are used by psychologists in a diagnostic capacity, to indicate where help might be needed. But during the decades which intervened between Binet's publications and the present, IQ tests were

used very differently, and in ways which were diametrically opposed to Binet's intentions.

From intelligence testing to IQ testing

Binet's test was translated, and imported to the United States and to Britain. Immediately, it came to be regarded, and used, as something very different from the diagnostic indicator which Binet had intended. Psychologists in both countries asserted that the IQ score represented a fixed, unchanging quality, and that this was established purely by genetic inheritance. Furthermore, these psychologists went on to argue that it was possible to rank-order individuals according to their IQ score, and that the large observable differences between social groups and even between races were attributable to innate genetic differences. In order to understand these dramatic changes in IQ theory, it is necessary to look at the social and psychological context in which they took place. Part of this context can be found in the views of two highly influential psychologists: Galton in Britain, and Goddard in America.

Galton

Francis Galton was a firm believer in the hereditarian perspective and, as we have seen, a proponent of the eugenics movement. Galton had repeatedly expressed his view that human beings could be classified according to the upper limits of their capacity, and that no matter how much effort was expended, such limits could not be overcome (see, for example, Galton, 1869). Furthermore, he argued, these limits, whether physical or mental, conformed to a **Gaussian distribution**. This pattern of results is also known as a **normal distribution**, and is illustrated in Figure 6.1.

Galton had come to these conclusions as a result of a study involving taking the chest

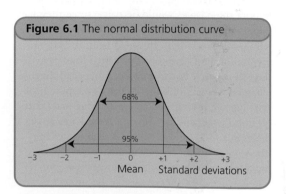

Figure 6.1 The normal distribution curve

68%

95%

−3   −2   −1   0   +1   +2   +3
         Mean   Standard deviations

measurements of 5700 Scotsmen, and the heights of members of the French army, but he also believed it to be true of mental characteristics. He said:

'Now if this be the case with stature, then it will be true as regards every other physical feature – as circumference of head, size of brain, weight of grey matter, number of brain fibres, &c.; and thence, by a step on which no physiologist will hesitate, as regards mental capacity.'

(Galton, 1869; reprinted 1961: 13)

The quotation is noteworthy, as it reveals Galton's assumption that mental characteristics are dependent on physical ones: an idea rejected by both physiology and modern psychology. Despite the invalidity of this assumption, however, the idea that intelligence must be normally distributed has remained axiomatic ever since. Incidentally, you may also have noticed that Galton referred to the 'physiologist' rather than the psychologist. In 1869, psychology was not yet an established discipline in its own right, or at least not in Britain, although it was becoming so in Germany.

Galton backed up his argument by opening an 'Anthropometric Centre' in South Kensington, where, for an admission charge of 3d, members of the public could come and assess their physical characteristics – height, strength of grip, diameter of upper arm, and many others. This gave Galton data about the physical characteristics of thousands of individuals (as well as a certain amount of income). The results of these tests confirmed Galton's observations that the measurements of human physical characteristics in a large enough sample produced a normal distribution (Galton, 1888).

Some rather more limited data on officer-level army entrance examinations also seemed to support Galton's idea that intelligence was normally distributed, although, naturally, this did not span the breadth of the population in the same way as the anthropometric measures did. But Galton's work meant that, when the IQ score was devised, there was a strong theoretical undercurrent which was more than ready to accept a numerical score of intelligence as being fixed and normally distributed; and a strong social undercurrent committed to the eugenics movement.

Goddard

Galton's rigid hereditarianism had its effects on other researchers. In America, Goddard (1912)

produced a study of a particular family, to whom he gave the name 'Kallikaks'. This study was widely reproduced in psychology and biology textbooks for the next few decades, as examples of how the outcomes of 'bad heredity' could spread through society if people who were 'genetically degenerate' were allowed unlimited breeding. One branch of the Kallikak family supposedly derived from an illicit liaison of the sire, Martin Kallikak, with a feeble-minded barmaid, while another branch came from his later marriage with a respectable Quakeress. The textbook accounts traced the progeny and social progress of each branch of the family.

Goddard's account demonstrated that the first combination had produced a family line of feeble-minded social degenerates, while the second line had produced highly respectable members of society. He attributed all these differences to the influence of a single gene for feeble-mindedness, possessed by the barmaid and transmitted to all her offspring. A later examination of Goddard's textbook (Gould, 1981) showed that in almost all the photographs of the feeble-minded Kallikaks, the faces had been crudely retouched to make them appear more degenerate. The sole exceptions were the photographs of the one Kallikak being cared for in Goddard's institution. Institutional confinement, Goddard argued, should be society's solution to the problem of widespread and increasing genetic degeneracy, partly because it would prevent a potentially criminal element being at large in society, and partly because it would also prevent them from breeding, and so perpetuating their undesirable genetic characteristics. Left at large in society, Goddard claimed, such people would produce moral and social squalor.

The Americanisation of IQ tests

Other American psychologists, in particular Louis Terman and Robert Yerkes, converted the Binet test into a form in which it could be used for classification. They too began from a committed eugenic standpoint, and saw intelligence testing as offering the possibility of measuring innate intelligence. Since they assumed that innate feeble-mindedness and/or degeneracy was the source of most social problems, including poverty and unemployment, these researchers welcomed intelligence testing. In particular, they saw it as offering possibilities for identifying what they referred to as the 'concealed high-grade' mental defectives (those whose IQs were in the 70s or 80s). Since such people were generally perfectly capable of living ordinary lives, they were not as easy to detect as those who were clearly sub-normal or mentally retarded.

The eugenic beliefs of these researchers were not hidden. When Terman produced the first Americanised version of the Binet test, the **Stanford–Binet** (Terman, 1916), he wrote in the introduction:

'In the near future, intelligence tests will bring tens of thousands of these high-grade defectives under the sur-veillance and protection of society. This will ultimately result in curtailing the reproduction of feeble-mindedness and in the elimination of an enormous amount of crime, pauperism and industrial inefficiency.'

(Terman, 1916: 6–7)

It would be hard to get a clearer statement of eugenic intent: in so many words, this states that people who were deemed 'inferior' according to the IQ test were not to be allowed to reproduce.

Goddard administered versions of Terman's converted Binet test to immigrants newly arrived in America, and still confined in the immigration centre on Ellis Island (Goddard, 1913). Despite protests from interpreters, who argued that they themselves would not have been able to do the tests when they first arrived in the country, Goddard and his assistants diagnosed large numbers of Jews, Hungarians, Italians and Russians as being incurably 'feeble-minded' – an outcome which resulted in the development of immigration restrictions, and which subsequently meant that large numbers of Europeans who were seeking asylum after the rise of the Nazi party in Germany were refused entry to the United States.

The US army tests

Although the original Stanford-Binet test had been individualised, designed to be administered to just one person at a time, a series of **group tests** based on the same principles was developed by another influential American psychologist, Robert Yerkes. The group tests had two forms: a written one known as 'Alpha', and a pictorial, performance-based version for illiterates, known as 'Beta'. Their advantage was that they were paper-and-pencil tests, with standardised instructions which meant that one tester could administer them to many people at the same time.

In 1921, Yerkes published the results of the administration of these new IQ tests to 125,000 young men who had been drafted into the American army. The outcomes of these tests showed very large group differences. In particular, those who were born in foreign countries scored lower than those who were born in America. Taken along with Goddard's work, the information obtained from the army data was heavily influential in the American laws restricting immigration from Central and Southern Europe.

An examination of these tests, however, shows that the questions were extremely culturally biased, so it was not surprising that those born in foreign countries should have been less successful with them. They included such items of 'general' knowledge as knowing the nicknames of American baseball teams, or, in the pictorial version, drawing a spoon in the right hand of someone sitting at a table, when drawing it in the left hand was marked wrong; or drawing a bowling ball in the hand of a man in a bowling alley, when drawing it in the hand of a woman in the same picture was marked wrong, as was drawing it in motion (see Figure 6.2).

Interestingly, both Goddard and Terman later changed their fixed hereditarian beliefs. From his institutional work, Goddard came to believe that feeble-mindedness was definitely curable, and also that he had set the criteria for feeble-mindedness too highly among the immigrant groups (Goddard, 1928); while Terman later explored environmental hypotheses to explain both differences and changes in the IQs of rural children as an outcome of schooling (Terman and Merrill, 1937). However, by then the damage was done. Hereditarian views had become enshrined not just in psychology textbooks, but also in immigration restrictions and social assumptions, in Europe as

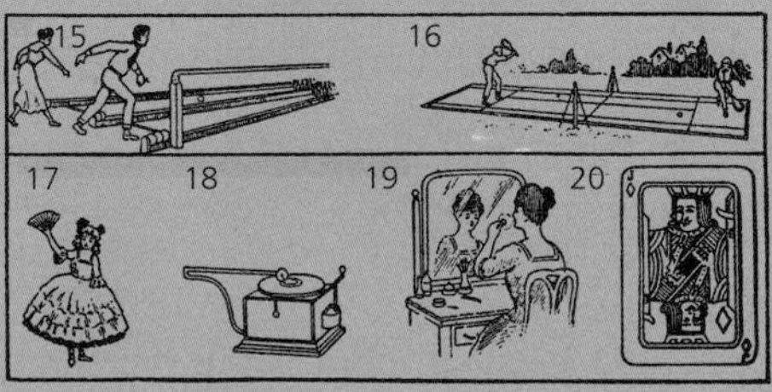

Figure 6.2 Some items from the Yerkes figure-completion test

well as America. However inaccurate, the idea that intelligence represented a fixed, genetic quality had become a fundamental concept in the development of IQ testing, and a powerful social belief.

Factor-analytic tests of intelligence

While the hereditarian approach to understanding IQ was just as strong in Britain, an alternative to the age-correlation view of intelligence testing was developing here. In 1904, Spearman produced a paper arguing that applying the statistical technique of **factor analysis** to the scores obtained on the numerous small tests gave statistical evidence for a general factor, which was common to success in solving all or most of the problems. Spearman named this the **g** factor, and argued that it represented a measure of general intelligence, which was what was being measured by intelligence tests. There were also specific learned skills which could influence intelligence performance, which Spearman classified as **s factors**, relating to specific skills.

Since psychologists working in the field were in no doubt that such tests measured intelligence (although many other psychologists were more critical), the implication that intelligence could be identified by a single score, and represented a concrete 'thing' in its own right, was readily accepted. Spearman himself fully expected that a biological substrate of the brain would be discovered, which would produce the 'mental energy' involved in **g** (Spearman, 1923).

Following this line of thought Burt (1955) and Vernon (1971) described a number of group factors occurring in between **g** and **s**. They identified a cluster of verbal skills and educational ability (which they referred to as **v:ed**) and a different cluster of spatial and mechanical abilities (which they referred to as **k:m**). Burt and Vernon saw **g** as being inherited, and therefore fixed, but they saw these group factors and **s** as resulting from training. Cattell (1971) identified a distinction between what he described as 'fluid' and 'crystallised' intelligence – in other words, between aspects of intelligence which could be improved by training and could therefore be regarded as 'fluid', and aspects of intelligence which would not be likely to change significantly, and were therefore fixed, or 'crystallised'.

The factor-analytic approach was heavily criticised by Gould (1997). Factor analysis is a statistical technique which is designed to investigate whether the scores produced by a number of different measures have anything in common. The mathematical aspects of factor analysis are complex, and it is not appropriate to go into them here, but one of the important features of factor analysis is how any grouping of the scores is identified. This involves taking a vector and seeing how the scores cluster around it. If they do, it is assumed that they probably come from a common source: Spearman argued that the fact that a number of scores from different intelligence test items clustered around a particular vector showed that there was a general factor, of **g**, underlying all of them.

Gould (1997) showed how the decision about which vector should be taken in factor analysis is an arbitrary one. He pointed out that the **g** factor apparently underlying the different tasks used in intelligence testing appears only if the vectors which are used in the analysis are oriented in a particular direction. If they are oriented in a different way, then these general factors disappear. For that reason, Gould argued that evidence from factor analysis cannot be taken as 'proof' that there really are underlying common factors in intelligence tasks.

The g factor as heritability

Spearman's **g** provided a powerful tool for the hereditarian theorists. The idea of a single, general factor underpinning the outcomes of intelligence tests provided a theoretical justification for their use of IQ in rank-ordering individuals and groups in society, because it supported the idea that intelligence was a fixed, measurable ability of which people had more or less. Those who developed intelligence tests had generally selected items, not on the basis of prior theory, but because they seemed to work – an issue which we shall return to later in this chapter, when we look at Sternberg's theory of intelligence. But Spearman argued that the identification of **g** could greatly enhance the conceptual and theoretical unity of intelligence tests, and so increase their efficiency.

Spearman's work was taken up by Cyril Burt, who championed the factor-analytic approach to intelligence testing. A highly influential figure in both British and American psychology, Burt too was a eugenicist, and argued throughout his career that intelligence was a fixed, inherited quality (see, for example, Burt, 1912, 1972). He argued that the existence of **g**, as indicated by factor analysis, proved that a common factor existed in intelligence, and that, moreover, this factor was inherited and could be assessed numerically.

The case of Cyril Burt

As the first British educational psychologist, Burt's views were directly instrumental in the adoption of intelligence testing to determine educational access. This resulted in the 1944 Education Act, which introduced a system of selection at age eleven to different types of secondary schools, depending on how the child performed in a selection examination known as the eleven-plus (Burt, 1959). The eleven-plus was heavily criticised in later years, as leading to a rigidly elitist system which labelled children at an early age. But it is important to realise that before this system was introduced, working-class children had virtually no access to grammar school education. Following the introduction of the eleven-plus examination, it became possible for a 'bright' working-class child to obtain a full education, and even get to university. Although in later years this system was seen as inadequate, it needs to be viewed in the context of its own time — and in its own time, it provided opportunities for many working-class children who would not otherwise have had educational opportunities. Kamin (1979) viewed Burt as having systematically sought to limit the opportunities of working-class children; but realistically, this is not a justifiable assertion.

That said, though, there are many other serious criticisms which have to be made of Cyril Burt's work. When Hearnshaw, an admirer of Burt, came to write his biography, a careful examination of Burt's papers and the testimony of those who had known him revealed that Burt had been involved in some serious scientific fraud (Hearnshaw, 1979). Hearnshaw's conclusions centred on three cases: first, and most important, Burt's data on twins; second, some data on the decline of educational standards; and third, his assertions about the history of factor analysis.

Burt's use of twin studies
Much of the source of Burt's influence in both Britain and America came from the apparently highly convincing data which he produced in support of his arguments. For the hereditarians,

the most convincing studies were those concerned with separated identical twins. If two twins are genetically identical, the argument ran, then if they are brought up in separate environments, any differences between them must be due to the effects of their environment. If they are still similar despite different environments, that similarity must result from genetic influences. We will be returning to look more closely at some other twin studies later in this chapter. It is worth noting, though, that the idea that inherited traits are fixed and unchanging is rather a questionable assumption biologically (see Box 6.1).

Separated identical twins, however, are rare, and the studies which have been conducted on them have tended to rely on very small samples. Burt, though, reported a study of 53 pairs of separated identical twins — an exceptionally large number. Moreover, he reported an extremely high correlation between their IQs (.86), which he asserted was definite evidence that intelligence was directly inherited. However, Hearnshaw found that the number of twins which Burt claimed to have tested was highly suspect. In a paper in 1955, Burt reported data from 21 pairs of separated identical twins. But in a paper published in 1966, this number had increased to 53. Burt had kept meticulous diaries throughout this period, recording even trivial events and routine visitors, and Hearnshaw's examination of these diaries showed that there was no evidence of any further testing of any pairs of twins during that period.

Miss Conway and Miss Howard
Burt's additional data was apparently collected by two research assistants: a Miss Conway and a Miss Howard. But Hearnshaw's enquiries revealed that these were regarded by several of his colleagues as simply 'pen-names' which Burt adopted. His secretary recollected, for instance, that he had signed a letter supposedly from Miss Howard himself, and also that at least one article which Burt had written and she had typed had gone out under this name.

In 1976, Oliver Gillie reported in the *Sunday Times* that an extensive search for Burt's two research assistants had met with no success: nobody who had worked regularly with Burt could remember ever meeting them, although a couple of not so close colleagues thought they had faint memories of one of these women. Moreover, there was no record of them on payroll

ox 6.1 Biological fallacies in nature-nurture debates

The nature-nurture debate is really a fallacy. Although it was very popular in psychology, and in medicine, during the 1950s and 1960s, it has never been particularly popular with geneticists and biologists – mainly because they understand the interaction of genes and the environment much more accurately. One major problem, for example, is that the nature-nurture debate ignores how organisms actually develop. Nature-nurture debates assume that development is caused either by genetic factors or by environmental ones. But to phrase it in terms of either/or, is to create an artificial distinction. The biological distinction which this idea draws on is that of **genotype** and **phenotype**. The genotype is the inherited design, or 'blueprint' which is represented in the individual's gene pattern, and which has been passed on from both parents. But the phenotype is the set of characteristics which the individual actually develops: if we look at a child or a grown person, what we see is the phenotype, not the genotype. The genotype is fixed, but the phenotype is much more malleable.

It is not possible for the genotype to determine what a person is like. The person emerges as a result of the interaction between genotype and experience – someone may inherit tall stature and blonde hair, for instance, and this may result in her being treated in a manner which is different from those with short stature and dark hair. In that sense, the genotype is influential in her experience. But the nature of that influence will vary depending upon the kind of society in which she lives, the subculture within that society and the family relationships which she has. One person with that kind of genotype may grow up confident, poised and socially reassured; another may attract sexual abuse while still a child, or grow up in a culture where these attributes are despised; and so become timid, lacking confidence and unwilling to attract attention.

D.O. Hebb tried to bring home this point in 1949, when he showed how both nature and nurture are essential to the development of an egg. As he pointed out, if we take the genotype away, there is no egg; but if we remove the warm supporting environment the egg dies. Nature cannot be regarded as distinct from nurture, because there is a constant interaction between the two – each is totally dependent on the other. Nor does it make any sense to claim that the egg is 80% inherited or 60%, or any other percentage: both sides are completely essential. It is not an either/or question but a **dialectical interrelationship**.

Many geneticists, therefore, see psychology's nature-nurture debates as arising from a biological misunderstanding. The genotype is the state of the genes, but it is the phenotype which is actually manifest in any organism, since there is always a continual environmental interaction with the genotype from conception. The phenotype is continually developing and interacting with its environment, so genetic influence is not static, or fixed. Different characteristics of genes come to the fore at different stages of development, and different experiences allow different aspects of the individual's genetic potential to be realised. As Rose *et al.* (1984) pointed out, the whole idea of some 'fixed' innate component apparent in the developed organism is pure biological myth. So trying to argue that intelligence is mainly a result of heredity – or, for that matter, entirely a matter of environmental influence – involves a complete failure to understand how developmental biology actually works.

lists, or of them visiting his house. The information which Burt himself provided, before his death, was contradictory. For example, at one point he said that one of the researchers had emigrated to Australia, but the date that he gave for this was before the time when, according to his own published papers, they were collecting data for his studies in London. Gillie concluded that it was questionable whether these women had actually existed.

The heritability of intelligence

From his twin studies, Burt developed the concept of **heritability**: the idea that the proportion of variation in intelligence which was due to fixed inherited factors could be assessed numerically.

According to Burt, the heritability of intelligence was 80% – in other words, the variability which people showed in their levels of intelligence was 80% from genetic sources, and only 20% due to environmental influences (Burt, 1955).

In 1974, Leon Kamin published an analysis of Burt's work, in which he revealed that the scientific and statistical basis of Burt's evidence was completely implausible. Burt had published many papers between 1909 and 1972, but when they were looked at closely these contained quite a lot of contradictory statements. In particular, references to the same data were described quite differently from one paper to another.

Other oddities, too, implied that at least some of the data had been fabricated. For example, one of the most obvious problems was the way that the correlations provided matched to the third decimal place, even over two decades and incorporating the inclusion of additional pairs of twins. Such accuracy was implausible in its own right – studies of real people just do not work out that precisely! In addition, Burt failed to provide accounts of the tests which he had used, and sometimes even admitted to having sized up a person's IQ informally during the course of an interview! Kamin was forced to the conclusion that much of Burt's data were spurious.

The evidence for fraud

On the basis of this, and much more evidence, it was concluded that at least some of Burt's work was fraudulent: that he had invented much of his data. In a careful professional enquiry investigating the charges, two of his ex-research students, by then respected academic psychologists, also reported that, at the time, Burt had altered papers which they had written, in ways which seriously distorted their findings, and then published the papers in their names without letting them know what he had done (Clarke and Clarke, 1977).

Other evidence as to his questionable practices also emerged. Hearnshaw (1980) described a set of figures produced by Burt in 1969 which, he claimed, showed that there was a systematic decline in educational standards. Hearnshaw argued that these figures were, without doubt, at least partly fabricated. In addition, Burt had made claims about the application of factor analysis to intelligence, claiming that he himself had discovered it, and not Spearman. Hearnshaw described how he had first made this claim in

1937, when Spearman was still alive: Spearman objected, and Burt retracted his claim. But after Spearman's death, he brought it up again, and insisted repeatedly that it had been he who had recognised the potential of the factor-analytic method for intelligence.

Recent disputes

More recently, Fletcher (1991) and Joynson (1989) argued that Burt had been misrepresented, and that the evidence for fraud was less convincing than it had been presented. They argued that what Burt had done had been deliberately distorted to make it appear worse than it was, whereas his positive achievements had been ignored. But while it is undoubtedly true that some of Burt's critics may have minimised some of his positive contributions – like the question of the eleven-plus examination described earlier – this cannot be said for all of them. Hearnshaw, in particular, was an admirer of Burt, and sought to exonerate him from many of the accusations which were made. But he regarded the conclusions which he had come to about Burt's fraud as inescapable in the face of the evidence.

Fletcher and Joynson asserted that Hearnshaw, in his biography of Burt, had failed to take account of the views of those who supported him, and instead had focused only on his detractors. This had meant that the picture which Hearnshaw had presented was extremely biased. But Hearnshaw (1992) disputed this strongly, reiterating the point that he was, himself, an admirer of Burt, and stating that he had been careful to pay as much attention to Burt's many admirers as to those who suspected his work. Certainly many of those who expressed strong feelings against Burt felt that Hearnshaw had, if anything, tried too hard to give credit to him, particularly with respect to his earlier work (for example Clarke and Clarke, 1980; Gillie, 1980).

Fletcher and Joynson also argued that there were substantive gaps in Burt's diaries, and that these gaps could account for the missing research assistants' work. But Hearnshaw (1992) pointed out that these gaps appeared for the years 1953–5, but did not cover the critical years between 1955 and 1966 when the twin data had suddenly increased so sharply. During that period, the diaries were virtually complete, except for occasional gaps during 1959. Moreover, the amount of detail which was contained in these diaries, in which even very routine visitors to the house were noted, made it highly unlikely that Burt could have been visited by either of the research assistants during the time.

Although there seems little doubt that Burt committed a major scientific crime with respect to his scientific research, it is equally true that his achievements as an educational psychologist were praiseworthy, and that he would exert his professional efforts wherever possible to help children who needed it. To attempt to paint him as an out-and-out villain is to overstate the case unfairly. But it is important to realise that Burt's statistics were not trivial: they provided the bedrock for almost all the powerful hereditarian claims about intelligence – and continue to do so.

To take just one example, Burt's statistics underpin the claims of Jensen (1969) that race differences in IQ were inherited and that therefore widespread educational opportunity has only limited value. His figures continue to appear in the racist National Front literature, and similar material. Burt was one of the most influential psychologists in the history of the discipline, so the fraudulent nature of his work is not something which can be quietly brushed under the carpet. The recent efforts to re-establish Burt's reputation have failed to answer all the criticisms of his work, and do not even begin to account for the internal contradictions in his own published papers, as identified by Kamin (1974) and Hearnshaw (1979).

Moreover, the existence of fraud in other hereditarian studies, like the 'doctoring' of Goddard's Kallikak photographs described earlier, or the flaws in Kallman's research into schizophrenia (see Chapter 8), suggests that, all too often, the strongly held eugenic views of researchers about the nature-nurture issue, rather than the search for scientific truth, were directing what they did. Burt in that sense was not alone. But fraudulent research is still by far the exception, and we will now look at some of the more reputable studies which have been undertaken in this area.

Twin studies of intelligence

The importance of **twin studies** is that, in theory, they have the potential to indicate how important inheritance is for the development of IQ. If two people are genetically identical, as is the case with monozygotic twins, and are then brought up entirely differently, it would be reasonable to suppose that any differences in their intelligence would be due to the effects of environmental factors. It would be less easy, however, to assume that any similarities are due to the effects of inherited factors, unless one could be absolutely sure that the environments in which the twins had grown up were completely different. If they *were* completely different, though, the argument could be made that similarities showed the influence of genetic factors.

Burt argued that the high correlations found between separated identical twins could be used to calculate the heritability of intelligence – the proportion of intelligence which was inherited. He concluded that, judging from the statistical evidence, the heritability of IQ was 80% – in other words, 80% of the variation in the individual's intelligence derived from genetic factors, and only 20% was environmental. As we saw in Box 6.1, this view contains a number of biological misconceptions about genetic influences; but there were additional problems which became apparent with this argument.

Most of the evidence for the heritability of IQ came from Burt's own studies, and we have already seen that these cannot be taken as convincing scientific data. But there have been three rather more respectable studies which have compared the intelligence of separated identical twins, and those of twins who have been brought up together. The first of these was conducted by Newman, Freeman and Holzinger in 1937, the second by Shields, in 1962, and the third by Juel-Nielsen, in 1965. In each of these studies, the IQs of pairs of separated identical twins were correlated. Table 6.1 overleaf gives the correlations obtained.

As can be seen from the table, the correlations vary widely, from a correlation of .62, which is not particularly convincing as evidence for heritability, to a correlation of .77, which is higher than would have been expected by chance. A **correlation coefficient** is a number between −1 and +1, which indicates whether, and how strongly, two measurements vary together. The closer the figure is to one, whether positive or negative, the stronger the correlation. So a figure which is close to 0 indicates that there is no relationship worth thinking about, whereas a correlation of .9 or −.9 is very strong. The interpretation of correlation coefficients will be discussed later in this chapter.

Table 6.1 Correlations obtained from separated twin studies

Study	Correlation	No. of pairs	Test used
Newman *et al.* (1937)	.67	19	Stanford-Binet
Shields (1962)	.77	37	Mill Hill
Juel-Nielsen (1965)	.62	12	Wechsler

Source: Kamin, 1974

The earliest of these twin studies, by Newman, Freeman and Holzinger, was used by Burt in his arguments – but their baseline correlations were not used. Instead, their data received two statistical 'corrections', at different times, supposedly to compensate for testing artefacts. McNemar (1938) applied a double statistical correction to these data, which raised the correlation coefficient to .77. This, as Kamin (1974) pointed out, was based on some very questionable statistical assumptions. Following this, an additional 'correction' was added by Jensen, in 1970, which raised the outcome to .81 – a figure which fitted nicely with the .86 supposedly obtained by Burt. So the outcome of a study which had apparently provided evidence for an environmental influence in intelligence was adjusted by others until it seemed to provide evidence in entirely the opposite direction.

Sampling problems of twin studies

There are other reasons, too, why the hereditarian argument derived from twin studies is less than convincing. In particular, there were sampling problems in each of the studies. In the Newman *et al.* study, the identical twins were obtained from responses to radio and newspaper appeals, and came from all over the country. Since this was the time of the Depression, and each pair of separated twins had to be brought to the Chicago centre for study and testing, which was expensive, the researchers were anxious to make sure that they really were genetically identical. So any twins which were not 'so strikingly similar that even your friends or relatives have confused you' were excluded from the study.

The problem is that these strict criteria may have created what is known as a **Type I error** – a false positive result. It is possible that genuine MZ (monozygotic, or identical) twins, who were different as a result of environmental factors, were excluded from the study. For example, one pair

was excluded, even though they were so similar as to be often confused with one another, because they reported that they were unlike 'in disposition' – a difference which might easily have arisen because of their environmental separation. So it is important to recognise that the sampling problems in the study made the pairs appear, if anything, more similar than they really were – which makes the relatively lower correlation obtained by the researchers very interesting indeed.

The Shields study showed a much higher correlation between the separated identical twins, but again this study showed distinct sampling problems. In particular, the pairs of 'separated' twins used in the study had often not been separated very much. Most of the time, the twins went to the same school, and stayed with relatives: one of each pair with a different relative. They often knew each other, and spent time together. Of the 37 pairs of twins in the study, only ten pairs had never attended the same school, at least for a period, and had not been reared by relatives. According to Kamin (1974), when the data from these ten pairs alone are analysed, the correlation obtained from them is very low – only .47.

There are other problems with the Shields study, as well. Certain pairs of twins with low scores were included in some assessments, while others were not. In one case, a pair of twins was dropped from the analysis of a particular set of scores (the Dominoes test) because one twin had scored only 1, while her twin had scored 27 – a difference of three standard deviations. It was concluded that the first had evidently not understood the instructions, although she did not give an impression of low intelligence. Yet another pair of twins also scored very low on the same test, gaining scores of 4 and 2, but they were included, even though they were both natural Welsh speakers and it could equally well have been argued that they too had not understood the instructions. Shields reported that the decision was based on whether the twins concerned had given an 'impression' of low intelligence. But again, dropping twins who produce very different scores would have the result of making the correlations higher than they should have been.

Sampling problems similar to those in the Shields study were also apparent in the Juel-Nielsen study. For example, one pair of twins had been cared for by relatives until they were seven years old, but then lived together with their mother until they were fourteen, so it was questionable how intensive their 'separation' really was. Another pair of twins in the study was reared by aunts, each married to farmers. As a general rule in this study, the homes of the separated twins were similar in housing conditions, socio-economic status, and often parental occupation as well, so their environments were not really all that different.

We can see, then, that the evidence provided by twin studies for the heritability or otherwise of IQ is equivocal. Although these studies form the basis for the hereditarian argument, they rarely stand up to close scrutiny. As evidence for existence of a heritable **g** factor, they must be taken as having very limited value.

Adoption studies

A different group of studies involves making comparisons between children who have been adopted or fostered, and their natural and adoptive parents. The idea behind **adoption studies** is that if the child's IQ correlates more closely with those of its adoptive parents than it does with those of its biological ones, an environmental influence will be indicated; but if the child's IQ correlates more strongly with those of its biological parents than it does with those of its adoptive ones, the implication is that genetic factors are most active.

There are some serious problems with these arguments, which mainly centre on the idea that a high or low correlation can indicate the cause of intelligence. We will be looking at these, along with some other statistical problems raised by studies of inherited intelligence, later in this chapter.

In 1938, Snygg reported a comparison of the IQs of 312 adopted and fostered children with those of their biological mothers. The correlation obtained was the extremely low figure of .13, indicating a strong environmental factor. As Snygg

pointed out, this low figure was even more remarkable because, as has been found with the studies of separated twins, adoption agencies tend to place children in homes which are similar to those they came from, so the environments are often not very different. But despite its findings, or possibly because of them, this study was completely ignored in favour of a different study, which appeared to show the opposite effect.

The Skodak and Skeels study

In 1949, Skodak and Skeels reported a study of 100 adopted children, making comparisons between the children's IQs, their biological mothers' educational levels and their adoptive mothers' educational levels. When making a comparison between these figures, Skodak and Skeels found a correlation of .32 between the child's measured IQ and the educational level of the biological mother, but one of only .02 between the child's IQ and the educational level of the adoptive mother. Skodak and Skeels also obtained IQ measures for 63 of the biological mothers, and found a correlation of .44 between these and the IQ of their children; although, oddly, they did not obtain IQ measures for the adoptive parents. Since the children had not lived with their parents since infancy, this seemed to be a very high correlation, and the Skodak and Skeels study received extensive publicity as a supposed 'proof' that intelligence was inherited.

This was a longitudinal study, conducted originally on 180 children who were given Stanford-Binet intelligence tests on four occasions. The average age of the group on each occasion was two, four, seven and thirteen years. Since a number of families dropped out during the period of study, the sample size by the fourth occasion – the one which provided the statistics which were so widely cited – was down to 100. But on earlier occasions, when the sample was larger, the data had provided rather different information. For example: when the children were tested at average age seven, there were 139 children in the sample. At that time, the correlation between the biological mothers' education and their IQs was .24, while the correlation with their foster mothers' education was .20. These were not significantly different from one another, although both of them were significant correlations in their own right (Skodak and Skeels, 1945).

While it might be possible to argue that the

apparent change in correlation occurred because of maturation, and is therefore genetic in origin, Kamin (1974) pointed out that there were also changes in the nature of the sample which could have influenced the final results. In particular, it was apparent that the drop-out rate for adoptive parents included a high proportion of those who had not been to college. This meant that, by the final study, the adoptive parents were very much more similar to one another, in terms of educational level, than the other group were. For that reason the correlations would have been weaker than they would have been in a more diverse sample – such as was found in the other group.

Problems with adoption studies

This brings up a serious methodological weakness of adoption studies, which centres on the use of correlation coefficients. A **correlation coefficient** indicates how much two variables vary together: whether one is likely to be high when the other is high, and so on. But it does not tell us anything about the actual value of each set of figures. In fact, using correlation coefficients does not really allow us to compare the two groups very well, because it does not tell us anything about the mean scores of the two groups.

In fact, the means of the two groups in the Skodak and Skeels study were very different. The mean IQ of the adopted children in the Skodak and Skeels study was 117; whereas the mean IQ of the 63 biological mothers was 86. This is an enormous difference, and one which is completely concealed by the use of correlation. Similarly, there was a large difference in the mothers' educational levels: over 50% of the adoptive mothers had attended college, whereas only about 8% of the biological mothers had done so. So the implication is that in terms of their absolute values, the children's IQs were actually similar to their adoptive mothers.

The problem is that using correlations only allows us to compare the relative values within the two groups, in terms of who was higher or lower in the group as a whole. Although correlations tell us that a child with a relatively lower IQ may have been likely to have had a biological mother with a relatively lower IQ, the 'relatively lower' in each case relates only to the other group of children, or to the group of biological mothers. We still need to explain how the scores of the two groups were so very different from one another.

Comparisons of IQ and home environment

Other adoption studies have taken a different approach: looking at the way that children's IQs correlate with the type of environment provided by their adoptive homes. There are three studies which are particularly significant in this respect. One, which like the Snygg study is rarely mentioned in the literature, was conducted by Freeman, Holzinger and Mitchell, in 1928. These researchers looked at the IQs of 401 children living in foster homes. They compared these scores with a 'home rating', which looked at six factors: (1) material environment; (2) evidence of culture; (3) occupation of foster father; (4) education of foster father; (5) education of foster mother; and (6) social activity of foster parents. These dimensions were each assessed on a scale of 1–5, giving a total score out of 30 for the quality of the home environment. Freeman, Holzinger and Mitchell found that there was a significant correlation of .48 between the child's IQ and the quality of their foster home, suggesting that a significant environmental influence was taking place.

A second study of this type was reported in the same publication by Burks in 1928, but this one received much more publicity. Burks correlated the IQs of 206 adoptive children with the quality of their adoptive homes, using a standard 'home rating' test known as the Whittier scale. This gave a single score of 1–5 for the quality of the home, with 1 representing very poor homes, using criteria such as 'the basement of a cheap tenement house, ragged dirty clothes and little food', and 5 representing very high-quality homes, using criteria such as 'modern home, fine carpets, rugs and pictures, abundant food, well-to-do'. Using this scale, Burks found that there was a correlation of .21 between the adoptive child's IQ and the foster home environment, but a correlation of .42 between the child's IQ and its home environment in the natural families. Burks argued that this provided strong evidence for the idea that intelligence was inherited.

One problem with this study, however, is that there was far less variation between the different adoptive homes than there was between those of the natural families. Although the means for the two groups were very similar (4.7 for the adoptive homes and 4.6 for the natural families), the standard deviations were significantly different: .4 for the adoptive homes and .6 for the control ones. Kamin (1974) argued that this difference in the variances of the two samples could account for the weaker correlation between the child's IQ and the adoptive environment. Since the adoptive homes were very like each other, the correlations with the children's IQs would be less powerful. This issue is also discussed in Box 6.2.

Although Burks had claimed that the homes were matched, and later writers had claimed them to be 'perfectly' matched, in fact they were matched only on age and sex of the child, occupational category of the father and neighbourhood. This, Kamin argued, had left scope for a considerable amount of variation in other respects,

---

Box 6.2 Reliability, validity and standardisation

There are several kinds of psychometric test. Psychometric means, literally, 'measuring the psyche', and any systematic attempt to assess mental characteristics comes into this category. Psychometric tests include tests of personality, aptitudes, creativity, attitudes or intelligence. And any psychometric test needs to conform to three criteria: reliability, validity and standardisation.

Reliability
Reliability refers to the consistency of a particular type of measure. When people are assessing the reliability of traditional psychometric tests, there are three main techniques which are used. The first is the test-retest method: the same test is given to the same people after a period of time, and the two sets of data are correlated. This is fine if the test is something that is not going to be affected by practice – for instance, if you were looking at individual differences in how often a Necker cube appeared to change its orientation.

But people might remember the answers that they gave the first time, so an alternative is the alternate-forms method. In this, two exactly parallel versions of the same test are drawn up, so that one version of the test can be used on one condition, and another the second time. Most commercially available psychometric tests have at least two different forms for this reason. The third technique for assessing reliability is the split-half method, in which the test is carefully divided by choosing alternate questions, so that each half is exactly equivalent. Half the test is given on one occasion, and the other half later; then the results are correlated.

Validity
Validity refers to how far the measure actually measures what it claims to do. There are different types of validity, which can be broadly classified into four: face validity, criterion validity, construct validity and ecological validity. Face validity is sometimes known as surface validity, and it is essentially just a superficial assessment of whether the measure looks as though it is measuring what it is supposed to.

Criterion validity is when validity is assessed by measuring it against some kind of external standard, like comparing IQ scores with success in school exams. Criterion validity can be of two kinds – concurrent validity, in which the measure is assessed against some other criterion happening at the time; and predictive validity, in which the measure is compared with something in the future.

Construct validity refers to whether the measure forms an accurate assessment of the theoretical construct that it is supposed to be measuring – does it accurately reflect the theory underlying the idea? And ecological validity is concerned with how a measure compares with its equivalent in the real world – like whether intelligence test scores correlate with people acting intelligently when they need to.

Standardisation
The idea of standardisation rests on the principle that abilities, both mental and physical, are distributed throughout the population according to a Gaussian distribution, or normal distribution curve. Standardising a test means establishing how the scores of this test are distributed among the population, and making sure that the test, if administered to enough people, would produce a Gaussian distribution. This makes it possible to identify much more accurately what would be an average score, what would be above average and what would be below average.

Because the Gaussian distribution curve has ● ● ● ▶

Box 6.2 continued

very precise properties, once the mean and the standard deviation of the curve are known, it is possible to use it to predict exactly what percentage of the population would be expected to gain any particular score; and so standardisation allows us to judge how typical, or uncommon, someone's result may be.

The process of standardising a test or an attitude measure involves developing sets of **population norms**, by applying the test to large numbers of people and therefore gaining an idea of what the normal scores for those types of people might be. Population norms for a psychometric test or attitude measure can vary, depending on the group of people who are taken as the population. For instance, intelli-

gence tests have different sets of norms for people of different ages, because what people can be expected to do successfully is different for different ages.

It is possible for population norms to reflect social bias, as well as the test items themselves. For example: IQ tests have different population norms for men and women, because ever since the very first IQ tests were devised, women have scored more highly than men. So the population norms were adjusted in order to make sure that the IQs of males and females could be fitted to the expected distributions: a woman has to answer more questions correctly to gain the same measured IQ as a man (Preston Brooks, 1984).

and this additional variation was apparent in the differences between the two groups.

The third study of this kind was conducted by Leahy, in 1935. Leahy compared the IQs of children with an 'environmental status score' composed of a combination of different measures, including parents' occupational status and education, the economic status of the family and their degree of social participation, and cultural aspects and child-training facilities within the home. The correlation between the two which Leahy obtained was .19 between adoptive children and their foster home environments, but .53 for the natural families in the study. Leahy concluded that this showed that environment had little effect on intelligence.

Kamin (1974) pointed out that, as with the Burks study, this study also showed far less variation between the adoptive homes than was apparent between the natural homes. But in this study, the adoptive children too showed less variation in their IQs than the control children, which suggested that, despite the low correlation, there might be an environmental influence taking place. Kamin also suggested that the reason why a similar difference in variation did not occur in Burks's study was because the adoptive group included a number of children who had very low IQs indeed – in the 50s – and who were suspected of having organic brain damage. Their presence in the sample meant that the variation in IQ

within the adoptive group might have been artificially enlarged.

We can see, then, that these data can be taken two ways. Although the Freeman *et al.* study suggested an environmental influence in the relationship between the child's IQ and its home environment, the studies by Burks and Leahy both suggested an inherited influence. But Kamin argued that this apparent influence was more of a statistical artefact than a real effect, brought about by the fact that adoptive homes tend to be very carefully vetted by social workers, and so are often very much more similar to one another than ordinary families are.

Comparison of child's IQ with foster parents

There are other outcomes of these three studies, as well. Freeman, Holzinger and Mitchell (1928) obtained IQ scores for many of the foster parents in the study, so that it was possible to compare the IQs of children directly with those of their adoptive parents. Some of these adoptive parents also had children of their own, and so the researchers were able to examine how adoptive parents' IQs correlated with those of their own children. These results are given in Table 6.2, and show no significant differences between the correlations for adoptive children and those for natural children, which again suggests an environmental influence.

Burks (1928) compared the IQs of 174 adopted children with the 'mental ages' of their foster

Table 6.2 Correlations from three adoption studies

	Adoptive m-p own child	Adoptive m-p adopted child	Family m-p own child
Freeman et al. (1928)	.35 (N=28)	.39 (N=169)	no data
Burks (1928)	no data	.20 (N=174)	.52 (N=100)
Leahy (1935)	.36 (N=20)	.18 (N=177)	.60 (N=173)
All studies	.35 (N=48)	.26 (N=520)	.57 (N=273)
(m-p = mid-parent scores)			

Source: Kamin, 1974

parents; and also compared the IQs of a separate set of 100 ordinary children living with their biological parents with the 'mental ages' of those parents. The correlations obtained from the two groups were significantly different (see Table 6.2). Burks argued from these findings that IQ was clearly inherited, and that only about 17% of environmental variability could be seen as owing to differences in the home environment.

Leahy (1935) compared the IQs of 177 adoptive children with those of their foster parents, but made comparisons with two other groups: one of twenty children living with their own parents, who had also adopted other children (like the group in the Freeman *et al.* study); and a group of 173 ordinary children living with their natural parents. These findings, too, are given in Table 6.2.

Each of these studies used the **mid-parent score** – in other words, the average of the father's and mother's IQ scores for the purposes of comparison. As with the comparisons with home environment, the picture from the three studies appears to be contradictory. The Freeman *et al.* study shows little difference between the adopted child and the own child for adoptive parents, implying a strong environmental influence. The other two studies, on the other hand, show a considerable difference between the two, implying a strong, inherited difference.

There are some other findings which also emerge from Table 6.2. The final row of the table gives the pooled scores from all the studies, as provided by Kamin (1974). One thing which is very apparent in this, as well as in the data from the specific studies, is the difference between the IQs

of 'own' children in adoptive families and in control families, who have not adopted a child. Despite the fact that the children in each case are the genetic offspring of the home's parents, there is a significant difference between the two correlations. In the adoptive families, there is a lower correlation between parent and child than is usually the case, whether that child is biologically related to the parent or not.

The second point which becomes apparent when the data are pooled is that the correlations between 'own' child and adoptive child within the adoptive families are not significantly different. Although they are very different from the control families, it is only within the adoptive families that a properly matched control can be said to have been established; and in these cases one study shows a higher correlation while the other shows a lower one. The two cancel each other out. A non-significant difference in this case would imply, if anything, an environmental influence rather than the strong evidence for heredity often claimed for these studies.

We can see, then, that the evidence for the heritability or otherwise of intelligence which can be gleaned from adoption studies is equivocal. One of the biggest problems is that the studies have very rarely looked at exactly the same things, and, when they have, they have rarely used the same tests to look at them with. So it is hard to make definite comparisons. But another problem has been the way that researchers in this field – and, more important, those people who have quoted their findings – have often had very definite preconceived ideas about the nature of intelligence. This has meant that implications of studies, and sometimes even studies themselves, have often been overlooked if they point in the other direction.

Problems of IQ testing

All these studies, of course, rest on the assumption that the IQ test is a precision instrument which can accurately reflect an individual's intelligence. Differences of just a couple of points in IQ were treated as if they were precise data, although the reliability coefficients of the tests indicate that much larger differences could occur by chance alone. IQ tests are not precise instruments, and it is also questionable whether they are accurate indicators of intelligence.

Validity and standardisation

There are three fundamental requirements for all psychometric tests: validity, reliability and standardisation. Some of the detailed aspects of these criteria are discussed in Box 6.2 (page 143). In summary, however, **validity** refers to whether a test really measures what it is supposed to measure – in this case, whether an IQ really measures intelligence; **reliability** refers to whether a test would give a consistent result if the same individual were to be tested on two different occasions; and **standardisation** is concerned with how the test results compare with results from other tests, and the typical results likely to be obtained by various groups in the population.

Intelligence tests are also expected to be reliable, valid and standardised. But there are a number of issues which arise when we begin applying these concepts to IQ testing. For example: as we saw earlier in this chapter, Galton (1869) showed how human physical characteristics within a population could be plotted along a normal distribution curve (shown in Figure 6.1), and then applied this distribution to 'intelligence' on the grounds that intelligence is presumably dependent on some physical characteristic of the brain. The assumption that intelligence is normally distributed is one which underpins all intelligence tests, and has **face validity**, in that it seems plausible.

This idea also has **construct validity**, since most theories of intelligence have also been based on

the idea that intelligence is normally distributed. But it is a concept which has been used as a basic assumption, rather than one which has been directly investigated. This means that any new test of intelligence which does not show a normal distribution is automatically assumed to be invalid. So there is no way of finding out whether intelligence really is normally distributed in real life or not, since all the measures of intelligence have been developed and adjusted until they produced a normal distribution. It is a completely circular process, based entirely on Galton's assumption that intelligence is dependent on physical characteristics.

In terms of **criterion validity**, defenders of intelligence testing have argued that IQ tests have predictive validity: that they are reasonably successful in predicting subsequent success at school. But there is more than one way to interpret the data on this issue. The correlation between intelligence tests and school examination success is generally about .6, which implies that roughly 36% of the variance between IQ scores and educational success can be accounted for by some relationship between the two measures. But this still leaves 64% of the variance to be explained. Since these data are obtained from school students doing paper-and-pencil IQ tests, performed under time-pressure and in the same kinds of conditions as school examinations, it is hardly surprising that there should be some similarity between the two scores. This statistic, therefore, although regarded as convincing by the pro-testing school of thought, is regarded more sceptically by those who are unconvinced of the value of IQ testing.

There are doubts about the standardisation of intelligence tests, as well. New tests have to ensure that they give scores which correlate with existing tests, in particular the Stanford-Binet. If they do not, they are assumed, automatically, to be invalid measures of IQ. If the Stanford-Binet test were unassailably a valid measure of intelligence in its own right, that might be acceptable. But as we have seen, the reality of intelligence testing is rather more controversial. So to insist that any intelligence test must measure up to an older test is questionable, to say the least! There is also some debate about how the population norms for IQ tests have been established, but since they directly concern issues of race and gender, we will look at them later on in this chapter.

Statistical problems in intelligence testing

As we have seen, intelligence testing, and in particular discussions about the heritability of intelligence, have always depended heavily on statistics. But often, researchers have used statistical tests to draw conclusions about the nature of intelligence which are not necessarily valid. And the conclusions that people draw about the nature of intelligence can sometimes have widespread and extremely unpleasant effects.

The normal distribution and parametric testing

We have already identified a number of statistical problems, as we have looked at the evidence for heritability of IQ. But there are others, too. One of them as we have seen is the assumption that intelligence is normally distributed – a concept which has been challenged, but not really tested, except by using tests which were designed to give a normal distribution as part of the outcome. This assumption led to the use of parametric tests to analyse IQ scores. But this, too, is dubious statistically.

A parametric statistical test assumes (1) that the populations of the scores being tested are normally distributed; (2) that they have equal variances – in other words, that they spread out around the mean about the same amount; and (3) that they are measured on an equal-interval or ratio scale of measurement. IQ scores do show normal distributions and equal variances, because intelligence tests have been developed to make sure that they produce those results. But IQ scores are not equal-interval or ratio data. In equal-interval and ratio scales, the difference between the points on the scale are the same, no matter whereabouts on the scale they come. A centimetre is the same length, no matter whether you are measuring the distance between 1 and 2 cm, or between 2012 and 2013 cm. A ratio scale differs from an equal-interval scale in that it has an absolute zero: you cannot have a shorter distance than 0 centimetres, so length is a ratio scale; whereas you can have less than £0, because you can be in debt, so money is an equal-interval scale.

But there are no grounds at all for claiming that the difference between an IQ of 105 and 115 is the same value as the difference between an IQ of 60 and an IQ of 70. In fact, they are very different, since at one level we are talking about whether the person has just about enough intelligence to cope with the demands of everyday living, and at the other we are talking about differences which are relatively unimportant in terms of how someone lives their life, or in terms of what they are likely to achieve. Nor is it realistically possible to achieve a measured IQ of zero. So using parametric statistics to compare IQ scores is a rather dodgy practice.

Problems with correlations

Correlations are another problem. One of the first things which a psychology student learning about correlations is taught is that correlation is not the same as **causality** – just because two things vary together does not mean that we can assume that one causes the other. All we can say is that when one changes so does the other one. As Kamin (1974) showed, there can be more than one reason for a correlation. Yet, throughout the history of IQ research, correlation has been taken as proof of causality.

Another fallacy is the way that similarity of correlation coefficients has been taken to imply that scores were similar too – but all that tells us is that the scores varied together. Similar correlation coefficients have often been concealing very large differences between the scores themselves – making it appear that there were more similarities between different groups than there really were. The arguments about within-group and between-group variance (page 148), which became so important in the race and IQ debate, often depend on this fallacy.

There are concerns, too, about what correlation coefficients actually mean. When interpreting correlation coefficients, we can obtain a rough approximation of how much of the variance they account for, by squaring the digit of the correlation and taking it as a percentage. So a correlation of .8, for example, accounts for about 64% of the variance between two sets of scores. And this, too, has been used to mislead. For example, protagonists of IQ testing claim that they correlate with school performance – and so they do. But this correlation is actually about .6. Although it is statistically significant, it still means that something like 64% of the variance is still unaccounted for. The correlation may sound high, but what it really tells us is that most of the factors affecting school success are unrelated to measured IQ.

The outcome of these problems can be very significant. Misunderstandings about the nature of correlation can give us a very severely distorted picture of how close a relationship is, if we rely on concordance rates (correlations) alone. Assumptions about parametric distributions might have seriously distorted our picture of the nature of intelligence. And, as we shall see, some researchers have used statistical evidence of this type to make dogmatic and often unwarranted assertions about the nature of intelligence in different social groups.

Race and intelligence

Sternberg (1985) argued that any definition of intelligence must recognise the cultural context in which the definition is being applied, since an act which is an intelligent thing to do in one cultural context could be completely inappropriate in another. But as we saw earlier in this chapter, ever since the first group IQ tests were developed, they have contained a cultural bias which ensured that white middle-class individuals score more highly than other social groups. The group versions of the Stanford-Binet test used by US immigration authorities to control entrance to the United States at the beginning of this century were not only culturally biased, assuming a prior knowledge of American culture; they were also unashamedly racist, asking such questions as: 'The number of a Kaffir's legs is: 2, 4, 6, 8 …?'

The bias inherent in those tests was extreme, and the revised versions of the tests excluded such items. On the surface, at least, IQ test items seemed fair. But they still contained cultural values and assumptions. For example, an item of the Wechsler Intelligence Scale for Children, one of the most widely used individual IQ tests in this country, asks: 'What is the correct thing to do if you find a stamped, addressed letter in the street?' If a child responds by saying 'Post it', it gets two marks. If the child says 'Give it to a policeman', or someone in authority, it is given one mark. But the child gains no marks at all if it says 'Open it' or 'Leave it'.

The marking system which is being used here is a measure of social conformity, and not, strictly speaking, a measure of intelligence. It is not the only question of its kind in the test. While no one would dispute the morality of the required answer, it is a moot point whether a measure of social conformity is the same as a measure of intelligence. This, of course, is not an example of ethnic bias: black children are as likely as white children to have been brought up with a strict sense of honesty. But it is an example of the way that social conventions and cultural assumptions affect IQ test items.

Perhaps not surprisingly, given the cultural biases in IQ tests, many researchers have argued that standard IQ tests discriminate strongly against certain populations, such as black Americans or people from working-class backgrounds. In America they have been successfully challenged in the courts: Judge Peckham, in 1979, ruled that education authorities who used IQ tests to place black children in special schools for the mentally retarded were discriminating against ethnic minority students, because standardised intelligence tests are racially and culturally biased, and because they were being misused in this diagnostic role.

Jensen's arguments

But these are factors which are completely ignored by those putting forward the hereditarian theory of IQ. When Arthur Jensen revived the race and IQ controversy in 1969, he argued that because American blacks scored an average of fifteen IQ points lower than American whites, they were therefore lower in intelligence. Moreover, Jensen argued that since Burt had shown that intelligence was 80% inherited, this difference between blacks and whites was fixed and lasting. Therefore blacks, Jensen argued, should receive different schooling from whites. On the basis of what we have already covered in this chapter, many of the fallacies in this reasoning should be obvious. But there are some additional ones worth spelling out.

One serious fallacy in Jensen's argument concerns the confusion between within-group variance and between-group variance. Burt's heritability estimate was an attempt to explain how intelligence varies within a single population. It was looking at **within-group variance**, and seeking to explain how that happens. But Jensen was looking at differences between two entirely different populations: **between-group variance**. The two types of figures are entirely different, and to try to use one to explain the other is completely inappropriate.

Gould (1997) gives the example of height, to make this point. Within any given human population, the heritability of height is about 95% – tall parents tend to produce tall children, and short parents produce short children. That is common within all human populations. But differences in nutrition make a great deal of difference to human height, so if we compare, say, people in an impoverished village in South America with middle-class Americans, we would find large differences between the two populations. We would not conclude, though, that these differences are inherited. And yet, that is precisely what Jensen did. He took a figure obtained (however questionably) to describe individual differences within a single group and used it to account for differences between groups.

There is considerable evidence that between-group variation in IQ scores arises from environmental, not inherited factors. Labov (1972) showed how there are systematic differences between the black and white populations of the United States: black families are more likely to suffer economic hardship and environmental deprivation than white people, and this can easily account for such differences. And Tyler (1965) showed that there were considerable differences between American black populations: black people living in the northern United States, where there was traditionally less social discrimination, scored systematically higher on IQ tests than those coming from the south – and scored higher, too, than several southern white groups.

There is another question which is raised by Jensen's argument, and this concerns population norms. As we saw in Box 6.2, ever since the very first IQ tests were developed, girls have scored more highly than boys, and women more highly than men. This difference was dealt with by adjusting the population norms of the tests: females must answer more questions correctly to gain the same IQ score. So if the IQ difference between blacks and whites was so important, why did they not simply adjust the population norms for those groups too? It is in the answer to this question that the implicit racism of the argument really becomes apparent. It was considered perfectly acceptable to adjust the population norms so as to compensate for men's lower performance, because that is a change which maintains the supremacy of the white middle-class male. But to adjust those same norms in order to compensate for blacks' lower performance would be to challenge the idea that the white middle-class

male is superior, and so, for the racists, it is out of the question.

Jensen's arguments relied almost entirely on Burt's statistics; and we saw earlier in this chapter that there is considerable doubt as to their reliability. But the reason why he achieved such acclaim was because he was putting a pseudo-scientific gloss on a political issue: he was legitimising the views of racists that black people were 'inferior', and providing a rationalisation for those who were objecting to their children attending mixed schools. Despite their spurious nature, his views are still quoted as 'proof' of the supposed inferiority of blacks in racist propaganda in both Britain and America.

The Bell Curve

In 1994, Herrnstein and Murray published a controversial book, *The Bell Curve*, in which they claimed that IQ was not only inherited, but that it also accounted for a significant proportion of social problems, among which they included poverty, crime, illegitimacy (i.e. single mothers) and dependency on welfare. The reference to the bell curve in the title of the book was the curve of the normal distribution, and their argument was that the normal distribution of intelligence in the population correlated with social problems, in that those of higher IQ were less likely to present social problems, of criminality etc., in society.

Herrnstein and Murray went on to revive Jensen's arguments about race and intelligence, arguing that the American African populations in the United States were disproportionately represented in the lower half of the bell curve, and that this reflected a genetic influence, rather than an environmental one. However, their arguments were no stronger than Jensen's had been. The confusion of between-group and within-group variance remained, as did the complete disregarding of the huge amount of evidence for the influence that upbringing, social values, and environment can have on intelligence test scores.

Those factors, of course, also have a huge effect on the individual's social **engagement** – the extent to which they feel that society's values and opportunities are relevant or achievable in their own lives. If one grows up in a subculture which sees only poverty and social inequality, it is difficult to acquire a conviction that working hard and getting educated will make much difference. But, of course, like many other such matters, social engagement was not considered by Herrnstein and Murray.

They did, however, purport to counter environmental arguments about intelligence – or at least, selected environmental arguments. For example, they did, reluctantly, admit that the gap in IQ between black and white American populations was narrowing, as education and social conditions for American black populations had improved. However, they also asserted dogmatically that this trend had ceased before 1990, and that a consistent gap between the two populations would remain. Williams and Ceci (1997), however, found that the gap was continuing to narrow. Other evidence against their arguments was dealt with in a similar manner. Effectively, like other books of this type, the authors ignored the important scientific challenges to what they were saying.

The book, of course, produced a storm of protest. The authors welcomed the storm and, rather sanctimoniously, represented it as attempted censorship. But as Gould (1997) and many others pointed out, the protests were nothing to do with censorship. They were to do with sloppy science masquerading as social concern, and having major social implications in the process. Herrnstein and Murray's arguments were superficially plausible, but they did not offer new evidence – indeed, they suffered from exactly the same inadequacies as other extreme hereditarian arguments had done before them.

Heritable factors

The environmentalist position on intelligence is often challenged as being unrealistic. It is clear that children do develop differently, and that there is considerable variation in temperament from one child to another. Bringing children up in the same way does not produce identical children. But in reality, there are very few modern environmentalists who would claim that it does. What environmentalists do challenge is the illogical reasoning and pseudo-biology of the extreme hereditarian position (such as their arguments about between-group differences, which are questionable both statistically and biologically); and the idea that intelligence, social success, crime, or just about anything else can be 'explained' by inherited factors.

Individual differences exist in every species of animal, and human beings are no exception. Babies differ from one another in all sorts of ways,

and variation in factors such as patience, curiosity, and observation are highly likely to influence the eventual intelligence of the child. But they do not produce the outcome on their own. Howe (1998) discussed how these variables are also shaped by parental interaction, by social values, and by the ways that the society which the child encounters foster or repress its abilities or talents.

It is not inconceivable, as psychologist Robert Plomin believes, that specific genes which have an influence on intelligence may eventually be identified. But the discovery that a particular gene code for a particular set of proteins which facilitate the development of abilities which may help an individual to produce intelligent behaviour is rather different from the idea of a 'gene for intelligence', as represented by hereditarian extremists. The abilities which such a gene may facilitate still have to be fostered, shaped, and channelled through the child's development, and in adult life; and the way in which that takes place is powerfully influenced by the social context in which the child grows up, the opportunities which it experiences, and, most importantly of all, the way that those opportunities are perceived and valued by the child and its 'significant others'.

As we have seen, and will continue to see throughout this book, human beings are highly social animals; and those social factors permeate both our development, and our adult lives. As a result there are, of course, correlations between measures such as those provided by IQ tests, and social success or its converse. But correlation is not causality. Both are influenced by widespread social factors – not just simplistic measures of income and socio-economic status, but also group differences in how social opportunities are perceived, social values, and personal attributions about causality. Any theory which fails to take account of these factors, and looks only for mechanistic correspondences between genetics and behaviour, cannot fail to be inadequate as an explanation for how human beings function, even though it may succeed in making its authors famous.

Theories of intelligence

As we have already seen, the position that a researcher takes regarding what intelligence is, determines how that researcher goes about investigating it, and what questions are asked. But intelligence is an elusive thing to pin down, as can be seen from the number of theories of intelligence that have been put forward by psychologists.

Defining intelligence

One of the first definitions of intelligence was developed by the psychologists responsible for the development of the first intelligence test, Binet and Simon (1905). They argued that the essence of intelligence is: '*to judge well, to comprehend well, to reason well*'. This is a very general view of intelligence, and one which does not try to be specific about actually defining what intelligence is, for reasons which will become apparent. Another general definition was provided by Heim, in 1970, who argued that '*intelligent activity consists in grasping the essentials in a situation and responding appropriately to them*'.

Other researchers, however, held different views. The factor-analytic theorists argued that basic aspects of intelligence could be pinned down: Spearman, as we saw earlier, believed that intelligence consisted of a general ability **g**, together with a number of different learned aptitudes, which he referred to collectively as s (Spearman, 1904). Terman (1916) described intelligence as '*the ability to carry on abstract thinking*', whereas Burt, as we have seen, regarded it as a fixed, inherited cognitive ability (Burt, 1955).

If we look closely at these general definitions of intelligence, we can see that they fall into two camps. Spearman, Terman and Burt quite clearly regard intelligence as an ability in its own right, with an independent existence. But both the Binet and Simon definition and that proposed by Heim describe intelligence in terms of how intelligence affects the way that people do things. There are other psychologists who share this view: for example, Estes (1982) argued that to think of intelligence as an independent entity in its own right is seriously misleading.

Intelligence, according to Estes, is a property of behaviour, jointly determined by cognitive functioning and motives. We perform an intelligent act, or ask an intelligent question. In other words, intelligence is an adjective, not a noun. This may seem like just a debate about words, but it actually represents an important distinction, concerned with the question of reification. Reification is the process of elevating a psychological property into a 'thing', as if it were some kind of ability in its own right, as opposed to a description of how something happens.

Rose, Kamin and Lewontin (1984) pointed out that reification is a familiar phenomenon within nature-nurture debates, and a significant one. It influences the direction which debates are likely to take. For example: if we regard a psychological property like intelligence or aggression as a separate, independent 'thing', the implication is that different people can have different amounts of it. If people have different amounts of it, then it becomes more plausible to argue that the amount they have is fixed (although we saw in Box 6.1 that the idea that an inherited property is fixed is questionable biologically). But if we regard intelligence or aggression as a property of behaviour, rather than as a 'thing' – as part of *how* people go about doing something – then the emphasis shifts. It becomes much more plausible that we could train people to act differently. So there are hidden political implications in the process of reification.

In reality, of course, what we consider to be intelligence is always associated with doing something. We do not look directly at intelligence – we look at intelligent behaviour, in some kind of context, even if that context is only how people tackle intelligence tests. This is why we might regard someone as highly intelligent in one way – say, very intelligent at computer programming, or academic work – yet not at all intelligent in other ways – say, being taken advantage of by other people. If intelligence were just one single ability, this would not be as likely.

Another problem with reification is that it does not really let us know where to go next. Howe (1990) questioned whether the concept of intelligence has any real value, arguing that using it as an 'explanation' does not actually tell us anything. Saying, for example, 'Jane is better at solving problems because she is more intelligent' may describe a state of affairs at the most, but it does not really help us to understand what is actually going on. Following a detailed study of **idiots savants** (people who have serious learning difficulties except for an exceptional intellectual ability in just one narrow area), Howe argued that such people simply represent extreme versions of normal skills (Howe, 1989). Most people, he argued, have a number of separate, independent skills, and to try to lump them all together as if they were all part of the same abstract phenomenon of 'intelligence' is not at all helpful.

The question of multiple intelligences

Howe's argument raises another issue in the attempt to define intelligence. Even researchers who believe in intelligence as an independent entity do not agree as to what that independent entity is like. This debate, which still exists today, centres on the existence of **g**. Is there a single **g** factor underlying apparently different forms of intelligence? Or does intelligence consist of a number of different, independent skills, operating independently of one another?

Thurstone

The debate has a long history. Thurstone (1938) saw intelligence as consisting of a set of primary mental abilities, all independent of one another. There were seven of these: verbal comprehension, verbal fluency, number, spatial visualisation, memory, reasoning, and perceptual speed. Tests based on this type of model, therefore, produce **profiles** rather than a single IQ score. This model is common in many of the individualised intelligence tests, like the Wechsler intelligence scales (see Table 6.3) which are commonly used in clinical assessments of intelligence.

Guilford's multifactorial theory of intelligence

Guilford (1967) argued that intelligence consisted of 120 different and independent skills, which he later expanded to 150 (Guilford, 1982). Each mental task, according to Guilford's model, consists of three kinds of components: a mental operation, a content, and a product. A **mental**

operation is concerned with how the mind goes about the task: the style or approach which it adopts. A **content** concerns the type of mental representation which is involved. And a **product** is concerned with the type of outcome which can result from the mental task. It is the different combinations of each of these which produces the 150 different cognitive skills involved in intelligence.

Guilford argued that there are five different types of mental operations, which he identified as being: (1) cognition; (2) memory; (3) divergent production; (4) convergent production; and (5) evaluation. Contents, in Guilford's model, are also of five types: (1) visual; (2) auditory; (3) symbolic; (4) semantic; and (5) behavioural. And there are six kinds of products: (1) units; (2) classes; (3) relations; (4) systems; (5) transformations; and (6) implications. Multiplying these together to produce all the possible combinations gives 150 different cognitive factors, each of which can be assessed by a different type of task. The model, Guilford argued, should be visualised as a kind of cube, composed of 150 smaller cubes (Figure 6.3).

Gardner's theory of multiple intelligences

A modern multiple-component theory of intelligence was proposed by Gardner (1985), who took a rather more extreme view. Instead of identifying independent skills working together to produce a general intelligence, Gardner proposed that we actually have different intelligences. This theory is based on the idea that the mind is not a holistic entity, but instead consists of distinct, independent modules. Intelligence, Gardner argued, is the com-

---

Table 6.3 Sub-tests of the Wechsler intelligence scales

Verbal scales	Performance scales
Information	Digit symbol
Comprehension	Picture completion
Arithmetic	Block design
Similarities	Picture arrangement
Digit span	Object assembly
Vocabulary	

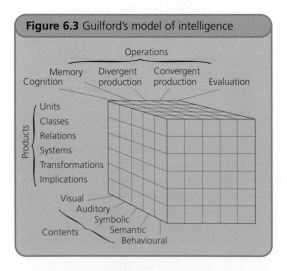

Figure 6.3 Guilford's model of intelligence

posite name that we give to reflections of the activities of those modules, but intelligence is not a single entity.

Gardner uses four main types of evidence on which to base this argument. One of these is **developmental** evidence, which outlines how the various aptitudes or skills develop as the individual ages. A second source is evidence from **brain damage** which affects specific functioning but not other functions. There is also evidence from **extreme cases,** such as idiots savants or those whom society perceives as 'geniuses'; and Gardner also included **evolutionary evidence** and accounts which indicate how a specific ability or aptitude might have evolved. According to Gardner, the evidence indicates that there are seven entirely different types of intelligence (see Table 6.4). Gardner proposed that each of these was an independent entity, having its own distinct biological source in the brain.

There are a number of criticisms which can be made of Gardner's approach, ranging from the methodological (for example, he tends to fall back on anecdotes as part of his evidence) to the conceptual – such as seeing calculation, mathematics and hypothesising as being effectively the same type of thing, which seems simplistic to some other psychologists. But perhaps one of the main problems is the acontextual nature of the theory – in other words, the way that the different intelligences are treated as though their social and cultural context is unimportant.

Language, for example, is treated entirely as if it were an individual cognitive skill – the social functions of language are entirely ignored. Yet, as we saw in Chapter 4, this is unrealistic: social factors are an essential aspect of both language acquisition and language use. In fact, social factors are generally ignored in Gardner's theory, except for interpersonal intelligence itself. There is no consideration of social factors as they concern other skills: the assumption seems to be that the intelligences are independent, individual abilities which develop in the individual as if they were independent of any context, and which can be assessed formally using psychometric tests.

However, there are several advantages to Gardner's theory, as well. In particular, it seems better able to encompass some of the oddities about human intelligence than other theories such as the existence of musical genius or idiots savants. Any theory needs to be able to explain how people can differ from the norm, as well as how people conform to it. Gardner makes a serious attempt to do just that.

Sternberg's triarchic theory of intelligence

An alternative model of intelligence, and one which seems to offer the possibility of integrating a number of very different aspects of intelligence, is the **triarchic theory of intelligence**, developed by Sternberg in 1985. This theory proposes that there are three distinct aspects to human intelligence, working together to produce what we consider to be intelligent behaviour or intelligent action on the part of a given individual. So Sternberg's theory consists of three separate sub-theories, each of which deals with one of these aspects.

Contextual intelligence

The first sub-theory is that of **contextual intelligence**, which is concerned with intelligence

Table 6.4 Seven types of intelligence	
Linguistic intelligence	used when reading, writing or comprehending speech.
Musical intelligence	used in musical appreciation, composition and performance.
Mathematical-logical intelligence	used in arithmetic, numerical calculation and logical reasoning.
Spatial intelligence	used in arranging objects spatially, as well as in visual art and finding one's way around.
Bodily-kinaesthetic intelligence	used in sport, dancing or simple everyday movement and dexterity.
Interpersonal intelligence	used in relating to others, interpreting social signals and predicting social outcomes.
Intrapersonal intelligence	used in understanding and predicting one's own behaviour, and in identifying aspects of the self and one's own personality.

Source: Gardner, 1985

within its socio-cultural setting. Within this sub-theory, intelligence is treated as mental activity which is directed towards purposive activity in the real world. In other words, it helps people to select appropriate stimuli or contexts for living, to shape their environment to fit personal or cultural needs or to adapt themselves to the relevant environments and contexts which they encounter during everyday life. This sub-theory proposes that intelligent acts cannot be seen as abstract, context-free actions: they take place within a context, and we do them for a reason. Those contexts and reasons shape the kinds of acts which we perform, and also how we go about performing them.

This aspect, therefore, makes the triarchic theory distinctive among theories of intelligence, in the sense that it is far more capable than most of dealing with the diversity of cultures and environments in which human beings live, and of acknowledging cultural differences in what constitutes intelligent behaviour. Indeed, Sternberg argues that it is not possible to understand intelligence outside a socio-cultural context. Although there may be aspects of intelligence which are universal, transcending cultural boundaries, the culture will determine whether these are emphasised or valued, or whether they are minimised and devalued. Quickness of thought and action, for instance, might be valued in Western culture, but is regarded far less favourably in some Asian cultures. So even universal properties of intelligence can manifest themselves differently in different cultures.

Also, the same underlying cognitive skill may manifest itself entirely differently from one culture to the next. So, for example, the cognitive skill concerned with spatial perception might be involved in two very different cultural contexts: travelling from island to island in a traditional Polynesian culture which utilises navigation by the stars, or a Western architect's design work. But that basic skill would have developed quite differently in the two cultures, and could not be assessed without taking this into account. Some fundamental elements of intelligence may, Sternberg argues, be found universally; but since their expression, development and social weighting will differ, their practical manifestations will be very different.

Experiential intelligence

The second sub-theory of the triarchic model is that of **experiential intelligence,** which is all

about how someone's own past experience influences how they go about a given task or situation. In other words, it addresses the way that we accumulate skills and knowledge as a result of our personal life-experiences. The way this life-experience manifests itself in intelligence, according to Sternberg, can be summarised in terms of the development of two fundamental skills. The first of these is the ability to deal with situational demands, and the second is the ability to automatise information-processing.

Different types of life-situations make different demands on us, and the experience we have had will affect our ability to handle them. Someone who has led a very narrow, restricted life with very little exposure to unusual or unexpected events is likely to have a limited range of options to choose from, if they are faced with something that is unusual or different. Within their accustomed situation, they may be perfectly competent, but if a situational demand, as Sternberg called it, is entirely outside your previous experience, it stands to reason that you are not likely to grasp the best way of handling it immediately. Someone who has experienced a variety of situations and circumstances, on the other hand, will have a greater knowledge of options and alternatives, so they are likely to be able to deal with a wider range of unusual or different events.

Coping with situational demands also includes handling interactions between different circumstances, and here too our personal experience is helpful. For example: an experienced teacher may use their knowledge of their students in judging which ones can work under pressure and which ones cannot. So if a school event is coming up at the same time as some coursework deadlines, they may choose only those who are good at working under pressure to help out with the organisation, knowing that they will be able to cope with the additional tasks. A judgement like this involves balancing knowledge about the students with two other circumstances: the nature of the tasks to be done, and the time-factor. For Sternberg, situational demands include the demands produced by interactions between tasks, situations and people, as well as the demands produced by novel tasks and situations.

The second fundamental skill developed as part of experiential intelligence is the ability to automatise information-processing. This involves the development of a range of habitual routines, so that task requirements do not represent such a great cognitive demand on the individual (see Chapter 2). For example, when we are first learning to drive, each sequence of actions is novel, and needs concentration, so the whole process involves a considerable cognitive demand. That is why people who are just learning, or have only just passed their driving test, do not generally find it very easy to talk as they drive. But as it becomes more familiar, these processes do not demand as much attention, because they have become automatised routines. As we saw in Chapter 4, purely cognitive skills can also become routinised, and the reason why it is important for children to have a great deal of practice in reading is because in fluent reading, word-recognition and scanning processes have become automatised. Because they are cognitively easier, they free the child's attention, so that it can be devoted more to the content of what is being read.

The personal life-experiences which someone has had will have provided the opportunity for a number of different skills to have become routinised. If you watch people playing darts, for example, you may notice that some people can perform complex subtractions from 301 or 501 almost instantaneously, whereas others have to work it out more slowly. For some, the calculations have become routinised, so they do not represent as much of a cognitive demand. For others, they are more demanding. And, of course, the more **practice** we have at such skills, the more likely we are to routinise them. Sternberg argues that, since individuals vary so much in how much their lives have allowed fundamental skills to develop, it is important to take this into account when looking at intelligence. A full theory of intelligence, he argues, needs to be able to recognise and explore the nature of this variation.

Componential intelligence

The third sub-theory in the triarchic model is that of componential intelligence. Componential intelligence is all about the cognitive mechanisms which underlie intelligent functioning. This sub-theory actually represents an older theory of intelligence (Sternberg, 1977), in which he classified the components of intelligence in two ways: function, or what they actually did, and level of generality, or how specific or general their targets were. This model proposed that there were three types of cognitive components which go to make

up componential intelligence: metacomponents, performance components and knowledge-acquisition components.

Metacomponents, in Sternberg's model, are the higher-order processes involved in mental actions such as planning and decision-making. So they would include things like working out what it is reasonable to do in the time available, or taking into account different factors influencing a problem. Performance components are those components which are involved in actually carrying out a task – like the ability to count or calculate, or reason logically. Knowledge-acquisition components are concerned with how we go about acquiring or learning new information: strategies for identifying important features or patterns, curiosity, and so on.

The important thing about this sub-theory is the way that it addresses the problem of what intelligence tests should contain. As we have seen in this chapter, the history of intelligence testing suggests that items in intelligence tests have often reflected social assumptions or used culturally specific problems. Partly, this happened because of the rather ad hoc nature of the tasks involved: for the most part, IQ test developers tended to include items in tests because they seemed to work. That does not mean that just anything was included, of course, because the need for extensive reliability checks meant that some items were systematically weeded out. But for the most part, the selection of test items was pragmatic rather than being informed by theory.

Sternberg's model, on the other hand, suggests what types of test items should be included in the development of a given test. Test items, Sternberg argues, should be chosen on the basis of what they will tell us about the components of intelligence, not just on a pragmatic or operational basis. According to Sternberg's model, an IQ test would need to include items to assess each of the different components. Some test items would need to assess planning, decision-making or other aspects of metacomponents; others would need to look explicitly at performance components, by assessing how people go about specific tasks; while a third group of test items would need to look at knowledge-acquisition components. To assess componential intelligence properly, these items would need to be evenly balanced throughout the test.

Although it is the componential sub-theory within Sternberg's triarchic model of intelligence which is most highly developed, the theory allows for a much greater recognition of the way that intelligence works in practice through its emphasis on contextual and experiential aspects as equally important parts of intelligence. It also suggests that it may be possible, in the future, to develop ways of assessing intelligence which might acknowledge more fully the importance of culture and experience. Any fully comprehensive model of human intelligence needs to be capable of acknowledging the diversity and multiplicity of human cultures and experience, while at the same time recognis-

ing that human beings all over the world do have something in common. It is possible that Sternberg's triarchic model may provide the opportunity to do that. At the very least, it leaves these possibilities open.

In the next chapter, we will go on to look at some of the models of human personality which have been proposed by psychologists. While some theories of personality, like some theories of intelligence, have a basis in psychometrics, others have stemmed from rather different origins, and make very different assumptions.

Key terms

alternate-forms method A system for judging how reliable a psychometric test is, which involves comparing the results produced by two different versions of the same test, if they are given to the same subjects.

between-group variance The general variation which is apparent between different samples of scores, such as the difference in height between, say, Pygmies and Europeans.

componential intelligence The part of Sternberg's triarchic model of intelligence which is concerned with, and consists of, mental process and skills.

concurrent validity A method for assessing whether a psychometric test is valid (i.e. really measures what it is supposed to) by comparing it with some other measure which has been taken at the same time – i.e. which is occurring concurrently.

construct validity A method for assessing whether a psychometric test is valid (i.e. really measures what it is supposed to) by seeing how it matches up with theoretical ideas about what it is supposed to be measuring.

correlation coefficient A number between −1 and +1 which expresses how strong a correlation is. If this number is close to 0, there is no real connection between the two; if it is close to +1 there is a positive correlation – in other words, if one variable is large the other will also tend to be large; and if it is close to −1, there is a negative correlation – in other words, if one variable is large, the other will tend to be small.

criterion validity A method for assessing whether a psychometric test is valid (i.e. really measures what it is supposed to) by comparing it with some other measure. If the other measure is assessed at roughly the same time as the original one, then the

type of criterion validity being applied is concurrent validity; if it is taken much later, it is predictive validity.

dialectical An interrelationship in which two apparently opposite or opposing entities or ideas combine to form an entirely new synthesis. Each influences the other and is influenced by it, such that together the relationship produces something new.

ecological validity A way of assessing how valid a measure or test is (i.e. whether it really measures what it is supposed to measure) which is concerned with whether the measure or test is really like its counterpart in the real, everyday world. In other words, whether it is truly realistic or not.

eugenics The political idea that the human race could be improved by eliminating 'undesirables' from the breeding stock, so that they cannot pass on their supposedly inferior genes. Some eugenicists advocate compulsory sterilisation, while others seem to prefer mass murder or genocide.

experiential intelligence The part of Sternberg's triarchic theory of intelligence which is concerned with what the individual has learned from their own personal experience.

face validity Whether a test or measure looks on the surface as though it probably measures what it is supposed to.

factor analysis A method of statistical analysis which examines intercorrelations between data in order to identify major clusters or groupings which might be caused by a single common factor.

g The abbreviation for 'general intelligence': a kind of intelligence which is supposed to underpin all different types of mental operations, as opposed to more specific types of talents or aptitudes.

Gaussian distribution A statistical distribution illustrated by a bell-shaped curve. Also known as the normal distribution.

genotype The total set of potential inherited characteristics present in an individual's chromosomes.

heritability A numerical value assigned to intelligence on the misleading assumption that it is possible to separate and quantify inherited and learned components.

idiots savants People who appear mentally retarded with respect to general intellectual abilities, yet show outstanding mental ability in one narrow area – like being able to add up extremely rapidly and accurately, or calculate the days of the week of any specific date in the past few thousand years.

intelligence quotient (IQ) A numerical figure, believed by some to indicate the level of a person's intelligence, which indicates how well that person performs on intelligence tests.

normal distribution curve A pattern of scores, distributed on a graph, which appears on that graph as a bell-shaped curve. Also known as the Gaussian distribution, this has mathematical properties which mean that the probability, or likelihood, of a given score can be calculated, simply by knowing the value of the mean and the standard deviation.

parametric test A statistical test which is used on the assumption that the data would, if a large enough sample were obtained, produce a normal distribution.

phenotype The physical characteristics which an individual develops, as evidence of the interaction between their genetic structure and the environment in which they have developed.

predictive validity A method of assessing whether a psychometric test is valid (i.e. really measures what it is supposed to) by seeing how well it correlates with some other measure, which is assessed later, after the test has been taken.

reification The process of treating an adverb as if it were a noun – e.g. seeing 'acting intelligently' as if it were a manifestation of some kind of entity called 'intelligence'.

split-half method A system for judging how reliable a psychometric test is, which involves splitting the test into two, administering each half of the test to the same people, then comparing the results.

standardisation (a) The process of making sure that the conditions of a psychological study or psychometric test are always identical; (b) the process of establishing how the results of a psychometric test will usually come out in a given population, by drawing up sets of population norms; (c) the process of comparing a new psychometric test with older, more established measures of the same thing.

test-retest method A system for judging how reliable a psychometric test or measure is, which involves administering the same test to the same people on two different occasions, and comparing the results.

triarchic theory of intelligence A theory of intelligence developed by Sternberg (1985) which argues that intelligence needs to be understood from three distinct viewpoints: (a) the cultural and social context in which an intelligent act occurs; (b) how the person's own previous experience has shaped their responses; and (c) the mental skills and abilities involved in solving problems.

validity The question of whether a psychometric test or psychological measure is really measuring what it is supposed to.

within-group variance Individual differences in behaviour, physique or abilities which occur among members of a given social group or category; e.g. the natural variation in height among members of the same group of pygmies.

Summary

1 The psychology of intelligence has developed in a highly political social context, as the outcomes of psychological research have been used as justification for social stratification, educational policy and eugenics.

2 The first IQ tests were developed by Binet at the beginning of the century, and aimed to identify those who would benefit from special schooling. Binet did not believe they could or should be used as labels.

3 The first IQ tests combined Binet's work with that of Galton, and were used to classify and compare individuals. This led to a number of questionable social applications.

4 Binet's tests had adopted the age-correlation method, but Spearman's work on factor analysis produced a new form of IQ testing, which led to debates about whether there was a general intelligence, as opposed to several specific skills.

5 Cyril Burt's data on twin studies were highly influential, but appear to have resulted from scientific fraud. More reputable investigations of nature-nurture issues in intelligence include twin studies and adoption studies, but their overall results are equivocal.

6 There are several possible criticisms of validity and standardisation in IQ testing, and also of cultural bias in IQ tests. Arguments that differences between black and white Americans arise from inherited factors, have been thoroughly discredited.

7 Theories of intelligence have tended to be of two kinds: those which see intelligence as an adjective, or a property of action, and those which see it as a reified, abstract entity. Gardner took the latter idea further, proposing that there may be several different, independent intelligences.

8 Sternberg proposed the triarchic theory of intelligence, which argued that any account of intelligence must deal with cultural and social factors and personal experience as well as mental components.

Self-assessment questions

1 Describe the age-correlation approach to assessing intelligence.

2 What can twin studies tell us about intelligence?

3 What are the three subtheories in the triarchic theory of intelligence?

Practice essay questions

1 'The development of intelligence testing directly contradicted Binet's original intentions'. Discuss.

2 Discuss, giving evidence, the idea that intelligence is genetically determined.

3 Compare and contrast Sternberg's triarchic theory of intelligence with Gardner's multiple intelligence theory.

Test your knowledge of this chapter with our online quizzes and games at: http://www.psych.co.uk

Explore intelligence further at:

Intelligence testing
http://www.queendom.com/tests.html – Links to assorted tests and related pages. Lots of fun.
http://www.apa.org/science/test.html – Frequently asked questions are answered in this helpful tutorial.
http://ericae.net/ – Links to resources, research, bibliographies and tests. Very useful as a starting point.

History/theories
http://www.ed.psu.edu/ – Penn State University Website. Searching for Gardner leads to useful information on multiple intelligences and related topics.

http://www.theatlantic.com/issues/95sep/ets/grtsort1.htm – First part of Richard Lenman's instructive article on the history of the Educational Testing Service. The second part is at http://www.theatlantic.com/issues/95sep/ets/grtsort2.htm

http://www.apa.org/journals/bell.html – Two views of the impact of *The Bell Curve*.

http://www.gwu.edu/~tip/theories.html – Links to articles on several intelligence theories including the triarchic theory and the structure of intellect theory.

Theories of personality

```
                    Issues                          Theories

Early      Narrow band    Types of    Psychoanalytic   Trait   Behavioural   Phenomeno-
approaches  approaches     theory                                             logical
```

Everyone is different, yet we also have things in common. Coming to terms with human individuality and what makes an individual personality is one of the most fascinating questions in psychology. The model of personality which we hold is crucial for our perception of human beings – it gives us our underlying beliefs about what human beings are really like. As with many other aspects of psychology, there is no one single answer – no model which is able to account for everything about human beings. Rather, different theories of personality adopt different levels of explanation, and seek to explain different features of human beings. In this chapter we will be looking at a number of different theories of personality. As you read through these theories, it is worth asking yourself what this theory is saying about what human beings are really like, and what the proponents of the theory think is the most important question about human beings.

There are a number of philosophical issues, too, which are raised by the various theories of personality. One of these is the question of **determinism**. Determinism, as we saw in Chapter 1, is all about whether human beings have free will or not. We all feel, for the most part, as if our behaviour is under our own control; but at the same time we recognise that we are influenced by other things as well. So, to phrase the question in an extreme form: are we free agents, or are we just the puppets of some external agency?

Determinist thinking within personality theory can take a number of different forms, depending on what is seen as the influencing agent or agents. So if we are examining a theory for determinism, we need to ask: are people regarded as being able to make genuine choices, and to direct their own lives? Or are the choices that they make seen, in this theory, as being pre-determined in some way, by forces or agencies outside their control?

Another issue to look out for in theories of personality is the question of **reductionism**. Reductionist accounts of human behaviour are often very popular, because they seem attractively simple. They consist of arguments which reduce the subject matter to its constituent parts, and then assert that there is nothing more to be explained. So a reductionist account of human personality, for example, might look for the basic units or factors which make up personality, and say that this is all there is.

As we saw in Chapter 1, however, reductionist modes of explanation have serious limitations. Simply taking a clock apart and examining the components may tell us a great deal about precision engineering, but it cannot tell us anything about what the clock did when it was working, or what the symbols on the clock face meant, or the significance of twelve o'clock. There is more to understanding the whole than simply analysing its parts, although looking at the parts can often be helpful.

Just identifying component parts does not automatically make a theory reductionist: any phenomenon will have many different aspects, ranging through cultural significance, personal meaning and components. But a theory which sees personality as *nothing* but its components, arguing that once these have been identified there is nothing else to be explained, is a reductionist theory – and often far too limited to be of much value in understanding human beings.

At the end of this chapter we will look at some of the other general issues that have arisen from the study of personality, but for now we will go on to examine some of the theories that psychologists have put forward.

Early theories of personality

People have been interested in personality from the very earliest times. Most psychological knowledge with regard to the history of psychology comes from the European tradition, in the Greek and the Roman cultures. Different theories about the nature of the human being emerged in the ancient Asian, Indian and African cultures, but the lack of recognition of these meant that it was the early European models which influenced the thinking of the personality psychologists.

Personality domains

In the second century BC, the Greek physician Galen outlined a theory of personality which stated that there were essentially three domains of the human psyche: the **cognitive**, or intellectual domain, the **conative**, or intentional domain, and the **affective**, or emotional, domain. Each of these was important in human functioning: the image which Galen used was of a charioteer driving two horses. The conative and affective domains formed the driving force of human behaviour, and the cognitive domain guided and directed how these energies were expended. In later years, when the behaviourist tradition focused psychological attention on behaviour rather than intentions, the conative domain became renamed the behavioural domain, and in that form this distinction is still used in attitude theory today. We will be coming across it again in Chapter 17.

The theory of the humours

Throughout the Middle Ages, the popular model of human personality was the theory of the humours. This was also one of the first examples of **physiological determinism** in personality theory – the idea that personality was shaped by physiological factors. The idea inherent in this theory was that the body contained different humours, or fluids; and that different personality types arose from one of the four fluids predominating in the body. As we can see from Box 7.1, many of the words that we still use to describe moods or personality come from this

theory – even the way that we use the word 'humour'!

Phrenology

An alternative model of personality, which gradually superseded the theory of the humours and became extremely popular in Britain and Europe, was **phrenology**. This theory, put forward by Gall at the beginning of the nineteenth century, and later modified by his colleague Spurzheim, was the idea that the human mind consisted of various 'faculties', located in particular areas of the brain. These faculties could be highly developed or less so, and it was the extent to which they were developed which determined whether the individual possessed that particular personality trait, and to what degree.

There were three main types of mental faculty described by Gall's theory: **affective faculties**, which were concerned with emotional responses towards other people, such as 'amativeness' (a

---

Box 7.1 The humours

One of the earliest theories of personality, dating from the Ancient Greeks and very popular throughout mediaeval Europe, was the idea that personality depended on the balance of fluids in the body. The idea was that there were four basic body fluids: blood, phlegm, black bile and yellow bile. Some people characteristically had a higher proportion of one fluid than of the others, and this was thought to produce their different personalities. Cheerful, energetic and lively personalities were thought to have a greater preponderance of blood, while those who were calm and placid were deemed to have a greater proportion of phlegm. A high proportion of black bile was believed to produce gloomy, 'melancholic' characters, whereas a high proportion of yellow bile, or choler, was believed to produce hasty and hot-tempered individuals. These four basic types of personality were thought to account for individual differences in temperament and personality.

There are references to this theory in Shakespeare – Hamlet was a classic melancholic – and in many other writers, right up to the last century. We can see how very influential this theory was, in the traces it has left in our language. It is even the source of the word

'humour', meaning mood, since body fluids were referred to as humours. Many other personality or personality linked words come from this theory too: the word 'sanguine' describes the characteristics of someone who was thought to have an excess of blood, coming as it does from the French word *sang*, meaning 'blood', and the word 'ruddy' originally had the same meaning. The extreme behaviours produced by high fever and raving were thought to come from an excess of blood, and it was from this idea that the practice of blood-letting arose.

The other humours were not left out. Calm, placid individuals are still described as 'phlegmatic', while intolerant and hot-tempered people are still referred to as 'choleric'. The word 'melancholic' originally referred to an individual with a preponderance of black bile, and is now still used to describe the mood that this humour was believed to produce. Also, we commonly refer to someone who is melancholic as being in a 'black' mood. These common phrases and idioms in our language show how very well-known and widespread this theory was.

tendency towards being loving); sentiments, such as hope or reverence; and reflective powers and perceptual capacities, such as musical tune, language and sensitivity to visual forms. There were some 37 different faculties in all, distributed in different locations on the skull (see Figure 7.1). Gall argued that it was possible to tell how highly developed any given faculty was by means of the bumps and indentations on the surface of the skull, and expert 'phrenologists' were even consulted as character witnesses in court!

Somatotypes

In the first part of the twentieth century the emphasis shifted to **somatotypes**: theories of personality which were based on bodily shape. Of several such theories, the most well known are those of Kretschmer (1925) and Sheldon (1954). Kretschmer argued that specific mental illnesses tended to be associated with specific bodily shapes: schizophrenia was most commonly found in people who were frail and thin, known as 'asthenic' types. 'Pyknic' types, or people who were plump and rounded in shape, were more likely to be suffering from manic-depressive psychosis, whereas Kretschmer asserted that the third type of physique, the strong muscular type that he called 'athletic', rarely suffered from mental illness (Figure 7.2).

Sheldon (1942) conducted a study which involved photographing the body shapes of 4000 college students, in which he first classified them according to physical type and then looked for temperamental correlations. (There was some controversy about this in the 1990s, when it emerged that the American President Bill Clinton and his wife Hilary had been among the students photographed in their underwear, and that the photograph negatives still existed.) Sheldon maintained the basic distinctions of somatotype outlined by Kretschmer, referring to them as ectomorphs (thin, frail people), mesomorphs (robust, muscular people) and endomorphs (plump, rounded people). He argued that ectomorphs showed pronounced tendencies to be introspective, restrained characters; mesomorphs tended to be hearty and insensitive; while endomorphs tended to be jolly and easy-going. However, the fact that Sheldon did all his own classifications and personality judgements means that these results, although from an exceptionally large sample, are open to question.

Psychoanalytic theories

Psychoanalytic theories of personality originated with the work of Sigmund Freud, in the later half of the nineteenth century and the beginning of the twentieth, but Freud's work was followed by that of many others. Unlike most modern psychological research and theory, the psychoanalytic approach adopts different methodological criteria. In particular, it emphasises the notion of 'psychological truth' – the idea that material reality is largely irrelevant in understanding the human

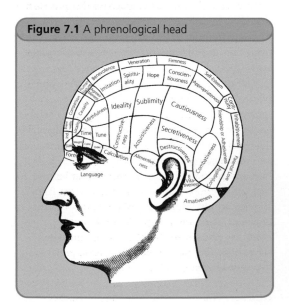

Figure 7.1 A phrenological head

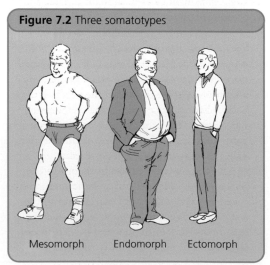

Figure 7.2 Three somatotypes

Mesomorph   Endomorph   Ectomorph

psyche, since much psychological reality is concerned with unconscious wish-fulfilment and memories of early experience. As a result, what counts as evidence in psychoanalytic theory is rather different from that which counts as evidence in the rest of psychology.

Freud

Freud developed his theory in the last century, strongly influenced by the work of Charcot in Paris, who used hypnosis to produce psychological 'cures' of difficult conditions which would not respond to other forms of treatment. Freud was also influenced by an older colleague, Josef Breuer, who had shown that some serious physical symptoms could be alleviated if the patients were allowed to talk freely about themselves and their lives (Breuer and Freud, 1895). Both Charcot and Breuer were specifically concerned with the illness known as hysteria, in which serious, often very painful, physical symptoms occurred, mainly in women, with no detectable physical origin. The common theory of the day was that it originated as a disease of the womb (the term 'hysteria' reflected this, having the same linguistic root as 'uterus'), but Freud's theory presented an entirely different explanation.

Freud used what were then some very new methods of **free-association** – the analysis of minor slips of the tongue and interpretation of dream symbols – to identify aspects of the unconscious mind. Freud was, essentially, a materialist, even though his notion of what was material evidence was rather different from what might be accepted today. Because of this, he considered that the interesting, and sometimes apparently inexplicable, responses which resulted from these methods provided material evidence of the working of an unconscious mind, which operated in an entirely different way from the conscious mind.

As his theory developed, Freud formulated a model of the mind as being constructed a bit like an iceberg, with four-fifths of it buried under the surface. The **conscious mind** represented the part of the iceberg above the surface, clearly visible and apparent to the individual. The part of the iceberg immediately below the surface, sometimes revealed by the ebb and flow of waves, was the **preconscious** mind. This consisted of thoughts, ideas and beliefs which might temporarily be forgotten but which could be retrieved easily when

they were wanted. But there was also a large, invisible, submerged part of the iceberg, which represented the **unconscious** mind. This contained all kinds of disturbing and emotionally significant ideas and memories, and exerted a powerful, though unseen, influence on the conscious and preconscious minds (Freud, 1901).

The concerns of the unconscious mind were not normally accessible to consciousness. There was no point, Freud reasoned, simply asking people about their deeper motivations or anxieties, because these were lodged in the unconscious mind, so the person would not be able to describe them – and generally would not even know anything about their existence. But these deep motivations and anxieties exerted a continual pressure on the conscious mind nonetheless, and could be detected in a disguised form, when the conscious mind was off-guard. The techniques of free association, dream analysis and the careful examination of minor slips of the tongue, in Freud's view, allowed these concerns to surface, providing material evidence of the contents of the unconscious mind.

Id, ego and super-ego

Freud saw the adult personality as having three basic components: the id, the ego and the super-ego. The id and the super-ego were both unconscious, but exerting pressure on the ego, which was the part of the mind in direct contact with reality. According to Freud, a young infant has only an **id** – the other two parts of the personality develop later. The id was the primaeval, impulsive part of the personality, demanding instant gratification of all of its demands. It was unrealistic, selfish and demanding, working on what Freud described as the **pleasure principle** – the idea that every impulse should be satisfied, immediately.

As a young child grows older, though, reality intervenes. The imperious demanding of the young child gives way to a realisation that some things are simply not possible, or not going to happen, and that it is necessary to make some adjustments in order to achieve any of its desires. At this point, in the Freudian model, an offshoot of the id develops which is in touch with the realistic demands of the outside world, and tries to pacify the id by compromising with reality. This part of the mind becomes the **ego**. The ego, according to Freud, operates according to the **reality principle**, trying to balance the demands of the unconscious mind with what is practical.

As the child grows older still, it comes into contact with authority. Freud, it is important to remember, was developing his theory in Victorian times, when strict discipline was enforced on virtually all middle-class children, and the father of the family was generally a remote, disciplinarian figure (the lack of a welfare state structure meant that working-class children grew up entirely differently, and their development was not really considered in this model). The developing middle-class child's life, then, became filled with rules, principles and duties, generally imposed by a strict and austere parent. As the child matured, these rules became internalised into the personality: rather than an external one, the child developed a kind of internalised, unconscious 'parent', which contained strict ideas of propriety, duty, conscience and obligations. This is known as the **super-ego**.

In its own way, the super-ego is as unrealistic as the id. Where the id is impulsive and over-reacting, for example reacting with murderous rage rather than anger, the super-ego would demand total commitment to the most rigid demands even at the cost of health and self. The role of the ego is, therefore, to maintain a balance between their conflicting pressures, and also to keep on an even keel with the demands of reality. According to Freud, the ego maintained a state of **dynamic equilibrium** between these different pressures – a kind of balancing act, giving in a little to one source and then compensating by giving in a little to another.

In Freud's model of the mind, then, the unconscious parts of the mind are continually trying to break through to dominate the consciousness, but they are held back by the ego. The ego, therefore, experiences three sources of threat: those from the id, those from the super-ego and those from reality itself. In order to cope with these, it uses **defence mechanisms**. Some of the major ego defence mechanisms outlined by Freud are described in Table 7.1.

Table 7.1 Some ego-defence mechanisms

Denial	Where the conscious mind refuses to acknowledge the existence of the potential threat, e.g. living in San Francisco and refusing to think about the possiblity of a serious earthquake, because the implications of taking the idea seriously are too traumatic to acknowledge.
Repression	Where a past event was so deeply traumatic that the memory of it becomes buried, and the person has no recollection of it happening, e.g. in some particularly unpleasant cases of child abuse, where the adult has no conscious recollection of the event, but is nonetheless powerfully influenced by it.
Regression	Reverting to an earlier state, generally in response to frustration or inability to cope, e.g. bursting into tears at moments of crisis, which may be an example of regression to a childhood dependency, when such behaviour would be answered by an adult stepping in and making things better.
Projection	The externalisation of internal unconscious wishes, desires or emotions on to other people, e.g. someone who feels subconsciously that they have a powerful latent homosexual drive may not acknowledge this consciously, but it may show in their readiness to suspect other of being homosexual.
Reaction-formation	Where a powerful unconscious impulse is repressed so strongly that the person reacts against it by becoming deeply hostile to anyone else manifesting the same impulses. The classic example of this is homophobia, where the person is actively hostile to homosexuals, in a reaction formation against their own unconscious homosexual drives.
Identification with the aggressor	Where the conflict and anger caused by being powerless against an aggressor is coped with by a kind of reaction-formation in which the individual comes to identify strongly with that person or style. The classic example here is that of the authoritarian personality, in which the child's anger in response to rigidly authoritarian parents is repressed so strongly that they come to identify with those parents and project their hostility on to other targets.

Early experience and personality

Freud argued that adult personality was set by experiences which had occurred during infancy and childhood. He saw the first five years of the child's life as being crucial in determining sexual orientation and other aspects of personality. One of the key concepts in that area is that of **fixation** – the idea that the individual may become 'stuck' at some early stage of development rather than progressing through it and on to a later stage.

For Freud, sexual energy, or **libido**, was the main life-affirming force in the human psyche. Later on in his career he also described a negative, life-destroying tendency in the human psyche, which he called **thanatos**, and which he postulated in an attempt to explain the carnage of WWI (Freud, 1920). But in the early years of his theory, it was the libido which was all-important, and the source of all pleasurable experiences.

In the young infant, Freud believed, the libido was focused on the mouth, and infants could derive great satisfaction from oral activity: at this time, the young child would automatically put anything new to its mouth. Freud called this the **oral stage**. A child which became orally fixated at this time, through weaning which was either too early or too late, would, according to Freud, be likely to become an adult with an excessive interest in oral stimulation. They might become a gourmet, enjoying the taste of food, or they might smoke, or be constantly chewing on pencils, fingernails, and the like.

In addition, the nature of the pleasure which the child experienced in the oral stage could leave a lasting effect on personality. Essentially, the child could derive pleasure from two types of activity: sucking and swallowing, or biting and chewing. Too much of either, Freud considered, could have lasting effects. A child which derived excessive pleasure from sucking and swallowing would become highly gullible and trusting (liable to 'swallow' any story); while a child which derived excessive pleasure from chewing and biting would be likely to become verbally aggressive and sarcastic.

Once the infant was weaned, the libido moved to focus on the anus, and the child began to derive great pleasure from defecating. This was known as the **anal stage**, and fixation on this stage too could result in an excessive interest in this physiological function in later life. Moreover, if parents were too strict during toilet training,

Freud argued, then the child could become an **anal-retentive** personality. The infant seeking to hold on to its faeces would eventually become the adult seeking to hold on to its possessions, and it would develop into a miser, or perhaps an obsessional collector. But if the parents were too lenient, the child would become **anal-expulsive**, becoming overly generous and giving in adult life.

It can be seen, then, that Freud's theory presented infant care as a tortuous path: mothers had to ensure that the child was not weaned too early or late, and that it was toilet-trained at exactly the right age, and so on. They were told, moreover, that failure to achieve these things could result in lasting damage to their child. Ehrenreich and English (1973) argued that this aspect of Freudian theory represented the first major step in the alienation of mothers from the process of bringing up their children. By inculcating such extreme anxieties, it devalued traditional child-rearing practices and encouraged the intervention of external 'experts': a development which ultimately resulted in a whole industry of child-care experts, and a systematic denigration of traditional female knowledge.

Sex-role identification

At the age of five or so, Freud saw the young child as having to resolve its sexual identity. The male child did so, he argued, through the **Oedipal conflict**. The libido was now in the **phallic stage**, focused on the genitals, and at this time the young boy developed an unconscious longing to possess his mother. The father, however, was a rival for his mother's love, and very much larger and more powerful than the small child. This meant, according to Freud, that the young boy developed an unconscious **castration threat anxiety** – worried that his father would deal with competition by these drastic means.

Since living with such anxiety was intolerable, the boy had to resolve it in some way. This was achieved by the ego-defence mechanism known as identification with the aggressor. Working unconsciously on the principle that his father would be less likely to be hostile to him if he saw him as being an ally, the boy stressed how similar he was to his father, and tried to become as 'masculine' and like his father as possible. In this way, he came to adopt his gender role, and to identify as male.

Little girls, on the other hand, were supposed to

become aware (unconsciously) that they had been born without a penis and to develop **penis envy**. This, according to Freud, was eventually resolved by their wishing to bear children for their father – the child being a penis substitute. There is considerable contention as to whether Freud meant this concept to be taken literally, or used as symbolic of the powerlessness of women in Victorian society. It is also open to question as to how young girls were supposed to come to such an awareness in an era when middle-class children were even bathed in their shifts so that they would not catch sight of their own bodies – let alone anyone else's!

Later psychoanalytic theorists added the idea of an **Electra conflict**, in which the young girl was supposed to see herself, unconsciously, as having been castrated. She blames her mother for this, which produces a conflict similar to that of the young boy and his father: the mother is bigger and more powerful, and therefore a threat. The young girl resolves the unconscious anxiety and aggression resulting from this conflict by identifying with her mother and emphasising her femininity.

After the resolution of the Oedipal conflict, Freud argued that the libido becomes diffused throughout the body and the child enters a **latency period** which lasts until puberty. At puberty, the libido again focuses on the genitals, and the child enters the **genital stage**, during which time it seeks satisfaction in relationships with the other sex.

These accounts of the development of personality are not really susceptible to normal psychological evaluation, since what is considered to count as evidence is so very different from the normal empirical evidence required in psychology. Although some psychologists see them as providing useful insights, others see them as little more than elaborate stories. For example, Champness (1980), in an amusing article, showed how it was equally possible to use these forms of reasoning to construct a theory of early experience based on the idea of 'deumbilification' – the severing of the umbilical cord at birth.

Refutability

One of the criteria of a scientific theory identified by Popper (1959) is that it should be possible to support or refute it, by the systematic collection of material evidence. Eysenck (1985) showed that, in

material terms, there seemed to be little evidence for psychoanalytic theory. But the notion of 'psychological truth' means that there are different criteria being applied by most of its supporters: Kline's (1984) defence of Freudian theory covered different material from Eysenck's attack on it.

A further problem with trying to apply the criterion of refutability is that psychoanalytic arguments tend to be circular. Attempts to disprove psychoanalytic explanations are often seen by psychoanalysts as defensive reactions, with the critic's ego defending itself against the psychological threat of accepting psychological theory by denying the validity of the theory itself. With this circular logic, it is not possible ever to refute the approach.

Freud's methodology

There are other weaknesses of psychoanalytic theory. One of these concerns the methodology, in which dreams or slips of the tongue are seen as indicating unconscious wish-fulfilment. Freud, as we saw earlier, was a materialist, and took these as clear evidence of the workings of the unconscious mind. But a modern psychologist would tend to be less confident of these. Freud also believed that the different aspects of personality which he described had distinct biological origins, and that it was only a matter of time before physiological research would reveal the physiological substrates of the id, ego and super-ego. One hundred years later, this picture looks rather different.

Another criticism of Freudian theory concerns the very limited sample of women, and just one child, on whom Freud based his theories. This criticism has two aspects. The first is the idea that generalising from such a limited sample may mean that the concerns of this sample may not have been those of the general population. This is the weaker aspect of the criticism, since individual cases can sometimes provide unique insights into more general principles, and Freudians argue that these cases have been supported by many others subsequently.

What is more important about the fact that the sample was so limited, though, concerns its particular society, and the suggestion that Freud's sample of clients may really have been very different from 'ordinary' people. When Freud was exploring his female clients' early memories, he concluded at first that he was coming across evidence for widespread sexual abuse, since so many of them had traumatic memories of sexual encounters with their fathers. He was persuaded by colleagues that his conclusions could not be correct, and that in any case to publish them would cause a social scandal. Although he would probably have faced up to the scandal if he had been absolutely certain, Freud was aware that there was a possibility that his clients' memories were not real, and eventually allowed himself to be convinced that the abuse had not actually happened.

As a result, he looked for other explanations for his clients' traumas, and came to the conclusion that if the events had not actually happened, they must represent some form of unconscious wish fulfilment. Recent evidence on the prevalence of child sexual abuse, though, suggests that Freud's initial explanation could have been accurate: it is now much more plausible that those clients really had suffered sexual abuse from their fathers. In which case, it becomes unnecessary to invoke unconscious wish-fulfilment as an explanation for the highly emotionally charged memories.

Cultural specificity

Freud, undoubtedly, was a seeker after truth. He believed he had found valuable insights into human personality. But the psychological realities which he was seeking to explain may have been very much more culturally specific than he realised. For example, in Victorian society, death was a commonplace event and frequently discussed, but sex was never mentioned, whereas in our society the reverse holds true. Freudian theory emphasised sexuality as a prime unconscious concern, but it is possible that this reflected the social prohibitions of the time, rather than a universal truth about human nature.

That does not mean, of course, that the whole theory should be rejected out of hand. The concept of ego defence mechanisms, for instance, is a part of the theory which has been very useful in psychotherapy, and which can be applied to other models of personality as well. But it does mean that many modern psychologists (though not all) treat psychoanalytic theory with a certain amount of scepticism.

Freud's pupils and colleagues developed many other forms of psychoanalytic theory. For reasons of space it would be impossible to cover them all here, so in this chapter we will look at just two more personality theories from the psychoanalytic school of thought: those developed by Carl Gustav Jung and Erich Fromm.

Jung

Jung was a Swiss psychologist who studied with Freud for some time – in fact, Freud regarded Jung for many years as his most promising pupil. He left the Freudian group, however, owing to a disagreement with Freud about the importance of sexuality, and formulated his own theory about personality.

Like Freud, Jung saw libido as being the basic energy of all motivation and pleasure. Unlike Freud, however, Jung's concept of the libido was as a non-sexual life-force, which encompassed religious awe and mystical life-affirming experiences as well as sexuality. While accepting Freud's model of the conscious, the preconscious and the unconscious, Jung also believed that there was a further level to the unconscious mind, which he referred to as the **collective unconscious**. The illustrative metaphor that he used was of a chain of islands, which seem to be separate and distinct, but are actually linked together on a deep level (see Figure 7.3). The deepest levels of the unconscious, Jung thought, were shared by all humans, and date back to our primaeval ancestry. Although this is sometimes referred to as the 'racial' unconscious, Jung himself included all members of the human race in his use of the term, not just a subgroup within it.

Sexual development

Jung outlined three stages of sexual development, which were very different from those described by

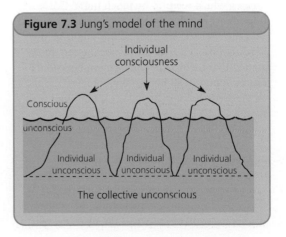

Figure 7.3 Jung's model of the mind

Individual consciousness

Conscious

unconscious

Individual unconscious

Individual unconscious

Individual unconscious

The collective unconscious

Freud. The first stage was the **pre-sexual stage**, which lasted from birth until the child was about five years old. During this stage, Jung argued, the infant is primarily concerned with nutrition and growth – a powerful contrast with Freud's theory. While Jung accepted the idea of an Oedipal conflict, he saw it as being based on love for the food-providing mother, and only developing sexual connotations later on, during the second stage of sexual development. The castration complex for Jung was symbolic rather than literal, representing a renunciation of infantile wishes and desires as the child grew older.

The second stage of sexual development outlined by Jung was the **pre-pubertal phase,** which lasted from age five to puberty. This, Jung argued, formed the real beginning of sexuality, and again this represents quite a contrast to the Freudian view, in which the child is seen as in the latency period at this age. The third stage of sexual development was **maturity**, from puberty and onwards through adulthood.

Synchronicity

Jung believed that certain events or circumstances strike reverberating chords which penetrate through all our levels of consciousness. When this happens, these things strike us as being deeply meaningful or significant – much more so than the material circumstances would warrant. He called this **synchronicity**. What is happening in these cases, Jung argued, is that the event or circumstance is connecting with something in the collective unconscious – a powerful symbol or meaning, which we cannot ignore.

The most famous examples of this are what he described as **archetypes**: powerful and recurrent images, which seem to be much more important than their physical expression would warrant. A classic example of this might be the idea of 'mother', or of the sea, or the sun. Jung argued that these archetypes are symbols which can be found in all human mythologies, and in all these mythologies they have a profound significance. The reason why they are so common, Jung argued, is that they are rooted deep in the collective unconscious, in a powerful, elemental form. Some examples of the archetypes identified by Jung include: the earth-mother; the all-powerful father; the sea as the symbol of rebirth, representing the primaeval womb; the symbol known as the mandala, which

represents the sun, or growth; the wise fool; and so on.

Jung believed that the reason why we react so strongly to something like the sea is because of synchronicity. The connection between the conscious experience and the collective unconscious means that we do not just encounter these phenomena on their own, as it were, but as symbols of the deep-rooted archetype. We do not just regard the sea as a large, splashy bit of water. Instead, we experience a very powerful emotional reaction to it, because it strikes a synchronous chord to its underlying archetype deep in our collective unconscious.

Jung's model of personality

It was Jung who originated the now-common psychological description of people as 'extroverts' or 'introverts'. He used these as general descriptions of the **persona** – the name he gave to the outward personality which people show in day to day interactions. Some people, he argued, are naturally more sociable than others, and are most at their ease when with other people. Jung referred to these people as extroverts. Others are less sociable in nature, preferring their own company, and these he described as introverts. The concept of extroversion-introversion became widely accepted in psychology, although there is some question among modern psychologists as to how consistent these types are: people behave very differently in different situations, and someone who is apparently extroverted in one type of situation may react as an introvert in another.

For Jung himself, that was less of a problem than it became for those who attributed fixed qualities to the persona, since he saw the persona as responsive to situational demands as well as to general inclinations. Moreover, Jung saw the unconscious mind as being a mirror-image of the conscious. So, for instance, a person with an extrovert persona would have an introvert unconscious. Each individual, he argued, has an opposite 'inner self', known as the **anima** or **animus**, which is masculine in a woman and feminine in a man. We all contain our opposites within ourselves, so the timid person is unconsciously brave, the strong person is unconsciously weak, and so on.

Jung saw personality as being complex and many-sided, including aspects which are concerned with intuition, emotion, thought and intentionality. The personality characteristics which Jung described were taken by some of Jung's successors to provide an indicator of personality type, and a very popular personality test, the **Myers–Briggs Type Indicator** (**MBTI**) was developed on that basis. But Jung did not see them as fixed qualities, more as indicators of potential temperament. The important thing, he believed, was that people should be able to develop the different facets of their personality evenly, and in congruence with one another. If personality development was uneven, such that only one side of the personality was able to develop and others were repressed, this could produce neurotic conflicts.

The solution to these conflicts was to be found by putting the individual into contact with the collective unconscious, which would act in a healing manner, restoring the individual's psychological integrity. Since the collective unconscious was a link back to the primaeval past, this meant that Jung saw the process of **regression** as an adaptive, helpful process, not as the maladaptive defence mechanism which it was construed as in Freudian theory. The process of Jungian therapy was seen as a co-operative venture between therapist and client, in which both together explored the collective unconscious and allowed the idea to surface and to synchronise with everyday experience, until psychological harmony had been restored.

Fromm

Erich Fromm was also a psychoanalytic theorist, but differed from both Freud and Jung in the importance which he ascribed to society and social factors. Both Freud and Jung had seen personality development as happening as a result partly of maturation, and partly of interaction with members of the close family. Fromm recognised both individual development and family as important, but also included society as a third factor in the formation of personality.

The individual, the family and society
Fromm argued that there was a dialectical relationship between the individual, the family and the wider society, with each interacting with, and influencing, the others. For example, he saw personal relationships as being crucial to the development of personality; while at the same time these personal relationships were being influenced by

wider social and economic factors. On the other hand, Fromm saw broader changes at the social and economic levels come about, in the end, through the efforts of individuals.

In Fromm's view, personality arises in its own social and economic context, and is shaped by it. Someone's attitudes, values and ideas are usually consistent with, and shaped by, their family's social class and background; but they are not totally determined by it. Nor are they static: over time attitudes, values and ideas change, and both society and individuals will be different as a result. '*It steam-engines when it's steam-engine time*', as the saying goes – in other words, the inventors and developers of the steam engine were personalities who were characteristic of their age, and developed their ideas in that social context. Other societies produced different kinds of personalities, and themselves were shaped by those people's efforts.

The productive character
This does not mean, however, that personality is totally fixed and unchanging. Fromm believed that people are able to change themselves, and also to change the family relationships which form the source of their character. The goal of such change is what he described as the **productive character**. People who are productive characters, according to Fromm, value themselves and others for what they are, are creative and loving, are able to experience security and inner peace, and manage to avoid loneliness and alienation by loving others and through creative work. They are open and receptive to new ideas and relationships, and not defensive in their approach to others. This is Fromm's ideal, and in his view, the only personality orientation in which the person can truly enjoy freedom.

Negative personality orientations
A positive childhood will produce a productive character, Fromm believed. But family relationships, economic forces and the like often combine to produce more negative personality orientations. Fromm described four of these: the receptive character, the exploitative character, the hoarding character and the marketing character.

Receptive characters, in Fromm's theory, typically feel that the source of all good things is external – outside themselves – and that being inoffensive and lovable will bring them a positive life. Such people tend to be very dependent on others – Fromm described them as 'masochistic' in their approach. They tend to show excessive devotion and loyalty, whether that be towards another person, or an organisation of some kind; and they avoid self-determination by passing all the responsibility on to an external source.

Exploitative characters, by contrast, see the world in competitive, 'dog-eat-dog' terms; and gain great satisfaction from outsmarting or controlling others. Fromm described them as 'sadistic' in their approach, having contempt for people that they feel are beneath them, and little sympathy or fellow-feeling for others. He described them as often being entrepreneurial and ambitious people, who have a strong desire to dominate and to be successful.

Hoarding characters, according to Fromm, are often avid collectors, and very protective of what they have, so they do not tend to be open to new ideas or to sharing their lives with other people. They have little faith in anything new, seeing their personal security as being based on hoarding and saving what they already own. Interestingly, Fromm argued that people of this type can often be very destructive, because their dominant tendency is to want control over their lives and the people and things in it. Being destructive is one way of achieving that control.

Marketing characters, in Fromm's model, are concerned with image and style, and tend to judge their personal worth in terms of social success. If they are not popular or admired, they feel inadequate and useless, so they go to great lengths to maintain themselves as desirable commodities, perhaps by adopting fashionable ideas or being a source of entertainment. Fromm argued that such people tend to be very conformist in terms of the prevailing social trends – they would not be able to risk being seen as holding an unfashionable attitude.

The individual within society

Fromm saw each of these non-productive character types as being typical of certain kinds of society. While every society produces some individuals of each type, the interaction between personality and society means that in any one particular society, some types are likely to be more

common than others. So, for instance, the receptive character type would be particularly common in a feudal or slave-based society, while the exploitative character might be typical of a newly capitalist or colonial society. The hoarding character would be typical of highly authoritarian societies and the marketing character of the consumer society. But since society is complex and families are all different, all types of personality orientation are possible within a modern society.

An important part of Fromm's theory was the distinction he made between animal and human nature. Fromm saw organisms which have only an animal nature as being at one with the natural world. But human beings have another side, which makes them separate from nature – they can stand aside and see themselves in relation to the rest of the world. Once an organism is endowed with such knowledge, according to Fromm, it is inevitably separate from nature and the other animals. Seen positively, this separateness gives us our freedom; but equally it makes us alone, and therefore potentially lonely and alienated.

The freedom and independence stemming from our human nature can allow us to rise to great heights of creative achievement. But if we look at society, Fromm argued, we find that people often deliberately forgo their birthright of freedom. By voluntarily placing themselves in obedience to some other person or organisation, they cease to act independently any more. So, for instance, those people who followed the German Nazi party before WWII deliberately surrendered their personal freedom and autonomy of thought in following their leaders. That is only one example – the same applies to people who identify completely with their work organisation, or who follow a religious leader blindly. Fromm saw this as coming from a **fear of freedom**. He argued that being free involves a certain amount of loneliness and isolation: acting autonomously and making your own decisions is a frightening responsibility, which some people prefer not to have.

Perhaps the main weakness in Fromm's theory is the account of the productive character. Fromm appeared to ignore the fact that creative work simply is not an option for everyone; and his theory has been described as having a rather 'Californian', middle-class orientation as a result. He is vague about the productive character, and seems to suggest that self-fulfilment arises simply from 'feeling good' about oneself. It can be argued, however, that some of the most productive characters in society seem to have broad social ideals which they work towards rather than just expressing themselves. But Fromm's theory does make the crucial point that personality does not arise in a vacuum, but is intimately linked with the society in which it was formed.

Trait theories of personality

An entirely different set of personality theories is concerned with identifying and quantifying distinctive **personality traits**, or characteristics, of personality. These theories are sometimes referred to as **psychometric theories**, because of their emphasis on measuring personality by using psychometric tests. In this section, we will look at three trait theories of personality: those developed by Eysenck and Cattell, and the more recent 'five-factor' model of personality.

Eysenck's theory of personality

Eysenck developed a theory of personality which argued that the most distinctive aspects of human personality could be grouped into two major traits, and that these traits could be effectively measured using psychometric tests. Eysenck's approach took a largely **nativist** stance, seeing personality as arising for the most part from inherited physiological tendencies, and regarding environmental influences as playing a very minor part. Eysenck himself claimed to be a behaviourist, but his use of the term was rather different from most. His claim to behaviourism rested mainly on his emphasis on the sampling of behaviour instead of opinions and attitudes by means of personality questionnaires, rather than from an emphasis on S–R learning.

The development of Eysenck's model

Eysenck developed his theory of personality by compiling a large battery of questions about behaviour. He applied these questionnaires to 700 soldiers who were being treated for neurotic disorders at the Maudsley Hospital in London. Eysenck (1947) found that the answers to these questions seemed to link naturally with one another, suggesting that there were a number of different personality traits which were being

revealed by the soldiers' answers. He called these first-order personality traits, and they included types of behaviour such as impulsiveness, anxiety and intolerance.

Eysenck then applied the statistical technique known as **factor analysis** to the soldiers' responses. This method of looking at general trends in the data showed that the first-order personality traits seemed to cluster together into two main groups. Eysenck argued that these groups implied that there were two major personality dimensions underlying the data, which he referred to as second-order personality traits, or sometimes personality dimensions.

Introversion-extroversion

One of the two personality dimensions which Eysenck identified related to how sociable or unsociable people seemed to be. But this was not just about liking to interact with people. The responses to those questions also seemed to link with the answers to questions about impulsiveness, risk-taking and stimulus-seeking. Eysenck argued that the personality dimension underlying this cluster of traits was all to do with the amount of stimulation which an individual required. He named the dimension **introversion-extroversion**, terms which had been originally developed by Jung to describe characters who were either withdrawn and self-sufficient (introverts), or outgoing and sociable (extroverts).

Eysenck argued that the introversion-extroversion dimension had a physiological basis. It occurred, he argued, as a result of inherited individual differences in the part of the brain known as the **reticular activating system (RAS)**, which we will be looking at in Chapter 10. The reticular activating system acts as a general 'switching' mechanism for large areas of the cerebral cortex – which is the part of the brain concerned with thinking and attention, among other things. The reticular activating system can either act in an excitatory manner, stimulating brain activity, or it can act in an inhibitory manner, which means that the activity of nerve cells is damped down.

Eysenck proposed that introverts inherit a nervous system in which the reticular activating system has a bias towards excitation rather than inhibition. This means that incoming information tends to excite more nerve cells, and the excitation does not die away so quickly. The consequence is that introverts do not need as much stimulation to maintain their optimal level of brain activity, since the neural activity resulting from a set of stimuli will last for much longer with these people than it does with others. Extroverts, on the other hand, have inherited a nervous system which tends to produce inhibitory responses. This means that they need much more stimulation than introverts, to achieve the same level of brain functioning.

The consequence of these physiological differences, Eysenck argued, is that extroverts can quickly become bored, and will tend to seek out novel sources of stimulation. They like to be with other people, because other people represent an ever-changing source of stimulation. Introverts, on the other hand, are happier with a less intense level of stimulation: an introvert would be happy settling down with a book for an evening, whereas an extrovert would be restless and bored.

The physiological differences between introverts and extroverts also, Eysenck argued, affect how readily the individual would become conditioned to particular stimuli. He was talking here about the process of **classical conditioning**, which we will be looking at in detail in Chapter 21, and which was seen in 1947 (when Eysenck was developing this theory) as being pretty well the basis for all learning. Classical conditioning involves the forming of learned, automatic associations between a stimulus and a response. According to Eysenck, introverts will condition to a stimulus more easily than extroverts, because of the additional amount of neural activity produced by the stimulus in the first place. Once their conditioning has been established, it will last a long time. Extroverts, on the other hand, are less ready to form new associations between stimulus and response, and, according to Eysenck, condition less rapidly. Their weaker conditioning also dies away relatively easily.

There has been a certain amount of experimental evidence which seems to support this theory. For example, Harkins and Green (1975) found that introverts seem to do much better at long boring vigilance tasks than extroverts do: extroverts find it hard to maintain concentration for lengthy periods of time. The explanation for this was that introverts can maintain an optimal level of cortical functioning more easily under conditions of limited stimulation. But these results are not necessarily evidence for differing levels of cortical activity: it might simply be that the extro-

verts become bored and careless because of learned habits: since they are used to being with other people and having a lot going on, they find it harder to adjust to a task which involves minute concentration for long periods of time.

Neuroticism-stability

The other second-order personality factor, or dimension of personality, identified by Eysenck (1947) was one which seemed to result from the grouping together of a number of different first-order traits, including anxiety, hostility and a trait which Eysenck called hypochondriasis, which was a susceptibility to 'nervous' ailments like headaches or panic attacks. Eysenck described this personality dimension as **neuroticism-stability**, and, like introversion-extroversion, he saw it as having a biological basis.

Neuroticism, according to Eysenck, is a function of the type of autonomic nervous system that the individual has inherited. The autonomic nervous system, which we will be looking at in Chapter 13, is concerned with the body's reaction to stressful or threatening events: one section of it becomes activated if we are threatened or angry, while the other is active in calm, peaceful situations. Eysenck argued that neurotic individuals have a highly labile (easily activated) autonomic nervous system. This means that they react very readily to alarming or stressful stimuli. People who are stable, on the other hand, take longer to react to alarming or stressful events, and do not react as strongly to them. So neurotic individuals are much more likely to become anxious, to suffer from 'nervous' ailments, and to over-react to threat than stable individuals.

Eysenck argued that, taken together, the two dimensions of extroversion and neuroticism could account for many different personality traits. The dimensions were orthogonal to one another – in other words, they were completely independent, and could be portrayed as crossing one another at right-angles on a graph. The theory has sometimes been represented as a type theory of personality, because when the four corners of such a graph are considered, they seem to map on to the four basic 'personality humours' which we looked at earlier (Figure 7.4). But in fact, there are so many in-between points on each of the scales that only people who would obtain extreme scores could be seen as fitting into the four 'types'. Most people, on these scales, tend to come somewhere in the

Figure 7.4 Eysenck's model of personality

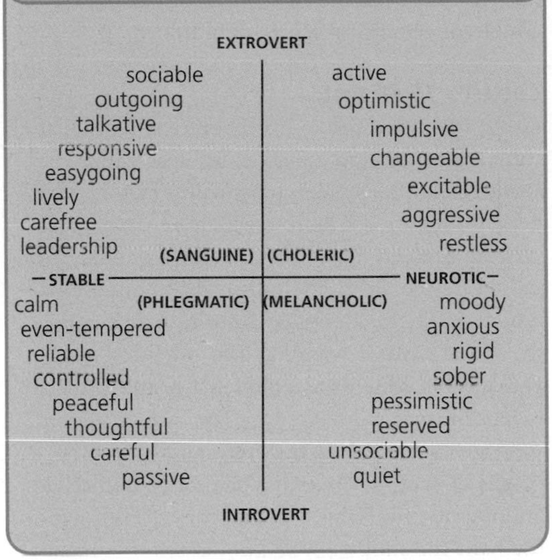

	EXTROVERT	
	sociable	active
	outgoing	optimistic
	talkative	impulsive
	responsive	changeable
	easygoing	excitable
	lively	aggressive
	carefree	restless
	leadership (SANGUINE)	(CHOLERIC)
— STABLE —		— NEUROTIC —
calm	(PHLEGMATIC) (MELANCHOLIC)	moody
even-tempered		anxious
reliable		rigid
controlled		sober
peaceful		pessimistic
thoughtful		reserved
careful		unsociable
passive		quiet
	INTROVERT	

middle – an important point, to which we shall return.

Psychoticism

In later years, Eysenck and Eysenck (1976) added a third personality dimension to the model, although this one was rather different from the others. The third dimension was called **psychoticism**, and related to how prepared the individual was to conform to society's rules, and to act in conventional ways. Eysenck also proposed that people who scored highly on the psychoticism scale had a higher level of the hormone androgen than normal people (who are expected to obtain low scores); but there does not seem to be much empirical evidence for this idea.

The main way in which this scale differs from the others is that it does not seem to be normal distributed throughout the population. The other two personality dimensions, Eysenck argued, were normally distributed: although there would be a few individuals who achieved extreme scores, most people would come somewhere in the middle. In terms of the Eysenck Personality Inventory, which has a possible score of 24 for each of the two dimensions, this meant that the majority of people tend to score somewhere between 9 and 15, and the numbers achieving each score tail off towards the ends of the scale. But the distribution of the psychoticism scale was quite different, with most people achieving very low scores, and only a few gaining

scores which were higher than, say, 6 out of a possible 24.

There are many criticisms of Eysenck's theory. One of these is the suitability of applying highly sophisticated analytical techniques like **factor analysis** to data which in the end consist of only 'yes' or 'no' responses to questionnaire items. There is also some question as to whether these scales have long-term reliability, over several years. The short-term reliability coefficients are very good, in the sense that they tend to give consistent measures if they are used to assess the same people over a few weeks or months. But it is uncertain how they respond to long-term assessments, taken over years. Eysenck, of course, believed that these scales are consistent in the long term as well, but that is because he believed the traits have inherited biological origins. As we will see later in this chapter, other psychologists take a different view about the ways that human beings can grow and change through life. But the basic model of personality, at least (ignoring the later addition of the psychoticism scale), seems to have proved fairly robust in many experimental situations.

Cattell

Like Eysenck, Cattell developed a theory which described personality in terms of consistent traits, measurable by means of a personality inventory. However, Cattell's theory differs from Eysenck's in two important respects: in terms of the number of traits which he considered to be appropriate for describing the personality, and in terms of the source data from which the traits were identified.

The development of Cattell's model

Where Eysenck's original data had consisted of questionnaire items administered to hospitalised servicemen, Cattell collected data about a much wider range of people, and obtained it from three different sources. One type of data was referred to as **L-data**. The L stands for life-record, and this data included such information as the individual's school grades, records of their absence from work and other recorded indicators of personality. These data were mainly derived from observation and from consulting official records.

A second type of data was referred to as **Q-data**. This was obtained by asking the research participants to rate their own personalities and likely behaviour, by completing pre-set questionnaires.

So Q-data was questionnaire data which gave personal information about the individuals themselves. The third type of data which Cattell used as source material for his model of personality was **T-data**. T-data involved the use of objective tests, in which the person responds to questions but, unlike the Q-data questions, does not know which aspect of their personality is being measured by any given question, or by the test as a whole.

Cattell analysed the information which he received from the L-data and T-data sources, using the statistical technique known as factor analysis. In this case, the analysis involved comparing the different pairs of measurements which had been obtained from each individual in the study, and seeing what relationships could be identified between them. The analysis of each pair of measurements would then be further analysed, so as to find out how strongly the scores correlated with one another. Cattell reasoned that if two measures showed a high correlation, then they were probably measuring related aspects of personality. This is very similar to the way that Eysenck identified his first- and second-order personality traits.

Source and surface traits

Cattell came to the conclusion that there are two distinct kinds of personality trait. One type of personality trait is very obvious, and can easily be identified by other people. Cattell referred to these as **surface traits**. A second type of personality trait is much less visible to observers, and seems to underlie several different aspects of the person's behaviour. Cattell referred to these as **source traits**. Of the two, Cattell considered source traits to be of far greater importance in describing the individual's personality than surface traits were, even though most people would be likely to notice surface traits first.

Having identified surface traits and source traits from L- and T-data, the second part of Cattell's research strategy was to show that comparable factors could also be identified from Q-data. By comparing the Q-data results from the same individuals with the trait scores obtained from L- and T-data, Cattell eventually concluded that sixteen major personality traits were needed to produce an adequate description of personality, not just one or two. This, he argued, implied that a psychometric test of personality should provide a

personality profile, which would give a more fully rounded picture of the individual, than a couple of numerical scores could do.

Cattell's *16 PF* test

Using these findings as his theoretical basis, Cattell went on to develop a personality test which would assess the sixteen personality factors which he had identified. The test which he developed was the Sixteen Personality Factor Inventory, now known as the 16PF. The personality dimensions which had been identified from L-data formed the initial basis of twelve of the 16PF test items, and another four were added as a result of the extension to include Q-data. The names which were given to each of the factors reflected the origin of each of the traits. The traits themselves are described in Table 7.2, and they also provide the basis for another well-known psychometric test: the Minnesota **Multiphasic Personality Test**, or **MMPT**.

Cattell argued that his sixteen personality factors would provide a 'picture' of someone in terms of the common traits, but that such a picture should not be taken as a complete description of personality. Everyone, he argued, shows some unique traits as well, which cannot be measured using personality tests. So a personality profile should always be accompanied by an individual description of the person's unique traits, if the

Table 7.2 Cattell's 16 personality traits

reserved	A	outgoing
less intelligent	B	more intelligent
affected by feelings	C	emotionally stable
submissive	E	dominant
serious	F	happy-go-lucky
expedient	G	conscientious
timid	H	venturesome
tough-minded	I	sensitive
trusting	L	suspicious
practical	M	imaginative
forthright	N	shrewd
self-assured	O	apprehensive
conservative	Q1	experimenting
group-dependent	Q2	self-sufficient
uncontrolled	Q3	controlled
relaxed	Q4	tense

picture is to form a comprehensive description of someone's personality.

Some researchers have argued that Cattell's test measurements were derived on a largely intuitive basis, from rather limited data. They argue that the model overestimates how much one can generalise from the data: that the traits are only superficial, and do not justify the wide-ranging way that Cattell interprets them. But on the other hand, Cattell did draw together several different sources of data in formulating his model, and to that extent it seems likely that his model provides a more accurate description of personality than, say, Eysenck's theory. By establishing the concept of a personality profile as the appropriate description, rather than a simple 'type' classification, Cattell opened the way for more detailed psychometric assessments of personality – and of other aspects of human behaviour too.

The 'five robust factors'

As psychometric techniques for assessing personality developed, other psychologists began to investigate numerous other traits, and to develop techniques for measuring them. More than 50 personality traits have been identified in this way. The number grew so large that eventually researchers again began to feel the need to establish some common ground by looking for second-order factors which might underlie groups of traits. In 1963, Norman described how almost all the different traits identified by personality theorists could be combined to form a simpler, more usable, model.

By applying factor analysis to the outcomes of different personality tests, Norman concluded that the various traits which were being measured could be grouped into five basic factors: (1) **surgency** (a trait similar to extroversion, but a bit wider than Eysenck's measure); (2) **emotional stability** (similar to neuroticism but again broader in scope); (3) **agreeableness** (including measures of generosity, stubbornness, tendency to criticise, etc.); (4) **conscientiousness** (including whether the person was hardworking, negligent, disorganised, dependable, etc.); and (5) **culture** (including scales of curiosity, creativity, intelligence, perceptiveness and knowledgeability). Norman argued that pretty well all personality traits assessed using psychometric tests could be seen as falling into one or other of these groups.

Other researchers too were looking at how personality traits might be grouped together. In 1976, Costa and McCrae outlined a model of personality which they named the **NEO model**. The initials summarised the three major personality factors which they saw as necessary for an adequate description of personality: N for neuroticism, E for extroversion (both much as discussed by Eysenck), with an additional O dimension which stood for openness to experience. Costa and McCrae argued that the 'openness' factor revealed itself through several different and well-established tests, like Rokeach's (1960) 'dogmatism' scale, which we will look at again later in this chapter, or Holland's (1966) 'artistic interests' scale.

In 1985, however, the two researchers published another paper which described how they had found it necessary to add two more basic dimensions to their model, making five personality factors in all. McCrae and Costa (1985) found, from factor analysis of the 16PF and other personality scales, that their NEO model did not quite account for scales assessing conscience, super-ego strength or persistence. Accordingly, they argued that another dimension, which they named **control**, was needed.

In the same paper, they discussed how their four-factor model fitted with Norman's five-factor one, and concluded that they were very similar – in fact, that they were probably assessing the same basic dimensions. The one difference was that their model did not include any measures of 'agreeableness'. McCrae and Costa suggested that this might be because the personality scales that they were analysing did not include any explicit measures of behaviour relevant to this dimension. When they included some scales which did measure these behaviours in their analysis, they found that they too seemed to form a fifth personality factor, which did not fit with any of the other four.

These five factors emerged from general analyses of different personality traits so often that they came to be known as the **five robust factors**. For example, Noller, Law and Comrey (1987) compared responses to test items from Cattell's 16PF, the Comrey Personality Scales and the Eysenck Personality Inventory, and also found that the items clustered into five basic factors. Other research produced similar outcomes. Interestingly, although the five factors identified in the different studies were always similar, they were not identical. Some researchers (for example Digman and Inouye, 1986) described a basic factor of 'will' or 'determination' instead of 'conscience' or 'control', while others debated about whether 'culture', 'openness to experience' or 'sensation-seeking' were the same factors, or different ones (see, for example, Zuckerman, Kuhlman and Camac, 1988).

In 1985, Eysenck, Barrett and Eysenck argued that Norman's 'culture' factor emerged as an important dimension only when research participants from largely academic settings were being tested. When personality tests were applied to the real world, they said, 'culture' did not appear as an important distinguishing factor. However, McCrae and Costa (1985) challenged this view, arguing that the 'culture' dimension was not just about middle-class artistic pursuits, as the Eysencks had implied. Rather, it was a kind of composite between the 'openness to experience' dimension and intelligence. If all the items to do with intelligence or intellectual skills were taken out of 'culture' factor measurements, what resulted, McCrae and Costa argued, was a dimension which was pretty well identical with 'openness to experience'. For this reason, they claimed, intelligence should be seen as a separate mental skill, and not as a dimension of personality – although it might, of course, affect how other personality traits showed in the individual's behaviour.

Temperament

As we have seen, there is not an absolute agreement about which five factors are basic to personality. But there does seem to be a recurrent finding that the different items from psychometric tests can be gathered into five groups. The frequency of this finding suggests that these five groups may possibly be tapping into some basic differences in temperament between individuals, even if these differences manifest themselves in different ways in the person's behaviour.

Claridge (1988) suggested that looking at underlying **temperament** may be more useful in the long run than trying to identify fixed personality traits. One of the main reasons for this is because traits can be affected so strongly by our social experiences throughout life. Every baby is different in temperament, and reacts in its own way to what it encounters. These initial differences are then shaped and modified by experience – including the expectations of other people, as we

will see in the later chapters. This means that different basic temperaments can result in adults who have the same surface personality traits.

Behaviourist and social behaviour theories

A different group of personality theories has seen personality as being largely the product of learning. These theories range from the extreme behaviourist stimulus-response theories, which see personality as simply the result of the numerous small bits of conditioning which the child receives through its life, to the more complex social behaviour and social cognition theories, which see social experience as the crucial determinant of personality.

The behaviourist view of personality

As we saw in Chapter 1, behaviourism as a school of thought was developed on the basis of Locke's associationism. It was assumed that human behaviour consisted of combinations of learned associations, combined into ever-larger chunks. Like Locke, the founder of behaviourism, J.B. Watson, argued that the child's mind was a *tabula rasa* at birth – a blank slate, waiting to be written on by its experiences. Personality, Watson asserted, was the product of those experiences, and in the quotation in Chapter 1, we saw how he believed that any child could be brought up to any vocation, as long as it experienced the right stimuli and environment. Personality, in Watson's view, formed the sum of the total learned stimulus-response associations which the individual developed through interaction with the environment. These could come from many different sources, deliberate or accidental.

B.F. Skinner (1972) adopted a similar approach to personality, although the underlying learning mechanisms which he identified were different. Rather than classical conditioning occurring mainly through the repeated associations of stimulu and response, Skinner saw learning as happening mainly through the **Law of Effect** – the principle that actions with pleasant consequences are more likely to be repeated (see Chapter 18). This, he argued, meant that the individual was continually being manipulated by the things which would bring it rewards, or allow it to escape from unpleasant consequences. Such notions as freedom and human dignity were, in Skinner's view, an illusion, since everyone was being unconsciously and randomly controlled in this way.

Skinner, like Watson, considered personality to be simply the sum of learned behaviours. People could be distinguished from one another because they acted differently, and their behaviour was different only because each person experienced subtly different reinforcement contingencies throughout life. Both Watson's and Skinner's approaches denied the existence of the mind, or any kind of internal 'self' – they were both **black-box theories**, emphasising the input of stimuli from the environment and the output of behavioural responses to those stimuli. And they were also extremely **reductionist** views of personality, which few modern psychologists would be prepared to accept unequivocally.

Social learning theory

Bandura (1977a) considered that social factors were more important in the formation of personality than either Watson or Skinner had acknowledged. Bandura identified **social learning** as the crucial process involved in personality. Social learning, in Bandura's view, included classical and operant conditioning, but more important it also involved the child learning through the processes of **imitation and identification**. These are rapid forms of social learning which allow an individual child to acquire complex units of behaviour quickly and efficiently, and without the dangers inherent in trial-and-error learning.

Bandura saw imitation as being a first stage, in which the person copies specific actions or behaviours from a model. The type of behaviours shown by the model are important in establishing a range of possible behaviours for the child. In 1963, Bandura and Walters showed how children can store patterns of aggressive behaviour which they observe, not reproducing them immediately, but showing them when they are in a later situation which seems to mean that these behaviours would give them an advantage. Imitation, then, involves the replication of specific behaviours or actions.

Role models
At first, the child learns almost entirely by imitation, but this soon leads on to the second stage of

social learning: identification. In this, the learning becomes assimilated into the child's self-concept, and this means that whole styles of interaction or behaviour can be adopted, not just single actions. In the identification process, the child adopts certain individuals as **role models**. By identifying with such models, the child becomes able to extrapolate its learning to novel forms of behaviour: it acts in a way it imagines the role model might act in that situation. So, unlike imitation, where the child can only replicate existing behaviours, through identification the child can produce novel behaviour.

Personality, in Bandura's theory, is seen as being the product of the individual's unique experiences and learning. It is learned, in the sense that it arises from the individual's distinctive experiences, but it includes patterns of interaction and mechanisms of social learning which were not included in the behaviourist models. Bandura's work provided an important link between the strictly behaviourist perspectives of Watson and Skinner, and the most socially oriented theories of Mead and Mischel.

Symbolic interactionism
For G.H. Mead, as for Bandura, it was the social nature of the human being that gave the key to understanding personality. Mead's **social behaviourism** emphasised how human behaviour is directed towards social goals. We are all socialised into appropriate social roles from our earliest moments, Mead argued. These roles determine how we interact with one another, and therefore the types of behaviour which we will acquire. It is society, and the social roles that we play in it, which forms the foundations for personality.

According to Mead (1934), personality develops through three stages. The **preparatory stage,** during infancy, involves the small child imitating the behaviour of those around it; but without any underlying comprehension of what the actions are about. So, for instance, an infant may spread out a magazine and copy mother as she reads; but the pages can just as well be upside down as the right way up. Imitation, though, gradually gives way to a more general internalisation of social roles, and the child moves on to the second stage.

The second stage outlined by Mead is the **play stage**, in which the child acts out whole social roles rather than simple actions. By playing the parts of the people in its world, the child develops its understanding of what is appropriate and in-appropriate role behaviour. The roles that the child acts out will be those of the significant others in its world: the people who have a decisive impact on the child's life. Mead thought that it was significant how children in this stage often referred to themselves in the third person when they were playing, such as: 'Emma feed baby now' or 'Emma hungry'. He thought that this showed how children of this age do not have a unified sense of self, but experience several different selves which can be called up when appropriate.

The third stage outlined by Mead involves inte-grating all the different roles that the child plays, and the many different representations of the self, into one coherent whole. We develop a **core self** which can cope with a number of different situa-tions, rather than adopting a different self for each situation that we are in. The origins for this common self, though, lie in the social roles that we have learned to play, so according to Mead, the **self-concept** is ultimately created by society, and needs social support to maintain it.

It is this core self which allows us to make our own, personal interpretation of the social roles that we play. Although such roles may determine the general form of our interaction with others, there is a range of role behaviour available to us: a doctor may be sympathetic, remote or dictatorial in deal-ing with his or her patients, while still conforming to the expectations surrounding the social role of doctor. We each adopt our own styles, and interpret our roles individually, and according to Mead it is this that makes each individual person unique. But we also internalise society's norms, so that the interpretations we make of our roles are not so totally different as to challenge other people's understanding of what the role is all about.

This model of human behaviour is known as **symbolic interactionism**, because it emphasises how we interact, not so much with individual personalities, as with the role that someone is playing, and what is symbolised by that role. Mead regarded this categorisation and the way that people interact with one another as symbols of their role as more or less inevitable. Even people who choose to drop out of orthodox society become socially categorised, and end up playing social roles of their own, like 'drop-out', 'tramp' or 'hippy'. Personality in this theory, then, results from the social roles that a person plays, and the way that they interpret those roles.

Social cognition

The theory put forward by Walter Mischel (1968) stated that it is people's understanding of the cog-nitive and social aspects of their situation which determines their personality. Rather than assuming that their behaviour is symptomatic of underlying dispositions or traits, Mischel focused on how people react to the different stimuli in their environment.

Although **social behaviour theory** developed out of the behaviourist approaches to personality, Mischel saw the strictly behaviourist perspective as being far too limited. In particular, Mischel argued, it did not look carefully enough at the concept of **discrimination**. Human beings, Mischel argued, are capable of recognising and learning from very subtle distinctions in stimuli; which means that even a slight variation on a situ-ation can produce totally different behaviour. The behaviourists tended to present the types of responses which people will produce in similar situations as being pretty consistent: a certain type of situation will produce a certain type of behav-iour. But Mischel argued that people discriminate in a more sophisticated way than that. They will act consistently across situations only if similar acts are likely to lead to similar consequences.

Increasingly, research into social influences on behaviour demonstrated the importance of per-sonal cognition in understanding personality. In 1973, Mischel showed how **expectancies** and **values** are crucial in guiding people's choices between alternative courses of action in any given situation. Following this, Bandura (1977b) identi-fied a special form of expectancy, known as self-efficacy. This refers to our beliefs about our own personal effectiveness – in other words, whether we feel able to measure up to what is needed in a given situation. In Mischel's view, personality resulted from a combination of social learning, expectancies, values and self-efficacy beliefs.

In 1989, Bandura argued that **self-efficacy beliefs** are important mediating agents in how and whether people feel in control of their lives. This in turn means that they link very strongly with self-concept and self-confidence; it is what we feel capable of doing which influences whether we feel helpless in certain situations, or whether we feel in control. Bandura argued that it is often quite a good thing when people have very high self-efficacy beliefs, even if they seem a bit unrealistic, because if you have high expectations about yourself you tend to rise to them; whereas people who have low, or 'realistic', self-efficacy beliefs tend to under-achieve because they do not go in for things that they know will be challenging. You never know what you can do until you try!

Modern social behaviour theory, then, concentrates both on the behaviour itself and on the person's understanding of their social situation, rather than seeing personality in terms of underlying traits or dispositions. Both the consistent and the uncommon aspects of personality are seen as depending on the individual's previous experience and their current situation. But both current cues and previous learning are seen as being extremely subtle and complex, bearing little resemblance to the mechanistic models of human behaviour and personality put forward by the behaviourists.

Phenomenological and humanistic theories

From the 1950s onwards, a new set of approaches to personality grew up. These emphasised that in order to understand a person's behaviour, it is necessary to look at how people themselves see their situations. This is known as a **phenomenological** approach. According to this way of thinking, human beings are actively interpreting and making sense out of their worlds, and the conclusions which they draw affect how they act. So a theory of personality which does not take someone's own perceptions into account is always going to be inadequate in explaining behaviour. There have been several different personality theories which have adopted a phenomenological approach, ranging from the humanistic theory outlined by Carl Rogers to the existentialism of R.D. Laing, which is actually included in Chapter 9 in view of its particular focus. All these theories, however, share the idea that a phenomenological understanding of the person and their situation is essential to the understanding of that individual's personality.

Rogers

Carl Rogers developed his theory of personality as a result of his clinical work, in which he found that the fragmented stimulus–response model of

the behaviourists was simply inadequate for explaining his clients' experiences. His theory emphasised the importance of the self-concept, and of personal growth, and argued that both of these are essential to healthy personality development.

Rogers (1961) argued that all human beings have two basic needs. The first is a need for **self-actualisation**, which Rogers saw as an active striving for personal development. Self-actualisation is making real, or actual, the different aspects of the self. This might involve exploring one's talents, educating oneself or perfecting physical skills. It could show itself in a number of different ways in different people, but Rogers saw it as a fundamental need in everyone, which had to be satisfied, or psychological problems would result.

He described the second basic need as the need for **positive regard** – affection, love or respect from other people. Rogers saw healthy personality development as occurring through relationships – usually in childhood, though not always – which provided the individual with **unconditional positive regard**. This is positive regard which does not depend on the person showing 'good' or 'approved of' behaviour: the person is loved anyway, even if some of the things which they do are not liked very much. The security of having a relationship like this frees that individual to explore their potential. So they can satisfy their need for self-actualisation quite safely, exploring the different things they feel they might like to try, because they do not have to risk losing positive regard through disapproval.

Some children, though, have parents who only provide **conditional positive regard** – they make their love dependent on good behaviour, perhaps insisting that they do not love the child when it is naughty or disobedient. This, according to Rogers, is very psychologically damaging for the child. Partly, this is because it grows up feeling that it is an ideal, never-naughty child that the parents like, and not the real child. Partly also, it stops the child from risking doing anything different, in case it brings disapproval. And this means that the child is unable to satisfy its need for self-actualisation.

Rogers argued that the neurotic clients that he had encountered during his clinical work had all experienced conditional positive regard from their parents or caretakers throughout their childhood. This meant that obtaining approval from other people had become all-important to them. These children had grown up striving for approval from others, and neglecting their own self-actualisation in the process. But self-actualisation is not just an option, Rogers argued: it is a need, which has to be satisfied if we are to remain psychologically healthy. If we ignore it we become psychologically damaged. So part of the therapeutic task was for these people to get back in touch with their inner selves, and begin to explore their own personal talents, inclinations and abilities.

This was not as easy as it sounded, however, because these people were very frightened of risking social disapproval by acting less than perfectly. As a result of the way their parents responded, they had developed an idealised set of **conditions of worth** – standards which they used to judge what type of behaviour would be likely to gain approval from others. These conditions of worth also represented their **ideal self-concept** – the self which they thought they ought to try to live up to. But this ideal self was unrealistically perfect, and simply not possible to achieve. So these clients felt continually anxious because they were unable to live up to the standards which they felt were necessary for social approval. It was this which produced the anxiety and neurosis which had eventually brought them to the clinic.

We will be looking at Rogers' form of therapy in Chapter 9. But we can see here how the model of personality put forward by Rogers centres on the two basic psychological needs of self-actualisation and positive regard. It assumes that people are continually growing and developing, and that a healthy personality is one which is striving for personal growth – a very different picture of personality from some of the theories we have looked at earlier in this chapter.

Kelly's personal construct theory

George Kelly was also a clinical psychologist, who saw the human being as essentially a rational, reasoning person. Unlike many other therapists, Kelly believed that people were often well aware of their problems and what they implied. He always said that after his death, if he was remembered for anything, he wanted to be remembered for **Kelly's first principle**, which was: '*If you don't know what's wrong with the patient – ask him. He may tell you*' (Kelly, 1955).

The underlying model of the human being in Kelly's theory is that of the person acting like a scientist, constantly making and testing hypotheses and developing theories to explain their observations. Where a scientist is trying to explain what was happening with laboratory material, however, ordinary people are trying to explain what is happening in their everyday life and the people they encounter in it. The process is the same, but the subject matter is different.

One of the most fundamental principles of Kelly's theory is the idea of **constructive alternativism**. Kelly argued that people do not react to objective reality as it stands. Instead, each of us reacts to the world as we understand it – we carry around with us our own, distinctive alternative universes. Through our everyday experience, Kelly argued, we develop a whole set of individual, personal theories about what the world is like, which we use as a guide for our own actions and responses. These individual theories are known as our **personal constructs**.

Personal constructs

Personal constructs, according to Kelly, can be seen as statements with two opposite ends – as **bipolar** statements, like 'kind-cruel', or 'intelligent-stupid'. But these constructs are individual and distinctive, so each person will have developed their own set, and they will express it in their own ways. The set of constructs which someone uses is distinctively personal: another person may never use those particular categories when they think about the people that they know – they may use a totally different set of constructs instead.

Since constructs are so very personal, it is also important to remember that although the words which one person uses to describe their constructs might be the same as those used by someone else, the construct itself might have an entirely different meaning. We do not normally express our constructs in words, so we tend to draw on our own personal mental imagery when we are trying to express them. This means that the same word will have different connotations. If you ask a number of different people to give a word that means the opposite of, say, 'aggressive', you are quite likely to find that you end up with a wide variety of answers, ranging from 'passive' or 'submissive' to 'calm' or 'gentle'. Each of these opposites implies that the person is understanding the word 'aggressive' in a slightly different way.

According to Kelly, most of us typically use about seven or eight major constructs when we are trying to understand the people that we come across, but we have a lot of minor ones as well. Some constructs that we use are more general than others, and can be applied to a wider range of circumstances or things. The construct 'good-bad' is one of these, and it often appears as a superordinate construct in people's personal construct systems. Other constructs are subordinate and relate to more specific information (for example 'likes animals–cruel to animals'). The **repertory grid technique** which Kelly developed, described in Box 7.2, provides a systematic way of examining an individual personal construct system.

Construct systems

There are many individual differences in the way that personal construct systems operate. Kelly made a distinction between 'tight' and 'loose' construct systems. 'Tight' construct systems are clearly defined and make very definite predictions. 'Loose' construct systems are vague, and can be used flexibly. Tight constructs are therefore useful in making specific predictions, but they cannot handle ambiguous situations. Loose constructs are good at coping with ambiguity, but are not very precise in letting the person know what to expect.

This is an important distinction, because the fact that we act like scientists means that we are constantly testing out whether our understanding of the situation is correct. So if a construct makes a prediction which does not come true, it is **invalidated**, and we have to seek an alternative explanation. A loose construct is not likely to be invalidated, but on the other hand, since it is so vague, it is not likely to be much use to us in guiding our behaviour either. The alternative to a construct being validated or invalidated, of course, is that the experience may turn out to be outside the **range of convenience** of the construct. The construct is completely unable to explain what is happening, and we become bewildered in the face of entirely new phenomena.

Kelly's theory, then, argues that what is distinctive about personality is the individual constructs which people use to make sense out of their experiences. Since everyone has their own unique set of constructs, they act differently from one another, and that is what makes them individuals.

---

ox 7.2 The repertory grid

The repertory grid was a psychometric technique devised by Kelly in an attempt to develop a systematic method of examining the personal constructs which people use to make sense of their worlds. There are two stages to devising a repertory grid. The first stage involves eliciting the constructs which the individual uses, and the second is to see how those constructs would apply to a number of different elements. The second stage allows us to identify patterns or themes in the way that the person interprets their world, and how they respond to other people or other circumstances.

Constructs can be elicited by asking the person to name eight or so **elements**. These are usually people who are in some way important to them, but market researchers have used other items – models of cars, buildings, brands – instead. Often, each element is given a reference letter. Then the person is given sets of three letters at a time, and asked to state in what way any two of them are similar, and different from the third. They do this for several different combinations of letters – ADF, BCH, and so on. Each pair of similarity and difference which they identify is taken to represent the opposite ends of a personal construct.

In the second stage, the constructs are arranged as a horizontal line on a grid, with each of the elements representing a column. Then the person is asked to indicate, by putting ticks and zeros on the grid, how each construct applies to each element. This is the repertory grid itself.

Repertory grids have been used extensively in a wide range of areas, ranging from psychotherapy to the analysis of consumer perceptions. It has been argued that they provide a unique opportunity for examining how people see their worlds. The outcome is particularly special because it is not just idiosyncratic, but allows for systematic comparisons between people while still acknowledging individuality.

Narrow-band theories of personality

Narrow-band theories of personality are theories which do not attempt to provide overall accounts of human functioning, but rather are concerned with just one or two distinctive features about people, and how they differ from one another. They leave other aspects of personality open, and concentrate on just one particular area of individual difference.

The authoritarian personality

WWII showed dramatically how extreme social prejudice could become, and with what tragic effects. Naturally, this led to a number of psychological investigations of prejudices such as anti-Semitism and other forms of racism; and of the emergence of fascism as a political viewpoint. Some of this research focused on how groups perpetuate intergroup hostility, and we will be looking at this in Chapter 16. Some other research, however, focused on the cognitive styles and personalities of those who subscribed to the extreme right-wing ideology which had produced fascism.

Research quickly showed that people with extreme right-wing beliefs had distinctive features in their cognitive styles. They seemed to have two distinctive characteristics. The first of these was **rigidity**. People with this type of attitude would maintain their beliefs even if they were faced with direct evidence showing that they were untrue or inadequate to explain what was going on. They were not open to changing their minds in the face of new information. The second characteristic cognitive style was **intolerance of ambiguity**. Such people found it very difficult indeed to cope with ideas that were equivocal, or did not have a clear 'right-and-wrong' solution. If faced with a debate, they would adopt one side or another of the question very quickly, and then automatically dismiss the arguments of the other side.

Adorno *et al.* (1950) proposed that these two cognitive styles actually reflected a specific kind of personality. They argued that there was a cluster of personality traits which made up what they called the **authoritarian personality**. This was a rigid personality pattern, characterised by extreme right-wing political beliefs, punitive approaches to social sanctions and high levels of prejudice towards 'outsiders'.

From interview data with large numbers of people holding right-wing political beliefs, Adorno *et al.* showed that people with authoritarian personalities tended to have been brought up by extremely strict authoritarian parents. These parents refused to allow their children to oppose their ideas, or even to show any resentment or aggression when things were unfair – unfairness was not all that uncommon since they did not listen to the child's point of view at all. This meant that the child would feel angry about the unfairness of this, but would have to suppress its anger and make sure that none of it showed. Experiencing such extreme feelings while still remaining outwardly an obedient, cheerful child would eventually become intolerable. So Adorno *et al.* argued that the child would **repress** its hostility – pushing it out of consciousness so powerfully that the child would become unaware of feeling any anger at all.

Adorno's theory was based on the Freudian model of the conscious and unconscious mind. In this instance, the hostility to the parents' arbitrary authority would become lodged in the unconscious mind, and not accessible to the child's consciousness. But this, of course, meant that the conscious mind would have to be very careful to make sure that the repressed hostility did not come to the surface again. Adorno *et al.* argued that the authoritarian personality structure was produced as a result of the defence mechanisms which were needed to keep this hostility buried.

Adorno came to the conclusion that the cognitive rigidity and intolerance of ambiguity which had been observed in highly authoritarian people were also due to defence mechanisms. These people were very hostile to conclusions or decisions which were ambiguous or unclear, because that left them too open to new ideas. Being open to new ideas might also mean that they became open to thinking the unthinkable – that they were angry with their parents. So by making sure that they kept their thinking rigid and definite, they unconsciously avoided anything that might make them vulnerable to their own inner conflicts. Rigidity of thought and opinions was, therefore, a way of preventing any unwelcome disturbance or mental re-thinking which might give these feelings an opportunity to come to the surface.

Evidence for authoritarianism

There was quite a lot of evidence to support these ideas. In 1948, Rokeach tested how authoritarian or politically right-wing research participants performed on puzzles which involved the formation of mental set (Einstellung), of the sort that we looked at in Chapter 5. Rokeach found that such people were unable to adapt their thinking from a previous mental set, to tackle a new problem. Moreover, once they had adopted a particular thought pattern, they found it much harder than ordinary people (those with more moderate views) to change their approach, even if the thought pattern they were using could be seen to be inadequate.

Authoritarian individuals were also shown to be characterised by an exaggeratedly high level of deference to authority figures. Adorno explained this as being a **reaction-formation** against the inner hostility laid down in childhood. Defending against facing up to their hostility meant that suppressing any aggression towards authority figures had become highly important, and this produced an attitude where they became extremely deferential. This was also the reason why they found challenges to established know-

ledge or authority so disturbing, and tended to be so hostile towards out-groups. But their hostility was also a way of displacing their inner anger: by making a racial group the target, they expressed some of their anger without having to face up to their inner conflicts.

Adorno *et al.* (1950) developed a psychometric test for measuring the extent of authoritarianism in an individual's personality. This became known as the F-scale – the F stood for fascism. The **F-scale** assessed nine personality traits which combined to form the authoritarian personality, and which were the direct result of the defence mechanisms produced by authoritarian parents. The traits are listed in Table 7.3.

Dogmatism

In 1960 Rokeach took this work even further by describing another, but strongly related, personality style. Adorno et al. had argued that the authoritarian personality was really only characteristic of people with extreme right-wing political views. But Rokeach argued that many (though not all) of its characteristics were also shared by those who subscribed to extreme left-wing political positions. The important dimension in

Table 7.3 Traits of the authoritarian personality

Conventionalism	Highly authoritarian people tend to be extremely conventional in their approaches to things, and very suspicious of anyone who is different from the majority.
Authoritarian submissiveness	Highly authoritarian people tend to be extremely deferential to those who are in authority, and expect others to be deferential as well.
Authoritarian aggression	Such people are extremely hostile to anyone who challenges authority, or suggests that it is inadequate in any respect.
Anti-intraception	Highly authoritarian people tend to adopt a very tough-minded and punitive approach to any form of social misdemeanour: they usually regard leniency as weak and socially corrupting.
Superstition and stereotype	Such people tend to believe that events are 'fated', inevitable, or externally controlled, and cannot be controlled by individuals, except through luck.
Power and 'toughness'	Authoritarian personalities tend to behave in a dominating and sometimes bullying manner towards other people.
Destructiveness and cynicism	Highly authoritarian personalities tend to show high levels of hostility and aggression towards other people and towards ideas which they disagree with.
Projectivity	Authoritarian personalities show a powerful tendency to project their own unconscious impulses onto others.
Sex	Authoritarian personalities tend to show an exaggerated concern with sexual misbehaviour, regarding it with extreme hostility.

Source: Adorno et al., 1950

this respect, he argued, was whether the individual was open- or closed-minded: whether they could entertain new ideas and ambiguities, or whether they insisted that everything should be seen in strict 'black and white' terms.

Rokeach named this personality style **dogmatism**. A series of studies showed that these dimensions could apply to those on the left as well as those on the right – although Rokeach accepted that dogmatism was much more common among right-wing individuals. The research also showed that dogmatic individuals tend to glorify authority figures, and are very intolerant of criticism towards them. Their rigid approach also limits their ability to deal with novelty: when tested, they were less good at analysing new situations, or at adopting new approaches or new strategies when they became necessary.

We can see, then, that the personality theories put forward by Adorno and Rokeach do not attempt to encompass all possible aspects of human personality. Instead, they just address one particular, very significant, dimension, looking at how it comes about in the individual, and how it manifests itself.

Type A and Type B personality

Another well-known narrow-band theory of personality concerns how people respond to stress. We will be coming back to this theory in Chapter 13, when we look at some of the general issues concerned with stress and ways of reducing it. But since the model represents another example of the narrow-band approach, it is worth mentioning here.

In 1959, two researchers, Friedman and Rosenman, observed that there seemed to be two distinctive ways that people went about working in high-pressure environments. They were particularly concerned with managers and executives in stressful occupations. One group of managers seemed to respond to their situations by acting very intensively. They were typically rushed and hasty, highly competitive, found it hard to delegate responsibility and tended to be extremely alert, even at times nervous. Friedman and Rosenman referred to this type of behaviour as **Type A**.

A second group of managers, however, went about their work in a very different way. They tended to be much more relaxed, and found it easier to delegate responsibility. Although they

were just as concerned with getting the job done as Type A individuals were, they were less competitive, seeing setbacks as obstacles to be overcome rather than as challenges or races. If something could not be done on a particular working day, they accepted that it would have to be finished the day after, rather than fretting about it: they did not take their cares and stresses home with them. In all, they tended to live at much lower levels of stress than the other group did, although they were just as productive. Friedman and Rosenman described this group as **Type B**.

The researchers developed a personality questionnaire, designed to assess these personality characteristics. They then began a longitudinal study of over 3000 managers and executives, which lasted for eight-and-a-half years (Rosenman *et al.*, 1975). They found that the Type A individuals in the group were almost twice as likely as the Type B people to develop stress-related diseases, and particularly coronary heart disease, even after differences in other factors, like age and smoking, had been controlled.

Glass (1977) proposed that what distinguishes Type A people from Type B people more than any other single characteristic is the way that they respond to being helpless. In one study, research participants who came into either the Type A or the Type B category were given puzzles to solve, but in fact some of the puzzles that they were given were unsolvable. Glass found that the two groups responded quite differently. The Type A individuals became much more stressed when they found that they were not able to control the situation, and made a number of attempts to regain control. When they found that this was impossible, they gave up altogether, not even managing to solve later problems which were similar, but solvable. Type B people, on the other hand, tackled the problems more calmly, and continued to try new approaches with further problems that they were given.

The implication, then, is that the difference between personality Type A and personality Type B is a cognitive – emotional one: it is partly to do with cognitive style, but that style in itself comes from differences in emotional orientation to pressures. Again, this is not a complete theory of personality in itself: it is a partial theory, which can work together with other theories of personality in providing a picture of an individual. In the same way that Adorno's theory of the authoritarian personality drew on Freud's model of the unconscious and conscious minds and defence mechanisms, so other theories might be drawn on to explain how Type A and Type B personality traits come about. Rogers' work on conditions of worth, for example, might be used to explain just why it has come to be so vital to Type A people that they should be successful every minute of the time.

Narrow-band theories of personality, as we have seen, do not seek to present a general model of human nature, unlike some of the more general theories. Instead, they focus on one area of human functioning and describe what is happening there, often working hand-in-hand with more general models as they do so.

Types of personality theory

In this chapter, we have looked at several different approaches to the understanding of human personality. They can be grouped together in a number of different ways. Here, they have been grouped into psychoanalytic theories, trait theories, social-learning theories, phenomenological theories and the more limited narrow-band theories. But there are several other classifications which could have been used.

Idiographic and nomothetic theories
One possibility, for example, might be to distinguish between **idiographic** and **nomothetic** theories of personality, because they are trying to do very different things. Nomothetic theories of personality operate by looking for general criteria on which all individuals may be measured and compared. They are concerned with identifying the general aspects of personality which all people have in common, and measuring how people differ with respect to those general aspects.

Idiographic theories of personality, on the other hand, do not concern themselves so much with making comparisons between people. Instead, their focus of interest is how the single individual works – with how psychological processes produce individuality, not similarity. Freud's model of the unconscious, for example, is an idiographic approach: what Freud is interested in is what is happening within the single individual's mind. Eysenck's trait theory, on the other hand, is nomothetic – Eysenck is

interested in how people measure up on these general scales.

Ipsative and normative tests
This distinction is also reflected in the different types of psychometric tests which have been derived from personality theories. **Normative tests** are those which can be used to compare one individual with other people. They give results on standard scales, which are then compared with tables of population norms provided in the test manual, to give the tester an idea of how typical that person's result is. Standard personality tests like the Eysenck Personality Inventory or Cattell's 16PF are normative tests.

By comparison, **ipsative tests** are used to provide detailed information about someone's own individual personality structure. They do this by looking at which characteristics are strongest or weakest within a person, but not in a way that allows for comparison with other people. For example, an ipsative test assessing a person on, say, the five robust factors of emotional stability, conscience, extroversion, agreeableness and openness to experience would give a result which indicated which of these was the strongest and the weakest quality in that particular person's character. So the test would be helpful to people who wanted to use it as the basis for counselling or careers advice. But a normative test based on the same traits would give a measure which showed how 'normal' the person's score was on each of these.

Johnson, Wood and Blinkhorn (1988) argued that it was important for all users of personality tests – occupational psychologists as well as other people who had been trained to apply them – to be aware of the difference between ipsative and normative tests. It is too easy, they argued, for ipsative tests to be treated as if they were normative, so that measures intended to describe the relative strengths and weaknesses of a single individual are used to compare different people. But this, they argued, produces extremely misleading results.

For example, using an ipsative instead of a normative test for interpersonal comparisons could mean that someone who scored highly on, say, openness to experience would seem to be more open than someone with a low score on the same test. But that need not necessarily be the case. The high score might mean only that it was the strongest of a generally weak set of traits, and the person might actually be quite low on the trait by comparison with others. Similarly, a low score might just mean that other traits were stronger, and that individual could still be far more open to experience than the other person. If the aim of the testing is to make comparisons between people, Johnson *et al.* argued, it is essential to make sure that a normative test and not an ipsative test has been used. Otherwise, the results will be useless.

The importance of qualified testers

Issues like these show how important it is that people who use personality tests should have training in applying them. As with intelligence tests, it is far too easy to misunderstand their results, and for them to be used in inappropriate ways. Personality tests are particularly popular for occupational selection, and are sometimes used by non-psychologists. So in recent years the British Psychological Society has established formal qualifications whereby non-psychologists, like managers and personnel officers, can be trained to administer and interpret occupational tests properly.

In this chapter we have looked at a range of approaches to understanding personality. Most of the theories originated from the work of clinical psychologists. They were developed to enable us to understand and help people who showed some form of abnormal behaviour, or mental illness. Theories of personality all contain an implicit model of human nature, and it is often useful to compare the underlying assumptions of what people are like with those used by other theories. These assumptions are also reflected in the different ways that psychologists and others have sought to explain abnormal behaviour. In the next chapter we will be looking more closely at abnormal psychology and some of the issues which it raises.

Key terms

affective To do with feelings or emotions, such as the component of an attitude concerned with feelings.

affective dimension The aspect of an attitude which is concerned with feelings and emotions which are directed towards the attitude's target.

anal stage The second of Freud's psychosexual stages, in which libido focuses on the anus.

anal-expulsive The Freudian idea of an adult character trait produced by children enjoying the act of defecation too much, and so becoming overly generous and giving.

anal-retentive The Freudian idea of an adult character trait produced by children experiencing over-strict potty training, resulting in their developing mean or miserly characters.

archetypes Symbolic figures or objects which, according to Jung, resonate in the collective unconscious and produce powerful mystical responses in the human being.

authoritarian personality A collection of characteristics found by Adorno to occur together, producing a rigid approach to moral and social issues.

bipolar Having two opposite ends, or poles, with a continuum running between them. For example, the bipolar personal construct of 'kind-cruel' has the two ends represented by the words used to describe it; but some individuals may fit somewhere in between the two extremes – e.g. being mostly kind but not always.

black box theories Theories which are concerned purely with stimulus input and behavioural output.

castration threat anxiety Freud's idea that the young boy is secretly afraid that his father will castrate him.

cognitive dimension The aspect of an attitude which is to do with thoughts, opinions and beliefs held in relation to the target of the attitude.

conative dimension Also known as the behavioural dimension, this is the dimension of an attitude which is concerned with the tendency to act – how likely it is that the person will take action in accordance with their expressed attitudes.

conditions of worth Internalised ideas about what personal qualities or achievements will make someone a valuable or worthwhile person, which are developed as a result of experiences with other people. According to Carl Rogers, the realism of the individual's conditions of worth are a main factor in the maintenance of self-esteem, or lack of it.

constructive alternativism The principle that each person's psychological reality is constructed on a personal basis, from their own distinctively individual experience.

defence mechanisms Protective strategies that the mind uses to defend itself against unwelcome or disturbing information.

determinism A style of thinking in which all human action or experience is assumed to be directly caused.

discrimination The skill of distinguishing one stimulus from another, usually learned through selective conditioning.

dogmatism A rigid personality trait similar to authoritarianism, but one which can be left-wing too (authoritarianism is always right-wing). Like authoritarianism, it includes intolerance of those who differ from the established view, a rigid 'black-and-white' approach to issues, and an extreme and personal categorising of 'us and them'.

dynamic equilibrium A balance between two opposing pressures which is achieved by constant movement and adjustment between them.

Electra conflict A Freudian attempt to explain female gender-role identification by means of a supposed penis envy on the part of the young girl, and rivalry with the mother.

extroversion A general tendency towards outgoing, social behaviour.

five robust factors The recurrent finding that personality questionnaires produce results which, when factor analysed, fall into five groups, thought to represent basic personality traits.

fixation In Freudian terms, the process of becoming 'stuck' in an early phase of psychological development.

genital stage In Freudian theory, a stage of psychological development around puberty in which libido becomes focused on the genitals and the individual develops an interest in the other sex.

identification The process of social learning which involves feeling oneself to be the same as, or very similar to, another person and basing one's styles of interaction on that comparison.

imitation Copying someone else's behaviour and specific actions.

introversion A general tendency towards solitary, withdrawn behaviour.

ipsative tests Tests which are used to show the balance of different characteristics within one individual, but not to compare people with one another.

latency period In Freudian theory, a period of childhood during which the libido becomes diffused throughout the body and the child is supposed to become sexually passive.

Law of Effect The learning principle that actions which have a pleasant effect on the organism are likely to be repeated.

libido The sexual and life-affirming energy which Freud initially saw as the energising factor for all human behaviour. In later work, he added the idea of a destructive energy: thanatos.

nativism An approach which assumes that knowledge or abilities are innate, and do not need to be learned.

normative Representing the norm; typical.

Oedipal conflict In Freudian theory, the idea that the young male child wishes to possess his mother sexually, and therefore perceives himself as the direct rival of the larger, more powerful father.

oral stage In Freudian theory, the period in infancy in which the infant derives pleasure solely from the mouth.

personal constructs Individual ways of making sense of the world, which have been developed on the basis of experience. Personal construct theorists argue that getting to understand the personal constructs which someone uses to make sense of their experience is essential for effective psychotherapy, as well as for effective interaction in day-to-day living.

phallic stage In Freudian theory, a stage in which pleasure for the young child supposedly becomes focused on the genitals, and the child's sexual attention is drawn to the other-sexed parent.

phenomenological Concerned with the person's own perceived world and the phenomena which they experience, rather than with objective reality.

phrenology A nineteenth-century belief that character and other qualities were revealed by systematic irregularities on the skull.

physiological determinism The approach which states that human and other behaviour occurs as a straightforward consequence of physiological systems.

pleasure principle In Freudian terms, the way that the id operates by demanding instant gratification of its impulses, regardless of social convention.

positive regard Liking, affection, love or respect for someone else.

psychoticism A form of mental illness which involves the individual losing touch with reality.

reaction formation A defence mechanism in which a repressed impulse turns into its opposite, e.g. repressed homosexuality turning into aggressive homophobia.

reality principle The name given by Freud to the way that the ego attempts to balance the demands of the id and superego with the practical demands of reality.

reductionism An approach to understanding behaviour which focuses on one single level of explanation and ignores others. The opposite of interactionism.

regression A defence mechanism which involves reverting to adaptive behaviour learned during an earlier period of development.

repertory grid technique A system for eliciting personal constructs and showing how individuals use them to interpret their experience.

reticular activating system The part of the brain which mediates sleep, wakefulness and alertness.

self-concept The idea or internal image that people have of what they themselves are like, including both evaluative and descriptive dimensions.

self-efficacy beliefs The belief that one is capable of doing something effectively. Self-efficacy beliefs are closely connected with self-esteem, in that having a sense of being capable and potentially in control tends to increase confidence. But the concept is often thought to be more useful than the generalised concept of self-esteem, since people may often be confident about some abilities, or in some areas of their lives, but not in others.

social learning The approach to understanding social behaviour which emphasises how people imitate action and model their behaviour on that of others.

somatotypes Types of body shape, once thought to indicate personality.

symbolic interactionism The approach to social understanding which looks at how people perceive and respond to one another as social symbols, such as roles, rather than as individuals.

synchronicity In Jung's analytic psychology, the idea that some events reverberate with more than everyday meaning because they tap into deeper meanings in the collective unconscious.

temperament The term used to describe basic differences between infants and people, in terms of their tendencies to respond differently to stimuli, and thought to be a precursor to personality.

thanatos The negative, destructive energy proposed by Freud as a counterpart to the positive sexual energy known as libido, and invoked in order to explain the destruction and carnage of WWI in psychoanalytic terms.

type A and B personality Personality syndromes in which A is characterised by impatience, intolerance and a high level of stress, while B involves a relaxed, tolerant approach and noticeably lower personal stress.

unconditional positive regard Love, affection or respect which does not depend on the person's having to act in particular ways.

Summary

1 Early theories of personality included personality domains, the theory of the humours, phrenology and somatotypes.

2 Freud's psychoanalytic theory of personality emphasised the importance of the unconscious mind, and asserted that early experiences in child-hood could produce lasting effects on the adult personality.

3 Jung believed that human beings had access to a shared collective unconscious, which could operate in a healing way; whereas Fromm believed that society, as well as family and maturation, was important in shaping character.

4 Trait theories of personality include Eysenck's two factor theory, Cattell's sixteen factor theory, and the 'five robust factors' identified by Costa and McCrae.

5 Learning-oriented theories range from the behaviourist stimulus-response model to social-learning theory, emphasising imitation and identification, symbolic interactionism emphasising social roles, and social cognitive theory which emphasises social learning, expectancies, values and self-efficacy beliefs.

6 Rogers argued that people had two basic needs: a need for self-actualisation and a need for positive regard from others. Both of these had to be satisfied for healthy personality development. Kelly argued that understanding personality meant understanding people's personal constructs.

7 Narrow-band approaches to personality include the authoritarian personality, which aims to account for extremes of social prejudice; and Type A and Type B personalities which describe approaches to work and stress.

8 Nomothetic theories of personality present general criteria but idiographic ones account for individuality. Similarly, normative psychometric tests are used for comparison, but ipsative tests only give an individual picture.

Self-assessment questions

1 Briefly describe the model of personality proposed by either Jung or Fromm.

2 Describe the sources of data which Cattell used in the development of the *16PF*.

3 Outline Rogers' theory of personality.

Practice essay questions

1 'Trait explanations of personality are intrinsically inadequate'. Discuss.

2 How far do the concepts of social learning, symbolic interactionism and social cognition make the concept of personality redundant?

3 Can phenomenological approaches provide us with a full understanding of personality?

Test your knowledge of this chapter with our online quizzes and games at: http://www.psych.co.uk

Explore theories of personality further at:

General
http://www.psych.nwu.edu/personality.html – The best site on this subject with excellent links to other websites, further reading, major theorists, etc.

History/theorists
http://www.wynja.com/personality/theorists.html – Links to information sites on the key theorists.

Personality tests
http://www.iglobal.net/psman/prstests.html – Serious and fun personality tests. Even when you find out which Star Wars character you are most like, there is an educational slant, explaining in great detail why they have come to the conclusion.

The medical model of abnormal behaviour

```
The medical model of abnormal behaviour
├── The medical model of psychiatric disorder
│   ├── Diagnosis
│   ├── Criticisms of the medical model
│   └── Abnormality
└── Specific disorders
    ├── Schizophrenia
    ├── Depression
    ├── Anxiety disorders
    └── Eating disorders
```

Learning objectives

8.1. Historical approaches
a name historical theories of abnormal behaviour
b describe early theories of abnormal behaviour
c evaluate early therapies of abnormal behaviour

8.2. Early classification systems
a identify underlying assumptions of the medical model
b describe the different categories of mental illness
c criticise the early classifiction system

8.3. DSM-IV
a describe the five axes of DSM-IV
b link problems of diagnosis to the emergence of DSM-IV
c evaluate the medical approach of psychiatric diagnosis

8.4. The medical model
a describe early approaches to somatic therapy
b outline reasons for the acceptance of the medical model
c evaluate the concept of mental illness

8.5. Normality and abnormality
a describe definitions of abnormality and normality
b evaluate definitions of abnormality
c list criteria for defining the concept of normality

8.6. Schizophrenia and depression
a distinguish between different types of depression
b describe a study of learned helplessness
c evaluate competing theories of schizophrenia

8.7. Eating and anxiety disorders
a identify types of eating disorder
b evaluate theories of eating disorder
c describe the symptoms of post-traumatic stress disorder

8.8. The diasthesis-stress model
a define terms relating to explanations for psychiatric disorders
b list factors which can influence the onset of a psychiatric disorder
c describe the diasthesis-stess model of psychiatric disorder

What do we mean if we say that someone is 'insane', or 'mentally ill'? Why do we think of them as 'ill' in the first place? The answer lies in the type of theory that we hold about why a person has come to act strangely, or in a way that is different from other people and not helpful to that person in living their life. In modern society, we tend to assume that abnormal behaviour of this kind happens as a result of some kind of illness: that is the theory which is most common. But it is not the only possible explanation. Throughout history, abnormal behaviour has been explained in a number of different ways, and there are also a number of different contemporary models, which people apply when they are trying to help those who show abnormal behaviour.

Historical approaches to abnormal behaviour

Nowadays, we tend to take it for granted that if someone acts so oddly that they are not able to meet the everyday demands of living in society, then they must be 'mentally ill'. But people who acted abnormally have not always been seen like that. In ancient times, the Egyptians, Greeks and Hebrews generally took the view that deviation from the normal could be attributed to the work of good or bad spirits – variations in the weather were seen in much the same way. Disturbed or abnormal behaviour was interpreted as being a sign of mystical or demonic intervention.

If someone's disturbance seemed to be mystical, then they would be viewed with respect, as if they had been visited by a 'good' spirit. But if their disturbance meant that they acted in ways which were contrary to the teachings of the priesthood, that was another matter. In such cases, it was thought that the disturbance came from the actions of evil spirits, which needed to be driven from the body. Some very unpleasant treatments were used to drive them out, such as flogging, starvation or prolonged chanting over the afflicted person as they lay motionless. Sometimes, too, ancient societies practised 'trepanning' – a technique which consisted of drilling a hole in the skull and draining off fluid, supposedly allowing the evil spirits to escape.

The theory of the humours
This general notion of abnormality as resulting from the actions of spirits seemed to be universally accepted until the time of the Greek physician Hippocrates. Hippocrates produced the first theory of abnormal behaviour as having a physical origin, arguing that these disturbances should be regarded as a sign of illness rather than a sign of possession. Hippocrates thought that the causes of the disturbance probably lay in brain pathology, produced by a disturbance of the four major body fluids, or humours – black bile, yellow bile, blood and phlegm. The treatment which he recommended consisted of drugs and purgatives to restore the fluid balance in the body, and also exercise.

According to this theory, the person's symptoms showed which body fluid was out of order, and therefore suggested which type of remedy would be most appropriate. If they were irritable and restless, then they were considered to have an excess of choler – hence our adjective 'choleric'. If they were gloomy and depressed, they were thought to have an excess of black bile, and this is the origin of our term 'melancholic'. Those who were overly cheerful to the point of being manic were thought to have an excess of blood, which is where our word 'sanguine' comes from; and those who were staid and unresponsive were thought to have an excess of phlegm – hence our word 'phlegmatic'.

As we saw in Chapter 7, this model, which became very popular, was used to account for personality as well as abnormal behaviour. It was distinctive, because it suggested that it was possible to adjust abnormal behaviour by using physical remedies, and in that sense was entirely different from the religious explanations which had previously been used.

The 'possession' theory
Although the theory of the humours did not die out completely, the Middle Ages in Europe were dominated by the Christian Church. As a result, physiological explanations of abnormal behaviour became less popular, and religious explanations again became common. This period saw the return of the 'possession' theory. While the Church was establishing itself, the general assumption was that people who showed disturbed or abnormal behaviour had 'troubled souls', and the cures which were used were gentle, like the 'laying on of hands' from a holy person. Later, however, as the Church consolidated its domination over the population, possession by demons or the devil

became the usual explanation, and more punitive methods were used to drive them out. The torturing and burning of 'witches' became commonplace, and the belief that witchcraft caused mental illness came to be so strong that eventually a Papal Bull was issued, officially confirming this belief.

There are political dimensions to these changes too. Ehrenreich and English (1973) describe the witch hunts of this period as an attempt by the increasingly influential medical profession to discredit the practitioners of traditional herbal remedies for illnesses. Ehrenreich and English argue that since the people who practised folk medicine were mainly older women of the poorer classes, devaluing their knowledge helped to establish the supremacy of the male-dominated medical profession.

The idea of 'mental illness'

The beginning of the idea that people who acted strangely were actually 'mentally ill' began to arise during the Renaissance. In the sixteenth century, the Dutch physician Johann Weyer suggested that many mental disorders required treatments other than exorcism. But the Church was still very powerful: his books were banned and burned by James 1 of England. The religious explanation, that abnormal behaviour arose as a result of possession by demons or the devil, was a powerful tool for maintaining control of the population, and the Church was not going to let go of it easily.

The times, though, were changing, and gradually institutions arose to care for those with mental disorders. One of the first of these institutions was the monastery of St Mary of Bethlehem, which had been converted to a hospital by Henry VIII in 1547, and which began to specialise in the treatment of people who showed disturbed or abnormal behaviour. Similar institutions also arose on the Continent. St Mary of Bethlehem became shortened to 'Bedlam' – a word which still survives in our language as signifying a situation of noisy chaos, and reflects the howls and shrieks of despair produced by the inmates. Good treatment for such people was still a long way away. Bedlam itself was open to members of the public as a sideshow, and was particularly renowned for its cruel practices and dreadful living conditions.

Moral therapy

After the French Revolution, Pinel, a radical French reformer, pioneered a new humanitarian approach in one of these institutions. He persuaded the revolutionary government to allow him to free some of the inmates of a notorious asylum, keeping them under his responsibility. There was some nervousness about this, since such people were regarded as uncontrollable and violent; and society in general was surprised when they did not go on the rampage. On the contrary, under Pinel's caretaking technique, the freed inmates behaved in a quiet and restrained manner. This led to a change of social attitude towards such people, and Pinel was encouraged to continue his work.

Pinel called his technique **moral therapy**. The essence of moral therapy, Pinel argued, was that the patients should always be treated as people with dignity – irrespective of whether they needed to be treated firmly or gently. Pinel considered them to be normal people who had lost the power to reason properly owing to environmental stress. Bringing them into the institution relieved the stress, and allowed them to recover their equilibrium. Pinel also introduced the first 'occupational therapy' techniques, giving the patients simple work to do. At its peak, Pinel's moral therapy achieved a success rate of 70%, which is a remarkably high figure in this field. A similar approach was undertaken in the famous Retreat at York, a caring institution run by Quakers.

Pinel's approach is distinctive in that it represents one of the first of the environmental stress explanations for disturbed behaviour. The success of his treatment is also rather special, in the sense that it is quite different from the outcomes of the other early theories. Explanations of abnormal behaviour as arising from spiritual sources had produced largely punitive treatments, and were inextricably linked with questions of social control. Explanations of abnormal behaviour as arising from physiological imbalances had produced confinement and restraint, as the disturbance was seen as largely inevitable. But explanations of mental disturbance as arising from environmental stress had resulted in a type of treatment which seemed to be able to produce some very definite improvements in these people's ability to cope.

The rise of the medical model

As time wore on, advances in the medical sciences led to a decline in the use of moral therapy. The idea of mental disturbance as representing a kind of illness or ailment again became popular. Success in curing physical illness led to the belief that success in curing 'mental illness' was only just around the corner. As the medical profession became more powerful, attendants were replaced by nurses and medical treatments replaced other forms of therapy. Moral therapy was considered to be 'unscientific' in its approach, and became unfashionable.

Further support for the medical model came from the discovery that brain damage or disease could lead to bizarre behavioural symptoms. Perhaps the most influential discovery was that syphilis, in its tertiary stage, led to a severe psychosis in which the person lost all touch with reality and ended up acting very strangely indeed. The discovery that this disorder, which was not at all uncommon in the population at large, had a physical origin encouraged the assumption that all such problems would eventually be explained as having their origins in physical disorders. This led to the idea that **somatic therapies** – therapies which are concerned with adjusting the state of the body, such as drugs or other physical treatments – would be appropriate for this kind of problem.

The development of somatic therapies

The development of somatic therapies was, in the early years, very largely a matter of trying things out to see what might happen. 'Mentally ill' people had no civil rights, or at least none which could be effectively enforced, and experiments could be conducted quite freely. Various types of therapies became popular, and then fell into disuse. For example, at the beginning of this century, **insulin shock therapy** was regarded as a useful treatment for those with extreme disturbance. The patient was given an injection of insulin which lowered the body temperature dramatically, putting the patient into a coma. After a while, they were gradually brought round.

The problem with many of these therapies was that they seemed to be very effective when they were new, but then ceased to be so as they became more routine. In part, this is thought to have come about because of the increased attention which patients received when they were taking part in a new treatment. As the treatment became ordinary, patients receiving it did not receive special attention, and so did not respond to the treatment. But the assumption that this type of

behaviour had a physiological origin meant that this phenomenon could not be explained – social and personal explanations were ruled out, since they were 'unscientific'.

A number of other treatments for mental disorder were explored, including the use of various types of drugs, the induction of artificial epileptic fits through the application of **electro-convulsive therapy (ECT)**, and various types of brain surgery. Although many of these were serious scientific investigations, and produced positive results, others, particularly some of the physical interventions (as opposed to the chemical ones), were conducted on very flimsy theoretical reasoning. In Chapter 10, we will be looking more closely at the use of brain operations such as lobotomy and leucotomy as attempts to reduce abnormal behaviour.

The theory underlying all these treatments, then, was the idea that mental disturbance and abnormal behaviour arose as a result of some kind of medical problem. These problems became known as **psychiatric disorders**. The medical model of psychiatric disorder became fully articulated at the beginning of the twentieth century, and is the main way that modern society interprets disturbances of this kind. We will therefore look at this model, and at some of the criticisms which have been made of it, very closely.

The medical model of psychiatric disorder

The medical model of psychiatric disorder assumes that the origin of abnormal behaviour lies in some kind of malfunction in the body or the brain. It assumes also that different types of malfunctions will produce different types of 'disorders', or mental illnesses. The full development of the medical model is often considered to have occurred with the first widely accepted **classification systems** of mental illnesses. In a medical context a classification system to identify the different types of disorders is useful since it provides some clue as to possible causes and treatments for an illness. It is not really surprising, therefore, that the earlier religious approaches did not bother with classifications – they felt that they already knew the cause of the problem, and the course of action which they should take.

Kraepelin's system

One of the first widely accepted classifications of mental disorders was developed by Kraepelin, in 1913. According to Kraepelin, 'mental illness' itself could be broadly divided into psychoses and neuroses. Psychoses are mental disorders which involve a lack of contact with reality: the person may suffer from delusions or hallucinations, or may react abnormally to apparently innocuous events. Neuroses, on the other hand, are disorders in which the person has only too much contact with reality: some aspect or aspects of living produce extreme anxiety, and the mental disturbance results from the individual trying to deal with or reduce that anxiety.

Although he regarded psychosis and neurosis as the two main forms of mental illness, Kraepelin also included other forms of mental disorder in his system. They were not illnesses as such, but in his view they seemed to be examples of mental processes which were disturbed or not functioning properly in some way. Kraepelin identified five types of mental disorder altogether: neuroses, personality disorders, organic psychoses, functional psychoses, and mental retardation.

Neuroses are disorders which involve excessive anxiety in 'normal' situations. The anxiety is usually contained by the person avoiding its source, which can lead to extremely odd behaviours at times. A neurosis may develop into: a **phobia**, which is an overwhelming, irrational fear of something; an **obsessive compulsion**, in which the person feels obliged to repeat actions or perform rituals repeatedly, or even a case of **multiple personality**, in which the person constructs several different independent identities, with their own separate memories and personalities, keeping each one cut off from the others. (Multiple personality is often called 'schizophrenia' in popular speech, but it is actually quite different from the clinical disorder known as schizophrenia.)

The category of **personality disorder** involves ways of thinking which are socially unusual or deviant. It includes: **paranoia**, which is a delusion that other people are conspiring against the individual; **obsessive personality**, which generally manifests itself in a rigid adherence to rules and regulations; **schizoid personality**, in which the person is not mentally ill but nonetheless prefers fantasy and avoids reality as much as possible; and psychopathy, which is a syndrome in which the individual is lacking in social conscience. Psychopaths are not necessarily criminals or under psychiatric care: they are also found in careers which value such attributes, such as entertainment, politics or big business, and can be extremely likeable people

The word 'organic' in **organic psychoses** implies that these disorders are the result of identifiable physical causes, such as brain infections, brain tumours, injuries to the nervous system or degenerative neural diseases like Huntington's chorea. Perhaps the most well known of these is tertiary syphilis, where the brain is invaded by spirochetes, and the person's ability to function normally and keep in touch with reality becomes increasingly impaired.

Functional psychoses are disorders in which the person is clearly disturbed and not in touch with reality, but there is no apparent organic cause of the problem. According to Kraepelin, there are two general types of functional psychosis: **schizophrenia**, in which the mind becomes split off from contact with reality, and the patient may have hallucinations or delusions; and **manic-depressive psychosis**, in which the patient experiences uncontrollable and extreme changes of mood, sometimes being triggered off by events, but sometimes occurring in a regular cycle

Mental retardation is not actually a mental illness, but it was classified by Kraepelin as a mental disorder. Mentally retarded patients were characterised in this system by an extreme slowness to respond to stimuli, a general lack of interest or curiosity and low IQ scores

Somatic therapy

The general acceptance of the medical model produced an emphasis on somatic therapy. Somatic therapies are therapies which take a physical or physiological approach. Somatic means 'to do with the body', and these therapies focus on adjusting the way that the body works, in order to reduce or get rid of the symptoms which the person is showing. The three major groups of somatic therapy represent the three main approaches to research and intervention in the brain: chemical, electrical and physical.

The approach to psychiatric treatment known as **chemotherapy** is the one which has been the most successful of all – although, as we shall see in the next chapter, there are those who believe that it may not be so helpful for some kinds of problems in the long run. Chemotherapy is concerned with correcting the balance of chemicals in the body through the application of drugs. In Chapter 11, we will be looking in some detail at the ways that some of the different drugs used in psychiatric practice work, in terms of the effects on brain chemicals. The advent of chemotherapy, and the discovery that highly disturbed and agitated patients could be calmed using chemical means, may truthfully be said to have transformed psychiatry, as it eliminated the need for the forceful, and sometimes brutal, restraints which had previously been used.

Electro-convulsive therapy, also known as **ECT** in Britain and **EST** (electric shock therapy) in America, was first developed as a psychiatric treatment during the 1930s, and became commonly used – and abused – during the 1950s and 1960s. Research showed it to be effective with some forms of depression, but Clare (1980) discussed how it fell into disrepute because it was so often used to treat other kinds of psychiatric disorders during that period, often completely inappropriately.

Broadly speaking, ECT works by inducing an artificial epileptic fit, by passing an electric current through the brain. Patients who experience ECT show muscular convulsions and tremors, which are controlled by the administration of muscle relaxants, followed by a period of extreme disorientation. The treatment is repeated on half a dozen occasions, usually administered every other day. This often has the effect of alleviating depression, possibly because of the amnesia which results – it can take several hours for the person to achieve full memory recovery after an ECT session.

The use of ECT has been systematically refined over the years: the range of problems for which it is considered suitable is more limited, and less extreme versions of the method itself have been developed. Some therapists, for example, adopt a technique known as **unilateral ECT**, in which the electric current is applied to only one side of the brain. This reduces some of the side-effects, particularly speech problems if it is administered to the right side of the brain (see Chapter 11), but there is some doubt as to whether the treatment is as effective as **bilateral ECT**, administered to both sides of the brain at once (Abrams et al., 1983).

The other type of intervention in the working of the brain is physical: the use of brain surgery to remove parts of the brain or to sever links between one part of the brain and another. Some of these, such as the operations known as **lobotomy** and **leucotomy**, were attempts to produce general changes in behaviour. Others were addressing more specific problems, like the operation of severing the corpus callosum, which was developed in an attempt to control epilepsy. We will be looking at the outcomes of these operations in terms of their psychological effects, in Chapter 10.

Problems of psychiatric diagnosis

Although it became very widely accepted, it gradually became apparent that there were a number of problems with Kraepelin's classification system, and the later systems which were based on it. Some of these seemed to involve the categories which were used, but others were more general problems to do with the medical model itself.

One of the main problems with a system of psychiatric classification which works by categorising disorders is that it uses a very narrow-band view of normality which does not necessarily apply to all human beings. We will be looking at the problem of defining normality later in this chapter. But it is important to recognise that what counts as 'normal human behaviour' can be very variable in different cultures and in different social groups – there is no definite, absolute list of 'normal' behaviours.

In terms of these lists of symptoms, the difference between normal and abnormal behaviour is elusive, because most of the symptoms are ones which everyone experiences to some degree. For example, we all have days or times when we feel happy or elated, and other days when we feel gloomy or depressed. Similarly, most people have panic attacks at times, or adopt rituals which they feel obliged to carry out, but this does not make them 'neurotic'. Many people like to immerse themselves in fantasy worlds when they read books or watch films, but they are not necessarily 'schizoid personalities'. People break speed limits and fiddle expense accounts or travelling expenses with the nonchalance supposedly characteristic of the psychotic.

So, if all these behaviours occur in everyday, normal life, then where do we draw the line? The answer is that in the end clinical intuition is used to determine whether an individual is 'sick' or not. But since this is a subjective judgement, it is also open to unconscious value-judgements – which can mean that a person is labelled 'sick' if he or she does not conform to the middle-class standards of the psychiatrist doing the assessing.

Problems of reliability

This means, of course, that different psychiatrists may end up applying different standards. In 1956, Schmidt and Fonda arranged for two psychiatrists to diagnose the same 426 patients using the official diagnostic categories which were based on Kraepelin's original system, although revised and extended. They found that the psychiatrists came up with widely varying diagnoses, particularly on questions of schizophrenia and mental deficiency. Similarly, Beck et al. (1962) presented identical clinical data to the same psychiatrists, on two different occasions. The only difference in the information they were given on the two occasions was that the names of the patients had been changed, and there was slightly different phrasing in the reports. Beck found that the psychiatrists tended to make different diagnoses on the different occasions.

The most famous of these studies was conducted by Rosenhan in 1973. Rosenhan arranged for eight 'normal' people (a psychology student, three psychologists, a paediatrician, a psychiatrist, a painter and a housewife) to present themselves to the admissions offices of assessment mental hospital (these are mental hospitals which admit patients for initial diagnosis, as opposed to long-term care). Each of the research participants pretended to have just one symptom: they said that they heard voices. Apart from providing false names and occupations, every other detail that they gave to the medical staff was true.

All the research participants were admitted to the hospital for treatment, and seven out of the eight were diagnosed as having schizophrenia. As soon as they were admitted, each of the research participants acted completely normally, but they were still regarded as disturbed by the medical staff. One of the research participants kept a diary, and this was entered as an example of their abnormal activity in the ward notes 'the patient engages in writing behaviour'. The research participants also said, from the first day of admission, that the voices which they had been hearing had ceased, but it took between 7 and 52 days before they were discharged from the hospital. The fraud was never suspected, and the diagnosis when the seven supposedly schizophrenic patients were released was that they had schizophrenia 'in remission' – in other words, still there, but lying dormant.

In a follow-up study, Rosenhan (1975) informed the members of a teaching hospital about the previous study, and told them that they could expect to see several 'false' patients over the next few months. In fact, no false patients presented themselves, but each member of staff was asked to rate each new patient on the likelihood of his or her being an impostor. Out of 193 new patients 41 were alleged to be 'normal' by at least one member of staff. Of these, 23 were alleged to be normal by at least one psychiatrist, and nineteen were alleged to be normal by at least one psychiatrist and one other person. Rosenhan's two studies cast some grave doubts on whether the psychiatric profession was seriously able to distinguish between 'normal' and 'abnormal' behaviour.

Problems of validity

Another set of problems identified by critics of the medical model is the way that symptoms are used as indicators of a disorder. Wittenborn (1951) used factor analysis on the different symptoms used to identify the diagnostic categories, and found that people sharing the same diagnostic category had widely different symptoms. Similarly, Bannister (1968) showed that it is possible for one person to have some of the primary symptoms of schizophrenia while another person has others. This results in both of them being labelled as 'schizophrenic', even though they do not actually have anything in common. What this really means, say the critics, is that these types of diagnostic categories are simply justifications or guesses, but not valid scientific classifications.

DSM-IV

The low reliability of the standard psychiatric diagnostic categories, together with a number of challenges which emerged during the 1960s and 1970s, resulted in the development in 1980 of a new system of psychiatric diagnosis, known as DSM-III, which is short for the Diagnostic and Statistical Manual of Mental Disorder, 3rd edition (American Psychiatric Association, 1980). A revised version, known as DSM-IV, was produced in 1994. These diagnostic systems aimed to address many of the weaknesses of the previous classification systems, such as the way that they had tended to deal with psychiatric problems as if they originated purely within the individual, and had nothing to do with anything else that was going on in the patient's life. DSM-IV is described in Box 8.1.

It is apparent that DSM-IV encourages the medical practitioner to take a much more 'rounded' view of the patient than original diagnostic systems did. Although the first three axes are about medical classifications, the last two encourage

---

Box 8.1 DSM-IV

One of the major characteristics of DSM-IV, which distinguishes it from earlier versions, is its use of **multi-axial assessment**. It does not try just to pigeonhole the patient's disorder into a single category. Instead, it gathers information about the presenting illness (the problem for which treatment is being sought) in terms of five general factors, or axes. These axes direct the practitioner's attention to different factors, so that they get a more complete picture of the possible relevant influences, and can direct relevant treatment accordingly. The five axes consist of:

Axis I: clinical disorders
Axis II: personality disorders and mental retardation
Axis III: general medical conditions
Axis IV: psychosocial and environmental problems
Axis V: global functioning.

The first two axes are fairly standard psychiatric diagnostic categories. Axis I includes the familiar list of psychiatric disorders, such as schizophrenia, mood disorders, and anxiety disorders. It also includes more controversial categories, such as sexual and gender identity disorders, and adjustment disorders like school phobias and work stress. Axis II relates closely to Kraepelin's second and fifth categories. The disorders which occur here are ones which are not the main problem as such, but which could contribute to making the problem worse, such as a tendency to paranoid thinking, or an inability to cope with solitude.

Axis III is concerned with any medical disorders which might influence the patient's behaviour. Problems like having high blood pressure or a heart condition might contribute to the overall stress which the patient is suffering, as could the physical stress of a recent illness or accident. Axis IV involves looking at issues such as bereavement, marital discord,

illiteracy, debt problems, or other personal circumstances which could add to someone's stress and so affect their psychiatric problem.

Axis V represents a general or global assessment of how the person is actually functioning in their life. This axis looks at positive aspects of functioning during the past year, in three areas: psychological, social, and occupational. People often return to their highest level of adaptive functioning once an immediate period of psychological difficulty is over, so this axis can provide guidance as to what should be aimed for in therapy. The assessment involves a rating, on a scale from 1 (meaning persistent danger of serious harm to self and others), to 100 (meaning that the person shows superior functioning in a wide range of activities).

Problems of DSM-IV
It is still open to question how far this type of diagnostic system really achieves a balanced, non-culturally-biased view of mental illness. It is noticeable, for example, that the five diagnostic axes do not allow for cultural variation, and yet cultural norms can vary so widely from one group to another that what is perfectly ordinary behaviour in one society can be regarded as seriously deviant in another.

The DSM-IV manual states '*Neither deviant behaviour (e.g. political, religious or sexual) nor conflicts that are primarily between the individual and society are mental disorders*'. It goes on to add '*unless the deviance or conflict is a symptom of a dysfunction in the individual*'. But the problem is about people being diagnosed – by psychiatrists – as having a dysfunction when really they are acting in accordance with different beliefs or cultural norms. So adding the caveat at the end, which effectively says '*unless the psychiatrist has diagnosed a dysfunction*' makes the statement about deviance not being mental disorder, effectively meaningless.

psychiatrists to consider social and personal information which could have contributed directly to
the stress that the individual is under, and which
therefore could have influenced how the person's
main problem originated or developed. In part,
this new approach to diagnosis came about
because of the challenges presented by alternative
ways of conceptualising abnormal behaviour,
which we will be looking at in the next chapter.

Psychiatrists argue that DSM-IV represents a
more reliable diagnostic system than did the earlier
psychiatric classifications, and that it continues to
be improved. There are claims that it has better
reliability than previous classification systems,
although these are still pretty low – between 50%
and 60%. Considering how important a psychiatric diagnosis is for someone's social future,
the fact that there is still such a degree of unrel-
iability in diagnosis remains a cause for concern.

In addition, of course, DSM-IV is still an
expression of the medical model, which assumes
that one of the major sources of disturbed and
abnormal behaviour is that of some kind of
mental 'illness'. This whole approach to understanding abnormal behaviour has been seriously
challenged by some critics, and it is worth looking
at the nature of their criticisms.

Criticisms of the medical model

One of the most vociferous critics of the medical
model of psychiatric disorder was Thomas Szasz
(1961). Szasz asserted that the whole concept of
'mental illness' was a myth, which could not stand
up to close examination. Although people used
medical terms to describe mental illness, Szasz
argued, they used social criteria to define it, not
medical ones – like how well the person was
coping with family and friends, or keeping up
with their social responsibilities. Psychiatric
diagnosis, unlike physical diagnosis, was all about
social judgements. But despite the fact that these
were social problems which were being identified,
Szasz argued, the medical profession assumed that
it would be sufficient to use medical methods to
'cure' or treat the disorder.

Mental illness or neurological disease
Szasz argued that the whole use of the term
mental illness was misleading, because it referred
to things which were not mental illnesses at all.
He maintained that if a supposed mental illness

arises from neurological defects, then it is, in fact,
a neurological disease, and should be classified as
such, not as a 'mental' illness. So the types of
'mental illness' which have specific organic origins
are not actually mental illnesses at all, and it is
misleading to call them that. They are physical illnesses. On the other hand, 'mental illnesses' which
do not have organic origins are not illnesses at all,
but problems which people have in living their
lives.

Szasz described **problems of living** as a more
useful concept than 'mental illness', because this
directs attention towards how the patient can be
helped to come to terms with, or resolve, their
problems. He argued that what we mean when we
refer to 'mental illness' is actually a set of communications which express unusual ideas, framed in
an unusual manner. But the medical profession
(and often the patients themselves) judge these
ideas within a value-laden context – the idea of
'normality'. This distracts attention away from the
main issue, which is that the patient has problems
in living their life. Instead of taking that as the
most important thing, the medical approach
means that their problems are simply seen as an
example of the consequences of 'mental illness'.
So treatment focuses on 'adjusting' the person,
rather than trying to sort out the problems.

Another problem, Szasz argued, is the way that
the medical model attempts to treat 'physical' and
'mental' well-being as if they are the same thing,
when really they are entirely different. According
to Szasz, physical symptoms are manifestations of
physical disturbances, whereas mental symptoms
are to do with how a patient communicates with
other people, or with society in general. So Szasz
saw the medical model as confusing two entirely
different contexts of human action: the physiological context and the social context.

The influence of the medical model
Szasz argued that there were four reasons why the
medical model, with all its weaknesses, was so
widely accepted within modern society. First, it is
to do with the dominating influence of the
medical profession, which results in alternative
viewpoints being ridiculed or discouraged.
Second, the model helps to reduce the uncomfortable ambiguity which other people experience
when they are faced with someone acting oddly.
Third, the model justifies taking such people out
of society and into psychiatric care, where they

will not embarrass their relatives or other people. And fourth, the patients themselves often welcome the opportunity to see themselves as 'sick', because that means they do not have to feel responsible for what is happening to them. All these factors, according to Szasz, work together to produce a powerful picture of 'mental illness'.

Szasz's views were criticised by Ausubel (1961), who challenged a number of his assumptions. Ausubel argued that it was a mistake to claim that mental symptoms are simply problems in living and therefore cannot be regarded as a result of a pathological condition, since it is possible for a particular symptom to be a reflection of problems in living and at the same time a manifestation of disease.

Ausubel also challenged Szasz's idea that diagnosing physical illness involves clear-cut, non-subjective criteria, whereas diagnosing mental illness involves social judgements. Most symptoms of physical illness, Ausubel argued, involve some element of subjective assessment, either on the part of the patient or the physician. At what point, for instance, do you consider yourself unwell enough to need to see a doctor? At what point does the doctor consider that your symptoms are severe enough to justify your having time off work? Diagnosis, Ausubel maintained, was always partly a social exercise, but that did not make it useless.

Mental illness as a useful concept

Certainly, Szasz's point that mental illness is not strictly the same type of thing as physical illness does seem to be valid. But on the other hand, the term 'mental illness' may be useful because it serves as an indication that certain people need psychiatric help. Sarbin (1967) pointed out that the concept of mental illness started out as a metaphor – that one should treat such people *as if* they were sick. Over time, though, the metaphor has been lost, and the idea of 'illness' has been accepted as if it were fact, and people really were ill. Szasz asserted that personality disorders are a result of moral conflict and ethical choice, but Ausubel felt that there is a distinction between ordinary cases of social deviation, like immoral behaviour, and mental illness. These qualitative differences, though, are hard to pin down, and depend entirely on what we consider to be 'normal' behaviour.

Moreover, the judgement is wide open to social

or political abuse. At the beginning of this century it was not uncommon for some women to be confined in psychiatric hospitals because they had offended society by becoming pregnant while unmarried: in the 1970s, some of these women still remained in psychiatric hospitals as long-term institutionalised patients. In Russia under Stalin's regime, political dissidents were diagnosed as psychiatric patients, and confined indefinitely. Cohen (1988) showed that millions of psychiatric patients all around the world are still seriously neglected and abused. So we need to look very carefully at the way that we define behaviour as normal or abnormal.

Defining abnormality

The question of what is, and what is not, abnormal behaviour is an important one, because to a large extent our society is based on such concepts. The right to vote, and legal rights of inheritance, for example, rest on the assumption that someone can be clearly defined as 'normal' or as 'insane', since those who are 'insane' have fewer legal rights and are not permitted to vote. But drawing the line between the two is not so easy. There are many problems inherent in trying to define what behaviour is 'normal' and what is 'abnormal'.

Deviation from the norm

One way of trying to define abnormal behaviour is to take the word 'abnormal' according to its literal dictionary definition. This means defining abnormal behaviour as behaviour which is different from the 'norm'. This idea is also closely related to the **statistical approach** to defining abnormality, which rests on the idea that differences in human behaviour tend to fall into a normal distribution curve (see Chapter 6). According to this view, abnormal behaviour is behaviour which is uncommon. If we were talking about introversion–extroversion, for instance, most people would be 'average' – somewhere in the middle of the scale – and we would define those who were at the extreme ends as abnormal.

This approach seems as good a way of defining abnormality as any other, until we start to look at other measures. For instance, intelligence test scores are also normally distributed. If we apply the statistical definition, we find that people of extremely low IQ would be defined as abnormal. But equally, people of extremely high IQ would be defined as abnormal too – and yet not many people would consider this to be the type of 'abnormal' which needs psychiatric help.

Even if we take a less precise view of deviation from the norm, in the sense of seeing it just as acting differently from the way that most people act, defining abnormality is not clear-cut. There is, for example, the fact that people are all individuals. As we saw when we looked at personal construct theory in Chapter 7, each of us interprets the world differently, and we have our own individual past histories. This means that we act in different ways, we have our own personal habits and hobbies and our own ideas. Some people are individua to the point of being regarded as 'eccentric': many of the great thinkers and social reformers of society have had personal lives which were quite different from those of most people. In that respect, they are certainly different from the norm, but most of us would hesitate to call them abnormal.

Some psychologists have argued that the decision about whether a particular behaviour is 'eccentric' or 'abnormal' has more to do with living space than any other factor. Someone who lives on their own, or in a large house with plenty of space, is not going to affect other people by acting unconventionally; but someone who shares their living space with other people will be required to act in a much more socially conventional manner. So we can see that it is not just a matter of looking at behaviour which is different from the norm: judgements about what is socially acceptable are also involved.

Social conformity

The **social conformity approach** to defining abnormality is the idea that a behaviour is abnormal if it does not conform to what society expects. It is not just a matter of what the person does – behaviour which is considered normal in one situation might be considered outrageous, or ridiculous, in another, even though it might involve the same group of people. It is a matter of what people are expected to do. A group of men at a football match may act in a certain way, but if one of their number were to start acting in the same way while standing on a platform waiting for his train to work, his companions would probably consider it distinctly abnormal behaviour, and would quite likely advise him to seek psychiatric help.

The problem with this approach, though, is that it can easily lead to a form of **social determinism**, whereby the person's abnormality is defined in terms of their audience, rather than in terms of what they as individuals are like. We cannot use this type of definition to tell us anything about the characteristics of the abnormal individual: all it tells us is whether that individual is conforming to what is expected of them. Moreover, it can then become very open to political abuse – indeed, some theorists argue that attempting to define abnormality at all is an inherently political act. Allman and Jaffe (1976) argued that basic divisions such as 'normal/abnormal' can be regarded as attempts by society to structure and regulate the world. What these concepts really mean, they say, is 'acceptable/non-acceptable' – whether the behaviour is such that the society is prepared to tolerate it or not.

For example, some researchers have become extremely concerned at how the terms 'hyper-active', or 'minimally brain-damaged', became popular in schools to describe children who were not amenable to traditional control. Children who are quiet, sit still in their seats and never say anything may be just as 'abnormal', but because they do not present their teachers with problems, they are not considered as such. In such circumstances, the psychiatric label is being used as a form of social control, drawing attention away from the actual situation that the child is in, or from any consideration of the wider problem, by claiming that there is something wrong with the child.

Cultural relativity

Definitions of abnormal behaviour also vary from one culture to another. Some cultures will accept and tolerate behaviour which would be considered totally unacceptable by another. Society does not consist of a single homogenous mass of people. It is divided into many different subcultures, each with its own view of what is normal and what is not. Many adolescents' problems with their parents, for instance, come from the fact that the adolescent is moving in two different social groups with two entirely different definitions of what constitutes normal behaviour.

Horsford (1990) argued that psychiatric diagnoses of black people in Britain often fail to take account of the fact that there are different cultural norms in what are considered to be normal everyday styles of interaction. Since psychiatrists tend to be white and middle-class, and to have had little experience of black culture, this means that black patients are all too often diagnosed as abnormal when in fact their behaviour is perfectly conventional for the subculture in which they live.

The fact that normal behaviour varies so much from group to group is one of the biggest problems in attempting to define abnormality. An individual is usually encouraged to ask for psychiatric help by other people, like family, teachers, friends or GPs. But some families will tolerate eccentric behaviour, whereas other families will regard behaviour which might be normal in most parts of society, as being 'sick'.

Abnormality as coping

Freud (1901) regarded abnormal behaviour as only quantitatively different from normal, not as a different kind of behaviour altogether. He considered that behaviour should be defined as abnormal when it begins to interfere with the person's normal functioning – in other words, when it becomes **maladaptive**. Most symptoms, he said, have an underlying adaptive quality to them, because they serve to reduce the individual's unconscious tensions and conflicts. In this respect, they are no different from normal behaviour, which is also geared to reducing tensions and conflicts.

Many other psychological theories see deviant behaviour as an attempt to cope on the part of the patient. Presenting oneself for psychiatric treatment can also be seen as a positive strategy. Melzack (1973) suggested that there are three main types of judgement which people make when they come to see themselves as being 'in need of help'. These are: first, comparisons with other people; second, comparisons with accepted social norms (or the person's idea of what accepted norms are); and third, the person's common states, like boredom, perfectionism or the presence of psychiatric symptoms. But there will be wide variation in how people use these criteria – one person may decide that the reason that they are habitually bored is because the society they are living in is intrinsically boring, while others may think it is because there is something wrong with themselves.

Rosenhan and Seligman (1984) suggest that there are seven properties that we can use to help us decide whether a person or a behaviour is abnormal. The first of these is **suffering**: whether

the person is experiencing distress or discomfort in going about their life. The second is **maladaptiveness**: whether the person engages in behaviour or thought patterns which make it more difficult for them to live their life, rather than helping them. The third is **irrationality**: if the person is incomprehensible, or unable to communicate in a reasoned manner with other people. The fourth is **unpredictability**: if the person acts in ways which are entirely unexpected to that person as well as to others, or which they feel unable to control.

The fifth property of abnormality which Rosenhan and Seligman identified is **vividness and unconventionality**: whether the person seems to experience sensations which are far more vivid and intense than those of other people, or if they experience things in ways which are very different from most other people. The sixth is **observer discomfort**: whether the person acts in ways which other people find embarrassing or difficult to watch. And the seventh is the **violation of moral and ideal standards**: whether the person habitually breaks the accepted ethical and moral codes of society.

From looking at these criteria, we can see how there is a fine line between defining abnormality in ways which focus on distress to the individual, and defining it in terms of what is or is not acceptable to society. The first four of these properties are criteria which are concerned with how the person concerned is living their own life. The fifth is borderline: 'unconventionality' is a social judgement, after all, because it depends on what is conventional. And the sixth and seventh are clearly ones which are about what behaviour is considered to be socially acceptable and what is not.

The danger in such social judgements, as we have seen, is that they can all too easily fail to take account of pluralism and diversity in how people live their lives. There is an increasing awareness of how psychiatric diagnosis of women and of some ethnic minorities has been misapplied, as a result of white, middle-class and predominantly male psychiatrists failing to comprehend the cultural norms of the groups that their clients have come from. History also suggests that it is the unconventional fringe which, in the long run, may contribute most to society's progress, through ideas which may seem radical or deviant in their time but eventually come to be recognised as necessary or useful.

There are other ways of looking at abnormality. The **humanistic** school, for instance, such as in the work of Carl Rogers, defines 'normal' behaviour in terms of positive psychological growth, and the struggle for self-actualisation. As we saw in Chapter 7, Rogers emphasises the positive striving aspects of psychologically healthy behaviour, and not simply the absence of negative symptoms. Accordingly, humanistic psychologists regard abnormal behaviour as the failure to achieve self-actualisation; and their therapy reflects this. The humanistic approach, therefore, casts the problem in a different light: not as that of defining abnormality, but as that of defining what constitutes normal behaviour.

Defining normality

Defining abnormality, as we have seen, is a tricky task. An alternative approach has been to try to define normality, rather than abnormality; although in a lot of ways, normality is even more difficult to define. Jahoda (1958) suggested that the best way to tackle defining normality might be to look at what qualities were required for 'optimal living' – in other words, for the person to gain the most satisfaction, enjoyment and fulfilment out of their life, while also making a positive contribution to society.

The six 'elements for optimal living' identified by Jahoda are given in Table 8.1. Using criteria like these avoids specifying precise behaviours too closely, which means that the criteria are capable of encompassing a greater diversity of cultures and lifestyles. But inevitably, psychiatric diagnosis is a form of social judgement. So some awareness of cultural pluralism on the part of the person making the diagnosis is essential, in view of the power of psychiatric diagnosis to influence the course of people's lives.

We can see, then, that the process of defining abnormality is not a straightforward one, and that it has a lot to do with the implicit theories that people hold about what is and is not normal. The medical model itself, although very widely accepted, is a theory about abnormal behaviour, and there are several other theories which have been proposed. Each of them makes different assumptions about what constitutes abnormal behaviour. In the next chapter, we will look at some of the alternatives to the medical model which have been put forward by psychologists working with disturbed people.

Specific disorders

In the rest of this chapter, we will look at some of the most frequently occurring specific disorders which have been identified by the medical model, and at some of their characteristics.

Schizophrenia

Schizophrenia is one of the most serious types of psychiatric disorder. As we saw earlier in this chapter, it is classified as a psychosis, but there is considerable variation in how long it persists and the forms that it can take. The name schizophrenia

Table 8.1 Elements for optimal living (Jahoda)

Positive attitudes towards the self	That the person has a reasonably positive level of self-esteem.
Growth and development	That the person should not be static or passive in their life, but should be active in utilising and developing their individual abilities and talents.
Autonomy	That the person should be able to act independently and make their own reasoned judgements.
Accurate perception	That the person should have a realistic view of what is happening in their world.
Environmental competence	That the person should be able to deal effectively with the demands of their situation and circumstances.
Positive interpersonal relations	That the person has fulfilling and warm relationships with other people.

Source: Jahoda, 1958

refers to a split between the mind and reality: the idea is that the schizophrenic has retreated from reality into a private world, which might include hallucinations, delusions or irrational perceptions of real events.

The classification system DSM-IV identifies three major subtypes of schizophrenia. **Catatonic schizophrenics** are characterised by disturbances of movement, with people either becoming unable to move, locked in what is known as a **catatonic fugue**, or being hyperactive and showing excessive physical activity. **Paranoid schizophrenics** typically suffer from the delusion that people are conspiring against them, or from grandiose delusions that they are really extremely important and influential people. And **disorganised schizophrenics** (formerly called hebephrenic schizophrenics) show disturbed behaviour which appears strange or strikingly inappropriate to the situation they are in, and are often extremely socially withdrawn.

The origins of schizophrenia have been studied for more than a century, and as we have seen the various explanations put forward at different times have tended to reflect the general concerns of society at those times. Overall, there seem to be four main factors involved in the onset of schizophrenia. Each of these four factors has at some time or other been proposed as the sole cause of the disorder, but modern thinking tends to see them as combining their effects rather than acting independently. The four factors are: genetics, family influence, brain chemistry and the role of society.

The genetic theory of schizophrenia

In 1938, Kallmann argued that schizophrenia was a genetic disorder, passed on by heredity. In 1946 and 1952, he reported evidence from twin studies: 691 pairs of twins in 1946 and 953 pairs in 1952, which he claimed produced convincing evidence for his theory. Kallmann found that monozygotic (identical) twins showed a concordance rate of 86.2% for schizophrenia, whereas dizygotic twins showed a concordance rate of only 14.5%. This implied strongly that schizophrenia was largely genetic in origin.

Kallmann's work was widely accepted, and proved to be extremely influential. No other studies had achieved such large sample sizes, nor such high concordance rates. The genetic theory of schizophrenia became widely accepted within

the medical profession, and Kallmann's very convincing statistics were quoted in most texts. They had social effects too, the most dramatic of which was the way that they were used to justify the Nazi policy of exterminating schizophrenics in concentration camps.

However, as with some of the twin study evidence which we looked at in Chapter 6, much of the research on which these statistics were based was seriously flawed. Marshall (1984) pointed out that Kallmann had tended to make judgements about whether twins were identical or not after he had already diagnosed schizophrenia. Kallmann claimed to be able to identify members of the family who were prone to schizophrenia, even though they had not experienced such problems, and in fourteen cases he changed the hospital diagnosis to conform to his ideas.

The problem with this is that, like Cyril Burt's dodgy statistics on intelligence, Kallmann's statistics powerfully influenced the views of other researchers in the field. The results from later researchers are far less dramatic, and there is a striking difference between the outcomes of studies conducted before the 1960s and those conducted afterwards. The later studies seem to have used more systematic criteria in their diagnoses of schizophrenia, which reflect developments in the system of diagnostic classification which was being used. Table 8.2 shows the outcomes of many of these studies.

It is important to remember, too, that many of the cautions necessary when interpreting the findings from twin studies of intelligence also apply when interpreting the same sorts of studies of schizophrenia. For example, the observation that identical twins have more similar experiences than fraternal twins do is as pertinent for the interpretation of twin studies of schizophrenia as it is for the interpretation of twin studies of intelligence.

As we can see from Table 8.2, the largest of the recent twin studies also gives the lowest concordance rates between monozygotic twins. We can see, then, that although there may be some hints that schizophrenia may perhaps have a genetic component, there is nothing like the kind of evidence which would be needed to describe schizophrenia unequivocally as a genetic disorder.

Family influences

Observing that a trait or disorder runs in families does not automatically mean that it is inherited: it

Table 8.2 Twin studies of schizophrenia

Researcher(s)	Date	Concordance rates for:		N	
		MZ twins	DZ twins		
Fischer	1973	24	10	MZ =	21
				DZ =	41
Gottesman and Shields	1972	42	9	MZ =	24
				DZ =	33
Tienari	1971	16	5	MZ =	19
				DZ =	20
Pollen et al.	1969	14	4	MZ =	95
				DZ =	125
Kringlen	1967	25	4	MZ =	55
				DZ =	90
Inouye	1961	60	18	MZ =	55
				DZ =	11
Slater	1953	65	14	MZ =	37
				DZ =	58
Essen-Moller	1941	64	15	MZ =	11
				DZ =	27
Rosanoff et al.	1934	61	13	MZ =	41
				DZ =	53
Luzenburger	1929	58	0	MZ =	19
				DZ =	13

Source: Adapted from Rosenhan and Seligman, 1984

Notes: *N* refers to the number of cases involved in research. In this case, it means the number of pairs of twins involved in each study. MZ stands for monozygotic twins, and DZ stands for dizygotic twins. So, for example, the study by Fischer involved 21 pairs of monozygotic twins, and 41 pairs of dizygotic twins.

Concordance rates are all about whether a pair of twins share a particular trait or not. If both twins have a particular trait in common, then they are said to be 'concordant' for that particular trait. The concordance figues in the table are percentages: they show what proportion of the twins in the study were concordant for schizophrenia. In the Fischer study, therefore, 24% of the MZ twins in the study were both diagnosed as having schizophrenia; while in the case of the DZ twins the figue was 10%.

can just as well mean that members of the family influence one another in consistent directions. In 1956, Bateson et al. proposed that certain families tended to induce schizophrenia in their members, by placing them repeatedly in intolerable situations, which Bateson *et al.* called **double-binds**. These are discussed in detail in the next chapter. Effectively, someone experiencing a double-bind is placed in a situation where they have to choose between two conflicting injunctions, and are unable to side-step the issue. Bateson *et al.* proposed that some families use these techniques repeatedly, and that they are often targeted on particular members of the family, who may develop schizophrenia as a result.

The theory of schizophrenia proposed by Bateson et al., then, was that schizophrenia is caused by disturbed family interactions. Some families were **schizophregenic**, having disturbed patterns of interaction which made them particularly liable to induce schizophrenia in their members.

Lidz (1975) distinguished between two types of schizophregenic family. The first of these is the **schismatic family**, in which the family is divided in a power game conducted between the two parents. Children in the family become caught up as pawns in the game. The conflicting demands arising from the two sides can mean that the child who is caught in the middle suffers intolerable psychological pressure as a result. The second type of schizophrenogenic family identified by Lidz is the **skewed family**. In this, the family is not actively divided, but one parent is noticeably dominant, and imposes their own view on the whole family, ignoring the emotional needs of other family members but imposing on their day-to-day lives.

There was a considerable amount of support for the idea that schizophrenia arises from disturbed family interactions, notably from the psychiatrist R.D. Laing (1961). We will be looking in more detail at Laing's work, and at the emergence of family therapy, which resulted directly from this approach to the understanding of mental illness, in Chapter 9.

The dopamine hypothesis

Many of the symptoms of schizophrenia are strikingly similar to the symptoms shown by people who take hallucinogenic drugs, such as LSD. Accordingly, some researchers have proposed that schizophrenia occurs as a result of an imbalance of chemicals within the brain, much like the imbalance produced by these drugs. Since the neurotransmitter dopamine seems to be very active in the influence of psychedelic drugs like LSD, Iversen and Iversen (1975) argued that schizophrenia may arise from too much dopamine within the brain.

In Chapter 11, we will be looking at how many groups of drugs have their effects in the brain, but it is worth noting here that the dopamine hypothesis is supported by observations that the drug phenothiazine is often effective in treating schizophrenics – at least in the sense that people who take it are less likely to show disturbed and aberrant behaviour. Neurophysiologists have found that phenothiazine seems to work by blocking the main dopamine receptor sites in the brain, so that dopamine cannot be used as a neurotransmitter chemical. This means that, for someone taking phenothiazine, there is less dopamine activity in the brain.

Another observation which appears to support the dopamine hypothesis involves comparisons with a specific neural illness: Parkinson's disease. People who suffer from this illness show stiffness and muscle tremors, which can become progressively worse. If they are treated with L-dopa, a drug which increases the amount of dopamine in the brain, their symptoms are alleviated. Psychiatric patients who have been receiving long-term treatment with phenothiazine often show physical symptoms of muscle tremor and stiffness which are very similar to Parkinsonism, and which may result from a chronic depletion in dopamine levels brought about by the drug.

The problem with the dopamine hypothesis as the cause of schizophrenia, though, is that it focuses purely on one level of explanation, and ignores everything else that is happening. But human behaviour very rarely arises just from one single cause – there are almost always multiple factors all working together to produce an effect. As we have already seen, family influence may be important in the development of schizophrenia, and other psychosocial stressors may also play their part.

Social factors

A number of studies have shown that schizophrenia is not evenly distributed throughout the population. Instead, it seems to concentrate in those sectors of the population with the lowest socio-economic status. Srole *et al.* (1962) showed that the highest rates of schizophrenia come from inner-city areas, and Clark (1948) showed that low-status occupations have much higher rates of schizophrenia than high-status ones. However, this relationship would seem to be more to do with social and economic stress than socio-economic status, since Clausen and Kohn (1959) showed that the strong relationship between schizophrenia and social class evident in large cities does not seem to hold true for those in small towns.

Kohn (1973) suggested that the link between social class and schizophrenia evident in the large cities might be something to do with personal strategies for coping with stress. Arguing that working-class people emphasise conformity more than do middle-class people, Kohn suggested that this might mean that they have fewer personal resources when faced with stresses. Other researchers, however, regard this argument with some scepticism, on the grounds that working-class people tend to experience more real stress in their day-to-day lives anyway, and this is more likely to be a source of the problem than just how they cope with it.

The diasthesis-stress model of schizophrenia

The idea that there is a link between stress and schizophrenia has become the cornerstone of the more recent approach to understanding the disorder. Rather than taking any one of these four possibilities as being 'the cause' of schizophrenia, modern theorists argue that it is the **interaction** between them which is significant.

Strauss and Carpenter (1981) argued that, taking all the various types of research into schizophrenia into consideration, it is possible to regard someone as having a genetic predisposition towards schizophrenia, which will develop if the person finds themselves in certain kinds of environments, like one which involves extreme family stress; but which will not develop in different circumstances. The way that the genetic predisposition operates might easily be by producing higher levels of certain neurotransmitters in the brain.

In the **diasthesis-stress model**, which used to be known as the vulnerability model of schizophrenia, no single agent is seen as the 'cause' of schizophrenia. Instead, schizophrenia is seen as resulting from several different factors, all combining together. It is possible that the individual has inherited a genetic predisposition which makes them particularly vulnerable to social and interpersonal stressors. In the normal run of things, such a person would be able to cope with day-to-day living quite well. But they are vulnerable, and when faced with excessive stress, either through disturbed family interaction, occupation or unemployment, or some other strain, they become unable to cope, and schizophrenia develops. Leff (1992) discussed how this model can explain a great many observations about recovery from schizophrenia, including the effectiveness of family-based interventions after the patient has been discharged from hospital.

There are still differences of opinion within the vulnerability model of schizophrenia. For example, there are those who believe that an inherited predisposition may be a specific genetic tendency towards developing schizophrenia. Others believe that an inherited predisposition need be little more than an oversensitivity to social stressors, with the person retreating into illness as their only coping strategy.

What is particularly interesting about the vulnerability model is the way that it mirrors one of the very earliest, and still one of the most successful, ways of treating mental disorders: Pinel's moral therapy. The idea that such people are able to lead normal lives but need to be protected from excessive strain is completely in accord with what Pinel was trying to achieve. It would not be true to say that the wheel has gone full circle, since we now know a great deal more about schizophrenia than we did before, but certainly the spiral of knowledge seems to have come round to a point which is very close to Pinel's original position.

Clinical depression

Depression is something which most people encounter at some time in their lives, in a mild form at least. It is not uncommon to feel depressed, tearful or hopeless after some upsetting or disturbing life-event, like the end of a love affair, or failing an important examination. This type of depression is just part of normal living: nobody lives their life on an even keel the whole time, and we all have some periods when we are more or less happy than at other times. Sometimes, however, depression can become more serious, and develop into what is known as a **depressive disorder**, or clinical depression.

Types of depression

Clinical depression can take several different forms. Some people's experience of clinical depression is of a combination of periods of depression with periods of what is known as **mania** – excessive elation, talkativeness, inflated self-esteem, and so on. This type of depression is known as **bipolar depression**, since the person's mood swings between the two poles, or extremes of mood. Another term for this problem is **manic depressive psychosis**, and it is often classified among the psychotic disorders.

For other people, however, their experience of depressive disorder is quite different, consisting only of the depression, with no manic periods. This type of depression is known as **unipolar depression**, and is one of the most common forms of mental illness. It is often characterised as a neurosis rather than a psychosis, although this can vary. Unipolar depression is characterised by an overriding state of apathy, lack of energy and a general feeling of sadness. Depressed people often find it hard to concentrate, and tend to feel that it is futile to make any effort to change their circumstances. They often take a very negative view of themselves, and believe that the future is hopeless.

The **Beck depression inventory**, a measure of depressive symptoms, lists eight different symptoms of depression, which are shown in Table 8.3. Not everyone experiences all symptoms, and some people experience the symptoms without being clinically depressed, so the inventory is not intended as a way of diagnosing depression. Instead, it is intended to allow a clinician to evaluate how strong a depression may be, and what symptoms it includes, after depression has been diagnosed.

There are generally considered to be two major kinds of depression, relating to their onset. These are known as exogenous and endogenous depression. The names relate to the theory about what has produced the depression: exogenous means 'coming from outside', while endogenous means 'coming from within'. So an exogenous depression is a depression which has an identifiable external cause, like being depressed after the death of a parent, or after rape or sexual abuse. For that reason it is sometimes also called reactive depression. Endogenous depression, on the other hand, is depression which appears to be coming from within the body, rather than from an external life stressor.

In terms of clinical diagnosis, a diagnosis of endogenous depression has often, in practice, amounted to a depression which seems to have come on without a single identifiable cause. But, as we have seen, diagnosis can be influenced by a number of cultural and social factors. Brown and

Harris (1978) showed that endogenous depression was a common problem in a large sample of London housewives, but that it linked closely with social isolation, such as the lack of a friend or supportive spouse, and other social factors. Similarly, Leff, Roatch and Bunney (1970) showed that endogenous depression is preceded by many stressful life-events, but that these are often combinations of whole sets of continuous problems rather than single dramatic events.

There do, however, seem to be differences in the symptoms associated with exogenous and endogenous depression, in that endogenous depression is more likely to include severe symptoms such as apathy and loss of interest in life, early-morning awakening and suicidal behaviour, than does exogenous depression. So it is possible that the two types do represent different forms of depression, even if the theory implicit in the names which they have been given does not seem to be appropriate.

Genetic explanations of depression

There have been a number of different attempts to explain why some people become depressed while others do not. One suggestion is that depression is genetic in origin. Studies of close-knit family communities which have been isolated from the modern world, like the Amish communities of America, have shown clearly that manic-depression runs in families. Since these communities have records which go back for several generations, it is possible to identify which individuals experienced manic-depression in

---

Table 8.3 Elements for optimal living (Beck)

The Beck depression inventory identifies eight symptoms of depression. These are divided into four categories: moods, thoughts, motivations, and physical symptoms.

Moods	**Sadness**	Feeling sad or unhappy.
	Interest in others	Feeling unsociable, lacking interest in other people.
Thoughts	**Pessimism**	Feeling that the future is gloomy or hopeless.
	Failure	Feeling oneself as having accomplished nothing in life, or failing as a person.
Motivation	**Work initiation**	Finding it hard to push oneself to do anything.
	Suicide	Feeling one would be better off dead.
Physical	**Appetite**	Losing interest in food, having no appetite.
	Sleep loss	Being unable to sleep, waking early.

Each of the symptoms is scored from 0–3 depending on its severity, and can therefore give a clinician an idea of how general or specific the type of depression which the person is experiencing is.

Source: Adapted from Beck, 1967

which families. The claim has been made that these family trees provide evidence which shows that depression is transmitted genetically.

There are several problems with studies of this type, of course, not least of which is that they are retrospective. Diagnosing a clinical syndrome in someone who is no longer alive runs up against problems of social exaggeration, dramatisation and all the other difficulties of relying on memory. Given that, as we saw in Chapter 3, people tend to recall information which is salient to them and ignore the rest, it is likely that extreme swings of mood would be recalled while more placid behaviour would not. It is also likely that these memories would tend to become exaggerated, both in recall of the frequency of the episode, and in memories of their severity. This happens even in contemporary records, and is even more likely in retrospective data, so we cannot really regard such data as reliable.

Another problem concerns the observation that the characteristic runs in families. Such an observation cannot be taken as evidence that a problem is genetic in origin, although this is a common misconception. Families also provide nurturing environments for their offspring, and part of growing up in a family involves learning appropriate ways of reacting to events – through imitation, identification and latent learning. (See Chapter 18.)

It is not at all uncommon for children to adopt their parents' ways of reacting to circumstances as they grow older. So if a child is growing up with a parent who shows extreme swings of mood in response to circumstances, it is highly likely that the child, whether consciously or not, will come to see such emotional responses as appropriate behaviour and will respond in that way to its own life-circumstances as they happen. Family-tree studies provide no method for disentangling these factors, and leave us no nearer knowing whether depression has a genetic component or not. All they can really do is hint that such a thing might be a possibility.

Learned helplessness and attributional style

A number of other theories have been put forward to explain depression. Seligman (1975) compared the apathy of clinical depression with the effects of learned helplessness in laboratory animals. Seligman had found previously that if an animal is exposed to an unpleasant event, like an electric shock, and given no way of escaping from it, then if it is later placed in a situation where it could escape the shock by taking action, it will not learn to do so. It is as if the animal has learned to be helpless, and simply accepts what happens to it. Moreover, such animals tend to be very passive and unwilling to move, and show little curiosity.

In the same way, Seligman argued, people suffering from depression show very little curiosity and spend a great deal of time doing nothing. Often, too, they do not take action which could improve their circumstances, because they 'cannot be bothered', or because they see it as pointless. Seligman claimed that what has happened here is that their previous life-experiences placed them in a position where they were unable to take any action to relieve their stress, and that this led to a 'learned helplessness' response where they do not take any action even when circumstances have changed.

Abramson, Seligman and Teasdale (1978) reformulated the concept of learned helplessness in terms of how people explain why uncontrollable events happen. Weiner (1979) had shown how different types of attributions (the reasons which people give for why things happen) can affect people's motivation. Abramson et al. proposed that there is a distinctive depressive attributional style, which characterises people who are suffering from, or liable to suffer from, depression. This attributional style perceives uncontrollable events as happening for reasons which are global (wide-ranging in their effects), stable (likely to recur in the future) and external (coming from factors outside the person, not internal ones). Because these people tend to construe everything that happens to them in these ways, they become apathetic and depressed, feeling that any efforts they might make would be useless.

Cognitive factors in depression

Earlier, in 1967, Aaron Beck had also produced a cognitive model of depression. Beck particularly identified negative styles of thinking as the important factors producing depression. These negative thinking styles focused on what Beck described as the cognitive triad: beliefs about the patient's own self, beliefs about the person's life-experience and beliefs about their future. Beck showed that depressed people respond selectively to things that happen to them. For example, they pick out negative events which confirm their depressed perceptions, interpret neutral events as negative and ignore events which suggest that life could be brighter or less negative. As a result, Beck argued, depressed people get into a self-fulfilling cycle of negative cognitions, in which they see the world as excessively demanding and unlikely to change.

Beck also argued that depressed people make errors in logic, and these also confirm their negative cognitions. One of these types of errors is **arbitrary inference** – the way that depressed people will often jump to a negative conclusion on the basis of very little evidence. Depressive people also focus on minor negative details of things and ignore major, positive ones: refusing to look on the bright side even of good news. This process is called **selective abstraction**. Depressed people are also likely to overgeneralise from failures, drawing wide-ranging conclusions about worthlessness or lack of ability. They magnify small, bad events and minimise good, large ones, and they personalise the bad things which happen to others, feeling as if they themselves are somehow responsible.

Beck's theory that depression arises largely as a result of these self-defeating cognitive strategies, led him to develop a form of cognitive therapy for depressive patients, which we will be looking at in the next chapter. Cognitive therapy uses argument and behavioural exercises to guide the patient into recognising their errors in logic, and helping them to reorganise their thinking. Although Beck's approach was developed independently from that of Seligman, the two are frequently combined in the general idea that depression has cognitive origins.

Social factors and vulnerability

Other researchers, however, have emphasised the social origins of depression. Depression is most common among those groups of people who lead the most highly stressful lives. For example, Brown and Harris (1978) found that working-class people were four times more likely to suffer from depression than middle-class people, and related this directly to the sources of social stress which the different groups encounter.

The statistics also show that women are more likely to be diagnosed as 'depressed' than men. Some medical researchers have argued that this suggests that women are predisposed towards depression in some way, possibly biologically. But other researchers point out that doctors are more likely to diagnose a woman as 'depressed': if men present with the same symptoms, they are more likely to be told that there is nothing wrong with them and to 'snap out of it'.

Another issue which arises from this observation is that women, particularly working-class women, lead more stressful lives anyway, and so are vulnerable to depression for that reason. Brown and Harris interviewed 539 women living in the Camberwell area of London, and found that those who had experienced prolonged periods of depression tended to have some or all of four vulnerability factors. The first of these was that they had three or more children living at home. The second was the loss of their mother before the age of eleven. The third vulnerability factor was a low level of self-esteem, and the fourth was the lack of a close confidant, either a personal friend or a supportive partner.

It seems likely that physiological, cognitive and social factors are all significant in the onset of clinical depression. Akiskal and McKinney (1973) proposed that depression should be seen as a combination of a biological predisposition towards the disorder with the effects of psychosocial stressors, like personal loss or social circumstances. The biological predisposition, as with schizophrenia, does not mean that the individual will inevitably develop depression, but does mean that they may be less able than others to overcome the effects of stress. This model does not include the cognitive explanations for depression which have been developed in more recent years, but it is easy to see how they might be integrated into such a model.

Eating disorders

The eating disorders anorexia nervosa and bulimia nervosa have attracted a considerable amount of attention in the past few years. They are classified in DSM-IV as neurotic disorders, although they can still be very serious. It has been estimated that something like one in five anorexic patients succeed in starving themselves to death; and many others do themselves lasting physical harm.

Anorexia nervosa

Anorexia nervosa occurs when someone deliberately restricts their food intake beyond a point where the body is able to sustain itself. Technically someone is defined as anorexic at the point at which they have lost 25% of their body-weight; although, of course, in order to get to that point the person must have had the problem for quite a long time. Anorexics are often teenage girls, although not always. It seems to have been quite a common syndrome among monks and nuns in mediaeval times, for example, although then it was interpreted as a mystical religious experience rather than a neurotic illness.

Anorexics tend to be preoccupied by their weight, and seem to have a severely distorted body-image, such that they regard themselves as 'fat' even when they are quite emaciated. This means that they refuse to eat, and may go to extreme lengths to ensure that they do not have to. Anorexics will often hide food away to avoid eating it, or deliberately make themselves sick in order to get rid of food that they have been forced to eat. In addition to the physical emaciation which results from starvation, anorexics find that menstrual periods stop, and that they have disturbed sleep patterns, often waking early in the morning and feeling restless.

Anorexic patients often have to be hospitalised, and closely watched to make sure that they start eating again. Sometimes, the treatment will follow a **behaviour shaping** pattern, in which any privileges are dependent on their eating something, and keeping it down. However, since anorexic patients can be extremely stubborn, this is not always successful, and successful treatments also include counselling or cognitive therapy in order to help patients to learn new ways of regarding themselves.

Bulimia nervosa

Bulimia nervosa is an eating disorder which is closely related to anorexia, and which also mainly affects teenage girls. Like anorexia, though, it can affect older people too. In this syndrome, the person is still extremely concerned about their weight, but they also become obsessed by food. For this reason, bulimia is sometimes considered to be an example of **obsessional neurosis**. Bulimic people tend to alternate between 'binges', in which they eat excessively, and 'purges', when they frantically try to get rid of what they have eaten, by using laxatives or making themselves sick.

Not surprisingly, the combination of starvation, vomiting and laxative abuse can result in physiological damage. The Royal College of Psychiatrists produced an information sheet listing some of these effects. Starvation can lead to brittle bones, the stopping of menstruation, difficulties with concentration, broken sleep, and depression. Vomiting can produce muscle weakness, arrhythmia of the heartbeat, damage to the teeth as stomach acid dissolves enamel, epileptic fits, and kidney damage. Laxative abuse can produce long-term damage to the bowel muscles, which can lead to serious constipation, persistent stomach pain, and swollen fingers and toes owing to circulation problems.

A bulimic problem often seems to originate from 'comfort eating' – the person turns to food to compensate for loneliness, temporary stress or feelings of social inadequacy. As a consequence, the treatment of bulimia often involves stressing that what has been learned can be unlearned, and teaching the patients new ways of living, such as social interaction skills and alternative ways of handling stress.

As a general rule, bulimics tend to hide their behaviour from others, and often feel very ashamed of it. For this reason, they can become very solitary, without any close personal friends. This leaves them alone with their problem, and focuses attention on it more and more. Because of this, **group therapy** is often quite a successful treatment for bulimics: the experience of sharing the problem with others allows them to overcome their shyness. By developing supportive relationships, they gain the personal resources to overcome their problem.

There have been a number of attempts to explain both anorexia and bulimia. Some of these are physiological explanations, which draw on neurological, genetic or physical reasons for the disorder. Some are social explanations, which see the problem as originating in the person's own social context and way of interacting with other people; others draw on behavioural analysis, seeing it as something which can be challenged by re-learning better habits and behaviours; and some are psychoanalytic explanations, which see the problem as a manifestation of deeply-buried conflicts and traumas.

Physiological explanations for eating disorders

Gelfand, Jensen and Drew (1982) suggested that anorexia might have a physiological cause, rather than a psychological one. Physiological researchers have established that among the self-regulating mechanisms of the hypothalamus is one which regulates body-weight (we will be looking at this more closely in Chapter 13). Animals, including people, appear to have a **set weight**, which is the 'correct' weight for them personally. If they fall below it, they will feel hungry and eat until they reach it again. If they go above it, they will eat less until they are back to normal, all things being equal. Of course, all things are not equal in modern human societies, because we are surrounded with advertising which encourages us to eat when we are not hungry. But the theory is that if we only ate in response to our bodily signals, we too, like laboratory rats, would keep our own weight close to the set-weight point.

Experiments using laboratory rats have shown that damage to certain regions of the hypothalamus can result in changes to the set weight. One type of damage can result in the animal over-eating and becoming obese; whereas damage to another area results in the animals starving themselves almost to death. Gelfand *et al.* suggested that anorexia comes from a similar source – that it happens because of damage to the hypothalamus. This means that hunger signals become inappropriate, and the person does not eat enough to stay healthy.

This is a contentious view, because it seems to ignore social factors. In modern society, people are not only surrounded by advertisements advertising food; they are also surrounded by images of ideal body shapes, and very distorted bits of information about what constitutes a 'healthy' or a 'fattening' diet. Our social expectations and habits seem to be perfectly capable of overriding physiological mechanisms, and many psychotherapists believe that the social pressures to achieve an ideal form, conveyed through advertising, have much more to do with the process than physiological mechanisms.

Another physiological explanation is the idea that eating disorders may have a genetic origin. There is some suggestion that it may run in families – for example, Holland *et al.* (1984) found that if one identical twin developed anorexia, the other was much more likely to do so as well than happened with fraternal twins, and similar findings have been reported for bulimics. But, as we have seen, families transmit cultural values and social beliefs as well as genes; and the environment for identical twins is often much more similar than that of fraternal ones. Moreover, DSM-IV states that people from families who have emigrated to Western consumer societies from cultures which do not have eating disorders, are just as likely to develop eating disorders as those who have lived several generations in Western society. So a direct genetic cause for eating disorders seems somewhat unlikely.

Social and socio-cognitive explanations for eating disorders

Both anorexia and bulimia are much more common in developed Western societies with consumer-oriented lifestyles; which supports the idea that anorexia and bulimia have largely social origins. Some researchers have suggested that anorexia results from distortions of the self-image, resulting from the person internalising extreme advertising using excessively slim models. Instead of taking these people as exceptional, they take them as the norm, and regard their own bodies as extremely fat as a result. Anorexics do often have a highly distorted body-image, which means that when they are looking at themselves in the mirror, they simply do not perceive just how gaunt and emaciated they have become.

Another explanation holds that anorexia has its origins in family disturbances, which may not be visible to the outsider. By refusing to eat, the patient exacts revenge on the family – particularly on the mother – and so gains power over the parents and also expresses the anger and frustration which they have developed during their childhood. Liebman, Minuchin and Baker (1974) suggested that **family therapy** could be used to deal with the problem of anorexia, and that the most successful form of such therapy was that which focused on establishing positive communication between all the different members of the family.

Agras *et al.* (1974) produced a socio-cognitive explanation for eating disorders, seeing it as a result of faulty attributions (we will be looking at attribution theory in Chapter 15). They suggested that anorexia can arise from a failure on the part of the patient to identify their hunger pangs correctly. Since the patients do not 'label' the feeling correctly, they do not recognise the signal for what it is, and so do not eat when they need to. Not eating then becomes a fixed habit, which is hard for them to break.

Behavioural explanations for eating disorders

The behavioural explanation for eating disorders is that the person has developed a number of behavioural habits, brought about by positive reinforcement for dieting. When one dieting experience produces a result which others admire, and which the person themselves feels pleased with, other, more extreme diets follow. As a result, dieting becomes an addictive habit. For both anorexics and bulimics, the attention which they receive as a result of their problem can be reinforcing. Some teenage girls seem to use their bulimia as a way of controlling their families, making sure that they can remain the centre of attention even though they are supposed to be growing up and becoming more independent. This, too, can mean that the behaviour of dieting/vomiting receives powerful reinforcement.

There are a number of ways that behaviour therapy has been used to treat anorexic and bulimic patients. In the most extreme cases, where the individuals have brought themselves so close to dying that they have become hospitalised, the therapy can be equally extreme, with basic privileges having to be 'earned' by appropriate behaviour. Other forms of behaviour modification can include the use of appropriate modelling to teach the person better ways of interacting with other people, or programmed learning schedules which will help them to learn to eat more and be more relaxed about retaining what they do eat.

Psychoanalytic explanations for eating disorders

Several explanations for eating disorders have drawn on psychoanalytic modes of thought. In classic Freudian theory, eating is seen as a substitute for sex; and one explanation is that anorexia is a way of repressing, or rejecting, sex. This is closely linked to the idea proposed by Bruch (1979), that girls who become anorexic are unconsciously trying to hold back the onset of maturity, because they do not want to face up to their full social role as women in modern society. Another view, which Bruch also discussed, is that it is unconsciously seen as a way of avoiding pregnancy, because 'fatness' and pregnancy are unconsciously perceived as the same thing.

Although these symbolic interpretations of anorexia may not seem particularly realistic, there does appear to be some evidence that childhood trauma makes people more vulnerable to anorexia later in life. It is not uncommon for both anorexics and bulimics to have suffered sexual abuse during childhood. The trauma and self-disgust which children feel as a result of this invasion of their bodies lingers on if the child does not receive appropriate psychotherapy. In adolescence, or even later, the individual expresses their self-disgust punitively, by ignoring the demands of the body and taking satisfaction out of the deprivation of their bodily needs.

As we can see, there are no absolutely conclusive theories of eating disorders. But there is very little evidence for any medical condition producing the problem; and quite a lot that suggests that family disturbance has a role to play. Most successful forms of therapy for eating disorders has been either based on behaviour modification, or on some type of family therapy.

Anxiety disorders

Some forms of abnormal behaviour appear to have their origins in anxiety. Anxiety – an emotion which includes feelings of disquiet, nervousness and apprehension – is something which everyone experiences from time to time. But for some people, the feeling persists for an unrealistic length of time, or occurs on inappropriate occasions. The point where inappropriate anxiety of this type begins to interfere with everyday living is the point where it is considered a disorder, rather than normal human variation. There are many types of anxiety disorder – indeed, it is one of the most common of all forms of mental disturbance in adults. The two we will look at in this chapter are phobias, and post-traumatic stress disorder, or PTSD.

Phobias

A phobia is an irrational, excessive fear of something which does not merit such an extreme reaction. Most people have some everyday things which they are nervous about – wasps, for example, or spiders. But some people are more than nervous. Their fear, or, more accurately, their anxiety about encountering the object which triggers off their fear, actually interferes with their ability to carry on with a normal life. An agoraphobic, with a fear of open spaces, may avoid going outside even when doing so is important. Or a phengophobic, with a fear of daylight, may attempt to live their whole life in darkness.

There are any number of possible targets for phobias. The medical profession grants them all interestingly obscure names. Some of these are familiar – most people have heard of arachnophobia (fear of spiders), claustrophobia (fear of enclosed spaces) or xenophobia (fear of strangers). Some, though, are less well known. Table 8.4 lists some of the more interesting ones.

Phobias are often accompanied by **panic attacks**. If the individual with the phobia feels that they are approaching the source of their fear – for example, if an agoraphobic needs to go outside – their anxiety may build up to the point where they develop a state of panic. This is an extreme anxiety reaction, in which the heart beats faster, thinking becomes disordered, and the person becomes unable to make decisions. Dealing with panic attacks – either through chemotherapy, or through psychotherapy – is an important aspect of treatments for phobias.

Explanations for phobias

Phobias have been explained in different ways by different groups of researchers. For the psychoanalysts, for example, phobias developed as a result of deeply buried early traumas, which were hidden and repressed by the unconscious mind. But, since their emotional content was so powerful, they still exerted an influence on the conscious mind, coming through in a disguised form, as a phobia.

Freud's main case-study illustration of this was a small child, called Little Hans, who was the son of a colleague of his, and who developed a phobia of horses. His father, who was well-acquainted with Freud's theories, wrote to Freud about him, and questioned him closely about his fears. They concluded that the fear was a disguised expression of the child's Oedipal conflict (see Chapter 7). Horses represented his large, powerful father, whom the child unconsciously feared as being in competition for his mother's affections. Since he could not express that fear directly, it had become manifest in his phobia of horses (Freud, 1909).

To a modern eye, reading this case-study, what is most striking is the way that the adults concerned completely ignored the fact that the child had been terrified while out walking with his nurse, when an overloaded horse had collapsed and died nearby, making loud noises as its hoofs struck the cobblestones. But this case-study occurred several decades before learning-based explanations for phobias were put forward.

Many medical researchers see phobias as a primarily physiological disorder, in which physical anxiety responses are triggered inappropriately. Their focus is on developing drug therapies – chemotherapy – which can reduce the anxiety, and so allow the patient to ignore the source of their phobia. Gray (1985) reported how research into tracing the anxiety mechanisms of the brain had resulted in the development of effective drugs, now commonly known as **beta-blockers**, which block the anxiety pathways and so prevent the experience of anxiety.

Identifying physiological mechanisms, though, is not the same as identifying causes of phobias. Other medical researchers attempt to explain phobias in genetic terms, mainly by showing that disorders such as agoraphobia often run in families. But genetic explanations for that observation are somewhat dubious, since children learn so much from how the people around them react to everyday objects; and they are particularly strongly inclined to learn about things which trigger off fear reactions.

Slater and Shields (1969) showed that monozygotic twins, with the same genetic inheritance,

Table 8.4 Some common phobias

acrophobia	irrational fear of heights
ailurophobia	irrational fear of cats
apiphobia	irrational fear of bees
astraphobia	irrational fear of lightning
cynophobia	irrational fear of dogs
ergasiophobia	irrational fear of work
helminthophobia	irrational fear of worms
hippophobia	irrational fear of horses
hydrophobia	irrational fear of water
keraunophobia	irrational fear of thunder
musophobia	irrational fear of mice
necrophobia	irrational fear of death
ochlophobia	irrational fear of crowds
oneirophobia	irrational fear of dreams
ophidiophobia	irrational fear of snakes
phasmophobia	irrational fear of ghosts
pyrophobia	irrational fear of fire
sciophobia	irrational fear of shadows
spermophobia	irrational fear of germs
tachophobia	irrational fear of speed

were more likely than dizygotic twins to develop agoraphobia. The implication is that there may be some genetic predisposition to anxiety responses. But that is very different from a genetic cause for the development of a phobia. What is likely is that the individual inherits a tendency to strong anxiety responses, but that they then learn from others around them to express their anxiety towards a particular target.

There are social factors operating in many phobias. One of the clearest examples of this is in agoraphobia. This is the most common phobia among women with children, for example, and it is thought to reflect the way that many women have very few opportunities to get out of the house while they have infants to look after – and even fewer opportunities to do so alone. This period can carry on for several years, particularly if there is more than one child; and so the external environment begins to appear strange and threatening by comparison with the known, safe world indoors. When it becomes necessary to go outside more, most women make the transition reasonably easily – though not without a little discomfort. But others find it more difficult, and experience panic attacks. If they do not overcome these, their anxiety may well continue to develop until it becomes a full-blown phobia.

There are other examples of social factors operating in phobias, too. For example, spermophobia – an irrational fear of germs – was an unknown disorder before the advertising profession began to emphasise the importance of sanitisers and disinfectants. Advertisers, understandably enough, attempt to inculcate anxiety about dirt and germs in their consumers – if people did not mind about these things, they would not buy the product. (And our general health would be likely to be rather less robust, too.) But sometimes, they succeed too well. Some individuals take these advertising messages to heart so strongly, that they become deeply phobic about the possibilities of infection.

The fifth type of explanation for phobias is also the one which has been most successful in treating them. This explanation was put forward by the behaviourists, and argues that phobias develop as a result of inappropriate learning. For example, many children acquire phobias as a result of their parents modelling fear and anxiety for them. Learning of this type can be deep, powerful and unconscious. It can also be acquired while the

child is very young. Small children respond very strongly to emotional states in adults, and seeing one's parent terrified at the sight of a spider or mouse is likely to make a very deep impact indeed on the child.

Reasoning that faulty learning can be replaced by more appropriate learning, the behaviourists developed treatments for phobias which concentrated on training the individual to develop new habits and ways of acting in response to the thing which they feared. These treatments were often remarkably successful. We will be looking at them in the next chapter, when we look at behaviour therapy.

Post-traumatic stress disorder

Post-traumatic stress disorder, or **PTSD**, is another problem which is commonly labelled an anxiety disorder, although researchers differ in whether they consider that to be an adequate classification. PTSD occurs as a result of deeply traumatic experiences, such as being in a war, or some other type of disaster such as an air crash, or an earthquake. PTSD is not new. During the two world wars, it was called 'shell shock', and a great many veterans experienced it. But it was only

Table 8.5 Explanations for Post-Traumatic Stress Disorder

Behavioural	PTSD is a form of intense classical conditioning brought about by traumatic events.
Neurological	PTSD produces long-term neurological change, increasing autonomic reactivity and increasing noradrenaline levels in the brain.
Cognitive	Vivid sensory imprinting of the event means that memories are cued by anything resembling the event.
Socio-cognitive	Survivor guilt produces feelings of self-blame, leading to unhelpful coping mechanisms such as avoidance, catastrophising, and alcohol abuse.
Psychodynamic	The immediate trauma is Buried in the unconscious, but surfaces later owing to its powerful emotional content.

classified as a specific disorder after the Vietnam war.

Post-traumatic stress disorder is not the same as the normal stress which people suffer from after a seriously disturbing event – everyone experiences some kind of reaction after something like that, and that is perfectly normal. But for some, the trauma of the experience produces disturbed sleep, 'flashbacks' (in which the person re-lives their experiences vividly, over and over again), and panic attacks. Post-traumatic stress disorder of this kind can happen soon after the event, or not begin for some time afterwards. But once it begins, it can persist for years if the person does not receive appropriate psychotherapy.

Several explanations have been put forward for PTSD, and a few of them are listed in Table 8.5. The most practical view, however, is not that there is any one specific cause, but that PTSD arises from a combination of psychological, physiological

and environmental factors, all acting together. As with so many other disorders, most researchers favour a **diasthesis–stress** model – some people may be physiologically more vulnerable to experiencing stress disorders than others, but it is the trauma of the psychological experience, their coping strategies, and the nature of their environment which will determine whether or not they develop the problem.

As we have seen in this chapter, there are rarely single causes for what used to be called 'mental illness'. What happens to a single individual is the result of interactions between many different factors, only some of which are physiological. It is for this reason that many psychologists challenge the medical model of psychiatric disorder, and have developed alternative approaches to the treatment of 'mentally ill' people. We will look at some of these alternative approaches in the next chapter.

Key terms

bilateral ECT Electro-convulsive therapy which is administered to both cerebral hemispheres simultaneously.

bipolar depression A disorder in which the person swings from a 'manic' state to a depressed one. Previously known as manic-depressive psychosis.

catatonic fugue A psychotic state in which the individual's body becomes rigid and they become unable to undertake voluntary movement.

chemotherapy Treatment for physical or psychiatric disorders which involves the use of drugs.

depressive attributional style A distinctive pattern of making attributions which is often shown by those who are chronically depressed, and which helps to perpetuate the depression.

disorganised schizophrenia A form of schizophrenia in which the person's thoughts and speech become apparently irrational.

dopamine A major neurotransmitter found in the central nervous system.

double-bind A disturbed pattern of social interaction in which a person becomes trapped by two conflicting and equally unpleasant injunctions, with a third implicit injunction preventing them from escaping from the situation altogether.

electro-convulsive therapy (ECT) A psychiatric treatment which involves passing an electric current

through the brain, producing an epileptic fit. Believed by some to lift endogenous depression.

endogenous depression A form of depression which appears to occur without any obvious precipitating factors.

exogenous depression Depression which is believed to have occurred as a result of external precipitating factors, such as bereavement.

family therapy An approach to psychotherapy in which individual dysfunction is seen as a family problem, rather than a personal one, and in which communication patterns and alliances within the family are explored and sometimes challenged.

group therapy A form of psychotherapy in which several patients interact with one another and the therapist, as opposed to the one-to-one situation of individual therapy.

insulin shock therapy An antiquated form of psychiatric treatment in which the patient was subjected to a coma through an overdose of insulin.

learned helplessness The way that the experience of being forced into the role of passive victim in one situation can generalise to other situations, such that the person or animal makes no effort to help themselves in unpleasant situations even if such effort would be effective.

leucotomy The cutting of the fibres leading from the frontal lobes of the cerebrum to the rest of the brain.

lobotomy The surgical removal of the frontal lobes of the cerebrum.

mania A form of psychosis in which the person experiences an elated mood and a high level of energy, and often makes wild plans and proposals.

moral therapy One of the earliest successful forms of treatment for mental patients, developed by Pinel after the French Revolution and based around treating such people with respect.

multiple personality A personality disorder in which the person seems to have more than one distinct 'self', each with its own memories and abilities. Brought about by severe childhood trauma.

retrospective study A study which involves collecting data about events which happened in the past.

schismatic Liable to cause a schism, or rift, between two parties.

schizophrenia A mental disorder in which the person experiences a separation or split from reality.

set weight The phenomenon detected by physiological studies of obesity, that the body appears to have an internal established ideal weight, and that eating or fasting behaviour will happen to maintain that weight.

social determinism The belief that human behaviour and experience are entirely produced by social and cultural factors.

somatic therapies Forms of treatment which are based entirely around the body, e.g. using drugs to suppress disturbed behaviour rather than attempting to deal with the disturbance using psychotherapy.

unilateral ECT Electro-convulsive therapy applied to one side of the brain only.

unipolar depression Depression which does not have any manic phase.

Summary

1 Explanations for why someone is acting oddly have changed through the centuries. The medical model is the form of explanation current in modern society.

2 Systems of classifying mental illness began with a distinction between five kinds: neuroses, personality disorders, organic psychoses, functional psychoses and mental retardation. This led to a number of problems with reliability of diagnosis.

3 The current system of psychiatric diagnosis is known as DSM-IV. It examines the problem by looking at five axes: clinical syndromes, personality disorders, general medical conditions, psychosocial and environmental problems and global functioning.

4 The medical model of abnormal behaviour resulted in somatic therapies, which involve chemical, electrical or physical forms of intervention with the body, designed to alleviate or cure mental disorders. It has attracted considerable criticism.

5 Abnormality is an elusive concept. It does not conform to statistical or normative criteria for abnormality, and may vary in social groups and cultures. Its conventional nature can lead to bias in psychiatric diagnosis.

6 The medical model identifies specific disorders, such as schizophrenia and depression. Explanations for these disorders include genetics, neurochemistry and social stressors.

7 Eating disorders such as anorexia nervosa and bulimia nervosa can ultimately result in the individual starving to death. Anxiety disorders include phobias and post-traumatic stress disorder.

8 Modern explanations for almost all specific disorders reject single cause-models, and adopt the diasthesis-stress model: that the problem arises from a combination of personal or physiological vulnerability and the action of external stressors.

Self-assessment questions

1 Describe the five early categories of mental illness.

2 What are the axes of DSM-IIIR?

3 Outline the cognitive approach to depression.

Practice essay questions

1 Discuss some of the problems of psychiatric diagnosis. To what extent can the system of diagnosis represented by DSM-IIIR overcome these problems?

2 Is 'problems in living' a more useful concept than 'mental illness'? Give reasons for your answer.

3 Is schizophrenia inherited?

Test your knowledge of this chapter with our online quizzes and games at: http://www.psych.co.uk

Explore the medical model of abnormal behaviour further at:

General

http://www.mentalhealth.com/ – Links to pages on specific disorders, offers assessments and possible treatments as well as detailing the latest research developments.

Medical models

http://www.psych.org/clin_res/q_a.html – Detailed answers to Frequently Asked Questions on DSM-IV. Also links to other sites.

Alternatives to the medical model

| Psychoanalysis | Behaviour therapy | Humanistic and existentialist techniques | Cognitive therapies | Other therapies |

Until the rise of the medical model, in the early nineteenth century, it was considered to be self-evident that someone's 'mental' state would be likely to have an effect on their physical health. Psychological factors like the death of a parent, or being disappointed in love, were accepted quite naturally as playing a part in the causation of disease. But, as we saw in Chapter 8, with the growing awareness of pathology, and the new discoveries in microscopy which led to the discovery of viruses, germs and the like, it became apparent that diseases had physical causes, which could be treated on the physical level.

This new knowledge led to a kind of **physiological determinism**, in which only physical causes were considered to be possible for any illness. The medical profession paid little attention to psychological factors, and concentrated on identifying and, wherever possible, treating physical ones. As we have seen, the discovery that a well-known mental illness known as 'general paresis of the insane' could be traced to a tertiary stage of syphilis confirmed this approach, and enhanced the medical belief that physical causes for all mental disturbances would eventually be found. We have already looked at the somatic therapies which resulted from this approach.

In Chapter 7, we looked at a number of different theories of personality, many of which were developed by psychologists engaged in clinical work. These different models of human personality also produce different explanations of what is happening when someone becomes psychologically 'ill', and therefore different ideas as to the best way to treat them. Other therapists also developed models of what was happening when people showed disturbed or abnormal behaviour, and developed their therapies accordingly. In this chapter, we will look at some of the different forms of therapy which represent an alternative to the medical model as a form of understanding and dealing with disturbed behaviour.

Psychoanalysis

At the beginning of the twentieth century, the influence of Freud and the other psychoanalytic theorists brought the idea of psychologically produced illness to the forefront once more. In Chapter 7, we looked at psychoanalytic ideas of personality. Freud's approach focused attention on **psychosomatic disorders** – problems which seem physical but have psychological origins – and presented an explanation of them in terms of the deep inner conflicts which are contained in the unconscious mind.

The psychoanalytic approach to therapy is known as psychoanalysis. Psychoanalysis involved the attempt to bring to the surface the motives and concerns of the unconscious mind, in order for the ego to develop more effective coping strategies in dealing with them. Freud used several different techniques to bring these hidden concerns to the surface, including, as we saw in Chapter 7, hypnosis, free-association, the analysis of verbal mistakes and the analysis of dreams. The process of uncovering these hidden conflicts would, he argued, be a lengthy one, as the patient brought defence mechanisms into play. But by uncovering them, the patient would become able to recognise them, and to develop new and less damaging coping strategies.

Some of the techniques used in **psychoanalysis** were partly designed to encourage the patient's defence mechanisms to emerge. Freud argued that therapists, for instance, should impose their own personalities as little as possible – they should remain neutral and detached. By doing so, they would make it easier for the patient to use them as a focus for projecting emotions, like the anger or jealousy which they felt towards a parent. The emotion would come to the surface more easily if there was a target for it, and the less the psychoanalyst imposed a different personality on the interaction, the better.

Freud's approach to psychotherapy was heavily criticised by Eysenck, in 1952, who published a paper arguing that there was actually very little evidence that psychoanalysis was successful, since the proportion of patients who recovered from their problems after psychoanalysis was very little different from the rates to be expected from **spontaneous remission** (recovering just as a result of time, without treatment being needed). About 30% of a sample of patients who presented with neurotic problems recovered from their problems spontaneously; this matched, Eysenck said, the 30% success rate of psychoanalysis in a similar sample.

Eysenck was widely construed to have argued in this paper that psychoanalysis was ineffective, although in fact he had merely argued that there was little evidence for its effectiveness. Rosenzweig (1954) challenged Eysenck's argument on several grounds, in particular arguing that there were differences between the two samples, in that the problems of those who recovered spontaneously were less severe than those who had been admitted for psychoanalysis.

The criticism, however, produced a spate of studies investigating the effectiveness of psychotherapy, as psychoanalysts realised that there had been, in fact, little systematic enquiry as to the effectiveness of their treatment. In a review of these studies in 1985, Eysenck concluded that there was still little evidence of its being any more effective than eclectic forms of psychotherapy (see Box 9.1). Moreover, he argued, since psychoanalysts tend only to accept YAVIS patients for treatment (YAVIS stands for young, attractive, verbal, intelligent and successful), they had loaded the dice in their favour, as this was the group of patients most likely to recover anyway. These conclusions, of course, are hotly disputed by psychoanalysts; although even Kline (1984), in his defence of Freudian theory, had to conclude that it was difficult, if not impossible, to obtain definite evidence that psychoanalysis really was more effective than any other kind of therapy.

Eysenck's criticisms were largely aimed at Freudian psychoanalysis, but other forms of psychoanalytic theory carried different implications for psychoanalysis. In Chapter 7, for example, we saw how Jungian therapy is based on the idea that putting the patient in touch with the collective unconscious is a healing mechanism, which restores an internal harmony and balance in the individual. Other psychoanalysts have developed different methods, stemming from their different ways of understanding the individual. Evaluating such therapies is extremely difficult, since they are aiming for more than simply the absence of symptoms: how does one assess harmony with one's inner self?

Psychoanalysis and physical illness

Freud was largely concerned with the type of psychosomatic problem which used to be known as **hysteria**, in which the disorder does not have a physical source – the disorder has been 'constructed' by the unconscious mind in order to

---

Box 9.1 Eysenck's criticism of psychoanalysis

In the review of several different studies investigating the effectiveness of psychotherapy which he conducted in 1965, Eysenck drew the following controversial conclusions.

1 If untreated groups of neurotic patients are compared with groups of neurotic patients treated by psychotherapy, the recovery rate is essentially the same in both cases.

2 Soldiers who have suffered a neurotic breakdown are just as likely to return to duty whether they have received psychotherapy or not.

3 Neurotic soldiers who have separated from the service also have an equal chance of recovery whether they receive psychotherapy or not.

4 Civilian neurotics receiving psychotherapy recover or improve to about the same degree as similar people who are not receiving any psychotherapy.

5 Children who are suffering from emotional disorders and receiving psychotherapy

recover or improve to the same extent as those not receiving any treatment.

6 Neurotic patients improve significantly more quickly if they are given psychotherapy based on learning theory than if they receive psychotherapy based on psychoanalytic or eclectic principles.

7 Neurotic patients undergoing psychoanalysis do not improve any more quickly than those receiving eclectic psychotherapy. When account is taken of the large proportion who break off treatment, it may even be considered that they improve less quickly.

8 Apart from psychotherapy based on learning theory, research into the effectiveness of psychotherapy for neurotic patients, whether civilian or military, adult or child, suggests that its therapeutic effects are small or non-existent, and not noticeably different from non-specific effects resulting from everyday life or routine medical treatment.

Source: Adapted from Eysenck, 1985

deal with some deep inner conflict. But there is another form of psychosomatic disorder, in which the illness is identifiable in physical terms – such as an infectious disease – but has been brought about, or at least strongly influenced by, the patient's unconscious attitudes. Although Freud was interested in this, as well as the problems of hysteria, he does not seem to have looked into the question particularly deeply.

One of the first of the psychoanalysts to look at this second form of psychosomatic illness was Georg Groddeck (1866–1934). Groddeck believed that people did not consciously control their own lives, but rather were governed by an unconscious entity which he called the 'It'. The 'It' decided when people would be born and die, how and whether they would succeed in life, and how and whether they would become ill.

Groddeck's 'It' seems to be similar to a mixture of the Freudian id and the Jungian unconscious – in tune with both the instinctive compulsions and the primaeval wisdoms of the individual and of the human race. What this idea also implied was that illness, in Groddeck's view, served a functional purpose for the individual. People become sick because it satisfies some unconscious need. According to this model, it is therefore possible to treat every illness – even physical ones – using psychoanalytic techniques.

Groddeck's approach has been largely discredited now, although there are several 'alternative' therapies which also operate from the implicit theory that illness is psychologically functional for the individual. One such therapy, the Bach flower remedies, takes the view that there is a form of mental disturbance or problem which corresponds to every form of illness, and that therefore treatment of physical illness should begin by identifying the underlying psychological cause. Flower essences are then used to treat the psychological problem, and this in turn is believed to tackle the physical one.

Interestingly, the more we learn about how stress, and particularly long-term stress, affects the body, the more we are finding that psychological factors can sometimes contribute to the development of physical disorders (we will be looking at this further in Chapter 13). Whether one accepts the psychoanalytic model or not, it may be that the psychoanalytic process of bringing hidden problems to the surface and looking for ways of dealing with them more

effectively is a good method of reducing stress, and it may be helpful in treating psychosomatic disorders for that reason.

Behaviour therapy

Behaviour therapy is a form of therapy which operates from a behaviourist viewpoint. That is, it ignores any possible underlying causes of disturbed behaviour, concentrating simply on the disturbed behaviour which the individual is showing. Abnormal behaviour is assumed to have resulted from faulty or inappropriate learning. Therefore, according to this model, it can be helped by new forms of learning – alternative patterns of behaviour which are more constructive for that person's own life.

The groundwork for the advent of behaviour therapy was set in 1920, when Watson and Rayner conducted the famous 'little Albert' study, which showed that phobias could be induced by conditioning. In one of the most ethically questionable studies in the history of psychology, a nine-month-old child, described as 'stolid and unemotional' at the beginning of the study, was startled by a sudden, loud noise caused by striking a sharp blow to a steel bar every time he played with a white rat. Very quickly, the child would show every sign of fear of the rat, crying and attempting to crawl away from the animal. To all intents and purposes, Albert had been trained into a full-scale phobia, which even generalised to similar objects, like a furry rabbit.

However, the implications of this study – that if phobias could be learned, they might also be amenable to being unlearned – were not followed up until the 1950s. At that time, clearly, the therapeutic world was ready for a change. In addition to Eysenck's criticisms of psychoanalysis, which we looked at above, other developments were taking place. In 1950, Dollard and Miller showed how psychoanalytic principles could be re-interpreted in terms of learning theory; in 1953 B.F. Skinner published his book Science and Human Behavior, which argued that all human behaviour could be explained in terms of conditioning principles; and in 1958, Wolpe published the first accounts of the application of systematic desensitisation as a treatment for phobias.

Forms of behaviour therapy

Broadly speaking, there have been three distinct strands of treatment which have emerged within the behaviour therapy paradigm. The first consists of those forms of therapy which are based on classical conditioning – straightforward associations of stimulus and response. The second consists of treatments based on operant conditioning, and the third consists of treatments based on social learning theory. We looked at the models of personality implicit in these concepts in Chapter 7, and these models contain the underlying assumptions on which the therapy is based.

Classical conditioning

Treatments based on classical conditioning include the phobia treatments of systematic desensitisation and implosion therapy, and the avoidance-inducing treatment of aversion therapy.

Systematic desensitisation involves gradually acclimatising phobic patients to a very weak form of their feared object, by teaching them relaxation techniques. When they are able to relax in its presence, the stimulus is changed, so that they now have to learn to relax in the presence of a slightly stronger form of the feared object. By slowly working their way up a list of feared situations and learning to relax with each one in turn, the patient becomes able eventually to tackle the most feared situation without becoming terrified. A new set of learned behaviours has been built up, to replace the old maladaptive ones.

Implosion therapy is a more extreme approach, which works on the principle that maintaining fear is physiologically and emotionally demanding, and so cannot be sustained indefinitely. So a prolonged exposure to the feared stimulus will eventually produce **habituation**: the person will become so used to the stimulus that it no longer provokes fear. Using this technique, a person who has developed, say, a fear of traffic after an accident may sit in a room surrounded by video screens showing cars coming at them from all directions. Although they will initially be very frightened, the idea is that after a while the fear will die down: the learned association between fear and the stimulus will become extinguished.

Aversion therapy aims to induce avoidance of the stimulus, rather than habituation to it. In this treatment, exposure to the stimulus is accompanied by an unpleasant experience. The idea is that eventually the two will become associated, so the individual will avoid the stimulus. Perhaps the most common example of aversion therapy in clinical practice is the treatment of alcoholics with Antabuse – a drug which produces violent sickness and nausea if the person drinks alcohol. The drug is administered as an implant, which can take some weeks to wear off: by the end of that time (in theory, if not always in practice) the alcoholic has learned new behaviours and is unlikely to want to drink alcohol again.

Operant conditioning

A second strand in behaviour therapy applies the operant conditioning approach. In this strand, new learning occurs because it is reinforced, or rewarded; and the treatment techniques involve methods which will do this. One of the first applications of operant conditioning in the clinical context involved the development of token economy systems to help in the rehabilitation of highly institutionalised psychiatric patients.

Since these people had often been in psychiatric hospitals for many decades, teaching them to become self-reliant rather than passively dependent on ward staff was a complex job. In some hospitals, a token economy system was introduced, in which patients showing the appropriate behaviours were rewarded with tokens, which could be exchanged for additional privileges, or sometimes for goods at the hospital shop.

Token economy systems also make use of behaviour shaping to train individuals in complex sequences of behaviour. The method involves building up to the complex behaviour by first rewarding behaviour which is a step towards it. So, for example, it might be unrealistic to expect a severely institutionalised patient to sweep a room effectively straight away, if they have never performed such an act before. In such a case, the patient will first be rewarded for any attempt at holding the broom and making sweeping motions. When the patient is used to that, they will be expected to achieve more before they are rewarded. The criteria for receiving tokens will be adjusted gradually, as the patient becomes more and more capable of the desired behaviour, until eventually they have learned it effectively.

Social learning

A third strand in behaviour therapy involves teaching new behaviours through the processes of **imitation** and **modelling**. This principle is based on Bandura's social learning theory. There are two core ideas: imitation, as a way of learning whole units of behaviour without the need for trial and error, and identification, as a method of generating entirely new behaviours consistent with social expectations.

There have been many behaviour modification programmes which have been based on imitating models, or which have used techniques like role-play to act out modelled sequences of behaviour. Bandura (1969) argued that abnormal behaviour could usefully be thought of as a problem of social learning, in the sense that many people who showed abnormal behaviour had failed to learn appropriate social skills and actions. Applying these techniques, therefore, in a process which Bandura described as **behavioural psychotherapy**, would allow the individual to learn more appropriate ways of acting and so remove the distress caused by social isolation.

There have been a number of criticisms of behaviour therapy – mainly criticisms that are applicable to the underlying approach of behaviourism itself, which was very strong in the early years of behaviour therapy. Behaviourism claims to maintain a 'black-box' approach to understanding people – applying the principle that what is going on inside the head is unimportant, and only the stimuli to which people are exposed, and the behaviour which they show as a result, matter. But Breger and McGaugh (1965) criticised these claims made by behaviour therapists, on the grounds that their treatments were not based truly on behaviour. They argued that 'relaxation' and 'imagining a scene' are not behavioural events, but mental ones, so it was inconsistent to claim that the therapeutic technique was focusing only on behaviour.

In addition, Breger and McGaugh argued about the importance of the client-therapist relationship in behaviour therapy. Even using a behaviour therapy approach, it seems that people will only recover if they have a positive relationship of some sort with their therapist. In strict behavioural terms, of course, the person who is doing the therapy should not matter, since the theory holds that only the stimulus input is important. In theory, a machine could equally well be used to manipulate the treatments. In practice, though, it does matter.

These criticisms are less relevant for the behavioural psychotherapy of Bandura and others, since this takes into account socio-cognitive phenomena like imitation and modelling. The important issue for its time, however, was the contrast which behaviour therapy provided to psychoanalysis. Before the 1950s, psychoanalysis was the dominant form of psychotherapy. Behaviour therapy operated from an almost entirely opposite perspective, and proved to be extremely useful for some very specific problems, like phobias, although less so in the treatment of more broad-ranging 'mental illnesses'. By opening up the field, as it were, the advent of behaviour therapy also provided opportunities for other forms of psychotherapy to develop.

Humanistic and existentialist therapies

The 1950s also saw the emergence of the **humanistic** school in psychology, in large part as a reaction to the mechanistic approach of the behaviourists, but also partly as a reaction to what was perceived as the negative picture presented by psychoanalysis. The essence of this, at least in the clinical field, was to do with what constitutes mental health. For the behaviourists, positive mental health consisted only of the absence of pathological symptoms. For the Freudian psychoanalysts, it consisted of keeping a balance between unconscious pressures and the demands of reality. But the humanistic school of thought believed that positive mental health involved psychological growth and development, not just refraining from acting oddly and keeping a lid on unconscious conflicts.

Client-centred therapy

As we saw in Chapter 7, Carl Rogers (1961) believed that psychologically 'healthy' people were those who were able to satisfy both their need for positive regard from others and their need for self-actualisation. This meant that they would be continually actualising (making real) more parts of themselves, and that maturity was a continuous, dynamic process of self-development and psychological growth.

Balancing essential needs

In Rogers's view, 'mental illness' originated from the patient's attempts to cope with a lack of positive regard from others. If someone had never experienced unconditional positive regard from anyone, they would always feel that they needed to try to gain positive regard from the people around them. So they would not be able to take risks by exploring their own inclinations, in case other people disapproved. This would mean that their need for self-actualisation was not being fulfilled at all. Also, as we saw in Chapter 7, they would develop unrealistically high standards of behaviour for themselves, and feel anxious because they could not live up to their ideal self-concept.

In the long term, this would produce a rift between what they felt to be their true inner self, and their outer self, which was acting a part in order to gain social approval. It is the anxiety produced by this rift which, in Rogers's view, produces neurosis: the person is aware of their inner and outer selves, and anxious about the lack of congruence between them. Psychosis, Rogers believed, occurs when the inner and outer selves become so split that there is no longer any point of contact between them. Rogerian psychotherapy, however, deals mainly with neurotic problems rather than with psychotic ones.

Unconditional positive regard

Rogers believed that if someone is able to become more secure in the positive regard which they receive from others, then they will be able to find their own ways towards solving their 'problems in living', as part of the drive towards self-actualisation. So according to Rogers (1951) the role of the therapist is to provide a relationship of unconditional positive regard, which will free the person to explore their own life-options and satisfy their need for self-actualisation.

Rogers believed that people would be perfectly able to help themselves, once they felt secure and able to explore possibilities without risking their source of positive regard. Moreover, he believed that they were really the only people who could ever know what was important, and they had to be helped to find their own answers, not given answers by someone else. Rogers described this therapy as client-centred therapy, because he was emphasising that it was the clients, not the therapist, who knew what was best for themselves.

He used the term 'client' particularly, because he wanted to reject the implications of dependency and passivity which are inherent in the use of the term 'patient'. The job of the therapist was not to 'treat' the patient, but to provide a warm relationship which gave them the security of positive regard.

To engage in successful client-centred therapy, Rogers (1957) argued that the therapist must have three qualities. They must be **genuine**, because it is not possible to fake liking, or unconditional positive regard convincingly, and clients would always notice if the therapist was presenting a false front. The therapist must be **empathic**, because it is important that they perceive things as the client does, and that they respect the client's choices. If they have no empathy with the client, they are unlikely to respect them. Most important, Rogers argued, the therapist must be **non-directive** – able to interact with the client without imposing their own ideas or opinions at all. Otherwise the outcome of therapy would be likely to reflect the therapist's wishes, and not truly satisfy the client's needs. The client would go along with the therapist's suggestions – even pretending it was exactly what they wanted themselves – because they would fear disapproval if they did not. And since such clients had been approval-seeking all their lives, they could pick up on even the subtlest of cues.

Encounter groups

The important feature, above all though, was the provision of unconditional positive regard, so that the person felt secure in the relationship. Rogers later argued that the necessary unconditional positive regard could equally well be provided by other people, if they met in a non-threatening face-to-face encounter (Rogers, 1970). He set up the first **encounter groups**: groups in which people could encounter one another safely and openly. In such a situation, people could feel free to explore their potential needs in a relaxed and accepting environment. An encounter group would be led by a **facilitator**, who would assist the development of an open, trusting atmosphere, but who would be as non-directive as possible. As people came to know one another, they would give each other the support and positive regard which they each needed.

Encounter groups can last for varying periods of time. They may meet at regular intervals, or occur in a sustained fashion over, say, a couple of days. But it is important that the group lasts for long enough to allow the people in it time to overcome their initial resistance to encountering other people without defence mechanisms or self-protective strategies. The role of the therapist is to facilitate the development of this open atmosphere without actually deciding what happens. As such, engaging in Rogerian therapy requires a highly skilled therapist with a very genuine belief in their clients' abilities to decide their own solutions for themselves.

Client-centred therapy, then, is concerned with creating a warm, positive relationship between the therapist or group and the client. Using encounter groups to put the client in touch with other people in an intensive and non-threatening way, so that they will provide an atmosphere of positive regard for each other, is equivalent to providing it through an individual therapist.

Existentialist therapy

Existentialist theory argues that if we are fully to understand human existence, we also need to understand the choices which we make. Existentialists see people as being directly responsible for their life-choices, on the grounds that we are always free to say 'no' and take the consequences. It places a strong emphasis on an individual's free will, and their right to choose for themselves. Since existentialism maintains that a person is always responsible for their actions: it is not acceptable to use 'illness' as an excuse. So according to this view of abnormal behaviour, mental illness is seen as a choice on the part of the patient – the choice of retreating into illness when reality becomes intolerable.

Ontological insecurity

In his early work on this subject, Laing (1965) made a distinction between ontologically secure and ontologically insecure individuals. The word 'ontological' means to do with an individual's life-history, and how they, personally, have developed, and **ontological security** means that someone's life-experiences have allowed them to grow up with a positive sense of their own identity, and of their place in the world.

Depending on their early circumstances, people may grow up with this inner security, or without it. Laing saw **ontological insecurity** as coming

from disturbed patterns of family functioning. He based this idea on the work of Bateson *et al.* (1956), who showed that some families have patterns of interaction which actually encourage the development of schizophrenia among certain of their members. These disturbed families, according to Bateson, trap the individual in situations which he described as 'double-binds'. Broadly speaking, a **double-bind** is a sequence of interactions in which the person becomes trapped between two equally unacceptable sets of social expectations or demands, so that whatever they eventually do is a personal threat. (Double-binds are described in more detail in Box 9.2 on page 276.)

According to Laing, early experiences like this make the person feel very insecure, and someone who comes from a family of this kind has often had little opportunity to develop a strong and confident sense of self. Although they may be able to manage in a situation which does not make many demands on them, they are ontologically insecure, and their sense of self is very fragile.

Psychological threat

Laing argued that ontologically insecure people feel that they face three kinds of psychological threat. The first of these is the threat of **engulfment** – the idea that other people may over-whelm them, by their presence or their demands, until their own personality becomes completely swamped, and lost. The second type is the threat of implosion – because the person has not been able to form a secure self-concept, they feel 'empty' inside. As a result of this, they do not feel able to stand up to external pressures, and they become afraid that the outside world will crash in and obliterate their inner self. The third threat that Laing identified is that of petrification – the person feels powerless to resist other people, and becomes unable to act against their demands, or to assert themselves even when they do not want to do what is being expected of them.

These three sources of threat, according to Laing, can mean that ontologically insecure individuals end up with a rift between their 'outer' and their 'inner' self. Because they feel so easily threatened, and unable to be themselves safely, a lot of what they do is depersonalised, and nothing to do with how their real inner self might choose to act. Instead, the inner self remains hidden, and an entirely false outer self takes over.

Understanding schizophrenia

Laing rejected the idea that there could be such a thing as an 'objective' psychiatric diagnosis. He argued that the process of labelling someone as mentally ill, for instance as 'schizophrenic', involves social judgements on the part of society and the psychiatrist involved in the diagnosis. This makes it important to look at the process by which the psychiatric label is applied, which in turn should direct attention towards the nature of the interactions within the family, and towards the assumptions about patients made by the medical profession.

Laing's existentialism included the **phenomenological** stance that understanding the objective reality with which someone is faced is not particularly important. Instead, it is how the patient views the problem that matters. Laing argued from this that any attempt to deal with mental disorders, even extreme psychosis, needs to tackle the problem of understanding how the patient views their world. Although this might not seem to be such an unusual claim, it is important to remember that Laing was applying this approach to the understanding of patients who had been diagnosed as schizophrenic, and were thought to be totally out of touch with reality.

Laing felt that, in the case of schizophrenia, what had happened was that the false self which the person had developed in order to cope with the conflicting demands placed on them had become alienated from the person's 'real' self, so that the person felt unreal. This separation from reality produced the abnormal behaviour which is commonly described as psychosis. This split from reality also meant that the individual's feelings about what was happening to them became expressed in hallucinations or delusions. They were expressed that way because the person did not feel able to express them directly, but the conflicts which they generated had become too powerful to cope with. Laing believed that it was useful to examine the content of these delusions, instead of simply dismissing them because they did not seem to make sense. In that way, he argued, it was possible to gain an insight into the problem – into how the patient saw what was happening to them.

For example, one case history described by Laing and Esterson (1968) concerned a girl who was trapped in a situation where the family was split down the middle. There was a hostile rift between the girl's father and his mother, and her mother and grandmother, and the two sides were often at loggerheads. At such times they would only communicate by using the girl as a go-between, which distressed her greatly.

Eventually, the girl entered a **catatonic fugue** – she became apparently paralysed, unable to move a muscle, and was admitted to hospital. When she recovered from the fugue, the girl entered a delusion that she was constantly watching a game of tennis. Laing argued that in this case, both her paralysis and her delusion of the tennis game were symbolic of the conflict within the family, and the girl's position in it. Her catatonic fugue was unconsciously signalling her feeling that whatever she did would be wrong – so she ended up doing literally nothing at all. And the tennis game was a metaphor for the family's interactions. So the retreat into mental illness was an unconscious choice: a solution to an intolerable family situation.

In Laing's approach, then, we can see that 'mental illness' is seen as a choice. Laing's work on schizophrenia was concerned with describing the structure and meaning of the experience, and challenging the conventional border between madness and sanity. And the aim of therapy, Laing argued, should be to restore the split between the real self and the false self in a supportive environment. This would allow the person to explore different kinds of behaviour and express their inner conflicts, either through delusions or directly, without facing even more conflict or censure from other people. Because of the way in which abnormal behaviour was suppressed by medical treatment, Laing regarded the psychiatric hospital as the worst possible type of environment for this to happen. People, he argued, needed to be able to express their delusions or ideas freely, because only in that way could they work through them, and achieve their own balance.

Instead, Laing said, what such people need is to be able to live for a while in a warm, supportive therapeutic community, which would be tolerant while the person explored their inner conflicts, and would gradually help them to come to terms with being themselves in their world. The most famous of these therapeutic communities was probably the one that he set up himself, known as Kingsley Hall. Ken Loach's film *Family Life* was a graphic and sensitive exploration of Laing's ideas about the origins of schizophrenia, and the contrasting approaches of therapeutic communities and conventional psychiatric treatment.

The psychotic as pioneer

In his later work Laing came to describe the psychotic as a pioneer, exploring the 'inner reaches' of time and space, and achieving illuminating experiences which were not available to ordinary people (Laing, 1967). He argued that schizophrenia was an attempted breakthrough in dealing with an insane world, and that schizophrenic patients should not be seen as insane, but as hyper-sane. Laing felt that society could learn a great deal from such individuals about the condition of being human.

Laing had adopted a position similar to the very early beliefs which held that those who experienced trances, or had phases of being out of contact with reality, should be seen as having special insight. Many outstanding figures in history, such as Joan of Arc, who claimed to hear the voices of angels telling her to free France, would be deemed to be mentally ill according to modern standards. Laing's point was that by classifying people like this, society could be missing out on those who had something valuable to give.

As one might imagine, this idea was sharply criticised by other professionals, and this aspect of Laing's work was seen as too extreme to be acceptable. Critics argued that his work with therapeutic communities was effective only for certain kinds of schizophrenics, and that his ideas were too mystical to be of use in helping people who were seriously distressed about what was happening to them. In addition, and perhaps this was a more valid criticism, it was said that Laing ignored the often very real personal distress which was experienced by people undergoing a schizophrenic episode, and their wish to be relieved of their symptoms, rather than to 'explore' them. Laing, of course, responded that the distress originated from society's rejection, and people's bewilderment about what was happening to them, neither of which would be pertinent if his approach to schizophrenia was more widely accepted.

Nonetheless, by focusing attention on the family and the social context of schizophrenia, Laing drew attention to many of the serious problems inherent in psychiatric diagnosis and treatment (Laing, 1956). The contextual revisions of diagnostic categories, which we looked at in the last chapter, came about at least partly as a result of his emphasis on the social pressures on many schizophrenics prior to their retreat into illness. His insights into how disturbed family interactions could produce psychological disturbance in a single 'scapegoat' individual also formed an important basis for the later emergence of family therapy.

Cognitive therapies

In tune with the 'cognitive revolution' of the 1970s and 1980s, more and more forms of psychological therapy began to deal with how patients thought about themselves, their lives and their options. Clinical psychologists began to explore how patients could be helped to re-analyse their problems, and develop more positive styles of thinking, and how these new styles of thinking would enable people to develop better coping strategies or to go about changing those aspects of their situations which they found intolerable. As such, the rise of **cognitive therapies** marked a shift away from seeing the patients as passive receivers of treatment, and towards seeing them as active, thinking individuals who were capable of making their own decisions about their problems and their lives.

Cognitive therapy

Cognitive therapy itself takes the view that it is how we perceive things which determines how we act towards them. According to this view, abnormal behaviour, or 'mental illness', occurs because the individual has distorted perceptions, producing an unnecessarily disturbing interpretation of what is going on around them. These affect the person's behaviour in ways which are maladaptive or damaging. Cognitive therapy aims to identify and change these distorted cognitions, so that the person can begin to deal with their life more positively. Behavioural and other exercises are used as tools to effect cognitive change, rather than as an end in themselves.

Cognitive therapists generally concentrate on four aspects of the person's thinking. The first of these are the **expectations** that the person has – the predictions they make about what is likely to happen. Bandura (1978) divided expectations into two kinds: expectations about what the outcome of certain kinds of behaviour would be; and expectations about the self-efficacy of the individual – in other words, about how successfully that person can undertake the task or role concerned. **Self-efficacy beliefs** are important, because unless we believe that we are capable of doing something, we do not try to do it.

A second focus for cognitive therapists is on the individual's **appraisals**, or how the person evaluates a situation or event. Some people make very self-defeating appraisals, which means that they end up feeling much more upset about situations than they might otherwise have done. For example, students who are extremely anxious about an examination often appraise their performance very negatively, so that even very good students manage to convince themselves that they have failed. Beck (1976) showed how these negative appraisals induce anxiety, which in turn can exaggerate other problems. Cognitive therapists therefore aim to teach the person how to recognise and counteract negative appraisals as they happen.

Some cognitive therapists emphasise the **attributions** which the client is making. An attribution is a reason which somebody gives for why things happen (we will be looking at attribution more closely in Chapter 15). We make unconscious attributions all the time, and these

affect how we go about solving problems. Rotter (1966) distinguished between internal and external attributions. An **internal attribution** implies that the reason why something happened was because of the person's own efforts or abilities. An **external attribution**, on the other hand, implies that the reason lies in circumstances outside that person.

The type of attribution that we make can have a direct effect on our behaviour. For example: someone who attributes exam success to internal factors is saying that it is their own efforts which will cause them to do well or badly. Someone who makes an external attribution is saying that success in exams is nothing to do with themselves, but to do with external factors, like 'luck', or whether the paper was a 'good' one. But a student who makes internal attributions about exam success is likely to work harder and more effectively than someone who does not believe that what they do will have much influence on the final outcome.

There are other ways in which attributions can vary. The **Leeds Attributional Coding System** was developed for use in cognitive family therapy, to help therapists to identify the type of cognitions which different family members use (Stratton *et al.*, 1986). It analyses attributions in terms of five dimensions, which are given in Table 9.1. By identifying distinctive features of the

Table 9.1 The dimensions of the Leeds Attributional Coding System

Stable/Unstable	This dimension concerns how lasting the identified cause is regarded as being. Causes which are likely to recur reasonably consistently in the future are coded as Stable, while those which are unlikely to recur are coded as Unstable.
Global/Specific	This dimension is concerned with the range of outcomes of the cause which has been identified. Causes which cover a wide range of possible actions or implications are coded as Global, while those which cover only a narrow range are coded as Specific.
Internal/External	The Internal dimension concerns whether the cause is considered to originate from the dispositional characteristics (such as character or personality) of the person or people concerned, or whether it relates to factors in the situation. Dispositional attributions are coded as Internal, and situational ones are coded as External.
Personal/Universal	Stratton *et al.* (1986) describe the Personal dimension in terms of whether the outcome is likely to affect the speaker or not. Those which are likely to affect the speaker are coded as Personal, while those which essentially relate to a wider context are coded as Universal.
Controllable/ Uncontrollable	The Controllable dimension is coded according to whether the identified cause is seen as open to being influenced or directed by the person, or whether it is something which is seen as being not amenable to any influence or direction. Cause which can be influenced are coded as Controllable, but those which cannot, are coded as Uncontrollable.

Source: Adapted from Stratton et al., 1988

attributions which people are making, the therapists are then able to target their intervention in ways that are most likely to help the person to deal with their situation effectively.

A fourth focus for cognitive therapists is on the individual's **beliefs**. People often have long-standing theories about the world, which shape how they respond to it. Many cognitive theorists have focused explicitly on the long-term beliefs that their patients hold, and on how to go about changing these.

There are several, more specific, forms of cognitive therapy, which place a particular emphasis on the nature of people's beliefs and how they can be changed. Perhaps the best known of these are the two specific forms of cognitive therapy known as personal construct therapy and rational-emotive behaviour therapy.

Personal construct therapy

Personal construct therapy can be regarded as one of the first forms of cognitive therapy. It was developed by Kelly (1955), and involved the application of personal construct theory (see Chapter 7) to clinical practice. Personal construct theory, as we have seen, is concerned with how people develop their own theories about the world and interpret their lives in terms of those theories, or constructs. In this approach, psychological disorders are seen as originating from the types of constructs which the individual has developed, and therapy aims to change those constructs in order to help the individual to cope more effectively.

Kelly argued that people construe their worlds using an individual set of bipolar **personal constructs**. They evaluate people and situations using these constructs, and act according to the interpretation and predictions which their construct system allows them to make of events. If circumstances do not work out as predicted, then a particular construct has been disconfirmed, and the person will need to seek an alternative explanation.

Bannister and Fransella (1980) argued that neurotic clients often have very tight, inflexible personal construct systems. This means that they are often incapable of dealing with the uncertainties and ambiguities of everyday life. So the neurotic's constant anxiety can be attributed to the fact that they suffer frequent

disconfirmation of their personal constructs in day-to-day living. Since their predictions about what is likely to happen frequently do not come true, they are left uncertain and anxious about what is really happening.

Bannister and Fransella also asserted that schizophrenics could be characterised by the extreme looseness and flexibility of their construct systems. Because they were so very open to new ideas, and made such vague predictions about what would be likely to happen, they were able to accept apparently irrational or illogical reasons or explanations for events. But they were not very good at dealing with definite reality, because it was much harder for them to be certain of anything.

One of the aims of personal construct therapy, then, is to change the personal constructs which the individual uses so that they can develop more positive understandings of what is going on about them. It is not uncommon, however, for people to feel a considerable amount of hostility towards people or circumstances which end up invalidating their personal constructs. Part of the process of personal growth and change, according to personal construct theorists, includes showing people how they can experiment using different constructs to interpret their circumstances, without having to feel threatened or invalidated.

One technique which has been developed to achieve this is known as **fixed-role therapy** – one of several therapeutic techniques which have been developed on the basis of personal construct theory. In this technique, the client and therapist together create a 'role sketch', based on some character that the client would quite like to resemble. By talking it over, they arrive at a detailed picture of what someone playing that role would be likely to do, and how they would be likely to act.

Once the role has been drawn up, the client is asked to act it out for three weeks or so, in their everyday life. As they do this, they find out that people's reactions to them are different: that the way they act with other people is an important factor in the way that other people act towards them. On this basis, they begin to develop a new set of personal constructs about the nature of social interaction. Eventually, the whole experience shows the client that a personal construct system can be changed for the better; and that doing so can help them to lead a more positive life.

Rational-emotive behaviour therapy

This therapy was originally called 'rational-emotive therapy'; but in 1993, Ellis changed its name to rational emotive behaviour therapy. He did this to express the three major dimensions of the therapy: that it tackles problems at the rational level, at the emotive level, and also at the behavioural level.

Rational-emotive behaviour therapy, or **REBT**, is concerned with the irrational ideas which neurotic people often hold, and which seem to be instrumental in their unhappiness and problems. Ellis, in 1977, argued that these ideas tend to fall into three major groups. The first of these is the idea that the person absolutely must do well and win other people's approval. The second is the idea that other people absolutely must act considerately and fairly towards that person at all times. And the third is the idea that the world in which they live should always be an absolutely fair and unfrustrating place. These ideas, Ellis maintained, are totally unrealistic. They are also illogical and self-defeating, but they are nonetheless very common as the key to psychological problems.

Ellis's rational-emotive behaviour therapy aims to challenge these irrational beliefs, and to put the patient in touch with a more realistic, sensible and constructive way of evaluating their day-to-day experiences. Since these ideas tend to be very rigidly held, though, Ellis believes that they need a powerful form of therapy to redirect them. Rational-emotive behaviour therapy deals with unreasonable ideas in three ways. The first is by a process of logical argument and reasoning, directed towards showing the person the irrationalities in their beliefs. The second part of the approach involves encouraging the person to act and feel in ways that fit with their new rational beliefs. And the third part of the approach involves the person using a number of behavioural techniques which are designed to strengthen the new, psychologically healthy, mindset.

'Awfulising'

Ellis argues that clients tend to get into cycles of self-destructive arguments, which are self-sustaining, and which prevent them from making a rational appraisal of their situation. He argued that they tend to 'awfulise' events – imagining an event to be an 'awful' thing, so dire as to be unthinkable.

Instead of 'awfulising', Ellis argued, people need to be encouraged to think through what would really happen – recognising that even though things might be bad, that does not necessarily make them 'awful'. So, much of the job of the rational–emotive behaviour therapist consists of helping the client to see that their world is not going to collapse if one person does not like them, or if they fail to be absolutely perfect in some way.

Another part of the work of a rational-emotive behaviour therapist might include **behaviour therapy** – exercises which will allow clients to explore and try out new behaviours for themselves, so they can see their tendency to 'awfulise' as being the unrealistic cognitive process that it really is. For example, a client might be asked to be deliberately late for something, or not turn up on a date, so that they can learn how to deal with negative outcomes constructively.

The **emotive** side of the approach encourages people to use force and energy in developing their ideas. Rational-emotive behaviour therapists use a variety of techniques, designed to encourage their clients to get in tune with their own emotional reactions. For example: if somebody held an irrational belief very strongly, the therapist would encourage that person to argue against it even more strongly – they would not try to counter it using restrained or mild arguments. Humour is another useful emotive technique. Perceiving one's beliefs as ridiculous is often a useful way to get an insight into how irrational they are.

Homework assignments

Rational-emotive therapists often negotiate 'homework assignments' for their clients to work on in between visits. These are exercises directed at helping the client to feel able to deal with things that they have been 'awfulising', in a way which is more psychologically healthy – like encouraging them to feel sad rather than depressed, or concerned rather than anxious. So, for instance, a man might be asked to work on a persistent impression that being turned down after asking a girl for a date would be 'awful'. By visualising the situation, and thinking it through, he would try to accept it in a rational manner, realising that, although it would not exactly be a pleasant experience, it would not be a complete personal rejection which made him utterly worthless either.

The homework exercises can sometimes be accompanied by a kind of operant conditioning, encouraging a more rational approach. For example, in the case of the man described in the previous paragraph, he might also be asked to give himself a 'reward' each time he engaged in the exercise for a ten minute period. The reward should be some kind of treat, and the idea is that this acts as a form of operant conditioning which will make the person more likely to engage in the exercise again (see Chapter 18).

Rational-emotive behaviour therapy encourages clients to accept themselves fully as human beings, and to realise that they are too complex for any simplistic judgement about their self-worth. When clients apply this attitude towards themselves, they can sometimes disclose shameful personal secrets. This can be difficult for many people, and their defence mechanisms often come into play. But it can also be very liberating for them.

In rational-emotive behaviour therapy, the relationship between the therapist and the client is important, but not the most important thing. What is more important is that the client learns a set of rational beliefs that they can live by. So rational-emotive behaviour therapists see themselves as educators or guides. At times, this may involve bringing some unpleasant 'home truths' out into the open, and the client may even dislike the therapist thoroughly at some points. (One of the harder parts of learning how to be an effective rational-emotive therapist is emotionally accepting the idea that it is not necessary to be liked by all of your clients all of the time.)

What is important in rational-emotive therapy, then, is the cognitive restructuring that is going on, and also the learning of new behaviours and psychologically healthy beliefs, as the client explores the implications of their old habits and learns to adopt new ones. It can be an arduous form of therapy for both the client and the therapist at times, as it tends to confront negative cognitive habits and destructive beliefs head-on, rather than indirectly. However, this confrontation occurs within a constructive working alliance between client and therapist, not as a single mode of interaction. There are many therapists and clients who find it a valuable approach.

Other therapies

A myriad different forms of psychotherapy have emerged since the 1950s, and there is not sufficient space to cover each one here. It is worth, however, looking at some of the main examples of these therapies.

Gestalt therapy

As we saw in Chapters 2 and 5, academic Gestalt psychology was highly influential in our understanding of the processes of perception and cognition. Gestalt psychology was very much concerned with the way that we perceive the world and things about us as whole units, not in terms of fragmented parts. The idea is that it is the complete form, or *Gestalt*, which is the important thing, not its component features.

In 1951, Perls, Hefferline and Goodman described how Gestalt concepts can be applied in therapy. The central idea of **Gestalt therapy** focuses on the idea of **awareness**. Gestalt therapists see awareness as an active process, directing the person towards the construction of meaningful, organised, whole ideas or perceptions (Gestalts), in much the same way as visual perception is seen as an active process. These Gestalts form the interface between the person and their environment, and they include thought, feeling and activity – or the cognitive, affective and conative domains of the individual, as described in Chapter 7.

According to Gestalt therapists, we are continually engaged in forming Gestalts. Their formation is seen as part of the lawfulness of nature, and is deeply built into our nervous systems. This means that if we fail to complete them, we become distressed or neurotic. Gestalts are organised around the satisfaction of needs: if you need something, like food or companionship, your attention is focused on fulfilling it, so your awareness becomes centred on this Gestalt. When the need is fulfilled, the Gestalt loses its energy. However, if a need remains unmet, the Gestalt remains incomplete and pressing for attention. This interferes with the formation of new Gestalts, and so it interferes with the total functioning of the individual. Gestalt therapy, therefore, is concerned with teaching people how to experience things fully, focusing on forming and completing just one Gestalt at a time.

According to the Gestalt therapists, our awareness is strongest, or most effective, only when it is grounded in the dominant immediate need of the time. So, for instance, if you are thinking about tomorrow's work while you are eating your tea, you are unlikely to derive full satisfaction from your food because you are not fully aware of what you are eating. Gestalt therapists believe that complete awareness is only possible with a full knowledge of the situation. This means that denying or distorting the situation, through defence mechanisms, will prevent you from experiencing it fully. Awareness includes knowledge about choices and options as well as about what is happening in the immediate situation, so it also implies self-knowledge and self-acceptance.

Gestalt therapy relates neurotic problems to the patient having lost their sense of awareness: they have lost the sense of who they are, and who is living their life. In other words, they have lost the sense of involvement in what they are thinking, feeling and doing. Neurotic patients typically direct their mental energies against themselves; this interrupts their Gestalt formation, and so they do not manage to complete the process.

Group therapy

According to the Gestalt therapists, the neurotic's lack of awareness crystallises in a belief that they cannot really be self-regulating or self-supporting as people. Often, the neurotic will try to lean on the therapist, and to derive strength from the therapist instead of from their own awareness. Another way of looking at this is to say that they manipulate their environment so that they can remain 'crippled' more comfortably, and do not have to rely on themselves. This puts pressure on the therapist, who must resist these manipulations. One way of avoiding them is by using group therapy techniques, which put the individual into the role of **co-therapist** with the others in the group, and so emphasise their ability to act positively and independently.

Gestalt therapy aims to encourage clients to develop a better awareness of what is and what is not relevant to their immediate experience. This often focuses on getting clients to recognise their preconceptions. Since preconceptions interfere with direct perceiving, because the person is comparing what they perceive with what they expected to perceive, they prevent the person from fully experiencing what is there. So the Gestalt therapist attempts to provide new modes of experience and new uses of psychological energy to help the client become more able to perceive and experience things directly.

One typical Gestalt exercise intended to train direct perception might be to allow the group to choose pairs – people whom they would like to get to know better – and then encourage one person in each pair to get to know the other in any way except verbally. No words at all are to be used. Of necessity, this means that the exploration has to involve the other senses – sight, touch, smell, and so on. After a while, the partners change roles, and the 'explorer' becomes the 'explored'. The idea is that this exercise will encourage the person to become more aware of the information that they are receiving as part of the whole perceptual experience.

Another well-known Gestalt exercise involves getting to know an orange. Clients are each given an orange and asked to explore it in every possible way except by eating it. In this way, their awareness of the touch, sight and smell of the orange is heightened, because it cannot be overshadowed by the orange's taste. The purpose of these exercises is to open the client to new ways of experiencing things around them, so that they can develop a fuller 'awareness' in the Gestalt sense. Gestalt therapists believe that the emphasis on immediate experience encourages the person to a greater acceptance of who they are, and that this greater acceptance is the first step in personal change. Later, the client will build on that greater acceptance and begin to explore further.

The role of the therapist in this form of therapy is to direct these exploratory exercises, and to provide support for clients as they engage in new explorations. In Gestalt therapy, the relationship between the therapist and the client is emphasised as being a two-way process, in which each gets to know the other as a person. Like Rogers's client-centred therapy, Gestalt therapy does not rely on an assumption that the therapist is an authority – rather, the therapist is seen as sharing in the exploratory process and simply helping the person to develop their own innate awareness.

Transactional analysis

Transactional analysis, often referred to as **TA**, is a therapy which does not restrict itself to those individuals considered to be 'neurotic' or 'in need of help'. Instead, it maintains that it has something to offer everyone, as a way of understanding their everyday interactions better. In contrast to the Freudian or other psychoanalytic approaches, transactional analysis assumes that our behaviour is conscious and deliberate, or at least can become so once we know how to recognise our behaviour for what it is. Transactional analysis aims to provide the tools for recognising it.

The ego-state

The main concept of transactional analysis is that of the **ego-state**. According to this system, every person has three different ego-states within them, and these states are triggered by different situations. The three states are parent, child and adult. The **parent state** is controlling and authoritarian, although it may be well-meaning as well as critical. The **child state** occurs when the person is thinking and feeling like a child – being helpless, rebellious or conforming. And the **adult state** is the realistic, balanced and logical way of interacting with other people which most people consider desirable.

These three ego-states are distinct in their functioning, although the same individual may shift from one ego-state to another during the course of the same conversation, if the situation seems to demand it. Transactional analysts believe that someone can gain a great deal of insight into their own reactions and responses to others by recognising which ego-state they are in at a given time. But once they have done that, what happens is entirely their own responsibility: transactional analysis places the burden of interpretation and explanation firmly on the client, rather than on the therapist. Once someone has acquired the tools they need in order to analyse what is going on around them, it is up to them to make sense of it, and to change their behaviour in more positive ways.

Transactions

A second important concept in transactional analysis, as you might guess from the name, is the idea of the **transaction**. A transaction is a unit of human communication, between one person's ego-state and that of someone else. With two people, there are six possible ego-states in total, and a transaction may take place between any of them. A transaction may be as brief as an exchange of greetings as two people pass in the street, or it might be a whole episode, such as a manager reprimanding an employee for lateness.

Transactions can take place on two levels: the social and the psychological. The social level is the overt one, which seems to be what is happening on the surface. However, the psychological level may also be present, but in a disguised form. For example, a manager might say to a secretary: 'What time is it?', and the secretary might reply: 'Two thirty-five'. On the overt social level this is a straightforward request to know the time. However, at the psychological level, it could mean something very different – the boss's 'parent' saying: 'You're late', and the secretary's 'child' replying: 'You're always criticising me'.

Games

This would also be an example of a **game**, which is a third important concept in transactional analysis. Games are orderly series of transactions which are played on two levels, and which result in bad feelings as the payoff. Berne (1973) described a number of these in the book *Games People Play*. In games, people act in stereotyped ways, which lead to the payoff. In the example above, the boss is playing the 'Now I've Got You' game, while the secretary is playing another game, called 'Kick-me', and feels bad and picked on.

Berne identified numerous other games, such as the 'Why Don't You?...Yes, But...' game, in which someone asks for help but refuses to accept any suggestions as practical. This is a game, not uncommon with neurotic clients, which ends in all suggestions being dismissed and the person with the problem exulting that no one can solve their particular problem. After a series of these games, Berne argued, players have made a collection of bad feeling, and may allow themselves a 'free' depression or anger outburst as a 'reward'.

The concept of the game may sound trivial, but it provides people with a conceptual framework which allows them to understand the patterned nature of many types of interactions. Moreover, by coming to see it as a game, a client is encouraged to perceive that there are other ways of playing, and so they are more likely to identify practical ways of changing their behaviour.

Strokes

Another concept in transactional analysis is that of the **stroke**. Strokes are positive units of human recognition, like telling someone that they have done something well, or that you like them. Berne argued that strokes are essential to people's psychological well-being. They also help to dissipate the bad feelings produced by a series of games, to allow someone to escape from a cycle. A stroke might be something like a helpful comment, a word of praise, a smile – in short, any unit of interaction which helps the individual to feel better about themselves or about what has just been going on.

Berne argued that, from early childhood, people can develop patterns of stroking and interaction, which last throughout their lives unless they act directly to change them. These patterns are known as **life-scripts**. Someone who had a childhood in which they played a continuous game of 'Kick-me', for instance, would make life-choices which resulted in their continuing that game in adulthood. But the principle of transactional analysis as a form of psychotherapy is that this does not have to be the case. By recognising the pattern of their interactions, using the conceptual tools provided by transactional analysis, an individual can identify their life-script and decide whether they are satisfied with it. (In Berne's terms, they can decide whether they are essentially '**OK**' or '**Not OK**' as a person.) By becoming aware of their ego-states and the games that they are playing, they can decide to change this script, and adopt a more positive way of interacting with the world.

Transactional analysis, then, sees the individual as autonomous, responsible and able to make their own decisions. The therapeutic process is a service, provided by the therapist, which will not effect a magical cure. Rather, it assumes that the client is willing and competent to achieve the goals of the contract between the two of them, client and therapist – responsibility for the client's progress rests squarely on the shoulders of the client, but what the therapist does is to provide the client with the conceptual tools for effecting that progress.

Family therapy

As we saw earlier in this chapter, Laing's work in the 1960s focused attention on the way that some families as a whole are seriously disturbed. Part of this involved identifying how such families often create a climate in which one individual becomes the 'scapegoat' for this disturbance, by being deemed to be mentally ill.

Clinical psychology was receptive to this idea. Bowen, in 1960, had observed how many schizophrenic patients seemed to improve while they were in hospital, but then relapsed when they got home, and suggested that some families might be **schizophrenogenic** – actually liable to induce schizophrenia in certain family members. One of the central concepts in the relationship between family and schizophrenia was the idea of the double-bind, which Bateson *et al.* (1956) described as an unresolvable sequence of experience. Bateson *et al.* listed five necessary ingredients for a **double-bind**, which are described in Box 9.2 overleaf.

In 1958, Wynne *et al.* showed how disturbed families often insist on maintaining a facade of family harmony, denying that there is any problem between them. They called this **pseudomutuality**. Laing argued that these families use such courses of action to engage in a process of mystification, which involves insisting that everything is fine, and that those family members who do not join in are 'sick' (Laing, 1961).

As this work progressed, it became clear that there was a strong need for a form of therapy which did more than just look at the individual for signs of 'illness'. Following a discussion with the child psychiatrist John Bowlby, Bell, an American child psychiatrist, started seeing the parents, siblings and the referred child all together, rather than just the mother and child being seen separately. He found that this was more effective both in time and results. The practice spread quickly, and in 1962, Ackerman and Jackson founded a new journal called *Family Processes*, to explore how this approach, together with the ideas of Bowen, Bateson, Laing and others, might be developed further.

Family therapy draws much of its ideas from psychoanalysis, behaviour therapy, and personal construct therapy. Historically, four major schools of thought emerged in the development of family therapy: psychodynamic family therapy, structural family therapy, systemic family therapy, and strategic family therapy.

Box 9.2 Necessary ingredients for a double-bind

The double-bind is a common experience in highly disturbed families. It has six ingredients:

1 Two or more persons
One of these people can be designated as the 'victim'. The others are other family members, often, though not always, the mother.

2 Repeated experience
The double-bind is not a single event, but a recurrent theme in the experience of the victim.

3 A primary negative injunction
This can take one of two forms. It may be an injunction to avoid something: 'Do not do this or I will punish you'; or it may be an injunction to do something: 'If you don't do this, I will punish you'.

4 A secondary injunction
This secondary injunction conflicts with the first one at a more abstract level, and is also enforced by punishment or threat signals. It is often communicated non-verbally, and can be quite difficult to pin down – because it is often not made explicit, it is particularly hard for the 'victim' to challenge it, or even to identify it explicitly. It can take many different forms, such as: 'Do not see this as

punishment'; 'Do not see me as the punishing agent'; or 'Do not submit to my prohibitions'. If there is more than one other family member involved, then it could be that obeying the first injunction from one person involves disobeying a second injunction from the other.

5 An injunction preventing escape
The double-bind also includes a tertiary negative injunction, which prohibits the victim from escaping from the field or side-stepping the situation in any way.

6 Learned perceptions

Bateson *et al.* add a sixth point to their list, which is that once the victim has learned to perceive their family interactions in terms of double-binds, it becomes unnecessary for the whole set of ingredients to be explicitly present. Almost any part of the double-bind sequence will be enough to produce emotional disturbance – generally panic or rage. The hallucinatory voices experienced by the schizophrenic, they argue, constitute the pattern of conflicting injunctions of the double-bind which has been internalised.

Source: Adapted from Bateson *et al.*, 1956

Psychodynamic family therapy

Psychodynamic family therapy is based on psychoanalytic ideas which emphasise the importance of early experience for a child. The early psychodynamic family therapists focused particularly on the **object–relations theory** developed by Melanie Klein. Klein emphasised the importance of early experiences, which were seen as being passed on from other relationships with the earlier family. So disturbances in early experience resulted from disturbance which the parents experienced as children in their earlier families. The therapy therefore focused on coming to terms with the past, using psychoanalytic techniques in order to enable members of the family to develop more satisfying relationships with each other.

Structural family therapy

Structural family therapy (Minuchin, 1974) concentrates mainly on the boundaries and divisions which occur between subsystems within the

family. A subsystem in this framework might consist of **paired relationships**, such as mother-son, sister-sister or wife-husband, or of **triangles**. In healthy families, the boundaries between the subsystems within the family, and between the family and larger systems (work, school, etc.) are what the therapists refer to as 'clear but permeable' – in other words, the subsystems are not confused with other systems, but they can also influence and be influenced from outside. But in some families, subsystems become disturbed or outweighed by others, so that some come to dominate the family interactions at the expense of other family members.

Families with difficulties generally have boundaries which are either too rigid, or too diffuse. Sometimes, too, a family member gets caught in the relationship between two others. For instance, an adolescent may continually break the family rules, forcing her/his parents to come together to deal with the problem. Therapeutic intervention in such cases is directed at balancing the subsystems, often by strengthening alliances between individuals. Structural family therapy also maintains a strong emphasis on age-appropriate behaviour within the family, insisting that it is unrealistic to expect, say, adult behaviour and attitudes from a child.

Systemic family therapy

Systemic family therapy (Bowen, 1966) focuses on seeing the family as a working system, not just as a collection of individuals. It therefore includes recognising the influences of other family members, like grandparents, in the nature of the interactions going on within the current family. In one metaphor, a family system is visualised as a mobile, with each member being separate, yet attached by strings and rods to the others. When one member is disturbed, all of the others are affected. Also, outside forces such as economic problems or external social influences can upset, tangle or break up a family, in much the same way as the wind can tangle up or damage a mobile. The aim of family systems therapy is to teach members of the family to respond actively and sensitively to one another, rather than simply reacting to each other as a source of irritation or discomfort.

What became known as **Milan systemic family** therapy involves a very specific process of hypothesis-testing in the therapeutic environment. A team of therapists work together, with one member of the team working directly with the family and the others observing from behind a one-way screen. The team develop hypotheses about the function which the apparent problem serves in the family, and the therapist questions the family to test that hypothesis. For some teams, the questioning and the responses are dealt with directly; while for others, the responses are subjected to attributional analysis designed to investigate the hidden assumptions made by family members.

Strategic family therapy

The fourth approach to family therapy, known as **strategic family therapy**, uses many of the ideas of structural family therapy; but it focuses primarily on solving the immediate presenting problem – that is, the problem which the family have identified, and which has caused them to seek help, or present themselves to the therapists.

It is called the presenting problem for that reason, and to distinguish it from the other, deeper problems, which the family itself might not recognise.

Strategic family therapists often operate by intensifying the presenting problem, so that it is so dramatic that the family is obliged to deal with it. For example, a child who had caused damage and endangered others by lighting fires was encouraged by the therapist to practise making bonfires under her parents' supervision. Similarly, a couple who were at their wits end over the untidiness and childish demands of their adult son, were directed to clear up after him and give in to his slightest whim until it became obvious to them that the situation was ridiculous, and they took charge. By bringing issues out clearly, in this way, it is assumed that the family will learn its own ways of dealing with similar problems as they arise.

Modern approaches to family therapy

It is no longer possible to perceive these four schools of family therapy as distinct and separate, although traces of their origins can be seen in the various techniques and practices which family therapists adopt. Many modern family therapists adopt a systems approach to understanding what is going on, but they draw on the other schools of thought as well, and might often, for example, use a strategic intervention approach with a particular family. Basically, therapists use whatever seems most appropriate to the family and its problems, or what they feel most comfortable with themselves.

In modern family therapy, the tendency is for therapists to focus more on the positive coping aspects of family behaviour, and less on their dysfunctioning aspects. There are a couple of relatively new approaches which have emerged, although in these, too, the therapists will also adopt techniques developed through other forms of family therapy. In **solution focused therapy**, the therapist helps the family to identify the symptom which is causing them most distress, and helps them to work out when it is least distressing, and why. The emphasis is on solutions rather than on talking about problems as such. In **narrative therapy**, the focus is on the unhelpful 'narratives', or accounts, which people can develop about their own lives. For instance, someone may always think that they are unsuccessful, and as a result, they do not notice when they actually do achieve something. The therapist challenges their narrative, by helping them to recognise their real achievements and so begin to change their view of themselves.

Techniques in family therapy

The major aim of all family therapists is to help the family change its ways of relating, so that a better balance is achieved, and the presenting problem improves or is accommodated to by other family members. In general, family therapy tends to emphasise the wholeness of the family unit, and examines it as a working system – looking at such questions as how open or closed it is to others, how interconnected the interests and relationships of the family members are, and so on. Family therapists may also look at the various triangles of individuals which go to make up the family, seeing them as important in producing change. Above all, though, seeing the family as a working system emphasises the need to provide **feedback** within the family. By letting family members as a whole recognise what is going on, the family can develop ways of adjusting itself to a more psychologically healthy way of working.

The methods which family therapists use vary considerably. One technique involves re-enacting crucial events which have taken place, to let the participants re-examine how they and other family members reacted. Another approach involves charting the family systems, so that the family can see for themselves the various alliances and schisms which are occurring between them. That might include developing **geneograms**, or

family trees, which explore influences from the past and from extended families.

Another technique is that of **sculpting**, where families are asked to demonstrate their closeness to or distance from each other, by arranging themselves physically and without speaking. And, of course, like most therapists, family therapists use role-playing and modelling, as well as cognitive approaches such as discussions of the attributions or beliefs which have been revealed. Some therapists also find it useful to see several families together. The idea is that these families can gain insight into their own problems by seeing other people's – it is often far easier to recognise disturbed functioning in someone else's family than it is to see it in your own.

In this chapter, then, we have seen how a number of different forms of therapy have been developed by clinical psychologists and others. This is not an exhaustive list of therapies by any means: there are many more. But it can be seen from the examples given here that each different therapy contains its own implicit model of what is important about human beings. The therapy builds on that model, and attempts to apply it to help those who show disturbed or abnormal behaviour.

This section has explored some of the psychology of individuality and differences between people, and well as approaches to abnormality. In the next group of chapters, we will go on to examine some of the physiological aspects of human psychology, including looking at the human brain and how it works, and at our experiences of emotion and consciousness.

Key terms

attribution The process of giving reasons for why things happen.

behavioural psychotherapy Psychotherapy which aims to teach people new ways of coping with problems by learning new ways of acting, e.g. through imitation and modelling.

client-centred therapy An approach to psychotherapy developed by Carl Rogers, in which the client is regarded as the best person to understand and resolve their own psychological problems, and the therapist's role is to provide a supportive environment to enable that to happen.

cognitive therapy A form of psychotherapy which is based on changing people's beliefs, attitudes and attributions about their worlds, and so helping them

to act more positively and to change things for the better.

ego-state Modes of interacting with other people, described by Berne as falling into three types: Parent, Adult and Child.

empathy Sharing in someone else's feelings; being able to feel with them even though not undergoing the same experience.

encounter groups Self-help groups originated by Carl Rogers, designed to generate unconditional positive regard between their members in order to facilitate personal growth.

facilitator One who acts to encourage positive interpersonal processes to take place, e.g. in an encounter group.

feedback Knowledge about the effectiveness of one's performance on a task or set of tasks. Feedback appears to be essential in most forms of learning, and is more effective if it is immediate.

fixed role therapy A form of psychotherapy in which people act out roles different from those which they would normally adopt.

Gestalt therapy A form of psychotherapy which emphasised the importance of complete sensory experience.

habituation Becoming accustomed to a stimulus, such that it is no longer registered by sensory neurones.

implosion therapy A form of behaviour therapy based on 'overkill', in which the person is continually faced with the feared stimulus until their fear dies down.

internal attribution The judgement that a behaviour or act is caused by sources within the person – i.e. their character, personality or intentions. This is also known as dispositional attribution.

modelling Providing an example which a child can imitate in order to learn styles of behaviour.

non-directive Acting in such a way as to allow inter-action with another person to continue without actually indicating how the other person should act, or hinting, implicitly or explicitly, at what they ought to be saying.

ontological insecurity A form of insecurity which is to do with one's own personal development and sense of identity.

physiological determinism The approach which states that human and other behaviour occurs as a straightforward consequence of physiological systems.

pseudomutuality A process found in some dis-turbed families, in which family members insist that no conflict exists and maintain a veneer of affection which masks serious underlying hostilities and aggression.

psychoanalysis A form of psychotherapy in which the aim is to analyse the unconscious mind with a view to identifying hidden meanings and motives.

psychosomatic disorders Physical problems which have their origin in psychological stresses or other psychological sources.

Rational Emotive Behaviour Therapy (REBT) A form of psychotherapy which mixes rational argument with behaviour therapy techniques.

schizophrenogenic families Families which appear to encourage the development of schizophrenia in certain members through disturbed interactions such as pseudomutuality.

social learning theory An approach to child development which states that children develop through learning from the other people around them.

token economy A system involving the use of tokens as secondary reinforcers in the rehabilitation of long-term psychiatric patients.

transaction A form of behavioural exchange or interchange between two individuals.

transactional analysis A method of analysing social behaviour which looks at the patterns of behavioural exchange in terms of the ego-states which they reveal.

Summary

1 Psychoanalysis initially reflected Freudian theory, although other forms developed subsequently. Critics of psychoanalysis have argued that it has little effect, despite being extremely widespread and influential.

2 Behaviour therapy was developed by applying learning theory to problems of abnormal behaviour. Behaviour therapy techniques can be seen as those based on classical conditioning, those based on operant conditioning and those based on social learning.

3 Client-centred therapy is based on Rogers's theory of personality, and takes the view that if individuals are given unconditional positive regard, they will be able to sort out their own personal problems.

4 Existentialist therapy sees people as having chosen their own actions, including retreat into illness. It emphasises the context within which the person exists, and how they respond to the demands on them. Its emphasis on family interactions in schizophrenia led to the eventual development of family therapy.

5 Cognitive therapy aims to identify distorted cognitions, so that the person can understand their situation more positively and act to change it. It focuses on expectations, appraisals, attributions and beliefs.

6 Personal construct therapy is based on the idea that everyone has their own, unique way of construing the world. Therapy aims to encourage people to change their personal construct systems so as to understand events in a more positive way.

7 Rational-emotive therapy aims to counteract irrational and self-defeating beliefs, partly through logical argument, partly through learning new behaviour, and partly through retraining emotional responses.

8 Other approaches to therapy include Gestalt therapy, which emphasises the whole cognitive field within which an experience takes place; Transactional Analysis, which interprets social interaction in terms of games and other social patterns; and family therapy, which emphasises the person within their family context.

Self-assessment questions

1 Briefly outline the assumptions and ideas in the existentialist approach to therapy.

2 Describe the main types of cognition addressed by cognitive therapists.

3 Outline the basic principles of *either* Gestalt *or* rational-emotive therapy.

Practice essay questions

1 What are the advantages and disadvantages of psychoanalysis?

2 'Where behaviour therapy works, it does so for entirely different reasons than those assumed by the behaviourists'. Discuss, with reference to specific forms of behaviour therapy.

3 Compare and contrast client-centred therapy and personal construct therapy.

Test your knowledge of this chapter with our online quizzes and games at: http://www.psych.co.uk

Explore alternatives to the medical model further at:

General

http://www.primenet.com/~dannell/andy/psych/personality/pindex.html – Links to brief but useful summaries of the concepts and assumptions of all the personality theories.

http://www.grohol.com/therapy.htm – Tutorials on psychodynamic, cognitive/behaviour, humanistic/existentialist and eclectic therapies.

Specific therapies

http://www.umdnj.edu/psyevnts/psa.html – Links, resources and tutorials on the subject of psychoanalysis.

http://www.gestalt.org/wulf.htm – Article on the historical roots of Gestalt therapy.

http://mindstreet.com/cbt.html – Article on the basics of cognitive therapy with useful links and bibliographical and research details.

Physiological psychology

Brain development and clinical neuropsychology

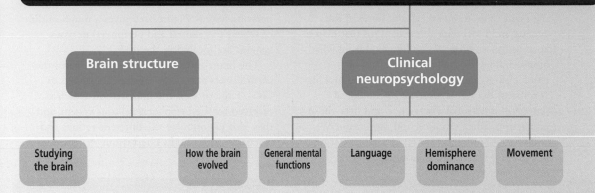

Brain structure

Clinical neuropsychology

Studying the brain

How the brain evolved

General mental functions

Language

Hemisphere dominance

Movement

Learning objectives

10.1. The nervous system
a define terms relating to the nervous system
b describe the three parts of the nervous system
c link parts of the nervous system with everyday experience

10.2. Methods of studying the brain
a describe methods of studying brain functioning
b identify limitations of different methods of studying the brain
c evaluate the use of animals in studying brain functioning

10.3. Brain evolution
a describe the main sub-cortical structures of the brain
b outline significant functions of sub-cortical structures
c link brain structure with evolutionary development

10.4. Genetic transmission
a define terms relating to genetic transmission
b distinguish between mitosis and meiosis
c assess complexities in the relationship between genes and development

10.5. Clinical neuropsychology
a define key terms relating to clinical neuropsychology
b link disturbances in brain function with memory disorders
c evaluate the relationship between brain function and personality

10.6. Language functions
a identify areas of the cerebrum involved in language
b describe language disorders resulting from cerebral damage
c apply knowledge of brain functioning to everyday experience

10.7. Hemisphere differences
a define terms relating to hemisphere differences
b describe Sperry's studies of people with split brains
c assess evidence for hemisphere differences and creativity

10.8. Brain mechanisms of movement
a outline the brain processes involved in skilled movement
b distinguish between the pyramidal and extra-pyramidal motor systems
c describe the neural basis of problems of movement

In the next few chapters, we will be mainly looking at that part of psychology known as **physiological psychology**, or sometimes **biopsychology**. We will be looking at how different parts of the brain and nervous system work, and what their functioning has to do with our experience. We will also be looking at how the brain came to evolve, and at some of the genetic and biochemical mechanisms that help to keep us functioning. We will be exploring what biopsychology can tell us about states of consciousness, and sleep. And we will be looking at some of the interactions of physiological systems and personal experience, and how those interactions affect emotion and motivation. We will begin, though, by taking a brief look at one of the main structures in biopsychology – the human nervous system.

The human nervous system

The human nervous system consists of a network of fibres running throughout the body. This net-work is composed of millions of special cells known as **neurones**, and these neurones are organised into different structures. The nervous system serves a vital communicative function for the body. Its network of nerve cells transmits messages from one part of the body to another, co-ordinates different activities at different times, and establishes when particular actions or respons-es are appropriate or inappropriate. All these messages allow the body to co-ordinate its

physical and physiological functioning, so that it can operate efficiently, and largely automatically.

The nervous system is often divided into three sections, although these sections are not completely separate (Figure 10.1). The three sections are: the central nervous system, the peripheral nervous system, and the autonomic nervous system. Figure 10.2 gives a rough outline of where the central and peripheral nervous systems are located in the body.

The brain and spinal cord together form the **central nervous system** (often shortened to **CNS**). They process the information which is received by the peripheral nervous system, and they also co-ordinate the different actions and reactions of the body. The various structures of the

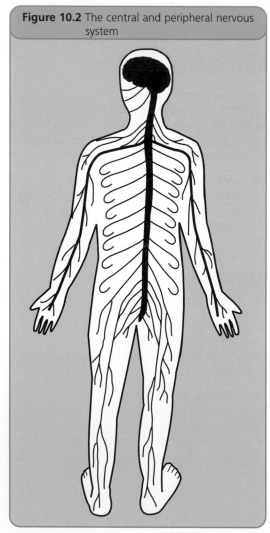

Figure 10.2 The central and peripheral nervous system

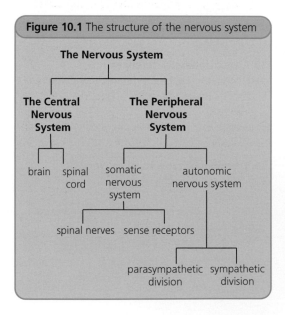

Figure 10.1 The structure of the nervous system

central nervous system communicate with one another and with rest of the body. Its operations are complex – sometimes involving specialised brain structures, and sometimes involving variations in the finely-tuned chemical balance of the brain.

The brain itself consists of millions of nerve cells, packed tightly together. Each of these nerve cells, or **neurones**, has connections with many others. Long fibres, known as dendrites (from the Greek word for branches) reach out from the cell body of the neurone, and stretch to make connections with neurones which may be either nearby, or located in other parts of the brain.

Within the brain, many of the neurones (though not all) take the form of **connector neurones**, or interneurones. These have tendrils, called dendrites, which reach out in all directions to form connections with other cells. The outer layers of the cerebral hemispheres consist of billions of these types of cells, together with billions more cells such as glial cells, whose functions appear to be to keep the neurones supplied with the nutrients that they need in order to keep functioning. These layers are referred to as **grey matter**. On the inside of the cerebral hemispheres is **white matter**, which consists of nerve fibres, covered by a fatty myelin sheath, so they appear white.

In the spinal cord (Figure 10.3), the order is reversed, so that the white matter is on the outside and the grey matter on the inside. In the very centre is a small canal, which contains cerebro-spinal fluid: a liquid which carries nutrients to the

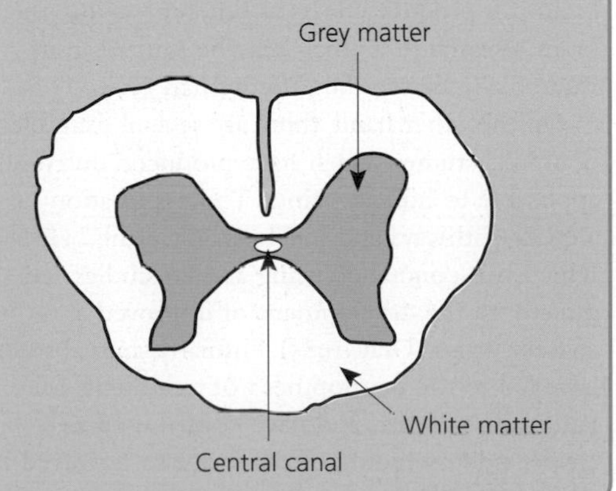

nervous system. The brain, too, has spaces filled with cerebro-spinal fluid. These are called ventricles. We will be looking at how brain structures work in the second half of this chapter, and at some of the chemical activities of the brain in Chapter 11.

The **peripheral nervous system** forms a network of neural (nerve) fibres, covering the whole body. Its role is to bring information about the body and the outside world to the brain and spinal cord, and to pass messages from the brain and spinal cord to other parts of the body. The receptors of the peripheral nervous system gather information about the external environment, and the nerves of that system communicate that information to the central nervous system and to the rest of the body – all of which allows us to perceive and respond to changes in our environment. We will be looking at the activities of the peripheral nervous system in Chapter 12.

The third part of the nervous system, the **autonomic nervous system (ANS)**, consists of glands as well as nerve cells, and is concerned with states of the body, like pregnancy, or emotional states. The glands and nerve fibres of the autonomic nervous system co-ordinate much of our general physiological functioning, using information from inside the body to do so. They also respond directly to some outside information, particularly stressful or emotional stimuli. We will be looking at the activities of the autonomic nervous system in Chapter 13.

Our human experience, though, amounts to more than just the actions of nerve, muscle, and gland networks. There will be many times in these chapters when we need to draw on other areas of psychology, in order to get a realistic picture of what is happening. The experience of emotion, for example, is partly physiological; but a full understanding of the psychology of emotion has to include personal and social dimensions as well. As we saw in Chapter 1, modern biopsychology takes an **interactionist** approach approach to understanding human experience, rather than a **reductionist** one. This means that biochemical, neurological and physiological levels of explanation all work alongside personal, social and cultural levels to contribute to our understanding of human experience.

Figure 10.3 A cross-section through the spinal cord

Grey matter

White matter

Central canal

Studying the brain

The brain is a tremendously complex structure. In human beings, there are two large cerebral hemispheres which overshadow almost everything else, so they are almost all you would see if you looked at a brain from the outside. But buried deep within the two hemispheres are many other structures, and also spaces called **ventricles**, which contain cerebro-spinal fluid. The cerebrum itself seems to be mainly concerned with what we know as the 'higher' mental functions – with thinking, reasoning, memory for events or for speech, and the like. We will look at some of the functions of the cerebrum later in this chapter.

From anatomical studies, we know that the rest of the brain is divided into a number of different structures. These are known as **sub-cortical structures**, because they are located below (sub) the cerebral cortex (cortical). They can be identified when the brain is dissected because of the way that the neural fibres bunch together. But anatomical studies can only tell us about dead tissue – about the brain's structure, not about its functions. There are a number of other methods which psychologists and psychobiologists use to find out how the brain works (Table 10.1). None of them is ideal on its own; but when we put all the evidence suggested by these methods together, we can begin to build up a picture of how the brain works – in some respects, anyway.

The difficulty in finding out which areas of the brain do what, is that the brain is a highly co-ordinated and integrated structure. Moreover, it is alive, and it is well protected. This produces a number of problems, because it has meant that techniques for studying the brain have traditionally tended to rely on looking at what happens when it goes wrong in some way. As we shall see, almost every technique that can be used to study the brain has its limitations or drawbacks, and we need to bear these in mind. That does not mean that all research is useless – just that we need to be cautious before we jump to conclusions.

Animal studies

Much of our knowledge of brain functioning has come from studies with animals. Some researchers, notably Gray (1985), argue that this work is ethically acceptable because it helps to develop effective medical treatments for human beings. Other psychologists argue against animal research, on the grounds that it is needlessly cruel, and to a large extent unnecessary. The debate is an intense one, and has at least had the valuable effect of making sure that any animal research which is undertaken in psychology is done for serious research purposes, and not just as a course requirement or a teaching illustration.

Some opponents to animal experimentation argue that it is inappropriate as a way of finding things out, since animal brains are not exactly parallel with the human brain. Fisher (1964) showed that injections of a neurotransmitter, acetylcholine, produced different reactions in cats and rats even when it was injected into exactly the same site within the brain. It provoked a hunger response in rats, but cats responded to the injection by producing all the signs of anger or rage. If the same substance in the same part of the brain can produce effects as different as this, then brain research in animals may be limited in its value for understanding the human brain.

On the other hand, there are several examples of animal studies which have produced outcomes applicable to human beings. The exploration of anxiety pathways and mechanisms in the brain, which was conducted using animal studies, led directly to the development of improved anti-anxiety drugs (Gray, 1985). Similarly, animal studies have led to the development of treatments for Parkinson's disease, and have contributed to a clearer understanding of the processes involved in Alzheimer's disease. So there are arguments to be

Table 10.1 Studying the brain	
Physical interventions	ablation
	lesion
	accidental injury
Chemical interventions	cannulae
	sampling
Electrical interventions	micro-electrode recording
	EEGs
	evoked potentials
	electrical stimulation
Scanning	CAT scans
	MRI scans
	PET scans

made on both sides: deciding between them is a question of moral choice and values, rather than one of simply weighing up the evidence.

Physical interventions

One set of methods for studying the brain involves physical interventions. These methods can involve the surgical removal of a part of the brain, which is a technique known as **ablation**, or they may involve damage to small parts of it, known as **lesions**. Lesions can occur accidentally, too, as can other injuries, and these accidental injuries are also used to tell us something about brain functions.

Some of the earliest information about the brain came from accidental injuries. The remarkable case of Phineas Gage, who suffered a dramatic brain injury yet still lived for many years, is a classic example (Macmillan, 1996); but there have also been less drastic ones. The large number of shrapnel injuries generated during WWI, for example, provided information about deficits arising from damage to a particular area. This information was collated by Holmes (1919), who identified the existence of the visual cortex from the observation that people with shrapnel injuries at the back of the brain had sight problems.

Trying to learn from accidental injury or brain disease has its drawbacks, though. If a patient has suffered some kind of lesion to a particular part of the brain, and then is no longer able to do something that they could do before, we still do not know what is going on. We know, of course, that the area of the brain which was damaged is involved in some way. What we do not know is how important it was, or whether it was part of a whole system. If the wires leading from a doorbell push to the bell itself are cut, then the bell will not ring; but that does not mean that the wires were the part that actually produced the noise. The whole **system** is involved in producing the effect, and damage to any part of it can interrupt its function.

Another problem that arises from trying to study human brain activity through accidental injury is to do with the social processes of attribution and social explanation (see Chapter 15). We often notice things only when they are drawn to our attention, but when we do, we like to explain them. If someone has had a brain injury, it draws our attention to how that person is functioning. This means that we may begin to notice things about them that we did not notice

before – even though they were exactly the same before the accident. It is very easy to attribute forgetfulness, for example, or a short temper, to the injury and to minimise our memories of what that person was like before it. Indeed, since we expect brain injuries to change people, we are particularly sensitised to do this: the injury sets up a **perceptual set**, which affects what we notice and what we disregard.

This does not just apply to observers: it also applies to the person who has had the injury. Everyone, for instance, is slightly forgetful at times, and we do not usually think anything of it. But someone who has just suffered a head injury will notice each time they forget something, and will tend to attribute their forgetfulness to the injury. In addition, they may not try so hard to remember things, believing there is no point in doing so. So their memory would get worse after the injury, but because of their expectations rather than because of the injury itself. Without very accurate records of what that person was like before (which we do not tend to keep) it is difficult to know what changes an injury has made.

Chemical techniques

Neurones transmit information from one cell to another by means of special chemicals known as neurotransmitters, which we will be examining in more detail in the next chapter. Different types of neurotransmitters are involved in different aspects of brain functioning. Some studies have involved **chemical injection** – inserting chemicals into the brain, using microscopic tubes called **cannulae**. They have revealed quite a lot about how some diseases, such as Parkinsonism, may be ameliorated by raising the level of specific neurotransmitters in the brain. Since many of these studies are undertaken with animals, however, it is uncertain how far the technique can be generally applied: the study by Fisher (1964), described above, suggests that there may be some variation in the functions of different neurotransmitters between species.

The use of **drugs** is another way in which the chemical aspects of brain functioning have been studied, although this is much more speculative, since we cannot see directly which parts of the brain the drug is affecting (at least in human beings). However, some drugs appear to have very similar chemical structures to certain types of neurotransmitters, and this may tell us something about the ways in which different naturally occurring chemicals operate in the brain. We will be looking more closely at the actions of drugs in Chapter 11.

Another technique involves **chemical sampling** – taking samples of neurotransmitters, in order to investigate which ones are active in the brain at any given time. Some research into the biochemistry of memory has used this technique. Because of the risk of damage, though, and the uncertainties about exactly whereabouts in the brain the sample was extracted, it is uncommon for this method to be used with human beings. Instead, it is mostly used with experimental animals.

Electrical studies of the brain

The nerve cells which make up the brain and nervous system work by generating tiny electrical impulses. So another way of studying the brain is to look at the electrical activity which takes place. Some of these methods involve collecting information about the electrical activity of single nerve cells. Other techniques allow us to look at general neural functioning – the electrical activity generated by whole regions of the brain.

Micro-electrode recording involves placing a highly sensitive microscopic electrode at or near a single neurone, so that the electrical activity when it fires can be detected. As might be expected, a high degree of precision is needed, and, since the brain consists of billions of neurones, the technique is not likely to tell us much about overall brain functioning – even though it is extremely useful for analysing specific information. It would take centuries to map out the whole brain in this way, and most areas do not respond to very specific and easily controlled stimuli. But, as we saw in Chapter 2 and will see again in Chapter 12, the technique has been used with considerable success by Hubel and Wiesel (1968, 1979), to map out the functions of some of the visual cells in the thalamus and in the visual cortex. They showed how the painstaking collection of thousands of different measurements could eventually be assembled to make a coherent pattern.

Another way in which we can measure electrical activity in the brain is by using **electroencephalograms**, or **EEGs**. These are obtained by attaching sensitive electrodes to the person's scalp. The electrodes record any changes in the electrical field which are produced by the electrical activity of brain cells. The information from these electrodes is passed to a **polygraph**, which consists of several pens resting on a roll of paper which moves along at a regular rate. Each pen receives information from one electrode, and moves up and down accordingly. A large movement, which would show up as a 'peak' on the paper, indicates a large burst of electrical activity, and a small movement indicates a smaller amount of firing. So we can tell from the EEG how much overall brain activity has taken place in each region of the brain. Figure 10.4 shows an EEG from a young woman who experienced a slight seizure while the EEG was being taken.

In Chapter 11, we will be looking at how EEGs have been used to study sleep. Alertness, relaxation, wakefulness and different levels of sleep all produce very different EEG patterns. But a major drawback of EEGs is that they can give us only a very general idea of what is happening in the brain – they do not tell us very much about specialised areas. In general terms, though, they can provide useful information about brain activity, and are often used to detect medical problems, like minor epilepsy or brain seizures.

A different, but related, method of studying the electrical activity of the brain consists of using **evoked potentials**, in which the electrical activity of a particular region of the brain is measured as a response to a particular event or stimulus. So, for instance, if we wanted to measure changes in the brain's activity in response to a particular sound, we would take a measure of the ordinary electrical activity of that person's brain, make the sound, while at the same time measuring electrical activity, and then compare the electrical records to see what changes in electrical activity were produced. In practice, the stimulus in an evoked potential recording is usually produced several times, and the average (mean) reaction is taken as the evoked potential recording.

Since the brain itself does not have any sensory receptors, there is no pain when it is cut or damaged – although of course the surrounding tissue of the scalp may feel pain. This means that it is possible to stimulate the brain directly, using small electrodes, and to observe what happens – or, in the case of human research participants, to ask them to say what they are experiencing. **Electrical stimulation** is sometimes used when surgeons are about to undertake brain surgery,

Figure 10.4 An EEG chart

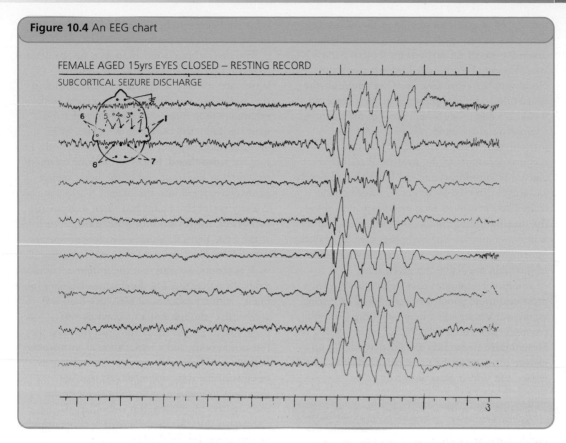

FEMALE AGED 15yrs EYES CLOSED – RESTING RECORD

SUBCORTICAL SEIZURE DISCHARGE

since the patient can be conscious, needing no more than a local anaesthetic for the scalp, and in this way the surgeon can find out which areas to avoid.

The most famous of these studies, reported by Penfield and Rasmussen (1950), resulted in the identification of the major sensory projection areas of the cerebral cortex, as well as the motor and somatosensory areas. While it cannot provide information about thinking and remembering, or about autonomic or unconscious processes, this technique has been useful in helping us to understand localised brain functions – particularly when it has confirmed insights obtained by other methods of study.

Brain scans

In recent years, some rather more sophisticated methods for studying the brain have emerged. These involve **non-invasive techniques**, which leave the individual relatively untouched, but nonetheless build up a picture of what is happening inside the brain, by scanning the brain and detecting any changes or areas of unusual functioning.

One non-invasive technique for examining the structure of the brain involves **computed axial tomography**, or **CAT** scans. This involves building up a three-dimensional X-ray picture of the brain, by using X-rays to photograph a series of 'slices' through it. The different images from the 'slices' are then combined using a computer. The picture which results can show areas of deformed or damaged tissue, and can identify the location of medical problems, such as blood clots or regions where the blood supply has been interrupted.

Magnetic resonancy imaging (MRI) involves a different technique, in which a succession of electro-magnetic waves – like radio waves – are passed through the brain. This causes the neurones of the brain to respond to the electro-magnetic stimulation by producing electro-magnetic waves themselves, and these are detected and recorded. As with CAT scanning, it is the computerised combination of a number of these measurements which results in an image of the brain, this time indicating active neurone bundles.

Each time a nerve cell fires it depletes its reserves slightly, and needs to be replenished from the supply of nutrients carried in the bloodstream before it can fire again. The blood vessels which distribute blood throughout the central nervous system respond to this need by increasing the blood supply to that area. So, if we could see the distribution of blood throughout the cortex, we would be able to see which areas of the brain were active at the time. **Positron emission tomography (PET)** scans allow researchers and medical personnel to do just that. Radioactive glucose is introduced into the brain's blood supply, and this is detected by receptors placed on the scalp. These receptors pick up information about the distribution of the blood in the brain, and feed it into a computer. The computer combines all the information to produce an image of which parts of the brain are active at a given time.

Scanning techniques have helped us to learn a great deal more about the functioning of 'normal' brains, but we are still a long way from getting a comprehensive understanding of what is going on. Nonetheless, researchers are slowly building up a picture of some of the principles of how the brain works, and which parts do what.

How the brain evolved

The human brain is a hugely complex structure. At first sight, it seems to be composed of a mass of different bits, doing apparently unrelated things in no particular order. But we can understand much more about why the brain is like it is, and how it came to be that way, if we look at how it has evolved, and what it is like in other animals.

The brain, as we have seen, is a part of the nervous system. A simple one-celled animal like an amoeba does not have a nervous system – it does not need one. But animals which are composed of different groups of specialised cells, which includes just about all of them except amoebae, need to have a way of co-ordinating the different parts of the body. That need for co-ordination is the evolutionary origin of nervous systems.

The very simplest form of nervous system is found in some flatworms, and this is simply a network of neurones that runs throughout the animal's body. Some flatworms, however, have slightly more complex systems, which are arranged in a ladder-like structure, running through the body, with more neurones at the front end (Figure 10.5). This arrangement resembles what we believe to be the evolutionary precursor of the mammalian nervous system.

The invertebrate animals, such as insects, tended to retain this ladder-like structure, but as vertebrates evolved, the number of neurones in the ladder-like nervous system increased, until eventually they formed a dense **neural tube**, running down the centre of the spine, with branches radiating out to the rest of the body. This tube, or **notochord**, began to produce enlarged structures at the front end of the body, which gradually evolved into the brain.

Early vertebrate brains had three sections: the **forebrain**, **midbrain**, and **hindbrain**. If we look at the basic brain structure of vertebrate species which have been around for a very long time, such as sharks, we find that these three sections are easily distinguished. The forebrain is largely a 'nose brain', with a pronounced olfactory bulb and cerebrum – though not a cerebral cortex; a thalamus, to relay sensory information from the rest of the body, and a hypothalamus to maintain homeostasis. The midbrain in the shark largely consists of the optic lobes, which regulate responses to visual stimuli; and the hindbrain includes the cerebellum, for muscular co-ordination, and the medulla, which maintains vital life processes for the body.

Although basic brain structure is usually reasonably consistent, different environmental requirements produce different adaptations. Most fish, for instance, rely on their chemical senses when they are detecting food, and so have large olfactory lobes. Birds, on the other hand, need

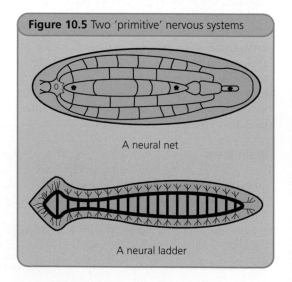

Figure 10.5 Two 'primitive' nervous systems

A neural net

A neural ladder

highly complex muscular co-ordination for flight patterns, and so they have highly developed cerebella. As mammals came to rely more on learning and adaptation, and on their complex sensory and motor systems, they developed a complex covering to the cerebrum, known as the cerebral cortex, and this becomes increasingly large and convoluted, as we move up the phylogenetic scale (Figure 10.6).

In human beings, the cerebral cortex is by far the largest and most complex part of the brain, and in dolphins it is larger still. Because it has expanded to cover over most of the rest of the brain, it overshadows the older structures, but they are still there, buried inside. Some researchers find it useful to talk of the brain as having three layers: an innermost 'primitive' **central core**, involving the thalamus, cerebrum and brain stem; an **old brain** involving the limbic system and its related structures, and a **new brain**, the cerebrum. It is also common to come across the cerebral cortex referred to as the **neocortex** – a term which reminds us that it is a relatively recent development, evolutionarily speaking.

The sub-cortical structures of the brain

If we look at the sub-cortical structures of the human brain – that is, the structures which lie below the cerebrum, which in human beings is the largest of all of the parts of the brain – we find that we can trace an approximate sequence to their arrangement (Figure 10.7, overleaf). As we have seen, the nervous system evolved gradually, from a simple neural tube with a ladder-like network of nerve fibres, to the immensely complex structure that it is in human beings and other mammals. As organisms developed methods of sensing their outside environments, comparable structures evolved in the brain to co-ordinate that sensory information, and as internal physiological structure grew in complexity, increasingly complex brain structures evolved to monitor and regulate their functioning. As we look at the human brain, the ordering of the structures is thought to reflect that evolutionary history.

Our equivalent to the primitive neural tube is the **spinal cord**, which runs through the centre of the spine. The spinal cord is still a tube, consisting of layers of neurones surrounding a central canal, containing cerebro-spinal fluid. The brain, too, contains spaces known as ventricles, which are also filled with cerebro-spinal fluid. They serve different functions nowadays, but these enclosed areas are an anatomic reminder that the brain, as well as the spinal cord, originally evolved from a neural tube.

The spinal cord receives information from sensors in the skin, and relays it to the brain. It also relays motor impulses from the brain to the muscles, thus producing movement of one kind or

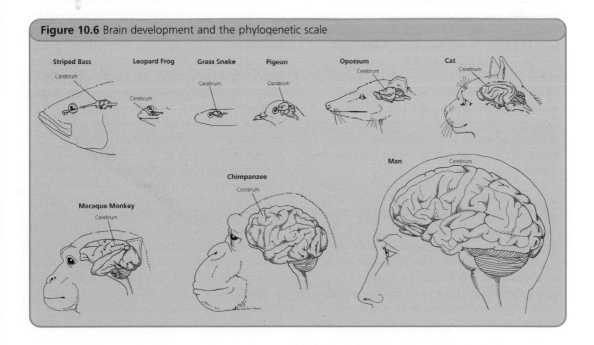

Figure 10.6 Brain development and the phylogenetic scale

Figure 10.7 Evolution of the brain

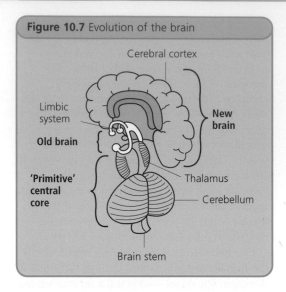

another. But the spinal cord also responds directly to certain kinds of stimuli – notably, painful ones which are likely to produce damage if action is not taken very quickly. Pulling your hand away from a burning surface is an example – the reflex action takes place before you are aware of it, because it is an act which is entirely mediated by the spinal cord. And withdrawing from painful or noxious stimuli would be likely to be one of the very first of all responses to evolve.

At the top of the spinal cord, where it joins the base of the brain, the spinal cord thickens into a structure known as the medulla. This part of the brain mediates the very basic and non-conscious body functions, like digestion, respiration and heartbeat. Again, these are basic responses, only slightly less essential than the ability to avoid things which might kill you, and ones which would reflect the internal evolution of the organism, as digestion becomes no longer a matter of direct absorption but begins to require co-ordinated muscle actions, and other functions too develop in complexity.

Above the medulla lies the region known as the midbrain, which contains the part known as the reticular activating system, or RAS. This part of the brain mediates alertness, attention, sleep and wakefulness. The evolving organism, now able to avoid pain and regulate its internal functions, develops a more sophisticated system for maximising benefit from its interaction with the environment, by becoming more able to pay attention to salient features; and also develops the

ability to enter quiescent, restorative states when no danger threatens.

At the back of the brain, bulging out from the midbrain, is a large, tightly-wrinkled structure known as the cerebellum. This is closely involved in balance and physical co-ordination. While the spinal cord and medulla mediate involuntary movements, so aiding the avoidance of noxious stimuli, the cerebellum ensures that deliberate actions are smooth and well-organised: a function which may have become more important to the developing organism through more efficient action in escaping from predators, or in hunting prey. As the animal itself became more complex, so too did its environment and other animals around it.

Above the midbrain, and just below the thalamus, is a small structure about the size of a baked bean, known as the hypothalamus. This structure has the task of maintaining homeostasis – a steady state in the basic functioning of the body. So, for instance, if the body overheats, this information is relayed to the hypothalamus, which then sends out signals to trigger off cooling mechanisms like sweating, until an optimal state is reached. If the body becomes too cool, the hypothalamus may initiate shivering. Temperature regulation, eating and drinking are all mediated by the hypothalamus, and reflect an increasingly sophisticated internal monitoring and functioning of the body. The maintenance of an internal 'steady state', in its turn, provides an environment in which even more subtle internal mechanisms can evolve.

In the very centre of the brain is the thalamus: a part of the brain which acts as a sensory relay station for information coming in from the sense receptors. In human beings, information is partially decoded in the thalamus, but is then also transmitted to the cerebrum for further interpretation. But it is in the thalamus that the nerve fibres carrying information from the sense organs synapse, which suggests that decoding in the thalamus was the primitive brain's technique for dealing with sensory information.

All around the thalamus, and just below the cerebrum, lie a collection of small structures known collectively as the limbic system. Although our knowledge of the limbic system is limited, we do know that it is involved in at least three sets of functions: in the storage of new information in memory; in play – an important method of skill-learning for young mammals; and in emotional activity. By now, we are beginning to find these parts of the brain mediating functions which are distinctively mammalian in character – or at least, which are more important to mammals, with their increased behavioural flexibility, than they are to other types of species.

Although this link between evolutionary development and brain structure is partly speculative – we must not lose sight of the fact that other groups of animals, with more 'primitive' brains, show equally sophisticated adaptation to the needs of their environments – we can trace a progression in brain functioning in the sub-cortical structures. This progression reflects, very generally, the evolutionary development of mammals. As their internal functioning and behavioural adaptation became more sophisticated, so too the structures of the mammalian brain evolved to mediate and co-ordinate those functions.

Evolution and genetics

As we have seen, a great deal of the brain's structure derives from its evolutionary history. In order to understand this, we need to know something about how evolution happens. Evolutionary theory as we understand it today began with the publication of Darwin's *Origin of Species*, in 1859. This proposed that the huge diversity of animals and plants in the world occurred as a result of a developmental process over many generations, which resulted in the species becoming better adapted to its environment. These changes happened through the ordinary process of genetic variability, and they were consolidated if they helped the individual who possessed them to cope better with their environment.

Darwin suggested that if a genetic difference proved beneficial, there would be a good chance that the individual possessing it would be stronger and healthier than the others. So it would be more likely (a) to survive in difficult conditions, and (b) to find a mate and reproduce. It would therefore be likely to pass on its beneficial genes to its offspring; and both it and its offspring would be more likely to survive hard times. Gradually, the population would come to contain a greater proportion of those sharing the beneficial characteristic, as natural phenomena such as severe winters meant that the weaker ones died out and the stronger ones survived. Eventually, many generations later, all the members of that particular population would share the beneficial characteristic.

Evolutionary theory is complex, and we will be looking at it again in Chapter 22. But there are a number of concepts in evolutionary theory which have particular relevance for the study of the brain. One of them is the concept of **neoteny**. Bolk (1926) suggested that the human infant is born prematurely, by comparison with the stage of development at which other apes, and indeed other mammals are born. Effectively, when it is born, it is not an infant, but a foetus, albeit a very large one. Most animals give birth when brain growth is pretty well complete and the bones are beginning to harden. But these processes continue for some months after birth in human beings.

According to Gould (1977), this makes it possible for the human brain to develop far more than it could have done otherwise. The brain is able to grow, without being confined by a hardened skull. And the prolonged period of dependency gives the young human much more time to learn and absorb information than a comparable animal would have. Moreover, according to Bolk there are many similarities between human beings and juvenile apes. Young chimpanzees, for example, are much more similar to human beings than adult chimpanzees are, and Bolk argued that the human ape reveals a kind of arrested development, which has kept it in the juvenile stage.

The idea of the human being as an underdeveloped ape may not appear too flattering on the surface, but Bolk's arguments are becoming increasingly accepted among biologists. The consequences of neoteny for brain development, and also for adaptability, are profound. Gould (1977) argued that what makes human beings distinctive is our massive capacity for learning. Neoteny, he argued, allows us to increase our potential and to continue learning throughout life.

Mechanisms of inheritence

Evolution, whether it involves neoteny or not, depends on genetic inheritance. In 1866, Gregor Mendel put forward his genetic theory, which is the model which is largely accepted today, although it has been extended and augmented by scientists ever since. Mendel proposed that each cell of the body contains units of heredity, or

genes, which direct growth and development in the body. Relatively uncomplicated characteristics, such as eye colour, are directly transmitted by genes. But most characteristics result from an interaction between the genes and the environment. The particular set of instructions for development which is contained in the genes themselves is known as the **genotype**. The animal, human or plant which actually develops, though, is the **phenotype** – resulting from the interaction of the genotype with the environment.

Genes consist of coded strips of DNA (deoxyribonucleic acid), arranged in a ladder-like structure that forms a double helix shape (Figure 10.8). When a gene is activated, it issues an instruction that a particular cell should synthesise a particular protein at a particular time. The combined effects of millions of genes working together, in a complex and ordered fashion, mean that this process of protein synthesis eventually results in the development and growth of a living creature. The 'genetic blueprint' contained in the coded strands of DNA contains the codes which, given the right environmental conditions and resources, will produce the individual.

Genes are arranged in pairs, known as **alleles**, and thousands of genes are combined in sequence to form thread-like chromosomes, which are also paired. During sexual reproduction, the pairs of chromosomes are separated, producing cells which have only half the required number of genes. This process is known as meiosis. But cells can also reproduce by cell division, and when that happens, the gene pairs are not separated. Instead, the cell produces a complete replica of itself, including the pairs of genes, which are replicated by a process known as mitosis.

Meiosis

The process of **meiosis** produces cells with half the required number of chromosomes, known as haploid cells. This occurs as the ladder-like DNA parts in the middle, producing two separate 'threads' that each go into new cells. Appropriate sexual activity between a male and female member of the same species results in two haploid cells combining, to produce a new organism with a full set of genes. Those genes will ensure that the new organism develops into the same species as its parents; but because half of its genes have come from the female parent and half from the male, it will not be exactly identical to either.

Since the new animal acquires an entirely new combination of genes, it is always possible that two alleles might contradict one another. One gene might contain information that its fur should be brown, while the other contains information which would produce white fur. This is resolved by **genetic dominance**: one of the genes is likely to be dominant over the other one, and will determine which colour fur the animal actually develops. The other gene will be recessive: it will not show up in the phenotype, but it will still be there, and passed on to some offspring. Which means that an unexpected genetic trait can show up even several generations later. In addition, the copying process is sometimes not quite exact, which leads to random changes, known as **mutations**.

Genetic variation is important, because it is what makes evolution possible. Sexual reproduction means that each new organism is slightly different, since the genes have been shuffled around and recombined. This opens the door for new combinations of characteristics to emerge, and for natural selection to work. The

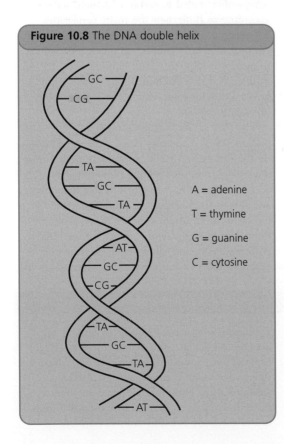

Figure 10.8 The DNA double helix

GC
CG

TA
GC
TA

AT
GC
CG

TA
GC
TA

AT

A = adenine

T = thymine

G = guanine

C = cytosine

production of mutations, too, is an important factor in evolution – although severe mutations are almost always sterile, small ones are not, and if the mutation gives the animal a survival advantage, it may eventually become the norm in that particular population of animals.

One particular pair of chromosomes determines the sex which the new animal will acquire. Females have two X chromosomes, and males have one X and one Y, although sometimes the copying is not exact, and someone might have an XYY pattern, or XXY. There were a few simplistic attempts by earlier psychologists to link these aberrant patterns with aberrant social behaviour – for example, linking XYY patterns with criminality – but the evidence for these connections was always extremely tenuous, and extrapolated from extremely small samples. There has been more concern about forms of **androgeny** which have resulted from unusual combinations of X and Y chromosomes, and we will be considering these when we look at gender identity, in Chapter 20.

These chromosomes are known as the X and Y chromosomes, because although the X chromosome is similar in shape to others, the Y one is shorter, lacking the bottom part of the X. As a result, there are some genes on the X chromosome which do not have alleles on the Y chromosome. This can lead to **sex-linked genetic disorders**, such as colour blindness, which is extremely rare in women but occurs much more commonly in men. This disorder is caused by a faulty gene on the X chromosome, which in women is balanced out by a normal one on the other X chromosome. Since 'healthy' genes are usually dominant over faulty ones, women only develop colour blindness if they have the faulty gene on both X chromosomes, and that does not happen very often. Men who inherit the colour blindness gene, though, do not have a 'healthy' gene to balance it. So they develop the disorder.

Mitosis

Every cell in the body carries a full set of chromosomes and genes in its nucleus. When cells divide, the chromosomes contract until they appear as X-shaped threads, and then they copy themselves through a process known as **mitosis**, forming two entirely new sets. The cell nucleus divides into two as well, and each half gains a completely new set of chromosomes which is identical to the chromosomes in the previous set. After that, the whole cell divides into two.

Mitosis is the process which is used in asexual reproduction, where a species reproduces itself by budding or some other mechanism which just involves making exact copies. It is also the process which is put to use in **cloning**. By encouraging cells to multiply through providing the right environmental conditions (not a simple business), scientists have been able to clone mammals, such as the famous Dolly the sheep, as well as many varieties of plants. The advent of Dolly generated a flurry of debates about the ethics of cloning, and attempts to regulate genetic research. The generally accepted view is that it would be entirely unethical to try to clone a human being, although many people see it as only a matter of time before the attempt is made.

There are, of course, large commercial applications for cloning, and it is widely used in agriculture. Kiwi fruit, for example, are all cloned, which is why they are so similar in shape and appearance. The problem, though, is that cloned fruits or vegetables are also very vulnerable to disease, since a disease is likely to run rampant very easily. Having each member of a species slightly different increases the probability that some will have characteristics which will help them to survive in difficult times, but clones are genetically identical, and have usually been reared in identical conditions too, so each clone is equally susceptible.

Genetic engineering is another recent development which has caused a storm of both ethical and ecological debate. In genetic engineering, tiny strips of DNA are cut out of one organism, and spliced into the DNA of another. As the cells reproduce through mitosis, the new DNA sequence is also replicated. The technique has been used to produce fruit and vegetables with what the retailers consider to be 'appropriate' qualities (although chefs and restauranteurs are vocal in their objections, since appropriate qualities usually have more to do with colour and keeping than with taste). It has also been used to culture bacteria or breed animals which can produce special proteins needed for medical treatments, and other new uses are emerging all the time.

The **human genome project** is a massive research venture aimed at mapping out the whole of the human genome – to identify and categorise the millions of genes involved in human heredity. It has already proved of value in medical terms, for example in identifying the genetic sources of illnesses such as cystic fibrosis, and it may in time lead to better medical treatments as a result. The project is complex, because the amount of information carried on just one chromosome would take thousands of books to describe.

In psychological terms, though, there is some doubt how far the type of knowledge obtained from the human genome project is likely to be useful. Some psychologists worry that the extreme emphasis on genetics may blind the medical profession to the importance of environmental and psychological influences in both physical illness and mental disorders. It is important to remember that genes interact with environment: there is no such thing as a genetic influence which has not come through that interaction, and as a result, the same genetic influence may have very different manifestations, in different circumstances.

Clinical neuropsychology

The human nervous system is one of the many results of the developmental process triggered off by our genetic heritage – and its chief, and most important organ, is the brain. The human brain is immensely complex, and it serves a myriad functions. For the rest of this chapter, we will be looking at how psychologists have studied brain functioning. As you might imagine, though, studying how the brain works can be tricky – after all, we cannot see it working directly, and we cannot exactly take it apart and put it back together again, or at least, not if it is alive. And although dead brains can tell us lots about structures, they cannot tell us very much about function.

In fact, most of our knowledge about the working brain comes from the area of psychology known as **clinical neuropsychology**. Clinical neuropsychologists use information from people who have experienced brain damage of one form or another, and also from ordinary people participating in psychological research projects, to draw conclusions about how the brain functions.

The history of clinical neuropsychology goes back a long way. The **phrenologists** of the eighteenth and early nineteenth centuries claimed

that mental 'faculties' were detectable as specifically localised areas of the brain, which could be detected because the highly developed areas caused the skull to protrude (see Chapter 7). Obviously, there is no sustainable scientific evidence for this sort of thing: despite its popularity at the time, phrenology was little more than a set of cultural myths. But the idea that particular mental functions were located in particular areas of the brain – the idea known as **localisation of function** – was one which lasted for a long time.

We can learn a great deal about the physical structure of the brain from anatomical studies. Figure 10.9 gives a picture of a human brain, showing how the rest of the brain is almost entirely covered by the **cerebrum** – a large, folded structure, divided into two halves down the middle, and covered in grooves and fissures. The two halves are often referred to as the cerebral hemispheres, and it is the outer layer of the **cerebral hemispheres** – known as the **cerebral cortex** – which is responsible for our 'higher' mental functioning – perception, learning, memory, and so on. Because they are mostly interested in this sort of function, psychologists often refer to 'the brain' when what they are really meaning is 'the cerebral cortex'.

Some parts of the cortex have been shown to have very specific functions. Over the years, brain researchers gathered information from accidents and surgical investigations, and this eventually allowed them to identify a number of **sensory**

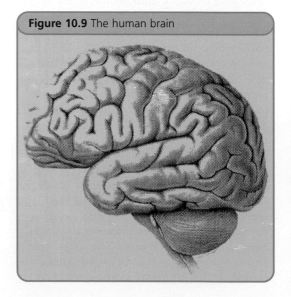

Figure 10.9 The human brain

projection areas on the cortex. If these areas are damaged, the person experiences problems with the specific sense associated with that area. The major sensory projection areas are shown in Figure 10.10, together with the four major lobes of the cerebral hemispheres.

At the very back of the brain, in the occipital lobe, there is an area known as the **striate cortex**. This is the visual area: it receives information from the retina, and is concerned with our awareness of visual information. At the side, at the top of the temporal lobe, is the **auditory cortex**, which mediates our awareness of sound; and at the bottom of the same lobe is the **olfactory strip**, which is concerned with smell and taste. In some animals which depend heavily on smell, this area is extended into a large bulb; but smell is not our primary sense – we depend much more on vision and hearing – and so in human beings this area does not take up so much of the brain's resources.

At the top of the cerebral hemisphere, there is a large groove, known as the **central gyrus**, which marks the boundary between the frontal lobe and the parietal lobe. The area on the frontal lobe edge is the **motor cortex**, concerned with conscious movement of the body. The parallel area, on the parietal lobe, is the **somatosensory cortex**, which is concerned with awareness of being touched. Different parts of these areas correspond to different parts of the body, and the more active, or sensitive, the area is, the more cortex it has devoted to it.

The cerebrum is not the whole of the brain. Far from it: there are many other brain structures, which are mostly hidden underneath the cerebrum. Table 10.2 lists some of these structures, and gives an indication of each of their functions. Simply listing functions, though, gives us a very over-simplified picture of what is really happening. In reality, as neurologists and clinical neuropsychologists have shown, several different parts of the brain will interact, making working systems which allow the body and brain to function appropriately together. We can see that more clearly if we look at some of the specific brain functions studied by psychologists.

Table 10.2 Functions of the Central Nervous System

Forebrain	
Cerebrum	Thinking, planning, perception, memory
Thalamus	Sensory processing and relay
Hypothalamus	Maintaining homeostasis
Pituitary gland	Co-ordination of endocrine activity and brain function
Limbic system	The four-Fs of motivation; emotion
Midbrain	
Tectum	Visual and auditory fibres
Tegmentum	Sensorimotor fibres
Hindbrain	
Cerebellum	Co-ordinated movement, skill learning, including speed of language and cognition
Reticular formation	Attention, arousal, movement, sleep
Pons	Sleep, dreaming, attention
Medulla	Breathing, heartrate, digestion, autonomic functions
Spinal cord	
White matter	Somatosensory nerve fibres
Grey matter	Pain responses, spinal reflexes

Figure 10.10 Sensory projection areas of the brain

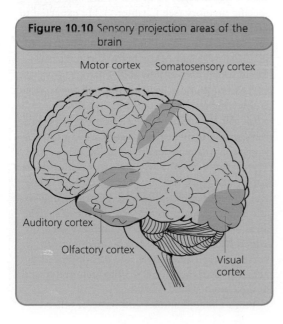

Motor cortex   Somatosensory cortex

Auditory cortex

Olfactory cortex

Visual cortex

General mental functions

One of the most famous cases in clinical neuropsychology is the remarkable case of Phineas Gage. Gage was a railway worker who had a tamping iron blown right through the frontal lobes of his cerebrum. The accident occurred in 1848, but Phineas Gage lived for many more years, earning a living by exhibiting himself, and his tamping iron, in a travelling fairground. Although his left frontal lobe had been almost entirely removed, he could still function effectively. Macmillan (1996) describes how contemporary reports state that he showed an increase in impulsiveness and became more aggressive than he had been before. On the whole, though, apart from these apparent differences in personality (which could have partly resulted from the accident itself and its consequences, rather than the damage to the brain) and some other minor effects, Gage showed surprisingly few deficits from the injury.

Lobotomy and leucotomy

These outcomes led to the suggestion that the frontal lobes were important in controlling personality and impulsiveness. In 1936, Moniz introduced the frontal lobotomy as an operation to treat schizophrenic patients. **Frontal lobotomy** involves the surgical removal of the frontal lobes of the brain. Having shown that chimpanzees who had experienced this operation became more docile and obedient, Moniz proposed that the frontal lobes were the source of aggression and socially irresponsible behaviour, and that their removal would make psychiatric patients more tractable, and cure the disturbed behaviour symptomatic of some types of schizophrenic.

A less drastic operation soon replaced the frontal lobotomy, as neurosurgeons realised that there was no need to remove the frontal lobes entirely. Instead, it was enough to cut the major neural connections between the frontal lobe and the rest of the brain, in the sense that this seemed to produce much the same effect. This operation, known as **leucotomy**, rapidly became popular as a means of controlling violent or highly disturbed psychiatric patients, although there was little explanation for why this effect took place.

Blundell (1975) reported that more than 6000 frontal lobotomies were carried out on schizophrenic patients between 1936 and 1946, and over 20,000 leucotomies by 1951. But these operations were performed with little or no follow-up studies of the patients, despite the lack of evidence that they were at all effective in treating the illness (although they were, of course, effective in keeping patients quiet, since many became virtually unable to act for themselves at all). The popularity of the operation said more about the lack of available treatments for schizophrenia than it did about the value of the operation itself, as was shown by the fact that the operation became very much less popular when chemical treatments for schizophrenia were developed (see Chapter 8).

Learning and memory

The idea that complex aspects of psychological functioning, like personality or learning, could be localised in one particular part of the brain was seriously challenged as a result of a series of studies undertaken by Lashley (1929). Lashley performed a set of lesions of the cortex in experimental rats, and correlated these with the rats' performance on maze-learning tasks. He would train a rat to run a particular maze, destroy 15% of its cerebrum and test it again. Then a further 15% would be destroyed, and the rat would be tested to see if it remembered the maze again, and so on. Lashley was actually looking for evidence of the 'engram' – the physiological trace which was thought to be left in the brain by a specific memory (see Chapter 3). He expected to find that specific items of learning, like the solution to a particular puzzle, would be located in a particular part of the brain. But in fact he found something entirely different.

As a result of the large number of studies which Lashley undertook, he concluded that no particular area of the cortex was more responsible for learning than any other: each area was just as important as any other area. This he termed the **Law of Equipotentiality** – all areas of the cerebral cortex had equal potential for retaining learning. But Lashley had also discovered that learning was affected by damage to the brain – not to specific areas, but in terms of the total amount of cortex which had been removed. It seemed that the cortex worked as a whole, and this produced the ability to learn and recall. Lashley referred to this as the **Law of Mass Action**.

From Lashley's studies and those of other

researchers, it was concluded that a large part of the cerebral cortex serves a general function, linking together different bits of information and containing the generalised associations which we know as learning. For this reason, it became known as the **association cortex**. More recently, though, and since the advent of brain-scanning techniques, researchers have discovered that a great deal of what originally seemed to be unspecialised cortex actually has very specific functions.

Amnesia

Although Lashley showed that memories do not relate in a one-to-one manner with areas of the cortex, it is nonetheless clear that damage to the brain can at times result in memory disorders. Memory disorders are known as **amnesia**, which is a general term referring to the failure of some part of the memory system. There are several different ways that amnesia may occur, ranging from brain damage and head injuries to problems arising as a result of the ageing process. We looked at some of these in Chapter 3 – in particular post-traumatic amnesia, the amnesia which results from injury to the head.

Another type of memory loss which has been studied extensively by psychologists is known as **proactive amnesia**, or sometimes **anterograde amnesia**. One of the most famous of these cases was of a patient known as H.M., studied by Milner in 1966 and any number of other psychologists thereafter. During brain surgery, H.M. suffered a bilateral lesion of the hippocampus – a structure which forms part of the limbic system of the brain. Although he showed no impairment in short-term memory, or in procedural memory, involving skills like using language or co-ordinated action, it rapidly became apparent that H.M. was for the most part unable to store new memories. The discovery that there were different forms of amnesia led to a reappraisal of many assumptions about how memory was stored (see Chapter 3).

The neuropsychological implication was that the hippocampus is directly involved in memory storage, but not in memory retrieval – H.M. had no difficulty recalling information which he had known before the accident. As one of the most-studied cases in clinical neuropsychology, H.M. has contributed a great deal, both to our theoretical understanding of memory, and also to our knowledge of its neuropsychology. Parkin (1996)

discussed how this was partly because the particular type of amnesia which H.M. experienced was so specific and so 'pure'; and partly because, unlike many other patients of this kind, neuropsychologists knew exactly what the brain injury was, and when it had occurred.

The psychiatric treatment known as **electro-convulsive therapy (ECT)** also produces a kind of amnesia. ECT involves passing a brief electric current through the brain, producing a simulated epileptic spasm. The type of amnesia which follows ECT is retroactive for immediate events – what happened just before the ECT is forgotten – and produces a more general amnesia as well, for a period after the treatment. For the most part, however, it is claimed that ECT leaves longer-term memories intact.

There tends to be some proactive amnesia resulting from ECT too, in that patients often have some difficulty in absorbing new information for a period following the treatment. Williams (1968) found that this proactive amnesia could be reduced by familiarity. If people had previously been shown test items, they were more likely to pick them out in a recognition test after having ECT, even though they did not consciously recall seeing the material before. One suggestion is that ECT may interfere with the retrieval of information rather than with learning and consolidating information.

It can be difficult, though, to tell exactly how ECT affects memory, because it is always accompanied by chemotherapy. Patients who are about to receive ECT are given tranquillisers and muscle relaxants as a routine (and necessary) part of the treatment, and it is possible that these drugs in themselves may contribute to the memory disturbances which these people show. So we cannot tell whether the changes to memory occur as a direct result of the ECT, whether they occur as a side-effect of the chemotherapy or whether they result from some interaction of both.

Paramnesia

Memories may not be totally lost through head injury or brain damage. Instead, they may become distorted: a condition known as **paramnesia**. This type of amnesia sometimes develops as a result of the types of central nervous system diseases which result in premature ageing, such as Alzheimer's disease, or Huntington's chorea. This seems to be a very exaggerated version of how people's memories normally adapt to their expectations and assumptions, as we saw in Chapter 3.

As with personality, however, we need to remember that our awareness of effects on memory can be affected as much by social expectations as by the injury itself. People who have suffered brain damage expect to show some effects, and they, or those around them, are quite likely to attribute even the everyday lapses of memory which most people suffer to the accident. Williams (1969) showed that in normal people the ability to describe in detail events leading up to a particular event is very dependent on what happens afterwards, so taking a failure to do this accurately as a sign of brain damage is questionable. It is easy to mistake normal, everyday forgetfulness for symptoms of physiological damage.

Some studies have investigated brain activity involved in different types of memory. For example, Wood *et al.* (1980) used measures of cerebral blood-flow – the amount of blood flowing to different parts of the brain – to compare episodic and semantic memory (see Chapter 3). The episodic memory task involved participants first being read a list of words, and then being asked to lift a finger when they heard a word that had been drawn from that list. The semantic task involved the participants lifting a finger when they heard a word that represented a concrete object. The researchers found that there were very different patterns of blood flow in the left hemisphere as a result of the different activities.

Brain mechanisms of language

One of the first questions in clinical neuropsychology was whether particular psychological functions are located in particular parts of the brain. The first empirical evidence that some of the higher functions of the brain were localised – found in a specific region of the cerebrum – came from a report by Broca, in 1861. He studied a patient who had been admitted to hospital with severe speech difficulties, but who had later died. When the post-mortem was performed, Broca found that there was a damaged area at the base of the left frontal lobe, but little evidence of damage to the rest of the brain. This very specific damage was mirrored by a very specific language deficit. Although the patient had

difficulty producing speech – a condition known as **motor aphasia** – he did not have any problems in understanding what was said to him. Broca concluded that this area of the brain must have the specific language task of formulating words for speech.

The region of the cerebrum which Broca had identified became known as **Broca's area**. His work was soon followed by a report about a different type of speech problem, which seemed to result from specific damage to a different region of the brain. Wernicke (1874) described a syndrome in which patients had problems understanding what was said to them, although they had little difficulty speaking perfectly fluently themselves. Post-mortem examination of the brains of these people again showed localised damage, but this time to a specific area at the top of the temporal lobe. This area became known as **Wernicke's area**.

As research into clinical neuropsychology continued, another specifically localised area of the brain concerned with language was discovered. This area, known as the **angular gyrus**, is located in the parietal lobe not far from the visual cortex (Figure 10.11). A fourth area, not very far away from the angular gyrus, also seems to be associated with reading. This is the **supra-marginal gyrus**, located just above the lateral fissure.

Both of these areas seem to be directly concerned with the process of reading: the angular gyrus receives visual information about written language from the visual cortex, and seems to interpret it as equivalent to spoken words. People

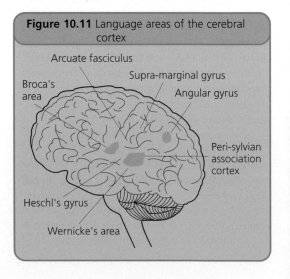

Figure 10.11 Language areas of the cerebral cortex

Arcuate fasciculus

Broca's area

Supra-marginal gyrus

Angular gyrus

Peri-sylvian association cortex

Heschl's gyrus

Wernicke's area

who have suffered brain injury sometimes experience difficulties in reading as a result, which is known as **acquired dyslexia**. This can happen in the case of damage to Broca's or Wernicke's areas, but it also sometimes happens when there is no impairment to spoken language. When that happens, it is usually associated with damage to the angular gyrus or the supra-marginal gyrus. Sometimes, too, damage to these areas produces specific problems in writing, but not with other language functions – a problem known as **agraphia**. It, too, seems to be associated with damage to the angular gyrus and the supra-marginal gyrus.

Interestingly, if these areas themselves are not actually damaged, but instead become disconnected from the visual cortex, patients can suffer from the syndrome known as **alexia**, or word-blindness. This syndrome means that although they can often still write, and can understand spoken language perfectly well, they are no longer able to make sense of what they read.

Location and function

It is worth noticing that the locations of these very specific areas of the brain seem to reflect their functions. Broca's area – the region which seems to be concerned with making speech plans and formulating words – is located near to the motor cortex, as we saw in Figure 10.11. Since the motor cortex is the part of the brain which seems to direct physical movements, this arrangement makes functional sense.

Wernicke's area – the region concerned with understanding speech – is located near to the auditory cortex, which is of course the part of the brain which would receive spoken language first. Another part of the brain, the **peri-Sylvian association cortex**, is located very close to Wernicke's area and is also concerned with language comprehension. And the angular gyrus – concerned with reading – is the language area which is located nearest to the visual cortex.

As research continued into language functions of the brain, it became apparent that several other areas are involved in the mental processing of language as well. Beaumont (1988) classified these into four main elements. The first of these elements is to do with receiving spoken language in the first place, and here a particular area of the auditory cortex known as **Heschl's gyrus** appears

to be involved. Heschl's gyrus is the region of the brain where spoken language is perceived – in other words, it is where the information is first received and interpreted.

The second element in the language processing system, according to Beaumont, is a group of structures which are all quite close together, and which are collectively described as the **posterior language centres** – in other words, the language areas situated towards the back of the brain. These include Wernicke's area and the peri-Sylvian association cortex, the angular gyrus and the supra-marginal gyrus.

Broca's area forms the third element, and is sometimes referred to as the **anterior language centre** – in other words, the language centre located towards the front of the brain. And the fourth element consists of a group of nerve fibres called the **arcuate fasciculus**, whose main function seems to be linking together the major language centres.

The operation of these language areas can be visualised by imagining what happens if you are reading through a letter which you have just received. A companion asks: 'Who's that from?' 'Oh, it's from Jane,' you reply, scanning the letter. 'She's moving house.' This example shows us how each of these areas might be involved in normal functioning. The first thing was hearing your friend's question. The information here passed from the ears to Heschl's gyrus, and then on to Wernicke's area and the peri-Sylvian association cortex, so that you could comprehend what was said.

When you were reading the letter, the visual information from the page went to the visual cortex, and then to the angular gyrus and supra-marginal gyrus for interpretation as language (as opposed to just visual patterns and shapes). Then it went on to Wernicke's area for comprehension of its meaning. From there it would go – via the arcuate fasciculus – to Broca's area where you would formulate the speech plans and words which would express what you were wanting to say; and then on to the motor cortex which would direct the muscular movements of your lips, tongue and larynx. So each of the language areas would be receiving information from, or sending information to, other areas of the cortex.

Studying language functions

The major language areas of the brain have been identified mainly from two sources: firstly, from the experiences of people who have experienced specific injuries to the brain, usually through an accident or an illness like a brain tumour; and secondly, from anatomical examination which can show how nerve fibres connect the different areas together. The advent of brain scans, however has allowed us to examine areas of the brain while they are in action, and that too has helped us to understand something about these areas.

Wallesch *et al.* (1983) showed that reading a magazine story, for instance, produced a greatly increased blood flow to the left side of the brain, by comparison with when the brain was at rest. While people were speaking, Wallesch *et al.* found, they have an increased blood flow not only to Broca's area and the motor cortex, but also to the left thalamus and the basal ganglia deep in the centre of the brain – in other words, quite a number of different brain structures seem to be involved when we are talking.

Posner *et al.* (1988) used PET scans to explore what happens in the brain when people are undertaking different cognitive activities. They began by asking their research participants to stare at a blank card, and recorded their brain activity. Then they asked them to undertake particular cognitive activities, and compared their brain activity with the record produced by the blank card.

One of their more interesting discoveries was that reading, as a cognitive activity, did not involve any of the language areas located in the temporal lobe – the part of the brain associated with hearing. It actually produces activity in the occipital lobe – which is where visual information is processed – and it produces activity in the frontal lobe too, but nothing in the temporal lobe (see Figure 10.12). That is interesting, because fluent readers often think of reading as being equivalent to 'hearing' words mentally; but the brain itself evidently processes reading and hearing words differently.

On the other hand, when people were asked to read pairs of words and think about their sounds, by judging whether they rhymed with one another or not, Posner *et al.* found that there was quite a lot of activity in the temporal lobe. So the temporal lobe is used for thinking about the sounds of words, but not for reading words directly. This is interesting, because it provides some direct physiological evidence for the conclusions reached by other researchers into

Figure 10.12 Cognitive tasks and brain activity

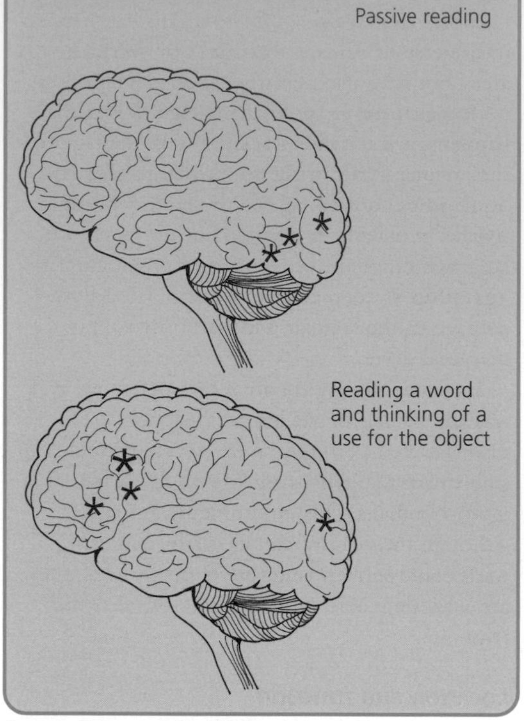

Passive reading

Reading a word and thinking of a use for the object

Source: Posner *et al.*, 1998

reading: that fluent reading does not involve converting words into their 'heard' equivalent, but is actually a much more direct experience.

Posner *et al.* (1988) used other tasks too, such as asking their research participants to read a word describing an object, and then to think about a way to use that object. This produced activity in Broca's area and in other parts of the frontal lobe, but not in the temporal lobe, and only a small amount of activity in the occipital lobe. When people were asked to listen to a word rather than read it, and then state its use, the results were very similar except for a slight activation of the temporal rather than the occipital lobe – presumably, as the sound of the word was received. But frontal lobe seemed to be much more closely involved in thinking processes than people used to believe.

Language difficulties

A different way of analysing how language is processed in the brain is to look at the different kinds of **aphasia**, or language deficit, which people experience. There have been many different ways of classifying aphasias, but one of the more useful ones is a system proposed by Kertesz, in 1979, in which five main types of aphasia are identified. These are: Broca's aphasia, Wernicke's aphasia, conduction aphasia, anomic aphasia, and transcortical aphasia.

Broca's aphasia, as we have seen, is when speech output is the main problem. People with this syndrome do not usually have any trouble understanding what is said to them, or reading. But they make errors when speaking and writing, may have difficulty naming things, and cannot talk fluently. Often, such people may use a form of telegraphic speech, in which they limit themselves just to the main words, and leave out all the adjectives and conjunctions which help what they say to make sense. Other people may get the sounds of parts of their words wrong, even though the words themselves are right. People with Broca's aphasia also tend to have problems repeating words or naming objects.

Wernicke's aphasia, as we have also seen, is to do with problems in language comprehension. These people can speak readily enough, but they have difficulty comprehending what someone is saying to them, or what they are reading. Sometimes, Wernicke's aphasia does seem to influence speech as well, usually by producing a tendency to use nonsense words, or to use words with the wrong meaning (like saying 'red' instead of 'green'). It seems that there is often a deficit in the system which allows them to monitor what they are actually saying, which produces these errors. People with this type of aphasia also have problems repeating words and naming objects.

Conduction aphasia is a problem in which the person can understand speech and read more or less normally, and can also, usually, speak normally, although sometimes with a slight impairment. But people with this type of disorder are entirely unable to repeat what has been said to them, or to read aloud accurately – even though they may understand the meaning of the material perfectly well. They can often produce an accurate paraphrasing of the information, so it is not about being unable to communicate it. Instead, it appears to be simply to do with repetition.

Anomic aphasia is when people have difficulty in finding the right words for what they want to say. It is probably the most common sort of aphasia, and for the most part people who suffer from it have no problems understanding speech or reading. Their speech, too, is more or less normal,

but they can encounter problems finding the right nouns, or in naming objects. One of the more interesting things about anomic aphasia is the way that someone can actually use the word they are looking for as a verb, while still being unable to find it as a noun, for example saying 'It's that thing you comb your hair with' but not being able to identify the object as a 'comb'. Some researchers believe that this is evidence for the specific word-stores proposed in some cognitive theories, such as in Morton's logogen theory (Morton, 1979).

Transcortical aphasias are ones in which all of the different aspects of language functioning are affected in some way. Some transcortical aphasias seem to affect speaking mostly, while some mainly affect comprehension – these are known as motor or sensory transcortical aphasias, respectively. But for the most part, transcortical aphasias produce a range of disturbances in using language. What they do not do, though, which is an interesting finding in itself, is affect repetition. People with transcortical aphasias can repeat what they are told parrot-fashion, even though they cannot paraphrase it, or have difficulty comprehending its meaning. In this respect, transcortical aphasias are almost the exact opposite of conduction aphasias.

The various forms of aphasias can be generally linked with their physical areas, as can be seen in Table 10.3 overleaf. Broca's area is associated with the anterior language areas; Wernicke's with the posterior language centres. Conduction aphasia seems to be to do with damage to the arcuate fasciculus, and anomic aphasia with damage to the angular gyrus. Motor transcortical aphasia seems to be linked with general damage across the anterior language centres, while sensory transcortical aphasia appears to link with the posterior ones.

Of course, this account makes it all seem very simple and very organised, but in reality things are almost certainly much more complex. As researchers discover more about the brain, we are bound to find that other parts of the brain are involved in language processing, and that the mechanisms are not nearly as straightforward as this model suggests. But so far, the evidence from both case studies and anatomical and brain scans does indicate that there is a remarkable congruence between the different language areas of the brain and the kinds of problems which can result if they are damaged.

Table 10.3 Types of aphasia

Aphasia	Fluency	Speech/writing	Repetition	Naming	Comprehension
Broca's	impaired	errors	limited	limited	OK
Wernicke's	OK	errors	limited	limited	impaired
Conduction	limited	OK	impaired	limited	OK
Anomic	OK	OK	OK	impaired	OK
Transcortical	impairøed	impaired	OK	impaired	impaired

Source: Beaumont, 1988

Handedness and hemisphere dominance

A considerable amount of research in clinical neuropsychology has been concerned with investigating the differences in function between the two cerebral hemispheres of the brain. Although they look similar, and although each hemisphere has roughly equivalent sensory projection areas, research has shown that there are some interesting differences between the two. We have already seen how language functions are usually located on the left hemisphere. But there are other differences, too, between the two halves of the cerebrum.

Left and right hemisphere functions

As we have seen, language is generally referred to as a left hemisphere function, since in the great majority of people (though not all) the main language areas are located on the left hemisphere. A number of studies have investigated whether there is any connection between being left or right-handed and having language functioning located on the left hemisphere. Since the left side of the brain controls the right side of the body, and vice versa, people who are strongly left or right-handed are often spoken of as having one hemisphere 'dominant' over the other.

However, although the majority of the population is right-handed, something like 25–30% of the population are formally classified as being mixed-handed, in that although they may use the right hand for complex tasks like writing, they can use either hand for a number of ordinary functions. Hardyck and Petrinovitch (1977) showed that estimates of how many of the population are left-handed can vary from 4 to 30%, depending on how strict the criteria are which are being applied.

Rasmussen and Milner (1977) performed studies which involved temporarily anaesthetising the left side of the brain by injecting sodium amytal into the major artery which supplies it. By observing whether or not their research participants lost speech functioning until the anaesthetic wore off, they were able to show that language functions (or at least speech production) are located on the left hemisphere for 95% of right-handed people.

In another study, Hardyck and Petrinovitch (1977) showed that left-handed people are slightly more likely to experience aphasia after damage to the right hemisphere than right-handers are, although this difference is only a small one. Most people, whether right or left-handed, do seem to be left-hemisphere dominant for language.

Motor and sensory functioning

Some early studies into the working brain showed that motor and sensory functioning are lateralised – in other words, that these functions are mainly located in different hemispheres of the brain. Penfield and Rasmussen (1950) showed that the motor and somatosensory areas on the right cerebral hemisphere relate to the left side of the body, while those on the left cerebral hemisphere relate to the right side of the body. They used small electrodes to stimulate different parts of the cerebral cortex in patients about to receive open-brain surgery, and found that electrical stimulation in the somatosensory area of the right hemisphere produced physical sensations on the left side, and vice versa.

Penfield and Rasmussen also showed that there was a correspondence between how sensitive a part of the body was, and the amount of somatosensory cortex which responded to it. Only a small part of the somatosensory area responded to information from relatively insensitive parts of the body, like the back or the legs. But highly sensitive parts of the body, like the lips and tongue, had larger areas of response on the somatosensory cortex. From this information, it is possible to devise a 'homunculus' – a distorted human shape – which reflects the sensitivity of different parts of the body. Looking at this figure we can see that, as a general rule, areas lower down the somatosensory strip relate to areas higher up the body, like the head, lips and tongue; whereas the part nearer to the top of the brain relates to the feet and legs.

A similar pattern is found in the motor cortex, the strip of cerebral cortex which runs parallel to the somatosensory area, on the other side of the central fissure. Stimulation of this area corresponds with movement: for example, when Penfield and Rasmussen stimulated one part of the cortex, the person moved their arm; stimulation of another part produced leg movement. The researchers found that motor functions too are lateralised: the motor cortex on the left hemisphere controls movement on the right side of the body, and vice versa. As with the somatosensory area, the more mobile a part of the body is, the greater the area of motor cortex it has devoted to it. So highly mobile parts, like the tongue or the hands, correspond to a larger area of motor cortex than the thighs or the back. Motor functions in different parts of the body can also be represented as a homunculus, which differs from the somatosensory one, but is also similar in some respects. Figure 10.13 shows both homunculi.

The lateralisation of motor and sensory functioning becomes particularly apparent in the case of 'strokes' – momentary interruptions in the blood supply to a particular region of the brain. Since a constant blood supply is essential to keep neurones alive, an interruption means that the neurones in that area of the brain die, often producing partial paralysis or similar problems. By looking at the effects of the stroke, it is possible to make a good judgement about where it happened: an interruption of the blood supply to the somatosensory area on the right hemisphere, for example, will produce a 'dead' feeling on the left side of the body. If there is interference with speaking, or with language comprehension, then it is likely that the stroke was located on the left hemisphere, since that is where the language functions are mainly located.

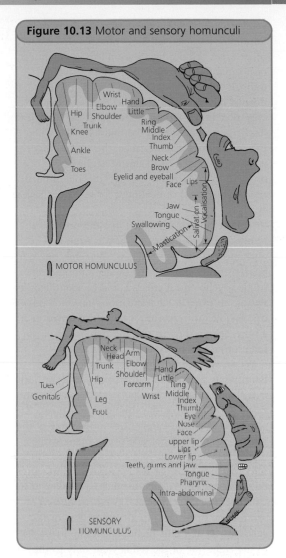

Figure 10.13 Motor and sensory homunculi

MOTOR HOMUNCULUS

SENSORY HOMUNCULUS

Spatial and analytical functions

There is also some evidence that spatial and analytical functions are, at least partially, lateralised. In 1961, Sperry published a paper describing a series of studies of patients who had experienced an operation in which the corpus callosum – the fibres joining the two halves of the cerebrum – had been severed. The results showed that the two cerebral hemispheres seemed to differ in the way that they responded to spatial and analytical information.

The patients who had experienced what came to be known as the **split-brain** operation were severe epileptics. Epilepsy is an uncontrolled electrical discharge which begins in the temporal lobe of the brain but then spreads across the cerebral cortex. Some types of epilepsy are very minor, having relatively little obvious effect, but other types can produce a complete interruption of normal functioning, which makes it very difficult for the person to live anything like a normal life. Surgeons reasoned that severing the corpus callosum would at least limit the electrical discharge to one side of the brain. In fact, when the operation was undertaken, they found that the epilepsy was reduced to almost negligible proportions. As a result, the operation became an accepted method of treatment for recurrent, severe epilepsy.

On the surface, it seemed that the operation resulted in virtually no side-effects from the separation of the two halves of the cerebrum; but Sperry's paper showed that in fact a number of subtle psychological effects could be identified. By setting up experimental situations in which only one half of the cerebrum received information at a time, Sperry showed that the two halves of the brain often responded quite differently.

As we will see in Chapter 12, each cerebral hemisphere receives visual information from both eyes. These messages are **ipsilateral**, which means that they come from the same side. In other words, information falling on the right side of the retina goes to the right side of the brain, while that falling on the left of the retina goes to the left side. This is because of the crossover of fibres at the optic chiasma, which we will be looking at in Chapter 12. The split-brain operation, however, severed the optic chiasma as well as the corpus callosum, so in a split-brain patient, the messages to the right side of the retina went only to the right cerebral hemisphere, while messages to the left side of the retina went to the left cerebral hemisphere – they could not cross over to the opposite eye.

What this means is that it is possible to feed information to one half of the cerebrum only. This formed the basis of Sperry's experiments. For example, one of the first findings from the split-brain studies was that when these research participants were presented with words to the right of the visual field (so that the images of the words fell on the left side of the retina), they could read them; but if the words were presented to the left of the visual field, they could not. Given what we know about language areas generally being located on the left side of the brain, this is not really surprising.

What was more surprising, however, was the fact that the right hemisphere, although unable to 'read', did seem to have some understanding of very simple words. For example, if the word 'key' was presented in the left visual field, the research participant would be unable to say what word it was. But sometimes, even at the same time as they were saying that they did not know what it was, their left hand would be selecting a key by touch from among a set of objects. (Remember that the left hand is controlled by the right side of the brain.) This implied that the right side of the cerebrum did seem to have a limited comprehension of simple words, even though it did not seem to have full speech functions (see Figure 10.14).

At times, the two halves of the brain seemed to be acting as if each were an entirely independent 'brain'. Sperry performed one study in which photographs of people's faces were cut down the middle, and pasted to halves from other faces. Each of the faces used was easy to describe – that of a young man might be pasted to that of an old woman, for example. The person was then shown the combined images, in such a way that one half of the image was shown to one eye (and therefore to the matching hemisphere), and the other half of the image was seen by the other eye.

When the research participant was asked what they could see, they would describe the half of the image received by the left eye. Since this had gone to the left hemisphere, they had no difficulty using language to say what they had seen. But when they were asked to use the left hand to point to an image of what they had seen, they would point to the image received by the right eye. What the mouth said, and what the left hand pointed to, were entirely different.

In another of Sperry's studies, research participants were presented with two faces simultaneously, one to each hemisphere. When

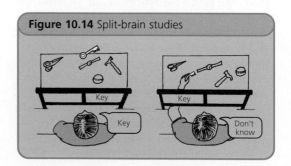

Figure 10.14 Split-brain studies

they were asked afterwards to select the face that they had seen from a set of pictures, they would choose the one which had been processed by the right hemisphere. This was one of several indications that the right hemisphere seems to be better at processing spatial and graphic material; whereas the left hemisphere seems to be better at processing words and numbers.

Problems of split-brain studies

One of the problems with using split-brain patients as research participants, though, is that they quickly become used to the fact that the two sides of the brain are separate, and the two hemispheres sometimes use tiny body movements to communicate with one another. For example, a patient who has been shown a word to the right hemisphere and asked to say what it is might give the wrong answer, then immediately give a slight shake of the head and correct it to the right answer. What has happened is that the right side of the brain (which knows the answer) has heard the wrong answer, and caused the head-shake to inform the other hemisphere. This cross-cueing can be very subtle, and almost undetectable, but it does create a problem for split-brain studies.

Another problem is that the split-brain operation is undertaken only with people who are suffering from extreme and chronic epilepsy. Severe epilepsy of this kind makes it very difficult for the person to live a normal life, because several times a week they find that consciousness, memory and motor functioning are dramatically interrupted. Since this was the early experience of most of these patients, we have no way of knowing how split-brain research participants compare with members of the 'normal' population.

Normal brain lateralisation studies

Although there are some limits to how far we can generalise from research with split-brain research participants, other types of research have also supported Sperry's findings about hemisphere functioning. For example, the arrangement of the neurones in the visual pathways of the brain means that a message flashed to the left visual field will reach the right hemisphere first, and will take longer to be passed to the left hemisphere via the optic chiasma.

Some studies have used this phenomenon to investigate differences in hemisphere functioning.

Although the time difference involved is only fractions of a second, it can make all the difference when two stimuli are presented at the same time, one to each eye, since one of them will reach the relevant hemisphere first. If these research participants are asked to report what they have seen using language, the right visual field has an advantage over the left, in the sense that its message will reach the left hemisphere first, and will therefore be more likely to be put into language. But if the research participants are asked to point, or to pick out the relevant stimulus from a set of pictures, then that difference disappears.

Rasmussen and Milner (1977) performed a number of studies of this kind. They confirmed that many of Sperry's findings seemed to be true for normal (that is, non-epileptic) research participants as well. In particular, they showed that the left hemisphere is usually more concerned with language and analytical functioning, in the sense that it is quicker to respond to this type of problem, and more accurate. The right hemisphere, on the other hand, seems to be more concerned with spatial and artistic functioning.

Ornstein (1986) argued that these differences in hemisphere functioning were so extreme as to represent almost entirely different types of consciousness. He said that the right side of the brain was the creative side, dealing not just with spatial and artistic functions but also with mystical and religious functioning. The left hemisphere, Ornstein claimed, was purely materialistic and logical. Other writers went on to link these with femininity and masculinity, the Oriental concepts of yin and yang and a number of other dualisms, arguing that many of the world's problems were caused by society overvaluing left-hemisphere functioning and undervaluing the mystical and creative aspects of the right hemisphere. There are few clinical neuropsychologists, however, who have much time for these kinds of speculations, and the evidence seems to be that the distinction between the two halves of the brain is not nearly as clear-cut as the mystics would like to think.

Creativity and bilateral hemisphere use

It seems, in fact, that many of the activities which we think of as 'creative' involve both hemispheres. For example, Bever and Chiarello (1974) showed that there was a difference between trained musicians and non-musicians in how they recognised melodies. When they were presented with an auditory task similar to the visual field ones (a task which uses the fact that a sound from one side arrives at the nearer ear fractionally faster than at the farther one), the non-musicians showed a left **auditory advantage**, implying that their response was being processed by the right hemisphere. The trained musicians, on the other hand, showed a right auditory advantage, implying that their response was being processed by the left hemisphere. Since one would normally think of trained musicians as being more creative than non-musicians, this finding implies that a one-to-one link between the right hemisphere and creativity is not really very tenable.

Some researchers have suggested that the difference comes from the complexity of the task: trained musicians are more likely to analyse the sound into its constituent parts, whereas non-musicians may be content just to experience it. Shanon (1980) found in one study that all research participants, whether they were musically trained or not, showed left hemisphere functioning for complex musical tasks, and suggested that perhaps the left hemisphere becomes involved when the person has to attend to details, rather than just receiving the whole melody as a complete unit. So, although it is clearly the case that the two hemispheres of the brain do normally address different functions, there is not necessarily an absolute distinction between them. Which hemisphere does what seems to be more variable than some researchers initially believed.

Neural plasticity

Children who suffer language problems resulting from brain damage to the left hemisphere often transfer their language functioning to the right hemisphere. This flexibility is known as **neural plasticity**. After puberty, though, the transfer of language from one side of the brain does not seem to happen. It is generally assumed that by this time the brain is pretty well fixed in its abilities and functions.

This general assumption, however, has been questioned. Four cases studied by Gooch (1980) involved patients who had been given a complete left **hemispherectomy** – in other words, the whole of the left hemisphere had been removed – rather than having split-brain operations. In these patients, Gooch reported, language functioning had gradually returned as they recovered from the operation. Although the left hemisphere was

entirely gone, the patients gradually acquired speech again, remembered songs and poems which they had known earlier and eventually achieved more or less complete language functioning, mediated by the right side of the brain. Gooch (1980) argued that the dissociation between the two hemispheres observed in split-brain patients might actually be a product of the operation itself, resulting in the functions of the hemispheres seeming to be more different than they really are.

This surprising finding suggests that perhaps there is more neural plasticity in the brain than has been thought. It also says something about the way that memory for linguistic information must be stored in the brain. Even though the left side of the brain may contain language functions, it obviously cannot contain language memories, because if it did they would have been removed too. Gooch suggested that language memories might be stored as diffuse, holographic mental images across the whole of the brain. In a hologram, the whole image can be re-created from just a part of the picture, and something similar might apply to language memories. The reason why normally brain-damaged patients do not recover language functions, Gooch suggested, might be because the damaged part of the brain is left in place. It might be that its presence somehow inhibits the right hemisphere from adopting left hemisphere functions.

Although these ideas are only speculative, it is noticeable that the brain can show remarkable properties of recovery. People who have experienced severe head injuries may be left without speech and with very little motor functioning, but with sustained effort they can often recover both language and movement to the extent that they are able to live normal lives again. The same has been observed with recovery from strokes. It is not known exactly how this recovery happens – one theory is that the effort forces the brain to use 'dormant' neural pathways to take over these functions. Another possibility is that the neurones themselves may recover their function: some very recent evidence suggests that nerve cells can repair themselves after having been damaged. At the moment, though, it is unclear which mechanisms are involved.

What does seem to be most important in all these cases, though, is **motivation**. In order to recover brain functioning, it seems that the person needs to keep up a sustained effort, sometimes for a very long period of time. If they are not highly motivated, they are unlikely to keep up the effort, and so they may find that the damage remains with them. But clinical evidence suggests that those who are determined that this is what they intend to do can recover from brain injury to quite a surprising extent.

Brain mechanisms of movement

We take movement very much for granted. In reality, though, being able to move about or move parts of the body is a complex ability which involves many different parts of the nervous system. It is possible, even, to argue that movement provided the basis for the evolution of the nervous system in the first place – a creature which is sessile, or immobile, does not need all that much communication between different parts of its body, and does not need to respond to outside stimuli in anything like the same kind of way as one which is mobile.

Movement in animals, including ourselves, takes place through the contraction of muscle fibres, pulling on the skeleton and producing movement as a result of its hinges. In vertebrates – animals with a backbone – there are three main types of muscle fibre. The one which we commonly think of when we think of muscle is known as skeletal muscle. This is the type of muscle which contracts when we move an arm or a leg. It consists of long, cylindrical fibres, bunched together into groups. Smooth muscles, which are the ones found in the internal organs, consist of long thin cells, which contract less than skeletal muscle cells do. Cardiac muscle, the third type, is similar to skeletal muscle except that the fibres are fused together at various points, so that when one fibre contracts all the rest do as well. This is what allows the heart to beat in time.

The message for the muscle to contract comes from a particular type of nerve cell known as a **motor neurone**. As we will see in Chapter 12, motor neurones begin in the spinal cord, where they receive electrical messages from the motor control systems in the brain. They pass these messages on down long, elongated axons to their other end, where the axons spread out to form what is known as the motor end plate. This releases a chemical, acetylcholine, which is picked up at special receptor sites on the muscle fibres, and stimulates the muscle to contract.

Reflex and voluntary movement

One of the main distinctions is between voluntary and involuntary, or reflex, movement. **Reflexes** are immediate bodily responses to specific stimuli, and are not really mediated by the brain at all. In a reflex action such as pulling your hand away from a hot surface, what happens is that the message is picked up by sensory neurones, and passed up to the connector neurones in the spinal cord. From there, it passes to motor neurones which send a message to the arm muscles, causing them to contract and pull the hand away. The whole action is known as the reflex arc. It is entirely mediated by the spinal cord, and the brain is not involved at all.

Effectively, then, in reflex movement the spinal cord responds automatically to an incoming message, and routes a response to the appropriate muscles. But in **voluntary movement** – movement that we make deliberately – the brain sends a message to the muscles to move, and the muscles do so. The system for the control of movement in the central nervous system involves two different, but co-ordinated systems. The first of these systems is known as the pyramidal motor system, and the second the extrapyramidal motor system.

The pyramidal motor system

The **pyramidal motor system** begins in the cerebral cortex, with a group of brain cells known as pyramidal cells, which run throughout the motor strip, alongside the central fissure. Fibres from these cells pass the neural impulses down to the midbrain, where they form connections with neurones which pass the impulses on down the spinal cord. In the spinal cord, they synapse with motor neurones, which transmit the message out of the central nervous system and out to receptor sites in the muscles (Figure 10.15).

It is not quite as straightforward as that, of course. For one thing, the message which reaches the midbrain has a certain amount of input from the sensory cortex as well, and also from some of the nerve cells in the secondary premotor area of the cortex. But, for the most part, the pyramidal motor system involves a message which is generated in the cerebrum, and passed through the midbrain and spinal cord out to the muscles of the body. If it becomes damaged, the person is usually still able to move, but their movements are weak and imprecise.

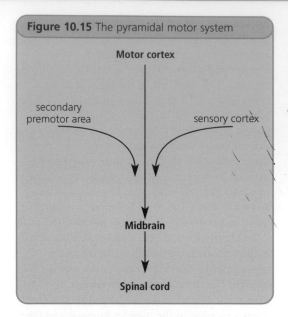

Figure 10.15 The pyramidal motor system

Motor cortex

secondary
premotor area

sensory cortex

Midbrain

Spinal cord

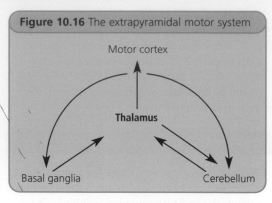

Figure 10.16 The extrapyramidal motor system

Motor cortex

Thalamus

Basal ganglia

Cerebellum

The extrapyramidal motor system

The **extrapyramidal motor system**, on the other hand, appears to be much more complicated (Figure 10.16). It involves four main structures: the motor cortex in the cerebrum, the thalamus, the cerebellum, and the basal ganglia, which are a group of cells buried deep in the centre of the brain. There are other areas of the brain involved as well, of course – few systems in physiological psychology are really that simple – but these seem to be the main ones.

The motor cortex passes information to the basal ganglia and the cerebellum. These two structures pass information to the thalamus, and the thalamus in turn passes messages back to the cerebellum, and also to the motor cortex. It seems likely that this arrangement represents the co-ordination and feedback systems which are needed to ensure smooth voluntary actions.

Skilled movement

It is one thing knowing how a particular act is generated by the central nervous system, but much of what we do actually consists of a large number of different acts, integrated into one smooth sequence. The process of integrating the different acts involved in smooth handwriting, for example, or stirring a sauce, is all to do with establishing nervous system units known as **motor programmes**.

A motor programme is a complete sequence of actions which results in the carrying out of a purposeful act. Some motor programmes are not learned, but innate – for example, walking involves a motor programme which requires co-ordination of muscular activity in the limbs, feet and torso. Other motor programmes are acquired through systematic practice. Learning highly complex physical skills, such as those involved in musical performance or exhibition skating, involves the development and combination of large numbers of different motor programmes, into new complete units.

The role of the cerebellum

One of the most important parts of the brain in the acquisition of learned motor programmes is the cerebellum. The cerebellum is active in the co-ordination of skilled movement; but it is also active in the planning and organisation of movement as well. Cells in the cerebellum become active before we actually begin to make the movement. People who experience damage to the cerebellum often have to plan each movement that they make consciously, even when they are doing things which the rest of us do automatically.

Animals which engage in a great deal of highly co-ordinated movement, such as birds, have a cerebellum which is proportionately larger than the cerebrum. The cerebellum comes from the term 'little brain', and it contains a vast number of neurones and connections. Some neuropsychologists argue that its capacity for information processing is as much as the cerebral cortex. The cells which seem to be most closely involved with the duration of movement are the **Purkinje cells**: a set of cells which control the output from the cerebellum to the rest of the nervous system. They act to inhibit target cells within the cerebellum, and by doing so, make sure that a given movement is smooth and controlled, not unsteady or jerky.

Movement and brain damage

We can learn something about movement using evidence from clinical neuropsychology. It has been known since WWI that the cerebellum was an important element in the co-ordination of voluntary movement. Holmes (1919) found that people with shrapnel damage in this region of the brain had problems co-ordinating their actions, and would make a series of jerky, disconnected acts rather than a smooth continuous movement.

Wilder Penfield's investigations of patients undergoing brain surgery showed that stimulation of the area of the cerebrum immediately in front of the central fissure produced movement, and that stimulation of different areas involved the movement of different parts of the body. By mapping out just where these different areas were on the **motor cortex**, Penfield was able to show that the area seemed to contain a kind of upside-down representation of the body (Penfield, 1959).

Stimulation of the part closest to the other hemisphere, just above the corpus callusom, produced movements of the feet. Just above that produced movements of the ankle, and above that were areas which responded to the calf and knee. The trunk and neck followed, and then a large part of the motor strip was dedicated to movements of different parts of the hand. Below this, coming down the outside of the brain, was a large area which encompassed movements of the various facial muscles, and at the base of this region were the areas which produced movements of the lips and tongue.

Penfield, and others, showed that the amount of cortex devoted to each different part of the body corresponded closely to that part's mobility: there was relatively little cortex devoted to the trunk, for instance, because that part of the body is not all that mobile. But there was a large area of cortex devoted to each finger, and to the tongue, because these are extremely mobile parts of the body.

The role of the **basal ganglia** appears to be to do with the organisation of movement. People who suffer from Parkinson's disease, which seems to produce damage to the basal ganglia, suffer from what is known as a resting tremor – a steady muscle tremor which occurs all of the time, unless they are engaging in deliberate action. If they are actually concentrating on a particular act, they can usually carry it out fairly smoothly; but if they are not attending, they experience constant muscular tremors and shakes.

The problem, of course, is that we cannot tell from this exactly what the basal ganglia do – whether the resting tremor is a basic property of muscle action, and the basal ganglia suppress it, for example, or whether their absence actually produces the tremor somehow. Identifying that a part of the brain is a component in a system is a very different thing from knowing what that part of the brain actually does – and the different parts of the brain are so interconnected that all we can really do is to try to make sense out of the general systems which are involved in behaviour or experience.

Spinal cord problems and movement

Damage to the **spinal cord** also produces impaired movements. One of the later stages of syphilis involves impaired sensation in the legs and pelvic regions, and also loss of bladder and bowel control. This arises because the dorsal roots of the spinal cord have gradually deteriorated through the action of the spirochetes. By contrast, poliomyelitis produces complete paralysis of various parts of the body, because the virus damages the motor neurones themselves.

Damage to different parts of the spinal cord and to the motor neurones can produce different forms of movement disorder. **Paralysis** consists of a lack of voluntary movement in part of the body. It generally results from damage to, or interference with, motor neurones in the spinal cord or peripheral muscles. **Flaccid paralysis** involves a lack of voluntary movement in part of the body, low muscle tone, and weak reflexes. It is usually produced by damage to the motor neurones in the spinal cord, although it can sometimes be an initial result from damage to those neurones which pass messages from the brain to the spinal cord. A third type of paralysis, **spastic paralysis**, involves problems with voluntary movement, but the person has strong jerky reflexes, and often muscle tremor. It tends to be the long-term consequence of damage to the neurones which pass from the brain to the spinal cord, with flaccid paralysis being the short-term result.

Severing the spinal cord produces different outcomes depending on where the break takes place. **Paraplegia** involves loss of feeling

Box 10.1 Modularity, localisation of function, and neural plasticity

Research into brain functions raises all kinds of questions about the relationships between the physiology of the brain and our personal experiences. One of the questions which has attracted a lot of attention is that of modularity: Fodor (1983) proposed that the human mind is structured in such a way that we have discrete, relatively independent information-processing modules, each of which deals with a different type of task. The research into face-recognition which we looked at in Chapter 2, for example, seems to imply that we have a special capacity for processing information about people's faces, which appears to be quite independent of our other perceptual processes.

There is also some clinical evidence for modularity, in that people have been found who have deficits in one specific mental area, such as face-recognition, or naming, but who are apparently normal in all other respects. Campbell (1973) compiled reports of several cases of patients with very specific problems, but whose mental functioning was unimpeded in all other respects. These, too, seemed to suggest that the brain might use a modular approach to processing information.

There are, however, still major gaps between our understanding of neural activity, and the proposed modularity of mind. Although researchers have been able to trace neural pathways which seem to be involved in particular skills – such as the various areas of the brain which are stimulated by exposure to language – there certainly is not a simple, one-to-one relationship which states, for example, that this area of the brain does face-recognition, while this one does naming. And more recently, researchers have been discovering that there seems to be more interaction between apparently independent modules than researchers had previously thought.

The question of localised functions in the brain is as old as the study of the brain itself. At first, researchers believed that each different mental 'faculty', such as memory, understanding, compassion, or impatience, would have a separate area of the brain. Then, as we have seen, researchers discovered that there only appeared to be a few specific brain

areas, and that the rest of the cerebral cortex, at least, appeared to operate as a whole.

Modern research, though, suggest that there may be many more specific areas for brain activity than used to be thought. Scanning techniques allow researchers to look at the areas of the brain which are stimulated when people engage in different types of mental tasks, and it appears that different types of thinking do involve different areas of the cerebral cortex after all. Decision-making tasks stimulate certain areas of what used to be known as the 'association cortex', while quiet reflection involves a different area, and reading another still.

The fact that there are areas of the cerebral cortex which are specifically concerned with reading may give us a clue to what is going on. Reading is too recent a human activity to have evolved as a specific skill – it is only in the last century that mass literacy has become at all commonplace. But the functioning of the angular gyrus and other such areas suggests that specific areas of the cerebral cortex may have the potential to develop specific functioning, if the individual received the kind of training which will encourage those skills to develop. That, of course, begs the question of what other potentials the human brain may have; and it will be interesting to see what emerges when researchers are able to engage in systematic studies of people with exceptional ability.

It appears, from the evidence available, that both the body and the brain can respond to the demands of experience – if those demands are serious enough. People with brain damage can re-train neurones to take over functions which have been lost – but only through sustained, intense effort, in the same way that injured sportspeople regain functioning through sustained, intense practice. The evidence suggests that it is the interaction between the person's mental experience and their neural potential which produces the active brain, in the same way that the interaction between a person's physical experience and their genetic potential leads to the development of healthy muscles. But we have much yet to learn about mental training, and how it may affect brain functioning.

(sensation) and voluntary muscle control in both legs, although reflexes – including sexual ones – remain. It results from a cut through the spinal cord above the segments with links to the legs. **Quadriplegia** involves loss of sensation and muscle control in all four limbs, and results from a cut through the spinal cord above the level with links to the arms. And **hemiplegia** involves the loss of sensation and muscle control to one side of the body, and can result from two sources. Most commonly, it results from damage to one of the cerebral hemispheres. Sometimes, though, hemiplegia can be produced by a cut halfway up the spinal cord.

The cerebellum, as we have seen, co-ordinates physical action, and this includes actions in different parts of the body. Some forms of damage to the cerebellum result in the person finding that they can move one part of the body but cannot make corresponding movements with other parts. For example, someone might make the correct arm movements for throwing a ball, but without adjusting the rest of their body for the throw. Since eye movements are also muscular actions, the cerebellum is also necessary for hand-eye co-ordination, and some kinds of damage may mean that people are unable to undertake this type of activity successfully.

Overall, the symptoms of severe cerebellar damage often resemble those of being drunk: a person's movements are unco-ordinated, their speech is slurred, and eye movements are inaccurate. One way of testing for cerebellar damage is to use the 'finger-to-nose' test. A normal person has no problem holding their arm straight out, and then touching their nose when asked. But someone with damage to the cerebellar cortex (the outer layers of the cerebrum) finds it difficult to move their finger to the correct place, either not bringing it far enough, or hitting themselves in the face.

We have seen, then, that the human brain is an immensely complex structure, and that studying its functioning is also fairly tricky. Nonetheless, by gathering evidence from brain injuries, and by developing research techniques which allow them to study an active brain, researchers have been able to identify a considerable amount about how the brain functions. The use of scanning techniques has been particularly valuable in that respect, since these are methods which allow researchers to investigate the brain's activity while it is actually taking place. This has already dramatically extended our knowledge of how the brain works, and that is likely to continue in the future. In the next chapter, we will look at the question of consciousness, and at some of the ways that psychologists have investigated different states of consciousness.

Key terms

ablation The removal or destruction of part or parts of the brain by means of surgical techniques, usually involving cutting or burning away the tissue concerned.

alexia Word-blindness, or the inability to identify written words as words, even though the person has no problem with spoken language.

allele The name given to one of a pair of matching genes, with one of each pair found on each of a matched pair of chromosomes.

amnesia The loss of memory, usually through physical causes.

angular gyrus That part of the cortex which decodes visual stimuli for reading.

anterograde amnesia The loss of memory for events taking place after the damage producing the amnesia.

aphasia A specific disorder to do with being unable to form words in producing speech.

association cortex The general name given to those parts of the cerebral cortex which do not seem to have a specific, localised function.

auditory cortex That part of the cerebral cortex involved in hearing.

autonomic nervous system (ANS) A network of unmyelinated nerve fibres running from the brain stem and spinal cord, which can activate the body for action, or set it into a quiescent state.

Broca's area A specific area in the left frontal lobe, in which damage produces aphasia.

central nervous system The brain and spinal cord.

cerebral cortex The outer covering of the cerebral hemispheres, consisting of six layers of nerve cells, in which information is processed.

cerebral hemispheres The name given to the two halves of the cerebrum.

cerebrum The part of the brain responsible for cognition, the co-ordinating of information and the initiation of voluntary action.

clinical neuropsychology The branch of psychology concerned with investigating how the brain works by studying the effects of brain damage, disease or injury.

cloning The process of creating genetically identical animals artificially, by causing the cells of parent animals to reproduce and develop into whole animals based on genetic information in the cell nucleus.

Computed Axial Tomography A method of detecting brain abnormality by examining a series of X-ray 'photos' taken successively through the brain.

connector neurone A nerve cell found in the central nervous system which links together other nerve cells.

cross-cueing Using one sensory mode to provide information which makes sense of stimuli being received through another mode. In split-brain patients, cross-cueing refers to clues given by one cerebral hemisphere to the other using slight movements of the body.

electrical stimulation of the brain (ESB) Direct positive reinforcement delivered to the brain by means of electrodes implanted in the hypothalamus.

electro-encephalogram (EEG) A record of the brain's electrical activity obtained by attaching electrodes to the scalp.

evoked potential A characteristic pattern of electrical activity in the brain which shows up on EEGs (electro-encephalograms), and is produced in response to a particular stimulus.

frontal lobotomy The removal of the front part of the cerebrum, once thought to reduce aggression and now known to damage planning and decision-making abilities.

genetic engineering The process of altering genetic characteristics through microscopic intervention.

hemispherectomy The surgical removal of a complete cerebral hemisphere.

homeostasis A state of physiological balance or equilibrium in the body.

ipsilateral Occurring on the same side.

Law of Equipotentiality The principle that all of the association cortex (those parts of the cerebral cortex without specifically localised function) are equally important in learning and memory.

Law of Mass Action The principle that it is the amount of cerebral cortex available which determines effective learning and memory, not the location of that cortex.

lesion Some form of damage to an area of the brain or body. Lesions may be accidental or surgically induced.

localisation of function The way that some psychological functions such as language seem to be mediated by very specific areas of the cerebral cortex.

Magnetic Resonancy Imaging Scanning the working brain by passing a series of electro-magnetic waves through it, causing neural activity which is then recorded.

medulla The part of the brain just above the spinal cord, concerned with autonomic bodily functions.

micro-electrode recording The method of studying the brain by inserting microscopic electrodes to particular sites, and recording the activity of individual nerve cells.

motivation That which drives, or energises, a human being or animal's actions – that which makes it be active rather than quiescent.

motor aphasia A speech disorder which comes about because the person is unable to move their lips and tongue in the necessary way.

motor cortex The area of the cerebrum which mediates physical movement of the different parts of the body.

motor neurone A nerve cell which carries instructions from the brain or spinal cord to the muscle fibres, so producing movement.

mutation A spontaneous change, usually used to refer to genetic changes which produce new heritable traits.

neural plasticity The ability of nerve cells and brain tissue to re-grow or to acquire alternative functions in response to damage.

non-invasive techniques Methods of studying the brain or body from the outside, such as the use of brain or body scans.

paramnesia A clinical condition in which memories become distorted, rather than lost altogether.

peripheral nervous system The part of the nervous system which links the rest of the body with the brain and the spinal cord.

polygraph A machine often used to measure stress or anxiety – sometimes known as a 'liedetector' –

which works by measuring many ('poly') different physical indicators that the person is under stress, such as blood pressure, pulse rate, heart rate, and GSR.

positron emission tomography Scanning the brain by monitoring the uptake of blood by active neurones. Blood distribution is identified by the radioactive labelling of glucose molecules in the bloodstream.

proactive amnesia A memory disorder in which the person becomes unable to store new information.

reflex A response which occurs automatically, and is not mediated by the brain.

sensory projection areas Areas on the cerebral cortex which receive information from particular senses.

somatosensory cortex The area of the cerebral cortex which receives information from sense receptors in the skin.

sub-cortical structures All of the structures of the brain, with the exception of the cerebrum.

thalamus The sub-cortical structure in the brain which receives sensory information and relays it to the cerebral cortex.

Wernicke's area An area of the cerebral cortex which, when damaged, produces problems in comprehending verbal information.

Summary

1 The human nervous system consists of the central nervous system, which includes the brain and spinal cord; the peripheral nervous system, which includes the nerves and senses; and the autonomic nervous system, which includes glands and hormones. Between them, they co-ordinate the activities and states of the body.

2 Methods of studying the brain include: physical interventions, such as lesion and ablation; chemical interventions; electrical interventions such as micro-electrode recording, EEGs and evoked potential recordings; and scanning techniques.

3 The brain evolved from a primitive neural tube, and traces of its evolutionary development can still be detected in the organisation and function of the various brain structures.

4 Genetic transmission occurs as a result of DNA codes which are passed from one generation to the next through sexual reproduction and meiosis. Growth occurs mainly through binary fission of cells, and mitosis. The human genome project aims to map out the whole set of human genetic codes.

5 Clinical neuropsychology is the study of how the brain functions. One of its concerns is how functions are localised in the cerebrum. Some characteristics, such as personality, learning and memory, do not seem to be specifically localised.

6 Studies of language functioning show that there are several distinct language-processing areas in the brain, which are generally located on the left hemisphere. Problems with these areas can lead to aphasia, alexia, and other disorders.

7 Motor and sensory functions are located on the opposite cerebral hemisphere from the relevant side of the body. Split-brain studies indicate that spatial and analytical functions tend to be located in different hemispheres, with some crossover between the two.

8 Brain mechanisms of movement involve complex interactions of brain structures and movements involve different neural pathways.

Self-assessment questions

1 How does genetic transmission occur from parent to offspring?

2 How has the evolution of the human brain influenced the organisation of its main structures?

3 What are the main areas for language processing in the brain, and what do they do?

Practice essay questions

1 Giving examples, critically evaluate the main methods of studying brain functioning.

2 To what extent are the functions of the cerebrum localised?

3 How valid is the idea that the two halves of the cerebrum operate as two distinct brains?

Test your knowledge of this chapter with our online quizzes and games at: http://www.psych.co.uk

Explore brain development and clinical neuropsychology further at:

General
http://www.neuroguide.com/ – A comprehensive guide to neurosciences on the internet, links to journals, images and resources and a handy search engine.

Images
http://anatomy.uams.edu/HTMLpages/anatomyhtml/neuro_atlas.html – For the strong of stomach, a complete pictorial atlas of the brain.

Nervous system
http://www.cc.emory.edu/ANATOMY/AnatomyManual/nervous_system.html – Detailed and well illustrated tutuorial on the nervous system.

Brain issues
http://williamcalvin.com/bk2/bk2.htm#TOC – On-line book *The Throwing Madonna* covers pertinent topics on the brain in 17 essays, including some on laterality.
http://serendip.brynmawr.edu/ – Very good links page for articles and information on the brain and behaviour.

Consciousness

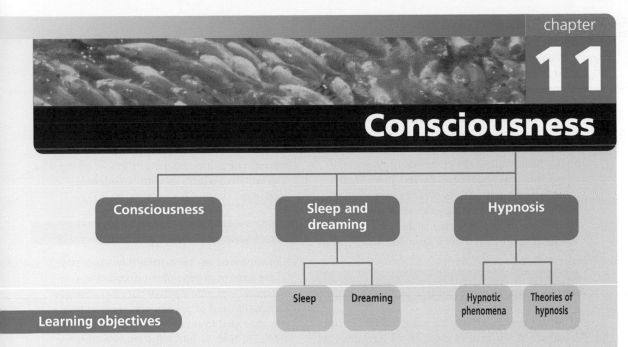

| Consciousness | Sleep and dreaming | Hypnosis |

| Sleep | Dreaming | Hypnotic phenomena | Theories of hypnosis |

Learning objectives

11.1. Studying consciousness
a define terms relating to the study of consciousness
b describe methods of studying consciousness
c evaluate methods of studying consciousness

11.2. Drugs and neurotransmitters
a describe the functions of the synapse
b outline the types of psychoactive drugs
c show how drugs may affect consciousness

11.3. Biological rhythms
a identify features of human circadian rhythms
b apply knowledge of human circadian rhythms to shift work
c link human circadian rhythms with everyday life

11.4. Types of sleep
a define terms relating to different types of sleep
b describe features of sleep cycles
c distinguish between explanations for sleep cycles

11.5. Physiology of sleep
a identify major physiological structures involved in sleep
b describe a study of sleep processes
c outline the major effects of sleep deprivation or restriction

11.6. Theories of dreaming
a describe a study of dreaming
b outline major theories of dreaming
c evaluate theories of dreaming

11.7. Theories of hypnotism
a describe Hilgard's model of hypnosis
b evaluate evidence for hypnosis as a special state
c identify social mechanisms contributing to hypnotic experience

11.8. Hypnotic phenomena
a identify types of hypnotic phenomena
b describe a study of hypnotic phenomena
c evaluate evidence for different types of hypnotic phenomena

One of the distinctive features of human beings, so it is claimed, is that we are aware of our own consciousness. But trying to identify and classify consciousness is not easy. In this chapter, we will be looking at some of the research into different forms of consciousness, and at the way that psychoactive drugs can affect the brain. We will also be looking at the controversial question of hypnosis – at what it can do, and at whether it really is a special state of consciousness, or not. And we will be looking at some of our ordinary variations in consciousness, including psychological research into sleep, dreaming and hypnosis.

Consciousness

We are continually experiencing changes in consciousness. We have all experienced how different moods can affect how we see the world; we have all experienced the changes in consciousness brought about when we are sleeping; and most of us have experienced the changes in consciousness brought about by at least some drugs – if only the use of caffeine to help us wake up in the morning. In many ways, consciousness is one of the most mystical of all human attributes – or at least, there has been a great deal of mystical writing about it.

In the early days of psychology, consciousness was regarded as the core of the discipline. The introspectionist psychologists regarded the study of the mind as the key to understanding everything about people, and they believed that the careful analysis of conscious experience would allow them to discover the workings of the mind.

As we saw in Chapter 1, this idea was challenged by a number of theoretical developments, and in particular the two opposing ideas of **psychoanalysis** and **behaviourism**. The Freudian idea that much of the mind's operation is unconscious, taking place without the individual being aware of it, questioned the idea that the contents of consciousness can be reached by introspection; and the behaviourist insistence that human behaviour could be seen as the result of stimulus–response conditioning questioned the importance of the concept of consciousness in an even more fundamental way.

In more recent times, psychologists have grown away from the behaviourist's total rejection of the idea of consciousness, and there have been a number of attempts to investigate it. As you might imagine, though, it is an elusive concept. Consciousness appears to serve an important function in allowing us to choose our actions. By weighing up a situation we can select what we would like to do. Consciousness also helps us to change or modify our behaviour, if we find that we are acting inappropriately. But identifying what it actually is, presents us with considerable challenges.

Studying consciousness

Consciousness has been studied in many ways. There have been physiological studies of consciousness and neural activity; studies of sensory deprivation and of people who seem to be able to react to visual stimuli even though they are blind; studies of how various consciousness-affecting drugs have their effect; and even studies of hypnosis, which may (or may not) be a special form of consciousness. We will look at these various ways of studying consciousness in some detail, before returning to the tricky question of theories of consciousness.

Consciousness and neural activity

Observations of people using **electro-encephalogram** recordings (**EEGs**) have shown that different kinds of subjective awareness are reflected to some degree in EEGs. People who are in a highly alert state show EEG patterns with a great deal of irregularity, whereas those who are daydreaming or in a conscious but relaxed state show regular patterns of EEG activity known as **alpha rhythms**. EEG traces obtained when research participants are concentrating extremely hard also show a distinctive form, which is referred to as a pattern of **theta rhythms** (Figure 11.1). And, as we will see later in this chapter, people in different levels of sleep also show different EEG patterns. So there is some indication that EEGs may be useful for identifying general states of alertness, at least; although they are unlikely to provide us with much more than an approximation.

Another technique for investigating consciousness arose from the brain studies of Penfield and Rasmussen (1950), who showed that stimulating different areas of the brain could produce distinctive forms of behaviour or experience in a conscious patient. Penfield proposed that the control

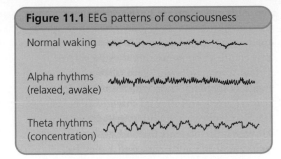

Figure 11.1 EEG patterns of consciousness

Normal waking

Alpha rhythms
(relaxed, awake)

Theta rhythms
(concentration)

of consciousness was mainly located in the
thalamus and the upper part of the brain stem.
This was on the grounds that animals with the
cerebral cortex removed still showed consciousness, whereas those with the brain stem removed
did not. But, as we have seen elsewhere, it is not
really possible to determine exactly what removal
of a particular part of the brain means for a
certain function; the area might simply be part of
a more complex process, rather than being the site
in the brain where that particular function is
localised.

In support of the idea that consciousness is
more concerned with the overall functioning of
the brain, Gazzaniga and Sperry (1967) conducted
a number **of split-brain studies**, which showed
that the two halves of the brain appear to be able
to act more or less independently, and that each
seems to have a distinct form of consciousness (see
Chapter 10). Anecdotal accounts from split-brain
patients give a number of examples of one part of
the brain making decisions independently of the
other. For example, one woman who had experienced this operation found that she would sometimes go to her wardrobe with a conscious, verbal
thought about what she would wear (which was
presumably from the left hemisphere), only to find
that her left hand (controlled by the right hemisphere) would choose something entirely different. This type of dissociation does not seem to be
uncommon in split-brain patients, although it is
hard to study systematically. It does not really help
us to analyse what or where consciousness is, but
it does tell us that consciousness is unlikely to be
simply a function of the brain stem.

Sensation and consciousness

In the late 1960s and 1970s, a number of experiments were conducted on **sensory deprivation**.
In these experiments, research participants floated
in tanks which were specially designed to reduce,
and where possible cut out, sensory information.
So, for example, participants wore ear-pads to
prevent them hearing sounds; they floated in fluid
and wore padding to remove tactile sensations;
they were blindfolded and closed off from smell or
taste sensations. People who went through this,
reported experiencing several different levels of
consciousness, and a deeper sense of self-awareness
(Lilly, 1977).

Other research participants taking part in
sensory-deprivation studies reported hallucinations
and other sensory or emotional experiences, and
there was considerable controversy about the
reasons why these happened. One hypothesis was
that these experiences took place because the
brain was unable to maintain consciousness without having continuous sensory input, so it created
that sensory input synthetically when it had to.
Other psychologists argued that not all research
participants had hallucinatory experiences, and
that those who did, had them because of their
pre-existing inner anxieties, or because they
expected to have them.

Research into sensory deprivation for its own
sake became less popular over time, but the idea
that restricting sensory input could allow the brain
to access deeper levels of consciousness was taken
up by researchers into parapsychology. Some
modern parapsychological researchers use what is
known as the **ganzfeld technique** to produce
conditions of near-sensory deprivation. There has
been a suggestion that reducing irrelevant stimuli
in this way allows the research participant to focus
more clearly on any extra-sensory information or
impressions. We will be looking at this research in
more detail in the next chapter.

Blindsight and amnesia

A different approach to the understanding of consciousness has emerged from research into the
phenomenon known as blindsight. **Blindsight**
occurs when the visual cortex, which is also called
the striate cortex, is damaged. As Holmes showed
in his studies of shrapnel injuries in soldiers,
damage to this area produces blindness, and the
amount of blindness corresponds to the amount of
damage the area has received. The location of the
blindness – whether it is in the left or right visual
field, or towards the top or the bottom – also
depends on where the damage is.

The striate cortex, though, is not the only part
of the brain which receives visual information.

The retina has five or six other pathways for the visual information that it projects, and these go to other structures in the brain. So visual information about the blind area is still being received; but not in the striate cortex. Early studies with monkeys showed that they were still able to respond to visual information even if the striate cortex had been completely removed. They could detect visual events, and even carry out simple pattern discrimination, although not as well as a fully sighted individual.

This led to investigations of human beings with damage to the striate cortex. Pöppel, Held and Frost (1973) found that these people were often able to respond to visual stimuli in their blind area. But they could not do so consciously. Instead, the researchers needed to make their investigations into a game, asking the participants to 'guess' what they might be able to see if they could. They quickly found that people, too, were able to detect visual events, discriminate between patterns, say whether a grid pattern was vertical or horizontal, and track moving objects by pointing. Other researchers took up the same approach, with similar results.

Even though they can do these things, people with striate cortex damage are completely unaware of what they are responding to. The phenomenon was called blindsight, because such people are blind in the sense that they are completely unaware of seeing anything, but they can still detect and respond to stimuli in that area. Weiskrantz (1980) looked at a number of cases of people with blindsight, and found quite a lot of variation in what they were able to do; but this variation appeared to correlate quite closely with the damage to the area surrounding the striate cortex (brain injuries are not often precisely located).

Blindsight is not the only case where people can reveal abilities which they do not think they possess. Paillard, Michel and Stelmach (1983) investigated a 'blind-touch' case where the person had a lesion in the sensory-motor cortex, which made her unaware when the corresponding area of her skin was touched. But if she was asked to 'guess' whether there was skin contact, her responses were far more accurate than they would have been if there had really been a lack of sensation.

People who have become **amnesiac** as a result of cortical lesions show a similar set of characteris-

tics. Although they are unable to remember new information consciously, they often show good memory retention as long as the task does not involve them knowing that they have remembered! Warrington and Weiskrantz summarised the range of memory tasks which amnesiac patients had achieved, and showed that it was an impressive list. Some of them are listed in Table 11.1. However, the patients themselves were entirely unaware of the information that they had remembered.

The thing that characterised all of these memory tasks, and others which produced similar findings, was that they could be conducted without asking the person directly whether they remembered the information. Asking them to report what they remembered showed that there was no conscious memory of the experience; but asking them to perform specific tasks showed that some memory certainly existed, but it was entirely unconscious.

Theories of consciousness

As we have seen, there are many ways that consciousness can be influenced. These range from the purely physiological effects of drugs, to the complex issues involved in sleep and dreaming, and the even more complex ones of hypnosis. Explaining what consciousness actually is, however, is another matter.

Table 11.1 Some memory tasks achieved successfully by amnesiac patients

motor skill learning (e.g. pursuit rotas)

visual discrimination learning

cued recall of words and pictures

rule-governed verbal paired-associate learning

stereoscopic perception of random-dot stereograms

solving jigsaw puzzles

arranging specific words into specific sentences

classical eyelid conditioning

mathematical problem-solving

mirror reading

Source: Warrington and Weiskrantz, 1982

Elements of consciousness

The introspectionist Wilhelm Wundt (1862) attempted to analyse consciousness by training research participants to describe their own mental sensations, feelings and images. Wundt argued that there were two different kinds of 'elements' making up consciousness. The first of these were **external elements**, or sensations coming from the outside world, which included social experiences as well as interactions with physical objects and processes. The second were **internal elements**, which consisted of feelings and emotions originating within the person.

Wundt believed that awareness arises from a creative synthesis between these two kinds of elements, forming new compounds which he described as **complexes of experience**. This model was a deliberate analogy with chemistry: Wundt saw the external and internal 'elements' as being like chemical elements, and the 'complexes of experience' as comparable to the molecular compounds that make up everyday matter as we know it.

Evolutionary approaches to consciousness

Some researchers argue that consciousness must have developed within an evolutionary context, providing an advantage for the organism which possessed it. According to this view, consciousness would provide a survival advantage for human beings by allowing us to monitor the environment for threats, and to anticipate them. This would make it possible to develop more effective ways of coping with such threats or avoiding them. If this were so, we might perhaps expect consciousness to be more likely to evolve in a rapidly changing environment, where new kinds of threat might develop and rigid inherited behaviour patterns were no longer appropriate.

Humphrey (1976) argued that consciousness evolves as a result of social complexity. Human beings are deeply social creatures, and the demands of our social lives are extremely complex. Typically, we retain memory of, and person-schemata for, a couple of hundred individual, each of whom may react to events in their own idiosyncratic way. We are able to use our knowledge of these individual people to predict their reactions; and we are also (usually) able to use our social knowledge to engage in role-playing and to ensure that interactions proceed reasonably smoothly. All this, Humphrey argued, led to the evolution of self-awareness and consciousness.

Consciousness as monitoring

Weiskrantz (1988) disagreed with Humphrey's view, pointing out that much of our social behaviour, even though it is complex, is carried out automatically, without thinking. Moreover, there are plenty of creatures which engage in complex social societies without consciousness, ants being a typical example. Drawing on the studies of blindsight and amnesia that we looked at earlier, Weiskrantz proposed that consciousness is actually a separate monitoring system, which allows us to become aware of what we are doing or experiencing. But most of our everyday activity takes place without involving that monitoring system.

Moreover, Weiskrantz argued, as activities become familiar, the monitoring system becomes disengaged: we do not consciously think about the automatic muscle routines involved in walking; but at first, we are very likely to think about the similar muscle routines involved in ice-skating. As we become more skilled at the activity, however, we become less and less aware of the muscle actions involved, until, with enough practice, it comes more or less automatically. Weiskrantz argued that the sensory projection areas of the cortex are actually the monitoring system for our experiences, not the neurological control centres for the activities themselves; and it is they which are involved in consciousness – or at least, in conscious awareness of sensation or action. And, as we saw in Chapter 10, they are also in the part of the brain which evolved most recently.

Sommerhoff's theory of consciousness

Part of the problem in understanding consciousness, as we have seen, is that it requires us to be able to take account of the fact that much of what we do is unconscious. Sommerhoff (1996) developed a model of consciousness which draws together a range of biological, neurological and psychological information. Like Weiskrantz, Sommerhoff acknowledges that there are layers of mental activity which do not occur in consciousness; and which can either contribute directly to our conscious experience, or can direct our physical activities without our being consciously aware of it.

Sommerhoff proposed that the brain has several layers of representation of reality, with the conscious layer at the top. Sommerhoff defines consciousness as '*awareness of the surrounding world, of the self, and of one's thoughts and feelings*'. (Sommerhoff, 1996: 142). But mental activity is not all concerned with awareness: there is a great deal of activity happening in the other layers as well. Sommerhoff proposes that the bottom layer, or base level, consists of inputs. Some of these are sensory inputs, coming from the external world. Some are physical inputs, coming from the movements and actions of the body. Others are physiological and drive inputs, which derive from the general state of the body.

The brain converts the information from these inputs into mental representations. Sommerhoff describes three categories of these. The first, category A, consists of representations of actual objects, events, or situations. These are drawn largely from the external sensory inputs received from the base layer. Category B representations are representations of imagined objects, events or situations. They consist largely of mental images, but they also include representations of the intended results of our actions. Category C representations, on the other hand, are concerned with the current state of the organism. They relate to internal representations or individual stimuli, which are part of that current state. They also include A or B-type representations of particular brain-states, or brain-events, which also become integrated into a general awareness of the state of the self.

Consciousness itself, according to Sommerhoff, consists of an **integrated global representation (IGR)** of the world. This is a functional model of the world, which allows an individual to act in ways which are appropriate to the current situation, even if that situation is unanticipated, or unexpected. Indeed, it is in dealing with the unexpected that the IGR particularly comes into play: we do not pay attention to those aspects of our environment which occur exactly as we predict. But if something is different from our expectations, our attention is drawn towards it, and we instantly become conscious of it.

In Sommerhoff's model, the IGR consists of category C representations. The IGR is the conscious level of the brain's activities: it is our self-awareness, and that awareness is all about how we are located in the world, how we are functioning, and how we are likely to continue functioning. But our consciousness also draws on representations which occur at a lower level, and

are not conscious. As Figure 11.2 shows, Category A and B representations are maintained at the subliminal level: they are not directly part of consciousness, although as we have seen, they can contribute input to category C. But they can also link directly with actions, without having to pass through the conscious level, and this is how automatised actions such as driving can be unconscious, yet still effective.

Modelling consciousness is a tricky task, and any model which is developed now will need to be adjusted to take account of new information being discovered by researchers. But Sommerhoff's theory does allow us to develop a general picture of how consciousness might be working in the brain, and how we can be conscious, yet simultaneously unconscious of so much that is going on around us. It also, importantly, allows us to integrate emotional and motivational states into our picture of consciousness.

Psychoactive drugs and consciousness

Psychoactive drugs are drugs which affect an individual's mental state: they may directly change our moods or how we respond to the environment. In general, psychoactive drugs produce their effects because they affect the way that neurones communicate with one another at the synapse. So if we are to understand this process fully, we need to look at how neural impulses are transmitted from one neurone to another. This means understand-

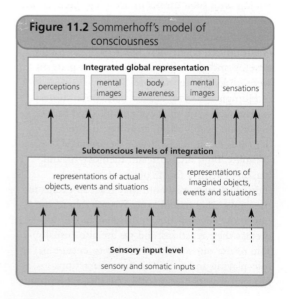

Figure 11.2 Sommerhoff's model of consciousness

ing something about the chemistry and activity of the synapse.

The synapse

Each neurone has a set of branches, known as dendrites, which are used to pass messages from one neurone to the next. Typically, a dendrite will have a small knob at the end, known as a **synaptic knob** or a **synaptic button**; and it will also have one or several special places along its length known as **receptor sites**. These areas are matched up from one neurone to the next: a synaptic button on one neurone will be located immediately opposite a receptor site on another neurone.

When the neurone is stimulated, an electrical impulse travels along the dendrite to the synaptic button, causing several small **synaptic vesicles** on the button to break open and spill out the chemical which they contain. The chemical, which is known as a **neurotransmitter**, passes into the synaptic cleft, or the gap between the two neurones, and is then picked up at the receptor site on the next neurone (see Figure 11.3). Once it has been picked up, any neurotransmitter which remains in the synaptic cleft is removed. Sometimes it is broken down by an enzyme. On other occasions it is picked up again by the synaptic button and 'recycled'. Psychoactive drugs are drugs which affect these processes.

When it is picked up at the receptor site, a neurotransmitter can have two main effects. It may stimulate the action of the receiving neurone,

making it more likely to fire; or it may inhibit the action of the receiving neurone, making it less likely to fire. Any particular synapse will always have the same general effect, so the first type of synapse is known as an **excitatory synapse**, and the second type is known as an **inhibitory synapse**.

If enough neurotransmitter is picked up at an excitatory receptor site, it depolarises the neuronal membrane, rendering it more permeable, and so allowing electrically charged particles to pass through. This results in a rapid exchange of sodium and chloride ions from outside the cell, with potassium ions from inside, and produces an **action potential** – a minute electrical charge of about 40 millivolts, which occurs for about half a millisecond (we will be looking at this more closely in Chapter 12). Inhibitory receptors have the efffect of increasing the polarisation of the cell membrane, rather than reducing it, so the action potential is less likely to happen.

There are three main categories of neurotransmitters: biogenic amines, amino acids, and amino peptides. Many of these are chemicals which fulfil an entirely different function when they are used in different parts of the body – the body often uses the same chemicals for many different purposes. Although there seem to be over 90 different substances which can be used as neurotransmitters, the best-known, and perhaps the most common, neurotransmitters are listed in Table 11.2 overleaf.

Where neurotransmitters come from

Neurotransmitters are synthesised by the neurones, often from chemical substances found in the diet which have passed into the brain. Acetylcholine, for example, is synthesised from choline, which is found in cauliflower and milk. Choline in its turn can be synthesised from the lecithin present in many other foods, such as egg yolks, liver, soya beans, peanuts and butter.

Similarly, the neurotransmitter serotonin is synthesised from the amino acid tryptophan. This is found in protein-rich foods, such as meat. But that does not mean that eating meat will necessarily increase the amount of serotonin in the brain. If meat is eaten on its own, the level of tryptophan which actually reaches the brain can be quite low, because the tryptophan has to compete with several other amino acids present in the same kind of food. The way round it is to combine eating

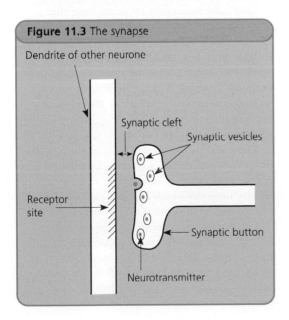

Figure 11.3 The synapse

Dendrite of other neurone

Synaptic cleft

Synaptic vesicles

Receptor site

Synaptic button

Neurotransmitter

Table 11.2 Some major neurotransmitters

Acetylcholine	This is the neurotransmitter found at the motor end plate, passing messages from the brain to the muscles. Its action can be inhibited or disturbed by various drugs, ranging from nicotine to toxic nerve gases.
Dopamine	This is found in the central nervous system, and associated with motivational and reward pathways. The disorder known as Parkinson's disease is associated with depleted levels of dopamine in the brain.
Noradrenaline and serotonin	These are associated with emotion, and with affective disorders like manic depression. Large amounts of these neurotransmitters are released during epileptic seizures. They also seem to be effective in treating long-term depression: tricylic antidepressant drugs have their effect by preventing these neurotransmitters from being reabsorbed, so that they stay active for longer.
Endorphins and enkephalins	These are associated with the action of the sympathetic division of the ANS. Subjectively, they produce a feeling of euphoria and well-being, and it is because of the actions of these neurotransmitters that people sometimes do not feel pain at moments of extreme arousal, or during strenuous activity.
Glutamates	These are very common neurotransmitters in the brain – perhaps the most common of all. They appear to act as general excitatory neurotransmitters, activating neurones to fire. The effects of the drug caffeine are linked with the effects of increased glutamate levels in the brain.

meat with eating carbohydrates. Carbohydrates stimulate the body to produce insulin, which 'captures' amino acids and transports them out of the bloodstream and into the body for various uses. As a result, there is less competition for the tryptophan, and so more of it eventually reaches the brain.

Some kinds of neurotransmitters pass through a more complicated sequence in their synthesis. For example, the three neurotransmitters known as catecholamines all have the same chemical origins, but have passed through different numbers of steps. Some neurones are able to synthesise dopamine from the amino acids phenylalanine and tyrosine. Some other neurones do this, but also have an extra enzyme which converts dopamine into noradrenaline, while a third set of neurones produce noradrenaline but then convert it into adrenaline.

Most neurotransmitters are actually synthesised in the synaptic button – although not always in the vesicles. It appears that sometimes, the neurotransmitter oozes through the cell membrane into the synaptic cleft. Other neurotransmitters are synthesised in other parts of the neurone: the peptides, for example, are always synthesised in the cell body, so they may have to travel quite a long way before being released into the synapse.

How psychoactive drugs work

Drugs can influence synapses in several different ways. Some drugs influence the presynaptic neurone – the neurone which is releasing the neurotransmitter. As a result, either more or less of the neurotransmitter is produced. Others act at the synaptic button to inhibit the release of neurotransmitters into the synaptic cleft. Other drugs (for example, most antidepressants) act to destroy the enzyme which breaks down the neurotransmitter after it has been released. This means that the neurotransmitter stays around in the synaptic cleft, and continues to affect the next neurone for much longer than it would otherwise have done. And some drugs (for example, the opiates) have their effect by 'mimicking' the neurotransmitter chemical, and being picked up at the receptor site. Each receptor site is sensitive to the chemical structure of one particular neurotransmitter, but if a drug has a very similar chemical structure, it can sometimes fit into the receptor site as well – rather like the way that a key will sometimes fit a lock designed for a different key, if the two are similar enough.

There are several different types of psychoactive drug. They include drugs which act on the peripheral nervous system – the network of motor and sensory neurones which link the sense receptors and muscles to the central nervous system; sedative and depressant drugs; stimulants, opiates and narcotics; and the hallucinogens (see Table 11.3). Each of these can have its effect on consciousness, so we will look at how they work before coming back to consider the tricky problem of working out what consciousness might be.

Drugs acting on the peripheral nervous system

There are a number of drugs which act on the peripheral nervous system, either by suppressing sensory activity, as the local anaesthetics used by doctors do, or by affecting motor activity. Curare, military nerve gases, some insecticides and the botulinum toxin which is sometimes found in contaminated meat, all have directly toxic effects produced at the motor end plate – the point on the muscle fibre which receives the message from a motor neurone.

The motor end plate works in a similar way to the synapse: the neurotransmitter acetylcholine is released by the synaptic knob of the motor neurone and picked up at special receptor sites on the motor end plate of the muscle fibre. Curare and botulinum toxin paralyse the muscles by being picked up at the receptor sites and so blocking the uptake of acetylcholine. Military nerve gases and some insecticides produce uncontrollable muscular tremors and jerks, because they prevent the neurotransmitter from being broken down once it has released, so it remains active for a long period of time.

The common, but highly addictive, recreational drug nicotine also has an effect at the motor end plate. Nicotine, like curare (but not as dramatically), is picked up at acetylcholine receptor sites, both in the brain and in the motor end plate. In the brain, nicotine locks into acetylcholine receptors and stimulates them, much as acetylcholine does. As a result, it produces an increased heart rate, and arouses parts of the cerebral cortex. In the motor end plate, it inhibits the uptake of acetylcholine in the motor end plate, producing muscular lethargy. It is this action which many nicotine addicts interpret as 'helping them to relax'. However, muscular lethargy and relaxation are not necessarily the same thing, and there is some evidence that overall feelings of tiredness are increased by nicotine consumption.

It is for this reason too that people who are withdrawing from nicotine dependency often feel restless and fidgety: they are having to acclimatise to an increased muscular responsiveness as the drug wears off. A similar effect appears to occur within the autonomic nervous system, in that people withdrawing from nicotine often

Table 11.3 Mechanisms of psychoactive drugs

Drug	Mechanism	Neurotransmitter involved
Motor system drugs		
curare	blocks acetylcholine receptor site	acetylcholine
botulinum toxin	blocks acetylcholine receptor site	acetylcholine
nerve gases and insecticides	prevent breakdown and recycling of acetylcholine	acetylcholine
nicotine	picked up at acetylcholine receptor sites	acetylcholine
Sedatives and depressants		
alcohol	inhibits noradrenaline receptors and facilitates GABA binding	noradrenaline and GABA
diazepam	facilitates binding of GABA at inhibitory synapses	GABA (gamma-aminobutyric acid)
chlorpromazine	blocks dopamine release	dopamine
marijuana	picked up at anandamide receptor sites	anandamide
beta-blockers	prevent re-uptake of beta-endorphin	beta-endorphin
Stimulants		
caffeine	inhibits adenosine release, increasing glutamate activity	glutamate
amphetamines	increase release of dopamine and noradrenaline	dopamine
MDMA (Ecstasy)	prevents re-uptake of serotonin in synapse	serotonin
cocaine	blocks re-uptake of noradrenaline and dopamine	noradrenaline and dopamine
Opiates and narcotics		
opium	picked up at endorphin receptor sites	endorphin
heroin and morphine	picked up at endorphin receptor sites	endorphin
Hallucinogens		
mescaline	picked up at serotonin receptor sites	serotonin
psilocybin	picked up at serotonin receptor sites	serotonin
LSD	picked up at serotonin receptor sites	serotonin

experience heightened emotional reactions. This can produce both increased irritability and increased levels of humour and euphoria. They may become more easily annoyed, but they are also more easily amused or happy.

Sedatives and depressants

The most commonly used sedative drug is undoubtedly the drug **alcohol**. Like caffeine, alcohol is a very powerful drug which we often overlook because it is in everyday use. Sedatives have their effects by lowering the activity level of noradrenaline receptors in the brain, resulting in drowsiness and impaired sensory functioning. Alcohol particularly interferes with nervous system activity, by inhibiting the flow of sodium ions across the cell membrane and expanding the cell membrane surface. It also acts on certain receptor sites – those for GABA neurotransmitters – which act as inhibitory synapses, producing calmness.

It has also been suggested that alcohol suppresses inhibitory synapses first, with excitatory synapses being suppressed later. If this is so, it might account for the exhilarating effects that small doses of alcohol can have, and the sedative effects produced by larger doses. Other psychologists, however, interpret the stimulating effects of alcohol as being produced by a lessening of social inhibition as the sedative produces increased relaxation. A third possibility is that the apparently stimulating effects of alcohol come from the amnesiac properties of the drug: alcohol encourages people to forget things, and so they may be forgetting their troubles and becoming more playful.

A very obvious effect of the drug alcohol on consciousness is the way that it impairs critical judgement. Many people, for instance, believe that they can drive adequately even when under the influence of the drug, although when they are tested on a driving course even very small amounts of alcohol result in many misjudgements. It seems that one consequence of the inhibitory effect of alcohol consumption is that people 'shrug off' minor errors, and forget that they happened, so they convince themselves that they can drive as well as ever, even though this is not true in reality.

The popularity of alcohol as a social drug is partly because of its amnesiac effect. Under the influence of alcohol, people tend to forget their immediate worries, and therefore find easier to relax. But if alcohol is taken in larger quantities, these amnesiac effects of alcohol become stronger, and addiction can lead to **Korsakoff's syndrome**, in which, as we saw in Chapter 3, the person loses the ability to retain new memories altogether. Prolonged heavy drinking can produce physical addiction, too, which has extremely unpleasant side-effects if the person tries to withdraw from the drug. At their worst, these effects can include hallucinations and convulsions, and even in a milder form they are likely to involve irritability and a general feeling of debilitation.

Other kinds of sedatives include the psychiatric drugs **diazepam** (Valium) and **chlorpromazine** (Largactyl). Diazepam is a tranquilliser, dampening down autonomic activity and producing feelings of calmness. It was seriously over-prescribed during the 1960s and 1970s, and only later discovered to be addictive, producing unpleasant withdrawal symptoms in those who tried to stop taking it suddenly, without phasing it out. Diazepam works by facilitating the uptake of GABA at the receptor sites.

Chlorpromazine is a very powerful sedative, which induces lethargy and even unconsciousness. Traditionally, it was used to sedate potentially violent psychiatric patients, although it has been used much more widely than that. It works by blocking the release of dopamine from the presynaptic neurone.

The widely used recreational drug **marijuana** is also a depressant drug, which slows reaction time and induces drowsiness. It was used as a tranquilliser during the nineteenth century, and for over two thousand years in China and on the Indian subcontinent, although owing to the development of more specific drugs, it is no longer used medically in the Western world. Marijuana does not seem to be as powerful as most other psychoactive drugs. Expectation and setting have a great deal to do with what people experience from it, and many of those who try marijuana once as a recreational drug report that they find little or no effect. Heavy users sometimes report **time dilation**, in which time seems to pass very slowly, and enhanced sensory effects. Long-term heavy use also appears to correlate with lethargy and depression, although this may partly result from the use of tobacco as a medium for taking the drug.

We are a long way yet from understanding exactly how marijuana works, since, for social and political reasons, it is difficult for scientists to get research funding to investigate this particular drug. But one important clue emerged when researchers in Israel discovered a chemical, anandamide, which seems to be a natural substance that has the same effect in the brain as THC (tetrahydrocannabinol, the active ingredient of marijuana). Not long afterwards, American researchers discovered that there may be specific receptors for anandamide in brain cells, which implies that these would also respond to THC (Mestel, 1993).

Stimulants

The category of stimulant drugs includes the drugs caffeine, amphetamine and cocaine. **Caffeine** is a far more powerful drug than many people suspect. It acts directly on the central and autonomic nervous systems, heightening arousal and increasing neural excitation. The way that caffeine works is that it inhibits the release of the neurotransmitter adenosine, which acts to inhibit the release of excitatory neurotransmitters such as glutamate. So by blocking the release of adenosine, the glutamates stimulate the nervous system in a general sort of fashion.

It is for this reason that many people take caffeine to 'see them through the day'. Like most drugs which have this type of effect, though, prolonged and heavy use can produce addiction, and also can have a debilitating effect. It is not good for anyone to live 'on their nerves' continually, which is the effect produced by heavy doses of caffeine.

Amphetamines are more dramatic in their effects than caffeine, producing an immediate increase in alertness and a decrease in fatigue. They have their main effect by increasing the release of stored dopamine and noradrenaline in the brain. If the levels of these neurotransmitters are lower than normal, then it has very little effect; but normally the brain has stores of both noradrenaline and dopamine, so it increases their release, increasing alertness and producing arousal.

Moderate doses of amphetamines were used during WWII to allow pilots and radar scanners to sustain their performance over very long periods of time. Amphetamines are sometimes used as recreational drugs, and in small doses can produce a pleasant sensation of confidence and increased sociability. However, the recreational use of amphetamines tends rapidly to lead to larger doses, as the user builds up a tolerance very

quickly, and it is very easy to become dependent on the drug. Moreover, after a large dose of amphetamine, people often enter a **rebound state** of depression, which is thought to arise because the brain has not had time to resynthesise noradrenaline fast enough to replace that which was released so suddenly.

Continuous or very frequent use of amphetamine produces unpleasantly distorted perceptions of reality, sometimes leading to severe paranoia and other psychotic symptoms. In many respects, these are similar to acute schizophrenia. Another danger from frequent use of amphetamines is the physical debilitation brought about by the fact that they suppress appetite, so the individual does not eat for long periods of time. All this means that amphetamines, or 'speed' as the drug is sometimes called, are extremely dangerous for recreational purposes.

A drug which has recently become popular is the drug **MDMA** (short for 3,4-methylene-dioxymethamphet-amine), also known as **Ecstasy**. In large doses, this drug can also induce heightened perception, and apparently even hallucinations, although as a general rule it seems to produce a strong feeling of euphoria and sociability. Abbott and Concar (1992) described its action as being like a mixture of LSD and amphetamine. It acts directly on the serotonin pathways of the brain, blocking the recycling of serotonin by the synaptic knob. This causes the serotonin to build up in the synaptic cleft, and continue to stimulate the receptor site on the next neurone.

MDMA was first synthesised as early as 1914, but only came into widespread use as a recreational drug in America in the 1970s. Because of its powerfully **prosocial** effects, it was even prescribed by marriage guidance counsellors to encourage couples to become closer to one another. Nowadays, however, it is illegal in both Britain and the United States. In America, MDMA was used as a quiet, social drug: in a survey of its use at Stanford University in 1988, Peroutka found that the students tended to use it sitting quietly with friends, much as they would use marijuana.

In Britain, however, MDMA is associated with dancing and nightclubs. MDMA produces autonomic arousal, and when this is combined with vigorous exercise, it has been known to produce overheating, dehydration, and even death through heat stroke. Abbott and Concar (1992) report that, as with many other psychoactive drugs, regular users of MDMA quickly become 'tolerant' to its action, and need increasing doses to gain the same effects. The frequent use of MDMA can also produce effects which are similar to amphetamine psychosis, although most use of MDMA seems to be intermittent, which allows the body to recover between doses. There is, as yet, no knowledge of possible long-term effects from taking this drug.

Cocaine produces an immediate effect of increased energy and self-confidence, particularly in those who are tired or physically run-down. It achieves this by blocking the re-uptake of noradrenaline and dopamine, so that the general levels of these neurotransmitters are higher than usual. But it also seems to have a more general effect, decreasing the overall amount of brain activity. Although the moderate use of cocaine is considered to be safer than other 'hard' drugs, like heroin or amphetamine, cocaine is an addictive drug, and its effects in masking tiredness or ill-health can produce further physical debilitation in the long run.

Cocaine was popular as a recreational drug in the last century and the early part of this one, and was used extensively by Freud, among others. Sir Arthur Conan Doyle was very explicit about Sherlock Holmes's habit of taking cocaine, in the detective novels which have become so popular, and this indicates how readily it was accepted in society at the time that the books were written. Recently, cocaine has again become popular, particularly in the form of a highly addictive derivative known as 'crack'. The long-term use of cocaine produces withdrawal effects which include feelings of emotional pain or anguish, and heavy use can produce hallucinations and distorted perceptions of reality.

Opiates and narcotics

Opiates are drugs which reduce physical sensation, and also slow down the brain's response to external stimuli. Many opiates are used therapeutically, as analgesics (pain-killers); and it is an interesting observation that it seems to be precisely those drugs which can reduce physical pain which have been used by addicts to reduce what Eugène Marais (1969) – an insightful ethologist, but also a morphine addict – referred to as 'the pain of consciousness'.

Possibly for this reason, most opiates are highly addictive drugs, and illegal consumption of them is regarded as a serious social problem. The initial effects of opiate consumption tend to include a feeling of euphoria and well-being, which entices the individual on to more regular use. However, with regular use, the individual builds up a **tolerance**, and needs increasingly large doses in order to produce the same effects. It is this cycle which produces the social deprivation visible among heroin addicts in Western society, and which so often results in their turning to crime to support the financial demands produced by their habit.

Opiates include the drugs opium, heroin and morphine, and several derivatives which have been obtained using these as the base material. They have their effects by keying into specific **endorphin receptor sites** in the brain, because they have a similar chemical structure to naturally occurring endorphins. Endorphins (and the related neurotransmitters known as enkephalins) are produced when the body has been engaging in prolonged energetic exercise. Their pain-killing properties may have evolved as a survival mechanism: if an animal is involved in a vigorous struggle to stay alive, or a flight for its life, then it would be an advantage to delay the experience of pain until the struggle is actually over. That way, it can put more effort into the fight.

This is also the secret of 'jogger's euphoria' – it explains why people who take regular and sustained exercise so often seem to be very cheerful. The exercise means that they produce high levels of endorphins and enkephalins in the brain. This means that they get the same feelings of euphoria and well-being as someone who has just had a dose of a powerful opiate, but they get this naturally and without the risks involved in taking dangerous chemicals. So if you have been wondering what taking opiates feels like, try taking up vigorous cycling or swimming, instead. You will have the same feelings, but with none of the dangerous side-effects!

Hallucinogens

Some drugs can produce a dramatic change in awareness, by either enhancing or distorting our perceptions. Although this can also be achieved by the long-term addictive use of some other drugs, the group known as hallucinogens produce such effects very quickly and directly. Some hallucinogens occur naturally, such as **mescaline** (derived from the peyote cactus) and **psilocybin** (obtained from psilocybin mushrooms). Others, though, notably the drug **LSD** (lysergic acid diethylamide) are manufactured synthetically. But all of these hallucinogens appear to be picked up in serotonin receptor sites within the brain – they have a chemical structure which is similar to that of the naturally occurring neurotransmitter.

Mescaline and other hallucinogens were frequently used as a source of inspiration by writers and artists in the early part of this century, but such use ceased to be described openly, for obvious reasons, when recreational use of these drugs was declared illegal in the 1960s. In mild doses, the drugs produce enhancement of sensory experiences like colour perception, and sometimes mystical or semi-religious experiences. Some studies, e.g. Aaronson and Osmond (1970), suggested that LSD could be effective in psycho therapy with mildly neurotic individuals, but such research is far less common now.

This situation arose partly as a result of incidents in which recreational use of the drug produced tragic effects, which were widely publicised. Some users experienced severe hallucinations, resulting in, for example, the belief that they had supernatural abilities, like being able to fly, and some injuries and deaths occurred in the process. Leary (1965) argued that hallucinogenic drugs allowed the individual to explore areas of consciousness which were not previously accessible, but that in doing so it was important for the individual to use the drugs in a responsible and informed manner. Leary said that it was important to take two factors into account: **set** – that is, the person's own mental state of readiness; and **setting** – ensuring that their environment was pleasant and relaxing. It was the lack of consideration of these factors, Leary claimed, which had produced the tragic 'bad trips'.

Leary, Alpert and Metzner (1965) argued that hallucinogenic drugs could provide a unique key to understanding different levels of consciousness within the human psyche. They proposed that consciousness involves several distinct layers, and that although we use some of these layers in everyday living, others are only accessed by extremes of experience of one form or another. Hallucinogenic drugs, Leary believed, allowed people to access different levels of awareness, as did the mental and physical disciplines involved in yoga and meditation.

Sleep and dreaming

Part of the study of consciousness includes the study of sleep and dreaming. Sleep raises a number of questions. What is going on when we are asleep? Why do our bodies need to have these regular periods when normal everyday behaviour seems to be turned off, and we remain quiescent for hours on end? What happens when we do not get enough sleep? And why do we dream? Researchers have been investigating the phenomenon of sleep throughout the second half of this century, looking at the physiology of sleep, and at sleep cycles, at how it is controlled by the brain, and at what happens when we dream.

Biological rhythms

It may seem obvious, but one of the reasons that we sleep is because it is night-time. Human beings, for the most part, tend to be awake during the day and asleep at night – they are what is known as **diurnal** animals. Other animals are awake at night and asleep during the day, and they are known as **nocturnal** animals. Cycles of activity which relate to being awake during the day are known as **diurnal rhythms**.

We have a number of natural cycles, which form part of our everyday lives. Some of these operate over several weeks, such as the human menstrual cycle, while others are much more rapid, such as the cycles involved in digestion and food intake. Some rhythms, called **circadian rhythms**, are based on the 24 hours of the day, and perhaps the most obvious circadian rhythm is to do with consciousness. We alternate, throughout life, between periods of wakefulness and periods of sleeping. By the time we are adult, most of us have adjusted to a 24-hour cycle which contains either one or two periods of sleep. In some societies, the cultural pattern is of one long period of sleep, during the night, followed by a longer period of wakefulness.

In other societies, though, particularly those in hot climates, the night-time sleeping period is shorter since there is a regular 'siesta' period in the middle of the day, when it is assumed that everyone will sleep again for a couple of hours. Biologically, we seem to be adjusted to either possibility. Measurable variations in human alertness and wakefulness show that, in addition to slowing down and becoming ready for sleep at night, we also tend to have a low efficiency period in the early afternoon – which is the time when many people (even in non-siesta societies) take naps. At this time, body functioning becomes more quiescent, and it is easier to fall asleep than at other times during the day.

Sleep-waking cycles correlate with other factors too. One of these is body temperature. This is at its lowest in the very early hours of the morning, when we are generally most deeply asleep. At such times, body temperature decreases to its lowest point, but then gradually increases again as we approach waking-up time. Through the morning, it remains fairly constant, but then shows a distinct dip in the early afternoon, before increasing again slightly. Of course, this is only a general pattern, not an invariable law: some people have stronger rhythms than others, and some, as we will see later, have adjusted to different time sequences.

Psychological measures of alertness and performance also show systematic changes throughout the day. These have involved tests of memory and attention (see Chapters 2 and 3), such as working memory speed, short-term memory span and the speed taken to search for a particular piece of information through a series of numbers or letters. Folkard (1983) argued that these changes in performance occur because of variations in the person's level of **autonomic arousal** during the course of the day, although this idea has been challenged by a number of other researchers. We will be looking at the concept of autonomic arousal in Chapter 13.

Zeitgebers

Our sleep-waking patterns are not just automatic, 24-hour cycles, occurring like clockwork. Instead, they are powerfully influenced by external events, known as **zeitgebers**. The most powerful of these is daylight: have you ever stayed up all night and found that as full daylight came you felt less tired? Miles, Raynal and Wilson (1977) studied a young blind man, who turned out to have a natural rhythm of a little more than 24 hours – 24.9 hours, to be precise. He had been blind from birth, which meant that he did not receive daylight as a zeitgeber, so he was unable to adjust his personal rhythm to external circumstances. Since he had a demanding professional job, he sometimes had to resort to tranquillisers and stimulants

to make sure that he was alert at the appropriate times.

In another study, Aschoff (1965) asked a number of people to stay in a cave for several weeks. The cave was well heated, with plenty of artificial lighting. But there were no external zeitgebers to indicate the time of day to the research participants. As a result, they operated their sleep-waking cycle purely according to internal, physiological cues: falling asleep when they felt tired, waking without alarms or other signals, and so on. Like the blind man studied by Miles, Rayner and Wilson, Aschoff found that the research participants tended to fall into a 25 hour sleep-waking cycle, rather than a strict 24 hour one.

Adjusting to new times

The phenomenon known as **jet lag** happens when we need to adjust quickly to different circadian rhythms. Because modern methods of transport mean that we can move across time zones very quickly, modern international travellers often find that their internal clock is 'set wrong' when they arrive in a new country, and that it takes them a few days – sometimes as many as ten, although it is usually less – for their systems to adjust. In the meantime, they feel fatigued when they should be alert, and wakeful at times when other people are quiescent. Travelling the same distances from north to south does not produce anything like the same effects.

Social factors, too, can influence the sleep-waking cycle, as you may already have discovered. If most of your social activity takes place in the evening or night-time, you will find it easier to be awake then and to sleep in the day than someone whose main activities take place during normal daylight hours. Webb (1975) showed that people's circadian rhythms can vary considerably: some are at their best in the morning, others at their best in the afternoon. But for many people, it is a question of lifestyle, and when they are most active in their day, which determines when they are likely to be at their most alert.

There are a number of influences which can help us to adjust to different circadian rhythms. Some travellers find that using natural daylight as much as possible helps them to adapt to the new time-cycle, particularly if they are moving from night into day. Kowet (1983) showed that time adjustment is easier if we move forwards rather than backwards in the 24-hour cycle. This applies to people travelling from east to west or west to east; but it also applies to people who regularly work different shifts.

One problem which **shiftworkers** face, and international travellers do not, is the fact that the external zeitgebers remain the same. This makes it more difficult for shiftworkers to adapt to a new time than for travellers. Akerstedt (1985) showed that the time people spend sleeping during the day when they are working a night shift can be anything between one and four hours less than their normal sleeping time would be. What type of sleep they had was also affected: such people spent less time in REM and Level II sleep (we will be looking at types of sleep in the next section) than they did during night-time sleeping.

Czeisler, Moore-Ede and Coleman (1982) showed that it is less fatiguing and produces easier adjustment for people if shifts are rotated in such a way as to get later each time. So, for example, a pattern of rotating shifts which goes from early shifts to late shifts to night shifts and then to early shifts again is easier than a pattern which moves backwards, or jumps about, like going from an early shift to a night shift to a day shift. Following a positive sequence of shift rotation also helps to reduce industrial accidents – possibly since people are more alert when they are working, so they are less likely to make serious errors.

Accidents and errors

Changes in sleeping patterns and adjustment are significant because of the higher rate of industrial accidents and errors which occur during night-time work. It used to be thought that allowing workers to remain on the same shift for a long period of time would minimise such problems, because it would allow them to adapt to a different rhythm. Nowadays, however, it is recognised that for many people the influence of external zeitgebers like natural daylight is too powerful for this to happen. Some individuals seem unable to adapt to night-time shifts no matter how long they spend doing them. Monk and Folkard (1985) showed that the best pattern for shift work involves frequent shift changes, so that people do not build up too much of a 'sleep debt'. It seems to be better in two ways: both in physical terms for the people concerned, and by reducing the number of industrial accidents.

It is not just industrial accidents which are affected by circadian rhythms. Motorway accidents too have been shown to occur mostly during three periods, which also correlate closely with human circadian rhythms. The three high-risk periods are from midnight to 2 am, from 4 am to 6 am and between 2 pm and 4 pm. Horne (1992) showed that most of these accidents happen as a result of drivers falling asleep at the wheel, sometimes just for a few seconds. They were detectable because the traces left by the accident were quite different from traces left by accidents when drivers are awake. For example, if a car crashes into a barrier when the driver is awake, there are skid marks on the road from the braking. But if the driver has fallen asleep, there are no skid marks.

Horne found that accidents between midnight and 2 am mostly tended to involve people who were driving later than their habitual bedtime. Those which happened in the early afternoon often concerned drivers who had had irregular sleep, frequently because of shift work. But most accidents of all occurred in the early morning period, with people who had been awake all night, or who had got up very early, often without having had much sleep the night before.

Horne also found that the time since the driver had last slept was very important indeed. Most sleep-related accidents seemed to occur when the driver had been awake for more than 18 hours at a time. The only practical remedy for those who found themselves tired at the wheel, Horne argued, was to pull over and get a couple of hours' sleep, because other remedies, such as black coffee or trying to keep awake, could only hold off the sleep for a few minutes or so. Trying to keep awake made the driver very vulnerable to 'micro-sleeps', where the person just dozes off for a few seconds, without realising that this is what is happening.

Rhythms of sleep

As well as being part of our behavioural circadian rhythms, sleep has its own internal rhythms. We are aware of some of the general changes which happen when we sleep. The muscles become flaccid, the 'attention-monitoring' systems of the brain seem to shut down, and we experience a lengthy period of passivity and inaction. But that is not all that is going on.

If we monitor people's brain activity as they sleep, we find that they show distinct changes in electro-encephalogram recordings during the course of a typical night. Berger (1929) was the first to show how EEG recordings could be associated with different levels of consciousness. Following on from this work, Dement and Kleitman (1957) described four basic types of EEG pattern which happen during sleep, and others which are associated with differences in the waking state (Figure 11.4).

Dement and Kleitman also showed that, during the course of the night, we pass through the different levels of sleep several times, moving from higher to lower levels of sleep, and back to higher levels again. They argued that this cycle is repeated several times during a typical night, although the deeper levels of sleep tend to be reached only during the first few cycles. Towards the end of the night, sleep cycles become shallower, which Dement and Kleitman interpreted as the person being more liable to wake up. Their conclusion, then, was that the changes in EEG pattern reflected how deeply the person was asleep.

REM sleep

Dement and Kleitman, as we have seen, believed that the pattern of the EEG trace for the most part reflected how deeply the person was sleeping. By waking people up when their EEG recordings moved to a different level, they found that for the most part this seemed to be the case. But in the case of Level I sleep, they found a paradox. When this type of sleep occurred during the course of the night, it was generally accompanied by rapid eye-movements, and so became known as **REM sleep**. Although the EEG trace for sleepers in this type of sleep seemed to indicate that they were only lightly asleep, they were actually very hard to wake up – as if they were at a much deeper level. For this reason, REM sleep also became known as **paradoxical sleep**, while ordinary sleep was referred to as **orthodox sleep**. Some modern researchers regard REM sleep as being so different from Level I sleep that it represents an entirely different fifth level.

Meddis (1979) argued that the distinction between several different levels of sleep was relatively unimportant, since what is essentially important in the different states of sleep is whether the sleeper is relaxed and quiescent, or active and showing REM. When we are awake, Meddis argued, we produce an EEG pattern which is distinguished by fast, desynchronised (i.e. irregular) activity. When we are in REM, we are in **active sleep (AS)** and show an active EEG pattern. But when we are in **quiet sleep (QS)**, the EEG pattern shows synchronised activity – a regular, patterned wave-form.

The synchronised activity involved in quiet sleep can be of two kinds. One of these is **light quiet sleep (LQS)**, in which the signals are synchronised but have a similar amplitude to that of waking sleep – in other words, the variations in brain activity are of roughly the same strength, but show regular patterns. In **deep quiet sleep (DQS)**, the amplitude of the wave-forms is much greater: the EEG shows large, regular wave-like patterns. Meddis argued that significant changes in EEGs during the course of the night show that people move between LQS, DQS and AS several times during the course of a night's sleep (see Figure 11.5). On average, most of us have four or five periods of active sleep a night.

Active sleep and dreaming

Dement and Kleitman (1957) found that sleepers who were woken from REM sleep also tended to report dreaming, and for this reason REM sleep is

Figure 11.4 EEG patterns of sleep

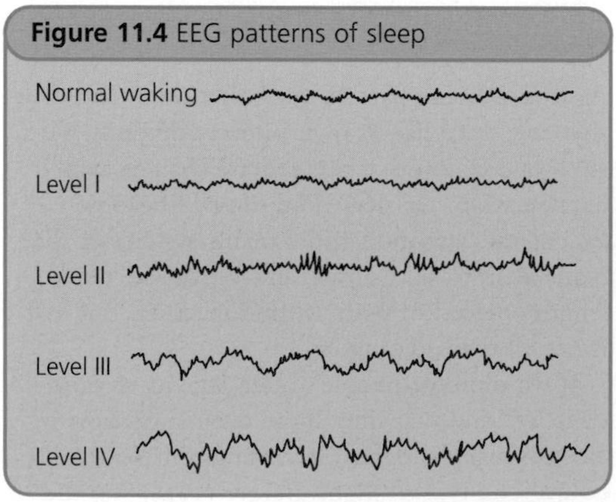

Normal waking

Level I

Level II

Level III

Level IV

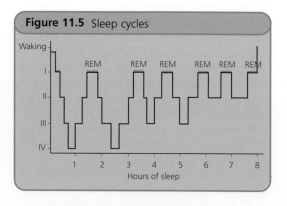

Figure 11.5 Sleep cycles

sometimes referred to as dreaming sleep. But there are two problems with this label. One of them is that there is some evidence that dreaming can happen at other times too. Jacobson and Kales (1967) investigated sleepwalking, and found that almost all **sleepwalking** incidents took place during quiet sleep, and mostly happened during the first third of the night when the person was in the deeper levels of the sleep cycle. Although sleepwalkers did report dreaming, the dreams that they described did not seem to correlate with their actions while they were sleepwalking.

Arkin *et al.* (1970) investigated people who talked in their sleep, and found that **sleeptalking** was not so strongly associated with quiet sleep, since some sleeptalking did occur during active sleep. Even so, the great majority – roughly 80% – of sleeptalking or sleepwalking incidents took place during quiet sleep. Also, if those who were sleeptalking were roused, the content of their dreams did not particularly match what they said while they were sleeptalking. The implication runs contrary to what we intuitively expect, and it seems that active sleep, dreaming, sleepwalking and sleeptalking do not inevitably happen together.

The physiology of sleep

As we have seen, circadian rhythms and the process of falling asleep seem to be very closely linked. There are a number of physiological mechanisms associated with this, and one of them seems to involve the **pineal gland** – a small gland tucked between the cerebral hemispheres, at the top of the brain stem. It is often referred to as the 'third eye', because it is located behind the centre of the forehead. Until recently, the functions of the pineal gland were extremely unclear to us. The philosopher Descartes believed it to be the seat of the soul, controlling the movements of the body through its links with the rest of the brain; but more empirical research has not revealed quite that much about its functions.

It seems that the pineal gland receives information from the eyes about the existence or absence of light. When the pineal gland receives messages that we are in darkness, it secretes a hormone known as melatonin, which has the effect of producing drowsiness. **Melatonin** also stimulates the production of the neurotransmitter serotonin, which also seems to be involved in sleep. It is possible too that longer-term rhythms may also

involve the pineal gland: some studies of birds have shown that seasonal changes, and in particular the behavioural changes associated with springtime (courtship, territory defence, and so on), may be associated with increased activation of the pineal gland due to the effects of increasing daylength.

The reticular activating system and the pons

The release of melatonin may also be associated with the amount of activity in the sub-cortical structure known as the **reticular activating system**, or **RAS** (see Chapter 10). The reticular activating system seems to act as a kind of 'switching system' for the cerebrum, affecting the general level of arousal across the cerebral cortex. As early as 1949, Moruzzi and Magoun showed that low levels of activity in the RAS, as measured by electro-encephalograms, were associated with the onset of sleep. Conversely, increased activity in this region signalled wakefulness. This was supported by a study by French (1957), who showed that electrical stimulation to a particular region of the RAS would gently rouse a sleeping cat.

French also found that surgical removal of the reticular activating system would produce deep comas in cats, from which they could not be roused. French, Verzeone and Magon (1953) suggested that this might be mirroring the deliberate unconsciousness induced by medical anaesthetics. They suggested that the drugs which are used to induce anaesthesia in medical operations have their effects by acting directly on neurotransmitters, to block the neural pathways of the reticular activating system.

The RAS is not the only sub-cortical structure of the brain to be involved in sleep, as is shown by Table 11.4. Jouvet (1967) found that lesions to a particular region of the **pons** changed the amount of REM sleep in animals, who would spend a much higher proportion of their time in REM sleep than they had before the operation. On the other hand, a lesion in a different area of the pons – lower down, closer to the **medulla** – would decrease the amount of time they spent in REM sleep. There is some evidence that this also holds true for human beings who have suffered accidental injury; but we have no way of knowing whether the increased amount of time in REM sleep arises directly from the brain injury itself, or

Table 11.4 Brain structures involved in sleep

the cerebrum

the pineal gland

the recticular activating system

the pons
(locus coeruleus)

the medulla
(raphé nuclei)

neurotransmitters
serotonin
noradrenaline

from the brain's efforts to restore psychological integrity after the injury.

Neurotransmitters and sleep

In 1972, Jouvet reported that lesions to a region of the brain known as the **raphé nuclei** produced serious insomnia in cats. Although the animals could occasionally manage a light doze, they did not sleep easily at all. Some researchers have suggested that certain kinds of insomnia experienced by human beings may come from the same source: some people may have naturally occurring lesions to the raphé nuclei, which result in their finding it difficult to get to sleep.

This finding was one outcome of a series of studies by Jouvet, which eventually resulted in a model of how neurotransmitter chemicals were involved in sleep. Jouvet (1972) identified two areas of the brain which seemed to be involved in sleep. One of these was the raphé nuclei, which has already been mentioned, and is a set of eight groups of neurones which spread from the medulla throughout the midbrain, through the pons and the reticular formation. The other area is located in the pons, and is known as the **locus coeruleus.**

Jouvet found that lesions to the raphé nuclei produced lower levels of the neurotransmitter serotonin in the brain, and also resulted in the loss of quiet sleep. As we have already seen, these lesions produced a general insomnia, although there were sometimes periods of active sleep. Lesions to the locus coeruleus, however, seemed to produce lower levels of the neurotransmitter noradrenaline, and resulted in loss of REM sleep. Jouvet proposed that the two different kinds of sleep were mediated by these two different areas of the brain, through the production of these neu-

rotransmitter chemicals. A link between the posterior areas of the raphé nuclei and the locus coeruleus would trigger the shift from quiet sleep to active sleep, and back again.

Jouvet also found that these two areas have slightly different connections with the rest of the brain. Both of them have links with the limbic system and the cerebral cortex, but the raphé nuclei have links with the hypothalamus as well, while the locus coeruleus has links with the cerebellum. (It may be worth looking back to Chapter 10, to remind yourself about these areas of the brain and what they do.) If quiet sleep is really to do with restoration of bodily tissues and temperature regulation, then links with the hypothalamus would make sense. Similarly, the cerebellar connection in active sleep may link with the rapid eye-movements and muscle flaccidity observed in active sleep.

A number of experimental studies supported Jouvet's model of the operation of the raphé nuclei, as being a mediator of quiet sleep states through the action of the neurotransmitter serotonin. But Ramm (1979) reviewed a number of studies on the functions of the locus coeruleus, and concluded that lesions to this area, or to the pathways leading to or from it, had little or no effect on REM sleep. Instead, Stern and Morgane (1974) proposed that the function of REM sleep is actually to restore the brain's levels of the neurotransmitters noradrenaline and dopamine. This hypothesis explained how some drugs, such as tricyclic antidepressants, increase the levels of noradrenaline in the brain while reducing REM sleep – the opposite to the effect which would be predicted by Jouvet's model.

Sleep-deprivation studies

People can do without sleep for very long periods of time, and often manage surprisingly well on most tests of psychological and physical functioning. But this does not mean that sleep deprivation has no effect: there are other, more general, consequences which seem to result. For example, although they can perform perfectly well on simple tasks, like reaction-time tests or responding to an immediate situation, many people report that they become more irritable, and less likely to notice additional details of what is happening around them. Junior doctors, who may have to be on duty continuously for up to 48 hours at a time, report concern that their decision-making ability is affected, in that they look only at the immediate problem without considering other, wider factors involved.

Unfortunately, most of these reports are relatively anecdotal, although they are very common. One of the problems seems to be that people who are seriously sleep-deprived can often rouse themselves successfully for short-term tasks, but find themselves losing awareness when undertaking routine or repetitive activities. They are able to do the kinds of controlled tasks which provide experimenters with precise measurements, like reaction-time exercises or decision-making simulations. However, it is harder to measure something like the focus of one's awareness, or one's ability to engage in continuous professional activity or interpersonal relationships.

Oswald (1970) reported that serious sleep deprivation can produce other psychological effects, like hallucinations and paranoia. Research participants who had been without sleep for up to five days at a stretch often reported that they experienced mild visual hallucinations, like the impression that a pattern on the wallpaper of the room was swirling around. They also often became deeply paranoid about the study, and the motivations of the experimenter, imagining that they were being manipulated for sinister purposes. In many respects, Oswald observed, these symptoms were identical to those of schizophrenia. Unlike schizophrenia, however, they disappeared completely once the person concerned had a chance to get some sleep.

Green (1987) argued that evidence from sleep-deprivation studies points to the striking similarities between what happens when people are deprived of sleep and what happens when they are deprived of another biological necessity – food. We can go without food for several days without suffering permanent damage, in the same way as we can go without sleep – but in both cases there are likely to be stresses on the body. When we eat again, after a period of starvation, we do not need to eat as much food as we have missed before we are back to normal, although we do eat more than usual. Similarly, when we sleep again after sleep deprivation, we do not need to sleep through the full amount that we have missed, although we do sleep more than usual. Sleep, then, shows similar homeostatic (regulatory) mechanisms to those of hunger. Like hunger, sleep

deprivation can be coped with in the short term. In the long term, however, both sleep and food are essential to life.

Deprivation of active sleep

A number of studies have investigated what happens when quiet sleep is allowed, but active sleep is prevented. Studies using both human beings and animals show that if they are woken up whenever they fall into active sleep, they show a **rebound effect** when they are able to sleep normally. In other words, their subsequent normal periods of sleep show increased REM activity, as if to make up for the time that they have lost. Dement (1970) showed that subjects who had been woken from REM sleep for five nights running spent up to 60% more of their sleeping time in REM sleep when they were finally allowed to sleep normally.

Dement also reported that the people taking part in this study developed a number of psychiatric symptoms, similar to those found in Oswald's total sleep-deprivation studies. But this finding is not a particularly reliable one, since Dement had informed his research participants beforehand that a psychiatrist would be present, in the event of such problems developing. This, he argued, probably led them to expect that they would develop such symptoms, as a kind of self-fulfilling prophecy.

Gillin, Buchsbaum and Jacobs (1974) suggested that a difference between schizophrenics and normal people might be the lack of a rebound effect: that schizophrenics who have been deprived of REM sleep do not seem to make up for it later, as ordinary people do. But Vogel (1975) reviewed a number of studies of REM deprivation, and concluded that there was no evidence for a link between schizophrenia and abnormalities of REM sleep.

There does, however, seem to be a link between endogenous depression (see Chapter 8) and REM sleep. Vogel (1974) showed that people with endogenous depression seemed to show an alleviation of symptoms if they were deprived of REM sleep. Antidepressant drugs also produce a dramatic reduction in REM sleep, and Vogel suggested that this is the main way in which they have their effect. An important feature of these drugs is that they do not produce a rebound effect: the amount of REM sleep really seems to be reduced. Other drugs which suppress REM sleep do show a rebound effect when the person stops taking them, and Vogel suggested that this is why they do not show a similar antidepressant effect.

Drugs which suppress REM sleep and do not show a rebound effect are thought to be those whose actions are a substitute for the normal functions of REM sleep. Those drugs which do produce a rebound effect are thought only to suppress REM sleep, but not to replace it. The idea behind this argument is to do with a connection between the drugs and the neurotransmitters which are involved in sleep.

Antidepressant drugs have their effect by raising the levels of what are known as the **catecholiner-gic** neurotransmitters in the brain – the neurotransmitters noradrenaline and dopamine. Since they do not show a REM rebound effect, it is thought that they might be mimicking the physical effects of REM sleep. As we have seen, Stern and Morgane (1974) proposed that the function of REM sleep is exactly the same: to restore the levels of noradrenaline and dopamine in the brain after they have been depleted during waking activity. Other drugs, which do show a rebound effect, simply suppress REM sleep without restoring these neurotransmitters.

Why do we sleep?

Almost all kinds of animals sleep. Fish, reptiles, birds and mammals all show very clear periods of sleep, while even molluscs and insects show periods of quiescence which seem to be very similar to sleep. Green (1987) identified three types of hypothesis which have been put forward to explain why people and animals sleep, and we have already looked at some of the evidence for each of these. **Physiological hypotheses** argue that the main function of sleep is that of physical restoration of the body, after the day's activity. **Psychological hypotheses** argue that the purposes of sleep are to do with processing and storing the experiences of the daytime. And **ecological hypotheses** are to do with the functions of sleep concerned with the survival of the species and its relationships with other organisms.

Horne (1988) conducted an extensive literature review, and came to the conclusion that there was little evidence for physiological hypotheses with respect to sleep. Although there are a great many physical restorative processes which take place while we are asleep – digestion, protein synthesis, removal of waste products from the body's systems, and so on – these will work just as well

when the body is simply relaxing and resting. If we have had a particularly demanding day, physically, we may fall asleep more quickly, but we do not seem to sleep for much longer than we would do normally (Horne and Minard, 1985). HERE IS some evidence that extreme physical exertion might increase sleep time slightly: Shapiro et al. (1980) studied people the day that they had run a marathon, and found that they slept less well the night after their race, because of aching muscles, but that they did sleep a bit longer on the next three nights.

However, when it comes to brain functioning, Horne's review of the literature showed that there do seem to be some quite extensive psychological reasons for sleeping. Sleep-deprivation studies indicate a range of effects, which in human beings can go as far as some of the more extreme symptoms of schizophrenia, and in animals can even produce death. During the Cultural Revolution in China, when Mao decreed that birds were enemies of the people because they stole grain, the entire population began a continuous scaring of the birds through an incessant banging and noise-making, day and night. At the end of the two-day period, the sparrows fell dead off the trees. Similarly, Rechtshaffen et al. (1983) showed that prolonged sleep deprivation led to rat deaths. It seems likely that the greater survival of humans derives from the fact that they were volunteers and largely informed about the study, which allowed them to control their stress levels better.

Hartmann (1984) suggested that non-REM and REM sleep serve different functions in the organism. In particular, Hartmann argued that non-REM sleep is particularly associated with physical restoration: the amount of non-REM sleep in a typical night has been shown to increase after strenuous physical exercise. It is possible that this might be what we are feeling when we talk of 'sleeping better' after a day walking in the open air. On the other hand, Hartmann argued, REM sleep is more necessary for psychological restoration. During periods of heightened tension, such as when they are premenstrual or after stressful life-events, many people show increased levels of REM sleep. It is possible that the explanation for this is directly concerned with what is going on when we are dreaming.

Ecological hypotheses of sleeping are often linked with evolutionary arguments about the need for sleep. Some researchers, such as Webb

(1974), argue that sleep is a kind of mini-hiberna-
tion, in which the basic processes of hibernation
are mimicked by the body – lowered metabolic
rate, blood pressure, body temperature. Many
mammals hibernate during winter months when
food is scarce, which has a clear function of saving
body resources and conserving heat energy. It
makes evolutionary sense to consider that this
type of ability is likely to have evolved gradually –
indeed, many animals such as squirrels and bears
wake frequently during the winter – and the evolutionary theory of sleep proposes that, effectively,
hibernation is a particularly deep, long-lasting
form of sleep.

Active and quiet sleep

One of the problems with describing REM sleep
simply as dreaming sleep comes from the fact that
both animals and foetuses show REM sleep. Stern,
Parmelee and Harris (1973) showed that foetuses
have periods of EEG activity which indicate waking, quiet sleep and active sleep. Moreover, they
show regular patterns as they alternate between
the three, and the patterns in a 36-week-old foetus are similar to those of an eight-month-old
infant. Active sleep seems to be important for
babies. new-born babies spend between 70% and
90% of their sleeping time in active sleep. This
gradually declines to something in the region of
20% – 25% of their sleeping time, during their
first year after birth.

Birds and mammals also show both active and
quiet sleep. They alternate between these two
while sleeping, as humans do. Some researchers
have taken this to imply that this shows that quiet
sleep evolved first, and that active sleep is a relatively recently-evolved phenomenon which
evolved only in warm-blooded animals. But other
researchers disagree with this argument, on the
grounds that the evidence that other animals do
not have active sleep is less clear-cut.

Meddis (1977) argued that cold-blooded animals have slower metabolic rates than warm-
blooded animals do, and therefore would show less
obvious changes in EEG and eye-movement patterns. In reality, Meddis stated, it is quiet sleep
which is more likely to have evolved later, because
of the demands of temperature regulation in
warm-blooded animals. Temperature regulation is
a significant feature of quiet sleep, but is unimportant for reptiles, fish and amphibia. This also,
Meddis argued, might explain why active sleep

seems to precede quiet sleep in foetuses: for the
initial growth and development of the foetus, it is
active sleep which is important, but as it develops
its internal organs and system of temperature regulation, quiet sleep becomes more necessary, and
so its incidence increases.

These two different views of the evolution of
active and quiet sleep are not easily resolved. Stern
and Morgane (1974) showed that, at least in adult
mammals, active sleep seems to require a period of
quiet sleep first, which might suggest that the
quiet sleep preceded active sleep in evolutionary
terms. But this pattern is in mature mammals only,
and so it might be a later adaptation, and not really be reflecting a basic evolutionary link.

On the other hand, Czeisler et al. (1980)
showed that sleep and body temperature were
closely correlated. By studying sleep patterns in
people who had spent months in isolation with
no indication of the time of day, Czeisler found
that their body temperature could be used to predict how long they were likely to sleep. People
who fell asleep when their body temperature was
low would sleep for seven or eight hours, but if
they fell asleep when body temperature was high,
they might sleep for up to fifteen hours, or even
more. But to say that body temperature and sleep
are connected is not the same as saying that quiet
sleep evolved for temperature regulation. we
would need much more evidence before we could
accept one or the other of these hypotheses.

Sleep disorders

There are a number of abnormalities of sleep,
which can result in considerable discomfort for
someone who is experiencing them. Perhaps the
best known of these is the sleep disorder known as
insomnia, in which people experience difficulty
getting to sleep or remaining asleep. Insomnia can
arise for many reasons, but is frequently associated
with physiological states of anxiety and tension.
Often, identifying the source of the tension can
resolve the insomnia. Most people will experience
a certain degree of insomnia before or during
particularly stressful times. For example, the period
before a house-moving is commonly associated
with insomnia, as is the period before exams.
Systematic attention to stress management
techniques can often deal with this quite
successfully.

There are three types of insomnia (see Table
11.5), but these really only describe when it takes

Table 11.5 Types of insomnia

Onset insomnia	This occurs when people have difficulty getting to sleep.
Maintenance insomnia	This occurs when people have difficulty staying asleep, and wake up frequently during the night.
Termination insomnia	This occurs when people wake up early and are unable to get back to sleep again.

Table 11.6 Symptoms of narcolepsy

1 Gradual or sudden attacks of sleepiness during the day.

2 Cataplexy – sudden muscle weakness during waking, often set off by strong emotions.

3 Sleep paralysis – an inability to move while falling asleep or waking up.

4 Hypnagogic hallucinations – dreaming states at the onset of sleep which the person finds it hard to distinguish from wakefulness.

place. Interestingly, though, there is some evidence that insomniacs actually sleep far more than they believe that they do. Kales and Kales (1984) found that, from EEG records, people who claimed that they had spent most of the night awake actually slept for most of the time. However, they seemed to have dreamed that they were awake, and subjectively reported that they felt extremely tired.

Sleep apnea is a respiratory disorder in which the person suddenly ceases to breathe while they are asleep. Something between 10% and 15% of adults experience periods of sleep apnea, which can last for as long as ten seconds. Those with extreme apnea, however, can wake up panicking, and gasping for breath. As a result, their sleeping patterns are seriously disturbed, and the person does not experience a restful night – even though they often do not actually recall waking up during the night.

Drug withdrawal is another common source of sleep disturbance. People who take barbiturates and tranquillisers regularly can come to induce a physiological dependence, which means that they experience withdrawal when they do not take them. As a result, their bodies go into a state of heightened arousal, which prevents them from being able to fall asleep. Often, this produces a vicious cycle, in which the person then takes more of the drugs in order to fall asleep again, and so heightens their dependency.

Narcolepsy is a relatively rare condition, affecting about one person in a thousand, which appears to run in families. Essentially, a narcoleptic is liable to fall asleep unexpectedly during the day. Narcolepsy has four common symptoms, which

are listed in Table 11.6. It seems to be associated with the intrusion of REM sleep into wakefulness (each of these symptoms, such as muscle paralysis, vivid dreaming etc. is associated with REM sleep). The drugs which are used to suppress narcolepsy are also ones which reduce REM sleep, which also implies that there is a connection between the two.

Most people experience **cataplexy** – muscle paralysis – while they are in REM sleep. However, those people who have what is known as **REM behaviour disorder** appear to be suffering from a problem which means that cataplexy is suppressed. As a result, they act out their dreams, perhaps punching or kicking about, and sometimes injuring themselves or others. In animals, this disorder seems to be associated with damage to the pons and midbrain, where the brain cells which inhibit motor activity are located. It is speculated that a similar mechanism may be at work with human beings.

Dreaming

Everybody dreams during the course of the night, although some people claim that they never do. This seems to be because they have no recollection of having dreamed when they wake up. Dement and Kleitman (1957) conducted a study in which people were woken up during the course of the night. They showed that whether we recall dreams or not seems to depend on whether we wake up out of dreaming or non-dreaming sleep: if someone is woken up out of a non-dreaming sleep phase, then they do not have any recollection of having dreamed, but if they are woken up out of REM sleep, then they are likely to recall their dreams.

Dreams, as we know, are fascinating things, and explaining dreaming has been a major preoccupation of human cultures for as far back as we can possibly know. Some cultures, such as the Native Australian cultures, have taken such understandings to a fine art, and have developed the skills of exploring within dreams as well as describing them after they have happened. Such dream exploration is known as **lucid dreaming** – the person concerned knows that they are dreaming, and, with practice, can learn to influence the content of the dream directly.

Dement and Wolpert (1958) showed that we are not totally unaware of the external world while we are dreaming. They sprayed sleepers lightly with cold water when they were in REM sleep. After a while, they woke the sleepers up and asked them what they had been dreaming about. Almost all of them had experienced dreams associated with water in some way, such as walking in the rain or being in the shower. So the real stimulus of the water had been incorporated into the dream, but not exactly as it was experienced. Like many other aspects of things which can appear while we are dreaming, it occurred in a disguised form.

Lucid dreaming is rather different from that kind of experience, because the essence of lucid dreaming is that the person is aware that they are dreaming, at the time that they are having the dream. Sleep researchers have shown that these types of dreams have several characteristics which are different from ordinary, non-lucid dreams. Table 11.7 (see page 264) lists some of those differences. Not everyone experiences lucid dreams, but Green and McCreery (1994) discussed how conscious attempts to become aware of dreams – for example, trying to recognise illogical events as odd, or getting into the habit of regularly asking whether an experience might be a dream – are often successful in inducing lucid dreams.

Hearne (1981a) used a different method. He reported a series of experiments with lucid dreaming, in which people learned to control their own dreams by being made aware that they were dreaming. Hearne's studies involved people spending the night in a special laboratory, where their REM activity could be observed. When REM began, the research participants were given an external signal (a very mild electrical buzz to the wrist) to tell them that they had entered REM sleep. As a result, they became aware that they were dreaming.

Table 11.7 Differences between lucid and non-lucid dreams

1 Lucid dreams show little difference between manifest content and the latent content: unlike ordinary dreams, they do not seem to use symbolism to disguise their meanings.

2 The dreamer feels in control of events during lucid dreams, but feels passive or unable to control ordinary dreams.

3 Lucid dreamers are able to reflect on, and think about, what they are doing at the time they are dreaming it.

4 Lucid dreamers are able to use imagination during the dream, and to think about other things as well as the immediate situation.

5 Lucid dreams appear to be much more memorable than ordinary dreams: details are retained more easily when the dreamer wakes up.

Source: Green and McCreery, 1994

We move our eye-muscles while we are dreaming, even though the rest of the body is passive. Schatzmann, Worsley and Fenwick (1988) found that participants' eye movements corresponded with their subjective experience – when a lucid dreamer dreamed he was drawing a triangle on the wall, his eyes moved in a corresponding triangular direction. Moreover, researchers found that people who were having lucid dreams were able to control their movements voluntarily – by agreeing on a prearranged set of eye-movement signals, Hearne's research participants were even able to let the experimenters know something of the content of what they were experiencing. They developed a special code for common dream events, like flying, and for signalling 'yes' or 'no' in response to questions.

One of the most interesting things about lucid dreams is the way that dreamers report that they can, at least partially, control them. But Hearne (1981b) reported that attempts to control the dream have to be plausible: there is no point in trying to make impossible things happen, because it simply will not work. Even certain plausible things, like turning lights on, can be tricky. And lucid dreams do not lend themselves to unrestricted fantasy either: Green and McCreery (1994) found that lucid dreamers experienced powerful inhibitions against injuring either the self or others, even when they tried hard, on the grounds that they knew it was a dream, so it was safe. They found that they were almost entirely unable to damage other people physically, or to injure themselves.

One of the very few exceptions to this was a case of a woman who reported attacking someone at a dinner party. However, the dream made it clear that the incident was a symbolic defence of her personal values: the woman who was attacked had appeared to symbolise a particularly cold and inhuman version of psychology, and the dreamer's attack was in defence of a more humanistic stance. As the dream continued, the person she had attacked reappeared, smiling, and they embraced fondly. So this example has more to do with expressing symbolic conflicts, than with direct aggression against another person.

Lucid dreamers also report difficulties with some other aspects of dream control. One of these concerns reading text: when the dreamer tries to read something, they may seem successful at first, but if they return to it they find that the text has changed, or is now just a set of hieroglyphics. Doing arithmetical or mathematical exercises can also be unusually difficult, and some researchers, notably Green and McCleery, used this to argue that lucid dreaming must involve a high level of right-hemisphere activity. But their arguments rest on an assumption that the two hemispheres of the brain have entirely opposing functions, whereas, as we saw in Chapter 10, their functions are not as separate as all that. Other researchers, notably Cohen (1979) argue that, if anything, lucid dreaming is a left-hemisphere activity, so the question of what is actually happening during a lucid dream is still wide open. But then, so is the question of what is actually happening during an ordinary dream. What lucid dream researchers do seem to agree on, though, is that the experience of lucid dreaming appears to be extremely refreshing to people who do it. There is no evidence that controlled lucid dreaming is any less effective, in terms of sleep or mental rest, than ordinary dreaming, and many researchers argue that it is, if anything, an improvement.

Freud's theory of dreaming

There have been a number of explanations put forward as to why people dream. Perhaps the most well known of these is the theory put forward by Freud, of dreaming as unconscious wish-fulfilment; but other researchers have taken very different views.

Freud (1901) asserted that, during dreaming, the unconscious mind comes to the surface, and expresses its needs and wishes. In order to ensure that the ego is not directly threatened by these, however, these needs and wishes appear in a disguised form. Freud saw dreams as consisting almost entirely of hidden meanings and symbolism. He referred to items and events in the dream as the **manifest content**, whereas the hidden meanings of the dream were its **latent content**. The unconscious, Freud believed, converts latent content to manifest content through a process which he referred to as **dreamwork**.

Since Freud considered that the human unconscious was fundamentally centred on sexual energies, he interpreted most dream symbolism in terms of hidden sexual content. There are, however, a number of ways of interpreting this. One is that, even if Freud's interpretations were valid, a preoccupation with sex would have been expected in the very sexually repressed Victorian period when Freud was developing his theory. (Of course, not all sectors of Victorian society were sexually repressed, but Freud was dealing with members of the middle classes, where sexual repression was a major feature of everyday life.)

It seems quite possible, therefore, that many of Freud's patients were expressing unconscious sexual wishes in their dreams, but this does not necessarily mean that the same would hold true today. A society in which eating had to be done in private and was never talked about would be likely to produce people who had dreams about eating – and if the social prohibition were strong enough, those dreams might involve symbolism and hidden implications rather than straightforward examples of eating, so as not to cause the person too much anxiety!

Many researchers, however, seriously doubt the interpretation which Freud placed on his patients' dreams and anxieties. Schatzman (1992) argued that Freud's own accounts of his therapeutic work contradicted one another – the early reports were quite different from Freud's later accounts of the same work. These differences, Schatzman pointed out, suggested that Freud may have been over-interpreting what his patients reported to him. A further, but related, problem of the Freudian approach to dream analysis is that analysing dreams is always retrospective: the person has the dream first, and then looks for a meaning – and most dreams are so complex that almost any meaning can be found in them if you are prepared to be imaginative enough. So although Freud's theory of dreams is an interesting one, it does not lend itself very well to scientific investigation.

Dreaming as forgetting

An alternative approach to dreaming was proposed by Crick and Mitchison, in 1983. Instead of dreaming being something which expresses unconscious wishes or desires, Crick and Mitchison suggested that dreaming is an almost accidental by-product of neuronal brain activity. They argued that, during the day, the brain encounters a myriad sensory impressions and makes numerous spontaneous memory associations. Taken together, these represent a massive sensory overload for the mind. As we sleep, the brain sifts through these sensory impressions and discards them. The process of doing so means that neural circuits are activated, and we accidentally re-experience some of those experiences and associations. According to Crick and Mitchison, then, we dream as much to forget things as for any other reason.

Certainly there does seem to be some evidence that dreaming is associated with psychological restoration. Hartmann (1984) found that women who were suffering from premenstrual tension engage in more REM sleep than they do at different times of their menstrual cycle, and suggested that this is a response to the higher level of psychological stress which they have at such times. Hartmann also found that psychiatric patients seemed to have very high levels of REM sleep, by comparison with similar individuals who were not undergoing psychiatric treatment. But we cannot really say whether such observations support the Crick and Mitchison view or not, since there are so many alternative reasons why such people may dream more. Perhaps, for instance, dreaming is associated with psychological restoration because it helps people to come to terms with their problems: a view expressed in the next theory that we will look at.

Dreaming as making sense of experiences

Evans (1984) took a different view. Evans also saw dreaming as providing a mechanism by which the brain can sort through the sensory impressions and other kinds of information that it has received during the day. But, unlike Crick and Mitchison, who suggested that we do this in order to forget it, Evans suggested that dreaming allows the brain to reorganise this information, and so helps us to sort it out and make sense of it. Moreover, by bringing up associations with previous fragments of knowledge, the brain is also able to organise memory storage so that similar themes are linked together.

This model seems to be quite a useful one, if only because it makes sense of a number of features of sleeping which are familiar in everyday life. For example, it is well known that it often helps to sleep on a problem, because by the time you wake up, a solution has often occurred to you, or at the least the problem often seems much clearer than it was before. If, during the time that you are dreaming, your brain is sorting information and linking it with other things that you know, then it is easy to see how this could happen. (Of course, it may equally well be an effect of mood: it may help to sleep on a problem because we rarely see the positive sides of things when we are tired.)

Evans's theory of dreaming may also link with the unconscious problem-solving that seems to be such a feature of creative thinking. For example, the chemist Kekulé reported that he was able to identify the ring-like structure of benzene molecules after dreaming of a snake entwined in a continuous loop, so that it seemed to be eating its own tail. When he woke up, he realised that the idea of a continuous ring could make sense out of his puzzling experimental data. Although it had been in a disguised form, he was sure that the dream had somehow been telling him the answer to his problem.

This theory may also provide us with an explanation of why we are more likely to have bad dreams when we are troubled. Partly, of course, we are likely to sleep more restlessly because the baseline state of arousal which we are experiencing will be higher (see Chapter 13), and this will make us more sensitive to extraneous stimuli or disturbances. But also this model suggests that the brain will be trying unconsciously to work out solutions to our difficulties: re-running scripts to try to find alternative options or aspects of the problem that have been ignored. In cases where a solution can be found, as we have seen, we may wake up feeling refreshed and knowing what to do; but where problems are deeper and more serious, the brain's unconscious efforts may simply result in frustration, reflected in nightmares or bad dreams.

Hypnosis

Some psychologists have argued that hypnosis represents a special state of consciousness – although, as we shall see, not everyone agrees. In the late eighteenth century, Franz Mesmer produced some spectacular public demonstrations of what he referred to as 'animal magnetism'. This, he believed, originated from invisible influences flowing like fluids from the hypnotist to the research participant, and making the latter obedient to the will of the former. Mesmer was one of the first people to popularise the phenomenon of **hypnosis**, and for many years it was referred to as **mesmerism** after him.

In the nineteenth century, the French neurologist Charcot discovered that hypnosis could be a valuable therapeutic technique in the condition known as hysteria – an apparently intractable condition, often very painful, which seemed to affect many women of that time. Freud spent some time studying under Charcot, and frequently used hypnotic techniques in his early work. Charcot believed that what occurred during the hypnotic state was symptomatic of an underlying neurological disturbance in the patient. Freud himself went on to suggest that hypnosis was a form of partial regression, in which the individual person goes back to a more infantile state, and therefore escapes from the controls imposed on the psyche by the ego. This formed part of Freud's theory of human personality, which we looked at in Chapter 7.

Since then, hypnosis has taken hold of the public imagination. It has been dramatised by stage magicians, used as pivot concepts for dramatic thrillers, and even used to 'uncover' forgotten memories. But in the process, hypnotic phenomena have been fictionalised and exaggerated, until the image of hypnosis presented by films, stage magicians and the like bears no resemblance to the real thing. The 'Hollywood theory' of hypnosis, as represented in films and less realistic fiction, suggests that: (1) people who are hypnotised are totally under the control of the hypnotist; (2) they can be made to do things which they would never do in their normal state – even to the extent of committing murder; and (3) people can be hypnotised against their will.

None of these is true. People co-operate voluntarily with their hypnotist even while they are hypnotised; they cannot be made to act against their own consciences; and they cannot be hypnotised without their co-operation.

So, having settled what hypnosis is not, we can move on to what psychologists think it is. The two main schools of thought about hypnosis are discussed in Box 11.1 on page 346. But perhaps the first point to make is that susceptibility to hypnosis is much less inevitable than people think. In 1965, Hilgard performed a study involving 533 university students, to assess their susceptibility to hypnosis. They were asked to undertake various tasks, ranging from relatively straightforward ones, like closing the eyes after staring continuously at a target and being told that they were getting sleepy, to more complex ones, like post-hypnotic visual hallucinations. The first session showed that only about one-quarter of the students responded as if they were deeply hypnotised, and only 5% or so achieved the maximum score. Most people tended to respond only to those tasks which will work whether someone is hypnotised or not, such as swaying backwards when standing with one's eyes closed.

Hypnotic phenomena

If we are to evaluate the two explanations for hypnosis – whether it is a special state of consciousness or a powerful response to social cues and suggestion – we need to investigate some of the main hypnotic phenomena, and see what systematic research (as opposed to stage magic) has shown. Hypnotic phenomena can be classified into five groups, listed in Table 11.8. We will look at whether the psychological evidence for these indicates that hypnosis is a special, distinctive form of consciousness.

Unexpected abilities

The alternative explanation for these phenomena is the fact that people usually under-estimate their capabilities to an astounding degree, and what the stage hypnotist actually does is put them in a situation where they do not have any doubts about it. Morris *et al*. (1993) discussed how stage hypnotists are very skilled at selecting those individuals who are most likely to comply with their requests. Most people prefer to be co-operative rather than confrontational, and there are unconscious signals

Table 11.8 Types of hypnotic phenomena

Unexpected abilities
A favourite trick of stage hypnotists is to get people doing things which the people themselves are surprised at, and would not have believed possible.

Hypnotic memory
A second group of hypnotic phenomena concerns hypnotic memory, in which the person seems to be either able or unable to retrieve memories from a hypnotised state. In **post-hypnotic amnesia**, people appear to 'forget' and to 'remember' on command.

Pain control
Other psychologists have investigated how hypnosis helps people to control pain. Hypnotic techniques have been shown to provide considerable relief to patients in a variety of clinical settings, including pain relief, the treatment of skin diseases like warts, and anxiety conditions like asthma.

Hypnotic reincarnation
A fourth set of hypnotic phenomena concerns **age regression**. Sometimes, hypnotised research participants appear to be able to go back to earlier lives. They produce very specific and detailed memories, and are often described as having had absolutely no access to that information in their current life.

The hidden observer
The fifth category of research into hypnosis concerns the matter of the **hidden observer**. Hypnotised research participants, or research participants who believe that they have been hypnotised, frequently report that, although they were complying with the hypnotist's requests, another part of their mind was dispassionately observing what was going on. That part was aware of what they were doing and objectively critical of it. But it did not affect what they did: they still conformed to the wishes of the hypnotist.

which particularly co-operative people give as they watch the magician on stage. Stage hypnotists have trained themselves to be particularly sensitive to these signals.

In a typical stage show, the hypnotist will begin by conducting a small exercise in which all the audience participates, and which gives the hypnotist hints as to who to choose from the audience. On stage, there is usually a further selection process (disguised as an exhibition of the power of hypnosis) allowing the hypnotist to pick out the most suggestible individuals. These people are anxious to comply with the magician, even though

they do not realise it – they have been chosen for that reason. So it is not altogether surprising that the hypnotists can produce such dramatic results.

There has been some interesting research on simulated hypnotism, in which non-hypnotisable research participants were asked to act as if they were hypnotised. Orne (1979) showed that these people show some differences from 'normal' hypnotised research participants, in terms of their **trance-logic** – the credibility of their performance. For example: if hypnotised people are told that they cannot see a chair in front of them, they will still tend to walk round it. But simulators tend to bump into it.

Similarly, Nogrady et al. (1983) showed that people simulating hypnosis, if asked to 'regress' to childhood, would write like children and spell incorrectly. Hypnotised research participants, on the other hand, write complex adult sentences, although they still report feeling like a child. In other words, people who are only pretending to be hypnotised actually produce a more credible response than those who are 'truly' hypnotised! And that response often seems to reveal unexpected abilities.

Hypnotic memory

In 1961, Hilgard *et al.* showed that highly suggestible individuals tend to be particularly good at post-hypnotic amnesia. In this study, research participants were asked to forget events which occurred during a hypnosis session, until they were given a pre-arranged signal from the hypnotist. About one-quarter of their student sample forgot more than 14 items out of a possible 20, but recalled them when they were given the signal.

An alternative explanation for these findings, though, is **motivation**. Wagstaff (1981) suggested that what actually happens in post-hypnotic amnesia is that the research participants try not to remember. This involves a number of strategies, like thinking about something else, deliberately withholding the information so as not to 'spoil the experiment', or making no effort to think back over what happened. Wagstaff also found that there would still be **interference** between two lists, even when research participants claimed to have 'forgotten' one of them. Words from the apparently forgotten list interfered with memory for words from the other list. If the list had really been forgotten, that would not happen.

Box 11.1 Theories of hypnosis

There are two modern schools of thought about hypnosis. On one side are those psychologists who believe that the phenomenon of hypnosis represents an altered state of consciousness. **State theorists** see hypnosis as a special condition, giving access to hidden parts of the mind. The alternative view is that hypnosis is not in itself a special state of awareness, but that it can be explained by social psychological phenomena. Members of this school of thought – **non-state theorists** – argue that all the observed phenomena of hypnosis can be understood by looking at how people operate psychologically in social situations.

The state theory of hypnosis

One of the main proponents of the state theory of hypnosis is Hilgard (1977), who proposed a model of hypnotism in which he described the mind, or consciousness, as being organised into vertical columns, or segments. Hilgard argued that these vertical divisions in the mind channel our awareness and our memories. We cannot usually cross over between these columns consciously, because of amnesiac barriers – if we are in one column, then we will have forgotten about the others. But, according to Hilgard, when someone enters a state of hypnosis, they become able to tap more than one of these columns of awareness.

Much of Hilgard's argument rests on the concept of the hidden observer. This is a distinctive phenomenon of hypnosis, which is the way that a part of our awareness remains independent, even if we are deeply hypnotised. This part of awareness – the hidden observer – is conscious, rational and to some extent critical of the person's actions. It may also be contacted through, for example, the person being asked to write while their attention is concentrated on something else.

Studies of the hidden observer in hypnosis are central to Hilgard's model of hypnosis – in fact, it was Hilgard (1977) who originated the term. He argued that the hidden observer represents a column of consciousness that is observing and commenting on the experience of another part of the mind – that which is in the hypnotic state. In Hilgard's view, hypnosis allows the individual to move between different columns or sections of the mind, when instructed to do so by the hypnotist.

For example: in one study, research participants were asked to immerse their hands in ice-cold water (a very painful experience). They were then hypnotised, told they would not feel any pain, and asked to repeat the action. When they were asked out loud if they felt any pain, they reported that they did not. But the written record of what was going on produced by the hidden observer, reported that the experience was very painful indeed. Hilgard explained this in terms of the hidden observer having access to a different column of consciousness from the hypnotised part of the research participant's mind. There are, however, other ways of explaining these phenomena.

Non-state approaches to hypnosis

Non-state theories of hypnosis point out that the full range of hypnotic phenomena can be explained without reference to special altered states of consciousness. They do not dispute evidence that people may become 'hypnotised', or that hypnosis can relieve pain. But they consider that the phenomena concerned can be explained more simply and parsimoniously using social psychological factors like role, compliance, expectancies, attitudes, imagination and relaxation.

All of these have their place in explaining hypnosis. Concepts about roles and role expectations come into play in the kind of hypnotic situation where people undertake tasks which they had not previously believed possible. Compliance features in the area of retrieving hidden memories, where the individual is trying to comply with the perceived demands of their situation. **Expectancies** and relaxation are major factors in explaining how hypnosis appears to be able to control pain. And **imagination** and attitude are major factors in the explanation of 'reincarnation' through hypnosis. Non-state theorists argue that the hidden observer phenomenon can be also explained through social psychological constructs of compliance, expectancy and self-attribution.

• • • •▶

Some researchers, then, retain a belief that hypnosis is, in fact, a special state of consciousness. Other theorists are more equivocal; and all we can really say at this stage is that the evidence is uncertain. Interestingly, the question of whether hypnosis does really exist as a special state has not been investigated directly. Studies of hypnosis give results which are open to both kinds of interpretation. It may be that there really is a special state of hypnosis: nobody can tell for sure. But the argument of the non-state theorists is not really about that. Rather, they are saying that we can explain all the observed hypnotic phenomena quite adequately, using our existing knowledge of social psychological mechanisms. We do not need to invoke a special state to explain them.

We do know, though, that despite extensive physiological tests there is no evidence for any special physiological state associated with hypnosis (Sarbin and Slagle, 1972). The evidence for the social phenomenon of hypnosis, however, is much clearer. It is certainly true that people can convince themselves that they have been hypnotised, and it is certainly the case that, when people enter the hypnotic situation, they will act as if they were hypnotised.

Of course, if we just take a behavioural perspective, the end result is the same. Many chronic and acute pain sufferers could not care less whether hypnosis is a special state or not – the demonstrable fact is that their pain can be relieved using hypnotic techniques, and that is what really matters! It certainly appears that using these techniques allows us to access psychological mechanisms which are both therapeutically and socially valuable.

Hypnosis has been used for some time in America to aid police investigations. Some people, and particularly those who use it, believe that it allows details to appear that are not normally accessible to everyday memory. This relies on a theory of memory which suggests that memory works like a factual tape-recorder, and all we need to do is to find the right part of the tape. But as we saw in Chapter 3, memory does not work like that: it is an active, constructive process, not a factual tape-recording. Gibson (1982) argued that using hypnosis in police investigations should be regarded as equivalent to tampering with evidence, since people in a hypnotic state are notoriously suggestible and often create memories in order to co-operate with the social expectations of the police.

It appears, too, that research participants reporting hypnotically constructed memories are actually more convincing to juries than people reporting factual experiences. As they convince themselves, they become very persuasive about the accuracy of the statement they are making. Ever since Bartlett's study of serial reproduction (see Chapter 3), psychologists have shown how people will produce plausible stories rather than incomplete accounts. The stories make sense in terms of their knowledge of the situation, but do not necessarily accord with the facts.

It seems, then, that it is possible to explain hypnotic memory phenomena using two psychological constructs: willingness to comply with the hypnotist's expectations, and the use of imagination to construct a plausible account of what is going on. Both of these are common psychological events. So non-state theorists (psychologists who do not believe that hypnosis is a special state of consciousness) feel that this is a perfectly adequate explanation for what is going on.

Pain control

There is a considerable amount of wide-ranging and clear evidence that hypnosis can be very helpful in controlling pain (Wadden and Anderton, 1982). Few psychologists would dispute this. What they do dispute is the mechanism by which hypnosis works to achieve these results. State theorists argue that hypnotised research participants feel less pain because they are in a special state of consciousness. But non-state theorists argue that hypnotised research participants are tapping into pain control mechanisms which are also accessible in other ways. Of course, for a clinician using these techniques, or a patient whose pain is being relieved, these debates are irrelevant – if the pain goes, it goes, and that is what matters most.

Subjective pain is very susceptible to the expectancies and beliefs that people have about it.

It is almost always enhanced by anxiety, for example, but relaxation and anxiety-reduction are a major feature of hypnotherapeutic treatment. In fact, hypnotherapy aimed at the relief of chronic pain is directly aimed to improve relaxation and reduce anxiety. Non-state theorists believe that this is why they are effective.

Wagstaff (1987) pointed out that patients who are given hypnosis for operations, for example, are very carefully chosen. Medical evidence suggests that local anaesthetics could be used for many operations. This does not happen, because patients, understandably, become very anxious about major surgery and do not want to be conscious while they are undergoing it. But internal organs do not sense pain from incision (although they are sensitive to being pulled about). Most of the pain associated with operations comes from cutting through the skin, and this can be controlled by local anaesthetics. There have been relatively few cases of major operations undertaken by hypnosis, but the few operations which have used it have also included local anaesthetics.

So, according to Wagstaff, there are two reasons why hypnotism can produce an apparent absence of pain in patients undergoing operations: first, the local anaesthetic, which reduces the pain anyway; and second, the patients' belief that they have been hypnotised. This produces an expectation that they will not feel pain, which in turn lessens the state of anxiety. Since the anxiety is lower, the pain is lower, and the person can accept the treatment quite comfortably.

Most modern hypnotherapists teach their clients how to enter a hypnotic state by themselves. **Autohypnosis** – also known as self-hypnosis – can be a valuable therapeutic tool, and many psychologists regard it as the best way of using hypnotism therapeutically. It has been shown to be helpful in all sorts of situations, ranging from giving up smoking to dealing with traumatic life-events.

Bliss (1980) showed that a high susceptibility to hypnotism is characteristic of patients suffering from **multiple personality disorder**. These people have generally experienced extremely traumatic events in their early childhoods, ranging from deliberate murder attempts, to mutilation or other forms of severe abuse. Their 'other' personalities develop to help them to cope with this. Several of the patients treated by Bliss described how they had discovered autohypnosis – or something very

similar – as children. Rosenhan and Seligman (1984) suggest that multiple personality is actually formed through self-hypnosis, as the child attempts to cope with severe trauma. The new personality relieves the emotional stress, so the child produces further personalities to cope with other stressful events.

Hypnotic reincarnation

Sadly, accounts of hypnotic **reincarnation** tend to be highly sensationalised, and important details are frequently omitted or changed when they are reported in the popular press. When these cases are studied in more detail, they often turn out to be much less persuasive than they seemed. For one thing, almost always the people concerned are misreported as having had less access to prior information than they really had.

One very famous case concerned a woman who remembered an earlier life in York, although she was supposed never to have been to York in her life. In fact she had previously worked in York library. Another example was of a man who believed he had been a member of Nelson's navy. The account was reported to be sprinkled with nautical terms to which the man would not normally have had access. However, when the case was fully investigated, it turned out that every single one of the terms was available in the popular Captain Hornblower stories, which he had read as a child (Wagstaff, 1981).

Similarly, the many apparently plausible reconstructed accounts from mediaeval York or Roman Britain generally show serious anomalies, which are rarely included in reports of the phenomenon. One woman who believed she had been living in Roman Britain reconstructed a plan of the villa in which she had 'lived'. However, the type of villa that she drew, although common in Rome, did not occur in Britain, where Roman villas were built to a different layout. This detail cast considerable doubt on the plausibility of her account. Other such accounts have shown similar anomalies.

Wilson and Barber (1983) investigated people's abilities to produce interesting and plausible accounts from **age progression** rather than age regression. In these studies, research participants were invited to project themselves forward into the future and to imagine what would constitute an ordinary life. They found a strong correlation between research participants who could produce

plausible 'future' accounts, and research participants who could produce plausible accounts from
'regressing' into the past. They suggested that these
people might be examples of the fantasy-prone
personality. They were good at inventing detail,
and particularly susceptible to suggestions,
whether they were made under hypnosis or not.

The hidden observer

Spanos and Hewitt (1980) argue that the phenomenon of the hidden observer can be explained
using our knowledge of the social mechanisms
involved in compliance, obedience and self-attribution. For example: when someone agrees to
participate in an undertaking with a hypnotist,
they see it as a kind of **social contract**, and their
co-operation and compliance is expected. In a
public demonstration, on a stage, they feel that
failing to comply would be letting down the hypnotist, or making themselves look silly. So the
social pressures to comply are very strong.

In 1962, Orne conducted a series of research
studies which were originally designed to see if it
was possible to distinguish between people who
were really hypnotised and people who were just
pretending. Orne was trying to find a task which
ordinary people would not do, but hypnotised
people would. He hit on the idea of asking people
to add up long strings of numbers, and then to
tear up the paper and throw it in the bin. This, he
thought, was a task which nobody would comply
with voluntarily. If people were asked to do it,
casually, they would do it once or twice, and then
refuse to do it any more.

However, when Orne told them that they were
taking part in a psychological study, he found that
people would carry on with the task for hours on
end. One research participant carried on nonstop
for six hours, and in the end had to be stopped by
the experimenter, who wanted to go home! The
study shows the power of social expectations in
determining human behaviour. The **demand
characteristics** of the situation were such that the
research participants produced quite unexpected
behaviour, which was not at all typical of what
they would do normally. They wanted to co-operate with the experimenter and to give the 'right'
answer. Agreeing to go on stage with a hypnotist,
Orne argued, has many of the same demand characteristics.

Many people, when they are interviewed after
hypnosis, report that they deliberately complied

with the experimenter, so as not to 'spoil things'
for them. During the experience, they feel completely normal, and are aware of what they are
doing. Hilgard argued that this was a separate 'hidden observer', or another 'column' of consciousness, but Spanos (1982) argued that people feel
like this because they really are completely normal. It is normal for human beings to avoid
unpleasant confrontations, which is why people
tend to comply in a social situation of that kind.
Spanos argued that we constantly underestimate
the power of social conformity, social expectations
and demand characteristics when we are apprais-
ing events of this kind.

The second variable that needs to be taken into
account in explaining the hidden observer phenomenon concerns people's beliefs about themselves. Some people, as we have seen, do not
believe that they have been hypnotised, but comply because they do not want to 'spoil it' for the
hypnotist. Others, however, believe very strongly
that they have been hypnotised. Belief in the state
of hypnosis is very common, both within the professions and among the general population. Given
that, and the relative lack of knowledge that people have about the power of social expectation, it
is not surprising that people look for external
explanations for their behaviour, particularly when
they find themselves undertaking tasks they did
not expect to do, or putting themselves in unexpected situations.

The search for explanation means that people
will create a **self-attribution**, explaining their
odd behaviour to themselves as being 'because
they were hypnotised'. This self-attribution
strengthens their faith in hypnosis, so they
attempt to convince others accordingly. But
believing that you have been hypnotised is not
really very good evidence that you actually have
been. Self-attribution can be a major factor in
explaining both the prevalence of belief in
hypnotism, and how people augment or exaggerate their compliance to the social demands of the
hypnotic situation.

As we can see, then, the evidence can be construed in either way; but many psychologists tend
to think that it is not really a special state.
Ornstein (1986) argued that what the phenomena
associated with hypnosis really show us is that we
are far more capable of controlling our experience
and our physiology than is normally thought. And
in this respect, what we call hypnosis is probably

closely related to yoga and meditation, and other such techniques.

In the next chapter, we will be looking at sensation – how we receive information from the outside world through our senses. And we will also be looking at research into whether we are also able to receive information in other ways, in addition to normal sensory channels. Parapsychological research poses a number of difficult challenges for psychologists, so in Chapter 12 we will explore some of its research evidence, and some of the debates regarding parapsychology.

Key terms

action potential The electrical impulse produced by a neurone when its stimulation crosses the threshold, and causes it to fire.

alpha rhythms Patterns of electrical activity of the brain which appear in an electro-encephalogram (EEG) when the subject is in a relaxed state, and/or daydreaming.

amphetamines Drugs commonly used for losing weight, or to provide additional short-term energy in demanding situations.

autohypnosis Self-hypnosis.

catecholinergic A term used to describe nerve fibres which use the neurotransmitters dopamine, noradrenaline or adrenaline.

circadian rhythms Biological rhythms based on a 24-hour cycle or near equivalent.

compliance The process of going along with other people – i.e. conforming – but without accepting their views on a personal level.

curare A nerve poison which works by blocking the reception of acetylcholine at the model end plate, so causing paralysis.

demand characteristics Those aspects of a psychological study (or other artificial situation) which exert an implicit pressure on people to act in ways that are expected of them.

diurnal rhythms Biological rhythms, based on the day/night cycle, and shown by animals which are generally awake during the day.

dreamwork The process of using hidden symbolism in dreams to express inner conflicts and unconscious desires.

evolution The process of species development through small genetic changes leading to adaptive fitness for the individual.

excitatory synapse A synapse which, when activated, makes the receptor neurone more likely to fire.

ganzfeld An entirely featureless perceptual field. Ganzfelds were used by the Gestalt psychologists in early research into the nature of perception, and are currently used by parapsychological researchers, as the technique is thought to facilitate ESP.

hidden observer A phenomenon observed in hypnosis, in which part of the mind remains detached and observes dispassionately.

hypnosis A condition of extreme suggestibility, in which a person voluntarily co-operates with suggestions made by a hypnotist. It is questionable whether hypnosis is a 'special state', or merely a normal extension of human sociability.

inhibitory synapse A synapse which, when activated, makes the receptor neurone less likely to fire.

jet lag Disruption of the circadian rhythms of the body caused by the need to adjust rapidly to different time zones.

latent content The Freudian term for the hidden content of dreams – the meanings which are concealed by the dreamwork.

lucid dreaming Dreaming in which the person is aware that they are asleep and dreaming.

manifest content The Freudian term for what actually happens in a dream, as opposed to its latent content.

mesmerism An old term for hypnotism.

motor end plate The part of the muscle fibre which receives messages from motor neurones, telling the muscle when to contract.

neurotransmitter A chemical which is released by one nerve cell and picked up by a neighbouring one, making the latter either more or less likely to fire.

nocturnal Active and alert at night, sleeping or resting during the day.

paradoxical sleep Sleep in which the EEG indicates light sleep but the person is difficult to ake up, and is often dreaming. Also known as REM sleep.

pineal gland A hormonal gland in the brain, thought to be particularly involved in biological rhythms.

pons The part of the brain situated above the medulla and thought to be involved in sleep and dreaming.

post-hypnotic amnesia When a person has come out of a hypnotised state but nonetheless continues to forget information because they were instructed to do so while hypnotised.

prosocial Altruistic, helpful, friendly, or otherwise acting in ways that are beneficial to others.

receptor site A location on the dendrite of the neurone or muscle fibre which is particularly sensitive to specific neurotransmitters, and therefore receives signals from other neurones.

REM sleep Sleep which involves rapid eye movements, and usually dreaming.

role A social part that one plays in society.

self-fulfilling prophecy The idea that expectations about a person or group can become true simply because they have been stated.

sensory deprivation The cutting out of all incoming sensory information, or at least as much of it as possible.

synaptic button See synaptic knob.

synaptic knob The structure at the end of each neuronal dendrite, which contains vesicles that release neurotransmitters into the synaptic cleft.

synaptic vesicle Small pockets or reservoirs found on the synaptic button which contain the neurotransmitter chemicals before they are released.

zeitgebers External signals of daily time-changes, such as daybreak and dusk, which influence human diurnal rhythms.

Summary

1 Methods of studying consciousness have included studies of neural activity, sensory deprivation, blindsight and amnesia, brain surgery and psychoactive drugs. Theories of consciousness include Wundt's description of elements of consciousness, evolutionary perspectives, and Sommerhoff's layered IGR model.

2 Psychoactive drugs directly affect the mind, by influencing the actions of neurotransmitters at the synapse. They include sedatives and depressants, stimulants, opiates and narcotics, and hallucinogens. Recreational drugs, whether legal or illegal, are psychoactive.

3 The body has many natural rhythms, including circadian rhythms which incorporate alternating periods of sleeping and waking. These are strongly influenced by external zeitgebers.

4 While we are asleep, we alternate between periods of quiet sleep, which appears to be concerned with tissue restoration, and active sleep, during which we are more likely to dream.

5 Physiological structures involved in sleep include the locus coeruleus and the raphé nuclei of the reticular activating system. Sleep disorders include insomnia, sleep apnea and narcolepsy, but physiological connections with these are not yet well understood.

6 Theories of dreaming include the idea that dreaming is disguised unconscious wish-fulfilment, that it is simply a by-product of neural activity, and that it allows the brain to sort out new information and link it with prior knowledge.

7 State theorists of hypnotism see it as a special state of consciousness, allowing access to parts of the mind which are otherwise inaccessible. Non-state theorists of hypnotism see it as a social phenomenon, which can be explained in terms of well-known social psychological mechanisms.

8 The main types of hypnotic phenomena are unexpected abilities, hypnotic memory, pain control, apparent reincarnation, and the hidden observer. None of these provides reliable evidence for one theory over another.

Self-assessment questions

1 Describe the physiological processes involved in the experience of jet lag.

2 Outline the different types of sleep, and their physiological characteristics.

3 What are the main methods which have been used to study consciousness?

Practice essay questions

1 Critically evaluate experimental evidence for, and theories of, dreaming.

2 How far can the actions of drugs be understood in terms of physiological brain processes?

3 Is hypnosis a special state of awareness?

Test your knowledge of this chapter with our online quizzes and games at: http://www.psych.co.uk

Explore consciousness further at:

General
http://members.tripod.com/~BilgiNet/index.htm – Links to articles on all topics and debates in the area of consciousness.

Drugs and consciousness
http://www.uwsp.edu/acad/psych/tdrugs.htm – Very good site for articles, links, topics and laws regarding the use of drugs and their effects upon the brain.

Sleep/dreaming
http://www.sfu.ca/~mcantle/biorhyth.html – Detailed tutorial on biological rhythms with a useful reading list.
http://www.sleepnet.com/index.shtml – Very useful and entertaining page containing links, tests, research, resources and details of sleep disorders.

Hypnosis
http://goinside.com/97/4/barber.html – Long tutorial with everything you could possibly want to know about hypnosis.

Sensation and parapsychology

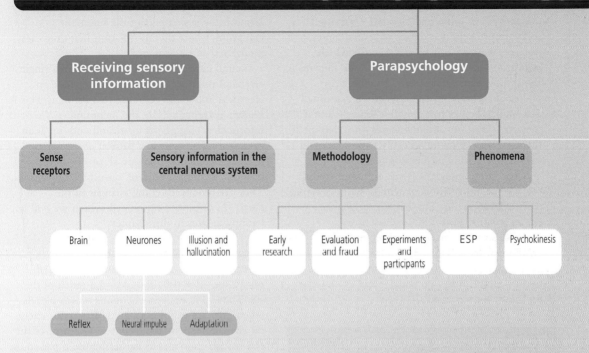

In this chapter, we will be looking at how the nervous system gathers information from our external environment. We have many more than five senses which convey information to the brain: at the very least, we have sight, hearing, touch, taste, smell and proprioception (the sense which tells us about the internal state of the body, such as the position of joints and muscles) – although really proprioception consists of several senses, not just one. We have one set of receptors which inform us about balance, another which informs is about movement, and so on. The empiricist philosophers were mistaken when they assumed that human beings had only five senses – and if they had taken our internal senses into account at the same time, they might easily have developed a very different kind of philosophy.

Sometimes, though, it seems as though people can receive information, or send it, without using their external senses. This has been given various names, ranging from ESP (extra-sensory perception) to psi, to parapsychology. In this chapter we will be looking at how psychologists have gone about studying ESP, and what it has told us about human potential – and the human capacity for deception!

Receiving sensory information

The process by which we receive information is known as **sensation**. Human beings possess a number of specialised systems which allow us to receive different types of information. The peripheral nervous system includes one system which receives that form of electro-magnetic radiation which we refer to as light; another system receives rhythmic changes in air pressure which we know as sound; a third system receives information about physical contact with the skin; a fourth about changes in the body; and we also receive information about the chemical composition of the air around us and of food that we eat, through the senses of smell and taste.

How sensory receptors work

The brain receives information from a number of sensory receptors, each of which is specialised to receive certain types of stimuli. Whatever type of stimulus they receive, these receptors change the information into electrical impulses that can be transmitted by sensory neurones to other parts of the nervous system. These **neural impulses** travel from the sensory receptor to the brain, usually going straight to the part of the brain known as the thalamus, which acts as a kind of sorting and relay station for the information which is coming in. From there they pass to the specialised sensory areas on the largest part of the brain, the cerebrum, where the information that they carry is analysed and interpreted.

Neural information takes the form of a single electrical impulse. Receptor cells generate an electrical impulse in response to a stimulus. This is known as **transduction**: the incoming information changes its form, and ends up as an electrical impulse, or as a pattern of several impulses. These impulses are all of the same strength, forming a kind of 'on-off' binary system. They are produced by the changes in the electrical potential of the cell, which we will be looking at later in this chapter.

Receptors in the visual system

The receptors in the visual system are special photo-receptor cells found in the retina of the eye. These cells contain chemicals which bleach when they are exposed to light. When this chemical change happens, the electrical potential of the cell changes, and an electrical impulse is passed on to the bipolar neurones which form the next layer of the retina (Figure 12.1). From there it passes to the **ganglion cells**. These have extremely elon-

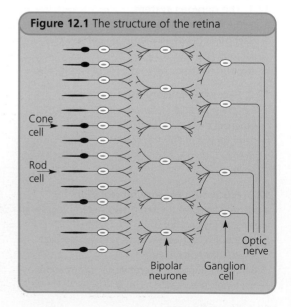

Figure 12.1 The structure of the retina

Cone cell

Rod cell

Bipolar neurone

Ganglion cell

Optic nerve

gated stems, or axons, which lead completely out of the eyeball. The axons collect together at a point on the retina known as the **blind spot**, and form the **optic nerve** which passes to the brain.

There are two kinds of photo-receptors: **rod cells** and cone cells. Rod cells contain a chemical known as rhodopsin, which is extremely sensitive and responds to minute changes in light. This means that rod cells are the cells which we use for night vision, when there is very little light available. Rod cells can also detect very slight movements, so we find that the edge of the retina, which is the extreme edge of our visual field, is entirely composed of rod cells. This helps us to react quickly to anything appearing at the edge of our field of vision – a mechanism which evolved to warn us of possible sources of danger.

As we move towards the centre of the retina, we find that there are fewer rod cells and increasing numbers of cone cells, until we find that the fovea, at the centre of the retina, is made up entirely of cone cells. The fovea is the point where we focus our vision. Cone cells contain a different chemical, known as iodopsin, which allows them to detect colour. This makes them very effective for detailed inspection of objects. There are a number of theories about how colour vision actually works, and these are discussed in Box 12.1 on the following page.

The effects of this arrangement of cells in the retina become particularly noticeable at night, or under conditions of very low illumination. Cone cells need quite a lot of light in order to function.

So, oddly, in dim light we can see things more clearly if we do not actually look straight at them. When we try to focus on an object in these conditions, it seems fuzzy because there is not enough light to see properly with the cone cells in the fovea. But to the side of the fovea, there are rod cells, and these can pick up dim light accurately. The constellation known as the Seven Sisters, or the Pleiades, in the northern hemisphere, contains one star which is too faint to be detected by cone cells, but just bright enough to be picked up by rod cells: if you look directly at this constellation you can count only six stars, whereas if you look slightly to the side of it you can count seven.

Receptors in the auditory system

The auditory system contains the specialised receptors for sounds, which are picked up as rhythmic changes in air pressure, arriving in waves which we refer to as **sound waves**. The outer ear collects the signal, and the outer and middle sections of the ear together amplify it. But the changes in pressure are actually transduced into electrical impulses by tiny **hair cells**, which lie between two membranes in the inner ear (Figure 12.2). When pressure waves pass through the fluid above and below them, the membranes are squeezed. This produces a change in the electrical potential of the hair cells, and they generate electrical impulses. These impulses are picked up by special ganglion cells in the **basilar membrane** (the lower one), and their long axons form the

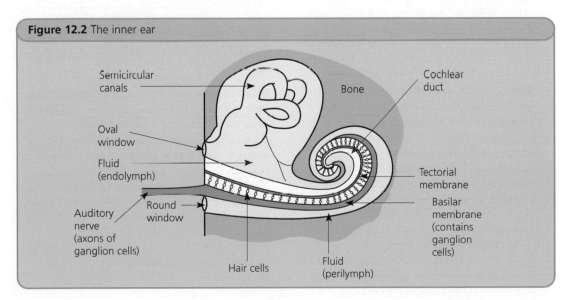
Figure 12.2 The inner ear

Box 12.1 Theories of colour vision

If we mix coloured lights, we find that any colour can be produced by varying the proportions of three colours: red, blue and green. The different shades which we see on a colour television are produced by tiny coloured dots in these three colours, lighting up in varying combinations to produce the colours of the TV image. The observation that different combinations of lights could produce all the different colours, formed the basis of the first attempt to explain colour vision, known as the **Young–Helmholtz principle**, after the nineteenth-century researchers who developed the ideas.

The Young–Helmholtz theory of colour vision proposed that we have three different types of colour-detecting cells – cone cells – in the retina of the eye. One type is sensitive to red wavelengths of light, another to blue, and a third type to green. By firing in different combinations, depending on the light which is reaching the eye, they signal the colour which the brain should perceive.

Although this seems a plausible enough explanation for how we see colour, it hits problems when we are trying to explain two phenomena: colour blindness and visual after-effects. **Colour blindness** occurs when the person – who is usually male, since colour-blindness is a sex-linked genetic disorder – is unable to distinguish between certain wavelengths of light. In the majority of cases of colour blindness, the person confuses certain shades of red with certain shades of green: a disorder not surprisingly referred to as red-green colour blindness. This is actually quite common, affecting about 7% of men, although less than 1% of women. In some cases, much less common than the red-green ones, the person may have no colour vision at all, seeing everything as shades of black, white and grey; and in a very few extremely rare cases, the person may confuse some shades of blue and yellow, but have accurate red-green colour vision. It is hard to see how these observations can be explained simply in terms of different cone cells for red, blue and green light.

A related issue is the question of negative after-effects. If you stare at a red patch for a period of time – say, 90 seconds or so – and then look at a blank sheet of paper, you find that you see an after-effect of the patch – but a green one. If the patch you stare at is green, the after-effect is red. Similarly, if you stare at a blue patch, you get a yellow after-effect; a bright patch produces a darker after-image; and so on. In other words, after-effects reflect the opposite of the stimulus to which they have been exposed – the opposite colour in the pairs red/green and blue/yellow; and the opposite brightness in the pair light/dark.

In an attempt to explain both negative after-effects and colour blindness, Hering (1878) proposed the **opponent-process theory** of colour vision. Hering argued that to explain human colour perception just in terms of the three primary colours for light – red, blue and green – was not enough: that in terms of human perception there are four primary colours, because yellow is also experienced as a pure colour and not a mixture. Hering believed that we have three types of receptor cells in the retina, which process information in opposite ways. When the receptor is in its anabolic phase, it responds to one colour of a pair; when it is in the opposite phase, which Hering called the the catabolic phase, it responds to the opposite colour. So the same cells respond to the pairs of colours, and the three types of receptor are red/green, blue/yellow, and light/dark. Negative after-effects are produced by the cells becoming fatigued by prolonged stimulation in one direction, and so working in the opposite way for a period after the stimulation ended, as they recover.

Although these may seem like opposite ideas, in fact there is some physiological evidence for both of them. MacNichol (1964) showed that there are different types of cone cells in the retina, which respond maximally to the three different wavelengths of light represented by red, blue and green – as predicted by the Young–Helmholtz theory. And De Valois, Abramov and Jacobs (1966) showed that bipolar cells, in the second layer of the retina, and also some cells in the thalamus, show opponent processing. So both types of mechanisms appear to have relevance in making sense out of how we see colour.

auditory nerve, carrying information to the brain.

Since a neural impulse is either on or off, and of the same strength each time, information about the volume and pitch of a sound has to be sent as a kind of code. Volume is signalled by the number of hair cells which are stimulated: loud sounds stimulate more hair cells. Pitch, however, is signalled in a rather more complex manner. In part, pitch seems to be indicated by the location of the hair cells which were stimulated. Von Bekesey, in 1960, cut tiny holes in the basilar membranes of guinea pigs, and found that the hair cells near the middle ear end of the cochlea responded to higher frequencies, while those at the other end of the cochlea responded to mid-range frequencies. But low frequencies seem to be picked up all over the cochlea, and these are indicated by how rapidly the hair cells fire. At low frequencies, hair cells fire less often than at high frequencies.

Several species of animals can detect sounds that are outside the range of human hearing. Dogs, bats and rats, for instance, can detect **ultrasound** – sounds which are too high for human ears to hear. Some dog owners train their animals to respond to 'silent' whistles, which produce ultrasonic signals. Bats use sonar to detect the insects that they eat, sending out an ultrasonic call which bounces off the insect, making an echo which informs the bat about the location of its prey. And male rats are known to produce a high-frequency, ultrasound shriek after they have just copulated, which warns other rats to keep away.

Some species can detect very low frequencies of sound too. Low sounds carry a very long way, and whales are thought to be able to pick up **infrasound** (sound which is too low for human beings to hear) through hundreds of miles of ocean. Blakemore (1984) described how pigeons can detect sounds so low that they can even hear the very low rumbles of mountain ranges. One theory about how homing pigeons find their way is that they can detect these distinctive, very low patterns of infrasound, although pigeons have other homing senses as well. And there is a theory – although evidence for it appears to be lacking – that some of the ancient stone circles and mystical sites are located over rock formations which produce distinctive infrasound patterns.

Receptors in the olfactory system

Smell is often described as a 'primitive' sense, because it was one of the first to evolve – but that does not mean that the information we receive from it is simple. On the contrary, the olfactory system is capable of analysing highly complex information. Unlike the other sense receptors, olfactory receptors are in direct contact with the external world – they do not need special collecting equipment, like ears or eyes. Hair cells protrude directly from the olfactory area in the nose – known as the **olfactory epithelium** – into the air flow created when we breathe. The ends of the hair cells are coated with a fatty substance. Chemical molecules in the air stick to this substance, which generates an electrical impulse in the cell. That impulse is passed directly to the olfactory cortex of the brain, and to the limbic system (see Chapter 10). So the cerebrum receives olfactory information directly, whereas most other sensory information is relayed through the thalamus.

The direct connections of the olfactory system indicate that in evolutionary terms it is a very ancient sense: more recently evolved systems tend to have more elaborate physiological structures. This direct contact, and the olfactory system's connections with the limbic system, may explain how smells can be so powerful in evoking memories or emotions from a long time ago. Many aromatherapists believe that the sense of smell and feelings of emotion are directly linked, and so they aim to help people who are distressed or depressed by using essential oils to evoke more positive moods.

Perhaps because it is a **primary sense** for many animals (the sense that they depend on most in their day-to-day lives), the olfactory sense is quite robust. New olfactory receptor cells are continually being grown, and a whole set can renew itself completely over a period of six weeks or so. So even if the olfactory receptors are damaged, they can recover quickly.

Although we tend to think of vision and hearing as our most important senses, human beings are far more sensitive to smells than we often suspect. Wallace (1977) showed that people can distinguish between males and females by smell; and professional wine-tasters or others with a highly trained sense of smell can make quite sophisticated discriminations between stimuli which seem to smell the same to most people.

People who grow up in societies where the sense of smell is systematically trained from an early age, as in the Native Australian societies, can detect a tremendous amount of information using smell.

A number of attempts have been made to classify smells. In 1895, Zwaardemaker proposed that all smells could be reduced to nine main types (see Table 12.1). Crocker (1945) suggested that there were four, not nine, classes of smell: fragrant, or sweet; acid, or sour; burnt, or empyreumatic; and caprylic, or 'goaty'. Crocker developed a system for numbering smells according to these components. The number was on a scale from 1 to 8, so, for example, the smell of a rose was given the number 6423, which meant that it was strongly fragrant, had some acid odour, and also just a little of the other two. Vanillin was numbered 7122, whereas the smell of ethyl alcohol was given the code of 5414. This type of numbering system did help researchers to identify some of the basic similarities between smells; but nowadays it appears rather over-simplified.

Modern researchers take the view that it seems rather unlikely that the sense of smell will be reduced to just a few basic components in the way that early theorists imagined, since the range of different chemicals which can be identified by the olfactory system is so large. Many recent attempts to describe smells use the idea of **notes** – the idea that a smell is a bit like a musical chord, composed of combinations of different notes. Some smells are thin and sharp, and these are mainly composed of high notes, whereas others are richer and deeper, as if they contain more low notes. Using this musical metaphor, researchers have been able to identify similarities in how people perceive different kinds of smells, and these do seem to correlate to quite a high degree with the chemical constituents that go to make up the substance which is being smelled.

Receptors in the gustatory system

We cannot taste anything without first dissolving it in saliva, a saline-like fluid produced by special glands in the mouth. Some chemical food additives, such as monosodium glutamate (E621), have their effect by increasing the flow of saliva from these glands, which makes the food taste more flavourful. The sense of taste and the sense of smell are very closely linked – so much so that if the sense of smell is impaired in some way, for example by a bad cold, we find it more difficult to taste food properly.

Taste receptor cells are grouped into **taste buds**, forming little bumps on the surface of the tongue and on the soft palate of the mouth. These cells end in short hair-like structures, which come into direct contact with the saliva in the mouth, and react to the different chemical combinations produced by dissolved food. The chemical causes a change in the chemical balance of the taste receptor cell, which produces an electrical impulse.

The strength of a flavour is signalled by faster or slower firing from the nerve fibre, but the way that different tastes are coded is rather more complex. Different parts of the tongue seem to be sensitive to different tastes, with those at the very front of the tongue being in general more sensitive to sweet foods, those at the sides and front responding best to salty tastes, those at the side but to the rear responding best to sour tastes, and those at the back of the tongue and on the soft palate responding most to bitter tastes.

For some time, it was thought that these regions simply contained different types of receptors. However, it is now clear that most taste receptors will respond to other tastes as well; but that they have different **thresholds of response** for different chemicals – in other words, different chemicals need to be of different strengths before they will depolarise the cell membrane enough to produce an electrical impulse. It is thought that the brain decodes the impulses being received from the taste receptors by assessing how often different nerve fibres in an area are stimulated, and

---

Table 12.1 Types of smell

In 1895, Zwaardemaker proposed that all smells could be reduced to nine main types:

1   *Ethereal* – e.g. fruits, resins and ethers.
2   *Aromatic* – e.g. camphor, cloves, lavender, lemon, and bitter almonds.
3   *Fragrant* – e.g. flowers, violet, vanilla.
4   *Ambrosial* – e.g. amber or musk.
5   *Alliaceous* – e.g. hydrogen sulphide, chlorine.
6   *Empyreumatic* – e.g. benzenes, roast coffee.
7   *Caprylic* – e.g. cheese, rancid fat.
8   *Repulsive* – e.g. deadly nightshade, bedbug.
9   *Foetid* – e.g. carrion, faeces.

how sensitive the different groups of receptor cells are.

As with the sense of smell, taste receptor cells are constantly renewing themselves, such that each taste bud is completely renewed every seven days or so. Sensitivity to taste seems to decline with age, although as with most age-changes this is highly variable. And, of course, individual sensitivity differs: a trained chef or food analyst, for instance, can detect very slight nuances of taste in the flavour of a particular food, whereas many other people are content with far more general assessments of flavour.

There are differences between species in terms of which tastes they can detect. Cats, for example, do not have taste receptors for sweet things, whereas dogs do. You may have observed this if you have pets: dogs are often very fond of chocolates or other sweets, but cats will tend to ignore them. In humans, our response to taste varies with our physiological state: a solution of zinc sulphate heptahydrate, for example, is used by dieticians to detect zinc deficiency, because it seems completely tasteless to those who have zinc deficiency, but has a strong and unpleasant flavour to people who have not. Similarly, the 'cravings' for the taste of a particular food which many women experience during pregnancy is thought to relate to a shortage of a relevant mineral or other substance, which can be found in that food.

Receptors in the tactile system

Sensory receptors in the skin are of three major types: those which respond to pressure, those which respond to temperature and those which respond to painful stimuli. The sensory receptors which respond to pressure are located just under the skin, and seem to be quite variable: some of them enclose the nerve ending in a small capsule, while others leave it free.

Some areas of the skin are more sensitive than others, because they have different numbers of pressure receptors. This can be tested by touching the skin with two points, close together, and seeing whether the person feels the two separate points or just one. The **two-point threshold** is set at the point where the person experiences the pressure as one point on 50% of the trials. Those areas of the skin that have the lowest two-point threshold tend to be the most sensitive parts of the body: the lips, fingertips, tongue and genitals. The

back, thighs and calves have very high thresholds, and are the least sensitive parts of the body.

Temperature is picked up by free nerve endings in the skin. These sensory receptors react when the temperature of the skin changes. 'Warm' receptors respond when the skin surface warms up gently, but both cooling and rapid heating activate the 'cold' receptors. One well-known tactile illusion which illustrates this involves passing warm and cold water through two intertwined tubes. A person grasping both tubes together in one hand, so that both kinds of stimulation are received, will feel a hot sensation (Figure 12.3).

Pain receptors

Although pain receptors are also part of the tactile system, they are important enough to warrant being discussed separately. When a stimulus which is powerful enough to cause damage contacts the skin, chemical substances are released within the skin itself, and these flood the immediate area. These chemicals are picked up at the specialised receptor sites of pain receptor cells, which have

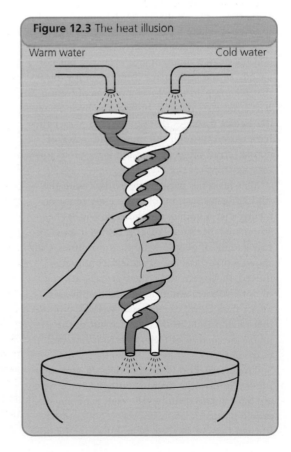

Figure 12.3 The heat illusion

Warm water   Cold water

free nerve endings in the skin. The chemical causes a change in the electrical potential of the cell, producing an electrical impulse which is transmitted rapidly to the spinal cord, stimulating a reflex response such as pulling the limb or body away from the stimulus.

As a general rule, the impulses carrying pain information are simultaneously transmitted to the brain, so that we become aware of it. There are times, however, when we can experience pain and not notice it – particularly if we are engaged in strenuous physical activity. Melzack and Wall (1982) proposed the **gate theory** of pain, which argues that the nerve impulses which produce pain pass through a series of 'gates' as they travel up to the brain. These gates do not automatically let the pain messages through: they are influenced by other types of information too. So the gate can be closed by neural impulses coming down from the brain, such as those produced during extreme arousal. And other kinds of stimuli, like pressure, can sometimes close the gate; which might explain why rubbing a painful spot sometimes relieves the pain slightly.

Interestingly, we do not always feel pain in the exact spot where an injury is located. Particularly with internal injuries, we may feel the pain to be coming from a different area – nearby, but not exactly in the same place. The reason for this is that feeling pain is not just a matter of feeling the nerve impulses directly. Instead, the brain receives the neural messages that signify pain – after they have passed through the appropriate gates, of course – and projects these messages on to its own internal 'map' of the body.

This becomes particularly evident with the study of **phantom limbs** – the experience of feeling that a limb is still there after it has been amputated. Melzack (1992) reported a series of case studies of people with phantom limbs, and showed that these are extremely common – indeed, they seem to be the normal outcome of both deliberate and accidental amputations, rather than being exceptional. Melzack proposed that phantom limbs occur as a result of the brain's projection of feeling on to its internal body-image.

The internal body-image, Melzack argued, is pre-wired into the nervous system: people who are born without limbs still often experience whole phantom limbs, but they could not have learned that. In the case of amputation, the body-image is still complete even though the body itself is not, and the feelings are often so real that the person acts on them. It is not uncommon, Melzack reported, for someone who has lost a foot to try to get out of bed using that foot to stand on – and to remember that it is missing only when they fall over.

Perhaps more disturbingly, Katz and Melzack (1990) showed that phantom limbs can also carry the memory of pain which happened before the amputation. Such pain can be extremely strong, and, of course, is very difficult to treat. In one case, a man on his way to hospital to have a painful splinter removed from underneath a fingernail was involved in an accident which crushed his arm. He still felt the pain of the splinter in the phantom limb he developed after the arm was amputated. Katz and Melzack reported that anaesthetising painful injuries for a period of time before an amputation is carried out seems to produce much less pain in a phantom limb. It seems to allow the brain's body-image enough time to get used to an image of a reasonably painless limb, so that when the brain is generating the phantom, that too is reasonably painless. Katz and Melzack recommended that this should become standard medical practice.

Receptors in the proprioceptive system

When the empiricist philosophers argued that we can know the world only through the evidence coming to us from our senses, they identified just five: sight, hearing, smell, taste and touch. But this meant that they ignored a very important set of senses: the ones which tell us about our own bodies. These senses, which we can loosely term the **proprioceptive senses**, provide an important source of information, which we often take for granted.

There are a number of different types of receptors for this type of information. Proprioceptive receptors carry information from our muscles, tendons and joints along internal nerve fibres to the sensory area in the cerebral cortex of the brain. Sacks (1985) reported a case in which a woman experienced complete loss of proprioception, quite suddenly. This was brought on by a sudden inflammation of the proprioceptive sensory nerves, and it left her feeling 'disembodied', and unable to co-ordinate or control her actions. She described it as feeling as though the body were suddenly 'blind' – unable to 'see' itself doing anything.

Another source of information is the **sense of balance**. The receptors for this are located in the vestibular apparatus of the inner ear, above the cochlea. They consist of a number of hair cells, which protrude into a thick viscous substance containing tiny pieces of calcium crystals, known as otoliths. When the body is not upright, or if the head is tilted, the otoliths exert pressure on the hair cells. The pressure produces an electrical impulse which is then transmitted to the brain. These sensors also allow us to detect constant, linear motion, like the kind of motion we feel in a train or aeroplane.

Body movement, or **kinaesthesia**, is also detected in the inner ear, but this time using another part of the vestibular apparatus known as the semicircular canals. These are three loops, each containing fluid, which lie perpendicular to one another in the three dimensions (see Figure 12.2 on page 355). When the body is moved suddenly, or changes direction, the fluid swirls around in the semicircular canals, and this movement is detected by small hair cells. Different types of movement produce different amounts of swirling in the canals, so the brain detects what movement is happening. The dizziness that we feel after going on a roundabout or rollercoaster is due to the fluid in our semicircular canals still moving.

Some recent evidence has identified special cells containing small metallic granules which seem to act as **magnetic receptors** in some animals, such as pigeons. This is thought to help them with their sense of direction. It has been suggested that human beings also might possess these magnetic orientation receptors; but so far the evidence is inconclusive. Some people believe that they have a good 'sense of direction', which might result from such receptors, but systematic evidence for this seems to be limited. And, of course, there is also the problem that we may need to be sensitised to such a sense from an early age in order to use it fully, as with the sense of smell.

There are many things that we still do not know about human beings and their 'minor senses', and it seems likely that conducting research among people from non-technological societies might help us to throw more light on the subject. For example: Dodd (1989) discussed the olfactory training system for Native Australian children, which was mentioned earlier. These children are explicitly trained in the identification and recognition of different smells from a very early age, so they become much more proficient at using smell as a major source of information than most Western people do. When it is trained, the human sense of smell is extremely sensitive, and can detect infinitesimal concentrations of some types of substances.

Similarly, in 1959, Witkin showed how people from traditional African societies were less dependent on vision as their main sense than were Europeans. They utilised their kinaesthetic senses far more in adjusting their balance, so they were less easily tricked by illusions which would unbalance Europeans. We may have a great deal to learn from people in non-technological societies about just what the human sensory system can achieve.

Sensory information in the central nervous system

The nerve fibres and neural structures which make up the brain and the spinal cord are known collectively as the central nervous system, or CNS. One important part of the functioning of the central nervous system concerns the processing of sensory information: sensory information is received through the specialised sense organs, as we have just seen, but the information then travels to the central nervous system in order to be analysed, and in order for action to be based on its implications.

Decoding in the thalamus

The neurones from most sensory receptors form synapses at the part of the brain known as the thalamus. A synapse occurs when a neurone comes to an end and passes its message on to other neurones, which carry the information on to other parts of the brain. (We looked at how synapses work in Chapter 11.) The thalamus acts as a sensory relay mechanism for the brain, in the sense that it receives sensory information and sorts it out before channelling it to the appropriate area of the cerebral cortex. The optic and auditory nerves, which as we have seen, began in the eye and the inner ear, end in the thalamus. Here, they make connections with other neurones which pass the information on to the visual and auditory areas of the cortex.

There are special sets of nuclei in the thalamus which process visual and auditory information. Those which process visual information are known as the **lateral geniculate nuclei**. In 1968, Hubel and Wiesel reported on the outcome of a series of studies involving **micro-electrode recording** – recording brain activity by using electrodes so small that they could record the electrical impulse of a single nerve cell.

Hubel and Wiesel found that cells in this area of the brain responded to very exact stimuli – a roughly circular spot of light in a particular part of the visual field. Each cell was excited by a stimulus in the centre of its receptive field, but inhibited by stimuli falling on the surrounding area. So a light directly in the centre of the cell's receptive field would cause the cell to fire, but one which only just missed it would not. The researchers also found that these cells reponded just as strongly to a bar of light: the stimulus did not need to be a dot, but the bar of light did have to cover the centre of the cell's receptive field.

In addition to this, Hubel and Wiesel found that binocular comparisons of information seem to begin in the thalamus. Lateral geniculate cells were arranged in alternate layers, depending on whether they received information from the left or the right eye. Those cells closest to one another in the different layers also responded to stimuli from the same part of the visual field. So the implication is that some preliminary processing of the visual information takes place in the thalamus, even though the processing becomes much more sophisticated when the information reaches the visual cortex.

Decoding in the cerebrum

The **cerebrum** is a large structure that, in human beings, overshadows all the rest of the brain. It consists of two large, heavily folded hemispheres, separated by a deep groove down the centre, and containing grey matter on the surface, and dense white matter underneath. The white matter consists of the myelinated axons of tightly packed connector neurones, which carry messages backwards and forwards between the different areas of the cerebrum. The grey matter, on the outside, consists of cell bodies and unmyelinated nerve fibres, and it is about six layers of cells deep. It is in the grey matter, known as the **cerebral cortex**, that most of the activity of the cerebrum seems to take place.

As we saw in Chapter 10, there are specialised areas on the cerebral cortex which process the information picked up by specific sense receptors

The sensory receptors are listed in Table 12.2. The special areas on the cerebral cortex are known as **sensory projection areas**, and they are listed in Table 12.3. In Chapter 2, we saw how Hubel and Wiesel (1968) found three different kinds of neurone in the visual cortex. One type of cell, which they called **simple cells**, responded to small, highly defined units of information coming from just one place in the visual field, for example a dot or a line at a particular angle. **Complex cells** received information from several simple cells, and this meant that they would fire in response to more complex information – like a line at any angle, or a line at a particular angle anywhere in the visual field. And **hypercomplex cells** received information from several complex cells, and would

Table 12.2 Sensory receptors	
The retina	This responds to light information entering the eye. The receptors are of two kinds, detecting brightness and colour.
The cochlea	This reponds to sound information received through the ear. It detects intensity and pitch.
The olfactory epithelium	This responds to chemicals carried in the air and entering the nose. Researchers are uncertain as to how many different types of olfactory receptor exist.
The taste buds	These respond to chemicals dissolved in saliva. They respond to salt, sweet, sour and bitter tastes.
The skin receptors	These detect information being received by the skin. There are different receptors for temperature, pressure, and pain.
The proprioceptors	These respond to information which comes from within the body. Some respond to proprioception itself – that is, the positioning of the muscles and limbs. Other receptors respond to information about balance; while the kinaesthetic receptors respond to information about movement.

Table 12.3 Sensory projection areas

The striate cortex (visual cortex)	Processes visual information.
The olfactory cortex	Processes information from smell receptors in the nose, and may possibly also be involved in gustatory (taste) processes.
The auditory cortex	Processes information from the ears.
The somatosensory area	Processes information about the surface of the body, which is picked up by sense organs in the skin.
The motor cortex	Concerned with voluntary movements of the muscles.

fire in response to simple shapes or patterns (see Figure 12.4).

The implication of this finding is that some very basic kinds of visual information-processing – at least, the processing involved in sorting out simple shapes and figures and distinguishing them from their backgrounds – may be 'wired in' to the nervous system itself. So it provides physiological evidence which can be taken as supporting the Gestalt psychologists' argument that figure-ground perception is a fundamental, innate part of visual perception. And it also tells us something important about the relationship between the structure and arrangement of nerve cells in the brain, and our perceptual experience.

Ocular dominance columns

In 1979, Hubel and Wiesel reported the outcomes of thousands of micro-electrode recordings in the visual cortex of the cerebrum. By presenting a simple visual stimulus, like a dot or a line, and recording which neurones fired in response, they gradually built up a picture of the way that the cortex was organised. One of their findings was that this part of the cerebral cortex seems to be organised into columns, which they referred to as **ocular dominance columns**. Each column responds to information from just one eye, and all the cells in a particular column are activated in response to the same stimulus.

Hubel and Wiesel found that there are roughly six layers of cells in each column, corresponding to the layers of the cerebral cortex. Also, different layers contain cells which seem to have different functions. For example, layer IV is where the cells bringing information from the thalamus end, forming synaptic connections with other cells. Other layers have cells which form connections with different parts of the cerebral cortex.

The arrangement of the columns is interesting too, because Hubel and Wiesel showed that they are organised in such a way as to alternate information from the left and right eyes. So a column which contains cells responding to, say, a line at a certain angle, in a particular part of the visual field as seen by the right eye, would be situated next to a column which responded to exactly the same stimulus but seen by the left eye. The next column along would respond to a stimulus seen by the right eye, which was only slightly different from the previous one – the angle might have shifted by just one or two degrees, say. And the column after that would respond to the same stimulus, but from the left eye, and so on (see Figure 12.5 overleaf).

Crossover points

Both hearing and vision are directional senses, which means that we use them to locate where things are. Ocular dominance columns alternate the same information from the right and the left eye, and this may be because it allows the brain to compare the slightly different images received by the right and left eye. As we saw in Chapter 2, the difference between the two tells us how far away something is: closer objects show more disparity in the visual image than objects which are further away. So comparing the stimuli received by the two eyes gives us an important cue to distance. Having information from different eyes next to one another may help the brain to process this information.

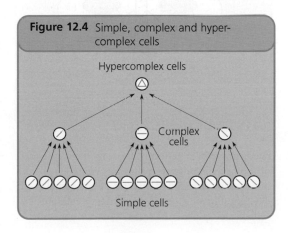

Figure 12.4 Simple, complex and hyper-complex cells

Hypercomplex cells

Complex cells

Simple cells

Figure 12.5 Ocular dominance columns in the visual cortex

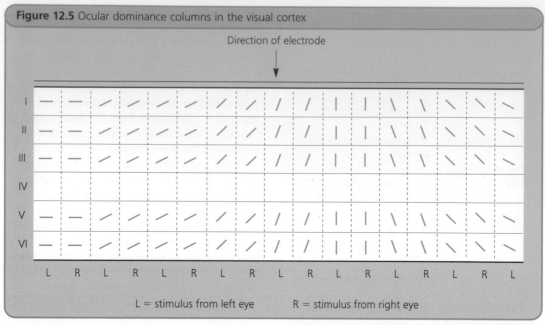

L = stimulus from left eye   R = stimulus from right eye

In order for the information from each eye to be compared, it needs to be matched up at some point. The matching up occurs at the **optic chiasma** – a crossover point in the brain where the optic nerves carrying information from the two eyes meet (Figure 12.6). At the optic chiasma, fibres carrying information from the left side of each retina pass to the left hemisphere, and those carrying information from the right side of each retina pass to the right hemisphere. So the left hemisphere receives information about what is to the right in the visual field, while the right hemisphere receives information about what is on the left of the visual field. We looked at this in Chapter 10, when we look at what happens when the two are separated, in split-brain studies.

A similar mechanism exists for hearing. We tell which direction a sound is coming from by comparing the signals received by our two ears. A sound from the right-hand side will reach the right ear fractionally before it reaches the left. There is a crossover point at which information coming from the two ears is matched and crossed over, and this means that by matching up the information coming from the two ears, the brain is able to identify where the sound is coming from.

Sensory information in the spinal cord

Not all processing of sensory information occurs in the brain itself. If the information is serious and

Figure 12.6 Visual pathways of the brain

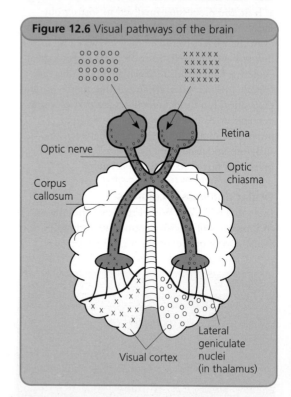

Retina

Optic nerve

Optic chiasma

Corpus callosum

Lateral geniculate nuclei (in thalamus)

Visual cortex

needs immediate action – like a message that part of the body is in acute pain or burning – then the information is handled directly by the spinal cord. The combination of receptors, nerve cells and cells in the spinal cord make what we generally refer to as the **reflex arc**. The reflex arc may be the most basic form of sensory processing which occurs in the nervous system, so studying the nerve cells which are involved can give us a simplified picture of how nerve cells work together (Figure 12.7).

The reflex arc

The reflex arc has nothing to do with the brain. When you pull your hand away from a hot object, you do not really think about it – it happens automatically, almost as soon as the sense receptors in your skin register the heat. This is because the stimulus is detected by the pain receptors in the skin, and stimulates a **sensory neurone**. The neurone stretches all the way from the sense receptor to the spinal cord, and the electrical impulse which it generates passes right along its length. When it reaches the spinal cord, the neurone ends at a synapse, where it passes its message on to a connector neurone.

Connector neurones are many-branched neurones that are found within the spinal cord and the brain. They make connections with several different nerve cells, but in the case of the reflex arc, what is important is that the connector neurone passes the message on to a long motor neurone, which begins in the spinal cord and stretches all the way down to the muscle fibres of the arm. The action of the motor neurone stimulates the muscle, which contracts and the hand is jerked away from the painful stimulus.

In reality, of course, a reflex like jerking your hand away from a hot object involves several of each type of neurone, and not just one, but talking about it as if it were just one makes the reflex arc easier to understand. Also, the connector neurone will send a message to the brain, as well as to the

muscles, so that you realise what you have done. But it is not the brain which decides to make the movement – the situation is too urgent for that. Instead, the information is processed by the most rapid means, so that the action can take place as quickly as possible.

Sensory information, then, is processed in the spinal cord as well as in the brain itself. But the kind of information which is processed there is very basic, survival-oriented information – avoiding pain – which needs to be dealt with as fast as possible. And the nerve cells involved are also designed to make sure the message gets where it is going as quickly as possible. In order to understand this, we need to look more closely at the way that neurones work.

How neurones work

The three types of neurones involved in the reflex arc – sensory, connector and motor neurones – are the three main kinds of neurones which make up the nervous system. **Sensory neurones** carry information from the sense receptors to the central nervous system – usually either to the spinal cord or to the thalamus, which is the main sensory relay centre (Figure 12.8 overleaf). **Connector neurones** are found inside the brain and the spinal cord, and have many dendrites connecting them to other nerve cells (Figure 12.9 overleaf). Most of the brain itself and the spinal cord are made up of connector neurones. And **motor neurones** carry the central nervous system's instructions to the muscle fibres, so they have one end in the brain or spinal cord, and the other in the muscle fibres (Figure 12.10 overleaf).

What we know as 'nerves' are actually the elongated fibres of sensory and motor neurones, bunched together. Some nerve fibres are **afferent**, which means that they carry information from the senses towards the brain. So they are composed of sensory neurones. Other nerves are **efferent**, carrying information from the brain or spinal cord to the muscles. They are composed of motor neurones. The two types of nerves are spread in a complex network throughout the human body.

The neural impulse

Because it is important that sensory information should travel quickly, the axons of both motor and sensory neurones are covered with a special coating known as a **myelin sheath**. This sheath

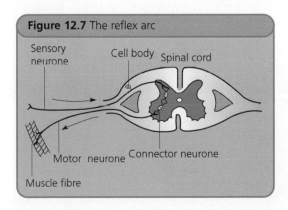

Figure 12.7 The reflex arc

Sensory neurone

Cell body Spinal cord

Motor neurone Connector neurone

Muscle fibre

Figure 12.8 A sensory neurone

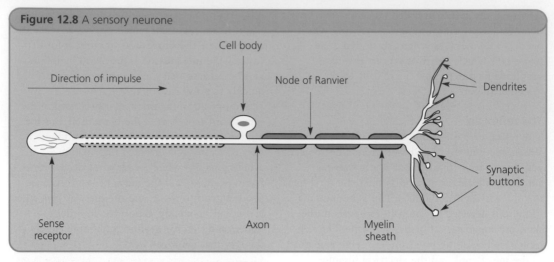

Cell body

Direction of impulse

Node of Ranvier

Dendrites

Synaptic buttons

Sense receptor

Axon

Myelin sheath

Figure 12.9 A connector neurone

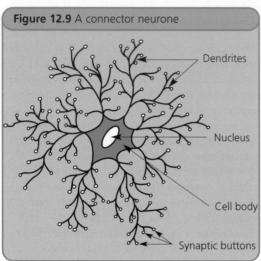

Dendrites

Nucleus

Cell body

Synaptic buttons

(Figure 12.11 opposite), which wrap themselves around the axon of the neurone. But they do not cover it completely. Instead, they leave small gaps which are called **nodes of Ranvier**. The myelin sheath acts as an insulator, preventing the electrical impulse from being generated at that point. But in order to understand this, we need to look a little more closely at the chemistry of the nerve cell.

Nerve cells fire by producing a brief electrical impulse which travels down the axon to the cell's dendrites. The electrical impulse results from an interaction between different chemicals inside and outside the cell. This interaction is possible because the membrane which covers the axon of the nerve cell is semi-permeable – that is, it lets some molecules through but blocks others out.

Figure 12.10 A motor neurone

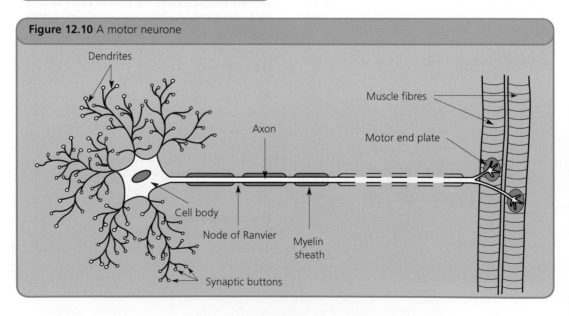

Dendrites

Muscle fibres

Axon

Motor end plate

Cell body

Node of Ranvier

Myelin sheath

Synaptic buttons

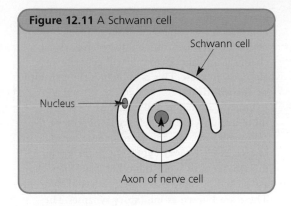

Figure 12.11 A Schwann cell

Schwann cell

Nucleus

Axon of nerve cell

either positively or negatively, and these are known as **ions**. The electrical impulse of the neurone results from an interaction between sodium and potassium ions.

When the nerve cell is resting, there are more potassium ions outside the axon, and more sodium ions inside it. 'Gates' in the cell membrane open to let them pass through. Potassium ions pass through the cell membrane much more quickly than sodium ions do, which means that effectively, three potassium ions pass outside the cell for every two sodium ions which pass into it. Since both sodium and potassium ions are positively charged, this produces a lower electrical charge inside the nerve cell than there is outside it – the inside of the cell is negatively charged with respect to the outside (see Figure 12.12). When it is at rest – a state known as the **resting potential** – the neurone is ready to fire, but it can remain that way for a long time before it is triggered off.

As the electrical impulse travels down the cell, the cell membrane becomes depolarised. This

opens special sodium 'gates', which allow sodium ions to flow through into the cell. If the membrane is only slightly depolarised, then potassium ions flow back to keep things at rest. But sometimes, the amount of depolarisation reaches a **threshold**, and so many sodium atoms rush through that they create a brief positive electrical charge in the neurone – what we call an **action potential**.

The action potential does not last long, because the sodium gates begin to close again as soon as it happens, while the potassium gates stay wide open. So potassium rushes into the cell again while the sodium is shut out. Sometimes, this reaction leaves the cell with such a strong negative charge that it needs a short period of time to recover before it can fire again. This period is known as the **absolute refractory period**. It is followed by the **relative refractory period**, during which time the cell can fire, but only in response to a particularly strong set of signals.

The myelin sheath

The action potential moves gradually along the axon of the neurone, depolarising the axon's membrane as it goes. But, as we have seen, some nerve cells are covered by a **myelin sheath** – a coating made of special fatty cells which wrap themselves round the axon. Schwann cells insulate the cell membrane, so that depolarisation cannot happen, and the ions cannot pass through. But there are gaps between the Schwann cells, known as nodes of Ranvier, and depolarisation can happen at these points. So in a myelinated nerve fibre – one which is covered by a myelin sheath – the

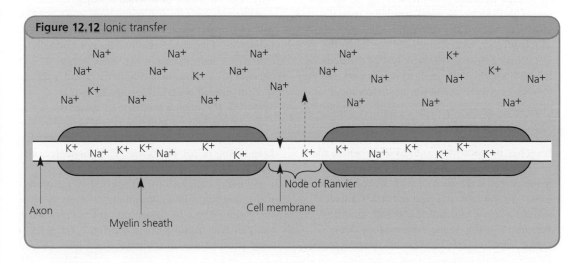

Figure 12.12 Ionic transfer

Na+　Na+　Na+　Na+　K+
Na+　Na+　K+　Na+　Na+　Na+　Na+
K+　Na+
Na+　K+　Na+　Na+　Na+　Na+　Na+　Na+

K+　Na+　K+　K+　Na+　K+　K+　K+　Na+　K+　K+　K+
　　　　　　　　　　　Na+　　　　　K+

Node of Ranvier

Cell membrane

Axon

Myelin sheath

impulse has to jump from one gap in the cell membrane to another. Travelling in large jumps means it travels much faster, and so signals can be passed around the body and to the brain far more quickly.

Sensory and motor neurones are all myelinated, which allows us to respond quickly to sensory stimulation – like pulling a hand away from a fire. But neurones in the autonomic nervous system are not, which is why it takes us a bit longer to feel the physical reaction to an alarming stimulus – increased heartrate and so on. Some neural diseases, like multiple sclerosis, produce a gradual demyelination of the motor neurones, which leaves the person with a progressive disability of movement, and is eventually fatal. One of the main areas of research into multiple sclerosis is looking for ways to encourage Schwann cells to re-grow in these damaged areas of the nervous system.

The neurones which do not have myelin sheaths tend to be mainly concerned with general states of the body, like those generated by the actions of the autonomic nervous system (see Chapter 13). These are longer-term states of being rather than immediate reactions to stimuli, so it does not seem to be quite so important if the nerve impulse carrying the signal takes a second or two longer to travel to the brain. But if your hand is in a flame, an extra second or two can do a lot of damage.

Synapses

The electrical impulse, as we have seen, passes along a neurone by electrochemical means. The way that a neurone passes its message to the next one is also electrochemical, involving special chemicals known as neurotransmitters. As we saw in Chapter 11, what happens is that when the electrical impulse reaches the end of the neurone, it causes a special chemical to be released into the **synapse** between it and the next neurone. This chemical is picked up at a receptor site on the next neurone.

Each neurone ends in a number of small branches, or **dendrites**, and these are where the receptor sites are located. This means that each neurone can make contact with a large number of others. In the case of a pain reflex, for instance, you do not just pull your hand away from the stimulus. You also realise what you are doing – neural impulses have been passed upwards to the brain as well as back to the muscles. But because neurones receive messages from so many other neurones, each neurone has to receive several chemical messages before it will generate an electrical impulse. This is known as the **principle of summation**.

Usually, a synapse will make the next neurone more likely to fire, by helping to depolarise the cell membrane. For this reason, these synapses are known as **excitatory synapses**. Some synapses, though, seem to work the other way. When they are picked up, they make the cell less likely to fire. These are known as inhibitory synapses. The combination of excitatory and **inhibitory synapses** means that the brain can direct impulses towards particular sets of neurones, and avoid stimulating others. This allows it to generate **neural pathways** – special routes for nerve impulses which are involved with particular functions or activities. We looked at some of these **neural pathways**, such as those involved in movement of the body, in Chapter 10.

Neurone activity and sensation

Repeatedly stimulating any nerve cell produces **habituation**. This means that the cell simply will not fire any more in response to that stimulus, although it might respond to a different one. In psychological terms, habituation means that we cease to be aware of the information that we are receiving, and become aware of it again only when the stimulus changes. You may have noticed this already – for example, in the case of the continuous humming of a refrigerator. We usually become so used to a stimulus like this that we only become aware of it when it stops.

Although we adjust to continuous noise, we can still look at the same visual stimulus without it fading out. The reason why we do not normally experience habituation in the visual system is because of the continual tiny tremors and jerks that the eyeball makes. These are known as **saccades**. By making sure that an image is constantly falling on different retinal cells, the saccades produce continual stimulation, so we can keep seeing things even when they themselves do not change.

All nerve cells become habituated to a stimulus if they are stimulated continuously – even those in the visual system. In 1961, Pritchard reported on a study in which miniaturised projectors and screens were attached to contact lenses (see Figure 12.13).

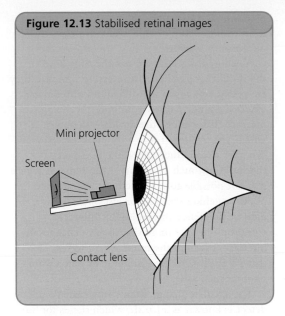

Figure 12.13 Stabilised retinal images

Mini projector

Screen

Contact lens

This meant that the volunteers who wore them received a stabilised image on the retina: the projector moved whenever the eyeball moved, so that the image always fell on exactly the same part of the retina each time. Pritchard found that the image which the research participants saw disappeared within just a few seconds, as the rod and cone cells became habituated to the stimulus.

We seem to habituate quite quickly to olfactory information. You may have had the experience of entering a room or a building and noticing that it had a slightly strange smell. Usually, by the time you have been in that room for a few minutes, you do not notice the smell any more – you have become habituated to it. Similarly, we can adapt quickly to different tastes, but we can recover from this adaptation almost equally rapidly. Much of the enjoyment of having more than one course in a meal involves precisely that kind of adaptation, and many people will have had the experience of being unable to taste something properly because they have just eaten something quite different: a classic example here is the effect of peppermint flavoured toothpaste, which can make orange juice taste completely different.

We can also become habituated quite quickly to some kinds of tactile information, especially temperature. You may have noticed that it does not take long to adjust to the temperature of a normal swimming pool – it may feel cold when you first dive in, but within a very few minutes your skin sensors adjust, and you feel quite comfortable in the water. Similarly, we become habituated to light pressures, like the feel of clothes, very quickly; although not when the pressure is so strong as to become painful. Given the role of pain receptors in alerting us to dangers and problems, it is probably just as well that we do not become habituated to pain stimuli very quickly.

Recovering from habituation can produce some interesting effects; we often experience a sensation which is exactly opposite to that which we have just been experiencing. **Negative after-effects** are particularly pronounced in the visual system. If, for instance, you spend a couple of minutes gazing continually at an area of red, and then you look at a white surface, you will experience an after-image of a greenish colour. Similarly, watching a continuous, linear movement produces an after-image of movement in the opposite direction – an effect known as the **waterfall effect** (see Chapter 2).

Adaptation

Adaptation is another factor in sensory perception. Our sense receptors tend to adjust themselves to the background stimulation that they are receiving. If the background stimulation is low, then the sensory stimulus can seem exaggerated, or much higher than usual. For example, a noise which seems quite ordinary in the daytime, such as a telephone bell, can seem extremely loud at night, when background sensory information is lower.

The process of adaptation is even more apparent when it comes to the way that our visual sense is able to adapt to low light levels. We have already seen how we have different types of receptor cells: cone cells providing colour vision, but not being very sensitive to dim light; and rod cells which are much more sensitive, but only detect black and white. Cone cells can react quite quickly to changes in illumination, but they do not allow us to see much in dim light. Rod cells take much longer to adapt, but when they have done so, we can see much more than we might have thought possible.

Researchers have investigated dark adaptation using perceptual thresholds. A **perceptual threshold** is the point at which a measured stimulus – in this case, a flash of light – can be detected 50% of the time. Varying the brightness of the flash of light, and measuring how long the person had been in the dark, allowed researchers to detect the way that rod and cone cells adapt to darkness.

When we go from a lit room into darkness, it takes real time for our visual system to adapt fully. At first, we cannot see anything at all, because our eyes are not adapted at all. After five minutes, our cone cells have adapted as much as they can, and we can see more than before – our perceptual threshold has fallen, so that a lower stimulus is required. The adaptation pauses at this point, and it would be easy to think that we had achieved full adaptation. But the rod cells only begin to adapt fully after about 11 minutes, and they do not reach their full sensitivity for about 40 minutes (Figure 12.14). So if you are in the country, away from street lights, do not be too impatient to switch on your torch – you will be surprised at how much you can see if you give your eyes long enough to adapt!

Sensory thresholds

When our sensory systems are fully adapted to low stimulation conditions, it is astounding how sensitive they become. The **absolute threshold** for a sensory system is the minimum stimulus that it can detect, under conditions of full adaptation. Psychologists have investigated the absolute thresholds of our five external senses, and Table 12.4 gives a description of how remarkably sensitive these are. But in real life, of course, we rarely give our nervous system a chance to extend its capabilities fully: street lights, traffic noise, air pollution and so on all combine to prevent us from experiencing the full adaptative capacity of our sensory systems.

Absolute thresholds are not the only kind of threshold that psychologists measure – in fact, they are pretty rare, given the difficulties of reducing external stimuli. More commonly, psychologists measure **difference thresholds** – the point at which we can detect that a stimulus has changed. We have already mentioned the two-point threshold of touch sensitivity – the point at which it is not possible to tell whether there are two points touching the skin, or just one. That is a kind of difference threshold. But the more common ones are those that involve changes in intensity – such as the point where we can detect that a light has become brighter, or that a sound has become louder.

The smallest change in intensity that we can detect is known as a **j.n.d.**, which stands for 'just noticeable difference'. A j.n.d. is the amount of change in physical energy that is necessary for someone to detect a difference between the two stimuli 50% of the time. This amount is not always the same: it varies according to the level which is already going on. If you are in conditions of very dim light, you will detect a slight increase in light energy. But if you were in bright light, you would not detect such a slight increase. You would need a much greater increase in light energy, so the j.n.d. would be proportionately larger.

The proportions are expressed by a number known as **Weber's constant**. There is a Weber's constant for loudness, for pitch, for brightness, for pressure on the skin, for detecting salt solutions, and many more. The constants are not all the same as each other, but they stay the same in any one scale. For example: to detect an increase in the weight of something that we lift, we need it to go

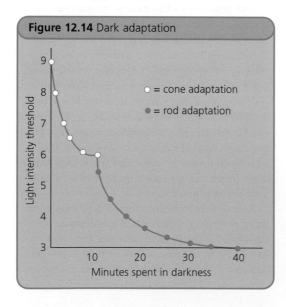

Figure 12.14 Dark adaptation

○ = cone adaptation
● = rod adaptation

Light intensity threshold (y-axis)
Minutes spent in darkness (x-axis)

Table 12.4	Absolute sensory thresholds
Vision	A candle flame 30 miles away on a clear, dark night.
Hearing	The tick of a watch 6.5 metres away.
Taste	One teaspoon of sugar in two gallons of water.
Smell	One drop of perfume in the volume of a three-bedroomed house.
Touch	The wing of a fly falling one centimetre onto your cheek.

up by approximately one-fiftieth of its weight. In other words, we would not detect the difference between 100g and 101g, but we would detect the difference between 100g and 102g. The **decibel scale**, which we use to measure sounds, approximates to human j.n.d.s for sound (Figure 12.15). Weber's constant for sound is roughly one-tenth, which means that the energy of the sound has to increase by a tenth before we can detect that it has become louder. So the difference between 95 and 96 db is much larger than the difference between 33 and 34 db.

Illusion and hallucination

Disturbances in the reception of sensory information usually take the form of illusions or hallucinations. There is often some confusion between the two. As we saw in Chapter 2, **illusions** are produced when a stimulus is misinterpreted, so that it is perceived as something different. If you see a human figure in the distance, but on moving closer you find that it is really a tree, you have experienced an illusion. But if you are in a wide-open field, with nothing near you, and you believe that you see a tree next to you, that is a **hallucination**. Hallucinations are sensory experiences which occur when there is no direct initiating stimulus: they are produced 'out of the blue', so to speak, by the nervous system.

Visual and auditory illusions are not uncommon – we often think that we have heard a particular sound which, on examination, turns out to have been something else. But visual or auditory hallucinations are frequently regarded as a sign of mental disturbance. If somebody sees and responds to visual images or sounds which are not there, they are often regarded, at least in modern technologically oriented societies, as being in need of psychiatric treatment. The experience of hallucinations, such as hearing voices, is regarded as a symptom of the psychiatric disorder schizophrenia (see Chapter 8).

Inducing hallucinations

There are a number of ways to induce hallucinations. In 1950, Penfield and Rasmussen conducted a series of investigations involving direct electrical stimulation of different areas of the brain, using small electrodes while the patient was conscious. (There are no sensory nerve endings in the brain itself, so the patients did not feel any pain.) When a particular region of the visual cortex was stimulated, one patient reported seeing balloons floating upwards into an infinite sky. Others reported seeing other visual images. These were hallucinations induced by direct stimulation of the visual cortex itself.

Sometimes hallucinations can be induced by drugs like LSD, mescaline and, in a milder form, psilocybin. Hallucinogenic drugs produce an intense sensitivity to visual stimulation, such that colours and sounds become brighter and clearer. Many drug-induced experiences which are described as 'hallucinations' are really illusions, brought about by this extreme sensitivity. Such illusions begin with an external stimulus, although they can be very powerful and convincing, seeming as if they have come 'from nowhere'. However, in a very few instances full-blown hallucinations do seem to occur, and it is thought that these come from chemical stimulation of the visual cortex by the drug.

Illusions, and on rare occasions hallucinations, can also be produced by other experiences, such as excessive fatigue or stress. Oswald (1970) conducted a number of sleep-deprivation experiments, and found that one of the effects of prolonged loss of sleep was that illusions or hallucinations would occur. This often involved a false perception of movement: a wallpaper pattern might appear to be swirling around, for instance,

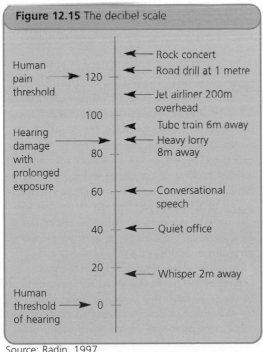

Figure 12.15 The decibel scale

Source: Radin, 1997

or an item of furniture might seem to shift its position when the person was not looking at it. People experiencing severely restricted sleep can have similar experiences, which is one reason, among many, why driving can be very dangerous under such conditions.

Synaesthesia

We know more about visual illusions and visual hallucinations than we do about any others, but these phenomena can occur with the other senses too. Most of us will have experienced tactile illusions, or auditory ones, where something sounds or feels like something else – there are a number of party games based on these experiences. The phenomenon known as **synaesthesia** involves the confusion of different sensory modes, such that someone might experience a sound as a taste, or a colour as a sound. In one case, a man who had been blind since the age of eleven experienced touch and sound in terms of colours: he had done this as a child, and as far as he was concerned, colours continued to be part of normal experience even though he could no longer see them (Wheeler and Cutsforth, 1925).

Vernon (1962) suggested that synaesthesia may be the normal state for infants, who only gradually learn to differentiate between the different sensory modes which make up experience. Other researchers have suggested that synaesthesia may result from neural confusions in the thalamus, perhaps occurring as a result of the action of neurotransmitters in neural pathways throughout that region of the brain. Essentially, though, such conclusions are mostly guesswork, based on our existing knowledge of how different functions are dealt with in different parts of the brain.

The study of illusion and hallucination is a fascinating one, which we have only touched the surface of here. It also has relevance for the next area which we will be looking at in this chapter, which is research into parapsychology. Both illusion and hallucination have been put forward as explanations for parapsychological phenomena, sometimes with reason. But many psychologists believe that they are not the whole explanation for all parapsychological experiences, and that there may genuinely be instances where we appear to receive or transmit information outside of the normal sensory channels.

Parapsychology

Throughout recorded history, human beings have described experiences which appear to have been impossible using ordinary sensory channels. They appear to be using what are loosely described as 'psychic' abilities – perceiving emotions or thoughts at a distance, influencing objects without actually touching them; healing people; predicting the future; and so on. The study of **parapsychology** involves investigating those aspects of human experience which seem to go beyond (*para* = 'beyond') the normal, conventionally accepted, types of experience.

What is psi?

Morris (1986) described parapsychology as the study of apparent 'new' means of communication between organisms and their environment. The term **psi** is used generally, to refer to all, or any, of these types of influence, which are described in Table 12.5. There are two sets of working hypotheses in modern parapsychology. The **pseudopsi hypothesis** states that most, if not all, of the evidence for **psi** is spurious, and comes from deception or misinterpretation. The **psi hypothesis** states that under certain conditions, human beings do seem to have access to genuinely new means of communication (Morris, 1991). Parapsychologists utilise both of these hypotheses.

The problem is that many, if not most, of the experiences that people think of as 'psychic' actually have much more mundane explanations. We have already seen, in Chapters 2 and 3, how important expectations are to our cognitive processes: we are very ready to perceive what we expect to happen, and our memories for what actually took place are a long way from being a factual tape-recording. Our perceptual systems are geared to 'filling in' gaps, which means that we can easily be tricked into failing to notice things. Also, as we saw in Chapter 5, most people have very unrealistic ideas about probability and coincidence. And as we will see in the next section of this book, our social representations and attributions mean that objective reality is much less important in determining what we think, than social consensus. And social consensus, for the

Table 12.5 Types of psi

Extra-sensory perception	
Telepathy	Information perceived by one (the 'sender') is obtained by another (the 'receiver') without using currently recognised sensory channels.
Clairvoyance	The person gains information about their environment, or things in it, without using currently recognised sensory channels.
Precognition	The person acquires knowledge about a future event when that knowledge could not have been deduced from existing information.
Psychokinesis (PK)	
Micro PK	The person is able to exert psychokinetic influence at microscopic or micro-electronic levels. Instrumentation or statistical analysis, or both, are needed to detect what is happening.
Macro PK	The person creates a psychokinetic effect which can be detected with the naked eye.
Direct mental interaction with living systems (DMILS)	The person is able to influence a living target – human, animal or plant.

most part, is fascinated by 'mystical' things, and very ready to believe in them.

Psychologists are very aware of these mechanisms, and of the way that members of the public are often hoodwinked by them into thinking things are more inexplicable than they really are. As a result, psychologists generally tend to be sceptical about experiences that are commonly claimed as paranormal. Blackmore (1996) described how many of these experiences can be explained much more easily by applying ordinary psychological mechanisms, and many other psychologists share this view.

However, most psychologists also retain an open mind when it comes to the possibility that people or animals really may have some forms of communication that we do not yet understand. The complexities of human experience are far from being fully understood, and it would be arrogant to assume that we knew everything there is to know. Although a knowledge of psychological mechanisms can explain a great deal of apparently parapsychological experience, most psychologists reserve judgement on the question of whether they can explain everything.

The Skeptical school

Some, however, do not. In addition to those who research parapsychological phenomena because they think there is really something that needs explaining, there are those who insist that there is absolutely nothing of the kind, and that positive research outcomes are the result either of deliberate fraud, or of inadequate research controls. Kurtz

(1985) described how scepticism about parapsychological phenomena has effectively become an entire school of thought in parapsychology. Skeptical parapsychologists (I use the American spelling of 'sceptical' to describe this school of thought, since that is what they call themselves) devote much of their research to challenging parapsychological theories and demonstrations. As a result, parapsychological methodology has had to respond to their criticisms, and we will be looking at some examples of this later in this chapter.

Exposing fraudulent activity, however, is also an essential part of parapsychological research. Many of the well-known and widely publicised 'psychics' have been shown to be fraudulent when exposed to careful and systematic laboratory investigation. But apparently successful 'psychics' can make a great deal of money, and so they are very reluctant to submit to rigorous investigation. Some of the tricks that they use to deceive people are described in Box 12.2 on page 374, and others will come up elsewhere in this chapter. A great deal of parapsychological research work, particularly in Britain where it is mainly based at the University of Edinburgh, is concerned with investigating these cases.

Early parapsychological research

Research into parapsychological phenomena of one sort or another took place throughout the nineteenth century, and continued into the twentieth. Mostly, this research was conducted by private individuals, or through organisations such

Box 12.2 Identifying parapsychological fraud

Evaluating whether either ESP or PK is really happening involves examining many different factors. It is important to be rigorous about this examination, because fraudulent 'psychics' who can convince the general public that they have 'real powers' earn a great deal of money. So, they put a great deal of effort and ingenuity into producing fraudulent psychic effects. The American stage magician James Randi has devoted a considerable amount of effort to exposing how psychic fraudsters work, and how they have tricked naïve parapsychological researchers (Randi, 1982). Parapsychology researchers at the University of Edinburgh and the University of Hertfordshire have also been active in exposing psychic fraudsters.

Some of these sources of fraud have been described in the text. But there are many ways that fraudulent psychics can deceive the public. One of them, for example, is to seem to gain information or exert influence across barriers, when really it is a matter of circumventing them using special techniques. For example: a magician with a highly trained sense of smell can often detect subtle characteristics in a person's smell, associated with fatigue, anxiety, or other emotional states, which they use as material for their apparent 'telepathy'. Or an accomplice may provide indetectable signals using a small hidden electronic pulser which informs the 'psychic' about crucial information.

Stage magicians are adept at the subtle 'peek' which allows them to gather necessary information even if they seem to be unable to see anything. They can also use sleight of hand, reflections, blindfolds with a loose weave that can be seen through, and even an odourless alcohol which makes an envelope temporarily transparent so they can see a hidden picture inside, and then evaporates leaving the envelope just as it was before.

Sometimes, of course, the barrier is not there are all – the connection between the psychic and the target results from a subtle application of the **self-fulfilling prophecy**, and people's gullibility. Since the majority of the public would quite like to believe that psychic phenomena exist, they are often prepared to see things as psychically influenced when there is no need to do so. Our tendency to notice the 'accurate' bits of horoscopes and ignore the irrelevant bits is a classic example of this – and it is no accident that horoscopes only make general predictions, not specific ones. Psychologists know this as the **Barnum effect**, after the circus entrepreneur P.T. Barnum, whose slogan was 'there's a fool born every minute'.

Morris (1991) discussed how observers can also be tricked. The most common methods for doing this are:

1 The observer may be given inaccurate information, e.g. through use of mirrors, echo devices, etc.
2 The observer may be led to misperceive the information, e.g. by means of camouflage, use of black threads, black-clad 'invisible' assistants, sensory overload, or skilful use of the laws of perception.
3 The observer's attention may be diverted, so that they are observing some irrelevant event at the crucial moment.
4 The observer may be led to misinterpret the information, through erroneous explanations, changes of props or illogically timed additions, or confusion of the natural sequence of events.
5 The observer may be led to misremember the information perceived, by using props such as 'doctored' photographs, or by skilful application of the principles of human memory.

Morris (1986) pointed out that each of these strategies involves a slightly different level of information processing, and this means that each level can be used to deal with situations that could not be dealt with adequately by the previous ones. Taken together, they amount to a considerable 'toolbox' that a skilled stage magician, or an equally skilled psychic fraudster, can use.

as the Society for Psychical Research (SPR). Beloff (1993) describes several of the case studies which SPR researchers investigated, some of which turned out to be fraudulent, but others of which seemed to have produced genuine, or at least inexplicable, phenomena.

One particularly influential investigation, as it turned out, was that of a 'Margery' Crandon, a medium who appeared to be able to summon and materialise spirits. The case attracted the attention of the influential psychologists E.G. Boring and William McDougall. It also attracted the attention of Joseph and Louisa Rhine: a couple who were actively involved in exposing the medium's fraudulent activity. When, later that year, McDougall was invited to head the psychology department at Duke University, North Carolina, the Rhines also joined his staff.

J.B. Rhine proceeded to develop an active research programme at Duke University. He had three principles for his research: firstly, that it would depend on ordinary people, not those who had made a living out of their supposedly 'psychic' abilities (Rhine had been deeply disillusioned by the discovery of 'Margery's' fraud, and he distrusted mediums and apparently spontaneous psychic phenomena as too open to manipulation); secondly, that it would involve simple and easily tested procedures, which would be more likely to show a reliable effect; and thirdly, that it would involve rigorous statistical assessment of the test results, and so take care of the problems presented by probability and chance effects.

The Zener cards

Rhine's research programme continued throughout the 1930s. He asked Karl Zener, a psychologist on McDougall's staff who specialised in perception, to design a set of cards which would provide clear, memorable imagery and could be used for ESP experiments. The result was a pack of 25 cards, now known as Zener cards, each of which had one of five symbols: a cross, a circle, a square, a star, and wavy lines (Figure 12.16). These cards were shuffled, and then the research participant would be asked to predict what the next card to be dealt would be. The statistical baseline was that the researchers could expect a 'hit' 20% of the time, purely by chance. But Rhine and Zener carried out 800 preliminary trials in the academic year 1930–31, and achieved a hit rate of nearly 26%, with 207

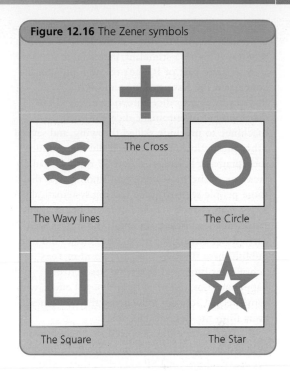

Figure 12.16 The Zener symbols

The Cross

The Wavy lines

The Circle

The Square

The Star

correct guesses as against the chance expectation of 160.

Rhine continued to research this phenomenon, and developed a series of rigorous testing procedures which became widely accepted for this type of research. His main concern at this time was to be able to distinguish between telepathy and clairvoyance, since the initial outcomes could have resulted from either. One way that he tested for clairvoyance tests was to use the 'Down-Through' technique, in which the participant had to call out the sequence of all 25 symbols before anyone had yet turned the cards over and looked at them – preventing any unconscious telepathic influence. Telepathy was more tricky, since it was hard to do objectively, but one approach was to provide the 'sender' with a set of numbers that told them which symbol to think of at a time.

Negative psi and the 'sheep-goat' effect

Rhine's belief that all human beings were likely to have parapsychological ability took a back seat as the research programme continued, because their results showed that they had certain people who were distinctive as 'high-scorers'. These people would typically score between seven and nine correct hits in a set of 25, as opposed to the chance score of five. Rhine investigated a number of variables, including the influence of drugs – finding, for example, that sodium amytal, a depressant, tended to decrease the level of scoring, whereas caffeine, a stimulant, increased it.

A separate part of Rhine's research programme concerned PK testing. Rhine and Rhine's investigations into dice-throwing involved the development of automatic dice-throwing machines, to preclude skilled throwing, and several other precautions. This research did not produce such dramatic findings as the ESP research had. In fact, one of the most consistent findings was that some people seemed to be scoring systematically lower than chance – to the point of being highly statistically significant. Although the studies were carried out during the 1930s, the Rhines did not publish these findings until 1943; and in 1945, Schmiedler proposed that what was actually happening was a kind of **negative-psi** effect, with some people actually influencing the outcomes away from the desired direction.

In 1943, Schmiedler reported that people who believed in psi were much more likely to produce positive findings on ESP tests than those who were avowedly sceptical. Indeed, the difference was so great that the sceptics – whom she called 'goats' – actually seemed to score at below-chance levels, while believers – referred to as 'sheep' – scored above chance.

Naturally, these results produced considerable discussion among parapsychologists, and further studies supported the general finding of the differences in outcomes between 'sheep' and 'goats', although not as strongly as Schmiedler's original ones. Lawrence (1993) performed a **meta-analysis** of 73 studies investigating this effect, conducted by 37 different experimenters. The results showed that there was a highly consistent significant difference between believers and non-believers in terms of how well they performed on experimental psi tasks.

The reliability problem

Rhine did, though, publish a report of his ESP findings in 1937, and the report attracted immediate and massive attention. It also stimulated a number of other research programmes in several American universities, and led to the establishment of the *Journal of Parapsychology* as a vehicle for reporting systematic academic research in the field. As research continued, however, it became apparent that the early findings could not be replicated consistently, either at Duke or elsewhere.

Critics argued that the Duke University findings had resulted from scientific fraud rather than rigorous research, and that the testing procedures used in the laboratory had been seriously flawed (Hansel, 1985) although other researchers challenged these claims.

The **reliability problem** appears to be a regular feature of parapsychological research. An initial phase of highly positive and convincing results tapers off into a period where results become elusive, and often has a third phase, where it is finally discredited when one or two high-achieving participants are detected in fraud. Beloff (1993) discussed how this reliability problem has occurred with almost all kinds of parapsychological phenomena, ranging from early demonstrations of mesmerism and clairvoyance, to the performances of spirit mediums, to demonstrations of Zener-card ESP.

For some, the reliability problem is evidence that the whole business of parapsychological research is fraudulent. Their argument is that initial demonstrations are less rigorously checked by sceptical investigators, since they involve new approaches and new techniques. As controls become more rigorous, those involved become less and less able to sustain the deception, and so their demonstrations are more erratic and less reliable. Dingwall (1965) argued that 60 years in psychic research had convinced him that almost all of the people involved were not seeking truth, but seeking to confirm their own personal agendas, and that this led to a powerful tendency towards either deliberate fraud, or negligent methodology. In the case of the Rhine experiments, for example, Dingwall argued that some of the Zener cards used in early studies were constructed of such flimsy material that they could be read even when face-down.

Other suggestions have been put forward to explain the reliability problem. One of these concerns the atmosphere in which the research is conducted. Rhine himself believed that the critical atmosphere engendered by sceptics interfered with psychic ability, which was why his results declined over time. The Duke researchers had discovered that the best mental approach to psi research was one of 'playful challenge', with the tasks being treated as pleasant and enjoyable. The Rhine ESP experiments were repeated in several American universities, with varying success but always lower than the Duke outcomes. They were also repeated in Britain, with absolutely zero results. However, one is tempted to speculate on the likelihood of British research psychologists of the 1930s managing to achieve an atmosphere of 'playful challenge' in their laboratories!

There is also the question of the immense pressure put on individuals who seem to have demonstrated psychic ability in the laboratory. The need to replicate their achievement over and over again is bound to produce boredom and decreasing interest, and it is not unreasonable to suppose that would affect ability as well. We have already seen how memory and perception – which are robust abilities – are affected by personal factors like hunger, emotion and fatigue; and there is no reason to suppose that parapsychological abilities are stronger. It may be that those individuals, faced with dwindling abilities from these factors but aware of the importance of their demonstrations, resorted to fraud in later years in an attempt to simulate their unfeigned earlier performance.

Evaluating parapsychological research

Parapsychology as a discipline experiences far more methodological criticism than any other area of psychology. But this is not because parapsychologists conduct sloppy work. On the contrary, the rigour with which modern parapsychological research is conducted would put to shame the work of many other psychological researchers. But parapsychologists, virtually by definition, are studying phenomena which challenge conventional materialist assumptions about how the world works. As a result, there are different standards applied to parapsychology than to other forms of psychological research.

Some psychologists argue that the **dual standard** is justified, on the grounds that parapsychology represents such a challenge to our general world-view that they need to produce findings which are absolutely incontrovertible. But there is also the problem of making what are known as **Type II errors**, by failing to recognise a significant phenomenon when it is really there. Radin (1997) argued that the extreme dual standard applied to parapsychology has resulted in stifling or suppressing very real findings, and also making it extremely difficult for parapsychologists to obtain research funds.

Experimental control

One source of these different standards concerns the adequacy of experimental controls. All psychoogical research which involves laboratory experimentation needs to be carefully controlled – and, as we will see, para-psychologists are perhaps keener than anyone else to ensure that happens. The main problem is to do with avoiding **sensory leakage**. This where a flaw in a study allows information to be transmitted to the participant through normal sensory channels, when that ought to have been impossible. For example, Dingwall's criticism of the early Zener card experiments was that they were so flimsy that participants could detect the symbol even when the card was face-down. If the ordinary senses could provide information which was supposed to be inaccessible by means of those senses, the results of the study are invalidated.

For this reason, as we will see, modern parapsychologists are meticulous in their attention to experimental control. In fact, they are far more so than many conventional psychologists. If we look closely at ordinary psychological research, we find that it is not the case that every single possible variable is normally identified and eliminated. An experimental cognitive psychologist, for example, will evaluate the potential contaminating variables of an experiment very carefully, and aim to eliminate those which are likely to affect the outcome. But with more obscure possibilities, the psychologist is likely to judge that the possibility of contamination is so remote that it can reasonably be ignored.

Parapsychologists on the other hand, must control any effect which could conceivably affect the outcome, even if it is distinctly unlikely that it actually did. They will also be rigorously scrutinised, to make sure that they do. A cognitive psychologist can uncover a psychological effect and be able to announce it to the psychological community relatively freely. But a parapsychologist who uncovers an effect of the same magnitude will need to respond to skeptics who are actively seeking to discredit their statements. The slightest flaw in the methodology will lead to the conclusion that the study is invalid as evidence. So the matter of **experimental rigour** is crucial for parapsychology.

Replication

A second aspect of the dual standard concerns the replication of experimental findings. Replication is an important criterion in scientific research – if a finding cannot be replicated, then it is considered invalid. But replication is not an absolute matter. Even physicists and chemists find that, on occasions, their experiments do not replicate. But if they can be replicated most of the time, that is considered adequate as evidence. Similarly, psychological findings are not invariably replicated – there are occasions when the researchers conducting the replication do not carry out the procedures exactly, or make some adjustment which means that the outcome does not happen according to prediction. But as long as the findings can be replicated by most other researchers, and as long as those researchers are working in different laboratories and not all part of the same research team, an effect is considered valid. An effect must be replicable to be accepted, but one or two failures to replicate do not matter – as long as the majority of replications are consistent.

The same holds true for parapsychology – except when parapsychological findings are being communicated to the rest of the world. Skeptics who argue against parapsychological research often seize on one or two failures to replicate, as evidence that a whole research finding is invalid – even when there are positive findings of the same effect being made in numerous laboratories around the world. Blackmore (1996) described how she became a skeptic as a result of experimental findings which were only positive in a minority of cases – about six experiments out of twenty – and not reliably replicable.

Radin (1997) challenges this argument, on the grounds that parapsychological abilities, almost by definition, are at the extreme end of human ability. A successful baseball player would not achieve peak performance in a replicable manner, and the team's fans would be very happy if he scored a 'home run' in six out of twenty attempts. It is unrealistic, Radin argues, to expect that level of consistency when dealing with exceptional abilities. And, of course, if parapsychological abilities were so robust that they could always be demonstrated experimentally under any conditions, they would not be a matter of debate in the first place.

Another problem is the fact that many parapsychological findings are not particularly strong. Some skeptics argue that the effects may be consistent, but that they are too weak to be considered valid. Yet the same standard is not applied to medical data. Utts (1991) compared the evidence for psi with the evidence that aspirin could be a useful tool for preventing heart attacks. In the latter case, the effect was only shown unequivocally in a study involving more than 22,000 people. A smaller study, involving only a couple of thousand individuals, would have only shown an extremely weak effect – and in fact, it was smaller studies with weak effects which had hinted that the large study was worth carrying out. But the larger study showed the effect was there, and that it was sufficient for medical action to be taken – aspirin is now recommended as a treatment for heart attacks.

Some parapsychological research, notably the **ganzfeld studies** which we will be looking at later, show effects which are up to four times stronger than the aspirin effect. But because of the way that parapsychological research is regarded, skeptics argue that they are still too weak to be considered adequate as evidence. The standards applied to one branch of scientific research are very different from the standards applied to another.

Meta-analysis

One solution to this problem has been to use the technique of **meta-analysis**. This is a research method which involves looking at the findings of all of the known studies in an area – or as many of them as practicable – and seeing how their results appear when taken as a whole. In a meta-analysis, researchers look at the scores obtained from different studies, and also at the standard deviations of those scores. Utts (1991) discussed how meta-analysis allows researchers to combine data using specific statistical techniques, and to explore the pattern of data across the various studies. This allows researchers to identify consistent findings, which may be less apparent in a single small study, and to evaluate just how reliable a given effect is.

Meta-analysis is used in many areas of psychology, and is one of the most powerful research tools available to us today. Radin (1997) showed how, in several different areas of parapsychological research, meta-analysis indicates that there are consistent effects. Because they are drawing data from a much larger pool of research participants, the overall reliability of an effect is much easier to estimate. Figure 12.17 shows the outcome of a meta-analysis of tests of micro-PK, in which participants attempted to influence a random number generator (Nelson and Radin, 1987). The points on the chart indicate the average result for the studies conducted during that year. The lines running through the points indicate the standard deviations of each year's findings. While the outcome of any one study on its own may not be particularly impressive, the small but consistently positive outcomes revealed by the meta-analysis give a very different picture.

The file-drawer problem

Another problem for parapsychologists, which is not faced by other psychological researchers (although perhaps it should be) is known as the **file-drawer problem**. This is the argument that only positive findings are submitted to journals for publication. Failed replications are not sent for publication, but instead are filed away in a drawer, with nobody knowing about them except the people who carried out the study. Skeptics argue that this effect seriously distorts parapsychological research findings, making them seem more convincing than they really are.

It is questionable, however, just how important the file-drawer problem really is. It is a problem which permeates all scientific research, not just that of parapsychology; yet in other fields it is accepted as unavoidable, and largely ignored. In the case of parapsychology, it is also possible for

the file-drawer problem to work in the opposite direction. Because of the fear of ridicule, or of seeming to be 'going out on a limb', some psychologists may not publish positive psi effects, even when they have obtained them. I personally know of at least one instance of an academic psychologist, working at a highly prestigious university, who conducted a set of psi studies out of curiosity, obtained highly significant results, consulted colleagues about publication, and was advised to keep quiet about them. He followed the advice, and the results of the study were relegated to the file drawer.

This is anecdotal, of course, and it is more likely that most 'file-drawer' studies are, as the skeptics argue, failures to replicate. But the use of meta-analysis also allows parapsychologists to deal with this argument, by calculating just how many failed studies would need to have been relegated to file drawers in order to cancel out the effect. In the case of the Nelson and Radin meta-analysis of micro-PK described earlier, there would have to be roughly 54,000 failed studies to cancel out the effects of the 832 studies analysed. A file-drawer problem of this magnitude somehow does not seem terribly likely.

Another factor in favour of parapsychologists on this matter is the way that – unlike other psychologists – parapsychologists have a policy of actively seeking out non-replications wherever they can. In 1975, the Council of the Parapsychological Association adopted a policy

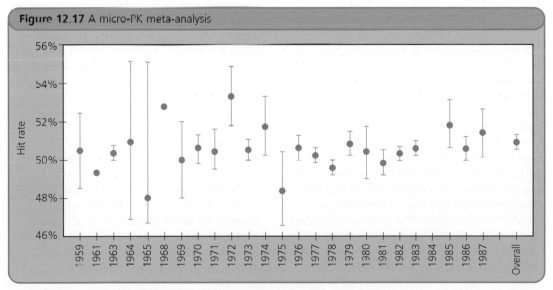

Figure 12.17 A micro-PK meta-analysis

Yearly hit-rate point estimates and 95% confidence intervals for RNG studies of mind-matter interaction. In some cases the confidence intervals are so small that they are obscured by the point-estimate dots. (Source: Radin, 1997)

aimed to counter the selectivity involved in only reporting positive outcomes. From then on, negative findings were reported routinely, both in their publications and at conferences. As a result, negative-finding outcomes are much more well-publicised in parapsychology than they are in other areas of psychology – and they are routinely included in meta-analyses.

Belief and gullibility

Schmiedler's distinction between 'sheep' and 'goats' included the observation that believers were much more likely to report psi experiences of their own than non-believers were. Schmiedler believed that non-believers do not report psi experiences because they subsconsciously avoid or suppress them; but others took the view that believers may simply be more gullible – too ready to accept fake psychic demonstrations at face value.

Besterman, in 1932, investigated this by asking people to attend a fake seance, and then asking them a number of questions about what had happened. Besterman found a number of differences between believers and non-believers. Believers tended to underestimate the number of people present; they failed to report major disturbances which took place if they seemed unrelated to the main subject of the seance; and they did not recall all of the conditions of the seance.

In another study, Jones and Russell (1980) set up a fake ESP demonstration in front of participants who were either believers or non-believers. In one of their conditions, the demonstration seemed to be successful, while the other showed an unsuccessful outcome. They found that believers often distorted their memories of the unsuccessful demonstration, remembering it as having successfully demonstrated ESP. The non-believers, on the other hand, recalled both of the conditions of the experiment accurately.

In 1995, Wiseman and Morris conducted a study to investigate whether believers and non-believers showed different recall for pseudo-psychic demonstrations. The participants watched a stage magician perform a number of apparently psychic manoeuvres. One was an apparent ESP task, in which the magician correctly identified cards taken from an ESP pack, without seeming to look at them. The second was a fake PK task, in

which the magician apparently bent, and then broke, a fork simply by stroking it. After they had seen the activities, the participants were given statements about the task, and asked to rate how far they felt them to be true. The questions were either 'important', such as 'the psychic handled the cutlery before the fork demonstration began', or 'unimportant', such as 'when the study was over, the psychic returned unbent cutlery to the pile'.

Wiseman and Morris found that the believers rated the demonstrations as being significantly more 'paranormal' than the non-believers did. The non-believers, however, recalled significantly more of the 'important' information, though there were no differences in recall when it came to the 'unimportant' information. Once that recall data had been collected, the participants were then told that the demonstration had not been of psychic ability, but of magic tricks. Then they were asked to recall information about the demonstration again. This time, there were no differences between believers and non-believers. It does seem, therefore, as though belief in psychic phenomena does predispose people to shape their memories of these events – something that is well-known, and deliberately manipulated, by fraudulent psychics.

ESP research

Modern parapsychological research is very different from the early Rhine studies. Parapsychologists have had to address the methodological challenges we have just examined, and as a result they make a great deal of use of rigorous measurement and computer-based controls. They also conduct research into a wide range of topcis: Table 12.6 lists some of the papers delivered at a recent parapsychological research conference. In this section, we will look at some of the specific research areas that have been investigated by parapsychologists.

We will begin by looking at studies of **extra-sensory perception**, or **ESP**. ESP research investigates cases where the person seems to receive information from some kind of target in the environment, across barriers which prevent that information from being transmitted in the ordinary way (see Figure 12.18). Modern research into ESP is mainly concerned with three areas: telepathy, clairvoyance, and precognition. We will look at research into each of these areas.

Table 12.6 The range of modern parapsychological research

*A sample of papers presented at the 1997
Annual Convention of the Parapsychological
Association*

Factors related to the depth of near-death
experiences: testing the 'embellishment over
time' hypothesis

Out-of-body experiences and dissociation

Emotion and intuition: unravelling variables contributing to the Presentiment Effect

Attention focusing facilitated through remote
mental interaction: a replication and exploration
of parameters

Exploring the links: creativity and psi in the
Ganzfeld

Psi and cross-cultural studies

Understanding misdirection: the pseudo-psychic's
invisible assistant

Quantitative investigation of a legally disputed
'haunted house'

Psi-Ping: an investigation of mental intention
and internet responsiveness via the World Wide
Web

An unbiased method for trial-by-trial sampling
of deterministic randomness sources for ESP
experiments

Ganzfeld at the crossroads: a meta-analysis of
the new generation of studies

Individual differences in blind psychic readings

Belief in the paranormal and attendance at
psychic readings

Experience of sleep paralysis

Relationship between childhood
hypnogogic/hypnopompic experiences, childhood fantasy proneness and anomalous
experiences and beliefs: an exploratory WWW
survey

Perceived luckiness and the UK National Lottery

Backwards causation, precognition and the intervention paradox

Human sensing of weak electromagnetic fields:
a possible relationship to psi?

Experiment One of the SAIC Remote Viewing
Program: a critical re-evaluation

Eyewitness testimony for 'seance room'
phenomena

'Broken' marital relations and claims of parapsychological experiences

Correlates of aura vision: the role of psi
experiences, dissociation, absorption, and
synesthesia-like experiences

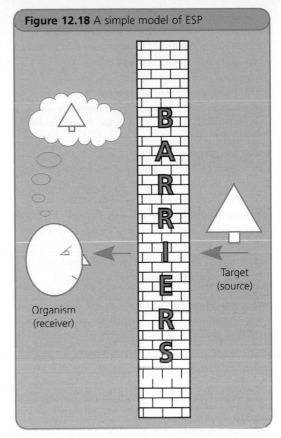

Figure 12.18 A simple model of ESP

Telepathy involves the sending of information
from the mind of one person (the 'sender') to the
mind of another ('the receiver'). As we have seen,
early research into this area used the Zener cards
as the material for sending information, and
perhaps as a consequence, the Zener cards have
come to symbolise research into telepathy, for
most people. However, just about nobody uses
them now. There were many criticisms of the
Zener card studies, and modern parapsychological
research involves very different techniques.

One of the main sources of dissatisfaction of
the Zener studies was the fact that they involved
forced-choice methods. In other words,
participants did not have free choices of what to
report – their answers were constrained to the five
symbols. As time went on, many parapsychologists
began to feel that this was a bit artificial, and
certainly remote from any manifestations of psi in
everyday life – a bit like Ebbinghaus's use of
nonsense syllables to study memory, which we
looked at in Chapter 3. So, they looked for
research methods which did not impose so many
limitations on the participant.

There had been a number of studies implying that psi seemed to be most associated with relaxed, or naturally meditative, states. Schechter (1984) conducted a meta-analysis of 25 experiments on hypnosis and psi, and found a strong suggestion that a hypnotic state could facilitate manifestations of psi. There was also a series of studies conducted at the Maimonides Medical Centre in New York, which suggested that the contents of dreams could be influenced by an image transmitted by a 'sender' in the next room (Ullman, Knipper and Vaughan, 1973). Although the Maimonides dream studies were criticised, and other researchers failed to replicate them (Child, 1985), there was enough to suggest that perhaps an experimental procedure which encouraged participants to relax and reduced sensory stimulation, might be a good idea.

The ganzfeld technique

The solution which researchers adopted was to use the **ganzfeld technique**. This is a long-established method of reducing sensory stimulation. We came across it in Chapter 2, since it was used by the Gestalt psychologists to investigate figure-ground perception. Establishing a ganzfeld means cutting off as many sources of external sensory information as practical, so that the person is relaxed and undistracted. Table 12.7 lists the features of a modern ganzfeld experience described by Bem and Honorton (1994).

In a typical ganzfeld study, a research participant – the 'receiver' – is settled in the ganzfeld, while a sender, in a separate, acoustically isolated room, is shown a randomly selected photograph, print, or video clip. The sender concentrates on the target, and the receiver keeps up a continuous verbal report of the sensory impressions and images that they are receiving. This carries on for about half an hour. After that time, the receiver comes out of the ganzfeld and is shown several (usually four) different stimuli of the same type as the one that the sender was looking at. The receiver rates each one according to how strongly it matches the imagery they experienced while in the ganzfeld. If the target image receives the highest rating, it counts as a 'hit', so if it were just chance, the hit rate would be 25%.

The results obtained using the ganzfeld technique were, for the most part, positive. But in 1994, Hyman, a convinced parapsychological skeptic, reported a meta-analysis of 42 ganzfeld studies, conducted between 1974 and 1981. He concluded that there were a number of statistical and methodological weaknesses in the way that the studies had been conducted. Honorton (1994), a parapsychologist, responded to the criticisms by conducting a parallel meta-analysis, which argued that even though these weaknesses had occurred, they were not enough to account for the strong psi effects shown in the ganzfeld studies.

As a result of this debate, and to the credit of both of them (it is rare for opposing academics to work together on anything), Hyman and Honorton produced a joint communiqué, which they released in 1986. This paper identified the types of weaknesses in the earlier ganzfeld studies, and recommended more stringent procedures for future experimenters, some of which are listed in Table 12.8.

The autoganzfeld studies

In 1994, Bem and Honorton reported a series of eleven new ganzfeld studies which followed the guidelines published by Hyman and Honorton meticulously. Their basic design was the same, but they used video clips as their material, and the experimental protocols were controlled by a computer. As a result, they became known as the **autoganzfeld studies**. These new, squeaky-clean studies produced very successful results.

Perhaps inevitably, the studies were criticised by Hyman (1994), mainly on the grounds that there was 'incomplete justification of the adequacy of the randomization procedures', but this was not a particularly strong critique, and was challenged as

---

Table 12.7 Establishing a ganzfeld

The room is acoustically isolated.

The research participant sits in a comfortable, reclining chair.

Translucent ping-pong ball halves are placed over the eyes.

Headphones are placed over the ears.

A red floodlight directed at the eyes creates an undifferentiated visual field.

White noise played through the headphones creates an undifferentiated auditory field.

Relaxation exercises are carried out to minimise somatic 'noise' from proprioception.

Source: Bem and Honorton, 1994

Table 12.8 Recommended procedures for ganzfeld studies

Strict security measures against sensory leakage.

Testing and documentation of randomisation methods for selecting targets.

Testing and documentation of randomisation methods for sequencing the judging pool.

Statistical correction for multiple analyses.

Advanced specification of the experiment's status (e.g. whether it was a pilot study).

Full documentation of experimental procedures in the published report.

Full documentation of the statistical tests used, including whether planned in advance or selected afterwards, in the published report.

Source: Hyman and Honorton, 1986

Table 12.9 Psi-conducive variables

The participant has had personal reported psi experiences.

The participant has had prior psi testing.

The participant obtains high scores on the Myers-Briggs Feeling-Perception scale.

The participant has studied mental disciplines.

The participant has a belief in psi.

The participant is extroverted rather than introverted.

The participant shows high levels of creativity.

The experimenters use dynamic rather than static targets.

The experimenters promote a 'warm social ambiance'.

The experimenters use a sender.

Source: Honorton, 1992

such by Bem (1994). Another criticism came from Wiseman, Smith and Kornbrot (1996) who suggested that there might have been some sound leakage between the two rooms containing the sender and the receiver. But this criticism, too, seems to have been speculative rather than based on evidence, and appears rather unlikely. The overall consensus was that the autoganzfeld studies conducted by Bem and Honorton provided strong evidence for a psi effect.

That effect, however, proved elusive. In 1997, Milton and Wiseman published another meta-analysis, this time of the ganzfeld studies which had been conducted since the publication of the Hyman and Honorton guidelines. It included 31 new ganzfeld studies, from ten different researchers. When they were taken together, their cumulative results were close to zero. Milton and Wiseman discussed a number of factors which might have explained why the Bem and Honorton studies had been successful, where other studies had not.

The main difference, they found, was in the way that the studies had been conducted. Bem and Honorton had paid particular attention to psi-conducive procedures. These are ways of carrying out a study which will make sure that the person feels at ease, and is likely to be able to utilise any psi abilities they may have. Honorton (1992) identified ten factors which could influence how effective the procedures were, and also how participants were selected (Table 12.9). Bem and Honorton had taken care to incorporate these factors into their study as far as possible, but the other ganzfeld studies examined by Milton and Wiseman had not. Milton and Wiseman concluded that it was necessary for researchers to address, and investigate, these factors much more closely – that just using a ganzfeld study without paying attention to psi-conducive procedures was not enough to produce reliable psi effects.

That was not, however, the end of the story, since at the same meeting at which Milton and Wiseman presented their findings, researchers reported four new ganzfeld studies, which would have produced a significant outcome in the Milton and Wiseman meta-analysis if they had been included. These studies had paid careful attention to their research procedures, and also to the selection of their participants – utilising highly creative individuals, or those with prior experience of mental disciplines which meant they were more likely to score positively (more about that later). The overall conclusion, then, seems to be that the ganzfeld technique does hold some potential for demonstrating psi abilities, but not with everyone, and not in every situation.

Clairvoyance

Clairvoyance is described as happening if a person gains information about their environment, or things in it, without using the currently recognised sensory channels. There is a major theoretical problem for parapsychologists in distinguishing between clairvoyance and telepathy, since a picture which is being 'sent' mentally by a participant in a telepathy study also has a physical existence, and could therefore, at least in theory, be perceived by a clairvoyant receiver. But there have been some experimental investigations which specifically relate to clairvoyance.

Some of the ganzfeld studies did not use a 'sender', on the grounds that the relevant images could be obtained by clairvoyance, rather than by telepathy. Honorton (1985) found that ganzfeld studies which used senders generally produced better results than those which did not; but only where the experimenters were already experienced in using both sender and no-sender methods. Where experimenters stuck to just one or other method, it was the no-sender studies which had produced slightly stronger results.

Morris, Dalton, Delanoy and Watt (1995) undertook a specific investigation of whether the sender mattered in autoganzfeld research. The study had three different conditions: sender absent (condition 1); sender present but receiver not certain whether they were present or not (condition 2); and sender present with receiver aware of the sender's presence (condition 3). At the beginning of the study, the receiver was introduced to their 'sender'. In conditions 1 and 2, they were told that the person might or might not be acting as sender for their study. At this point, nobody involved knew whether the person would be in condition 1 or condition 2. In condition 3, they were told definitely that this person would be their sender.

Once the receiver was settled in the ganzfeld, the sender returned to the room where the targets would be shown. At that point, for those in conditions 1 or 2, the computer system made a random selection as to which condition of the experiment was to be carried out. If it was condition 1, the 'sender' would be asked to leave; if it was condition 2, they would be asked to remain and focus on the images they would be shown.

The overall results were significant, indicating that there had been an effect. Interestingly enough, though, there was no significant difference between the three conditions – although the researchers did find a strong experimenter effect, which we will discuss later. They concluded that the presence of a sender was not actually necessary to obtain results in ganzfeld studies, since some participants seemed to be able to identify the target images whether another human being was consciously trying to transmit them, or not.

Remote viewing

Perhaps the most well-known studies of clairvoyance, though, are **remote viewing studies**, some of which caused quite a stir among scientists in the late 1970s and early 1980s. It began with a report in *Nature* by Targ and Puthoff, in 1974. They reported a series of field experiments using Pat Price, a former Californian police commissioner. The experiments had been investigating remote viewing – a form of clairvoyance in which the individual is able to 'see' a specific area or location some distance away, without receiving that information through conventional channels.

The target locations for Targ and Puthoff's studies were all in the San Francisco Bay area. They had a pool of 100 targets, twelve of which were randomly chosen for each experiment. Neither the experimenters involved, nor the research participants, knew the contents of the target pool, and the twelve locations for the study were chosen using a double-blind control. Price would be taken to the location from which he would work, accompanied by an experimenter. Two of the nine studies were conducted out of doors, one in an office, and five from a large copper-screen Faraday cage, designed to block any electrical transmissions. When Price was settled, a team of two to four experimenters would be given a target location. They had half an hour to drive to that location, and remained there for a further half-hour. During that second half-hour, Price described the sensory images that he was receiving, and these were tape-recorded.

Price showed a striking ability to describe the buildings, docks, roads, gardens and the like which formed the target locations. But he also made a number of inaccurate observations. So the researchers asked independent judges to assess the correlation between Price's descriptions, and the locations. The judges correctly matched six of the nine locations tested with Price's descriptions.

In 1978, however, Marks and Kammann wrote a letter to *Nature* challenging the Targ and Puthoff studies. They challenged the methodology, on the grounds that the experimenters had encouraged Price by referring to the previous successful trials, and that these remarks were on the tapes and could have cued the judges. Without these cues, they argued, independent judges obtained results which were little more than chance.

Tart, Puthoff and Targ (1980) in turn challenged Marks and Kammann's criticisms. They performed a re-analysis of the data, removing all phrases suggested as potential cues, and any others which might have been subsequently identified as having that potential. Then they submitted the material to a new, independent judge, who was unfamiliar with the Price study. This judge was asked to visit each target site, and to evaluate how closely the transcripts of Price's tape-recording matched the targets. This time, seven out of the nine targets were correctly matched, with a high match between the transcript and the target site, and a very low match between the transcript and other locations. So, Tart, Puthoff and Targ argued, their findings were not a cueing artefact. And also, the criticism did not apply to their several replication studies.

Marks (1981) responded by challenging the validity of their re-judging exercise, on two counts: firstly, that one of the researchers had carried out the editing of the transcripts, and secondly that the material which was being re-judged had already been published, and the new judge might have retained an unconscious memory of it. For good measure, he also challenged their statement about the replication studies, saying that they too had provided sensory cues in the transcripts. In their response, Puthoff and Targ (1981) said that his criticism was based on a misunderstanding about how the procedure had controlled for sensory cueing. They also performed yet another re-analysis of their data, taking Marks's argument about cueing and showing that, even if it had been true (which they did not believe) it still would not have had a large enough effect to account for the significance of the results.

The arguments about remote viewing carried on, and still carry on today. But the research was convincing enough for the US military to fund a considerable research programme into the field, and for a number of successful cases to be reported in the parapsychological journals. In one case, described by Radin (1997), a remote viewer was given the map co-ordinates of a particular site, and described a secret military facility in great detail, even identifying code words written on folders inside filing cabinets. A journalist heard about this, drove to the site, and reported that the experiment was obviously a failure, because all that was there was a hillside with sheep. The military people to whom he reported this eventually said that there had been a mistake with the map co-ordinates. The journalist, however, was unaware that the location was exact – but the military base was hidden deep underground.

In 1995, the CIA commissioned a review of the government-sponsored remote-sensing research. The committee came to six general conclusions. Firstly, that free-response remote-viewing studies were generally more successful than forced-choice ones. Secondly, certain individuals were consistently more successful than others – regardless of specific design conditions in specific experiments. Thirdly, mass screening showed that about 1% of those tested seemed to show consistent remote-viewing abilities. Fourthly, remote viewing did not improve consistently with either practice or training. Some people could perform effectively after only a few minutes of instruction; others still found it difficult or impossible after several hours. Fifthly, while it was unclear whether feedback was necessary, it did seem to enhance performance by providing a psychological boost. And sixthly, that remote viewing was unaffected by either distance or electromagnetic shielding (Utts, 1996).

There is, of course, still a great deal of dispute over remote-viewing studies. But there is also a considerable programme of research which has built up in this area, in several research locations. Like other parapsychological research, effect sizes seem to be larger when there is an atmosphere of trust and openness among participants. In 1997, Targ and Katra proposed a set of guidelines for researchers conducting remote-viewing studies, which are listed in Table 12.10. Despite the challenges, they regard remote viewing as one of the most reliable of the psi experiences currently being researched by parapsychologists, but they stress that it requires a sense of commonality of purpose, and mutual trust between viewer and experimenter.

Faking clairvoyance and telepathy

So far, we have looked at experimental evidence for telepathy and clairvoyance. But telepathy and clairvoyance are also popular areas for stage psychics, whose activities often involve appearing to perform ESP when really they are doing nothing

Table 12.10 Guidelines for remote-viewing

Use viewers who are open to and even excited about the prospect of psychic experience.

Pay attention to each viewer by giving consideration to his or her mental state at the time of the experiment.

Provide trial-by-trial feedback of only the correct target, and do it as soon as feasible.

Create trust by full disclosure, and no hidden agendas.

Psi is a partnership, not a master/slave relationship.

Seriousness of purpose provides motivation both to the viewer and the experimenter.

Targets should be physically and emotionally attractive, and uniquely different. No tarantulas for those who do not want to experience them.

Do not create large target pools. Have two to four items at most.

Take enough time to achieve rapport, plus 10-30 minutes for each trial. One trial per day is plenty. One trial per week is better, to maintain seriousness of purpose.

Practice allows viewers the opportunity to recognise mental noise and separate it from the psi signal.

Source: Targ and Katra, 1997

Table 12.11 Some common general responses

A European city	Paris
One of a list of five items	The second or fourth in the list
Number between 10 and 20	17
One of the Zener symbols	the star
Number between 1 and 100	37
A vegetable	carrot

of the kind. Sometimes, it is simply a matter of being sensitive to highly subtle forms of information. People who have come asking for psychic readings often give away a lot, without realising it. The 'clairvoyant' will pick up cues from clothing, from the way that someone sits and talks, from information that they have unconsciously revealed earlier in the interview, and from many other cues.

If the person has made an appointment to see the 'psychic', the latter is likely to have learned as much as possible about them beforehand, and many well-known 'psychics' subscribe to information-gathering services about their specialist areas. Their supposedly psychic observations are based on their specialist knowledge, and so have a reasonable likelihood of being fairly accurate. There are also many general observations which can be made reasonably safely, because people tend to choose them as a general rule. A few of these are listed in Table 12.11, but there are many more.

Precognition

Precognition, as its name implies, involves acquiring knowledge about a future event, in situations where that knowledge could not have been deduced from existing information. There are, obviously, many anecdotal accounts of precognition – someone may dream about a fire, for example, and then discover that a friend's house has burned down. Too often, though, these apparently convincing examples have other explanations. As we saw in Chapter 11, for example, we all have five or six dreams a night. It is not uncommon, either, for people to dream about fires. Statistically, it is entirely likely that sooner or later, someone will have a dream about a fire and then encounter a real-life one. Moreover, the dream may have taken place some time before, and only be recalled when news of the fire is received.

That does not, however, mean that all evidence for precognition can be discounted. Sometimes, precognitive experiences are dramatic and very difficult to explain in that way. Those experiences often seem to involve powerful events such as death, accident or severe illness happening to very close friends or relatives. But the problem for parapsychological researchers is gathering the data, and seeking independent sources of verification. Occasionally, these predictions are well-documented; but since they are real-life events, researchers are more often dependent on the participant's own accounts. And, as we saw in Chapter 4, people's accounts are not factual records of what happened, but constructions of events shaped to fit in with their social understandings – including their personal understandings of the paranormal.

Physiological measures of precognition

There is, however, some intriguing experimental evidence for a different kind of precognition. This evidence involves taking physiological measurements of changes in skin conductivity. As we will see in the next chapter, skin conductivity changes in response to emotional or stressful stimulation. It is a well-established and reliable response, which, among other things, forms the basis for lie-detectors. But it can also form a useful measure of people's involuntary emotional reactions.

Radin (1997) reported a set of studies which looked at people's responses to emotional stimuli. In a typical study, the participant would sit in a comfortable chair, facing a colour computer screen. Electrodes for measuring changes in skin conductivity and a heartrate monitoring device were attached to the fingers of the left hand. The participant was able to control the computer display using a mouse with the right hand. Pressing the mouse button caused the computer to make a random selection from a large set of photographs. The screen remained blank for five seconds, then the photo was displayed for three seconds, then the screen went blank again for another five seconds. Finally, a message indicated that the participant could start again when they were ready.

Some of the photos, which were high-quality digitised images, were of pleasant images, such as landscapes or happy people. Others were designed to be disturbing or shocking, including images of autopsies and erotic photos. (Because of this, only adults were used in the study.) The participant's physiological reactions were monitored and recorded for the whole period of the study.

Not suprisingly, the emotional pictures produced a powerful physiological reaction. But what was more interesting was that they seemed to produce a reaction in the participant before they had actually appeared. Figure 12.19 is the combined results from 24 research participants in this study. It shows how there was a measurable difference between the physiological reactions before pleasant pictures, and the physiological reactions obtained before emotional ones. Radin's research suggests that the research participants were somehow able to anticipate what type of image they were about to see. However, when they were asked whether they had any idea about what was coming up, almost all of the participants responded negatively.

This is a very new approach to precognition research, and it remains to be seen what it will produce. However, Radin states that the results have been independently replicated in at least one other laboratory, located in a different continent. The unconscious nature of the physiological reactions involved make this approach to parapsychological research a very interesting one.

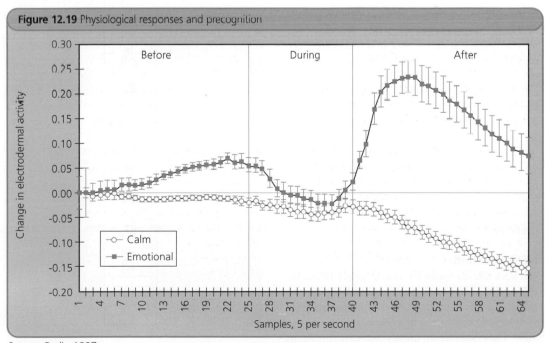

Figure 12.19 Physiological responses and precognition

Source: Radin 1997

Fraudulent precognition

There is, however, a large discrepancy between the type of precognition identified by Radin's research, and the kind that appears in supposedly 'psychic' demonstrations on TV or stage. Sadly, these offer many opportunities for fraud. Many supposed 'predictions', for example, consist of a note in a sealed envelope, or a note written on a pad. But there are devices for inserting new notes into apparently sealed envelopes, and also ones which allow a stage magician to write rapidly and inconspicuously on a pad of paper, once the information has become known. These devices are also used by fraudulent psychics, to add to their credibility.

Fraudulent psychics also have our selective perceptual mechanisms on their side. Psychics often make a number of 'predictions', but they only home in on the successful ones. The others are disregarded, and any records of them which might exist are rarely offered as evidence. It is also very easy for us to become convinced that a prediction was actually quite similar to what has happened even when it wasn't – our tendency to adjust our memories and to disregard small details (see Chapter 3) does the fraudulent psychic a great favour.

Psychokinesis research

In research into **psychokinesis**, usually shortened to PK, the organism (which means the animal or human being researched) is able to exert an influence on a target in the environment, across barriers which would normally prevent any such influence from happening (see Figure 12.20). Psychokinesis is generally split into two categories. **Micro-PK** deals with situations where someone has been able to exert psychokinetic influence at microscopic or microelectronic levels, where instrumentation or statistical analysis, or both, are needed to detect what is happening. **Macro-PK** is considered to occur if the psychokinetic effect can be detected with the naked eye.

Micro-PK studies

We have already looked at one example of micro-PK experimentation, in the form of the meta-analysis of **RNG studies (random number generator studies)** conducted by Nelson and Radin in 1987. These studies are usually automated trials, in which a research participant attempts to influence a random set of numbers generated by a computer. The computer produces random sequences of zeros and ones, and the research participant attempts to influence what it produces, so that there are, say, consistently more ones than zeros. Obviously these studies need to take careful account of the nature of randomness – sometimes there will be more ones than zeros naturally – but, as we saw earlier, there does seem to be some evidence that some people might be able to exert a microelectronic influence in this way.

Dice-tossing studies were a spin-off from Rhine's research, and have been conducted since the 1930s. These are very straightforward: a particular number is selected – not normally six – and the person tosses the dice while 'willing' that number to come up. A 'hit' occurs on those occasions when their mental intention coincides with the face that actually comes up. Again, it is necessary to take into account the probability of that number occurring randomly. It is also best not to choose the number six, since in ordinary

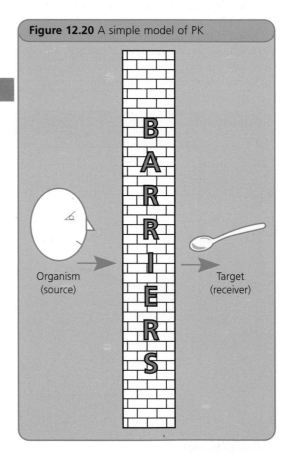

Figure 12.20 A simple model of PK

Organism (source)

Target (receiver)

dice, where the holes are scooped out of the face, the six is very slightly lighter than the other five sides, because it has more holes. So it is slightly more likely to turn up than the others.

In 1991, Radin and Ferrari conducted a meta-analysis of dice-tossing studies conducted between 1935 and 1987. Their analysis included every English-language study they could find, which produced 52 experimenters, in 148 different experiments, using a total of 2569 research participants who had tossed the dice about 2.6 million times. They compared these outcomes with just over 150,000 dice throws in 31 control studies, where people had tossed dice without attempting to influence them.

The overall hit rate for the control studies was 50.02%. The overall hit rate for the studies where participants had deliberately tried to influence the outcomes was 51.2%. Although this difference might not seem to be very large, given the huge numbers of participants involved, it works out statistically as giving odds of more than a billion to one against the results happening simply by chance. And when the researchers controlled for high-achieving individual researchers by eliminating their studies from the analysis, they still found odds of more then three million to one. Although individual studies of dice-throwing are often equivocal, their combined results do imply that micro-PK – or some other factor – might be influencing the outcomes.

Macro-PK

Macro-PK – psychokinesis which is visible with the naked eye – is one of the most popular of all of the apparent parapsychological effects, including as it does spoon-bending, and other dramatic effects. Unfortunately, however, it also seems to be the area of parapsychology which is most dogged by fraud and misdirection on the part of practitioners. Sadly, too, many television presenters (though not all, as Chris Evans recently demonstrated) collude with such people, allowing them to handle and adjust their material beforehand in order to create an apparently spectacular effect in front of the cameras.

Skilled fraudsters are able to exert highly subtle influences on their material, which are not apparent to observers. In one case, a purported 'psychic' appeared to be able to make objects move simply by 'thinking' at them. He could, apparently, turn the pages of a book without touching it, or make a piece of paper on a spindle turn round, also without contact. In reality, he had become extremely skilled at blowing out a fine jet of air without showing it, and the breeze that this generated produced the effect. The investigator learned to replicate the trick, and so demonstrated the fraud.

There are other ways of creating apparently psychokinetic effects. For example, holding the hands round an open cylinder heats up the air inside, and sets up an air current which can make paper or other light objects move. It is often possible to re-start a stopped watch by holding it in the hands, because the problem is often congealed oil inside the watch, or a small piece of grit. The oil in the watch becomes more fluid as it warms up, and this frees the mechanism – for a while, anyway. And, of course, the spoon-bending so beloved of some 'psychics' requires an opportunity to handle the spoon surreptitiously beforehand, so that the metal can be weakened, and only a very subtle, invisible pressure is required to produce the effect. Magicians have a range of tricks for creating apparently impossible events, and skilled psychic fraudsters learn how to use these to create apparently convincing paranormal phenomena.

It is also possible for psychic fraudsters to circumvent obstacles which have been set up. Magnets can be used to create apparent movement in objects, or invisible threads between the two hands can be used to move a small item backwards and forwards. The obstacle may be weaker than it appears, or not a barrier to some other factor, such as heat. It may even not be there at all: sometimes, stage magicians use perceptual illusions which lead the person to think that a barrier is present when it is not really. And psychic fraudsters do too.

The stage magician and skeptic James Randi has offered a 1,000,000-dollar reward to anyone who is able to demonstrate macro-PK unequivocally, under controlled conditions. But despite the large number of self-styled psychics making a living on TV and in other sectors of the entertainment business, his prize has not yet been claimed.

There are, of course, several areas of parapsychological research. One area concerns the type of research where a person attempts a direct mental interaction with another living system. This area used to be known as bio-PK, but more recently, researchers have preferred to use the category **DMILS** (direct mental interaction with living systems) instead. DMILS studies include research into remote staring – investigating the feeling of being stared at which many people experience – and other types of remote influence on the body. Another major source of research in this area concerns healing – the ability to induce positive physiological states in people which help them to recover from illness or injury. But there is not space to go into these areas here.

Experimenters and participants

Parapsychological research, as we have seen, has produced some interesting findings. But it also has some special requirements. Because researchers are investigating very subtle abilities of the human mind, they are particularly susceptible to small human influences which may not affect the more robust of our abilities.

Experimenter effects

One of the most consistent findings in parapsychological research is that some experimenters, using well-controlled methods, repeatedly obtain significant results from ESP or PK studies; whereas others, using exactly the same methods, consistently obtain negative findings. One of the main hypotheses which have been put forward to explain this is that the difference comes from **experimenter effects** – subtle differences in manner, tone of voice, and other slight factors which convey different expectations to participants.

Experimenter effects are powerful in all forms of psychological research. Their strength was first identified by Rosenthal and Fode (1963), who demonstrated how experimenters' beliefs about experimental rats' abilities in maze-running were sufficient to produce fast or slow maze-running in the rats concerned. These were not magical effects: the experimenters who believed that their 'maze-bright' rats would do well handled them more gently and stroked them when taking them to the maze, whereas those who believed that their rats were from a strain bred to be 'maze-dull' handled them more roughly, and spent less time with them. Rosenthal went on to demonstrate experimenter effects in many other situations, including a well-known field experiment involving manipulating teachers' beliefs, which we

will be looking at in Chapter 15 (Rosenthal and Jacobsen, 1968).

Experimenter effects are no less powerful in parapsychological research than they are in other forms of psychology. But since the differences are so very apparent in parapsychological research, they are recognised explicitly. Some experimenters appear to be able to facilitate psi abilities in their research participants, and these are known as **psi-permissive experimenters**. Others obtain consistently negative outcomes from parapsychological research, and they are known as **psi-inhibitory experimenters**.

Factors in experimenter effects

When the experimenter effect was identified in parapsychology, a number of researchers began to investigate it explicitly. They found that it was a combination of two sets of factors. The first was the pleasantness or unpleasantness of the experimental setting, for the participant. Crandall (1985) found that if the experimental participant was relaxed and found the atmosphere pleasant, they would be more likely to produce positive results. This, of course, also meant that people would respond differently depending on whether they liked the person who was dealing with them: it was not about achieving a single successful formula, but about having an experimenter who could get on well with that particular participant, and so help to create a pleasant, relaxed atmosphere.

The second set of factors concerned the expectations of the experimenter. Taddonio (1976) found that experimenters who expected to obtain positive results tended to do so, while those who expected the experiment to be unsuccessful tended to produce unsuccessful outcomes. But, as with Rosenthal's rats, it was not a magical effect. Experimenters communicated their expectations subtly, and those who expected the research participants to fail conveyed that message to them. As a result, any psi abilities which the individual might have shown were inhibited: not many people are able to do well in any task when it is apparent that they are expected to fail.

As we saw earlier, Morris et al. (1995) found a strong experimenter effect in their comparison of sender and no-sender conditions in autoganzfeld studies. Table 12.12 shows the different outcomes obtained by the three experimenters. The researchers identified four possible explanations for their findings. One of these was the possibility of fraud, which they had to consider as a

Table 12.12 Different success rates for experimenters in the same study

	Experimenter A	Experimenter B	Experimenter C
Hit rate	48%	24%	14%

Source: Morris et al., 1995

possibility. However, the experiment had included a great many controls designed to make fraud almost impossible, including a computer-automated procedure, the involvement of a second experimenter who had to sign off a hard copy of the experimental data before the end of the session, and several other safeguards. Given the sheer number of controls in the procedures, and the commitment to experimental rigour of the experimenters concerned, fraud in this instance seems an unlikely hypothesis.

Another possible explanation was psychological, in that one experimenter may have been better at adopting a style and manner which facilitated enthusiasm, comfort, trust, and confidence. As a result, participants may have felt more relaxed, and able to pay attention to internal states and imagery. A third possibility is that some experimenters might have additional psi capacities which could facilitate the occurrence of psychic events around them. And a fourth possibility which the researchers considered is the fact that the successful experimenter had also done much of the recruitment of participants, and so they were already familiar with her when they arrived. It could be that, unconsciously, this researcher had scheduled participants for herself who were more likely to perform well.

Psi-conducive experimenters

Schmiedler (1997) argued that some experimenters may influence experimental findings too much. There have been several cases where specific experimenters obtain remarkably high success levels with participants, but those same participants are unable to repeat their performance later, or even come close to it. These results, as far as anyone can tell (and they have looked) do not come from fraud, or conscious effort on the part of the experimenter, but seem instead just to happen.

Schmiedler suggested that, in situations where the experimenter is highly motivated and also has strong psi abilities of their own, they may somehow transfer those abilities to experimental participants, for the duration of the experiment. Schmiedler argued that it is important to distinguish between ordinary psi-permissive experimenters, who simply create a climate in which the participant's own abilities can come out easily; and these **psi-conducive experimenters**. It is important, Schmiedler argued, that psi-conducive individuals should be identified, and that they should not conduct routine psi investigations, since if they do, the experimental findings may become distorted.

Psi-responsive participants

There have also been some studies indicating that people with particular personality characteristics are more likely to produce positive psi outcomes than others. For example, Honorton et al. (1990) conducted a meta-analysis of free-response ganzfeld studies, and found that extroverts tended, as a general rule, to score more highly than introverts. However, in a further study using an artistic population, Morris et al. (1995) found a slight positive correlation between introversion and psi success, so evidently the relationship is not that simple.

When researchers had measured extroversion and psi success using the NEO model of personality (see Chapter 7), which has six different sub-factors, they had found that psi success correlated positively with the three factors of activity, excitement seeking and positive emotions; but not with the other three, which were warmth, gregariousness and assertiveness (Morris et al., 1993). They suggested that the correlation with extroversion probably came from extroverts enjoying the novelty of the ganzfeld experience, rather than coming from social factors, as such.

We have already seen how believers in psi tend to score more highly than non-believers. Honorton (1992) showed that taking part in other psi experiments was also correlated with successful performance, and it was suggested that this might have its effect by reducing feelings of anxiety or tension which could inhibit psi performance. Having previously practised a mental discipline, such as yoga or meditation, was also positively correlated with psi success.

Creative people also tend to score more highly

Table 12.13 Creativity and psi outcomes

Group	N (one trial per participant)	Hits	%	Significance level
Musicians	32	18	56	p<.0001
Artists	32	16	50	p<.002
Creative writers	32	13	41	p<.05
Actors	32	13	41	p<.05
Total	**128**	**60**	**47**	**p<.0001**

on psi tasks. Dalton (1997) performed a study comparing different types of high-creativity participants in an atuomated ganzfeld task. There were four groups: artists, musicians, creative writers, and actors. Each of the groups achieved significance on the task, with musicians scoring extremely highly. The results are given in Table 12.13. Dalton's findings agreed with those of an earlier ganzfeld study which used music students at the Juillard School of Performing Arts, who had produced similarly high success rates (Schlitz and Honorton, 1992).

Research into parapsychology, then, offers us some interesting challenges. Parapsychologists themselves distinguish between 'proof-oriented' research, which aims to establish whether or not psi exists, and 'process-oriented' research, which aims to explore the conditions and processes involved in psi demonstrations. But acceptance or rejection of psi is a matter for each individual. Psychology's official position, obviously, is of reserved judgement and some scepticism (though not, inevitably, skepticism). Psychologists know far too much about the way that people can be hoodwinked into believing that an event is mysterious when it is nothing of the kind, to accept psi unreservedly. But, as we have seen, parapsychologists are concerned about that too. And many psychologists, if approached privately, will express a personal belief that psi is not an impossibility; although the dangers of being misrepresented often mean that they are reluctant to say so in public.

Parapsychological research in many ways is very different from other areas of psychology. But its methods and approaches are similar – it is the emotions which the topic generates which makes it distinctive. In the next chapter, we will be looking at research into the psychology of emotion, stress, and motivation.

Key terms

absolute refractory period The period of a few milliseconds immediately after the firing of a neurone, when the neurone will not produce another electrical impulse, no matter how much stimulation it may receive.

afferent neurone A neurone which carries information from the sensory receptors towards the brain and spinal cord.

autoganzfeld studies Ganzfeld studies of ESP which involve a computer-controlled automated procedure to prevent sensory leakage or unconscious experimenter bias.

clairvoyance Gaining information about objects or the environment without using recognised sensory channels.

cone cells Cells in the retina which respond to different wavelengths of light, and therefore indicate colour.

dendrites Branches at the endings of the axons of nerve cells, which allow the cell to make connections with several other neurones.

dice-tossing studies Studies of psychokinesis in which the person aims to influence the fall of a dice.

DMILS An abbreviation for 'direct mental interaction with living systems', which is the term used in parapsychology to refer to psi phenomena such as telepathy or healing.

efferent neurone A neurone which carries information away from the brain and spinal cord.

electrical potential The burst of electricity produced by a nerve cell when firing.

experimental rigour The carefulness with which an experiment is conducted; the care taken when conducting an experiment to make sure that all procedures and controls are implemented effectively.

experimenter effects Unwanted influences in a psychological study which are produced, consciously or unconsciously, by the person carrying out the study.

extra-sensory perception Acquiring information from a target in the environment, without using normal sensory channels.

file-drawer problem The problem of selective reporting in psychological research, in that only studies with positive findings tend to be reported in journals, while unsuccessful studies tend to remain in the experimenter's filing cabinet and are not sent off for publication.

fovea The central part of the retina, where the visual image is most clearly focused.

habituation Becoming accustomed to a stimulus, such that it is no longer registered by sensory neurones.

infrasound Sound which is too low to be detected by human ears.

kinaesthetic senses The bodily senses which inform us about the position and state of the muscles, skeletal system and internal organs.

lateral geniculate nuclei An area of the thalamus where the cells forming the optic nerve synapse with those leading to the visual cortex.

macro-PK Psychokinesis in which the para-psychological influence on the target is visible by the naked eye.

micro-PK Psychokinesis in which the outcome of the psi influence is too small to be detected by the naked eye, and usually needs to be identified electronically.

myelin sheath A fatty coating around sensory and motor neurones which help the neural impulse to travel faster.

nodes of Ranvier Gaps in the myelin sheath of a sensory or motor neurone, which allow ionic transfer across the cell membrane and so produce the electrical potential which forms the nerve impulse.

ocular dominance columns Columns of nerve cells found in the visual cortex in which the cells at each level respond to the same stimulus, received by the same eye.

olfactory epithelium The layer of cells in the nose which responds to direct chemical stimulation, and so forms the receptor for the sense of smell.

optic chiasma The part of the brain where the optic nerve from each eye meets, and half of their fibres cross over.

parapsychology The scientific study of anomalous means of communication or of transmission of information. Parapsychologists conduct research into extra-sensory perception, telekinesis, and DMILS.

phantom limbs The name given to the phenomenon experienced by amputees, of still feeling the limb as present and alive even though it has been surgically removed.

photo-receptor cells Special cells in the retina (rods and cones cells) which respond to light by altering their chemical structure and so producing an electrical impulse.

precognition Knowledge of events which will happen in the future, which appears to have been obtained without using normal sensory channels.

pseudopsi hypothesis The idea that all evidence for parapsychological influence comes from deception or misinterpretation.

psi A general term used by parapsychologists to describe forms of communication which have occurred without the use of ordinary sensory channels.

psi-conducive experimenters Experimenters who generate high success rates from research participants, without using fraud, but with the same research participants being unable to repeat their success with other experimenters.

psi hypothesis The idea that human beings are able to use new, apparently impossible means of communication under certain circumstances.

psi-inhibitory experimenters Experimenters who seem to inhibit the demonstration of psychic abilities among their research participants.

psi-permissive experimenters Experimenters who seem to facilitate the demonstration of psychic abilities among their research participants.

psychokinesis A psychic ability in which the person exerts an influence on a target, across barriers which would normally prevent any such influence.

random number generator studies Para-psychological research into micro-PK, in which a research participant attempts to influence a random set of numbers generated by a computer.

reliability problem A problem in both para-psychology and psychotherapy, in which an initial research phase yields highly positive results, but these taper off with repeated studies, or treatments, until eventually, outcomes are little more than chance.

remote viewing studies Parapsychological studies in which the research participants describe scenes or physical objects located at considerable distances from them, and not perceivable by conventional means.

replication The repeating of a study by other researchers, in order to ensure that the findings are reliable, and not just an artefact of one particular experimental situation.

RNGS See random number generator studies.

saccades Minute, involuntary movements of the eyeball.

sensory leakage When a flaw in a para-psychological study allows the research participant to gain relevant information through normal sensory channels.

sensory neurone A nerve cell which receives information from sense receptors and passes it to the nerve cells of the central nervous system.

synaesthesia A condition in which sensory input becomes distorted and confused, such that sounds may be experienced as touch, etc.

synapse The junction between nerve cells which is bridged by neurotransmitter chemicals.

telepathy The transmission of information from one person to another without using normal sensory channels.

transduction The process of converting information from one form to another in physiological terms, e.g. converting the pressure waves which comprise sound into electrical impulses which can be passed to the brain.

two-point threshold A measure of skin sensitivity which is concerned with how far apart two pinpricks must be to be identified as separate stimuli.

ultrasound Sound which is too high-pitched to be detected by human hearing.

Summary

1 The peripheral nervous system consists of sensory receptors, which transduce sensation into electrical impulses; and neurones which transmit those messages to the central nervous system.

2 Different senses have receptors responsive to different types of information. There are visual receptors, auditory receptors, olfactory and gustatory receptors, tactile receptors which respond to temperature and pressure, pain receptors, and proprioceptive receptors.

3 Sensory information is processed and decoded in the central nervous system. Both the thalamus and the visual cortex of the cerebrum are involved in decoding visual information.

4 The reflex arc is a simple representation of the action of the three main types of neurone: sensory neurones, connector neurones and motor neurones. These convey electrical impulses generated by electro-chemical interactions.

5 Sensory systems show habituation and adaptation. Perceptual thresholds describe the minimal stimuli which can produce a perceptual response. Sensory systems may also become distorted, producing synaesthesia, illusion, or hallucination.

6 Parapsychologists conduct research into experiences which appear to involve information transmission which bypasses normal sensory channels. This includes research into fraudulent psychics, as well as experimental studies of apparent psi phenomena.

7 Experimental parapsychological research includes studies of ESP using the ganzfeld technique, remote viewing, and studies of micro-psychokinesis. Each of these areas has generated considerable debate, although cumulative research findings often imply some general effects.

8 Parapsychological investigations indicate that positive findings are closely linked to a number of experimenter and participant variables, and do not occur on every occasion. Although skeptics see this as a weakness, others argue that the same observations apply to most exceptional human abilities.

Self-assessment questions

1 Briefly outline how visual information is processed.

2 What is the reflex arc, and what types of neurones does it involve?

3 What is a ganzfeld and how has it been used in parapsychological research?

Practice essay questions

1 What problems do parapsychological researchers encounter when attempting to evaluate parapsychological phenomena scientifically?

2 How important are experimenter and participant effects in parapsychological research?

3 To what extent can behaviour be explained in terms of the activity of the nervous system?

Test your knowledge of this chapter with our online quizzes and games at:
http://www.psych.co.uk

Explore sensation and parapsychology further at:

Senses
http://ear.berkeley.edu/ – Diagrams, links and extensive research on the hearing sciences.
http://www.umds.ac.uk/physiology/jim/tasteolf.htm – Basic information and diagrams about taste and smell.
http://www.science.mcmaster.ca/Psychology/psych2e03/lecture11/touch.lecture.html – Tutorial and diagrams on touch perception.
http://www.ispub.com/journals/IJAMI/Vol1N1/motion.htm – Tutorial and reading list on motion interpretation.

Parapsychology
http://www.ed.ac.uk/~ejua35/parapsy.htm – Extensive links page to resources on the internet, includes all branches of parapsychology including sites where you can have your fortune told.
http://www.psiresearch.org/para1.html – Answers to frequently asked questions on this subject.

Emotion and motivation

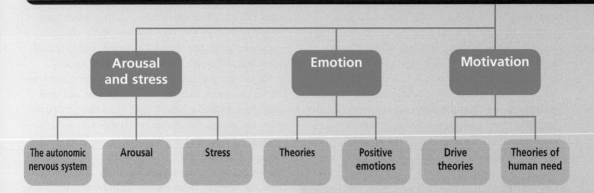

Arousal and stress			Emotion		Motivation	
The autonomic nervous system	Arousal	Stress	Theories	Positive emotions	Drive theories	Theories of human need

Learning objectives

13.1. Arousal
a describe methods of studying arousal
b outline the Yerkes-Dodson Law of arousal
c evaluate the concept of general arousal

13.2. Stress
a identify effects of long-term stress
b describe a study of long-term stress
c describe therapies for reducing long-term stress

13.3. Theories of emotion
a distinguish between early theories
b describe a study of emotion
c identify theories of emotion

13.4. Positive emotions
a describe a study of postivie emotions
b outline Argyle's model of positive emotion
c identify the major functions of humour

13.5. Drive theories
a define terms relating to drive theories of motivation
b describe processes relating to maintaining homeostasis
c identify limitations of drive theories of motivation

13.6. Hunger
a name physiological mechanisms involved in hunger
b describe a study of hunger
c outline evidence for a biological set-weight regulating hunger

13.7. Exploration and incentives
a identify implications of studies of exploration
b describe a study of electrical stimulation of the brain
c distinguish between incentives and rewards

13.8. Human motives
a describe a study of achievement motivation
b evaluate Maslow's theory of human needs
c describe the human needs identified by Rogers and Harré

The interaction of physiology with experience is a complex one, and we are still a long way from understanding how it operates. In some cases, we find what seems to be a strong connection between physiological mechanisms and human experience. In other cases, though, we find that we have to include other levels of explanation, including social and personal factors, to gain a realistic picture of what is going on. In this chapter, we will be looking at some of the physiological mechanisms which appear to be involved in the experiences of emotion and motivation, but we will also be looking at psychological research into these topics in a wider context – at cognitive, social, cultural and personal factors which can influence both our experience of emotion, and our motivation.

Arousal and stress

In order to understand something about the interactions between physiology and emotional experience, we need to begin by looking at the physiological mechanisms which are involved. Much of our experience of stress, and of negative emotions, is influenced by the action of the autonomic nervous system and what we refer to, very generally, as arousal.

The autonomic nervous system

The autonomic nervous system is the general name given to a network of unmyelinated nerve fibres, which run from the spinal cord and the lower regions of the brain to the internal and sensory organs of the body (Figure 13.1). This part of the nervous system is rather different from the central nervous system, which we looked at in Chapter 10. It is concerned with the general 'state' of the body, rather than with specific behaviours like talking or movement. The structure of the autonomic nervous system, or ANS, reflects two distinct types of 'state'. The sympathetic division is concerned with states which are highly activated and prepared for action, while the parasympathetic division is concerned with states which are quiet and restorative.

The sympathetic division of the ANS
Activation of the sympathetic division of the autonomic nervous system is often given the gen-

eral term of arousal. The reason for this is that it produces a number of different physiological changes in the body, each of which contributes to making the individual more alert and active. Fibres of the sympathetic division of the autonomic nervous system pass from the medulla and spinal cord to the viscera (the internal organs of the body), and change their mode of operating when they are activated in this way. Each of these changes contributes to the state of alertness and preparedness for action which we loosely call 'arousal'.

If we are preparing to be highly active, then we need to ensure that muscles are strong and well-supplied with the blood sugars and oxygen necessary for action. So the spleen releases stored red blood cells, so that the blood can carry more oxygen; the heart begins to beat faster, circulating the blood more rapidly round the body and replenishing the oxygen supply more rapidly; and breathing becomes deeper, taking more oxygen into the lungs. The digestive system also changes its mode of operation, so that sugar is metabolised much more quickly, to provide an instant energy supply, but foods which require longer-term digestion, like proteins and fats, take longer.

These changes are sometimes described as the **fight or flight response**. In evolutionary terms, it

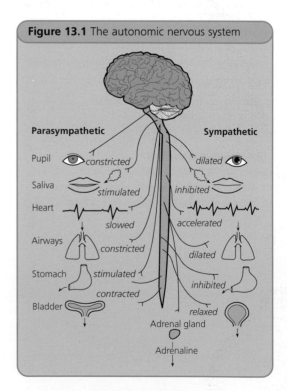

Figure 13.1 The autonomic nervous system

is a response which maximises an animal's chances of survival when danger threatens, by allowing the animal to produce as much energy as possible to help it either to fight or to run away. In that situation, the body would need to be prepared for tissue damage, so additional blood platelets, which help the blood to clot, are produced and distributed throughout the bloodstream, and the brain produces endorphins: neurotransmitters which block out immediate feelings of pain resulting from injuries. As with digestion, longer-term processes, like long-term immune system activity, are suppressed until the fight or flight response is over.

There are a number of other features of the fight or flight response, including an increase in the rate of sweating – one of the body's cooling mechanisms – helping to deal with the heat produced by active muscles. In a state of arousal, we also become more alert: the pupils of the eyes dilate, and perceptual thresholds are lowered, producing increased receptivity to external stimuli. Each of these changes helps the body to produce, and utilise, physical energy. Arousal responses are not always as dramatic as the fight or flight reaction, though – we can become mildly, as well as extremely, aroused.

The physiological changes involved in arousal are stimulated by neural impulses from the sympathetic division of the autonomic nervous system, but they are maintained by the action of the **endocrine system** (Figure 13.2). This is a series of glands which release hormones into the bloodstream, thereby helping to maintain consistent states within the body (Table 13.1). The hormones which are concerned with stress and arousal are released from the pituitary and adrenal glands following stimulation from the sympathetic nerve fibres of the ANS.

The pituitary gland releases **glucocorticoids,** which are concerned with the digestive and tissue repair functions – converting fat stores to glucose and suppressing the immune response – so physiological studies of stress reactions often involve measuring the amount of glucocorticoids in the blood or urine. Acting on chemical instructions from the hypothalamus, the pituitary gland also releases a 'messenger hormone', called **adrenocorticotrophic hormone (ACTH)**, which stimulates the adrenal gland to release adrenaline into the bloodstream. Adrenaline is mainly concerned with maintaining levels of muscular activity and an ade-

quate blood supply, so an injection of adrenaline will produce an almost instant increase in heartrate, blood pressure and sweating.

The parasympathetic division of the ANS

The activities of the parasympathetic division of the ANS are much less dramatic than those of the sympathetic division. Perhaps as an inevitable

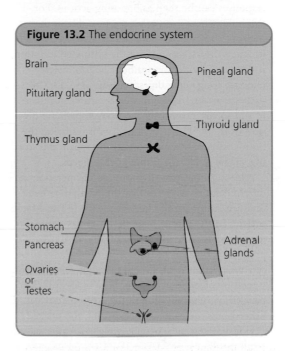

Figure 13.2 The endocrine system

Brain
Pituitary gland
Pineal gland
Thyroid gland
Thymus gland
Stomach
Pancreas
Adrenal glands
Ovaries or Testes

Table 13.1 Some endocrine glands and their functions

Pineal gland	Regulates seasonal changes and diurnal rhythms.
Pituitary gland	Acts as a 'central control' for all the other glands in the system. Also controls birth changes and lactation.
Thyroid gland	Regulates growth, and the metabolic rate of the body.
Thymus gland	Regulates the body's auto-immune system.
Adrenal gland	Controls blood sugar levels, and is involved in energy-releasing states and emotions through the hormone adrenaline.
Gonads	Release the hormones responsible for sexual development and secondary sexual characteristics.

consequence, they have received less attention from researchers. Parasympathetic nerve fibres run from the medulla and the brain stem to the internal organs, and stimulation from many of them has an effect which seems to counteract that of the sympathetic division, although it is not an exact mirror-image.

For many practical purposes, though, the two responses can be seen as opposing actions. For example: where sympathetic action dilates the pupil of the eye, parasympathetic action constricts it; where heartrate increases by sympathetic action, it decreases by parasympathetic action; where effective long-term digestion is inhibited by sympathetic action, parasympathetic action stimulates it, and so on. Essentially, the parasympathetic division of the ANS is concerned with restoring the body's resources: stimulating tissue repair and storing sugars as fats for future energy needs.

Although the two divisions are in operation at different times, it seems that the parasympathetic division automatically becomes activated as intense activity in the sympathetic division dies down. So, for example, an intensive exercising session would produce activation of the sympathetic division, but this would then be followed by a quiescent period which involves parasympathetic activity. But the parasympathetic division of the ANS is active at other times too: for instance, during the relaxed period which many people experience after eating a full meal.

Arousal

The concept of arousal relates to the activities of the ANS, and its effects on human behaviour. As we have seen, the two divisions of the ANS – the sympathetic and parasympathetic divisions – have different effects. The function of the sympathetic division (generally speaking) is to prepare the body for action, whereas the parasympathetic division (generally speaking) is concerned with resting, and storing energy for future use.

Psychological interest in arousal has tended to centre on the relationship between a physiologically aroused condition, and the experience of emotion. Periods of high physiological activity, such as happen when we take vigorous exercise, are accompanied by high levels of adrenaline and by all the other symptoms of the generalised arousal state. But aroused states also accompany the emotional states of fear and anger. Some evi-

dence suggests that the sensation of arousal appears to interact reflexively with these emotions, with each enhancing the other. We will look at some of this in more detail later in this chapter, when we explore some of the theories of emotion which have been put forward by psychologists.

Measuring arousal

As we have seen, changes in autonomic arousal levels produce a number of physiological changes. These are readily detectable, and can be measured in several different ways. The most visible changes, of course, concern the changes in facial colour which occur as a result of emotion – pallor, particularly in the case of fear, or flushing, in the case of anger or annoyance. There are other visible signs of arousal too, which are familiar to most people, such as muscle trembling and changes in breathing rate.

These outward signs of arousal, though, are highly variable: some people seem to show emotion more readily than others. A more reliable indicator of arousal is that of **galvanic skin resistance (GSR)**, which is a measure of how much the skin conducts electricity. When we are anxious or aroused in some other way, we sweat, and this changes the conductivity of the skin. Even a very slight anxiety-producing stimulus, like a worrying thought, produces a change in skin conductivity, and this can be detected by electrodes attached to the skin.

Another system for measuring stress or arousal is by using a **voice stress analyser**. Minute tremors of the vocal cords occur naturally, but when we are worried, anxious, angry or frightened, our vocal muscles become more tense, which changes the sound of the voice. Although with practice people can learn to hide most of the effects of that tension, so that their voice sounds virtually normal to the ear, there is still a slightly 'flattened' tone to the voice, because the natural tremors have been suppressed by the effort of maintaining control. This shows up clearly in an analysis of the voiceprint on a **sound spectrograph** – a visual image of a sound (Figure 13.3). Normal speech shows a general waveform, superimposed on the changes in pitch and tone of what is being said. Stressed speech does not – the pattern simply reflects the changes in speech and tone without any regular rhythmic variation.

The most practical instrument for gaining overall measurements of levels of arousal is known as a

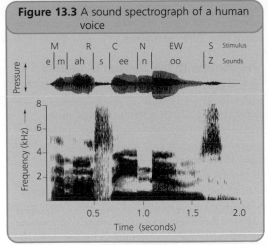

Figure 13.3 A sound spectrograph of a human voice

©MRC News, Source: Rosen, 1991

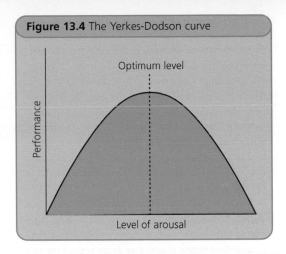

Figure 13.4 The Yerkes-Dodson curve

polygraph. 'Poly' means 'many', and this instrument is called a polygraph because it combines measures of several different indicators of arousal, such as GSR, pulse rate, heartbeat and blood pressure. It then combines the information to give a general estimate of the level of arousal. 'Lie detectors' are polygraphs which detect arousal levels. They work on the principle that people are more anxious when they are telling a lie than when they are telling the truth. Since anxiety produces arousal in the same way that other sources of stress do, the polygraph detects the difference in arousal level between the lie and more ordinary truthful statements that the person has made. But you will probably already have detected a problem with this: since it is only physiological arousal which is being measured, it is not possible to tell the difference between an anxiety-producing true statement and a lie.

The Yerkes-Dodson Law of arousal

There are degrees of arousal – we can be only mildly aroused, or extremely so. And the overall level of arousal which we experience can affect our performance. This relates to a principle known as the **Yerkes-Dodson Law of arousal**, which is concerned with describing the relationship between the state of arousal of a given individual, and how well that individual will perform on a given task. According to the Yerkes-Dodson law, this relationship can be expressed on a graph as an inverted-U curve (see Figure 13.4). In other words, arousal improves performance only up to a point, but beyond that point, performance will begin to decline. A moderate

level of arousal will help us to do things better; an extreme level will impair how well we do. So the best state to be in – the optimal state – is one in which the level of arousal is not too high or too low.

The optimal level of arousal varies for different tasks, with complex tasks showing an earlier **performance decrement** than simple tasks, for the same level of arousal. In other words, if we are performing a relatively simple task, then we can cope with a much larger range of arousal levels – the curve is flatter. So, for example, if you are doing the washing-up, you would not do it very well if your state of arousal was very low indeed, and you were half-asleep; but equally, you would have to be very upset indeed before you started to break things (accidentally, that is). But if you were engaged in a complex task, like trying to write an essay, you might need to be a bit more aroused – or at least, alert – before you could get started. Equally, however, getting upset would interfere with your ability to write the essay much more than it would interfere with your ability to wash up.

As we saw in Chapter 2, an illustration of the Yerkes-Dodson Law was provided by Stroh (1971) when investigating sustained attention using the alpha rhythms which occur spontaneously in electro-encephalograms to provide a measure of relaxation – people who are relaxed produce EEGs with more alpha rhythms than people who are aroused. Stroh found that, when research participants were undertaking a very boring vigilance task, some of them would show more alpha activity, while others would show less, before a missed signal.

It was understandable that those who showed more might miss the signal, since it indicated that they were more relaxed, and so they might not have been concentrating. But the other finding was puzzling. On investigation, Stroh found that those who showed lower alpha activity before a missed signal tended to be younger and more neurotic than the other group. Stroh surmised that what had happened was that their arousal levels had become too high for them to perform effectively. They had gone past the optimal arousal level on the inverted-U curve.

Hardy (1988) suggested a modification of the Yerkes-Dodson principle of arousal. Hardy suggested that work with athletes implied that the inverted-U shape is not a realistic reflection of the relationship between arousal and performance. An inverted-U implies that, if you become so upset or angry that it interferes with your performance, then just calming down a little bit will restore you to the high level that you had before. But in high-powered athletic performance, Hardy argued, it does not work like that. If athletes become so upset that it interferes with their performance, they need to calm down a lot, not just a little, before they can gradually work their way back to performing to the peak of their ability.

Hardy suggested that **catastrophe theory** provided a better model for describing the relationship between performance and arousal. In this model, a curve changes smoothly up to a point, but then there is discontinuity – a sudden and rapid change (Figure 13.5). This model, according to Hardy, reflects more accurately the sudden decline in performance produced by extremes of arousal during intensive competition, and it might also explain why it is often so hard for high-powered athletes to get back to peak performance once they have been upset.

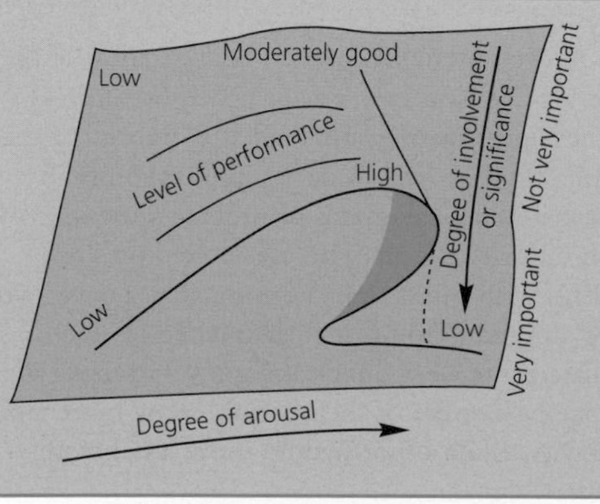

Problems with the concept of arousal

A number of questions have arisen to do with how useful the concept of arousal really is. These have come about as a result of some of the detailed investigations of arousal conducted by researchers, which have shown that, although they may seem superficially similar, arousal states produced by different types of stimuli or emotions can in fact involve quite different physiological effects. As early as 1955, for example, Funkenstein showed that there were physiological differences in the type of arousal produced by fear and anger, identifying the fear response as similar to that induced by adrenaline injections, and the anger response as similar to that produced by noradrenaline injections.

In discussing these problems, Gale (1981) pointed out that the term 'arousal' has been used in so many different contexts, and to describe so many different types of response, that it becomes almost impossible to state exactly what is being measured, and what the different forms of arousal that researchers have studied actually have got in common.

Green (1987) argued, however, that the general concept of arousal is one which is useful in many respects, particularly when we are trying to look at broad patterns rather than specific reactions, or when we are trying to understand everyday experience. We need to bear in mind, though, that the idea of autonomic arousal is a generalisation which encompasses a number of different types of response when examined at the level of fine-detailed research, and not an extremely precise concept.

Some critics have also queried just how closely an experimentally induced arousal state can replicate arousal which occurs in real life. For example: one of the main problems which psychologists studying anger have faced, is defining what we actually mean by 'anger'. Rose, Kamin and Lewontin (1984) pointed out that when researchers use the term 'aggression' they are often referring to several very different concepts, and the same thing applies to the way that we use the term 'anger'.

We can see this more clearly if we look at how other communities define the different experiences

Figure 13.5 A catastrophe model

which we call 'anger'. Lutz (1990), in an anthropological study of the Ifaluk people of Micronesia, found that their language includes words for at least five different types of anger, each of which is differentiated very sharply from the others. We can see from Table 13.2 that each refers to a different type of anger, and we can recognise the different experiences which they are describing. But in our language, each of these experiences would be lumped together under the same name, 'anger', whereas in the Ifaluk language, they are quite different.

This has implications for research, since the fact that we do not distinguish them clearly in our own language means that they can often become confused, so that researchers all investigate 'anger' but in reality examine experiences which are very different from one another. Alternatively, it can result in researchers investigating only one specific type of anger, and using those investigations to draw conclusions about 'anger' in general.

Stress

Immediate responses to stressful or anxiety-provoking events, as we have seen, generate a rapid high level of physiological arousal. But what happens when the threat simply does not go away? The 'fight or flight' response is very costly in terms of energy, and not the sort of thing that the body can keep up for very long. Yet, in modern living, perceived threats are rarely responded to by physical action. Moreover, they are often continuous and non-specific – a constant anxiety that financial problems will result in homelessness, for instance, represents an acute but ongoing perceived threat, which does not take a direct physical form.

The general adaptation syndrome

In 1956, Selye identified what became known as the **general adaptation syndrome (GAS)**, a model which described how people and animals respond to long-term stress (Figure 13.6). Selye was particularly interested in the effects that prolonged exposure to stressful situations has on the body's resistance to disease and illness. From studies with animals, Selye identified three phases to the general adaptation syndrome. The first of these is the **alarm stage**, involving 'fight or flight' reactions, and therefore the activation of the sympathetic division of the ANS. In animals, this stage has been shown to produce enlargement of the adrenal glands, shrinking of the thymus gland and lymph nodes, and sometimes ulceration of the stomach walls.

As the stress continues, however, the body attempts to revert to normal functioning, while at the same time coping with the additional adrenaline in the bloodstream and the effects which it produces. This is the second phase, which Selye described as the **resistance stage**. Rats which were exposed to long-term cold stress for long enough to have entered this stage survived much lower temperatures than rats which had not been exposed to this type of long-term experience.

Table 13.2 Types of anger	
tipmochmoch	The feeling of irritability which is often experienced by people who are ill.
nguch	The irritability which occurs when relatives have not fulfilled their obligations.
tang	The kind of anger which arises from frustration or helplessness in the face of personal misfortune, or some other unfairness which cannot be tackled.
lingeringer	The anger which builds up gradually when a whole series of little unpleasant events occur.
song	A sense of 'justifiable anger', or righteous indignation.

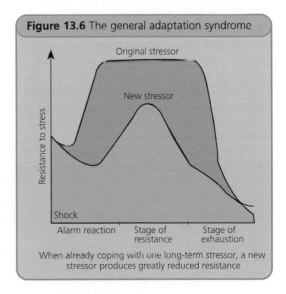

Figure 13.6 The general adaptation syndrome

When already coping with one long-term stressor, a new stressor produces greatly reduced resistance

The third stage occurs when the body has finally outstripped its reserves of energy, and **exhaustion** results. In this final phase, the general adaptation syndrome is characterised by a return to apparently normal levels of heartrate, blood pressure and the like, but is identifiable by an excessively high level of adrenaline remaining in the bloodstream. This produces an immediate and strong – sometimes excessive – reaction to even mild sources of additional stress. Selye showed that if an animal is experiencing the general adaptation syndrome, it will show much lower resistance to a stress-producing stimulus than would an animal which was not in this condition.

Selye's work led to the development of two new areas of research. One of these was the development of **psychoimmunology**, which is to do with the relationship between psychological factors and the immune system of the body. The second was the exploration of **locus of control**, and the types of coping strategies which can minimise the harmful effects of long-term stress.

Psychoimmunology

A number of researchers began to investigate how psychological factors such as long-term stress can make people (and animals) more susceptible to illness. One of the most important findings which emerged as a result of this interest was the mapping out of the physiological effects of long-term stress – which, as we have seen, turned out to be very different from the body's response to emergencies.

The immune system is one of the most complex systems of the body. It consists of a number of defences which the body has, to protect itself against disease. As the first line of defence, white blood cells patrol the body and lymphatic system, seeking out foreign organisms such as bacteria, fungi and viruses, while natural killer cells roam through body tissue, destroying cells which have become infected by a virus or transformed into cancer cells.

There are two types of immune reactions which the body produces. **Non-specific immune reactions** are general ones, which can deal with a range of different problems. One of them is the inflammatory reaction, in which damaged tissue becomes red and inflamed because the blood and lymph supplies to the area are increased. These secretions also attract white blood cells, which get rid of the debris produced by the body's own

cells, and any invading strange cells. Another non-specific reaction occurs when cells have become infected with some viruses. This causes the cells to release a chemical known as interferon, which prevents the virus from reproducing and infecting other cells. These general defences are the body's way of dealing with minor infection, such as from cuts and abrasions.

Specific immune reactions are targeted against particular invaders, such as the organisms which cause illnesses like measles, smallpox, or poliomyelitis. Many of these are chemically mediated: the immune system learns to recognise proteins known as antigens, on the surface of invading bacteria, and manufactures a set of anti-bodies, known as immunoglobulins, which seek out and destroy those particular bacteria. Immunisation works on that principle: by giving the body a mild and harmless exposure to polio or smallpox bacteria, the immune system is 'taught' to recognise those bacteria, so that if they enter the body again, they are sought out and destroyed.

Some specific immune reactions are mediated by the cells themselves. Special cells, known as T-lymphocytes, are produced by the thymus gland. These also produce antibodies, but instead of floating freely through the system, those anti-bodies remain stuck to the surface of the cell. When an invader, such as a fungus, virus, or para-site, comes into the area of the cell, the antigens on their surface stick to the antibodies on the surface of the T-lymphocyte cell, and the cell responds either by killing the invader directly, or by sending out a message which attracts other white blood cells to come and kill it.

The problem is that stress increases the secretion of glucocorticoids in the blood, and over a long period of time these glucocorticoids attach themselves to white blood cells, and lower their effectiveness. Solomon (1963) showed that a sig-nificant outcome of the general adaptation syn-drome seems to be a lowered resistance to illness, and a tendency to feelings of fatigue and general weakness. Long-term psychological effects have also been identified, taking the form of increased irritability and a tendency to a pessimistic out-look. Over time, too, this can lead to seriously negative thinking styles which can actually pro-long the stress which the individual is under.

It is thought that many of the characteristics of the syndrome known as **burnout**, which affects people in helping professions like social work, teaching or nursing, can be attributed to a combination of these factors. The long-term stress which these people are under produces the general adaptation syndrome, which reduces their mental and physical resilience, and their experiences mean that they feel powerless in the working situations, augmenting and exaggerating their stress.

Several studies have suggested a link between long-term stress and minor illnesses, although it is always difficult to be certain that it is the stress itself which is producing the effect. For example, in a study by Glaser *et al.* (1987), medical students showed distinct changes in their immune systems during exam times. They also reported that they were more likely to contract coughs and colds during exam times than at other times, but this aspect of the study was not really fully controlled: as Watson and Pennebaker (1989) pointed out, it is possible that the students expected to be ill at such times, or noticed it more because they found the experience of illness even more unpleasant when they had other stressors.

Other studies also showed changes in the immune system as a result of stress. For example, Irwin *et al.* (1988) took blood samples from women whose husbands had recently died, and found that they showed significantly less natural killer cell activity during the six months after their bereavement than at other times.

Treatments for illness in non-technological societies often shows a recognition of how long-term stress can lower resistance to disease. Horton (1967) discussed how traditional African medicine practitioners, sometimes derogatively called 'witch doctors', go about treating infectious illnesses. Typically, they will talk with the patient about what has been going on in their lives, looking for sources of social stress like quarrels or arguments with friends or relatives. To Western ears, this does not make any sense, because we 'know' that these diseases are caused by infection. But Horton points out that, in a country with a high infant mortality rate, the people who survive to adulthood are likely to have a high natural immunity.

So the real question is not whether the infection is around, but why the person has become susceptible to it – in other words, why their immune system is less efficient than usual. In this context, and given what we are finding out about psychological factors in illness, the idea that social stress might be an important factor makes much

more sense. Since much of the traditional medicine practitioner's approach is to deal with the source of this stress, by appeasing or reconciling the two parties, then taking such an approach to the treatment of illness, far from being primitive, is actually far more sophisticated than it appears on the surface.

Long-term stress has also been linked with **coronary heart disease** – an illness which has been observed to be common among certain kinds of patients, but rare for others. In 1959, Friedman and Rosenman drew up a summary of those patient characteristics which seemed to correlate with an increased likelihood of coronary heart disease. Their list included high competitiveness, a high level of achievement motivation, restlessness and hyperalertness, and a tendency to feel as though they were continually under pressure from time, and from their own responsibilities. As we saw in Chapter 7, the researchers concluded that there were, typically, two very different personality styles manifested by these traits. People who scored highly on these characteristics were described as Type A's, while those who scored low on this dimension were Type B's.

Friedman and Rosenman (1974) reported a longitudinal study of over 3500 healthy men aged between 39 and 59, which lasted for over twelve years. The men were assessed by means of structured interviews, which involved about 25 questions, like 'would your partner or a close friend describe you as a hard-driving person?' or 'how would you be likely to react if you were stuck towards the end of a slow queue?' The research participants were also observed as they answered the questions, and assessed in terms of how impatient or restless they seemed to be. Certain questions were deliberately asked very slowly, to see if the individual interrupted.

As the study progressed, more than twice as many Type A men as Type B's developed coronary heart disease: 178 out of 257. Even when the figures were adjusted for factors such as whether the Type A's smoked more, or had higher blood pressure, the risk for Type A's was 1.97 times as high as the risk for Type B's. In a more detailed analysis, Jenkins *et al.* (1978) found that there were different kinds of Type A behaviour, which correlated with different forms of heart disease: angina sufferers tended to be impatient with other people and very conscious of work pressures, but those with heart failure or likely heart failure tended to have hasty personal habits and schedules, inflicting the pressures on themselves rather than on others.

Long-term stress has been linked with a number of other illnesses too. One of these is cancer, although it is unclear just what the relationship actually is. Unfortunately, many of the studies which seemed to show a direct relationship between stress and cancer did not really control for other kinds of factors, like smoking, diet or alcohol intake; and it is also very difficult to sort out how far the stress people are under may be an effect of the disease, rather than a cause. Nowadays, most researchers working in this field tend to take the view that stress is unlikely actually to cause cancer, but that it may well influence the rate of growth of cancerous tumours, once the cancer has begun.

There are a couple of studies , though, which do seem to provide us with some good evidence on this question. One of them was reported by Spiegel *et al.* (1989), who were originally investigating whether psychotherapy would help women to cope with the experience of having a fatal illness – advanced breast cancer. They selected 86 women, all of whom were receiving the standard medical treatment for their illness, and offered an additional psychotherapy treatment to half of them. They found that the psychotherapy did seem to help the women: they became less anxious, and less depressed, and also learned to reduce their pain through self-hypnosis.

Originally, that was all that was planned for the study. However, about thirteen years later, the researchers decided to follow up the medical records of those patients, just to see if there had been any medical effects. They did not expect that it would have made any difference to the medical progress of the illness, but when they consulted the records, they found that those women who had received psychotherapy had lived on for an average of 37 months after the treatment, by comparison with only 19 months for the others. And three of them were even still alive.

We do have to be careful, though, about jumping to the conclusion that it was the reduction of stress which prolonged the patients' illnesses, even though the study does seem to suggest that kind of link. It is always possible that, because the women became a little more relaxed, they complied better with medical instructions, or might have been able to get more exercise because they were in less pain. But even though it may not be

absolute proof, the study does suggest quite strongly that stress reduction might be able to ameliorate the disease, at least a little bit.

Another illness which has been linked with long-term stress is that of **gastric ulcers**. This research began with some early studies on animals. In 1958, Brady conducted an experiment involving four pairs of monkeys, linked together as 'yoked controls' (in other words, each monkey received the same experiences as the animal that was paired with it). The monkeys were given regular electric shocks to the feet, but one of each pair was provided with a lever which allowed it to turn the shocks off for 20 seconds at a time (the shocks were given at 20 second intervals). The second monkey in each pair could do nothing but receive the shock passively. Brady argued that, in this set-up, both animals were subjected to the same physical stress but only the 'executive' monkey – the one which could press the lever – was subjected to the psychological stress of having to maintain the response.

The experimental sessions continued for six hours at a time, with an intervening six-hour rest period. Brady found that many of the 'executive' monkeys died of duodenal ulcers. Their yoked controls, on the other hand, did not show any gastrointestinal abnormalities. Following a series of investigations of different schedules, in which the experimental conditions were maintained for one-hour, three-hour and six-hour periods, Brady found that only the six-hours on, six-hours off schedule was sufficient to produce ulcers. He related this to the changes in stomach acidity brought about by long-term stress: there were fewer changes in acidity resulting from the shorter sessions.

In a different study, Weiss (1972) performed a similar study with laboratory rats. This time, the 'executive' rats were able to postpone an electric shock by turning an exercise wheel, while they also had a yoked control who experienced exactly the same shocks. Interestingly, though, Weiss found that it was the helpless rats which developed gastric ulcers, rather than the ones which had been able to take action – a finding exactly opposite to Brady's. Weiss explained this by arguing that what was important was not so much whether the animal had control over the stressor, but two other factors. The first was the sheer amount of stressor – the degree of stress the animal experienced. The second was whether there was any feedback, indicating to the animal that its actions were having an effect.

For Brady's monkeys, the rapid rate of the stimulus had meant that the rate of stressors was extremely high. In fact, when the pairs were being set up, the monkey which could respond most quickly was the one from each pair which was assigned as the 'executive' rather than as the control. So this high degree of stress meant that they were more prone to ulcers. But in addition, they had relatively little feedback about the effectiveness of their actions – just that the shock did not arrive on schedule. Weiss's rats, on the other hand had heard a warning tone to signal each shock, and so also became aware that the shock had been averted.

Another possible interpretation of these differences is to do with the degree of body movement involved in the animals' responses. As we have seen, the alarm response prepares the body for action. But Brady's monkeys were only required to perform **molecular actions** (actions involving a small part of the body), in the sense that all they had to do was to press a lever. Weiss's rats, on the other hand, performed **molar actions** to avert their shock – movements which involved the whole body, like running in the exercise wheel, or, in one condition, jumping into a shuttle box. These molar responses would utilise the bodily energy generated by the alarm response, so the animal was responding in a way that was appropriate to its physical state. But Brady's monkeys would have experienced the alarm response with no way of utilising that energy, and it is possible that this is why their stress was so much more.

Locus of control

The implication of Weiss's study is that there are two aspects to developing effective coping when faced with sources of stress. The first is that there should be some opportunity to exert control over the stressor – to reduce it in some way. And the second is, that there should be some feedback about the effectiveness of the action. It is not enough just to do something – you have to know that your actions have worked. This principle has formed the basis for much of the research into locus of control.

Rotter (1966) showed that the beliefs which people have about how much they can control situations can make a great deal of difference to the amount of stress which they experience.

People with an **internal locus of control**, who believe that control of their lives largely comes from their own efforts, experience less stress than those with an **external locus of control**, who believe that they are largely the victims of circumstance. And, of course, these beliefs can easily become self-fulfilling prophecies, since people with an internal locus of control are more likely to make more efforts to influence their lives, whereas those with an external locus of control are more likely to take a passive stance towards things.

Beck, Emery and Greenberg (1985) showed how people who believed they could exercise some control over potentially threatening events responded very differently to their worries. Although they were aware of them, they did not engage in continuous worry or feel anxiety over what might happen, to anything like the same degree as people who felt powerless. Beck, Emery and Greenberg (1985) argued that the kind of repetitive, circular thoughts involved in continuous worry actually heighten the person's feelings of anxiety and make it more difficult for that person to act effectively. This is closely linked with research into **learned helplessness**, which we will be looking at later in this chapter.

Therapies for reducing long-term stress

Levonkron et al (1983) investigated how useful therapy was for modifying Type A behaviour, and found that it often had quite a high degree of success. Some of the most successful therapies were based on behaviour therapy, training the client to develop coping strategies so that they could deal effectively with stress. They usually included relaxation training as well. A five-year intervention programme of such training for 1035 post heart attack patients showed that the recurrence rate for both fatal and non-fatal heart attacks was reduced to half that of the control group. The control group was equal on other factors but received just the normal cardiological treatment and not the additional therapy.

There is some evidence that Type A may be a cultural factor. Although it seems to be a reliable phenomenon in America, a study in Britain by Bass and Wade (1982) found that, among patients complaining of heart pain, those with Type A personality patterns tended to have normal coronary arteries – although they were also the most psychiatrically disturbed. Some other researchers, though, argue that Type A is not really a characteristic in itself. Instead, it is made up of a whole series of sub-characteristics like ambition and activity levels, so to treat it as if it were a single, complete character trait is misleading. What seems to be more important is the stress which the person is experiencing as part of their way of going about their life, rather than the style of activity itself.

Biofeedback

Some of the relaxation techniques which are used in programmes of stress reduction involve **biofeedback**. This is a method for teaching people to have some control over their autonomic responses. It used to be believed that autonomic activity was not susceptible to learning, until a series of studies by Miller and DiCara (1967) showed that rats which had been paralysed using curare could learn to lower or raise their heartbeat, if they received an incentive in the form of direct electrical brain stimulation. Since then, a number of studies have shown that human beings, too, can gain some control over autonomic functioning like blood pressure or heartrate. To do that, though, we need to have immediate feedback as to what our current heartrate or blood pressure is.

Typically, someone who is using biofeedback to learn to control stress responses will use some kind of equipment which gives them information about their physiological state. In its simplest form, this might simply be a GSR-sensitive pad which wraps around the finger, which is connected to a box which produces a tone. The higher the tone, the higher the level of autonomic activity. There are, of course, many more sophisticated biofeedback machines on the market, but the type described is fairly typical, and commonly available. By practising relaxation exercises, the person finds that they can lower the tone of the feedback signal, or that, alternatively, they can raise it by allowing themselves to become more agitated. This provides the feedback for learning how to relax effectively and reduce their level of autonomic arousal.

Attributional therapy

Solomon (1969) found that there were considerable variations between people in what constitutes 'stress'. An experience which is highly stressful for one person might be taken in their stride by someone else. Part of that seems to come from

how people explain what is happening to themselves. Maier and Seligman (1976) found that depressive people tend to have a consistent **attributional style**, which means that they tend to feel that they have no control over what is happening. This in turn increases their stress levels and so contributes to maintaining their depression (see Chapter 9).

As we have seen, locus of control – whether one perceives oneself as a victim, or as an agent in one's own life – appears to be a major factor in stress reduction. People who see themselves as being more in control of what happens to them experience far less stress than those who feel themselves as being victims of circumstances, even when their objective conditions are exactly the same. The cognitive therapies which we looked at in Chapter 9 aim to help people to develop new types of attributional style, which will help them to take more control over their lives and so reduce their stress levels.

Biofeedback and attributional therapies are two different ways of combating the effects of long-term stress. Another approach aims to utilise the relationship between arousal and physical exertion, by drawing on the high levels of adrenaline found in the body as part of the general adaptation syndrome. If someone experiencing long-term stress adaptation begins to engage in regular vigorous exercise, such as swimming or other forms of sport or dance, their adrenaline level becomes lower – not at the time of the exercise, but afterwards as the parasympathetic division of the ANS exerts its restorative influence on the body. The existing high adrenaline level becomes 'harnessed' into the adrenaline response produced by the exercise, and so the physiological outcomes of high stress can be reduced.

Emotion

Until relatively recently, almost all psychological research into emotion concentrated on negative emotions, and in particular on fear and anger. This is partly because these emotions appear to link much more closely with physiological arousal, but psychological research also reflects the values of the society in which it is located, and modern society also neglects or undervalues the positive emotions. So we will begin our exploration of the psychology of emotion by looking at some of the theories of emotion which psychologists proposed on the basis of studies of fear and anger, before going on to look at some of the positive emotions.

Theories of emotion

The activity of the two divisions of the ANS is intimately connected with some types of emotional experience. Each can feed into the other: if we are angry or frightened, we become aroused; as we calm down, so does our physiological state. But as we have seen, if we have been exercising, we are also aroused in physiological terms, and this can sometimes affect the emotions that we feel. For example: if you run for a bus and it pulls away, you tend to feel much more annoyed than you do if you have just strolled round the corner and seen it pull away. But which causes what?

The James-Lange theory of emotion

The introspectionist psychologist William James proposed that emotion occurs as a result of our perceptions of physiological changes taking place in the body: '*We do not weep because we feel sorrow: we feel sorrow because we weep*' (James, 1890). Essentially, James was arguing that we produce a physiological reaction to some emotion-producing stimulus, and we then notice this reaction and try to make sense out of it. He gave an example of tripping on the stairs and catching the bannister: at the time of tripping and grabbing the banister, no fear is felt; but afterwards, the heart starts beating faster, we sweat more and breathe more deeply. And it is then, according to James, that we begin to feel afraid. Our cognitions of the event at the time are not enough to frighten us; but when the emergency response of the body begins, we feel fear.

This approach to emotion became known as the **James-Lange theory of emotion**, because a similar idea was also put forward by Carl Lange, at roughly the same time. The theory has led to some experimental investigation. If we become aware of our emotions by perceiving physical changes in the body, this implies that different emotions would give rise to different changes. There would be a difference in the arousal response produced by fear, for example, and the arousal response produced by anger. In 1953, Ax carried out an investigation to see whether physiological differences between fear and anger could be detected in the laboratory.

The first thing to do was to set up experimental conditions in which research participants felt either fear or anger. The research participants were shown into a laboratory containing impressive-looking equipment and were connected to electrodes attached to the head, the hands, above the heart, and so on. This allowed Ax to take multiple recordings of various indices of arousal (blood pressure, heartrate, sweating, skin temperature). The research participants were told that the study was about hypertension – looking at the differences between people who suffered from hypertension and those who did not – and that all they needed to do was to relax and listen to their preferred music.

Research participants in the fear condition then experienced a number of small, but gradually increasing, electrical shocks to the little finger. When they mentioned it, the experimenter expressed surprise, checked the wiring, and pressed a key which produced sparks near to the research participant. At this, the experimenter exclaimed that there was a dangerous, high-voltage short-circuit in the apparatus. As you might expect, this condition induced fear responses in the research participants.

In the anger condition, the technician who operated the polygraph was involved. The research participants were told by the experimenter that the technician had been fired earlier for incompetence, but that they had been obliged to re-employ him because the regular operator was sick. When the experimenter left the room, the technician was sarcastic and insulting to the nurse and to the research participant, as he pretended to check the wiring of the apparatus. Like the fear condition, this lasted for about five minutes. (It is worth noting here that this type of research would not be considered at all ethically acceptable nowadays – fortunately, psychologists are no longer permitted either to terrify or to enrage their research participants. Nor are they permitted to lie to them, except under very special circumstances and only temporarily.)

Ax found that the research participants did show different physiological reactions to the two experiences, as well as reporting their feelings differently. In particular, blood pressure and face temperature were significantly higher in the anger condition. This resembled the effects of a combination of adrenaline and noradrenaline on the body. In essence, the research participants in the fear condition produced physiological responses similar to those which occur when people are injected with adrenaline; whereas those in the anger condition produced physiological responses similar to the reactions of people injected with both adrenaline and noradrenaline.

The Cannon-Bard theory of emotion

In contrast to the James–Lange model, Walter Cannon, the physiologist who first discovered the 'fight or flight' syndrome, saw the experience of emotion as entirely separate from its physiological correlates. Rather than emotions being caused by physiological changes, he argued, they both take place independently, albeit sometimes in response to the same stimulus. This became known as the **Cannon-Bard theory of emotion**.

In 1929, Cannon argued that the arousal response was general, not specific to different emotions. The same physiological changes, he said, occur in very different emotional states, and also occur in non-emotional states as well. According to Cannon's model, an emotion-producing stimulus produces a generalised fight or flight response. This occurs through a direct associative process which does not have anything to do with the feeling of emotion. At the same time (usually), we respond to the situation as we understand it, and it is this cognitive response which produces feelings of emotion. The two reactions – the experience of emotion and the physiological changes – have nothing to do with one another.

The problem with this, of course, is that we tend to use very similar words to describe both our subjective emotions and our physical reactions. Many of the early investigations into emotion found it very hard to separate the two. A study by Marañon (1924) involved injecting 210 research participants with adrenaline, and simply asking them to report how they felt. Most of the research participants (71%) reported how they felt purely in terms of their physical symptoms, like: 'My heart is beating faster'; 'I am sweating', etc.; however the other 29% used emotional analogies to describe their feelings, like: 'I feel as if I am afraid'.

Marañon also observed that a handful of the second group (the ones who used emotional analogies to describe their experience) really seemed to be experiencing the emotion, rather than simply using the words as labels to report physical sensation. This suggested that there might

be a closer link between the two than the Cannon-Bard model implied. However, later researchers, especially Schachter and Singer (1962), noted that these feelings were particularly likely to come to the fore if the research participants were reminded of a real emotional experience. It seemed likely that the appropriate cognition was necessary in order for the research participants to describe their experiences as 'emotions'.

Schachter's theory of emotion

Schachter (1964) argued that the experience of emotion is all to do with the **attributions** which people make about what is going on. These attributions include both the physiological reactions which are taking place and the social situation that the individual is in at the time. Essentially, Schachter believed, the social setting determines the type of emotion which will be experienced (fear, anger, happiness, etc.) whereas the physiological response determines the strength of that reaction (how extremely the person feels it).

In 1962, Schachter and Singer conducted a study which quickly became a 'classic' in psychology. They aimed to investigate three propositions. (1) That if research participants experienced a state of physiological arousal for which they did not have an immediate explanation, they would 'label' their experience according to the cognitions that they had available. (2) That if research participants experienced arousal but had a clear explanation for what was going on, they would be unlikely to 'label' their feelings as emotions in the same way. (3) That, in the same cognitive circumstances, research participants' experiences of emotion would depend on the amount of physiological arousal that they were experiencing.

The experimenters set up two general experimental conditions, one designed to induce feelings of happiness or euphoria, the other designed to induce feelings of anger. Both conditions involved the use of 'stooges'. In the euphoria condition, research participants were asked to wait with a stooge who appeared to be happy and playful, engaging in 'basketball' games with waste paper and making paper aeroplanes. In the anger condition, research participants were given a long and highly personal questionnaire to fill in, and the stooge expressed increasing annoyance at the intrusiveness of the questions, eventually tearing up the questionnaire and stamping out of the room. These conditions, then, were designed to provide cognitive contexts within which the research participants could make sense of their physiological feelings.

Immediately before entering the waiting-room, research participants were given an injection, and told that it was a vitamin compound. Some people received a placebo injection (a harmless saline solution). The others received an injection of adrenaline. Of those others, one group of people were informed about the likely effects produced by the adrenaline; one group (in the euphoria condition only) was misinformed, and told to expect symptoms which did not take place; and one group was not told anything at all about the possible effects (Table 13.3).

Schachter and Singer found that their findings conformed with the propositions that they had made. When people understood about the effects of the adrenaline injection, they conformed slightly, but not strongly, with the mood of the stooge – after all, they already had an adequate explanation for their feelings. The group who were misinformed, however, were much more strongly influenced by the mood of the stooge, as were those who were uninformed about the effects of adrenaline. So it seemed that some kind of internal 'labelling' was indeed going on. Also, those who were in a state of arousal (induced by the adrenaline injection) were much more likely

to react strongly than those who had been given placebo injections, suggesting that the degree of emotion was affected by the research participant's physiological state.

Schachter's work provided the impetus for the growth of the study of attribution, which has developed extensively in recent years, and which we will be looking at more closely in Chapter 15. Unfortunately, however, despite many attempts to replicate the study, there has been little success; and it has attracted a number of methodological criticisms. One of these concerns the way that Schachter and Singer dropped five research participants from the analysis when it appeared that they were insensitive to the effects of adrenaline. This may have produced an exaggeration of the effects of the drug. They also did not check the prior mood of the research participants before proceeding with the experiment, which again could have led them to an experimental error.

It sometimes happens that a particular study becomes well known as much because it summarises the view which is generally held, as because of its own merits. There were serious drawbacks to Schachter and Singer's work, as we have seen, but the researchers did establish that just studying physiology is not enough to tell us about emotional experience. Their argument that the cognitive and self-attributional dimensions of a situation need to be taken into consideration as well, was an important insight in its own right, and reflected the views held by many researchers in the field. Most theories of emotion which have been developed since then have taken this stance.

Lazarus's appraisal theory

Lazarus (1980) proposed that emotion happens whenever a situation is deemed to be relevant to the person's central life concerns. Essentially, this involves a quick **appraisal** of a situation in terms of whether it represents a threat or not. The initial appraisal is then followed by coping responses, which may be either cognitive or physiological, or both. They may also be unconscious. Defence mechanisms like denial or rationalisation (see Chapter 7), as well as the fight or flight syndrome, can be seen as coping mechanisms. Once the person has manifested these coping mechanisms, the threat is reappraised. This secondary appraisal involves a more sophisticated analysis, in which specific emotions are identified.

Lazarus's theory, then, proposes that feelings of

Table 13.3 Conditions in Schachter and Singer's study

Groups involved in the study

Euphoria	Anger
Adrenaline informed	Adrenaline informed
Adrenaline ignorant	Adrenaline ignorant
Adrenaline misinformed	–
Placebo group	Placebo group

Adrenaline informed research participants were given accurate information about the effects of the drug.

Adrenaline ignorant research participants were told that the drug would have no side-effects.

Adrenaline misinformed research participants were warned to expect mild numbness, itching or headache.

Placebo group research participants were given saline solution and told that it would have no side-effects.

Source: Adapted from Schachter and Singer, 1962

emotion are determined by an immediate evaluative judgement combined with the behavioural or cognitive reactions produced by the event. In effect, this model proposes a three-stage response in emotion: the individual begins by deciding whether there is a threat or not; takes immediate coping action to deal with the threat; and then takes a closer look to see exactly what was involved, which leads them to identify the emotions which they are feeling.

Weiner's attributional theory

Weiner (1985) also saw emotion as coming from the attributions which the person makes about a situation. The initial reaction to any emotion-producing stimulus, Weiner argued, is concerned only with whether it is pleasant or unpleasant – whether it is 'good' or 'bad'. Once that initial evaluation has been made, Weiner suggested, the person then looks at what has caused the event. The attributions of causality which they make can modify the emotion which they feel – the attributions might define it more clearly, or even cause a complete re-evaluation of it.

In one study, Weiner asked research participants to recall pleasant and unpleasant circumstances that they had experienced. When they were asked to recall an unpleasant event which they felt was due to their own lack of effort, the research participants reported feeling shame. But when they were recalling something similarly unpleasant which was not their fault, they were more likely to report feeling anger. This, Weiner argued, was because of the nature of the attributions which they had made about the event. If it had an internal cause, they experienced shame, but if it had an external cause, they experienced anger. However, this type of study has a number of methodological problems, not least that of validity – remembering an occasion when you have experienced an emotion may be quite different from feeling the emotion itself.

The facial feedback theory

Ekman, Sorenson and Friesen (1969) proposed that the facial expressions which people use to signify emotions may in themselves be involved in promoting those emotions, by providing feedback to the brain. The **facial feedback hypothesis**, in this sense, is similar to the James–Lange approach, but where James was concerned with central physiological states as the cause of emotion,

Ekman suggests that peripheral social signals, like smiling, are its cause.

Ekman, Sorenson and Friesen (1969) found that some facial expressions – those which signal 'basic' emotions, like surprise, happiness or fear – seem to be innate, in that they take the same form in all human societies. By detailed analysis of video records of facial expression, they could identify which facial muscles were involved in these basic emotions. Using this information, Ekman, Levenson and Friesen (1983) asked research participants to arrange particular muscles of their faces. The muscle changes which they were asked to make corresponded exactly to the apparently innate expressions of emotions, and they were asked to hold each combination for ten seconds.

During that time, various physiological measures of arousal were taken, and Ekman, Levenson and Friesen found that their research participants showed changes in these measures, depending on the emotion which they were signalling. For example, when they were simulating anger, fear or sadness, the research participants showed increased heartrate; but happiness, disgust and surprise produced lowering of the heartrate. Fear and sadness showed lower skin temperature, whereas anger showed a raised skin temperature. What was interesting, though, was that the differences in these measures produced by simulating appropriate facial expressions was actually greater than the differences in such measures which were produced when the research participants were asked to 're-live' the emotions.

Averill's social construction theory

Averill (1980) proposed that the experience of emotion is socially constructed. The combinations of genetic and physiological reactions which take place are organised and interpreted by the individual in terms of the social norms and social roles which are involved in the situation. Averill sees emotions as **transitory social roles**, which are all to do with how the person appraises the situation. They are roles, because they allow a range of social actions to take place within a context that is socially agreed and understood; but they are transitory, because it is expected that the emotion which someone is experiencing is not a permanent state of affairs.

One of the distinctive features of the role-behaviour involved in emotional expression, according to Averill, is that it breaks the conventional social norms, of not experiencing emotions. So, for instance, in the normal run of things it is socially unacceptable to state that you want to harm someone. If you are angry, however, this social taboo is suspended. Perhaps because of this, Averill argued, strong emotions are experienced as 'passions' – experiences which are not under the individual's control – rather than as the social roles which they are. Even when they are angry or upset, people will tend to express this in socially acceptable ways. Some societies, for example, permit people to express their grief at a bereavement by wailing aloud, but in other societies this behaviour is not acceptable. Although the experience of grief is no less for them, people who live in the latter kind of society manage to express their grief in other, quieter ways. So emotions, according to Averill, are not as uncontrollable as society likes to believe.

Averill argued that society adopts this external mode of thinking about emotions because it allows people to distance themselves from what is going on: they do not have to accept the full responsibility for their actions. The way that emotions are acted out involves a number of mechanisms, including the use of sophisticated signals like facial expressions, and often involving arousal as a result of the disruption of normal functioning. But the experience of emotion, Averill argued, is of the acting out of a social role.

It is not just negative emotions which Averill interpreted in this way. According to this theory, the same social processes apply to the positive emotions. In discussing love, Averill argued that this represents a social role which allows individuals to idealise, and be idealised by, another person. In Averill's view, this process provides a mechanism by which the person can preserve their feelings of self-worth, while at the same time

accepting that a single individual matters little in society at large.

We can see, then, that theories of human emotions have ranged from those which emphasise the purely physiological to those which emphasise the purely social, and in the process they have included the behavioural and cognitive levels of explanation as well. Cornelius (1996) identified four major research traditions in emotion research (Table 13.4): the Darwinian perspective, which sees emotions as having adaptive functions for the organism; the Jamesian perspective, which sees emotions as physiological responses; the cognitive perspective, which sees emotions as being based on cognitive appraisals; and the social constructionist perspective, which sees emotions as social constructions which serve social purposes.

In our study of emotion, we have looked at examples of each of these traditions, although our exploration of the social approaches to emotion will continue in the next chapter too. There, we will be looking at relationships and those emotions, such as loving and loneliness, which are directly related to them.

Positive emotions

It is worth noting, however, that relatively few theories of emotion have concerned themselves with positive emotions, such as happiness, love or serenity. It is only recently that researchers have become seriously interested in investigating some of the more positive aspects of human emotions. In part, interest in positive emotions has come about as a result of some of the ethical problems raised by experimentation into emotion. As we have seen, some of the early experiments involved

Table 13.4 Theoretical traditions of emotion research

Tradition	Key idea	Key researcher(s)
Darwinian	Emotions have adaptive functions and are universal.	Ekman *et al.* (1987)
Jamesian	Emotions are bodily responses.	Levenson *et al.* (1990)
Cognitive	Emotions are based on emotions.	Smith and Lazarus (1993)
Social constructionist	Emotions are social constructions and serve social purposes.	Averill (1980)

Source: Adapted from Cornelius, 1996

the free use of deception, and often caused research participants considerable (though temporary) distress. That type of research is far less acceptable nowadays, and so psychologists have had to re-evaluate their methodology.

However, there is still relatively little research into positive emotions, certainly by comparison with the amount of research into fear or anger. Partly, this is because we have relatively few ways of identifying positive emotional experience. In an attempt to address this issue, Argyle and Crossland (1987) performed a study of positive emotions. They asked research participants to think about 24 different pleasant situations, like: 'Spending a good social evening with friends'; 'Feeling overwhelmed by the beauty of nature'; 'Having a long hot bath'; or 'Being successful at work'. The research participants were asked to take each situation one at a time, think about it, and describe how the particular situation would make them feel.

From their answers, Argyle and Crossland identified four dimensions for positive emotions. They named the first dimension **absorption**, as it ranged from private, absorbing experiences to social experiences which were more superficial in terms of the amount of attention or concentration which they demanded. The second dimension seemed to involve feelings of **potency** – whether the person felt active and capable. At one end of this dimension were things like sport or success at work, while the opposite end of the dimension was concerned with experiences like enjoying a hot bath or listening to music.

The third dimension identified by Argyle and Crossland seemed to be concerned with **altruism**. At one end of the scale they found situations like conversations, or engaging in some kind of commitment activity (like church or charity work). At the other end, they found more self-indulgent situations, like receiving a valuable present or engaging in a personal hobby. The researchers named the fourth dimension **spiritual**, because it was concerned with personally meaningful experiences at one extreme, like solving a challenging problem or enjoying nature, while the opposite end of the scale was concerned with more trivial activities, like watching a television thriller or buying something nice for oneself.

Although there is, naturally, much more to be said about positive emotional experiences, Argyle and Crossland's work provides us with a framework within which some of that research might

take place. By showing how positive emotional experiences can be identified and classified, they have opened up the possibility that these different dimensions can be explored, perhaps modified, and at the very least elaborated more specifically.

Humour

Another of the positive emotions, and one which is easily overlooked, is that of humour. As with many of the positive emotions (and possibly the other emotions too, as we have seen) social factors are a very important facet of the experience. With humour, particularly, social factors are more than important, since humour is by definition a social phenomenon.

Emerson (1969) pointed out that humour, in the form of jokes or asides, is judged differently from other forms of social interaction, in that it officially does not 'count' as part of a serious exchange. This means that people find themselves able to take risks with humour which they would not feel able to take if they were required to make the comment or observation in a less protected way. As such, humour is an important social tool, for defusing tense situations or encouraging a fresh perspective on a problem.

Kahn (1989) identified five primary functions that humour serves for individuals and groups. The first is that of **coping**. Humour helps people to become detached from potentially threatening aspects of their situation, so that they can cope with it a bit better. So, for example, people who work in the emergency services often use humour in a way that appears to outsiders to be callous, but which in reality allows them to cope better with things that are happening. The second function is **reframing** – humour allows people to see things that they have previously taken for granted, in a new light; or to restructure their experience in such a way that it conveys different implications. Kahn also pointed out that **communicating** is an important role for humour. It allows people to deliver messages that they would otherwise not be able to say, particularly with reference to socially 'taboo' experiences like death or bereavement.

The fourth function of humour which Kahn identified is **expressing hostility** – it is not uncommon for hostile racist or sexist feelings, for example, to be expressed using a joking medium. Framing the comment like this makes it difficult for a recipient to protest, but such humour can sometimes be extremely vicious. Aggressive humour between different groups often reflects the existence of pre-existing group tensions. It may also, more innocuously, serve to ridicule or derogate members of the other group, or substitute for more blatant confrontation. For example, members of one department in an organisation may express their hostility towards those in another department by presenting them as caricatures: 'those paperheads over in accounting'.

The fifth function of humour that Kahn identified has to do with **constructing identities**. 'In-jokes' are often used to maintain or establish group cohesion, and to provide evidence that the person speaking is a member of that social group. As such, they are often used to help members of a group to draw the boundaries between their group and other people.

There are, of course, many more positive emotions than this, and some of them have even been the subject of research – for instance, the studies of love and loving which we will be looking at in Chapter 14. So far, though, researchers are only just beginning to explore the range of positive emotions in our lives. As Argyle's study showed, positive emotions are many, and complex. But, sadly, many of them are still regarded as relatively unimportant, at least when it comes to gaining research grants, and as a result, our understanding of them is still relatively limited.

The study of emotion, then, has taken many different forms, ranging from investigations of physiological mechanisms to explorations of the personal and social dimensions of experience. The same complexity applies to the psychological investigation of motivation. While early research into motivation emphasised the physiological dimensions, more recent investigations have spanned social, cognitive and cultural dimensions as well.

Motivation

In the early years of psychology, the question of motivation – why people, or animals, do what they do – was largely accounted for using the concept of 'instinct'. In Chapter 22 we will be looking more closely at some ideas about 'instincts'. But the trouble with trying to explain things by using the idea of an 'instinct' is that it is not really an explanation. It just raises more questions.

For a physiological psychologist, for example, it is not enough to say that something happens because of instinct, because even if that really was why it happened (which is questionable, since most definitions of instinct are too woolly to be much use), we would still need to know more. Somehow, for instance, this mystical 'instinct' causes muscles to contract, and actions to be performed – and that is just the beginning. When we are talking about human behaviour, motivation becomes far more complex than just the performance of acts and actions. Even for the simplest form of motivation, we need to be able to show how an 'instinct' might produce behaviour.

Drive theories of motivation

In the first half of the twentieth century, psychologists who were interested in motivation often used the idea of 'instinct', but addressed their efforts to trying to find out how instincts influenced behaviour. McDougall (1932) proposed that the study of motivation could usefully be approached by identifying a range of different behaviours engaged in by an animal, and assuming that each of these behaviours represented a manifestation of some kind of underlying **drive**, which provided the energy for the behaviour to take place. So, according to McDougall, the presence of a drive could be inferred from the behaviour that an animal was showing.

A number of attempts were made to classify different types of drive. Morgan (1943) drew a distinction between **primary drives** – those which satisfied a basic need within the organism – and **secondary drives**, which were learned or social. Morgan further subdivided the primary drives into two kinds: **physiological drives**, which were concerned with unavoidable physiological necessities, such as hunger, sleep, thirst and sex; and **general drives**, concerned with more wide-ranging or less specific goals, like exploration, fear, manipulation and affection.

Drive-reduction

Hull (1943) proposed that all animal learning was based on the need to reduce some kind of primary drive. **Drive-reduction**, in Hull's view, was what motivated and energised learning: a rat would learn to press a lever in a Skinner box only because it was hungry, and because the food reward reduced that hunger. Without the food to satisfy the primary drive of hunger, learning would not take place. Hull's theory was interesting, because it introduced an internal variable to the idea of stimulus–response learning. Strict behaviourists, such as Watson (see Chapter 1), had insisted that learning took place through direct links between stimulus and response (S-R). But Hull was arguing that the internal state of the organism was a necessary part of that learning – that the link was **stimulus–organism–response** (S-O-R).

Moreover, Hull argued, if a stimulus was consistently associated with the satisfaction of a primary drive – for example, if a mother was constantly present whenever her infant was fed – then that stimulus itself would become rewarding, through association. So, according to Hull, even complex behaviour could be traced back to a motivational origin in terms of the satisfaction of a primary drive. It was the internal state of the organism which determined whether it would learn or not.

The part of the brain known as the hypothalamus is responsible for maintaining **homeostasis** in the body – for keeping it in a steady state, so that it is functioning in an optimal way. In 1967, Grossman proposed that a distinction could be drawn between homeostatic and non-homeostatic drives. **Homeostatic drives** are triggered off internally, by the state of the body. Hunger, thirst and maintaining body temperature are all like that – they are internally initiated, and concerned with maintaining homeostasis. But **non-homeostatic drives** are triggered off by external events rather than internal states. For example: sexual activity, emotional arousal and overall levels of physical activity are types of behaviour which become relevant only in the presence of appropriate environmental cues. Grossman argued that it was important to distinguish between drives which were triggered by internal cues and those which were set off by external ones, since the physiological mechanisms through which these drives operated would probably be very different.

The concept of drive was a very popular one, common throughout the psychology of the 1950s and 1960s. Maslow (1954) even proposed that the higher forms of human motivation could be categorised in terms of 'needs', which energised human behaviour. According to Maslow's hierarchy, the more primitive or basic needs would have to be satisfied before the higher-order needs

became important. However, this type of approach to drive theory incorporates quite complex social and cognitive aspects of human behaviour; and as such it was rather different from motivation as studied by the physiological psychologists. Since most experimental research was conducted using animals as subjects, psychologists' attention at that time focused mostly on the basic, primary drives, and not on more complex social motivation.

The drive-reduction model of motivation was challenged on a number of fronts. Humanistic psychologists such as Carl Rogers argued that higher-order needs like the need for **self-actualisation** were fundamental to human beings, and not simply the outcome of an elaborate chain of associations from feeding in infancy or the sublimation of the sex drive (see Chapter 7). Physiological psychologists, too, discovered that animals would learn to press levers for non-nutritive rewards, like flashing lights or sounds, as we will see later in this chapter. So it gradually became clear that Hull's model of motivation as drive-reduction was not the whole story. But as research into the basic manifestations of hunger continued, it revealed a number of underlying physiological mechanisms, which we will look at before going on to consider some of the more complex forms of social motivation.

Hunger

One of the interesting things about both eating and drinking is that they are activities which are designed to satisfy needs which have not happened yet. As a general rule, we do not eat because we are actually starving. Instead, we eat in order to prevent such an extreme circumstance from arising – we begin to eat long before the body begins to suffer from starvation. This implies that we can in some way monitor our body's resources, and predict what will satisfy our needs in the future.

One of the first questions, then, is: how do we know when to stop eating? Le Magnen (1972) showed that when people eat, they do not actually keep eating for very long, and they stop eating long before the food can have been digested. Animals do the same: as a general rule, a hungry animal will eat up to a certain point, but will then refuse to eat any more, even though it is not possible for it to have digested what it has just eaten.

Drive theory assumes that the process of satisfying a need involves four major features. The first is the existence of a **need state** in the individual (or 'organism', as these researchers preferred to say): the individual should be hungry, thirsty or something similar. This need state then stimulates the **drive activity**, which directs the organism's behaviour towards the goal stimulus: food, water or whatever else is likely to satisfy the need. When the **goal stimulus** has been reached, a fast-acting feedback loop then reduces the drive activity. The messages which arrive via the **feedback loop** make sure that the behaviour stops at an appropriate time; but the need state itself, which initiated the whole process, is reduced very much more gradually (Figure 13.7).

Satiation

In 1942, Hetherington and Ranson showed that laboratory rats with a lesion in the ventro-medial nucleus of the hypothalamus (known as the VMH for short) would overeat dramatically, and become massively obese. The researchers suggested that this area of the hypothalamus must be the area which regulated hunger. The brain lesions had damaged this area, which meant that hunger was increased, and so the animals would overeat.

However, a series of studies by Miller, Bailey and Stevenson (1950) suggested that this was not really an adequate explanation for what was going on. For one thing, animals with VMH lesions would not make any effort to obtain food, although they would overeat if it was there. Hunger is a motivational state, so it is something which might be expected to generate effort: if the animals were really hungry, Miller *et al.* reasoned, they would be prepared to make an effort to obtain their food, as normally hungry rats do. Furthermore, whereas normally hungry rats will learn to tolerate unpleasant stimuli (like mild electric shocks) to obtain food, those with VMH lesions would not do this either. If there were any difficulties, they just did not bother with the additional food. It was simply that, in a situation where food was provided freely, they would eat far more than normally hungry rats.

Miller, Bailey and Stevenson (1950) suggested that perhaps lesions of the ventro-medial hypothalamus did not simply increase hunger. Instead, they proposed that the lesions interrupted the mechanisms which stopped eating: the **satiety mechanisms**, which assess when the animals have eaten enough. Because they did not receive an appropriate 'stop' signal from the brain, the animals just carried on eating.

In 1951, Anand and Brobeck showed that a lesion in a different region of the hypothalamus, the lateral hypothalamus (LH), produced the opposite effect – a complete failure to eat. Experimental animals with lesions in the lateral hypothalamus would literally starve themselves to death, or eat only very little so that they became malnourished. Anand and Brobeck suggested that the lateral hypothalamus is a kind of initiation centre for feeding, which triggers off eating behaviour. When it was destroyed by the lesion, these animals did not receive the appropriate message to start feeding, and so they simply did not begin to eat.

The implication of these studies, then, was that there are two distinct regions of the hypothalamus which are involved in regulating hunger. One of these regions is a 'feeding centre', which triggers off eating, and the other is a 'satiety centre', which stops it. This model received further support in 1967, when Arees and Mayer showed that there were neural fibres linking the two regions of the hypothalamus, so it was possible for the two to operate together to produce co-ordinated feeding behaviour.

Neurotransmitters and feeding

Grossman (1960) found that, often, the same neural pathways seemed to be involved in both eating and drinking. There were differences, though, in that the two behaviours seemed to involve different neurotransmitters. For example: if noradrenaline was injected into a particular site in the hypothalamus, rats would show feeding behaviour; but if acetylcholine was injected into the same site, they would drink. The drug amphetamine was also found to suppress feeding activity, and this too seemed to link with neurotransmitter functioning: amphetamine appears to be taken up at the receptor sites of neurones involved in feeding behaviour (see Chapter 11 for an explanation of how drugs and neurotransmitters work).

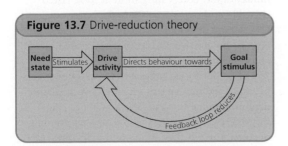

Figure 13.7 Drive-reduction theory

Need state → Stimulates → Drive activity → Directs behaviour towards → Goal stimulus

Feedback loop reduces

Following Grossman's suggestion, other researchers began to investigate the role of neuro-transmitters in motivation. Leibowitz (1970) suggested that there are two different types of receptor site in the hypothalamus. One type is **noradrenergic** – responding to the neuro-transmitter noradrenaline – and this type triggers off or excites feeding behaviour. The other type, Leibowitz proposed, responds to amphetamine, inhibiting feeding. In 1973, Gold showed that the lesions which produced obesity in animals are located just behind the ventro-medial nucleus, not actually in it, and suggested that what these lesions really involve is the cutting of the noradrenergic pathways rather than damaging the ventro-medial nucleus itself.

A problem with this idea is that one of the effects of the drug amphetamine is actually to increase the production of noradrenaline, not reduce it; yet at the same time, amphetamine suppresses appetite. If noradrenaline stimulated feeding, as Leibowitz's early model proposed, it should not be possible for amphetamine to reduce appetite. But in 1973, Leibowitz proposed that there are different types of noradrenergic receptors. Some noradrenergic receptors, Leibowitz argued, have an excitatory effect, and so will stimulate eating, whereas others have an inhibitory effect and will make the organism disinclined to eat. This helped researchers to make more sense of the complex neurochemical processes which were going on.

All these findings involved experiments with animals – usually laboratory rats. But some studies with human beings also supported the model which was gradually being developed. For example: in 1969, Reeves and Plum reported on a clinical case of a young woman who had developed a brain tumour. She had doubled her body-weight over the two years in which the tumour developed, through eating excessively. After her death, an autopsy showed that the brain tumour was located near the ventro-medial nuclei of the hypothalamus, which suggested that similar mechanisms might be operating in human beings.

As a result of some of these findings, some surgeons performed lesions of the lateral hypo-thalamus as a last-resort treatment for excessive obesity. Quaade, in 1971, reported on some of these cases. As part of the surgery, the patients had undergone brain stimulation, while they were conscious (partly to help surgeons make sure that they had reached the right area). Quaade showed that when this region was stimulated during brain surgery, patients' verbal reports of what they felt included descriptions of feeling very hungry.

The set weight

In 1972, Nisbett suggested that a key to under-standing how hypothalamic lesions had their effects might be that the body has an internally regulated **set weight**. With the set weight in operation, eating would be triggered off when the body-weight fell below it, and satiation would occur when the organism had eaten enough to regain the set-weight point. Both mechanisms would operate through homeostatic mechanisms in the hypothalamus.

Nisbett suggested that hypothalamic lesions, whether in the ventro-medial nucleus or in the lateral hypothalamus, altered the body's set weight. Lesions in the VMH raised the set weight, whereas lesions in the LH lowered it. So the animal would then begin to eat either a great deal more, or eat less, until its body-weight reached the new set point. Something like this, Nisbett suggested, might also be what was happening in human beings who suffered from obesity.

Obesity which has been experimentally induced by VMH lesions shows some distinctive characteristics. Weingarten, in 1982, discussed how rats with this kind of obesity were finicky in what they would eat: although they ate more in one meal than normal rats did, they did not just eat anything. For instance, they would eat chocolate biscuits incessantly, but would refuse food which had been very lightly adulterated with quinine (so that it had a slightly bitter taste), and which would be eaten by normally hungry rats. These animals were also less active, both generally and sexually, and more easily irritated. Schachter (1971) observed similar characteristics in obese human beings, showing that they ate more food at one sitting than ordinary people, and also were more finicky about taste, eating more if food tasted palatable and much less if it had a bitter taste. Obese human beings too, Schachter pointed out, tend to be inactive, and to show increased emotionality.

This is not to say, however, that all obesity can be explained in terms of impaired hypothalamic malfunctioning. In 1976, Sclafani and Springer showed that normal rats would also eat enough to become obese if they were continually presented with novel and highly palatable food. They react strongly to the smell and taste of the food. Powley (1977) pointed out that any attempt to produce a general theory of the motivational mechanisms of hunger needs to take these external factors into account as well. The sensory and cognitive mechanisms involved in taste and smell may be just as important as internal homeostatic mechanisms. In our consumer society, where people are constantly being presented with images of highly desirable food of all different kinds, we may not need to look to hypothalamic functioning to explain why some people become obese.

Hunger and thirst are intimately linked with the process of maintaining homeostasis. The main role of the hypothalamus seems to be to keep the body functioning at an optimal level. In order to do this, it receives messages about the internal conditions of the body, and initiates actions designed to correct those conditions if they become less than optimal. As we have just seen, the hypothalamus has mechanisms which can produce eating or stop eating. It also has other nuclei which seem to do much the same thing with respect to thirst; and others which are concerned with maintaining body temperature and other essential functions. By initiating action which will correct the imbalance or non-optimal state, the hypothalamus can bring the body back to optimal functioning. So for this type of motivation, at least, the research suggests that physiological mechanisms are heavily involved in the primary drives.

Exploration

As we saw earlier, the drive-reduction theory proposed by McDougall (1932), and later by Hull (1943), assumed that all behaviour was 'energised' by drives. But both animals and human beings also do many things which are not directly involved in reducing a primary drive. Hebb (1955) showed that monkeys would learn to solve manipulative puzzles for no specific reward, apparently deriving some intrinsic reward from the task itself. They would also find it rewarding if they were allowed to watch a roomful of other monkeys rather than just sitting on their own. So it is difficult to see how all types of behaviour can be explained as drive-reduction. Some research, however, suggested that much animal behaviour could in fact be linked with more basic types of drives, such as exploration, even when that did not seem to be the case on the surface.

Welker, in 1959, showed how rats would take any opportunity to escape from even a new maze that they had not explored before, and proposed that the exploratory impulse in rats is closely linked with the motivation to escape. Blanchard, Kelly and Blanchard (1974) showed that this type of response could have survival value. Two groups of rats were used, one of which had experienced the opportunity to explore a complex maze, and the other of which had not. Both groups were placed in the maze with a cat. Blanchard et al. found that the group which had previously explored the maze froze when they saw the cat, remaining perfectly motionless. But those who had not explored it before ran into the maze and through its passages. They suggested that the first group, through their previous exploration, had learned that they could not escape from the maze, and were applying that knowledge to modify their response to the cat – which would increase their chances of survival.

Cognitive maps

O'Keefe and Nadel (1978) suggested that exploratory behaviour may be linked with the activity of the brain structure known as the **hippocampus.** Using micro-recording techniques, they found that the pattern of electrodes which fired while rats were exploring a maze seemed to record the position of the animal within the maze itself. (In order to avoid unwanted visual effects, they used a special maze which did not allow the rats to look into the distance.) For the first time, this view provided some physiological support for Tolman's idea of **cognitive maps**, which we looked at in Chapter 5, and will be meeting again in Chapter 18. Tolman (1932) had found that rats seemed to develop an internal representation of a complex maze if they were allowed to explore it, and that they could apply this knowledge when it became advantageous to do so.

Exploration is a complex form of motivation which can be affected by a number of factors. In the 1960s, a number of researchers suggested that exploration might be linked to the general arousal level of the organism, but the experimental research designed to investigate this idea proved highly contradictory. In some studies, rats which had experienced stresses (to produce high arousal levels) explored more, but in others, they explored less. Some research suggested that there might be no connection at all between the two. Although some of these apparently contradictory outcomes might have resulted from different experimental conditions – like the amount of novelty with which the animal was faced all at once – it became obvious that any relationship between arousal and exploration was not likely to be a simple one.

Electrical stimulation of the brain

In 1954, Olds and Milner discovered that electrical stimulation to certain specific parts of the brain seem to be highly rewarding. Rats would learn to press levers just to 'earn' a brief electrical stimulation through electrodes implanted in these areas. Moreover, they would work very hard to obtain this stimulation, producing up to a thousand presses an hour for several hours on end. Spies (1965) showed that, if it was faced with a choice between **electrical stimulation of the brain (ESB)** and food, a hungry rat would choose ESB even to the point of starving itself to death.

Initially, Olds and Milner proposed that the electrodes which they had implanted tapped into a **pleasure centre** in the brain, which represented the central neural pathways for all the different reward systems of the organism. Most of the 'pleasure centre' regions seemed to be near to the hypothalamus, so the idea that there might be general motivational pathways to do with experiencing pleasure, linked with some of the findings which had already been made about the role of the hypothalamus in motivation.

Rapidly, though, researchers began to discover that ESB differed from ordinary rewards in several significant ways. For one thing, as we have already seen, it did not show satiation: experimental animals would continue to work for it without ever seeming to have had enough. But on the other hand, it extinguished very quickly. Where most types of reward produce learning which dies out slowly, ESB-rewarded lever-pressing would die out more or less as soon as the animal stopped receiving the reward – sometimes only two or three fruitless lever-presses were enough for the animal to stop trying. Nor did it re-start after a break. Gallistel (1973) showed that rats which had been engaging in frenzied lever-pressing only an hour previously would ignore the same lever when they were put back in front of it. They would resume lever-pressing for ESB stimulation only if they were given a few 'samples' first. This is quite different from ordinary learning based on

food rewards, which dies out slowly, and often shows spontaneous recovery even after it has extinguished (see Chapter 18).

One possible explanation for the difference between ESB and ordinary rewards may be to do with the amount of time which elapses between the action and the reinforcement. With ESB, of course, the reward happens straight away, whereas with ordinary food rewards, there is a delay while the animal gets the food pellet from the delivery chute and eats it. Mogenson and Phillips (1976) showed that rats which were rewarded for pressing a lever by receiving an immediate intravenous glucose injection responded in a way which was similar to ESB: their lever-pressing was persistent, extinguished rapidly, and did not survive unrewarded intervals easily.

Incentives and rewards

One possible solution for these differences was to distinguish between **incentives**, which would act to encourage behaviour but did not reduce drives, and **rewards**, which would directly reduce internal drives. Crow (1973) suggested that there might be a difference in the neural pathways of rewards and incentives, with incentives exciting dopamine pathways in the brain, and drive-reducing rewards (like food) exciting noradrenaline pathways. Gallistel (1973) suggested that sensory stimuli like smell and taste might act as incentives, but become rewarding because they are generally associated with stimulation of the reward pathways. Gallistel went on to suggest that perhaps ESB stimulates incentive pathways but not drive-reduction pathways, which might explain why it does not act in the same way as conventional rewards.

There was some experimental support for this idea. For example, Valenstein (1967) showed that the pattern of lever-pressing in rats who were allowed to taste a mixture of saccharine and sucrose, but without it going to the stomach (the incentive of taste, but without the reward of hunger satiation) was the same as the pattern for ESB lever-pressing. The weakness, though, of the incentive explanation for ESB is that it does not explain why the animal does not become habituated to ESB, as it does to taste and smell. It is possible, though, that habituation is a property of the sensory receptors rather than of the internal motivational system, in which case this might not be so much of a problem.

ESB in humans

As you might imagine, there has been only a limited amount of investigation of ESB in human beings, but there has been some. In 1963, Heath reported on two patients who had minute electrodes implanted into various regions of the brain. They were able to operate these by pressing buttons on a control box, which they wore attached to their belts. One of the patients frequently pressed the button which would stimulate the septal region of the limbic system, and reported that he did so because it felt 'good', like the build-up to a sexual orgasm. The other patient did not show any clear preference, but reported that several of the buttons made him feel good.

In 1973, Campbell reported on surgical patients who were given ESB to the septal region of the limbic system. They described it as making them feel 'wonderful', 'happy' or 'drunk'. If they were given a rapid rate of stimulation (approximately 1000 per hour) they seemed to be quite happy to do nothing else for the whole six-hour period (the longest time allowed). In some of his science fiction books, the writer Larry Niven suggested that 'wireheading' could become the addiction of the future, replacing addictive drugs like heroin or amphetamine. But we need to remember that these patients were also experiencing extremely serious physical problems – like extreme and continuous pain brought on by terminal cancer, or recurrent and uncontrollable epilepsy – so it could be that their reactions were affected by their relief at freedom from their immediate condition, rather than purely reflecting the ESB itself.

Theories of human needs

When we look closely at human motivation, we can identify a number of different ways that human behaviour could be motivated, some of which do not seem to have much to do with physiological mechanisms at all. Most explanations of human motivation, however, still tend to be framed in terms of 'needs' and 'drives', even though the needs which have been identified are often personal or social rather than physiological.

Achievement motivation

McClelland (1961) believed that human motivation could be understood in terms of 'needs', but not physiological ones. Instead, McClelland emphasised the importance of social needs, and particularly the **need for achievement** (often referred to as **nAch**) and the **need for affiliation** (which is *not*, strangely enough, referred to as nAff!). McClelland proposed that achievement motivation was the reason why some people seem to be very keen to do well, while others seem to be reluctant to make an effort, and do not seem to mind whether they are successful or not.

A large part of McClelland's contribution to the study of motivation consisted of the methodology which he developed to try to measure underlying levels of achievement motivation. One technique was to ask children to tell stories, or to complete stories which had been begun by someone else. By looking at the content of the child's story, and the imagery which it used, McClelland could calculate a score of achievement motivation. This score, he found, also correlated with other measures, like parents' or teachers' reports of that child's tendency to persevere at a given task.

McClelland (1961) also argued that different societies, as well as individuals, showed different levels of achievement motivation. These were reflected in the literature and imagery used in those countries, and McClelland felt that it accounted to some extent for those countries' economic success. For example, there was an extremely high correlation between measures of economic growth and the imagery and ideas prevalent in the literature and drama of those countries: high levels of achievement-oriented imagery correlated with times of economic prosperity, whereas low levels of achievement-oriented themes tended to occur at times of economic recession or depression.

It is interesting to speculate about cause and effect here: McClelland demonstrated a correlation, and assumed that there was an underlying motivation which could explain it. But it would be possible to argue the case both ways. One might say, for instance, that there were high levels of achievement imagery because people were achieving so much during prosperous times, and their achievement was being reflected in the imagery. Alternatively, one could argue that the achievement-oriented literature or art inspired people to make more effort, and, as a result of that, they contributed more to economic growth. What is more likely, of course, is an interactive relationship, with each contributing to the other. By looking at imagery and pervasive themes, McClelland was tapping into the **social**

representations of the societies concerned. We will be looking more at social representations in Chapter 15.

Other researchers also investigated achievement motivation in children and found that it correlated very highly with parental **expectations**. Winterbottom (1953) showed that achievement motivation as measured by story-completion tasks correlated with parental expectations of their children, obtained from interviewing mothers. Parents of children with high levels of achievement motivation expected their children to achieve developmental tasks (like tying shoelaces) earlier, and were more likely to reward their children with affection.

Rosen and d'Andrade (1959) asked parents to watch their child trying to build a tower of blocks while blindfolded, and found that parents of children with high levels of achievement motivation set high standards, but also praised the child's efforts more. Again, we cannot really say which causes what (perhaps the parents had developed high expectations because their children always tried so hard), but this does tie in with other work on the power of expectations, such as the research into self-fulfilling prophecies by Rosenthal and Jacobsen (1968), which we will be looking at in Chapter 15.

Maslow's hierarchy of human needs

Maslow (1954) proposed that human beings have a number of complex needs, but not all of these needs are equally important at any one time. Instead, they are organised hierarchically, with each different level of needs resting on the assumption that the ones underneath have been satisfied. As each group of needs becomes satisfied, the next level becomes important. At the bottom of the pyramid (Figure 13.8) are **physiological needs**, which are essential for the body's survival. If we are in a situation where these needs are not being met, according to Maslow, our energies are devoted towards satisfying them: obtaining food, drink or shelter becomes more important than anything else. But if those needs are satisfied, we do not think any more about them, and social needs become more important then. At the very top of the pyramid is **self-actualisation**: the point where all the needs of the human being are satisfied, and that person is operating at their absolute peak.

Maslow's theory became very popular as an explanation for motivation at work, mainly because it seems to be able to explain how it is that employees' needs never seem to be entirely satisfied: once adequate levels of pay have been achieved, people will be looking for increased job satisfaction, and so on. The hierarchical approach of Maslow's model seems to be able to account for this, and to give managers some guidance as to what types of issue are likely to become important.

But although it may be useful in some respects, there are several serious flaws in the theory, and in particular with the idea that lower needs have to be satisfied before higher needs become important. There are many instances which show how people do not always conform to this. Perhaps the most extreme is the case of the starving poet, whose search for beauty and symmetry has led to the neglect of basic physiological needs. Similarly, some people will put up with unemployment and financial insecurity rather than abandon family, home and friends to go to look for work in more prosperous areas. For such people, social or family needs override others. And the teenager who develops anorexia as a result of an extreme and unrealistic image of her ideal body-shape is showing that higher needs (for social approval or respect) can directly override physiological ones, even to the point of actual starvation. These cannot be explained by Maslow's model. Although

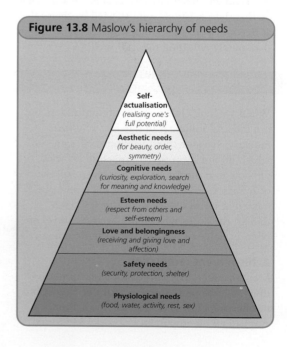

Figure 13.8 Maslow's hierarchy of needs

Self-actualisation
(realising one's full potential)

Aesthetic needs
(for beauty, order, symmetry)

Cognitive needs
(curiosity, exploration, search for meaning and knowledge)

Esteem needs
(respect from others and self-esteem)

Love and belongingness
(receiving and giving love and affection)

Safety needs
(security, protection, shelter)

Physiological needs
(food, water, activity, rest, sex)

they are extreme examples, a theory which purports to explain human motivation should be able to explain what people do. Maslow's model may provide a rough working generalisation about most people in most situations, but it is not really adequate as an explanation of human motivation.

Rogers' theory of human needs

As we saw in Chapter 7, Rogers (1961) believed that human beings have two fundamental needs, and that the satisfaction of each of these needs is essential for psychological health. The first of these is the **need for positive regard**: the idea that each of us needs to be seen positively by others, in some way. For most people this means love – from a loving family, or a loving relationship in later life. But Rogers argued that it was possible for people to settle for respect or approval: as long as they were regarded positively by someone, that need could be assuaged, although loving relationships were more fulfilling. The need for positive regard, in Rogers' view, is a basic need, and one which could not be left unfulfilled without psychological harm to that person.

Satisfaction of the second need, the **need for self-actualisation**, is equally indispensable for psychological health. This need is concerned with the human tendency for personal growth. If we look at the pastimes and hobbies which most people engage in, we find that they are almost always concerned with learning or developing skills – even if it is only in computer games, darts in the pub or knitting. Rogers argued that to develop oneself, and to make real (actualise) one's abilities and talents, is a basic need in all human beings, and that psychological harm would result if this need is not expressed in some way.

The need for social respect

In 1979, Rom Harré argued that obtaining social respect from others is an important, and much under-researched, human motivator. If we look at how people interact, it is possible to argue that it is the most important motivator of all: people want to be noticed, acknowledged and respected, and many social actions can be construed in these terms. Human dignity, no matter where it appears, is crucial to human interaction. Harré argued that it is more important for people to avoid being laughed at or made to look ridiculous than almost anything else.

Harré also pointed out that although a consid- erable amount of research has gone into investigating darker motives, like aggression, they are not really the most important motivators for human social behaviour. Instead, if we look at, for example children playing in school playgrounds, most of their behaviour is directed towards getting attention: 'Look at me!' Aggression is actually much less common in situations of this kind than showing off, although we are much more likely to notice it. As with the study of emotion, which as we saw earlier in this chapter, society's emphasis on the darker side of human nature has tended to minimise research into its more positive aspects, even though these may reflect far more of what people usually do.

The need for respect identified by Harré also ties in with another aspect of social motivation: **social identification**, which we will look at more closely in Chapter 15. Tajfel and Turner (1979) showed that belonging to social groups and cate- gories is an important part of an individual's self- image. Since these groups occur in a real society, with real inequalities and values, belonging to some groups carries more status than others. Tajfel and Turner argued that it is important for group membership to provide the person with a positive source of self-esteem, since seeking positive self- esteem is such a fundamental motivation for human beings. If we can feel proud of belonging to our group, then we will tend to identify with it; if not, then we will try to leave the group, or to distance ourselves from the other people in it ('I'm not really like the rest of them').

Learned helplessness

Another aspect of human motivation has to do with perceived effectiveness and agency. Research into this area combined findings from animal studies with observations from clinical psy- chologists. In 1967, Seligman and Maier showed that if dogs were exposed to unavoidable electric shocks, they would become very passive, and remain passive even when they were in a situation where taking action would allow them to avoid further pain. Seligman referred to this as **learned helplessness**, and argued that the experience of being a victim and being helpless, unable to do anything about the problem, produced a kind of general apathy, in which no efforts at all would be made to do anything.

Some studies suggest that helplessness also happens with human beings. De Vellis (1978) gave

Box 13.1 Studying motivation

Behaviourist and experimental psychology have traditionally had problems trying to come to grips with broader questions about human nature. As a result of the dominance of these two traditions in British and American psychology for most of this century, many aspects of human life remain very little researched, although with the increasing acceptance of qualitative methodologies, many of these areas have recently been coming into focus. This is a recent development, however, and their omission has left many gaps and distortions in accepted psychological knowledge.

Motivation is one of those areas which became distorted as a result of the emphasis on laboratory studies of overt behaviour. A look at psychology textbooks of the 1960s and 1970s shows a chapter on motivation which will almost inevitably be devoted to research into physiological drives such as hunger and thirst, some discussion of neural mechanisms underlying these drives, and possibly some discussions of maternal and/or exploratory drives in the albino rat. If the authors were being really radical, they might even include Maslow's hierarchical model at the very end – or the beginning – of the chapter.

But what about all the other reasons why people do things? In fact, a great deal of psychology has to do with human motivation. But those aspects of human motivation which are to do with social or personal motives tend not to come under the same heading – they are treated as social psychology, or personality theory, or something quite different. If they are all brought together as aspects of motivation, though, they produce a very interesting, and much more well-rounded, picture of why people do things. Let us look at what such a collection of psychology of human motivation might include.

If we wanted a poetic starting point, we could take the model of domains of experience held by the early Greeks, in which the cognitive domain was viewed as the charioteer, holding the reins and being pulled along by the affective and conative domains. Emotion and intention are the driving force behind (or rather, pulling) the chariot.

Physiological motives and brain mechanisms are, of course, important, and as a result of the rigorous research of the past few decades we know a great deal more about them than we did before. They would, of course, be included in our collection, because they make a definite contribution to our knowledge. But we would also include cognitive motivation, including, for example, the drive to avoid cognitive dissonance identified by Festinger, the use of psychological defence mechanisms to conceal unconscious impulses as identified by Freud and Rogers, and the way that our personal construction of reality may influence the decisions we make and the way that we interact with people – as discussed by Kelly in his theory of personal constructs.

As in this chapter, we would also look at aspects of motivating personal actions, learned helplessness, attribution, locus of control and self-efficacy. People (and animals) with experience of their efforts being continually futile may become passive, and not recognise when the situation has changed and they really could do something. People are more likely to take action if they think that their actions will be effective; those with an internal locus of control are more likely to believe this. So these models can help us to understand not just why people take action, but also why they sometimes do not.

We would also include affiliative motives: the need for positive regard from other people identified by Carl Rogers, questions of empathy and the need for social respect, and the very deep need that people seem to have to identify with the in-group that they belong to, and to distinguish it from others. The formation of 'them-and-us' groups permeates all levels of society, and the process of social identification is a very important human motivator. And there are other processes linked with that: questions of status, the formation of shared group beliefs and social representations; identification with cultural and sub-cultural values; loyalty towards one's own.

When we scan even very quickly through modern psychology, then, we find that it has a great deal to tell us about human motivation: why people do things. Physiological and behavioural drives are only part of the story. That they were the dominant part of the study of motivation for so many years tells us more about the limited scope of behaviourist methodology than anything else.

college students a series of unsolvable puzzles, and found that when they were later given a set of similar, but solvable, puzzles, they performed much worse than students who had not had the earlier, demoralising experience. As we saw in Chapter 8, Seligman (1975) drew a connection between learned helplessness and the passivity that accompanies human **depression**, arguing that one reason why people become depressed is the feeling that whatever efforts they might make are doomed to failure.

This idea has several implications for our understanding of human motivation. One is that it may explain why people sometimes do not seem to try to improve things, when making some effort would help considerably. But it also contains implications for human motivation when we turn it around: it implies that people will be most likely to be active and positive when they feel that their actions are having an effect – when they feel a sense of personal agency in their dealings with the world. This ties in with Bandura's findings about

self-efficacy beliefs, which we will be looking at in more detail in Chapter 14 – the finding that the beliefs which people have about how effective or competent they are at doing things are important factors in how much they achieve, since they affect how much effort they put into a given task.

Although this is only a very superficial look at human motivation, we can see that it is both complex and varied: some types of motivation may be heavily influenced by physiological factors, but for other motives they are less important. Many of the chapters of this book contain implications for human motivation, in one way or another (see Box 13.1 on page 329). It is the task of the professional psychologist to bring all these different factors together when looking at motivation on a personal or organisational level. Inevitably, when we do this, we move into the social domain. The next few chapters of this book deal with social psychology, and how the social level of analysis can help us to understand human behaviour.

Key terms

adrenocorticotrophic hormone A hormone produced by the pituitary gland, which stimulates the release of adrenaline into the bloodstream.

altruism Acting in the interests of other people and not of oneself.

arousal A general physiological state in which the sympathetic division of the autonomic nervous system is activated.

attributional style The distinctive pattern of attributions which an individual makes, in terms of whether events are usually perceived as external, stable, controllable, etc.

biofeedback The use of electronic signals as indicators, in order to learn voluntary control of autonomic responses.

burnout A problem incurred by voluntary workers, social workers and others in which consistent and frustrating hard work over years produces a sense of emotional numbness, lethargy, and a lack of motivation.

Cannon-Bard theory of emotion The idea that physiological responses and emotional experience are entirely separate.

catastrophe theory A mathematical model used to illustrate how gradual increases in the intensity of a stimulus can produce sudden and dramatic discontinuities.

drive theories Theories of human motivation which explain why we do things, using the idea that our behaviour is directed towards reducing some inner need. The need then sets up an internal tension, and the desire to reduce this tension forms a pressure to act (the drive) which is only reduced when the need becomes satisfied.

electrical stimulation of the brain (ESB) Direct positive reinforcement delivered to the brain by means of electrodes implanted in the hypothalamus.

endocrine system A network of glands and ducts which release hormones into the bloodstream, and so induce or maintain physiological states of the body.

external locus of control The feeling or belief that events are caused by situations or by others, and cannot be influenced by oneself.

fight or flight response A physiological reaction produced by the sympathetic division of the ANS in response to threat or anger, which results in the body being activated for energy.

general adaptation syndrome The process of physiological adaptation to long-term stress, resulting in lowered resistance to illness and other negative outcomes.

hippocampus One of the sub-cortical areas of the brain.

internal locus of control The belief that important life events are largely caused by one's own efforts, abilities, etc. as opposed to being caused by external circumstances.

James-Lange theory of emotion A theory which states that our experience of emotion derives from our perceptions of physiological changes in the body.

locus of control Where control of what happens is perceived to come from. An internal locus of control means that the person sees it as coming from within themselves – so they are largely in control of what happens to them, or at least in a position to influence it. An external locus of control means that it is perceived as coming from sources outside of the person, and so is not something which the individual can influence.

molar actions Movements involving the whole body, e.g. standing up, walking.

molecular actions Movements involving particular parts of the body only, such as shrugging the shoulders.

need for achievement An internal motivation to succeed in life, or in attaining particular goals.

need for affiliation An internal motivation to belong to a group or family, or at least to be accepted by others.

need for positive regard An internal motivation to be loved, approved of, or respected by other people.

need for self-actualisation An internal motivation to develop one's own talents and abilities to the full.

noradrenergic receptor A receptor site on a nerve cell which responds particularly to noradrenaline.

physiological drives Motives which are concerned with satisfying physiological needs, such as hunger, etc.

pleasure centre The part of the limbic system which, when stimulated electronically, appears to provide feelings of intense pleasure.

primary drive A motive which is concerned with satisfying a basic human need, such as hunger, thirst, or possibly affiliation.

satiation The experience of having eaten sufficiently to quell hunger.

secondary drives Motives which do not relate to biological needs, but instead are concerned with acquired or learned preferences.

set weight The phenomenon detected by physiological studies of obesity, that the body appears to have an internal established ideal weight, and that eating or fasting behaviour will happen to maintain that weight.

sympathetic division The part of the autonomic nervous system which produces a state of arousal when activated.

voice stress analyser A method of analysis which identifies the slightly flattened tones of an individual under stress, by analysing the sound of the voice using a spectrograph.

Yerkes-Dodson Law of arousal The principle that performance of any given task can be improved if the person is aroused; but that if the arousal increases beyond an optimal point, performance then declines.

Summary

1 The arousal response results from the action of the sympathetic nervous system and the endocrine system. Studies of arousal resulted in the Yerkes-Dodson Law of performance and arousal, and some debate about the usefulness of arousal as a generalised concept.

2 Selye identified a general adaptation response to long-term stress, which could produce gastric problems and lowered resistance to illness. Long-term stress has also been linked to locus of control, and to Type A and B behaviour patterns.

3 'Classic' theories of emotion include the James-Lange theory of emotion, the Cannon-Bard theory of emotion, and Schachter and Singer's model. Later theories of emotion include appraisal theory, attribution theory, the facial feedback theory and the theory of emotion as transitory social roles.

4 Research into positive emotions has identified the four dimensions of absorption, potency, altruism and spiritual experience.

5 Drive theories of motivation were popular in the first half of the century. One distinction was between primary drives, satisfying basic physiological needs, and secondary drives, which were more wide-ranging and sometimes cognitive.

6 Physiological studies of hunger identified two areas of the hypothalamus, one concerned with feeding and the other with satiation. These have been linked with neurotransmitter activity, and with the concept of a neurological set weight for the body.

7 Exploration is a complex form of motivation which may link with some brain activities, but is also strongly influenced by environmental factors. Studies of direct electrical brain stimulation led to a distinction between incentives and rewards in motivation.

8 Theories of human motivation have identified several psychological needs, including needs for achievement, for positive social regard, for self-actualisation, for respect from others and for control over the effects of one's actions.

Self-assessment questions

1 Giving examples, briefly describe the concept of homeostasis.

2 How do studies of exploration challenge drive-reduction theories of motivation?

3 Identify sources of individual difference which can make people more or less susceptible to stress.

Practice essay questions

1 What can a knowledge of physiological mechanisms tell us about human motivation?

2 Describe physiological and alternative explanations of the experience of emotion.

3 Compare and contrast psychological research into negative and positive emotions.

Test your knowledge of this chapter with our online quizzes and games at: http://www.psych.co.uk

Explore emotion and motivation further at:

Motivation
http://ear.berkeley.edu/psych2/lecture10/lecture10.html – Well laid out and clear summary of all the theories of what motivates us and why.
http://pavlov.psyc.queensu.ca/~symonsl/motivation/motivationnotes.html – Tutorial on motivation, deals with hunger in great detail.
http:// www.xula.edu/%7Ergougis/PsychDrill3/drilleig.htm – Discusses the terms of sexuality, motives and emotions and provides essay questions and model answers.

Emotion

http://trochim.human.cornell.edu/gallery/young/emotion.htm – Tutorial and reading list on emotions and emotional intelligence.

http://www-white.media.mit.edu/vismod/demos/affect/AC_research/emotions.html – Links to research sites on human emotion and summaries of the main theories.

http://psych.wisc.edu/faculty/pages/croberts/topic8.html – Tutorial and diagrams on the subject of emotion.

Stress

http://www.stress.org.uk/ – Information on the causes and management of stress, at home and in the workplace.

Social psychology

Self and others

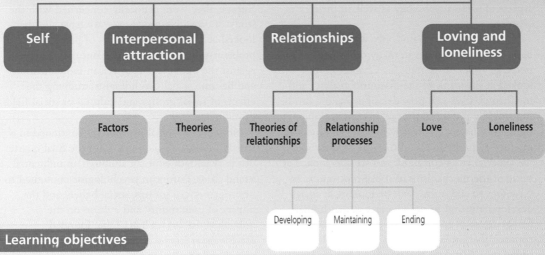

Self

Interpersonal attraction

Relationships

Loving and loneliness

Factors

Theories

Theories of relationships

Relationship processes

Love

Loneliness

Developing   Maintaining   Ending

Learning objectives

14.1. Self-concept
a define terms relating to processes of the self-concept
b identify mechanisms contributing to the self-concept
c describe a study of the self-concept

14.2. Social identification
a describe the basic processes of social identification
b evaluate methods of studying social identification
c apply concepts of social identification to everyday life

14.3. Cultural concepts of self
a identify social and cultural influences on the self-concept
b distinguish between different cultural conceptions of self
c evaluate the idea of the independent self-concept

14.4. Interpersonal attraction
a describe factors influencing attraction
b identify theories of attraction
c evaluate the psychological study of attraction

14.5. Theories of relationships
a define terms relating to the study of relationships
b describe theories of relationships
c identify problematic assumptions in early studies of relationships

14.6. Relationship processes
a list Hinde's dimensions for studying relationships
b describe strategies of relationship maintenance
c identify reasons for relationship breakdown

14.7. Loving
a describe a study of investigating loving
b differentiate between love and limerence
c outline different theories of loving

14.8. Loneliness
a distinguish between situational and chronic loneliness
b identify social differences between lonely and non-lonely people
c describe cognitive aspects of loneliness

In the next four chapters, we will be looking at social psychology. Social psychology is concerned with how people interact with, and understand, one another. It covers a range of different topics, including our concepts of self, our relationships with other people, communication and social understanding, and our social beliefs and actions. We will be looking at all of these, and some other aspects of social psychology as well, in these chapters.

Social psychology is not only what is described here, though. It appears in many other parts of this book, as well. For example, in Chapter 4, we looked at the work of the discourse analysts, and in Chapter 5 we saw how decision-making can be distorted by the social process known as group-think. In Chapter 13 we saw how social processes interact with physiological ones to produce what we experience as emotions, and we also looked at some of the mechanisms of social motivation. In Chapters 19 and 20 we will be looking at social development, and so on. The fact is, that human beings are so deeply embedded in their social contexts that interacting with other people is one of the very first skills that an infant human being develops. And our social experiences influence our cognitive processes, and sometimes even our physiological reactions, far more than we think.

The development of social psychology

Social psychology is as old as psychology itself. For example, although the pioneering psychologist Wilhelm Wundt is generally thought of as having been concerned with cognitive processes such as attention, in fact he was also extremely interested in social psychology. In his Völkerpsychologie, a ten-volume work published between 1900 and 1920, he studied language, religion, customs, myth, magic, and aspects of social knowledge and social cognition (Farr, 1996).

The advent of behaviourism in America resulted in a change of focus for social psychology. Partly, this came about as a result of the behaviourist insistence on studying social behaviour, rather than feelings, thoughts and experiences. Partly, though, it came about as a result of the powerfully individualistic views maintained by the majority of American social psychologists. These were perhaps best expressed by F.H. Allport, in 1924, who firmly insisted that social psychology was fundamentally the study of the individual, and

that studying how individuals operated would provide the answers to all of our fundamental social questions.

To those who had experienced Europe in the 1930s and 1940s, this approach was clearly inadequate. Many Gestalt psychologists emigrated to America as a result of the political disturbances in Europe in the first half of this century. While in Europe, they were primarily concerned with the study of cognitive processes – we have already looked at Gestalt investigations of perception and problem-solving, for example. But they reacted against the extremes of American individualism, and became social psychologists, studying the effects of social groups and cultural or social fields of influence.

Nonetheless, social psychology continued in a largely individualistic mode until the final quarter of the twentieth century, although an influential strand of ex-European psychologists continued to investigate social groups, social beliefs, and the impact of community and culture on the individual. In 1972, Henri Tajfel founded the *European Journal of Social Psychology*, which recognised these new developments, and provided a forum for publishing them. It also crystallised the approach into the school of thought now known as European social psychology, a school which emphasised the influence of community, group membership and cultural distinctiveness on social cognition.

Perspectives in social psychology

Modern social psychologists go about their research in many different ways, using a number of different perspectives. I have already mentioned one of these: the perspective known as European social psychology. But there are others, too: experimental social psychology; discursive social psychology; applied socio-cognitive psychology; evolutionary social psychology; and critical social psychology. It is worth taking a brief look at these.

European social psychology
European social psychology, as we have seen, developed as a reaction to extreme individualism, and emphasises the influences of group membership and cultures on social understanding. There are two psychological theories which lie at the heart of European social psychology: Social Representation Theory (SRT), and Social Identity

Theory (SIT). We will be looking at them both in Chapter 15. In essence, social representations are the shared beliefs which are transmitted through society, and act as explanations for why things are like they are; while social identifications are the aspects of group membership which result in the kind of 'us-and-them' consciousness which is so common in human societies. Researchers in European social psychology, then, operate within a strong theoretical framework, using both qualitative and quantitative research methods to explore meaningful social issues.

Experimental social psychology

Griffin (1997) described how experimental social psychology is primarily concerned with identifying causes of social behaviour. For that reason, it leans heavily on experimental methodology, and on the use of quantitative measurements of social behaviour. Although experimental social psychologists are interested in the personal ways that people construct their social worlds, they are nonetheless concerned with gathering objective, measurable data, and so their focus is generally on the behavioural aspects of social experience, rather than on its internal or cognitive aspects.

Discursive social psychology

Discursive social psychology, on the other hand, is concerned with how people construct their social worlds through conversation and other forms of social discourse. We looked at discourse analysis in Chapter 4, and this is an important part of discursive psychology. Potter (1997) discussed how discourse analysts are not particularly concerned about investigating any objective reality. Instead, they are interested in how people use discourse and descriptions to construct, and reconstruct, their experiences. This means that discursive psychology is inevitably relativistic – that is, it looks explicitly at multiple forms of discourse, and rhetorical frames, and how these act to shape human understanding; without assuming that any one form of discourse or explanation is 'correct'.

Applied socio-cognitive psychology

Abraham (1997) described how applied socio-cognitive research is interested in how people form mental representations of their reality, which shape both how they describe their understanding and also how they see, and manage, social actions. These mental representations can be changed through new learning, particularly from social

influences. One type of research which Abraham described examined how people understand health education messages. It involved looking at people's understanding of the messages, their actual behaviour, changes in understanding of those messages which happened as a result of direct interventions, and any changes in practice which correlated with changes in understanding. Like the discursive approach, it is interested in what people say about their understanding; but unlike discursive psychology, it is also concerned with how that understanding maps onto reality and social practice.

Evolutionary social psychology

Evolutionary social psychology is concerned with the way that our biological evolution, as social animals, has come to shape our activities and behavioural choices. It takes the view that the complexity of our minds and bodies is an outcome of genetically inherited adaptations, which have built up through cumulative natural selection, over many generations. (We will be looking at evolutionary theory more closely in Chapter 22.) These adaptations have given all human beings some mental and cognitive attributes in common – human universals, which occur across all cultures and societies. Evolutionary social psychologists aim to bring together and integrate biological, psychological, geological, and cultural knowledge, in order to understand the fundamentals of human nature.

Critical social psychology

Parker (1997) described how critical social psychology (and critical psychology in general) has two parallel tracks. One of them is concerned with critiquing and challenging orthodox scientific psychology – mainly in terms of examining its theoretical framework, and demonstrating how much of its knowledge is socially constructed rather than being some kind of scientific truth. The second is concerned with developing what Parker referred to as 'unscientific psychology' – in other words, developing theoretical frameworks drawing on philosophical perspectives such as postmodernism or the work of Wittgenstein, which can be used to generate alternatives and challenges to the conventional approaches to psychological knowledge.

We can see, then, that the work of social psychologists varies to a tremendous extent, and that the assumptions made by each perspective can be very different, and even contradictory. That does not mean, however, that social psychology itself is fragmented. As we saw when we looked at the development of European social psychology, there have always been different approaches and perspectives within the discipline, and these have, if anything, only enriched how social psychologists go about studying human beings. Social psychologists have a wide range of theoretical perspectives and analytical tools available to them, and this means that modern social psychology is both wide in scope, and flexible in its orientation. We will begin our explorations of social psychology by looking at research into concepts of self, then go on to explore ideas about interpersonal attraction, relationships and, finally, the social emotions of loneliness and love.

Concepts of self

The Western concept of the 'self' as an individual, entirely separate from social context and relationships, is a relatively recent development. It first began to emerge with the work of the seventeenth-century philosophers Descartes, Locke and Hume (see Chapter 1), and became increasingly popular as European society moved out of mediaeval feudalism and into merchant-based economies, and ultimately capitalism. Gradually the concept of the individual rather than the community became dominant in society, and the idea of the 'self' continued to develop, until now it is regarded by people in Western societies as self-evident.

However, as we shall see, the idea of the 'self' as independent of the social context is one which is not shared by all human societies – indeed, most other cultures in the world at the present time tend to perceive people rather differently. Rather than being seen as an isolated individual, the human being is perceived as embedded in its cultural, social and family context. These differences are reflected in psychological theories of the self. When looking at the idea of the self-concept, then, we will first examine some of the ideas common in traditional Western psychology, and then go on to look at some of the broader dimensions of self which have emerged as psychologists have become more aware of the importance of culture and social context.

The self-concept

Seeing the self as an independent individual, however, does not mean that social influences can be entirely discounted. From the very beginning, psychological theories of the self have recognised how important other people are in influencing the ideas which we develop of ourselves. William James (1890) argued that the self-concept develops from **social comparisons**. He argued that we compare ourselves with 'significant others', and use this information to develop an idea of what we are like.

This idea was developed further by Cooley (1902), who saw **feedback from others** as being crucially important in the development of the self-concept. According to Cooley, the self-concept is like a looking-glass, reflecting what we believe other people think of us. This looking-glass self includes both evaluative and illustrative dimensions. Evaluative dimensions are the judgements that we believe other people are making about us, and illustrative dimensions are what we believe they see when they look at us. So it is not just a question of how people respond to our actions – we are also forming our opinion of ourselves on the basis of what we think other people think. Cooley believed that feelings such as pride, embarrassment and even anger arise directly from these ideas we have about how other people are perceiving us.

G.H. Mead (1934) also emphasised the importance of **social interaction** in the development of the self-concept. Mead saw the self-concept as being formed directly through social experience. Social experience, however, was much broader than simply the reactions of individual people. It also included social norms, personal values and cultural patterns. According to Mead, these dimensions of social interaction become internalised as we develop psychologically. This means that they are used as standards for evaluating our own behaviour – regardless of whether there are other people present or not.

Goffman (1959) saw the self-concept as reflecting the collection of **social roles** played by the individual. We all play a large number of social roles as we go about our daily lives. Initially any new role is 'acted out', as if it is just a game that the person is playing, but after a while the role becomes internalised as another part of the person's own self-concept. According to Goffman, therefore, any one person will develop a number of facets to their personality, reflecting the number of different social roles which they play in life. Which one is to the fore at any given moment depends on the social roles which the person is playing at the time.

Self-image and self-esteem

The self-concept is often regarded as consisting of two components: the **self-image** and the self-esteem. The self-image is a factual self-portrait, including information about the body, such as height, weight and build; the person's likes and dislikes; their past experiences, and so on. Self-esteem, on the other hand, is the evaluative component of the self-concept, and is concerned with internalised social judgements and ideas about how worthwhile a trait or personal quality is.

Coopersmith (1968) investigated levels of self-esteem in 'normal', middle-class American boys aged between ten and twelve. The boys were classified into three groups, of high, medium and low self-esteem. This was done on the basis of self-evaluations by the boys themselves, teachers' reports and psychological tests. Coopersmith found that levels of self-esteem varied systematically with other aspects of the person: a high level of self-esteem was found in active, expressive and successful individuals, whereas low self-esteem correlated with low ambition, and also less physical fitness – these boys were more likely to suffer from insomnia, headaches and stomach upsets.

There were also differences in **parental styles** between the three groups. Those boys with high self-esteem tended to have parents who were fairly strict and set clear limits for their children, but were also interested in them and expected them to reach high standards. Parents of low self-esteem boys, on the other hand, tended to be much less involved, often not even knowing the names of their sons' friends. They also had low expectations for their children. Coopersmith concluded, as have many psychologists since, that positive self-esteem is an important aspect of good psychological health, and that parental treatment can be influential in the way that the self-esteem develops.

Carl Rogers (1961) also saw self-esteem as a significant factor in psychological health. Rogers believed that self-esteem develops through childhood as we internalise social standards, or **conditions of worth**, which we learn about through everyday social interaction. The important thing in maintaining a positive self-esteem, Rogers argued, is that these conditions of worth should be realistic.

As we saw in Chapter 7, Rogers argued that people have two fundamental psychological needs, and each of them is just as important as the other. The first of these is that we all need some sort of **positive regard** from other people – like love, affection or respect. The second is that we all need to explore and develop our own abilities and potential – which Rogers referred to as the need for **self-actualisation**. Most people manage to satisfy these two needs in a reasonably satisfactory manner, but some people find that one conflicts with the other. They do not feel free to develop their own abilities or potential because they feel that to do so is to risk disapproval from others, and so to lose positive regard.

Typically, Rogers argued, people like this develop unreasonably high standards for their own behaviour – unrealistic conditions of worth. They expect themselves to be able to do everything perfectly, and overreact to even the slightest failure. This means that they end up with very low levels of self-esteem, because they set their personal standards so high that they cannot help failing – nobody can be perfect in all ways. Even people who are high achievers in society can sometimes feel this way. This, Rogers argued, could only be set right by the experience of unconditional positive regard from someone, whether in childhood or adulthood. We saw in Chapter 9 how this formed the basis for Rogers' therapeutic model: the ultimate goal of such therapy is to raise the person's own self-esteem, and to allow them to develop more realistic conditions of worth so that it can remain that way.

Self-perception

Bem (1967) suggested that how we perceive ourselves is an important part of the self-concept. **Self-perception theory** argues that we observe how we are acting, and draw conclusions from this about what we are like. In one study which illustrated this, Valins and Ray (1967) showed snake-phobic research participants pictures of snakes. As they watched, they sometimes saw the word 'shock', which was followed by a mild electric shock. All the research participants experienced this, but the experimental group were also played a recording of a heartbeat, and informed that it was their own heart being monitored. The heartbeat beat faster at the shock slides, but not at pictures of snakes – inferring that the shock was more disturbing.

At the end of the study, Valins and Ray asked the research participants to approach a tame boa constrictor, and found that the people who had been in the experimental group could get much closer to the snake than those people who had been in the control group. During the study, they had looked at the snake but heard what they believed to be their heartbeat remain undisturbed. From this, the research participants had inferred that they were not being particularly upset by the snake. This effect is similar to that found by Schachter and Singer (1962), which we looked at in Chapter 13. They too showed that the way in which people perceive and interpret their physiological state can be important in their experience of emotion.

Self-efficacy

Bandura (1997) argued that one of the most important features in self-perception is what we believe that we are capable of achieving. **Self-efficacy beliefs** are beliefs about our own perceived competences – what we believe we can do well, or at least adequately. These differ greatly from one person to another: some people see themselves as competent in a wide range of activities or tasks, while others do not see themselves as particularly efficacious at all. According to Bandura, self-efficacy beliefs are not just about how we interpret what we have done in the past. They are also instrumental in determining how we interact with our environment and other people. Bandura (1989) identified four psychological processes which are affected by self-efficacy beliefs, and these are described in Table 14.1.

Collins (1982) looked at children who had varying mathematical abilities, and either high or low levels of self-efficacy beliefs. Collins found that those children who had high self-efficacy beliefs solved more problems more quickly than those who had low self-efficacy beliefs – regardless of how good they actually were at sums. The children with high self-efficacy beliefs were more prepared to go over problems which they had done wrong, and more likely to correct themselves a second time. Because they believed they could be competent, they put more effort into the problems, whereas the children with low self-efficacy beliefs gave up quickly and did not regard making more effort as being of any use.

In a study of physical endurance, Weinberg, Gould and Jackson (1979) raised research participants' self-efficacy beliefs by giving them false feedback on how well they had performed in competitive tasks. The feedback was designed to raise or lower their self-efficacy beliefs with respect to those particular tasks. The researchers found that those people with raised self-efficacy beliefs performed better at the endurance tasks, and when they failed, they tried harder to recover. Those with lowered self-efficacy beliefs, on the other hand, tended to be put off by failing, and did not do as well overall.

In an interesting second part of the experiment, the experimenters deliberately manipulated self-efficacy beliefs and gender, such that female research participants' self-efficacy beliefs were raised while those of male research participants

---

Table 14.1 Psychological processes affected by self-efficacy beliefs

Cognitive processes	Self-efficacy beliefs can be shown to affect the thought patterns people use, which in turn affect behaviour. Weighing up a situation in terms of what we are capable of, influences what we are then prepared to attempt.
Motivational processes	Our self-efficacy beliefs directly influence how long we will keep trying at something after we have failed once or twice at it.
Affective processes	Our self-efficacy beliefs can directly affect feelings such as stress or anxiety. For example, research into locus of control shows how people experience lower levels of stress if they feel they are in control of a situation. Having high self-efficacy beliefs is directly linked to feeling capable, and in control of things.
Selection processes	People tend to choose those activities and situations which will present them with challenges, but which they will nonetheless be capable of managing. So one's beliefs about one's personal efficacy will directly affect what one chooses.

Source: Bandura, 1989

were lowered. When they did this, they found that the normal gender differences in physical endurance tasks disappeared almost entirely. Bandura (1989) pointed out that this raises the question of how far traditional sex differences are a product of lowered self-efficacy beliefs, since most societies traditionally raise girls to believe that they are not as good at doing things as boys are.

Bandura (1986) suggested that it is often a good thing if people's self-efficacy beliefs are slightly higher than previous performance would suggest, because this means they will put in extra effort and go for new challenges, which will mean that their abilities will develop even further. Overconfidence may be good for you!

Social identification

Tajfel and Turner (1979) proposed a different way of looking at how people see themselves. They argued that **social groups** are the basic units that people use for making sense out of their social worlds, and it is our membership of social groups which affects how we see ourselves. Society is largely composed of different groupings of people, and these groups differ from one another in terms of their relative power, status and influence, as well as in terms of their functions and areas of relevance. Social groups, in Tajfel's theory, form an important part of human thinking because we have such a powerful tendency to categorise and classify our experience. We categorise ourselves as well as other people, so the social groups to which we see ourselves belonging become a part of our self-concept, as well as affecting how we relate to other people.

Social identity theory (see Chapter 15 for more detail) proposes that people do not simply relate to each other as individuals, on an independent one-to-one basis. Instead, sometimes we interact with other people as representatives of our social group: the group acts as an interface, colouring our interactions. This does not always happen – you are unlikely to see a personal friend as a member of a social category. But social groups are such an important part of society that, a lot of the time, we are interacting as representatives of our groups too. It depends on what is salient at the time. For example, a chemistry student might interact with student friends from other courses as an individual, until the conversation turns to

something like the difference between a science and an arts education. Then, they are likely to identify with their own social group – as science students – and argue from that point of view. His or her social identity as a scientist has become salient for that particular conversation.

Social identity and self-esteem

Sometimes, of course, we do not identify with the social group that we belong to. Instead, we try to separate ourselves from other members of the group ('I'm not like the others'), or leave it and join some other social group instead. Whether we actually identify with the group that we belong to depends on what it has to offer us. According to Tajfel and Turner (1979), people will come to identify with their social group if it provides them with a source of positive self-esteem. Belonging to a group must give you some reason to be proud of it. If it does not, you are likely to try to leave the group, or, if that is impossible, to distance yourself from it.

Given a choice, Tajfel and Turner argued, people belong to groups because this enhances their own self-image. Moreover, we remain members of any particular group only for as long as this continues to be the case. But sometimes we do not have such a choice – it is not easy to change your gender or skin colour, for example. In such cases, ensuring that your group membership reflects positively on your self-image requires a rather different approach. One option is to compare your group only with others which are similar or lower in status, and to ignore or disparage groups which have a higher social status. In this way, people can identify with their own group without feeling inferior.

Another option is to change the perceived status of the group. A major breakthrough in combating American racism was the 'Black is Beautiful' movement in America in the 1960s. This made an enormous difference to many people's lives, by redefining being black as a positive experience, and not the negative experience which the racist mainstream American culture had been portraying. Highly visible representatives of this belief, such as Angela Davis and Malcolm X, allowed the message to reach many black people, so that more and more people were able to identify with the movement and feel proud of belonging to their social category.

In-groups and out-groups

The process of social identification has a number of outcomes for how we perceive and interact with other people. One of these outcomes is that the identification with our own group leads to a tendency towards 'them-and-us' thinking, and this in turn has been shown to lead to an exaggerated view of the differences between groups. 'We' are the in-group and 'they' are seen as the out-group, and different from us. This is a powerful social process, which can be seen in many walks of life, and it seems to result from the mental process of classification.

Tajfel and Wilkes (1963) showed that even such simple measures as judgements of line lengths were affected by an arbitrary classification of the lines as A or B. Unlabelled lines were perceived reasonably accurately, but lines which had been put quite randomly into the same category were seen as being more similar than those in different categories – even when people knew how arbitrary the categories were. Social differences are accentuated in much the same way. Sherif (1935) showed in his experiments on group norms, which we will be looking at in Chapter 17, that accentuating or exaggerating the differences between groups can also lead to intergroup rivalry and social prejudice – although it does not always do so.

Tajfel *et al.* (1971) discussed how simply being a member of a group often seems to produce in-group favouritism at the expense of the out-group. In one study, they classified teenage school-boys into two groups on the basis of obviously arbitrary criteria, like tossing a coin, or asking the boys which kinds of paintings they preferred. These were known as **minimal group studies**, due to the fact that the grounds on which the boys would see themselves as belonging to one group or another were quite minimal. Once they had been allocated to a group, the research participants were asked to allocate points, either to themselves, or to other boys. Each boy worked alone, and the only information they had about the others was which group they had been placed in. Even though the game was set up in such a way that co-operation between groups was sometimes a winning strategy, Tajfel *et al.* found that the boys always favoured their own group at the expense of the others.

More recent research, however, has questioned whether intergroup conflict or competition is inevitable. There seems to be much more scope for intergroup co-operation than the early studies suggested, particularly when one looks at how groups interact in the real world as opposed to in artificial situations like minimal group studies. There has been some suggestion, too, that the participants in minimal group studies are responding to the **demand characteristics** of the situation and trying to do what seems to be expected of them, so it is unclear just how valid these particular demonstrations are. What does seem to be clear, however, is that to see the social world in terms of social groups, and ourselves as taking part in that social world, is a fundamental part of the self-concept.

Cultural contexts of identity

As I mentioned at the beginning of this chapter, most psychological research into the self has tended to take for granted Western concepts of the self as a separate, independent entity. Social identity theory challenges that idea, discussing as it does how the membership of social groups affects our perceptions of ourselves. But most of the other Western theories tend to assume that the 'self' is in some way independent of its social context. Marsella, Devos and Hsu (1985) argued that this means that much of the psychological research into the self is completely irrelevant to a large part of the human world.

Although from the start, as we have seen, psychologists have acknowledged social influence as a factor in the self-concept, they have still regarded it as an 'influence' – as if, somehow, the self could exist without it. But in many cultural groups, both within and outside the Western world, it is not a question of 'influences', but more the whole location of the experience of self. For example, Mbiti (1970) described how African philosophical tradition locates the individual self firmly within the collective self of the tribe or people. The context for 'being' is the ongoing tribal life of the people and the rhythms of the natural world. To try to separate out any of these is regarded as nonsensical – they are all part of the whole. So, while every person is of course different, the idea of the 'individual' as an independent entity which can be somehow separated from its context is regarded as simply unrealistic.

It may be worth noting a couple of points here. First, stating that the individual is part of the collective self, as Mbiti does, does not involve denying that people have their own special thoughts and ideas. Every human being is unique, and recognised as such. It is the idea that the self can exist independently of its social context which is being challenged. People need to be understood in the context of their families, their social groups, their friends and their culture if that understanding is to make any sense. Take those away, and the 'individual' would be quite different, and not a fully independent entity at all.

This brings us to the second point, which is that while Western philosophy and psychology has often regarded the self as if it were independent, the reality of Western social life is that social contexts – families, religious groups, friendship groups – are actually crucially important in how we see ourselves too. We have seen this as we have looked at some of the more practical research in the field. It is simply that this is formally recognised in African traditional thought, whereas traditional Western philosophy does not acknowledge its importance. In part, we can trace this back to the Cartesian tradition which we looked at in Chapter 1 – the separation of mind from body, and the concept of the body as a machine, had a number of consequences, including a denial of the importance of the social context.

Nobles (1976) argued that the different views of self in Western thinking and African thinking link with their assumptions about the world. Nobles argued that the European view rests on the two guiding principles of 'survival of the fittest' and 'control over nature'; whereas the guiding principles in traditional African thought are 'survival of the tribe' and 'one with nature'. Hayes (1983) pointed out that these guiding principles form a fundamental part of traditional African education systems, which is in direct contradiction with the idea of individualism. Individualism, in this view, is seen as being irresponsible and virtually uncivilised, since individuals are not simply responsible to themselves, but are interdependent members of the community.

This is not to say that all non-Western cultures perceive self similarly. In a discussion of the Hindu concept of self, Bharati (1985) described how the emphasis is on selfhood, rather than society, but with the indivisibility of the 'true' self – the *atman* – with the one-ness of God. This innermost self needs to be reached through meditation and self-discipline: everyone contains it, but we need to learn how to access it. Bharati also described other aspects of self in Hindu thinking, some of which contain the more negative aspects of personal experiences, and so form obstructions to the realisation of the atman. Others are concerned with the personal thoughts and ideas which the individual does not communicate to other people – the 'unexpressible consciousness' – or with those aspects of self which engage in conscious interaction with other people.

DeVos (1985) argued that Japanese people are reared in such a way as to become highly sensitive to interpersonal guilt, and also to social shame, and that this forms an important feature of the Japanese perception of self. Belonging to a group, and forming part of the group identity, is important in Japan, because it means that the painful self-awareness which is associated with existing as a separate individual can be avoided. So personal thoughts tend to be kept very private, in case they should disturb the social balance. The personal sense of identity is rooted much more strongly in social relationships and appropriate social behaviour in Japan than it is in American or European culture.

This very cursory look at some alternative conceptions of self show that the idea of the self-concept as portrayed by Western psychologists is not the whole story. The self can be conceptualised in a number of ways, but almost all the Western theories have had to acknowledge the importance of social influence. It seems likely that the recurrent identification of social factors in the self-concept may be tapping into something very much deeper about the human need for context and social identity. Who we are, and who we regard ourselves as being, seems to be firmly linked with our culture, our subcultures, our friendship and occupational groups, and – perhaps most important of all – our families. It makes sense, therefore, to look at how we go about forming relationships with other people, and we will begin this by looking at research into interpersonal attraction.

Interpersonal attraction

Attraction forms a major aspect of our social lives: not just in terms of the intimate relationships which we form with other individuals, but also in our friendships and working companionships. We try to spend time with people that we like, and we prefer to avoid people that we do not like. We get into relationships with people, which are sometimes very intimate, and sometimes casual or formal friendships. And most of us do our best to get on with the people that we work or study with. So how does attraction happen? What are the factors which make us more or less likely to like someone else?

Factors influencing attraction

Psychological research has identified a number of different factors which seem to influence whether we are attracted to someone or not. These factors include physical attractiveness, similarity and complementarity, familiarity and propinquity, reciprocal liking and perceived fallibility. We will look at the empirical investigations into each of these before going on to examine some of the theories which psychologists have put forward to explain attraction.

Physical attractiveness

There are a number of studies which show that we react more positively to people that we find physically attractive. In particular, we tend to act much more favourably towards such people. This has a number of social implications. One of them, for example, is that attractive children are often treated much more leniently than unattractive children when they are naughty.

Dion (1972) asked 243 research participants to complete questionnaires about children, on the basis of record cards which described the child's behaviour. Each child was described as having misbehaved, either mildly or severely, in one of two ways – by acting aggressively towards another child, or by acting cruelly towards an animal. Each card also had a small black-and-white picture of a boy or girl. The picture had been rated by independent observers as either attractive or unattractive. The questionnaire included questions about whether the child was likely to have acted similarly in the past, how serious the misbehaviour was, how harshly the child should be punished, whether the child would be likely to behave like this in the future, and so on. The research participants were also asked to suggest a reason why the child had been so naughty, and to assess how that child would normally behave.

Dion found that the attractiveness of the child made a considerable difference to the judgements which people made. Unattractive children were judged to have more anti-social characteristics. They were described as being more likely to commit serious offences habitually, to have behaved badly in the past, and to be likely to behave badly again. Also, the research participants viewed the misbehaviour of the attractive children as being far less serious than the same misbehaviour committed by an unattractive child.

It is not just in childhood where attractiveness counts. These differences in judgement affect how we assess adults as well. Sigall and Ostrove (1975) asked 120 people to recommend sentences for a crime. The crimes which they had to consider were either fraud (a crime likely to be related to attractiveness) or burglary (no connection with attractiveness). Again, research participants were presented with the information on a small record card. One set of cards – given to members of the control group – had no picture of the criminal; another set had a photograph of an attractive woman; and a third set had a photograph of an unattractive woman. The research participants were told that there was no doubt about the person's guilt, but they were to recommend the sentence which the person should receive.

The results of the study are shown in Table 14.2. We can see from the table that in the case of burglary, the average sentence recommended for the attractive research participant was much less than that for either the control or the unattractive research participant. It is interesting, though, that the sentence for the fraud crime was more severe for the attractive criminal: perhaps the research participants thought that she deserved more because she had been deliberately using her attractiveness.

Physical attractiveness itself is not always so easy to judge. When using a simple ten-point scale,

Table 14.2 Sentencing an attractive criminal		
Control (no information)	**Attractive**	**Unattractive**
Average length of sentence, in years.		
Burglary 5.10	2.80	5.20
Fraud 4.35	5.45	4.35

Source: Sigall and Ostrove, 1975

there is often a surprising amount of agreement between judges on which people are more attractive than others. But Garwood *et al.* (1980) showed that people's judgements of attractiveness can be influenced by very small factors – like someone's name. They asked research participants to rate photographs for attractiveness, and gave each photograph either a 'desirable' first name, like Kathy, Christine or Jennifer; or an 'undesirable' first name, like Gertrude, Ethel or Harriet. They found that their research participants judged those pictures with the 'better' names as being more attractive than the others.

In terms of the effect of attractiveness on more intimate attraction, Walster *et al.* (1966) suggested the **matching hypothesis**. This proposed that people tend to form their longer-term relationships with those who are about equal in physical attractiveness to themselves. Some support for this view came from Murstein (1971), who showed that marriage partners were often rated as being very similar to one another in attractiveness.

Walster *et al.* set up a 'computer dance' for students, in which they were allocated partners at random. As each student arrived to buy their ticket for the dance, independent judges rated their physical attractiveness. Halfway through the dance, the students were handed questionnaires and asked to evaluate their partners. They were approached again six months later, to see if they had been out with their partners at all since the dance.

Before the dance, each of the student research participants had completed questionnaires on aptitude, personality and self-esteem, but when the researchers compared the questionnaires with the ratings, none of these seemed to affect their judgements of their partners. Nor did the matching hypothesis really seem to hold up: more attractive partners tended to be liked more, regardless of whether they matched with their partner in attractiveness. But, in defence of the matching hypothesis, Walster *et al.* suggested that this was because a short-term dating situation like a dance was a different matter from a long-term relationship, and that people would use different criteria to evaluate partners in the two cases.

Consequently, in 1969, Walster and Walster set up another 'computer dance', but this time the research participants were able to meet each other beforehand, and were also able to indicate what sort of a partner they would like to have, in terms of physical attractiveness. They found that in this case, people were more attracted to those who were judged as being equally attractive (the judgements were made by independent raters), which appeared to support the matching hypothesis.

Huston (1973), however, argued that this result did not really come from matching, but because people were afraid of being rejected by their prospective partners. So somebody who was only averagely attractive would deliberately choose someone similar, not because they really found them most attractive, but because they did not want to be rejected by somebody who was more attractive than they were. Huston performed a study in which research participants were asked to choose a partner from a group of people who had already seen their photograph and indicated that they would accept them as partner. In this situation, research participants often chose partners who were rated as more attractive than themselves, which seemed to support the idea that the choices made in the Walster study were based on avoiding possible rejection. Whether this really challenges the matching hypothesis, though, is open to question, since the effect would still mean that, in an uncertain situation, people would tend to pair up with others of approximately equal attractiveness. And real life is usually pretty uncertain.

Similarity and complementarity

We also tend to like people who are like ourselves – who have the same kinds of attitudes and ideas that we do. Winslow (1937) compared the attitudes and opinions of groups of friends, and found that they were far more similar to each other than they were to randomly matched pairs. There are several possible explanations for this: for one thing, it might be that friends grow more similar as they get to know one another better. Because they understand one another's point of view more clearly, they might come to share more and more of the same attitudes. But there does seem to be some evidence that people are attracted to people with the same attitudes in the first place: it is not just that people change as a result of their friendships.

Byrne (1961) asked students to complete a questionnaire which assessed their attitudes to a number of different topics, like musical tastes, participation in sport, religious attitudes, and so on. Two weeks later, each of the students was handed a copy of the same questionnaire which, they were told, had been completed by someone else that they did not know. They were then asked to use the completed questionnaire to rate that person for attractiveness, knowledgeability, morality, adjustment, how much they thought they would enjoy working with the person, and how much they would like to meet her or him.

In fact, the scales had been completed by the experimenter, and were carefully balanced with the student's original attitudes. There were four groups of research participants in all. One group of students received questionnaires which revealed exactly the same attitudes that they themselves had shown. Another group received questionnaires which were exactly opposite to the ones that they had completed. A third group received questionnaires which matched their own attitudes on important issues but not in areas that they rated as less important, while the fourth group received questionnaires which revealed attitudes which differed on important issues but matched the research participant on less important ones.

Byrne showed that strangers with similar attitudes were liked better and rated as being more intelligent, knowledgeable, etc., than those whose questionnaire responses indicated that they had different attitudes from those of the research participants. The strangers who agreed only on important issues were judged as being more moral, better adjusted, and slightly more likeable than those who agreed only on unimportant issues.

It is open to question, though, how important similarity is in longer-term relationships. Kerchoff and Davis (1962) interviewed engaged couples who had been going out together for more than eighteen months, and found that they did not see similarity of attitudes as particularly important to their relationship. But engaged couples who had been together for less than eighteen months did think that it was important. Kerchoff and Davis found, though, that couples together for less than eighteen months who had similar attitudes also tended to have firmer relationships than those who had different ones.

One explanation for this may be that our interactions with other people are less vulnerable to misunderstandings or disagreements if our attitudes are basically similar. There is a strong human tendency to avoid direct confrontation in social interaction, so it may be that choosing our friends from people who are essentially similar to ourselves is a good way of avoiding social conflict.

But that does not mean that we only like people who are mirror-images of ourselves. Sigall (1970) found that people were more attracted to those who seemed to have changed their attitudes, and come round to the person's own way of thinking, than they were to those who had similar attitudes to start with. Also, some people seem to be attracted to partners or friends who come across as the exact opposite to themselves.

Winch (1958) proposed the **complementary needs hypothesis**. This suggests that people deliberately choose partners whose personal characteristics will compensate for their own personal deficiencies. By analysing data on the needs of married couples, Winch concluded that most couples have two main pairs of complementary needs: nurturant-receptive and dominant-submissive. Dominant people, they argued, would choose submissive partners, and nurturant people would choose receptive partners in order to complete these needs. But many psychologists since then have argued that this model is rather too simplistic: often a partner will be nurturant in one situation and receptive in another, or dominant in some areas but not in others.

Familiarity and propinquity

In 1961, Newcomb reported a study in which male students were offered free accommodation in return for participation in the research. The students shared rooms, allocated at random. When Newcomb examined the friendships which had developed between the students during the first year, it emerged that the students held similar attitudes and values, which suggested that this had been the basis of their friendship.

In the second year of the study (and with a different group of research participants), students were allocated room-mates according to their attitudes. Some shared rooms with people who were very similar to themselves, while others shared with people whose attitudes were very different. When Newcomb came to look at the friendships which had developed, though, it emerged that **propinquity** (being nearby physically) was the main factor, not attitude similarity. The students generally became close friends with their room-mates, regardless of their personal differences.

Propinquity refers to physical proximity, and there is a considerable amount of evidence that we like people that we see frequently. In 1974, Segal studied the personal friendships of new recruits and longer-term students at an American police academy, and found that almost half their friends were people who appeared next to them on their alphabetical class list. They had become friends because they had been placed next to each other in dormitories and classrooms, on the basis of their surnames.

Festinger, Schachter and Back (1950) examined the friendship patterns which had developed in a block of university flats for married couples. They found that 41% of the research participants had become friendly with the people who lived next door to them, while people who lived a few flats away from one another almost never became friends. Also, people who lived near to the stairs leading to and from any particular floor tended to have more friends and know more people than those who lived further away from the stairs. Zajonc (1968) proposed that simple exposure, or contact with others, was enough to produce liking. People became friends purely because they often came into contact.

Saegert, Swap and Zajonc (1973) asked research participants to participate in an experiment which they were told was about tasting different drinks (some fairly unpleasant, but harmless, laboratory solutions). They were each assigned to closed cubicles for the tasting, either alone or with someone else, and the researchers varied how often they were with the other research participant or alone. Afterwards, each research participant was asked to complete a questionnaire. One of the questions was designed to evaluate how favourably they regarded the person who had been in the cubicle with them. Saegert, Swap and Zajonc found that the more contact the research participants had with their partners, the more favourably they regarded them.

There is such a thing as too much closeness, though. We tend to dislike people who invade our **personal space**, by sitting or standing too close to us. Felipe and Sommer (1966) performed a study which involved invading the personal space of people who were working in a university library. They chose people who were working on their own at a table, and then deliberately sat at varying distances from them, and made notes. In the closest condition, the researcher would sit right next to the research participant (at an otherwise nearly empty table), and move the chair such that

there was a shoulder-to-shoulder distance of only about 30 cm between them. They reported that this was not easy, because the person who had been selected would tend to sit on the farthest edge of the chair and lean away from the intruder. In the most distant condition, the researcher would sit opposite the person, or two chairs away from them.

Felipe and Sommer timed how long the person would continue to work in the library under these conditions. As a control, they also timed how long people worked in similar conditions, if they were not interrupted. They found that 55% of the unwitting research participants in the first condition packed up and left within ten minutes, compared with almost none in the control conditions. By the end of half an hour, only 30% of the people were still working in the same place, by comparison with 73% of people in the intermediate conditions and 87% of the controls. Many of the people who had stayed had set up a 'defensive barrier' of books and papers between themselves and the intruder. The researchers then went on to perform a similar study in a mental hospital, sitting next to people who were otherwise alone, and timing how long they stayed, with very similar results.

Incidentally, apart from their implications for the study of attraction, these two studies raise some interesting issues about the ethics of disrupting people in their day-to-day activities. How would you feel if you were working in a library, or sitting out on a fine day, and were treated in this manner? Our modern code of ethics emphasises respect for experimental research participants, but many of the older studies do not seem to have considered this issue very much.

Reciprocal liking

Often, a major factor in whether we like someone seems to be whether they like us. We tend to avoid people who say unpleasant or hurtful things about us, and to spend more time with people who show that they feel positively towards us. In 1965, Aronson and Linder asked research participants to participate in what they were told was an experiment in verbal conditioning. They were asked to have a conversation with a stooge whom they believed was a genuine research participant, while at the same time counting the number of plural nouns which the person used (they were told that this was part of a conditioning study).

After this, the research participants 'overheard' the stooge giving an evaluation of them to the experimenter.

This continued for seven sessions altogether. The research participants were then asked to say how much they had liked the stooge. In order to disguise what was really happening, the researchers used an ethically dubious 'double-bluff'. They said that the research participants were being asked questions about how much they liked the stooge to deceive the others into thinking that the study was about interpersonal attraction. So although the study really was about attraction, the research participant was misled into the idea that attraction was only the disguise, and it was really about verbal conditioning.

There were four conditions in the study, and these reflected the reward–cost principle outlined by Aronson in 1976. This suggests that reciprocal liking or otherwise can be described in four conditions, listed in Table 14.3. Although superficially it seems as though we might be more likely to like people who always like us, Aronson (1976) argued that the strongest attraction comes from people in condition 3. Perhaps we feel that if we have 'won someone round', their positive comments are worth more than those from someone who has been positive all the time!

The outcome fitted with the predictions of the reward–cost principle: research participants gave the most positive ratings to those people who had evaluated them negatively at first but more positively later on. Their next highest ratings went to those who had been consistently positive about them, and the people whom they disliked most were the ones who had initially been positive in

their comments but had later changed to being negative.

Clore, Wiggins and Itkin (1975) asked people to evaluate how attracted a woman was to a man on the basis of videotaped non-verbal reactions. They had the same four conditions as appeared in the Aronson and Linder study. Again, research participants rated the woman as being more attracted to the man when she initially acted very coolly towards him and later became warmer. Aronson and Linder suggested that liking people better if they begin coolly towards us but then change their attitude to become more positive is a general principle of interpersonal attraction, which they described as the **gain–loss model of attraction**.

Perceived fallibility

We often find people more attractive when they have shown themselves to be fallible. The British ski-jumper Eddy Edwards became nationally popular as a direct result of his cheerfulness in the face of his spectacular lack of success in the international Olympic competition. However, there is some evidence that we are tolerant of mistakes only from relatively high-achieving people – it seems that they give us something to identify with. If less high-achieving people make mistakes, it seems, we are far more likely to dislike them.

In 1966, Aronson, Willerman and Floyd played recordings of interviews, supposedly from a contestant in a top-level national university quiz contest, to research participants. They varied the conditions, such that the person in the recordings appeared to be either an outstandingly high-achiever and got 90% of the quiz questions correct; or appeared to be more average, and only got 30% of the questions right. The research participants reported that they found the high-achieving contestant more attractive.

In a second part of the study, research participants heard a scraping of chairs halfway through the recording, and the contestant exclaiming that he had spilled coffee all over his new suit. When research participants rated the contestants in this condition, they liked the 'superior' contestant even more as a result of the blunder; although when this occurred in the presentation of the 'average' contestant, their liking was less.

This finding seems to apply only for research participants whose self-esteem is in the 'average' range, though. Helmreich, Aronson, and Lefan (1970) showed that research participants with

---

Table 14.3 Conditions of Aronson's study

Condition 1	The person is entirely positive towards the research participant.
Condition 2	The person is entirely negative towards the research participant.
Condition 3	The person is negative at first but then becomes positive towards the research participant.
Condition 4	The person is positive at first but then becomes negative.

Source: Aronson, 1976

either very high or very low self-esteem liked a 'superior' person much less when they made a mistake. It seems that people with very low self-esteem like to put people on a pedestal, and to be able to look up to them, so they find it uncomfortable when mistakes are made. People with high self-esteem, on the other hand, appear to expect high standards from high-achievers, and are not sympathetic to those who do not keep up to them. Since most of us are, by definition, average, though, the general finding seems to be pretty valid: we like our heroes and heroines to be human!

Theories of attraction

Many of the factors that we have looked at so far have provided their own explanations for attraction; and many could support several different theoretical explanations of it. Some of these theories, such as social exchange theory, deal with maintaining attraction in longer-term relationships, and so we will look at them later in this chapter. But we will discuss some of the other theories of attraction here.

Attraction as evaluation
Berscheid (1985) proposed that all attraction ultimately depends on our evaluating the other person. If we decide that they are 'good' (used in a very general sense), we like them; but if we see them as 'bad', then we do not. The different factors in liking and attraction, Berscheid argued, have their effect because they make us more likely to evaluate someone positively: it is the evaluation which provides the key.

Berscheid argued that our basic feelings of attraction and repulsion are rooted very deeply in our biological needs. According to Berscheid, we interpret our approach–avoidance tendencies in terms of evaluations: we see things which are safe to approach, on a primitive level, as 'good'; whereas we see things which we need to avoid as 'bad'. Human beings are dependent on one another right from the earliest moments of life, so survival depends on being able to approach and get on with one another. Similarly, avoiding people we dislike may be traced back to the idea that they may represent a threat to our survival. So attraction and dislike, in this model, are essentially all about weighing up and evaluating other people, in response to very basic, primitive survival demands.

Berscheid's evaluation theory of attraction forms a kind of 'meta-theory' in this area: it does not actually contradict other theories of attraction, but instead provides a general, overarching statement about what may be happening when we are attracted to someone else. So it can be seen as working alongside other explanations for attraction, rather than opposing them.

Attraction as reinforcement
Some theorists argue that attraction is all to do with the **positive reinforcement** we get from the other person's company (we will be looking at reinforcement in detail in Chapter 18, but for now it is adequate to think of it as reward). Lott and Lott (1968) set up a study in which they observed children either being systematically rewarded by their teacher or being ignored or punished. When they tested the children's attitudes to the other children in their class, they found that the children who had experienced most rewards liked their classmates much better than those who had been ignored or punished liked theirs.

Lott and Lott argued that we come to like other people if being with them is associated in our minds with pleasant experiences. In the same way, if someone we know is continually associated with unpleasant experiences, we will come to dislike them. The children who had been rewarded by their teachers were experiencing pleasant events in the company of their classmates, so they liked them more than the other children did. The reasoning behind this idea is association: Clore and Byrne (1974) argued that if we experience pleasant events in the presence of someone else, then we come to associate that person with our positive emotional reactions, and so are more likely to like them.

This theory implies that liking can depend on the circumstances and associations connected with people, and this idea does seem to be supported by some evidence. Griffith and Veitch (1971) showed that people who meet for the first time in a hot, crowded room are quite likely to dislike each other, regardless of whether they have compatible personalities or not. However, this study, like many of the other studies of attraction, concentrates on initial attraction to strangers – it does not investigate what happens over a longer period, and long-term relationships may not work in quite the same way. For instance, there is a great deal of anecdotal evidence that people who go through a difficult experience together often retain a camaraderie and long-term friendship as a result.

Attraction as cognitive similarity

Byrne (1971) proposed that one of the main sources of interpersonal attraction is whether two people have similar attitudes. If they do, then each partner in the relationship will receive positive reinforcement for their own ideas and opinions through the other person's agreement. Byrne and Nelson (1965) argued that the higher the proportion of attitudes that are shared between two people, the higher the level of attraction. But it is the proportion that counts, not the absolute number of attitudes that they share, because contradictory attitudes are likely to lead to interpersonal clashes, producing unpleasant, negative outcomes instead of reinforcing the relationship.

Another angle to this type of approach comes from **personal construct theory** (Kelly, 1955). Kelly proposed that people interpret their worlds by means of their own, special 'mini-theories' or constructs; and that two different people may construe the same events very differently if their social worlds are very different (see Chapter 7). Bannister and Fransella (1980) argued that we choose our friends from among those whose personal construct systems are similar to our own. We feel that they are inherently 'in tune' with us, and so find them more attractive. Taking this approach, we might expect that this would work in a similar way to attitude similarity.

Rubin (1973) proposed that similarity is rewarding for a number of different reasons. Receiving agreement from other people helps us to increase our own self-confidence, and it also flatters our vanity – if someone agrees with us, we tend to see them as being intelligent and perceptive, by contrast with people who challenge our views. Agreement also makes it easier for us to communicate with other people, and provides common ground for doing things together; and similarity also suggests a basis for reciprocal liking, because it suggests that the other person will be like us and approve of the same things that we approve of.

Duck (1977) made a clear distinction between social attraction and interpersonal attraction. **Social attraction** is a short-term thing, strongly influenced by the membership of social groups, and factors such as similarity and proximity.

Interpersonal attraction, on the other hand, is based on a much deeper knowledge of the other person's personality and ideas. When we first meet other people, Duck argued, we tend to react to them mostly in terms of the effect that they have on us. In other words, we treat them mainly as stimulus objects ('He makes me laugh'). But if we get to know them better, we come to react to them much more as people ('He's a very gentle person when you get to know him'). According to Duck, it is this attraction to the individual person which forms the basis of long-term relationships.

One of the problems of the traditional studies of attraction is that, by and large, they have concentrated on how people are attracted to strangers (see Box 14.1). But attraction to strangers is not always such an important feature of many people's lives, and more recent studies of relationships have tended to take a different emphasis, looking at the factors which are involved as we form longer-term relationships – at the different types of relationships, like friendship, 'best friends' and courtship; and at how relationships are maintained, at how they can be repaired and at how they end.

Relationships

Other people form such a significant part of our day-to-day experience that most people regard their personal relationships with others as the most important thing in life. The experience of being a parent, for instance, is one which can transform someone's life entirely; and the trauma of losing someone who is close to us can disrupt our personal stability for some time. Often, too, we find that people define themselves in terms of their relationships with others, like saying 'I'm John's father' or 'I'm Susan's friend' when they are meeting someone who knows John or Susan. In the rest of this chapter, we will look at some of the ways that psychologists have investigated the relationships that we develop with others.

Theories of relationships

Early approaches to the study of relationships generally adopted an 'economic' approach – seeing relationships in terms of costs and benefits, and suggesting that we engage in those relationships which provide us with the most 'profit'. In 1959,

Box 14.1 Problems of studying attraction

Studying attraction can be a tricky process, for a number of reasons. One of these involves the ethical problems of investigating long-term relationships: it is easy enough to conduct experiments to see which of a group of, say, first-year students at a university will be attracted to one another; but much more difficult to investigate a long-term relationship without the investigation itself either intruding into people's personal privacy, or putting strains on the relationship simply because of the investigation.

In addition, people have many different kinds of relationships. Huston and Levinger (1978) argued that research into attraction only dealt with a very limited range of just three types of social relationships. These are: same age, same-sex friendships; cross-sex romantic relationships; and marriage. The types of relationships which are missed out (and it does seem as though their criticism is almost as relevant today as it

was in the late 1970s) include cross-sex friendships, friendships between older and younger people, homosexual partnerships, extra-marital relationships, and relationships between workmates or relatives.

Berscheid (1985) argued that another problem with research into attraction has been that it has usually involved studying attraction in American college students, and therefore may not be relevant for people from different subcultures, or with different occupations or ages. The way in which college students meet and come to like one another is likely to be very different from the way that, say, two divorcees in their forties meet. Bearing these problems in mind, then, we will go on to look at some research into the different factors involved in attraction, and then at some of the theories of attraction which have been put forward.

Thibaut and Kelley proposed a four-stage model of long-term relationships, which is described in Table 14.4. Their model has the potential to explain, for example, why a very active social life is so important to most adolescents and young adults, for instance, who will mainly be in stage 1, while both children and people in middle age tend to be satisfied with a less frenetic social life. Stage 2 suggests that factors in interpersonal attraction, like similarity of attitudes or personal constructs, will become important because they provide indications as to whether the relationship is likely to be worthwhile or 'profitable' in the end.

Kiesler (1971) suggested that commitment increases a couple's ability to predict each other's behaviour, which leads to a higher level of attraction between them. Thibaut and Kelley suggested that this is because they find it easier to elicit rewards from one another when each can predict how the other is likely to react (stage 3). A stage 4 couple will not necessarily live together or get married – this model can be applied just as well to a developing close friendship – but it means that there is no longer any need for the couple to test out similarity, or to bargain about the basic assumptions of their relationship (although, of course, some degree of negotiation will always

Table 14.4 Thibaut and Kelley's four-stage model of relationships

Stage 1 **Sampling**
People explore the costs and rewards of associating with different people in different ways, either by trying out a number of different friendships and relationships themselves, or by observing other people in their relationships.

Stage 2 **Bargaining**
This takes place at the very beginning of the relationship, taking the form of giving and receiving various types of reward – effectively, seeing whether the relationship can be seen as profitable.

Stage 3 **Commitment**
The individual reduces the amount of sampling and bargaining with others, and devotes their attention more to the relationship itself.

Stage 4 **Institutionalisation**
In this stage, a couple 'settle down' together and establish norms and mutual expectations.

Source: Thibaut and Kelley, 1959

take place as two people grow psychologically through life).

Thibaut and Kelley's model is based on social exchange theory, which argues that people see relationships (and social behaviour generally) in terms of a kind of 'social contract', involving bargaining for the best deal. We receive social rewards in exchange for our social actions, and we try to organise them so that we can maximise our reward (or positive reinforcement) and minimise punishment – in other words, so that we can obtain as much 'profit' as possible. This approach assumes that we enter into relationships voluntarily, and that we will withdraw from them if the costs become greater than the rewards that we gain from them.

Homans (1974) argued that one of the most powerful social reinforcements available to us is esteem, or social approval, and that we are attracted to people who can provide this for us: we give our own approval in return for something that we value. Moreover, as in economics, the shorter the supply of something, the more it is valued – this is known as the **principle of satiation** – so that we are more likely to appreciate someone who gives us reinforcement in an area in which we feel inadequate than someone who reinforces us in an area where our confidence is already high. For example: if I feel that my tennis playing, say, is reasonably adequate, but I feel very much more apprehensive about my ability to play chess, then I would respond more positively to someone who commented on an improvement in my chess playing than I would to someone who complimented my tennis game.

According to this theory, then, we are most attracted to people who can provide us with social reinforcement in our areas of insecurity; and, over time, we tend to weigh up any given relationship in terms of 'costs' and 'benefits'. Homans (1961) proposed the **distributive justice hypothesis**, which argued that we expect the rewards that we get out of something to be proportional to the amount that it has cost us. If it does not, we become angry, because we feel that we have somehow been 'cheated'. Homans suggested that this may account for the way that some long-term relationships eventually break down.

Equity theory was developed further from Homans's idea of distributive justice. Essentially, equity theory is concerned with the way that relationships need to be 'balanced' if they are to survive in the long term. Walster, Walster and Berscheid (1978) summarised equity theory in terms of four principles, which are outlined in Table 14.5. The theory implies that it is not necessary for each partner to get the same benefits from the relationship, as long as the various rewards and costs involved balance themselves out between the two partners.

Many couples seem to have 'agreed to differ' about different aspects of relationships. For example, one partner may go away motor-racing every alternate weekend in the summer, but in return for this it may be agreed between them that that partner takes full domestic responsibility in the household on the other weekends. The arrangement maintains equity in the relationship, and would be an example of principle 2 in action. And many of us have seen, or perhaps even experienced, how an inequitable relationship can cause personal distress (principle 3).

Similarly, if we look at principle 4, there are many cases of couples who seem to be in relationships which are extremely inequitable, but where it is the 'put upon' partner who puts most effort into keeping the relationship together. But this only lasts for as long as that person feels that there is some chance of restoring equity. Sternberg (1987) described an example of a married couple where one partner had had an affair some time previously. The other partner would bring this up

---

Table 14.5 Equity in relationships

Principle 1	People will try to maximise reward and minimise unpleasant experiences in a relationship.
Principle 2	Rewards can be shared out in different ways, and a group or couple may agree on their own 'fair' system.
Principle 3	An inequitable ('unfair') relationship produces personal distress, and the more inequitable it is, the more distressing it is to the person on the losing side.
Principle 4	Someone in an inequitable relationship will try to restore the relationship to an equitable state; and the greater the degree of inequity, the more effort they will put into doing so.

Source: Walster, Walster and Berscheid, 1978

every time they had a disagreement, long after the whole thing was over. Eventually, the first partner felt that there was no choice but to leave, because no amount of requests to stop had made any difference, which meant that it was completely impossible to restore equity to the relationship.

Cognitive similarity

While social exchange and equity theory suggest that we develop our relationships on a 'trading' basis, there are alternative approaches to the understanding of human friendship. Duck (1977) argued that the crucial variable in long-term relationships is how similar the personal constructs of the two people concerned are. As we have seen, we tend to be initially attracted to people who share the same attitudes and beliefs that we have. Duck argues that this is because attitudes and beliefs form reliable cues, indicating what a person's underlying construct system is like.

As the relationship develops, and two people get to know one another well, they also get to know more about how the other sees the world, and what their private theories about the world and about human nature are. If these are similar, then they may find it easy to interact with the other person, and so the attraction is able to deepen into a longer-term relationship. So what is being emphasised in this model is the way that relationships develop as a result of the cognitive similarity between the two people.

Duck and Sants (1983) criticised many of the early studies of relationships on the grounds that they have derived from a set of ideas and assumptions which portray relationships as 'states' – in other words, as fixed and static – rather than seeing them as continually changing and developing. They identify this as having developed from four common assumptions made in early theories. The first of these assumptions is the idea that relationships can be viewed simply in terms of the personal characteristics of the two partners, without reference to the social context in which the relationship develops, and how the people in the relationship understand what is going on.

The second assumption which Duck and Sants challenged is the idea that what is important in a relationship are the actual incidents or events which take place, and not how people think about them or interpret them. Duck and Sants pointed out that what is important about events is how the people concerned make sense of them: taking

a purely behavioural stance and looking only at the event does not really get to what is important. People's strategies, plans, intentions and memories are crucial in the development of a relationship, they argued, and these are cognitive, not behavioural.

The third assumption identified by Duck and Sants as problematic is the idea that a relationship is something distinctive and separate, which can be studied as if it were an object in itself. A relationship, they argued, is not a separate object, but something which emerges from the interactions, and the thoughts about those interactions, between two people. To treat the relationship as if it were somehow separate from the people who are having it is unrealistic. Equally unrealistic is the fourth common assumption made in early theories of relationships, which is the idea that people act a bit like air-traffic controllers, processing information in a dispassionate, objective and fully rational way. People are human beings, and as such they engage in memory, perception and other cognitive processes in a human way (see Section 1 of this book), not like a computer, objectively weighing up costs and benefits.

According to Duck and Sants (1983) these four assumptions have tended to draw attention away from the interactive aspects of relationships, and away from the idea that relationships are ongoing social processes, which change and develop with time. More recent studies in this field have tended to adopt rather different assumptions, in particular about how relationships change.

Developing relationships

Defining exactly what a relationship is is not an easy task, since a great deal of it is to do with how the people concerned understand what is going on, and this is strongly influenced by the individual's own personal history. Hinde (1987) proposed eight dimensions which can usefully be applied in examining a number of different relationships, including those between parents and children, those between lovers and those between friends. The eight dimensions are shown in Table 14.6.

One of the most common experiences in the early stages of a relationship seems to be anxiety about whether the other person also wishes to have a relationship with us. Duck and Miell (1986) found that, when asked, people engaged in

Table 14.6 Dimensions of relationships

Content	What type of things or actions the participants do together.
Diversity	The number and range of different things that participants in the relationship do together.
Quality	How the participants go about engaging in the interaction – for example, to an infant's signals.
Patterning/relative frequency	Whether the relationship has a distinctive pattern in the type of interactions which it includes – like whether several different types of interaction within the relationship are distinctively loving.
Reciprocity/ complementarity	How far interactions are reciprocal, in that each partner will undertake similar actions in turn or as appropriate; or complementary, with each partner characteristically taking different roles, linking together to make a pair.
Intimacy	The extent to which the participants in a relationship reveal the different aspects of themselves to the other.
Interpersonal perception	How each person in the relationship sees and understands the other.
Commitment	The extent to which the partners recognise their relationship as continuing indefinitely, or as having some possibility of ending. Belief in the partner's commitment would also be included in this dimension, since that forms the basis of trust in many relationships.

Source: Hinde, 1987

developing friendships or in courtship took the view that whether the relationship continued depended on whether the other person wanted to continue it or not. What is interesting about this, though, is that both partners in such a developing relationship would tend to see things this way – seeing themselves as much less in control over what happens than the other person.

Self-presentation

In part, this seems to arise from a fear of rejection by the other person. One of the things which we often do to minimise rejection is to make ourselves as likeable as possible. Bell and Daly (1984) showed how we tend to take an active role in doing this, by showing our 'better sides', like being polite, making the most of our appearance, showing an interest in the other person's life and showing through other interactions that we are trustworthy and worthwhile people to know. According to Bell and Daly, it is through strategies like this that we show the other person not only that we are attracted to them but also that we are worthy of a relationship.

We also use a number of indirect **non-verbal signals**, particularly eye-contact and smiling, to indicate when we are attracted to someone. Kurth (1970) argued that the reason why non-verbal signalling becomes so important for this purpose is because it avoids the risk of a direct rejection. Asking the other person straight out, 'Do you like me?' runs the risk that they will respond with 'No', and that would be difficult to cope with. Signalling it indirectly, through non-verbal messages, means that we do not actually raise the question directly and so do not face a direct rejection. We will be looking more closely at non-verbal communication in Chapter 15.

Once interest has been established between two people, they then begin a period of gathering information. Sometimes we do this directly, by asking a third person about the other or trying to learn through indirect conversations; but we also try to learn more by re-analysing our own experience. Duck (1980) argued that a significant part of this information-gathering phase involves mentally replaying conversations or episodes, and making plans for the future. According to Duck, this allows us to reduce our uncertainties about the other person and to clarify our ideas about the likely success of having a relationship with them. It is important to note, though, that these evaluations are based on mental reflections and interpretations, rather than on an objective or dispassionate weighing up of circumstances or information.

Self-disclosure

One of the significant factors in a developing relationship is **self-disclosure**: the personal information which each person reveals. Sprecher (1987) found that we tend to monitor this quite closely, and try to match the amount of self-disclosure which we make with that of the other person. At some times, though, a relationship will 'turn a corner' – perhaps through some event which reveals a great deal more private information about one person than the other knew before. The other person then matches their level of self-disclosure to this, so that the relationship develops and becomes closer. Again, this mechanism is one which seems to apply just as much to developing friendships as to courtship.

There are, however, social and personal conventions about the amount of self-disclosure which is appropriate in a developing relationship. Knapp (1984) showed that at the early points in a relationship, people tend to stick to fairly neutral topics: engaging in too much self-disclosure at this time can be irritating for the other person and damaging to the future of the relationship.

Miell and Duck (1986) also showed that we tend to be careful about the amount of self-disclosure we make in a developing relationship, often 'floating' a topic in conversation first to see how the other person will respond, before making the full disclosure. Some topics, too, can have negative effects if they are raised in conversation too early in a relationship. This particularly applies to discussing the state of the relationship or asking too openly about the other person's commitment to it. Instead, the more socially acceptable strategy seems to be to approach such topics only very indirectly, if at all.

How the relationship develops past the initial stages tends to depend on the kind of relationship that it is. There are many factors involved in the development of close intimate relationships. Of these, the two most important ones which Duck (1988) identified are firstly, the couple's beliefs and expectations about relationships; and secondly, the joint patterns of activity which the couple develop together. Duck argued that the common view of seeing the progress of the relationship as an indicator of the couple's feelings about one another is actually only a small part of the story.

Maintaining relationships

Although, as we have seen, a considerable amount of research has gone into studying how relationships are first started, it is only recently that researchers have begun to investigate how relationships are maintained over time.

Ayres (1983) collected accounts from a wide range of adults of how they went about maintaining their relationships, and found that the tactics which they described could be grouped into three categories: avoidance, balance and directness. These are described in Table 14.7. Using this model, Shea and Pearson (1986) found that which strategy members of a couple chose to adopt in a relationship was influenced by a number of factors, including the partner's intentions and the sex of the individual. Women, for example, seemed more likely to employ directness in situations where a male partner wanted to escalate the relationship, and they were not interested in doing so.

Dindia and Baxter (1987) interviewed each partner of a set of 50 married couples about the strategies which they used to maintain their relationships. The couples identified 49 different strategies altogether, ranging from 'talking about the day', to paying each other compliments, 'reminiscing together' and 'spending time together with

Table 14.7 Strategies for maintaining relationships

Avoidance strategies	These occur when one person wants to develop a relationship further while the other does not: the one who does not want it to develop tries to maintain the previous level of relationship by avoiding discussion of the relationship's future.
Balance strategies	These tend to be adopted when one person wants the relationship to decline and therefore puts less effort into it. As we saw earlier, however, this often results in the other person attempting to balance the relationship, for instance by doing favours.
Directness	This often involves simply talking about the relationship and expressing a wish to keep things as they are.

Source: Ayres, 1983

friends'. It was noticeable that the strategies which couples used for maintaining their relationships tended to emphasise joint activities and contact, whereas strategies which they offered for repairing it once it got into difficulties tended to focus more on the relationship itself, like 'talk over the problem' or 'ultimatum'.

Dindia and Baxter also found that couples who had been married a long time tended to adopt fewer maintenance strategies than those whose relationship had lasted for a shorter period. One possible interpretation of this is that their relationships simply did not need as much active effort, either because the partners had come to understand each other so well or because the relationship had its own momentum and just kept going through force of habit.

A different explanation, however, may be that longer-married couples simply did not notice the aspects of their relationship which helped to bind them together, because they had become so familiar. Close couples often underestimate the importance of the trivia of day-to-day living in maintaining relationships. As Morgan (1986) pointed out, it is often only when a relationship actually breaks down that people begin to notice the amount of minor, unnoticed interaction with their partner which has gone on from day to day, often concerning very unimportant things. Although they are barely noticeable, these small things may play a significant part in maintaining a relationship, if they are satisfying for the two partners. Alternatively, they may contribute significantly towards its end if they are less positive.

One of the other factors in maintaining relationships comes from the social contexts and social networks that a couple are in. Hagestad and Smyer (1982) showed how the **social roles** which are involved in relationships can become significant forces in maintaining the relationship itself. Friends and relatives have expectations about the relationship, and society exerts expectations and social pressures on couples, which are different from those exerted on single people. Often, a couple whose relationship is breaking up will shrink from actually telling friends about it until it is unavoidable: telling friends involves a formal statement of the end of the relationship, which is often a painful process.

Friendships

Rose and Serafica (1986), in a survey of beliefs about maintaining relationships, found that differ-

ent types of relationships involve considerable differences. In particular, they found that best friendships are expected to last without the two parties having to put a great deal of effort into their maintenance, whereas people expect to have to make more effort to maintain other kinds of close friendships, and in marriages or similar close partnerships.

One of the drawbacks with this type of study, however, is that it is measuring only what people believe they do – and what they actually do may not be the same thing. In Chapter 15, we will be looking at how the shared social beliefs known as **social representations** can influence how we see things. There are generally accepted beliefs about how relationships 'ought' to be, and it is possible that the responses which were given in the survey were reflecting these, rather than describing how people really acted.

It is also possible in survey studies of this kind that people describe only the efforts which they actually notice themselves making, not the things which they do out of habit. As we have seen, people may easily overlook the importance of small, routine matters in maintaining relationships, and this applies to friendships as well as to couples. 'Best friends', for example, often communicate using a very condensed kind of speech, which contains references to shared knowledge which they refer to in shorthand terms. So each time they interact, even if it is relatively brief or does not seem to involve much conversation, they are reaffirming the shared understandings and shared experiences which they have developed. The use of that type of speech, therefore, is an unconscious maintenance behaviour for the relationship: even if they do not interact very often, the quality and personal meaning of their interaction can be very high, which serves to maintain the relationship.

Friendship also involves a certain amount of **reciprocal obligation** to the other person. Argyle and Henderson (1984) showed that, although the ways in which friendships manifest themselves may vary from one culture to another, there are certain expectations about friendships which seem to apply across all human societies. Argyle and Henderson identified six of these expectations, which are listed in Table 14.8. They observed that although simply adhering to these rules is unlikely to be completely sufficient to maintain a close friendship, breaking one or more of them certainly

Table 14.8 'Rules' of friendships	
Rule 1	Stand up for the other person in her or his absence.
Rule 2	Share news of successes with her or him.
Rule 3	Show emotional support for the other person.
Rule 4	Trust and confide in one another.
Rule 5	Volunteer help in times of need.
Rule 6	Strive to make her or him happy while in each other's company.

Source: Argyle and Henderson, 1984

seems to be enough to damage one. They seem to be an essential background for close friendship, in any human culture.

Support networks

Argyle and Henderson (1984) reported on a series of investigations into long-term social relationships, such as friendships. They found that these relationships seem to produce a number of benefits for the people who are involved. For example, one of their findings was that people who had strong and supportive social networks tended to be in better health than those who did not. Brown and Harris (1976), in their study of the social origins of depression, also found that strong social support at home could reduce or ameliorate many of the effects of stressful life events. It seems that having a good support network seems to give people a buffer against stress.

One of the ways that having a support network helps may be because it allows people to talk over their problems with someone else, rather than keeping it all 'bottled up'. However, Wellman (1985) showed that, although talking things over can sometimes be helpful, at other times it can make matters worse, having a 'negative buffering' effect. In one study, research participants were asked to talk to other people for ten minutes about the most depressing thing they had done recently. A control group were asked to think about it for the same period of time. The group who talked to others showed more negative mood change than those who had just been asked to think about it, suggesting that simply talking is not the most important thing.

Much of the positive effect of 'talking things over' seems to depend on what happens in the conversation itself. As we saw in Chapter 9, cognitive psychotherapy is concerned with encouraging people to make more positive attributions about their circumstances – helping them to look for ways that they can reduce the bad effects and maximise their own control over things. This often happens through conversation with friends as well, and it is these which seem to have positive, stress-reducing effects. It is not just the talking, but the **interaction** between the two people which causes the effect: the friend's point of view helps the person to see things differently. Just talking could make things worse if it simply ended up confirming negative viewpoints rather than helping the person to re-evaluate their situation.

Other kinds of relationships, too, may provide important sources of social support. Argyle (1990) proposed that the relationships which we form with people at work may be more significant than we generally assume. According to Argyle, there are a number of characteristics of work friendships which have been shown to be psychologically healthy. These include fooling about and teasing, and co-operation with routine tasks. Unfortunately there has been relatively little psychological research into this area, although the long-standing and highly structured nature of working relationships suggest that they may be quite special in many respects.

Ending relationships

Relationships, of course, do not remain static: they develop and change over time, and what has been a highly satisfactory relationship may become unsatisfying for one or both partners, in time. Rusbult (1987) looked at how couples deal with dissatisfaction in their relationships, and found that the kinds of behaviours which they report can be classified into four categories, which are described in Table 14.9.

The end of a close relationship is often one of the most painful experiences in people's lives. Naturally, research into this area has tended to focus on 'what went wrong', and often concentrated on identifying demographic or social factors in unstable marriages. For example, Bentler and Newcomb (1978) showed that marriages between young partners are less likely to survive than those where the partners are older; and Jaffe and Kanter (1979) showed that if people come from very different backgrounds their marriages are less likely

Table 14.9 Dealing with dissatisfaction in relationships	
The exit strategy	This involves either getting out of the relationship altogether, or doing so at least mentally, by thinking and talking about getting out.
The voice strategy	This involves talking things over and discussing problems.
Loyalty	This involves waiting for things to get better in the hope that they will sort themselves out in time.
Neglect	This involves responding to dissatisfaction by doing nothing to improve things, and just letting the relationship fall apart.

Source: Rusbult, 1987

to last than those between people who come from similar backgrounds.

This type of research, however, while it illustrates general trends, is not really very helpful in understanding what happens between particular individuals. Other psychological research has examined the social and interpersonal factors which seem to be involved in relationships which are disintegrating, and this research may be of more value in understanding how break-ups happen.

Noller (1985) showed that, very often, couples who are in a relationship which is coming apart show disrupted patterns of communication. They become less sensitive to non-verbal signals from the other person, and often enter 'negativity cycles' in which each person complains about the other without really paying attention to the other person's concerns. Instead of attempting to resolve issues by conciliation or discussion, both people engage in 'scoring points' off the other, which results in problems being perpetuated and exaggerated.

Breaking the rules

The rules which Argyle and Henderson identified as applying to close friendships apply to close relationships as well. At times, a relationship may be broken because one partner ceases to observe the rule of, say, loyalty to the other person. This

signals that the relationship does not matter enough for them to keep to these rules, and so indicates to the other person that there is little point in attempting to sustain the relationship. Argyle and Henderson found that the breaking of these rules was seen as a very important cause of relationship breakdown. In the case of married couples, the rules which were most frequently broken were those to do with intimacy and support: the partners each felt that the other had failed to provide trust or trustworthiness, or to provide emotional support when it was needed.

Miller, Mogeau and Sleight (1986) investigated the strain on relationships caused by **deception** or lying. They found that relationships change dramatically if a partner is found to be deceiving the other about something serious. This change often signals the beginning of a process which ends in the dissolution of the relationship altogether. Interestingly, Comadena (1982) found that people with close relationships were less able to tell when their partner was lying than those in newly developing relationships, despite the fact that they tended to believe that they would always know. Duck (1988) suggested that this might be because an established relationship has become secure, and is founded on a mutual trust which has been built up gradually over time. Because of this, both parties have ceased to expect deception from each other. When we are forming newer relationships, on the other hand, we feel that we are still learning about the other person and so are partly on our guard and aware that they might lie to us.

Baxter (1986) identified break-ups of long-term relationships as deriving from unmet expectations. There were eight expectations in all, which Baxter identified from analysing the accounts which were given by partners for why their relationship ended. The eight expectations are given in Table 14.10 opposite. Looking at this table, we can see that some of these expectations, and in particular the last one, may not be all that realistic: it can be argued that the last one derives directly from media representations of the 'ideal relationship' rather than from real life. It may also be culturally specific, in that not every culture views intimate relationships in the same way as Western culture does.

Another issue might be a failure to distinguish between 'love' and 'limerence'. We will be looking at this later in this chapter; but effectively there is

Table 14.10 Expectations about intimate relationships

1. Partners should each expect a certain amount of autonomy.
2. Partners should find a good basis of similarity between them.
3. Partners should be supportive of the other's self-esteem and feelings.
4. Partners should be loyal and faithful.
5. Partners should be honest and open with one another.
6. Partners should expect to spend time together.
7. There should be equitable shares of effort and resources between the partners.
8. There should be some 'magical quality' in the relationship.

Source: Baxter, 1986

a big difference between the kind of obsessive infatuation that we call 'love', but which researchers have begun to call 'limerence'; and the kind of long-term intimate closeness which we also call 'love'. Confusing the two can result in disappointment and a perception of unmet expectations in longer-term relationships.

Novelty

Duck and Miell (1986) found that another set of reasons why relationships break up is because they cease to provide stimulation for the partners. We tend to look to new relationships as a source of novelty and of new ideas about the world in general; the corollary is that existing relationships may not provide interest for the other person – or at least, may not seem to, by comparison. Duck and Miell found that many of the research participants whom they interviewed in an investigation of courtship gave the fact that it 'was not going anywhere' as the reason for breaking up. We expect those relationships to develop and to become closer and more satisfying as time goes on: if they do not, we feel justified in ending them. Since courtship represents a kind of 'experimental' phase for a deeper and longer-term commitment, perceiving the relationship as static may be considered sufficient reason to end it.

Physical circumstances such as distance may make a relationship difficult to maintain, although it is not at all certain that this is generally the case. Shaver, Furman and Burmester (1985) showed that 46% of pre-college attachments broke up in consequence of one partner's moving away to college. However, given the general age of college students, the number of distractions, and the fact that much of college life often centres on the formation of new friendships and relationships, what is probably more remarkable about this study is the 54% who did not break up rather than the 46% who did!

Rose and Serafica (1986) asked research participants to report on why their own relationships had broken up, and also to talk about why hypothetical relationships tended to break up. They found that the two produced quite a difference in emphasis. When people were speculating about the endings of hypothetical relationships, they identified distance or lack of effort as the causes. When they were describing the break-up of real relationships which they had experienced, however, they identified interference from other relationships and a gradual decline of affection as causes. Again, social beliefs about what is likely or what 'ought to' happen may have been influencing people's ideas – although it is difficult to tell from retrospective accounts of this kind how accurate the accounts of their own break-ups were. Duck and Sants (1983) found that people show a strong tendency to adjust their memories of relationship break-ups until they fit with their own emotional experience, so a retrospective story of what happened is not all that likely to be an unbiased and dispassionate account.

Processes in relationship breakdown

We can see, then, that a number of different factors may contribute to the breakdown of relationships. Duck (1988) described a process model, in which relationship breakdown is seen as passing through several different but connected phases (Table 14.11), each of which involves characteristic thoughts and actions.

The first phase, in Duck's model, is one of dissatisfaction with the relationship. It tends to begin at the point where one person thinks to themselves that they cannot stand the relationship any more. From that point, they begin to look very closely at their partner's behaviour, and to evaluate the costs and benefits of being in or withdrawing from the relationship. This is known as the **intrapsychic phase**, since it is going on within the person's own mind, and does not yet show in overt behaviour.

Table 14.11 Phases in relationship breakdown

The intra-psychic phase	One person is becoming dissatisfied and questioning the value of the relationship.
The dyadic phase	The other person becomes involved, and the couple express uncertainty or indecision about breaking up.
The social phase	The social and practical implications of the change are worked out, and close friends may be informed.
The grave-dressing phase	The relationship is ended, and both partners develop their own accounts of the break-up story.

Source: Duck, 1988

Should that person conclude that they would be justified in leaving the relationship, they then enter the second phase, which Duck calls the **dyadic phase**. This now involves the other partner: the person has to decide whether to confront the other or just to avoid them; whether to attempt repair or reconciliation or to withdraw altogether. Discovering the state of affairs may come as a shock to the other person, and often at this time couples will oscillate or express uncertainty at the idea of breaking up. They may also decide to try to renegotiate the relationship in some way, or they may come into open conflict with one another. If things develop to a point where it appears that repair or reconciliation are not practical or not worthwhile, the couple enter the third phase.

The third phase of Duck's process model is known as the **social phase**, since this involves working out the social implications of the change. At this point friends may be told, which means that the couple need to work out publicly acceptable accounts of the break-up. The effects on friendships and social networks need to be faced, and in some circles, family or religious elders may intervene in an attempt to promote reconciliation.

At some point, however, the break may become inevitable, in which case the couple move into the fourth phase. Duck referred to this as the **grave-dressing phase**: the erstwhile partners concentrate on getting over their emotional stress or distress, distributing their own versions of the break-up story to friends and family, and establishing the basis for any continuation of friendship with the other person despite the breakdown in the relationship.

We can see, then, how recent research into relationships has tended to concentrate much more closely on the cognitive and social factors which are involved, and to look at relationships as changing, dynamic processes rather than just as fixed states. Although there is much remaining to be investigated in this area, the new emphasis seems to give us the opportunity to look more closely at why it is that people feel as they do, at how relationships can become or cease to be satisfying for the people in them and at how social pressures and influences can affect them.

Loving and loneliness

One of the most significant aspects of close relationships, for most people, is the fact that they involve powerful emotions – both in their presence and in their absence. Although many researchers into the different aspects of relationships have tended to avoid dealing with the emotional dimensions, there has been a significant amount of psychological research into the emotion of love, and also into its opposite, the emotion of loneliness.

Love

Some psychologists see love as being simply an extreme example of attraction, or liking, which we looked at earlier in this chapter. They perceive it is drawing on the same psychological mechanisms, but perhaps more intensively. Other researchers, though, see love as being qualitatively different from liking, and we will look at some of their theories here.

For Freud (1901), all positive emotions were essentially manifestations of the life-affirming sexual drive which he referred to as the **libido**. He saw love as being a specially sublimated version, in which the sexual drive was channelled into a socially acceptable form. Romantic love, for Freud, included psychological defences and conversions: such as the transference of the young female child's affection for her father to her husband; or the husband's attempt to rediscover the mother-figure who had been the object of his affections in his early years, in the person of a nurturing wife.

Maslow (1954) distinguished between two kinds of love: **D-Love**, which stood for 'deficiency love', and **B-Love**, which stood for 'being love'. D-Love, according to Maslow, originates from the person's own unsatisfied need for security and belonging, and is the sort of love in which the individual looks to the other person to fulfil themselves. Maslow saw this kind of love as being ultimately destructive, in the sense that a relationship built on that degree of dependency would not be able to cope with how people change and grow over time, and also because the dependent person would be bound to be disappointed in some respects, as they found that their lover was only human after all. B-Love, on the other hand, was a more settled kind of love, in which both partners were essentially balanced, independent and secure, with all of their psychological needs largely fulfilled. They could therefore respect each other and enjoy being in each other's company.

Limerence

One of the problems which emerges quite quickly whenever we begin to talk about love is that we often mean a great many different things by the same word. The type of love which is shared by two people in a long-lasting, stable marriage is very different from the type of love in which two people have just met and are totally infatuated with each other. And that again is different from the love that a young couple who have been together for maybe three or four years may share. Tennov (1979) used the term limerence to refer to a kind of infatuated, all-absorbing passion   the kind of love that Dante felt for Beatrice, or that Juliet and Romeo felt for each other.

Tennov argued that an important feature of limerence is that it should be unrequited, or at least unfulfilled. It consists of a state of intense longing for the other person, in which the individual becomes more or less obsessed by that person and spends much of their time fantasising about them. The state of limerence also often involves the use of tokens, like photographs or small gifts, as a focus for the person's thoughts about the other. Tennov suggests that limerence can only really last if external conditions are such that it remains unfulfilled: it is not uncommon for people to maintain a state of limerence about someone who is unreachable for some years; but if

the desired person should actually come within reach, so that the desired relationship begins, then the limerence becomes extinguished and the attraction sometimes disappears very quickly.

In a sense, according to Tennov, limerence can only survive with occasional or intermittent reinforcement. It is the unobtainable nature of the goal which makes the feeling so powerful. This might provide us with one explanation for why teenage love-affairs which are banned or interfered with by parents often grow so much stronger. Because the parents are putting obstacles in the way of the relationship, the infatuation grows, and the tendency to idolise the other person increases. Also, because the two participants are limited in how often they can see each other, they tend to notice only the idealised 'good bits' of each other: faced with more routine contact, they can quickly become bored or begin to notice things that they do not like about each other.

Lee (1976) argued that there were several different styles, or 'colours' of love, and these are described in Table 14.12. Lee emphasised that the same person may adopt a different style, depending on the relationship that they are in; and the style of a relationship may change over time. But if two people are adopting very different styles within the same relationship, then it is quite easy for serious misunderstandings to arise.

Hendrick and Hendrick (1988) argued that it would be reasonable to expect that people who were currently 'in love' would hold different attitudes towards love from people who were not. Using Lee's 'colours of love' classification, they asked 789 research participants about their attitudes towards being in love. Roughly 63% of the research participants answered positively to the question 'Are you in love at the moment?', and Hendrick and Hendrick found that these people were more concerned with the erotic and agapic dimensions, and far less with the ludic dimension than research participants who were not in love.

In general terms, people who were 'in love' had a far more altruistic approach to their partners, and believed strongly in such phenomena as sexual communion – merging with the loved one – while being more inclined to disapprove of sexual permissiveness or a view of sex as simply being to do with physical stimulation. Hendrick and Hendrick argued that being 'in love' tended to colour their attitudes towards other people as well as towards each other, and argued that the

Table 14.12 Colours of love

Eros	This is where someone is searching for a partner who matches up to a physical ideal – they have a clear mental picture of the type of lover that they are looking for, and seek someone who fits it.
Ludus	This is a playful, gamelike form of love, in which the relationship is seen as a source of fun and enjoyment, but not necessarily of commitment.
Storge	This is a form of love based on the idea of a friendship which gradually increases in intimacy, affection, and companionship.
Mania	This is a very emotionally intensive love style, in which the person concerned is typically very possessive and very jealous of the partner.
Agape	This is an altruistic form of love, in which the person loves the other without any thought of payback: they do all the giving, and expect little in return.
Pragma	This is a hard-headed, practical style of loving, in which objective information like the partner's occupation or location, is seen as being just as important as emotional feelings.

Source: Lee, 1976

tendency to see things 'through rose-coloured glasses' which has often been referred to in literature seems to be a very real phenomenon.

The problem, though, is that these researchers did not seem to make any distinction between love and limerence, so their research seems to be mostly concerned with the type of romantic, infatuated love that Tennov referred to as limerence, rather than with steady, long-term loving relationships.

Sternberg's triangular theory of love

Sternberg (1987) proposed that love is made up of three components: intimacy, passion and commitment. Any given relationship may emphasise one or two of the three components more than the other(s), but in a lasting, fulfilling love-relationship, the three are likely to be fairly well balanced (Figure 14.1). Sternberg argued that different combinations of the three components could account for the different types of love which people experience.

Each of the three dimensions consists of several different aspects. So, for instance, the **intimacy** dimension includes aspects like seeking to promote the welfare of one's partner, having mutual understanding, receiving and giving emotional support and valuing the partner highly, as well as good mutual communication. **Passion**, on the other hand, concerns the expression and satisfaction of desires and needs – not always sexual ones, although these are involved too. Some of the sorts of needs concerned in the passion dimension of a relationship might be nurturance, personal fulfilment, or self-esteem as well as sexual fulfilment. The **commitment** dimension also has more than one angle: on the one hand there is the short-term commitment to the relationship as it stands; and on the other hand there is the prospect of longer-term commitment to the relationship. The two are not at all the same thing: someone could be entirely committed to a relationship in the short term, but be unwilling to make a longer-term relationship.

Some forms of experience which are referred to as 'love' consist of just one of the components in Sternberg's triangular model. For example: the type of infatuated love which Tennov described as limerence is very high on the passion dimension, but lacks either intimacy or commitment. By contrast, a relationship which is essentially one of mutual liking might be high on the intimacy component but not involve passion, and possibly not commitment either. Sternberg describes love which consists of commitment but little else as **empty love**.

Other forms of love have different combinations of the three components. The long-term companionate love that many couples develop

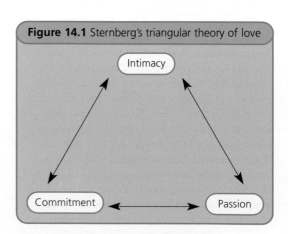

Figure 14.1 Sternberg's triangular theory of love

Intimacy

Commitment   Passion

over time is high on intimacy and on commitment, but often not on passion. Romantic love would be love which is high on intimacy and passion, but not on commitment; and Sternberg uses the term **fatuous love** to describe love which is high on passion and commitment but not on intimacy. Love which is high on all three components is referred to as **consummate love** in Sternberg's model.

Sternberg went on to investigate how relationships vary over time, and showed that relationships at different stages involve different aspects of partnership. His study involved 80 men and women, ranging in age from seventeen to 69, with the average age being 31. In terms of Sternberg's triangular theory, the findings suggested that it was the intimacy and commitment sides of the relationship which mainly continue to grow over time, whereas the passion angle seems to decline (see Table 14.13). However, since the passion component is primarily concerned with the satisfaction of unmet needs, this could simply reflect the idea that the needs which people had initially brought to the relationship had become satisfied, so that they were no longer important. Without much more detailed research it would be very difficult to know exactly what patterns were involved.

Either way, however, the picture that emerges is

that relationships do change over time, and that in the long term the important aspects of a relationship may not be the same as they were in the short term. Sternberg suggests that possibly one reason for the relatively high proportion of marriages that fail might be that people make decisions based on the short-term needs of the relationship, rather than looking at longer-term factors. But as we can see, there is a great deal yet to be investigated in this matter.

Loneliness

Most people have some experience of feeling lonely at some time in their lives. It may hit us when we have just moved house, or moved away from home for the first time, or when we are coming to terms with the ending of a close personal relationship. Loneliness is a complex emotion, and one which was not really studied by psychologists until relatively recently. During the 1970s and 1980s, however, psychologists made considerable headway in understanding some of the many aspects of loneliness.

Cutrona (1982) argued that it is important to distinguish between **chronic loneliness** and **situational loneliness**. The type of loneliness described in the previous paragraph would be situational loneliness: loneliness which occurs as a result of some kind of change in our personal situation. Cutrona found that this type of loneliness can happen to pretty well anyone. But some people seem to be lonely on a more long-term basis: they are chronically lonely individuals. This distinction led to research into what distinguishes these chronically lonely people from others.

It would be easy to assume that loneliness is simply an emotional state which occurs when people do not have enough social contacts with others. But one of the most interesting aspects of loneliness seems to be the way that the subjective state of loneliness does not always correlate with social isolation. In fact, a study by Jones (1981) showed that in some cases, people who experience high subjective loneliness may even have more social contact than people who do not feel particularly lonely. But it is the quality of that social contact which counts, not the sheer amount of it.

Social aspects of loneliness
Williams and Solano (1983) showed that lonely people tend to feel that they have a noticeable

---

Table 14.13 Changes in relationships over time

Increasing importance over time
Sharing values.
Having a willingness to change in response to each other.
Being prepared to tolerate each other's flaws.
Having matching religious beliefs.

Less importance over time
How interesting each partner seemed to the other.
How well each handled the other's parents.
How attentively each listened to the other.

Increasing importance at first, less importance later
Physical attractiveness.
The ability to make love.
The ability to empathise with the partner.
Having knowledge of what each other is like.
The expression of affection towards each other.

Unimportant at first, more important later
Having a matching intellectual level.

Source: Sternberg, 1987

lack of intimacy with other people. This also correlates with how they interact with others: in an observational study, Williams and Solano showed that lonely people are much less likely to engage in self-disclosure to their friends than are people who are not lonely. Since self-disclosure is one of the most distinctive features of intimate relationships, the lack of it in a relationship usually means that the relationship remains on a formal or semi-formal basis. For many relationships this can be quite a good thing – you would not want to reveal your personal secrets to everyone you meet, after all – but if all your relationships are formal or semi-formal, then it is understandable that you would feel rather lonely.

Jones, Hobbs and Hockenbury (1982) also found that lonely people tend to act differently in social situations from people who did not report themselves as lonely. From observational studies, they found that lonely people tend to give their partners less attention, ask them fewer questions and are less talkative generally. When Jones *et al.* gave their research participants training in conversational and partner attention skills, they found that this had the effect of reducing the person's reported loneliness significantly. Even quite small amounts of training seemed to be enough to have this effect.

Cognitive aspects of loneliness

There may be differences too in the attributions which lonely people make. Anderson, Horowitz and French (1983) found that lonely people are more likely to see interpersonal difficulties in terms of stable, dispositional factors than in terms of temporary situational ones. We will be looking at attribution more closely in the next chapter, but essentially this type of attribution means that they would be less likely to see loneliness as something that they could do something about, or avoid.

Horowitz, French and Anderson (1982) also found that lonely people are very passive when it comes to interpersonal problems. When they were given a series of problems and asked to think up possible solutions to them, lonely research participants generated noticeably fewer solutions to interpersonal problems than did non-lonely research participants, although there was no difference between the two in problems which did not concern people. It may be that they are experiencing a kind of 'learned helplessness' (see Chapter 13), by tending to see interpersonal situations as things which they cannot really influence much.

Shaver and Hazan (1985) argued that lonely people are particularly liable to experience limerence, as a form of loving, and to found their relationships on this emotion, as opposed to on a more realistic form of love. Not all lonely people do this, of course, but Shaver and Hazan argue that if people have a large number of unmet social needs, and are not aware of this, then a sign that someone else might be interested is easily built up in that person's imagination into far more than the friendly social contact that it might have been. By dwelling on the memory of that social contact, the lonely person comes to magnify it into a deep emotional experience, which may be quite different from the reality of the event.

All these studies are concerned with people who describe themselves as lonely. But Marangoni and Ickes (1989) argued that some chronically lonely people – particularly those with social skills and personal attention skills deficits – may be unaware that they are particularly lonely. As a result, they argue, these people may not describe themselves as 'lonely' when asked about it in a questionnaire, and so may be overlooked by the standard measures of loneliness which are used to distinguish between lonely and non-lonely people.

However, arguing that people may be lonely yet unaware of it may be getting a bit over-sophisticated: Peplau and Perlman (1982) described two basic points of convergence about research into loneliness as that it is, firstly, a subjective state, and secondly, one which is unpleasant, or aversive, for the individual. This definition contains a basic requirement that the lonely person does, to some extent, recognise what the problem is, even if they are not sure of what to do about it.

Although as yet research into loneliness has been mainly concerned with identifying characteristics of lonely people, we can see how the nature of the characteristics which have been identified has led directly to ideas about how loneliness might be reduced or even stopped altogether. Both social and cognitive approaches to loneliness have been effective in helping lonely people to overcome their state; and, of course, for the most part cognitive and social dimensions of the experience go hand in hand.

In the next chapter, we will be looking at some different aspects of social psychology, and in particular, focusing on how people come to make sense out of their social worlds. To do so, we will be looking at non-verbal communication, at the cognitive structures we use for organising our

social awareness, and at the attributions and social representations which we use to make sense out of our experiences.

Key terms

complementary needs hypothesis The idea that some couples are attracted to one another because they are opposite personalities, and therefore each can fulfil the other's personal needs – e.g. one is talkative while the other likes to listen.

dyadic phase The stage in the breakdown in a relationship where both members of a couple become involved – in other words, where the decision of one partner to end the relationship is communicated to the other.

equity theory The idea that social conventions and norms are based around a principle of fair, though not necessarily strictly equal, exchange.

grave-dressing phase The stage in relationship breakdown where the couple concentrate on recovering from the break-up, and elaborating their own version of what has occurred.

intra-psychic phase The first stage in relationship breakdown in which one person acknowledges to themselves that their increasing dissatisfaction with the relationship has got beyond the point where things can be salvaged, and makes the decision to end the relationship.

limerence The term used for a powerful infatuation, to distinguish it from long-term love.

matching hypothesis The idea that members of couples mostly match one another in degrees of physical attractiveness.

minimal group paradigm An approach to the study of social identification which involves creating artificial groups in the social psychology laboratory on

the basics of spurious or minimal characteristics (e.g. tossing a coin), and then studying the in-group/out-group effects which result.

personal space The physical distance which people like to maintain between themselves and others. This varies according to their relationship with, and attitude to other people, and according to norms and contexts.

positive reinforcement In operant conditioning, strengthening learned behaviour by direct reward when it occurs.

self-image The factual or descriptive picture which people hold of themselves, without the evaluative component implicit in the concept of self-esteem.

self-perception theory The idea that we develop an impression of our own personality by inferring what we are like from the way that we act.

social comparison The process of comparing one's own social group with others, in terms of their relative social status and prestige. Social comparison is important, in that people will tend to distance themselves from membership of a group which does not reflect positively on their self-esteem.

social exchange theory An approach to the understanding of social behaviour which sees social interaction as a 'trade', in which the person acts in certain ways in return for some social reward or approval.

social phase The stage in relationship breakdown where the couple acknowledge publicly that their relationship has ended or is ending.

Summary

1 Feedback from others, social interaction, the maintenance of self-esteem, self-perception and self-efficacy beliefs are significant factors in the maintenance of the self-concept.

2 Social identity theory argues that the social groups to which the individual belongs are important in how we see ourselves and how we interact with others.

3 The Western concept of the self as an isolated, independent entity is not one which is shared by most human cultures. Instead, the self is more likely to be seen as embedded within a social and cultural network.

4 Factors influencing interpersonal attraction include physical attractiveness, similarity and complementarity, familiarity and propinquity, reciprocal liking and perceived fallibility. Theoretical explanations of attraction have included evaluation, social reinforcement and cognitive similarity.

5 Early theories of relationships tended to use economic metaphors, such as applying social exchange or equity theory. Later theories tended to emphasise cognitive similarity and the way that relationships change over time.

6 Self-presentation and self-disclosure are important in early stages of relationships, while their maintenance involves reciprocal obligations and social support. Relationships may break down as a result of breaking rules, lack of stimulation or unmet expectations.

7 Research into loving suggests that it is important to differentiate between limerence – the intense experience of romantic infatuation – and long-term love, which may take several forms.

8 Studies of loneliness have shown that chronically lonely people may interact differently with others, using less self-disclosure and giving partners less attention. They also tend to see interpersonal situations as less easily influenced.

Self-assessment questions

1 Briefly outline the main factors in the maintenance of the self-concept.

2 Describe the major factors influencing interpersonal attraction.

3 Outline the four phases of relationship breakdown.

Practice essay questions

1 'The concept of the independent individual is a delusion'. Discuss.

2 Critically evaluate psychological theories of attraction.

3 'Studying relationships is more useful to understanding human beings than studying attraction'. Discuss.

Test your knowledge of this chapter with our online quizzes and games at: http://www.psych.co.uk

Explore self and others further at:

General

http://www.socialpsychology.org/ – Excellent site with a wealth of links to research sites, articles and journals on all aspects of soical psychology.
http://www.richmond.edu/~allison/glossary.html – Comprehensive glossary of related terms.

Self/social identity

http://www.canisius.edu/~gallaghr/pi.html – Excellent bibliographies on subjects relating to the self, as well as links to online articles and journals.

Relationships

http://www.isspr.org/ – The homepage of the International Society for the Study of Personal Relationships, features links to related sites and information on journals and articles.

Love/loneliness

http://psych-server.iastate.edu/faculty/drussell/uclalone.htm – UCLA's 'loneliness scale' explained with a useful reading list.

http://world.topchoice.com/~psyche/love/ – Links, tutorials, definitions and tests about love and relationships.

Understanding others

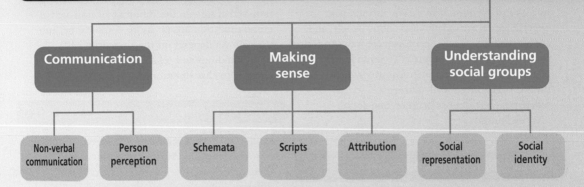

Communication
- Non-verbal communication
- Person perception

Making sense
- Schemata
- Scripts
- Attribution

Understanding social groups
- Social representation
- Social identity

In this chapter, we will be looking at how we come to make sense out of our social worlds. In dealing with other people, we do not just act blindly: we apply our past experience and social knowledge, using them to guide our actions. We use this knowledge to perceive messages in how people act – for example, in interpreting their non-verbal communication. We also use past experience to formulate ideas about people, and apply these when we meet someone new. And our social experience accumulates to provide us with cognitive structures and mechanisms which we use for organising social awareness – social schemata, social representations, and social identifications.

Non-verbal communication

Have you ever noticed how much you can say without words? We do it all the time. We communicate by gestures, tones of voice and facial expressions. And what about when you are choosing your clothes carefully for a special night out? What image are you trying to project? How is it different to the way you dress when you are going for a job interview?

Most, if not all, human beings are expert in non-verbal communication. Like other social animals, we spend most of our time in contact with other members of our species. Our non-verbal communication is usually specific to the context of the interaction. A shared glance with a friend can replace any amount of talking, but a glance exchanged with a stranger might not convey any message at all. So although researchers have been able to discuss the general meanings of non-verbal signals, the minutiae of non-verbal communication are far more complex, because they always depend on the shared social understandings and relationships which are relevant to that situation.

Non-verbal cues

Non-verbal communication can serve a number of social purposes. Argyle (1984) identified four of these, which are listed in Table 15.1. These different social purposes are complex, and involve conveying very subtle messages at particular times or in response to particular events. We achieve this complex communication by using a range of **non-verbal cues**, which are signals that we use to carry information. Some of these are listed in Table 15.2, and we will begin our study of non-verbal communication by looking at them in more detail.

Facial expression

One of the more obvious forms of non-verbal cue which we use is **facial expression**. We greet someone we like with a smile, frown if we are puzzled, or scowl if we are angry. Human beings have immensely mobile faces, and can produce a large range of different expressions. Sometimes, these expressions are idiosyncratic – habitual expressions adopted by just one individual, or

Table 15.1 Functions of non-verbal communication

Assisting speech	For example, emphasising important words by stressing them heavily, and saying them more slowly than other words.
Replacing speech	For example, shrugging the shoulders to say 'I don't know'.
Signalling attitudes	For example, adopting a bored facial expression when forced to listen to someone whose opinion you are not interested in.
Signalling emotions	For example, hugging a close friend that you have not seen for some time, to express your pleasure at seeing them.

Source: Argyle, 1975

Table 15.2 Major non-verbal cues

facial expression

eye-contact

posture

gesture

proxemics

touch

paralanguage

dress

possibly by people in the same family. Everyone has their own distinctive way of smiling, for instance. Some facial expressions seem to be cultural in origin, used by people in that society but not elsewhere. But other facial expressions seem to be universal, found in all human cultures, which suggests that they may be innate.

In 1872, Darwin argued that the expression of basic emotions, such as anger or fear, is innate, on the grounds that the same patterns occurred in other mammals as well as humans, implying that they had a common evolutionary origin. For example, the fear response in both humans and other mammals includes high-pitched whimpers and the **pilomotor response**, in which the hair stands on end. (In human beings, being relatively hairless, this shows itself as goose-pimples.) This response occurs in dogs, cats, chimpanzees and monkeys as well as in humans. Another of the distinctive features of fear is the 'fear-grin', in which the skin is pulled back from the teeth and the mouth is stretched wide, and this again is found in almost all mammals.

Other facial expressions may be inherited by human beings, but not necessarily by other animals. In an examination of several different films of social encounters made of people from different cultures, Eibl-Eiblesfeldt (1972) showed that a number of different facial expressions appeared in all these cultures. One of them was the eyebrow flash of recognition: if we are greeting someone that we recognise, we raise our eyebrows quickly and lower them again. Osgood (1966) found that there seem to be seven main groups of facial expressions signalling emotions, which also seem to be universal for all human cultures. The seven groups are: surprise, fear, happiness, sadness, anger, interest and disgust or contempt.

Facial expression is also a powerful signal of attitudes, and in some respects this too may show links with other species. Goodall (1974) observed that young chimpanzees have a 'play-face' which is very similar to the 'play-face' of children. It signals that what they are doing is a game (Figure 15.1), although human culture uses these signals in ways which seem to be rather more sophisticated than chimpanzee cultures. Friedman, DiMatteo and Mertz (1980) showed how the facial expressions of television presenters change to indicate approval or contempt, depending on the topic that they are discussing. This was particularly apparent during the 1976 American presidential elections, when presenters used different facial expressions when talking about Carter from those used when talking about Ford.

Eye-contact

Eye-contact is a powerful signal, which can signal both affection and hostility. Prolonged eye-contact with someone you love signals affection, but the same with a stranger is likely to be taken as a challenge. Ellsworth and Langer (1976) showed that prolonged gaze is very likely to invoke flight – people will withdraw from such a threatening situation. The fact that prolonged eye-contact is not easily ignored also tells us something about the power of non-verbal communication.

Eye-contact is also an important signal in regulating social interaction. Kendon (1967) observed pairs of students who were asked to 'get acquainted' with one another, and showed that there is quite a sophisticated set of social rules about eye-contact to regulate conversations. For example, a speaker will tend to avoid eye-contact while she or he is speaking, but will look up at the end of an utterance, as if to 'hand over' to the other person. The listener, on the other hand, will look at the speaker much more. Argyle, Lalljee and Cook (1968) showed that when normally sighted people were deprived of this cue because one of the pair was wearing dark glasses, their conversations were much more hesitant and included more pauses and interruptions.

Breaking the conventional pattern may also be a signal in its own right. Dovidio and Ellyson

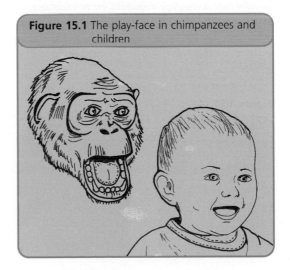

Figure 15.1 The play-face in chimpanzees and children

(1982) showed how maintaining prolonged eye-contact while speaking, and looking away while listening, is a strategy people use to maintain social control over the interaction, and is a signal of power and status in social interaction.

The eyes can also signal attraction, because the pupil of the eye dilates when we are looking at something we like (which is, of course, why the lighting in romantic settings like restaurants is usually dim). Hess (1965) asked male research participants to rate photographs of women for attractiveness. Some of the photographs were adjusted so that the pupils appeared dilated (as in Figure 15.2). These were rated as the most attractive, even though the research participants were unaware of the basis for their choice.

Posture and gesture

Gestures are specific actions, usually made with the hands and arms during communication. They tend to be used to amplify and illustrate speech, and may have very precise, culturally specific meanings. For example, most Western cultures have a specific gesture to indicate that someone is 'crazy'. In some cultures, this is expressed by tapping the side of the forehead, but in others it is signalled by twirling the forefinger in the air by the side of the head. There are cultural differences, too, in the amount of gesture which is used: people from some cultures have a more expressive conversational style than those in others.

Posture involves the whole orientation of the body. Where gestures are often used to signal specific messages, posture is a powerful signal of general attitude – so powerful, indeed, that we usually take a message conveyed by posture as a more reliable indicator of someone's attitude than what they say. We recognise, instantly, a casual posture, an aggressive stance or a relaxed, friendly position.

Figure 15.2 Attractiveness and pupil dilation

One of the more interesting uses of posture in conversation occurs with the phenomenon known as **postural echo**. If we are talking to a friend or listening closely to someone else, we often unconsciously adopt the same posture that they are showing. It is thought that this is an unconscious message that we are on the same wavelength as they are.

McGinley, LeFèvre and McGinley (1975) showed that the posture which someone adopts can make a difference both to whether we are likely to like them, and to whether they are perceived as powerful. An open stance, like leaning back in a chair with legs extended and knees and feet apart, tends to be interpreted as more likeable as well as being a signal of confidence; more closed postures, such as having the legs or arms crossed, are seen as indicating that the person is being less open and more self-protective, and so we are less likely to like them. Knapp, Hart and Dennis (1974) showed that minor self-grooming gestures, like running the fingers through the hair or touching the face, are often interpreted by observers as a sign of deception.

Proxemics and touch

Hall (1968) described how we all learn very specific rules about **proxemics** – the distance which we maintain between ourselves and other people during different types of social interaction. As part of growing up in a particular society, we develop clear ideas about what is an acceptable distance for different forms of interaction, and for different relationships. People in different relation-ships will signal their degree of closeness physically, by the distances they maintain between themselves and others. Lovers, for example, will sit very much closer together than will two friends, and they in turn will sit closer to one another than would two strangers sharing the same seat. The four main interpersonal distances which Hall identified are given in Table 15.3

There are cultural rules about situations which require physical closeness, and those which do not. In Western society we would signal that we wanted to tell someone something secret or intimate, for example, by moving closer to them; but if we were consulting a stranger – asking them the time, for instance – we would maintain a considerable distance between us. The fact that these distances vary from culture to culture can produce some problems in personal interaction:

Table 15.3 Interpersonal distances	
Intimate	up to about eighteen inches
Personal	up to about four feet
Social	up to about twelve feet
Public	up to about eighteen feet

Source: Hall, 1968

Watson and Graves (1966) showed that what is considered to be a comfortable speaking distance in some Middle Eastern cultures, for example, is considered to be a very intimate distance in America. People from Middle Eastern cultures, and people from South American ones, also were more likely to stand face-to-face, and to touch the person that they were speaking to.

Touch is a powerful non-verbal signal, and one which is often perceived as being deeply meaningful. Jourard (1966) performed a study in which college students described which parts of the body could be touched by various groups of people. Other-sex friends were allowed the most body contact, but in general it was only considered acceptable for family members or same-sex friends to touch the hands or sometimes the shoulders of the other person. Henley (1977) showed how touch is often used as a signal of power and status: higher-status individuals, such as senior managers, would often place an arm across the shoulders of a lower-status employee, to signal approval or inclusiveness; but lower-status employees never initiated touch contacts.

Paralanguage

Paralanguage is all about the way that we say things. We do not just deliver words in a flat monotone – we bring in tones of voice, vocal 'fillers' like 'er' or 'um', and we vary the speed with which we speak. These are all non-verbal signals which accompany speech, and which help us to clarify what we mean, or to convey additional information to other people. Davitz and Davitz (1959) showed that we have eight clearly distinguishable patterns of voice, which indicate to people the different moods that we are in. The moods to which they correspond are: affection, anger, boredom, cheerfulness, impatience, joy, sadness and satisfaction.

The tone of voice that we use can also be a powerful non-verbal signal about how competent or authoritative we are. Apple, Streeter and Krauss

(1979) showed that speaking with a high-pitched voice is often seen as reducing the credibility of what we are saying. Media advisers to Margaret Thatcher put this finding to work when she gained power as Prime Minister of Britain in 1979. Studies of her interview style showed that she had consciously deepened her voice and slowed down her rate of speech, as a strategy for enhancing media credibility.

The use of vocal 'fillers' in conversation, such as 'er' and 'um', also makes a difference to how what we are saying is perceived. Kasl and Mahl (1965) showed that speech errors increase dramatically when we are nervous or uncertain of what we are saying, and they are often picked up by the other person as a non-verbal signal. Similarly, Erikson *et al.* (1978) set up a study of how people judge what is being said in a court setting, and showed that the use of phrases like 'you know', 'kind of' and 'I guess' seriously reduces the credibility of what the person has to say.

Dress

Dress has always been acknowledged as a powerful medium of communication. Much modern fashion in Western societies is concerned with projecting specific images, which make statements about what type of person the wearer is (Figure 15.3). Comprehension and interpretation of image in consumer societies is highly sophisticated – we are all trained in it from the moment we become aware of advertisements, after all!

But dress is also used for other purposes. The uniform of a nurse or a security guard, for instance, makes clear statements about what that person does, and what social role they are playing. Religious figures often wear distinctive dress, and sometimes both religious and social beliefs are

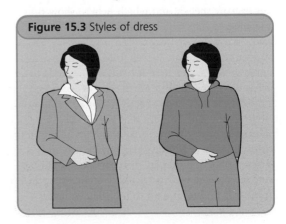

Figure 15.3 Styles of dress

indicated by costume – for example, the wearing of the chador by women in some Muslim countries makes a statement about the role of women in those societies, as well as about religious belief.

Functions of non-verbal cues

Ekman and Friesen (1969) classified the functions of non-verbal signals into five categories: emblems, illustrators, affect displays, regulators and adaptors. Each of these categories reflects a differing function: we may at times use the same signals, but for quite a different purpose.

Emblems
Emblems are signals which have a distinct and well-defined meaning, and which stand for a specific idea or concept. A policeman's uniform or a technician's coat makes clear statements about social role and areas of responsibility. Specific gestures, like putting a finger to the lips to signal for quiet, also fall into this category. There are less obvious forms of emblem too: adopting a particular style of dress (for example dressing as a 'punk') may indicate a social role just as much as a uniform does. Since people respond to these cues unconsciously, they often exert a considerable influence on the nature of our social interactions with other people. Many people, for instance, like to adopt a fairly formal style of dress if they are in a position of responsibility, because they feel (consciously or unconsciously) that it helps to promote a professional, task-oriented approach to what is going on.

Illustrators
Illustrators are non-verbal actions which accompany speech, and which help to show the meaning or intention underlying what is being said. So a wry facial expression may serve as an illustrator to indicate a 'well, I do not necessarily agree with this but here it is anyway' attitude to what is being said; or a warm tone of voice may underline a statement of approval or an expression of sympathy. The amount that people use illustrators varies both from culture to culture, and from individual to individual; but Ekman and Friesen observed that, in everyday speech, illustrators seem to be used particularly often when the speaker is finding it hard to put their thoughts into words.

Affect displays
Affect displays reveal emotional states, although the term is used very loosely to include attitudes – 'states of mind' – as well. They can involve many different cues: body posture to signal depression, resignation or confidence; tone of voice to indicate irritation or friendliness; a new style of dress to indicate a fresh approach; agitating fingers or feet to indicate nervousness or impatience. Many affect displays are unconscious, particularly when they concern the less obvious parts of the body. Part of the training that the police receive in interviewing techniques, for example, includes becoming aware of the small movements of the feet and legs. Although people can control facial expressions or posture, they are often unaware of tapping a foot rapidly, or shifting the feet about.

Regulators
Regulators are non-verbal signals which are used to help social interactions along. Eye-contact, as we have seen, is a powerful regulator of conversation: we use it to signal when we are listening, to check that a listener has understood or is still listening; and to 'hand over' when it is the other person's turn to speak. This applies to the teaching situation just as much as it does in other contexts: Beattie (1984) described a study of eye-contact in tutorials, showing in particular how skilled many students become at averting their gaze as the lecturer is coming to the end of an utterance, so that they can avoid catching the lecturer's eye and having to speak next!

Adaptors
Adaptors are non-verbal signals which are usually involuntary, personal behaviours, which we resort to at times of uncertainty. These might include biting your nails, fiddling with a ring or tapping your fingers. Essentially, adaptors are used to help someone to cope in a given situation. Many lecturers and teachers, for instance, develop ritualised adaptors, like clearing the throat in a certain way before speaking. This minor ritual helps them to cope with the teaching situation. Ekman suggested that many of these idiosyncratic behaviours are learned from childhood, and carry over into adult life without our really being aware of them.

As you will probably have noticed, any given type of non-verbal cue can serve several different functions. The most powerful ones, like tone of voice, eye-contact or facial expression, can serve as illustrators, affect displays or regulators, and we may use them interchangeably. Any social situation involves innumerable complex meanings, and non-verbal signals may be communicating messages on a number of different levels simultaneously.

The importance of non-verbal communication

Effective non-verbal communication is a skill, and like other skills, it becomes almost unconscious once we have mastered it (we will be looking at skill learning in Chapter 18). In fact, we tend to notice non-verbal communication only when it is wrong, or interrupted in some way. For example, people who are highly insecure or anxious sometimes develop a habit of avoiding eye-contact with other people – they find it threatening. Yet eye-contact is a normal part of everyday interaction, and if you are talking with someone who avoids it, you may feel uneasy yourself.

Often, in such cases, other people are unaware of just what it is that is wrong: all they know is that the person is a bit 'strange', and that they do not feel comfortable talking with them. But that is usually enough to leave that person even more lonely and isolated than before. Argyle (1981) argued that such people are helped considerably by **social skills training**, which teaches them the basics of non-verbal communication in normal social interaction, so that their contact with other people is more positive.

We place a great reliance on non-verbal communication, and if the non-verbal content of a message is not congruent with its verbal content, as a general rule we tend to ignore the verbal content and believe the non-verbal message. Argyle, Alkema and Gilmour (1971) asked actors to give a verbal message to research participants, while at the same time using a non-verbal style that contradicted it. For instance, if the words that the actor was saying were hostile or aggressive, the manner in which they said it might be friendly; or the other way round. They found that people were four times as likely to remember the non-verbal message than the words that were actually being said.

This is probably realistic. It is easy to tell lies using words, but it is much more difficult to lie non-verbally. Just think of how you feel when you have to talk to someone you do not like.

Automatically your muscles will stiffen up – you will not be as relaxed as you are when you are with your friends. You will also find it harder to smile; and the smile that you do manage can be shown using micro-photography to involve different muscles from a genuine smile. It is our non-verbal communication which usually give us away, not what we say.

Non-verbal episodes

As a general rule, the psychological study of non-verbal communication has been concerned with specific acts and actions, and the social functions which they might serve. But analysing social inter-action in terms of small acts may not be all that helpful to understanding social interaction in the long run. Harré, in 1979, pointed out that in everyday life, social experience takes the form of whole, meaningful **episodes**, not isolated acts or actions.

We need to look at the whole context, including the people concerned, the ways in which they express themselves, the background to what is going on, the setting in which events are taking place, and so on. So, for instance, instead of just looking at individual utterances in conversations, Harré suggests that we should look at whole conversations in terms of their social meaning – for the participants, and for other people too. Studying a single conversation out of context, Harré argued, is not likely to tell us very much.

Ritual

One area of non-verbal communication which would require Harré's **ethogenic approach** – looking at episodes and accounts to make sense of what is going on – is the area of ritual. Ritual is a deeply meaningful form of communication in any human society; but it is about complete episodes, not individual acts or actions. And rituals can only really be understood when we look at the social meaning of what is going on.

So, for example, although the form of the ritual varies from one culture to another, every human society has rituals to deal with death and bereavement. These rituals play an important part in structuring the bereaved person's experience, and giving them a way of expressing their grief in a familiar, yet special, setting. By prescribing what should happen and when, the rituals create a higher-order 'script' for the event. This script draws on any number of different verbal and non-verbal signals to make up a meaningful whole. A ritual is a complete episode of experience, in Harré's terms, and provides a framework within which that experience can be understood, with the minimal amount of explanation.

Ritual serves an important function in social life, because it gives us a clear structure within which interaction takes place. But ritual carries higher-order meanings too, and the nature of the ritual can tell us volumes about social organisation and power structures. The rituals associated with a formal examination, for instance, convey messages of distrust and suspicion. This distrust extends both to those conducting the examination (whose behaviour is rigidly prescribed by the regulations) and to the students taking the exams. For the most part, we perceive these messages unconsciously, but this does not mean that they are less powerful – in fact, unconscious messages of this kind can often be even more influential than messages of which we are consciously aware.

Everyday rituals

Berne (1973) identified a number of everyday rituals which people carry out. For example, a conversation involves verbal exchanges between two people. The formal rituals of religious ceremonies often also involve utterances and responses, although we would not describe these as conversations in any ordinary sense. Yet many of our everyday conversations are almost as ritualised. Berne pointed out that many conversations in everyday life actually have a ritual function, rather than a straightforward communicative one: they serve to affirm participation in social life, rather than to communicate information.

For example, think of the 'How are you?' conversations which you have with acquaintances that you meet when you are out shopping, or at the bus stop. There is a definite pattern to the enquiries and replies, and there is also a prescribed context – you are supposed to respond in a particular way. Although these may seem to be simply examples of brief conversations, they really are not anything to do with exchanging information. Instead, they are all about reaffirming the social relationship.

Environmental messages

Take a fresh look at the layout of an average class-room or lecture theatre. In a typical classroom, the teacher – one person – has about one-third of the space, while the students sit close together in the remaining two-thirds. In a lecture theatre, the lecturer has a wide open area, while the students sit closely packed in tiers. In both locations the teacher is the one who has freedom to move about, whereas the students are expected to stay in one place. The room is arranged in rows, and the students sit side by side, and are more or less forced to face the teacher (a signal of attention). These are powerful non-verbal signals, which are saying things directly about the power relationship between teachers and students.

One important message which they convey is that communication should be between teacher and student, and not between the students themselves. When we are talking to someone in everyday life – particularly if it is an intense or serious conversation – we tend to face the person that we are talking to, so that we can make eye-contact with them and signal that we are paying attention. In a typical classroom, eye-contact between students is made difficult by the physical layout, but eye-contact between teacher and student is made easy. Power and authority are also reflected in the relative amount of space which each person has. These environmental signals contribute directly to controlling the social interaction which goes on. That is why a teacher who is interested in group work will often re-arrange the layout of the room: arranging chairs in small circles helps people to talk to one another more freely, and tends to lead to a better discussion.

Non-verbal messages, then, are not just transmitted by specific cues. There are non-verbal messages in the use of ritual or regularity, or the lack of it; in the proportion of positive to non-positive interactions within a group or pair of people; in the provision or lack of information in a working setting; in the physical layout of a room or building; and in many other aspects of experience. In fact, almost anything can, and does, serve as a non-verbal signal in social interaction! Symbolism is a crucially important part of everyday living. We can see from this that non-verbal communication operates on a number of levels, ranging from specific signals to more general messages about social assumptions. It is a major factor in how we perceive other people, and how we respond to them.

Person perception

Perceiving other people is a complex process, involving our awareness of non-verbal signals, and also requiring us to draw on a broad range of implicit and explicit social knowledge. As we try to understand what any given person is like, we apply different ideas and assumptions about people in general, as well as cues about particular individuals. All of these help us to inform our ideas, and contribute to forming our impressions of that person. In this section, we will look at some of the psychological research which has been conducted in an attempt to tease out some of the implicit knowledge and principles that we use to form our impressions of others.

Implicit personality theory

Asch (1946) began an investigation of this area by showing that people will often develop highly complex ideas about other people simply by extrapolating from one or two items of information. This is because that information taps into our implicit theories about personality. We tend to believe, for example, that personality traits cluster together, so if we find someone who has one trait, we often assume that they will have a number of other personality traits too.

Central and peripheral traits

Some traits are more important than others in affecting how we perceive other people. In one of Asch's studies, research participants were provided with lists of adjectives, six of which were always the same: *intelligent, skilful, industrious, determined, practical* and *cautious*. A seventh adjective, however (which was always placed in the middle of the list), varied. It might be *warm, cold, polite* or *blunt*.

Asch gave these descriptions to four groups of research participants and asked them to describe the person, and to predict how that person would be likely to behave in certain situations. The two groups who received 'polite' and 'blunt' in their descriptions tended to make very similar judgements about the person who was being described – those characteristics seemed to be peripheral to the impression which was being formed. But the groups who received the terms 'warm' or 'cold' had completely different perceptions of the individual. The personality traits

of being 'warm' or 'cold', it appears, are central to our perception of other people. In a similar study, Kelley (1950) found that students who expected a visiting lecturer to be 'warm' were more likely to stay behind to talk than those who expected the lecturer to be 'cold'.

It seems, then, that some traits carry more weight than others. Maier (1955) showed that these central traits do not actually have to be personality descriptions. For example, when someone was described as being either a manager of a small business or as working for a trade union, people's assessments of what they were like and how they would be likely to act were both strongly affected. The question of whether a trait is peripheral or central seems to have everything to do with what our implicit personality theories are like.

Dimensions of traits

Using the technique known as **meta-analysis**, Rosenberg, Nelson and Vivekanathan (1968) showed that implicit personality theories seem to have two main dimensions. One of these, they argued, is concerned with mental ability, while the other is concerned with sociability. Each of these dimensions has evaluative weightings: 'good' examples of the intellectual dimension might include traits like persistent or skilful, for instance; while 'bad' ones might include cunning or naïve. Similarly, 'good' examples of the social dimension might include, say, helpful or sociable, while 'bad' ones might be, say, irritable or unsociable. Rosenberg, Nelson and Vivekanathan showed that these two dimensions could provide a key to understanding other personality traits. So, for example, someone who is seen as good-natured would also be seen as humorous, happy and popular, as these are traits which cluster in the 'good', social area of the scale.

Stereotyping

Stereotyping is another factor in how we form impressions of people. Stereotyping involves classifying people according to some superficial characteristic, like skin colour or sexual orientation. So, although it is related, it is not quite the same as implicit personality theory, mainly because it has a different starting point. Implicit personality theory begins from some information about that person and goes on from there, whereas stereotyping involves fitting the person into a category regardless of what they are actually like as an individual.

Karlins, Coffman and Walters (1969) studied stereotypes held by students, basing their study on an earlier one, conducted in the 1930s. They found that the stereotyping of different ethnic groups seemed to have changed quite a bit, or at least faded (see Table 15.4), although it is always possible that this could have resulted more from the students being more sensitive to the social unacceptability of stereotyping, than from changes in their views. But certainly, there have been changes in how many ethnic groups are perceived by society during that time, and it seems likely that the views of students would have changed too.

Gahagan (1984) asked research participants to read a passage about a woman, and tested them a week later to see how much they recalled. The research participants were then given some additional information about the woman. One group received 'neutral' information, the second group was told about a heterosexual relationship she had had in the past and the third group was told that she had had a homosexual relationship in the past. Gahagan showed that, in the third group, the research participants' stereotypes of lesbians directly affected their recall of the material. For example, unlike the other two groups, they did not recall that she had dated boys during adolescence, although that had been in the material which they had read.

While ethnic and gender stereotyping are powerful social mechanisms, almost any characteristic can engender some kind of stereotyping. Harari and McDavid (1973) showed that teachers stereotyped children according to their first names: they would expect different things from a 'Karen' or a 'David' than from an 'Adele' or a 'Hubert'. These stereotypes were also influential in their marking – the teachers in the

sample tended to give students with 'positive' names higher marks than the others. When we put this together with Rosenthal's work on the self-fulfilling prophecy, we can see just how powerful a process stereotyping can be.

The self-fulfilling prophecy

Rosenthal and Jacobsen (1968) investigated the **self-fulfilling prophecy**. They went to a school in a middle-sized American city, and gave the children there an IQ test as well as collecting information about their school achievement. Nothing was explained to the children, but the teachers were told that the researchers were testing out a new form of IQ test designed to identify children who were late developers, and who would be expected to make academic gains in their later school years even if they had not done very well before. The researchers selected a group of children randomly, and made sure that their teachers 'accidentally' overheard a conversation in which these children were identified as ones who had done well on the new test.

When they returned a year later, they found that the children they had selected had shown dramatic improvements in their school work, and had also improved their IQ scores. This applied whatever the age of the child, but initially it was with the younger ones that the changes were most dramatic (although in an even later follow-up the older ones' improvements seemed to be more lasting). It seemed that the teachers had changed their whole attitude to these children, so the children received more encouragement in their school work and had more friendly interactions with the teachers. Often, the difference was very subtle, showing itself only in tones of voice or the speed of noticing what the child was saying.

This study showed how dramatically our expectations can influence what we see and how we behave. It also highlighted the dangers of **labelling**, or stereotyping children. Many teachers working in schools in deprived areas tend to have low expectations about the abilities of their children – while still wishing their pupils well, they are acutely conscious of the problems which such children face, and so do not expect them to achieve very much. What Rosenthal demonstrated is that those expectations in themselves can become self-fulfilling prophecies and affect children's educational chances.

Table 15.4 Changes in student stereotypes

	% agreeing with descriptions	
Year	1933	1969
Germans 'solid'	44	9
Italians 'musical'	32	9
Black people 'superstitious'	84	13

Source: Karlins, Coffman and Walters, 1969

Personal constructs

Shared theories about personality seem to be relatively common in society – the idea that fat people are jolly, for instance – and these tie in with the theory of **social representations** which we will be looking at later in this chapter. But people also develop their own ideas about other people from their own experience. In Chapter 7, we looked at **personal construct theory** (Kelly, 1955), which shows how people form their own, personal theories about people on the basis of their own experiences, and how the constructs which one person uses to make sense out of their world may be entirely different from the constructs which the next person uses. We use personal constructs to make sense of other people too, so they are an important aspect of how we form impressions of others.

Primacy effects

The order in which we receive information can make a considerable impact on how we perceive someone. In Chapter 3, we saw how **primacy effects** can influence person perception, in Luchins's (1959) study of how a character, 'Jim', was perceived, when he was described as acting in both an introverted and an extroverted way. People's assessments of Jim's personality and likely behaviour depended on which description came first.

Similarly, Asch (1946), gave research participants a list of six adjectives, in the order: *intelligent, industrious, impulsive, critical, stubborn, envious*. A second group was given the same list, but with the first three traits at the end. They were asked to think about the person being described by the six adjectives, and to tick the ones in a further list that would also fit the person. Asch found that the order of presentation determined how favourably the target was perceived: those with the favourable description first ticked off more positive adjectives than those with the negative ones first. For instance, 90% of the first group ticked 'generous' on the list, as opposed to only 10 % of the second group.

These effects may extend to real-life situations as well. Most of us are aware of the importance of creating a favourable first impression when we are going for an important interview: we will take pains to dress ourselves neatly, for instance. And it is not just appearance: in a mock courtroom study, Pennington (1982) showed that research participants' verdicts on a rape trial were strongly affected by whether the prosecution's evidence was given before the evidence for the defence, or not. So we can see that primacy effects can be quite powerful in affecting how we perceive other people.

Halo effects

Another effect which is similar to the primacy effect in terms of the way that it operates is the **halo effect**. We often see people as being better than they really are because they are associated with positive experiences, events or people for us, or because we know that they have acted positively in the past. In such cases, we judge what they do in a better light – we can find ourselves excusing or overlooking shortcomings that we would think important in someone else, or we might assess something that they do as being of higher quality than the same standard of work by someone else.

Person perception, then, draws on our already-existing knowledge and ideas. But it seems to have surprisingly little to do with the actual information about the person that we are receiving – sometimes even to the extent that we will completely ignore the real characteristics of the person that we are perceiving. Instead, we draw on stored social knowledge and apply it as soon as we think it may be relevant. As a result, psychologists have also been concerned with exploring the different forms that this stored social knowledge can take, and we will now go on to look at some of this research.

Schemata and scripts

One of the most important ways that we store information is as guidance for appropriate action. We **organise** our knowledge into forms which will allow us to apply it when we are faced with unfamiliar situations that we have not met before. To do so, we need to be able to make generalisations, and we also need to have stored the information in a form which includes possibilities and strategies for action, as well as just factual knowledge or memories of experience. Schemata and scripts are examples of this type of storage.

Schemata

The concept of the **schema** is one which recurs in a number of psychological fields: in cognitive psychology (see, for example, the description of Neisser's theory of perception in Chapter 2); in developmental psychology (such as the Piagetian model which we will be looking at in Chapter 19); and also in social psychology. A schema is usually thought of as a cognitive framework which we build up through experience, and use to guide and direct our actions. ('Schemata' is the technical plural of the word, although recently, some people use the term 'schemas' instead. But whichever they are called, they can have quite a dramatic effect on our social perception.)

Since our expectations guide our behaviour, we can often set up self-fulfilling cycles of behaviour which end up simply confirming what we believe. For example, if we hold a view of somebody as being 'arrogant', or 'stuck up', then we are likely to pick out those aspects of their behaviour which can be interpreted that way, and to ignore completely any signs that they may not be like that.

Sagar and Schofield (1980) set up an experiment in which black boys and white boys from four different schools were told stories and shown pictures of different types of actions, which could be interpreted as either aggressive or non-aggressive. For instance, one event was of one student bumping into another in the corridor; and another described a student poking another one in class. The people in the pictures were either black or white. After they heard the descriptions the schoolboys were asked to rate the behaviour by choosing appropriate adjectives to describe it.

The ambiguous behaviour was interpreted (by both black and white schoolboys) as being far more threatening from black students than it was from whites, despite the fact that the descriptions had been exactly the same in every other respect. This shows how strongly expectations which we hold – which would be generated by our schemata – can affect our social judgements. And, of course, if we interpret an act as aggressive, we are far more likely to react in an aggressive manner than if we see it as accidental. This in turn makes the other person more likely to respond irritably, and so we get a self-fulfilling cycle.

Social scripts

Social scripts are another type of schema. Schank and Abelson (1977) described how much of our social understanding draws on social scripts, which we understand well, and which contain information about relevant knowledge as well as appropriate plans and sequences of actions. Social scripts can also exert considerable influence over what we remember – to the extent that we may remember different types of information when we are applying different scripts to the same event.

Zadny and Gerard (1974) performed an experiment in which research participants watched a videotape of two students wandering round a flat and discussing minor drug and theft offences. One group of research participants was told that the students were planning to burgle the flat; a second group was told that they were looking for drugs; and a third group was told that they were waiting for a friend. When the research participants were asked what they remembered later, they remembered information which was relevant to the script that they were applying. So, for instance, those who thought the students were burglars remembered vulnerable items in the flat, such as credit cards, and also more parts of the conversation which related to theft, than those applying different scripts.

Fiske and Linville (1980) argued that the concept of the schema is useful to human thinking because it allows us to simplify our social world. By providing us with a way of drawing together a vast range of information, and extracting general rules for directing action from it, the schema allows us to deal with many more different situations than would be possible if we were to treat each situation separately. Moreover, since the schema itself is continually being modified and adjusted as our social experience grows, it helps us to adapt our behaviour to complex and changing social demands.

Types of schema

Some schemata are very general, while others are much more specific. We have already seen how Schank and Abelson (1977) developed the idea of scripts, which are a special kind of schema, concerned with the immediate directing of action: they are sometimes referred to as **event schemata**. For example: if we go into a restaurant we already know roughly what to expect and what sequence it should happen in: we know the 'script', as it were. If the script were to be broken – if, say, the waiter brought coffee at the beginning of the meal – we would find it very disorientating. In reality, of course, scripts are almost never broken, and so social interaction is able to proceed smoothly on the basis of the shared understanding of the script that all the participants have.

Baron and Byrne (1984) identified some other types of schemata which are particularly common in social interaction (see Table 15.5). **Role schemata** are the frameworks we use when we are dealing with others in particular, pre-specified social relationships. So, for instance, some role schemata might include how we think about the likely behaviour and personality of a gardener, or of a teacher. Role schemata also allow us to draw out general principles concerning broad social groups, or categories of people in society. Hamilton (1981) described them as the basic cognitive processes which underlie stereotypes and prejudice, although they can also be much more open than that. Research into implicit personality theory also often taps into our underlying role schemata.

Another type of schema described by Baron and Byrne is the **person schema**. As we get to know somebody, we develop an increasingly clear idea about them, which allows us to make predictions, and which we use to guide our behaviour towards them. If you are going to buy someone a birthday present, you need to draw on the person schema you have of that individual,

and use it to predict (or at least make a reasonable guess at) what they are likely to appreciate. Usually, the more we interact with people, the more sophisticated our understanding of them becomes. The schema which we have of them accumulates more information over time – assuming that we are open to receive it, of course!

Person schemata can be more general too: if we decide, for instance, that someone is 'a typical career woman', then the person schema which we develop about them will focus on the particular traits which we believe such people are likely to have, and we may not actually notice aspects of their behaviour which are different. A person schema, then, may concern itself with the uniqueness of a particular individual, or it may involve a limited form of stereotyping – generalising about specific traits or characteristics of that person.

A fourth group of schemata relate to ourselves: our **self-schemata**. Some people experience themselves as having a stable self-concept, whereas others find it more elusive to identify; but all of us infer what we are like from our observations of own behaviour. From this, we can build up a range of self-schemata which we use to predict what we are likely to do. For example, the process of choosing a holiday involves predicting what sort of things we are likely to enjoy: some people like to have very active holidays, whereas others like the type of holiday in which they lie about in the sun all day. We are usually fairly good at predicting which kind we ourselves will like – although we can sometimes surprise ourselves too!

The idea of the schema has been criticised on the ground that it is too vague, and does not provide clear predictions. But Fiske and Taylor (1983) pointed out that the schema is a concept, not a full theory in itself. They argued that, in order to be useful, the concept of schema needs to be developed as part of a wider theoretical understanding of social processes. For example, they argue, the schema is to do with the knowledge that someone holds, whereas attributions are concerned with how people go about applying that knowledge. In this way, the idea of the schema and the idea of attribution can complement, rather than compete with, each other. We will go on to look at attributions, and how they can help us to understand social interaction.

Table 15.5 Types of schema

Event schemata	Concerned with the appropriate sequences of actions during a particular event or type of event.
Role schemata	Concerned with the appropriate behaviours and activities relevant to playing a particular social role.
Person schemata	Concerned with knowledge and predictions about a particular individual or group of people.
Self-schemata	Concerned with our knowledge and appraisals about our own selves.

Source: Baron and Byrne, 1984

Attribution

In 1958, Fritz Heider proposed that we are always striving to understand our social worlds, and that we do this by forming ideas and theories about what is going on. Some of the most important of these ideas and theories concern the causes which we attribute to actions or events: why did something happen, or why did someone act in a certain way? Heider (1958) proposed that there are five major **levels of responsibility**, which are all about how much the person actually intended the outcome to happen. These are described in Table 15.6. Together they make up different types of **attributions** or causal beliefs.

Correspondent inference theory

Correspondent inference theory is one of several forms of attribution theory. It explores the different factors which contribute to the inferences which we make about social responsibility. Whether we see someone as responsible for their actions or not depends on a number of factors, including whether we think they are capable or not, and how important the situation is to what they are doing.

Jones and Davis (1965) argued that attributing

Table 15.6 Heider's five levels of responsibility

Level 1	*Global association*	The individual is merely associated with the outcome.
Level 2	*Causality*	The person caused the outcome, but accidentally and in such a way that it could not have been foreseen.
Level 3	*Foreseeability*	The individual causes the action accidentally, but it could have been foreseen that such an accident could occur.
Level 4	*Intentionality*	The action was caused deliberately, but without justification.
Level 5	*Justification*	The outcome was caused intentionally, and with justification.

Source: Heider, 1958

intention is the first stage in working out reasons for why something happens. Once an act has been judged to be deliberate, we then look for the personal trait or characteristic which produced that person's intention – why would they want to do such a thing? By doing this, we are making what Jones and Davis called **correspondent inferences** – we are inferring personality, or disposition, which corresponds directly to the person's behaviour.

Stability, intentionality and disposition

Correspondent inference theory rests on three concepts, which were originally developed by Heider, in 1944. The first of these is our human tendency to look for **stable causes** for why things happen. Heider argued that our wish to make sense out of what is going on in the world means that we prefer stable, as opposed to unstable, causes for things. A stable cause is one which is likely to happen again, so this helps us to predict what is likely to occur next time. Unstable causes, by definition, do not give us any guidance for the future.

The second concept is concerned with **intentionality**. Heider stressed that it is important for us to be able to distinguish between intentional and unintentional behaviour, because otherwise we are unable to judge whether someone can be held responsible for their actions. We cannot interpret social action unless we know (or think we know) whether someone acted deliberately or not.

The third major concept contributing to correspondent inference theory is the distinction between dispositional and situational attributions. A **dispositional attribution** occurs when we conclude that someone in themselves is responsible for something happening – because of their abilities, their intentions or the efforts that they have made. But we make a **situational attribution** if we conclude that it was the situation, or external circumstances, which caused the person to act that way.

Correspondent inference

Linking these three concepts, Jones and Davis (1965) proposed that we have a powerful inclination to make dispositional attributions as opposed to situational ones. When we are attributing intentions, we make inferences about the person's knowledge of the likely outcome of what they were doing, and about their ability to undertake the action. By and large, we tend to assume that they have acted deliberately rather than accidentally, unless we have some reason to judge the person as being incapable – for example, because they are too young, or mentally inadequate. Once we have judged an act to be intentional, we look for a personal trait or characteristic which could have produced that intention. This is the **correspondent inference** for which the theory has been named.

The idea that attributing intentionality leads automatically to dispositional attributions was challenged by Eiser (1983), who pointed out that dispositions and intentions are not necessarily the same thing. An attribution of carelessness, for example, is a dispositional explanation, but making that attribution about a breakage does not imply that the person did it intentionally. Eiser argued that correspondent inference theory could therefore be applied only in circumstances which involved some element of choice, rather than with occurrences which were accidental or unintended (Eiser, 1983).

There is some evidence that the tendency to make dispositional attributions rather than situational ones can be changed with experience. Guimond and Palmer (1990) compared students' explanations of poverty and unemployment as they proceeded through their courses. At the beginning of the first academic year, there were no differences between social science, commerce and engineering students. However, by the end of the first year, significant differences began to appear, with social science students blaming the system significantly more than the others did.

In 1976, Jones and McGillis produced a modified version of correspondent inference theory, which took into account findings about how social factors could influence whether a dispositional attribution was made or not. For example, in a study by Jones and Harris (1967) American students were asked to listen to a short written speech indicating support for Fidel Castro, and to state what they believed the speaker's true attitude was. Even when told that the speaker had been allocated the topic, with no choice, roughly 45% of the research participants still rated the speakers as believing what they had said. This conformed to the original version of correspondent inference theory. But when the research participants were asked to judge a more

conventional speech, the effect was much smaller. It was clear that social norms were influencing the judgement which was being made.

Non-common effects, personalism and hedonic relevance

Correspondent inference theory identifies three major factors which affect whether we are likely to make a dispositional attribution or not. One of these is known as the **principle of non-common effects**. This is about the range of consequences which occur as a result of the action. Jones and Davis (1965) showed that if we do something which has a wide range of consequences (for example failing an examination on which our whole future depends) then people are more likely to think of situational factors as the reason than if the outcome is more limited, and has only a narrow range of consequences. So we are likely to identify dispositional causes for events which have limited outcomes.

How the act affects us is also something which influences our attributions. One factor in this is the degree of **personalism**. Personalism concerns whether an outcome deliberately affects the perceiver (the person who is making the attribution) or not. You are more likely to judge an act as intentional, and therefore dispositional, if it affects you personally. If someone breaks someone else's pen, then you are more likely to see it as an accident than if someone breaks your own pen, leaving you with nothing to write with.

Another way that an act can affect the perceiver is to do with its **hedonic relevance**. Hedonic relevance relates to whether the outcome of the act has pleasant or unpleasant consequences for the perceiver: if it has positive or negative outcomes (as opposed to neutral ones) then correspondent inferences are more likely – in other words, the action is more likely to be judged as deliberate. Hedonic relevance and personalism are independent of each other: for example, a reduction in the rate of income tax might have high hedonic relevance for someone who is working, but low personalism.

The fundamental attribution error

Perhaps one of the most well-known implications of correspondent inference theory, however, is the **fundamental attribution error**. This is our tendency to perceive our own actions as arising from situational factors while at the same time judging other people's actions as arising from dispositional causes. In 1973, Nisbett *et al.* asked male students to write a paragraph saying why they liked their girlfriends, and also why they had chosen their particular subject of study. They were then asked to write an equivalent paragraph about their best friend. The researchers found that the students tended to make situational attributions about their own course of study and girlfriends (such as referring to the job opportunities offered by their course of study); but dispositional attributions about their friends (for example 'He likes maths').

The fundamental attribution error has been subject to a considerable amount of investigation. Ross, Amabile and Steinmetz (1977) set up a quiz game, in which research participants were randomly given the role of questioner or contestant. Although both observers and participants knew that the roles had been randomly assigned, they nonetheless rated the questioner as being more knowledgeable than the contestant was, ignoring situational variables such as the fact that the questioner had free choice of subject, and so could choose questions from their own knowledge, whereas the contestant had no such choice.

The attribution error has been demonstrated in real-life situations, as well as in laboratory studies. For example, in a series of interview studies with 34 scientists, Gilbert and Mulkay found that the scientists explained their own theories by referring to direct physical evidence (in other words, situational factors), but explained the views of their opponents in terms of personality characteristics, or other such dispositional factors (Gilbert and Mulkay, 1984).

It has been suggested that the fundamental attribution error might arise simply because we take a different perspective on the situation when we are judging our own behaviour from that taken when we are looking at other people's. Storms (1973) videotaped a series of two-person conversations, taping each side of the conversation separately. Then the research participants who had taken part in the conversations were each shown what the other person had seen. Storms found that this produced a change in the attributions that they made. When people saw their own behaviour from the viewpoint of an observer, they produced more dispositional attributions; and when they saw the conversation from the other person's side, they produced more situational attributions for the other person's behaviour.

Although later studies of this phenomenon were less clear in their results, it does seem as though manipulating the focus of people's visual awareness can influence the attributions which they make, to some extent. But that does not necessarily mean that it is the viewpoint which causes the attribution error. It could be that asking research participants to look at things from both sides communicates to them that they need to try to be fair, and it may be this attempt to judge both sides equally which affects the attributions research participants make.

It has also been suggested that the fundamental attribution error may be culturally specific. In an attributional study undertaken with Hindu children and white American children of the same ages, Miller (1984) found that the Hindu children made fewer dispositional and more situational attributions than the American children did. Moreover, this difference increased systematically with age: while there was a slight difference with children of eight years old, the difference was more apparent with children who were eleven, and even more so with fifteen-year-olds. Miller proposed that causal attributions do not simply depend on the individual's personal history, but also result from socialisation in a particular culture. However, Lalljee (1991) argued that there were significant methodological flaws in the studies, in particular concerning whether the people that the children were asked to make attributions about were known to them personally or not. The Hindu children may have been trying particularly hard to be fair to the people that they did not know.

Guimond, Bégin and Palmer (1989) found that the attribution error was reversed in a study which compared the attributions about poverty made by social science students and by poor and unemployed people of the same age. Unemployed people tended to make dispositional attributions where the students made situational ones. Guimond and Palmer (1990) argued that this study shows how the types of attributions we make are directly relevant to the ways that our social group defines our reality, and linked this with the study of **social representations**, which we will be looking at later in this chapter.

The self-serving bias

A slightly different aspect of the way we make attributions, which is related to the fundamental attribution error but not quite the same thing, is known as the **self-serving bias**. This is to do with the way that we tend to make attributions which will help us to see ourselves in a favourable way, particularly when we are trying to explain why we have succeeded or failed at something. Miller and Ross (1975) described how several attribution studies have shown that we tend to attribute succes to dispositional causes, and failure to situational ones: 'I passed my biology exam because I'm good at biology, but I failed French because my Aunt Millie visited us that week and I did not get any time to revise'.

There have been several explanations for the self-serving bias. One possible explanation is that we like to present a favourable impression to others – to 'save face'. If we explain failure as being something that we could not help, it will mean that we can avoid looking stupid, or incapable; and explaining success as coming from our own personal qualities also makes us look good. Jones and Berglas (1978) argued that alcoholics may drink too much partly in order to avoid making personal attributions for failure – by attributing their poor performance to alcohol, they avoid having to attribute it to lack of ability. They described this as a **self-handicapping strategy**, which provides the person with a ready-made excuse for potential failure.

Another explanation is the idea that the self-serving bias allows us to protect our self-esteem. McFarland and Ross (1982) gave research participants false feedback about how well they had done at a fairly difficult task, and asked them to explain why they had done as well or badly as they had. They found that people might make either dispositional or situational attributions about their performance, but that those who attributed failure to lack of ability also tended to have very low levels of self-esteem. But, of course, this study shows only that self-esteem and the type of attribution we make might be correlated – it does not show that we change our attributions in order to protect our self-esteem.

Attributional dimensions

Correspondent inference theory identified a number of ways that attributions could vary. One of the first distinctions, as we have seen, was between internal or dispositional attributions, and external, situational ones. This distinction also led

to other ideas. In 1966, Rotter proposed that there are consistent and distinctive patterns in attributional style, and that people can be broadly classified into internal and external attributors in terms of the attributions which they generally make. This led to the concept of **locus of control**, which we looked at in Chapter 13, and which became very useful in therapeutic practice. Gradually, however, it became clear that internal attributions were not always controllable, and that controllability should be seen as a separate dimension. As research proceeded, additional dimensions emerged.

In 1976, Weiner, Nierenberg and Goldstein proposed that there was a need for an additional dimension of causality, which would distinguish between causes which were temporary and fluctuating (such as mood or weather) and causes which were stable and enduring (such as aptitude or ability). Mikulincer (1988) investigated the relationship between learned helplessness and the stability of attributions. Research participants drawn from Bar-Ilan and Tel Aviv universities were asked to solve a number of problems which looked as though they had a solution, but in fact did not. The instructions which they received encouraged them to attribute the outcome to either stable or unstable causes. Those who made stable attributions performed much worse on later, easily-solvable tasks than people who had made unstable ones.

Abramson, Seligman and Teasdale (1978) argued that it is important to distinguish between causes which apply to only one or two situations and those which could apply generally to several different settings. So, for example, you might attribute failing to solve a maths problem correctly to not being particularly good at maths, which would be a **specific attribution** that would be likely to apply only to maths problems; or you might attribute it to low intelligence, a **global attribution** that would be likely to be relevant in a number of other situations as well.

Pasahow (1980) manipulated whether research participants were likely to make global or specific attributions for failing to solve laboratory problems, and found that those research participants who were induced to make global attributions performed worse on later tasks than did the people who made specific attributions. Similarly, Mikulincer (1986) found that manipulating the attributions which people made about failing at a task only seemed to produce helplessness when the research participants made global attributions, and not if they made specific ones. However, this was also influenced by how much the research participants expected to be able to control their situation.

In 1986, Stratton *et al.* described a system for coding attributions which are made in the course of everyday conversation. They had developed this model from work in family therapy, which had provided them with a considerable amount of material in the form of conversations (all the families who were involved in the research had given permission beforehand for their data to be used for research, of course). Stratton *et al.* had found that analysing the attributions which people made had been very valuable in helping the therapists to identify useful areas to emphasise. From this material, they developed the Leeds Attributional Coding System (Stratton *et al.*, 1988). This lists five attributional dimensions, which were described in Chapter 9 (Table 9.1, page 208). Since its development, this system has been used in a number of different contexts, including organisational and marketing research as well as family therapy.

In one example, Stratton and Swaffer (1988) investigated whether parents of abused children made different attributions about their children from other mothers. They had three groups: one group of mothers with children who were known to have been abused; one group of mothers from the same kind of social background; and one group consisting of mothers of disabled children, who were included to act as a control for the general amount of stress experienced in the family. The mothers watched their children and talked about them while the children played with a special toy, known as a 'contingency house'. This was designed to provide a puzzle for the children to solve, so that the researchers could see how persistent the children were. It also gave the mothers something that would encourage them to talk about their child.

Stratton and Swaffer found that the mothers of abused children made very different attributions about their children in their conversation. They saw themselves as being less in control, and their children's behaviour as coming more from internal causes, than the other mothers. Stratton and Swaffer suggested that the beliefs which mothers hold about their children could be significant

causal factors in child abuse: if you see your child's behaviour as uncontrollable, you may be more likely to become frustrated and angry. The form of family therapy that these mothers received, therefore, focused on showing them how to influence their children's behaviour, so that they would feel more in control and less frustrated.

Covariance theory

The covariance theory of attribution was first outlined by Kelley in 1967, and then modified in 1973. Again, it is concerned with whether the person sees an action or event as happening as a result of external or internal causes. Kelley proposed that in order to decide whether the cause is internal or external, we look at three particular aspects of the situation: consistency, consensus and distinctiveness.

Consistency is concerned with how the person has acted on previous occasions – is what they have done this time consistent with what they have done in the past? **Consensus** is concerned with how other people act in the same circumstances – is what the person has done the same as anyone else would have done? **Distinctiveness** is concerned with the target of the act – does the person act in this way only towards that particular target, or do they act in this way towards other kinds of targets too? The pattern of covariance, according to Kelley, determines whether the cause of the event will be attributed to an internal or an external source.

In 1972, McArthur gave research participants the sentence 'John laughs at the comedian', and then manipulated each of these three variables to see what attributions the research participants would make. Table 15.7 uses a different example to explore some of the different ways that the three dimensions can be combined, and the types of attributions that they lead to.

Consistency refers to how the person has acted in similar situations on other occasions. So, if we know that Sheila always buys Ecover detergent, we will assess her action in a certain way; if we know that she has not bought Ecover detergent before, however, we will assess it in a different way. Consensus concerns whether other people react in the same way: if Sheila is the only person we know who buys Ecover detergent, we judge her behaviour differently from how we judge it if most people that we know buy Ecover detergent

Table 15.7 Patterns of covariance

Consistency	Consensus	Distinctiveness	Type of attribution
High (Sheila always buys Ecover detergent)	Low (The other people she knows do not buy eco-sensitive products)	Low (Sheila buys other eco-sensitive products)	Person (It is because of Sheila's personal commitment to ecological issues)
High (Sheila always buys Ecover detergent)	High (Other people buy Ecover detergent too)	High (Sheila does not buy other eco-sensitive products)	Entity (It is because Ecover detergent is particularly good)
Low (Sheila has not bought Ecover detergent before)	Low (The other people she knows do not buy eco-sensitive products)	High (Sheila does not buy other eco-sensitive products)	Circumstance (It is because there is something special about this occasion)

as well. Distinctiveness is about whether the action happens only with that particular stimulus and not with others. So if Sheila mostly buys non-ecological household products, but buys Ecover detergent, that is high distinctiveness. If, on the other hand, Sheila always buys ecologically sensitive products for the household, that is low distinctiveness, and would lead to a different attribution.

Seeking relevant information

Kelley proposed that people will tend to seek out information about these three sources of information, and form attributions on the basis of them. Different combinations of the three will imply either dispositional or situational attributions. So, for instance, if Sarah is the only person who asks questions in developmental psychology lectures (low consensus), she always does so (high consistency) and she does not ask questions in any other lectures (high distinctiveness), we would conclude that it is Sarah's interest in developmental psychology which causes her behaviour to be a dispositional attribution.

But if we found that Sarah asks questions in other lectures too (low distinctiveness), that she asks questions in developmental psychology lectures sometimes but not always (low consistency) and that everyone else asks questions too (high consensus), then we would be more likely to conclude that her asking a particular question in a developmental psychology lecture is produced by the situation – perhaps that the lecturer was not explaining things very clearly.

Criticisms of covariance theory

Lalljee (1981) challenged Kelley's assumption that distinctiveness, consensus and consistency form the basis of the attributions which we make, pointing out that people who are attempting to explain an event actually bring a great deal of their pre-existing knowledge to bear on the issue – they do not just apply a pre-set 'formula'. Although we might use the three criteria, Lalljee argued, we do not just use them mechanically. So, for instance, while we might accept 'They all dress like that' as an explanation for why a teenager dressed in a certain way, we would not accept 'They all do that' as an explanation for why someone engaged in theft. It would not be considered to be an adequate explanation. In the same way, saying 'He always does it' would be adequate to explain why someone habitually goes for a walk at six o'clock in the evening, but this would not do as an explanation if we were trying to explain why someone goes for a walk at midnight.

Lalljee argued that explanations are always given for a reason, and so it is unrealistic to look at people's explanations without looking at why they were given in the first place. Looking at attributions within their interpersonal context in this way means we have to take into account four different areas of social knowledge. The first of these is what we assume the other person already **knows** – are they aware of what is expected of them in this situation, for instance? The second is the **relationship** between the two people who are communicating, and this can include factors like social roles and affiliation. Saying 'I could not decide what to wear' might be a perfectly adequate explanation for why you were late if you were talking to a friend, but not if you were trying to explain your lateness to an employer or teacher.

The third area of social knowledge concerns the **topic** or activity implications of the explanation. For example, the reason which someone gives for moving house might be different depending on the interests of the person they are talking to. The fourth major area of social knowledge which Lalljee identified as influencing the kinds of attributions which we make comprises the interpersonal **consequences** of the explanation. If a particular explanation is likely to provoke misunderstandings or social unpleasantness, we will tend to look for a different one. By analysing the social context of the conversation, as well as the simple mechanics of the attributional process, Lalljee argued, we are much more able to come to terms with the real-life explanations that people use.

Lay epistemology

In 1983, Kruglanski, Baldwin and Towson argued that traditional research into attribution is too concerned with the mechanics of how people process information, and does not really look at their motivation and personal interests. It also does not take account of how people change their minds. Sometimes we rethink attributions that we make – we decide that there was a different reason for why something happened – and it is important to understand how this happens.

In 1980, Kruglanski proposed a theory of **lay epistemology**, which suggested that we need to look at how people seek knowledge, and how their ideas can become fixed or unfrozen. Epistemology is the study of what counts as knowledge, and how knowledge is formed, so lay epistemology is concerned with how ordinary people ('lay' people as opposed to experts) form and use knowledge in their everyday lives.

Like Kelly (1955) or Heider (1958), Kruglanski saw people as generating hypotheses to explain what they experience in the world around them. In practice, though, most people do not generate new hypotheses all the time. Instead, we take a lot of information for granted and do not think about it any further. When we are faced with new experiences, we can develop any number of alternative hypotheses to explain them. Water falling from the sky could be explained by a number of possibilities – rain, wet birds, someone spraying upwards with a high-powered hosepipe, a film studio special effects team on location, and so on. In practice, though, we do not generate all these different possibilities – we just conclude that it is raining, and question it only if something about it seems a bit odd.

Freezing on explanations

Even with more unusual events, Kruglanski argued, we generally develop only one or two ideas, and then settle on one particular hypothesis as an explanation. What happens is that the belief becomes **frozen**, and we accept that one and discard any alternative ideas. Ross, Lepper and Hubbard (1975) asked people to rate a series of suicide notes in terms of whether they were likely to be genuine or not. Then they gave the research participants false feedback about how accurate they had been. Later, the researchers admitted that the feedback had been false, and showed the research participants the experimenter's random allocation list. But when they were questioned, the research participants still believed what they had originally been told – they had taken no notice of the new information at all.

Kruglanski, Baldwin and Towson described a follow-up study, which successfully replicated these findings, but then told one group of research participants that their own evaluations, which showed that they still retained the false belief, would be publicly compared with their real scores, so other people would be able to see that they had not adjusted their beliefs. They were also told that it is important to be able to achieve accurate self-perception. Unlike the others, these research participants were able to 'unfreeze' their beliefs, and to learn how they had really managed to perform on the task.

Capacity and motivation

Kruglanski (1980) suggested that whether any specific belief becomes frozen or not depends on two factors: the person's **capacity** and their **motivation**. By someone's capacity Kruglanski meant their ability to generate alternative hypotheses on a given topic. This depends on how much prior knowledge they have, not on 'ability'. For example, someone whose hobby is tinkering with car engines will be able to generate far more hypotheses about what has made a car break down than someone who knows nothing about how engines work.

Capacity also depends on whether the hypotheses are currently available – in other words, whether we can bring them to mind at that particular moment. This in turn will be affected by factors like recency and relevance. If I had just been reading about levels of processing theory, for example (see Chapter 3), I would be more likely to give someone coming up to exams advice about how to study the information. On the other hand, if I had just done a course on stress management (see Chapter 13), I would be more likely to suggest advice about reducing the stress of revision.

Motivation, according to Kruglanski, depends on three factors, and these are listed in Table 15.8. Among other things, they show us that sometimes it does not really matter very much whether our beliefs are true or not, as long as they serve our own purposes. For example, if we know someone only very slightly, it does not really matter much to us whether they are clean in their personal habits. So we might generally accept, or freeze on to, a belief that they are OK, even though we see them looking a bit scruffy from time to time. In this example, we have a low **need for validity**, and so we can cope with a bit of inconsistency between what we observe and what we believe.

Table 15.8 Motivation for freezing beliefs

The need for structure	We have to organise what we know in such a way as to give us clear guidance for action. We may need to make a decision quickly, so we choose what seems like the most probable hypothesis, and act on it, ignoring the alternatives.
What we wish to believe	People have their own personal values, ideas and images of themselves, and will tend to select those beliefs which fit them.
The need for validity	As a general rule, we do not believe things if we know that they are not true; but sometimes it does not really matter very much whether they are true or not. Our need for validity can vary, depending on the situation.

Source: Kruglanski et al., 1983

But if we were about to share a flat with that person, the need for validity regarding that particular belief would become much more important, in that someone who is scruffy might also turn out to be untidy, lazy, and so on. So in that case, our high need for validity would unfreeze the belief, and we would be open to a number of different possibilities. A high need for validity, then, gives us the motivation to keep our belief options open and to gather more information.

Kruglanski, Baldwin and Towson (1983) argued that this theory of lay epistemology can provide a framework that allows us to draw together and make sense of the many different aspects of research into attribution. In particular, it allows us to look much more carefully at how motivation is involved. Rather than simply being an optional extra, as it were, motivation is built into the attributions and inferences that we make. While covariance theory presents the attributional process as if it was strictly rational, Kruglanski argued that attributions are both rational and motivational at the same time. They are rational because they have to be consistent and logically deduced, as shown by Heider and the other attributional theorists; but they are also motivational, because they reflect people's needs for structure, conclusions and validity too.

Social representation theory

What counts as an acceptable explanation is also strongly influenced by the shared beliefs which are held by society in general, or by the particular social group to which we belong. As we saw in Chapter 14, social representation theory emerged in the context of a need to understand the European experience of Nazism, in the middle of the twentieth century, and also in reaction to the behaviourally-oriented social psychology which was dominated by American individualism. But its origins can be traced as far back as 1898, with the distinction made by the sociologist Emile Durkheim between individual and collective representations of reality. Durkheim proposed that social life involved a level whereby collective interpretations of reality, developed within a social group or society, were shared and taken as 'truth' by those participating in social life. These ideas were taken up by the French psychologist Serge

Moscovici, who showed how collective understandings become adopted by the individual person and incorporated into their way of thinking.

Moscovici (1984) argued that the shared social representations held by a group or society are what allow people to communicate effectively, and to come to an agreed view about reality. They also guide social action, and are the link between individual cognitions and social ideology. The beliefs which we hold can make all the difference to how we act. For example, Herzlich (1973) showed how a doctor who believes that illness comes from physical causes may decide that someone who comes to their surgery complaining of pain without any physical cause is just a hypochondriac and does not merit treatment. Another doctor, who believes that illnesses can also have psychological origins, may arrange for treatment for such a patient, possibly in the form of psychotherapy. The underlying theory which each doctor holds determines how each treats the patient.

According to Moscovici, if we are to understand why people think and act as they do, we need to examine the deep representations of the social world – theories about human beings or the nature of reality – which underlie our thinking. And, over time, our social representations change, as society changes. Fischler (1980) showed how changes in social representations of what constitutes an acceptable diet reflect the social and economic changes which have taken place in Western society over the past half-century. Some of these changes have been concerned with the production, distribution and consumption of food, while others have been concerned with the adoption of new, consumer-based lifestyles which involve different modes of eating – such as more fast food and snacks rather than full meals. Similarly, Jodelet described how changes in social representations of the 'ideal' body could be interpreted in terms of the influence of youth movements, women's liberation and other social factors (Jodelet, 1991).

Social representations, then, provide the framework of social assumptions within which people are socialised. And this framework can take many different forms: for example, right-wing thinking tends to be characterised by internal attributions; whereas left-wing thinking tends to adopt external attributions in explaining human behaviour (Moscovici, 1984). An interesting study illustrating this was conducted by Echabe and Paez-Rovira, in 1989. They asked adults, of around 35 years old, to provide explanations as to the causes , spread and transmission of acquired immune deficiency syndrome (AIDS). The researchers found that the research participants separated into two groups. One group blamed the individuals: AIDS was deemed to originate and be passed on by immoral sexual behaviour, and the people concerned were argued to have brought it on themselves: an internal attribution. The other group gave a more liberal social representation, which saw the people who had caught it as the unlucky victims of an epidemic – an external attribution.

Echabe and Paez-Rovira also found that their research participants were extremely selective about the information they would adopt. When they were provided with technical information about AIDS, they recalled only information which fitted with their pre-existing representations, while memories of contradictory information were distorted. Their social representations had actually determined what they saw as valid explanation – they were causal factors, not just influences, of cognition.

Social representations and social cognition

Social representation theory rests on the principle that thinking forms a social environment and that it has the power to shape the reality that we experience. Moscovici (1984) argued that it is an illusion to think that we perceive reality directly, for the reasons listed in Table 15.9. But social representations are those theories about what the world is like, or how things happen which we use to interpret the world around us.

Some social representations are shared by large groups of people, and dominate their society's beliefs, while others are held by much smaller groups. For example, Carugati (1990) looked at what teachers, parents, and teachers who were also parents believed about intelligence. Carugati found that parents tended to think that intelligence could be trained, but that the teachers who were also parents were most likely of all to hold to the theory that intelligence was a 'gift'. The reason for this was that in this way, they could justify their own behaviour (encouraging capable children and giving less help to those experiencing difficulties)

Table 15.9 Problems perceiving reality

1 We fail to see lots of things that are right in front of our eyes.

2 Some things which we might take for granted turn out to be illusions – e.g. the earth going round the sun.

3 Our reactions to events are related to how we define what sort of event it is, and that is a social process. For example, we respond quite differently to the idea of child labour now, than people did in the nineteenth century. Society's definitions of what is acceptable have changed since then, and as a result, our own reactions have changed too.

Source: Moscovici, 1984

more readily. Carugati's study shows how the social representations that we adopt are often strongly linked to our personal motives, as well as to social ideology.

Social representations, then, are shared beliefs, held by social groups, which serve to organise and direct social action. Moscovici (1976) argued that the shared social representations held by a group or society are what allow people to communicate effectively, and to come to an agreed view about reality. They create a base of shared knowledge which allows us to communicate effectively with one another. But they are also closely linked to membership of social groups, and society itself consists of many different groups, cultures and subcultures. As a result, there can be many different social representations in any given society.

This can sometimes produce major misunderstandings. Di Giacomo (1980) examined the social representations in a student protest movement at a university in Belgium, by performing a content analysis on the students' free-associations to key words, as well as interviewing them about how they saw the issues. It turned out that there were major differences between the social representations held by the leaders of the protest movement, and those held by the majority of students. The differences involved concepts such as 'student-worker solidarity', which was talked about by the student leaders, but which had no place at all in the ordinary students' social representations. They saw 'students' and 'workers' as having very little connection with each other on this issue. This

meant that when the student leaders called for concerted student action against changes in the student grant system, there was very little support. It was the discrepancy between the social representations held by the two groups which resulted in the failure of the student activity.

Mechanisms of social representations

We do not swallow social representations wholesale. When someone gives us an explanation for something, we think about it, and see how it will fit into our own personal construct system. We also decide whether it is coming from a trustworthy source or not (which is where the link with social identification comes in – more about that later). But what this means is that any one person's social representations are a combination of shared, or **consensual** beliefs, and individual ones. And this also means that social representations are continuously changing, as they are passed on through society.

The structure of social representations

But how can social representations be simultaneously shared and individual? It happens because social representations have two parts: a central core and peripheral elements. The central core is known as the **figurative nucleus**, and it stays pretty consistent. Flament (1989) discussed how the figurative nucleus is the part of the social representation which virtually everyone in that group or culture shares, and it is also the part which is most firmly ideologically based. The **peripheral elements**, though, do change. They are the parts of the social representation which are negotiated and adapted through conversation. So they are able to adapt to an individual's own personal construct systems, to recent or unexpected events, or to society as a whole. Box 15.1 overleaf discusses how the peripheral elements of social representations of educability in Britain have changed over time, while leaving the central core largely untouched. The social representation has been negotiated to fit its time and social context.

How are social representations formed?

Social representations, according to Moscovici (1984), are formed by two processes: anchoring and objectification. Both anchoring and objectification help us to grasp the idea more easily – they make it more familiar and easy to understand. But

Box 15.1 Social representations and ideology

The sociological concept of ideology concerns the structure of beliefs and ideas which express the interests of the dominant class in society. In sociological terms, these beliefs and ideas are therefore the dominant ones in a given society, and form a significant factor in maintaining the status quo – in making sure that even if social change occurs, it will tend to be limited, and not make a significant difference to the established balance of power in that society, or the distribution of wealth.

This sociological argument, however, does not explain how individual people come to hold these dominant beliefs, even if they are not the people who directly benefit from keeping society the way that it is. Social representation theory represents a way that we might form links between the sociological concept of ideology, which is about the general beliefs of a society, and how those beliefs come to be held by an individual person. People are not robots: we have already seen how we sift through the information which we receive, and formulate our own ideas. Yet societies do differ, systematically, in what the people in them believe. This is more because of the things which are taken for granted in that society, than because of things which people are explicitly taught.

Social representations encapsulate a whole way of looking at the world, and make assumptions about how the world is and what human nature is like. A society which makes one set of assumptions about human nature is unlikely to accept a set of beliefs or social practice which do not fit with those assumptions. For example, England and America have rather different educational systems, and this has come about partly because the two societies have very different social representations about human nature.

England, like many other European societies, evolved from the feudal system into its modern social structure. This meant that it carried a number of assumptions about human beings with it, as part of its history. One of those assumptions is the idea that people are not born equal. Indeed, European writers who maintained that people were born equal were traditionally branded as 'revolutionary', which shows how very much that idea went against the assumptions of society. White America, on the other hand, was founded by people who were deliberately getting away from the feudal European traditions, and so the idea that all people are born equal has always been a favourite belief in America – whether or not it has turned out to be true in practice.

As a result of this, England and America have produced very different educational systems. The American system has always tended to emphasise social development above academic development, because it has seen becoming a responsible member of society as a primary goal of education. But it has also assumed that all children can benefit from having the opportunity to learn, and college courses are designed to be as open-access as possible. The assumption is that most people will be able to complete college and obtain a degree if they are given the chance.

The English system, on the other hand, was traditionally based on the idea that only a minority of the population are likely to benefit from academic education, and this commonly-held belief has always permeated British educational structures. That does not mean that the belief has always stayed the same: social representations do change over time. But in the first part of this century, the commonly-held belief – propagated by Cyril Burt and others (see Chapter 6) – was that intelligence was **inherited**. This argument held that it was a waste of time trying to teach the majority of the population any more than basics, since only a small minority had inherited the capacity for academic thinking.

In the more democratic 1960s and 1970s, however, this view fell out of favour (although it never completely died, especially in educational textbooks). Instead, **Piaget's theory** of cognitive development (see Chapter 19) became the dominant theory in education. Despite the fact that Piaget himself regarded it as almost totally irrelevant, it was the concept of biological 'readiness' which was taken as educational 'gospel' from this theory – not its

● ● ● ➤

message about the importance of stretching the child's understanding to facilitate schema development. Instead, the concept of biological readiness was used as an 'explanation' for why some children would not learn. In the hands of some theorists (e.g. Shayer and Adey, 1981), it was even argued that some children could never achieve the fourth stage of formal operations at all, so they would never become capable of abstract thought. This was a world away from Piaget's own ideas.

During the early 1980s, Piaget's theory became less popular, and **social deprivation theories** became more popular. According to this view, working-class children were not likely to learn in school because of the hardships which they endured at home: because they did not receive support, or anywhere to study, they were unable to do well at school. But the point about this view was that, despite the good

intentions of those propounding it, it was still putting forward the same message: that only a few could benefit from education. Most people, for one reason or another, were not able to do so.

English educational history is full of attempts to make the system more democratic, and to improve opportunities and access for more children. But each of these attempts has come up against the prevailing social representation, which has provided an 'explanation' for why it is that only a few can benefit from education. It is only when we look at other countries, and at the very different beliefs and assumptions which are held there, that we can see the belief that most children are unable to succeed in education is a social representation, which has changed its form over time, but not its general message.

they also mean that the idea gets changed quite a lot in the process. They are summarised in Table 15.10, but it is worth explaining them in more detail here.

Anchoring involves setting the ideas in a familiar context, so that people can grasp them more easily. This might involve deliberately connecting the idea behind the social representation with a well-known social event or process, like construing something as a 'mid-life crisis' or 'teenage angst'. Or it might mean classifying the idea in a particular way. The classification links what is being described with a

form of understanding that is already familiar, but in the process, it changes how we regard it – and even creates an entirely new way of viewing the idea. Describing protesters against a new motorway as 'eco-freaks' or 'rent-a-mob' changes the way that those protesters are seen, and makes their protest less likely to be taken seriously.

Objectification involves finding a way of making the idea easier to grasp, by making it more concrete and tangible. Expert knowledge tends to be a little obscure for most people, so part of the process of making it generally accepted as social knowledge involves presenting it in a way that makes it easy for most people to grasp. One way that this happens is through **personification**, in which theories or ideas become associated with particular groups or individuals – like the way that relativity theory is associated with Einstein, or like referring to Newtonian physics, or Thatcherite policies.

Figuration is another form of objectification. In figuration, images and metaphors are used to represent the concept. So, for example, popular Western concepts of medicine often present an image of the body as a machine, but if a metaphor is convincing enough, it can often be taken as if it were completely real. So, for instance, non-scientists often believe very firmly indeed that

Table 15.10 Forming social representations

Anchoring	Setting the idea in a familiar context; making comparisons with familiar patterns or sequences, or using familiar classifications.
Objectification	Making the idea more accessible either through personification or figuration.
Personification	Linking the idea with a specific well-known individual.
Figuration	Using images or metaphors to represent the idea.

atoms are real things – that they have an independent existence, rather than being theoretical constructs developed by physicists in order to explain their observations. But sometimes figuration involves just general images, such as describing ideas which relate to ecological awareness as 'green'.

Wagner, Elejabarrieta and Lahnsteiner (1995) studied the process of objectification in how people understand conception. They explored the views of 169 rural Austrian research participants, and found that the process of fertilisation was perceived in a way which made direct comparisons with stereotyped sexual attraction and behaviour between men and women. The sexual stereotypes of man and woman were mapped on to the sperm and the ovum: the 'successful' sperm was seen as active and dynamic (masculine), competing better than the other sperm by swimming faster and reaching the ovum first, while the ovum was perceived as passive and receptive (feminine), simply waiting to be penetrated by the sperm.

As Wagner, Elejabarrieta and Lahnsteiner pointed out, there were many other possible metaphors: magnetic attraction, cats and mice, armies conquering cities, mosquitoes and victims; but the sexual metaphor was the one which had become taken for granted. But adopting the sexual metaphor as the social representation of this complex biological process also led to some systematic misrepresentations of what was actually going on.

Social representations, then, are often expressed through metaphors, images or stories. These do not just provide pretty pictures: they also give us a way of understanding our own experience. Larsen and Laszlo (1990) described a study of social representations in which Hungarian and Danish research participants each read the same short story, which told of two peasants being abused by two armed men, but engaging in passive resistance. This story reflected the cultural history and traditions of Hungary, but not those of Denmark, which has a tradition of independence and autonomy among its peasantry. The research participants were asked to note down each occasion when the story reminded them of their own personal experience. Larsen and Laszlo found that the story had far more personal relevance for the Hungarians than it did for the Danes, since it related directly to an established Hungarian social representation.

Sometimes, though, social representations can be passed on without being expressed in words. Jodelet (1991) described a study of social representations of mental illness, in France. The policy of the area was to operate a kind of 'care in the community' system, with mental patients being boarded out among families. When the families were interviewed, they expressed the belief that it was better for these people to be with families, that they were just like anyone else, and that they needed support and help. But Jodelet observed that there was an implicit social representation, which was never expressed verbally, of mental illness as contagious. The patients' eating utensils were washed up separately and kept apart from those of the family; they had separate sheets and towels, and so on. The social representation was not expressed in words, but it seemed to be quite widely shared in the village.

Social representations and scientific ideas

Social representations also develop as scientific ideas become popularised. One of the first studies of social representations was conducted by Moscovici, in 1961, and was to do with the way that the theory of psychoanalysis had developed from a way of explaining human neurosis into a widespread explanation for society as a whole and how it operated – which was its status in France at the time that he conducted his research. Moscovici identified three phases in this process. The first was the scientific phase, in which psychoanalysis was elaborated as a scientific theory, and knowledge of its tenets and practices were largely restricted to professional scientists. This was followed by a second phase, in which the images and ideas of psychoanalysis became more widely known, and were adapted in the process to apply to a broader range of situations and events. The third phase was where psychoanalysis became applied even more widely, and was used as an explanation for why society was like it was. Moscovici named this the ideological phase.

More recently, a similar process occurred with split-brain research. Moscovici and Hewstone, in 1983, explored how split-brain research had become transformed into an explanation for the economic and social differences between human beings. Split-brain research was described in Chapter 10, and as any student who has studied the evidence is aware, it simply shows that the left side of the brain tends to process language functions, while the right side of the brain tends to be concerned with spatial functions, such as drawing. But, as these findings became popularly known, they were transformed into something very different.

In a study using attributions to explore social representations, Moscovici and Hewstone showed how the split-brain findings had become used to justify a folk-scientific belief that: (1) the two halves of the brain are two different, independent minds; (2) each side deals with opposite skills; (3) that these include major aspects of personality, e.g. intuition, masculinity, etc.; and (4) that this explains social differences, because society favours those with left hemisphere dominance. A set of limited scientific findings had become transformed into a much more widespread set of ideological beliefs – with no scientific justification at all!

How do social representations come to be shared?

One of the strengths of social representation theory is that it is firmly rooted in the everyday world, being directly concerned with what people do, think and say outside of the psychological laboratory. What this also means is that social representations in common currency often consist of traditional knowledge, which has been passed on through the family, through social institutions, or through the wider culture. But, as we have seen, newer scientific ideas can also become fitted into our social representations, even if they do become rather distorted in the process.

I have said several times that social representations are negotiated and adapted by the individual. This happens as we discuss ideas, observations and events with other people. The social representations which emerge from these conversations are really explanations for why reality is like it is: we use social representations to explain issues as diverse as why someone has moved away from the neighbourhood; why our politicians seem to be acting particularly incompetently; why the spring seems particularly hot/cold; or why there are people begging on the street. Through conversation and discussion, we negotiate shared ways of explaining these things.

The fact that social representations are negotiated through conversation means that they are not all identical. But they do have a lot in common. Many dimensions of a social representation are **consensual**, which means that

they are shared and agreed by all of the people who hold them, and that consensus can develop very quickly. Galli and Nigro, in 1987, explored the way that children's social representations of radioactivity changed as a result of the Chernobyl explosion. They asked the children to produce drawings and definitions of radioactivity, and also to comment on their own drawings and those of other children. Within just a few days, the children's drawings and explanations showed that they had developed a shared representation of radioactivity, and of the Chernobyl explosion itself. A major event like Chernobyl can produce a social consensus very quickly, because it generates so much conversation and discussion.

Social representations and social groups

As we have seen, social representations can be held at the cultural level, at the sub-cultural level, or within groups or professions. So whether we adopt a social representation or not depends to quite a large extent on whether it fits, not just with our personal beliefs, but also with the beliefs and ideas of the social groups that we belong to. We will be looking at social identity theory later in this chapter. But there are many ways that social representations and social identification connect.

Gervais and Jovchelovitch (1997) described a study of social representations among Chinese communities living in Britain. They were particularly interested in how traditional Chinese health beliefs were reconciled with the very different Western medical tradition of British society. Normally, traditional beliefs tend to be held less strongly by the second generation of a migrant community. But interestingly, Gervais and Jovchelovitch found that virtually all members of these communities – even when they had been born and socialised in Britain – shared the Chinese social representations of health and illness. They perceived these beliefs as complementary to Western ones, and as having more power to identify the root causes of illness or disease.

As Gervais and Jovchelovitch looked more deeply at this question, they found that, for many of the 'acculturated' people – those who had adopted Western beliefs and lifestyles – their acceptance of Chinese health and illness beliefs acted as a powerful statement of identification with their parents' community. Like many others born of immigrant parents, these people felt torn between their acceptance of Western lifestyles, and the cultural inheritance of their parents. For them, integrating the traditional understandings of health and illness with modern beliefs was also an assertion that they did, somehow, remain Chinese. The social representation was used to affirm their group identification.

Social representations and in-group beliefs

We have already seen how social representations develop through conversation and negotiation. But we do not treat everyone's opinions the same way. We consider the opinions of people who are 'like us' as much more important than the views of 'outsiders', and so we have a strong tendency to favour the beliefs expressed by other members of our particular 'in-group'. This is a powerful mechanism, which can operate either positively or negatively. If the beliefs of one group are particularly hostile to another group – as Nazis were towards the Jews, for instance – then members of the first group are likely to adopt social representations which foster prejudice and discrimination. But if the social representations emphasise prosocial values and tolerance, then, as we have seen, people will tend to co-operate with, and tolerate, their neighbours.

Many studies of social representations have been concerned with large-scale social representations, spanning cultures, societies, or large proportions of the population. But social representations can work on a smaller scale too, and it is here that the link between social identification and social identity can become most apparent. For example: the accepted aim of group psychotherapy sessions is to generate an identification with the group, in order for group members to be able to provide one another with mutual support. Kaës, in 1984, showed how group psychotherapy sessions also resulted in the development of shared explanations of social reality. These were social representations about people's problems and the way that those problems could usefully be addressed. As the therapy sessions continued, those social representations became the framework for ideas, explanations, or developments with respect to group members' problems. And they also became an important part of how the group defined itself.

In another study, Lorant and Deconchy (1986) studied the emergence of social identification in groups who were undergoing physical training

programmes. The identification with the group was strongest in the group whose training was particularly rigorous – possibly because they felt they had a special shared experience which differentiated them from the others. But Lorant and Deconchy also found that the group developed explicit social representations, in line with their strong in-group/out-group distinction. The social representations were tied in with the growth of social identification, and seemed to be part of the same process.

Social representations can also develop within working groups. Hayes (1991) described how distinctive organisational cultures can be seen as social representations, which come to be shared by members of the organisation as they come into long-term contact with the shared ideas, assumptions and traditions of particular organisations. And the processes of anchoring and objectification, through metaphors, heroes and organisational stories, apply just as much when we are looking at organisational cultures as they do when looking at social representations of other groups in society (Hayes, 1998).

The theory of social representations, then, allows us to look at the more generally accepted explanations which are common in society, and at how these explanations are used socially to explain why things are as they are. Every culture has its accepted assumptions, which become manifest in the shared social beliefs which we know as social representations. Often, too, these accepted assumptions contradict people's personal experience directly – for example, most people actively dislike confronting other people aggressively, and will do almost anything to avoid having to do so. Yet they accept social representations of human beings as inherently violent and aggressive. Social representation theory shows us how this can happen, and how our implicit cultural assumptions form part of our individual psychology.

Social groups and social identity

Social groups, in one way or another, are an essential part of our lives. Human beings are social animals: we have evolved as social creatures, and (apart from the occasional hermit) we have always lived in social communities. For most of our evolutionary history, those communities have been relatively small-sized ones, where everyone would know one another, and a stranger would be an object of some curiosity. But nonetheless, those communities contained other groupings – perhaps based on age and/or gender; perhaps based on skills and expertise; or perhaps based on kin and family. Belonging to social groups is an integral part of our evolutionary history.

In modern times, our communities are large and most of us encounter strangers every day. Indeed, we are often in situations where strangers are the norm, and it is unusual to see a face that we know. Within these large and complex societies, belonging to social groups is just as important as it ever was. It may even be more so. Group membership affects almost every aspect of our lives, ranging from conflicts between nations to the 'image' that we proclaim through our choice of clothes and consumer possessions. And, as we have seen, it can also result in conflict and prejudice. But what are the psychological processes that make group membership so important? How is it that other people can be so important to us?

Group norms

One aspect of group membership is the development of **group norms**. Group norms are the unspoken rules that develop between members of a group over time. They establish what is acceptable practice and what is not; and how the group's members are expected to behave. Groups which last for a significant period of time tend to develop their own norms, quite spontaneously, and they can become an extremely powerful part of how the group goes about its activities.

Evidence of how powerful group norms can be, emerged from the famous Hawthorne studies, conducted in Chicago in the 1930s by Elton Mayo and his colleagues, Roethlisberger and Dickson. They were organisational psychologists, investigating different ways of increasing production in the Hawthorne works of a large electrical company. For the most part, they found that interventions could make quite a difference to how well employees worked. But in one particular section, known as the bank-wiring room, nothing the researchers did made any difference. This working group consisted of a close-knit group of people with a well-developed

set of group norms, which regulated their working behaviour to a steady, consistent rate, which did not vary, no matter what external factors were changed by the researchers.

As a result of this experience, psychologists became very interested in the question of group norms and how they exert their influence. They found that group norms develop unconsciously, through force of habit for the most part, and are shared by all members of the group. They emerge from the implicit assumptions and beliefs which people hold about what they are doing, and they are maintained through informal sanctions – which may be informal but can be quite powerful. Group members who do not conform to the group's norms may be excluded from the group, or ridiculed – both of which can be very powerful social punishments.

Feldman (1984) argued that group norms serve four different purposes, which are listed in Table 15.11. We can see from the table that these purposes emphasise a number of facets: the distinctiveness of the group by comparison with others; the sense of cohesion or belonging among group members; and the way that the group defines itself. These are all factors which are important in social identification – the psychological phenomenon of 'them-and-us'.

Table 15.11 Purposes of group norms

To express the central values of the group
This gives the group members a strong sense of what the group is all about – and what is not acceptable to the group, as well.

To help the group to function smoothly
Group norms establish common ground, so that everyone knows what to expect. This means that people do not have to waste time checking that activities are appropriate, and streamlines social interaction in the group.

To define what counts as acceptable social behaviour
By doing this, people are able to avoid embarrassing or awkward situations, and avoid confrontations within the group which could threaten its cohesiveness.

To help a group to maintain its distinctiveness if it is under threat
This happens by allowing the group to reject deviant behaviour and preserve what the group 'stands for'.

Source: Feldman, 1984

But there is another side to social identification too, which, as we saw in Chapter 14, emerged particularly strongly in Germany before and during WWII. In that social environment, membership of particular social groups became quite literally a matter of life and death. It was so important that those belonging to groups which had been deemed 'inferior' were no longer perceived, or treated, as human by members of other groups. People were no longer seen as members of society, but as members of social categories: Jews, Aryans, Gypsies, Poles, and so on. The group membership which Nazi society assigned them overrode all other considerations.

Social identity theory

Social identity theory, as its name suggests, argues that part of how we see ourselves is closely tied in with the social groups that we belong to. Belonging to, and identifying with, social groups also exerts a tremendous influence on how we interact with others – to the extent that it can colour, and even determine, our interpersonal relationships. The reason for this is that our social identifications are closely bound up with our personal motivation for self-esteem and social respect (Tajfel and Turner, 1979).

In this sense, social identity theory is quite different from theories like Goffman's **symbolic interactionism** which emphasised social rules. According to symbolic interactionism, if I am asked to give a talk as a psychologist, I will be acting out a part: playing the role of psychologist. If I do it often enough, the role may come to seem natural, but it is still a role. According to social identity theory, though, what I am doing in behaving as a psychologist is expressing part of my own self: it is not an act that I put on for the occasion, but a part of me, which comes out in that type of situation.

Mechanisms of social identification

Social identification is extremely deep-rooted, and some of those roots lie far back in our evolutionary past. It is a universal human process, which happens across the whole human species. As Doise (1978) pointed out, that makes it quite different from most of the phenomena which are studied by social psychologists, which only relate to their own particular culture and time. It seems to be a fundamental part of being human that we see

other people in terms of 'us' and 'them' – although, as we shall see, that does not automatically mean that we see 'them' as being enemies.

Our culture and time determines what particular social groupings exist, of course, as well as determining socially acceptable ways of expressing group identification. But the psychological process of internalising and identifying with social groups is a fundamental adaptive mechanism, used by all human beings. We are, as has been said many times before, social animals, and identifying with our social groups is a straightforward psychological consequence of that.

There are three psychological mechanisms involved in the process of social identification: categorisation, social comparison, and the need for positive self-esteem. **Categorisation** is a cognitive mechanism. Our understanding of the world is based on categorising the events and phenomena that we come across: we live in a world of plants, animals, buildings, transport and so on. We need to classify in order to simplify our perception, and we categorise people as well as objects and events. Young people, children, mothers, football supporters, Europeans, Volvo drivers, golfers, doctors, yobs, eco-freaks: these are all social categories, and there are infinitely more. Moreover, any one person can belong to a lot of different social categories: the same person might be a mother, a European, a Volvo driver, a golfer, and a doctor. Social categories can complement one another, such as children and mothers; they can overlap; or they might have no connection with one another.

Social comparison is more evaluative than categorisation. It is all about comparing one group with another. In an equal world, whether we belonged to one group or another would not matter all that much. But the world is not equal. Social groups differ from one another in power and status, and those differences are tremendously important. And this brings us to the third mechanism of social identification, which is our human tendency to seek positive sources of **self-esteem**. This is a motivational mechanism. We need to feel good about ourselves, and we are highly motivated to obtain respect from other people. So the social status of our particular group is an important factor in social identification: we can become angry or defensive if someone criticises a group that we belong to, because it matters to us that our group should be respected.

Minimal group studies and their weaknesses

Early research into social identification seemed to suggest that simply being categorised into a group led to an 'in-group/out-group' bias. People would tend to favour their own group to which they belong, and to act less favourably towards those in a different group. This was particularly evident in the **minimal group experiments** which we looked at in the last chapter, where research participants were divided into groups on the basis of really trivial criteria, such as the flip of a coin or whether they preferred one modern artist to another; and showed an in-group bias, favouring their own group above others (e.g. Billig and Tajfel, 1973).

But even in minimal group studies, researchers found that there are personality differences in how people respond. Platow, McClintock and Liebrand (1990) found that research participants who were co-operative and prosocial tend to prefer fair distributions of resources, and unbiased evaluations of groups. Competitive participants, on the other hand, prefer to show a bias towards their particular in-group. What this implies is that people who come from a social context which emphasises prosocial values, are much less likely to favour their own groups at the expense of others. So in-group favouritism is not as inevitable as it seemed.

The minimal group studies have methodological weaknesses too. Mummendey and Schreiber (1984) suggested that the in-group bias which they showed was actually a methodological problem: it was all to do with how the minimal group studies were conducted. The early studies had all used forced-choice tasks: if one group received more, then others would receive less. And this suggested to the research participants (who, like all human beings taking part in psychological experiments, were trying to work out how they ought to behave) that they were expected to favour their own group. But Mummendey and Schreiber found that when the participants were allowed to make entirely separate assessments of the other groups, so that they could be judged as 'equally good', in-group bias virtually disappeared.

Mummendey and Schreiber found that in-group bias also vanished when research participants were allowed to choose the dimensions that they assessed other groups on, instead of being told what criteria to use by the experimenter. Forcing people to choose between either the in-group or the out-group does produce a high rate of in-group favouritism, but allowing them to make their own judgements, without setting up artificial competition between the groups, does not (Mummendey and Schreiber, 1984).

This is quite an important finding. It shows us, for instance, why highly prejudiced groups always make it appear that the disliked group is in direct competition ('taking our jobs', etc), even when it is obvious that nothing of the kind is happening. It also shows us that making people compete for limited resources is likely to produce intergroup hostility – which is a message for office managers everywhere. And it shows us why knowing more about a group reduces prejudice – because we become aware of more dimensions for evaluating that group, and are less likely to see the group in simplistic, competitive terms.

The importance of social status

Whether you favour your own group may also depend on the status of the group that you belong to. For example, in a study comparing the identifications made by undergraduate students, Spears and Manstead (1989), students attending Manchester University were found to be much more likely to identify with students from Oxford or Cambridge, than to identify with students from what was then Manchester Polytechnic. Their awareness of status differences between the various institutions of higher education led the Manchester University students to emphasise similarities with Oxbridge, and also to exaggerate the differences between themselves and the undergraduates studying at the Polytechnic.

But people do not always favour high-status groups. Sachdev and Bourhis (1987) asked research participants to judge items produced by different groups during a creativity exercise. The research participants came from high, medium or low-status groups themselves, and the researchers found that this directly affected their judgements. Although high and medium-status group members were much more likely to discriminate against the other groups, low-status group members did not. This is an interesting finding, because it suggests that it is not a matter of the lowest status groups being most prejudiced. And indeed, it fits with sociological observations, which show that the most prejudiced groups in society tend to be the lower middle classes, rather than those at the bottom of the social status ladder.

It is possible, also, for a clear group identity to generate social harmony rather than social conflict. What seems to be important in this, though, is that the groups concerned do need to be clearly categorised. Rabbie and Horwitz (1988) showed that as long as there is a clear distinction between them, and it is apparent who belongs to which group, even groups which are very similar and have comparable social roles can get along perfectly well.

So we can see that intergroup conflict is nothing like the inevitable thing that it appeared to be from the early studies. There are many factors which can reduce it, or even make it disappear altogether. Having clearly defined groups helps; as does having groups which are not in direct competition for resources. Coming from a culture which emphasises prosocial values such as co-operation also helps, and so does being able to choose your own ways of evaluating other groups. Intergroup conflict is something which is actively manipulated by some groups, and by the mass media, but it is not an inevitable part of our human nature. It is human to see the world as consisting of 'them' and 'us'; but that does not mean that we automatically see 'them' as enemies.

Group co-operation and self-categorisation

Moreover, social categories are not fixed and unchangeable. In 1990, Capozza and Volpato explored the way that doctors saw other groups, and in particular nurses. They found that if the doctors were encouraged to think about the work that nursing staff did before being asked to evaluate different groups, they tended to classify the nurses in the same category as themselves, instead of regarding them as an out-group.

In another study, Rehm, Lilli and Van Eimeren (1988) looked at the stereotypes held by women living in senior citizens' homes. The researchers looked particularly at the women's stereotypes of 'the old woman' – their own group – and 'the young woman', and measured how much those stereotypes had in common. By doing this, they could get a measure of the amount of **intergroup differentiation** – how different the two groups were perceived as being.

Some of the women in the study participated regularly in a course of gymnastics, while others did not. The researchers found that those who did gym showed significantly less intergroup differentiation then the others – in other words,

they could see more similarities between young and old women. The women who did not do gym saw 'older women' as being entirely different from 'young women'. The researchers suggested that belonging to another group (the gymnastics one) helped the women to compensate for the personal effects of belonging to a low-status group (old women), and to make less rigid distinctions.

In early versions of social identity theory, it was generally assumed that members of a social group felt they belonged together because the group members were basically similar. But more recent work implies that this is not the case. For one thing, researchers have found that we actually accentuate the similarities between out-group members much more than we do for our own group – we see 'them' as being all the same, whereas 'we' are individuals, and quite different from one another (Wilder, 1984).

Another thing that might make a difference is how large the in-group actually is, by comparison with the others. Simon and Brown (1987) showed that members of smaller groups saw their own people as more similar than 'outsiders', whereas people who belonged to large social groups did the opposite. So, for example, someone who belonged to the TV Test Card Appreciation Society would be likely to see the other TV test card enthusiasts as quite like themselves, whereas someone with a hobby like reading science fiction, which involves millions of people, would see sci-fi fans as much more variable. Simon and Brown also found that people who belonged to smaller groups identified with their groups much more strongly than people belonging to larger ones.

We also tolerate much more individuality from members of our own group than we will accept from someone who belongs to a different one. Sometimes, we will even tolerate a 'black sheep', who acts in a way which is quite deviant by comparison with the rest of the group. And we will often accept much more deviance or unusual behaviour from them than we would accept from anyone else. Marques and Yzerbyt (1988) showed that people make so many allowances for members of their own group that they will often overrate the performance of in-group members, even when it is quite obvious that they have not done at all well on things they have been asked to do. But if out-group members did the same, then they would be heavily criticised.

Group membership and self-esteem

A central tenet of social identity theory is that social identification is a fundamental, possibly essential, source of self-esteem for the individual (Tajfel and Turner, 1979; Turner, 1991). We can see this in the way that we react to insults to our particular group: Bond and Venus (1991) found that people reacted much more strongly to insults directed at their social group than they did to insults which were directed at them personally. And that was not just a matter of defending the group in public: it was equally strong whether they were insulted in private, with members of their own group, or with 'outsiders' present.

Social groups do not happen in a vacuum. They occur in the real world, and in the real world, everything is not equal. Groups differ from one another along many dimensions. But two of the most important dimensions in this respect are the dimensions of power and status. Some groups have more access to the resources of society than others. Some groups have more social status than others. Some groups are relatively powerless; others are relatively powerful.

Tajfel and Turner (1979) suggested that if a group cannot allow its members to maintain their self-esteem and derive some kind of social respect from membership, then they will look for ways of leaving or disassociating themselves. But not everybody belongs to high-status groups, and recently, researchers have devoted quite a lot of time to exploring how people belonging to low-status groups maintain their self-esteem. In essence, the alternatives are straightforward: you can leave the group, if that is possible, or you can try to change how the group is perceived.

Leaving the group for a higher-status one is known as the **social mobility** option. But this is not always possible: some social groups, like being female or being white-skinned, are not easily leavable. Whether a group is leavable or not (in technical terms, whether it has a **permeable boundary**) does not make any difference to people in high-status groups, which is not particularly surprising. Ellemers *et al.*, in 1988 found that the amount of identification shown by people belonging to low-status groups depends on whether it is possible to leave the group or not. People identified much more clearly with low-status groups if leaving was not an option.

If you cannot leave your group, then the alternative is to try to change its status. This is known as the **social change** option. It might involve challenging the status of the group through direct confrontation: a strategy which is evident, for example, in the increasing pressure for women to become accepted in top management circles. **Social creativity** is another possibility: making membership of the group more attractive in some way, such as by redefining the group or emphasising comparisons with alternative groups instead. This was the basis of the 'Black is Beautiful' movement in America in the 1960s, which formed such an important part of the racial equality movement.

When we look at social change and social creativity we find another link between social identity and social representation theory. Both of these strategies involve transforming the social representations held by society about that group, and also transforming how the group's members see themselves. These are not small tasks. The beliefs which a social group develops about itself and about other social groups are often a powerful source of self-esteem for that group's members, so they can be difficult to change. But history has shown time and time again that such change is not impossible.

Doise (1984) suggested that social identity and social representations represent linked social phenomena, explored at different **levels of analysis**. Social representations are studied at the level of general conceptions, or theories, about social issues, while social identification is concerned with the intergroup level: how groups within society interact with one another, and how individual people identify with their social groups (Table 15.12).

In this chapter, then, we have looked at some of the ways that we understand other people. We

Table 15.12 Levels of social analysis

	Level	Theory
IV	General conceptions of social issues	Social representations
III	Intergroup level	Social identification
II	Inter-individual level	NVC, relationships, attraction
I	Intra-individual level	Attribution, social schemata

Source: Doise, 1984

began by looking at some of the ways that people interact non-verbally, and went on to look at how people use social information to develop ways of conceptualising their social worlds, in the form of schemata, attributions, social representations, and

social identity. In the next chapter we will look at how people influence one another's behaviour: at research into social roles, leadership, conformity, obedience and helping.

Key terms

affect display A set of actions which is used to indicate an emotional state.

categorisation The first stage in the process of social identification, which involves grouping other people into social categories or sets. Research shows that such categorisation, even if based on minimal criteria, may lead to a strong bias in favour of the in-group.

consensus A factor in the covariance approach to attribution, which is to do with whether other people also act in the same sort of way.

consistency A factor in the covariance approach to attribution, which is to do with whether the person always, or usually, acts in that way.

correspondent inference theory A variant of attribution theory which looks at how people infer that an act came from dispositional or situational causes, by drawing on things like whether its consequences affected them personally or not.

dispositional attribution When the cause of a particular behaviour is thought to have resulted from the person's own personality or characteristics, rather than from the demands of circumstances.

distinctiveness A factor in the covariance approach to attribution which is to do with whether the person acts in the same way in similar situations to the one being considered, or not.

episodes Units of social action which are complete and meaningful in themselves while still forming part of an ongoing sequence – much like a scene in a play. Harré proposed that the study of episodes, rather than acts or actions, should form the basic unit of social analysis.

ethogenics An approach to studying social experience developed by Harré, which emphasises the importance of complete episodes and verbal accounts.

fundamental attribution error The way that people tend to apply different standards in attributing reasons for other people's actions than they do with their own. Specifically, people tend to assess their own actions as resulting from situational demands, but other people's as resulting from dispositional causes.

hedonic relevance The tendency that people have to be more likely to make a dispositional attribution about the cause of something if that something has either pleasant or unpleasant consequences for them. Acts which have neutral consequences are more readily judged to have occurred as a result of the situation.

labelling theory The approach to understanding social behaviour which is based on the idea of the self-fulfilling prophecy – that expectations can become self-confirming, because the people concerned act as if they were already true.

lay epistemology The study of how everyday beliefs and social representations are adopted, transmitted and changed, and of what counts as valid knowledge in socially accepted belief systems.

non-verbal cues Acts or signs which communicate information to other people, deliberately or unconsciously, but which do not involve the use of words.

paralanguage Non-verbal cues contained in how people say things, such as in tones of voice, pauses, or 'um' and 'er' noises.

person schema The set of memories, knowledge and intentions which someone holds about a particular person.

personalism The tendency that people have to be more likely to make a dispositional attribution about the cause of something if that something affects them personally. Acts which do not affect them personally are more likely to be judged as being caused by the situation.

pilomotor response The part of the fight or flight response which involves the hair standing on end, presumably to make an animal look larger and more fearsome.

postural echo The way that people who are in intense conversation or rapport will often unconsciously mimic one another's stance or posture.

role-schema The total set of memories, actions and intentions associated with a particular social role: the understanding of that role.

self-esteem The evaluative dimension of the self-concept, which is to do with how worthwhile and/or confident people feel about themselves.

self-schema The total set of memories, representations, ideas and intentions which one holds about oneself.

self-serving bias The idea that we judge our own behaviour more favourably than we judge other people's, mainly because of the fundamental attribution error.

situational attribution A reason for an act or behaviour which implies that it occurred as a result of the situation or circumstances that the person was in at the time.

social representation theory A theory which looks at how shared beliefs develop and are transmitted in social groups and in society as a whole. Such shared beliefs serve an important function in explaining reality, and in justifying social action.

stereotyping Classifying members of a social group as if they were all the same, and treating individuals belonging to that group as if no other characteristics were salient.

Summary

1 Non-verbal communication uses a range of cues, including facial expression, eye-contact, posture and gesture, proxemics, paralanguage, dress, and ritual. These non-verbal cues can serve a number of different functions.

2 Person perception can involve applying implicit personality theories about which traits are likely to be found together, as well as the application of stereotypes and labels, personal constructs and primacy effects.

3 People make sense out of their social worlds in a number of different ways. The concepts of schema, attribution and attitude have all been used to examine different aspects of social cognition.

4 Attribution theory concerns how people assign causes to events or actions. The fundamental attribution error is the way that we judge other people's behaviour as caused by their dispositions, but we see our own as being caused by the situation we are in.

5 Lay epistemology is concerned with the explanations and beliefs that people use in everyday living. In adopting particular beliefs, people are motivated by their need for structure, validity and specific conclusions.

6 Social representations are the shared beliefs which are held by society in general or groups in society. They can change over time, and can determine how information is accepted or applied in a social context.

7 Social representations are formed through a process of anchoring and objectification, which makes ideas more accessible but also changes them. They can occur at the level of social groups, as well as at society-wide or cultural levels.

8 Social identification develops as a result of social categorisation, social comparison, and the need for positive self-esteem. Intergroup conflict appears to result mainly from real or perceived competition for resources

Self-assessment questions

1 Briefly describe the main non-verbal cues used in communication.

2 Describe some of the basic mechanisms of person perception.

3 Outline the correspondent inference approach to attribution theory.

Practice essay questions

1 Give evidence for or against the idea that non-verbal communication is more important than language for human beings.

2 What psychological mechanisms do we use to make sense of the social world?

3 How important is an awareness of social representations for understanding human social action?

Test your knowledge of this chapter with our online quizzes and games at:
http://www.psych.co.uk

Explore understanding others further at:

General
http://clem.mscd.edu/~psych/intro/cncpsoci.htm – Table of clear definitions for terms such as attribution, schema,
   person percepton, etc.

Non-verbal communication
http://socpsych.lacollege.edu/nonverbal.html – Extensive links page with news, bibliographies, research and journals.

Attribution
http://www.as.wvu.edu/~sbb/comm221/chapters/attrib.htm – Comprehensive tutorial on attribution theory with
   reading list.

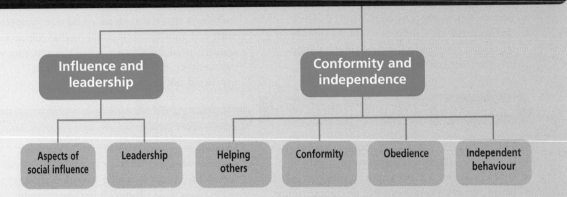

Social influence and social action

Influence and leadership

Conformity and independence

- Aspects of social influence
- Leadership
- Helping others
- Conformity
- Obedience
- Independent behaviour

Learning objectives

16.1. Coaction and audience effects
a describe a study of coaction or audience effects
b outline explanations for social loafing
c identify coaction or audience effects from examples

16.2. Groups and roles
a define terminology related to the study of roles and groups
b describe a study of social role or group behaviour
c outline explanations for group polarisation

16.3. Leadership
a distinguish between different types of leadership style
b describe a study of leadership
c outline major theories of leadership

16.4. Conformity
a describe a study of conformity
b identify factors contributing to conformity
c outline types of conformity

16.5. Obedience
a describe a study of obedience
b identify factors likely to increase or reduce obedience
c outline Milgram's theory of obedience

16.6. Bystander intervention
a define terminology relating to bystander intervention
b describe a study of helping behaviour
c outline explanations for bystander behaviour

16.7. Rebellion
a describe a study of rebellion
b identify factors likely to induce rebellion
c define terms relating to independent behaviour

16.8. Minority influence
a describe a study of minority influence
b identify key factors in minority influence
c evaluate research methods used to study minority influence

In this chapter, we will be looking at some of the ways in which people interact with one another, and how other people's behaviour, or the social setting in which we find ourselves, can influence how we behave. Psychologists have investigated this in many different ways, ranging from exploring group behaviour and leadership to looking at why we obey others or conform to society's demands. All of us influence, and are influenced by, others, even though we are often entirely unaware that this is happening.

Aspects of social influence

One of the first discoveries about social behaviour made by social psychologists was that people could influence the behaviour of others simply by being present when they were doing something. This became known as social facilitation. In 1898, Triplett performed one of the very first studies of **social facilitation**, when he set children to turning a fishing reel as fast as they could, for a set period of time. Triplett found that the children would turn the wheel faster and more energetically if there were other children doing the task in the same room, than they would if they were on their own.

Triplett interpreted these findings in terms of competition, believing that the reason why the children performed more quickly was because they were unconsciously competing with the others. But in 1920, Allport performed a similar study, this time setting multiplication problems for college students. This time, the students were directly instructed not to try to compete with one another, yet again the students completed more problems when they were working alongside other students than they did if they worked alone. They would even work better if they could just see other people working than if they were working on their own. It seems that **coaction**, or simply being active while others are also active nearby, can be a powerful social effect.

It is not always as clear-cut as this, though. Dashiell (1930) also investigated how quickly students would solve multiplication problems if other students were working in coaction with them. Unlike Allport, however, Dashiell found that if all rivalry was excluded from the task, and the students were aware that there was no competitive element at all, then the coaction effect dis-

appeared. The students completed the same number of problems as they did when they were working alone. One possible explanation for the difference between these findings might lie in the way that Allport's research participants were simply told verbally not to compete, whereas Dashiell was careful to adjust the situation to make sure that the students could not compete with one another. So it could be that Allport's research participants were actually competing with one another, even though they had been instructed not to do so.

Presence of others

In another part of Dashiell's study, the other students were not working in coaction; instead they were simply watching the other person undertake a task. Dashiell found that simply having an audience meant that students would complete a higher number of multiplication problems. On the other hand, it also meant that they tended to make more errors. Other researchers also discovered that **audience effects** tended to affect behaviour in this way, and went on to investigate a number of factors which seem to be influential in how much behaviour can be influenced simply by the presence of other people.

Cotterell et al. (1968) showed that if an audience was blindfolded and could not observe exactly what the research participants were doing, audience effects more or less disappeared. The implication they drew was that it was important that the audience should be in a position to **evaluate** the other person's performance. In support of this, Paulus and Murdock (1971) compared the effects of different types of audience on student research participants, and found that audience effects were much stronger when the audience consisted of an 'expert' (who was in a position to evaluate how well the person was doing), than they were when the audience simply consisted of curious psychology students.

Another factor influencing audience effects was to do with the **size** and **status** of the audience. Porter (1939) asked people who stuttered to read aloud to an audience, and found that the larger the audience, the more they stuttered. They were much more affected by large audiences than by small ones. In another study, Latané and Harkins (1976) asked their research participants to rate how nervous they felt when they were about to recite poems in front of audiences. The audiences varied in both size and status. They found that their research participants rated themselves as being much more nervous if the audience was larger or composed of people of higher status than they did with small or unimportant audiences.

Jackson and Latané (1981) compared ratings of nervousness from people who were about to perform on stage. They found that those who were about to perform solo, rated themselves as a great deal more nervous than those who were going to perform in a group with other people. Jackson and Latané argued that this was because of **diffusion of impact** for the group performers: the total influence of having an audience was shared between several different people on the stage, instead of being focused on one person.

Theories of audience effects

Zajonc (1965) proposed that the reason why audience effects result in more errors is that the presence of an audience puts other people into **a high drive state** (see Chapter 13). When an organism – animal or human – is in a state of high drive, they perform straightforward life-sustaining tasks (like eating or running away) very well indeed. If they are asked to undertake complex tasks, however, they tend to do less well. We have met this idea before, when looking at the Yerkes-Dodson Law of Arousal in Chapter 13. Applying this explanation to the studies of audience effects, Zajonc argued that studies like the one which Dashiell (1930) had reported would produce a high drive state in the students, so that they would be highly energised and working fast. But because of their high drive state, they would also perform less accurately – they would be more likely to make mistakes. Practice, too, means that people are less likely to make mistakes, and this may be because a well-practised task does not require as much conscious attention. Zajonc's argument also explains how the presence of others can enhance sustained attention, as we saw in Chapter 2.

Other researchers have proposed different explanations. Baron (1986) suggested that audience effects occur because the research participant is distracted from the task by the presence of the other people. This produces an internal conflict for the individual, because they have two sources which are making claims on their attention. The conflict between whether they should attend to the people in the audience or to the task that they

are doing produces tension, and this results in a high state of drive that leads to errors. This is known as the **distraction-conflict theory** of audience effects.

Both Zajonc and Baron were arguing that audience effects arise from some underlying drive, producing tension or arousal in the individual when faced with a difficult situation. But a third theory, put forward by Bond in 1982, does not use the drive model at all. Instead, it is concerned with how we present ourselves to other people. Bond suggested that audience effects occur because people want to present a **favourable image** to those who are watching. Easy tasks do not present any problem, because the individual can concentrate on the task at hand and be aware that they are doing it well. But when people are dealing with more complex or difficult tasks, things are more difficult.

In such cases, the person has two problems to cope with simultaneously: first, the demands of the task itself, and second, the awareness that any errors or mistaken strategies are visible to other people. This means that they can become embarrassed, excessively anxious or even withdrawn as a defence against social disapproval or ridicule. In turn, these reactions are likely to make concentrating on the task even harder, and lead to increased numbers of errors. Bond's theory is known as the **self-presentation** theory of audience effects.

Social loafing

Most of the time, coaction and audience effects seem to result in people working harder at the tasks that they are set. But this is not always the case. Latané, Williams and Hawkins (1979) showed that sometimes working with other people means that the individual puts less effort into the task, and not more. They called this social loafing. In one study, for example, Latané, Williams and Hawkins asked college students to generate as much noise as they could. They found that the students produced far less noise when they were acting with other people than they did on their own. In a group of four, the whole group would produce only twice as much noise as one individual. If there were six people in the group, they would produce only 2.4 times as much noise as a single person. Even allowing for sound combination effects, this result showed that the participants simply were not trying as hard.

Latané, Williams and Harkins (1979) then set up special 'pseudogroups', or false groups. In these experimental conditions, the students actually shouted alone but they believed that they were shouting with others. The researchers found that what had been implied by the group experiment findings was true: the students simply did not produce as much noise. A given research participant would produce only 82% of the noise that they produced alone, if they believed they were with one other person. If they believed that they were with five other people, they would produce only 74% of the noise.

Social loafing has been observed on a number of different tasks. In some ways it is almost the opposite of standard audience or coaction effects. But there are some noticeable differences between the two types of situations. One of them is how personally responsible the person feels for the end result. Williams, Hawkins and Latané (1981) suggested that social loafing might occur because of the relative anonymity of the individual's contribution. They performed a similar noise-generating study, in which the task was essentially the same. This time, however, they gave the students to understand that their own contribution to the shared noise would be personally identified. In this situation, the researchers found that social loafing did not occur at all. So it would seem that social loafing is much more likely to happen in situations where the person's contribution is anonymous, and just mixes with that of others. In more personal situations, coaction and audience effects seem to be more the rule.

Risky-shift

Being with other people can also affect the way that we think. It can affect the types of decisions that we make, and also how productive we are in producing ideas. Research into group polarisation, and into groupthink, shows how important an influence this can be.

For example: in 1961, a management student named James Stoner decided to investigate whether it was really true that groups and committees are inherently conservative, and always choose the more cautious options when they are making decisions. Stoner performed a study which involved getting both individuals and groups to make decisions. Typically, the people concerned would be given a series of problems and asked to decide what should be done in each case. The

decisions all involved some level of risk, and the research participants were asked to indicate what levels of risk they found acceptable. They would then discuss these problems with other people, in a group.

Stoner found that the group would tend to produce consensus decisions that were much riskier than the decisions which had been made by its individual members. Moreover, the group decisions affected how they saw the problems: when their individual judgements were obtained a second time, Stoner found that people tended to make riskier decisions after a group discussion than they had made before. Several social psychologists (for example Kogan and Wallach, 1967) replicated these findings. It seemed that what had become known as the **risky-shift phenomenon** really did seem to exist.

Wallach, Kogan and Bem (1962) suggested that perhaps it was **diffusion of responsibility** – the shared responsibility of acting in a group – which produced the effect. Each individual who made up the group would feel able to make risky decisions if they were not carrying the whole responsibility themselves: belonging to the group allowed them to feel safer than they did when acting alone.

Group polarisation

The diffusion of responsibility hypothesis was challenged when, in 1969, Moscovici and Zavalloni showed that groups can end up making more conservative decisions as well as more risky ones. They argued that what was happening was not risky-shift, but **group polarisation**. As a result of discussion, the group's views were becoming polarised – shifted towards one extreme or the other. Whether the group decision was riskier or more cautious depended on the original decisions which had been made by the members of the group. If the group, by and large, was in favour of approaching a problem cautiously, Moscovici and Zavalloni found that the shift would be towards caution. If it was in favour of approaching a problem in an adventurous manner, then the shift would be towards risk.

These observations link with the phenomenon of **groupthink**, which we looked at in Chapter 5. We saw there how committees and other groups can develop their own consensual definitions of what counts as important, which may not actually link with the real world at all; but which determines the kinds of decisions that the group will make. The assumptions and beliefs shared by the group are likely to have more influence on the decisions that they take than whether the decision is actually risky or not.

Lamm and Myers (1978) discussed two possible explanations for group polarisation. One of these is based on information availability. The idea is that, during the group discussion, members of the group receive additional information which clarifies the problem. That additional information will tend to represent the views held by the majority. So if most of the group are in favour of caution, then the group discussion will tend to centre on reasons to be cautious and provide each member with additional information in this direction. But in a group where most people favour risky decisions, then reasons for taking chances will be the ones that get most discussion.

Social comparison

However, although additional information through discussion may be a factor in group polarisation, it cannot be the whole reason, because Myers and Kaplan (1976) performed a study in which group polarisation occurred without research participants hearing any arguments at all – they were simply informed of the preferences of the other members of the group. This study, however, supported the second explanation, which was based on Festinger's (1954) theory of social comparison. Social comparison theory suggests that people are continually evaluating themselves, and trying to present themselves in the best way that they can. In a group polarisation study, people can find out from the discussion whether risk or caution is the more socially desirable quality for that particular group, and so they respond to the problem with that in mind.

Jellison and Davis (1973) showed that research participants also tend to evaluate those who have taken extreme positions more favourably than they do those who take more conventional ones. This provides some additional support for the idea of social comparison, in that once the socially desirable trend has been established, someone who expresses that trend clearly is likely to be approved of by the others. So how someone sees themselves in their social context is an important factor which needs to be taken into account if we are to understand their behaviour.

Social roles

One of the most important concepts which we can use in understanding human social interaction is the concept of the social role. When we are with other people, we do not just act randomly, or as the whim takes us. Nor do we work out what we are supposed to do each time a social action is expected of us. Much of our social life is conducted by playing well-understood parts, as if we were in a play. We know what type of behaviour is expected of us, and so do the other people we are dealing with. So, for example, if I go into a library to look for a book, I know what kind of behaviour I am expected to show, and I am likely to conform to it.

In addition, I would also have clear **role expectations** about how the librarian should act. I would probably be both surprised and uneasy if the librarian suddenly began to act very differently from this; and the librarian would probably become surprised and uneasy if I were to act in a manner which was very different from social expectations. If my behaviour was sufficiently different, I would be likely to encounter a number of social sanctions, or 'punishments' of some kind. Social sanctions can range from mild expressions of disapproval to more extreme ones, such as (in this case) being banned from the library, or even, in an extreme case, imprisoned.

Interestingly, people very rarely need to have roles explicitly taught to them. In Chapter 18 we will be looking at some of the ways that children engage in social learning, through processes like imitating other people, or identifying with people who are special role models. We all have people who mean more to us than other people do, and we learn most effectively from these significant others. But for the most part we absorb rules about expected social behaviour unconsciously, as we grow up – and we often internalise these rules quite deeply. This means that sometimes people respond to social pressures without any external authority figure telling them what to do at all – simply being aware of what is expected in a particular role is enough.

The Stanford prison study

In 1973, Haney, Banks and Zimbardo showed dramatically how powerful our implicit understanding of social roles can be. They showed that acting out well-known social roles could result in cruel and uncharacteristic behaviour in people who were otherwise quite ordinary. The researchers set up an experimental situation in which a basement at Stanford University was converted so that it resembled a prison. It had ordinary cells, a very small confinement cell (really a converted broom cupboard) and an observation room for the 'guards'.

Haney, Banks and Zimbardo (1973) selected 21 male research participants, all of whom had volunteered for the study and been previously assessed as emotionally stable. The researchers assigned nine of them to act the roles of 'prisoners', while the rest were to act as 'guards'. In order to make it as realistic as possible, the research participants were 'arrested' at their homes by the local police, and brought to the prison, where they were stripped and showered before being dressed in prisoners' uniforms. The 'guards' wore uniforms as well, which reflected their status. They had mirrored sunglasses, batons and whistles.

Originally it had been planned to run the experiment for two weeks, but the experimenters had to call a halt after just five days. The reason for this was how the prison guards acted out their roles, and the psychological effects which were developing from playing the prisoner role. Although they were not allowed to use physical violence, the guards entered into the spirit of their roles, and acted with increasing psychological brutality against the prisoners – for example, making it a 'privilege' to go to the toilet. Five of the prisoners had to be 'released' from the study because they were showing such acute symptoms of depression and anxiety.

There were a number of social mechanisms operating in this experiment. The main one was the expression of **role expectations**. Those people who were acting the role of prison guards knew that they were expected to behave brutally. But they had few role models for other types of behaviour on the part of prison guards, and so they were actually much more brutal than real prison guards would have been. In their own way, the prisoners' role expectations were as dramatic as those of the guards. They expected to be helpless and at the guards' mercy, and rapidly became depressed and dependent. This was so extreme that when one prisoner tried to organise a rebellion, the others saw him as a trouble-maker and refused to support him.

Another factor was the process of **deindividua-**

tion, which we will be looking in Chapter 17. The mirrored sunglasses which the guards wore meant that they felt anonymous and not recognisable as individuals, and this resulted in them acting in accordance with the role that they had been given.

What was particularly clear was that these outcomes were not just an effect of the individuals' personalities. As mentioned previously, all the research participants were selected as being emotionally stable, and yet the prisoners rapidly became depressed, anxious and compliant. The guards, when they thought over their behaviour later, were horrified at how brutal they had been: at the time it had not occurred to them, and in day-to-day life they saw themselves as being quite gentle people. But the social setting and their role expectations had produced quite different behaviour from them.

Group roles

Within a given social group, people often adopt very different roles. If you think of a group of people that you know who meet together fairly regularly, you may find that different people in that group adopt different roles. Someone may habitually be the joker, someone else the organiser, and so on – although in friendship groups, these roles often swap around a lot, with people just acting as the mood takes them rather than conforming to habitual expectations.

In working groups, however, group roles are sometimes more consistent. Bales (1970) argued that in most working groups two different kinds of specialist will emerge: a **task specialist** and a **social-emotional specialist.** The task specialist is the person within the group who is mainly concerned with specifying how the goals of the group can be achieved, and with co-ordinating the activities of the group. The social-emotional specialist, on the other hand, tends to be concerned with making sure the social relationships within the group run smoothly, and that people are motivated to accept the goals of the group. Although a good leader can combine both of these roles, Bales argued that they are more commonly carried out by different people. Bales also suggested that these two categories actually distinguish two different styles of leadership. We will be looking at leadership style later in this chapter.

In 1948, the organisational psychologists Benne and Sheats identified a number of group roles which could be detected through observations of social groups at work. Essentially, Benne and Sheats found that group roles could be divided into three main categories. Being organisational psychologists, they were naturally interested in roles which were concerned with how a group goes about tackling a task, a job, or a problem, so the first category that they identified were 'group task roles'. There were ten of these altogether (see Table 16.1), including roles such as the information-seeker who elicits facts and information from other people; the orientor, who guides the discussion, keeping it on track; the procedural technician, who handles routine tasks; and the evaluator-critic who assesses the group's accomplishments against external standards.

The second set of roles which Benne and Sheats identified were known as 'group-building or maintenance roles'. These were to do with making sure that the group could function well as a group: maintaining a cohesive, positive atmos-

phere and good working relationships between the group members. There were seven of them altogether (see Table 16.2), including that of the harmoniser, who tries to resolve conflicts between group members; the gatekeeper, who regulates conversation so that everyone can have a say; and the standard setter, who establishes standards and deadlines for the group.

Benne and Sheats described the third set of roles as 'self-centred': they were roles in which the person used their formal position in order to further their own interests, to express their own feelings or concerns, or for their own amusement. They listed eight of these (see Table 16.3 overleaf), including the aggressor, who attacks other people's ideas or contributions in order to maintain personal status; the recognition-seeker, who seeks to have their own contributions acknowledged by the group; and the playboy, who uses humour and irrelevant activities to distract attention away from the group's main activities or task.

Although these roles were given as if they described particular people, it is important to remember that Benne and Sheats were actually describing social roles: ways of interacting with the group rather than personalities. The same person might adopt several of these roles during a single meeting. Although people would be likely to have favourite types of role, playing some more

Table 16.1 Group task roles

Role	Description
Initiator-contributor	Recommends new ideas about, or novel solutions to, a problem.
Information-seeker	Emphasises facts and other information from others.
Opinion-seeker	Solicits input concerning the attitudes and feelings about ideas under consideration.
Elaborator	Clarifies and expands on the points made by others.
Co-ordinator	Integrates information from the group.
Orientor	Guides the discussion and keeps it on topic when the group digresses.
Evaluator-critic	Uses some set of standards to evaluate the group's accomplishments.
Energiser	Stimulates the group to take action.
Procedural technician	Handles routine tasks such as providing materials or supplies.
Recorder	Keeps track of the group's activities and takes minutes.

Source: Benne and Sheats, 1948

Table 16.2 Group-building and maintenance roles

Role	Description
Encourager	Encourages others' contributions.
Harmoniser	Tries to resolve conflicts between group members.
Compromiser	Tries to provide conflicting members with a mutually agreeable solution.
Gatekeeper	Regulates the flow of communication so that all members can have a say.
Standard setter	Sets standards and deadlines for group actions.
Group's observer	Makes objective observations about the tone of the group interaction.
Follower	Accepts the ideas of others and goes along with the group majority.

Source: Benne and Sheats, 1948

Table 16.3 Self-centred roles

Aggressor	Tries to promote own status within the group by attacking others.
Blocker	Tries to block all group actions and refuses to go along with the group.
Recognition-seeker	Tries to play up their own achievements to get group's attention.
Self-confessor	Uses group discussion to deal with personal issues.
Playboy	Engages in humour and irrelevant acts to draw attention away from the task.
Dominator	Attempts to monopolise the group.
Help-seeker	Attempts to gain sympathy by expressing insecurity or inadequacy.
Special interest pleader	Argues incessantly to further own desires.

Source: Benne and Sheats, 1948

Table 16.4 Belbin's team roles

The co-ordinator	Clarifies goals, allocates tasks and expresses the conclusions of the group.
The shaper	Pushes the group towards agreement.
The plant	Advances proposals and makes suggestions.
The monitor/ evaluator	Analyses problems and assesses each person's contributions.
The implementer	Gets on with the job at hand, transforming talk into practical activity.
The team worker	Gives support and help to others.
The resource investigator	Negotiates with outsiders to locate resources or information.
The completer	Pushes the group towards meeting schedules and targets.

Source: Belbin, 1993

often than others, they would be unlikely to adopt a single one throughout.

Towards the end of the twentieth century, the concept of teamworking began to replace the earlier interest in working groups (Hayes, 1997a). A team is a kind of group, of course, and often one with a very close structure; but teams often tend to be more task-focused than groups do. In 1981, Belbin developed a typology of **team roles**, which was arrived at through conducting a number of decision-making exercises at a management training college. The managers operated in groups, and each group was provided with a number of management case studies, and asked what they should do to resolve the problem. Their discussions were observed, and the ways that people contributed to the team's task were carefully noted and classified.

There were eight team roles altogether in Belbin's category, and these are listed in Table 16.4. Unfortunately, however, these descriptions of team roles lost quite a bit of their flexibility by becoming closely associated with personality types. This was partly because Belbin (1993) linked each of the role descriptions with a set of personality characteristics. For example, the shaper was

described as highly strung, impatient, and dynamic, while the chairperson was described as calm, self-disciplined and a positive thinker. So the emphasis moved from the way people interacted in the group, to the type of person that they were. Belbin argued that the empirical data showed quite a lot of consistency between personality and role; but since it had all been collected in the same situations and using the same type of task that was not very surprising. In more 'real-life' situations, people often act differently in different situations, so the link with personality type made the role-categories less useful.

Another way of looking at this is not to try to identify specific roles, but to look at the different ways that people interact within groups. In 1950, Bales looked at the interpersonal processes which go on within groups, and developed a list of different types of interaction. This list has been extremely popular with trainers and others, because it provides categories which can be used to highlight what is happening in particular social groups. The method is known as **interaction process analysis**, and includes eight categories, each of which lists a different type of activity which might happen in a committee or decision-making group. The eight categories are listed in Table 16.5.

Table 16.5 Categories for interaction process analysis

Giving support	Building on suggestions or showing acceptance of suggestions that other people have made.
Giving suggestions	Proposing particular directions, or making opportunities for other people to contribute to the discussions.
Giving opinions	Expressing one's own feelings or ideas, or evaluating those of other people.
Giving information	This does not just include contributing new facts, but also repeating or re-phrasing previous contributions, or clarifying issues.
Asking for information	This includes seeking clarification of particular points or issues.
Asking for opinions	This includes asking about people's feelings, wishes and evaluations.
Asking for suggestions	This includes looking for ways of taking action as well as seeking ideas or new directions.
Showing disagreement	Resistance or rejection of ideas, withholding help or attacking other people.

Source: Bales, 1950

Bales' interaction process model has been widely used for observing group processes. When it comes to identifying different types of verbal strategies, it can be very useful, as it highlights whether people are using one particular type of interaction habitually, or whether a particular committee or group is generally short of particular types of interaction. But it has also been criticised for over-emphasising consensual behaviour – or at least, for under-emphasising the importance of dissent. Classifying all challenges, disagreements, attacks and resistance to ideas together as if they were the same thing can be very misleading. There are times when challenges and disagreements can be very constructive group processes, and can have quite a different meaning or implication than an attack on someone's ideas for the sake of it.

Leadership

Perhaps the first ever psychological exploration of leadership, many centuries before psychology emerged as a distinct academic discipline, can be found in the writings of Niccolo Machiavelli (1513). In his book *The Prince*, Machiavelli outlined the different strategies and policies which a leader could adopt in order to ensure success at ruling a kingdom in a competitive and potentially hostile world. Although Machiavelli's advice was, to say the least, manipulative, many of the problems which he identified remain valid today. For example, Machiavelli identified the problem of how a ruler could obtain true information in a setting where flatterers would tend to say what they thought would please rather than the truth, and where admitting ignorance could be damaging to the ruler's credibility. Machiavelli's advice – that the ruler should think over advice obtained from 'wise men' who are prepared to disagree, and ignore the flatterers completely as sources of information – is as valid for people at or near the top of large organisations, surrounded by organisational 'yes men', as it was for mediaeval princes.

Types of leaders

Since Machiavelli, many other researchers have examined the basis of leadership. The sociologist Weber (1921) distinguished between three sources of a leader's authority, and these are listed in Table 16.6 overleaf. Other researchers focused on identifying different types of leader. As early as 1939, Roethlisberger and Dickson showed that some industrial supervisors tended to concentrate strongly on production, while others emphasised interpersonal matters more, making sure that staff in their departments got on well together and ensuring that problems were resolved. Interestingly, it was the interpersonally oriented supervisors who tended to have the most productive departments, not those who focused on production.

Stodgill and Coons (1957) produced a model of leadership which suggested that leadership styles vary along two dimensions: consideration and initiative structure. The **consideration dimension** is concerned with how the leader relates to other people – such as whether they believe that positive social relationships at work are important, and

Table 16.6 Sources of a leader's authority

Rational grounds	These rest on a belief in the legal authority of the leader as the representative of legitimate patterns of normative rules.
Traditional grounds	These rest on a belief that the continuity of social structures is important or even sacrosanct.
Charismatic grounds	These depend on the character and social recognition of a particular individual character.

Source: Weber, 1921

so on. The **initiative structure dimension** is to do with how the leader organises and structures the tasks that their team has to do, and with the amount of task-related organisation and guidance that they give. Stodgill and Coons suggested that in general managers tend to focus on one of these dimensions rather than the other: they are either primarily considerate or they are task-oriented, but rarely both. Bales and Slater (1955) applied this distinction to informal groups as well. They argued that as a general rule a typical functioning group would have two leaders, each of which would fulfil one of these functions but not the other.

Situation-dependent leadership

However, the idea that these were different and opposing factors in leadership was challenged by Blake and Moulton (1982), who argued that in fact the most effective leaders were those who scored highly on both dimensions, not just on one. Also, Blake and Moulton argued that Stodgill and Coons in their studies had not taken account of how the workers themselves might influence the leader's behaviour. So, for instance, a leader might be very considerate towards a worker whom they knew to work hard; but less so towards one whom they believed to be lazy. Making a general classification of someone as 'considerate' or 'task-oriented' was misleading, in that respect. Firestone, Lichtman and Colamosca (1975) also challenged the idea of a single consistent leader in an informal group, suggesting that, rather than just having a single leader (or even two), groups tend to choose whichever of their

members has the qualities required at the time. So a group may have several different leaders, depending on what the situation demands.

Lorzetta (1955) set up an experimental situation in which groups were increasingly pressurised to complete their experimental tasks in an unrealistically short length of time. This placed the groups under considerable stress, and Lorzetta found that in those circumstances aggressive individuals were much more likely to emerge as group leaders, by comparison with control groups who were not placed under the same amount of stress. This also suggests that groups directly select leaders which they consider to be appropriate to the task at hand.

Firestone, Lichtman and Colamosea (1975) used a method known as the **leaderless group discussion technique**, in which a group is set up without a formal leader and the leadership behaviour of each of the members is assessed by observers. From this, they obtained a leadership score (LGD score) for each of 195 research participants, organised into groups of five. They then made each group acquire a leader. One-third of the groups held an election, choosing their own leaders. These leaders also turned out to be those group members who had shown the highest LGD scores, which was convenient for the experimenters but not rigged. Another one-third of the groups held elections, but these were rigged so that the person with the lowest leadership score was appointed. The final one-third received leaders appointed by the experimenters, randomly divided between high- and low-scoring people.

Firestone *et al.* then set up a fake emergency, in which one of the members of the group (a confederate of the experimenters) appeared to become ill. The groups were observed to see if anyone would send for help within three minutes, which was the test of effective leadership adopted by the experimenters. Of the thirteen groups with genuine leaders, eleven sent for help within the allotted time; and the observers reported that the leader seemed to be in charge in all of the thirtee groups. But in the groups with low-scoring leaders, only three of them achieved the criterion, and only six of the groups with externally appointed leaders did so.

Fiedler's contingency theory

Fiedler (1978) emphasised how the effectiveness of the leader's style is contingent on the overall situation. The two types of leader – task-centred or relationship-centred – are most effective in different situations. The favourability of the situation for a given style, Fiedler argued, depends on three factors. The first of these is the quality of the leader's relationship with their subordinates. Clearly, if the subordinates do not trust, believe or like their leader, then the leader will be less able to lead effectively. It also depends on what the leader's formal position is, in terms of the power and resources that they can draw upon within the organisation or to aid them in performing the task. And it depends on how structured the task itself is. Fiedler argued that task-oriented leaders do best in highly favourable or highly unfavourable conditions; but relationship-oriented leaders do best in conditions that are in between the two.

Fiedler's theory was based on an assessment measure which became known as the LPC scale (the initials stood for Least Preferred Co-worker). In this, people were asked to think of the one person that they liked least, out of everyone they had ever worked with. Then they were asked to rate them on several eight-point scales, such as how friendly or unfriendly they were, or how co-operative or un-co-operative. People who scored highly on the LPC scale were those who had been able to rate their least preferred co-worker fairly favourably, and Fiedler concluded that they were relationship-oriented individuals. Those who obtained low scores on the LPC scale were considered to be more task-directed individuals.

There are problems, though, with the validity of the LPC scale, in that someone who was essentially relationship-oriented might still have very strong feelings against someone they had worked with. Green and Nebeker (1977) found that high-scoring LPC research participants were not always relationship-centred. They became task-centred under highly favourable circumstances, but changed to relationship-centred approaches when things were less favourable. Similarly, a low score on the LPC could mean that the person concerned perceived social relationships very intensely, rather than that they did not consider them to be important. So although Fiedler's theory was useful in analysing when relationship-oriented or task-directed behaviour might be relevant, the LPC scale itself appears to have some weaknesses.

Leadership style

A different type of leadership style was investigated in 1939 by Lewin, Lippitt and White. They used a boys' after-school hobbies club to investigate the effects of different approaches to leadership. The boys were making model aeroplanes, in three different groups. One group had an **authoritarian leader**, who dictated what the boys should do, and supervised them strictly and closely. A second group had a **democratic leader**, who would chat with the boys and discuss their work with them; and the third group had a **laissez-faire leader**, who left the boys largely to themselves. In order to make sure that any effects were not simply due to the personalities in the groups, the leaders were rotated after seven weeks, until each group had worked with each leader.

Lewin, Lippitt and White were particularly interested in patterns of aggression and co-operation. Those boys in the group with the authoritarian leader tended to work independently and in competition with one another: they did not help one another out. They also worked hard only while the leader was present – when he was out of the room they would stop working. Those in the group with the democratic leader worked reasonably consistently throughout: not as hard as the boys in the first group, but steadily. Moreover, they were interested in what they were doing, cheerful and very co-operative. Those in the group with the laissez-faire leader were quarrelsome and restless, and did not do much work at all.

Although Lewin, Lippitt and White concluded that this showed democratic leaders to be the most effective, Smith and Peterson (1988) pointed out that the effectiveness of the group leader depended on the criterion which was being used to assess leadership. If leadership was assessed in terms of productivity, then the authoritarian leader was the most effective, in that while he was supervising them (but not when he was not), the boys made more models and worked harder. But if the role of an effective leader was seen as maintaining good morale and a steady level of work, then the democratic leadership style was clearly more effective, in that boys in that group were more co-operative and cheerful, and more interested in what they were doing. That leadership was important was shown by the third group, in which very few boys did any work at all, and the lack of direction from the leader resulted in generally low morale and a lack of interest in the work.

Vroom's decision-making model

A refinement of this approach to leadership style formed the basis of Vroom's decision-making model, which was concerned with how leaders make decisions. Vroom and Yetton (1978) developed an approach to leadership decision-making in which they examined seven characteristics of situations that required decisions, and examined which types of leadership styles (autocratic, consultative or based on group decision-making) would be most appropriate for each situation. In 1984, Vroom extended the list of situational characteristics to eleven, which are given in Table 16.7. Different combinations of circumstances suggested that different styles of leadership might be appropriate.

In a study by Vroom and Jago (1978), 96 managers were asked to recall their successful and unsuccessful decisions: what they were and what they involved. These were then analysed in terms of the different characteristics of situation. Vroom and Jago found that 68% of the decisions which

conformed to the approach outlined in their model had been successful, as opposed to only 22% of the decisions which had not conformed to the model. This implies that the model might be useful in predicting how successful managerial decisions are likely to be, since none of the managers were acquainted with Vroom's ideas before the study took place.

Leadership, expectations and values

An alternative to the idea of leadership style is the idea that the quality of leadership is all to do with the **expectations** which a leader has about the nature of the task, and, most important, about the people who make up the team. McGregor, in 1960, proposed that industrial managers tend to hold one of two theories about their workers, which he called Theory X and Theory Y. Theory X was the idea that people are, as a general rule, lazy, and will work only because they have to. This means that they need to be made to work, and will avoid challenges if they possibly can. This theory, McGregor felt, was all too commonly held by managers. But some managers – the better ones, McGregor argued – held Theory Y, which was the idea that people basically like to work, and want to be respected for working, so if they feel that they are respected and trusted, they will tend to work hard and readily.

The self-fulfilling prophecy

McGregor's Theory X and Theory Y drew attention away from the 'personality' approach to management which was implicit in the early theories of management styles, and towards the idea that it was social expectations which mattered. This fitted with other work in social psychology which showed how strong the power of expectation could be. As we saw in Chapter 15, Rosenthal and Jacobsen showed that children's performance could be affected simply because their teachers expected them to do better. The statement that they would improve had become a **self-fulfilling prophecy**. It had come true simply because it had been made: the teachers had believed it and the children had responded to their teachers' expectations. Many researchers have argued that the same thing can happen in management.

Table 16.7 Vroom's situation analysis questions

A Is it necessary to produce a quality solution to the problem?

B Do I have enough information to make a high-quality decision?

C Is the problem structured?

D Is acceptance of the decision by my subordinates important for its effective implementation?

E If I were to make the decision by myself, is it reasonably certain that it would be accepted by my subordinates?

F Do my subordinates share the organisational goals to be attained in solving this problem?

G Is conflict among my subordinates over preferred solutions likely?

H How much prior information and ability do my subordinates have?

I Is there a time constraint on solving this problem?

J How important is my subordinates' development in this?

K How valuable is time in this situation?

Source: Vroom, 1984

The path-goal theory of leadership

The importance of managers' expectations was emphasised in the **path-goal theory of leadership** put forward by House, in 1971. This theory argues that people will tend to live up to the expectations that the leader has of them, and that therefore it is necessary for a good leader to see the people in their team as adult, responsible human beings. Moreover, as adult human beings they will respond most positively to an approach to leadership which respects them as individuals and recognises their own personal goals: that they are not just robots working for the company, but have their own ideas and aims for what they want out of life.

House suggested that, for this reason, the most effective leaders were those who set up the working environments in such a way that employees were able to fulfil their personal goals at the same time as working effectively for the company. House argued that the task of a good leader was not only to make it very clear to their subordinates what they were expected to do, but also to make sure that the subordinates also managed to satisfy their own personal goals in the process.

Although there have been a number of investigations into how effective path-goal theory is, they tend to have come up with rather inconsistent results. Smith (1983) suggested that this might have been because the theory was framed too generally, whereas the investigations of it in practice were looking at specific situations. As a general rule, however, the principle that people tend to act in accordance with the expectations that surround them seems to be a recurrent finding in social psychology.

Leaders as encapsulating group values

A related approach is to see effective leadership as the management of values within the group. Smith and Peterson (1988) argued that one of the most important tasks of a modern leader is to articulate and exemplify the goals and values of the group or organisation. In this way, the leader can provide common goals with which all the team members can identify. In other words, the leader is the person who encapsulates the group's values and gives it a sense of identity, or a vision of what it is supposed to be doing. Many of the earlier studies of leadership often manifested this idea, although implicitly. For example, the five characteristics of effective group leaders identified by Krech, Crutchfield and Ballachey in 1962, which are outlined in Table 16.8, can be construed as ways in which the leader 'stands for' the group as a whole.

From looking at the various theories, we can see that research on leadership has not come up with any 'magic answers' to the problem of creating good leaders; but many of the theories have proved to be useful in more limited ways. Smith (1983) pointed out that research on group leadership might benefit from adopting some of the ideas which have emerged from conformity studies of minority influence which we will be looking at later in this chapter. After all, a leader is by definition in a minority!

Helping others

Another area of research into human social interaction concerns helping behaviour, or **altruism**. As a topic, helping behaviour has not attracted nearly as much interest as has aggressive behaviour (like journalists, researchers are often far more interested in the 'darker' sides of human nature than they are in the positive sides) but there has nonetheless been some research into this area.

Bystander intervention

Much of the research into altruism has centred on the factors which encourage or inhibit people in

Table 16.8 Five characteristics of genuine group leaders

1 The leader should be seen as belonging to the group – not as an outsider.
2 The leader should have all the qualities and beliefs of the group, but to a special degree – a bit more than most people.
3 The leader should be able to serve as a model – not be so far ahead of the other members of the group as to appear remote or excessively advanced.
4 The leader should be seen as aiding in the attainment of goals, and giving rewards impartially.
5 The leader should represent the group positively to external bodies or those in higher positions.

Source: Krech, Crutchfield and Ballachey, 1962

helping strangers who seem to need it. Initially, this research was referred to as the study of **bystander apathy**, because it came to researchers' attention because of some tragic cases in which people did not offer help, even where it was obviously badly needed. But as researchers looked more deeply into the area, they found that in general people are more prepared to help than to stand by, and it is now more often referred to as the study of **bystander intervention**.

Factors contributing to bystander apathy

The study of bystander apathy was initiated as a result of a news case in which a young woman was stabbed to death in the presence of several witnesses, none of whom attempted to help her, or even telephoned the police. Milgram (1970) suggested that the experience of living in cities encourages people to withdraw from one another. We are all familiar with anecdotal evidence which suggests that people in small towns are friendlier, and Milgram suggested that this really might be true. In small towns, the faces around us are more likely to be familiar, and there are fewer strangers. The pace of life is often slower, which means that people tend to be a little less tense. And there is often more day-to-day interaction with others on a personal basis in a small town, whereas in a city such interactions are often more limited. All these factors, according to Milgram, combine to make people less likely to respond to strangers in a city.

Another factor which may link with Milgram's argument is the effect of being isolated from interacting directly with people. Coming into contact with others on a day-to-day basis appears to be important in ensuring that we have a realistic perception of the outside world. When people are isolated from such contact, perhaps because they only travel by car and do not go out much, they tend to see the world entirely as presented through the television or newspapers. Since journalists tend to report only unpleasant happenings and regard positive ones as less important, and since much television drama tends to focus on murder and other forms of anti-social behaviour, the picture which emerges is one of a world which is extremely dangerous – much more so than it is in reality.

Gerbner and Gross (1976) showed how heavy television viewers rate the outside world as being far more dangerous and threatening than it really is: they estimate rapes, murders or muggings, for example, as being extremely frequent events, whereas in reality they occur far less often than many people realise. This can also mean that they are less likely to help other people, because their imagination conjures up a series of 'What if …' situations, which make them see such behaviour as risky.

Helping strangers

Sometimes, though, we can be helpful towards strangers. Lerner and Lichtman (1968) asked people to choose which condition of a learning experiment they wanted to take. They were told that one condition, the 'experimental' condition, involved receiving electric shocks, while the other, the 'control' condition, did not. The research participants were informed that they would be paired with another research participant, who would be given the condition that they did not choose.

Understandably, perhaps, only 9% of research participants chose the experimental condition – at least, when they did not know anything about their partner. But another group was told that the partner had requested them to take the experimental condition, because they were 'really scared' of the shocks. In this case, 72% of the group chose the experimental condition. And when they were told that the other partner had been offered the choice first, but had decided to stand back and let them choose instead, 88% of the research participants chose the experimental condition. This study shows very clearly that human beings do not always act in their own self-interest. Even a very simple request from the other person was enough to result in most people choosing the less 'selfish' option, although it meant that themselves would suffer some pain.

Darley and Latané (1970) performed a study in which an actor approached passers-by in the street, and asked the passer-by to lend him ten cents. Sometimes the actor gave a reason: that he needed the money to make a telephone call. On such occasions 64% of the people asked gave him the money. Sometimes the reason was even stronger, in that passers-by were told that the man's wallet had been stolen, and on such occasions 70% of the people who were asked gave money. But even when no reason was given at all, 34% of the people who were asked gave him the money.

In another situation set up by the same researchers, coin dealers were asked to make an offer for a set of coins, which had been previously valued at \$12. When they believed that the person selling them was an impoverished student who had inherited the coins and wanted to buy text-books, the dealers offered more money than they did when they were just told that the coins had been inherited. The average offer for the first group was \$13.63, while the average for the second group was only \$8.72. It seems that the assessment that we make of the 'worthiness' of the cause affects how much we are prepared to help.

Factors affecting helping

So why is it that sometimes we will help others while sometimes we just stand by? Latané and Darley (1968) asked male college students to wait, either alone or in groups of three, for an interview. The research participants were secretly observed as smoke poured through a small ventilation grille as they waited. When they were alone, 75% of research participants reported the smoke within two minutes. But if they were accompanied by others, fewer than 13% of the research participants reported it, even though the room was eventually completely filled with smoke.

What seemed to have happened was that the research participants who were waiting with other people present had modelled their own behaviour on the reactions of others. This meant that nobody wanted to be the first to respond. But this obviously was not a very good reason for not doing anything, and when they were asked about it afterwards, the researchers found that the research participants had **redefined the situation** in order to justify their behaviour. Sitting still in a smoke-filled room would have produced a certain amount of **cognitive dissonance** – they would have been able to see that their behaviour was irrational (we will be looking at cognitive dissonance in Chapter 17). So to cope with this they had redefined the situation, seeing the smoke as steam, or fog, or something equally harmless, so they had not taken any action about it.

In a similar study, Latané and Rodin (1969) asked research participants to wait in a waiting-room. This time they heard the sound of a woman falling over, and calling for help, saying that she had sprained her ankle. Of those waiting alone, 70% went to the woman's aid; but of those waiting with others, only 40% did. When asked, it appeared that the research participants had again redefined the situation as not being serious. They

also said that they had been influenced by each other's calmness. The researchers called this mutual influence **pluralistic ignorance** – the research participants as a group had kept one another ignorant of the seriousness of the situation.

Darley and Latané (1968) asked research participants to participate in a discussion which used an intercom, with each research participant being alone in a booth. During the discussion, one of the participants appeared to have a seizure. Whether the research participant left their booth to report the incident depended on whether they thought they were alone or not. The results are given in Table 16.9. Darley and Latané attributed these findings to **diffusion of responsibility**. Since there were several other people who were also aware of the situation, the research participants felt that responsibility was shared between all the members of the group. This meant that each individual person felt less responsible. But if they were on their own, or just with one other person, they were more likely to perceive themselves as having a responsibility to do something about the situation.

'Real-world' studies of helping

Although these studies were cleverly devised, they were nonetheless laboratory studies. Piliavin, Rodin and Piliavin (1969) looked to see what would happen in a similar situation in the 'real world'. They chose the New York subway, as it is one of the places which traditionally has a reputation for being a source of bystander apathy. In their study, someone (actually an actor) would 'collapse' while travelling. Sometimes the 'victim' carried a cane and appeared to be weak and ill; at other times he smelled of drink. The other passengers were observed to see what they would do when the man collapsed.

Even when the 'victim' appeared to be drunk, he was helped 50% of the time. If he seemed to

Table 16.9 Reporting an accident	
Those who believed that they were the only person in contact.	85%
Those who believed they were one of a group of three.	62%
Those who believed they were one of a group of six.	31%

Source: Darley and Latané, 1968

be ill, then help was forthcoming 95% of the time, which is rather different from the apathetic picture of the travelling public which is so often presented by the media. It also made no difference whether the 'victim' was black or white – people were just as likely to offer help. But in this situation, there was no ambiguity: the person had collapsed, and there was no doubt that help was needed, so redefining the situation as a non-emergency was not really an option here.

The law of social impact

Latané (1981) proposed a model which presents the individual as operating within a kind of social force-field, with a variety of different social forces all acting on the same target person. Latané likened these to a number of different light bulbs all shining on the same target: how brightly the target is lit will depend on the wattage of the bulbs, how many bulbs there are and how close they are to the research participant (Figure 16.1). In the same way, Latané argued, social forces can vary in strength, number and immediacy.

The 'strength' of another person as a social force can depend on a number of factors. Latané suggested status, age and prior relationship with

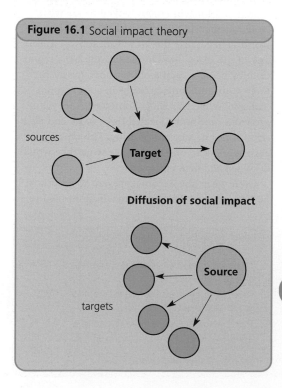

Figure 16.1 Social impact theory

sources

Target

Diffusion of social impact

Source

targets

the target individual; but it might also include factors such as whether the person was a 'significant other' or not, or whether they formed part of someone's special reference group in relation to that particular context. So, for instance, you might feel more anxious in an anti-racist argument if you had some militant black friends looking on than you would in the company of less militant white friends, because the latter would not form part of your special reference group for that topic.

A second aspect of social force, according to Latané, is the total number of individuals involved. The more people, the more powerful the force, but that does not mean that the increase proceeds steadily. In fact, there is a law of diminishing returns: if an extra person makes three instead of two, that would make quite a lot of difference, but an extra person making 254 instead of 253 would not make much difference to the social impact at all.

The third variable is the others' immediacy, or salience, to the target – how close they are in time and space, and also whether there are barriers in the way. So, for instance, someone might be very strongly influenced by what their mother might think of their behaviour, even though their mother actually lived a long way away; but this would be likely only if there were no psychological barriers between them – for instance if they were frequently in telephone contact. Another person, having less contact with their distant mother, might be far less affected: their mother's opinion would have much less salience.

Latané proposed that the total social impact on any one person would increase with the number of sources, their immediacy and their importance. We can use this principle to interpret data on both conformity and obedience – you might like to look over the studies we will be covering in the next section, and try to identify the sources of social impact which are operating on the research participants in the various studies. But Box 16.1 discusses some of the problems inherent in this type of theory.

Conformity and obedience

A substantial amount of psychological research has focused on the way that we generally tend to go along with people, rather than openly disagreeing with them. Some of this research has concerned

Box 16.1 Social reductionism

In other chapters of this book we have seen various manifestations of the approach to knowledge known as reductionism. Most of these have been examples of genetic reductionism, for example in the nature–nurture theories about intelligence and in debates about the origins of schizophrenia, in which those propounding the theory have insisted that all of the important aspects of the subject under discussion were caused by genetics. As we have also seen, the major weakness of reductionism as an approach is that it ignores other influential factors in what is going on.

Latané's social impact theory is a classic example of reductionism in social psychology. Having obtained some extremely interesting experimental evidence about bystander behaviour, Latané then put forward a theory to explain it. However, the theory adopts a reductionist approach – it assumes that social behaviour can be understood purely in terms of the interaction of individuals, without input from the wider society or the social context. So the key variables in Latané's theory are the number of people involved, whether they are in the immediate vicinity or elsewhere, and the type of relationship those people have with the individual undertaking the behaviour.

The assumption, therefore, is that the person acts purely in response to the other people around them. Latané does concede that it is possible for some of those other people not to be physically present, but insists that this would only be likely if the person had frequent contact with those absent others. It is the immediate interactions with other individuals, in Latané's model, which determine how someone will act.

These, obviously, are important factors in any social action. But there are other factors, too, which influence how people behave. One of the weaknesses in the theory, for example, is that it ignores the whole dimension of intentionality – what the Ancient Greeks called the conative dimension of the psyche. If someone is in a hurry because they are intending to reach a particular destination and have little time to do so, they may be less likely to stop to help someone than someone who does not have the same intentions.

But that is not the whole story either. A great deal will depend on the individual's past history, and their personal experiences. Someone who has had little experience of illness or of the way that people can incapacitate themselves through drinking is likely to respond differently from someone who has had considerable experience of it. Someone who has been taught to believe that helping others is part of their personal duty is likely to act differently from someone who has learned to consider their own interests first and foremost.

Their reactions will also be influenced by the repertoire of social scripts which they have at their disposal. If they have been exposed to social scripts in which helping behaviour meets with attack or other disastrous consequences, they are less likely to respond to someone who needs help than someone who has a different repertoire of social scripts, in which helping behaviour is rewarded or is considered to be morally commendable (it is for this reason that many psychologists are concerned about excessive exposure to TV violence – not because of the imitation of particular acts, but because of the way that these obviate or squeeze out more positive social scripts).

The social representations of their society and their sub-culture will also play a part in how prepared someone is to help others. Someone from a culture in which the dominant social representation is of an 'underclass', with drunks, thieves and murderers all being regarded as of the same type, and as effectively similar, is likely to respond differently to someone from a culture in which social representations are of drunkenness as a regrettable foible to which any member of the society might succumb.

The problem, then, with social reductionist explanations like social impact theory is that they leave out too much to be able to count as an explanation for the behaviour. Social impact processes, as described by Latané, may be involved, but they represent only one **level of explanation** out of many. That would be OK if the theory was open to the possibility of integration with other levels of explanation; but it stands alone, as if it were a complete

● ● ● ➤

Box 16.1 continued

explanation in itself, with no obvious way that other influences could be included. Social impact theory is not alone in this – it is typical of many social reductionist theories of its kind, and indeed, it was this type of social reductionism which led to the formation of European

social psychology. If we are to understand bystander behaviour – or any other aspect of human social interaction – fully, we need theories which can interact with several different levels of explanation, not ones which simply ignore large chunks of social living.

itself with how we conform – we fit our behaviour to that of others who are in the same situation. Other studies have looked directly at how we obey people who are in charge, or at what is involved on those occasions when we do not obey them.

Conformity

The study of conformity is all to do with how we go along with other people's behaviour, even when we sometimes feel like disagreeing. Psychological research into this area received a significant boost from research conducted by Sherif, in 1936. Sherif conducted a number of studies in which people were put into groups, and asked to estimate the amount of movement shown by a dot of light in a perfectly dark room. In reality, the dot did not move even though it seemed to: its apparent movement was an illusion known as the **autokinetic effect**. So there was no single correct answer to the question, and when people were asked individually to make estimates, their answers varied widely.

When people are in a group, however, Sherif found that they tend to establish a **group norm**, and then conform to it. Each person's estimate of the amount the light is moving, converged, until in the end they were very similar. When Sherif combined research participants in groups of three, with one person who made estimates very different from the other two, he found that the final group judgement was very similar to that made by the pair. The person with the minority view shifted their position to agree with the majority. Also, people who were new to the situation conformed to a group norm more quickly than people who had already had some experience with the task. Sherif argued that this shows how conformity is related to the degree of uncertainty which people feel. The more uncertain we are, the more we tend to conform to group norms.

Asch's studies

But people sometimes conform even when there is no uncertainty at all. In 1951, Asch undertook a series of studies in which research participants believed that they were being recruited for an experiment in visual perception. They were asked to undertake what seemed to be a straightforward line-judging task, making their judgements together with a set of other people. What each research participant was unaware of, though, was that the other people in the group were all confederates of the experimenter, and would deliberately give the wrong answer when secretly signalled to do so. The task involved judging which line from a set of three was the same length as a stimulus line (Figure 16.2), and it was obvious what each correct answer should be.

The situation was set up so that each member of the group answered in turn, and the real

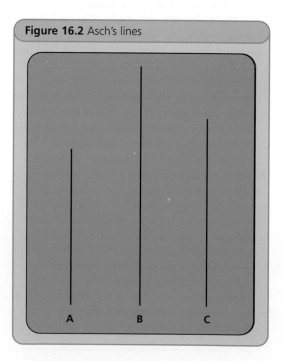

Figure 16.2 Asch's lines

research participant was either the last or the second to last to give their answer. Asch found that as the research participants heard other people give the wrong answer, they would become increasingly anxious – so much so that in one out of three trials they would give the same incorrect answer as the stooges had given, even though they knew that what they were saying was wrong. Most research participants conformed in this way at least once – only 24% of research participants did not conform in any trial. But when Asch carried out a control task, in which people were asked to write down their answers privately, mistakes were very rare indeed.

This was quite a dramatic finding. Sherif's earlier work had shown that people would conform in uncertain situations, but there was no uncertainty in Asch's task. The answers to the questions were easy and obvious. From what they said after the tasks were over, and from observations taken during the study, people made it clear that they had felt very uncomfortable being in placed in a position where they were a minority, and had to disagree openly with other people. Bogdonott et al. (1961) conducted some similar studies, this time measuring levels of autonomic arousal (see Chapter 13), and showed that people become measurably agitated when they are placed in this type of situation.

The effect of distance
In the wake of Asch's findings, a number of researchers began to investigate different aspects of conformity. In 1955, Crutchfield set up an experimental situation with different research participants, this time military personnel on a management training course. They were asked to respond to a simple task, working in booths on their own, but with a display of lights to indicate what answer other people looking at the same problem had given. Again, the tasks were very simple, and the right answer was obvious. From time to time, however, the display showed the other research participants all making the same, incorrect judgement in the task.

Even though the research participants did not have to confront other people in this situation, Crutchfield still found a surprisingly high degree of conformity. About 50% of research participants conformed to a wrong judgement at some point during the task. So although it does seem as though having to disagree publicly in the presence

of others may be a factor in why people conform, it certainly is not the only reason. One problem with drawing too many conclusions from Crutchfield's findings, though, is that, as we have seen, the study involved military personnel. Since the military place a very high value on conformity and obedience, it may be that the finding of 50% conformity is high, by comparison with the majority of the population.

The effects of disagreement
In his original studies, Asch found that if even one other person disagreed with the rest, then the research participant would not conform. The dissenter did not need to agree with the research participant – they could give a different but equally wrong answer. However, the fact that they were disagreeing seemed to be enough to encourage the research participant to stand by their own ideas.

Using a similar experimental set-up, Allen and Levine (1968) showed that the effect of dissent seemed to apply only when the task concerned physical judgements, like the length of a line. If the task involved making political or social judgements, then it mattered what answer the dissenter gave. If the other dissenter had similar views to the research participant, then their dissent would encourage the research participant to disagree openly. But if the research participant disagreed with the dissenter's social opinions as well as with those of the rest of the group, then they would tend to conform with the majority. Allen and Levine argued that this is because of the basic assumptions that we make about the physical and social worlds. We expect social opinions to differ, but we expect that people's perceptions of the physical universe will be more or less identical.

In 1971, Allen and Levine performed another study, which investigated how extreme a non-conformist had to be to have some degree of credibility. They set up an Asch-type task of judging line lengths, in which the research participants had previously been informed that one particular person had very bad eyesight. During the task, that person wore thick pebble glasses, and was the one who disagreed with the majority. In other words, that person had very little credibility as a judge of line lengths.

But Allen and Levine found that this did not matter – research participants still conformed less when someone else dissented, no matter how much the other lacked credibility. Another study, by Morris and Miller (1975), found that the timing of the disagreement mattered. Their findings are given in Table 16.10.

What about those who do not conform? A study by Stang, in 1973, assessed research participants according to whether they had high or low self-esteem, and found that those who had high self-esteem tended to conform significantly less than people with low self-esteem. A further study in this area, by Weisenthal *et al.* (1976), showed that people who see themselves as skilled or competent at judgement tasks tend to conform to the majority much less than those who do not see themselves in this way. This may relate back to Sherif's early findings about the way that uncertainty can increase the amount of conformity which can be expected.

Conformity and groupthink

The implication of all these findings is that there seems to be a lot of implicit social pressure to conform to other people's views rather than to disagree openly. Asch's interviews with research participants showed that people seem to hold two main beliefs about conflict. The first of these is that it is important to maintain group harmony, and that to disagree with other people could damage it. We might link this with the studies of groupthink which we looked at in Chapter 5, which showed how group problem-solving can become seriously distorted if a group creates a climate in which disagreeing is seen as 'disloyal'. The implication, really, is that if we want to have open debate in a group, we will need to take active steps to encourage disagreement – we cannot just assume that it will happen naturally. The second belief held by Asch's research participants was that it is more important to please other

people than to be 'correct' in one's assessment. This showed that research participants' judgements of what is most important in a given situation are highly significant, and will affect what outcomes a study produces.

A child of its time?

In 1980, a series of conformity studies by Perrin and Spencer seem to indicate that the Asch effect was 'a child of its time'. They had repeated the Asch procedures with students in the late 1970s, and found that very few of them conformed, even though the students appeared to be equally upset at finding themselves in a minority position.

Perrin and Spencer argued that perhaps society had changed, and no longer emphasised conformity as a socially desirable characteristic as much as it had in the 1950s, when Asch was conducting his research. But alternative explanations were put forward as well. Doms and Avermaet (1981) also replicated Asch's studies, and found that their research participants conformed just as much as the original people had. They suggested that the reason for the difference was all to do with the kind of people that Perrin and Spencer had recruited as research participants.

Since they had been trying to avoid research participants who had heard of the original Asch research, Perrin and Spencer had used engineering and medical students. Doms and Avermaet suggested that these were precisely the type of students who would consider accuracy of measurement to be very important. In their own studies, Doms and Avermaet had used students from less mathematical disciplines, and they argued that these students would not see making accurate line judgements as being that important. As we can see, this finding implies that the personal decisions which people make when they take part in psychology experiments can make all the difference to how they act.

In their own studies, Doms and Avermaet had found conformity rates of round about 35% (research participants conformed on 35% of trials), which were similar to Asch's original findings. Other researchers found lower rates, but still found that conformity happened. Nicolson, Cole and Rocklon (1985) compared British and American university students in standard Asch conformity tasks, and found that the rate of conformity which they found was lower than that of Doms and Avermaet, but still clearly detectable.

Table 16.10 Disagreement in conformity studies

	% of people conforming
Same wrong answer given by several people before any disagreement.	46
Disagreement occurred after most of the group had responded.	28
Disagreement before the majority of the group had a chance to respond.	23

Source: Morris and Miller, 1975

Moreover, there were no significant differences between the two samples, although Nicolson, Cole and Rocklon suggested that the similarities between the two groups of students might reflect the general similarities of university life in the two countries, and that perhaps a study done with non-students might produce different results.

Compliance, internalisation and conversion

Kelman (1958) identified three forms of social influence as manifest in studies of this kind: **compliance**, **internalisation** and **identification**. These are described in Table 16.11. Kelman argued that it is important to make a clear distinction between compliance and internalisation. Asch's research participants, Kelman argued, were complying with the experimental situation, but interviews with them afterwards showed that they had not believed what they had said – they had not internalised the judgements of other people.

Sherif's original research participants, by contrast, did seem to have internalised their group's judgements, since when they were tested individually after the group trials, they tended to stick with the group judgement rather than reverting back to their own original ideas. Since the task which Sherif had given them was ambiguous anyway, the research participants seemed to have concluded that their original judgement was probably wrong. In the Asch study, though, the research participants knew that it was the others who were wrong, and so their conformity had been purely at the behavioural level, and did not actually affect their private beliefs.

Moscovici (1976) argued that the Asch experiments were inadequate as a way of looking at social influence, because all they permitted was a one-way measure – the research participant could either conform to the majority or not. They could not influence the majority themselves. In real life, though, Moscovici argued, minorities as well as majorities can influence groups – particularly if they put over their ideas in a consistent fashion. Moscovici and Faucheux (1972) re-analysed Asch's data, and argued that it was the consistency of the judgements made by the stooges which influenced the research participants most, not simply the fact that the set-up invited people to conform.

In 1980, Moscovici produced a paper distinguishing between compliance and conversion. **Compliance**, he argued, tends to be what happens when a majority influences a minority. It is directly related to the fact that the majority has power on its side, and that it can use that power through rewards and sanctions. **Conversion**, on the other hand, is more indirect, and is the way that a minority will tend to influence a majority. Conversion mainly involves convincing members of the majority group that the minority's view is valid. In this process, it is consistency which counts the most. We will be looking further at Moscovici's research when we look at independent behaviour, later in this chapter.

Table 16.11	Compliance, internalisation and identification
Compliance	People act in accordance with the majority but do not change their private ideas and beliefs.
Internalisation	People change their private beliefs because they come to believe that the other view is the more valid one.
Identification	People change their attitudes or beliefs in order to become more like somebody that they respect or admire. For instance, if someone had a personal role model that they wanted to emulate as much as possible, they might adopt some of the attitudes and ideas expressed by that person.

Source: Kelman, 1958

Obedience

One of the most direct ways that we can influence someone else's behaviour is by issuing a command which they feel obliged to obey. People in our society are often placed in a position where **obedience** is expected of them – and yet at the same time, we expect each person to act according to the dictates of their own conscience. In cases where people are living in relatively ordered communities, this does not present a problem. But in a disturbed society it means that very real conflicts can arise far more easily. For example, after WWII, several Nazi war criminals were put on trial for the atrocities which had been committed. Despite their having been personally involved in these acts, their defence was almost always: 'I was only obeying orders'. As members of an organisation which placed a high value on military discipline and obedience, they had not perceived themselves as having any choice in their actions.

Arendt (1963) reported on the trial of one of the people responsible for the whole concentration camp programme: Adolf Eichmann. Arendt was particularly struck by what an ordinary sort of person he was. She argued that what was particularly horrifying about the Nazi war crimes was how such evil actions could be performed by ordinary people. Despite being responsible for the deaths of six million Jews, Eichmann was not particularly anti-Jewish: he had originally argued within the Nazi party for a separate Jewish homeland, and had personally helped his Jewish half-cousin to escape. But he saw himself as a good officer, obeying what he saw to be the demands of his duties. In so doing he directly perpetrated one of the most monstrous crimes that the world has ever seen.

Obedience to authority is not limited to members of the armed forces. In 1963, Milgram reported on a set of studies which showed that ordinary people – volunteers who had answered a newspaper advertisement – were prepared to administer potentially lethal electric shocks to another person, simply because they had been told to do so by an experimenter. Before he conducted the studies, Milgram undertook a survey, asking ordinary people and professionals such as psychiatrists and psychologists what they thought would happen in such a situation. The consensus was that less than 3% of people would be prepared to do this. But when he put the situation into practice, Milgram found that the real outcome was very different.

Milgram's basic study

Milgram's research participants were ordinary members of the population, recruited through a local newspaper. When they arrived at the university, they were introduced to another 'volunteer', who was in fact a confederate of the experimenter. They were told that it was a learning experiment, and asked to draw lots to see who would be 'teacher' and who would be 'learner'. In fact, the lots were rigged, so that the real research participant always took the role of 'teacher'.

The 'learner' was taken into the next room and strapped to a chair, with the research participant looking on. The 'learner' was then told that they would receive some electric shocks, which would not cause any permanent damage. The research

participant was given a sample low-voltage electric shock, to give an idea of what they were like. In fact, this was the only real electric shock used in the whole experiment, but the research participant did not know that. Back in the laboratory next door, the research participant was asked to sit in front of a console which held a row of 30 switches. The switch at the far left was labelled '15 V' and they increased by 15 V each time, until the extreme right-hand switch was labelled '450 V'. In addition, there were some descriptive labels above the switches, ranging from 'slight shock', 'moderate shock', etc., up to 'danger: severe shock' and finally 'XXX'.

The research participant was asked to read out words for a paired-associate task. When the 'learner' made the first mistake, the research participant was told to press the first switch, calling out the voltage of the shock. For the next mistake, they were told to press the next switch in line, again calling out the voltage. This continued, with the apparent voltage increasing for each mistake. During the whole experiment, the research participants were supervised by an experimenter who gave them verbal 'prods' when they hesitated or objected. These were pre-scripted, and included phrases like: 'Please continue', 'The experiment requires that you continue' and 'You have no other choice, you must go on'.

As the study progressed, different responses were heard from the 'learner'. These were actually pre-recorded, but again the research participants did not know that. At 75 V there was a slight grunt, which then continued until 120 V, at which point the 'learner' called out that the shocks were becoming painful. At 150 V the 'learner' yelled to the experimenter to get him out; at 180 V there were cries of 'I can't stand the pain'; and from 270 V there were increasingly severe screams. At 300 V the 'learner' refused to answer any more questions, but the research participants were told by the experimenter supervising the study that they had to treat silence as a wrong answer, and so continue giving the shocks. From 330 V the 'learner' was ominously silent.

In this basic experiment, Milgram found that all the research participants would go up to 300 V, and 63% of the research participants would carry on right up to the end – despite the silence from the next room. In other words, they would continue even when it seemed that they might have actually killed the other person. Other researchers found much the same outcomes in other countries; although there was some cultural variance. In Amman, Jordan, Shanab and Yahya (1977) showed that the baseline rate of obedience was as high as 80%; whereas Kilham and Mann (1974) showed that in Australia it was slightly lower than the usual two-thirds of the sample.

Variations on the basic study

In order to tease out exactly which factors were involved, Milgram performed 21 different variations of the study. Some of the main findings are illustrated in Figure 16.3. These include a condition in which there was no feedback at all from the 'learner'; one in which the 'learner' was visible in the same room; one in which the study was conducted in a downtown office block (to see if it was the prestige of Yale University which made research participants more likely to obey); one in which the 'teacher' forced the 'learner's' hand on to an electrode plate to give the shocks; one in which the experimenter gave directions by tele-

phone; and one in which the research participant was not told what level of shock to give at all (the mean level of shock which research participants gave in this condition was 50 V).

Among some of the other variations that Milgram set up was one in which the 'teacher' role was shared between three people, but only one was a genuine research participant. One person was asked to read out the word-pairs, the second pronounced the answer as correct or incorrect and the third (the real research participant) gave the shock. At 150 V, the first 'teacher' refused to continue with the study, so the experimenter (appearing exasperated), assigned their task to the real research participant. At 210 V the second 'teacher' refused to go any further, and so their task too was assigned to the real research participant. As we can see from Figure 16.3, in this condition only 10 % of the research participants continued to the highest shock level.

Other variations involved changing the role of the experimenter. In the baseline study, the experimenter had been deliberately chosen to present a remote, austere personality, with the 'learner' being a friendly, likeable person. Reversing these roles produced a slight decline in obedience, but not a particularly dramatic one. In another condition, the experimenter was apparently called away suddenly to take a telephone call; and a third 'research participant' (who was really another confederate) was asked to stand in. They were not told what level of shock should be used, and the stand-in pretended it was his own idea to raise the level each time. The much lower level of obedience showed that the authority of the experimenter was definitely an important factor.

Milgram did not find any gender differences in his study of obedience: both men and women obeyed to about the same level. Another study, by Sheridan and King (1972), involved asking research participants to give a small puppy real electric shocks of increasing severity. Like Milgram, they found extremely high levels of obedience, even though the research participants could see the puppy howling and yelping when it received the shocks. Although it had initially been thought that perhaps women would comply less than men in this task, because of the traditional female image as being more 'nurturant' and caring, the researchers found that women obeyed even more extremely than men, with every female

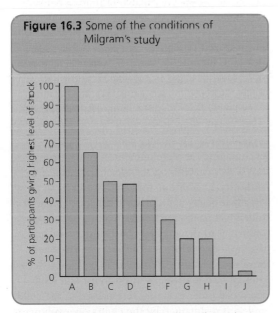

Figure 16.3 Some of the conditions of Milgram's study

A = No sound from victim throughout (100%)
B = Victim pounds on wall at 300 V (65%)
C = Friendly experimenter, impersonal 'learner' (50%)
D = Study conducted in town office block (48%)
E = Victim in same room (40%)
F = 'Teacher' forces victim's hand on to electrode (30%)
G = Experimenter gives directions by telephone (20.5%)
H = Experimenter seems just a member of the public (20%)
I = Others sharing 'teacher' role disobey (10%)
J = Teacher has free choice of shock level (2.5%)

research participant shocking the puppy to the maximum possible level.

Hofling's study of obedience

Milgram's research was conducted in the form of laboratory experiments, but Hofling *et al.*, in 1966, performed a real-life study of obedience in a hospital setting. In these studies, a staff nurse on night duty would receive a telephone call from somebody who claimed to be a doctor and who was supposedly treating a particular patient. The 'doctor' asked the nurse to check the medicine cabinet to see if it contained a particular drug. The container stated very clearly that the maximum dose for this particular drug was 10 mg. When the nurse returned to the telephone to say that she had found the drug, the 'doctor' asked her to administer 20 mg to the patient immediately.

This request challenged a number of hospital regulations. Officially, the nurse was not permitted to give medication on the strength of telephone instructions. In addition, it was an unauthorised drug for that particular ward, and the nurse did not know the doctor concerned. On the other hand, in normal medical practice, nurses are expected to obey instructions from doctors. Of the nurses in this experiment 95% actually poured out the medication and were prepared to administer it to the patient, before being stopped by a previously hidden observer.

In fact, disobedience would have been very difficult for the nurses in that situation. When they were interviewed afterwards, several of them said that doctors often gave instructions by telephone, and that they became very annoyed if the nurses attempted to go by the hospital regulations. In view of the unequal power balance between doctors and nurses within the medical profession, most nurses preferred to do what they were told, rather than annoy the doctors and possibly damage their future careers by playing it by the book. What the Hofling experiment showed was that this social pressure can result in a level of obedience which could lead to a nurse performing a dangerous act, just by 'obeying orders'.

Milgram's agency theory

Milgram (1973) suggested that the surprising degree of obedience which he had demonstrated could be explained in terms of the functions of hierarchical social systems, seen from an evolu-

tionary perspective. Within a hierarchical arrangement, some degree of control over one's actions is given up, as part of accepting control from a superior in the hierarchy. Milgram proposed that the normal inhibition of aggression towards other people, which occurs when people see themselves as free, autonomous individuals, becomes suppressed when people see themselves as agents acting on behalf of someone else.

The agentic state

According to Milgram's theory, conscience is an important factor when someone is working on their own. But it becomes suppressed when they are working as part of a social system, in what he described as an organisational mode. In that context, instructions are not evaluated against individual conscience in the same way as they are when the individual is acting independently. This suppressing of individual direction and control means that higher-level control from other people can operate more effectively. In other words, Milgram proposed, people are capable of shifting between two different states: the **autonomous state**, in which they see their actions as voluntary and self-directed, and in which conscience is fully operative; and the **agentic state**, in which people see themselves as being the agents of others, and in which individual conscience does not operate.

Milgram sees people as being trained into the agentic state from a very early age. A parent telling a child not to hit smaller children is partly encouraging the development of moral principles; but is also establishing the idea of obedience to authority. In addition, the child is trained to show organisationally appropriate behaviour at school. Individual needs and desires have to be subordinated to the 'general good' of the class, and the authority of the teacher must be respected. Similar mechanisms, Milgram argued, are reflected throughout other social institutions. As a result, the social order becomes internalised in the child, and so is maintained by the child's own voluntary action as well as by external control. Imperatives about the rightness of obeying authority become deeply rooted. They also become firmly associated with 'belonging' to the social group – something which seems to be a very basic need in human beings.

Milgram suggests that the agentic state manifests itself through a number of mechanisms. One of these is known as **tuning** – the person becomes 'attuned' to orders or instructions received from superiors, and these are seen as the items of information that matter. Information or requests from lower down in the hierarchy are not noticed so much. So in the case of the research participants in the laboratory study, the communications from the 'learner' were not particularly heeded (despite their emotionality), whereas those from the experimenter were.

People in the agentic state also tend to **redefine** the meaning of the situation, so that they can accept the definition of their actions which is provided by the authority under which they are working. Some of the research participants in Milgram's study mentally redefined the pain that they were causing as 'not dangerous', even though they themselves felt worried, because this was how it had been defined by the experimenter. When we look at studies of bystander intervention, we will see how the person's cognitive definition of the situation can be a major factor affecting how people will act.

A further, most important effect of the agentic shift is that people no longer feel responsible for their actions. Instead, they feel **responsible** to the higher authority, and are mainly concerned that they should 'do the job right'. This, according to Milgram, is how ordinary people – of the sort that Eichmann seemed to be when he was on trial in 1963 – can undertake tasks which involve killing, murdering or torturing other people. It is striking that the levels of obedience in Milgram's studies declined as the 'teachers' became closer to the 'learner', and were faced more immediately with the consequences of their actions. When Eichmann himself came face to face with the 'death trains' which he had been organising, he was physically sick. But he did not change what he was doing.

When we look at obedience, then, we need to look at the aspects of the situations which, according to Milgram, induce the 'agentic state' in people, and keep them in it. Milgram described this as happening through the formation of a 'social bond', which had three main features in the experimental situation which he had set up. These are discussed in Box 16.2 overleaf.

Moral strain

It was very clear throughout the studies that the research participants were under a considerable amount of **moral strain**. They argued with the

experimenter, tried to persuade him to call off the study and showed every sign of being highly distressed about what was happening. There were several aspects of the experimental situation which served to increase this moral strain. One of them was the cries of anguish of the 'learners'. Although research participants were attuned to the experimenter rather than the 'learner', they could not ignore these entirely. Similarly, the 'learner' was issuing demands – 'Let me out of here' – which directly contradicted the demands of the experimenter. Another was the possibility of later revenge or retaliation from the 'learner', either through the courts or through personal violence. Many research participants also felt their actions to be incompatible with their self-image, in that they were administering pain to an innocent victim.

Some research participants coped with this moral strain by using psychological **defence mechanisms**, which are listed in Table 16.12. Milgram argued that most situations which induce obedience in everyday life have **buffers** which reduce the level of moral strain. So, for instance, technology creates a distance between the perpetrator and the victim. The shock machine, with its precise switches and formal appearance, reduced the immediacy of what was happening. Physical

---

Table 16.12 Psychological defence mechanisms in Milgram's study

Denial	Some of the research participants minimised what was happening to their victims. (Denial was an overwhelmingly common defence mechanism in Nazi Germany too – most people simply refused to admit what was really happening.)
Avoidance	Many research participants tried not to look at the 'learner' or the experimenter.
Degree of involvement	Some research participants tried to flip the switches only lightly, as if they could somehow minimise the pain of the shock or their responsibility by doing so.
Helping the learner	A number of research participants tried to help the 'learner', for instance by stressing the correct answer as they read it out so that they would not have to get it wrong.

Source: Milgram, 1973

Box 16.2 The 'social bond'

Milgram's studies established what was perceived as a kind of **social bond**, which appeared to tie the research participants into the behaviour which was required of them. The social bond had several elements, of which the three most important were as follows:

1 *The sequential nature of the action* At any given moment, research participants were not being asked to do much more than they had already done. Going on therefore became more reassuring than stopping, because stopping meant that the person must acknowledge that what they had already done was also unsatisfactory.

2 *The implicit social contract* The demand characteristics of even fairly innocuous social psychological experiments are very high, because people feel that they have placed themselves in a situation where they have agreed to co-operate, and so they co-operate as much as possible. Research participants in the Milgram studies felt as though they would be breaking this social contract if they were to refuse to fulfil their role of 'good research participants'.

3 *Anxiety* People felt a strikingly large amount of anxiety at the prospect of disobeying the experimenter. Research participants in Milgram's study made several attempts to rebel, which usually consisted of arguments with the experimenter. In addition, they showed a number of other responses including extreme tension and defensive giggling. However, despite indicating that they wanted to rebel, they accepted the suggestion that the responsibility for their actions was not theirs, and so continued with the experiment.

What is interesting of course, is Milgram's observation that those who did actually rebel against his authority were able to do so calmly and without tension – at least, once they had reached the point of decision. One possibility is that by challenging the social bond, they replaced one set of values with another, which placed different behavioural constraints on them. For most people, though, the pressures exerted by these factors were so strong as to make them believe, at least at the time, that they really had no choice but to do what seemed to be required of them.

distance acts as another buffer – the pilot of a bomber does not see the people who are killed or maimed by the napalm bomb. Social distance acts as a buffer too: Eichmann took care to have as little direct contact as possible with the concentration camps, or those who worked in them, despite having overall responsibility for them.

Independent behaviour

Research into conformity and obedience suggests that people will tend to go along with others, rather than to assert themselves or act differently. But this is clearly not always the case. In some instances, people do rebel against authority – both openly, and covertly. And people do not always go along with the majority either – sometimes, minorities can exert a considerable influence. Recently, psychologists have become increasingly interested in **independent behaviour**, and how people resist pressures to conform to social norms, or to obey authority.

Rebellion

Not every research participant in Milgram's study obeyed the experimenters. Moreover, the reactions of those who disobeyed were quite different from those who obeyed. Milgram (1973) described Gretchen Brandt, a research participant who had refused to continue with the study. When the voltage level rose to 210v, she turned to the experimenter, quite composed, and refused to comply. Milgram commented that she showed few of the signs of nervousness and anxiety displayed by the other research participants, and seemed to be quite calm throughout. For her, conscientious disobedience was simply a rational act. When she was asked about her past background, it turned out that Gretchen Brandt had grown up in Nazi Germany. After the experiment, when she was asked to suggest how her background might have affected her, she said slowly: 'Perhaps we have seen too much pain'.

Another volunteer who refused to comply, Jan Rensaleer, had been in Holland during WWII.

Like Gretchen Brandt, he accepted personally the full responsibility for the shocks that the victim was getting, saying that he thought it was 'cowardly' to assign the responsibility to the experimenter or anyone else. The relative calmness of these two research participants when they disobeyed was very apparent – Jan Rensaleer only became angry when he was told by the experimenter that he had no other choice but to continue. He continued to refuse.

Milgram compared the agentic state to being equivalent to 'morally sleeping'. This meant, he argued, that research participants who are 'morally sleeping' will not notice small amounts of noise, but will be awakened by a loud one. People in an agentic state also retain residues of their own self, so if the situation is serious enough, in terms of their own experience, they will 'awaken' and act according to their own conscience. Gretchen Brandt and Jan Rensaleer perceived and acted on the moral implications of their actions because of their previous encounters with the social consequences of unquestioning obedience. For them, the characteristics of the situation as it developed passed their 'awakening' threshold.

The calmness of these people, by comparison with that of other research participants, was striking. According to Milgram, this is because they disobeyed – disobedience was the act that brought moral strain to an end. It followed a sequence that began with an inner doubt, which the research participant was careful to express to the experimenter. This shaded gradually into a clearer dissent, which then became a threat to withdraw from the situation and finally resulted in disobedience. Milgram was particularly impressed by the way that the tension built up only while disobedience was being contemplated, in the early stages. Once the research participants had made the decision to disobey, the tension dissipated completely, and they were composed again. Milgram explained this in terms of a psychological exit from the agentic state and a return to the autonomous state, in which the person is fully responsible for their own actions.

Inviting rebellion

Gretchen Brandt and Jan Rensaleer had particular life-experiences which seemed to influence their decision. But what of other people? In 1982, Gamson, Fireman and Rytina performed a study which was an attempt to set up a situation in which people would come to rebel against authority, rather than simply comply with it.

Setting up an experimental situation in which people are likely to rebel is not easy – particularly in view of the tendency which people have to co-operate with experimenters and do what they believe the experimenter wants them to do (Orne, 1962). However, in 1982, Gamson, Fireman and Rytina reported an experiment which investigated rebellion against authority. Inevitably, this involved a certain amount of deception, but the researchers got round this by asking each member of their pool of participants to respond to a telephone survey beforehand. Among the questions was one which asked whether they would be prepared to participate in a study in which they were misled about the purpose until it had been completed. So the deception was considered permissible by the ethics board who reviewed the experimenters' plans, because the participants had agreed to it.

The research participants were assembled in groups, nine at a time, and asked to complete a number of attitude questionnaires. Among many other questions, they were asked about employee rights, the behaviour of large oil companies, and extramarital affairs. The research participants were told that the study was being conducted by a company called MHRC (Manufacturer's Human Relations Consultants), and that it was investigating legal cases and how they were affected by community standards. They were told that they would be asked to discuss these issues, and that their discussions would be videotaped. Each participant signed an agreement to be taped, which stated explicitly that the tape was the property of MHRC.

The participants were then asked to discuss a particular case. Mr. C., the manager of a gas station, had been living with someone to whom he was not married. The oil company had investigated this, using a private detective, and had revoked his franchise on the grounds that he had broken a clause in his contract. That clause said that the franchise could be revoked in the event of arrest, drug addiction, insanity or similar condition, and the oil company argued that living with someone to whom he was not married was immoral, and counted as a 'similar condition'. Mr. C. had responded by suing the company for invasion of privacy, and breach of contract.

As the participants discussed the case, it became

increasingly apparent that the discussion had been set up purely to obtain evidence for the oil company. After they had talked for about five minutes, the co-ordinator came into the room, turned the videotape off, and asked three members of the group to pretend to be offended by Mr. C.'s conduct. He turned the tape back on as he left the room. This type of event occurred more than once. Also, each person was asked to spend a few minutes explaining to the camera why they would not do business at a gas station with such an immoral manager, and saying that they thought he should lose his franchise. The final stage of the procedure was for the research participants to sign an affidavit saying that the videotapes could be edited as MHRC saw fit, and used as evidence in court.

Gamison, Fireman and Rytina tested 33 groups, but only one complete group continued right to the end. The other groups all rebelled at some point or another, as it became increasingly apparent that they were being asked to collude in distorting evidence for the benefit of the oil company. Not everyone in each group rebelled, of course: some people continued to the end and signed the affidavit even though other members of their group had refused to continue. In some groups, though, people became extremely angry – so much so that the researchers feared that some personal distress might be caused to the participants, and decided to end the study early, running only 33 groups instead of the 81 that they had originally planned.

Factors inducing rebellion

One of the first questions that the researchers investigated was whether it was only people with anti-authority attitudes who rebelled. The questionnaires and attitude tests completed at the beginning of the experiment had provided them with a considerable amount of this type of information, and they had used it to arrange many of the groups. They did find a correlation between anti-authority attitudes demonstrated in their initial assessment and rebellion during the study, in that those groups composed of people with anti-authority attitudes tended to rebel quite quickly, and to perceive what was happening earlier.

But that correlation did not account for all of the rebellion. Ten of the groups had been constructed entirely of people who did not hold anti-authority attitudes. Their personality profiles had indicated that they were actually very pro-authority, and would be likely to take the side of the oil company against the manager. But even in these groups, although most of the group members did complete the procedure, there was some rebellion, and a great deal of heated argument. In less extreme, more ordinary groups, rebellion became a group norm, and all of the group members refused to continue with the procedure.

Modelling and personal integrity

This study raises a number of interesting questions about the nature of rebellion against authority. One point which is reinforced by other studies is the way that the presence of other people taking a similar position is important. This had also been evident in Milgram's studies, in which the presence of other people disobeying had been sufficient to enable many of the research participants to disobey themselves. In most of the groups, rebellion became an established response: people were indignant about what they were being asked to do, and expressed that indignation openly. It is a small step from a point where outrage is being openly expressed by the whole group, to an individual feeling able to act in accordance with that outrage.

Modelling is not the whole answer, though. As we have seen, some rebellion happened even in groups with pro-authority attitudes, although it was not as widespread as in the other groups. If some people are pressed hard enough, it seems, their personal moral integrity asserts itself, and they decide to take a principled stand even if they are in the minority. Milgram would explain it in terms of the re-awakening of the autonomous state, challenging the unacceptable demands of the agentic state. The person eventually comes to the conclusion that the issue has become a matter of personal integrity, which causes them to leave the agentic state and act autonomously.

There are difficulties in trying to draw exact parallels between this and Milgram's study, of course. For one thing, it was taking place at a later time than Milgram's studies – since then, America had experienced the Watergate enquiry, which made the value of challenging established authority much more clearly recognised – and there had been other social changes too. One research participant even cited Milgram's work as a reason why one should not conform in studies of this kind!

So far, there are very few psychological theories explaining independent behaviour. Milgram's model is about the best that we have available, and that, given its weaknesses, indicates a considerable gap in this area. We do, however, understand much more about independent behaviour than we did a couple of decades ago. The research by Gamson, Fireman and Rytina can tell us a little more about the nature of rebellion; but we have come to understand much more from the developments which have emerged from research into conformity and minority influence.

Minority influence

In their appraisal of Asch's research, Moscovici and Faucheux (1972) argued that conformity researchers had entirely neglected the social context within which the studies were carried out. In fact, they argued, Asch's studies actually demonstrate the influence of the *minority*, not of the majority. What Asch and the others had forgotten was that people do not suddenly abandon the rest of their lives when they agree to take part in a psychology experiment. Rather, Asch's lone research participants could really be considered as representatives of a much larger majority. They could see the correct answer to the line-judging task very clearly. So would other people, they knew. The majority view, therefore, would be to judge the lines accurately. But because of the social pressure set up in Asch's study, participants gave in and conformed to the minority, who were there at the time, and giving a different solution to the problem.

In 1969, Moscovici, Lage and Naffrechoux set up a study to investigate the question of minority influence. Like Asch, they conducted their study in small groups. The participants were shown blue slides, which were always of the same hue but varied in brightness, and they were asked to call out what colour the slides were. Although the slides were obviously blue, sometimes confederates of the experimenter would call out 'green'. This was a minority view, different both from the majority in that group, and also from the accepted view of society as a whole.

In total, there were three conditions in the study: the control condition, the inconsistent minority condition, and the consistent minority condition. The control condition involved six real research participants, while the others had four

real research participants, and two confederates. In the inconsistent minority condition, the confederates called the slides green two-thirds of the time, and blue one-third of the time. In the consistent minority condition, the confederates called out 'green' all of the time.

Not surprisingly, the six real research participants all responded 'blue' on more-or-less all of the trials: there was no evidence that their perceptions were anything other than might be expected. The inconsistent minority did not have much effect either (see Figure 16.4). But the consistent minority had a surprising effect. Even though the task was obvious, nearly 10% of the responses from the research participants in the consistent minority condition identified the colour as 'green'.

After the experiment, Moscovici, Lage and Naffrechoux tested the **colour thresholds** of the research participants. The colour threshold is the point where someone judges that one colour has turned into another. People are not machines: their responses to stimuli vary. So in psychophysical measurements, the threshold is set at the point where 50% of the stimuli are identified. In this case, the threshold was set at the particular shade of colour which the person named as blue on 50% of the occasions that they were shown it, and named as green for the other 50%.

What Moscovici and his colleagues found was

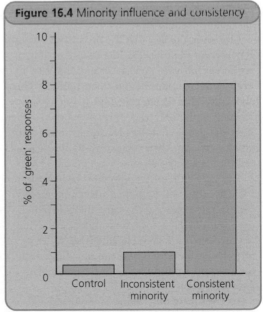

Figure 16.4 Minority influence and consistency

Source: Adapted from Moscovici *et al.*, 1969

that the participants in both experimental groups showed a lower threshold for green than the people in the control condition did. In other words, they were more ready to say that blue-green stimuli were green than they had been before. While the thresholds of those in the control condition had not changed, it seemed that participating in the experiment had affected the participants' perceptions of colour. Interestingly too, the people who were most affected in this way were those who had been in the consistent minority condition, but had not given in to it. Although publicly they had continued to call the colour blue, their own perceptual judgements had been slightly affected by the consistent minority.

Consistency and plausibility

Consistency, in fact, turns out to be one of the most important factors in minority influence, and this has been confirmed by several other studies. Hogg and Vaughan (1995) outlined a number of reasons why this should be so. One of them is that having a consistent minority disrupts the comfortable continuity of the majority viewpoint, and so it produces a degree of uncertainty and doubt. It also shows that there can be an alternative to the accepted point of view, which is something that people may not have realised before. And it tends to draw attention to itself, which means that people do notice its existence. So a minority viewpoint, simply by being consistent, can make people re-evaluate their own beliefs, and explore alternative possibilities.

Moreover, the fact that the minority viewpoint is consistent indicates that the people holding it are certain of what they are saying, and have an unshakeable commitment to their position. This also shows that taking the minority viewpoint seriously is the only way of resolving the conflict, since the people who hold it are obviously not going to change their minds lightly, or just as a result of majority pressure.

Consistency, then, is important for minority influence. But consistency involves a bit more than simply repeating the same thing over and over again. What a consistent minority is saying also needs to be believable. If it is not at least plausible to the others who are in contact with the minority's position, then it is not likely to have any effect.

To investigate this, Nemeth, Swedlund and Kanki (1974) set up a 'blue–green' experiment which was almost exactly the same as those performed by Moscovici and his colleagues. They had one control condition, with no confederate input, and five experimental conditions with four real research participants, and two confederates. The first two experimental conditions involved simple repetition: the confederates responded 'green' to all the slides in the first, and 'green-blue' to all the slides in the second. The idea was to use these conditions to investigate whether it was enough for a minority simply to repeat the same answer over and over again.

The third was described as the random condition. The confederates still disagreed with the others, but this time they responded either 'green' or 'green-blue' on a purely random basis, with no consistency in their answers. In a sense, this was like a second control condition, but this time it was the content of the answers which the minority gave which was being controlled, rather than whether there was a minority viewpoint at all.

The fourth and fifth experimental conditions investigated a different type of consistency, which was correlated with the brightness or dimness of the colours. In the fourth condition, the confederates said 'green' to the bright slides, and 'green-blue' to the dim ones. In the fifth condition, it was the other way round. So the consistency in the fourth and fifth experimental conditions related to the actual stimulus which was being shown.

Nemeth et al. (1974) found that the fourth and fifth conditions, which they referred to as the 'correlated conditions', showed a higher rate of minority influence than all of the others. The control condition, the random condition, and the repetitive 'green' condition – the first one – all had virtually no influence on the participants. In all of these conditions, the number of responses which conformed with the minority was either zero, or very close to it. In other words, nobody was particularly affected if other people responded randomly, or insisted on an unlikely answer.

The second condition, in which the confederates had said 'blue-green' repeatedly, produced an average of four conforming responses out of 28, implying that a plausible, consistent answer from a minority can have an influence. But it was in the fourth and fifth conditions, where the answers were correlated with variations in the stimulus, where the effect of the minority was most pronounced. These conditions produced an average of 5.84 conforming responses out of a total of 28. In other words, the minority were able to influence the research participants by producing consistent responses which fitted with the stimulus in some way. Even though their responses may not have seemed particularly plausible at first, they were nonetheless able to have an effect.

What this study tells us is that the most influential circumstances for consistency are when what is being said is a consistent response to the environment. Consistency is much more subtle than simply repeating the same thing over and over again – and in fact, a rigid position can be either an asset or a hindrance, depending on whether the minority's position seems to be plausible or not. Repetition can work if what is being repeated is already slightly plausible, as in the repeated 'blue-green' condition. But if repetition appears both dogmatic and implausible, as in the condition where confederates simply insisted that the colour was green, it is not likely to have much effect.

Flexibility and dogmatism

While it is important to be consistent, it also seems that a minority with a flexible approach to the topic can be more influential than a minority which simply insists on its position dogmatically. Nemeth and Brilmayer (1987) investigated this idea by asking groups to decide on compensation for the victim of a ski-lift accident. The groups were made up of three 'real' research participants and one confederate of the experimenters. In one condition, the confederate argued consistently for a very low amount. In the other conditions, the confederate began by arguing for a very low amount, but then shifted towards the majority viewpoint, either quite early on in the sessions, or towards the end. Nemeth and Brilmayer found that research participants were much more likely to side with those minorities who had shifted their positions, than with those who had stuck rigidly to one position.

This finding has been supported by many other psychologists, as well as by real-life evidence. Although minorities are expected to be consistent in terms of the position and approaches which they hold, they are also more effective if they are prepared to negotiate with the majority. Rigid minorities, according to Mugny (1982) lose their influence, because they become labelled as dogmatic, unrealistic and extreme. Friends of the Earth, for example, became more effective in changing industrial attitudes towards pollution when it began to work with industrialists to minimise industrial damage to the environment, rather than simply insisting that industrialism was a bad thing and should not happen. The environmental values which FOE held remained consistent, but showing that they were prepared to negotiate how those values were to be expressed in action with the industrialists, meant that they had much more influence on the industries concerned.

Implicit responses to minority influence

It seems, however, that minority influence does not always show up immediately. Maass and Clark (1983) set up an experiment in which the discussions were all about gay rights. In each trial the majority would express one view (either being in favour of gay rights or against them), while the minority would argue for the opposite view. Maass and Clark measured how their participants responded in the experimental sessions, but also took private measures of their attitudes to the question. What they found was that people would side with the majority during the discussions, but privately, their opinions would change. When their attitudes were measured afterwards, the participants showed that their personal opinions had moved towards the minority viewpoint, even though their behaviour had indicated agreement with the majority.

It is not always a matter of conscious decisions, either. In a different set of studies, Moscovici and Personnaz (1980) found that the influences of minorities can run deeper than we think. To investigate this, they used negative after-images. If we look at a single coloured shape for a long time, and then look at a white piece of paper, we see a shape appearing on the paper. The shape is the same but it has the opposite colour. This is known a negative after-image, and it is believed to come from nerve cells being over-stimulated, and compensating by producing the opposite effect until they return to normal (Chapter 12). A deep blue shape will produce an after-image which is yellow, while a vivid green shape produces an after-image which is purple. After-images have always been considered to be simple, physiological processes. But Moscovici and Personnaz's research suggests that this might not be the case.

The researchers began by ensuring that their participants did not know that after-effects are supposed to be the opposite colour to the stimulus colour. There was just one confederate in these studies, who consistently called the blue colour 'green'. One group of participants, however, was led to believe that the confederate's response was typical of quite a lot of people (82%), while the others were led to believe that only a minority of people (18%) would see the colour as 'green'. So some of them interpreted the confederate's answer as typical of a minority response, while others saw it as a majority one.

The study itself followed the same pattern as the other 'blue-green' experiments, but this time, as well as measuring what the research participants actually said, Moscovici and Personnaz asked them to look at the after-image produced by the stimulus. They were asked to rate its colour on a scale from 1 = yellow to 9 = purple. When the participants were shown the blue slide, they looked at it and publicly called out its colour. That was the first phase. Then the slide was removed, and the research participants wrote down the colour of the after-image that they were seeing. The confederate was still present at this time, although each participant's response was private. That was the second phase. In the third phase of the study, the participants were shown the blue colour again and asked to rate the colour of the after-image that they could see. During this phase, the confederate was absent.

The response from this study was intriguing. At the start of the study, all of the research participants produced the same ratings for the after-images which they saw, and these ratings all fell roughly in the middle of the scale. Also, they all described the colour of the slide as 'blue', and they all continued to do this throughout the experiment. In terms of overt behaviour, then, there was no indication of any minority influence caused by the one confederate.

When it came to the ratings of the after-images, though, it was a different story. When the confederate's answer was apparently representing the majority viewpoint, ratings of the after-images did not change. But in the conditions where the confederate's 'green' answers were seen as representing a minority influence, the judgements of after-images shifted towards the purple end of the rating scale. And, as Figure 16.5 shows, they were even more extreme in the condition where the confederate was absent than when they were present.

These effects were very small, but they were significant, and they were re-confirmed in a further set of studies conducted by Moscovici and Personnaz in 1986. What they imply is that a minority, in certain circumstances, can be even more influential than a majority – a surprising finding, and one which directly challenges the assumptions made by most researchers into conformity. One interpretation of these research findings is that influence produces behavioural compliance: we act in accordance with the majority, but it does not really affect us very much. But minority influence, even though it does not affect our behaviour, produces an indirect, latent change in our perceptions. It is possible that this sets the foundations for conversion at some later date.

Majority and minority views

Moscovici (1980) suggested that majorities and minorities affect us in quite different ways. We accept majority views passively, and do not bother to think about them very much. But minority views, even if we do not accept them, involve a certain amount of cognitive restructuring. We think about them, and what they mean, and sometimes that means that eventually we become converted to that point of view, even if we rejected it at first. This also implies that conversion as a result of minority influence would take longer to show up in our behaviour than compliance to the

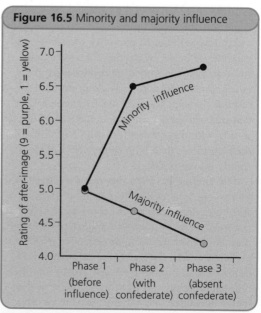

Figure 16.5 Minority and majority influence

Rating of after-image (9 = purple, 1 = yellow)

Phase 1 (before influence)   Phase 2 (with confederate)   Phase 3 (absent confederate)

Source: Adapted from Moscovici and Personnaz, 1980

majority. Given that many psychological studies only measure immediate responses, this might account for some of the apparently contradictory findings in the experimental evidence for minority influence.

The picture which develops from studies of minority influence, then, can tell us a number of things about research into independent behaviour. It tells us, for a start, that context is important. Research into conformity cannot be separated from its cultural and social context; and participants in a laboratory experiment bring that context with them. It is naïve to assume that those participating in such studies abandon all prior experience and social knowledge; and unless research is seen as a contextualised activity, then research findings are unlikely to make much sense.

Studies of minority influence also tell us that it is overly simplistic to assume that influence is manifest openly and immediately. As history tells us, even apparently extreme minority viewpoints may exert an influence over time. The movement for the abolition of slavery was an extreme minority at one time; but over time and with consistent effort from those committed to that cause, society's views changed completely, until what had been a small minority view became a dominant majority. The social influence exerted by a minority may be hidden, invisible to simplistic behavioural measures, but it may nonetheless be present.

In this chapter, we have looked at a number of different aspects of social interaction. People influence one another in a myriad different ways, ranging from obedience, to helping, to coaction and audience effects. In the next chapter, we will look at people's attitudes towards one another, and at the ways that psychological research has helped us to understand some of the darker side of human nature: prejudice and aggression.

Key terms

agentic state A mental condition proposed by Milgram in which, he suggested, independence and autonomy and, most importantly, conscience, are suppressed as the individual acts as an agent for someone else.

audience effects The way that people will often act differently when there are others present or observing, than they would if they were alone and unobserved.

authoritarian leaders Leaders who act in an autocratic fashion, giving commands and directing action without showing interest in the views of their subordinates, unlike democratic leaders.

autonomous state A mental condition proposed by Milgram, in which the person is acting and thinking as an autonomous, independent individual, and in which individual conscience is fully active. In this condition, the individual will not do things which go against their conscience; in the agentic state, they will.

bystander intervention The issue of when and under what circumstances passers-by or other uninvolved persons are likely to offer help to those who look as though they need it.

cognitive dissonance The tension produced by cognitive imbalance – holding beliefs which directly contradict one another. The reduction of cognitive dissonance has been shown to be a factor in some forms of attitude change.

deindividuation The idea that riots and other types of crowd behaviour can be explained in terms of a kind of 'mob psychology' in which the anonymity produced by the lack of individual identifiers causes people to abandon such aspects of individuality as conscience, consideration, etc.

democratic leaders Leaders who make decisions only after consulting with subordinates and discussing issues with them.

diffusion of impact The observation that bystanders are less likely to intervene to help someone if there are several others present who would be equally likely to be able to help.

diffusion of responsibility The idea that people are less likely to intervene to help someone who seems to need it if there are others present (see diffusion of impact) because they perceive responsibility as being shared between all present, and therefore see themselves as being less personally responsible.

group polarisation The observation that people will often make more extreme decisions when they are working in a group than the members of such a group would make as individuals. Such decisions may be more extreme in either direction: they may be more risky or more conservative.

high drive state A condition in which a particular drive is thought to be very strong – in other words, a drive-theory explanation for when an individual is strongly motivated to do something.

pluralistic ignorance The way that a group of people will tend to define a situation in such a way that they all appear to be unaware that some emergency or other event which requires attention, is going on.

risky-shift phenomenon A form of group polarisation which involves the observation that some people will tend to make riskier decisions when acting as members of a group or committee than they would when they are acting as individuals.

social facilitation The observation that the presence of other people can influence how well they perform on a task, often improving their performance.

social loafing The observed tendency in some situations for individuals to devote less effort to a group task than they would give to the same task if they were doing it on their own.

Summary

1 Research into coaction and audience effects shows that the presence of others affects what we do considerably. Social loafing can occur when efforts are shared with no individual recognition. Arousal, drives and distraction have been suggested as explanations for audience effects.

2 Social roles are important influences in both individual and group behaviour. One explanation for group polarisation is that group members adopt the position which they feel will present them most favourably to others.

3 Studies of leadership have focused on different types of leader, leadership styles and the idea that effective leadership is about managing the expectations and values of the team.

4 Studies of conformity show that people tend to conform to group pressure rather than assert individual judgements even when they know that the group is wrong.

5 Milgram's studies of obedience showed that many people will act cruelly if ordered to do so. Milgram proposed that people in hierarchies adopt an 'agentic mode' in which their personal conscience is suppressed.

6 People often act to help others. Bystander intervention is strongly influenced by people's definition of the situation, pluralistic ignorance and diffusion of responsibility.

7 Studies of rebellion show that past experience, or obvious manipulation, may lead people to rebel against authority in accordance with their conscience. Such rebellion typically involves high levels of tension beforehand, but calmness when it has been carried out.

8 Studies of minority influence show that consistency and plausibility are both important influences on people's judgements. Minorities may also have implicit, or time-delayed, effects.

Self-assessment questions

1 Briefly describe research into group polarisation.

2 What are the main factors in minority influence?

3 Outline Milgram's theory of obedience.

Practice essay questions

1 What is the psychological evidence for the idea that our behaviour is determined by the presence of other people?

2 Under what circumstances will people obey authority, and under what circumstances will they rebel?

3 What are the distinctive features of successful leadership?

Test your knowledge of this chapter with our online quizzes and games at:
http://www.psych.co.uk

Explore social influence and social action further at:

Social influence
http://www.influenceatwork.com/intro.html – Online book detailing the influence of advertising, cults and the resulting mindlessness of letting our 'framing' slip.
http://www.vcu.edu/hasweb/psy/psy633/read.html#readings – Useful links to articles and books on group dynamics.

Conformity/obedience
http://home.vicnet.net.au/~aragorn/holocaus.htm – Links to resource sites on the Holocaust, showing how obeying orders can make us perform atrocities that conflict with what our conscience tells us is right.
http://www.washingtonpost.com/wp-srv/national/longterm/cult/cultmain.htm – Articles and chronology debating the influence of cults and the question of free will versus mind control/brainwashing.

Helping
http://www.usi.edu/libarts/socio/socpsy/helping.htm – Lecture with images and charts detailing the likelihood of bystander intervention or general altruism, with case studies and particular focus on homelessness.

Attitudes, prejudice, and crowd behaviour

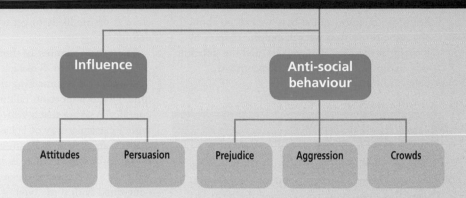

Learning objectives

17.1. Attitudes and values
a identify distinctive features of attitudes
b distinguish between attitudes and values
c list the major functions of attitudes

17.2. Dimensions of attitudes
a distinguish between the three dimensions of attitudes
b outline the theory of reasoned action
c evaluate studies of attitudes and behaviour

17.3. Attitude theories
a outline the processes of cognitive balance
b identify examples of social judgement mechanisms
c describe a study of social judgement in attitudes

17.4. Persuasion
a identify factors which can influence persuasion
b outline the process of cognitive dissonance
c describe a study of persuasion

17.5. Prejudice
a describe a study of prejudice
b evaluate different explanations of prejudice
c outline social and cognitive processes underlying prejudice

17.6. Principles of ethnic prejudice
a list the principles of ethnic prejudice
b describe a study illustrating principles of prejudice
c evaluate studies of ethnic prejudice

17.7. Theories of aggression
a outline the major theories of aggression
b describe a study of aggression
c apply models of aggression to everyday examples

17.8. Crowds
a describe a study of crowd behaviour or deindividuation
b evaluation the deindividuation approach to crowd behaviour
c identify strategies for minimising aggressive behaviour in crowds

In this chapter, we will be looking at how the attitudes and ideas which people hold can influence how they act towards other people. We will also look at the process of persuasion: how do we manage to persuade other people to adopt a different attitude, or to act in a different way? We go on to look at the fixed attitudes which we know as prejudice, and at how we can go about changing those. And we will end the chapter by looking at theories of aggression, and the different way that psychologists have studied crowd behaviour.

Attitudes

What is an attitude? It may be worth beginning this section by looking at some of the different ways that researchers have defined the term. In 1935, Allport defined an attitude as: '*a mental and neural state of readiness, organised through experience, exerting a directive or dynamic influence upon the individual's response to all objects and situations with which it is related*'. Other researchers have defined attitudes in different ways. Rokeach (1948) defined it as: '*a learned orientation or disposition … which provides a tendency to respond favourably or unfavourably to the object or situation*'.

One difficulty with academic definitions is that they have to try to take account of all possible examples of the thing that they are defining. When we are dealing with terms and ideas which we use in everyday life, this can sometimes make them a bit obscure. Also, the theoretical view which we take of human nature will influence how we define what we are talking about. For example, researchers who took a more behavioural stance defined attitudes as '*predispositions to act in certain ways*'. As with so many other areas of study in psychology, it is difficult to pin down exactly what we mean by the term 'attitude', although most researchers seem to work out what they are studying clearly enough!

Attitudes and values

Reich and Adcock (1976) argue that it is important to distinguish very clearly between attitudes and **values.** Although some theorists have argued that they are really the same thing, we tend to regard attitudes as broader, and at times less personal, than values. An attitude is like a combination of beliefs and values together. But it is as difficult to produce a clear definition of a value as it is of an attitude. Rokeach (1973) defined a value as: '*an enduring belief that a specific mode of conduct or end-state of existence is personally or socially preferable to an opposite or converse mode of conduct or end-state of existence*', which is probably as close as we are likely to get to an acceptable definition.

There are a number of things to notice about this definition. First, Rokeach described a value as 'enduring' – it is something that lasts for a long time. That is important. Talking of the 'mode of conduct' is saying that a value may be concerned with a particular way of behaving (for example, that it is important to be unselfish or kind). Rokeach described this as an **instrumental value**. 'End-state of existence' means that the value is concerned with some type of goal (such as that of world peace). Rokeach called this a **terminal value**. And some values are very personal to us, while others are more socially important: for example, someone might not be particularly concerned with whether they dressed neatly or not, but they might take the trouble to do so because it is socially valued.

Functions of values and attitudes

Rokeach argued that values serve two important functions for us. The first is that they serve as **standards**, which allow us to weigh up our behaviour, and to decide what is praiseworthy or blameworthy as appropriate. The second function is that they **motivate** our behaviour – we try to live up to our values, and to act in accordance with them if we possibly can. So values have a very direct influence on our attitudes. Although they are more abstract, they act as underlying standards and motives, which means that our attitudes towards specific ideas or objects can often be seen to be related to the values that we hold.

Katz (1960) argued that attitudes serve four different functions, which are listed in Table 17.1; and which imply that some of our attitudes will be very close to our inner selves, and we are likely to resist changing them; whereas others will be much more 'optional' and amenable to change.

In a similar vein, Smith, Bruner and White (1956) argued that there are three different functions which attitudes serve for us. The first of these is **object appraisal**. Our attitudes help us to assess different features of our environment, so that

Table 17.1 Functions of attitudes

A knowledge function	Attitudes can give meaning to our experiences.
An adjustive, or utilitarian, function	Holding certain attitudes may make us more socially acceptable and so help our social interaction.
A value-expressive function	Allowing us to express what we experience as the more positive aspects of our own 'inner selves'.
An ego-defensive function	Allowing us to defend and protect our unconscious motives and ideas.

Source: Katz, 1960

we know how to act towards them. If you are a militant environmentalist, for example, you would not be likely to be impressed by advertisements for new cars, and so you probably would not pay much attention to them. Attitudes allow our past experience to guide our reactions, so that we do not have to go through the process of learning how we should react each time. Because we develop a positive attitude to things we have found beneficial in the past, or a negative one towards things which we have found harmful, we know immediately whether we should be approaching something, or avoiding it.

Another function of an attitude is **social adjustment**. Holding certain attitudes rather than others can help us to identify with, or affiliate to, particular social groups. Holding the same attitudes as other members of a particular social group is a way of stressing how much you are like them, and therefore also of defining your own place in society. In other words, holding particular attitudes can help the process of social identification.

Smith, Bruner and White identified a third function of attitudes, which they called **externalisation**. This is to do with how we match up our inner, unconscious motives with what is going on around us. Attitudes, they argued, allow us to externalise our inner fears or anxieties. For example, if we have an inner fear of becoming too personally involved with someone, we might manifest that fear in a cynical attitude towards close relationships in general. In other words, we treat external objects as if they were relevant to an internal problem – although Smith,

Bruner and White emphasised that this is an unconscious process, not a conscious one.

Smith, Bruner and White suggested that one reason why attitudes are often quite difficult to change might be because any given attitude can be serving any one of these functions, or even a combination of two or three. As a general rule, they argued, we try to understand the world better, and so we will change our attitudes as our experience grows. But some attitudes will be resistant to change, because they are serving a personal function for us.

This also has implications for how we go about trying to change people's attitudes. It implies that some attitudes will be more central – serving more personal functions for the individual – than others, and the person will tend to hold on to these attitudes strongly. So it will be more effective to try to change peripheral attitudes at first rather than central ones. It also implies that it is better to try to change attitudes just a little bit at a time, so that the person does not have to cope with too much disruption all at once, and does not become defensive about it very tense or anxious, so another implication of Smith, Bruner and White's model is that people are more likely to change their attitudes when they are feeling relaxed and secure, not when they are feeling under threat or attacked.

Attitudes and behaviour

One of the very earliest models of the human personality, dating back to the Ancient Greeks, involved the idea that the human psyche consisted of three basic domains: the cognitive, conative and affective domains (see Table 17.2 overleaf). One metaphor used to describe this was that of a charioteer driving two horses: the forces which provided the power to move the human spirit were the conative and affective domains, and the charioteer guiding them along was the cognitive domain. It is an enjoyable metaphor, although it does not fit very well with many of the theories of personality which we looked at in Chapter 7.

The idea of cognitive, conative and affective domains of the human psyche has been kept alive in attitude theory. Attitudes have been seen as having three dimensions: a cognitive dimension, which includes the reasons and explanations which people will give for why they hold a particular attitude; an affective dimension, which

Table 17.2 Domains of the human psyche

The cognitive domain	This is the thinking, reasoning part of the individual.
The conative domain	This concerns the individual's will and intentions.
The affective domain	This is concerned with feelings and emotions.

includes the way they feel about their attitudes; and a behavioural, or conative, dimension, which is to do with how likely we are to act on the attitudes that we hold.

We can see how these three dimensions would work together if we look at them in relation to a particular attitude – for example an attitude towards eating caterpillars. The cognitive component in this attitude might be a belief that to eat caterpillars is, say, unhealthy, or likely to do you harm, or at any rate the sort of thing which would make you appear abnormal to others. The affective component would be feelings of disgust or nausea at the thought of eating the things; and the conative component would be how likely you would be actually to eat caterpillars if someone asked you to, or how likely you would be to refuse to do it.

Inferring attitude dimensions

Rosenberg and Hovland (1960) argued that the different dimensions of an attitude can be inferred from different signals. For instance, the cognitive dimension of an attitude is often signalled by what someone says. The affective dimension can be assessed from people's verbal descriptions of how they feel, or from their physiological reactions to the attitude object, or from facial expressions, posture or other forms of non-verbal communication (see Chapter 15). For instance, our pupils tend to dilate when we look at something or someone that we like, so measuring pupil dilation would give us an idea of whether someone liked a given object. The behavioural dimension can be measured by observing how people actually behave towards the particular object.

One of the problems with the Rosenberg and Hovland model, though, is the fact that people often do not act in a way which is consistent with their attitudes. A famous study by LaPière, in 1934,

showed this very clearly. LaPière travelled around America with a middle-class Chinese couple, at a time when there was a considerable amount of racial prejudice towards Chinese people. Together they visited 250 hotels and restaurants, and were only refused service once. LaPière reported that on every other occasion, the service they received was extremely courteous and considerate. However, LaPière subsequently sent out a questionnaire to the owners of each of the establishments that they had visited; and 92% of them responded that they would not accept Chinese guests. This gives a clear indication that people do not act consistently when it comes to expressing their attitudes.

There are problems with these conclusions, of course. One of them is that we have no knowledge of the **attributions** that the hotel proprietors were making when they received the questionnaire. Since anti-Chinese feeling was so common at that time, they may have believed that expressing more liberal sentiments would lose them custom. Alternatively, they may not have been prepared to engage in interpersonal confrontation when the couple were actually on the doorstep, but preferred to dissuade Chinese people from arriving in the first place, by stating in the questionnaire that they were not welcome.

Specific versus general attitudes

Another possibility is that the hotel and restaurant owners may have been quite prepared to express themselves as prejudiced against Chinese people in general, but found that they quite liked, or at any rate had no objection to, the particular couple in LaPière's study. There have been several other studies which have shown such a discrepancy between the attitudes that people hold and the way in which they act.

Eiser (1979) argued that this is an important weakness in studies of the attitude/behaviour discrepancy. Typically, a study in this area assesses attitudes in general. But then, it compares them with very specific forms of behaviour. The Chinese couple in the study were middle-class, well-dressed and accompanied by a non-Chinese American companion. This meant that they were not likely to have been typical of the stereotypical 'Chinese' that the hoteliers would have thought of when answering the questionnaire.

In a meta-analysis of studies of attitudes and behaviour, Ajzen and Fishbein (1977) assessed 109 studies which showed differences between the attitudes which people expressed and the behaviour which they actually showed. (Box 17.1 overleaf describes some of the main techniques for measuring attitudes.) Ajzen and Fishbein showed that 54 of the studies had assessed general attitudes and then attempted (with a noticeable lack of success) to use these to predict specific actions from research participants. This does, of course, still leave 55 studies which did seem to show a discrepancy between attitudes and behaviour, but it suggests that perhaps the problem is not as clear-cut as all that.

The question of intentionality

Fishbein (1963) argued that it is not attitudes as such which determine how people are likely to act, but the **intentions** which they help people to form. Behavioural intentions, Fishbein claimed, are arrived at from a combination of three different factors, of which the person's attitude towards performing the appropriate behaviour is only one. A second factor which has to be taken into account is what the person believes other people expect them to do in that particular situation. They may, for instance, believe that it is more socially acceptable to act in a way that is different from their attitude. And a third factor is how strongly motivated the person is to comply with those norms: they might wish to appear 'daring' or unconventional, for instance, or they might have very strong personal values which mean that they do not feel able to avoid acting in a certain way.

For instance, if someone did not like cats, but, on visiting a neighbour, felt that they were expected to stroke their neighbour's cat, and also felt that the neighbour would be offended if they did not, then they would probably stroke the cat, albeit slightly reluctantly and probably not for very long. The attitude alone would not predict their behaviour, because it is a combination of all three factors: not just stroking the cat, but also acting socially acceptably and avoiding a confrontation.

This model also allows for the idea that we might choose not to conform to the expectations that other people have of us. So, for example, if the person just described was proud of being a non-conformist, or wanted to surprise their neighbour by acting unpredictably, they might refuse to stroke the cat. The negative attitude and the motivation not to comply with expectation

together would outweigh the social expectation. Someone who was very keen indeed on refusing to conform to social expectations might end up avoiding or refusing to do things that they really quite enjoyed!

The theory of reasoned action

Ajzen and Fishbein (1980) developed the **theory of reasoned action**. This theory is based on the assumption that people usually behave in a sensible manner, taking account of information and considering the implications of their actions. As a result of this, the theory argues that statements of intention are more informative than attitudes in predicting whether or not people will act in certain ways.

Ajzen, Tinko and White (1982) collected a set of attitude measurements from a group of students about the smoking of marijuana. They also asked the students to predict, on a seven-point scale, how likely it was that they would be smoking marijuana in the next couple of weeks. Four weeks after the experiment, the students were contacted and asked if they had smoked marijuana during that time. The students' attitudes correlated with their actual behaviour with a score of .53, but their ratings of their intentions correlated at .72, which was significantly larger. (There is an explanation of correlation coefficients in Chapter 6, but the principle is that, the closer the number is to +1 or −1, the stronger the relationship is between the two variables.)

Sources of intentions

So where do intentions come from? Intentions, in Ajzen and Fishbein's model, arise from a combination of two basic factors. The first of these is the person's attitude towards the behaviour – as opposed to their attitude towards the object or idea. The second is the person's perception of social pressure to perform or not to perform the action. This is known as the **subjective norm**. In other words, in Ajzen and Fishbein's model, we intend to perform a behaviour if we evaluate it positively, and if we believe that it is socially a good thing that we should perform it.

The attitudes which we develop towards a behaviour arise mainly from our own beliefs, based on past experiences, which link the behaviour to a particular outcome. In other words, they are based on what we think is likely

Box 17.1 Measuring attitudes

Many studies have taken for granted the idea that attitudes can be measured. There have been a number of different techniques which have been proposed for doing this. Four different examples are described below.

The Likert scale

In its final form, the **Likert scale** is a five-point scale, which is used to allow the individual to express how much they agree or disagree with a particular statement, such as:

'I believe that ecological questions are the most important issues facing human beings today'

agree – agree – don't know – disagree – disagree

strongly   strongly

Likert scales have the advantage that they do not expect a simple yes/no response from the respondent, but rather allow for degrees of opinion, or even no opinion at all.

The semantic differential

Developed by Osgood (1952), the semantic differential asks the respondent to express how the target would rate on a number of dimensions, such as:

Friendly

angular	rounded
weak	strong
rough	smooth
active	passive
small	large
cold	hot
good	bad
tense	relaxed
wet	dry
fresh	stale

The semantic differential, therefore, represents an attempt to assess the emotional and associative nuances of an attitude – its conotative meaning – rather than asking about its literal (denotative) meaning. As such, it tries to capture more of the depth in someone's attitude than can be measured by conventional scales.

Sociometry

This method of assessing attitudes was developed by Moreno, in 1953, and can be used with any 'natural' group. Each group member is asked to name another, either as a friend, or as a preferred partner for some activity. From this, a **sociogram** is drawn up, which charts the friendship groups. The individuals are represented on the sociogram as circles, with letters in them to indicate which circle stands for whom. The choices which have been made are then drawn in as arrows linking these circles. Each arrow originates from the person making that particular choice, and points to the person that they have chosen. The resulting diagram indicates which members of the group are the most popular, or the natural leaders; and also shows which members of the group are socially isolated.

The Bogardus social distance scale

This is a measure of racial and other forms of ethnic prejudice, comprising a series of statements which represent how much perceived 'social distance' there is between the person whose attitude is being obtained, and a number of different social groups. Through this, the scale indicates the relationships which the individual finds tolerable. For each social group asked about on the scale, the research participant is asked to tick or cross a number of statements, for example:

Doctors

would admit to close kinship by marriage
would admit to citizenship in my country
would exclude from my country
would admit to my street as neighbours

The outcome of the scale is primarily used to identify prejudiced attitudes of one form or another.

Problems of attitude measurement

As can be seen, each of these methods of measuring attitudes has its limitations, as well as its advantages. Measuring attitudes is a difficult task, for several reasons. One of these is the problems of response bias: most attitude scales are fairly transparent to the respondent, and people may deliberately seek to present themselves as socially acceptable. There is some evidence, for instance, that people will give different answers to black and white questioners, if they are being asked about social attitudes in a survey. Some attitude tests include

● ● ● ➤

a 'lie scale' to detect social desirability bias; but sometimes this simply is not practical.

Another common source of bias is the way that people sometimes give consistent answers regardless of the question. For instance, there is a pronounced tendency for respondents to answer 'yes' rather than 'no' to questions: so the way that the question is phrased can make quite a lot of difference to the answers it gets. In the case of an atttitude scale, people tend to 'agree' rather than 'disagree', which means that the scale must be carefully designed to balance out the questions.

Essentially, attitude scales make three basic assumptions:

(1) That attitudes can be expressed by verbal statements.

(2) That the same statement has the same meaning for all participants.

(3) That attitudes, when expressed in the form of verbal statements, can be measured and quantified.

Each of these statements is more controversial than it may appear. We have already seen, for example, that what people say may not correspond with what they actually do. In Chapter 7, when we looked at personal construct theory, we saw that people may interpret the same words or statements entirely differently, depending on their own personal way of interpreting the world. And some researchers (e.g. Sherrard, 1997) believe that the only realistic way of capturing meaning in attitudes is to look at them qualitatively, not to try to reduce them down to a set of meaningless numbers.

to happen if we perform that behaviour. We can see that this contains an assessment of probability – our attitude towards going on a diet will be affected by our estimate of how likely it is that going on that particular diet will actually produce the weight-loss outcome that we want. Behavioural beliefs, then, are ways of expressing what the person expects to happen.

Subjective norms, on the other hand, are externally focused. They develop from the person's beliefs about social judgements and how they operate in a particular group of people. So they are all to do with what we believe the social norms are in a particular group. Both behavioural beliefs and subjective norms combine to form the intentions. So Ajzen and Fishbein's theory of reasoned action is directly concerned with how our beliefs and our perception of social norms influence our behaviour. They see intentions, rather than attitudes, as being the central focus in this.

Heider's balance theory

Heider (1944) believed that understanding people's cognitions, or ideas, about relationships would provide the key to understanding social behaviour; and that there is a strong tendency for people to prefer their attitudes to be consistent

with one another. If our attitudes are inconsistent, Heider argued, a state of cognitive imbalance will occur, producing tension and a certain level of stress. Unbalanced attitudes will leave us with unpleasant feelings of tension, and so we will strive to balance them in some way. So, in general, we seek a cognitive balance between our different attitudes. We find it much easier to believe that people we do not like have unpleasant qualities, and to like people who have the same kinds of ideas as we do.

Dyadic and triadic balances

Heider applied this principle both to the understanding of personal relationships and to the understanding of attitudes. A pleasant, tension-free relationship between two people would involve a **dyadic balance**: both members of the couple would, for instance, like each other about equally. If the relationship was unbalanced, then tension and misunderstandings would result.

In a similar way, Heider's view of social attitudes was based on the concept of **triadic balance**: the three elements being either three different people, or two people and an attitude object. So, for example: if I like Sally, Sally likes Ann and I also like Ann, the relationship is balanced, which is a pleasant, tension-free situation. Similarly, if I like Sally and both of us support the environmental movement Greenpeace (the attitudinal object), then the relationship is balanced and tension-free. This model, of course, provides an explanation for the way that we often seek out friends with similar interests and values.

But if I like Sally but dislike Sally's best friend Josephine, then there is an imbalance in the triad, which produces tension. Or if I like Sally but find that she supports what I think of as repressive social measures against unemployed people, then again there is tension and the relationship is unbalanced. When all three of the relationships in the triad are negative, the situation is more ambiguous. If I dislike Josephine, and also Sheila, and if Sheila and Josephine dislike each other too, then it could work either way. We might regard the triad as balanced – there is no tension because we might just have nothing to do with one another. But most researchers who use balance models of attitudes regard such situations as unbalanced, because of the tension that is generated by the negative relationships.

Heider argued that the tension generated by unbalanced triads produces pressure to change, so that we can get the cognitive balance back. But this assumes that we see ourselves as directly involved in the situation. Mower-White (1977) asked research participants to rate a number of situations for pleasantness. Each of the situations involved a triad of some type, but half of them referred directly to the research participant (the person was referred to as 'you'), while the other situations described other people. The research participants rated balanced situations as 'pleasant' and unbalanced ones as 'unpleasant', as balance theory predicted, but only when the situation referred to them personally. If it concerned other people, they saw the situation as neutral.

Newcomb's theory of interpersonal balance

Newcomb (1968) proposed a modification of Heider's original balance theory, which concerned how suitable other people are as sources of information in the triads. In this model, an imbalance will produce tension in a triad only if it is highly relevant. If I believe that Sally is an authoritative source of information on social affairs, or influential in deciding government policy, then I may be disturbed by our lack of agreement regarding the treatment of the unemployed. But if I perceive Sally as knowing very little about such things, and

having little influence, then her attitude is unlikely to trouble me very much.

Using Newcomb's model, some researchers (for example Zajonc and Burnstein, 1965) found that we have a **positivity bias** towards triads: we prefer positive attitudes to negative ones. We also find triads which involve a positive relationship between a person and an attitude object much easier to learn and to remember. This applies even when we are comparing an unbalanced positive relationship with a balanced negative one – the positive one is easier to grasp. An unbalanced positive relationship might be one in which, for instance, I approve of Greenpeace and like Janet (both positive), but Janet disapproves of Greenpeace (negative). A balanced triad with negative relationships might be, for instance, in the event of Sarah and I both agreeing that we disapprove (negative) of blood sports.

Social judgement theories of attitudes

A different group of theories sees attitudes as being forms of social judgements, much like the physical judgements we make when estimating size, or how far down the road something is. These theories originated with the work of Thurstone, in 1928, who argued that people could assess how favourable or unfavourable a statement was towards its target object, without being particularly affected by their own personal views. So, for instance, faced with a statement about the Church and its relationship to religion, people can say whether the statement is favourable or unfavourable, and how favourable or unfavourable it is, regardless of their own personal views about religion. This assumption also underlay Thurstone's work on measuring attitudes.

Assimilation and contrast theory

Where Thurstone had implied that people can make totally independent and impartial judgements about the favourability or unfavourability of various attitude statements, Sherif and Hovland (1961) argued that people generally use their own personal views on an issue as a standard for evaluating other statements. So a statement which someone finds personally acceptable will be rated as more favourable – closer to their own position – than it might do if they were assessing it on a more general scale. This is known as the **assimilation effect**.

So, for instance, if I hold an attitude of extreme concern about the state of the environment (which I do), and I read that phosphate-free detergents are being used more and more, I am likely to rate that statement as being a favourable one. On the other hand, someone who regarded the environmental issue as unimportant might rate it differently (for instance, as evidence of the gullibility of the detergent-buying public).

Sherif and Hovland also predicted that there would be a **contrast effect**, whereby statements will be seen as more extreme if they differ markedly from someone's own personal views. This contrast will be made stronger by the amount of personal involvement which the person has with the area. If someone feels very personally involved, then they will be inclined to define very clearly whether they agree or disagree with the statement. So, for example, somebody who felt very strongly about environmental issues would have a larger range of statements that they either agreed with or disagreed with. But somebody who did not care much about the environment one way or the other would not respond as strongly.

The range of statements which we agree with, with respect to a particular issue, is known as our **latitude of acceptance**, and the range of statements that we disagree with is known as our **latitude of rejection**. Sherif and Hovland argued that statements which fall within someone's latitude of acceptance can be quite effective in producing attitude change. Because people will tend to rate these statements as being already quite similar to their own views, it means that they can easily shift their own attitude to fit with the statement.

For instance, imagine someone who is in general against the death penalty but not altogether certain about it. They then hear a strong statement (which falls within their latitude of acceptance) about the number of cases in which people are wrongfully judged guilty when in fact they are innocent. This statement is likely to be quite influential to them: that person's view would probably shift towards being strongly against capital punishment. But such a statement would have no effect on someone who was rigidly in favour of the death penalty, because it would fall within their latitude of rejection.

Oddly enough, though, sometimes statements which are really extreme can produce what Sherif and Hovland called a **boomerang effect**. The contrast which is formed by the difference between the statement and the person's own values is so strong that it produces an attitude change which is the exact opposite of the one that is intended. For the most part, though, boomerang effects are uncommon: we tend mainly to be influenced by statements which fall into our latitude of acceptance, because we can assimilate them more readily.

Accentuation theory

Although there seemed to be quite a lot of experimental support for the idea of assimilation effects, the contrast effects which were identified by Sherif and Hovland were much more elusive. For example: Selltiz, Edrich and Cook (1965) asked research participants with highly varying attitudes towards black people to rate the favourableness or otherwise of a number of different statements about 'the social position of the negro'. While they found that fewer racist research participants gave extreme ratings to favourable statements, they did not find that highly racist research participants gave extreme ratings to the extremely unfavourable statements. Instead, such people tended to rate the statements more moderately than would have been expected.

Eiser (1975) explained this in terms of the social context in which the study took place, and the evaluative language that was used. The experiment was done in an American university in the 1960s, when social norms were powerfully directed towards increasing racial toleration. This meant that statements about 'the social position of the negro' were highly evaluative – they were not just simple, factual statements. Non-racist research participants could use the extremes of the rating scale for their judgements, because they would be using the end of the scale which was evaluatively positive; but racist research participants would be expected to admit that the statements with which they agreed were the ones at the 'socially disapproved of' end of the scale. So they showed less extreme judgements than they might have done if the context and phrasing had been different.

Eiser's **accentuation theory** emphasised that the evaluative judgements implied in how people are asked to indicate their attitudes is crucially important. As we saw earlier, attitudes and values are closely linked; and often the words which someone uses can reveal their underlying attitude. For instance, if we are describing someone who takes a lot of risks and we refer to them as 'foolhardy', that implies that we disapprove; whereas if we refer to them as 'adventurous', it implies that we approve.

Eiser and Mower-White (1974) performed an experiment which began by assessing teenagers' attitudes towards authority. The teenagers were then sorted into three groups, and each given an attitude scale to complete which was similar to the one which they had just done. The control group was told that the second scale was a check on the first measure. The second group was told that the scale was to assess 'how polite, obedient, helpful and co-operative you are'; and the third group was told that the second scale was to assess 'how bold, adventurous, creative and with-it you are'. By comparison with the control group, the second group's scores showed that their attitudes had shifted towards a more pro-authority stance, whereas the attitudes of the third group had shifted towards a more anti-authority stance. In other words, the descriptions which the teenagers had been given had accentuated these tendencies in their answers.

Another aspect of accentuation theory is the importance of **labels**. People tend to categorise statements into different types – such as pro- or anti-authority statements, or right- or left-wing ones. Once they have categorised them, they will then decide whether or not they are prepared to see their own ideas as fitting into that category. This relates back to Tajfel and Wilkes' findings about how strongly research participants respond to arbitrary classifications. Tajfel and Wilkes found that people made more extreme judgements about the length of the lines if they had been classified into groups, even though the groups were quite arbitrary.

Eiser (1971) found that ratings of statements about recreational drugs varied according to the source from which the statements were supposed to have come. The sources which were used in the study were newspapers which took particular approaches towards the idea of recreational drugs and unconventional behaviour. By comparison with ratings from a control group who received the statements unlabelled, research participants who had been told about the source of the statement produced more extreme views. Whether those views were favourable or unfavourable

depended on the source from which the statement had come.

Eiser's theory, then, shows that how we describe our attitudes – the words we choose and the labels we give to the sources of particular attitudes – can be highly influential. This is particularly significant if we look at media communication: many researchers regard the choice of words used in documentaries or news reports, for instance, as being clear attempts to manipulate public opinion. We looked at some of these effects of language in Chapter 4.

Persuasion

In the modern world we are constantly surrounded by attempts to persuade us to do one thing or another. Advertisers try to persuade us to buy certain products rather than others, political parties try to persuade us to vote one way rather than another and public health organisations try to persuade us to change to a more healthy lifestyle. All of these are attempts to change the attitudes that we hold, on the grounds that this is likely to make us act differently. As you might imagine, there has been a considerable amount of research into the factors which are likely to be most successful in persuasion.

The information-processing approach to persuasion

Most psychological research into the effectiveness of persuasion has looked at it in terms of how we process information. In this, there seem to be four groups of factors which are relevant. The first group is those factors which relate to the source of the communication; the second is those factors which concern the message itself; the third group of factors concern the person who is receiving the message; and the fourth group is to do with the context in which the whole process takes place. We will look at each of these in turn.

The source of the communication
One very important factor in the persuasiveness of a communication concerns the **credibility** of the sender of the message. Kelman and Hovland (1953) performed a study in which people heard a talk about juvenile delinquency, given by one of three speakers. One of the speakers claimed to be

a juvenile court judge, and therefore was thought to have high credibility; one speaker was described as a random member of the studio audience, whose credibility was thought to be neutral; and one speaker was described as a 'dope peddler', and so was thought to have low credibility.

Kelman and Hovland found that the more credible the communicator was, the more influence their talk had exerted on the listeners. However, when they retested the research participants four weeks later, they found that the **source effect** had entirely disappeared. People remembered what had been said, but not who had said it. So it is possible that the credibility of the source is important only in the short term.

Friedman and Friedman (1979) compared the effects of different types of testimonials – personal recommendations – in television advertisements. They compared recommendations from celebrities, professionals and typical consumers. The research participants were asked to watch advertisements for 360 different household products. They were asked to rate each advertisement by judging the appropriateness of each of twenty adjectives, such as 'honest', 'likeable', 'informative' or 'powerful', in describing them. They were also asked how believable they found the advertisement, and whether they were likely to buy the product concerned; and they were telephoned 48 hours later to see if they still remembered the products that they had seen advertised. Friedman and Friedman found that the celebrities were far more effective as endorsers of the products than were the other two types of people. The only exceptions to this were one or two specific cases where a professional's advice was judged to be highly appropriate.

If we believe that people are deliberately trying to influence us, we can sometimes become **resistant** to what is being said. Walster and Festinger (1962) set up an experimental situation in which research participants either 'accidentally' overheard information, or heard messages which they knew were directly aimed at persuading them. Walster and Festinger found that the 'overheard' messages were more persuasive, but only in situations which had a high degree of personal relevance for the individual. If it was about something which did not concern them at all, then it did not make any difference whether the message was overheard or received directly. For instance, an overheard discussion of how

husbands should spend more time at home had more impact on married male research participants than it did on single ones.

Another aspect of persuasiveness is to do with whether we believe that the person who is communicating is saying things which fit with their own personal goals. Walster, Aronson and Abrahams (1966a) found that if communicators seem to be arguing against their own interests, people find their messages more persuasive. In one study, adolescents were given newspaper interviews to read, about the amount of power that prosecutors and the courts should have. Some of these reports argued that the courts should have more power, and others that they should have less. Half of the children were told that the report came from a man serving a prison sentence, while the rest were told that it came from a particularly successful prosecutor. Walster, Aronson and Abrahams found that most attitude change was produced when the criminal argued in favour of more power for the courts, and when the prosecutor argued for less power. In the 'more power for the courts' condition, the research participants also rated the criminal as being more honest then the prosecutor.

The message itself

Have you ever been irritated by advertisers who insist that their product is definitely the best, phrasing things in such a way as to imply that there is no room for doubt? They do this because the confidence with which a message is communicated has been shown to be an important factor in how persuasive it is. Maslow, Yoselson and London (1971) gave people written documents from legal cases, and also a written argument in favour of the accused person. Half of the research participants read arguments which were tentative in tone, using phrases such as: 'I'm not certain' or 'I do not know'; whereas the other half read statements written in very definite tones, including confident terms such as: 'I believe' and 'obviously'. Research participants were asked to assess the guilt or innocence of the accused person, and significantly more of those who had received the confident statement recommended that the person be regarded as 'not guilty'.

As advertisers and propagandists know very well, language can have quite a dramatic effect on attitude change. In 1977, Eiser and Ross asked research participants to write essays on the topic of capital punishment. Half of the research participants (who were Canadian students) were asked to include in their essays a number of words with anti-capital-punishment overtones, such as 'callous' or 'barbaric'. The other students were asked to include words which were linked with pro-capital-punishment attitudes, like 'over-sentimental' or 'irresponsible'.

Eiser and Ross found that the students shifted their attitudes towards the stance suggested by the words that they had used in their essays. Eiser (1979) suggested that language communicates a specific **thematic framework**, which gives the person guidelines for interpreting information. We might also link this finding with the schema model of social cognition which we looked at in Chapter 15: it is possible that emotive words have their effect by triggering off particular schemata, and allowing the information to be fitted into that context. As we have already seen, Eiser's accentuation theory of attitudes emphasises how important words can be in directing and emphasising our attitudes.

There is some debate as to whether it is better to spell out a message very clearly, or not. Heller, in 1956, presented research participants with complete and incomplete advertising slogans, and found that they remembered those which they had completed themselves much better than the ones which they were simply given, and which left them little to do. MacLachlan (1983) suggests that this finding may be to do with **levels of processing theory** (see Chapter 3) – the more cognitive processing which research participants perform on the material, the more likely they are to remember it.

Janis and Feshbach (1963) performed a study in which they investigated the effects of different levels of **emotionality** in a message. They gave American high-school students a health survey, which assessed attitudes towards care of teeth. Then they sorted them into four groups, and gave three of the groups an illustrated talk about dental hygiene. (The fourth group was the control group, and was given a talk about the eye.) The talks were varied according to how much fear they were designed to induce in the people who heard them. When Janis and Feshbach repeated the health survey a week later, they found some quite surprising results, which are given in Table 17.3.

This finding suggests that a message can sometimes be too powerful to achieve its purpose.

The rejection of very emotional messages particularly seemed to apply to high-anxiety research participants, and it was suggested that there may be a link between this and the **Yerkes-Dodson law of arousal** and performance (Chapter 13). This law states that very extreme levels of arousal can actually interfere with effective action, because the person becomes too aroused or upset to act effectively. In this case, the highly emotional messages might have resulted in the person avoiding the whole topic, because it caused too much anxiety to even think about it!

The receiver of the message

Not everyone responds in the same way to persuasive arguments. In 1949, Hovland, Lunsdaine and Sheffield investigated whether people were more likely to be influenced by being given just one side of an argument, or by a message which gave both sides but also countered the arguments of the other side. They found that the effectiveness of the strategy was affected by the person's **level of education**. People who were more highly educated were more influenced by being given both sides of the case; people who had only a basic education were more influenced by just being given one side of an argument.

What the person already believed also made a difference. If they were being given information which essentially supported their own views, then one-sided arguments were more effective; but if they were being given information which ran counter to what they already believed, then two-sided arguments were better. This finding might fit with the accentuation theory of attitudes which we looked at earlier in this chapter.

Himmelfarb and Eagley (1974) argue that one important factor in how likely people are to

Table 17.3 Effects of emotionality in attitude change messages

Condition	No. of references to unpleasant consequences of neglecting dental hygiene	% of people changing their behaviour
'low fear'	18	37
'medium fear'	49	22
'high fear'	71	8

Source: Janis and Feshbach, 1963

respond to persuasive messages is the degree of ego-involvement that they experience. People who are highly personally involved with a particular viewpoint will be very resistant to changing their attitudes, whereas those who regard the issue as relatively unimportant will be able to select arguments much more freely, depending on the persuasiveness of the way that the argument is presented.

McGuire (1968) argued that there was evidence for a persuasibility factor in personality – that some people seem to be consistently more persuadable than others. However, Ajzen (1988) argued that there is very little evidence for such consistency in how people respond to different situations, and that personality trait approaches to persuasion have been largely discredited. Education, beliefs and ego-involvement seem to be more important, and these are very much a function of the person's own past experience, rather than a personality trait.

The context of the message

Gorn, in 1982, performed a study in which it appeared that musical background can directly influence consumer choice. Gorn showed research participants slides of coloured pens while playing music in the background. The music had been rated as either pleasant or unpleasant. When they were given a free choice, research participants chose the colour of pen which had been associated with the pleasant music. However, Kellaris and Cox (1989) challenged Gorn's findings, on the grounds that the demand characteristics of Gorn's study could have directly influenced the research participants' choices (see Box 17.2 overleaf).

Kellaris and Cox replicated Gorn's study, but with some important modifications. First, where Gorn had told the research participants that the study was about 'evaluating music for a pen commercial', their research participants were told that it was about 'assessing perceptions of various products'. Secondly, they matched the music more carefully than Gorn had done, using music which involved the same instruments, tempo and modality, but which had been rated by independent judges as pleasant or unpleasant (the 'pleasant' piece was by Mozart; the 'unpleasant' one by Milhaud).

Thirdly, they arranged a different way for research participants to select the pens. In Gorn's study, research participants had been asked to walk to different sides of the room, which made the selection decision a little obvious, so Kellaris and Cox arranged that both the pens would be available, but that the pens would contain either blue or black ink. This meant that they could check on the person's choice of pen when they filled in a questionnaire at the end of the experiment. In this way, Kellaris and Cox were careful to make sure that their research participants remained unaware of what the study was all about. When they did this, they found that the background music seemed to have no effect.

This is not to say that the context of a message does not have any effect at all. A study by Murphy, Cunningham and Wilcox (1979) compared the effectiveness of humorous advertisements in different television 'environments'. They found that if a humorous advertisement was shown in the middle of an action-adventure programme it had far more effect than if it was shown in the middle of a situation comedy show. So clearly context can have some influence, but that influence may be more subtle than some of the early research suggested.

Cognitive dissonance

A different type of research into persuasion did not use an information-processing approach, but rather looked at how people become motivated to change their attitudes – why they want to change them in the first place. This research began with the idea of cognitive balance, as put forward by Heider (1944), which we looked at earlier in this chapter. Basing his work largely on Heider's ideas, Leon Festinger (1957) went on to develop the theory of **cognitive dissonance**.

Cognitive dissonance is directly concerned with how we change our attitudes when we find that they are unbalanced. Cognitive dissonance theory states that if a cognition (such as an attitude) that we hold is in direct conflict with another one, and if the two are related in some way, then we will experience tension. We deal with this tension in one of two ways: either we change one of the cognitions, or we add an extra one to 'explain' the apparent discrepancy.

For example, you might see a friend as being a kind person, but then come across them expressing what appear to be very callous attitudes towards someone else. These two cognitions – your knowledge of the kindness of the friend and

Box 17.2 Demand characteristics of attitude change studies

A major difficulty with attitude-change studies is that when people are acting as research participants in psychological experiments they will often try to be co-operative, and produce the results that they feel the experimenter expects. Silverman (1977) described a study in which research participants were given a standard attitude-change task, with an introductory statement, and then some messages and opinion items that they were asked to complete. There were two groups, but each group performed the same task. In one group, though, the research sponsor was listed on the front of the material as 'Institute for the Study of Propaganda Effects'; whereas the second group had material which purported to come from the 'Institute for the Study of Communication and Information Processing'.

The researchers found dramatic differences between the two groups, with the second group showing far more attitude change than the first. Silverman and Shulman (1970) argued that research participants in attitude research tend to respond to the demand characteristics of the experiment: people feel that some sort of response is expected of them and they do their best to co-operate and produce the right one.

Rosnow (1968) performed a study in which American students were presented with pro- and anti-fraternity arguments. Some of the students received papers giving just one side of the debate, and some received both sets of papers. Research participants who received one-sided arguments changed their attitudes in the appropriate conditions, but those receiving both arguments showed a strongly significant trend towards the anti-fraternity attitude. When they were questioned later, it emerged that the research participants had been aware that the experimenter conducting the study held strongly anti-fraternity views. Since they had no other indicators as to how they should behave, they had geared their responses in the direction they thought was expected of them.

your perception of their callous behaviour – are in direct conflict. One seems to contradict the other, and that produces cognitive dissonance. To deal with the dissonance, you may change one of the cognitions. For instance, you may decide that your friend is not really a kind person, or that the behaviour only appears to be callous but is not really. Alternatively, you may add another cognition: your friend has put up with a great deal of trouble from this particular person and given them lots of sympathy in the past, to no avail, so they are justified in acting this way now.

Mrs Keech and the end of the world

In 1956, Festinger, Riecken and Schachter reported on a natural experiment in cognitive dissonance which they had been able to observe. A celebrated medium, Mrs Keech, received a 'message' that the whole of a large US city would be destroyed by a great flood on a particular date, but that she and her faithful followers would be saved and taken away by a flying saucer, if they renounced their material goods, went to a particular hill and spent the night in prayer. She and her followers duly sold all their possessions and went along to the hill to wait for the fateful day. Festinger, Riecker and

Schachter went along too, interested to see what would happen when the predictions failed to come true.

Interestingly, when the city remained intact, the followers adopted a second strategy. Rather than concluding that the original prediction was wrong, they added a new idea, arguing that their actions and prayers had saved the city. Festinger explained this by pointing out how concluding that the original prediction was wrong would have produced more cognitive dissonance, raising awkward personal conflicts about why the person had believed the prediction in the first place. Rather than face up to the tension which this would have caused, the cult members preferred to believe that their actions had been effective.

Attitude change through cognitive dissonance

Festinger saw cognitive dissonance as an extremely influential factor in inducing attitude change, and his model stimulated a great deal of experimental research. Most of these experiments took the form of **forced compliance studies**, in which conflicting cognitions were generated by asking experimental research participants to comply with something that they did not really believe in.

In one of these studies, Festinger and Carlsmith (1959) paid research participants either $20 or $1 to perform some extremely tedious tasks for half an hour at a time. One of the tasks involved giving a quarter-turn to each of a large number of wooden pegs in a peg-board, individually. As you might imagine, this was an extremely boring task indeed. When they had completed the tasks, the research participants were asked to go out to the waiting-room, where there were other people waiting for their turn, and to tell the others that the task was really interesting. After that, their own private attitude towards the task was assessed.

Festinger and Carlsmith found that the group which had been paid $20 did not change their attitudes significantly: they still maintained that the task was extremely dull. But the research participants who had only been paid $1 appeared to have changed their attitudes: they did not think that the task was as bad as all that. The researchers argued that this was because these people had experienced more cognitive dissonance than the other group. The $20 group could justify lying to the other research participants on the grounds that they were being paid for it; but the amount that the $1 group members were being paid was simply too trivial to provide an adequate justification for lying. So, this group dealt with the cognitive dissonance by rationalising their actions – believing that the task was not as bad as all that.

Cooper and Worchel (1970) replicated the Festinger and Carlsmith study, but this time varying how the people in the waiting-room responded. If these people acted as though the research participants had convinced them that the task was interesting, then research participants showed attitude change similar to that found by Festinger and Carlsmith. But if they looked unconvinced, research participants' attitudes were unaffected. In other words, if people felt that it did not matter whether they had lied or not, then they did not experience the cognitive dissonance.

In another study, Collins and Hoyt (1972) asked students to write an essay arguing in favour of a case which they actually disagreed with – for example, someone who believed in legal abortion might be asked to write an essay giving a case for its abolition. They found that research participants who were allowed to sign a disclaimer stating that they were not responsible for the contents of the essay showed no attitude change, but those people who were not permitted to sign such a disclaimer did show some change. However as we saw in Box 17.2, there is always a distinct possibility in studies of this kind that the results which the experimenters obtain come from the **demand characteristics** of the study and not from what the researchers believe they are investigating.

We can see, though, that attitude change is a complex area, influenced by a number of different factors. In addition, as the theories about attitudes which we examined earlier showed, the wider context of expectation, consistency and intentionality have a significant impact on how attitudes manifest themselves, and how we change them.

Prejudice

When we describe someone as prejudiced, we mean that they hold a certain attitude or mental set towards some target, which has become fixed in such a way that the person is reluctant to change. Prejudice means, literally, 'pre-judgement': in other words, the issue has already been judged, and the person is no longer weighing up alternative possibilities or explanations.

Prejudice can take a number of forms, including positive ones: we can be prejudiced in favour of someone, so that we interpret everything they do positively. Extreme patriotism, for example, involves a strong prejudice in favour of one's own country – 'my country right or wrong' – and someone who feels that way will tend to interpret every action of their government as positively as they can.

Team loyalty is an example of this too: in 1954, Hastorf and Cantril showed a film of a football match to students at two American universities, Dartmouth and Princeton. The match was between their two university teams. The researchers found that students from each university thought that their own team had committed fewer fouls than the other side. They also judged the other team's fouls to be more flagrant than those committed by their own team. This highlights one of the more dramatic effects of prejudice, which is its ability to affect how we receive information. Strongly prejudiced people look for information which will confirm their views, as in Hastorf and Cantril's work.

We also regard the same information differently, depending on whether we are prejudiced towards its source or not. In 1948, Asch gave two groups of American students the same political quotation, but told each group that it had come from a different source. One group was told that the quotation had come from John Adams (a hero of the American Revolution), and the other that it had come from the writings of Karl Marx. (The quotation was: '*Those who hold and those who are without property have ever formed two distinct classes*'.) The students were asked whether they agreed or disagreed with the statement. Those who believed it came from Adams tended to agree with it, but those who thought it came from Marx tended to disagree.

Theories of prejudice

For the most part, when we talk of prejudice we are referring to negative conditions: being prejudiced against other people. A number of different theories have been put forward in an attempt to explain prejudice. Broadly speaking, they can be classified into four groups: biological explanations; psychoanalytic explanations; cultural explanations; and socio-cognitive explanations.

Biological explanations of prejudice

This approach derives from extrapolations from animal behaviour put forward by writers like Ardrey, Lorenz, Morris and, more recently, the sociobiologists Dawkins and Wilson. Essentially, this approach consists of the view that human social behaviour is basically identical to that of animals. In this view, our social motivation and behavioural styles are 'caused' directly by genetic influences, inherited through evolutionary selection. (In the last section of this book, we will be looking at some rather less reductionist approaches to understanding both human beings and evolution.)

Ardrey (1966) proposed that people act according to a **territorial imperative**. He stated that it was a basic instinct in human nature to defend a certain territory against all comers, and that both wars and racial prejudice should be seen as inescapable outcomes of this basic drive. Lorenz, too, saw aggression and the tendency to attack strangers as being fundamental to human nature, and, following on from his work, Morris (1967) saw the human being as simply a 'naked ape', and argued that intergroup conflict and prejudice was essentially the same phenomenon as one group of baboons engaging in a territorial dispute with another group.

With the advent of sociobiology the theory became slightly more subtle, but the overall message was the same: that conflict between groups, and the prejudice ensuing from such conflict, was an inescapable outcome of the genetic structure of human nature. In sociobiological theory, as proposed by Wilson (1975) and popularised by Dawkins (1976), **xenophobia** (fear of, and hostility towards strangers) arises from a powerful tendency to protect those who share the same genes. This kin selection, according to sociobiological theory, ensures that people with different genes will automatically be regarded with suspicion and hostility.

There are a number of criticisms of this type of perspective, some of which we will be looking at in Chapter 22. Hayes (1995) pointed out that one of the distinctive features of this type of biological determinism is that the biological cause – whether it be the 'gene' or 'natural selection' – is used as a 'magical' concept, as if it could explain everything. But if we are to examine complex social issues, like prejudice, we need to look at what is going on at a number of different levels, rather than proposing simplistic causes. Moreover, as Rose, Kamin and Lewontin (1984) point out, similarity is not homology: just because something looks similar, we are not at all justified in concluding that it is homologous – that it is the same thing. An aggressive action by an animal may be quite different from an aggressive act by a human being, both in terms of its causes and the way in which it manifests itself.

Psychoanalytic explanations of prejudice

Essentially, psychoanalytic models see prejudice as arising from deep-seated motives within the individual. Explanations for these motives differ: Freud (1920) argued that we all have a fundamental 'death-instinct', which he named thanatos. This is the opposite of the life-affirming energy libido, and leads us into destructive and negative courses of action. Wars and prejudice were explained as manifestations of the destructive energy of thanatos, since Freud saw the wider society as reflecting the psychological characteristics of the individuals who make up that society.

A different approach, also based on psycho-analytic principles, was put forward by Adorno *et al.* in 1950. They proposed that the basis of social prejudice lay in the particular personality formation which certain individuals show. They called this the authoritarian personality. We looked at this theory of personality in some detail in Chapter 7, but, broadly speaking, it states that certain types of people are more inclined than others to be prejudiced and punitive in their attitudes towards out-groups. The origins of this lie in their childhood experiences: such people have parents who exerted a rigid and unyielding discipline. This produced a defence mechanism known as a reaction-formation, which meant that they found ambiguities very difficult to cope with and had to see everything in very black-and-white terms. As a result of this, they were very intolerant of people who were 'different', or did not behave in what they considered to be a 'normal' fashion.

Adorno's explanation was very popular for some time. Several studies showed that people with an authoritarian-style personality were much more inclined to engage in prejudiced behaviour than others. In 1960, Rokeach put forward an extension of the theory, arguing that another personality characteristic which could be linked with prejudice was dogmatism (we also looked at this in Chapter 7). This form of personality applied just as much to people who were politically left-wing as it did to those who were politically right-wing (Adorno's work had largely concerned itself with the form of right-wing authoritarianism known as fascism). Rokeach argued that people who are highly dogmatic and rigid in their thinking are more liable to show extremely prejudiced behaviour than people who have a more balanced outlook.

However, any approach which serves to explain social phenomena entirely in terms of what individuals are like has limitations as an explanation for social prejudice. It may well be true that someone with that particular personality profile will direct hostility towards out-groups, but different groups are identified as the target at different times: prejudice is not always directed at the same group. In addition, differing cultures show different degrees of social prejudice, even though they show a variety of personality types. The social context of the behaviour and the choice of target are important factors in understanding prejudice.

Cultural explanations of prejudice

Middleton (1976) showed that, among people with high F-scale scores (the F-scale is Adorno's measure of authoritarianism), those from southern states in the USA expressed more extreme attitudes against black people than they did against Jewish or Catholic people. This, however, was not the case for highly authoritarian people from northern states, who did not single out blacks so strongly. The culture and social practices as a whole were less prejudiced, and this was reflected in the attitudes of individuals.

Racism also shifts its focus as society changes. In Britain over the past century the main focus of racism shifted from Jewish people to black people (specifically West Indian groups) and then to Asians (specifically Pakistani groups). In Germany, the main focus in recent years has been Turkish people who have come to Germany to work, whereas it was directed mainly against Jewish people in the first half of the twentieth century. Other groups still experience racism, but these specific targets have received the most hostility from racists at these times. A full theory of prejudice needs to be able to explain the choice of target as well as the personality of the originator.

It is clear that the culture of a society has considerable influence on individual people's prejudices. If one group in a society has privileges and the other does not, those who have them may feel defensive, while those who do not will feel frustrated and envious. Rogers and Frantz (1962) found that white immigrants to what was then Southern Rhodesia and is now Zimbabwe developed more anti-black attitudes the longer they stayed in the country. This suggested that their attitudes were adjusting to the racist white culture in which they found themselves.

Positive cultures can have their effect too: Bagley and Verma (1979) showed that levels of racial discrimination were considerably lower in Holland than in Britain, despite the fact that the proportion of black to white people is roughly the same. Dutch society and culture frowns on prejudice, so that although it does exist to some extent, mainly among older or more working-class people, it is not accepted or expressed openly – with the result that there is much less of it.

One cultural explanation of prejudice is known as the scapegoat theory. This theory sees prejudice as arising because certain social minority groups are made scapegoats for general economic or socially deprived circumstances. Racial prejudice tends to be higher among less educated and less well-off members of society; and it rises at times of high unemployment or social deprivation. Hovland and Sears (1940) analysed the number of lynchings in the southern states of the USA each year, and found that they correlated with the price of cotton. There were more lynchings in years when cotton (which was the main crop of those states) was at a lower price than expected, and fewer in years when the price was higher. Hovland and Sears explained this in terms of the scapegoat theory: the aggression generated by the economic frustration of the cotton farmers was displaced on to the black population.

Although it is obviously important to look at the influence which culture has on prejudice, it is clear that, as an explanation, culture too tells only part of the story. Not everyone in a given society is prejudiced to the same extent, and cultures themselves can change over time. Brown (1985) saw societal and cultural norms as being far more important than personality in determining prejudice, and Bagley and Verma's findings seem to suggest that this may be so. But on a social level prejudice can manifest itself in small, individual incidents: a black person being turned down for a job here; a woman being ignored as having nothing to contribute to a meeting there; a racially motivated attack on a specific individual somewhere else. If we are really to understand how prejudice works, we also need to look at what is going on in the minds of the people who perpetrate it.

Socio-cognitive theories of prejudice

In Chapter 14 we saw how Tajfel proposed that our membership of social groups forms a signifi-cant part of our identity. Tajfel proposed his theory in an attempt to explain how the intergroup con-flicts and prejudice which were apparent in Europe before and during WWII could have taken such extreme forms, when many of the people involved were decent, ordinary individuals when they were acting on their own.

In 1969, Tajfel identified three cognitive mechanisms which operate as the basis for social prejudice. The first of these is **categorisation**: the way that we classify information into sets or groups. This Tajfel saw as basic to human cognitive

functioning, drawing on, for example, the research into concept formation which we looked at in Chapter 5. In 1954, Allport had pointed out that prejudice operates on the basis of stereotypes. Stereotypes also depend on our cognitive tendency to categorise.

The second process outlined by Tajfel in 1969 is the **assimilation** of social knowledge. According to Tajfel, evaluations like 'good', 'bad', 'like' and 'dislike' become firmly fixed as factual impressions at a very early age, and retain their effect in adult life. This is social knowledge, which the young child learns from those around it. The child's social reality – including evaluative judgements – is defined by the central source of information about the world provided by the family, and there is no room for alternative viewpoints. So the child will pick up evaluative ideas from its family, and apply those to its growing knowledge of the world.

Tajfel and Jahoda (1966) asked British children about their attitudes to other countries, by means of a number of indirect games (such as giving the children a number of black plastic squares of different sizes and asking them to choose a square representing their own country, and then squares which would correspond to the size of America, France, Germany and Russia). They found that at ages six to seven the children agreed more about which countries they liked and disliked than about their size, and that even at ages ten to eleven, there was as much agreement about preferences as there was about factual information.

When this tendency to assimilate social knowledge is combined with the tendency to categorise, it implies that there is a powerful tendency to evaluate groups of people even from a very early age. According to Tajfel, categorisation provides the mould which gives it shape, and the assimilation of social norms provides the content.

The third cognitive mechanism outlined by Tajfel involves a **search for coherence**, which is to do with how a particular individual explains what is going on to themselves – and to others. We like to understand what is going on around us, and we look for reasons for why things are as they are. In this, the mechanisms of situational and dispositional attribution which we looked at in Chapter 15 come into play. In the case of social prejudice it is the group (already stereotyped and disliked because of the other two mechanisms) which is likely to be considered as having distinctive and stable characteristics.

These observations about the cognitive dimensions of prejudice formed the basis for the development of social identity theory (Chapter 15). In this theory, Tajfel and Turner (1979) argued that one of the most important aspects of group identification is concerned with how group membership reflects on the individual's own self-esteem. People do not just classify themselves as belonging to one group or another. Their group membership means something personal to them – they identify with their group. Since, in the real world, social groups differ in relative power and status, social comparison means that people compare their own group with others, and look for reasons why their group is 'better'. This may involve denigrating those who are 'different'.

Intergroup prejudice, according to this model, develops through three mechanisms. First, as before, there is the process of categorisation, in which various groups are identified and individuals are classified as belonging to one group or another. This is followed by the process of **accentuation**. Differences between groups become exaggerated, and members of other groups may be regarded as being 'all the same', or stereotyped. In conditions of social rivalry, such as occurs in periods of economic depression, this accentuation leads on to the third stage, of **intergroup conflict**. The groups are seen as being in direct competition with one another, and rivalry between social groups can become very intense (Tajfel, 1981).

One of the important things to remember about this process is that the individual's group membership has become **internalised** – it is part of their own self-concept, rather than just an external 'role' which they adopt, and a significant part of how they think of themselves. But people also respond to one another as individuals, not just as representatives of their social groups. It is in this way, according to social identity theory, that someone can be prejudiced against another social group as a whole, while still having a personal friendship with an individual member of that group.

Originally, Tajfel argued that the simple existence of different groups was sufficient for prejudice between the two to develop. But more recent research suggests that intergroup conflict is not as inevitable as all that. Mummendey and Schreiber (1984) argued that studies show inevitable intergroup conflict only because they force people to make choices between different groups. If people are allowed to act co-operatively, or to rate one another as 'equally good', then intergroup conflict often simply does not appear. Capozza and Volpato (1990) found that in real life, too, group conflict can be reduced if the different groups are seen as distinctive, and not in competition with one another.

Social identification, then, does not inevitably lead to prejudice, although it can do so if the groups are seen as being in conflict with one another. One common argument of racists in almost every society is that members of the disliked group are 'taking all the jobs' – an argument which, factually, is often entirely the reverse of the truth. Using social identity theory, we can see how this type of argument is directly aimed at encouraging intergroup hostility, by presenting the disliked group as being in direct conflict with other groups in society.

Allport's stages of social discrimination

Social discrimination does not just happen all at once: it builds up, if it is not directly challenged by society. In 1954, Allport identified five stages by which prejudice can manifest itself in people's behaviour. Each of these five stages was seen in Nazi Germany, in terms of that society's treatment of Jewish people, and much of it can also be seen in the racist system of apartheid practised in South Africa until recently. The stages are listed in Table 17.4 overleaf. By looking at Allport's stages in terms of the way in which they have manifested themselves in society, and still do today, we can see how the study of prejudice – particularly ethnic prejudice – remains very pertinent, with serious implications for society.

Principles of ethnic prejudice

A considerable amount of psychological research into prejudice in our society has concentrated on ethnic, or racial, prejudice. This is partly because this type of prejudice is extremely visible and blatant, and partly because Nazi Germany's treatment of the Jewish, Polish and Gypsy peoples showed, in such a horrifying way, where extreme racial prejudice can lead. Bethlehem (1985) identified ten principles of ethnic prejudice, which summarise much of the research in this area. Table 17.5 overleaf lists the ten principles, and we will briefly discuss each of them in turn.

Table 17.4 Allport's stages of social prejudice

1	*Antilocution*	Hostile talk and verbal denigration, like the anti-Jewish propaganda which was common in pre-war Germany.
2	*Avoidance*	Keeping at a distance, although without any actual harm. We can see this in the development of racial ghettos today. In Nazi Germany, Jewish people were singled out and made to wear a yellow 'Star of David' so that they could be easily identified as different from other German people.
3	*Discrimination*	Exclusion from civil rights, employment, housing and the like. This became a matter of State policy in Nazi Germany and South Africa; but it can also be seen in underprivileged minority groups in the West – although unemployment affects both groups, black people are far more likely to be unemployed in Britain than white people are.
4	*Physical attack*	Violence against property and people was common in Nazi Germany, and also occurs both in South Africa, and in some areas of Britain.
5	*Extermination*	Indiscriminate violence against the entire group of people, reaching its most horrific manifestation in the attempt by the Nazis to annihilate Jewish people altogether, through the gas chambers of Auschwitz and the other concentration camps.

Source: Allport, 1954

Table 17.5 Principles of ethnic prejudice

1 There are two interacting kinds of prejudice: one based on personality, and the other based on misinformation and the need to minimise cognitive processing.

2 When groups are in competition or conflict, discrimination in favour of the in-group and against the out-group becomes a social norm.

3 The less information we have about somebody, the more likely we are to fall back on stereotypes.

4 Socially accepted attitudes and stereotypes are widely known and have widespread effects on people's behaviour.

5 Prejudices can become self-fulfilling, generating their own 'evidence'.

6 The category of people towards whom prejudice is directed varies from one group to another.

7 Prejudices remain stable as long as norms remain stable, and change when social norms undergo change.

8 Intelligence, education and social class show a negative relationship with prejudice.

9 Children acquire attitudes and prejudices from their parents and families.

10 Children discriminate between different ethnic groups from an early age, but do not develop stable attitudes and preferences until they are older.

Source: Bethlehem, 1985

1 There are two interacting kinds of prejudice: one based on personality, and the other based on misinformation and the need to minimise cognitive processing.

We have already looked at the theory of the authoritarian personality developed by Adorno *et al.* in 1950. Bagley *et al.* (1979) asked secondary school pupils about their attitudes towards people in other racial groups. They found that those who were prejudiced towards one group were often prejudiced towards others as well. So, for instance, if someone disliked blacks, then they would also tend to dislike Pakistanis. This provides some support for the idea that certain types of people are more likely to be prejudiced than others – the basis of the 'personality' approach.

But there is also evidence that people try to reduce their cognitive load, and that they may use stereotyping to do this. Taylor *et al.* (1978) tape-recorded several versions of the same conversation, such that each part in the conversation could be presented to listeners as if they were coming from different people. As the research participants listened to the conversations, a picture of the speaker was shown briefly on a screen. The speakers varied as to skin colour, and might be of either sex. The research participants were given several conversations to listen to, and later asked to recall who said what. Taylor *et al.* found that research participants tended to mix up people in the same category. For instance, if the original speaker was a black woman, then if the research participant made a mistake, it would be by attributing the remark to another black woman. This suggested that stereotyping was being used to ease the amount of information which had to be retained.

2 When groups are in competition or conflict, discrimination in favour of the in-group and against the out-group becomes a social norm.

This was illustrated very clearly by Sherif's 'Robber's Cave' study (Sherif *et al.*, 1961). Sherif argued that, ultimately, prejudice arises from two groups competing for the same goal. To illustrate this, Sherif *et al.* set up two competing teams from a group of 22 boys attending a summer camp. At first the boys were unaware of each other's existence, because they were staying in huts out of sight of one another. They were allowed to meet only after a few days, when they would have had time to begin developing good relationships with other members of the in-groups.

The organisers arranged a major competition between the two groups, and the boys quickly developed a powerful 'in-group' and 'out-group' mentality. They saw their own team members as being 'brave' and 'tough', while the boys from the other team were seen as 'unpleasant' and 'underhand'. This rivalry became intense and often quite bitter. However, the organisers were able to break down the prejudices which had developed when a problem occurred with their transport which meant that all the boys had to co-operate to solve it – all working together to pull a truck out of the mud. Following this, the organisers arranged for a number of co-operative events, and this meant that the boys quickly became friends.

However, Tyerman and Spencer (1983) argued that Sherif's study was not an adequate illustration of conflict and prejudice, because the ill-feeling between the two groups was largely manufactured. The boys had known each other beforehand, and were friends again at the end of the study, so it is unlikely that they experienced the same kinds of divisions or emotions as occur in racial prejudice.

3 The less information we have about somebody, the more likely we are to fall back on stereotypes.

Hepburn and Locksley (1983) asked research participants to complete a questionnaire asking about the characteristics of different social groups: blacks, whites, overweight people and others. The questionnaire asked for estimates of the proportion of people in each group who were likely to conform to a specific characteristic, like

being impulsive, athletic, and so on. These characteristics were chosen to reflect common stereotypes. The people participating in the research were also given varying amounts of information about the groups which they had to judge.

Hepburn and Locksley found that the more information people had been given, the less likely they were to use conventional stereotypes. However, a similar study by Quattrone and Jones, in 1980, showed that this applies only to research participants who were not highly prejudiced. People who were highly prejudiced used stereotypes just as strongly, regardless of the amount of information that they were given.

4 Socially accepted attitudes and stereotypes are widely known and have widespread effects on people's behaviour.

Many studies have shown that there is widespread agreement between people about the characteristics and expected behaviour of people from certain social groups. Buchanan (1951) looked at national attitudes of people in nine different countries including: Britain, France, Germany, Italy, Netherlands, Norway, Mexico and the USA. Research participants were asked to select from a list which was supplied to them, the most appropriate adjectives to describe people from various groups.

Although the research participants were allowed to say that they did not think it was possible to characterise national groups in this way, or to reply 'do not know', most people were quite confident about their judgements. Buchanan also found considerable agreement between people: Americans were rated as practical, Russians as hardworking, domineering, brave, cruel and backward; and English people as intelligent, self-controlled and conceited. The amount of agreement showed that people were well aware of the common stereotypes in use at the time.

5 Prejudices can become self-fulfilling, generating their own 'evidence'.

Word, Zanna and Cooper (1974) asked white students to interview other students, who were either black or white. Although their research participants were not particularly prejudiced individuals, when they examined recordings of their non-verbal behaviour, they found that the students sat further away from the black interviewees than they had from the white ones. They had also made more speech errors, and ended the interviews more quickly. One suggestion was that their relative lack of contact with black people had made them more nervous than they were when interviewing white students.

Such slight differences in non-verbal behaviour can transmit significant messages to the other person. If someone is 'labelled' in a certain way, and knows it, then they become likely to act accordingly – it becomes a **self-fulfilling prophecy**. Aronson and Osherow (1980) reported on a demonstration conducted by a schoolteacher, which was initially devised to help the class to learn about what social prejudice was really like. It has been replicated a number of times. The demonstration involved the teacher announcing to the class one day that from now on the brown-eyed children were superior and would be the 'ruling class'. They were given extra privileges and more free time, whereas those with blue eyes had to sit at the back of the class, wait at the ends of lines and had less time for free play.

Very soon, the blue-eyed children began to do less well at their work, to describe themselves more negatively and to become depressed or angry. The brown-eyed children became arrogant and bullying, and made nasty comments about the others. The next day things were changed around, so that it was the blue-eyed children who were the 'rulers'. Quite soon the entire pattern had reversed itself. This was a powerful demonstration of how the process of institutionalised discrimination could result in the poor achievement and lack of motivation which is sometimes found among members of oppressed minority groups, and it showed how the existence of prejudice can become self-fulfilling.

Snyder, Tanke and Berscheid (1977) asked research participants to have telephone conversations with a stranger. They were mixed-sex pairs, who did not know each other. The male research participants were given photographs which were supposedly of the person they were talking to. The conversations were tape-recorded, and later the halves of the conversations spoken by the female research participants (not the males) were played to a separate group of people. They were asked to rate the women whose voices they heard. The ratings showed that the women had 'lived up' to the stereotype that the men had of them from the photographs. Those women whose partners had been given attractive photographs were rated as more sociable, poised, warm and outgoing than those women whose partners had been given unflattering photographs.

6 The category of people towards whom prejudice is directed varies from one group to another.

As we have already seen, if we look around the world we can see that the targets of social prejudice are different in different places. In Northern Ireland, for example, the major distinction on which prejudice is based is religion – whether one is Catholic or Protestant. In South Africa it is skin colour which forms the basis of social prejudice and discrimination. Economically, though, these characteristics tend to be linked to more general issues, since such rigid classification of people into groups is usually associated with one group having better access to socially desirable assets than the other. So, for example, one group will tend to have better housing, better access to employment and higher social status than another.

This also implies that members of the discriminated group who do not fall into the same social class category will be regarded with less prejudice by members of the other group. There is some evidence to support this. For instance, Feldman and Hinterman (1975) found that, in America, upper-class black people did not experience anything like the same amount of prejudice as lower-class blacks did. Brigham (1971) examined the prejudiced attitudes of American whites towards blacks, and found that these were often based on characteristics of social class rather than skin colour as such.

7 Prejudices remain stable as long as norms remain stable, and change when social norms undergo change.

Since prejudices reflect social norms, we can expect them to change if social norms change. These in turn will depend on the wider political context. For example, Buchanan (1951) compared American perceptions of Russians in 1942, when they were allies in fighting Hitler, with their views in 1948, when the war was over. The Americans showed very much less favourable attitudes towards the Russians in the post-war years than they had done during the war.

Two studies conducted in Zambia illustrate this point very clearly. Both studies were concerned with the social attitudes which people held towards the different tribal groups in the country. Mitchell (1952) reported on a study conducted in 1957, when the country was still called Northern

Rhodesia. Their investigation involved a measure of social distance, which allowed them to place the different tribes in a kind of 'league table' of popularity. In 1976, Bethlehem and Kingsley performed a similar study, and found that the order had changed considerably. During the intervening years, Zambia had become independent; and the tribe which had formerly been most popular was now least so, as it was largely suspected of cornering all the best jobs in the civilian government. On the other hand, the Chewa tribe, who were previously only averagely popular, had become much more so. The change in social awareness brought about by national independence had produced changes in racial awareness as well.

This applies to more subtle social attitudes too. Clark and Clark (reported in 1968) asked children to pick out 'the doll of the nice colour' from a pair of white and black dolls. They found that very few children picked out the black doll. But when the study was replicated nearly 30 years later, Hraba and Grant (1970) found a marked difference in the findings. Far more of the children chose to play with the black doll, and chose it as 'the doll of the nice colour' than had happened in the earlier study.

8 Intelligence, education and social class show a negative relationship with prejudice.

Many studies have supported this idea, in America, Britain, Europe and Africa. Grabb (1979) performed a large-scale investigation involving 1499 research participants in the USA. This involved looking at the factors which correlated with prejudice most closely. Grabb found that education, rather than income or social status (measured by occupation), was by far the strongest correlation, with educated people being far less likely to be racist. Interestingly also, the authoritarian personality explanation of prejudice seemed to be more valid for educated or middle-class people than it was for those from the working class. Weima, in 1964, found that although prejudice was strongest in the more working-class sectors of Dutch society, authoritarianism was weaker. This seemed to provide support for the scapegoat theory of prejudice that we looked at earlier.

9 Children acquire attitudes and prejudices from their parents and families.

Pushkin and Veness (1973) reported a study in which white London children were given a free choice of black or white dolls to play with. Children from families with low levels of racial prejudice tended to choose either black or white dolls freely, but those children with highly racist mothers consistently preferred playing with just the white dolls.

In an early American study, Horowitz (1936) found that children with communist parents showed very little racial prejudice, whereas those with more right-wing parents showed higher levels of racism. And a study by Marsh, in 1970, investigated the attitudes of white English children who had been placed with black foster parents, and found that they showed more favourable attitudes to black children than those who had been fostered with white families.

10 Children discriminate between different ethnic groups from an early age, but do not develop stable attitudes and preferences until they are older.

Milner (1973) asked 300 five- to eight year-old children from two large British cities to identify dolls which represented 'English', 'Jamaican', 'Indian' or 'Pakistani' people. (Notice the implicit racism here, in the assumption that only white people are 'English'. The experimenter did not indicate what proportion of the ethnic minority group samples were English, too.) One-third of the children came from white English families, one-third from families of Jamaican origin and one-third from families of Asian origin. The children had no difficulty with the task. Milner also noted several spontaneous racist comments made by the children. However, Porter (1971) found that the expressed attitudes which children showed did not appear to affect their behaviour all that much: even children who produced racist statements when asked about their attitudes, played with children of other ethnic groups quite happily.

Aggression and crowd behaviour

Aggression is a topic that has attracted a considerable amount of attention, from non-psychologists as well as psychologists – far more, indeed, than helping behaviour or any of the more positive aspects of human interaction. And this is partly because models of aggression can serve an important social function. I mentioned in Chapter 15 how social representations of aggression are often directly contradictory to people's own experience; yet models of society as being dangerous, and of people as being aggressive and violent are continually being propagated by the media. So it is worth looking at the main theories of aggression which have been put forward by psychologists, and at some of their implications.

Aggression as a biological trait

One of the popular explanations for aggression is that it is some kind of innate biological trait. Biological explanations for aggression have taken several different forms. Freud (1920) argued that, in addition to the life-giving positive energy which he had initially described in his model of personality, people also had a negative, destructive energy, which when released produced aggression and other aspects of the 'dark side' of human nature. He called this dark energy thanatos, while the positive energy was known as libido. The apparent contradictions of human nature – how we can be affectionate and caring to some yet vicious and cruel to others – were produced, in Freud's theory, by the conflicts between these two energies.

Lorenz (1950) also described aggression as a biological trait – in this case, an internal energy which builds up within the individual and has to be released. If it is not released safely, in ritualised aggression such as sports, then, Lorenz argued, it will spill out in anti-social aggression. Human nature, in Lorenz's model, included a continually-filling reservoir of aggression, which therefore had to be controlled and safely released. Unfortunately for this theory, though, the concept of 'safe release' of aggressive energy has been rather challenged by the finding that allowing people the opportunity to discharge aggression actually seems to make them more aggresive – not less, as Lorenz would have predicted (e.g. Buss, 1966; Loew, 1967).

Jacobs, Brunton and Melville (1965) found a higher percentage of individuals with XYY chromosomes in prison than in the general population (1.5% as opposed to about .01% in the general population), and went on to argue that aggression might be genetically determined – that such people were just 'born criminals'. But despite the widespread publicity received by this theory, Witkin et al. (1976) tested over 4500 men and found no evidence at all that XYY individuals were more aggressive than others. Other studies, similarly, have found little support for this idea.

Aggression as social learning

Bandura (1977) suggested that people behave aggressively because (a) they are imitating behaviour which they have seen modelled by other people, and (b) they have learned, vicariously from watching others, that aggressive behaviour pays off. In a series of demonstrations, Bandura and others (Bandura and Walters; Bandura, Ross and Ross) showed that children were very quick to pick up aggressive styles of acting from watching a film, but did not necessarily show them immediately in their behaviour. However, they would produce these behaviours if they were put in a situation where it was advantageous for them to do so.

It is this finding which lies at the root of the concern about the extremely violent picture of society which is generally portrayed through the television screen. TV demonstrates a range of aggressive behaviours and interactions which can lead children to believe that these behaviours are justifiable options (Eron et al., 1972), which desensitises people to violence (Thomas et al., 1977), and which leads those who watch TV heavily to believe that the world is very much more dangerous than it really is (Gerbner and Gross, 1976). Many police officers have expressed the fear that it also produces 'copycat' crime. Some recent studies suggest that, by contrast, many soap operas, particularly ones such as *Neighbours*, are very good for children, because they teach them a positive set of social skills, and prosocial values.

Aggression as a response to frustration

Dollard et al. (1939) proposed that aggressive behaviour results from frustration in our attempts to achieve personal goals. These personal goals may be explicit, such as failing to reach something that we are aware that we are aiming for; or implicit, such as a desire to get on quietly with our own lives. For the most part, Dollard et al. argued, people are non-aggressive; but frustration causes their motivational energies to become displaced and therefore results in aggression. There has been some criticism of the extreme version of this theory, which was the proposition that all frustration will inevitably lead to aggression. It centred around three main arguments: (a) that people sometimes respond in other kinds of ways (Bandura, 1977); (b) that extreme frustration can sometimes produce passivity and helplessness, not aggression (Seligman, 1975); and (c) that in many cases aggressive behaviour happens which does not actually result from aggression, e.g. a professional boxer, or a Mafia 'hit-man' (Berkowitz, 1978).

Aggression as a response to the environment

Another set of explanations has seen aggression in terms of environmental factors. Donnerstein and Wilson (1979) showed that noisy conditions were more likely to produce aggressive interactions than quiet ones, but that this effect was noticeably less if people felt that they had control over the amount of noise that they were experiencing. Similarly, Aiello, Nicosia and Thompson (1979) showed that people are more likely to be both competitive and aggressive if they have been crowded together in a confined space. Zillman (1979) suggested that both of these factors serve to heighten arousal, which then makes the individual more susceptible to stimuli which may be potentially irritating.

Some environmental explanations for aggression have a deeply political flavour to them. The classic examples here are those studies which relate aggression to temperature, such as Baron and Bell (1975), who showed that inner-city riots only tended to happen on long hot summer evenings, and went from there to suggest that temperature actually causes the aggression. These theories are often used in the media to distract attention away from the real social issues underlying such conflicts; and the idea that there might be other explanations for the correlation between temperature and rioting – like, for instance, the way that people tend to be out on the street, so news of social injustice travels very much more quickly around the community – does not get much of a hearing.

Social constructionist theories of aggression

Social constructionist approaches to aggression argue that aggression is effectively in the mind of the beholder. Often, what we think of as aggressive behaviour can be construed quite differently by people who have a different perspective on the situation. It will depend on the cultural background, the personal constructs, and also the social representations, of the individuals concerned. Reicher (1984) discussed how the varying social identifications of people participating in or witnessing the St Paul's riots in Bristol, in 1981,

affected the way that they interpreted events. The media view was unequivocally of the rioters as engaging in purely aggressive behaviour. But Reicher showed that the different standpoints of the participants led to very different interpretations of what had been happening.

Hewstone (1989) argued that just about any type of behaviour could be construed either as aggressive, or as its opposite, depending on the social construction which people place on the event. An event described as an aggressive attack by 'terrorists' by one group of people, may be described as justifiable action from 'freedom fighters' by another group in society. A fight in a pub may be construed as mindlessly aggressive by some, or as a justifiable response to provocation by others. But the view that people take will depend on their own social and political viewpoints. Potter and Reicher (1987) argued that judging whether behaviour is aggressive or anti-social is a social construction, which does not come from nowhere, but has an established basis in the person's individual conceptions of social categories and the attributions which they make about social justification.

Problems with theories of aggression

One striking feature of explanations for aggression is the way that it is those which propose innate or physical 'explanations' for aggression which get more publicity, despite the availability of research evidence for the other views. The implication here is that they are actually being used as justifications for the status quo, rather than as real explanations for why things happen. Theories which suggest that aggression happens because 'people are like that', or because of the weather, are more comfortable for society than theories which suggest that there are social causes for aggression which we could (and should) do something about.

Another problem in this area is the confusion of terminology. Rose, Kamin and Lewontin (1984) pointed out that researchers are often using the term 'aggression' to mean very different things, ranging from mouse-killing behaviour on the part of a laboratory rat, to ritualised athletic events like the Olympics. The problem is, Rose argues, that the whole concept has become reified into some abstract concept, when really it is just a description. Just because people can act aggressively, does not necessarily mean that there is an actual 'thing' called aggression. Like intelligence, their argument is that the concept should be treated as an adjective, not a noun.

Crowd behaviour

Aggression has also often been linked with crowd behaviour, even though most of our experience of crowds is far from aggressive. In ordinary public life, it is not unusual to find yourself part of a crowd. Whether it is in a packed railway station, attending a sporting event or concert, or simply shopping, large masses of people are not an uncommon experience in a modern society. For the most part, these crowds are uneventful: we accept them as an ordinary part of modern life, and think no more about them. However, there are some times when crowds seem to become more than simply a temporary mass of people. A particular event brings people together with a common purpose, and at such times the crowd seems to take on a life of its own. And of course, at its most extreme, a crowd can erupt into violent public disorder: a 'riot'.

Disorderly crowds, though, are very rare by comparison with the sheer number of peaceful crowds that occur every day. The sociologist Emile Durkheim saw peaceful crowds as serving a valuable social purpose: drawing people together and strengthening social solidarity and social cohesion. This was particularly so of crowds centred on large-scale public events, like a royal wedding or a state funeral. Benewick and Holton (1987) interviewed members of the large crowd who attended the open-air mass at Wembley Stadium during the Pope's visit to Britain in 1982, and found that they viewed the event as being a very powerful and meaningful experience. An important part of this was the way that people felt themselves to be part of a wider unity, all sharing the same experience together.

Unfortunately, peaceful crowds, although they occur much more frequently than non-peaceful ones, have not been studied in nearly as much detail. Perhaps it is precisely because they are so common that we do not even notice them very much. Or perhaps it is simply the fact that peaceful crowds do not present a social problem. Typically, psychological theories about crowds have regarded them as dangerous 'mobs', liable to break out into almost any kind of anti-social activity. In part, this links with some of the theories of aggression which we have just looked at. But there are also specialised theories of crowd psychology which have helped to maintain this impression.

Mob psychology

One of the most influential early theories of crowd behaviour was put forward by Le Bon, in 1895. Le Bon viewed crowds as inherently pathological, seeing them as having reverted to a kind of animal psychology, acting according to primitive impulses and almost totally lacking in rationality or reasoning power. Le Bon saw people taking part in crowds as becoming easily aroused or agitated, and descending into barbarism. Individual conscience would disappear, and the crowd would operate as one vicious animal, following what Le Bon described as a 'law of mental unity'.

As with many theories which reflect the spirit of their times, Le Bon's 'mob psychology' became a very popular theory, despite its relative lack of evidence. Immediately, it took on political overtones, being used as a justification for heavy-handed police action against the political demonstrations of the time. As a model of how crowds are, it remained a powerful social influence, and is still believed in many sectors of society. Banyard (1989), discussing the Hillsborough tragedy in which nearly a hundred football supporters were crushed to death against barriers, argued that it was the belief in mob psychology held by the police who were controlling events which meant that they made no attempt to explain or reason with the crowd and therefore made the situation very much worse than it need have been.

Deindividuation

Basing his approach largely on Le Bon's general perspective, Zimbardo (1969) proposed that people in crowds experience **deindividuation** – a loss of their own personal identity, such that they merge anonymously into the mob. This means that they are prepared to act in ways that are very much more cruel or impulsive than they would do if they were acting as individuals. Zimbardo performed a study in which groups of college women were asked to deliver electric shocks to another woman. Half of them were dressed in bulky lab coats and hoods which hid their faces, and were never referred to by name. The other half were dressed in their own clothes and wore large name-tags. Zimbardo found that the de-individuated women were prepared to give shocks which were twice as strong as those given by the individually identified women.

Johnson and Downing (1979), however, criticised Zimbardo's study, on the grounds that the nature of the 'uniform' that the deindividuated research participants wore was very similar to that of the Ku-Klux-Klan, an extremely violent American racist group. They suggested that this would encourage the research participants to feel that violent behaviour was expected of them in this situation. When the experiment was repeated with three groups – a group wearing Ku-Klux-Klan-type costume, a group wearing their own clothes and a group wearing nurses' uniforms – Johnson and Downing found that those wearing nurses' uniforms gave fewer, and less severe shocks, than the others. So it appears that the outcomes were produced by the costumes, rather than deindividuation as such.

Following Zimbardo's work, Diener (1979) proposed that deindividuation is centred on a lessening of self-awareness. When a person is a member of a crowd which is focused on some external goal (say, a crowd watching a football or cricket match), they feel very different and much less aware of themselves than they usually are. This means that they can act more impulsively, and feel less restrained by normal social conventions. Diener proposed that there are five general outcomes of the deindividuated state, which are listed in Table 17.6.

Prentice-Dunn and Rogers (1982) modified Diener's theory, by arguing that there are two different aspects of self-awareness: public and private. Only private self-awareness, they argued, is

important to the process of deindividuation. Public self-awareness concerns our awareness about the impression we are making on others – for example by our behaviour or our dress. A lessening of this does not seem to have any effect on individual identification. But private self-awareness is concerned with the attention that we pay to our own thoughts and feelings, and in certain situations this can decrease.

Prentice-Dunn and Rogers argued that private self-awareness decreases in the type of situation where our attention is centred elsewhere, such as on a football match or public speaker; where there is a high level of group cohesiveness, such as is shared by supporters of the same sports team; where the people concerned are experiencing a high level of arousal, like the excitement produced by a match or the intensity produced by a sense of social injustice; and where there is effective anonymity for group members. In such situations, they argued, deindividuation might be likely to occur.

Deindividuation is a controversial perspective, mainly because of its implicit value-judgements about crowds, and its assumptions that people in crowds become incapable of rational thinking. It seems likely that deindividuation does have a role to play in understanding why people act as they do, but at the same time research into crowds and the way that people in the crowd perceive what is happening suggests that 'mob psychology' is not nearly as powerful as Le Bon described.

Football crowds

Even in crowds which are widely considered to be violent, there is evidence that deindividuation is very much less than we might think. Marsh, Rosser and Harré (1978) performed an ethogenic study of football fans – observing social behaviour and analysing the accounts that the participants gave of what was going on. By talking with the fans and analysing their descriptions of what went on on the terraces, Marsh, Rosser and Harré concluded that, rather than coming from a de-individuated mob, aggressive behaviour among football fans in fact operates according to clear rules; although it involves a great deal of ritualised aggression, it very rarely results in actual damage.

While the fans were talking, their choice of language implied very violent behaviour indeed: they would talk about people getting 'murdered' if they were caught by opposing fans; or about

---

Table 17.6 Outcomes of the deindividuated state

1 Normal restraints against impulsive behaviour are weakened.

2 Sensitivity to current emotional states and immediate situational cues is increased.

3 The person becomes unable to monitor or regulate their own behaviour.

4 There is less concern about what other people will think of their actions.

5 The person becomes less capable of engaging in rational planning.

Source: Diener, 1979

someone having their 'head smashed in'. But when they were questioned further about what actually went on, and when what they said was compared with observations and videotapes of their behaviour, it emerged that the actual aggressive behaviour which went on was very limited. For instance, it was not uncommon for fans to 'see the others off' – to chase rival fans to the railway station after the match. But although the chase was pursued vigorously, the fans were careful not to catch up with the others. To do so would have produced a potentially embarrassing situation, because it was the ritualised gesture of aggression – the chase – rather than the actual acts of violence which were important.

There were many other examples of ritualised fighting observed by the researchers, and although there were occasional cases of people getting seriously hurt, these were seen as 'breaking the rules', and not at all as the normal state of affairs. The fans' aggressive talk was really more of a language metaphor – much as people might talk of a 'battle of wits' or a 'barrage of questions'. However, the media and other sectors of society took the fans' violent language literally, and therefore interpreted the aggression as being very much more serious than it actually was.

That is not to say that seriously violent events never happen – there is clear evidence that they do. But Marsh, Rosser and Harré suggested that outbreaks of uncontrolled violence become much more likely when the ritual is upset through over-reaction by external agencies, resulting in over-control. This has the effect of removing the security of known, ritualised patterns of behaviour and sequences of prescribed responses, leaving individuals to react without internal or immediate social inhibitions.

Marsh, Rosser and Harré also found a very strong social pattern and social structure among those fans who tended to be described by the press as 'hooligans'. Over time, the fans tended to follow a 'career' path by becoming part of different groups of supporters: graduating from a junior group into a different one by proving themselves to be good at the rituals and rules of being a football fan. This picture of how football fans behave is one which is very different from the one generally presented by the media.

Political crowds

Similarly, political crowds have often been presented as acting much less rationally than they usually do. The political demonstration is an established, and at times very effective, system by which members of the public can make known their feelings about a given political issue. Public demonstrations against the poll tax in Britain, for instance, were highly influential in reversing that policy, both in historical times and more recently. Most political demonstrations are peaceful affairs, which pass off without incident, but others sometimes result in violent altercations, usually between police and demonstrators. Similarly, inner-city 'riots' are generally sparked off by a specific event – a flash-point – but then erupt into a more generalised disturbance.

Waddington, Jones and Critcher (1987) argued that it is too simplistic to perceive riots or political disturbances as caused by these flashpoint incidents. Instead, they argued, the flashpoint incident serves to provide an example, which is regarded as typical of more general problems in the community by the crowd at the time. Smelser (1962) argued that disorderly crowds emerge only under particular social conditions, which include general social tension, the social perception of a grievance or grievances, people who will initiate action and some kind of precipitating incident. A flashpoint always has a context.

Waddington, Jones and Critcher proposed a theoretical model which could be used to analyse a variety of different types of social disorder. In view of the complexity of what is happening at this type of event, they proposed that the situation should be analysed at six different levels of analysis. No single level can be taken as a 'cause' on its own, but together the six levels, they argued, provided a reasonable index for charting and analysing crowds and crowd disturbances. The six levels of analysis in their model are given in Table 17.7 overleaf.

Using this model, Waddington, Jones and Critcher went on to analyse two public rallies which occurred during the miners' strike of 1984 in Britain. One of these was disorderly, with outbreaks of violence between police and demonstrators. The second, occurring in the same town a week later, was not. The researchers collected data by participant observation both during the events and in the run-up to them, and by interviewing members of the crowd about how

Table 17.7 Levels of analysis of social disorder

1	*Structural*	Waddington, Jones and Critcher (1987) argue that it would be naïve to ignore wider issues of social structure in looking at public disturbances. For example, the fact that black people in the inner cities experience higher levels of unemployment than white people means that they have less of a stake in social institutions and experience higher levels of frustration.
2	*Political/ ideological*	A sector of society may have a political grievance about some form of legislation; social control may tighten to what is felt to be unacceptable levels; or society may have what Cohen (1973) described as a 'moral panic' about, say, hippies or unemployed youth.
3	*Cultural*	This includes shared ideas about the world, such as the social representations described by Moscovici (1984), which we looked at in Chapter 15. Beliefs about rights, the likely outcomes of actions, and definitions of the nature of the problem will all contribute to the crowd's reaction.
4	*Contextual*	The particular context in which the event takes place will also have its effect. This includes the temporal setting: the sequences of happenings which have led up to this particular event (like, say, the police being sensitised to expect certain forms of violence, as they were in the case of the 'Mods and Rockers' clashes in the 1960s, according to Cohen (1973)).
5	*Spatial*	This includes the physical setting, in which particular areas may have a symbolic significance for participants in the disturbance, or the layout of open spaces and buildings may serve to precipitate or reduce the likelihood of confrontations.
6	*Interactional*	The final level at which large-scale public events need to be examined concerns the nature of the interactions between people involved. For example: the police or official agencies may be seen as over-stepping the established 'norms' for dealing with a given group or community; or the arrest or rough treatment of a local politician or trade union official may be considered to be 'out of order' by the crowd. Waddington *et al.* pointed out that conflict can be prevented or intensified by interpersonal style as much as by the political context.

they saw what was going on. When they came to apply their model to the two demonstrations, it was clear that the structural, political/ideological and cultural levels were the same for each; but that there had been major differences between the two events at the contextual, situational and interactional levels.

On the contextual level the second, peaceful, demonstration had been systematically planned, with appropriate consultation with the local police. The situation, or setting, was organised carefully, with speakers and entertainments to channel the responses of the crowd, and with barriers being set up beforehand, to prevent the need for police force to contain the crowd's movements. And on the interactional level, crowd control was undertaken by the organisers themselves rather than the police, and the police carefully avoided confrontational behaviour. Ironically, but probably typically, the peaceful second rally received virtually no press coverage, whereas the more confrontational demonstration was widely reported.

Waddington, Jones and Critcher argued that – by contrast with Le Bon's 'mob psychology' approach – public disorder is not unpredictable,

and that a careful examination of the factors in a given situation can predict when such disorder is more or less likely. They identified five practical courses of action which would contribute to successful crowd control (Table 17.8). Moreover, they argued, even if all the factors point to

Table 17.8 Practical action in crowd control

1 The crowd should be allowed to be self-policing.

2 There should be effective liaison between police and organisers.

3 A policy of 'minimum force' should be applied by the police (being seen to be 'tooled up' for trouble means that people will expect trouble, and act accordingly).

4 Those involved in managing and controlling crowds should have training in effective interpersonal communication.

5 Police and enforcement agencies should be seen as accountable for their actions to the community (a belief that the police can do exactly what they like is likely to encourage resentment and hostility).

Source: Waddington et al., 1987

disorder being imminent, action at the relevant levels – including the interactional and situational levels – can produce a positive effect. It needs a lot of things all going wrong together to produce a riot, it seems, and even then it usually can be ameliorated.

In this chapter, then, we have looked at some of the psychological research into attitudes, prejudice, and aggressive behaviour. In this, many of the social mechanisms which we have looked at in the previous three chapters also come into play, such as the mechanisms of social representations, attribution and social expectation. In the next few chapters, we will go on to look at the psychology of development, including the development of social knowledge.

Key terms

intergroup rivalry Competition between different social groups, which can often lead to powerful hostility.

scapegoating The process of putting the blame for difficult economic circumstances or other sources of frustration onto some disliked but 'inferior' social group, and so increasing prejudice and intergroup hostility.

search for coherence The way that members of an in-group look for ways to justify or rationalise their beliefs about the positive attributes of the in-group and the negative attributes of the out-group.

semantic differential A form of attitude measurement which involves asking people to evaluate a concept by weighing it up according to several different verbal dimensions.

Summary

1 Attitudes are distinct from, but strongly linked to, personal values. An attitude may serve several different functions, including object appraisal, social adjustment and the externalisation of inner conflicts.

2 Attitudes have three dimensions: a cognitive dimension, a conative (behavioural) dimension and an affective dimension. There is often inconsistency between attitudes and behaviour.

3 Fishbein and Ajzen argued that intentionality and expectations are important in directing behaviour, as well as attitudes. Other attitude theories have emphasised the importance of cognitive balance, assimilation and contrast, accentuation, and labelling.

4 Factors in persuasion include the source of the communication, the message itself, the person who is receiving the message and the context in which the message is presented. Cognitive dissonance can also be a major factor in attitude change.

5 Theories of prejudice include biological explanations, psychoanalytic explanations and cultural explanations. The scapegoat theory sees it as arising from the need to blame others, while social identity theory sees it in terms of intergroup conflict.

6 Bethlehem's ten principles of ethnic prejudice show how cognitive mechanisms, social learning, intergroup and cultural factors all contribute to the manifestation of prejudice in society.

7 Theories of aggression include biological approaches, social-learning approaches, the frustration-aggression approach, the model of aggression as a response to the environment, and social constructionist approaches.

8 Early theories of crowds suggested that they acted as a primitive mob. Deindividuation theory is a modern version of this idea, but more recent studies suggest that crowd behaviour is more rational and structured than it is usually presented as being.

Self-assessment questions

1 Describe the major functions of an attitude.

2 Explain the concept of cognitive dissonance, and describe a study which illustrates it.

3 Outline the cognitive dimensions of prejudice, as described by Tajfel.

Practice essay questions

1 How far can the concept of attitude dimensions further our understanding of persuasion?

2 Outline and discuss psychological evidence for or against the idea of 'mob psychology'.

3 How can prejudice between different social groups be reduced?

Test your knowledge of this chapter with our online quizzes and games at:
http://www.psych.co.uk

Explore attitudes, prejudice, and crowd behaviour further at:

General
http://www.carleton.ca/~rthibode/summary.html – Links to seminar notes on the important topics; persuasion, prejudice, group behaviour and attitudes.

Prejudice
http://members.aol.com/markr13/RtsofRacism1.html – Tutorial on the roots of racism and the factors that lead us to think in this way.

Attitudes
http://www.police.wayne.edu/~wpott/cor/grp/attitude.html – Useful tutorials with illustrations of attitudes, and related topics.
http://www.fmdc.calpoly.edu/libarts/cslem/Wizdemo/16 ChapterD.html#Components – Clear summaries of the related issues surrounding attitudes.

Persuasion
http://www.swix.ch/clan/ks/CPSP17.htm – Part 1 of a comprehensive bibliography for attitudes and persuasion topics. Part 2 is at http://www.swix.ch/clan/ks/CPSP9.htm.

Developmental psychology

Learning and skill development

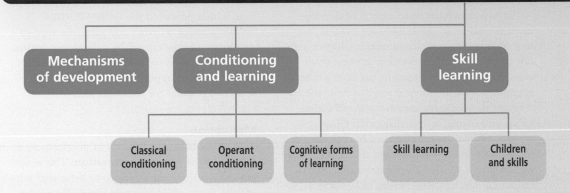

Mechanisms of development

Conditioning and learning

Skill learning

Classical conditioning

Operant conditioning

Cognitive forms of learning

Skill learning

Children and skills

Learning objectives

18.1. Mechanisms of development
a define terms relating to mechanisms of development
b describe individual mechanisms of development
c outline social mechanisms of development

18.2. Achievement motivation
a identify factors in achievement motivation
b describe a study of achievement motivation
c distinguish between trait and social theories

18.3. Classical conditioning
a define terms relating to classical conditioning
b describe the processes involved in classical conditioning
c evaluate behaviourist explanations for classical conditioning

18.4. Operant conditioning
a define terms relating to operant conditioning
b describe features of operant conditioning
c link principles of operant conditioning to specific examples

18.5. Types of learning
a outline different types of learning
b describe a study of genetically prepared learning
c apply concepts of learning to everyday examples

18.6. Skill acquisition
a list the features of skilled behaviour
b describe theories of skill acquisition
c identify factors which can influence skill acquisition

18.7. Models of skill acquisition
a define terms relating to theories of skill acquisition
b outline the mechanisms involved in skill acquisition
c contrast different models of skill acquisition

18.8. Metacognitive development
a outline different types of metacognition
b describe a study of metacognitive development
c define terms relating to metacognitive development

Development involves change over time. We all change as we grow older: some of those changes are a result of our particular experiences, while others are the outcome of physiological change. Developmental psychology is all about studying patterns, regularities and processes in the way that people change over time.

We have looked at some aspects of development elsewhere in this book – for example, we looked at language development in Chapter 4. In this section, we will be looking at some other ways that human development has been studied, beginning with the identification of basic mechanisms of development, and the study of various forms of learning, in this chapter. In Chapter 19 we will look at the development of cognition and social awareness in children, and in Chapter 20 we will look at research into children's attachments and social development. Finally, in Chapter 21, we will look at development through the lifespan, from adolescence through to old age.

Mechanisms of development

In this chapter, then, we will be looking at some of the basic mechanisms of development. There are a number of different mechanisms by which children learn, or by which their behaviour changes as they grow older, so we will begin by summarising the main ones, very briefly, and looking at how they can manifest themselves by taking the example of achievement motivation. We will then go on to look in more detail at specific forms of learning, beginning with behaviourist research into conditioning, and going on to look at the processes of skill learning, and meta-cognitive development.

Mechanisms of development range from those which appear to be internally, physiologically determined, to those which occur as a result of the types of experience which the child has. Although each child's experience will be different, some of the underlying mechanisms are basic to everyone, so it is worth looking briefly at these.

Maturation and conditioning

In the first half of the twentieth century, part of the influence of modernist ideas, and the 'machine age', was reflected in the types of theories of development which were put forward by

researchers. Psychologists of that time expected to find straightforward mechanisms which would produce human behaviour and development, without complications or interactions between different processes – an expectation which seems naïve to modern psychologists, but which fitted with the Zeitgeist of their times. This was also the time which produced the **nature-nurture debates,** about whether any particular type of development was 'caused' by genetic maturation, or by learning. As we now know, the two act together, not in opposition; but the debates remained popular for many decades.

Maturation

One of the basic mechanisms of development is the process of **genetic maturation.** This is the gradual development of forms of behaviour which emerge as the child becomes physically mature enough for that behaviour to be triggered. For example, all physically normal human infants, no matter what culture they grow up in, will begin to walk at a certain point in their physical development, usually at around twelve to fourteen months. It varies a lot from one individual to the next, though: some will begin earlier and some later. Typically, we speak of children learning to walk, but in practice this is a genetically determined behaviour which appears when the child has reached a certain stage of physical development. It is part of being a human being, and comes directly from the genes which we have inherited from our parents.

That does not mean, though, that it is unaffected by the child's environment. Super (1976) found that Kenyan children from the same tribe – who had therefore inherited the same basic genetic mechanisms – varied a great deal in the age at which they started walking. In traditional villages, they were deliberately taught these skills, but those brought up in urban environments were not. Super found that the children from traditional villages developed walking on average a month before their counterparts in the towns.

As we have seen in earlier chapters, all genetic influence affects development by interacting with environmental pressures, and even walking is something which can be influenced in this way. Early developmental psychologists did not recognise this interaction, and tended to think that genetic maturation was automatic, regardless of experience. For example, in 1929, Gesell and

Thomson reported a study of twin girls, one of whom was given training in motor skills, including climbing stairs, at the age of ten months. The training was for twenty minutes a day, over six weeks. Her twin was given the same training, but over seven weeks. Gesell and Thompson reported that there were virtually no differences between the two in the age at which they learned motor skills.

However, in 1983, Fowler re-appraised the evidence, and found that the difference in training had produced some differences between the girls. The child who was taught earlier was more dextrous in handling toy blocks, and generally better at other motor skills – and these differences persisted for several years. When they were teenagers, the twin who had been given the early training was consistently better at motor skills such as running and walking, and also tap-dancing. Howe (1998) discussed several other examples of research which imply that early training in physical skills can have long-lasting effects. Given the way that environment interacts with genetic influences in other areas of human experience, it is not really surprising to find the same thing occurring with basic motor skill development.

Conditioning

Although we have genetic predispositions towards certain kinds of behaviour, it is our experiences which will affect how those tendencies manifest themselves. The basic forms of learning known as classical conditioning and operant conditioning are also important mechanisms of child develop-ment. We will be looking at the fine detail of these types of learning later in this chapter, but since they form an important part of the way that children develop, a brief description is appropriate here.

Classical conditioning, essentially, is learning by **association**. If two things happen together, we come to associate the two, and so we expect to encounter one when we encounter the other. For example, many people feel anxious when they walk into a room which is set out for students to take an examination, even if they are not taking an examination themselves. This is because the feeling of anxiety has, in their previous experience, always been associated with rooms arranged in that particular way. When they enter a room like that, people feel anxious purely because of learning by association.

Operant conditioning, on the other hand, is learning by **effect**. If an action has a positive out-come, in terms of allowing us to gain something we want, or to avoid or escape from something which is unpleasant, then we are more likely to repeat that action. If we do something which earns us approval from other people – such as a smile or a friendly nod – then it is likely that, in similar situations, we will do the same thing again.

Social learning mechanisms

During the first half of the twentieth century, developmental researchers tended to believe that the three mechanisms of maturation and classical and operant conditioning were fully adequate to explain all the different aspects of child develop-ment. Nowadays, however, we take a less simplistic view of human nature. Psychologists are aware that there are many other mechanisms involved in how the child develops. Since most of these are to do with the child's social experience, they are often grouped loosely together under the heading of **social learning mechanisms**.

Imitation

One of the most fundamental social learning mechanisms is the process of **imitation**. As any parent knows, children learn by copying other people's behaviour. Imitation is a very useful shortcut for gaining information about how to act in the world. If we learned everything by operant conditioning, for example, then it would be a long and tedious process. We would have to try out a number of different possible activities, see what the consequence was for each one and repeat only those activities which had pleasant consequences. But imitation is a much quicker way of learning whole patterns of behaviour.

Imitation also allows us to see quickly which actions are likely to have pleasant consequences. It involves watching other people's behaviour and then doing the same thing ourselves. So as part of the first stage, we are able to select which behav-iours we will imitate. Bandura (1969) showed that children are much more likely to imitate people whom they see receiving rewards, or people whose actions result in a pleasant outcome, than people who are not rewarded. In this type of learning, we do not have to get the reward ourselves: we can learn vicariously, by seeing other people rewarded. It is therefore known as

vicarious reinforcement. Imitative learning, particularly when it is coupled with vicarious reinforcement, is a powerful mechanism of social learning for children.

Identification

Another social learning mechanism is that of **identification.** Children make comparisons between themselves and other people. In doing so, they see some people as being like themselves and some as different. Often, we will identify with other people whom we see as in some way similar to ourselves: we will emphasise similarities, and try to act in the kinds of ways that we believe the other person would act. Identification is different from imitation, because imitation concerns the copying of very specific acts or actions, whereas identification is more concerned with general styles of behaviour – so identification can guide our behaviour even in entirely novel situations.

We tend to identify with people who are important to us. A young child, for example, may identify with its mother and act how it believes its mother would act. As we saw in Chapter 15, we may also identify with whole social groups, and act according to the social identity which is involved. Although social identification does not appear as early as learning through personal identification, as the child begins to learn more about society, through school and the mass media, it will often identify with one social group (e.g. 'children who go to our school and not that other one') rather than another.

Metacognition and social cognition

Yet another aspect of the way in which children learn concerns how they think about learning – the area of **metacognition**, which we will look at towards the end of this chapter. As we have seen, children develop an understanding of how the mind works as they develop. They learn, for instance, how to go about learning something; they learn how their memory works; and they learn what they can or cannot do. A considerable amount of recent research has shown that the metacognitive skills which children have are very important in determining how they interact socially with other people – and this, in turn, will affect which type of social reinforcement a child receives.

The child also develops a **theory of mind** as it grows older, and it uses this to interpret other people's behaviour. We will be looking at this in Chapter 19. The process of recognising that other people have minds, and trying to predict what may be going on within them, is a fundamental aspect of human interaction – we all do it. So this type of social cognition is an important learning mechanism for the child as it learns to adjust its own behaviour to socially acceptable norms and values. It also forms an important basis for the social mechanisms of conformity and obedience to social norms, which we looked at in Chapter 16.

Self-efficacy beliefs

The types of beliefs which children hold about themselves are also important in development. Bandura (1988) argued that **self-efficacy beliefs** are important to us because they express what we believe we are capable of. If we believe that we are able to do something successfully, then we are more likely to put effort into doing that thing, and because of this, we are more likely to succeed at it. This applies to adults as much as children, but it is particularly apparent with children, since positive beliefs about self-efficacy are necessary if we are to put the effort into learning the necessary skills in the first place.

Several psychologists have shown how beliefs about their own abilities directly affect how children interact with their worlds, and therefore how they learn from them. As we will see in the section on achievement motivation, children's beliefs about intelligence, for instance, have a direct bearing on the amount of effort they are prepared to put into challenging tasks – and so therefore they affect directly how successful any one child is likely to be.

Social expectations

A further social mechanism by which children learn concerns other people's **expectations.** Children pick up the expectations that other people have of them, whether they are directly told about them or not. These can often become self-fulfilling. When we look at child-rearing styles, we can see how parents who express high expectations of their children in terms of honesty and conscience tend to have children who live up to those expectations. The self-fulfilling prophecy (see Chapter 15), in which a certain form of behaviour occurs simply because it is believed to be true, is a very important mechanism in a child's development.

The complexity of social learning also implies that children need to have appropriate **models** to learn from, and appropriate social expectations around them, if they are not to find themselves later in opposition to their society. Bronfenbrenner, in 1974, performed observational studies of child-rearing practices in Russia and America, and argued that, at that time, Russian society was very much more efficient in transmitting expected social norms and ideas to its children than was American society.

In Russia, adults tended to consider themselves committed to the general goal of bringing up socially responsible children, whether they were parents themselves or not, and children were included in social practices as much as possible. By contrast, American children tended to inhabit a separate world from adult society – often a very individualistic, consumer-oriented one, dominated by television and peer-group pressures. This meant that society's goals were not systematically re-inforced, and the child was largely left to its own devices.

According to Bronfenbrenner, the separation of American children from the adult world resulted in American youth often growing up to become alienated and disaffected from its society. While Russia, of course, had its own problems, their young people as a general rule were much less alienated from the society as a whole. Bronfenbrenner was not suggesting that everything in Russia was wonderful. Rather, he was arguing that social expectations and the social mechanisms which encouraged the child to feel part of its society and to share in it are important goals in any society; and that some systematic approach to the way in which children are socialised is likely to be beneficial, both to the individual and to the society.

We can see, then, that the basic mechanisms of child development are much more complex and sophisticated than the early psychologists believed. Children acquire their knowledge and skills through a variety of social processes, which help them to learn how to act appropriately in their society. One of the best ways of seeing how this happens is to look at some of the psychological research into achievement motivation.

Achievement motivation

Children differ from one another in terms of how ambitious they are, how keen they are to learn and how hard they try to achieve things. Having a high level of achievement motivation can make all the difference to how well someone does in society. Although some people seem to sail through life with everything handed to them on a plate, most of us encounter difficulties and dis-appointments along the way. If we are put off by these, then we are unlikely to be able to overcome obstacles and achieve our personal ambitions. But if we remain ambitious, we are likely to persist in our efforts, and so we become more likely to achieve our own personal goals in life.

Early psychological research into **achievement motivation** tended to refer to children having dif-ferent levels of achievement motivation, as if it were an internal trait of some kind. In fact, even now achievement motivation is often referred to as **nAch,** standing for 'need to achieve'. This is based on the observation that some children seem to be more keen than others to succeed in minor and major tasks, and will try very hard to achieve any goals that they are set. It is questionable, though, how far achievement motivation really is an internal trait.

Origins of achievement motivation

There is a certain amount of research which shows how children from parents with high expectations tend to achieve far more than children whose parents have low expectations of their likely success. In a classic study of this kind, Rosen and d'Andrade (1959) asked children to build a tower of building blocks while they were blindfolded. The parents looked on as they worked, and were allowed to talk to the child. The researchers found that the children with highest achievement motivation – those who kept trying and aimed further – had parents who expected a great deal from them, and also who encouraged the child as it proceeded with the task.

Atkinson (1964) argued that achievement moti-vation can be seen as arising from three elements: motive strength, expectancy and incentive. These are not separate factors, though, because the strength of the motive to succeed – one of the elements – depends on the expectancy of success held by the child, and the incentive value of suc-ceeding or failing. A child who does not expect to be able to succeed, and who has little incentive because it is not particularly encouraged or praised, would not tend to be very highly motivated.

There is a considerable amount of research evidence linking high levels of performance on challenging tasks with high expectations. Children can be powerfully affected by the expectations of their success which their parents hold, as well as by their own expectations of success. High expectations, or expectancies, according to Dweck and Elliott (1983), come from three sources, which are given in Table 18.1.

Atkinson also emphasised other aspects of the incentive value of success or failure. This draws on the idea that every task involves a certain amount of conflict between approach and avoidance. Atkinson argued that there is an **approach-avoidance conflict** in every task, between achieving success, which is a positive sort of goal that we would want to approach, and avoiding failure, which is a negative sort of outcome that we would want to avoid. So although achieving success may appear attractive, risking failure can appear equally unattractive. If the child does not value the task particularly highly, or if they regard themselves as unlikely to succeed, then avoiding failure may become more important than trying to succeed.

Effort and attribution

More recent theories of achievement motivation have emphasised the beliefs about likely outcomes which children hold. The idea is that the **attributions** which children make about effort and achievement will affect how much effort they put into succeeding. For example, if children attribute failure to a lack of ability of some kind, then this will result in their not expecting to be able to achieve much in the future. As a result of this, they will be unlikely to persist in a task which requires effort, because they feel that their effort will not help them to greater success. On the other hand, if children attribute failure to some other cause, such as lack of effort, then, faced with a similar task, they will put more effort into it, and so will be more likely to succeed in the long run.

Dweck and Elliott (1983) reported a study by Bandura and Dweck, in which they investigated the different **theories of intelligence** and achievement that children held. Broadly speaking, these theories could be divided into two sets. One group of children tended to see intelligence as a repertoire of learned skills, which increase with effort. The other group of children tended to see intelligence as a global, stable quality, of which people have a fixed, unchanging amount. For this group, success in performing a task showed whether the amount of intelligence the person possessed was adequate or not.

Bandura and Dweck showed that these two theories resulted in the children having very different perceptions about whether it was worthwhile making any effort when undertaking a difficult task. Children from the first group saw

---

Table 18.1 Sources of achievement motivation

1	*A realistic analysis*	of the tasks or skills which are involved when planning strategies. Without a realistic appraisal of the situation and the type of skills that the problem is likely to need, then any effort is unlikely to be worthwhile.
2	*The self-efficacy beliefs*	which people hold about their own capabilities. These directly affect how much effort they are prepared to put into things. Bandura argued that it is often good for people to have beliefs about their self-efficacies which are slightly higher than the evidence would suggest, because this encourages them to aim high, to try hard, and therefore to develop their skills even further.
3	*The standards*	which an individual maintains. For optimum performance, these standards should be personal rather than normative – in other words, they should be concerned with that individual's own goals, rather than what other people achieve or do not achieve. In addition, such standards need to be flexible, so that they can adapt to the demands of the situation. Expecting total success all the time in every situation is unrealistic; but if somebody has learning goals, then if a task turns out to be something different from their previous experience, they will be able to modify their standards accordingly.

Source: Adapted from Dweck and Elliott, 1983

effort as an investment that would be likely to increase their intelligence, whereas the second group saw effort as a risk that might reveal that they had an inadequate level of intelligence. So the second group of children were far less likely to try hard at tasks, and tended to set themselves very low goals. We can see how these findings can be linked with the social mechanisms of attribution and social representations, which we looked at in Chapter 15.

Learning and performance goals

In the Bandura and Dweck study, the **personal goals** of the two groups of children were different too. The first group of children tended to have learning goals – as a general rule, they aimed to do better at any task which they attempted. They saw doing things as a continuous process of self-improvement. But the second group of children tended to have performance goals. They judged a task as being valuable or not by whether it had a successful outcome. They did not really take into account, or value, any learning or personal development that might arise from attempting to do the task.

Another study, reported by Dweck and Elliott in 1983, showed that children with learning goals do not tend to show any decline in performance if they undertake a series of tasks where they end up with repeated failures. Instead, they will carry on undertaking these tasks at a high level of motivation. But children who have **performance goals** tend to show marked deterioration in their behaviour if they undertake tasks and are unsuccessful. They will quickly stop trying, and give up. So having learning goals and a belief in intelligence as a set of acquired skills tends to make children more likely to be successful at long-term tasks which involve some initial frustration. This includes tasks like basic literacy – learning to read is very difficult and frustrating at the beginning and grows easier only with effort and practice – as well as longer-term achievement in school and work.

We can see, then, that the child's cognitive appraisals and beliefs about the situation seem to be the most important factors in determining whether that child is likely to persevere at any given task. We can also see how what initially seemed to psychologists to be an internal character trait – achievement motivation – now appears quite differently, as a sophisticated application of the child's world-knowledge to the situation in front of them. The study of achievement motivation also reflects how the emphasis in developmental psychology has shifted from simply classifying and describing traits which children seemed to possess, to identifying how children understand their worlds. Box 18.1 overleaf discusses how developmental psychology changed during the twentieth century, and how different approaches became popular at different times.

Conditioning and learning

Many of the studies of the basic mechanisms of learning have been conducted using animals rather than human beings. This is not accidental, particularly when it comes to the study of conditioning. Conditioning appears to be the most fundamental form of learning, and many psychologists of the first half of the twentieth century believed that it was the basic mechanism underlying all other learning. Studying animal learning, they believed, would reveal those mechanisms more clearly, because animals learned less complicated things than human beings.

Conditioning was investigated in considerable depth by the behaviourists, who argued that learning was, essentially, a change in behaviour brought about as a result of experience. The new behaviour would appear under appropriate environmental conditions, which is where the term 'conditioning' originated. The behaviourists studied two fundamental forms of conditioning: classical and operant conditioning.

Classical conditioning

Classical conditioning developed from two parallel sets of investigations into associative learning. In America, J. B. Watson (1903) developed the **Law of Exercise**, which proposed that a learned link – an association – between a stimulus and a response could be forged simply by repeating the two together often enough. At the same time, in Russia, Ivan Pavlov was investigating how involuntary responses – reflexes – could become conditioned to appear in response to new forms of stimulus. Pavlov's work on **conditioned reflexes** is one of the classic texts of psychology and medicine.

Box 18.1 Changing perspectives in developmental psychology

The history of ideas in developmental psychology reflects, in many ways, the way that ideas have changed in society as a whole, during the course of the twentieth century. At the beginning of the century, and represented particularly in the work of Gesell, one of the founders of developmental psychology, we find an emphasis on **genetic maturation** as the source of development. This emphasis on innate qualities was very typical of the psychology of the time – it is at this time that we find the vigorous insistence on intelligence as genetically determined, for instance. In many ways, it was a hangover from the Victorian mode of thinking, which by and large took the view that society, and the status of the individuals in it, was pretty much ordained by God, and not something which would be easily changed.

After WWI, things changed considerably – not all at once, obviously, since paradigm shifts take time to develop. But this was the time of **modernism** – a belief in progress, and that it was possible for the human being to create a brave, new world in which the legacies of old social problems would vanish in the face of scientific progress. Science and technology would find the answers to all social problems, and to biological and physical ones too. This, in psychology, was the era in which the philosophy of **behaviourism** – with its emphasis on the human being as a *tabula rasa*, wide open to experience – really took hold. And in developmental psychology, it was the period of exploring the conditionability of young children, and how they responded to various forms of stimulus-response training.

After the war, although behaviourism was still dominant, new voices began to emerge. The modernist view was gradually giving way to a sense that things might not be quite so simple. Although British psychology at the time was largely dominated by psychometrics and behaviourism, other perspectives were beginning to emerge. Rogers, Maslow and Bruner all offered alternative ways of understanding human experience; and in the developmental field, the vital work of Bandura legitimised recognition that children used more complex forms of learning than just conditioning. Adherents of Bandura's social learning approach began to look at the effects of child-rearing: conducting research into achievement motivation, the development of aggression, and even raising the almost heretical idea that perhaps gender roles were learned, rather than being part of the instinctive and unquestionable natural order.

The 1960s and 1970s saw the emergence of the **structuralist movement**, both in social life as a whole, in academic theory, and in developmental psychology in the form of the adoption of the Piagetian approach to child development. Piaget's grand theory dominated social psychology for some time. But the paradigm changed again, as researchers became increasingly aware of the subtlety and importance of social interaction and social awareness. As in psychology as a whole, social factors began increasingly to impinge on developmental psychology – ironically, exemplified in the work of Vygotsky, a Russian psychologist of the 1920s, whose approach seemed to express most clearly the current emphasis on social interaction and educability.

In a series of experiments with dogs reported in 1927, Pavlov showed that they could learn to produce the salivation response to the sound of a bell, if that sound was repeatedly paired with the presentation of food. This was significant, since salivation in response to food is an involuntary response, and not the sort of thing which an animal can produce deliberately. Moreover, Pavlov found that the response would generalise the response to similar stimuli. However, an animal could also be trained to discriminate between similar stimuli, if one stimulus was reinforced while the other was not. Repeated presentation of the learned stimulus without the original unlearned one would lead to extinction of the learned response.

Reinforcement

Reinforcement is one of the central concepts in this form of learning. According to both Watson and Pavlov, learned associations are strengthened, or reinforced, by repeating the association between the stimulus and the response several times. Watson called this the Law of Exercise: by exercising the connection between the stimulus and the response, the association between the two would be strengthened.

Pavlovian theory described reinforcement as repetition of the pairing of an unconditioned, or unlearned, stimulus with a conditioned, or learned, one. Since the unconditioned stimulus, which was the presentation of food in Pavlov's example, brought about an unconditioned response – in this case salivation – the pairing of the two meant that the response of salivation also became associated with the conditioned stimulus of the sound of the bell. So, with repeated pairings, the association between the bell and the response would be strengthened, until eventually the conditioned stimulus on its own was enough to elicit salivation (Figure 18.1). Salivation had become a conditioned response.

Autonomic responses

Perhaps a better example of classical conditioning can be seen in an experiment using human research participants by Menzies in 1937. Menzies studied **vasoconstriction** – the way that the blood vessels contract and withdraw from the surface of the skin in cold conditions. Vasoconstriction operates as one of the body's automatic temperature-regulating mechanisms, preventing the body from losing heat through the skin. But it is not a response which is under conscious control – it happens involuntarily. Menzies elicited vaso-constriction by plunging the research participant's hand into ice-cold water. At the same time, they heard a buzzer. After a number of trials, it was found that the sound of the buzzer in itself would elicit the response of vasoconstriction.

This experiment is particularly interesting, not just because it contains a number of the distinctive features of classical conditioning, but also because it emphasises the **autonomic** nature of this form of learning. Classical conditioning is concerned with direct associations between stimulus and response, and as such it is not mediated by cognitive mechanisms – you do not have to think about it. It is much more to do with basic autonomic responses which are mediated by the spinal cord and medulla (see Chapter 13). When we are applying the concept of classical conditioning to human

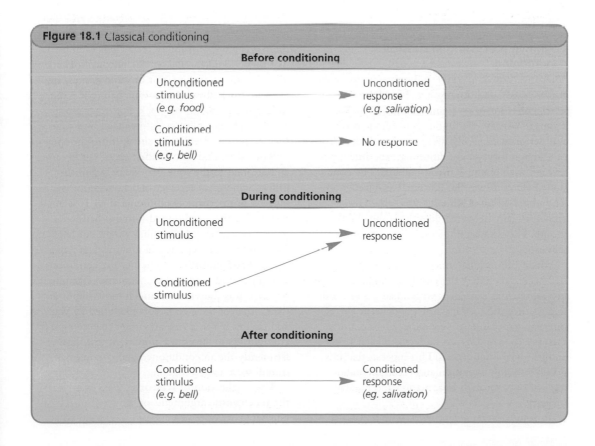

Figure 18.1 Classical conditioning

Before conditioning

Unconditioned stimulus (e.g. food) ⟶ Unconditioned response (e.g. salivation)

Conditioned stimulus (e.g. bell) ⟶ No response

During conditioning

Unconditioned stimulus ⟶ Unconditioned response

Conditioned stimulus ⟶

After conditioning

Conditioned stimulus (e.g. bell) ⟶ Conditioned response (eg. salivation)

behaviour, therefore, it is important to bear in mind that it operates on a non-cognitive level. It is not easy to break a conditioned response by thinking or reasoning – they tend to be extinguished only by breaking the stimulus-response connection.

Behaviour therapy

Since classical conditioning operates at an autonomic level, it is frequently associated with anxiety or fear reactions. Several of the techniques used in behaviour therapy, such as systematic desensitisation, implosion therapy and aversion therapy (see Chapter 9), adopt a classical conditioning framework to create new associations between the stimulus and the response.

There is some doubt, however, as to whether it is really the strict stimulus-response learning that is important in this type of therapy. The criticisms focus on two areas: first, the relationship which builds up between the therapist and the client; and second, the fact that human beings often strengthen traumatic responses by **cognitive rehearsal:** 'What would happen if …'. Strictly behaviourist models of learning leave no place for cognitive factors of this type.

Cognitive processing in classical conditioning

There are, however, some studies which do imply that classical conditioning may be able to link with higher forms of cognitive processing. For example, a study of stimulus generalisation which was performed by Volkova in 1953 took the form of a straightforward conditioning experiment performed with young Russian children. The conditioned stimulus was the Russian word for 'good'. The unconditioned stimulus was spoonfuls of cranberry jam, delivered directly to the child's mouth. The measured unconditioned response was salivation.

Volkova found that, once the basic conditioning had been established, the children would salivate just as much to sentences which had 'good' meanings, as they did to the word 'good' itself. This is interesting, because to generalise the response in this way, the child has to understand each sentence and its social implications. This suggests that it is possible to link cognition and classical conditioning – if only through imagination and mental imagery.

To some extent, recent work within classical conditioning has broken free from traditional behaviourist assumptions, and is now able to accept the idea that some cognitive factors may be relevant. This particularly applies to the idea of **expectation:** Pearce (1987) discussed how current models of conditioning involve the idea that the presentation of a conditioned stimulus causes the animal to retrieve a mental representation of the unconditioned stimulus from memory, and act accordingly.

Pavlov and many of the traditional behaviourists had assumed that the critical factor involved in classical conditioning was **temporal contiguity** – the fact that the unconditioned stimulus and the conditioned stimulus both happened at about the same time. However, in 1972, Rescorla argued that what is important in the conditioning process is not temporal contiguity, but the fact that the conditioned stimulus allows the animal to predict what is going to happen next. According to Rescorla, it is the animal's expectation which produces the conditioned response.

In one experiment, in 1968, Rescorla investigated whether it was important that the conditioned stimulus should predict the unconditioned one. Several groups of rats were subjected to an experimental procedure in which, if they heard a tone, there was a 0.4 probability (two chances in five) that they would receive an electric shock. This was the same for all groups. But in some groups, any electric shock always had a tone before it – the tone was a predictor of shock. For other groups, shocks were not necessarily preceded by a tone – they could not predict the shocks from the tones.

Rescorla found that the first set of rats became conditioned to the tone very quickly. But the others, which had received shocks without warning, did not become conditioned at all. It seemed that, unless the conditioned stimulus had some predictive power, conditioning would not happen. This finding was repeated in a number of experiments. **Predictability** – whether the conditioned stimulus could predict the unconditioned stimulus or not – was shown to be much more important than either of the two factors identified by Watson and Pavlov. It was more important than temporal contiguity, and also more important than how frequently the unconditioned and conditioned stimuli were paired together.

The implication of Rescorla's work was clear: the mechanistic arguments of the traditional behaviourists were not enough to explain what was happening during the process of classical conditioning. What the animal expects to happen is all-important, and this depends on whether there are features of the situation which allow for prediction. Seligman (1975) suggested that the conditioned stimulus is being used as a 'warning' signal by the animal, so that it knows when to relax and when to be fearful. He showed that rats which have no reliable predictor that a shock is coming become continuously fearful, and may even develop ulcers from the stress. **Uncertainty** about what to expect can induce anxiety in rats as well as in human beings.

In another study, Kamin (1969) showed that having a conditioned stimulus which can predict an unconditioned one is not just necessary, it also seems to be sufficient. If an animal learns that one conditioned stimulus is a reliable predictor of an unconditioned stimulus – for example, if a rat learns that a light will reliably predict a forthcoming electric shock – then it will not become conditioned to a different stimulus. Such a rat, for example, would not learn that a tone would also predict the shock. Kamin described this as **blocking**. Once the animal has learned one reliable association, it blocks out further associations because it does not need them.

Preparedness in learning

Although classical conditioning itself rests on the idea of reinforcement through repetition, it has frequently been observed that, at times, a single exposure to a particularly powerful or traumatic event seems to be able to effect a very strong form of associative learning. Seligman (1971) investigated this **one-trial learning**, which he dubbed the 'sauce Béarnaise phenomenon', following a visit to a restaurant at which he had eaten sauce Béarnaise, subsequently been sick, and found himself unable to face eating sauce Béarnaise again.

One-trial learning has shown itself to be particularly resistant to extinction. Seligman discussed this in terms of a basic survival mechanism. If we take a comparative perspective, and look at one-trial learning as a mechanism which has evolved through natural selection, then it makes sense to enquire into the potential function of such a response. If something makes you sick, that is quite a reliable indicator that it (or a larger dose of it) would be poisonous to your system. The sickness means that your body is getting rid of toxic substances which might harm it. So, in survival terms, it makes sense for an animal to avoid food which has made it sick in the past. That way, it will avoid the risk of poisoning itself again. Feeling a strong aversion to such food therefore becomes a valuable survival mechanism for any animal, including a human being.

This argument has interesting implications, though. Traditional classical conditioning, and behaviourism in general, was based on the premise of **equipotentiality** – the idea that conditioning will be just as effective whatever stimuli are paired together, because the organism started off as a *tabula rasa* – a blank slate. But Seligman (1970) argued that the survival concept implies that some stimuli will be more easily paired together with others – that there is a state of 'preparedness' to learn some kinds of things in preference to others.

A considerable amount of experimental work emerged to support the idea of **preparedness**. Garcia and Koelling (1966) performed a study in which thirsty rats were allowed to drink salty water. The water was accompanied by a light and a clicker. Subsequently, one group of the rats was injected with a mild poison, inducing illness, and the second group was given an unpleasant electric shock. Garcia and Koelling found that the rats which had been ill would not drink the salty water again (although they would drink salt-free water), whereas those which had been shocked would. But the animals which had been shocked would not drink in the presence of the light and the clicker.

In another study, Shapiro, Jacobs and Lolordo (1980) showed that pigeons would connect the presence of a red light with food quite easily, but learned to connect it with electric shock only with great difficulty. But they would connect a sound with a shock more readily than with food. It seems that pigeons are prepared to associate sounds with aversive stimuli and visual information with food. These, and several similar studies, produced a considerable amount of support for Seligman's preparedness hypothesis.

What we find, then, when we examine recent work in classical conditioning, are two strands of thought which are at variance with traditional behaviourist models. On the one hand, we find that it may be necessary to invoke cognitive mechanisms like expectancy in order to understand what is happening, instead of simply taking an external, 'behaviour-only' point of view. And we also find that animals may have an innate preparedness to learn some things in preference to others, which challenges the 'blank slate' concept. Operant conditioning research, too, has shifted towards a more cognitive perspective, as we will see.

Operant conditioning

In 1911, Thorndike reported on a series of investigations of trial-and-error learning. Thorndike used cats, which he put in a specially constructed **puzzle box.** He placed food outside the box, but the cats were shut in, and in order to escape had to pull on a loop of string suspended from the roof of the box (Figure 18.2). Thorndike noted that the amount of time which the cats took to escape from the box became steadily less as they had more experience of the puzzle. Plotting the data on a graph produced a characteristic **learning curve,** which showed that the more often a given cat had been in the box, the less time it took to escape.

Clearly the cats were learning how to escape from the box, through trial and error. But how was this learning taking place? Thorndike argued that the cats were learning to pull the cord because of what happened once they had pulled it. Being released from the box was a pleasant outcome for the animal and so was reaching the food. From this work, Thorndike formulated the **Law of Effect,** which proposed that a given

behaviour is likely to be repeated if it produces a pleasant effect.

This idea was developed further by B.F. Skinner, in 1938. Skinner investigated the Law of Effect in detail, teasing out the different factors which affected learning. One of the most important pieces of equipment which he used for this was a device which became known as a **Skinner box.** This was a box in which an animal could be deliberately trained to produce a response. Typically, a Skinner box would contain a lever for the animal to press (this would be the behaviour which was being trained), a food delivery chute for giving the animal a reward when it performed the behaviour correctly, a light to signal when the response should be made and sometimes, though not always, a grid floor which could be electrified to give the animal a light shock (Figure 18.3).

From numerous studies involving training animals to produce specific behaviours, Skinner (1938) proposed the theory of **operant conditioning.** As part of this theory, he proposed that this type of learning, could account for virtually all human behaviour. Eventually, as we saw in Chapter 4, he even extended the theory to explain the acquisition of language (Skinner, 1957).

Reinforcement

The central idea of Skinner's theory was that any given organism will emit **operants** – small actions which have an effect on the surrounding environment. If these operants have some kind of a pleasant effect, they can be shaped into large and increasingly complex units of behaviour.

Skinner's investigations included the different ways that this learning could be reinforced, or strengthened. For Thorndike, the cat's escape from

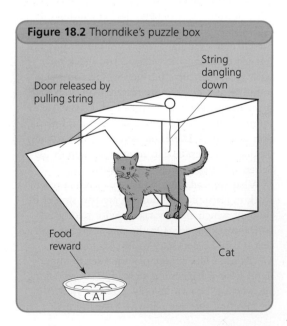

Figure 18.2 Thorndike's puzzle box

String dangling down

Door released by pulling string

Food reward

Cat

CAT

Figure 18.3 Skinner box

Photographer: Colin Smith

the box and its receipt of food were equivalent – he saw them both as having a pleasant effect. But Skinner distinguished between the positive reinforcement of receiving a reward (like food) and the negative reinforcement of escaping from or avoiding something unpleasant (like escaping from the box). Although both of them strengthened learning and fitted with the Law of Effect, Skinner argued that the two produced different behavioural consequences.

As with classical conditioning, operant conditioning will become extinguished, or die away, if it is not reinforced. But Skinner (1969) described how different ways of administering reinforcement can produce differences in extinction rates. These are listed in Table 18.2. And negative reinforcement which takes the form of avoidance learning, so that the animal avoids the unpleasant consequence altogether, can be very hard indeed to extinguish.

Behaviour shaping

One major difference between classical and operant conditioning is the type of behaviour with which each form of learning is primarily concerned. Classical conditioning, as we have seen, tends to be concerned with autonomic responses like emotional reactions, or with reflexes. Operant conditioning, on the other hand, is mainly con

cerned with **voluntary behaviour:** acts which can be deliberately controlled (although, as we saw in Chapter 13, there has also been some work on the use of operant conditioning to control autonomic processes through biofeedback). The emphasis on voluntary behaviour means that operant conditioning can be used to create new forms of behaviour, by a process known as successive approximation, or behaviour shaping.

Perhaps the best way to look at how behaviour shaping works is by means of a simple example. Suppose that, for some obscure motive of your own, you wished to train a laboratory rat to salute each time it pressed a lever. First, you would train it to press the lever by providing a reward (usually a food pellet) when it did so. Gradually, the animal would come to press the lever more and more often. Then you would begin to reward the rat only when it lifted both front paws from the ground before it pressed the lever. Once that new learning was established, you would reward it when the non-pressing paw was raised, but not when it was only just off the ground. In this way, the animal would come to raise its paw higher and higher each time it pressed the lever, until eventually it looked as though it was saluting.

Using this technique, animals can be trained into quite complicated forms of behaviour. Breland and Breland (1966) showed how circus animals are often trained using behaviour-shaping techniques. One of Skinner's own demonstrations of the power of this technique was to condition a pair of pigeons to play a version of ping-pong, using specially adapted ping-pong bats which they could hold in their beaks.

Behaviour shaping has some less trivial applications, though. It has been used in the training of autistic children to encourage them to produce sounds, by offering pieces of fruit or other rewards, and then gradually altering the **reinforcement contingencies** (what the child has to do to obtain the reward) until the child is forming words. Another use for behaviour shaping is in token economy systems for institutionalised psychiatric patients. This is a system in which appropriate behaviour is rewarded immediately with tokens which the patients can later exchange for privileges. By doing this, they can be trained into more independent behaviour, to help them to cope with looking after themselves in a hostel or flat.

Table 18.2 Variable reinforcement schedules

Schedule	Rate of response	Resistance to extinction
Continuous (reward given after each response)	fast	low
Fixed interval (reward given only after a set period of time)	very slow	high
Fixed ratio (reward given only after a set number of responses)	very fast	low
Variable interval (reward given after a variable period of time)	regular and steady	very high
Variable ratio (reward given after a variable number of responses)	very fast	moderate

Secondary reinforcement

Token economy systems also use another feature of operant conditioning: the idea of **secondary reinforcement.** Essentially, this is the finding that a reinforcing event does not have to be something that satisfies a primary need, like food or water. Instead, other kinds of stimuli can acquire reinforcing properties, through being associated with a primary reinforcer. So if a laboratory rat always hears a click each time it obtains a food reward for pressing a lever, after a while the sound of the click will become enough to reinforce the lever-pressing, and the food will not be so necessary.

In token economy systems, the tokens are needed because traditional operant conditioning works on the principle of **immediacy of reinforcement.** This is the idea that behaviour must be reinforced as soon as it happens if the conditioning is to be effective. By using secondary reinforcements (which are sometimes called conditioned reinforcers), many different types of stimulus can be used to reinforce human behaviour. The most obvious secondary reinforcer, of course, is money, which does not satisfy any primary need directly, but nonetheless appears to be reasonably effective in reinforcing several kinds of human behaviour.

Premack's principle

Premack (1959) explored the range of different secondary reinforcers which would have an effect on human behaviour. According to Premack's model, it is the activity itself rather than the stimulus which is reinforcing. So, for example, it is eating the food rather than the food pellet itself which strengthens the rat's behaviour. Premack suggested that we each have a kind of hierarchy of preferred activities, with those that we are most likely to do (if we get the chance) at the top and other, less preferred, activities lower down.

The hierarchy of reinforcers is not always the same. Timberlake and Allison (1974) found that an activity will acquire much stronger reinforcing properties if the individual has been deprived of it for some time. And Premack (1962) found that the same rats would treat different activities as reinforcement, depending on their physical state. If they had been inactive for a long time, then they would drink in order to get a chance to run in an exercise wheel – the exercise had become reinforcing, rather than the drink. But the same rats would run the wheel in order to get a drink, if they had been thirsty for some time. Because they had been deprived in different ways, different activities had become reinforcing.

Premack went on to propose that any activity in the hierarchy could be reinforced by activities which are above it. It is possible to make the less preferred activity more likely to happen, by using a more preferred one as the reinforcer. So, to use a human example, you might train yourself to stay at home and study for longer periods of time by using something that you like doing much more (for example going swimming) as your reward.

Homme *et al.* (1963) used Premack's principle to encourage three-year-old children to sit quietly and attend to a blackboard. The reinforcement which the children were given was the opportunity to run around the room and scream, which they enjoyed much more. By using these opportunities as reinforcement for the behaviour of sitting quietly, they managed to get the children to attend for quite long periods of time.

Premack's work is interesting because many of the reinforcements involved are quite different from the strictly behaviourist notions of reinforcement. Skinner insisted that reinforcement must be immediate, on the grounds that what was happening was a basic association between action and outcome. But Premack's model implies that deferred rewards will work just as well. It includes the idea that **cognitive processing** (like expecting a reward, or promising it to yourself) is involved. As with classical conditioning, much of the more recent research within the operant conditioning framework has broken free from 'pure' behaviourism, and is able to integrate the insights gained from the behaviourists' work with a broader awareness of cognitive factors.

Superstitious learning

Another example of this comes with research into **autoshaping.** Skinner noticed that sometimes an experimental animal would perform an odd action before it pressed a lever – for example, a pigeon might briefly preen its wing, or a rat might lift its head in a certain way before responding. Moreover, the animal would repeat this action each time that it pressed the lever or pecked the key. This was particularly likely to happen if the animal was being trained according to a highly variable reinforcement schedule, and Skinner described this as **superstitious learning,** which has also became known as autoshaping.

The traditional explanation for both secondary reinforcers and autoshaping is that they work by means of classical conditioning mechanisms – they acquire reinforcing properties through their association with a primary reinforcer. Superstitious learning occurred because on one occasion the animal, coincidentally, performed the action before receiving a reward, and the action had then become linked with the reward, in the same way as a gambler may blow on a pair of dice before throwing them, because this action once preceded a win.

In 1968, Brown and Jenkins observed that pigeons would peck at a light that signalled that food was coming, even though the action did not affect whether the food was actually delivered. This is an interesting finding, because it challenges the Law of Effect. In this case, the action is being learned simply because it is associated with reward, not because the action produces the reward. Schwartz and Gamzu (1977) went on to show that such birds appear to expect the food. By photographing pigeons as they pecked at a signalling light, they showed that a bird would have its beak open in a feeding position if the light normally signalled food, but in a drinking position if the light normally signalled water.

This finding suggested that **expectation** plays a significant part in the learning process. As with Premack's principle, the idea is that some cognitive processing is going on as a routine part of operant conditioning. This idea of cognitive processing also occurred in explanations for negative reinforcement, which we will look at later.

Punishment

Punishment and negative reinforcement may seem similar at times, but the crucial distinction between them is whether the behaviour is strengthened (made more likely to happen) or suppressed. Within the operant conditioning framework, behaviour is strengthened only if the outcome fits in with the Law of Effect. Avoiding threatened punishment may be reinforcing, because it leads to a pleasant outcome (no punishment). But actually receiving punishment for doing something is, by definition, unpleasant, and so is not reinforcing.

Skinner (1972) argued that punishment is a very bad technique for controlling behaviour, because all it does is suppress what the person or animal is doing. It does not strengthen the right behaviour:

all it can do is suppress the wrong one for a while. So punishing a child for doing something wrong does not stop that child from going off and doing something else equally wrong, or even worse. But rewarding a child for doing something right encourages that child to continue doing it, or to do it again.

Skinner believed that society could be a far better place if we would learn to use reinforcement effectively, and therefore guide people into socially acceptable behaviour, instead of simply punishing them for wrong-doing. His theory, though, was deeply controversial. It presented a rather totalitarian model of an ideal future society, in the sense that he felt there was no room for human dignity or freedom. Everyone was simply the product of their reinforcement contingencies, in Skinner's view, so society should manipulate those reinforcements to produce desirable behaviour. Punishment would then become unnecessary, since people could be manipulated into acting in a socially acceptable fashion.

Negative reinforcement

Negative reinforcement occurs when behaviour is strengthened because an aversive stimulus – one which is unpleasant for the organism – has been escaped from or avoided. So an experimental rat may learn to jump into a shuttle box to escape from an electric shock. In this case, the behaviour of jumping is reinforced because the shock stops – a pleasant effect. This is not the same as punishment, because in punishment the intention is to stop a behaviour from occurring, rather than to make it more likely to happen.

Escape learning of this kind is reasonably straightforward, and conforms to other aspects of operant conditioning: it will become extinguished if it is not reinforced, it can be generalised to other situations, and so on. But the other kind of negative reinforcement, **avoidance learning,** is rather different. In avoidance learning, the animal or human being learns to perform a behaviour because doing so allows it to avoid something unpleasant. This time, the experimental rat learns to jump into a shuttle box when a light comes on, if the light has previously been followed by an electric shock. It does not do it to escape from the shock, it does it to avoid getting the shock at all.

Although it may look similar, this type of learning has two differences from other operant techniques. One of them concerns the nature of the reinforcement – in other words, the question of what it actually is that strengthens the behaviour in avoidance learning. One suggestion, put forward by Rescorla and Solomon in 1967, was that there is a two-stage conditioning process going on in avoidance learning. The first is a classically conditioned association, between the stimulus and a response. This is then followed by a different response, learned through operant conditioning in the form of escape learning. In the first stage, the animal learns to associate the warning light with the emotional reaction of fear, which is classical conditioning. In the second stage, it removes that fear by jumping into the shuttle box, which is operant conditioning. So the behaviour of avoidance learning is a combination of two different types of conditioning.

The explanation suggested by Rescorla and Solomon fits in with **Lloyd Morgan's canon,** which we will be looking at in Chapter 22. It follows the canon by attempting to explain what is happening using the lowest-order mechanisms available – in this case, keeping strictly within traditional notions of classical and operant stimulus-response conditioning, and avoiding more complex processes such as cognition.

But in order to do so, the explanation has become quite convoluted, and does not accord with the principle of parsimony known as **Occam's razor,** which states that the best explanation is the simplest possible one. We can achieve a more elegant explanation if we are prepared to invoke the slightly higher-level, cognitive mechanism of expectancy. If we are prepared to say that the animal learns because it *anticipates* the shock, then we can explain what is going on in a much less elaborate manner. It is an example of how trying to explain everything using strict behaviourist interpretations of conditioning may lead us into quite convoluted, and clumsy, explanations.

The idea of expectation may also help to explain why avoidance learning is so difficult to extinguish. We carry on acting to avoid an aversive situation long after that situation has ceased to occur, partly because avoiding the aversive situation altogether leaves us with no knowledge of whether the aversive stimulus would have recurred or not. According to classical and operant conditioning, both forms of learning should become extinguished eventually. The fear induced by the first stimulus should die down after enough occasions in which there is no cause for fear. But there

is less reason to suppose that an expectation will become extinguished, since that does not come from an external stimulus, but from the internal representation, or cognitive map, which an animal or human holds about the situation.

Learned helplessness

Another indication of possible cognitive factors in conditioning comes from Seligman's work on **learned helplessness** (Seligman, 1975). Seligman proposed that learning will occur only if the animal or person concerned is able to exert some degree of control over the situation. If no control is possible, Seligman argued, then the animal will become passive, and will remain so even if the circumstances change so that effective action becomes possible.

Maier and Seligman (1976) performed a number of experiments which showed how learned helplessness can occur. In one study, they linked dogs in pairs and arranged the situation such that one dog in each pair could push a panel which would turn off an electric shock. The other dog received the same shocks, but was not able to do anything about them. After a while, both dogs were placed in a new experimental situation. This time, they were given a signal that a shock was likely to occur, and could avoid the shock by jumping over a barrier. The dogs which had been 'active' in the previous condition quickly learned to jump over the barrier to avoid the shock. But those which had been 'inactive' previously, did not try to jump over the barrier. They became more and more passive as the shocks continued. It seemed that their previous experience had taught them to be helpless. Seligman (1975) compared this with the passivity and inaction which is often shown by very depressed people. He argued that one characteristic of such people is a belief that they will be unable to control whatever happens to them, and claimed that this too could represent a form of learned helplessness.

Seligman's research ties in with other work, such as that on **locus of control,** which we looked at in Chapter 13. It suggests that people will only emerge from their depression by learning that they really can have an effect on their environment, or their lives. Another implication of Seligman's work, of course, is the idea that control is important in learning. Seligman's findings are difficult to explain within a strictly behaviourist framework, but it makes sense if we are prepared to invoke the cognitive concepts of anticipation and expectation.

In both classical and operant conditioning research, then, we find that the focus has shifted away from the purely behavioural interpretations of learning – the insistence on 'pure' stimulus-response connections – and towards the idea that conditioning mechanisms work together with cognitive factors in controlling both human and animal behaviour. There are other forms of learning, too, which seem to draw on cognitive mechanisms.

Cognitive forms of learning

Although it is relatively recently that psychologists investigating classical and operant conditioning have come to accept a possible role for cognitive factors, the idea that animal learning may also involve some cognitive capacity is not a new one. There has been research into several cognitive types of animal learning since the early part of the century.

Insight learning

As early as 1925, the Gestalt psychologist Wolfgang Köhler argued that animals do not learn everything simply through trial and error, or stimulus-response association. Instead, he argued, they can also show **insight learning** – they can learn by obtaining a cognitive understanding of the important elements within the problem and the relationship between them. One example cited by Köhler was that of a dog, who watched him as he threw some food out of the window and shut it. The dog jumped up once at the glass, then wagged her tail, spun round, ran outside and round the house to the food. This, Köhler argued, was not trial-and-error learning, but rather showed that the animal had an insight into the nature of the problem.

Köhler also performed a number of studies of problem-solving in chimpanzees, in which they solved problems in ways that were not subject to trial-and-error learning. A typical problem of this type involved suspending a piece of fruit from the ceiling, and leaving boxes lying around the cage. The apes would have to pile the boxes on top of each other in order to reach the fruit. Another example involved a piece of fruit placed out of reach outside the bars of the cage. Inside the cage was a short stick, which was not long enough to

reach the fruit but was long enough to reach a longer stick, which could be drawn into the cage and used to reach the fruit.

In each of these experiments, Köhler noted, there was a period of intensive but fruitless (literally!) activity. The animal would try to reach the fruit by jumping up and down underneath it, or trying to reach through the bars. This would be followed by a relatively quiet period, in which the animal would rest for a while, as if having given up on the problem. Then, suddenly, the animal would jump up and begin to pile boxes together under the fruit, or seize the sticks and poke them through the bars. This, in Köhler's view, was insight learning. The quiescent period was while the animal was thinking – or engaging in cognitive restructuring of the problem, as psychologists of the time preferred to call it. It would produce a sudden insight into the nature of the problem, which would result in the animal suddenly becoming active and performing the solution.

Unfortunately, Köhler's studies were not very well controlled, and they left room for a number of alternative explanations. For example, he did not record the prior experience which the apes had before the study. Also, there were often several chimpanzees in the cage at the same time, and they might have learned from imitating one another. But although his evidence cannot be taken as conclusive, there has always been a great deal of anecdotal evidence that some cognitive processing is involved in animal problem-solving.

The role of prior experience

Although it was cited as a criticism of Köhler's work, prior experience with the elements of a problem does not actually rule out the possibility of insight learning. It may be that insight involves the combination of familiar elements into a new synthesis. Epstein *et al.* (1984) reported a study in which pigeons were given two kinds of prior training. They were taught to push a small box towards a spot on a wall; and they were also taught to stand on a box and peck at a suspended plastic banana. Then they were placed in a situation with the banana hanging from the ceiling, but the box some distance away from it.

Epstein reported that at first the pigeons appeared to be 'confused' by the task, but then suddenly they would begin to push the box until it was under the banana. At that point, they would climb on the box and peck the banana. Pearce

(1987) observed that the 49 seconds which one bird took to solve this problem compares very favourably with the five minutes taken by Köhler's ape Sultan to solve a similar one!

Learning sets

In 1949, Harlow investigated the possibility that insight learning might originate from previous experience with direct trial-and-error learning. It could appear to be insight, he argued, if the trial-and-error learning had resulted in the formation of learning sets. Harlow performed a number of experiments using rhesus monkeys, in which they were trained to solve particular types of problems by repeatedly presenting them with similar ones. So, for instance, a monkey might be faced with two shapes on a tray, and have to pick the one with corners – which might sometimes be a triangle, sometimes a square, sometimes a hexagon, and so on. If it did so, it would receive a reward – usually a raisin or a peanut.

Harlow showed that the more of these problems they were given, the more quickly the monkeys solved them. It was clear that they were not simply developing a stimulus-response association with the solution of the problem, because the solution changed each time. Instead, they had developed a learning set – a state of readiness to solve such puzzles. In some cases, these learning sets could be quite complex. For example, a monkey might be presented with three coloured shapes on a coloured tray. With the right training, it could learn to pick, say, the object with the odd shape if the tray was orange, but the object with the odd colour if the tray was blue.

Harlow argued that this finding challenged Köhler's idea of insight learning. To all intents and purposes, it looked as though the animal had an insight into the nature of the problem, but they had learned these abilities entirely by operant conditioning. However, although this was certainly true, it was not the pure stimulus-response form of operant conditioning which the animals were showing, since a learning set has to involve some degree of cognitive **representation.** At its simplest, it implied that the animals had learned to remember what had occurred on previous trials and apply it to the current one. At a slightly higher level, it could be argued that the monkeys had extracted the principle of 'oddness' from the tasks. Either way, it implies that there is a cognitive element in this type of learning.

Latent learning

Tolman, in 1932, also challenged the behaviourist idea that all learning would always be manifest in behaviour and did not involve cognitive elements. He set up an experiment in which he set up a complex maze in which he trained three groups of rats. The first group was directly rewarded from the outset, by receiving a food reward when they reached a goal box. For the first nine days of the experiment, neither of the other groups received any reward. Instead, they were simply allowed to wander the maze freely, and the amount of time that it took them to reach the goal box was recorded. From the tenth day, the second group of rats was rewarded for reaching the goal box, but the third group remained as a control, receiving no reward.

The first group of rats, as might be expected, showed a progressive decrease in the amount of time it took them to reach the goal box, which formed a standard learning curve. Until they were reinforced for reaching the goal box, the second group showed no such improvement, but when they began to receive reinforcement, they learned to run the maze. The third group's time remained at a high level throughout the study (Figure 18.4). Tolman argued that, in order for the second group to learn as quickly as they did, they must have been learning during the period when they were not being reinforced. Since this learning had not shown in their behaviour, he described it as latent learning.

Cognitive maps

Tolman (1948) went on to propose that the animals had been able to complete the maze more quickly because they had developed a mental representation – a cognitive map – of the maze, during their period of exploration. There has been research on cognitive mapping in human beings which we looked at in Chapter 5. But this seems to be a form of learning used by other types of animals too, which suggests that it may be a very basic part of how we appraise our worlds.

Gould (1986) described a study in which foraging honey-bees, whose hive was near to a lake, were provided with food from a boat on that lake. When they returned to the hive, they would perform a 'dance', to indicate to other hive members where the food was to be found (we will be looking at bee dancing in Chapter 24). When the boat was moored next to the lake shore (on the

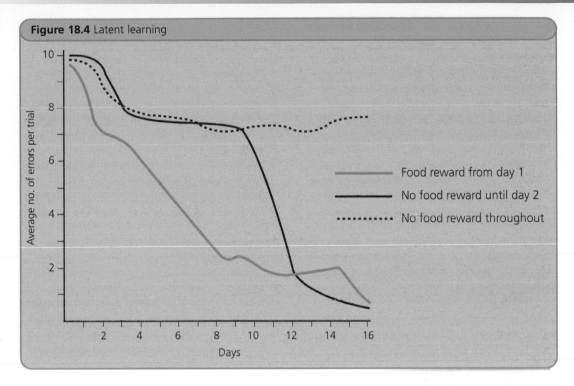

Figure 18.4 Latent learning

opposite side from the hive), other bees would fly out to it in response to the forager's messages. But when it was moored in the middle of the lake, the other bees would ignore these messages. This implied that the bees must have had some kind of cognitive map of the area, which included the knowledge that food was not to be found in the middle of a large expanse of water.

Olton (1979) performed a study in which experimental rats learned a multiple maze, in which the passages radiated out from the centre. The rats had to visit each arm of the maze without visiting any of them twice. Once the task had been learned, the rats would very rarely make a mistake, even though they would visit the arms in random order. Olton argued that this implied that they had formed a cognitive map of the maze, which allowed them to recall and identify the passages that they had not yet visited.

Imitation

Earlier in this chapter, we looked at how imitation and identification are two of the basic mechanisms of human development. Imitation, as we will be seeing in Chapter 20, is something which the human infant seems to do almost from its earliest days. As the child grows older, imitation represents a valuable short-cut in its learning, removing the

need for learning everything through painstaking trial and error conditioning processes, and allowing the child to learn indirectly, from the experiences and actions of others.

Of course, the child's readiness to learn through imitation is a mixed blessing, as any mother will tell you. Children pick up undesirable behaviour just as quickly as they pick up desirable activities. In 1963, Bandura, Ross and Ross showed how children can learn to imitate aggressive behaviour, purely from seeing someone else act in that way.

Their study involved 96 children aged between three and six years old, separated into four groups, with 24 in each group. Each group was then shown a different scene. The first group watched an adult behaving aggressively towards a large rubber 'bobo' doll. This included punching the doll, shouting at it, and hitting it with a hammer. The second group watched the same adult behaving in exactly the same way, but this time instead of seeing it in real life, they saw it on film. The third group saw the same sequence of actions towards the doll, but they were shown it as a cartoon, set in a fantasy land. And the fourth group was a control group, who were not shown any violent behaviour at all.

Following this, the children were put into a playroom, and the researchers observed them through a two-way mirror. It contained a number of toys, including the ones which had been represented in what the child had seen, and in particular, including the 'bobo' doll. The children were allowed to play freely with the toys for a while, before the researchers deliberately frustrated them by taking the toys away from them just as they were getting involved with their games.

Each child's behaviour was rated by the hidden observers, who counted the number of aggressive actions that they made. The results are given in Table 18.3, which shows how the children who had seen an aggressive model performed many more aggressive actions than those who had not. Also, many more of their actions were specifically copied from the model than the aggressive acts copied by those who had seen either the film or the cartoon. And the children did not imitate all the models equally. They were far more likely to imitate models who they saw as similar to themselves – particularly if the model was another child – than to imitate those they perceived as very different.

Vicarious learning

In another study which formed part of the same research programme, Bandura and Walters (1963) investigated whether a child's tendency to imitate was affected by observing the consequences of aggressive behaviour. They divided children into three groups. One group saw the model being rewarded for showing aggressive behaviour, either by approval from an adult, or by being given sweets. The second group saw the model being punished for showing aggressive behaviour, and the third group observed the model, but were not shown any consequences for the model's aggressive behaviour.

The observers found that what they had seen was reflected in the children's play. Those who had

seen the model being rewarded for aggressive acts showed a high level of aggression in their own play. Those who had seen the model punished showed a low level of aggression in their own play, while the no-reward, no-punishment control group were inbetween. Bandura referred to this as **vicarious learning** – the children were learning about the likely consequences of actions, and adjusting their imitations accordingly.

But when the researchers began to reward the children for copying the model, all of the children imitated the model's aggressive behaviour, showing that they had learned those aggressive acts, even though they had not shown that they had learned them straight away. There were no differences, either, in how well the various children imitated the model's aggression. It is studies like this which lie at the core of concerns about what children learn from television. Whether they saw aggressive behaviour rewarded or punished, the children still learned from seeing it; and when they were in a position to gain an advantage from that learning, they produced the behaviour.

Status envy

Bandura, Ross and Ross (1963) also investigated the question of **status envy** – whether a child would be more likely to imitate people who had high status, or seemed to be in powerful positions. The children watched a film which showed two adults playing together. One of the adults had a lot of expensive, complicated toys. The other adult seemed to want to play with them, so the toys' 'owner' shared some of them with the other adult. Then both adults played with the toys, but they behaved quite differently.

When the children were allowed into the playroom to play with the same toys, they were carefully observed to see which adult they copied most. Although both adults had played with all of the toys, it was the powerful adult which the children imitated most. The implication was that the children were attracted towards high-status, powerful role models, and would be more likely to imitate them than others who had less control over resources.

Identification

The second-stage process of identification is another aspect of observational learning. In this, the child adopts a whole style or pattern of behaviour, producing novel acts which seem to be

Table 18.3 Imitating an aggressive model	
Condition	**Average no. of aggressive acts**
Child observes a real-life model	83
Child observes a filmed model	92
Child observes a cartoon model	99
Child has no model to observe	54

Source: Bandura, Ross and Ross, 1963

in keeping with the model who the child is identifying with. This seems to be one of the most important roles for childhood heroes – super-heroes, pop stars and sporting heroes all allow the child to develop its own learning, but in accord with a generalised model. Identification takes place over a much longer period of time than imitation, and it is thought to be a key process in the learning of social roles. As a result, social learning theorists have emphasised the need for appropriate role-models. Children, and adults as well, need to have positive role-models with whom they can identify, as a way of structuring their ambitions and development. For many black children in Britain, for instance, the social visibility of high-achievers such as Trevor McDonald, or Linford Christie, has provided them with important role-models for their own ambitions.

Imitation is an intriguing form of learning, used by many animals – even ones which we would not have thought capable of engaging in mental representations. Allott (1997) discussed how understanding what is going on during imitation presents a great many challenges for those who aim to understand cognitive processes, and partic-ularly for those who are trying to develop artificial intelligence systems which can replicate them. For human beings, it is such an everyday form of learning that we pretty well take it for granted; but unpicking its elements and understanding what is actually happening when a small child imitates its older sister, or a chaffinch learns mobbing behaviour from other chaffinches, is a distinct challenge to researchers.

We have seen, then, that research into the fundamental processes of learning suggests that all, or at least most, animals, including human beings, use some kind of cognitive learning, as well as behavioural associations. These basic forms of learning are extremely important mechanisms for human beings – much more so than we often realise. Anyone who has tried to give up smoking will recognise the power that associative learning can have; while cognitive maps form a part of our daily experience. But human beings have more sophisticated learning mechanisms available to them as well. Kolb (1985) argued that human learning is a cyclical process, which is shown in figure 18.5. It begins with **concrete experience** – that is, with our experiences in the real world. In itself, though, just gathering experience isn't enough for learning. Learning only begins to

happen when we reflect on our experience, which is the second phase of the learning cycle: **reflective observation.** Reflecting on our experi-ence – thinking about it, and trying to understand what was happening – leads us into the third phase, which Kolb refers to as **abstract conceptualisation**. It is in this phase that we draw out the general principles and meanings from our experience, and relate these to other things we may have learned. The **abstract conceptualisation** phase in turn encourages us to engage in Active Experimentation – testing out new ways of gathering experience, based on what we have learned. And that experimentation in turn pro-vides us with a fresh batch of concrete experience to reflect on, which means that the cycle begins all over again. **Kolb's learning cycle** refers to both cognitive and physical types of human learning.

In the rest of this chapter, we will look at the development of both physical and mental skills, as they, too, form a significant aspect of human development.

Skill learning

Annett (1989) defined a skill as an item of behav-iour which has three characteristics. First, it is directed towards the attainment of a specific goal: a skill is all about **intentional,** or deliberate, behaviour. Second, the behaviour is organised in such a way as to be reliably achieved with economy of time and effort – it is something which the person carries out **efficiently** and reasonably

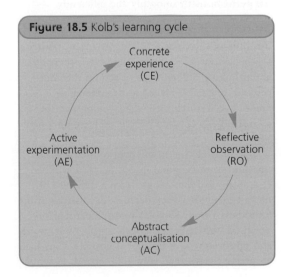

Figure 18.5 Kolb's learning cycle

Concrete experience (CE)

Reflective observation (RO)

Abstract conceptualisation (AC)

Active experimentation (AE)

quickly. Third, the behaviour has been acquired by **training** and practice. We would not call a behaviour a skill if we just performed it automatically, like a reflex. Although Annett is talking here about physical skills, we can see that the important three features of the definition could be applied just as well to cognitive or mental skills, such as the skill of reading which we looked at in Chapter 4.

Learning new skills is an important part of development, and one which we continue to do throughout our lives. There has been a considerable amount of research into how we go about acquiring physical skills. Although much of this research has been done with adults, the principles of skill acquisition are considered to be similar throughout the lifespan – we just acquire different skills at different times. Learning to manage a co-ordinated skipping routine, or to master a complex computer game, involves a similar pattern of skill acquisition as learning to drive a car, but the learning takes place at different ages. In this section, therefore, we will begin by looking at some research into skill acquisition, and at some of the theories which have been developed, before going on to look specifically at skill development in infants and children.

Acquiring skills

Psychologists have studied several different features of skill acquisition. These include the effects of different types of practice, the effect of knowing what the results of our actions have been, and the study of how actions become automatic, so that we perform them smoothly and efficiently.

Massed and spaced practice

To some of the early psychologists – particularly the behaviourists – skill learning was essentially all about linking different bits of actions together through practice. This led to a considerable amount of research into what type of practice seems to be best when people are learning a new skill.

The main debate in this area centred on the question of massed and spaced practice. Kimble (1949) showed that people learn a difficult task more effectively if they practise for relatively short periods at a time. Kimble's research participants practised writing letters of the alphabet backwards and upside-down, as quickly as possible. They had 21 practice trials each lasting 30 seconds in which

to learn this skill, but they were sorted into five groups, which had 5, 10, 15, or 30 seconds' rest between sessions, or no rest at all. Kimble found that those research participants who had the longest rest between trials learned more quickly than those whose sessions were grouped closely together.

The problem with this study, though, was that how well people had learned was judged entirely by how well they performed the task as they were learning it. But there might be a difference between the process of learning, and the final outcome. Perhaps those experiencing massed practice sessions would end up just as good, even though they did not seem so while the learning sessions were going on.

In 1954, Adams and Reynolds set up a study in which people were asked to keep the end of a bent rod on a dot near the edge of a rotating turntable – a piece of equipment known as a **pursuit rota.** Their five groups of research participants all ended with spaced practice, but only one group had spaced practice throughout. The other groups had five, ten, fifteen or twenty massed trials first, then a five-minute rest before going on to the spaced practice sessions. Adams and Reynolds found that the groups performed very differently while they were in the early stages of the task; but by the third spaced practice trial, their performance was equivalent – they had all learned the task equally well. So although immediate performance was worse with massed practice, in the long term the effects of massed practice had balanced out.

Baddeley and Longman (1978) studied postal workers who were learning to type postcodes, using a keyboard – a task which was needed in order for the Post Office to introduce automatic letter-sorting machinery. They arranged the schedule so that four groups of workers each had different training sessions. Each person had the same amount of training in the end, but one group had just one session a day, of one hour at a time, a second group had two one-hour sessions each day; a third group had one two-hour session a day, and a fourth group had two two-hour sessions a day. The outcome of the study is shown in Figure 18.6.

It is important to remember, though, that although spaced practice means that the person needs less learning time to acquire a new skill, the overall amount of time which they take to learn it

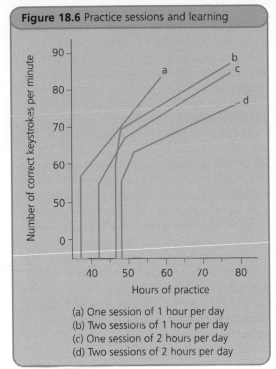

Figure 18.6 Practice sessions and learning

(a) One session of 1 hour per day
(b) Two sessions of 1 hour per day
(c) One session of 2 hours per day
(d) Two sessions of 2 hours per day

Source: Adapted from Baddeley and Longman, 1978

may actually be longer. Although the postal workers in the Baddeley and Longman study who just had one 1-hour session a day required fewer training hours to learn the skill, they did not feel as though they were getting on very fast, because their learning involved more days. So they actually felt as though they were learning more slowly than their colleagues.

Whole or part learning

Another aspect of research into practice is the question of whether it is better to practise separate sub-units which go to make up a skill, or to practise the whole skill all at once. Niemeyer (1959) compared people who were learning swimming, badminton, or volleyball, and found that whether whole or part learning was better, depended entirely which skill they were trying to learn. Swimming was learned best with the **whole method,** volleyball was learned best with the **part method** and badminton was learned equally well with either approach.

Naylor (1962) performed a meta-analysis of research into whole or part learning, and came to the conclusion that which was better was all to do with the complexity of the task and whether it

required a lot of organisation – in other words, whether the different units were closely inter-related. As we can see from Table 18.4, whole learning was better when the task was complex, and required a high degree of physical organisation. But a less complex task was often learned more effectively using a part method of learning.

Visualisation

Sports psychologists have also found that **visualisation,** or mental practice, can make a great deal of difference to how well people perform. When Ainscoe and Hardy (1987) asked gymnasts to practise their performance mentally, visualising themselves undertaking each task successfully, they found that a visible improvement could be achieved using this technique.

In a much earlier study, Twining (1949) asked male students to practise throwing rings at a target. One group practised every day for 22 days, another group practised on the first day, and then was asked to practise mentally for the next 19 days before being tested physically on the 22nd day; and the third group was tested only on the first and 22nd day. Twining found, perhaps not surprisingly, that the group which had practised physically performed best when the students were tested. But the mental practice group performed much better than the control group, even though neither group had had any physical practice since the first time.

Practice does not just apply when we are learning a new skill. We continue to practise skills even after we have learned them, and this can often make a difference to how well we learn the skill.

Table 18.4 Comparisons of whole and part learning

Complexity	Organisation	Results of studies
High	High	Whole method better
High	Low	Part method better most of the time (63% of cases)
Low	High	Part method better most of the time (75% of cases)
Low	Low	Part and whole methods equally successful

Source: Adapted from Naylor, 1962

Overlearning has been shown to have a very positive effect on how well we remember skills. Melnick (1971) asked research participants to practise a balancing task until they reached a set standard. When they did so, one group was told that they need not practise any more, and the other three groups were given varying amounts of overlearning. One group had 50% more practice time, another had the same amount of overlearning time as they had spent learning the task in the first place, and a fourth group had twice as much. Melnick found that when they were tested one week and one month later, the amount of overlearning directly affected how well they could do the task. Those who had practised more after the task had been learned could do it better.

We can even improve skills which have been learned to a very high standard. Crossman (1959) studied women who were operating cigar-making machines, and found that even after a vast amount of experience – in some cases they had made over ten million cigars – they were still showing signs of improving as a result of practice. But that does not mean that just doing things over and over again will mean that we automatically get better. To improve with practice, we also need to know how well we did in the first place.

Knowledge of results

Knowledge of results, often abbreviated to **KR,** is an essential feature of skill learning. Without knowing what the results of our actions have been, we are unable to modify them in order to produce the precise behaviour needed for the performance of a skill. The combining motor units to produce complex skills is entirely dependent on continuous feedback: crossing a road involves a continuous assessment of the distance between yourself and a car in the distance, and a modification of your speed accordingly.

Knowledge of results is sometimes called **feedback,** although, strictly speaking, feedback is a term which refers to information coming from the internal parts of a system, rather than to information which comes from the outside world. Some psychologists, therefore, make a distinction between **intrinsic feedback,** which comes from internal systems (like the information coming from proprioceptive nerves which respond to the positions of our muscles), and **extrinsic feedback,** which comes from the outside world (like the information about the approaching car which we

receive through our eyes). In this section, though, we will use the word 'feedback' as a general term to describe knowledge of results, as many psychologists do. Psychological research into the importance of feedback has resulted in the development of three general principles, which are summarised in Table 18.5, but which are worth discussing in more detail here.

The first principle is one which we have already stated: that feedback is essential to learning. To a large extent this is self-evident. After all, you would not expect to get any better at throwing darts at a target if you were blindfolded, would you? But this principle relates to the acquisition of complex cognitive skills as well as physical ones, and it is remarkable how often, particularly in some types of education, people are expected to get better at doing things without being told when they are doing them well or badly. Some of the most successful modularised and computer-based learning systems achieve their success precisely because they present students with consistent and regular feedback.

The second principle is that continuous feedback is better than intermittent feedback. Bilodeau and Bilodeau (1958) asked research participants to learn to pull a lever through a 33° arc. They were divided into four groups. One group was given feedback on their performance after each attempt. A second group was given feedback after every third attempt. A third group was given feedback after every fourth attempt, and the last group was given feedback after every tenth attempt. They were not actually told what they were aiming for: instead, they were told what degree of arc they had managed to achieve, and whether it was too high or too low.

The researchers found that the research participants improved with practice, but only after those attempts in which they were told how well they had done. They showed no improvement at all after the attempts for which they had been given no feedback. This meant that the group which

---

Table 18.5 Principles of feedback

1   Feedback is essential to learning.
2   Continuous feedback is better than intermittent feedback.
3   The more precise feedback is, the better the learning will be.

received continuous feedback learned the skill much more quickly than those who received intermittent feedback. The more frequently research participants received feedback, the better they learned.

The third principle, as the table shows, is about precision: the more precise the feedback is, the better the learning will be. Trowbridge and Cason (1932) asked people to draw a three-inch line while they were blindfolded. The control group was given no feedback at all, and, not surprisingly, they did not show any particular improvement. A second group was given irrelevant feedback: they were given a nonsense syllable after each response. They too did not improve their performance.

A third group was given qualitative information about how well they were doing, being told that it was 'right' if they were within one-eighth of an inch of the goal, and otherwise 'wrong'. They improved their performance steadily over a block of ten trials. The fourth group were given quantitative feedback, being told whether their line was longer or shorter than the target, in terms of units of one-eighth of an inch at a time; so, for example, they would be told 'plus two' if their line was a quarter of an inch too long. This group improved dramatically, becoming very accurate even after two trials, and remaining so for the whole block of ten.

The speed-accuracy trade-off

One of the criteria which we use to judge whether someone has achieved expertise at a particular skill is whether they are able to perform that skill both quickly and accurately. For the most part, if we are learning a skill, we will tend to become less accurate the faster we do it. This is a basic principle of skill performance, which is known as the **speed-accuracy trade-off:** greater speed leads to more error.

Woodworth (1899) asked people to rule lines of equal length in time to a metronome. Not surprisingly, Woodworth found that the accuracy of the research participants' performance depended on how fast they were doing the task. At 20 beats per minute, they were largely accurate, but as the speed increased to 200 beats per minute, they became less and less accurate. What was interesting, though, was that it was not a steady decline. People were just as accurate at 40 beats per minute as they were at 20, and equally inaccurate when the speed was 140 beats per minute or higher.

In 1954, Fitts showed that the relationship between speed and accuracy is **logarithmic:** the degree of inaccuracy increases by an ever-greater proportion as the speed increases. The factors which influence this are the amplitude of the task – the amount of movement which is required – and the width of the target. This relationship became known as **Fitts' law**, and it can be expressed mathematically according to the formula:

$$MT = a + b \log_2 (2A/W)$$

MT in this formula is the time of movement, a and b are both constants, A is the amplitude of the task and W is the width of the target.

This formula, however, only really applies to tasks which are about movement of greater or lesser extent, and the amount of error which people will make in undertaking that movement. Different types of tasks show a different relationship between speed and accuracy.

For example, Begbie (1959) asked people to throw pencils at targets, and calculated their errors on the basis of what angle they threw the pencil at. This was different from the errors of extent described in Fitts' law, because those had been only about whether a line was too long or too short: they were overshoot or undershoot errors. Begbie found that, in the pencil-throwing task, the more quickly people were asked to do the task, the less accurate they became. The speed-accuracy trade-off showed a steady relationship: if people were performing the task very quickly they were very inaccurate; if they were doing it very slowly they were very accurate; if they were throwing it at an intermediate speed they were moderately accurate. In other words, the relationship between speed and accuracy was **linear,** not logarithmic.

Moreover, in the performance of some types of skill, errors are not acceptable. A typist, for example, is not expected to make errors in typing at all, or at least is expected to minimise those errors. So the type of training which is involved in typing emphasises accuracy over speed: someone who is learning to type is expected to learn to do it accurately but slowly at first, and only to increase their speed when they can do so without creating more errors. So we can see that the relationship between speed and accuracy is complicated, and seems to be highly dependent on other factors, like practice and overlearning.

Automatisation

Virtually all approaches to understanding skill acquisition, however, have involved some idea of **automatisation.** This is the idea that a unit of behaviour, or motor unit, will become so well learned that it can be performed without any conscious control at all. Automatisation involves a shift in the neural control of the activity, from the cortical levels of the brain to the sub-cortical structures which are involved in voluntary movement.

As we saw in Chapter 10, conscious movement is mediated by the area of the cerebral cortex known as the **motor cortex,** which is located in the frontal lobe of the brain, along the central fissure. If we decide, say, to lift an arm, it is this area which will send the message to the arm muscles telling them to contract. But when we are undertaking a skilled action, we do not think about each individual movement as we do it. Indeed, thinking about it can mean that we do things in a very slow and jerky fashion. With skilled behaviour, however, we perform the necessary actions unconsciously and smoothly. The part of the brain which is responsible for co-ordinating this type of action is the sub-cortical structure known as the **cerebellum:** a large cauliflower-like structure located at the back of the brain, below the occipital lobe of the cerebrum.

Learning a skill involves gradually shifting control of the activity from the motor cortex to the cerebellum. This happens as a result of practice. When we are first performing any new set of actions, like learning to drive, we have to think about each action, and so our movements are often un-co-ordinated: they are being controlled by the motor cortex. But gradually, as the combination of action becomes more and more familiar, less concentration is needed, and control shifts to the cerebellum. At that time, we find that we can, say, change gear without thinking about it: the activity has become automatised.

Of course, that does not mean that the cerebellum is the only part of the brain which is involved. As we have seen, performing a skilled activity involves continuous feedback, which means that we need to have links between the **sensory input systems**, like the thalamus, and the **motor systems** in the brain. Other parts of the brain are involved too. Brooks (1986) showed how the brain stem, the limbic system, the cerebellum and the cerebral cortex are all involved in produc-ing and co-ordinating skilled movement (see Figure 18.7).

Models of skill acquistion

Theories explaining what is happening as we acquire various skills have changed with the development of psychology as a whole. One of the first models of skill acquisition, and one which became very widely known, was based on the idea that skill development consisted of forming **stimulus-response links,** so that the skill would be performed more or less automatically in the presence of the right stimulus. Fitts (1964) expressed this theory in terms of three stages of skill acquisition, which are listed in Table 18.6.

An alternative approach to skill learning which became increasingly popular as the computer age developed, from the 1960s onwards, was to see skill learning in terms of **information-processing.** According to this model (see, for example, Welford, 1958), the human being is seen as acting like a computer, receiving information through sensors, processing that information, and, as a result of the way that the information is processed, producing an output in terms of behaviour. This model is therefore different from the stimulus-response approach, because it places more emphasis on what is happening internally, as the skill is

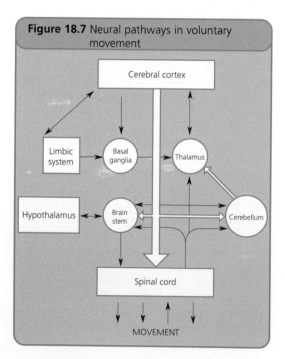

Figure 18.7 Neural pathways in voluntary movement

Table 18.6 The stimulus-response model of skill acquisition

Stage 1	*Cognitive* The person who is learning the skill comes to understand what is required, and how to go about achieving it.
Stage 2	*Associative* The person practises the skill in order to develop the necessary sensorimotor connections.
Stage 3	*Autonomous* The link between the presence of the appropriate stimulus and the motor performance of the skill becomes automatic, and the skill is performed with very little voluntary control.

Source: Adapted from Fitts, 1964

Table 18.7 The information-processing approach to skill acquisition

1 *Plan formation*	In this stage, the person who is learning the skill identifies what is required, and develops a cognitive plan in order to guide and organise the necessary actions.
2 *Perceptual organisation*	The person acquiring the skill learns to filter their sensory inputs, so that they can distinguish between sensory information which is irrelevant to the skill, and that which is essential. Redundant sensory information is filtered out, leaving significant information active.
3 *Economy of motor action*	The person acquiring the skill learns to perform the actions required in the skill efficiently, in such a way that the amount of conscious control and sensory input required to perform the skill is minimised.
4 *Timing*	The sequencing and co-ordination of sensorimotor patterns and chains of responses are gradually fitted together until they form a smooth pattern: the performance of the behaviour forms a continuous, unbroken act.
5 *Automatic execution*	The learned skill is transferred from conscious to unconscious control – from the cerebral cortex to the cerebellum and spinal cord – so that it makes few cognitive demands on the individual who is performing it.

Source: Adapted from Taylor et al., 1982

performed. According to this model, there are five stages of skill acquisition, which are listed in Table 18.7.

Skills as hierarchical schemata

A more recent approach to skill acquisition, proposed by Annett in 1989, is that skills should be seen as the hierarchical organisation of motor programmes, or **schemata**. A schema, as we saw in Chapter 5, is a form of cognitive representation which incorporates programmes of activity as well as mental description and classification. According to this model of skill acquisition, skills consist of a number of different sub-units of behaviour, each of which has been learned, to become a complete unit in itself. These units are then combined into groups, and patterns of co-ordination and motor control are also developed at the higher levels. Each successive level in the hierarchy is concerned with the organisation and performance of a higher level in the skill.

Perhaps the best way to interpret this model is in terms of a complex skill like typing, or learning to play the piano. As we saw in Chapter 5, when we learn to solve a problem or to undertake a simple task, the pattern of learning will typically show a **learning curve** – the time which we take to solve the problem or undertake the activity becomes gradually less and less, following a reasonably smooth sequence. But when we are learning to perform a complex task, development proceeds in a different way. Typically, we will improve for a while, and then reach a **plateau** – a period of time when we do not seem to improve much. But if we carry on practising, we then reach another period when we begin to improve again, followed by another plateau (see Figure 18.8 overleaf).

When somebody is first learning to type, for example, they will tend to be very slow while they get used to the positions of the individual

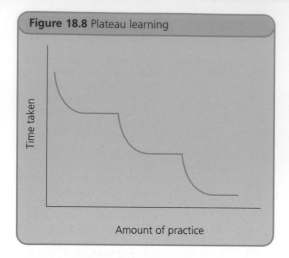

Figure 18.8 Plateau learning

Time taken (vertical axis)

Amount of practice (horizontal axis)

letters on the keyboard. For a while, as they learn these, they will get faster each time that they practise. Then, typically, they will hit a plateau and not appear to get any faster for a period of time. But after a certain amount of practice, the patterns made by particular words which they type a lot will become familiar to them, and they will begin to type these faster than unfamiliar words. At this point, they will have another period in which their typing becomes faster, before they hit another plateau.

Rumelhart and Norman (1982) argued that what is happening in this second stage is that the person is beginning to develop a schema for particular words, which is a higher-order level of motor co-ordination than when the person was just developing schemata for the location of individual letters. Developing a complex skill, in this model, involves not only developing schemata for particular actions, but also organising them in hierarchical sequences.

Rumelhart and Norman (1982) developed a computer simulation program based on this approach to typing. They set arbitrary activation values (the conditions under which each schema would become activated), and then set the simulation to type 2000 words. As a result of the activation values, the system made occasional mistakes in the typing. Interestingly, these were very similar to the errors which human beings often make when they are typing. One type of mistake, for instance, was when one simulated 'hand' would respond faster than another, producing errors like 'hte' instead of 'the'. Another was that the system would sometimes double the wrong letter in a

word, such as typing 'bokk' instead of 'book'. Human beings often do this too, and it suggests we have a higher-order schema for doubling letters, which is sometimes applied inappropriately.

Schemata can inhibit or activate other schemata, which is part of how they become linked into higher-order groups. If someone habitually types the word 'behaviour', for instance, the schema for that word will become very well established, and as each letter in the word is typed in sequence, it will tend to activate the next one. This means that if the person is typing a related word, such as 'behave', it will be easier for them to make a mistake and type 'behaviour' instead. Typing the pattern of letters up to the 'v' would activate the schema for 'behaviour', and inhibit the schemata for other letters. Someone who did not habitually type the word 'behaviour', on the other hand, would not be at all likely to make this mistake.

A very skilled typist, however, is not likely to make a mistake like this. Partly, this is because they have well-developed schemata for a greater range of words and combinations, but also it is because a significant part of skilled activity is to do with continuous **feedback**. Part of the hierarchical model of skill acquisition is the idea that there are feedback loops for each schema, which inform the person about the result of each action, and allow them to modify and correct what they are doing more or less automatically.

The hierarchical model of skill control depends very strongly on the idea of feedback. We have already seen how important feedback is for the initial learning of skills. But it is equally essential in complex skill learning. Annett (1989) proposed that feedback in complex skill learning operates according to the **TOTE** system (test – operate – test – exit) identified by Miller, Galanter and Pribram (1960), which we looked at in Chapter 2.

According to Annett's model, each unit in a complex skill has a goal state, which is how the situation should end up. In performing each unit, the individual continually compares the current state with the goal state. This is the 'test' phase of the TOTE model. Then they act, or modify their behaviour, which is the 'operate' phase in the model, test it again, and either repeat the operate phase before testing again, or exit from that sequence if the goal state has been achieved. So each motor unit involves a continuous pattern of feedback and activity.

Skill learning in children

The research which we have looked at to date has been mostly concerned with skill acquisition in adults – although it may have something to tell us about the way that children acquire skills, as well. But children, too, acquire skills – indeed, one might look on the whole period of infancy and childhood as being a period for acquiring the skills which the child will need throughout life.

Bruner's theory of infant skill development

Some developmental theorists have argued that cognitive development is essentially all about skill learning. Bruner (1973b) argued that infant cognitive development is all about the skills which the infant develops, and the way in which these skills become automatised. Like adults, Bruner argued, infants develop skills deliberately: they express **intentionality**, and learn because they are trying to do so.

Bruner argued that studies of infant reaching, which we will be looking at in the next chapter when we look at infant perception, show that intentionality is present from a very early age. The reason why it is possible to use reaching to study perception is because the infant *intends* to try to reach the object. Moreover, Bruner argued, the purpose of infant action is very clearly pre-adapted to the infant's intentions and needs: infants are more predisposed to reach out for things with their hands than they are, say, to kick them.

What this means is that the actions which are most likely to be of value to the child in the long run are those which receive most practice. The component parts of any action become better established by repeated use. For example, the more an infant attempts to grasp things, the more co-ordinated its grasping becomes, and the more that action becomes automatic and less variable. So, as the action becomes automatised, the infant can begin to predict what will happen when it closes its fist in a certain manner. At this point, the behaviour has become **modularised** as a skilled unit.

Once a behaviour has become modularised, Bruner argued, it is no longer necessary for the infant to pay attention to it – it can do it automatically, as it were. So this allows the infant's attention to be freed for other things. Bruner sees cognitive development as being very much a matter of increasingly modularising components of physical skill, in such a way that the child's attention is then freed to deal with novel stimuli. We could draw a parallel with the process of learning to drive, in an adult. The initial stages of learning to drive require a great deal of attention to be given to actions like changing gear, but with increased practice these become modularised and are done more or less automatically, freeing the driver's attention to concentrate on more difficult perceptual features of the road ahead, or to hold a conversation.

Bruner saw the components of skilled activity as being similar to the units of language, in the sense that they can be reorganised and creatively re-combined in different ways. This means that the child will be able to discover new combinations of actions – new skilled behaviours – because it has the basic components already established in modular form. So, according to this model, physical play becomes an exploration of how modularised actions can be put together into new combinations.

Fischer's theory of cognitive development

As we have seen, the current approach to understanding skilled behaviour is to see it as a hierarchical structure of modular units. Interestingly, one of the main developmental theories of cognitive skill learning also adopted this approach, even though it has entirely different theoretical roots from the research into adult skill learning. Fischer's skill theory is a developmental model which applies a hierarchical, skill-based approach to the understanding of cognitive development.

Until the late 1970s, theoretical perspectives on cognitive development were relatively few and far between. The main ones were essentially the Piagetian and the behaviourist approaches – and the latter saw cognitive development as arising mainly as a result of combinations of stimulus-response links in behaviour.

But the problem with the behaviourist perspective of cognitive development, Fischer argued, was its over-emphasis on environmental influences. Seeing cognitive development as arising purely from the individual's experience implies that people are only likely to have anything in common with those who have experienced a similar environment. It implies that if someone has had a different type of personal environment and experience, then their cognition will be entirely different. But there do seem to be some similarities and regularities in human cognitive development, and these, Fischer argued, need explanation.

Fischer's skill theory (Fischer, 1980) was an attempt to form a synthesis between the two main approaches: Piagetian theory, which we will be looking at in the next chapter, and behaviourism. From Piagetian theory, Fischer took three main ideas: construction, control and structure. **Construction** is the idea that the individual actively constructs their cognition through interacting with the environment. Cognitive development is not passive, nor is it automatic; rather, understanding of the world is systematically put together by the individual as a result of the operations which are performed on the environment.

Control refers to cognitive control, rather than manipulative control. It is about the level at which we understand events, and how variations in our world come to be seen as systematic rather than random. When Fischer or Piaget says the child can 'control' the shape of a rattle, they mean that the child has acquired such skills as size and shape constancy, so it is not confused by the fact that the rattle has different appearances from different angles, or that it seems a different size when viewed from across the room. The child can represent the rattle cognitively, and use its representation to link the variations together. So in that sense, it has achieved cognitive control.

Fischer also adopted the idea of **structure** from Piaget. But instead of the schema, which Piaget saw as the basic unit of cognitive structuring, Fischer saw cognitive structures in terms of **hierarchical systems** of skills and higher-order skills. Fischer believed that the child's environment was all-important, with environmental experience resulting in a corresponding variation in cognition. So this theory was able to deal with the phenomenon of uneven development, which was quite a problem for Piagetian theorists.

From the behaviourist side, Fischer saw the type of **experience** which someone has had as leading directly to the type of skills which they develop, and so to the type of cognitive structures which emerge. Moreover, Fischer argued, the **differentiation** of the child's environment increases with age. The environment for very small children, and the

cognitive control which they need to acquire, does not vary particularly from one child to another. Environments for children or adolescents, however, are much more variable, and so give rise to large differences in cognitive development.

The process of skill development

In essence, then, Fischer saw cognitive development as arising from collections of specific skills, hierarchically organised, and acquired through interaction with the environment. In Fischer's theory, it is the individual's increasingly effective ability to control variation which forms the source of that cognitive development.

As the infant's sensorimotor skills develop, so there is more control over variation in movements. As experience grows too, variations in the appearances of objects and people become better understood – more cognitively controlled. Objects in the perceptual world come to represent a whole class of stimuli: the face of someone we know may involve different expressions each time we see them, or the same cup may be viewed from a different angle each time. In psychophysical terms, the effective stimulus may be a completely different one; but cognitive development consists of identifying and controlling these variations where they relate to the same object.

This applies to adults, as well as children. For example, if we see someone we know well, we will recognise them regardless of a new hairstyle or a different state of health. But we may fail to recognise someone whom we have only met once before. In the former example, we have cognitive control over the variation in stimuli, but in the latter example this control is not yet developed, so the different stimuli are not effectively linked. Each time we master some new source of variation in stimuli, we have developed what Fischer termed a **set**. The infant may develop a set concerning its rattle, for instance, or its teddy. An adult may develop a set concerning the recognition of a new public figure, or the route to a particular place.

Skills, according to Fisher, result from the linking of sets to produce units of behaviour. The structure of that skill depends on the number of sets which are involved. Control of variation does not just include control of stimuli; it also includes control of behaviour, so a cognitive skill, in Fischer's terms, includes both the stimuli and the behaviours concerning a particular event or experience.

Levels of skill organisation

Skills have differing levels of complexity, and one skill may be subsumed into a higher-order skill. For example, the set which a toddler develops concerning 'leaves' may initially simply involve the control of variation in the appearance of the thing which is called a leaf. But at the same time the child may be gathering information concerning the feel of leaves, or the way that sometimes there are lots of them around. Each of these will form a further set. As the child's experience grows, these will link to form a higher-order skill which the child can then apply to new stimuli, and which may result in a complex, many-sided cognition to do with leaves, autumn, trees, etc.

Fischer considered that there were ten hierarchical levels in all, which could be roughly grouped into three types of skill (see Table 18.8). The highest level of sensorimotor skill is also the lowest level of representational skill; while the highest level of representational skill is also the lowest level of abstract skill. Each skill builds on previous ones, so there is a progressively higher level of generality.

At the lowest level, the skills are concerned with basic co-ordination of movement and interpretation of sensory stimuli. As their order of generality increases a more complex form of skill arises, which includes a variety of related skills. By the time we reach the highest level of sensorimotor skills, we are talking about highly sophisti-

cated combinations of actions, and there comes a point where these may also form the first representations. As the basis of mental imagery in the child, they can simultaneously be the highest level of co-ordination and the basic level of mental imagery. Mental imagery eventually becomes subsumed into more complex forms of representation, and later into the basic levels of abstract symbolism and cognition.

Fischer argued that, although the environment determines which skills are developed and how sophisticated a level the child will reach, there is nonetheless an upper limit to how sophisticated a child at a given age is likely to become. So, according to Fischer, observed regularities in cognitive development in children of different ages, normally explained in Piagetian terms, may be explained in this way.

Fischer developed a set of **transformational rules,** by which the child comes to organise skills hierarchically. There are four basic transformations in this model, which are described in Table 18.9 overleaf. Together, these form the overall process of inter-co-ordination, whereby skills become transformed from one level to the next as they become compounded, differentiated or transformed in other ways.

Fischer's theoretical model, then, is an attempt to develop a synthesis between the behaviourist emphasis on environment and experience, and the structural approach of Piagetian theory. It also shares some similarities with the models of physical skill development which we looked at earlier, and which see complex physical skills in terms of a hierarchical structure of modular units.

The theory does have some problems, though Perhaps the most serious of these is the way that Fischer, like Piaget, tended to regard cognitive development as independent of the child's social experience. There is a gathering body of evidence which suggests that social experience is qualitatively different from other kinds of experience for the child, and that its influence needs more emphasis if we are really to understand cognitive development.

Metacognitive development

The child does not just acquire sensorimotor, representational and abstract skills. It also develops metacognitive skills – skills which enable it to develop an understanding of its own cognitive

Table 18.8 Types of skill

Levels 1–4 *Sensorimotor skills*
Learning to use and co-ordinate actions; learning to interpret sensory information, and utilise it in interacting with the environment.

Levels 4–7 *Representational skills*
Learning to use sensory imagery, and to develop more complex forms of representation based on imagery. The development and use of symbolic representation.

Levels 7–10 *Abstract skills*
The manipulation of symbols and concepts in problem analysis or synthesis. The development of metacognitive and other complex cognitive skills.

Source: Fischer, 1980

Table 18.9 Transformational rules in skill acquisition

Compounding	This is the combination of different skills to produce a new skill, but at the same level as the others. For example, the child may have control of 'which way up' variation for cups, plates, and pieces of paper. It may compound this cognitive skill by linking it with the skill concerning furniture. In this case, there is no difference in the type of skill, but it has wider application – much like Piaget's concept of assimilation.
Focusing	This involves the orienting of attention towards different stimuli from moment to moment. The child learns to transfer its attention, in sequence, from one thing to another, and this may eventually result in connections. In this model, the hand and the rattle become connected as a result of successive focusing of attention. Similarly, an adult learning a new video game, or other complex skill, will learn to pay attention to different stimuli in sequence, and eventually to connect focusing sequences.
Substitution	This is the term given to the way that a skill becomes more complex because it is generalised to apply to a wider range of objects. A skill which has previously been learned with one stimulus object may also be demonstrated with another. So a piece of blanket may substitute for a pillow, indicating 'sleep' in a toddler's game, or an adult may apply the skills learned in one type of game to a different one. The level of the skill does not change, but other objects may be substituted for its normal target.
Differentiation	This involves the skill becoming more sophisticated and broken up into more and more subsets – like, for example, the skill of walking becoming developed into running or skipping, as the child becomes more adept at motor co-ordination. This is not a change of level, but an example of the increasing differentiation of the skill.

Source: Adapted from Fischer, 1980

processes. Flavell (1979) described **metacognition** as the way that an individual is able to monitor memory, comprehension, and other cognitive enterprises and products. This monitoring itself then becomes part of that person's knowledge about cognitive phenomena. Metacognition is knowing about cognition: knowing about thinking, knowing about memory, knowing about how we use language and ideas – in short, knowing about knowing.

There is a considerable amount of recent research which has shown that children develop increasingly sophisticated **metacognitive skills** as they grow older. This research suggests that it is these metacognitive skills which help them to understand both the physical and the social world. Metacognitive skills are also crucially important in helping children to pass successfully through the educational process.

Metacognitive abilities can begin at quite an early age. In 1981, Hayes, Bolin and Chemelski showed that even pre-schoolers knew that it was easier to learn new information in certain circumstances rather than in others. When presented with a choice, for instance, they knew that it was easier to learn when you are happy as opposed to when you are sad. They also knew that it was easier to learn when you were feeling alert and not tired.

So even children of four and a half have some awareness of the nature of learning, and what it is like to learn. This is a metacognitive awareness.

Not surprisingly, children's metacognitive skills become increasingly sophisticated as they grow older. A study by Markman in 1977 investigated the aspect of metacognition which is perhaps best described as knowing that you do not know something. Children of five, six and seven years of age were given incomplete instructions about how to play a game and how to do a magic trick. Before beginning the task, the children had been asked to let the experimenter know if she had forgotten to tell them anything, or if their instructions were not clear. So recording whether the children asked questions when they were attempting to do the task on the basis of inadequate information, indicated whether the children knew that they did not know what was necessary.

In this study, Markman found that the five-year-old children carried on trying to do the task unsuccessfully – they did not appear to realise what, if anything, was wrong, but simply became aware that they could not complete the task. But the seven-year-olds would ask about the task when they discovered that they needed more information. Moreover, they often discovered this right at the beginning. Observations showed that they seemed to be more likely than the five-year-olds to run through the task mentally before starting it, and they would sometimes point out to the experimenter that they had not been given adequate instructions. In other words, where the five-year-olds simply knew that they did not know enough, the seven-year-olds were beginning to realise what it was that they did not know – a higher level of metacognitive skill.

Metacognition and overlearning

Shatz (1978) suggested that one explanation for the way that metacognition becomes more sophisticated as children grow older might be that it is linked with how well-learned a task is. If children have had more experience undertaking a given cognitive task, then they are more likely to be able to think about it. In one study, Shatz asked five-year-olds and four-year-olds to choose a toy suitable for another child to play with. The child was either younger than the one making the choice or the same age. Then they were asked to explain why they had made that choice.

When the range of toys was limited, both groups of children performed equally well. But when there were a large number of choices available, the five-year olds did better. Shatz argued that the greater experience of the five-year-olds with different types of toys, and with choices of this kind, meant that the circumstances were more familiar to them. So they found the metacognitive task of giving appropriate reasons for their choice easier, because the choice imposed less strain on their cognitive capacity.

Metacognition, then, is a higher-order cognitive ability, which may depend on having some of its basic units so well-learned that they have become almost automatic. In this respect, metacognitive development seems to resemble the development of other kinds of cognitive skills.

In this chapter, we have looked at mechanisms of development, and at the processes involved in learning and skill development. In the next chapter, we will go on to look at some of the psychological research into cognitive development: how the infant first develops its perceptual skills, and the child's growing understanding of its world. This will also take us into the way that the child develops its social awareness. We will be exploring the theoretical models put forward by Piaget and Vygotsky, and looking at how recent research evidence can build our own understanding of the child's cognitive development.

Key terms

approach-avoidance conflict When a goal is attractive but also has some drawbacks, it often seems more attractive while it is a long way in the future, but less so the nearer it comes. A person may become torn between wanting to achieve the goal and wishing to avoid it.

autonomic To do with the actions of the autonomic nervous system; sometimes used vaguely as a general term for unconscious, automatic neural functioning.

autoshaping The way that an animal may develop 'superstitious learning', performing an irrelevant behaviour before or with the desired one in an operant conditioning task.

behaviour shaping A process whereby novel behaviour can be produced through operant conditioning, by selecting naturally-occurring variations of learned responses.

cognitive processes Mental operations, such as thinking, remembering, forming concepts, perceiving, or using language.

insight learning Learning which takes place as a result of making a sudden mental connection, and

seeing the solution all at once; as opposed to more gradual forms of learning in which the solution is arrived at a little bit at a time, like trial and error learning.

latent learning Learning which takes place without producing an immediate change in behaviour.

Law of Exercise The principle that if a stimulus and action occur together regularly, they will come to form a learned association.

Lloyd Morgan's canon The principle that animal behaviour should always be explained using the lowest possible level of explanation.

negative reinforcement Encouraging a certain kind of behaviour by the removal or avoidance of an unpleasant stimulus.

Occam's razor A principle which states that, faced with two equally possible explanations, the scientific option is to choose the least complex one.

one-trial learning A rapid form of learning, which only takes one event to be learned, such as avoiding a food which has made you sick.

secondary reinforcement Something which reinforces learned behaviour because it has previously been associated with a primary reinforcer.

successive approximation See behaviour shaping.

temporal contiguity Juxtaposition in space and time – in other words, occurring together, or in rapid sequence.

vasoconstriction The constriction of blood vessels which occurs as a response to cold.

vicarious learning Learning through observation of what happens to others.

Summary

1 The basic mechanisms by which children develop psychologically include genetic maturation, conditioning, imitation and identification, metacognition and social cognition, the formation of self-efficacy beliefs and responses to social expectations.

2 The study of achievement motivation has moved from early attempts to identify internal personality traits, to approaches which emphasised child-rearing styles and on to the way that the child's own attributions and goals can affect their efforts.

3 Classical conditioning occurs as a result of association of a stimulus with an involuntary response to a different stimulus. Recent research into classical conditioning suggests that expectation is also important in this form of learning.

4 Operant conditioning occurs when behaviour has a pleasant effect, either through reward or by escaping from or avoiding an aversive stimulus. Reinforcement is a central concept in operant conditioning. Recent research suggests that it too involves some cognitive processing.

5 Studies of one-trial learning show that some forms of learning are easier than others. This appears to be an indication of genetic prepared-ness to learn survival-oriented behaviour. Other forms of learning include insight learning, the formation of learning sets, latent learning and cognitive maps.

6 Early models of skill acquisition saw it as stimulus-response links or as information-processing. Recent ones see complex skills as hierarchies of motor schemata. Research into skill acquisition emphasised the effects of types of practice, the need for knowledge of results, explorations of the speed-accuracy trade-off and the process of automatisation.

7 Bruner and Fischer both proposed that cognitive development proceeds through the acquisition of skills. Bruner emphasised the roles of intention-ality, automatisation and modularisation in cogni-tive skill development. Fischer emphasised the hierarchical organisation of skill acquisition.

8 Metacognitive development is concerned with how children develop a higher-order awareness of their cognitive processes and how they are using them.

Self-assessment questions

1 What are the main mechanisms of social learning?

2 What factors influence achievement motivation in children?

3 Outline Fischer's theory of skill development.

Practice essay questions

1 Is reinforcement a sufficient explanation for human learning?

2 Discuss the relationship between genetic influence and mechanisms of learning.

3 What are the main processes involved in human skill acquisiton?

Test your knowledge of this chapter with our online quizzes and games at: http://www.psych.co.uk

Explore learning and skill development further at:

Child development
http://www.nncc.org/Child.Dev/child.dev.page.html – Information and articles (largely aimed at parents) dealing with the stages of development from infancy to puberty.
http://idealist.com/children/cdw.html – Summaries and book lists for theories and theorists of child development.

Learning/conditioning
http://www-hcs.derby.ac.uk/tip/index.html – Links to detailed articles on all of the major theories about learning.
http://www.biozentrum.uni-wuerzburg.de/~brembs/classical/classical.html – Tutorial on all aspects of classical conditioning.
http://www.uwm.edu/People/jcm/psy551/skinner.1/ho3 A lecture handout outlining the differences between operant and classical conditioning.

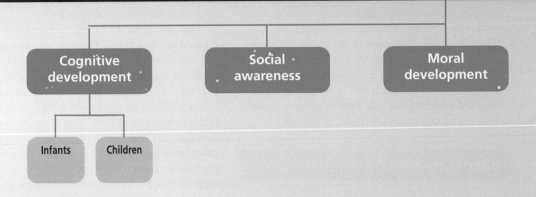

Cognitive development and social awareness

Cognitive development

Social awareness

Moral development

Infants   Children

Learning objectives

19.1. Infant reflexes
a identify common infant reflexes
b distinguish between theories of infant reflexes
c link infant reflexes with later development

19.2. Theories of infant cognition
a define terms relating to theories of infant cognition
b outline the four major theories of infant cognition
c describe a study of infant perception

19.3. Piaget
a define terms relating to Piagetian theory
b describe Piaget's basic studies of cognition
c explain basic Piagetian processes

19.4. Reappraisals of Piaget
a describe a study reappraising Piagetian ideas
b evaluate the Piagetian approach to cognitive development
c outline alternatives to Piagetian theory

19.5. The child's theory of mind
a identify features of social interaction in the home
b describe a study of the child's theory of mind
c outline age-related changes in social awareness

19.6. Autism
a list features of childhood autism
b distinguish between behaviours shown by normal and autistic children
c link an absence of theory of mind with autistic behaviour

19.7. Moral development
a outline how children perceive friendship
b list stages of moral development
c describe a study of socio-cognitive development

19.8. Vygotsky's theory of development
a outline Vygotsky's theory of development
b define terms relating to Vygotsky's theory
c apply the concept of a zone of proximal development to real-world examples

In this chapter, we will be looking at the development of the child's awareness of its world. We will begin by looking at infant cognition, and at how psychologists have studied cognitive development in babies. Then we will go on to look at the Piagetian approach to cognitive development, which was so influential in developmental psychology for many decades. We will look at some of the recent re-appraisals of Piaget's approach, at some of the research into the child's developing social awareness and theory of mind, and at the child's moral development. Finally, we will look at how Vygotsky's approach to child development may help us to make sense of the various research findings.

Infant cognition

How do infants think? Anyone who has observed a small child repeatedly patting or hitting a toy must have wondered what was going on behind those intent eyes. We know that the period of infancy involves a great deal of learning, but exactly what is being learned is not so clear. In this section, we will begin by looking at some of the research into infant reflexes, then go on to look at research into the perceptual development and abilities shown by infants, before considering four general theories which have been put forward as models of what is occurring during infant cognitive development.

Infant reflexes

Traditionally, the study of the foetus before birth focused purely on physical development, on the assumption that there would not be any psychological development until the infant was in contact with the outside world – until it had been born. But recently researchers have begun to examine the movements which the foetus makes in the womb. As any expectant mother will tell you, a foetus in the womb makes a number of movements, including turning around and kicking. Ianniruberto (1985) suggested that these movements provide important stimulation for the foetus, which helps to make sure that the nervous system develops the right kinds of connections.

Some of these actions of the foetus may provide useful groundwork for future, post-birth activity. For example, Dawes (1973) charted the

phenomenon of **foetal breathing**, in which a foetus in the womb produces rhythmical movements of the chest and abdomen, similar to the later breathing activity which it will show after birth. This behaviour begins as early as ten weeks after conception, and it is thought that it may be important for the development of lung tissue and the intercostal muscles.

It has also been shown that a foetus is able to respond to stimulation. The very first responses take the form of reactions to brushing around the region of the nose and lips. Hooker (1952) showed that in response to such stimulation, a foetus will turn its head away. A further study by Humphrey (1969) showed that as the foetus develops, this response becomes increasingly complex until it eventually includes the infant extending its arms and rotating the pelvis. This suggests that the foetus's nervous system is becoming better co-ordinated and organised.

Theories of infant reflexes

Neonates – newborn babies – are born with a range of reflexes. Testing reflexes is one of the main forms of assessment of infants born in British and American hospitals. If the usual range of infant reflexes is present, then it is judged that the infant's nervous system is probably functioning normally. These reflexes include actions like the **stepping reflex**, whereby if a young baby is held up by the armpits and a gentle pressure is applied to the soles of the feet, it will appear to step. Similarly, there is the **Moro reflex**, whereby the infant will stretch its arms wide and then bring them together suddenly, in response to its head suddenly dropping. These reflexes die out a very few days after birth.

The usual explanation for infant reflexes is that they are precursors of future activity. The stepping reflex, for example, has been proposed as a precursor to the later behaviour of walking. As the infant becomes more co-ordinated, it is thought, reflexes become unnecessary, so they die out through lack of use. There have been some studies that have indicated that infant reflexes can be maintained through practice; Zelazo (1976) gave infants regular practice in the stepping reflex, and showed that the period during which it lasts could be extended.

But an alternative explanation for infant reflexes is simply that they are leftovers from pre-birth activity. For instance, Prechtl (1984) suggested that the stepping reflex is a behaviour which allows the foetus to turn around in the womb, and that this alternative left-right movement with the foot is the way in which the foetus moves around. So observations of the way that neonates behave and respond to stimulation in the womb, and suggestions as to how this may help the development of the nervous system in response to actions by the foetus, may give us important clues as to the function of infant reflexes.

These two theories of infant reflexes are not necessarily mutually exclusive. It may be, for instance, that the co-ordination which the infant develops as an adaptation to the womb is also connected with the development of walking in later life. Perhaps the womb activity establishes a basic left-right co-ordination pattern which the child will then apply later. It is possible that movements by the foetus may provide the background, and the neural co-ordination, for later development.

Infant reflexes and psychological development

On the surface, it may seem that infant reflexes do not have much to do with psychological development. However, there has been a considerable amount of research which has shown how important activity can be to later development. In a famous study by Held and Hein (1963) young kittens which were given visual stimulation but no opportunity to move, using a 'kitten carousel' apparatus, did not develop appropriate perception. But 'control' kittens, who were given the opportunity to move and to act on their environment, did. It is equally possible that these pre-birth activities help to set some kind of framework for later cognitive development.

Piaget's theory of cognitive development, which we will be looking at later in this chapter, also assumes that the child is able to act upon its environment. These actions provide the infant with the data on which it bases its cognitive organisation. So the ability to act on the environment, and to respond to stimulation, may turn out to be important precursors of the development of infant cognition.

Perceptual development

Another aspect of understanding infant cognitive development concerns the development of perception. Some cognitive theorists (for example Neisser, 1976) have argued that perception forms the basis of all cognition. It is certainly the way in which we receive the information which is the raw material of cognition, so being able to perceive the world around us does seem to be a primary requirement for other cognitive activity. This means that infant perceptual development has been of major interest to psychologists.

Pattern perception

As we saw in Chapter 2, one of the primary features of our kind of perception is the way that we can perceive patterns and figures against backgrounds. In 1961, Fantz showed that even quite young infants have a preference for looking at patterns which are complicated, rather than simple ones. Most of all, Fantz showed, infants like to look at patterns which resemble human faces (see Figure 19.1). Fantz suggested that this implied an innate predisposition towards sociability in infants.

However, the study was criticised, since there were important differences between the stimuli which the infants preferred and those which they did not. For one thing, the face-like figure was symmetrical, whereas the scrambled face was not. When Fantz and Miranda (1975) investigated different kinds of patterns which infants preferred, they found that infants would look longer at patterns with curves, especially if those curves were round the outside of the figure. When they were presented with the same figures but embedded in a standard surrounding, it made no difference whether the figure had curved or straight lines (see Figure 19.2 overleaf).

While it is not clear whether infants really do prefer face-shapes to other shapes, there does seem to be a certain amount of evidence that they prefer complex stimuli to simple ones. This preference also develops as they grow older. Brennan, Ames and Moore (1966) showed infants chequerboard patterns, with 2 × 2, 8 × 8 or 24 × 24 squares. They found that at one month old,

Figure 19.1 Fantz's face shapes

Figure 19.2 Stimulus patterns for infant perception

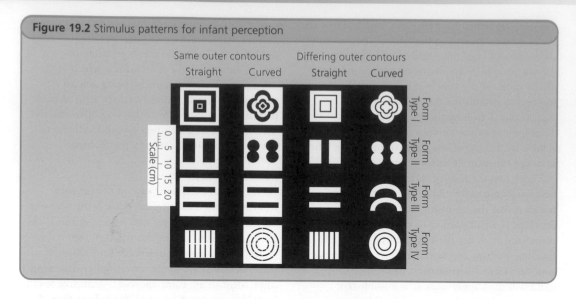

infants preferred the 2 × 2 stimulus, at two months old, infants preferred the 8 × 8, whereas three-month-old infants preferred the 24 × 24 stimulus. In other words, infants prefer increasingly complex stimuli as they grow older.

Functions of pattern perception

So if infants prefer complex stimuli to plain ones, and this preference increases as they grow older, what functional purpose does this serve? Banks and Ginsberg (1985) suggest that it is their preference for patterns which encourages children to look for features of the environment, and it is noticing features of the environment which will help their visual systems to develop. Banks and Ginsberg argued that, although the basic 'wiring' of the human infant's nervous system is completed at birth, any refinements will depend on what kind of stimulation it receives. So preferring increasingly complex patterns will encourage the infant to 'fine-tune' its visual system in accordance with the demands of the environment.

This idea appears to be supported by physiological evidence. Blakemore and Cooper (1970) showed that kittens which were brought up in a 'vertical world' – an environment in which they could perceive nothing but vertical lines – developed a visual system which was more adapted to dealing with vertical lines than those brought up in a normal environment. This suggests that the kind of perceptual stimuli we receive affects the development of the nervous system. Reporting later research, Blakemore (1984)

showed that kittens reared in this way showed adjustment of the neurones in their visual system, so that they had more cells that responded to vertical lines than a normal kitten would have (see Chapter 12).

Depth perception

One of the most well-known studies of infant depth perception was conducted by Gibson and Walk in 1960. Gibson and Walk developed a piece of apparatus known as the **visual cliff** (see Figure 19.3). This was a platform on which babies were placed, one side of which appeared to be very much lower than the other side. The whole platform was covered with a sheet of thick glass. Although it was safe, Gibson and Walk showed that infants of crawling age were very reluctant to crawl on the deep side of the visual cliff, whereas they would quite happily go on the shallow side. They concluded from this that infant depth perception was innate.

But since the infants were six months old when they were studied, and so were able to crawl, it is uncertain whether this was a valid conclusion, at least for human beings. They could easily have learned about depth through experience, rather than have inherited the ability to perceive it. Young kittens whose eyes had just opened, small ducklings and other **precocial** animals (animals which can get around independently soon after birth) refused to go on the deep side straight after they were born, and this suggested that they did have innate depth perception. But human infants

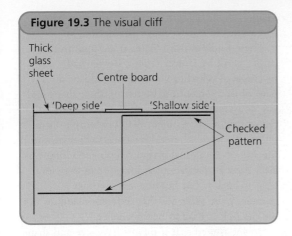

Figure 19.3 The visual cliff

Thick glass sheet

Centre board

'Deep side'   'Shallow side'

Checked pattern

are not precocial, so there is no reason to assume that the same mechanisms of development occur in the visual systems of infants. The longer period of dependency gives the human infant more time to learn depth perception gradually.

Campos, Langer and Krowitz (1970) measured the heart rate of infants who were placed on the visual cliff. Their surprising finding was that two-month-old infants placed on the visual cliff showed a *decrease* in heart rate. If they had been frightened, one would have expected their heart rate to increase, but a decrease in heart rate is usually associated with interest rather than fear. So this implied that the infants could see something which interested them, but they were not particularly frightened of it.

In a further study, Schwartz, Campos and Baisel (1973) compared five-month-old and nine-month-old infants on the visual cliff, also measuring heart rate. They found that the younger infants showed a drop in heart rate, suggesting that they found it interesting, whereas older infants showed an increase in heart rate, indicating fear (or at least wariness). They suggested that fear of depth occurs at the point where the child becomes capable of independent movement. Once a child is able to crawl around on its own, it would be a good survival mechanism if it were then to become wary. Before this point, Schwartz *et al.* proposed, the child is able to perceive a difference, which stimulates interest, but it does not interpret what that difference actually means in terms of the possibility of falling.

Reaching and defending

Other studies of infant depth perception have looked at how infants reach for things. Bower

(1972) presented very young infants with two different kinds of objects: one of them only just out of reach, and the other one twice as far away but twice the size (and therefore presenting the same sized **retinal image**). Bower found that infants would reach for the close object twice as often as they did for the further one, which suggested that there is some innate component in infants' depth perception. Unfortunately, other researchers found it difficult to replicate this study with very young infants. But Bower argued that, in those other studies, the very young infants had not been supported in such a way as to free their arms for suitable movement.

A study by Field (1976) compared infants of two and five months old. They were offered objects at variable distances – some within reach, some just out of reach and some quite a long way away. The objects were also of variable size, and carefully arranged so that the same-sized retinal image was produced by each. What they found was that the two-month-olds would reach out indiscriminately, regardless of how far away the object was, but five-month-old children tended to reach for objects which were closer, implying that their additional experience had helped them to refine their depth perception.

A third set of studies investigated infant depth perception by looking at how infants defend themselves against objects that appear to be approaching them on a collision course. Bower, Broughton and Moore (1970) tested infants of less than two weeks old, and showed that if infants are faced with such an approaching object they will raise their arm and their head, as if they were defending themselves against the object. The infants in their study also seemed to be able to distinguish between small objects that were very close to them and other objects which were larger but further away and cast the same-sized retinal image.

Ball and Tronick (1971) replicated these findings, and also showed that infants do not make defending actions if the approaching object is on a trajectory that is likely to miss them. This observation implies that infants have quite a sophisticated form of depth perception. Some researchers have criticised these studies on the grounds that, since the reactions which the infants make are very small, there is a great deal of room for misinterpretation – tiny movements of the arm or the head may be interpreted as defensive, whereas in reality they may simply be random movements. The issue, as you can see, is controversial, and the debate about whether infants do or do not have depth perception continues.

Neonatal depth perception

Bremner (1988) suggested the possibility that there may be some kind of neonatal depth responses, which exist for the first couple of weeks but then die out, in much in the same way that infant reflexes die out. Bremner thought that one reason for this might be to do with the 'fine-tuning' of connections within the cerebral cortex. Much neonatal behaviour, it is thought, is controlled by the primitive part of the brain known as the **midbrain** (see Chapter 10). As the infant grows older, more sophisticated cortical structures become increasingly important in controlling behaviour. This change, Bremner suggested, might account for how some behaviours appear as infant reflexes in the very early stages of life, but then disappear and re-emerge as learned skills later on.

This explanation certainly might help us to account for the conflicting evidence which appears to emerge from research in this area. In the last chapter, we looked at skill development, and at how new abilities become controlled by different parts of the brain as we become practised or expert at them. Although this probably does not happen in exactly the same way in infants as in adults, it is apparent that control of different types of movement can shift from one part of the brain to another, and so it is not inconceivable that a similar process might happen at an earlier stage of development.

Object perception

In 1961, as part of the study on infants' visual preferences, Fantz presented infants with a real sphere and a picture of a disc of the same size, and found that infants preferred to look at the three-dimensional object rather than at the two-dimensional image. This could not be taken as clear evidence that infants could perceive objects, however, since Fantz had not controlled for differences in shading and texture. In 1984, Slater, Rose and Morison replicated this study, but this time controlling for these two factors. They found that newborns still preferred to look at a solid object rather than a two-dimensional image, which suggested that infants may have some kind of innate object perception.

These findings from Slater *et al.* supported earlier work by Bower (1966). Bower had investigated whether young infants do or do not have object perception, by testing their shape and size constancy. Shape constancy is the ability to recognise the same object despite seeing it from different angles, whereas size constancy relates to the size of the retinal image. An object a long way away casts a smaller retinal image than the same object close by, but because we have size constancy, we allow for that difference, and do not see the object itself as being smaller.

Bower argued that if infants have size and shape constancy, this would imply that they have an innate ability to perceive objects. He tested infants using an **operant conditioning** technique. Infants of less than two weeks old were conditioned to turn their heads every time they saw a 30 cm cube, by giving them a reward if they did so. The infant was placed in a special chair which had padded pillows on either side of its head, which could detect very small changes in pressure. During the training procedure, if the infant turned its head when it saw the cube, an experimenter who had been crouching down out of sight would jump up and play peek-a-boo, which the infant evidently enjoyed (Figure 19.4).

When the infants had learned to respond to the 30 cm cube, Bower presented them with other cubes of different sizes. These were presented at distances which meant that they would cast the same-sized retinal image – such as a 30 cm cube from 1 m away and a 60 cm cube from 2 m. Bower found that the infants would respond to the original cube, but not to the others. They would also respond to the original cube seen from several different angles.

Other researchers investigated infant depth perception using **habituation** – if an object is presented continually, after a while the infant will cease to look at it. McKenzie and Day (1976) found that if a baby had become habituated to an object, and was then shown the same object at a different distance, the baby would become dishabituated and look at it again, which implies that the infant could tell the difference between the two distances. But McKenzie and Day also found that infants responded in the same way whether the same object was presented, or a larger object projecting the same-sized retinal image. In

Figure 19.4 Studying infant perception

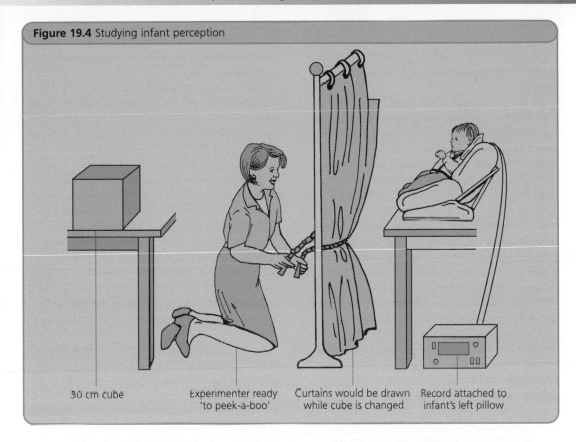

| 30 cm cube | Experimenter ready 'to peek-a-boo' | Curtains would be drawn while cube is changed | Record attached to infant's left pillow |

other words, they did not find evidence for size constancy, but they did find that objects at different distances tended to generate a lot of spontaneous attention from infants. However, in a later study, Day and McKenzie (1981) reported that there was some weak evidence for size constancy in four-month-old infants, although this is not as early as Bower had suggested.

The increased sophistication of infants' perceptual abilities with regard to depth perception and constancy again suggests that the environment may be 'fine-tuning' the innate capacities with which the child is born. Given the flexibility of infant behaviour, and the notable human capacity to adapt to a range of environments, it seems unlikely that any abilities in the human infant are totally innate. Rather, it seems probable that there are strong tendencies towards certain kinds of abilities and capacities which are present at birth, but which are then acted on and refined by the child's experience.

Models of infant cognition

Researchers into infant cognition have developed a number of different models in an attempt to describe and explain what is happening as infants come to understand their worlds. Harris (1983) summarised four theoretical approaches which have been proposed to make sense out of the data on infant cognition: the approaches developed by Piaget, Kagan, Gibson and Bruner. We will look at each of these in turn.

Infant cognition as operating on the environment

According to Piaget (1952), infants acquire their knowledge of the world by performing **operations** – by acting upon the world. Using the results of their actions, they gradually develop internal representations of the world, which become increasingly sophisticated and are used to direct the child's activities. In infancy the process of schema-formation is started by motor activity, and is based on what Piaget called **circular**

reactions. A circular reaction is an organised act which leads to stimuli which then re-elicit that act. So, for example, sucking produces sensations in the child's mouth which then lead to more sucking.

As the child's experience develops, circular reactions become increasingly differentiated from one another, depending on the operation which the child is performing on the environment. For instance, when a child is grasping something like a pencil, its grasping circular reaction is different from when it is grasping something like a ball. Circular reactions may also become integrated with one another, for example as they do when the two actions of reaching out for something and grasping it become combined into one sequence. These combinations and differentiations eventually produce internal representations known as schemata, which in turn become able to direct the child's operations on the environment.

The process of imitation, according to Piaget, operates in a similar manner to circular reactions. Imitation initially involves simple repetition, but then gradually becomes more and more differentiated, and integrated into the child's understanding of the world. Eventually, this results in abilities such as **delayed imitation**, which also depend on the infant's ability to form mental representations of the world.

The development of the capacity for mental representation also helps the infant to grasp how the physical world is organised. This in turn produces the distinctive characteristics of child cognition which Piaget identified as milestones in cognitive development, such as the development of the object-concept and the reduction of egocentricity. We will be looking in more detail at Piaget's theory of cognitive development later on in this chapter.

Infant cognition as distributed attention

Kagan (1970) argued that what is important about infant cognition is how the child pays attention to things. Kagan believed that during the first months of life, an infant's attention is mainly drawn to the physical aspects of a stimulus: change, movement, boundaries and textures. Several of the findings from the research into infants' perceptual abilities which we looked at above could be taken as supporting this idea. Kagan argued that, later on in the infant's life, stored experiences begin to lead to **internal rep-**

resentation. The child forms schemata – representations which in turn direct the child's attention, and encourage it to pay attention to other things.

Once an original schema has been formed, the child's attention becomes drawn to features of the physical environment which are a little different from the schema which the child already possesses – but not too different. This is known as the **discrepancy hypothesis**. At about eight months of age, Kagan argued, a further change occurs. At this time, infants begin to compare current input to their stored representations, as opposed to just noticing different things. They try to understand the nature of the difference, which is why they sometimes seem as though they are no longer paying much attention to the external environment. It is possible, if one adopts Kagan's explanation, to see this as perhaps the very beginnings of **metacognition**, which we looked at in Chapter 18.

Kagan's theory is different from that of Piaget, although both emphasise the importance of internal representations in cognitive development. However, Piaget was mainly concerned with how the child uses representation in order to transform its world – to perform operations on it – whereas Kagan was concerned with how the infant's internal representation of the world results in the infant distributing its attention to the different objects or people around it. As you can see, this could be regarded as more of a difference in emphasis than a contradiction between the two theories.

Infant cognition as fine-tuning pre-adapted mechanisms

As we saw in Chapter 2, J. J. Gibson (1979) argued that inferential theories of perception involve unnecessarily complex explanations, since there is already enough information in the visual world for us to perceive things directly. According to Gibson's ecological model of perception, we use information about texture and locomotion directly, to perceive the nature of the physical world without having to guess at it or form hypotheses. Gibson also applied this theory to the development of infant perception. According to Gibson's model, the role of experience in the young child is to enable the child to 'fine-tune' its perceptual discrimination and to develop an increasingly accurate awareness of the features of the physical universe – not, as both Piaget and Kagan argued, to develop increasingly complex cognitive structures which will eventually mediate in perception.

E.J. Gibson (1969) also saw the child as seeking information about the stimuli around it in a very direct, systematic manner. Stimulus information would enable the child to gather information about the world, and to interpret its perceptual data accordingly. Both Gibsons, and E.J. Gibson in particular, interpreted evidence about the young child's perceptual abilities as indicating that the child is ready and pre-adapted to respond to direct features within the visual environment. The model held by both Gibsons, then, denied any role for mental representations or schemata in early perceptual development, although they did not deny that there may be a role for imagery and other more complex forms of representation in other kinds of cognition, later in the child's life.

Infant cognition as the acquisition of skills

A fourth approach to infant cognition was put forward by Bruner (1973b), who argued that cognitive development in infancy could be interpreted, like most other kinds of development, in terms of the growth of skills. Skilled activity, we saw in the last chapter, is a goal-oriented activity which consists of a number of constituent components. These occur in definite sequences, and tend to be pre-adapted to meet familiar or expected events. Bruner sees infant responses as pre-adapted to the kinds of actions which will be required for later skilled activities. But the action is not yet developed, because it is not produced in the right sequence.

For example, a young infant might open and clench its fist when looking at an object which it could hold. This is an indication of the right kind of activity, but it is not an action which is successful, because the child has not yet developed the component of the skill which involves reaching towards the object and making tactile contact with it. Bruner takes the opening of the fist as evidence that the components of the skill are present, but argues that the child needs experience of the world and practice in motor co-ordination before it can bring the necessary components together in the right sequence.

We can see that these four theories represent rather different approaches to understanding infant cognition. Piaget sees the purpose of infant cognition as allowing the child to operate on and change its environment, and sees infant cognition developing further as a result. Kagan is concerned with how the development of internal representation means that the child will distribute its attention to different features of the environment. Gibson (1969) sees the child as being like an astronomer, making increasingly 'fine-tuned' observations, and Bruner sees infant cognition as allowing the child to acquire an increasingly complex repertoire of skilled behaviours, on which it can draw as necessary. Each approach makes use of some of the evidence for infant cognitive development in order to justify its own emphasis; and each may have some value in helping us to understand the different aspects of infant cognition.

Cognitive development in the child

The way that thinking develops in the young child is a topic which has been of interest to psychologists for most of the history of the discipline. Perhaps one of the most influential of all psychological theories was the theory of cognitive development proposed by Piaget, and this is the theory which we will look at first.

Piaget's theory of cognitive development

Piaget has often been referred to as the pioneer of research into cognitive development in children. His overall approach to understanding cognitive development was known as **genetic epistemology**. Genetic epistemology was based on the nineteenth-century biological concept of **recapitulation**. This was the belief that 'ontogeny recapitulates phylogeny'. Ontogeny means the development of the individual, and phylogeny means the development of the species, so this phrase implies that, during its development, a growing organism will go back over, or recapitulate, all the different stages of its evolution.

This idea was proposed when it was observed that a foetus goes through a stage in which it has external organs similar to gills. Some early biologists believed that this represented a throwback to the early stage of evolution, before mammals emerged from amphibians. Although this idea is no longer in common currency among biologists, it was very influential at the time that Piaget formulated his ideas, and it is why he became interested in cognitive development in children.

Piaget was interested in how knowledge and understanding – cognition – had evolved in human beings. Using the biological principle that ontogeny recapitulates phylogeny, he argued that how cognition develops in the child would indicate how cognitive development had evolved, to reach its current peak. The peak, in Piaget's view, was the use of formal, abstract logic. Piaget regarded this as the highest form of thought, and therefore the ultimate stage in the evolution of cognition. He was therefore interested in showing how the young child could move from the 'primitive' state of infant cognition up to the state of having an 'advanced' ability to handle abstract, formal logic.

The theoretical model which he applied to this included, as a central idea, the concept of the **schema**. A schema is a theoretical construct which is generally understood as being an internalised representation of the world, or at least some part of the world. It relates to a particular area of activity, and encapsulates the stored knowledge and experience we have which relates to that activity. We looked at some of the different types of schemata in Chapters 5 and 15.

A schema is not the same as a concept, because it is used as the basis for action. For instance, if I were to sit at a desk and write, the action of writing would call into play a large amount of prior knowledge, for example about things that make marks on pieces of paper, pieces of paper which are appropriate for writing on (as opposed to paper that is suitable for reading, like pages of a book), suitable places on which to rest the paper, places to sit, and so on. But it would also include expectations: what the writing is for, how I should go about it, who, if anyone, is likely to read it. All this knowledge is combined into a meaningful whole. It would be contained in a schema about writing and used as a basis for my actions.

Piaget argued that the very first schema which an infant develops is the **body-schema**. When it is first born, the child is unable to differentiate between itself and the outside world: everything is just a mass of sensation. Gradually, though, the child draws a distinction between 'me' and 'not-me' – things which are always part of the child's experience, and things which are sometimes not there. This is the very first schema – the body-schema – and it forms the basis from which all

the future, more sophisticated schemata develop.

This view of schema development implies that the primary cognitive process which is occurring in cognitive development is the reduction of **egocentricity**. At the beginning, the child is totally egocentric, in that it has no conception that there might be any world outside itself. The development of the body-schema is the first stage in reducing egocentricity, as the child gradually distinguishes the existence of an outside world. Nonetheless, the 'me' part of experience remains the most important part to the child, and determines the essence of its reactions to that outside world. Piaget believed that this egocentricity is gradually reduced throughout infancy and childhood, until the child eventually becomes capable of the detached, objective thinking represented by formal logic.

All thinking, according to Piaget, is based on the application of schemata. Schemata develop through two processes: assimilation and accommodation. **Assimilation** occurs when new information is absorbed into the schema without fundamentally changing it. So, for instance, the child may have a number of experiences that fall into the category of 'not-me'. One of them might represent 'mother', another might be to do with being placed in a different room, another might represent the feeding bottle. In the very early days, when the child has only the two schemata, these different experiences might all be assimilated into the same 'not-me' schema, without changing it much.

The second process is known as **accommodation**, and Piaget (who was a biologist by profession) used this in a biological sense – that a schema would accommodate itself to fit new information. It would stretch or change its shape or otherwise adapt itself to the information. So, for instance, the child might initially include its wrappings and bedclothes as 'me', as opposed to 'not-me'. But gradually it would come to distinguish between those parts of itself which were there all the time, like hands and feet, and those parts of itself which were sometimes not there, like its bedclothes. So its body-schema would have to accommodate itself to include this distinction. Eventually it might even subdivide into two different schemata, which is an extreme form of accommodation.

Piaget argued that the reason why the child is motivated to develop its schemata is through the process of **equilibration**. Experience which cannot be included within existing schemata, he argued, sets up a state of anxiety in the child. The anxiety is reduced through the processes of assimilation and accommodation, so that the child's schemata become able to deal with the information. Once this has happened, the previous state of equilibrium is restored. The process of reducing tension through equilibration is important to Piagetian theory, because it is this, according to Piaget, which provides the incentive for the child to continue to try to understand the world.

Another central concept of Piagetian theory is the idea that all cognitive development proceeds as a result of the child performing **operations** on its environment. An operation is anything the child does which produces some kind of an effect. In infants, as we saw earlier, these operations take the form of circular reactions – a sequence of actions in which a given act produces a stimulus that leads to a further act, as a continuous cycle. Circular reactions are the building blocks of operations, because they gradually become differentiated and refined so that the infant can adjust to different types of experience.

In the older child, operations are just as important as they are to the infant, but they are not as concerned with circular reactions. Nor are they necessarily concerned with physical actions – an operation in Piagetian terms is as likely to be mental as physical. By the time it enters childhood, as opposed to infancy, a child has developed its knowledge of the environment, and a wider repertoire of schemata, and can perform a large number of operations on the environment.

Piaget concluded from his observations that children perform different kinds of operations at different stages in their cognitive development, as their egocentricity gradually reduces. He also argued that these stages had a biological basis – that they occurred as a result of genetic maturation. Once the child had acquired a certain level of maturity, it would then be biologically ready to move on to the next stage. In fact, the concept of biological readiness was a very minor part of Piagetian theory, although unfortunately some educationalists applied the concept in a manner that was far more rigid than Piaget had ever intended.

Piaget grouped the different types of operations into a set of four cognitive stages, which are described in Table 19.1. The first, the **sensorimotor stage**, is the stage during which the child is acquiring skills – acquiring cognitive tools, ready for the second stage. The second stage is the **pre-operational stage**, during which period the child can perform some operations, but not fully. During the third stage, the **concrete operational stage**, the child is able to perform most kinds of operations, but only if they relate to the world, whereas in the fourth stage, the **formal operational stage**, the child has acquired the ability to deal with abstract problems as well as to engage in formal logical reasoning, which Piaget regarded as the highest point of cognitive development.

Piaget's evidence

Piagetian theory was always very firmly based on empirical demonstrations. The child's lack of an object concept, of the ability to 'decentre', or of

Table 19.1 The Piagetian stages	
The sensorimotor stage	*From approximately 0–2 years* The child has to learn to organise and interpret sensory information and to co-ordinate motor activity.
The pre-operational stage	*From approximately 2–7 years* The child's egocentricity is gradually reducing, but its operations on the environment are limited. It can only take account of one feature at a time in conservation problems, and is unable to decentre.
The concrete operational stage	*From approximately 7–11 years* The child is able to undertake adult-style cognitive operations; but these are mainly limited to targets which exist in material form in the world.
The formal operational stage	*From approximately 11 years* The child is now fully decentred, and can undertake abstract reasoning and perform logical operations.

the ability to conserve volume, mass or number was demonstrated repeatedly, with each demonstration adopting a particular formula developed by Piaget. These studies reliably indicated consistent age differences in the child's responses, and these age differences were taken as evidence of the existence of Piagetian cognitive stages.

Piaget obtained the evidence for his theory by performing a number of studies on children at different ages, on his own children and on others. He did so using a **clinical interview** technique – he would chat with them, sometimes set them informal problems and sometimes just ask them what they thought about things. The problems which he asked children to solve were ones which would allow him to investigate how the child performed operations on its environment.

One set of problems was designed to investigate the child's awareness that the world might continue to exist even when the child is not paying attention to it. These studies focused on the development of an **object concept**. The question Piaget was asking was: if a child sees an object, and then that object is covered up so that it can no longer be seen, does the child still know it is there? If it does, we can assume that the child has an object concept – that it knows that objects have an independent existence. Piaget found that young infants did not seem to have an object concept – they were too egocentric to be able to think that a separate world existed. But by the time they were about eighteen months or two years old, the object concept had begun to develop.

A further set of studies which investigated egocentricity directly concerned the child's ability to **decentre** – to see things from someone else's point of view. In a typical study of this type, Piaget would place dolls at various points around a model of some mountains laid out on a table, and invite children to choose, from a series of photographs, what the doll could see. Younger children would tend to pick out their own viewpoint from the set of pictures, because, Piaget believed, they were too egocentric to be able to see things from someone else's point of view, whereas older children could complete the task accurately.

In Piaget's **conservation** experiments, he investigated a different aspect of egocentricity, which was concerned with whether the child would focus only on the main attribute of what they were looking at, or whether they would be able to take into account other features as well. Piaget invited children to explain or describe the consequences of changing an object's shape or form. In a typical study, for example, children would watch coloured liquid being poured from a short, fat glass into a tall, thin one, or a row of counters being stretched out so that the row was longer. Then they would be asked if the amount of liquid, or number of counters, remained the same. Piaget found that younger children tended to assert that it had changed – that there was more liquid in the taller glass, for instance – because they would pay attention to only one attribute, such as height, and not take the others, like width, into account as well.

In some of Piaget's investigations into children's **moral development**, he asked them to explain to him the rules of the game of marbles. This was on the grounds that marbles is an entirely child-centred game, in which rules are very rarely taught by adults. He used these investigations to explore such concepts as fairness, the importance of abiding by rules, how inflexible rules were, and so on; and again found that moral development tended to go through a definite sequence, as the child grew older. We will be looking at Piaget's ideas about moral development later in this chapter.

Piagetian theory was tremendously influential throughout developmental psychology, not least because of its scope. As a grand theory of development, it portrayed a unified approach to understanding development, which allowed more specific phenomena or findings to be absorbed and interpreted in terms of the theory. Most developmental psychologists explored single aspects of cognitive development, such as the development of object constancy or the child's understanding of number in some detail. Piagetian theory provided the overall context within which these smaller aspects of development could be incorporated. Its influence was so strong that even alterna-tive models, such as Kohlberg's theory of moral develop- ment, tended to adopt a form which meant that they could be easily incorporated into an overall Piagetian framework.

Problems of Piagetian theory

There were, however, a number of weaknesses in the Piagetian approach, and as time went on, the theory attracted an increasing number of criticisms. Some of these were epistemological, in that the criticis were challenging the whole rationale underlying his approach. Some were theoretical, addressing problems in the theory itself. And some were methodological, challenging the evidence he had used to derive his theoretical conclusions, and eventually led to a complete re-evaluation of the cognitive capabilities of children.

Epistemological criticisms

Some criticisms have involved challenging many of the basic assumptions of the theory. For instance, Boden (1979) pointed out that the concept of genetic epistemology applied by Piaget, which, as we have seen, forms the basis of the whole theory, derived from two biological assumptions, both of which are now discredited. One of these is the idea that ontogeny recapitulates phylogeny, which has already been described, and the other is Lamarckian genetics.

Lamarckian genetics is the idea that it is possible for organisms to pass on to their offspring characteristics which have been acquired during their own lifetimes – for example, that the giraffe had acquired its long neck because its ancestors had stretched theirs upwards while gathering food. Although it was a popular theory in its day, Lamarckian genetics is now regarded as false by most scientists. (We will be looking at theories of evolution in more detail in Chapter 22.) Evidence which has been used – even quite recently – to suggest that Lamarckian mechanisms may be at work has often been shown to be fraudulent: some recent studies on colour pigmentation in mice, for example, were shown later to have been faked.

Of course, it is not possible to state absolutely that Lamarckian genetics is completely impossible, since some studies of the action of messenger RNA in the cell nucleus suggests that there may be more activity in the cell's chromosomes than was previously believed. But this appears to be at the molecular level only: scientists are reasonably certain that such influences could not affect the major characteristics of a developed individual.

In Piaget's day, though, Lamarckian genetics was a fairly well-known theory, and a popular alternative to **Mendelian genetics**, which proposed that inheritance worked through the action of genes and chromosomes which were fixed at conception. Piaget, like several other scientists of his time, believed that the major learning experiences which 'primitive' peoples had

experienced could have been passed on through genetic transmission, and later reflected in the individual child's development.

Another epistemological problem concerned Piaget's assumptions about the individual nature of development. Piaget regarded development as effectively a matter between the individual and its environment. He ignored social influences to an extreme degree, or at least, did not consider them to be fundamentally different from any other kind of environmental influence. But this left unanswered a number of other questions in child development research.

One of them, for example, was the question of **feral children**, or 'wolf children' (see Chapter 20). Although these cases were rare, studies of severely deprived children such as Genie (Curtiss, 1977) or the Koluchova twins showed that both social contact and social influence seem to be essential for development – an issue which was not fully addressed in Piagetian theory. Although some Piagetians tried to deal with this by treating social influence as another set of environmental demands, for the most part these studies were sidelined or ignored by those specialising in cognitive development.

A different problem with the Piagetian approach concerned unevenness in development. Piaget argued that cognitive development arose as a maturational process within the individual, and involved distinct stages. So his theory assumed that development would be regular – that as a child developed cognitive abilities, it would manifest those abilities in different contexts, as appropriate. But many researchers observed that children did not necessarily produce the regularity of development within the stages that Piaget had identified. Children who could do some concrete operational tasks in one area, for example, might only manage pre-operational thinking in other areas. Fischer's skill theory of cognitive development, which we looked at in the last chapter, was one of the suggestions put forward to deal with this problem.

Theoretical criticisms

One of the biggest theoretical problems presented by Piaget's theory was the question of the reduction of egocentricity, which Piaget viewed as the core of cognitive development. Piaget proposed that the young child begins life by being totally egocentric, and that this only reduces very gradually. There have been a number of studies of the mechanisms of infant sociability, which we will be looking at in the next chapter, and these indicate that the behaviour of the infant, from almost the first few days of life, is geared towards the early development of social relationships.

The first attachments, for example, develop when the infant is far younger than the age at which Piaget claimed they develop an object concept. Yet attachment would be impossible if the Piagetian view were correct, and infants were really totally egocentric. Since the reduction of egocentricity is such a central concept to the whole process of cognitive development in Piaget's model, these studies represent quite a serious problem for the theory. Some other issues about social influences in development are discussed in Box 19.1.

Interestingly, though, there have been few criticisms, if any, of the Piagetian concept of schema, and the idea of cognitive development as proceeding through the development of schemata through assimilation and accommodation is widely accepted. As we have seen throughout this book, the idea that we use schemata to store information and to direct action has proved useful in several different areas of psychology, and so have the ideas of assimilation and accommodation. The concept has been applied far more widely than just to child development.

Empirical criticisms

Piaget's sampling has sometimes been criticised, in that it comprised a relatively small number of children. However, this does not appear to be as powerful a criticism as some others, particularly as modern psychology is coming to accept the value of **case-study methods** for exploring issues in depth, which more general surveys may not do. In addition, the replication of Piaget's findings by

---

Box 19.1 Social influences on cognitive development

Traditionally, cognitive development in its several guises has been treated as if it were an individual event, dependent only on the stimulation which the individual child receives from its environment. But more recently, the evidence has been accumulating that what is involved is much more than simply environmental stimuli. Increasingly, attention has become focused on the importance of social influences and social interactions in the child's cognitive development.

In the 1960s, research into what were considered to be personality traits like the need for achievement (nAch) showed that the expectation of parents seemed to be exerting a considerable influence on the way in which this trait developed in children. Research into language acquisition, too, developed from the two extreme nature/nurture positions represented respectively by Chomsky and Skinner, to an emphasis on the importance of language as a means of social communication (e.g. Vygotsky, 1962), and on the need for social interaction while the child is acquiring language (e.g. de Villiers, 1978).

In terms of the formal theory of cognitive development developed by Piaget, recent evidence shows that many of the outcomes of traditional Piagetian tasks came about because of the social demands of the situation: rather than being cognitively incapable of doing anything as difficult as solving the tasks which were presented to them, children were actually applying a sophisticated social awareness to the situation and presenting the adult experimenters with the answers which they believed the experimenters wanted (e.g. Rose and Blank, 1974).

The recent interest in the child's theory of mind also shows that the child's understanding of other people is very much more highly developed than a strict interpretation of the Piagetian model of cognitive competence might allow. And research into moral development, too, has come increasingly to emphasise the importance of social interaction.

The picture which is emerging from all of this is congruent with the picture which emerges when we look at the young infant: of a child whose prime focus is on social interaction and social adaptation. The human infant is born predisposed to interact with people, and to learn from that interaction. And this predisposition forms the basis for child development as well.

many researchers suggests that criticisms of the sampling involved are fairly superficial.

More important, however, have been studies which have cast doubt on Piaget's own research. It is possible to question whether the answers provided by children in Piagetian tests have really revealed their true cognitive abilities. As with so many other aspects of child development, when we take our investigations into the real, social world in which the child lives, we find a different picture from that found when investigations are limited to more structured, formal techniques. Virtually all Piaget's 'classic' studies lend themselves to reappraisal when they are redesigned so as to take into account the child's 'real' world.

The object concept

One of Piaget's observations of the development of the object concept in the child was that a baby will not look behind a cushion for a ball that it has been playing with if the ball has rolled out of sight. Instead, it seems to forget entirely about the ball's existence. But a re-evaluation of how babies look for objects by Butterworth, Jarrett and Hicks (1982) showed that whether a baby will look at all is very dependent on the cues which are available. Moreover, babies tend to be more inclined to look in certain directions: they prefer to look down rather than up, for example.

In one study, Bower and Wishart (1972) used infra-red photography to show that if an infant was playing with a toy and the room was plunged into darkness while the toy was out of the infant's grasp, the child would still reach for the toy as if it knew it was there. These studies, and others, combined to suggest that the object concept is rather more highly developed than Piaget had suggested: whether an infant will reach for an object or not depends much more on the individual circumstances and environmental cues, than on some general cognitive ability, or lack of it.

Decentration

The 'mountain' studies, on which Piaget based his idea that children were unable to decentre, also showed similar flaws. Part of the problem seemed to involve the child's understanding of photographs rather than whether or not it could really imagine what things looked like from someone else's point of view. When Hughes (1975) recast the task into something with which children were more familiar – a puzzle which involved hiding a

boy doll from a policeman doll, behind a series of tabletop walls – the children had no problems with the task.

Hughes argued that, rather than showing the child's lack of cognitive capacity, Piaget's original task had been unclear to the children, and so they had not fully understood what they were expected to do. They performed much better with a task that they understood, or even at the original task once it was explained more clearly to them. In a replication of Piaget's mountain task, with clearer instructions, Hughes found that 64% of five-year-old children completed it correctly: Piaget had found that very few children of that age could manage it.

Conservation

Piaget's conservation experiments, too, were re-evaluated, using methods which connected more with the child's experience in everyday life. One of the most famous of these studies was by McGarrigle and Donaldson (1974), in which the experimenters pretended that a **naughty teddy** – a small toy teddy bear – was responsible for pouring the water into a different container, spreading out rows of counters or performing any of the other operations in a typical conservation test. McGarrigle and Donaldson found that when the conservation test was treated as a game like this, over 70% of the children whom they tested gave the right answer if they were asked which container or row contained more. But in a formal conservation test, the same children were just as likely to get the answer wrong as to get it right.

Greco (1962) argued that part of the reason for the wrong answers in standard conservation tests is because young children do not always use the term 'more' in the same way as the psychologist does. When shown two rows with five counters in each, but one row more spread out, the children would count the rows and state that there were five counters in each, which was the same. But they would still say that the spread-out row contained 'more'. Greco suggested that they were using the word 'more' to mean 'having more length', not to mean that there were more counters.

Other studies focused on methodological issues. Rose and Blank (1974) suggested that the design of the study might accidentally call upon the child's social knowledge to encourage the wrong answer. In a traditional conservation task, the child is asked twice to state whether the two rows, containers, etc., are the same. It is asked once before the experimenter has manipulated the materials and again afterwards. Rose and Blank pointed out that, normally, children are only asked the same question twice if they have got the answer wrong the first time. So the experimenters performed the standard conservation tests, but asked the child whether the two were the same only once, after the materials had been manipulated. When they did so, they found that a far higher percentage of children got the answer right.

These methodological challenges to traditional Piagetian theory suggested that rather than demonstrating underdeveloped cognitive abilities, children in the Piagetian studies were actually demonstrating a sophisticated social knowledge, tailoring their responses to what they believed were the social demands of the situation. Researchers began to investigate child cognitive development in its social context; and in doing so, they discovered that the child's understanding was far more sophisticated than had previously been believed. Although children were as bad as ever at understanding abstract, decontextualised problems, within their own familiar environments they demonstrated an intriguing level of social and cognitive competence.

Developing social awareness

The growing interest in social influences led to the emergence of a body of research which deliberately explored the importance of social contexts and social demands on the child's understanding. Researchers began to explore the way that small children interact in their family contexts, rather than in clinical interviews, and found an intriguing picture of growing social competences.

Family interactions

Dunn (1988) pointed out that children are born into a complex social world, and they become active participants in that world from a very early age. Family interactions are a central part of the young child's world, and it is through family interaction that the child is able to develop its world-knowledge, and its awareness of what

counts as acceptable or unacceptable behaviour. Moreover, Dunn argued, the emotions and conflicts of family life, as well as the play and humour, are crucial features of the way that the child learns. The child's socio-cognitive development is not just a matter of responding to demands or sanctions: it involves active intentions, emotions, and dynamic exchanges.

Hinde (1987) argued that all relationships need to be seen in their social and cultural contexts. Although, as social animals, we have biological tendencies towards forming relationships with other individuals, the way that interaction occurs within a given society will also tend to shape the kinds of relationships which we develop. This cultural framework in its turn will influence which biological propensities are nurtured and which are played down. In other words, there is what we call a **dialectical relationship** between the individual, their interactions with others and their culture. Each influences the other and is influenced by it.

As we saw in Chapter 14, Hinde also suggested that when we are looking at human interpersonal relationships it is useful to examine them in terms of the eight basic dimensions: content; diversity of interaction within the relationship; quality of the relationship; their patterning or relative frequency; reciprocity or complementarity; intimacy; interpersonal perception; and commitment. These dimensions are explained more fully in Table 14.6, on page 348, and each of them can give us a useful perspective to help in comparing different relationships. Hinde's dimensions have been helpful to several researchers investigating the nature of relationships within families.

The Cambridge project

In a series of studies conducted in the mid-1980s, Dunn and her colleagues carried out ethological observations of family life in a range of homes in the Cambridge area. The families who participated in the research were carefully selected to represent a range of income and social class backgrounds. Most lived either in council houses, or in turn-of-the-century semis, and at the time that the researchers began the study, none of the mothers were working full-time; although several worked part-time and some obtained full-time work as the study progressed. The main focus of interest was the second child in the family, and its pre-school development, so the ages of children ranged from 14 months to 36 months. Since the studies were longitudinal in nature, though, each child was observed on more than one occasion.

The observers tried to be as unobtrusive as possible; although, of course, it would be unrealistic to think that they had no effect at all on the way that the families behaved. But the same researcher visited the family each time, so that the children (and parents) could get used to them, and they visited quite often. Also, although they did not interrupt or interfere, the observers did try to be as natural as possible, so they would respond if a child spoke to them rather than remaining silent.

Altogether 52 families took part in the project, which was divided into three 'studies'. The first involved six families, and the observations were conducted at two- or three-month intervals from the time that the second child was 14 months old, until it was 24 months; then the children were visited again at age 36 months. The second study was larger, involving 40 families, and these were each observed when the second child was 18, 24 and 36 months old. The third study involved a further six families, beginning when the second child was 24 months old, and continuing at two- or three month intervals until they were 36 months old. This programme of observations gave Dunn and her colleagues a wealth of material about the socio-cognitive development of pre-school children.

What emerged was a direct challenge to the assumptions about children's cognitive and moral development which had been made by earlier researchers. As we have seen, Piaget considered cognitive development to be based on a gradual reduction of egocentricity, which had only just begun by the age of two or three. Yet Dunn and her colleagues found that even from 18 months of age, children understood a variety of interpersonal and moral issues, which would not have been possible if the child were as egocentric as had been assumed.

Teasing

As many mothers know to their cost, it is not at all uncommon for older children to tease their younger siblings, and deliberately provoke them to distress. Younger children too sometimes deliberately provoke their older siblings. Each family seems to produce its own style of interaction, and these can be very different from one family to the next.

Dunn and Kendrick (1982) found that in some families anything up to 50% of the interactions can consist of mutually hostile encounters, such as quarrels. But this depends on the family: some families show far fewer mutually hostile encounters, and in some cases these were virtually non-existent. Similarly, the researchers' observations showed that the proportion of mutually friendly encounters can also be anything from zero up to about 85%, depending on the family.

Dunn and Munn (1985) showed that children become increasingly more sophisticated at teasing, and tend to do it more often as they grow older. When a child is 16 to 18 months old, their teasing of an older sibling is likely to involve removing or destroying something which belongs to the older child. Dunn and Munn found that these children are often very sophisticated in their choice of object to remove – it is usually something that the older child is particularly fond of. By the age of two, children become more adept at the type of teasing that they can do to their siblings, and their techniques begin to vary much more.

Dunn and Munn also found that children increasingly tend to tease their mother during their second year. This teasing frequently took the form of doing something which they knew to be forbidden, while looking at the mother and laughing. Dunn suggested that behaviour of this type is one of the ways in which children learn about their social world and its limitations. By teasing, they find out how people react, and what the consequences of particular actions are. Depending on how people respond to their teasing, they may also learn about the acceptable boundaries of social interaction.

Dunn and Kendrick (1982) pointed out that most children in families show a mixture of friendly behaviour and aggression. However, they also suggested that some children seem to be particularly inclined to cause distress to others. They suggested that this could be connected to the type of child-rearing style used by the child's parents. Zahn-Waxler, Radke-Yarrow and King (1979) showed that children seem to be less inclined to cause distress and more inclined to try to make amends in families where parents reprimand the child by making statements of principle such as 'You must never poke anyone in the eye' or 'You might talk about biting but you must never do it'. Children who were reprimanded by physical abuse, like being slapped or beaten by their parents, on the other hand, were noticeably less aggressive than other children, but also tended to be less likely to share things with, or help, others.

Comforting

Dunn, Kendrick and MacNamee (1981) looked at how children comfort older or younger siblings in the home. They obtained reports from mothers about the behaviour of their eldest child towards a younger brother or sister. The older children were usually between two and four years of age, while the younger siblings were between eight months and fourteen months old. The researchers found that about one-quarter of the older children comforted their siblings frequently, about one-third did so occasionally, and one-third did so rarely. It was also apparent that the younger children tended to turn to their older siblings for comfort – by fourteen months, almost one-third of younger children would do this. And by fourteen to sixteen months of age, younger children tended to reciprocate by comforting their older brothers and sisters when they were upset, or by trying to comfort their parents when they had accidents or minor upsets.

In a similar study, Dunn and Kendrick (1979) observed children interacting during the researchers' house visits, and found that something like 80% of older children tended to make helpful or sympathetic actions towards a younger child when the younger child was upset. This often took the form of offering food or toys, or helping out the younger child in some task or other.

Zahn-Waxler and Radke-Yarrow (1982) observed how children's reactions to other people's distress changed over time. They asked mothers to keep records of what their child did when someone was distressed nearby. They also observed the child's reactions in response to feigned distress from mothers or investigators. Their results are given in Table 19.2, and show that by the age of eighteen months the children's behaviour often showed quite a sophisticated understanding of what the problem was. One child that they studied had upset its mother by making a mess. The child tried to placate its mother by saying, 'I want Mummy'; it hugged her and then said, 'I wipe it up', and tried to do so. Here, the child was clearly responding to the mother's distress in quite a complex fashion, and trying to make amends for it.

Main and George (1985) showed that abused children often tend to respond differently from other children when they encounter distress in another child. The researchers observed two groups of children, both of which came from disadvantaged families (the mothers were mainly on state benefits, and fathers were often absent). In one group, the children were known to have been abused and battered to varying degrees of severity. The other group had no known history of maltreatment.

The two groups of children were observed during day-care sessions, and it was clear that their responses to distress in other children were different. The non-abused children tended to try to comfort other children when they saw them in distress, but the abused children very rarely did so. Sometimes they simply looked on, or mechanically patted or tried to quieten down the crying child. More often, however, they would

Table 19.2 Children's reactions to other people's distress

Approximate age	Typical reaction
10–12 months	Children tended to simply observe other people's distress. However, in about half of those incidents, the children also showed some kind of distress themselves. They did not, however, try to comfort the person concerned.
12–18 months	Children showed fewer signs of being upset themselves when they saw someone in distress, but tended to make far more active interventions. Typically, they might approach the person and touch them or pat them.
18–24 months	These efforts became more complex – children might bring objects to the distressed person that they thought might help, they made suggestions about what they could do, expressed their sympathy in words, sometimes went and found a third party who might be able to help, and sometimes even tried to protect the person in distress.

Source: Adapted from Zahn-Waxler and Radke-Yarrow, 1982

become hostile and threaten the child. Occasionally they became upset and showed fear or distress themselves, or a mixture of both. The non-abused children very rarely made threatening gestures and never showed this sort of distress or fear in this situation.

It is clear from this study that simply coming from a disadvantaged background does not in itself result in problems with relationships. The non-abused children in this study responded in the same concerned, comforting way as children from intact, stable, working-class families, or children from middle-class families. However, the abused children reacted to other children's distress in much the same way as ordinary children react to anger – by becoming upset, ignoring it or becoming aggressive.

It is possible that this is one of the ways in which a **cycle of abuse** is maintained, in which children who have come from abusing homes sometimes abuse their own children when they grow up. This is not inevitable: as we will see, many people recover from distressing early experience, and develop normal, psychologically healthy adult relationships. But there do seem to be some occasions when a family may show such a cycle of abuse. One suggestion is that abusing parents provide role models, which mean that their children learn to see distressed behaviour as a signal for aggressive reactions. It has also been suggested that abusing parents inhibit the natural empathic tendencies of their children, which in turn could produce these effects. This means that the child does not really come to see events from the other person's point of view, and this links with some of the recent research into children's understanding of people's minds.

Features of social competence

It was evident from the observations made by those involved in the Cambridge project, and others, that small children often had a far more sophisticated social understanding than had previously been thought. Although they were unable to express this understanding in hypothetical terms – such as by responding to a problem set by an experimenter – the nature of their interaction within the family showed that they understood the issues very well, and were able to apply them within their family interactions.

Understanding others' feelings

One of the distinctive features of the child's social awareness was that they revealed some understanding of others' feelings. Researchers into infant behaviour, such as Stern (1977), had observed that even in their first year of life, children seem to 'tune in' to the moods of others, responding to distress, but also to amusement. This ability, which Stern referred to as **affective tuning**, became even more highly developed as the child entered its second and third years. Dunn's research showed that children respond empathically to their parents', or their older siblings' distress, and often make attempts to comfort and distract them (Table 19.3). Moreover, both their non-verbal behaviour and their comments showed that they were deeply interested in emotional states, showing increasing curiosity about pain, distress, anger, pleasure, comfort and fear as they grew older.

Understanding others' feelings, though, does not necessarily mean sparing them. As most mothers rapidly discover, small children often take a great delight in teasing or upsetting their siblings. Although the children in the study clearly understood distress, they might respond in any one of five ways: ignoring, watching, trying to comfort, laughing, or acting to make things worse. Which option the child took also appeared to have quite a lot to do with how old the child was. For example, those closer to 36 months were more likely to comfort their siblings, particularly if they had not caused the distress in the first place, than children of 18 or 24 months (Figure 19.5).

The overall conclusion, then, is that pre-school children are very ready to learn to understand other people's feelings, and that they show a great deal of interest in doing so. They will joke about them, tell stories in which other people's feelings

---

Table 19.3 Understanding others' feelings

Family R (Study 2). Child 18 months.

(Older) sibling is crying bitterly, lying on mother's knee, face down.

Mother attempts to comfort. Child watches soberly.

Mother to child: 'What's wrong with Kelly?'

Child, with concerned expression, bends down, turns his head to look face to face at sib, strokes her hair.

Source: Dunn, 1988 © Judy Dunn, 1988

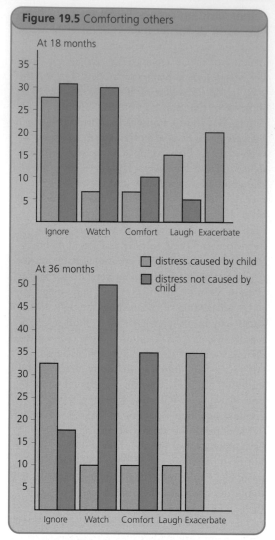

Figure 19.5 Comforting others

At 18 months

At 36 months

☐ distress caused by child
☐ distress not caused by child

(Categories: Ignore, Watch, Comfort, Laugh, Exacerbate)

Source: Adapted from Dunn, 1988 © Judy Dunn, 1988

Understanding others' goals

Dunn's observations of pre-school children showed that they are also developing an understanding of other people's intentions and personal goals. As Dunn and Kendrick (1982) showed, young children are able to co-operate in play with their siblings from a very early age – well before they are two years old. This requires a sensitivity to the other person, which seems slightly at odds with the total egocentricity of the Piagetian model; and it also requires an understanding of what the other child intends to do, and a fitting in with their play.

Many researchers into infant behaviour have shown how readily they will engage in games with the mother, such as 'peek-a-boo', or 'hide and seek'. These games involve sustained co-ordination between the mother and the child, and they have been studied in considerable depth (e.g. Bower, 1966; Kaye, 1982). The various studies all show that by the time they are one year old, children are able to engage in games which involve two or more individuals working towards a mutual goal. So the basis of co-operation is well established for the pre-school child.

Dunn and her colleagues looked at examples of the child co-operating with a sibling's play in a way that showed that they understood the other person's goals. Some children demonstrated this from as young as 14 months (Table 19.4, example 1), but it became more common between 18 months and 24 months (Table 19.4, example 2). Interestingly, though, it did not become any more common between 24 and 36 months, but stayed at

are the most important part, and even play with other people's feeling states (particularly those of their brothers and sisters. In doing so, they learn about the states themselves, but also about what their particular culture (personified in the mother, for the most part) considers to be acceptable or unacceptable in dealing with them. This responsivity, Dunn argues, shows that even though abstract moral reasoning is some way away, by the time the child is three years old it is already capable of caring, considerateness, and kindness: a sound basis for future social, and moral, development.

Table 19.4 Understanding others' goals

Example 1
Family B (Study 1). Child 14 months.
Sibling begins to sing. Child goes to toybox, searches, brings two toys to sibling, a music pipe and bells.
Child holds out pipe to sibling and makes 'blow' gesture with lips.

Example 2
Family P (Study 2). Child 18 months.
Sibling is acting out a fairystory with puppets. Child watches, laughing.
Child goes to shelf and finds other puppets, appropriate to the play, and brings them to sibling.

Source: Dunn, 1988 © Judy Dunn, 1988

about the same level. Although the children had become more skilled at co-operating during this time, it appeared that their motivation for co-operating remained at about the same level.

Understanding social rules

Another characteristic underlying socio-cognitive development which emerged from Dunn's studies was the way that children between one and three years of age develop their understanding of social rules. Interaction with other members of the family – not just the mother, but also with siblings – produces an increasingly sophisticated know-ledge of what is and is not permitted, when rules will or will not apply, the idea of responsibility, and the use of excusing and justifications. In other words, children of this age do not just learn about social rules: they also learn to use them, and even to manipulate them for their own ends. But this is all practical knowledge, used within the family – extracting abstract principles or dealing with hypothetical problems is quite another matter.

The conclusions of Piaget and other researchers had been based on requiring the child to deal with hypothetical examples: 'stories' of one form or another. This research implied that, by and large, young children were unable to grasp social rules and principles. But Dunn, working within the family and analysing the real interactions which took place, found that the child's ability to understand and use social rules actually develops steadily throughout the third year of life.

By the time they reach two and a half, or three years of age, children are demonstrating a sophisticated awareness of rules, authority and responsibility, which indicates that their comprehension of the social world is really much subtler than was previously thought. Dunn's observations showed that children are able to apply different sets of rules appropriately in different circumstances, and that they understand issues which relate to the wider society, as well as the patterns within their own particular family.

Understanding social rules, though, is not the same as obeying them. In part, the children's understanding of the rules was evidenced by the way they used them: taking great delight in pretending to break rules in joint play with their siblings; putting the blame on other people (Table 19.5, example 3), challenging mother's authority by applying the rule to her as well (Table 19.5, example 4), and so on.

Perhaps one of the most significant findings which emerged from Dunn's research was how quickly children learn about rules when the context has some emotional significance for them. At 18 months, children have developed a strong idea of their own rights, and become extremely angry and emotional when they feel these are being infringed. By the age of 36 months, the tantrums have died down somewhat, but they are much more inclined to argue and dispute about issues. But as we can see from Figure 19.6, it is precisely those issues that they become most angry about, that the child argues most about later. Dunn argues that the role of emotional

---

Table 19.5 Understanding social rules

Example 3
Family A (Study 3). Child 30 months.
Child (Annie) and sibling (Carol) are playing with hose in garden, previously forbidden. Child turns it on again.
Child to sibling: 'And it got some water out spraying.'
Sibling to child: 'Make some out of this.' (pull other end of hose)
Mother enters garden: 'Who's put the hosepipe out again?'
Child to mother: 'Carol.'
Sibling to mother: 'No it was Annie.'
Mother to both: 'Why did any of you put the hosepipe out again? Cos I'd packed it all away to go in the shed.'
Child to mother: 'Ummm. Carol did it.'
Sibling: 'I didn't. She did it.'
Child to mother: 'Carol did it.'
Sibling: 'No she didn't. (to M:) Oh no I didn't. She done it.'
Child to mother: 'Carol did. Carol did.'
Sibling: 'No she didn't. (to M:) Oh no I didn't. She done it.'
Child to mother: 'Carol did. Carol did.'
Sibling to child (shouts): 'I did not!'
Child to mother: 'Umm. Carol – I'
Mother to both: 'Well, whoever it was is a naughty girl.'
Sibling to mother: 'It was Annie.'

Example 4
Family H (Study 2). Child 36 months.
Mother, sibling and child in kitchen. Mother organising (play) cooking.
Mother: 'Would you two like to go and wash your hands?... Go and wash your hands please.'
Child: 'Why don't you wash your hands?'
Mother: 'Well, it's you two doing the cooking.'

Source: Dunn, 1988 © Judy Dunn, 1988

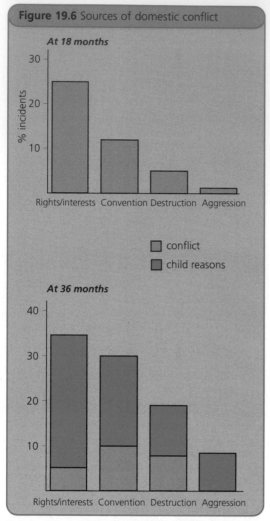

Figure 19.6 Sources of domestic conflict

At 18 months

% incidents

Rights/interests   Convention   Destruction   Aggression

☐ conflict
■ child reasons

At 36 months

Rights/interests   Convention   Destruction   Aggression

Source: Adapted from Dunn, 1988 © Judy Dunn, 1988

involvement in socio-cognitive development is one which has been seriously overlooked; and that it may provide an important key to understanding both the motivation and the mechanism for the child's developing sophistication in this area.

The child's theory of mind

A fourth finding of the Cambridge studies concerned the young child's growing awareness of other people's minds, and their moods. This observation links very closely with another area of research into children's socio-cognitive development, which investigated how children develop a 'theory of mind' between the ages of

two and four. What Dunn's research showed was that family interactions provide a rich developmental context for that theory of mind to develop. And much of the development of social understanding revealed by the children acts as a foundation for their growing sophistication in matters of social interaction.

Understanding people's minds means knowing that other people might do things which are different from what you yourself might do. But children also develop a **theory of mind** – an idea that other people have independent minds of their own. Developing a theory of mind allows the child to begin to understand other people, and to predict what other people are likely to do and to believe.

Understanding false beliefs

One set of investigations into the nature of children's theories of mind concerns how they understand false beliefs. Perner, Leekam and Wimmer (1987) showed that three-year-olds found it very difficult to understand that other people may hold false beliefs. In this study, three-year-olds were shown a Smarties box and asked what they thought it contained. All of them answered 'Smarties'. The children were then shown that the box in fact only had a pencil inside it. After that, the box was closed, and the children were asked a number of questions. First, they were asked what was still in the box, just to make sure that they remembered the situation. This presented no difficulties – they knew that the box contained a pencil. Then they were asked, 'What did you think was in the box when you first saw it?' which they also answered correctly. Finally, they were asked to predict what would happen if a friend of theirs, who was waiting outside, was brought in and asked what was in the box.

Perner *et al.* found that, of the 29 children in the study, sixteen succeeded in the first two questions, but failed to predict their friend's false belief. To the question 'What do you think is in the box?' they predicted that the friend would answer, 'a pencil'. The children who succeeded in the task as a general rule were older – they were from three to four years old, rather than being only just three years of age. The researchers had found that the younger children could report their own false beliefs – that they had originally thought Smarties were in the box – but they did not really understand where that belief had come from, so they did not understand that another person might also share that false belief.

By the time they are four years old, however, children are becoming more sophisticated about other people's false beliefs. Wimmer, Gruber and Perner (1984) investigated how children understood lying, and their moral judgements about true and false assertions. This study involved stories in which a speaker was led to a false belief. A typical story involved three dolls, representing an older girl, a younger girl and a young boy. The story went like this: the older girl and the younger girl were walking past a wall, and the older girl could see a lion on the other side. The younger girl could only see the tail of the animal, and asked the older girl what it was. The older girl lied and said it was a dog. After that, the young boy asked the younger girl what the animal was, and the younger girl also said that it was a dog.

The children were tested first in terms of whether they understood that the younger girl held a false belief. Almost all the children did. When asked, even four-year-olds judged the speaker according to their intentions, rather than according to whether they had acted truthfully, which implied that they were able to distinguish to some extent between intention and truth. They knew that the younger girl was not intentionally deceiving, whereas the older girl was.

But when they were asked whether the younger girl had lied, most four-year-olds judged that she had. Some six-year-olds did too, but virtually no eight-year-olds did. Younger children, it seemed, held a 'realist' concept of lying, judging it purely according to whether the statement was true or not. Older children, on the other hand, tended to judge lying according to the intention of the speaker. This implies that, as they grow older, children do become better at understanding how other people can hold false beliefs.

Perner and Wimmer (1985) showed that six-year-olds' understandings of other people's beliefs are even more sophisticated than just knowing that someone may hold a false idea. In this study, stories were acted out for children aged between five and ten years old. In the stories, two characters were told, separately, that an ice-cream van had moved to a new place. Each character knew where the van was, but they did not know that the other person knew as well.

The researchers then asked children about this story, using questions like: 'Where does John think that Mary will go for ice-cream?'. They found that children as young as six and seven years old could infer second-order beliefs. In other words, they would predict that John would think that Mary would go to the old place for ice-cream. On the other hand, five-year-olds were unable to do this, which support the view that children become increasingly sophisticated in their social understanding as they grow older.

Perner (1988) summarised the research into children's understanding of false beliefs as implying that children seem to be directly attuned to social situations as a whole. Children can, for instance, answer questions about mental states much earlier than they can draw moral judgements, and before they can distinguish between different kinds of false beliefs. So they do at least understand that social interaction is based on understanding the mental states of the actors – they have the beginnings of a theory of mind. But children also become increasingly proficient at understanding the more complex implications of a theory of mind, and this proficiency seems to appear between six and nine years of age.

Understanding emotion

Some studies have looked at how young children conceal emotion, since hiding your emotions from other people also involves having a theory of mind. A study by Cole in 1986 involved surreptitiously observing children of three to four years old when they received a very disappointing gift. (The researchers knew that they would find the gifts disappointing, because the children had previously been asked to rate a number of objects in order of their attractiveness.) There were two conditions in the study: some of the children were given the gift in the presence of observers, while others were given the gift on their own.

Cole found that, when other people were present, the children were careful to attempt to conceal their emotions from them. They tried to smile and say 'Thank you', even though they were disappointed. When they were alone, though, the children openly expressed their disappointment in their facial expressions. This implied that the children had understanding of how their emotional responses would feel to the giver. However, it is of course possible that the children were responding in this way simply because they had been thoroughly trained in good manners by their parents!

Harris *et al.*, in 1986, performed a study to investigate how children understand deception and emotion. In this case, the children were presented with stories in which the character would feel upset but try to look cheerful. For example, they used stories like: '*David wants to go outside, but he has a tummy ache. He knows that if he tells his Mum that he has a tummy ache, his Mum will say that he cannot go out. He tries to hide the way he feels, so that his Mum will let him go outside.*'

All the children understood what the boy's real feelings would be. But the four-year-olds found it difficult to describe what he would pretend to feel, and how other people would interpret it. The six-year-olds, on the other hand, were able to predict the boy's behaviour, and also realised that adults would be likely to be misled by it. So the four-year-olds had developed a theory of mind, in that they were able to understand one other person's point of view, but the six-year-olds were more sophisticated, and able to appreciate more than one person's point of view simultaneously.

Harris (1988) suggested that these studies imply that three- and four-year-olds are not particularly aware of the gap between real and apparent emotion, whereas six-year-olds are. When Harris *et al.* asked, for instance, about how David's mother might interpret David's behaviour they found that the six-year-olds, unlike the four-year-olds, realised that other people would be misled by David's behaviour, and believe that the feelings that he expressed showed what he really felt. This implies that six-year-olds are capable of taking two different viewpoints at the same time: what is actually going on and what is apparent to an onlooker. Again, this is evidence of an increasing sophistication in the child's developing theory of mind.

Autism

One of the things which children need to do as they grow older is to develop a clear sense of themselves, and also a sense of other people as independent, active agents. Developing a theory of mind is a crucial part of this. Quite early on, children learn about other people, and become able to predict how they are likely to respond to events. There are a few children, however, who never seem to become able to respond to other people in this kind of way. These children are known as **autistic children**.

Autism is a very rare condition – only between two and four children in ten thousand suffer from it. When it was first diagnosed (Kanner, 1943), four major symptoms of autism were identified, and these remain the basic criteria for diagnosis today. They are listed in Table 19.6. Kanner came to the conclusion that autistic children have an innate emotional difficulty, which means that they are unable to form the usual affective, emotional relationships with other people that normal children can do.

Interpreting emotional signals

However, Sigman *et al.* (1986) showed that autistic children do not necessarily fail to feel emotions. When they are briefly separated from their mother or caretaker, they act on her return in the same way that normal children do – they will move closer to her and touch her more, and appear to be anxious about her absence. It is not, then, that autistic children cannot feel emotion themselves. Instead, Harris (1988) suggested that

Table 19.6 Criteria for childhood autism

1 *Inability to form relationships with other people.*
   Autistic children do not appear to form attachments or relationships, and seem to remain cut off from other people.

2 *Lack of spontaneous play, especially pretend play.*
   Autistic children rarely initiate play, although they may respond to others at times. They do not appear to utilise imagination at all.

3 *Serious abnormalities in the development of language and communication.*
   Some autistic children never learn to speak, but simply echo what other people have said to them. Others learn to speak, but fail to learn to reverse pronouns, so they use the phrases that other people have said to them. This means that an autistic child will often refer to itself as 'you', and refer to its mother as 'I', because that's how its mother has spoken when talking to the child.

4 *An obsessive insistence on particular routines or interests.*
   Autistic children often seem to become very attached to systematic, routine methods of doing things, which often involve quite a lot of repetition, and they can become very distressed if these routines are interrupted.

Source: Adapted from Kanner, 1943

the problem lies in their inability to interpret emotional signals from other people. Autistic children may lack a theory of mind which enables them to understand and respond to others.

Hobson (1986) showed autistic children videotapes in which standard emotions such as happiness, anger, fear and sadness were shown in different ways: by facial expressions, by gesture, by sound and by portraying events which would be likely to bring on that emotion. The children would be shown a videotape, and would then be given, say, five drawings of facial expressions. They would be asked to pick out the drawing that fitted with the video that they had just seen. So, for instance, if they had seen somebody who was looking very happy, then they would be expected to pick out the drawing which showed somebody looking happy.

Hobson found that autistic children could perform this task quite easily if it involved matching the same condition. So if they had seen facial expressions on the videotape and were asked to pick out photographs of facial expressions, they had no difficulty matching the task. However, when they were asked to relate some other characteristic, like relating the sound of someone moaning and sighing to a picture of somebody looking unhappy, then the autistic children made a great many mistakes. In fact, they performed significantly worse than children with learning difficulties, or than normal children. Hobson argued that this inability to interpret other people's signals of emotion might be directly responsible for the other peculiar symptoms which autistic children show.

Autism and theory of mind

Other studies of autistic children have shown that they do indeed seem to lack a theory of mind. A study by Leslie and Frith (1988) involved situations in which an autistic child would be in a room with two experimenters. In full sight of the child, a coin would be placed in a hiding-place on the table. When one of the experimenters went out of the room, the coin would be moved – again in full sight of the child. Then the child would be asked, 'Where do you think So-and-so [the other experimenter] will look for the coin when they come back?'.

Leslie and Frith found that, unlike normal children, autistic children being tested in this way would name the place where the coin already was,

rather than the place where the coin had been when the experimenter left. In other words, they seemed to find it difficult to imagine what would be going on in the mind of the other person. Other children, however, had little difficulty with the task.

Baron-Cohen, Leslie and Frith (1986) asked autistic children to place sets of pictures in order. When they were asked to do this with simple sets involving a physical event, like a man kicking a boulder which ran down a hill and into some water, the children had no difficulty. But when the task involved intentions or understanding states of mind, like a set which showed a boy stealing a girl's teddy while her back was turned, and then her turning round to discover the loss, autistic children were unable to complete the task. Normal children, again, had no difficulty, but the autistic children did not seem able to understand what the story was about.

Beliefs and desires

Harris and Muncer (1988) investigated the understanding of beliefs and desires shown by both autistic and normal children. In some stories, two children, John and Mary, were described as wanting different things: John might want to go to the fair while Mary might want to go to the swimming-pool, for example. These were designed to investigate children's understandings of **desires**. In other stories, the two children expected different things to happen: Mary might expect that they were going to have an ice-cream while John expected a bar of chocolate. These were designed to investigate understanding of **beliefs**. At the end of the story, mother would announce what was going to happen. Each time, one of the children, but not the other, would have its desire or its belief confirmed.

The children were then asked to say which character had been right, and whether the character would have been pleased with the outcome. Since the autistic children, who averaged eleven years old, were of the same verbal intelligence level as normal five-year-olds, Harris and Muncer compared their understandings of these stories with a control group of normal five-year-old children. Despite being so much older, the autistic children performed much worse than the five-year-olds at both tasks. They were equally bad at judging beliefs and desires.

Understanding what other people are likely to

believe is an important part of everyday social interaction. Understanding other people's wishes is an important part of relating to others. Since autistic children seem to be unable to do either of these things, Harris (1988) proposed that lacking a theory of mind is a social-cognitive deficit – a problem with the child's understanding of social interaction – which lies at the heart of the autistic syndrome, and may give rise to all the other symptoms which have been observed.

What all of these studies about children's theories of mind show us is that the child's social understanding is much more sophisticated than earlier theorists had perceived. Perner (1988) argued that children are directly attuned to social situations: they are able to answer questions about mental states long before they can make moral judgements, and also before they can distinguish between different kinds of false beliefs. From a very early age, children have the social awareness which supports the later development of a theory of mind. The theory of mind itself appears sometime between age three and four; and that form of social understanding continues to become increasingly sophisticated and complex throughout childhood.

Moral development

Harris (1988) argued that the findings about children's social-cognitive development also have implications for understanding moral development. He argued that children's moral judgements are inextricably bound up with the way that children understand other people's emotions, and this in turn suggests that their social-cognitive understanding, in particular the theories of mind which they apply in their interactions with others, is an important facet of moral development.

Children's friendships

The friendships which children form are also an important background to their moral development. From the time that they start school, children form friendships with others of their own age. Youniss (1980) reported on a large-scale interview study with children of various ages. In these interviews, children were invited to tell stories about how a child might let another

child know that they liked them. The children in the stories were always the same age as the child who was being interviewed, and so it was assumed that these stories would reveal something about the child's own understanding of friendship.

Youniss found that several distinct themes emerged from the stories told by children in different age-groups. From about six to eight years old, the children's stories involved giving and sharing, especially valued possessions like toys or sweets. Such stories also involved 'playing nicely', and other such ideas which were clearly derived from adult interactions. When they were asked to suggest how they would indicate an even stronger degree of liking, these children tended to make suggestions which involved increasing the amount of the goods which were shared.

From about nine to eleven years of age, children were more likely to mention inequality between people, and talked of sharing to equalise the position. For example: 'In a class, if someone does not have a pencil or a book, you would give them one'. Their stories emphasised an awareness that friendship would involve levelling out inequality. From roughly twelve to fourteen years of age, the children talked more about giving psychological support to friends than about the physical exchange of toys, books or pencils. For children of this age-group, friendship might be shown by not laughing at someone who does something stupid; or by comforting someone, or giving them advice.

Youniss argued that the differences in these themes show that children develop an increasing awareness of the needs and demands of the individual. This is emphasised by the way that the descriptions shift from the physical to the psychological domain, and by the increasing recognition of inequality and discrepancy of opportunity. The descriptions given by the children also showed an increasing assertion of mutuality – a recognition that friendship is reciprocal, and involves giving and taking, rather than being a one-way affair – as the child grows older.

Selman (1980) also examined how children view friendship, this time using a Piagetian approach, by posing the children a friendship dilemma and asking children of different ages how they would resolve it. The dilemma was: '*Debby and Cathy have been best friends since they were five years old. A new girl, Jeanette, invites Cathy to the circus. Debby does not like Jeanette; she thinks she's a show-off. What should Cathy do?'*

Selman analysed the themes which emerged from children's answers. This analysis revealed a series of steps in their perceptions of friendship. The levels of friendship identified by Selman from children's responses to the problem are given in Table 19.7. As the table shows, Selman did not identify ages for these levels of friendship, emphasising that this depended on the child's own range of experiences and how much the child was able to reflect on them.

The studies of both Selman and Youniss show that there is an increasing sophistication in children's understandings of friendship as they grow older, particularly in terms of their awareness of the demands of the wider social context and social conventions. This growing understanding links with other aspects of their growing social awareness.

Piaget's theory of moral development

As we have seen, stage theories of development dominated psychological research for some time, and moral development was no exception. There are two major stage theories in this area of developmental psychology: one by Piaget, put forward in 1932, and the other by Kohlberg, in 1969. Each theory emphasised the idea of different stages in the development of the child's understanding of moral situations and questions.

As we saw earlier in this chapter, Piaget used clinical interview techniques to investigate how children of different ages understood their worlds. In investigating moral development, he used two main lines of questioning. One of them was to ask children to explain to him the rules for playing marbles. Since this is a game which passes from child to child and is very rarely taught by adults, Piaget believed that it could be useful in illustrating some of the underlying ways in which children understood concepts like 'fairness' or the application of rules.

The second technique which Piaget adopted, and one which has been used by many investigators since, was to set the children a problem, arising from a story or a situation, and ask them to decide what was the right thing in such a case. One of the stories which he used, for instance, was about a little girl who was playing with her mother's scissors and accidentally cut a

Table 19.7 The child's perceptions of friendship

Level 0
Friendships are seen as momentary, and based simply on geographical proximity.
Example:
If Cathy happens to be with Debby at the time, that is enough – there is no particular opinion about anyone else's feelings.

Level 1 One-way assistance
Children talk about one-way assistance and the longstanding relationship – strength is in reducing conflicts. There is an increasing recognition that the conflict has psychological effects, but a very simplistic view of how those effects can be sorted out.
Example:
Cathy might be expected to give a present to Debby to make up for her bad feelings about Cathy going to the circus with Jeanette.

Level 2 Two-way fair weather co-operation
The solution to the dilemma involves appealing to each person's responsibility. Children at this level often saw the different levels of intimacy in the various friendship-pairs as being very important, and talked about who was the closer friend. (Selman described this as typical of pre-adolescents.)
Example:
Cathy might be expected to present her own point of view to Debby, and try to get Debby to change her mind about the situation.

Level 3 Intimate, mutually shared relationship
Friendships at this level are seen as deeper and more enduring. Conflicts are not always necessarily seen as a bad thing, because they are seen as having the possibility of cementing or deepening the relationship. The child tends to reject superficial resolutions and to realise that long term relationships are of a very different order than short-term, transitory ones, and therefore require behaviour which will respect the long-term relationships more.
Example:
Children tended to perceive that the conflict is something to do with the relationship itself. For example, some saw it as to do with personality, and they saw one way of resolving the conflict as a change of personality. So a typical suggestion was that the new girl, Jeanette, should try to be less of a show-off.

Level 4 Autonomous interpersonal friendships
At this level, the child recognises that there are limits to mutuality, and that sometimes even a long-term relationship, important though it may be, might need to be abandoned in the quest for autonomy and personal choice.
Example:
The child recognises that just because Debby and Cathy have been friends since they were five years old does not necessarily mean that Cathy has the right to tell Debby what to do. The conflict will be seen as highlighting this, and providing an opportunity for Debby to go her own way.

hole in her dress. By varying the outcomes in the story, like the amount of damage and whether the child was represented as being disobedient (having been forbidden to play with the scissors), Piaget was able to identify what seemed to be some of the key factors in children's moral judgements.

In 1932, Piaget argued that the child's moral development passes through three main stages, reflecting the other types of cognitive development shown by the child. The stages which he identified are described in Table 19.8, and show how the child's understanding of the moral nature of the problems which Piaget was presenting grew increasingly sophisticated as its experience in the world developed.

Moral development as gradual change

It is important to remember, however, that although Piaget talked in terms of stages, he did not see moral development as occurring with a series of sudden discontinuities. Instead, he saw it as a gradual development, from a **heteronomous morality**, dependent on external rules or laws, to an **autonomous morality**, decided by the person applying their own, internalised principles of right and wrong. Like the stages of cognitive development Piaget saw this development in moral think-ing as an outcome of the gradual reduction of **egocentricity** in the child's thought.

The child would begin from a completely egocentric point of view, and only gradually accept that the outside world had an independent existence. In Piaget's view, the child's initial understanding of the outside world was therefore relatively limited, and tended to be expressed in terms of the application of external rules and principles, often applied quite rigidly. But as the child began to be able to decentre, and to see things from other people's points of view, it would begin to develop a more complex view of the process of moral reasoning, until eventually it could make autonomous decisions about particular situations.

We can see from this that Piaget's view does not fit particularly well with the research into the development of a theory of mind – at least in terms of the ages at which children are supposed to be able to undertake certain kinds of reasoning. One problem may be that Piaget expected children to be able to *explain* why they had made particular decisions. This is often a difficult task even for adults, particularly because being asked to explain something is often taken as having an implicit social meaning of being asked to justify it. This makes it more difficult, as the person then

---

Table 19.8 Piaget's stages of moral development

1	Moral realism	*Until the age of 7 or 8* During this stage, the child's judgements of morality entirely reflect what is allowed by adults. The child judges acts as being 'bad' if they are not permitted, and makes no attempt to see beyond the restriction to intentions underlying the behaviour, or to more general issues. When presented with a problem in which a child had to choose between getting a 'fair' outcome in a situation, or obeying its parents, these younger children argue that the morally correct thing to do is to obey the parents.
2	Egalitarianism	*From about 8 to 11 years* Children in this stage will opt for solutions which give the fairest, and most equal treatment to all participants. It is on this basis that an act is judged to be morally correct or incorrect. Egocentricity has reduced to the point where the child can see that other people's needs are important too, and the types of moral judgements which the child makes reflect this.
3	Equity	*From about 11 onwards* The child has now grown beyond simplistic egalitarian solutions, as its social under standing becomes more sophisticated and it begins to realise that not everybody's needs are the same. At this point, Piaget argued, the child will begin to develop the idea of **equity**: for example, that some people might need a larger share, in order to compensate for the fact that they did not all start off the same. Judgements of justice and moral correctness have to reflect this, to make sure that the solution which is developed in the end is appropriate.

Source: Adapted from Piaget, 1932

searches for an explanation which the other person will accept, and it may be for this reason that the younger children in Piaget's study tended to invoke external rules and principles as strongly as they did.

Kohlberg's theory of moral development

A second, more sophisticated stage theory of moral development was put forward by Kohlberg (1969). Like Piaget, Kohlberg developed a series of problems which he would put to children and ask them to decide whether the actions concerned were right or wrong. One of Kohlberg's most famous examples was an account of a man who broke into a chemist's shop to get essential medicines for his dying wife. The children would be told about the situation, and then asked to judge whether the man had been right or wrong to break into the shop. By asking children of different ages, Kohlberg identified three major stages of moral development, as Piaget had done. These stages are described in Table 19.9.

Like Piaget, Kohlberg argued that each of these stages represented a continual transition: the child's beliefs in the first part of the stage were different from its beliefs in the later part. In Kohlberg's view, the child progresses from a state in which moral judgements are entirely based on the need to avoid being punished, to a condition in which the individual becomes able to apply universal ethical concepts according to its own autonomous judgement. This, according to Kohlberg, represents the highest form of moral reasoning.

The socio-cognitive approach to moral development

Both Piaget's and Kohlberg's theories of moral development argued that the child gradually passes through these stages, almost as a natural consequence of its individual cognitive development. But in many respects they take little notice of the social context within which the child's experience is located, and do not appear to come to terms with the growing sophistication of the child's social cognition. More recent research into the child's developing social awareness has looked at how children develop moral ideas as a result of their increasingly sophisticated understanding of the social world.

Table 19.9 Kohlberg's stages of moral development

Stage 1 *The pre-moral stage*
The child identifies obedience to rules as the most important part of moral correctness.
Part 1 This is initially seen in terms of the need to avoid punishment: a child would argue that it was important not to be disobedient because otherwise you might get into trouble.
Part 2 As the child moves through the stage, the focus changes: rather than avoiding punishment for disobedience, it will identify the good things which happen as a result of obedience. Moral judgements are still based entirely on external proscriptions or commands, but the reasoning for why such commands should be obeyed becomes more sophisticated as the child progresses through the stage.

Stage 2 *Conventional morality*
At this time, moral judgements are made in terms of the social consensus: how it fits with what 'ought' to be done.
Part 1 In the early part of the stage, the emphasis is on intentionality: an act will be judged as good or bad depending on the intentions of the individual committing it.
Part 2 By the second part of this stage, the child has come to focus more on the general good, and an act is judged as good or bad in terms of the wider needs of society in general. If it was disruptive, or harmful to society in some way, then it would be judged as morally incorrect.

Stage 3 *Autonomous morality*
In this stage, the child is beginning to thread its way through the complexities of social convention and individual responsibility, and is gradually developing an internalised, autonomous form of moral reasoning.
Part 1 There is an increased awareness that social rules and laws may differ, and that some groups of people have different ideas of what is right than others. The child – or rather, adolescent – is also developing the idea that there may be more general underlying principles of right and wrong, and exploring how that works in terms of laws and rules. This often provokes an interest in how a rule which appears to be wrong can be changed, in accordance with the appropriate principles and procedures, so as to make it better.
Part 2 The second part of this stage continues this development, and goes on to identify abstract, universal principles of justice which may be applied generally, but which take into account differing conventions and pluralistic society.

Source: Adapted from Kohlberg, 1969

Understanding wrongness

Smetana (1981) studied how three- and four-year-olds understand 'wrongness'. The children were given descriptions of a child doing things wrong – putting toys away in the wrong place, taking another child's apple, not saying grace before a meal, hitting another child, etc. Some of the problems were **moral transgressions** – acts which broke a moral code, such as acts involving stealing or aggression. Others, though, were **conventional transgressions** – milder violations of rules about tidiness or similar conventions.

Smetana found that the children were very sensitive to this difference. They judged the moral violations as being much more serious than the conventional ones. So when they were judging hitting another child, they described it as being very bad, but when they were judging putting toys away in the wrong place, they described it as only a little bit bad. The children in Smetana's study also insisted that moral transgressions, like hitting another child or taking things, would be wrong whether there were rules about it or not. But in the case of minor deeds, like putting toys away in the wrong place, the children were more likely to say that these things were wrong only if there was a rule against them – if there was no rule, they would be all right. This implied that even at three and four years old, children have quite a sophisticated understanding of different kinds of transgression, or 'wrongness'.

The understanding of different types of wrongdoing seems to develop regardless of the personal experiences which the child has had. Smetana, Kelly and Twentyman (1984) investigated children who had experienced very different family interactions. One group had suffered from physical abuse, another group had suffered from neglect, and they had a control group of children who, as far as the researchers were aware, had not been maltreated. The researchers made sure that in other respects, like socio-economic background, the children's families were equivalent. But all three groups of children reached very similar conclusions about the seriousness of moral transgressions, and about the relatively minor nature of social convention transgressions. There was a very clear-cut consensus about what type of transgression was serious and what was not.

In a similar vein, Song, Smetana and Kim (1987) investigated the moral judgements of pre-school children in Korea and found very similar outcomes. The children all judged hitting another person to be wrong, regardless of whether or not it was forbidden by rules, whereas they would consider that a conventional transgression, such as eating with one's fingers, was all right unless there was an explicit rule against it.

Responses from adults

How do children know what acts are wrong and what acts are socially acceptable? One way of finding out is to examine how parents respond to what small children do, to see if this provides the child with a guide as to which acts are acceptable and which are not. One might expect, for instance, that children will be reprimanded for acts which are morally wrong, and not reprimanded for acts which are socially acceptable. But the picture is not always as simple as this, though, because parents also reprimand children for relatively minor misdemeanours.

Dunn and Munn (1987) kept notes about all the disputes which occurred either between children or between parents and children, during their ethological studies in family homes. They found that the disputes which emerged in the families were based on a number of different types of rules. Politeness rules, for instance, were based on things like saying 'Please' and 'Thank you' at appropriate times, while house rules were concerned with what you should do when and where. There were also rules about possession, sharing and turn-taking with siblings, and rules about disorderly or disruptive behaviour.

Dunn and Munn found that household disputes between parent and child tended to be about house rules and disorderly behaviour, whereas disputes between siblings tended to concentrate on rules about possession, turn-taking and sharing. These kinds of issues were likely to cause more serious problems, in the sense that when children were involved in them, they were more likely to end up in tears or very angry. But what was really noticeable from their findings was that the parental behaviour tended to be concerned with relatively minor kinds of events, or at least events which were not causing active personal distress.

Smetana (1984) observed young children playing at pre-schools, and found that although teachers reacted to both moral and conventional violations, if anything, they responded much more often to violations of convention than to moral transgressions. So it seems that children do not acquire their judgements about how serious an action is from their teachers' or parents' reactions.

Judging the seriousness of an action

So how does a child judge how serious an action is? Since research implied that parents reprimanded children more for conventional than moral transgressions, Siegel and Storey (1985) thought it possible that children acquire these values from external contacts, at school or pre-school. Siegel and Storey reasoned that children who had been exposed only to adults in the home would be less likely to differentiate between moral and conventional offences than those who had spent more time with other children. They looked at children who had attended pre-school for about nine months, whom they referred to as 'veterans', and compared them with children who were attending pre-school for the first time: 'novices'. The veterans, they argued, would have learned more about what causes distress and what does not from their contact with other children, so they would have learned to discriminate between serious actions and those which are less serious.

In fact, the researchers found no differences between the two groups of children in judging moral transgressions. Both groups, for example, would judge hitting another child as serious. But there were differences in how the two groups saw conventional transgressions like untidiness. The 'novices' saw those as also being serious, whereas the 'veterans' regarded them as minor or trivial. Siegel and Storey suggested that pre-school experience allows children to clarify the rules that they have learnt at home, and to learn which rules apply more generally in the wider social context and which are specific to the demands of their own homes.

In order to investigate this idea, Davidson, Turiel and Black (1983) asked children to justify the moral rules which they knew about. What they found was that children's justifications of why moral transgressions were wrong invariably mentioned the harm and distress that it would cause to others. When they were dealing with conventional rules, however, they did not mention harm or distress. In fact, children seemed to categorise an action differently if they learned that it would cause distress. Davidson et al. argued that it is this awareness of the consequences of actions which affects the judgements that children make. This seems to be yet another manifestation of the increasing sophistication of the child's social understanding as it grows older.

We can see, then, how research into moral development has changed its focus, shifting from stage models of development to enquiries into how the child understands its social world, and its own actions within that world. This fits with the shift in emphasis of research into the child's cognitive development, as well as with that in the study of achievement motivation, and also of language development, which we looked at in Chapter 4. Increasingly, we are becoming aware that the child develops its own, very sophisticated social understanding which it applies to the situations within which it finds itself.

Vygotsky's theories of child development

The modern picture of the child's cognitive development, then, is a far cry from the Piagetian image of the egocentric child, struggling to make cognitive sense of its world through problem-solving and rules. Modern psychological research tells us that when it comes to interpreting social situations, the child is infinitely more capable than it appears to be when presented with physical or abstract puzzles. Moreover, the knowledge and awareness which the child displays in 'real-life' social situations is exactly the kind of knowledge which will ultimately allow it to develop an understanding of the cultural and social rules which it requires to operate within its society.

Making sense of all this requires a perspective on child development which can take into account the interaction between the individual and society, and the way that the child's social life provides the basis for, and amplifies, its cognitive development. This type of perspective can be found in the work of the child psychologist Vygotsky, a Russian psychologist of the 1920s, whose work only became available to the West in the 1960s. In recent years, Vygotskyan perspectives have become extremely popular among modern researchers into child development.

Vygotsky's main emphasis was on the way that culture influences the course of human development. For many Western theorists, including Piaget, **organic maturation** was seen as the prime motive power for development. From Gesell onwards, psychologists had viewed the biological maturation of the child as determining what the child would develop and when, and the influence of culture and society was seen as something which would, at best, channel that development. For Vygotsky, the picture was very different.

As far as Vygotsky was concerned, organic maturation was a condition rather than a motive power for cultural development. Of course the child requires the biological maturity to be able to achieve certain levels of development; but in Vygotsky's model, it is the child's culture, expressed through **social interaction** and **language**, which provides the motivation for that development to happen. Both intellectual and socio-cognitive development require social interaction, social demands, and social stimulation if they are to take place. And the child, as we have seen, is powerfully predisposed to engage in that social interaction and to respond to those social demands.

The zone of proximal development

One of the central concepts in Vygotsky's model of development is that of the **zone of proximal development**. Essentially, the **ZPD**, as it is often known, is all about the difference between what the child can manage on its own, and what it can achieve when it has help and guidance from other people. Bruner, in his introduction to Vygotsky's book *Thought and Language*, referred to the way that social interaction provides the child with a kind of 'scaffolding', which supports the child as it develops cognitive skills and understanding.

As we learn from Judy Dunn's studies (and those of many other researchers), parents, siblings and others all interact socially with children, and children learn to respond appropriately in those interactions. This involves a considerable amount of learning: sometimes from people explaining things or stating rules; sometimes from others amplifying their statements or making games a little more elaborate; and sometimes from sanctions or rewards which communicate social expectations to the child. All of this is 'scaffolding' for the child's developing understanding. Without it, the child's cognitive development would be very much more limited.

What Vygotsky was saying, then, is that what the child achieves on its own, without social interaction, is essentially a basic, 'primitive' form of knowledge which allows it to survive in the material world, but not to understand general principles or abstract concepts. Organic

maturation alone cannot provide more than this. But there is also a wide area of potential development which is stimulated by social interaction and language: the zone of proximal development. The child's readiness to respond to other people also makes it ready to learn from that interaction. And learning from that interaction ultimately involves developing sophisticated social knowledge, cognitive skills, and abstract reasoning.

Vygotsky's theory allows us to make sense out of a great deal of modern developmental psychology – which is, of course, why modern developmental psychologists have shown so much interest in it! Using this model, we can understand modern language acquisition studies, which emphasise the importance of human social interaction; we can make sense of the accounts of feral or severely deprived children, reared without human contact, and see why those children were like they were when discovered; and we can understand why converting Piagetian studies into contexts which are socially meaningful for children can make so much difference to their cognitive abilities.

Piaget and Vygotsky approached child development from two very different sides. Piaget was a biologist, whose main concern was with organic maturation. His theory, like those of others with similar backgrounds, emphasised the maturational aspects of development but did not attribute much importance to socio-cultural factors. Vygotsky was a psychologist, with a wide-ranging literary and historical background; and his concern was with the social environment of the child, and its implications for the child's development. As a result, the two developed very different theories. Butterworth and Harris (1994) expressed some of those differences in terms of development at different ages (Table 19.10).

Although Vygotsky was aware of Piaget's work, he was also aware of the work of other psychologists of the time, such as Binet, who took a rather different approach to social influences. Moreover, he was working in a society with many different languages and cultures, and one which was in a period of revolutionary change. As a result, Vygotsky was able to explore an area which many developmental psychologists have found too complex to tackle directly. By converting those explorations into a specific theoretical model, Vygotsky has given us a valuable tool for

Table 19.10 A comparison between Piaget and Vygotsky

	Piaget *Sensorimotor*	**Vygotsky** *Affiliation*
Infancy 0–2 years		
Early childhood 2–7 years	Pre-operational	Play
Middle childhood 7–12 years	Concrete operational	Play
Adolescence 12–19 years	Formal operational	Peer group
Adulthood 19–55 years		Work
Early old age 55–70 years		Theorising

Source: Adapted from Butterworth and Harris, 1994

understanding the developing child – and its family and culture.

We have seen, then, that research into child psychology shows how social experience and cognitive development are increasingly being seen as more and more interlinked. The child's cognitive development is facilitated, amplified and even directed by its social understanding. In the next chapter, we will go on to look at research into the social development of the child: beginning with the formation of attachments and relationships, and going on to look at play, and the development of gender identity.

Key terms

autistic children Severely disturbed children who withdraw from reality and contact with others.

autonomous morality The third of Kohlberg's stages of moral development, in which the individual is making independent moral judgements.

clinical interview A technique used by Piaget in studying children, based on asking them questions in an informal setting.

concrete operational stage The third of Piaget's four stages of cognitive development, characterised by a need to relate problems to real circumstances or events.

conservation The ability to recognise that volume, number or mass do not change when presentation changes.

decentre To take another person's point of view.

egocentricity The assumption that the entire world centres about the self, and that nothing exists except that which impinges directly on the person.

equilibration The process by which schemata are developed, to take account of new information.

formal operational stage The fourth of Piaget's four stages of cognitive development, emphasising abstract thinking and logical reasoning.

heteronomous Subject to the laws of others.

object concept The idea that objects continue to exist even when you are not paying attention to them.

pre-operational stage The second of Piaget's four stages of cognitive development, characterised by an ability to focus on only one attribute of an object at a time, and an inability to 'decentre'.

retinal image The pattern of light which falls on the retina of the eye as an image of the external world.

sensorimotor stage The first of Piaget's four stages of cognitive devlopment, characterised by receptiveness to sensory information and the development of the very first schemata through explorations of movement in the environment.

zone of proximal development Vygotsky's concept of the extent to which the child can learn and develop skills, if aided and taught by others, preferably adults.

Summary

1 Infants are born with a number of reflexes, which may be precursors to future behaviour, or simply left over from foetal activity in the womb. Some developmental psychologists see infant reflexes as providing the basis for future psychological development.

2 Theories of infant cognition include cognition as resulting from operations on the environment, as distributed attention, as the fine-tuning of pre-adapted mechanisms and as skill acquisition.

3 Piaget's theory of cognitive development emphasised the formation of schemata through the results of operations on the environment. Different types of operations became possible as a result of the gradual reduction of egocentricity.

4 Empirical reappraisals of Piaget's work uncovered a number of methodological weaknesses, which may have resulted in a serious underestimation of children's cognitive abilities, and also of the child's developing social awareness.

5 Teasing, comforting and responding to distress are important aspects of forming relationships with other people. Children develop a theory of mind – an awareness that other people have minds of their own – which is an important feature of social interaction and relationships.

6 Autistic children may not develop a theory of mind. Research shows that they find it difficult to interpret social situations which require such knowledge, and that they interact very directly with their world without taking into account what other people may know or believe.

7 Stage theories of moral development were put forward by both Piaget and Kohlberg. More recent research, however, has emphasised the social-cognitive aspects of moral development rather than documenting stages in its development.

8 Vygotsky emphasised the zone of proximal development, which is concerned with the way that interactions between adults and children can enhance and extend the child's cognitive development.

Self-assessment questions

1 Can infants perceive depth?

2 Describe the basic processes involved in the formation of schemata.

3 Describe the characteristics of autistic behaviour.

Practice essay questions

1 What can experimental evidence tell us about infant cognition?

2 Critically evaluate Piaget's theory of cognitive development.

3 Compare stage theories of moral development with socio-cognitive approaches.

Test your knowledge of this chapter with our online quizzes and games at: http://www.psych.co.uk

Explore cognitive development and social awareness further at:

General
http://muextension.missouri.edu/xplor/hesguide/humanrel/ – Links to tutorials on all aspects of developmental psychology, particularly good for tips on how to promote social awareness and moral and motor development in children.

Autism
http://www.nacd.org/articles/autchild.html – In-depth article on the causes and consequences of autism.

Development theories
http://www.wpi.edu/~isg_501/nsushkin.html – Tutorials on some of the major theorists, including an outline of Piaget's work, with a bibliography.

Social development

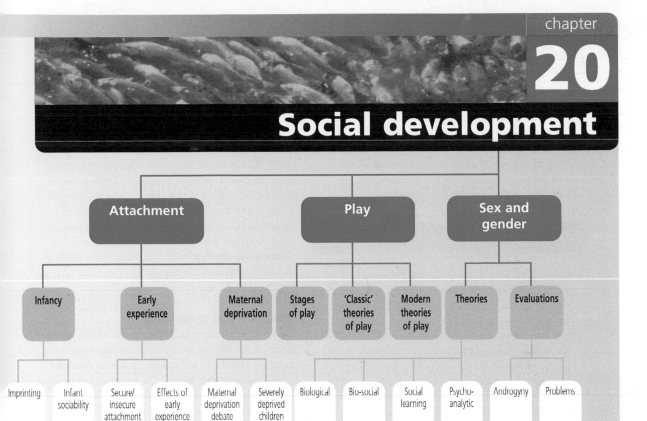

Attachment			Play			Sex and gender	
Infancy	Early experience	Maternal deprivation	Stages of play	'Classic' theories of play	Modern theories of play	Theories	Evaluations

Imprinting | Infant sociability | Secure/ insecure attachment | Effects of early experience | Maternal deprivation debate | Severely deprived children | Biological | Bio-social | Social learning | Psycho-analytic | Androgyny | Problems

Learning objectives

20.1. Imprinting and monotropy
a identify key concepts in early models of attachment
b describe a study of maternal deprivation
c evaluate evidence of maternal deprivation

20.2. Parent-infant interaction
a identify distinct features of infant sociability
b describe a study of infant sociability
c outline aspects of parenting behaviour

20.3. Secure and insecure attachment
a list the short-term response to separation
b identify aspects of infant behaviour in cases of insecurity
c describe underlying mechanisms in infant relationships

20.4. Recovery in later life
a descibe a study of recovery from disturbed childhood
b identify important features of recovery from disturbed childhood
c evaluate evidence for recovery from severe deprivation

20.5. Classifications of play
a list different types of play
b describe distinctive features of play
c evaluate definitions of play

20.6. Theories of play
a define terms relating to theories of play
b describe different theories of play
c evaluate theories of play

20.7. Theories of gender role
a define terms relating to the study of gender role
b describe the main theoretical approaches to gender role acquisition
c evaluate the concept of androgyny

20.8. Gender role research
a describe a cross-cultural study of gender role
b evaluate evidence for flexibility in gender role
c appraise gender role research using levels of explanation

In the past two chapters, we have seen how children develop their skills and understanding as they grow older. Much of this research has indicated how the young child's social awareness is constantly growing and developing. In this chapter, we will look at some different aspects of the child's social development, beginning with a look at the way that the child forms attachments, and then going on to look at play, and the development of gender role socialisation.

Attachment

One of the first stages of becoming socialised into human society comes about through the formation of emotional attachments to other people. Interest in the development of human relationships and attachments first began as a result of naturalistic investigations into attachments in some kinds of animals, which showed a phenomenon known as imprinting. We will be looking at **imprinting** research in more detail in Chapter 22, but since it influenced theories of attachment a great deal, it is worth looking more closely at it here.

Imprinting

Imprinting is a rapid, special form of learning, which is shown by some young animals shortly after birth. The young animal is born strongly prepared to receive a certain type of stimulus, which is normally provided by its parent – whether it is the mother or the father depends on which species of animal it is. The stimulus might be a visual image, a sound or a combination of several sensory stimuli, but typically it results in the young animal following around its parent (or whatever else is providing the stimulus). This produces a rapid attachment – the young animal becomes distressed if its parent is not nearby, and contented when it is.

The attachment resulting from imprinting is very sudden and very striking, and is most clearly shown in **precocial animals** – animals which can move about freely very soon after birth. By causing the young animal to develop a firm bond with its parent, imprinting means that the young animal is less likely to stray, because parting from the parent causes distress. This naturally maximises the young animal's chance of survival: young ducks which are following their mothers around are less vulnerable to predators or accidents than they would be if they were wandering off alone.

The discovery of imprinting in animals led researchers to ask whether a similar process was taking place with human infants, as they developed attachments with their parents or the people who were looking after them (usually referred to as their **caretakers** (or caregivers), which allows for the fact that it is not always their mothers). One of the first researchers to investigate this question was John Bowlby, who was commissioned by the World Health Organisation to investigate whether young children were likely to be harmed if they are separated from their mothers in the early years.

The theory of monotropy

In 1951, Bowlby produced a report which argued that infants form a special relationship with their mother, which is qualitatively different from the relationship which they form with any other kind of person. He described this as the process of **monotropy**. By a mechanism which he saw as very similar to imprinting, Bowlby considered that the young infant developed a firm attachment to its mother within the first six months of life, and that if this attachment or bond was then broken, either by the mother's death or by other kinds of factors, the infant would suffer serious consequences. This led to the maternal deprivation debate, which we will be looking at later in this chapter.

Infant sociability

As a result of Bowlby's theory of monotropy, the way in which attachments are formed in human infants rapidly became the subject of extensive psychological research. In 1964, a paper by Schaffer and Emerson produced new evidence for the attachment process. Rather than using clinical interviews and retrospective data from hospital and school records, as Bowlby had done, Schaffer and Emerson performed **ethological** observations of mothers with their young babies. Ethological studies are observations of behaviour in its natural environment – in this case, observations of how mothers and infants interacted in their own homes.

Schaffer and Emerson found that attachments did not automatically result from the mother simply being with the baby and looking after it, as

Bowlby had thought. Instead, they seemed to develop as a result of the quality of the **interaction** which the baby and mother engaged in. This meant that in some circumstances, an infant might form a relationship with someone who was not their primary caretaker (the person who looked after them most of the time). In some cases too the infants formed multiple attachments, developing relationships with more than one person. These findings seriously challenged Bowlby's idea of monotropy, since an important feature of it was that there could be only one special relationship for any one child.

Perhaps because of the political nature of the maternal deprivation debate, the findings by Schaffer and Emerson did not receive much attention in the popular media. They were, however, very influential in opening up a wide range of research. What Schaffer and Emerson's research had shown was that babies are **sociable.** They respond best to those people who interact with them, not just to the people who take care of their physical needs.

Evolutionary perspectives on attachment

Bowlby's theory of monotropy had been based on the idea that human infants develop their attachments through an imprinting process, like the one which Lorenz had observed in animals. But in human infants, Stratton (1983) pointed out, imprinting is not so appropriate as an explanation for how attachments develop. Stratton discussed how behaviours like imprinting do not just occur randomly. They are appropriate to the circumstances that the infant or young animal is likely to encounter after birth or hatching. Imprinting is a special case of a biologically pre-programmed sequence of behaviours, which results in a helpful outcome for the animal because it prevents the young from straying.

Human beings live in some very different environments, and behaviour which helps you survive, say, in the tropics might easily kill you if you were living in the Arctic. So inheriting a response which told you how to act in your physical environment would not be a good idea, even if the human infant was physically capable of independent action, which it is not. What is consistent in all human cultures, though, is that human infants are looked after by human beings. So infants are biologically pre-programmed to pay attention to their human caregivers.

Since they have such a long period of dependency, and because infants can do so much learning during that time, attachment can take place much more slowly than it does with imprinting. In human infants, the interactions which take place between parent and child combine to produce a gradual development of attachment between the infant and the caregiver. Stratton (1983) pointed out that the biologically pre-programmed behaviours which human infants show are not at all the same as the kind of pre-programmed behaviours shown by animals which imprint. Instead, they are behaviours which encourage the infant to interact with the people around them, and to learn the patterns and roles of that interaction.

The emphasis on the sociability of infants produced by Schaffer and Emerson's research was followed up by a number of investigations into how infant sociability happens. Using ethological as well as traditional observational techniques, psychologists began to observe how infants make contact with, or signal to, their parents, and also to identify the underlying sociability mechanisms which they use.

Contingencies and transactions

A study by Watson and Ramey in 1972 showed that infants are particularly sensitive to events which result from, or are contingent upon, their own actions. If an infant performs an act which has a direct consequence, which the infant then notices, it will tend to repeat that act – and derive a great deal of enjoyment from it, as anybody who has played the game of 'throw your teddy out of the cot and watch someone pick it up' with an infant will realise. Infants demonstrate an apparently endless capacity for enjoying repetitive games, in which some consequence is contingent on their actions. Stratton (1983) suggested that it is through **contingencies** of this kind that infants manage to gain some sense of control over their environment. It helps the infant to develop a sense of self-as-agent, and this forms a basis for the child to learn from its actions and experience.

Another important concept in looking at the development of infant sociability which Stratton identified is the idea of **transactions**. These are exchanges of behaviour in which what one person does depends on what the other does. The interactions which occur between infant and caregiver are transactions in the sense that they form whole sequences of behaviour, where each individual's action is contingent on what the other person does. So, for instance, the mother talks to the baby, which means that the baby responds by gurgling, which means that the mother will talk again, the baby will respond again, and so on. The whole pattern of interaction forms a transaction: an exchange between mother and baby. These transactions are understood mutually between mother and infant as social exchanges, and are also believed to form the basis of later social relationships.

Crying

Wolff, in 1969, showed how infant crying is a far more sophisticated signalling system than had previously been supposed. From recordings, interviews and observations, Wolff showed that babies can produce at least three different types of cry, and that parents, or at any rate most mothers, can usually recognise what the cry means (see Table 20.1). Since crying is the infant's long-range signalling system, this increases the infant's chances of survival. The action which needs taking if a baby is hungry is quite different from that which is needed if the baby is in pain, or angry, and having different signals helps the infant to attract the right kind of assistance from its caretaker.

Smiling

In 1954, Ahrens had shown that infants seemed to have an inbuilt tendency to smile at a relatively simple shape which resembled a human face from as early as one month. As the child grew older,

however, it required a more sophisticated stimulus to elicit the smiling. The stimulus needed to have greater detail, and to resemble a human face more accurately, as the child grew older (see Table 20.2). But what was interesting in Ahrens's study was that infants did not smile at similar stimuli which had no similarity to faces. Effectively, the human infant seems to be pre-programmed to smile at something which resembles a human face. As its perceptual abilities become more complex, it requires a correspondingly lifelike stimulus.

Perceiving faces

Ahrens's observations led to a considerable amount of research into the way that infants perceive and respond to human faces. As we saw in Chapter 19, Fantz, in 1961 showed that babies seem to have an automatic preference for stimuli which resemble faces, as opposed to stimuli which are simply complex patterns of black and white. Given a choice, Fantz showed, infants will look for a longer time at stimuli which resemble human faces than they will at other images.

In 1965, Haynes, White and Held showed that newborn infants' eyes have a fairly set focus at about 19 cm. This is the same as the approximate distance of the mother's eyes from the child's face when the child is breast feeding. Infants often watch their mothers' faces while they are breast feeding, and Haynes *et al.* suggested that this fixed focus is precisely that which will encourage the

---

Table 20.1 Patterns and meaning in infant crying

The hunger cry	This begins unevenly, and reasonably quietly, but gradually increases in volume and becomes more regular in rhythm.
The pain cry	This begins with a sudden, very loud cry, followed by a silence, and then a set of short, gasping breaths, before the sequence is repeated again.
The anger cry	This has a loud cry, followed by a pause and an inward breath, followed by another loud cry, in cycles.

Source: Adapted from Wolff, 1969

Table 20.2 Stimuli required to elicit smiling from infants

Age of infant	Details
1 month	An oval shape with two dots in the position of the eyes.
2–3 months	Some additional contour detail around the eyes such as indicating nose or eyebrows is needed, but the mouth is still not necessary.
4 months	All the usual features of eyes, nose and mouth must be present to elicit smiling.
5 months	The image must contain all the usual features, but must also be shaded so as to appear three-dimensional.

Source: Adapted from Ahrens, 1954

child to learn to recognise its mother most easily, and to respond to her face.

To describe an ability as 'pre-programmed' invites the question of how it comes about. One likely explanation is that there are special cells within the visual cortex of the infant which are most sensitive when they receive certain kinds of stimuli. This fits with the work of Hubel and Wiesel (see Chapter 12), which showed that complex and hyper-complex cells in the visual cortex will respond to specific patterns or shapes. Haith (1980) suggested that babies act in such a way as to provide themselves with maximal stimulation from these nerve cells, because they find that these give them the clearest experience. This is what encourages the infant to look at the mother and to make eye-contact with her.

In turn, looking at the mother and making eye-contact is a useful **survival skill**, since the mother will find eye-contact rewarding, and will therefore be more inclined to take care of the baby. The smiling response which the infant also shows, as identified by Ahrens, will also strengthen the inclination of the mother to take care of the infant. Very young babies are extremely dependent on their human caretakers, so a mechanism of this kind maximises the infant's chances of survival.

Interacting with people

Smiling also enhances the likelihood that the child and the caregiver will engage in transactions, and these transactions often develop into quite complex exchanges. Stern (1977) videotaped parents and children interacting, and observed that they often tend to **imitate** each other's facial expressions. Also, as the baby gains control over its vocal apparatus, it will imitate sounds. In this way, Stern argued, the baby acquires the basic physical abilities needed for future social interaction: it learns to interact with its mother by producing appropriate facial expressions and appropriate sounds in an appropriate social context.

In 1974, Newson argued that the reason why human babies become human beings is because adults tend to treat them as if they already are. Adults often attribute meaningful intentions to babies: they talk to babies as if they understand what is going on, and they interpret babies' actions as if they were deliberate responses to their questions. As a result of this, the child learns appropriate styles of interacting, and develops its social understanding and its capacity for deliberate action.

Snow (1979) showed how mothers often have 'conversations' with their young infants. During these conversations, they pause, as if the child were answering them, and they interpret gestures and actions from the baby as if they were verbal responses. A mother will often have a whole 'conversation' with a very young child. Snow argued that it is this type of interaction with the child which sensitises the child to important features of social behaviour, such as the way that interaction involves taking turns in conversations. It also, Snow argued, establishes the basis for later language development.

A number of other researchers, such as Trevarthen (1969), suggested that mothers are not just acting one-sidedly when they have a conversation with an infant. Babies, in their turn, respond to the actions of their mothers. Using slowed-down videotape, Trevarthen showed that infant behaviour can be seen as consisting of a series of small episodes, which form meaningful, complete gestures. This behaviour might include, for instance, a fleeting smile or a stretch, or something which produces a co-ordinated response; and infants produce them most often during conversations or interactive sequences with the mother.

Newson used Trevarthen's evidence to suggest that human infants are biologically pre-programmed to produce signals which are designed to attract the mother's attention. Perceiving these signals, the mother then ascribes social significance to them, and proceeds to treat the young child as if it were a sophisticated human being. This in turn encourages the infant to acquire more sophisticated skills, and also serves to convey to the young child meaningful social dimensions for interpreting the world.

Fathering

Newson (1974) also argued that mothering skills are not in any way innate or instinctive. Instead, they are skills which are acquired through practice in communicating with that particular individual baby. As you get to know a baby, and see it as having human sensibilities and a 'personality', you also become more able to detect and understand that baby's responses. Babies, on their part, learn very fast, and respond more to those people who are sensitive to their actions. They are also, as Schaffer and Emerson showed, more likely to form attachments with people who respond sensitively to them. The implication here is that interacting with babies is a learned skill; and that fathers can acquire these skills just as mothers do, given motivation and opportunity.

It has long been known that fathers and infants often develop very positive attachments. The early study by Schaffer and Emerson (1964) showed that infants could develop multiple attachments – several of the infants in their study were just as strongly attached to their fathers as to their mothers. Some, too, had developed an attachment to the father but not to the mother, even though it was the mother who was looking after them most of the time. In such cases, always, it was the father who responded most sensitively to the child.

Parke and O'Leary (1976) observed mothers and fathers in a maternity ward. What they found was that, contrary to the popular stereotypes, fathers tended to be very keen on interacting with their infants, and were neither inept nor uninterested in what their newborn children were like. Instead, they were often as sensitive in interacting with their infants as the mothers were.

Parke and Sawin (1980) observed mothers and fathers each feeding their three-month-old infants. They also found that the fathers responded just as sensitively to infant cues as the mothers did, responding in terms of both social interaction/conversational or gestural – and by adjusting the pace of feeding according to the signals being put out by the child. However, they did find that fathers tended to hand the responsibility for caretaking to their partners rather than adopting that responsibility themselves. The skills that fathers had in parenting became apparent only when they were asked to demonstrate how they would go about interacting with their children for the investigators: much of the time they did not seem to exercise these skills at home.

Differences in interaction styles

Yogman *et al.* (1977) suggested that there may be some differences between how mothers and fathers interact with their infants, particularly concerning the timing of their interactions. They videotaped fathers in face-to-face interaction with infants ranging from two to 25 weeks old, and found that, while fathers provide both physical and social stimulation for the infant, they do so in bursts, intermixed with quieter periods, whereas mothers tend to be very much more rhythmic

and continuous in their approach to the child. While either style of interaction seems to be just as good for the child, it may be that this difference in pacing is why some mothers feel unsure about whether the fathers are actually interacting appropriately with their infants. But, of course, these are generalisations: there are fathers who interact rhythmically and continuously, just as there are mothers who interact more intermittently with their children.

Lamb, in 1977, conducted observations of fathers playing with infants aged seven to thirteen months, and found that they generally tend to engage in play that is quite physically stimulating, and that also tends to be more unpredictable or idiosyncratic. This type of play generally produces positive responses from the infants, with the consequence that, in general, infants interacted more positively with fathers than they did to the play approaches made by their mothers. Lamb also found that mothers were less likely to hold infants during the routine business of looking after them, whereas fathers were more likely to hold them. In Lamb's study, it was noticeable that infants responded more positively to being held by their fathers than they did to being held by their mothers.

Working mothers

Interestingly, a study by Pedersen, Cain and Zaslow (1982) showed that there seems to be a difference in this when both parents are employed. In this study, the researchers found that mothers who are in full-time jobs tend to stimulate their infants when playing with them more than mothers who did not go out to work. They also tend to be far more active in interaction with their infants than their husbands are. Fathers with partners who did not go out to work played with their infants more, whereas those with partners who did go out to work played with their infants less. In both types of family, though, the mothers retained the overall responsibility for child care.

The implication of this finding is interesting, because it suggests that the quality of parental play may have something to do with contact with the baby being less routine. It may be that mothers who are away from their children during the day appreciate the company of their children more, and so are likely to engage in very intensive interactions. Those who are with them all the time may be more likely to value peaceful times, and therefore to avoid stimulating their children into excited behaviour. But, of course, this depends on the individual people involved.

Secure and insecure attachment

As we have seen from research into parent-infant interaction, the infant is born with a number of abilities which serve to structure and organise the relationships between itself and other people. In turn, other people may be more or less sensitive to the signals that the child is putting out; and, as Schaffer and Emerson showed, the infant will develop its main attachments with the people who are most sensitive.

Typically, human attachments appear at round about the seventh month: before that, infants generally show little distress at parting from a parent (although the parent may become distressed at such a parting, which may affect the child). The child will express recognition and pleasure at interacting with a less familiar person much earlier but at about seven months or so, this changes: if the parent leaves, the child may cry or otherwise indicate that it is unhappy about the separation. Research into parent-infant interaction suggests that although the full attachment does not appear until that age, the basis for the attachment has been established steadily throughout the preceding months, through the interaction which the infant has experienced with its caretakers.

Nash (1978) argued that individual development proceeds most efficiently if the environment fosters the inherent tendencies of the individual, rather than requiring adaptations from that individual. In other words, an infant will be more able to grow and to develop in its own way and at its own pace if the social and physical environment fosters and encourages its own inherent tendencies. So if the infant is with someone who is sensitive to its signals and responds to them, it is in a better position to go on and develop its social abilities. As a principle, we could argue that this also applies to the development of talents in older children and in adults. Every human being is uniquely individual, and we all do best in an environment which fosters and encourages our particular and special talents.

Short-term effects of separation

One of the findings which emerged from research into attachment and parent-infant interaction was that there are different types of attachment, and that these can be influenced by parental behaviour as well as by the immediate circumstances and situations. In 1980, Bowlby described the short-term effects which occur when a child is separated from the person with whom it has formed its main attachment. (Bowlby referred to this as the mother, but as we have seen, this may not always be the case.) By studying children who had to go into hospital, or whose parent had needed to go away for some reason, Bowlby identified a three-stage sequence in what became known as the **separation response.** This is shown in Table 20.3.

How a given child actually proceeds through these three stages will be affected both by their past experience and by the external situation. When the parent or other attachment figure is reunited with the child after a period of separation, the child's response may be quite complex. It often includes a period of anger and rejection, as the child goes through an emotional readjustment at the return, and expresses its feelings of anger at having been abandoned. This may also be followed by a period in which the child is more 'clingy'

Table 20.3 Responses to short term separation

1	*Protest*	This stage involves clear signs of distress, particularly crying. The child is upset and agitated, sometimes seeking for the attachment figure, and calling.
2	*Despair*	When the protest does not result in the return of the attachment figure, the child enters a period of despair, in which its behaviour expresses misery and grief, and the child often becomes listless and apathetic in response to its immediate surroundings.
3	*Detachment*	The despair phase is often followed by a period of detachment, in which the child appears to have adapted to the situation and seems to be content and not particularly interested in the return of the attachment figure.

Source: Adapted from Bowlby, 1980

than usual, as it expresses its need for reassurance that the parent is still available.

Needs and security

Bowlby suggested that infants will seek the amount of parental contact which they need to feel secure. First, they **appraise** their needs, then they compare these with the current situation. If they find they need more contact than they have at the moment, they will move to be closer to the mother. But if the child finds that the amount of proximity it needs is equal to, or less than, the amount it currently has, then it will feel able to explore its environment, and interact with other people. So a child which feels secure in the proximity of its parent will also feel able to explore and interact with others.

The appraisal that the child makes of its current circumstances also depends on its past experiences. An infant which has had experience of insecurity – such as its parent by disappearing suddenly, for several days – will often need more proximity than one which has always experienced continuity. This might explain why insecure infants often cling to their mothers or caretakers, and may be reluctant to explore new situations. Other infants, who feel secure in the proximity, or in the certainty of predictable return, of their parental figures, will feel more confident and more able to explore.

Ainsworth *et al.* (1978) developed a set of eight episodes illustrating different degrees of separation, which they referred to as the **strange-situation technique**. These episodes are described in Table 20.4. They then used these situations in a series of studies which involved observing how mothers and infants interacted. Ainsworth *et al.* found that they could categorise the relationships which they observed between mothers and their infants as being of three kinds: avoidant, secure and ambivalent (see Table 20.5).

Ainsworth (1979) also showed that how children act in strange situations relates to a number of other variables to do with parent-infant interaction. For instance, they found that the mothers of securely attached infants tend to be more sensitive and more responsive to their babies, even during the first few months of their infant's life. They also tend to hold their infants more carefully than mothers of infants whose relationships had been classified as either avoidant or ambivalent.

A study by Main, Tomasini and Tolan (1979) found that mothers of infants with avoidant relationships showed more rejection and aversion

---

Table 20.4 Episodes involved in Ainsworth's 'strange situation' assessment

No.	Duration	Description of episode
1	30s	Observer introduces mother and baby to experimental room, and leaves.
2	3m	Mother remains passive while baby explores.
3	3m	Stranger enters, is silent for one minute, converses with mother for one minute, approaches baby for one minute. Mother leaves unobtrusively at end of three minutes.
4	3m *	Stranger responds to baby, playing, soothing, etc., as appropriate.
5	3m **	Mother re-enters, comforts baby, then settles baby in play again, then leaves, saying, 'Bye bye' to baby.
6	3m *	Baby alone.
7	3m *	Stranger enters room and interacts with baby.
8	3m	Mother returns, greets baby and picks it up. Stranger leaves unobtrusively.

* or less if the baby is too distressed
** or more if it is needed

Table 20.5 Behaviours associated with different relationships

	Avoidant	Secure	Ambivalent
Proximity-seeking	low	high	high
Contact-maintaining	low (if distressed)	high	high
Proximity-avoiding	high	low	low
Contact resisting	low	low	high
Crying (pre-separation)	low	low	occasionally
Crying (separation)	high or low	high or low	high
Crying (reunion)	low	low	moderate/high

to bodily contact than mothers of infants with ambivalent relationships. They also showed more controlled anger, and sometimes acted with their children in a manner which implied that although they were adjusting to the situation of having young children to look after, they were only doing it because they had to.

Ainsworth's three categories of attachment relationships proved to be useful in structuring research on how mothers and infants develop their attachments. However, Main and Weston (1981) argued that there are still a number of infants who do not fit the Ainsworth categories, although most of them do. Consequently, they argued that to place too much emphasis on these three types of attachments can be a bit misleading – it is important to bear in mind that the range of possible types of attachments varies a great deal. For example, some infants show behaviour appropriate to secure attachments in some situations, avoidant behaviour in other situations and ambivalent behaviour in others. Any one child can show a mixture of different kinds of responses, so we need to be careful not to categorise relationships too strictly.

Systems in infant behaviour

Bowlby (1973) highlighted four major systems in infant behaviour, which are described in Table 20.6. According to Bowlby, children use all four of these systems in their interactions with their environment and the people around them, but the powerful activation of any one of these at any one time tends to inhibit the rest. So, for example, the powerful activation of the attachment system will inhibit exploration and affiliation. The powerful triggering of the fear/wariness system will inhibit the affiliation system and exploration, and other similar behaviours.

This model, however, assumes that fear and wariness would be likely to inhibit attachment behaviour, and there is some suggestion from Ainsworth's studies that this may not be the case. Judging from what we know about the infant's earliest abilities, and from the importance of interaction for the young child, attachment seems to be a primary mechanism in human infants, overriding almost everything else.

Bowlby's early argument was that natural selection would tend to favour protective mothers; but there is also some evidence that many mothers actively promote their child's independence, and natural selection would tend to favour these parents too, in that such children would tend to be well equipped to deal with new or unforeseen experiences which they encounter. Drawing on animal studies of attachment as well as studies of human infants and parents (see Box 20.1), Hinde (1983) argued that the important requirement, in evolutionary terms, is that the child emerges from its relationships adjusted to the society in which it lives.

The effects of early experience

Ainsworth's research largely centred on the effects of temporary, short-term separation of the parent and the infant. But what happens if the separation lasts for a year or more, or if it is permanent, or if the child has never been able to form an attachment with another person at all? Bowlby suggested that the first five years of life are crucial to the child's later development. This represents what is known as the **continuity hypothesis:** the idea that a damaged infancy leads to a damaged childhood, which in turn will lead to a damaged adulthood.

The continuity hypothesis was first proposed by Freud, who argued that events even in the child's very first year of life could leave lasting effects on adult personality. It has been a recurrent theme of psychoanalytic approaches to understanding child development ever since. But some studies of early experience have brought into question whether

Table 20.6 Infant behaviour systems

The attachment system	This co-ordinates proximity-seeking, in order to ensure protection or care of the individual.
The fear/wariness system	This co-ordinates behaviour which involves the avoidance of people or events that could conceivably turn out to be dangerous to the individual.
The affiliation system	This controls behaviour such as playful social interaction with other people.
The exploration system	This controls the investigation of the non-social environment.

Source: Adapted from Bowlby, 1976

Box 20.1 An ideal mothering style?

A considerable amount of research has centred on Bowlby's idea that extremely protective behaviour on the part of the mother is an evolutionarily advantageous mechanism for the individual. Bowlby considered that a mechanism which promoted dependency of the infant upon the mother would be one which would make the infant more likely to survive.

There are some limitations to this idea, though. Hinde (1983) points out that, within the evolutionary context, there is also evidence that there may be evolutionary advantages for mothers to promote independence on the part of their infant, and also that some mothers may actively promote their infant's independence before the infant itself feels ready for it.

A study by Altman in 1980 showed that baboon mothers who were more restrictive and protective of their infants had infants which survived better in the early months of their lives, but were less likely to survive if orphaned.

Mothers who were less protective (there is a great deal of individual difference between baboons in a single troop) produced youngsters which could survive more readily on their own.

So we can see that there are arguments both for and against promoting intensive dependency. Hinde also emphasised that natural selection arguments are unlikely to ever produce just one ideal mothering style (such as promoting dependency). Within any society, the mothering techniques which will produce the 'best' infants will vary according to a number of factors: the position in the family, the social and material situation (like the food supply and whether there is competition for it), whether the child is male or female, and so on. In human infants of course, cultural differences also affect mothering strategies and their outcome, and what is considered desirable for the infant.

this really is the case – whether it is truly impossible to repair the damage which can be caused by harmful early experiences.

Institutional child-rearing

One way in which a young child may be deprived of the opportunity to form personal attachments through interaction is by its having been brought up in an institution, such as an orphanage or a children's home. Research into attachment has generally concentrated on the type of attachment which develops between parents and children in a family environment. But some studies have investigated the effects of institutional child-rearing, and the attachments which the children develop.

Tizard and Hodges (1978) studied children who had been born to unmarried mothers and placed in institutions before they were four months old. Although the institutions in which the children were cared for were good ones, the system of caretaking was designed to make sure that children did not become unduly attached to any one member of staff. Like many other such institutions, there was also a very high turnover of staff, so a child who was in the institution for, say, four years might have as many as 50 different caretakers during that time.

The children were studied on three occasions: first while they were still infants, and then at the ages of four and eight years old. They fell into four groups. One group consisted of children who had remained in institutions for the whole time. The second consisted of children who had been in the institutions and then been adopted. The third group consisted of children from the institutions who were returned to their natural mothers. The researchers also included a fourth control group of children from intact families with similar socio-economic backgrounds. For the most part, the groups were very similar with respect to age and socio-economic status, although the adoptive parents tended to be older and more middle class than the parents in all the other categories.

When the children were observed at four years of age, they showed a number of signs of their experience in institutions. Those who had been in the institution but were now in adopted or foster homes tended to be indiscriminately and excessively friendly towards strangers. The children who were still in the institution showed noticeable attention-seeking, and tended to be very 'clingy' towards adults. They also showed disturbed peer interactions – they were argumentative and quarrelsome with the other children. Despite their tendency to cling to adults, the children who had remained in the institutions showed only very shallow attachments to their caretakers. Of the 26 children in this sample, two of them showed no preference between different caretakers at all, and many of those who showed preferences were not at all disturbed when their 'special' person was off-duty or had left. Out of the group of 26, eighteen of them were said not to care very deeply about anyone.

When Tizard and Hodges looked at the same children at the age of eight, the ex-institutionalised children who had been restored to their own mothers seemed to be experiencing behaviour difficulties. Two-thirds of the sample had received professional help for behaviour problems, in comparison with less than one-third of the institutionalised and control group children, and less than one-tenth of the adopted children. They also tended to be far less attached to their mothers, and their mothers also said that they did not feel deeply for those children.

Only about half of the mothers of restored children and of the caretakers of institutionalised children said that they played with their children during the week. This contrasted sharply with the other two groups: 90% of the adoptive parents and 72% of the working-class parents said that they played with their children on weekdays. The children's teachers rated all the ex-institutionalised children, even the adopted ones, as having significantly more behaviour problems in school than the control group, but the children who had been restored to their natural mothers showed the most severe behaviour disturbances. However, it is always possible that the teachers knew about the children's individual case histories, which might have affected this last finding through the work ings of **self-fulfilling prophecies.**

Effects of disrupted homes

There is also some evidence that disruption in the family home during childhood can affect how parents interact with their children, which may influence the attachments which the children develop. A study by Frommer and O'Shea in 1973 found that mothers who had experienced highly stressful or disruptive homes during their childhood tended to be either abusive or very disruptive parents. But Rutter (1979) found that women who had been brought up in institutions, but who then married stable partners and had satisfactory marriages were likely to be better parents.

It seems unlikely that there is a simple relationship between parents' childhood experiences and their own parental style. Instead, parental style seems to depend on a number of factors. According to Rutter (1979) these include past factors, such as the existence of parental marital conflict and parent-child separation or rejection operating together, as well as current factors, such as the person's socio-economic situation, and psychological factors to do with the individual's own circumstances, such as their feelings of being in control (see Chapter 13).

The maternal deprivation debate

One consequence of Bowlby's view of monotropy – the idea that there was a qualitative difference between an infant's relationship with its mother and all its other relationships – was the implication that severe disturbance would result if this relationship was broken or damaged.

Part of Bowlby's evidence for this came from his study of 44 juvenile delinquents. These were adolescents who had been caught stealing, and who had come to a child guidance clinic for treatment. As a psychoanalyst, Bowlby believed it possible that the roots of anti-social behaviour might lie in an early disruption of the bond between mother and infant, and his investigations showed that seventeen out of the 44 delinquents had been separated from their mothers for some period before the age of five. Comparisons which he made with similar children who were emotionally disturbed but did not steal, showed that they were less likely to have been separated from their mothers. Bowlby concluded that **maternal deprivation** – being deprived of one's mother during the first five years of life – could seriously affect the child's social development, producing juvenile delinquency.

Among his sample, there were two children who were particularly delinquent, and who appeared to have very little in the way of social conscience. This syndrome was described by Bowlby as **affectionless psychopathy,** and he argued that this was the extreme consequence of maternal deprivation. If the child lacked a special relationship with the mother, it would grow up unable to form relationships with other people. Without relationships with other people, the child would be unlikely to conform to social norms in the usual way. Therefore, it would fail to develop a social conscience and would become a psychopath, acting out of self-interest without thought for others.

Other evidence cited by Bowlby (1951) did indeed seem to suggest that such harm could result, and moreover that it could last until adult life. Bowlby cited a study by Spitz (1945), who described how the depression a child felt at losing a parent could last until adulthood; and a study by Goldfarb (1943), showing how children who had lived in institutions for their first three years of life were less rule-abiding, less sociable, and less intelligent (as measured by IQ tests) than a comparable group who had been fostered.

Other evidence for 'maternal deprivation' accrued rapidly. Patton and Gardner (1963) introduced the concept of **deprivation dwarfism,** showing that deprived and neglected children were often undersized by comparison with others. And further study by Bowlby (1956) of 60 children who spent a period in a sanatorium before the age of four showed lower school achievement in later childhood, and a tendency to over-exciteability and daydreaming.

Political aspects of the maternal deprivation debate

Bowlby's work rapidly assumed a political dimension, as his arguments were seized by the post-war pressure groups, which argued that women should stay at home and look after children full-time. The reason why this had become a sensitive political issue was because at this time there were a large number of returning servicemen, and it was considered necessary that jobs should be freed for them. Since a large number of women had worked during the war and carried on working afterwards, some people argued that they should return to full-time child-care in the home, and free their jobs for the returning servicemen.

The political nature of this debate meant that Bowlby's work received a large amount of publicity, which was inevitably sensationalised. However, Bowlby himself had included, in his book *Child Care and the Growth of Love* (Bowlby, 1951), a table of the kinds of circumstances which were likely to damage children. These were mostly extreme circumstances, like 'war', 'famine', 'death', and so on, but he did include in this list 'mother working full-time', and it was this phrase which

fuelled the debate, until the term 'maternal deprivation' became a catch-phrase in society.

It was argued that mothers who went out to work were depriving their children of the care and attention which they needed, and thereby causing them lasting psychological damage. Other researchers also began to investigate circumstances which seemed to result in children being psychologically damaged. These were almost inevitably attributed to maternal deprivation, although later research, summarised by Rutter (1981), showed that in fact the evidence for these arguments was not always particularly sound. When the subject was examined closely, alternative explanations and mechanisms emerged.

Problems with the concept of maternal deprivation

It did seem clear that serious psychological disturbance could result from disruptive early experiences. In particular, such disturbances seemed to interfere with the capacity to form meaningful relationships with others, even at times resulting in Bowlby's 'affectionless psychopathy'. There were, however, three issues which were less clear. The first of these was whether these consequences really arose from disruption of the mother-infant bond. Rutter (1981) showed that other factors were always involved as well, such as physical and emotional neglect in general, the lack of any positive relationships with others, and/or the more generalised deprivation of institutional life. To attribute it strictly to disturbed mother-infant attachments was to go beyond the data.

The second debatable issue was whether such outcomes were permanent. As we have seen, Tizard and Hodges (1978) showed that late-adopted children could still develop positive relationships with others despite early deprivation. Similarly, Clarke and Clarke (1976) presented a number of case-studies showing how careful therapy could ameliorate the effects of even very severe privation.

The third debatable question was whether only the first few years of life mattered. As a psychoanalyst, Bowlby had assumed that these were the formative years of personality, and had therefore expected lasting effects from early deprivation. But Rutter (1979) showed that the delinquency attributed to early experience by Bowlby was more often attributable to immediate stress in the family home; and Power et al. (1974) showed that recidivism was linked to continually stressful home circumstances, whereas single offences were more closely associated with temporary disturbance.

The conclusion, then, was that although early experience could certainly cause damage, there was little evidence for such damage being irreversible, and even less for maternal deprivation in itself being the cause. That maternal deprivation had become such an issue may be attributed more to the socio-political context of the debate.

We can see, then, that the study of early experience involves many different variables. One problem is that such studies often have to rely on reports about the children from other people, like teachers or institutional staff, and this makes them very susceptible to self-fulfilling prophecies based on the staff member's own expectations of what is likely. Studies of this kind cannot really assess the **quality of care** within the family either, so it is difficult to identify just why the situations produced the outcomes that they did.

Studies of late adoption

The idea that early experience produces inevitable consequences for later life exerted a powerful influence on adoption policies. The usual belief of adoption agencies is that children need to be adopted during the first five years of life if they are to have any chance of making good the damage of early deprivation – a belief which stems directly from the psychological emphasis on the importance of early experience by researchers such as Bowlby. As a result of this, adoption agencies are generally reluctant to place older children for adoption, believing that such placements are likely to be unsuccessful: that it will be too late for the child to develop a sincere attachment to the adoptive parents.

Despite this belief, some people do manage to adopt older children. Kadushin (1976) studied 91 families who had adopted children who were more than five years old, and found that in by far the majority of cases these adoptions had been highly successful. Using measures of parental satisfaction derived from transcripts of interviews with the parents, Kadushin found that between 82% and 87% of these cases showed highly satisfactory outcomes: the children had developed close relationships with their adoptive parents, and showed little signs of their earlier experience of neglect or abuse. Only two out of the 91 adoptive placements had failed, with the child subsequently

leaving the adoptive home: in all the other cases the children and their families were still together when the study was conducted, six years after the initial placement.

Other studies of late-adopted children had found similar effects, although these had often been neglected in the face of maternal deprivation theory. For example, in 1945, Roe reported on a study of 36 young adults who had been fostered after the age of five, because of continuing neglect, abuse or chronic alcoholism on the part of their parents. Roe found that most of these children had established positive and successful lives in terms of establishing friendships, participation in their community and forming close personal relationships. Many of them were happily married. In fact, there were no differences between them and a control group of adults from ordinary homes which had been disturbed during their childhoods by the death or serious illness of a parent.

In a follow-up study of twenty children who had been removed from home in early childhood and placed in institutional care, Maas (1963) also reported that they showed no evidence, twenty years later, of any damaging outcomes. Studies of this kind directly challenge Bowlby's emphasis on the importance of early attachment in the first five years of life. Instead, they suggest that children are very much more resilient than such theories would allow, and that early damage may be overcome – but only if the child's later environment provides the emotional and social context for this to happen. For some children, the damaging circumstances remain present throughout later childhood and young adulthood, and so the children do not have the opportunity to recover from what has happened to them.

Kadushin (1976) suggested that one explanation for how children manage to recover is that they have the potential for a much wider range of behaviours than early studies suggested. Being in a different type of environment emphasises different facets of the personality and de-emphasises those which were needed during the stressful period. The social context, for example, which for most adoptive children emphasises social acceptability and participation in society, is in sharp contrast to the social context experienced by a neglected child, who may suffer social rejection by others as a result of the home background. These factors help to promote a more positive self-image for the child, and encourage the development of new attachments and positive social awareness.

Severely deprived children

The idea that, given the right environment, children can recover from even quite severe early experiences, is supported by studies of severely deprived children. Throughout the centuries, there have been numerous legends of **feral children** – children who were found wild, appearing never to have had any social contact – beginning with Romulus and Remus, the legendary founders of early Rome, who were said to have been reared by a she-wolf. Unlike Romulus and Remus, however, most of the individuals described in the accounts were thought never to have become really civilised. The idea was that such children were untreatable, because their early experience had produced permanent damage. However, studies of severely deprived children in this century suggest that perhaps these cases were not irreversible, although, of course, we cannot know the full details of those early cases.

The Czechoslovak twins

Koluchova (1976a) reported the discovery of a pair of seven-year-old twins in what was then Czechoslovakia. These twins had been severely neglected throughout their childhood. Their mother died shortly after their birth, they spent the next eleven months in an institution, and then returned to live with their father and his second wife. For the rest of the time, as far as is known, they experienced severe neglect and physical abuse, mostly from their stepmother, although the father was once seen beating them with a rubber hose until they lay flat on the ground, unable to move.

When they were discovered, it was found that they had spent much of their time locked in a small closet or in the cellar of the house. They had no toys except for a handful of building bricks and no social contact with other people. When they were found they could barely walk, they had no language, although they sometimes tried to imitate adult speech, and they were also (not surprisingly) very timid and mistrustful of other people. They did not play spontaneously and were unable to understand pictures, never having seen any before.

After some time in institutional care, which

helped to remedy some of the worst physical symptoms of their neglect, the twins were fostered with two middle-aged sisters, who understood their situation and could provide them with the right kind of loving care and stimulation. As they adapted to their new life they began to progress rapidly, and soon developed abilities and skills which they had lacked before. At school and with other children they were cheerful and popular, showing no sign of their previous experiences; their IQs changed from somewhere between 40 and 50 when they were first discovered, to 100 and 101 by the time they were fourteen; and they developed warm and loving relationships with their foster-mother and her sister.

L.H.

Some psychologists argued that the twins' recovery was possible only because they had been able to maintain an emotional bond with one another, which had kept alive their capacity for attachments. But Koluchova (1976b) attributed their recovery more to the relationship with the foster-mother. In support of this was another case of a severely deprived child, L.H., who was eventually fostered in the same family as the twins. This child had experienced severe neglect and vicious treatment from infancy, and was withdrawn from her home at the age of four. Since she showed agitated and aggressive behaviour in care, she was placed in a psychiatric institution, where she remained for a couple of years, until the twins' foster-mother heard about her and offered to attempt fostering.

Despite having been diagnosed as mentally defective and unlikely to recover, the girl made considerable progress in her new environment. Her IQ improved considerably, as did her social stability. She formed close relationships with the others in the family (the two sisters and the twins), she learned to read and write well, and also showed a musical talent which had not previously been suspected.

However, L.H. also suffered some lapses of memory and attention, which were thought to have resulted from brain damage caused by her early neglect, and she did not seem to recover as completely from her emotional traumas as the twins had. So it is possible that the twins' relationships with one another had ameliorated the effects of their experiences a little, although it does not seem to have been the determining feature in whether any recovery would take place or not.

Anna

Davis (1947) described two children who had also suffered severe neglect. One of them, Anna, was found at the age of six years old, having spent her first few months being shifted around unsuccessfully for adoption (she was a sickly baby, which meant that adoptive parents could not be found), before finally returning home to her mother. Since she was illegitimate and her grandfather, who owned the house, objected to her presence, she was kept in an attic and had little food except cow's milk, and no social contact. When she was discovered, she could not speak, walk or feed herself, and was totally apathetic.

After three years in care, however, she made considerable progress. She learned to speak, at least to the standard of a two and a half year-old (we looked at language development in Chapter 4); was physically capable and able to play with other children; and was able to dress and take care of herself. However, she remained sickly, and died at the age of about ten. One of the problems with Anna's case, though, is that little was known of her father, or even who he was, so it was impossible to rule out the possibility that she might have inherited some mental disability.

Isabelle

Davis (1947) also reported the study of another child, discovered at roughly the same time as Anna. Isabelle was discovered at the age of six and a half. She was illegitimate, and her mother was a deaf-mute, so the child had no experience of spoken language. She had been kept in a darkened room and had virtually no social contact with anyone. Consequently, she could not speak, did not recognise objects or people and acted almost like an infant. The impression she gave when she was discovered was that she was unable to learn, and would be unlikely ever to recover from her early deprivation.

Isabelle was given a great deal of prolonged and expert attention, as well as warmth and loving care. Her recovery was dramatic: a year and a half after her discovery she gave the impression to a visiting psychologist of being a bright, happy little girl. She did well at school, and was cheerful and popular with schoolmates. Davis observed that, far from being irreparably damaging, these years of arrested development seemed to have resulted in an accelerated recovery: she learned much more quickly than other children of her age, and quickly made up the skills which she had lacked before.

Like studies of late adoptions, studies of severely deprived children suggest that the first five years of life may not be as all-important as was once thought. Although it is clear that children can be seriously damaged by experiences at this time, it also seems that, if they have the right kind of later environment and suitable expert treatment, children do seem to be able to recover to some extent, even from deeply traumatic experiences. Such children can become able to form warm and close relationships with other people, as well as developing the skills and abilities they need for later life. But that does not mean that such recovery is easy, or that it will just happen without expert help and the provision of warm, loving relationships from others.

Play

Everyone knows that children play, and most of us believe that play helps children to develop. But what do we mean when we talk of play? How can we define it? This is not as easy as it might appear: trying to define play raises all sorts of questions, such as how much we should include. Should we include hobbies? Should we include adults who enjoy going down to the pub for a game of darts? Or should we limit our studies strictly to what children do? When we look at what children do, what we mean by play may seem very clear, but when we try to define it we can easily become confused about what counts as play and what does not.

Some psychologists have tried to define play by identifying distinctive features, which are not shared by other kinds of behaviour. Rubin, Fein and Vandenberg (1983) argued that an important feature of play is that it is **intrinsically motivated** – we do it because we feel like doing it. It comes from within us as an inclination, rather than as a response to some kind of need or external compulsion.

Rubin et al. also described playing behaviour in children as being distinguished by the child paying attention to the **means** rather than the **ends** of the behaviour – it is attending to how it is doing things, rather than what it is doing. So, for example, if a child is conducting a doll's tea party, the focus of that child's attention is on how it goes about the activity of setting out cups and saucers, and pouring out the tea. This would be different from an adult's perception of a tea party, which might focus more on conversation, or what there is to eat or drink.

Hutt (1970) argued that, during play, exploration is **organism-centred.** In other words, a child will approach a new object along the lines of 'What can I do with this?' rather than 'What can this do?' – the child is concerned with how it can interact with and manipulate the object, rather than the properties of the object itself.

Garvey (1977) argued that the behaviours which children show during play tend to be **non-literal** behaviours – they are behaviours which involve acting out, or pretending, rather than actually doing. Although these behaviours are related to real ones – a child might pretend to eat, and that behaviour is related to eating behaviour – they are not really the same thing at all. Another characteristic of play which Garvey identified, although not all researchers would agree with her, is that play requires the participant to be actively engaged – to be actively doing something. In this case, Garvey would distinguish play from other non-purposeful activities, such as daydreaming, although she recognises that they may sometimes be connected with one another.

Garvey (1977) also argued that play is free from externally imposed rules. In saying this, Garvey was drawing a strong distinction between children's 'natural' play and organised games, but there are some problems with this idea. For instance, there may be a connection between the kinds of play that young children engage in, and the more structured games which they play as they get older or in adulthood. Early play may form a developmental basis for these later kinds of play, so if we define one as play and the other as not play, where do we draw the line? Another criticism of this differentiation is that socio-dramatic play, where the child acts out different social roles that it has encountered, seems to have very distinct rules which children obey in terms of how it is carried out.

So looking at play in terms of its distinctive features is not as simple as it might appear. As we can see, there are some characteristics which all play seems to share, and other characteristics which are not necessarily shared by all kinds of play. Most people, for instance, would probably agree with the idea that play is intrinsically motivated – that people play for the sake of enjoyment rather than because of externally imposed reasons. But whether we can distinguish between play and organised games is a much more debatable question.

Stages of play

A number of researchers have attempted to categorise different types of play. In one early theory Spencer (1873), argued that the child goes through a series of developmental stages in terms of the type of play it engages in at different ages. The first of these is where the child's play largely consists of superfluous activity of the sensory and motor apparatus. At this time, the child is developing skills – enjoying looking at things, tracking things, catching things, perhaps experimenting with sensorimotor activity.

Once the child has developed its physical skills, it then moves on to a type of play which Spencer described as 'artistic' or 'aesthetic' play. In this, the child begins to create and manipulate things: it may engage in modelling, drawing, or building towers with bricks and similar activities. From there, according to Spencer, the child passes on to a higher level of co-ordinated play, such as play which involves structured games with rules. Spencer also identified mimicry as a fourth type of play: children imitate adults and animals as part of their play. Interestingly enough, this set of categories of play suggested by Spencer in 1873 is almost directly parallel to the categories of play described by Piaget in 1962.

Piaget's model of play

As we saw in the last chapter, Piaget argued that children pass through four stages of cognitive development: the sensorimotor, pre-operational, concrete operational and formal operational stages. He also argued that the type of play which children engage in is different during these cognitive stages. During the sensorimotor period, Piaget argued, the child engages in **mastery play** – play which will allow it to gain control of its environment, by learning to co-ordinate its muscles and actions and to interpret sensory information. This reflects the major developmental task of the sensorimotor stage, which is to gain control over the body and its actions with respect to the outside world.

During the pre-operational stage, Piaget argued,

the child is more likely to engage in **symbolic play** – such as make-believe and pretend games. Again, this reflects the young child's developing but incomplete understanding of the wider world, as is found in the pre-operational stage. As the child moves into the concrete operational stage, in which adult-type thinking begins to emerge but only within a highly specified and concrete context, the child starts to engage in **rule-bound play**. In this, it is beginning to see rules as constructs which can generate enjoyable activities: acting within a specified structure allows the child to obtain more enjoyment from competition or achievement.

Categories of social play

In 1932, Parten distinguished between five different types of social play, which are described in Table 20.7. Parten identified a gradual shift through these different types of play as the child grows older, although there is a great deal of overlap – they are not separate and distinct stages. Nonetheless, solitary play and onlooker play seem to be more usual for two-year-olds, whereas associative play and co-operative play are more usually observed in five-year-olds.

A number of other such categorisations of play

have been identified by researchers. However, Cohen (1987) argued that categorisations of play, although widely accepted by researchers, are extremely limited in their usefulness. One of the problems with them is their implication that the child engages in only one type of behaviour at a time, whereas most children will mix many different forms of play in the course of a typical day or week.

Perhaps the most serious problem of this type of approach to understanding play, Cohen argued, comes from the data which psychologists have used to develop the categories in the first place. Typically, these categories have been developed from observations of children in playgroups or nursery schools. But Cohen pointed out that this is an extremely artificial type of data. In reality, most of the play which young children actually engage in takes place within the family, not in playgroups or schools. This makes a big difference, because it means that most play consists of children of different ages playing together, and also of children playing with adults. The type of interaction and what is expected of the child are therefore likely to be entirely different.

In the family, it is rare for a child to have another child of its own age-group to play with, and so the types of play that the child engages in tend to be very much more sophisticated than the types of play which happen in conventional play groups, particularly if it is playing with older brothers or sisters. Even if it is playing with younger siblings, the child will be tailoring its play to their abilities, so again the type of play will be different from that which it might engage in with others of the same age. Both of these situations require a much higher level of social understanding from the child.

Cohen argued that unless play is actually studied in the family context a very unrealistic and quite limited perception of children's abilities emerges. Many of the classifications of different types of play developed by researchers rest on this limited and artificial set of observations. So simply developing typologies may not actually help us to understand very much about how play develops.

Table 20.7 Types of social play	
1 Solitary play	The child plays on its own and is largely unaware of other children.
2 Onlooker play	The child watches other children and may react to what they are doing, but does not actually play with them.
3 Parallel play	Two children perform the same sort of actions with similar toys, and are often side by side, but not actually sharing – they are acting largely independently.
4 Associative play	Two or more children interact, and they may share activities or speak to each other, but it is still not entirely for mutual gain.
5 Co-operative play	The child plays directly with others, taking turns, or engaging in complementary roles.

Source: Adapted from Parten, 1932

'Classic' theories of play

There have been a number of different attempts to explain what is going on when children play. When we look at these explanations, we can divide them roughly into the 'classic' theories of play and more recent approaches. Effectively, there were four classic theories of play: the surplus energy theory, the relaxation theory, the recapitulation theory and the play as practice model. We will look at these before going on to look at some of the more recent explanations for play which have been put forward by psychologists.

Play as surplus energy

The **surplus energy theory** of play was first put forward by Spencer in 1873. Spencer argued that play results from surplus energy being produced by the organism. As nervous tissues and cells are repaired, they revitalise the organism, generating energy. Once basic survival needs have been met, there is often energy left over, and this surplus energy makes the organism active, spilling over into play.

According to Spencer, animals which are higher in the **phylogenetic scale** (see Chapter 22) and therefore closer to human beings, produce more energy than lower ones. Because of this, they are more likely to play. The kind of play which is produced is an unconscious product of the animal's natural instincts. So according to this theory, rough-and-tumble play is an instinctive kind of play which allows the young animal or child to develop its survival skills.

There have been several criticisms of the surplus energy theory of play. One is that it assumes that there is a kind of 'tank' of energy that fills up and overflows in the young child or animal, and that this surplus is continually filling up and continually having to be drained away. This type of model is known as a **hydraulic energy model** of functioning, and is similar to Lorenz's theory of inherited behaviour, which we will be looking at in Chapter 22, and his theory of aggression, which we looked at in Chapter 17. Unfortunately, however, there is little empirical support for this type of model, in that no evidence has yet been found to support the idea that either energy or aggression is constantly building up and constantly needing to be drained away in activity. If anything, the opposite applies, in that those who are active appear to generate more energy than those who are less so.

A second criticism of the surplus energy theory of play concerns observations of the behaviour of children. In 1968, Miller observed that children will play to exhaustion – they will tire themselves

out completely – but then if some kind of novel or arousing stimulus is introduced, they will resume play – in other words, they will generate more activity. If play were simply a product of surplus energy, then once children had tired themselves out, they would be unlikely to begin to play again.

A third criticism of the surplus energy theory of play is that draining off surplus energy is not likely to provide a young animal with an evolutionary advantage. Although its basic survival needs have already been met, there are still unexpected dangers which a young animal can encounter. During play, an animal or child is relaxed, so it tends not to be very watchful of danger. This reduced vigilance can make the young animal very vulnerable, so it is unlikely to help the young of the species to survive.

A fourth criticism of the surplus energy theory of play is that it is a circular argument, in terms of whether energy is considered to be 'surplus' or not. Energy is judged as surplus only if it is expended on playing; but if the behaviour which the young animal or child is showing is 'serious', then the energy which it is using is not considered to be surplus. So we have no set way of telling whether play involves surplus energy or not, since if we accept the theory, any energy expended on play is by definition surplus. The argument is circular, so it becomes impossible either to refute or to support this theory.

Play as relaxation

The second classic theory of play is known as the **relaxation theory.** Patrick (1916) suggested that both children's play and adult recreational activities serve a restorative function, allowing us to replenish our energies. He argued that modern working conditions demand concentrated attention and co-ordination from the worker, which is a relatively new and sophisticated type of activity. Human beings, he argued, are not adapted evolutionarily to this type of activity, and therefore need to obtain relief from their fatigue. They do this by reverting back to the kinds of activities which they have engaged in in their evolutionary past – activities such as hunting, fishing, and so on.

Patrick argued that evidence for this idea could be seen in the way that children like very ancient, basic types of musical instruments – rattles, drums and horns – which are the types of instruments that have been used by human societies from their earliest days. It also, Patrick argued, showed in the way that children tend to be preoccupied with animals – children's toys are often very full of animal imagery. Both of these, Patrick argued, were a regression back to a more primitive past. Engaging in primitive activities restores the individual by allowing people to engage in evolutionarily familiar activities.

There are criticisms of this model too. First, it does not explain why people who are engaged in physical work play. If what Patrick claims were really the case, then we would expect only people engaged in modern types of occupations to have recreational activities, but there is very little evidence for this. It also cannot explain why modern children often spend a great deal of time engaging in high-technology activities: computer games, for example, can hardly be seen as a regression to a primaeval past. But Patrick was writing before computer games existed.

Ellis (1973) argued that the theory was invalid on the grounds that children actually play far more than adults. If play is to be seen as a way of recuperating from work, then adults should play more than children, since children do not engage in the same kind of formal work as adults do. Patrick explained this observation as being that it is 'natural' or 'instinctive' for children to play, but Ellis pointed out that this is not an adequate explanation, since it still leaves unanswered the question of why children play.

The third criticism of the relaxation theory of play is its dependence on the idea of some kind of **genetic memory**. Although, as we saw in Chapter 7, this idea formed an important part of Jung's analytical psychology, there is little modern evidence for it. In fact it is almost impossible to gather data on this systematically, apart from anecdotal evidence. So for many modern psychologists, invoking a genetic memory is not really regarded as being an adequate explanation for why some thing happens.

Play as recapitulation

A third theory of play is known as the **recapitulation theory**. This is based on the old, and now largely discredited, biological idea that the development of the individual in some way retraces the development of the species – that ontogeny recapitulates phylogeny (we came across this idea when discussing Piaget's theory, in Chapter 19). According to this view, children's play represents the evolutionary history of our species, so each individual child re-lives the species' development as it passes through childhood.

Hall (1920), who was the main proponent of the recapitulation theory of play, argued that children's play passes through five different stages, in which the origins of the human race can be traced. These are listed in Table 20.8. Hall also saw play as serving a **cathartic** role, allowing the child to release its unconscious 'primitive' instincts, and so let it move on to develop higher forms of behaviour. This, he argued, explained why young children play hunting games like tag, or why they enjoy climbing and swinging, whereas adults do not. According to Hall, the adults have got these 'primitive' urges out of their systems, and progressed to more advanced forms of play.

There are many criticisms of the recapitulation theory. One is that it is very selective in terms of the 'occupations' of earlier races, and it reflects a distinctly patronising approach to non-technological societies. Given what we know about the extent and depth of civilisation and culture in such societies, to regard them as 'primitive' is not exactly realistic. Most non-technological societies, for example, have highly developed verbal cultures,

Table 20.8 Evolutionary stages of play	
One of the earliest theories of play reflects the racist social assumptions of its time. Hall (1920) argued that the child's play passed through five stages, reflecting the evolution of the human species.	
1 *The 'animal' stage*	Children engage in climbing and swinging, and a great deal of motor-co-ordinating behaviour.
2 *The 'savage' stage*	The child's activities concern games such as hunting or 'tag' or 'hide-and-seek.'
3 *The 'nomad' stage*	Keeping pets was considered by Hall to reflect societies which moved around to pasture herds of animals.
4 *The 'agricultural' or 'patriarchal' stage*	The child's play concerns activities like digging in sand or looking after dolls, said to reflect an early agricultural culture.
5 *The 'tribal' stage*	The emphasis is on team games and mutual co-operation.
Source: Adapted from Hall, 1920	

and show a great deal more sophistication in the way of verbal record-keeping and social awareness than is apparent in more technologically based societies.

A second criticism of the theory is its assumption that children will pass through different kinds of play in a regular sequence. Yet there does not appear to be any evidence for such a sequence in the way that most children play. Children engage in different types of play at the same age – they may keep pets at the same time as engaging in hunting-games or tag, or they may have pets and dolls simultaneously.

A third criticism of the recapitulation theory of play is that, like the relaxation theory, Hall's model does not explain why children also play with highly technological, modern materials such as bicycles and toy cars, or, more recently, computer games. Although it may sound interesting at first hearing, the recapitulation theory of play has as many weak points as most of the other versions of recapitulation theory which were around at the time and are now no longer regarded as particularly plausible.

Play as practice

The fourth classic theory of play is known as the **practice theory.** First put forward by Groos in 1901, this theory has received support from several modern researchers. According to this model, childhood exists mainly in order to allow children to play. That play, in turn, serves a purpose by allowing young organisms – animals or children – to practise the kinds of skills which they will need in later life. Groos argued that during play children are far more interested in the processes of behaviour than in the products – an idea similar to the one put forward by Rubin *et al.* which we looked at earlier. Groos believed that this encourages the development of skills, as children learn how to perform necessary actions and activities through practice.

Groos also argued that complex animals, which play more, also have longer periods of immaturity, and this means that they can spend more time in learning. As we will see in Chapter 22, as we move higher up the phylogenetic scale, looking at animals which are closer to human beings, we find that the young animal tends to have a longer period of dependency on its parents. This suggests that the young animal does not have to be born with a repertoire of already-established inherited

behaviours to deal with the external world. Instead, it spends its time observing and imitating its caretakers, and learning skills through playing.

This view is supported by the work of J.S. Bruner (1972), who argued that the practice obtained through play allows us to perfect skills which will be required in later life. We looked at Bruner's model of skill learning in Chapter 18, and at his ideas of the development of mental representation in Chapter 5. These both form part of Bruner's approach to how children develop, cognitively and physically, by practising and developing physical and mental skills.

The practice theory of play was also supported by the social biologist Stephen J. Gould (1981), who argued that **neoteny** (being born at a 'premature' stage of development, and so having to spend additional time learning) is an important survival mechanism for the human being. Human infants are born at an earlier stage of development than are other animals, and have to spend a longer period dependent on their caretakers. This means that they can learn more about their surroundings, and are therefore better equipped to adapt to a wide range of environments.

By playing, young human beings use their period of dependency to learn the very wide range of skills and behaviours which will help them to survive as adults. Other animals, such as young monkeys, are much more capable when they are infants, and become independent more quickly. This means that they spend less time learning, and can adapt successfully to a relatively smaller range of environments – although, of course, the abilities of monkeys to learn new behaviours is far greater than the ability of many other animals.

Groos also distinguished between two different types of play: **experimental play**, which leads to the development of both physical and mental self-control; and **socionomic play**, which forms the foundation for the later development of interpersonal relationships. Both types of play change with development, and these changes are described in Table 20.9. According to Groos, each type of experimental play contributes to the development of self-awareness and self-control, while socionomic play eventually forms the basis for the child's understanding of the social world, and of interpersonal relationships.

Ellis (1973) criticised the practice theory of play on the grounds that seeing play as acquiring skills

Table 20.9 Experimental and socionomic play

Experimental play	This begins as **sensorimotor play**, in which the child explores its basic physical abilities. It later develops into **constructive play**, where the child is constructing or assembling different kinds of objects or ideas. Constructive play in turn forms the basis for **games with rules**, which Groos believed involved higher, or more sophisticated, mental capacity.
Socionomic play	This includes most types of play with other people. The most common examples of this type of play are **'rough-and-tumble' play, imitation**, and all kinds of **dramatic play** including social and family 'pretend' play.

for the future implies that there is some kind of implicit knowledge of which skills the person is likely to need. He also criticised it on the grounds that it is overdependent on the concept of instinct. But these criticisms may be countered by arguing that this type of play simply reflects the acquisition of a range of abilities – for instance, the strengthening of muscular co-ordination – which help the child to realise its genetic potential, rather than being developments which are aimed at specific potential goals.

Modern theories of play

The four classic theories of play formed the basis of most psychological research into play until about the 1970s. But, more recently, a number of other approaches to play have been influential in guiding research in the area.

Play as the expression of underlying conflicts

One of these approaches to the understanding of play has been to see children's play as an expression of the child's underlying psychological conflicts and complexes. This is known as the psychodynamic approach to play, and is based on the theories of Freud and the other psychoanalytic theorists, in particular Melanie Klein and Anna Freud. As we saw in Chapter 7, Freud outlined a number of psycho-sexual stages through which the child passes in childhood. Psychological conflicts, such as the Oedipal conflict, can arise as part of this process and need to be resolved. Other forms of threat to the developing ego also need to be resolved by the child.

This model led in particular to the development of a system for helping highly disturbed children, known as **play therapy**. According to the psychodynamic model, play provides a vehicle by which the young child can act out its conflicts and disturbances, and thereby explore alternatives and ways of resolving them. In play therapy, the therapist provides a secure environment within which this can happen, and observes the child as it plays in order to obtain a better awareness of the child's disturbance.

Axline (1971) reported the case of a highly disturbed child, Dibs, who was able to resolve his conflicts with respect to his family by expressing them and acting them out through playing with dolls. At one point, the child expressed his hostility towards his father by burying the doll which represented him face down in the sandpit. The child's behaviour as he played not only allowed the therapist to gain insight into the child's problems, but also allowed the child to express the hidden anger and distress which he could not express at home.

Play as stimulus-seeking

Another approach to understanding play is that it is a form of **stimulus-seeking**, based on physiological arousal (Ellis, 1973). Arousal is a physiologically excited state (see Chapter 13) which can have considerable effects on psychological and physical activity. Novel circumstances have been shown to stimulate arousal in individuals, as do high levels of activity, and the idea behind this theory of play is that children are drawn towards situations which will produce high arousal. Consequently, they are likely to engage in physical play and to explore new environments and phenomena. According to this model, play is therefore seen as some kind of stimulus-seeking behaviour, in which children look for forms of stimulation which will produce a state of physiological arousal.

There are a few problems with this theory, particularly since it does not explain the quieter forms of play. When a child is playing with a jigsaw, or taking care of its dolls, or acting out a tea party, it is just as much 'playing' as when it is running around and shouting. Assuming that only excitable or boisterous forms of play are the ones which count seems to be taking a rather limited approach.

Play as metacommunication

One of the features of play which seems to be missing from most of the theories is the idea that play is 'not really serious'. Yet most of us would recognise this as an essential element of play, if not its most important feature. In 1955, Bateson proposed that play should be seen as **meta-communication** – a higher-order type of communication, which sets a framework for the understanding of what is subsequently communicated. He argued that what play does is to provide a context or a **frame,** which we can use to interpret a number of different types of communications.

Children are aware when they are playing that what they are doing is 'not really serious', and they incorporate that knowledge into the activity. Cohen, in 1987, described the 'play-face' which is used in family play to signal when something which would normally be intended seriously is actually intended as a joke. Such signals form a type of metacommunication: 'What I am about to say is not to be taken exactly as I say it'. It is that which defines the action as play, and not serious.

According to Bateson, play and make-believe provide a groundwork for 'reality', producing cultural and personal images used in day-to-day living. But they do so within a framework which has been defined as exploratory and not really serious, and which is therefore 'safe'. Bateson's emphasis on internal representation and language as signs might help us to explain, not just the development of fantasy and imaginative play, but also perhaps the development of humour, and other types of play with words.

According to Bateson, then, the contribution which play makes to the young child's psychological development is that, through play, the child learns about the different ways in which social roles can be framed and re-framed. It is not so much that the child learns about the content of what it is playing at, but that, through play, the child learns about learning. In other words, play is a form of metacommunication, which the child develops and uses throughout childhood and

which sometimes continues into adulthood as well.

Play as social framing

A related theory of play was put forward by Vygotsky (1967). Vygotsky saw play as arising from social pressures – social needs and emotional needs on the part of the child. The process of play, in this model, allows the child to free itself from the constraints of the immediate situation by creating a mental situation instead. In this theory, then, play is defined as the child's creation of an imaginary situation. According to Vygotsky, even in physical play, mental representations are being developed: a child running away in a game of 'tag' will mentally exaggerate the consequences of being caught.

Vygotsky saw play as developing the basic framework for the child's social understanding. According to Vygotsky, the child's activity during play is concerned with practical problems, which involve direct action on the environment. So the first types of play which the child participates in tend to be physical, concerned with sensory or motor co-ordination. The child acts directly on the environment in some way, by running, hitting objects, banging rattles or drums, and so on.

Gradually, this kind of play is replaced by what Vygotsky referred to as **mediating technologies** – objects are used by the child as tools, so that the environment can be acted on more effectively. For example, a child may seize a spoon and bang its drum with it. Since in this way it will make more noise than it did when it just banged on its drum with its own hand, it is likely to use the spoon more and more. By using tools to operate on its environment, the child develops internal, mental **representations** about how objects can be manipulated.

Internal mental structures are also constructed and developed from the child's use of **signs.** Signs, in Vygotsky's terms, are things which stand for concepts or ideas. So, for instance, a child may use a cup as a sign, to indicate that its dolly is thirsty and it has now got a drink. By combining the use of signs and practical knowledge about tools and their effects, the child's internal representations become increasingly sophisticated. Speech is a powerful source of signs, and objects as tools can be organised or restructured by using speech. So speech, in Vygotsky's theory, becomes another powerful tool for controlling and organising the use of objects as tools.

Vygotsky believed that an important feature of language development is the way that the child uses language to engage in internal cognitive restructuring (we looked at this idea in Chapter 4). By playing, the child learns to structure its understanding of the world, and language is a very important tool for this process. As the child plays, it will often maintain a monologue – a commentary – about what it is doing. This monologue, according to Vygotsky, eventually becomes the **inner speech** which allows the child to monitor what it is doing, and forms the basis of verbal thought.

The combination of these different types of play allows the child to form a mental framework for understanding the world. Physical types of play allow for the understanding of physical possibilities and constraints, and the development of motor skills. The internal representations formed during the two earlier periods also form the basis for later imagination, and this, according to Vygotsky, is why the more 'mental' types of play, like pretend play, tend to develop after the sensorimotor and tool-using periods.

Play as meta-representation

A different approach to understanding play concentrates on the role of pretend play in helping the child to develop **metacognition** – knowledge about its own cognitive processes. Leslie (1987) described pretend play as having three fundamental forms, which are listed in Table 20.10. These three types of pretence seem to emerge at about the same time as the child matures, usually somewhere between 18 and 24 months of age.

Leslie argued that these three forms of pretence are actually meta-representations of the world. They are not simply concerned with the child's own mental representations of the world, but with the child's understanding of those representations. There is an important difference, for instance, between pretend play and play which is just talking about things being true or false. For example, take the case of a child and mother playing together at an imaginary tea party. The mother might say to the child, 'Oh, this cup is empty. We need to fill it'. When she says this, the reality is that the cup is empty, so it is true. But that does not make it a straightforward true statement, because both the child and the mother are seeing the remark in an overall context which includes the idea that the cup can be filled up with imaginary tea.

So pretending is not simply about whether a statement is true or false. It is about the way that both the infant and the mother are sharing a meta-representation – an overall understanding – of the situation. Leslie argues that the ability to pretend emerges when this ability to generate meta-representations develops in the child. Pretend play, in this sense, is not simply about having a better way of understanding the world, or a more advanced level of understanding events. Instead, Leslie sees pretend play as one of the first manifestations of the child's ability to understand cognition – to understand its own and other people's thinking – and it is in this sense that pretend play can be seen as the development of meta-representation.

This more recent emphasis on the need to understand play within its social and family context reflects the growing trend in research in child development to examine the child in its social context. We have already seen how this trend has manifested itself in studies of cognitive development, attachment and deprivation, and increasingly, it is apparent that such studies reveal a number of limitations of the older approaches. Many of the traditional approaches to child development examined the child as if it were largely context-free; and often, as a result of this, they produced a picture of the child's capacities

Table 20.10 Forms of pretend play	
Object substitution	Pretence is to do with types or identities, of objects. The child may use one object to represent another, like pretending that a banana is a telephone.
Attribution	This type of pretence is pretending that things have certain attributes, or properties, like where a child describes its doll's face as being dirty, or pretends that it is a fine day, so the dolls can go out to play.
Imaginary objects	In this type of play, children pretend that an object exists where there is none, like pretending that its toy teapot is pouring out imaginary tea.

Source: Adapted from Leslie, 1987

which turns out to have been much more limited than the child's real capabilities.

Sex and gender

One of the most important, and most controversial, aspects of child development is the question of sex and gender, and how it comes about that children – or some of them anyway – come to act in accordance with gender roles established by their culture and society. In discussing this question, we need to draw a clear distinction between sex and gender. Sex refers to the biological quality of the individual: someone is, biologically, either male or female. But gender refers to the social aspects of this distinction: to the behaviour and conduct which the individual engages in as they interact with other people.

A number of ideas have been put forward to explain gender identity. Broadly speaking, theories about gender differences can be divided into four types: the biological approach; the bio-social approach; the social learning approach; and the psychoanalytic approach. A fifth type of theory looks at the similarities between men and women, rather than focusing purely on differences between them, and this work usually comes under the general term of research into **androgyny.** We will look at each of these approaches in turn.

The biological approach

Biological theories of gender identity try to explain the differences between males and females in terms of the physical differences which appear in the brain and in the body. These are **reductionist** approaches, which consider that the human personality is entirely a product of physiological characteristics, as opposed to **interactionist** perspectives, which argue that biological propensities and social and cultural factors interact in determining gender identity.

The types of physical characteristics which are referred to by biological theorists are of three kinds. First, **chromosomal sex** – every human being has a special pair of chromosomes, which is known to be connected with sexuality. Females have two X chromosomes, while males have one X chromosome and one Y chromosome. These take their name from the shape of the chromosomes, when they are seen under a microscope

just before dividing. The Y chromosome is very much shorter than the X chromosome – it looks a little like a Y shape, but with a very short central stem. This short central stem means that there are genes on the X chromosome which do not have their counterpart on the Y chromosome, and this can sometimes result in sex-linked disorders, like haemophilia and colour blindness, which appear much more often in males than females.

The second physical characteristic which indicates femaleness or maleness are the **gonads** – ovaries in females and testes in males – which are the organs of reproduction. The third major physical characteristic consists of differences in the **hormones** which males and females produce. Males produce different hormones from females, and these different hormones result in different sexual characteristics. Male hormones are known as androgens, and the most important one of these is known as testosterone, because it is released by the testes. The two most important types of female hormones are oestrogen and progesterone, both produced by the ovaries. Both males and females can produce all the hormones, but males produce far more of the male hormones than women, and the reverse is true for females.

These are the three main characteristics by which physical gender is determined, and biological theorists in general argue that the ultimate progression of an individual – whether it grows to be either male or female – is dependent on these biological characteristics. It may seem obvious, but we need to establish clearly what the defining characteristics are, since not everybody has all the typical characteristics to the same degree. For example, although there are differences in external appearance between most men and most women, these distinctions can blur into one another: some women appear masculine, and some men appear feminine.

Hormonal influences

A case which occurs from time to time, in which biological characteristics become particularly significant, is known as **testicular feminising syndrome.** In this, a woman will appear to be completely feminine from her external appearance, but when she undergoes a detailed medical examination (which usually happens when doctors are exploring the reasons for her infertility) it may emerge that she is genetically male and possesses testes. This syndrome is a genetic disorder due to a recessive gene. People who have it grow up as female, and the condition is often not diagnosed until they are adult. There are other cases, such **hermaphroditism**, where someone has the physical characteristics of both male and female; and several cases where individuals have possessed one type of chromosomal structure, but have been reared as the other gender, apparently quite successfully.

Although the evidence from many animal studies suggests that sex-role behaviour can be induced by hormones – for instance, mothering behaviour can be induced in male rats by injecting them with the appropriate hormone prolactin – there is very little evidence to suggest that human behaviour is as easily influenced by biochemical events. As we will see in Chapters 22 and 23, many behaviours which seem fixed and inherited in animals are much more flexible when it comes to human beings. So looking at human gender behaviour purely as the result of biological sex is not very likely to provide us with a full explanation.

Perhaps the problem with adopting purely reductionist approaches to issues of gender identity (reductionist approaches are explanations which attempt to reduce human phenomena down to one single cause, such as genetics) is that to do so ignores the wider social factors within society. Not every culture or subculture expects the same differences in behaviour from the different genders, and individuals within any given culture differ widely in how such behaviour is expressed.

Throughout this book, we have found that human behaviour is influenced by context, and is amenable to learning, so it would be very strange indeed to find that this area of human behaviour was rigidly defined by biological characteristics – it would make it completely different from the rest of human psychology. A more reasonable approach than the strictly biological ones seems to be represented in the bio-social theories, which take biological factors into account, but also take a broader view of the human being in its social context.

The bio-social approach

Bio-social approaches to gender role argue that biological characteristics are mainly important because what they do is set up expectations on the part of parents, which determine how children are then treated. So the way that the child is labelled directly affects the way that it is going to be brought up. Money and Ehrhardt (1972) argued that gender identity follows this kind of **labelling** process. They argued that, during the first few years of life, there is considerable flexibility in how a child categorises itself. Children of between two and three years of age can adopt different gender identities quite easily, and often do in their play, unless they are sensitised to rigid role behaviour very early on. However, this becomes more fixed as the child grows older, and comes to identify more with its gender group.

Money and Ehrhardt based their approach mainly on studying hermaphrodites, pseudo-hermaphrodites and those with testicular feminising syndrome. What they showed was that the physical characteristics of sex seem to be relatively unimportant in terms of the ultimate gender-role characteristic that the individual eventually adopts. Out of ten individuals with testicular feminising syndrome, they found that eight showed a preference for the female role, and all of them reported dreams about raising children. This was despite the fact that, genetically at least, these people were male. Money and Ehrhardt argued that the human psyche, or the central nervous system, is so open to the effects of learning that it is possible to reverse completely the biological contributions to psycho-sexual identity.

Transsexualism

Money and Ehrhardt's approach accords with the experience of many transsexuals. A number of individuals find that they are unhappy with the physical sex that they are, and, if this unhappiness persists over a number of years, they may opt to undertake a long and arduous process which eventually results in changing sex. Typically, a transsexual will have to 'pass' as a member of the other gender for a period of at least two years, acting out the role and behaving as a member of the other gender, until they have satisfied those responsible for the case – doctors, psychiatrists and counsellors – that they are serious in their desire to change sex, and flexible enough in terms of their gender identity to be able to live with their future role.

Once a transsexual has managed to establish a lifestyle based on acting a different gender role to the satisfaction of those supervising her or his case, they will then undergo a course of hormone treatment. If they are female, they receive additional male hormones and, if they are male, regular doses of female hormones. These hormones stimulate the development of secondary sexual characteristics, such as breasts or facial hair. After an extended period on hormone treatment, the individual then undergoes a complex operation, in which the appropriate sexual characteristics are constructed by skilled plastic surgeons.

As can be seen, changing sex is an arduous process, and one which frequently involves social rejection from friends, family or employers, although fortunately, such prejudice appears to be becoming less extreme. It is apparent, then, that only those who feel very strongly that they have been born into the wrong sex, as it were, will be prepared to undergo this process. Most transsexuals report that they have felt very strong feelings of being born into the wrong type of body from quite an early age, and that the operation, including the treatment leading up to it, has given them an opportunity to express what they have always considered to be their true selves.

Cross-sex behaviour

One of the problems in studying sex-role behaviour has been that researchers typically look at the 'norm', rather than at the amount of variation which individuals show. Within the same society, and even the same family, people differ in how much they conform to traditional gender roles. Sometimes, even, they do not conform to them at all. There are many historical accounts of **cross-sex behaviour**: cases where someone has dressed and acted as a member of the other gender, and sustained the illusion for many years.

Cross-sex behaviour occurs in many human societies. An ancient tradition of Native American Indians, for instance, was of females who would take on male responsibilities and duties, joining in hunting parties and other traditionally male activities, and males who opted for the female role, caring for and looking after children. These cases, apparently, were not uncommon, and were recognised by the tribes concerned as a valid form of social being. The crossing was marked by a long period of preparation, and then an initiation ceremony, in which the individual would become accepted into the new gender. In modern Thailand, too, young boys sometimes choose to become dancing girls, and adopt a lifestyle and appearance in which they become extremely

feminine, and almost completely indistinguishable from women.

These circumstances support the idea that gender identity is more flexible than the traditional biological theorists may have supposed. Some researchers have also suggested that biological propensities may play a relatively minor role, and that what is really important is the social learning which the individual experiences throughout life.

The social learning approach

A third set of approaches to gender identity is **social learning theory**. This is based on the idea that people learn appropriate sexual behaviour from society and from the expectations of those around them. Since female children are treated differently from male children, they acquire role models and identifications which are different, by virtue of the social learning process that they have undergone. Observational learning and imitation shows that some behaviour is considered to be appropriate for girls in our society, while different forms of behaviour are considered suitable for boys. The process of social reinforcement, whereby appropriate behaviour is encouraged and inappropriate behaviour is discouraged, either subtly or explicitly, may serve to reinforce this.

Smith and Lloyd (1978) showed that mothers treat girl infants quite differently from the way they treat boy infants. In this study, mothers were given a chance to play with a young baby that they did not know. A baby was dressed in either pink or blue, as if it were a little girl or a little boy. From filming how mothers interacted with the infant, Smith and Lloyd found that mothers tended to stimulate the 'boy' baby much more than the 'girl'. If the baby 'girl' seemed restless, she would be soothed and petted and expected to lie quietly. If the baby 'boy' seemed restless, he was encouraged to bounce around, and jiggled up and down by the mothers. The mothers also gave the 'boy' baby more assertive types of toys to play with – for instance, a toy rubber hammer – whereas the baby 'girls' were given toys which were soft and cuddly.

These dramatic differences in the ways that 'boy' and 'girl' babies were handled shows that parents may be establishing different behaviour patterns in their children even from infancy. Given the capacity of human infants to respond to the people around them, and to learn new forms of behaviour, we can see that a mother who consistently treats a baby boy in such a different way from a baby girl is likely to encourage the child to higher levels of activity. This in turn can provide the material for a belief that the boy is 'naturally' active.

As early as 1957, Sears, Maccoby and Levin found that mothers allow boys to express aggression far more than they allow girls to do so. Boys were encouraged to be assertive and to fight back, but girls were severely punished if they attempted to do so. There are a number of studies which have shown that boy children tend to be more active, aggressive and intolerant than girl children, and that girl children tend to prefer quieter pursuits. It is possible that this arises from early socialisation. The social learning theory approach to sex-typing would argue that this is the case.

The psychoanalytic approach

Freud (1901) considered that traditional gender-role development was very important for the young child. In order to acquire this, Freud believed, the child would need to grow up in a home which provided traditional gender-role models: a strong, authoritative father and a warm, caring, nurturant mother. The way in which a child received its gender-role identification, according to Freud, was via the Oedipal conflict. Freud argued that the young boy feels a very strong warmth and passionate love for his mother. However, seeing his father as a rival for this affection, he then wishes his father dead, so that he can have his mother all to himself.

According to Freud, the child finds the inner conflict produced by these wishes to be intolerable. This is partly also because he is living with his father, whom he perceives as being very powerful, but at the same time a direct threat and rival. So the child needs to reduce this psychological threat, and does so using an ego-defence mechanism known as **identification with the aggressor.** In this, the boy comes to identify with his powerful father figure, emphasising how much the two of them are similar, and attempting to become as much like his father as possible. In this way, he and his father can form a team, and so he feels less vulnerable.

Freud regarded this mechanism as being crucial to the child's healthy sexual development. Later Freudian theorists, and possibly Freud himself,

argued that if this process did not occur, the child would grow up to be homosexual. For instance, if the child was brought up by a very powerful mother-figure, with a very weak father, or if the father was absent, then the identification with the aggressor would not occur, and the child would be at risk of homosexuality. However, although this idea received a considerable amount of publicity, there does not seem to be much evidence for it. Malinowski, in 1927, investigated the Trobriand Islanders, in which children were brought up by the mother's brother, rather than their father. Malinowski found that children had no problem with gender identification, despite the fact that it was not possible for them to resolve the Oedipal conflict successfully.

Another study, by Golombok, Spencer and Rutter (1983), assessed children who were brought up in lesbian and single-parent households. They compared 37 children aged between five and seventeen who had been raised in households with lesbian couples, with 38 children of the same ages who had been raised in heterosexual single-parent households. They found that there were no differences between the two groups in terms of gender identity, sex-role behaviour, sexual orientation or any other kind of gender-related characteristics. The researchers concluded that there was no danger to the child of sex-role confusion in the sense that psychoanalytic theory had implied.

Androgyny

Society has strong stereotypes for both male and female behaviour and, as we have seen, these stereotypes can directly affect how a child is brought up. But in 1975, Bem argued that highly sex-typed behaviour is psychologically unhealthy for the individual. Instead, behaviour which mixes psychological characteristics from both sexes – **androgynous behaviour** – is more psychologically healthy, because it leaves the individual free to engage in whatever behaviour is appropriate to their situation.

Bem asked 444 male and 279 female research participants to complete a sex-role inventory which contained both a masculinity scale and a femininity scale. From this, they were classified into six basic groups: three male groups, which consisted of 'masculine' males, 'feminine' males and 'androgynous' males; and three female groups consisting of: 'masculine' females, 'feminine' females and 'androgynous' females. The research participants were asked to participate in what they believed to be an experiment on humour, which involved them working individually in booths.

They were shown 92 different cartoons, previously rated by independent raters as to how funny each was, and they also listened to what they believed to be other people's responses, through earphones. In fact, this was a standard conformity test: those responses were manipulated by the experimenter, and the aim was to measure the research participant's independence, which is stereotypically considered to be a 'masculine' trait. Bem found that 'masculine' and 'androgynous' research participants conformed on fewer trials than 'feminine' research participants.

The second task assessed playfulness, considered to be a stereotypically 'feminine' trait. Research participants were asked to join in an experiment on mood, which involved four different activities. First, there was a block-building task which lasted eight minutes. The purpose of this task was mainly to equalise the research participants' moods. They were then asked to play with a small, friendly kitten for five minutes, then to perform a challenging game of skill. For the fourth task, the research participants were told they could do anything they liked – the room was full of interesting things, such as puzzles and games, and the kitten was returned to the room during that time. The playfulness of the research participants' behaviour was rated by hidden observers. The outcome of the study can be found in Table 20.11.

It was interesting that highly feminine females showed low measures on both independence and playfulness tests. The low playfulness score for 'feminine' females was consistent with findings

that femininity tends to be correlated with high anxiety and poor social adjustment, neither of which, Bem argued, are psychologically healthy traits. On the other hand, androgynous research participants, who did not conform to stereotypical notions of masculinity or femininity, scored highly on both tasks, regardless of whether they were male or female. Bem argued that androgyny is a psychologically healthy state for people to be in.

Problems with sex-difference research

One of the problems with much research into sex differences is that it has tended to make assumptions about sex-stereotypical behaviour, without really taking into account issues of similarity or androgyny. The problem is that research which is designed to uncover differences between groups of people almost always prevents researchers from identifying similarities, and there is some suggestion that this has resulted in psychological differences between men and women having been exaggerated.

In 1978, Hall performed a **meta-analysis** of 75 studies which looked at gender differences in people's abilities to decode non-verbal behaviour, such as facial expressions, tones of voice, posture and gestures. Hall found that overall the studies showed that women seemed to be better at decoding non-verbal cues than men were. But a similar meta-analysis by Eisenberg and Lennon (1983) suggested that, although there were such differences, they were not as extreme as Hall had suggested – that differences between genders were moderate at best, and in fact showed a great deal of overlap.

Table 20.11 Androgynous and sex-stereotypical behaviour

Experiment 1	Measures of independence in a conformity-inducing situation		
	Masculine	**Feminine**	**Androgynous**
Males	high	low	high
Females	high	low	high
Experiment 2	Measures of playfulness		
	Masculine	**Feminine**	**Androgynous**
Males	low	high	high
Females	moderate	low	high

Source: Adapted from Bem, 1975

Empathy

There is also some suggestion that gender differences in the traditionally 'feminine' trait of **empathy** may have been exaggerated by researchers. Eisenberg and Lennon (1983) performed a meta-analysis of studies of gender differences in empathy, looking particularly at the different measures, and the outcomes that they had produced. They found that studies of gender differences in empathy seemed to be highly dependent on the type of method that was used to study them. Research which had involved self-report scales tended to produce large differences between the genders, implying that women were more empathic. Studies which used reflexive measures in the laboratory produced more moderate differences. But, when 'hidden' or less easily modifiable measures were used, like physiological measures of empathy, or unobtrusive observations of non-verbal reactions to someone else's emotional state, no gender differences emerged.

Eisenberg and Lennon saw these findings as indicating that women were responding to the **demand characteristics** of the investigation. If they knew that the researcher was interested in people's empathic behaviour, women tended to present themselves in line with the stereotypical role, as higher in emotionality and nurturance, and men presented themselves as less so. But if it was less apparent what the study was about, the differences between the sexes did not appear. This suggests that men and women could be just as empathic as each other, but that the way in which the research is conducted makes such differences appear.

This is a slightly worrying conclusion for sex-difference research, since traditional 'masculinity' and 'femininity' measures include measures of empathy almost by definition. A man who scores as 'empathic' in a traditional masculinity or femininity rating scale will be classified as being more feminine; so it then becomes circular: it is not possible to find out how empathy is really distributed within the population.

Integrating levels of explanation

The question, then, is how biological, individual, social and cultural levels of explanation of sex differences may be integrated. One message which seems to come through fairly clearly, is that global measurements of 'masculinity' or 'femininity' are probably impracticable: it is better to look at specific traits, like empathy or independence, separately, and not try to get general ratings. Another message is that looking only for differences and ignoring similarities may produce an exaggerated picture. It seems likely that any given biological propensity will, like other biological characteristics, be normally distributed within a population; but that when it comes to traits associated with male and female gender roles, cultural and social pressures will act to skew that distribution in one direction.

This argument may become clearer if we take an example of the wish to bear children: an urge which clearly has a biological origin, but which also shows cultural variation in terms of the number of children which people want to have. If we could leave all the social, religious and cultural pressures aside, we would still find that some women feel such a powerful drive for motherhood that they would want to have a lot of children; but we would also find some women who were quite happy to have no children at all. These are the two extremes of the distribution, and the majority of the female population would fall somewhere in between. Most women would probably want at least one child, the majority two or three, and so on. But cultural, religious and social influences also act on the individual. Most women grow up assuming that they will have children one day, and do not regard childlessness as a practical option – indeed, in some cultures childlessness is even seen as a disgrace. These pressures act to produce a **skewed** distribution (Figure 20.1), so that fewer women opt for no children, and more opt to have large families.

Childbearing is an example with a clear biological origin; but similar mechanisms are also likely to apply to psychological characteristics. To that extent, it may be more useful to look at how a given trait, like independence, is distributed

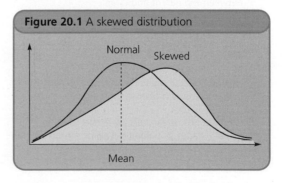

Figure 20.1 A skewed distribution

within the female population, and within the male population, than it is to look for general differences between males and females. Any given trait is likely to be normally distributed, and looking only at gender differences may obscure how much the two distributions overlap.

Child development, then, involves a complex interaction of biological and maturational processes, social learning, cognitive development, and growing social awareness. But developmental psychology does not stop with childhood. We continue to develop throughout life. In the next chapter, we will go on to look at development throughout the lifespan, and at some of the other aspects of development which have emerged as significant when we look beyond childhood.

Key terms

affectionless psychopathy A syndrome outlined by Bowlby, characterised by a lack of social relationships and also of social conscience.

catharsis The idea that aggressive or other energies can be safely discharged through harmless channels (e.g. highly competitive spectator sports). Although it has been a popular idea, dating from Plato, most research into catharsis implies that cathartic events may actually generate increased aggressive or other energies rather than reducing them.

imprinting A very rapid form of learning, shown by precocial animals soon after birth, resulting in a rapid and powerful attachment to a parent.

maternal deprivation A phrase used to describe a condition of being separated from the mother in the early years of life.

monotropy A theory put forward by Bowlby, that infants form only one very strong attachment to their mothers, different from their attachments with other people.

precocial animals Animals which can move about as soon as they are born or hatched.

social learning theory An approach to child development which states that children develop through learning from the other people around them.

Summary

1 Early theories of attachment were based on the idea of imprinting: that the infant forms a rapid, exclusive bond with its mother shortly after birth, and that other relationships are less important.

2 Later research into human attachments showed that they develop as a result of parent-infant interaction. The human infant is innately predisposed to respond positively to interactions with other human beings.

3 Depending on the quality of the interaction which they have with their parents, human infants may show secure, insecure or ambivalent attachments. These involve different behaviour and transactions between the parent and infant.

4 The continuity hypothesis states that early experience exerts a permanent effect on adult personality. However, research implies that it is possible to recover from even very severely deprived childhoods, as long as the person experiences help and warm relationships in later life.

5 A number of researchers have attempted to identify stages in children's play, or categories of different types of play. Other researchers have identified distinctive features of play, such as intrinsic motivation, its process-centred, rather than product-centred nature, its concern with non-literal behaviours and its self-directed nature.

6 Classic theories of play include models of play as surplus energy, play as relaxation, play as recapitulation and play as practice. More recent approaches see play as the expression of underlying psychodynamic conflict, as stimulus-seeking, as metacommunication, as social framing and as meta-representation.

7 Psychological research into how the child comes to acquire appropriate gender-role behaviour includes biological approaches, bio-social approaches, social learning approaches, psychoanalytic approaches and research which emphasises gender similarity and androgyny.

8 Cross-cultural and other studies of gender differences show that there is much more flexibility in human gender roles than research in one society might suggest. Gender role is best interpreted using multiple levels of explanation rather than looking for one single cause.

Self-assessment questions

1 Outline significant aspects of parent-infant interaction.

2 Briefly describe Ainsworth's research into secure and insecure attachment.

3 What is play therapy?

Practice essay questions

1 Using psychological evidence, discuss whether early experience inevitably affects the rest of one's life.

2 What have psychologists discovered about the child's theory of mind?

3 Critically evaluate psychological research into children's play.

Test your knowledge of this chapter with our online quizzes and games at: http://www.psych.co.uk

Explore social development further at:

General
http://www.parentingweb.com/index.htm – Tutorials and information aimed at parents about play, attachment and interaction.

Attachment
http://www.priory.com/psych/garelli.htm – Tutorials and bibliographies on aggression and attachment.
http://www.psychology.sunysb.edu/ewaters/Default.htm – On-line articles on the subject of attachment.

Lifespan developmental psychology

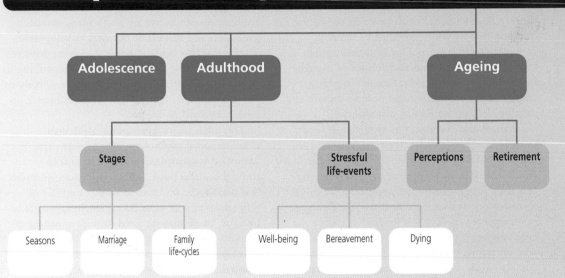

Learning objectives

21.1. The lifespan approach
a define terms relating to lifespan psychology
b list the four assumptions of the lifespan approach
c apply lifespan concepts to everyday experience

21.2. Adolescence as storm and stress
a outline mechanisms leading to emotional disruption during adolescence
b describe theories of adolescence as emotional upheaval
c evaluate the storm and stress model of adolescence

21.3. Alternative theories of adolescence
a define terms relating to role-transition models of adolescence
b list Eirkson's stages of development
c apply concepts of role-transition to everyday examples

21.4. Coleman's focal theory
a outline Coleman's focal theory of adolescence
b describe a study of adolescence
c define terms relating to the lifespan approach to adolescence

21.5. Stage theories of adulthood
a list stages of the family life-cycle
b describe theories of adulthood
c evaluate theories of adulthood and family life

21.6. Stressful life-events
a outline the stressful life-events model
b describe a study of stressful life events and/or coping
c evaluate the stressful life-events approach

21.7. Grieving and bereavement
a list the stages and components of grief
b distinguish between normal and abnormal grieving
c describe social factors which can influence the experience of dying

21.8. Ageing and retirement
a evaluate studies of ageing and ability
b identify factors which can mitigate the effects of ageing
c compare theories of retirement

For much of the twentieth century, developmental psychology focused almost entirely on childhood, and the changes which happen to human beings during that time. There was very little research into how adults develop, and what there was, tended to present rather negative pictures of ageing, senescence and death. But in more recent times, a number of factors have given rise to the question of how adults continue to develop throughout the lifespan. One of them was the influence of the **humanistic school** of thought in psychology, which, as we saw in Chapter 7, emphasised the continual and positive growth and development of the human personality.

Changes and choices in lifestyle and in family relationships have also left their mark, as researchers came to realise that the traditional family unit may not represent the real experience of a large proportion of the population, at least for some sectors of their lives. And also, the influence of feminist psychology has resulted in more emphasis being placed on the experiences of women throughout life. Even in the conventional nuclear family, these are marked by a number of very different stages, as children are born, raised and leave home.

Assumptions of lifespan psychology

Sugarman (1986) outlined a number of fundamental assumptions in lifespan developmental psychology. One of these, which is strikingly congruent with the emphasis of modern research into child development, is the way that development needs to be seen within its **social context**. People act within a social milieu consisting of other people: friends, family, schools. They also develop within a socio-cultural context – expectations of how people are likely to develop are affected by social class, the political setting and cultural assumptions as well as by immediate social demands. All these need to be taken into account when studying development.

Another assumption in lifespan developmental psychology is that of **reciprocal influence**. Families and the individuals within them influence one another reciprocally – each person or interaction in a family unit has an effect on the other people involved. Families are not static, and can sometimes change radically within a relatively short space of time, as in the case of a divorce. Expectations and relationships between parents

and children, or between siblings, have their influence even in stable families, and change with time through the actions of those same participants.

People do not simply receive influences: they are **active agents** in their own lives. Through making choices and through the influences that we have on others, we are all, to some extent, producers and shapers of our own development. To this end, the understanding which we have of that development can be crucial in determining its direction and nature – what we believe is likely to happen to us can have an important influence on what actually does happen.

The other major assumption of lifespan developmental psychology which Sugarman identified is **complexity**. As we have seen throughout this book, human beings are complex and need to be understood from a number of different points of view. So no single approach is likely to be all that we need to understand people. A multi-disciplinary approach, which examines development from the point of view of social and cultural, biological and psychological perspectives, is necessary if we are to come to grips with how human beings develop through the lifespan.

Lifespan developmental psychology, then, is a relatively new area. As yet, it is a long way from having comprehensive theoretical perspectives which will encompass the whole of people's experiences throughout life. In this chapter, we will look at some of the research and theoretical insights which have been developed in this field, looking first at adolescence, then at research into adulthood and maturity, and finally at the ageing process and the final stages of life.

Adolescence

Adolescence, in Western society, is a stage of development which marks the transition between the world and privileges of childhood and the world and privileges of the adult. As such, it is a stage where the experiences and beliefs which the child has gained during the childhood years need to be re-evaluated and re-formulated, in preparation for the individual's new status and increasing participation in society.

A number of different theoretical views have been put forward about the nature of adolescence. By far the most influential one has been the idea that adolescence is a turbulent period for the individual, involving conflict with authority, major emotional upheavals and social readjustment. We will begin, therefore, by looking at this model and at some of its weaknesses, before going on to look at some of the alternative models of adolescence which psychologists have developed.

Adolescence as a period of 'storm and stress'

This is the 'classic' theory of adolescence, which sees the adolescent as inherently rebellious, rejecting parental authority and substituting the authority of the peer group, and emotionally unstable, inclined to wild swings of mood. This view of adolescence has quite a long history, perhaps reaching the height of its popularity in the 1950s and 1960s. Throughout the century, a number of explanations have been advanced to explain how and why this aspect of adolescence occurred.

The biological perspective

The biological view of adolescence as a turbulent period was first put forward by G. Stanley Hall, in 1904. Like Piaget (see Chapter 17), Hall took the theoretical view that **ontogeny recapitulates phylogeny** – in other words, that ontogeny, or the development of the individual, passes through all the stages in the evolutionary development of the species (its phylogeny). As a result of this, Hall regarded the teenage years as being emotionally unstable, harking back to more primitive periods of human evolution characterised by tribal warfare and barbarism. Hall also suggested that, since this was an inevitable part of development, adolescents required a tolerant and supportive environment in order to work through their emotional upsets.

A different biological explanation emphasised **maturational change**. Sorenson (1973) took the view that the physical bodily changes which occur during adolescence produce an emotional instability, which manifests itself in disturbance and rebellion. Sorenson suggested that boys in particular experience a number of stresses as a result of the physical changes in their bodies and their developing sexual awareness. These stresses, according to Sorenson, produce tension, anxiety and an increased likelihood of confrontation with authority.

Maturation rates

A considerable amount of research investigated the effects of physical maturation rates on adolescent self-concepts and social identification. Lerner and Karabenick (1974) pointed out that adolescents who see themselves as physically different from cultural stereotypes often tend to have problems with their self-concept. The glamorous images which are constantly being received through the mass media portray certain types of physique as attractive. These images tend to be internalised and used as the standard for comparison, even if they are unrealistic.

Both boys and girls experience a **growth spurt** during adolescence, which makes others aware of how they are developing. An early developer will be noticeably taller than others of the same age; conversely, someone who develops late may be noticeably smaller than their peers, and this can last for a period of several years. Either comparison may induce feelings of inadequacy which produce emotional stress. Jones and Bayley (1950) found that late-maturing boys tended to be less relaxed and were more dependent on others than those maturing earlier. Peskin (1973) showed that early-maturing girls often showed more psychological disturbance and were less confident with their peers than those who matured later.

Petersen and Crockett (1985) put forward the **deviance hypothesis** to explain this discrepancy. This proposed that it is not the actual fact of late or early maturation which matters. Instead, what is important is the fact that early and late developers are deviant in some way from their peers. The various negative psychological effects which researchers have identified occur as a result of this feeling of being deviant. A study by Brooks-Gunn and Warren (1985) supported this idea. They compared girls attending dance schools with other girls of the same age. In this context, late maturing was an advantage, as the emphasis in the dance schools was on small stature and low body-weight. In these schools, those who matured 'on time' showed more personality and eating problems than those in the control group.

The psychoanalytic view

The psychoanalytic school of thought also regarded adolescence as a period of emotional upheaval. This, they argued, stemmed from the sudden eruption of genital needs during puberty, and the need to re-work many of the sexual conflicts which had been encountered earlier on in childhood. According to Anna Freud (1968), this resulted in violent swings of mood, from elation to wild despair to suicidal depression.

Blos (1967) argued that the process of disengaging from the family – in particular, of finding a 'love object' outside the family circle – meant that the adolescent had to go through a process of renouncing dependency and changing childhood relationships so that they became less of a tie. Blos also argued that in order to do this it was necessary for the adolescent to regress and work through the emotions of early infancy and childhood. It was this process which produced the wild swings of mood and dramatic emotional expression of adolescence.

Adolescent regression, according to Blos, could be seen in a number of facets of adolescent behaviour. For example, the idealisation of pop stars or sporting personalities could be seen as a regression to the idealised parent of childhood; or the tendency of adolescents to become absorbed in abstract ideals – political, religious or artistic – could be seen as a regression to an infantile state of 'merger', allowing them to become entirely submerged in another. Another example of adolescent regression, according to Blos, is ambivalence towards the parents, manifested in wild swings of mood. Blos interpreted this as a regression to the love–hate reactions of early infancy.

According to Blos, it was essential for the adolescent to work through this process. If they did not, it would not be possible for the adolescent to disengage effectively from the family and to form positive and meaningful relationships with others. From the psychoanalytic point of view, then, upheaval and rebellion were perceived as necessary for the psychologically healthy development of the adult.

Cultural relativity

In many respects, young people are segregated from adult society. Technically, at least, they are not supposed to engage in sexual activity; various recreations, like drinking in pubs, are at least nominally prohibited, as are some skills such as driving cars. This promotes the development of a separate 'youth culture', with independent standards and pressures and a whole range of products and recreational activities aimed specifically at adolescents.

Bronfenbrenner (1973) identified this segregation as an important contribution to anti-social attitudes held by American teenagers. In his study of child-rearing practices in the USA and USSR, Bronfenbrenner observed that Russian adolescents tended to be very much more openly pro-social, and did not respect anti-social behaviours from their peers. In America, on the other hand, juvenile delinquency, especially in boys, was seen as 'daring' by the peer group, producing a subculture of social approval for certain kinds of anti-social acts. Bronfenbrenner argued that the way that Russian cultures specifically included adolescents, offering numerous opportunities for them to become involved in adult society, meant that it was easier for peer pressure to work on the side of society rather than against its values.

Although in Western society adolescence is seen as an inevitable period, this is not so in all societies. Mead (1928) published a famous study of the adolescent period in Samoa, which presented adolescence very differently. According to Mead, even at the age of five or six, the child was participating in many of the tasks which it would undertake as an adult, and these would simply have increased in number and degree of responsibility as the child grew older. There was little discontinuity between childhood and adulthood, and so less need for a separate stage of adolescence.

Sexual relationships too, Mead reported, were able to develop gradually, which meant that by the time they were married, both partners would be sexually experienced. Mead observed that there seemed to be little 'storm and stress' in Samoan adolescent life, and attributed this to the gradual transition rather than sudden discontinuities.

Freeman (1984) challenged Mead's observations. From his own research in Samoa, he argued that, rather than sexual experience being commonplace among adolescents of both sexes, virginity in girls was highly prized among the higher-status families. Freeman argued that Mead's findings were biased, because she had obtained her information by talking primarily with the women and girls of the society. But critics of Freeman (for example Ballard, 1983) pointed out that his own information was obtained from talking primarily with high-status males, which represents an equally biased source of information. It seems likely that Samoan society, like other human societies, was, and is, characterised by considerable variation in attitude and behaviour. But it does suggest that 'storm and stress' in adolescence may not be inevitable.

Criticisms of the 'storm and stress' model of adolescence

Gradually, psychologists began to realise that the 'storm and stress' model of adolescence had been somewhat exaggerated. One of the first challenges to this view came from Bandura (1972), who investigated 'normal' adolescents and their families, rather than simply looking at those who were referred for psychological treatment. Bandura found that most adolescents did not show any particular opposition to their parents' values, nor did they engage in hostility and rebellion. On the contrary, for many people their adolescence was a period in which they developed greater trust and a better relationship in general with their parents.

Bandura argued that the classic view of adolescence was misleading on several counts. One of them was its idea that adolescence was a relatively sudden phase, in which a new autonomy from the parents had emerged. Bandura argued that, on the contrary, children increase their autonomy throughout later childhood, so that by the time adolescence is actually reached, it has been pretty well established – at least on the child's part, although the parents might still have some adjusting to do.

The classic model of adolescence also suggested that the adolescent simply transferred their earlier psychological dependence on the parents on to the peer group, arguing that adolescents would simply follow their peer group slavishly and without discrimination. Bandura's research showed that, on the contrary, most adolescents were extremely discriminating about their peer group and choosy about who they would take as role models.

Musgrove (1963) took the view that segregation from the adult world did not automatically produce adolescents with values which run counter to society. Musgrove argued that it depends entirely on what the person is doing during the period of segregation. If young people are cut off from the adult world and are held in low esteem by it (for example, like low achievers at school), then, according to Musgrove, a subculture will form which has values which run counter to the dominant culture. If, on the other

hand, adolescents are segregated from the adult world but regarded in higher esteem, or at least with respect, then the adolescent subculture will tend to adopt the values of adult society, using the time to explore and develop in readiness for fuller participation.

It is this view which underlies many of the various 'adventure schemes' for young people, like Operation Raleigh or the Duke of Edinburgh Award schemes. Providing young people with an opportunity to develop their skills through activities which, although separate, are in general respected by the adult world, allows them to use the period of adolescence to achieve a more positive integration with society.

Coleman and Hendry (1990) argued that the misleading emphasis on rebellion and rejection of parental authority had resulted from a number of social factors, such as the media emphasis on the rebellious adolescent, as portrayed in films and television. Possibly the most significant influence, they argued, was the fact that most of the psychologists theorising about adolescence had come from the clinical field. As a result of this, although they came into contact with a large number of adolescents, those whom they encountered almost always had some kind of psychological problem, or were experiencing stress. This meant that these researchers had developed an unrealistic perception of what life was like for the majority of teenagers in society.

Like Bandura, Coleman and Hendry argued that most adolescents progress much more smoothly through this period than was previously assumed. The 'storm and stress' model of adolescence, they argued, applies to only a minority of individuals, rather than to the majority. Of course, there are those for whom this model represents an accurate picture of adolescence, but Coleman and Hendry see their 'storm and stress' as traceable to other psychological factors, like earlier disturbance or pathological relationships within the family (see Chapter 9), rather than to adolescence itself. Most psychologists now recognise that the 'storm and stress' model does not represent the experience of the majority of adolescents.

Adolescence as a period of role transition

In more recent years, the view has been put forward that adolescence should be seen primarily as a period of increasing **role transitions**, which in turn lead to personality change. Transitions such as moving from school to work, or work experience, involve the adolescent in learning very different role behaviours. The role of child within the family is also abandoned at this time, and a different set of expectations takes its place – the teenager is expected to act differently within the family set-up than is the ten-year-old. At the same time, too, interactions with peers change, involving entirely different types of expectations and social behaviours from those of childhood.

Mead (1972) highlighted the lack of role models for adolescents in modern society. In stable, non-technological societies, those passing through adolescence can see examples of the future roles that they will be expected to adopt. But in modern society, changes in the nature of work, leisure and social demands take place rapidly, which can mean that it is no longer possible for parents to act as role models for their children. In more stable societies, older people can say: 'I have been young and know what it is like, but you have never been old', but in modern societies, young people can say: 'You have never been young in the world that I am young in'. This, Mead argued, leads young people to turn increasingly to their peers and to the media for role models, rather than to their elders within the family.

Types of role change

Elder (1968) distinguished two types of role change which take place during adolescence. First, the adolescent experiences changes in their existing roles – **intra-role change** – as the expectations of the other people around them change. An individual may still be an 'older sister', for instance, but that role will involve different expectations and different role behaviour when she is fifteen from that required when she was nine. Part of the adolescent task, therefore, involves becoming aware of these changes in their existing social roles, and learning to adjust to them.

The second type of role change involves the adoption of entirely new roles. Within school or work, at home and with the peer group, new roles are emerging, which the teenager needs to explore. For example, as a student moves through school, one of the new roles may represent increased identification with authority (such as the role of prefect) or its opposite (such as the role of

anti-school gang member). Within the peer group, childhood friendships become transformed into entirely new role relationships, with other factors like gender identity often becoming far more important than they were before.

Brim (1965) pointed out that a single individual may have several very different reference groups, and this means that their behaviour may vary widely, as a result of different role expectations emanating from these groups. What your peers expect from you as 'pupil' may not be the same as the behaviour expected from you by your teachers, or by your parents, while you are in the same role. Part of the task of the adolescent, then, is to balance out these different demands, and to come to terms with the disparity between the different 'selves' presented to different reference groups.

Adolescence as a developmental stage

Erikson (1968) saw adolescence as one in a series of developmental stages, which span the individual's whole lifetime, from infancy to old age. In Erikson's theory, the individual's psychological development is assumed to occur through the resolution of basic psychological conflicts, which form the foundation for later ones. The psychosocial conflicts which the individual must face at different ages are listed in Table 21.1.

Erikson began from a psychoanalytic orientation, but unlike most psychologists of this persuasion, he saw psychological development as a life-long process, rather than occurring mainly during the first five years of life. Psychological development, for Erikson, took place through the resolution of basic **psychosocial conflicts**, with each stage building on the successful resolution of conflicts in previous stages. The unsuccessful resolution of earlier stages could produce lasting consequences, in that they would leave unsettled conflicts remaining to interfere with current psychosocial development.

The psychosocial stage represented by adolescence, as we can see from Erikson's model, is the resolution of the conflicts raised by the profusion of role changes in adolescent life. Healthy resolution of these conflicts would mean that the person would be able to adjust to the changing role demands of the period of adolescence while still retaining a strong sense of

Table 21.1 Psychosocial conflicts in development

Early infancy	**trust** vs **mistrust** To gain a balance between trusting people and risking being let down, or being suspicious and mistrustful and therefore being unable to relate to others fully.
Later infancy	**autonomy** vs **shame and doubt** To develop a sense of personal agency and control over behaviour and actions, or to mistrust one's personal abilities and anticipate failures.
Early childhood	**initiative** vs **guilt** To develop an increasing sense of personal responsibility and initiative, or to develop increased feelings of guilt and doubt.
Middle childhood	**industry** vs **inferiority** To learn to overcome challenges through systematic effort, or to accept failure and avoid challenges, leading to an increasing sense of inferiority.
Puberty and adolescence	**identity** vs **role confusion** To develop a consistent sense of personal identity faced with the changes in social role and expectations of adolescence, or simply to become overwhelmed by choices and expectations and to fail to develop a sense of a consistent inner self.
Young adulthood	**intimacy** vs **isolation** To develop intimate and trusting relationships with others, or to avoid relationships as threatening and painful.
Mature adulthood	**generativity** vs **stagnation** To develop a productive and positive life incorporating recognition of personal achievements, or to stagnate and fail to develop or grow psychologically.
Late adulthood	**integrity** vs **despair** To become able to look back on one's life in a positive fashion, and to evaluate one's achievements, or to feel that life has been meaningless and futile.

Source: Adapted from Erikson, 1968

their own lasting personal identity. If the increasing role demands of adolescence placed too great a stress on the individual, then **identity diffusion** would result. This means that the individual would become confused about who they were, in view of all the different roles which they seemed to be acting out.

In Erikson's view, there are four elements to identity diffusion. The first is the problem of **intimacy**: the adolescent needs to be able to establish intimate relationships with other people without losing her or his own identity. The adolescent who fears intimacy because of the danger of being 'swamped' may become isolated from others, retreating either into stereotyped or formal relationships. Alternatively, they may become frantically involved in seeking intimacy with what Erikson described as 'improbable partners'.

The second element is that of the **time perspective**. Since so much of adolescent experience involves learning and preparing for adult life, it is important that adolescents can see themselves within a realistic time context.

Excessive anxieties about changing and growing into the world of adulthood may mean that the adolescent represses that fear into an inability to plan for the future, and so denies that times are changing. If this happens, the adolescent may not undertake the long-term projects or make efforts which are needed to form a secure basis for adult life.

The third element concerns **industry**: using one's energies productively and effectively Adolescents typically have a number of tasks to do, in terms of work and study. These, too, represent preparation for adult life, and Erikson regards it as important in this stage that the adolescent should learn to harness their energies realistically. But doing this involves a certain amount of commitment to the task in hand, which some adolescents find anxiety-provoking. In order to avoid facing these anxieties, they may become obsessively involved with one activity to the exclusion of everything else, or they may refuse to concentrate on any of them.

The fourth element of identity diffusion, in Erikson's theory, is the problem of **negative**

identity. Some adolescents will consciously choose an identity which is based on rejection of the values of others, rather than on a positive choice of their own – such as choosing an identity which is exactly the opposite to that which their parents would like them to adopt, purely in order to assert their own independence. In reality, of course, this type of reactive choice leaves the person just as psychologically dependent on the parents as before: without the 'opposition', the individual has no identity of their own. What is important is that the adolescent learns to make their own personal choices on the basis of their own inclinations, talents and abilities, not on the basis of reacting to what others want them to do.

Erikson saw the period of adolescence as forming a special stage, which he described as a **psychosocial moratorium**. During this time, major life-decisions are left in abeyance, and the individual is free to experiment with alternative possibilities without having to face up to the full consequences of those choices. In this sense, Erikson saw the explorations of adolescence as a special form of play. Instead of the overt physical play of childhood, the adolescent is playing with the more complex roles and identifications of society.

The identity crisis

Marcia (1966), working within Erikson's framework, saw Erikson's concept of **identity crisis** as being an important factor in the successful psychological resolution of this stage. This was the idea that the sheer variety of role demands and expectations would produce an identity crisis within the individual, which would enable that person to break free of the assumptions of childhood and prepare for their future adult identity. As part of that, Marcia identified different types of identity status, which could result as the person works through adolescence. These are listed in Table 21.2.

Marcia (1966) showed that those who had reached the stage of identity achievement tended to experience less stress in challenging situations, and also had higher and less vulnerable self-esteem than those in the identity diffusion category. A study by Toder and Marcia (1973) showed that college women who had reached this stage were less likely to conform to social pressure in a group situation.

Although many psychologists have found the analysis of identity tasks to be helpful, there has been some criticism of the approach. Working within the model, Matteson (1977) challenged the inclusion of the third stage of moratorium as an identity status, on the grounds that this is a process, whereas the others are outcomes. A more general criticism of the approach, however, is the assumption that an identity crisis forms the major vehicle by which positive social identity is obtained. While this is consistent with the 'storm and stress' model of adolescence, which was largely taken for granted at the time that Erikson was formulating his theory, as we have seen, such a model is not really supported by the psychological evidence.

Table 21.2 Types of identity status during adolescence	
1 *Identity diffusion*	In this, the individual has not yet made any commitment to a future identity, and there is no indication that she or he is about to do so.
2 *Identity foreclosure*	The individual has not experienced a crisis, but has nonetheless become committed in their goals and beliefs, mainly through choices made by others. So, for instance, someone with a committed religious upbringing in, say, a fundamentalist sect, might pass smoothly on to accepting the identity and goals consistent with that religious approach, rather than exploring alternatives and resolving the crisis on a personal level.
3 *Moratorium*	The individual is in a state of crisis, actively searching for an identity within a range of alternatives. There has been some criticism of the inclusion of this as an identity status, on the grounds that this is a process, whereas the others are outcomes.
4 *Identity achievement*	This is the final outcome of the successful resolution of identity crisis. At this stage, the individual has resolved their crisis on their own terms, and is now firmly committed to an ideology, social roles, and occupational goals.

Source: Adapted from Marcia, 1966

Offer (1969) reported on an extensive study of American adolescents, and found that only a very small minority indeed showed any signs of identity crisis. Similarly, Siddique and D'Arcy (1984) reported that less than one-quarter of a large sample of adolescents whom they interviewed showed psychological distress, whereas the majority appeared to experience a smooth transition through adolescence to adulthood.

However, these findings do not mean that Erikson's whole-life model is invalid for making sense of this period, since the majority in both studies adjusted well, developed meaningful relationships with others and achieved positively integrated identity as they passed through adolescence. There is role transition, but it is not necessarily accompanied by identity crisis. Coleman and Hendry (1990) argue that what is needed is a theoretical model of adolescence which can deal with the normal experience of adolescence, as well as with abnormal or minority experiences.

Other stage theorists have also attributed specific tasks to the adolescent period. As we saw in Chapter 19, Piaget characterised this as the period when formal thinking develops, and Kohlberg identified it as the time when moral reasoning has developed or is developing towards its final stage of autonomous morality. All these theories require that each stage will be worked through in order for progression to occur to the next stage, and imply that failure to complete one stage successfully will result in fixation or regression. However, other theorists take the view that development does not necessarily happen in the sequential way proposed by stage theories: rather, they argue that there are changes of several different kinds occurring within the period of adolescence, and the order in which they appear may vary from one person to the next.

The lifespan approach to adolescence

The 'storm and stress', social role and stage theories of adolescence all tend to portray the adolescent as passive – experiencing adolescence but not significantly influencing it. However, some theorists have seen people as more active in creating their own experience than these models imply. Lerner (1985) discussed how adolescents interact with their environment, and in so doing affect their own development. Lerner identified

three ways in which adolescents do this, which are listed in Table 21.3.

Lifespan developmental psychology insists that in order to understand people we need to see them within their social and personal contexts, and as agents in their own lives. Since human beings are complex, we also need to adopt a multi-disciplinary framework of study, rather than simply focusing on one angle or theoretical explanation. So, for example, a study of physical development in adolescent girls by Brooks-Gunn and Petersen (1983) involved looking at the effects of family influences, the girls' own career choices and even school influences, as well as simply looking at the issue from a biological perspective. By so doing, they were able to detect factors and influences at work which a more narrow perspective would have entirely missed.

Coleman's focal theory of adolescence

It is important to remember that there are very wide variations in adolescent experiences and expectations. While some people begin their working careers at sixteen, others prolong their education and may not expect to begin work until the age of 23 or even later, particularly if they are training for professional careers. Some people expect to leave home almost as soon as their education is over, others expect to remain

---

Table 21.3 The adolescent as interacting with its environment

1	As a stimulus to others	The adolescent produces different reactions or behaviour from different people.
2	As processors of information	Adolescents make sense out of the behaviour of other people according to their own understanding of what is going on, and adjust their own actions according to the sense which they make out of their experience.
3	As agents in their own lives	Adolescents act as active forces within their own environments, choosing, shaping and selecting what is likely to happen to them.

Source: Adapted from Lerner, 1985

within their parental family until their own marriage. Some people expect to marry early, others to remain single until their late twenties or even later. For each of these groups, the period of adolescence is experienced differently, and changes occur at a different rate.

Coleman (1974) put forward the **focal theory** of adolescence. This theory sees adolescence as involving a broad range of tasks of one kind or another. The individual has to adjust to biological changes in the body; to develop the self-image and sometimes cope with deviance through early or late maturation, or with having a non-idealised physique. The adolescent also has to develop satisfying peer relationships while at the same time maintaining and developing relationships within the family, to cope with demands from school and future career demands, to explore new demands for intimacy in relationships with others, and so on. The list could be much longer.

Each of these tasks represents challenges for the individual, and requires the person to make new adjustments. Unlike a stage theorist, who would see these tasks as occurring sequentially, Coleman proposed that the issues, problems and ambiguities of adolescence are present at all times. But they are not all equally important all the time. For some adolescents, for example, issues of specific career choice are immediate at age fifteen, because they expect to be leaving school in the next year. For others, who expect to go on to further or higher education, such choices are much less immediate – the educational choices which they make still allow a wide latitude, leaving specific choices for later.

The focal theory proposes that, as an individual passes through adolescence, their attention becomes focused on different aspects of the changes at different times. Once one set of issues is resolved, they recede into the background and other issues become prominent. Although the original challenges are still there, they have ceased to be quite such a problem. In other words, proceeding through adolescence involves focusing on one set of challenges at any given time, but changing that focus according to the situation and what has gone before.

Coleman's studies

Coleman and Hendry (1990) reported a series of studies in which 800 girls and boys were given identical tests at the ages of eleven, thirteen, fifteen and seventeen years. The tests included material on self-image, relationships of various kinds, being alone and large group situations. Coleman found that the anxieties expressed by the adolescents changed with time. Some types of anxieties, such as fears of rejection from the peer group, seemed to come to a peak fairly early on, while others, such as conflict with parents, peaked later.

Coleman suggested that each of these issues has its own distribution curve: some adolescents will come to them earlier than others, and some later. Taken as a whole through the years of adolescence, though, the curves will overlap: there is no need for one set of anxieties to be resolved before moving on to the next. This means that most adolescents are not faced with all their adjustments at the same time, and so they therefore keep some areas of their life relatively stable at any given time. This gives them a secure basis for tackling the tests presented by the other challenges of adolescence. According to this model, problems are most likely to occur in those adolescents who are faced with a number of different issues to resolve at the same time, and so are not able to retain stability in any part of life.

Coleman's model presents a view of the adolescent as an active agent in their own development. Most adolescents, Coleman argued, are able to manage the transitions of adolescence by dealing with one focus at a time, and influencing other aspects of their lives, in the ways which Lerner identified. A teenager can choose whether or not to confront their parents, to seek a relationship or the acceptance of a specific group of peers, to stand up to an authoritarian teacher or to resist persuasion from another person. By exercising those choices, many people pace themselves through the adolescent transition, rather than being overwhelmed by the 'storm and stress' of everything happening at once.

Adulthood

When we consider how many years of our lives we spend as adults, and compare it with the much smaller amount of time that we spend as a child, it is remarkable that there has been so little research into adulthood. To a large extent, however, this can be traced to the influence of the two dominant schools of thought in the earliest years of developmental psychology.

The **nativist** school of thought, as exemplified by one of the very first developmental psychologists, Arnold Gesell, believed that development was genetically determined, and that it was simply a matter of genetic abilities and characteristics 'unfolding' along with the biological maturation of the individual. For these psychologists, adulthood was uninteresting and unimportant, because they believed that genetic development was completed, and that the individual would therefore remain the same throughout their adult life.

The **psychoanalytic** school of thought, too, believed that the personality was essentially fixed by adulthood, because they saw it as having been determined by early experiences. For the most part, therefore, they did not think that personality would change in significant respects. Although many psychoanalysts were engaged in clinical work, and therefore actively involved in the phenomenon of adult change, very few of them saw the need to initiate research into this area.

In recent years, though, there has been a growth of interest in adulthood, and its developmental changes. In part, this arose from a recognition that people do change during this time; in part, too, the increasing demands and complexity of modern life, with its second marriages, double families and major career changes, has meant that we have had to rethink our ideas; and, of course, the increasing sophistication of the consumer culture has led people to consider the types of lives which adults lead, and how these change over time. All these influences, as well as those we considered at the beginning of this chapter, have contributed to the development of a psychology of adulthood.

Stages and phases in adult development

As we saw earlier in this chapter, and in Table 21.1, among the eight psychosocial conflicts which Erikson identified, two in particular need to be resolved during the course of adult life. The first of these occurs in early adulthood, and concerns the conflict between **intimacy** or **isolation**. At this point, according to Erikson, the young adult is developing intimate relationships with partners, and these may involve unsuccessful attempts and painful disappointments. The developmental challenge is to weather these and still remain capable of developing positive, open relationships, rather than to react to disappointment by retreating into isolation and loneliness.

According to Erikson, the intimacy–isolation conflict is at its most significant in the twenties, and by later adulthood has generally been resolved. At that time, a new conflict emerges, which is that between **generativity** or **stagnation**. Those in later adult life may find themselves in routine work, and with little novelty and excitement in the domestic sphere. At this point, they may simply settle for stagnation, believing that for them the interesting parts of life are over. But many others take a more positive view, and continue to develop their interests and skills; or they look for new ways to explore their potential. This, according to Erikson, is the more psychologically healthy resolution of the conflict, and forms a positive foundation for the successful resolution of the next conflict, of **integrity versus despair**, which arises as the person faces old age.

Levinson's eight 'seasons' of adulthood

Levinson (1978) identified eight 'seasons' of adulthood, which are listed in Table 21.4 overleaf. Levinson preferred the term 'seasons' to 'stages' because the notion of 'stage' also carries within it the implicit idea that things are continually improving. A developmental stage theory somehow implies that early stages are in some way inferior to later ones. Levinson argued that it is not a matter of 'worse' or 'better', simply a matter of the nature of what is going on being different at different ages.

A number of criticisms have been made of Levinson's model. One is that it is biased towards a middle-class perspective, in that it assumes that marriage will take place later on in adult life, rather than in the late teens or early twenties. Although some may do, not everyone spends their twenties exploring alternatives, and many people have made career choices and are engaging in full family life much earlier than Levinson's model would seem to suggest.

Another major problem with Levinson's model is that it is very male-centred, and therefore does not address the experiences of half of the adult population. There are different issues which arise for women at different ages. For example, Notman (1980) argued that one of the major problems for women to resolve as they reach the age of 30 is that of the conflict between career and

Table 21.4 Seasons of adulthood

1   *Early adult transition* (17–22)
    Adolescence is left behind, and the first choices about adult life are made.

2   *Entering the adult world* (22–28)
    The young adult is making initial choices about work, friendship, personal values and lifestyle, and relationships.

3   *Young adult transition* (28–33)
    The adult is now establishing the pattern of their adult life, based on a fuller knowledge of themselves and their relationship with others and with society. Some earlier choices may be reconsidered and changed.

4   *Settling down* (33–40)
    A stable life structure is now created, and the person establishes their niche in society and stable relationships within the family.

5   *Mid-life transition* (40–45)
    A 'mid-life crisis' may occur, causing re-thinking of general goals and values. The person re-examines their life, and how they have come to terms with their talents and aspirations. For most people, this is a time of consolidation.

6   *Entering middle adulthood* (45–50)
    The individual needs to commit themselves to new tasks, and to create a new life struc-ture; given, for instance, that children may now have grown up and departed, or that further advancement in a given career has become unlikely.

7   *Transition* (50–55)
    The individual may now engage in further questioning of how their life is organised; and those people who did not have a crisis earlier in their adult life may have one.

8   *Culmination of middle adulthood* (55–60)
    At this age, people start to build a new life-structure for themselves. This is often a time of great fulfilment and satisfaction; although of course some may take a more negative view.

Source: Adapted from Levinson, 1978

parenthood. For career-minded women who also want to have children, timing is crucial. As the age of 30 approaches, such women become acutely aware that they will need to make a decision soon. This puts considerable pressure on them to achieve a reasonably high level of success in their chosen career quite early on, in order that their necessary absences from it will not detract too much from their whole life-path.

For women who have children earlier on in their lives, the differences can be even greater. Where Levinson describes the period between the ages of 33 and 40 as a time of 'settling down', many such women find this to be exactly the age when their lives are opening out and offering new opportunities. The immediate demands of small toddlers are now behind them, and many women return to work or to college. They begin to look to developing a career for the first time, often as teachers, social workers or in other careers where maturity and interpersonal experience are valued. So far, there is relatively little data on the life-transitions of women who make such choices, although it seems likely that the growing impact of feminist psychology will result in such research becoming more important in the near future.

Gould's model of consciousness transformation

Gould (1978) put forward a different model of what happens during adulthood, suggesting that, between the ages of 16 and 45, people pass through a series of **transformations** in terms of how they see themselves, and these are closely linked with the way that they experience adult-hood. The transformations are listed in Table 21.5.

As we can see from the table, Gould's model places much more emphasis on the self as agent, active in determining its own experiences, rather than simply portraying the person as passing through a series of life stages or seasons. Gould is discussing changes in consciousness, rather than changes in the external persona or in the physical situations of the individual, and is therefore emphasising the importance of our own self-definition to how we go about interacting with the world.

Gould's model, too, is open to criticism, as is any theory which attempts to put dates to when specific life-events or life-transitions are likely to take place. Many of the criticisms which apply to Levinson can also be applied to Gould, particularly where the later periods are concerned. For example, the discovery of internal aspects of oneself is something which can continue throughout life, and often does.

The mid-life crisis

Sheehy (1976) argued that adults go through a **mid-life crisis** in their forties or fifties. This period, according to Sheehy and other theorists, produces a certain amount of anxiety and in-

Table 21.5 Transitions during adulthood

Age 16–22	The individual's primary task is that of leaving the world of the parents, and adjusting to the responsibilities which that change implies. Central to this is the change from dependency, with its implicit idea that someone is always there in the background, so that we are protected from the consequences of our choices, as mostly happens during adolescence; to the recognition that independence also involves taking responsibility for ourselves.
Age 22–28	The individual develops their adult competences, and learns to develop their own autonomy rather than simply blindly following rules or conventions which they learned at home. 'I'm nobody's baby now.'
Age 28–34	The adult is coming to know themselves better, and coming to terms with aspects of their nature which were not previously to the fore.
Age 35–45	The major psychological transition involves accepting a sense of our own mortality: perceiving that life is not going to go on for ever and that the end of one's working career is in sight.

Source: Adapted from Gould, 1978

security, as the individual comes to terms with the reality of growing older and evaluates the progress of their life so far. At this time, the individual may make dramatic changes to their life: perhaps moving into a totally different field of work, or re-evaluating their personal relationships with friends and family. Mann (1980) described the crisis as involving the individual in facing up to a fear that it may be too late for them to achieve some of their life-goals, and coming to terms with the realities of their life as opposed to the ideals and ambitions of young adulthood.

Sheehy regarded the mid-life crisis as an important transition, during which the individual generates a positive adjustment to the process of growing older. Other writers, however, have challenged the idea that a mid-life crisis is inevitable. Although some people undoubtedly do change direction in their middle years, others pass through adulthood more smoothly, and without facing crises at all. Brim (1976) argued that the mid-life crisis is actually far less common than many researchers had assumed, applying only to a relatively small proportion of people.

There is, however, some suggestion that middle life does generate a certain amount of **reappraisal**, even though people often re-evaluate their lives without going through the type of emotional upheaval characterised by the mid-life crisis. A longitudinal study of male Harvard graduates which began in the 1930s (Vaillant, 1977) showed that in their fifties, they had come to value family and work significance far more than the power and prestige they had valued earlier in their adult careers.

Brim (1976) discussed how many men engaged in intensive pursuit of their careers feel obliged to suppress the more nurturant aspects of their natures, but feel much more able to express these after the age of 50 or so, when the major career battles are over. Similarly, many women later in life express the more assertive and achievement-oriented facets of their personality. This does not mean that their original characters have changed: simply that they feel more able to express themselves fully, and less need to suppress the non-stereotypical aspects of their personality.

We can see, then, that stage theories of adulthood and those theories which have attempted to identify sequences in how adults proceed through their middle years have encountered some difficulties. These have mainly been concerned with the difficulty of making normative statements about what people are like: as with research into gender roles, researchers have too often neglected the wide diversity of lifestyle and possibilities which exist in modern society. But general stage-type approaches can be useful in highlighting some of the important features of development, and in directing attention to aspects of the adult experience which might otherwise be overlooked.

Marriage and family life

A different type of research into lifespan development has focused on typical experiences which form a part of adulthood for many people, such as the idea of the mid-life crisis which we looked at earlier. It also includes research into marriage and family life, life-events and bereavement, which we will look at later.

Most research into marriage has been conducted by interviewing couples who have been married for varying lengths of time to find out about their experiences. Swenson, Eskew and Kolheff (1981) found that, during the course of marriage, the types of interactions which partners experience changes over time. In the first few years, couples report a great deal of talking, spending time together, engaging jointly in recreational activities, and arguing and making up. But as the demands of child-rearing become more intense, the partners spend less time with each other, and the relationship becomes less intense. However, in many cases, couples reported that they became closer again when the children left home.

Not every couple decides to have children, of course, and it would be interesting to see how those marriages develop over time. In Chapter 14, we looked at the different theories of loving which have been put forward. Hatfield and Walster (1978) suggest that love in marriage can be divided into two types: **passionate love**, which is the sort of love that many couples feel when they first get married, and companionate love, which develops more slowly. It is possible that couples who do not have children have more opportunity to develop a close companionate relationship over time, as they are able to share more adult activities and interests than may be possible for child-rearing couples.

Marriages can develop in many different ways. Cuber and Harroff (1965) identified five basic types of marriage, which are listed in Table 21.6. In their own research, Cuber and Harroff found that about 80% of the marriages that they studied fell into the first three categories. However, it is worth noticing when the study took place and the social context in which it occurred. The 1960s were a time when the rigid conventionality of the post-war years was being rejected. As a result of this, many researchers held quite idealised views of relationships and how they could be. Nowadays, possibly as a result of many of the lifestyle explorations which took place during the 1970s and 1980s, we may see things a little more realistically.

Many modern psychologists, for instance, could argue that the type of marriage described as 'total', while an attractive idea, might in fact be psychologically cloying and unhealthy for the partners. Psychologists nowadays tend to emphasise the importance of people retaining their independent identities, rather than allowing themselves to become totally submerged in a relationship with another person. Retaining independence generally involves retaining a certain amount of psychological privacy. Nowadays, too, psychologists and other people tend to value companionate love more, and so many people would regard a marriage in category 3 as quite a positive thing, whereas Cuber and Harroff seemed to regard it as something to be avoided if possible.

Argyle (1990) reported a questionnaire study of the experience of marriage, from which a number

Table 21.6 Types of marriage	
1 *Conflict-habituated*	In this type of marriage, both partners argue and fight with one another, but as a routine part of their relationship. Often, the partners in such marriages have an implicit mutual understanding about their relationship – even though they find it stressful, they would not consider divorce.
2 *Devitalised*	Although the partners are still fond of each other, and will assert that they are still in love, many of their interactions are routine, and they share few activities and interests.
3 *Passive/congenial*	These partners find marriage comfortable and convenient. They are contented with one another, and accommodate readily to each other's interests.
4 *Vital*	In this type of marriage, both partners are equally involved in and committed to the family's activities. They will share economic, parenting and recreational activities together.
5 *Total*	Partners in this type of marriage are completely committed to one another, and share their emotional lives, fantasies, work interests and personal confidences as well as their family activities.

Source: Cuber and Harroff, 1965

of findings emerged. One of these was that married people appear to engage in far better health-promoting behaviour than those of equivalent age and background who are single. They drink less – and specifically get drunk less – they smoke less and they are better at obeying medical instructions. Married people are also much less likely to be admitted to a mental hospital.

Argyle also found that there is some evidence that the immune system seems to be more highly activated in people who are living in close family situations, although it is uncertain how this should be interpreted. Argyle suggested that this might be part of a biological system evolved by the family to aid survival, which is one possible explanation. It is also possible that this is a direct outcome of the social and emotional effects of living in families: if family life is all about looking after one another, then this might have an outcome of emotional stability and physical health; alternatively, the increased immune system activity could simply be a physiological result from the individual's close exposure to a wider range of potential infection. More research into how people respond to living in close non-family groups might be helpful here.

The family life-cycle

For many people (though not for all), entering marriage it is also the first step towards forming a new family of their own. Many couples expect to have children, and, after a few years of marriage, may experience considerable pressure from relatives in that direction. The task of raising children places distinctive responsibilities on the partners involved, and inevitably has its effect on the development of the marriage.

Duvall (1971) proposed that a family passes through eight distinct stages during the course of its existence (see Table 21.7). Some families will spend more time in one stage than in another, but the stage that a family is in is generally determined by the age of the oldest child. According to this model, each phase makes different demands on family members. For many, the first stage is the time which they remember as being the happiest – perhaps because of the rather dramatic change which ensues when the first infant is born.

Galinsky (1981) discussed how the demands of caring for an infant typically leaves both parents feeling tired and drained, even when both are participating in domestic responsibilities. Many of Galinsky's interviewees thought that they had underestimated how much effort would go into caring for the baby, even though they found the infant itself to be a delight. This second stage in the family life-cycle, then, is often remembered and experienced as an arduous one, although it is also seen as having many rewards.

In the third stage of the family life-cycle, the focus within the family becomes the issue of **authority**. Anyone who has dealt with a child between the ages of two and five will know how self-willed these children can be on occasions. The question of how the child will be managed, by both parents, becomes important at this time. In addition, the adult partners will be establishing patterns in the sharing of their responsibilities, which raises issues of authority within the partnership which need to be settled between them.

Table 21.7 Stages of marriage

1	The honeymoon period	Married couples, without children.
2	The nurturing period	Childbearing families (the oldest child being between 0 and two years).
3	The authority period	Families with pre-school children (the oldest child being between two and five years).
4	The interpretive period	Families with school children (the oldest child being between five and thirteen years).
5	The interdependent period	Families with teenagers.
6	The launching period	Families launching young adults (first child gone to last child leaving home).
7	The empty-nest period	Middle-aged parents, no children at home.
8	The retirement period	Ageing family members, retired from work.

Source: Adapted from Duvall, 1971

When the first child goes to school, the parental role changes, gaining an increased emphasis on **interpreting**, **broadening** and **adjudicating** the child's experiences. Typically, parents report that at this stage they begin to become a little more realistic about parenting and their family life – if only because they recognise that each stage is not going to last for ever. The fifth stage, when the first child becomes adolescent, raises different problems again, and often involves significant re-alliances within the family. Bengtson and Troll (1978) found that many partners in this stage report becoming closer to one another, perhaps in response to the new parenting demands raised by adolescent children.

The sixth stage, in which the children leave home and establish themselves in their own lives, may be either easy or stressful for the parents. Datan (1980) found that most stress seems to occur when the children do not leave on time, remaining in the parental home long after they would normally have been expected to leave. Once the children have gone, though, many parents report the seventh stage – the **empty-nest period** – as being the most satisfying of the whole marriage. At this time, couples often find themselves sharing new interests and enjoying one another's company in ways that have not been possible beforehand. For many, this enjoyment and interpersonal harmony lasts throughout the retirement stage as well. Argyle (1990) found that this is often the time of greatest marital happiness, particularly if the couple maintain contact with the children who have left home.

Although the age at which couples have children varies, Duvall argued that most families will tend to go through these stages. The normative model is that couples will spend their early adulthood in stages 1–3, and send the youngest child to school when the mother is round about 35 or so. Duvall's model has been useful in identifying the number of different phases involved in parenting, although it is notable that most people spend only about a dozen or so years in the first three stages by comparison with the many more years which they spend in other stages.

Criticisms of the family life-cycle model
The family life-cycle model has been criticised for a number of reasons. One of these is its limited scope – as can be seen, it really only describes

traditional families, and does not take into account the number of people who divorce, remarry, become widowed or have a second family. A significant number of people bring up children who are not their own, and a large number of people also spend some years as single parents. None of these everyday circumstances can really be encompassed by Duvall's model.

Duvall's model has also been criticised on the grounds that it fails to consider the overlap between families. By assuming that the family 'begins' in the first few days of marriage, little attention is given to the influence of the older families from which the partners have come. In real life, though, there is often considerable involvement with parents (whose own family will be in stage 7 or 8), particularly during the first three stages. Duvall's model contains an implicit assumption that families can be regarded as isolated and self-contained; but inter-generational influence can be important, regardless of whether the family remains in physical proximity or not.

However, despite the criticisms, the model has some value in giving structure to our ways of looking at the family, and in highlighting areas in which further research is needed. In particular, its emphasis on the way that the family unit is not a static entity, but is constantly changing in response to the different tasks facing the people involved, has been a useful one for the study of human development through the lifespan.

Stressful life-events

As we saw in Chapter 13, stressful experiences can have a serious effect on physical health. During the course of adult life, people encounter a number of stressful events, such as the death of a parent, moving house, coping with major illness, either in themselves or in someone close, and so on. In 1967, Holmes and Rahe proposed that such life-events could have very serious consequences for people's physical well-being.

Holmes and Rahe examined a number of medical case histories and conducted a series of interviews. As a result of this work, they developed a scale of stressful life-events, in which different types of events were assigned different values (see Table 21.8). The scale ran from 0 to 100, with an arbitrary value of 50 assigned to marriage, as a major life-change involving stress and adjustment.

Holmes and Rahe argued that the number of

Table 21.8 The Holmes and Rahe stressful life-events scale

Death of marriage partner	100	Change in work responsibilities	29
Divorce	73	Son or daughter leaving home	29
Marital separation	65	Trouble with in-laws	29
Prison sentence	63	Outstanding personal achievement	28
Death of parent, or close family member	63	Spouse begins or stops work	26
Personal injury or illness	53	Beginning or ending school/college	26
Marriage	50	Change in living conditions	25
Being sacked from work	47	Change in personal habits	24
Marital reconciliation	45	Trouble with boss at work	23
Retirement	45	Moving house	20
Change in health of family member	44	Change of school/college	20
Pregnancy	40	Change of recreation	19
Sex difficulties	39	Change in social activities	18
Gain of new family member	39	Change in sleeping habits	16
Business readjustment	39	Change in eating habits	15
Change in financial state	38	Holiday	13
Death of close friend	37	Christmas	12
Change to a different kind of work	36	Minor breaches of the law	11
Foreclosure of mortgage	30		

Source: Adapted from Holmes and Rahe, 1967

points which an individual collected in a given year according to this scale could be correlated with their physical health in the following year. For example, people who scored between 200 and 300 points in a given year were statistically very likely to develop major health problems during the course of the following year. Those scoring over 100 points were statistically likely to suffer a moderately serious period of illness. Holmes and Rahe attributed this to the physical drain on the body's reserves represented by the stress of these life-events, and the person's reactions to them.

It is important, though, to remember that a correlation between two measures does not mean that there is a causal relationship between them. Dohrenwend and Dohrenwend (1974) claimed that 29 of the items on the stressful life-events scale could be linked with a developing illness in some other way. Something like trouble with in-laws or changes in personal habits might be triggered by changes in physical health, so the two measures – physical health and stressful life-events – may not be completely independent of each other. So we should be wary of drawing the automatic conclusion that stress causes illness, even though we know that there is a connection between the two.

Furthermore, the correlations which Holmes and Rahe found, although significant, were small ones, which means that a great deal of the variation is still unaccounted for. Some people can survive a large amount of stress without falling ill, and they seem to be the ones who have good psychological **coping mechanisms**, and/or who engage in physical exercise. (We looked at the reasons why this might make a difference in Chapter 13.) So even though Holmes and Rahe's findings were statistically significant, there is quite a wide range of individual differences in terms of how likely any given person is to suffer physically as a result of a particularly stressful year.

Subjective well-being

Research into stressful life-events led to research into adults' feelings of subjective well-being, and in particular how this involves making comparisons with other people, and with the person's own past. Strack, Schwartz and Gschneidinger (1985) investigated what effect thinking about events in one's life had on judgements of subjective well-being. They found that thinking about positive past events tended to lead to lower ratings of general well-being than thinking about negative past events. It seemed to produce a mental contrast between 'me as I was then' and 'me as I am now', in which the current picture was far less favourable than the previous one. People who could look back on the past and think how their life had improved tended to have a much higher level of subjective well-being.

Interestingly, whether people judge themselves to be happy with their lives or not bears very little relationship to what their objective circumstances are. But it does depend on who we compare ourselves with. Strack *et al.* (1990) asked people to report their own subjective well-being in a situation in which they would be making comparisons with another individual. They found that the presence of someone who was worse off led people to make more positive judgements of their own happiness. This effect was enlarged when the research participant's attention was deliberately directed towards the comparison person, such as by making sure that they were sitting next to one another.

Strack *et al.* concluded that judgements of subjective well-being can often be a function of temporary influences. Who we are with, what our own situation is, how we look back on the past, our mood at the time of making the judgement and the social context in which the report is given can all affect whether we judge ourselves to be largely happy or not. Which is why, Strack *et al.* argued, the relationship between the objective conditions of someone's life and their personal reports of subjective well-being is not particularly strong.

Bereavement

At the opposite end of the emotional scale, one of the most difficult life-changes which we can face is that of **bereavement** – losing someone who is close to us. During middle life, many people experience a severe bereavement, sometimes through the loss of one or both parents. Others lose their partners, or sometimes children, accidentally or through illness and disease. The impact of modern medicine and more hygienic lifestyles, however, has meant that death is a much more uncommon event in most families than it used to be: people live for longer, and are less likely to succumb to childhood ailments or diseases in early adulthood.

Perhaps as a result of this, in modern Western society, death is often regarded as an unthinkable event: people dislike talking about death, and it is often regarded as psychologically unhealthy to want to do so. But the **death taboo** of Western society also means that we often avoid acknowledging what people are going through when they have recently been bereaved, and this can sometimes magnify the distress which they experience.

Grieving is an intense process, and many people feel overwhelmed by the complexity of the emotions which they feel. Ramsay (1977) identified nine different components of grief, which are listed in Table 21.9 opposite. The complexity of the emotion is in itself often extremely disturbing for those experiencing it, since they feel as though they have no sooner come to grips with one of the emotions involved, than another one threatens to overwhelm them.

As might be expected, all this emotional turmoil takes its physical toll. Severe bereavement is often followed by physical illness. Parkes (1964) found that widows consulted their doctors more often in the first six months after bereavement than they had done before, and Rees and Lutkins (1967) showed that widows and widowers were ten times as likely to die themselves in the year immediately following bereavement. Parkes, Benjamin and Fitzgerald (1969) explained this finding as coming about in three ways: through self-neglect, through suicide of one form or another, or as a result of cardiac illness brought on by severe stress.

Stages of bereavement

The experience of bereavement brings out a number of reactions in people. From work with widows and other bereaved people, Parkes (1972) described three 'stages' in the reaction to bereavement. Strictly speaking, however, these are not true stages, since they overlap considerably. The bereaved person will often oscillate wildly between one reaction and another. The first appearance of each part of the bereavement reaction, however, tends to follow the three-phase sequence which Parkes identified.

The first stage of bereavement, according to Parkes, is that of **denial**. In this, the bereaved person expresses disbelief that the death has really happened, refusing to see it as 'real'. This stage is more extreme and lasts for longer when death has been unexpected. It is a common reaction in

Table 21.9 Components of grief

1	*Shock*	A feeling of numbness, that it cannot be really true.
2	*Disorganisation*	Being unable to get even simple everyday tasks done.
3	*Denial*	Refusal to acknowledge the death.
4	*Depression*	This includes feelings of both desolate pining, and of despair.
5	*Guilt*	People often blame themselves for things which have happened, even when it is clear to an outsider that such guilt is unreasonable.
6	*Anxiety and/or panic attacks*	These may come about because the complexity of feelings is so strong and so unlike normal everyday behaviour that the person wonders if they are going mad.
7	*Aggression*	There is often considerable hostility and anger resulting from the bereavement, which may be focused inwards, or may be directed at others, like medical staff or relatives.
8	*Resolution*	This is a form of acceptance which begins to emerge as the worst of the grief dies down.
9	*Re-integration*	The person begins to re-organise their new life. Many people find it difficult to do this immediately, because it constitutes a formal acceptance of the loss which sometimes feels disloyal. But after a couple of weeks most people are beginning to re-integrate the structure of their lives.

Source: Adapted from Ramsay, 1977

people who have been bereaved through accidents, for instance, to remark that it took them some time before they could believe that it had actually happened. But even when death has been expected for some time, there is usually some element of denial: it seems to be a little unreal to people when they are first told about it.

The second stage identified by Parkes is a period of **pining**. At this time, the bereaved person longs for the other intensely, and can become very restless and fidgety. It involves a certain amount of unconscious searching for the dead person, and often, at this time, bereaved people will think they have caught a fleeting glimpse of the lost person in a crowd, or at a distance. When this happens, they can become very worried, thinking that they may be hallucinating, or losing their grip on reality.

In reality, though, what they are experiencing has a much more prosaic explanation. It is a real-life manifestation of the power of **perceptual set** (see Chapter 2), in which our mental readiness to see something makes us more likely to think that we have seen it. Because the individual is thinking about the person that they have lost so much, they are mentally prepared to see them. This means that anyone with a similar appearance, or way of walking, or similar mannerisms, can instantly look the same, and turn out to be different only when seen more closely. If someone does not know what is happening on these occasions, the experience can be very distressing.

The third stage of bereavement, according to Parkes, is **depression**. The process of accepting that the loved person really has gone and will not return is frequently accompanied by a period of intense apathy, which often includes elements of self-blame and sudden waves of anguish. This depression comes and goes, gradually becoming less frequent, until by three to six weeks after the bereavement it has largely abated. It will, however, still be easily triggered off by particular events like finding a special photograph or visiting a favourite place. Parkes also found that most people experienced a resurgence of grief on the anniversary of the bereavement, and at special times like Christmas.

Abnormal grieving

Parkes distinguished between 'normal' and 'abnormal' grief. Normal grief, he argued, follows the three-phase pattern outlined above, and the worst of it is usually over after six weeks or so. In some of Parkes's clients, however, the grieving process lasted much longer. They were still experiencing intense grief well over a year after the bereavement. One characteristic of these people which Parkes observed was that they had often spent a longer period of time in the first stage, denying the reality of the death, than most other people did.

In a later study, Parkes and Weiss (1983) identified two sets of factors which could cause prolonged or abnormal grieving. The first were factors concerned with how the grief is **expressed**. During the course of grieving, it is important for people to be able to express how they feel, and it helps them to work through the process and to come to terms with what has happened. Yet in our society, expressions of grief are discouraged: people are often not permitted, generally by well-meaning friends or relatives, to talk about their loss 'in case it upsets them'. This suppression can mean that the grieving process lasts for much longer than it would do otherwise, and means that the person is more likely to become abnormally disturbed.

Another consequence of our social taboo about death is that people are often encouraged to get everything over with very quickly. But it generally takes a couple of days for people to recover from the first, stunned phase of bereavement, which can mean that if the funeral is rushed, it can take place too early. Many people find that the rituals connected with funerals are helpful at this time; and it is not uncommon for bereaved persons to feel deprived or cheated later on, if the funeral has taken place too quickly, or they have no way of acknowledging the death. Other societies, which have different traditions for dealing with death, are often psychologically healthier in this respect (see Box 21.1).

The second set of factors has to do with the finding is that those who have had **disturbed relationships**, or unsettled ones, with the dead person often find that their grief is extremely intense, and even overwhelming. Relatives are often surprised at how keenly a family member may feel the death of someone close that they had never appeared to like much in life. This is not hypocrisy: the distress is genuine. It is thought that this arises from excessive feelings of guilt, or of 'unfinished business', mixed with the awareness that it is now too late to re-establish good relationships or resolve old conflicts. If someone has had a positive relationship with the person who died, or if they were able to resolve their relationship positively, then bereavement is less likely to become severe or abnormal.

Dying

Facing up to the fact that someone you know is going to die is something that many people find very difficult. Facing up to your own death,

paradoxically, is often rather different. In *Living While Dying* (1989) Owens and Naylor reported on the reactions from others which one of the authors had experienced while approaching death because of a terminal illness. When she found out that she was dying, Freda Naylor, a doctor studying clinical psychology, decided that her experiences should be used to inform and help other people. Together with a psychologist, Glynn Owens, she discussed different aspects of what was happening to her, and made suggestions to guide those dealing with dying people, or going through the experience themselves.

Telling people

One set of recommendations concerned the business of telling people that they are dying, or that someone close to them is about to die. Hinton (1967) identified this as a major problem for many people who are facing up to death. Owens and Naylor argued that trying to hide this knowledge from the dying person can place a great strain on that person, who wants to be able to discuss what is going to happen, and put their affairs in order.

Many professionals, such as nurses or doctors, also avoid telling people that they are dying, for fear of the emotional reaction which results. But according to Owens and Naylor, the immediate reaction is mainly a result of shock. In the long run people will almost always say that they prefer to have been informed. Owens and Naylor emphasised that it is important for a dying person to gain accurate information about what is likely to happen to them, so that they know what to expect. They need to be allowed to discuss what is happening, including being able to express emotional upset without being hushed up or having the subject changed.

Another problem which often occurs for people who are dying is that others may treat them as if they were already halfway dead. They sometimes find it difficult to allow a dying person to get on with living what is left of their normal life, even if they are expected to live for some considerable time. Feelings of awkwardness can also result in well-meaning friends avoiding the dying individual, perhaps communicating only with the partner or avoiding contact with the family altogether. All these factors, Owens and Naylor pointed out, are about adaptation to the new situation. It is relatively easy for problems of this type to be overcome if others

Box 21.1 Attitudes to dying and bereavement

Every society has its rituals and traditions associated with death, and they serve several valuable functions. One of these is that **bereavement rituals** provide the people who have been bereaved with an established structure within which they can act without the pressure of continual decision-making. Because what is expected of them is ritualised and conventional, all they have to do is to go along with it. To someone who is trying to cope with the re-adjustment and grief involved in losing someone who is dear to them, the presence of these rituals can be comforting.

Bereavement rituals also provide the bereaved person with an opportunity to express their grief. They provide a structure and a known sequence of activities, at a time when we are at our most disorganised and distressed. They also allow people to express psychological needs, such as the need to 'talk' with the dead person mentally, and to resolve the unfinished business that is almost always left behind when a human relationship is severed. In this respect the traditions in some societies are far more psychologically healthy than others. Secular Western society tends to be rather dismissive of grief: people are not provided with many opportunities to cry freely, and often feel as if, in some way, it is wrong for them to do so. Other societies are more realistic: in an Irish Wake, for example, it is completely acceptable to express extreme emotion, as it is in the mourning customs of many other cultures.

In addition, many traditional belief systems accept the psychological experience of bereavement far more fully. What Western colonial explorers interpreted as 'ancestor worship' in some African tribes, for instance, is very far from that. Instead, it is a method of acknowledging the continuing psychological reality of the people who have died. People who have been bereaved often report that they keep 'seeing' the dead person, walking down the street, among crowds; or feeling as if they were there when they enter the house. It feels to them as if that person were still alive. All Western belief systems can say about this is that it is not true – which is not very helpful to those who are going through it. But by providing a place where the bereaved person can take food and drink to the dead person, and can talk to them as if they were still alive, many traditional belief systems provide an experience which accepts the psychological reality of bereavement, and helps the individual to cope.

In the same way, Western society has a very extreme **taboo about death**. Despite filling its entertainment media with accounts of murders and killings (or perhaps because of it), the reality of death is considered to be unthinkable – and not something which should be talked about. To discuss one's own death is considered 'morbid'; to prepare for it by making a will or arranging things with relatives is often dismissed as unnecessary. The emergence of the hospice movement in Britain came about because there was such a need for places where dying people could go, which would acknowledge that they really were about to die, and would help them to cope. Most of the efforts of bereavement counsellors and others working in this area are directed towards helping people to admit openly the (to the Western mind) unthinkable fact that people, including ourselves, do die.

are prepared to be open and honest with the dying person.

Owens and Naylor argue that society needs to become more at ease with the subject of death, rather than trying to pretend that it does not happen. Everyone does die, after all, so making the subject more open would provide considerable relief for many who are suffering terminal illnesses, and would help their relatives as well. The treatment of death as a taboo subject simply creates more strain for everyone involved. This is the belief which also underlies the hospice movement, which has shown that the months or years when someone is dying can be a happy and productive time despite awareness of what is to come. As Owens and Naylor pointed out, our society's morbid fear of death too often means that, unthinkingly, we do not allow dying people to make the most of what is left of their lives.

Ageing

What does it mean to say that someone is old? How do we define ageing? Kastenbaum (1979) distinguished between five different kinds of age, which are listed in Table 21.10. These ages can be quite different, not correlating with one another at all. For example, it is quite common for someone's subjective age to be very different from their chronological age – many chronologically old people feel 'young inside'. Some people, through paying attention to exercise and fitness routines, may have a biological age which is also quite different from their chronological age, and biologically, of course, people age at different rates.

Unrealistic perceptions of ageing

In terms of social age, our society tends to be quite split in its attitudes. On the one hand, it tends to be **ageist**, regarding 'old people' in a range of negative ways – in one study, for instance, young children described old people as 'sad', 'dirty' and 'ugly'. Barrow (1976) found that college students experienced disgust and repulsion when they thought about growing old. The ageism of society is also shown in the way that we regard **retirement**. Even though we now live longer and are much healthier than used to be the case earlier in this century, we still regard people as being 'too old' for work when they reach retirement age.

Table 21.10 Types of age

Chronological age	This is the exact number of years that someone has lived.
Biological age	This is concerned with the state of the body.
Subjective age	This is to do with how old a person feels to themselves.
Functional age	This is to do with the kind of life that someone leads, the job that they do, their family responsibilities, and the like.
Social age	This is to do with how we are accepted by others, and the age-group of people with whom we mix.

Source: Adapted from Kastenbaum, 1979

On the other hand, many professional people in our society are not expected to retire at the same ages as are working-class people, and the most responsible jobs in society, like those of judges, politicians and even company directors, are often held by those who are well past retiring age. In these professions, older people are respected for their experience, an attitude which is similar to that found in traditional societies, in which old people are revered and respected for the knowledge and experience that they have accumulated over the years. Overall, modern consumer society tends to devalue age, but with these very interesting exceptions.

The ageing stereotype

The fact that we are prepared to entrust the most powerful social positions to older people should in itself show us that the negative stereotypes of old people which many of us hold are inaccurate. But old people are often 'invisible' in society – despite the fact that the population as a whole is growing older. In Britain in 1972 there were over eight million people over 65, and the proportion has increased dramatically since then. Given this, it seems odd that old people do not object more to their social status.

Dyson (1980) suggested that one of the main reasons why old people do not challenge the more negative stereotypes of ageing is because they hold them too. In interviews with elderly people, Dyson found that they were fully aware of the stereotype, and thought that most old people were really like that – but not themselves personally. So although they knew that the stereotype was unfair and unreasonable in their own case, they did not organise together with other old people to challenge it.

Another reason why old people do not object to the stereotype of the old person – or why people may not listen to them when they do object – may lie in the nature of the stereotype itself. The problems presented by Alzheimer's disease and senile dementia mean that people suffering from these conditions become confused and disoriented, and need to be cared for constantly. Although they represent only a small proportion of the elderly – fewer than 10% – it is a minority which makes up a significant part of the popular stereotype. This means that many old people who are suffering from nothing more than normal absent-mindedness are treated as if they were senile by others. So any protests which they make are dismissed as 'ramblings', and not to be taken seriously.

Physical weakness

Another problem is presented by physical weakness. As we grow older, bones become more brittle and joints become less elastic. This means that an old person can be quite vulnerable to everyday accidents, and may learn to move more slowly and to treat their body with caution as a result. In a society which is oriented towards youth and fitness, many people unthinkingly respond to those who are weak and disabled with contempt. It is not a pleasant reaction, but one which is very common.

For many, a decline in physical health means that they will eventually need to be looked after full-time. This often means that they will have to live in an institution, which in itself may produce changes which confirm the stereotype that people have of old people. Wigdor, Nelson and Hickerson (1977) asked college students to play the roles of staff and residents in a mock-up of a residential home for old people. After only 48 hours, the students who had been assigned roles as residents began to show personality changes including submissiveness, withdrawal and introversion; whereas those playing care staff roles became increasingly dominating.

The implication of this study, then, is that the dependency induced by the conditions of the home and the assumptions of care staff (for example that 'they're just like children') sometimes means that old people have very little chance of asserting their individuality without being seen as troublemakers. But of course, not all residential homes are the same. Studies of 'good' old people's homes show that they include practices like encouraging visits from relatives and contact with other groups in the community, encouraging people to go out of the home (for instance to go shopping, or to the pub in the evening), organising residents' committees and taking notice of what they say and encouraging people to bring in their own furniture and personal possessions. In short, a good old people's home, Hayes (1988) argued, is one which encourages its residents to lead as normal a life as possible. But although some are changing, many residential homes still follow the old model of encouraging dependency.

Changes in ability

One of the other problems produced by ageist stereotypes is that they tend to exaggerate the decline of ability which occurs with ageing. This tended to be reinforced by early research into the subject, which found that when people of different ages were tested, the results seemed to show a systematic decline as people grew older. Those in their twenties were more capable than those in their forties, who in turn showed higher abilities than those in their sixties.

But these studies were all done using a **cross-sectional research** method. The researchers took a cross-section of the population, of different ages, and compared them on various tests of ability. However, this meant that the researchers were unable to identify the effects of different experiences during the course of life, and these can be very considerable. For example, people who were born in the early part of this century had very different educational, nutritional and social experiences from those who were born later. So someone who was 60 in the 1960s could not realistically be compared with someone who was in their teens at the same time, because their early experiences would have been so very different.

When researchers started to investigate ageing using a longitudinal method – following the same people throughout the course of their lives, and testing them at intervals as they grew older – a different picture began to emerge. This picture showed that lifespan development, including ageing, had everything to do with practice and experience. The way in which people exercise their abilities plays an important role in whether those abilities decline with age or not.

For example, early cross-sectional studies of intelligence showed a decline in measured intelligence (IQ) as people grew older. They suggested that IQ reaches a peak in the early twenties and then declines steadily with age. But many of the older people in those studies had little experience with IQ tests, whereas the younger ones had often done them before, if only as part of the eleven-plus examination which was introduced after 1945 to decide which type of education each child should receive. The older people had experienced a different kind of education, and the kinds of abilities tested by the IQ tests were not ones which had been emphasised in their younger days. This too was quite unlike the experience of the younger research participants. So it was not really surprising that younger people did better on IQ tests than older ones.

Burns (1966) reported on a longitudinal study of intelligence, which followed a cohort of teachers from the time of their graduation from college through to when they retired. This study found that the teachers showed a general increase in IQ, rather than a decline, as they grew older. Moreover, when their scores on the IQ tests were analysed, Burns found that practice seemed to have had a great deal to do with what had happened. The teachers who taught science and mathematical subjects showed an improvement in the numerical and diagrammatical components of the IQ tests, whereas those who taught arts subjects showed an increase in verbal fluency and verbal reasoning.

Ability and motivation

Another unrealistic perception of ageing was generated by the methodology used by some of the psychologists who investigated changes in ability as we grow older. Some of the most significant studies in this respect were conducted by Welford, in 1958. Welford adopted the technique of testing people to the absolute limits of their abilities. By doing so, he found that short-term memory, reaction-time and decision-making seem to decline with age. But Welford emphasised that this did not necessarily mean that older people were less capable at their jobs or at day-to-day living, since it is very rare indeed that we use any of our abilities to their absolute limit. For all realistic purposes, older people were just as capable as young people.

Gradually, however, researchers began to discover that sometimes older people are even more capable than young people – particularly where real-life tasks to do with their working lives are concerned. Belbin (1958) found that if training methods were adapted to the needs of older workers – and in particular if they were made relevant to the job and did not involve abstract and disconnected instruction – older workers would learn faster than younger ones. Their greater experience and expertise gives them a wider range of resources to draw on, so that they can often learn more efficiently than those who have less experience.

Welford, in 1976, suggested that the lower performance which older people show in abstract laboratory testing may result, not from lack of ability, but from lack of motivation. Quite simply, if older people see a task as irrelevant, they do not try as hard at it as younger people do, and so they score less well. This connects with findings by Bromley (1966), that older people do better on tasks which make sense to them than they do on tasks which are meaningless and context-free.

Retirement

Perhaps one of the biggest life-changes which people face as they get older is that of **retirement**. Atchley (1976) proposed that retirement involves seven distinct phases, which are listed in Table 21.11. As we can see from the table, retirement can be a lengthy process and involve a number of different transitions. Although originally, when retirement was first introduced, the expected lifespan afterwards was only a few years, as a result of improved health and nutrition most people nowadays can expect to live for a considerable length of time – often as much as 30 years or even

---

Table 21.11 Phases of retirement

1 *The pre-retirement period*
 The person is enjoying and involved in work and does little to prepare for retirement.

2 *The period of work disengagement*
 This occurs immediately before retirement, when they begin to give up some of their work obligations to younger colleagues.

3 *The 'honeymoon' period*
 The person becomes very active, enjoying the 'holiday' from work and doing a number of planned activities.

4 *The disenchantment phase*
 Things are found to be less rosy, and the individual may become depressed.

5 *The reorientation phase*
 The person comes to terms with retirement, and again may take up activities, though usually less frenetically than before.

6 *The adjusted phase*
 The person settles into a long-term way of living. They may even return to employment at this time, or take up charity work.

7 *The final phase*
 This often involves illness: death is pending and the individual begins to prepare for it.

Source: Adapted from Atchley, 1977

more – after retiring from full-time employment. How they adjust to this is intimately linked with our perception of ageing in this society.

Because, to many young people, 'old' includes people in their forties and fifties, we have tended to ignore the fact that many people continue to be healthy and active for many years after they retire. But psychologists are increasingly aware that people in their fifties, sixties and seventies may be as active as they ever were. In some cases, people continue to be active and productive into their eighties, or even their nineties. So it is clear that our views of ageing and of what constitutes 'old' need some adjustment.

In view of this, it seems odd that society continues to reduce the retirement age: many people nowadays are offered early retirement from work, and will retire in their fifties. For some, early retirement is a passport into a second, more independent working career. It is not uncommon, for example, for an ex-policeman to take up a second career as, say, a security consultant, or for an experienced social worker to work as a consultant to social services project teams. But for others retirement involves a different type of life, which does not include external, paid employment.

Disengagement theory

In 1961, Cummings and Henry suggested that there is a biological process of **disengagement** which takes place as someone grows old. As part of this, they gradually come to withdraw from the wider society and participate in fewer aspects of it. The withdrawal is mutual, in that society too has less and less to do with the old person. Cummings and Henry suggested that this disengagement might have a biological basis, as a way of gradually preparing the older person for death once they had fulfilled their biological functions of reproduction and working to maintain species survival.

Disengagement theory became quite popular in the 1960s and early 1970s, because it seemed to explain how there could be so many old people in society and yet they could be so 'invisible'. It was also popular because it presented a genetic explanation for the phenomenon, and, as we have seen in other chapters (for example Chapter 6), genetic explanations for how human beings behave were generally popular with the media, at least in Britain at that time. However, there are a

number of criticisms which can be made of disengagement theory.

Perhaps one of the most significant problems is that disengagement theory does not take account of what happens in many other human societies. As we have seen, in non-technological societies, older people are respected and revered for their experience. Rather than withdrawing from their society, they become more involved than ever, as they are called on to make decisions and to adjudicate in social disputes between family members or different groups. If disengagement had been the inevitable biological process proposed by Cummings and Henry, then we would expect it, or a similar process, to be universal in human societies. In fact, though, we find that the withdrawal of old people from society tends be a feature of industrial societies and not the older types of human civilisation.

Another criticism of this theory is that it presents disengagement as if disengaging were a voluntary action on the part of the old person. But in practice, our society presents far fewer opportunities for involvement on the part of old people than it does for those in younger age-groups. Where opportunities for involvement exist, such as in some charity shops which are almost entirely staffed by people over retirement age, or in those professional careers which we discussed earlier, old people tend to show an active and healthy involvement.

So it is apparent that disengagement is not an inevitable consequence of growing older, even though it is equally clear that some people do seem to disengage from society. A more likely explanation for disengagement seems to lie in a combination of a lack of opportunities for involvement and an acceptance of the stereotype of ageing, which can mean that many people do not try to get involved.

Activity theory

Havighurst (1964) argued that it is important for old people to remain involved in society if they are to have a happy and healthy old age. In interview studies with people from different nationalities, Havighurst et al. (1969) found that, within a group of elderly people, those who were most socially active and involved with their families and communities were far more satisfied with their lives than those who were more segregated. Havighurst saw the process of a healthy retirement as being all to do with the number of social roles which an individual possesses.

Social roles, Havighurst believed, are important in determining someone's feelings of self-worth. Retirement usually involves a decline in the role-count, and this in turn produces a decline in personal feelings of self-worth. As a result, the person is less likely to put as much effort into taking care of themselves and is therefore likely to decline with age. Since the process of retirement means that people lose a significant number of social roles – all those connected with their working careers – Havighurst regarded it as important for old people to keep up their 'role-count' by replacing the social roles that they have lost through retirement with new ones.

This might involve taking on new responsibilities, perhaps by involvement with organisations like Age Concern or within the family and community. An increased role-count would mean that the person had a higher level of self-esteem, was more inclined to look after themselves and would be more likely to have a productive and happy retirement. As can be seen, the activity theory of ageing has been the model for a number of organisations concerned with providing opportunities for older people. It takes a positive view of ageing, seeing the old person as an active agent in her or his own life and as able to make their own decisions, and in this respect is very different from the rather negative picture presented by disengagement theory.

Social exchange theory

However, although many people clearly do benefit from the increased opportunities and additional roles offered by organisations adopting Havighurst's approach, there are other people who look forward to retirement as a time when they can deliberately take a rest, becoming less involved and disengaging themselves from society, at least to some extent. Both activity and disengagement, it would seem, are appropriate strategies for some people but not others. Dyson (1980) proposed that these differences might be explained by seeing retirement as a **social exchange**, between the individual and society.

According to Dowd (1975), who also looked at retirement as a social exchange, the two sides of the social contract are: the old person implicitly agrees to participate less in society's activities, thus freeing places in the work force for younger

people, while society agrees to grant that person an 'honourable discharge' from the Protestant Work Ethic. They gain social approval for their years of leisure, and the right to enjoy them as they feel inclined.

For some old people, this social exchange results in disengagement, as they feel themselves to be no longer fully part of society; while for others the social exchange means that they seek alternative activities in other fields. Atchley (1976) showed that there may be some social class differences in which choice is made. In a comparison between working-class men and male teachers reaching retirement, the working-class men tended to disengage, while the teachers would 're-engage' – looking for new activities in which to become involved.

Dyson suggested that the social exchange of retirement actually places the old person in a **double-bind** (see Chapter 9), in which they are trapped by their situation. As members of society, old people acknowledge the 'fairness' of the unspoken agreement. As individuals, however, often with many healthy and active years ahead, the contract is often seen as inappropriate for them personally. This makes it difficult for old people to challenge the way that society marginalises them, because any attempt to do so is seen as demanding special and unfair treatment.

This has the effect of reducing the possibility for social cohesion among older people. Since they implicitly accept the 'fairness' of the social contract, they conclude that, if they do not fit the accepted view of the older person, there must be something wrong with themselves – that they are not 'typical'. So where victims of other social prejudices have been able to challenge them by banding together and becoming more vocal, it is much harder for old people to do so.

A changing society

In modern society, though, it is apparent that attitudes are changing. In recent years, we have seen a certain amount of increased organisation for old people. Organisations such as the University of the Third Age have shown how the period after retirement can be a very positive one, bringing new opportunities to learn and to take up new hobbies. For many people, the experience of ageing is becoming broader in scope, offering greater possibilities. Increasingly, too, old people who are able to look after themselves are finding it possible to live in sheltered housing or remain in their own homes, rather than having to go into institutional care.

As longevity and good health increase, many more people are using their retirement to set up second careers, and to pursue interests and activities that they would not have expected before. Some firms are experimenting with employing only older workers, and others are recognising the value of having experience rather than youth on their staff. It also seems unlikely that the adults of the post-war baby boom, as they reach retirement age, will be prepared to settle for disengagement or social exchange, and already there are signs that things are changing. We may perhaps see ageism joining racism and sexism as an acknowledged and undesirable prejudice in our society.

Key terms

authority figure A person who represents power or status in some way.

companionate love A form of love which is based on mutual friendship and affection, which generally develops over a long period of time.

psychosocial stages The term given to Erikson's eight life-stages.

Summary

1 Lifespan psychology assumes that development needs to be viewed within its social context. It sees people as active agents in shaping their own lives, exerting a reciprocal influence on their physical and social environments.

2 One of the most influential views of adolescence has been that it is a period of 'storm and stress', producing disruption and emotional upheaval for the adolescent. But more recent research suggests that this applies to only a minority of adolescents.

3 Alternative perspectives on adolescence have emphasised the role transitions of adolescence, or seen it as a developmental stage in which a coherent identity must be built.

4 Coleman's focal theory of adolescence proposes that adolescence is a period which involves diverse changes in many, if not all, areas of life, and that the individual focuses on different changes at different times during the adolescent period.

5 Some studies of adulthood have looked at it in terms of stages, seasons, or in terms of changes in consciousness. The idea of the family life-cycle highlights different phases through which families pass, but has been criticised because it does not take account of single parenting, divorce or remarriage.

6 Stressful life-events may have deleterious effects on the individual's physical health. However, these can be ameliorated by lifestyle or appropriate coping mechanisms.

7 Bereavement has three stages: numbness, pining and depression. Abnormally prolonged grieving may result if the normal grieving process is interrupted or prevented. Research into dying suggests that openness is one of the most important psychological factors in coping with death.

8 Social stereotypes of ageing are unrealistic. Physical and mental skills can improve with age if they are practised. Explanations for why old people become less visible in society after retirement include disengagement theory, activity theory and social exchange theory.

Self-assessment questions

1 Describe Coleman's focal theory of adolescence.

2 Briefly describe research into stressful life-events.

3 Outline the stages of response to bereavement.

Practice essay questions

1 Is adolescence inevitably a period of 'storm and stress'? Give psychological evidence for your answer.

2 Compare and contrast stage, season and family life-cycle models of adult development.

3 'Ageing is nothing but disengagement and decline'. Do you agree? Give psychological evidence for your answer.

Test your knowledge of this chapter with our online quizzes and games at: http://www.psych.co.uk

Explore lifespan developmental psychology further at:

Adolescence

http://www.personal.psu/edu/faculty/n/x/nxd10/adolesce/htm – Tutorials on the major changes and issues surrounding adolescence. Features extensive bibliographies and selected links and resources.

Ageing

http://www.gl.umbc.edu/~vdotte1/index.html – Comprehensive links page to all matters regarding the social context of ageing. Links to tutorials, articles, bibliographies, and associations that care for the elderly and provide advice for the bereaved.

Comparative psychology

Introducing comparative psychology

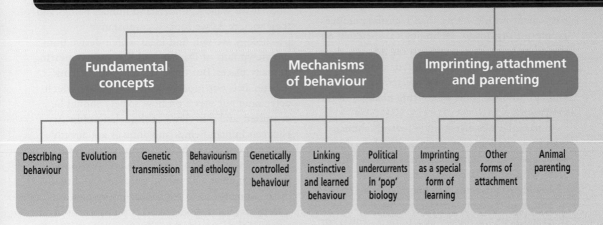

- Fundamental concepts
  - Describing behaviour
  - Evolution
  - Genetic transmission
  - Behaviourism and ethology
- Mechanisms of behaviour
  - Genetically controlled behaviour
  - Linking instinctive and learned behaviour
  - Political undercurrents in 'pop' biology
- Imprinting, attachment and parenting
  - Imprinting as a special form of learning
  - Other forms of attachment
  - Animal parenting

Learning objectives

22.1. Fundamental concepts
a identify significant issues in comparative psychology
b describe fundamental concepts in comparative psychology
c apply comparative concepts to examples of animal behaviour

22.2. Evolution
a describe the basic processes of evolution
b identify concepts in evolutionary theory
c evaluate the concept of the phylogenetic scale

22.3. Genetically controlled behaviour
a list criteria for genetically controlled behaviour
b describe mechanisms of genetically controlled behaviour
c apply principles of genetic control of behaviour to specific examples

22.4. Theories of inherited behaviour
a define terms relating to models of inherited behaviour
b describe hydraulic models of inherited behaviour
c evaluate hydraulic models of inherited behaviour

22.5. Control of behaviour
a outline types of genetic and environmental process in behaviour acquisition
b distinguish between critical and sensitive periods
c describe a study of preparedness in learning

22.6. Imprinting
a identify mechanisms involved in the process of imprinting
b describe a study of imprinting
c distinguish between critical and sensitive periods

22.7. Attachment
a describe a study of attachment in monkeys
b identify ethical considerations arising from investigations of attachment
c evaluate the concept of imprinting as the model for all attachment

22.8. Parental behaviour
a list stages of parental behaviour in monkeys
b describe forms of parenting behaviour in animals
c identify factors which can disturb or disrupt parental behaviour

Since the very earliest times, people have lived with animals, used them to help in day-to-day living, and been interested in their behaviour. But attitudes towards animals vary between different human societies. Many non-technological societies, for example, traditionally regarded both animals and human beings as participants in life, rather than regarding animals as inferior organisms. Technological societies, on the other hand, have tended to regard animals as inferior and there to be exploited, although recent changes in ecological awareness may perhaps produce some interesting changes in this viewpoint.

In part, the Western attitude towards animals goes back to an ancient concept: that human beings have souls whereas animals do not. This view was first put forward by the Greek philosopher Heraclitus, and continued as a strand in European thinking throughout the next two thousand years, eventually becoming a central part of the influential view of human nature put forward by the philosopher Descartes.

Descartes argued that what made human beings distinctive was the fact that they were able to think and reason ('I think, therefore I am') and that they had souls. Animals, according to Descartes, did not think, and their behaviour was governed by mechanistic instincts. Although human beings also possessed an animalistic side to their natures, and their bodies operated mechanistically as did those of animals, Descartes regarded the human ability to think and to act rationally as meaning that they were able to 'rise above' their animal nature in their actions.

According to Descartes, then, human beings were qualitatively different from animals – all animals. But the theory of evolution put forward by Charles Darwin in 1859 implied that in fact not all animals were the same; and that some might be quite similar to human beings. For example, as we saw in Chapter 15, Darwin (1872) showed how the expression of the emotions in some animals was very similar to the way that human beings express emotions. Essentially, Darwin's theory presented human beings as animals, albeit as highly sophisticated ones, and therefore challenged the idea that there were fundamental qualitative differences between people and all other animals.

Why study animal behaviour?

There are a number of different reasons why we might want to study animals. One of them, of course, is to learn more about ourselves. Comparative psychology is an important area of study if we want to understand human beings and their society. As we look at comparative psychology, we will find ideas which derive from the viewpoints of Darwin and Descartes appearing in many places. But these are not just academic debates. It is our models of human nature which determine our views on how society should be organised, and our views of the relationship between human beings and animals are directly linked to our ideas about human nature. Ever since Darwin, people have made comparisons between human and animal behaviour and used these comparisons to explain or justify political actions and social policies. So it is important to be aware of the scientific basis for these ideas, as well as their social implications.

Another reason for studying comparative psychology, of course – some would say the most important reason – is that animal behaviour is interesting in itself, as a subject of inquiry. There is a tremendous range of behavioural patterns and systems between different species, and each of these is of interest in its own right. Human beings have always explored their natural world, and sought to understand it, in their own ways. Comparative psychology is another way of doing that.

Accessibility

There are other reasons too. For example, one of the traditional reasons given for some kinds of comparative investigation is that studying animals allows us to gain access to physiological and behavioural systems which are not so easily studied in human beings. For example, experimenters in the behaviourist tradition saw animal learning as representing a 'pure' form of stimulus-response association, uncontaminated by memory or complex social habits. This, they believed, would allow them to understand the essential principles of learning more readily. Similarly, physiological researchers have found that a great deal can be learned about how nerve cells work by studying the neurones of the squid, because although these have the same form and operate in the same way, they are much larger than neurones from other species, and so can be investigated more easily.

Ethical issues

Another reason why some researchers have chosen to study animals, and one which particularly concerns the experimental tradition within comparative psychology rather than the ethological tradition, is to do with ethical issues. Although this attitude is now changing, for many years it was accepted that animals could be used for experiments which would not be possible otherwise. As we look at comparative psychology we will come across a number of studies which would have been unthinkable if they had been carried out on humans.

This, of course, is a highly contentious area: many people nowadays would argue that we should have as much respect for animals as we do for people, and it is certain that the number of such experiments is far fewer than in previous years. And as we look at comparative psychology it will also become clear that a great deal of insight can also be obtained from ethological observation – looking at animal behaviour in the natural environment. For many people this represents a far more acceptable way of studying animal behaviour.

The origins of comparative psychology

Comparative psychology as we know it today has developed from two entirely different strands of academic thought. The first is the European **ethological** tradition, which developed from the documented observations of amateur naturalists to become formalised into a more systematic and rigorous approach at the beginning of this century. This approach reached a peak with the work of Konrad Lorenz and Niko Tinbergen, which led to the full development of ethology as a scientific discipline in its own right.

The ethological approach was dominant in Europe, but in America the study of animal behaviour was mainly concerned with animal behaviour in the laboratory. The impact of **behaviourism**, under the influence of J.B. Watson and B.F. Skinner, led to a focusing of interest on stimulus-response connections in animal learning. This in turn led to extensive investigations of the behaviour of animals under artificial laboratory conditions. These were designed to allow researchers to investigate 'pure' learning without additional contaminating variables from the natural environment getting in the way. The approach was also widened to include other, more 'instinctive', forms of animal behaviour, such as the laboratory study of maternal behaviour or aggression in the rat.

For the first part of this century, these two traditions in the study of animal behaviour remained separate, but they came together in the 1950s. Since then, comparative psychology has retained the influences of both schools of thought. Although most of the comparative psychology that we will be looking at in this book derives from the ethological tradition, we will also be looking at some of the concepts and ideas which have come from the behaviourist school, and at some of the areas, such as the study of imprinting, where both experimental and ethological approaches have come together to further our understanding of what is going on.

In 1963, Tinbergen argued that comparative psychology was concerned with four areas of study: development, mechanisms, function, and evolution (see Table 22.1). The older forms of comparative psychology tended to concern themselves mainly with the question of how behaviour develops within the individual, and the mechanisms by which it takes place. More

Table 22.1 Areas of study for animal behaviour research

Development	How an organism develops from conception to death. This area includes the study of courtship, mating, and methods of rearing young as well as individual growth and maturation.
Mechanisms	How behaviour occurs in the animal, such as through genetic transmission, inter-individual exchange through ritualisation, communication and sensory patterns, and learning.
Function	What behaviour is for, in terms of how it aids the individual to survive, to interact with others of its species, and so on.
Evolution	How the behaviour is located within an evolutionary context, and what it can tell us about the processes of evolution itself.

Source: Adapted from Tinbergen, 1963

recently, though, there has been an increased emphasis on the function which behaviour serves for the animal concerned, and evolutionary arguments too have had a higher profile. The research which we will be looking at in these chapters reflects that recent emphasis.

Fundamental concepts in comparative psychology

There are a number of fundamental issues and concepts which underpin modern comparative psychology, and which influence the nature of the arguments and explanations in this area of study. In this section, we will take a look at some of these, and at how they relate to our understanding of animal behaviour.

Describing behaviour

Some of these fundamental concepts concern how we go about describing animal behaviour. It may seem as though describing behaviour is actually a reasonably straightforward thing to do, but in reality, our descriptions and observations are directly affected by our ideas of what the behaviour is all about. As we saw in Chapter 2, what we see is very strongly influenced by what we expect to see; and what we see when we look at animal behaviour is no exception to this.

Anthropomorphism and animism

Whenever we are observing animal behaviour, there is a tendency to ascribe meaning or purpose to what we are seeing – it is part of the way in which we make sense of the world. But we can find that we are unconsciously inferring purpose or intention to animal behaviour when it is not really clear that the animal is showing purpose or intention. Perhaps the most extreme example of this tendency is in **anthropomorphism** – the tendency to view animals as if they were human beings, and to project human emotions, ideas and intentions into our interpretations of their behaviour. In part, this is a way of thinking which human beings fall into very easily – it is similar to **animism**, wherein we treat objects in our physical world as if they too were alive and sentient. Talking to your car or your computer are modern-day forms of animism and, although we may laugh at them, they are strikingly common.

But although both animism and anthropomorphism are very common tendencies in human thinking, they do interfere with our ability to examine the world dispassionately and objectively. Comparative psychologists have spent a considerable amount of time developing rigorous techniques for observing animal behaviour, in an attempt to reduce the likelihood of this happening. Some modern researchers feel that this may have gone too far: that in some instances, some animals really do have plans and intentions, and that to understand what they are doing we need to identify and recognise these, without falling into the trap of anthropomorphism. But for the most part, comparative methodology concentrates on attempting to describe the behaviour with as little inference as possible.

In an attempt to clarify how researchers can get round this problem, Hinde (1970) distinguished two different ways of describing behaviour. The first is the description of **patterns of movements** – describing what happens as an animal's muscles contract. Descriptions like 'running', 'raising the head' or 'wagging the tail' come into this category: they are simply descriptions of actions undertaken by an animal (or a human being), and nothing more. The second category of behavioural description is when we describe behaviour in terms of its **effect on the environment**. Terms like 'drinking', 'pressing a lever' or 'retrieving a kitten' are behavioural descriptions which do not describe sequences of muscle actions, but instead focus on what is happening in terms of its effects. It is important to be clear about what we are describing, because confusing the different kinds of description may lead us into errors.

Lloyd Morgan's canon

One of the conceptual tools which comparative psychologists frequently use in their attempts to describe behaviour is a principle known as **Lloyd Morgan's canon**. In 1894, Morgan proposed that an action or sequence of actions should not be interpreted as the outcome of a higher mental process, if it can be interpreted in terms of more basic mechanisms. As part of this argument, Lloyd Morgan was using the idea that some behavioural mechanisms were lower on a kind of 'psychological scale' than others. Terms like 'understanding' or 'belief' implied a high level of psychological awareness, whereas 'learning' or 'habit' described psychological processes that were lower, and represent a more primitive level of evolution.

Morgan argued that animals represent more primitive forms of evolution than human beings (in itself a highly questionable idea), and so the psychological mechanisms which they used would also be more primitive. Moreover, to use a higher level of explanation when a lower level would be adequate was likely to make the observer fall into the trap of anthropomorphism. So Lloyd Morgan's canon states that descriptions of animal behaviour should always use the lowest level possible.

Occam's razor

Lloyd Morgan's canon is sometimes described as being equivalent to Occam's razor – the **principle of parsimony** developed by William of Occam in the fourteenth century. Occam's razor states that, faced with an equal choice between a straightforward, parsimonious explanation for something, and an elaborate or complex one, we should go for the parsimonious explanation. Some researchers have taken this as being the same thing as Lloyd Morgan's canon. But it is not really, because sometimes, trying to keep to the 'lowest' explanation in the psychological scale actually makes the argument much more convoluted and elaborate than it needs to be.

For example, stimulus–response explanations for some of the more interesting kinds of animal behaviour can become highly convoluted: the need to invoke lower psychological processes can make them much more elaborate than they would need to be if the theorist was prepared to invoke higher psychological processes. So it does not always coincide with the principle of parsimony. Nonetheless, Lloyd Morgan's canon has been – and still is – highly influential in guiding comparative psychology. And it was certainly essential at the time that it was first put forward, when many supposedly scientific accounts of animal behaviour were highly anecdotal and lacking in objectivity.

Evolution

Perhaps the most fundamental concept of all in comparative psychology is that of evolution. The theory of evolution was put forward by Charles Darwin, in 1859, and proposed that all forms of life on earth can be seen as linked together, through the development of species. Darwin went on to argue that species develop through a process of **natural selection**, whereby those individuals within the species which are best fitted for survival go on to breed and perpetuate their winning characteristics, while those which are less well suited to the demands that the environment makes on them are less likely to survive. Over very long periods of time, if environmental demands remain reasonably consistent, this means that the species gradually changes to become adapted to its environment. This is the process of evolution.

Natural selection

Darwin had come to his conclusions about natural selection through observing large numbers of animals and plants from all over the world. One of the examples which he gave concerned the various types of finches which he found on the Galapagos Islands, off South America. It was clear that, at some time or other in the past, these finches had originated as the same species, but Darwin found that the birds which inhabited different islands had changed subtly, in ways that made them better adapted to the food supply that they had available to them.

So, for example, those birds which were on an island where the main food supply was nuts or seeds with tough shells had developed thick, strong beaks, which helped them to crack open the shells more easily. The ones which had thicker beaks were more able to get food, and so had become stronger and fitter than the others, because they were better fed. This would mean that they were better placed to survive very severe conditions, like a hard winter or a serious drought, than birds with less strong beaks, so over time most of the finches on that island would come to be descended from these individuals.

Phylogeny

Darwin proposed that, over millions of years, organic life developed into species through the process of natural selection. His theory also implies that it is possible to detect relationships between different species, in terms of their evolutionary history. The evolutionary history of a species is known as its **phylogeny**, and the evolution of species in general is often portrayed in terms of a phylogenetic tree (see Figure 22.1 overleaf). In such a tree, species which are currently alive today would be represented at the

Figure 22.1 A phylogenetic tree

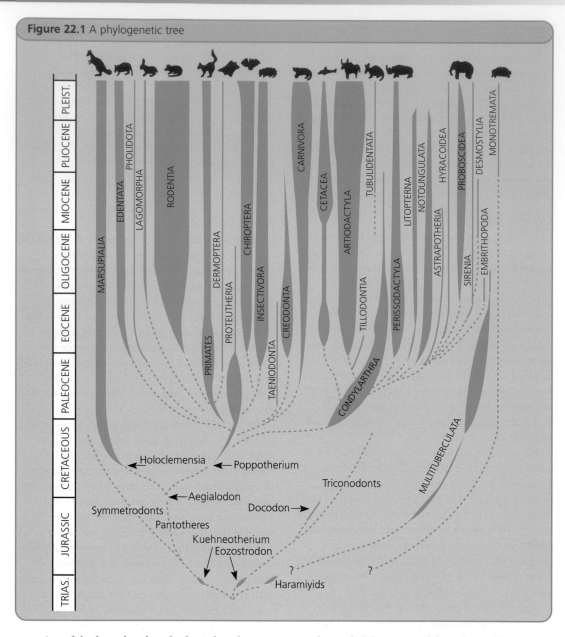

very tips of the branches, but the branches themselves would represent 'families' of species, which developed from common ancestors.

So, for example, in a general phylogenetic tree representing the phylogeny of mammals, human beings would find themselves at the tip of the 'primate' branch, with the other great apes – chimpanzees, bonobos (the animals which used to be called pygmy chimpanzees but are now recognised as a different species), gorillas and orang-utans – as their closest neighbours. But that would not mean that any of the current species

are descended from any of the others – we are not descended from chimpanzees, or any other living primate. What it means is that there was a **common ancestor** further down the tree – that is, a long time ago, just before the branches divided into separate species. Separate populations of that common ancestor, through natural selection, evolved into different types of great ape.

Moving further back down the branch (in other words, further back in time), we would find that it made other connections – or rather, that earlier divisions had occurred in different animal populations. The branch that led to the gibbon family would appear next, as they too are apes. Moving back further still we would come to the point where monkeys and apes had separated into distinct groups, and further back than that we would find the marmoset family, which branched off from the evolutionary tree even earlier than the monkeys.

Biodiversity and behavioural diversity

The concept of the phylogenetic tree carries the clear implication that species are not better or worse or more advanced than one another, just different. A cephalopod, such as a squid, represents just as complex an evolutionary development, and just as much adaptation to its environment, as a human being. Evolution takes different species in different directions. It does not really contain any idea of 'progress', or moving towards an ultimate goal – instead, it is just concerned with those adaptations which will help the species to survive.

Since every species shows different adaptations, one of the most important principles in current evolutionary theory is that of **biodiversity**. It is advantageous to a species to be different from other animals, particularly if its difference enables it to obtain a source of food which other animals do not eat, or to obtain food or rear young more efficiently than competing species. Since the animal and plant worlds are complex, the millions of years of evolution have produced tremendous diversity between different species.

Evolution has also produced tremendous diversity in animal behaviour, and we will be looking at some examples of this in the next two chapters. Although some comparative psychologists have tried to identify single rules of animal behaviour, and ignored diversity, others are concerned with exploring how the diversity of animal behaviour can inform us about the range of outcomes that the pressures of evolution can produce, and with using this diversity to look for underlying generative principles rather than superficial regularities or rules.

The phylogenetic scale

It is important not to confuse the concept of a phylogenetic tree with the idea of a **phylogenetic scale**. The phylogenetic scale is an idea which some, though not all, comparative psychologists have found useful. But it is an idea which needs to be treated with some caution, because it is very

easy to draw false conclusions from it. Broadly speaking, a phylogenetic scale is a scale which takes one single characteristic, such as the ability to learn, and places species in order according to this. Hodos and Campbell (1969) discussed how such a scale usually places human beings at the top, and then ranks other species in descending order from there.

The phylogenetic scale can be a very useful concept, as long as we take it for the broad generalisation that it is. For example, physiological psychologists (e.g. Green, 1987) have sometimes found it useful to look at brain development in terms of a gradually increasing competence in learning and adaptability. By examining the development of structures of the brain according to this framework, it is possible to see how they may have evolved, and also how they may relate to known psychological characteristics of the animal or human being.

Another example of how the concept of the phylogenetic scale can prove useful is to examine how the cerebral cortex (the part of the brain that deals with memory and association) varies in different groups of species. By charting those species on a rough phylogenetic scale, we can identify some systematic developments in the size and complexity of the cerebral cortex and we can also correlate those developments with what we know about how the nervous system mediates behaviour. In Chapter 10, we saw how Hubel (1979) showed that there is a progressive increase in the size of the cerebrum in vertebrates, with it increasing dramatically in mammals and particularly among primates. This increase in the size of the cerebrum correlates with an increased adaptability of behaviour and reliance on learning.

But this type of phylogenetic scale is only one way of ranking species, and it is far from being the only possible way. For example, it would be perfectly possible to construct a phylogenetic scale based on jumping distance relative to body size, and such a scale would probably end up with fleas and springtails at the top, and human beings very low down indeed – far below kangaroos and gerbils. So it is important to remember that the choice of scale is purely arbitrary: it is we, as human beings, who choose the variable, and who place ourselves at the top. Although it may have value in indicating which species most resemble us in some way, that does not mean that the phylogenetic scale can be taken as an abstract or arbitrary truth. It is only an extremely rough generalisation.

Genetic transmission

Genetic transmission is another fundamental concept in comparative psychology. It is also basic to evolutionary theory, since the whole of natural selection depends on the genetic transmission of favourable characteristics from one generation to the next. As we saw in Chapter 10, the nucleus of each cell of a living organism contains structures known as **chromosomes**. These are made up of long strands of DNA molecules (DNA is short for deoxyribonucleic acid), which carry information about how the plant or animal should develop – the physical possibilities which can develop if the environment is right for that development to happen. A section of DNA which codes a particular development is known as a **gene**. Chromosomes are found in pairs, and each gene has a matching pair, known as an **allele**, on the other chromosome.

This genetic 'blueprint' for development is established at the time of conception. From then on, it is replicated in every cell of the body as the organism grows. At various stages of development, particular genes – sequences of DNA – will trigger off the synthesis of a specific protein in a relevant part of the body, through the action of a 'messenger molecule' copied from the DNA, made up of RNA – ribonucleic acid. The RNA combines with amino acids in the body to produce the new protein, and the protein in turn triggers the development of new types of cells, such as bone or hair cells.

When a new organism is conceived, as a result of the combining of cells from the male and the female, the resulting embryo contains genetic material from each parent. But if it simply combined each parent's chromosomes, it would end up with twice as many as its parent. So the special reproductive cells – the sperm and ova – only contain half of each parent's chromosomes. When a reproductive cell fuses with another reproductive cell, a full set is produced.

Genotype and phenotype

What this implies is that each new organism formed through sexual reproduction is genetically different from its parents. It will inherit some genetic characteristics from one parent and some

from the other, and there are innumerable possible combinations which can occur. So this makes sure that within a given species, there is variation and diversity – each individual is different from the rest. Some of this variation, though, may not be very apparent, because some genes are **dominant** over others: if two alleles contradict one another in their message, one will habitually show in the development of the organism, while the other will not.

For example, there is a rare gene carried by some human beings which means that the individual will grow six fingers, rather than the usual five. It does not show up very often, though, because five-fingered genes are dominant, and will 'win out' if an individual inherits both. (The other reason why you do not see people with six fingers very often is because the extra finger is usually surgically removed at birth, but that is a social matter and does not have anything to do with genetics.)

We can see from this, though, that there is a difference between the full genetic complement which an individual has inherited, and the genetic characteristics which they show in their development. We call the full set of genetic potential which an individual contains in their cells, the **genotype**. The genotype is set at conception, and does not change through the individual's lifetime. It is the pattern of possibilities encoded in the DNA sequences of the individual's chromosomes.

But no gene acts independently of its environment. The individual's nutrition, the availability of amino acids, the physical demands of the individual's environment and a host of other factors mean that from the moment that the gene initiates the process of protein synthesis, the environment has an effect on what happens. The organism which actually develops is not a simple product of the genotype. It is a **phenotype**: a product of the interaction between the genes and the environment.

The phenotype of the individual, whether animal or human, is continually changing and developing, because the environment continues to interact with the organism's genetic potential. Goldspink (1992) showed how the changes in muscle development which occur after a period of athletic training occur as a result of the continual interaction of the genes with environmental demands. These can result in the development of different types of muscle fibre depending on whether the individual is training for a short burst of activity, like sprinting, or prolonged muscular effort, like weight training. Genes and environment interact continuously. As we saw in Chapter 6, some serious methodological problems have arisen because some researchers confused genotype and phenotype, and argued that some aspect of development is genetically determined and fixed. But it is far from being that.

The gene pool

But although individuals vary, the total possible traits available to them are only what is available within the gene pool. The gene pool is the sum of the genes possessed by the breeding population of members of that species. Effectively, it is all the genes which could possibly become expressed in development through all the possible matings over several generations. A gene pool contains recessive genes, which may become apparent only with interbreeding of related individuals, as well as dominant genes, which are expressed in the phenotype.

Although there can be a great deal of variation within a given gene pool, it would not be possible for a species to acquire a completely new trait without another mechanism. This mechanism is known as mutation. Every now and then a new gene emerges, which produces an entirely new characteristic. Mutations are usually thought to arise because of faulty copying – when the reproductive cells are formed, a sequence of DNA is not copied accurately, and so the characteristic which it produces is new. Most mutations do not help the organism to survive, and very extreme ones do not usually survive in the womb. Others render the individual that carries them sterile. But sometimes a mutation may represent a relatively minor change, which does not affect the rest of the organism's functioning.

If the mutation does not affect survival, then the young organism may develop to maturity carrying it, and may pass it on to its own offspring. And, of course, if it actually helps the individual to survive, then natural selection will come into play and the new gene will become a part of the gene pool of that species. One example of this was the emergence of a gene for short-leggedness in sheep, which occurred spontaneously round about 1800. It became an established trait in sheep, because farmers

deliberately bred from the short-legged sheep to produce a new animal. Although it was selected by human intervention rather than natural selection, the original gene for stubby-leggedness had mutated. It became an established variant in the sheep species, and was thereby added to the gene pool.

Behaviourism and ethology

It was mentioned earlier that comparative psychology was formed as a merging of two different schools of thought in studying animal behaviour: the American laboratory tradition, which took an experimental approach to studying animal learning and motivation and was powerfully driven by the behaviourist school of thought; and the European ethological tradition, which was much more concerned with studying animal behaviour in the natural environment, through observation. These two traditions also represent basic approaches in modern comparative psychology.

Behaviourism

Throughout most of the twentieth century, behaviourism, personified by the two influential behaviourists J.B. Watson and B.F. Skinner, dominated the experimental tradition in comparative psychology. As we saw in Chapter 1, behaviourism was an attempt to place psychology on a firm, objective, and supposedly scientific, footing. The behaviourist approach, however, made certain fundamental assumptions about the scientific method. One of these was reductionism: the idea that a science should proceed by identifying the smallest relevant unit, and study more complex phenomena through how those small units combine together. For the behaviourists, the smallest unit of behaviour was the learned stimulus-response link.

Another basic concept for behaviourism was the idea that the organism should be seen as a black box. Scientists should observe input, in the form of environmental stimuli, and output, in the form of behaviour, but should not speculate about what was going on inside. The behaviourists saw it as unscientific to infer that an animal was showing cognitive processes, such as thinking or reasoning. Since it was not possible to obtain direct evidence of thinking or reasoning – all that could really be seen was the animal's behaviour – such inference, they argued, could only be speculative. Only the direct observation of behaviour could be made rigorous and objective. Anything else, they argued, was unknowable and irrelevant.

This viewpoint dominated much of psychology for many years, although gradually, as we saw earlier in this book, methodologies were developed which allowed researchers to undertake systematic investigations of cognitive processes, at least in humans. Despite the advances in cognitive psychology, however, and the increased awareness of the serious limitations of the behaviourist approach, the behaviourist influence is still strong within some areas of comparative psychology, although there is increasing evidence for a cognitive component even in stimulus–response learning (see Chapter 18).

Ethology

The ethological tradition in comparative psychology is very different. As we saw earlier, it emerged from the European tradition of the study of natural history: for hundreds of years people had collected and documented their observations of the natural world. Ethology is the study of animal behaviour in its natural environment, uncontrolled by laboratory manipulation. ('Animal' in this case can include human behaviour – for example, we looked at some ethological studies of parent-infant interaction in Chapter 20.) Because of this, ethology operates from rather different principles of scientific explanation. Where behaviourism adopted reductionist forms of explanation, ethology for the most part uses what is known as **teleological explanation** – ways of explaining behaviour which are concerned with showing how that behaviour fulfils a distinct function for the organism. Ethology looks at behaviour in its evolutionary context, and tries to identify how a particular behaviour could have developed in such a way as to be useful to the animal's survival.

That does not mean, of course, that ethologists never use other methods as well. As we will see in the next chapter, for example, studies of imprinting in young birds began with ethological observation, and then also used laboratory investigations to single out the specific mechanisms which were involved. But it was the observation of the behaviour in the natural environment which initiated the study in the first place.

These basic concepts are fundamental to comparative psychology, and tend to be taken for granted by comparative psychologists. All comparative psychologists take evolution as a basic process, even though they may argue about which particular form evolution takes – whether they follow the sociobiological approach, the phylogenetic approach or some other version. And even psychologists who do not agree with behaviourism as an approach are influenced by behaviourist methodology when they are doing laboratory research. So in studying comparative psychology, it is important to bear these assumptions in mind.

Mechanisms of behaviour

How behaviour is controlled has always been one of the central questions of comparative psychology. For much of the time, this took the form of a **nature-nurture debate**, with some researchers, like Lorenz or Morris, insisting that animal behaviour was instinctive – in other words, genetic in origin – while others, like Skinner or Pavlov, saw it as learned, having been acquired through the learning mechanisms of classical and operant conditioning.

However, as comparative psychology developed, it became obvious that there is no clear either/or issue here. Ethologists showed that some behaviours are clearly genetically determined (in other words, entirely caused by genetic influences). But then further research showed that other forms of behaviour are quite clearly learned. The discovery of critical and sensitive periods in development showed that there are also halfway stages in between – behaviour which is neither entirely genetically controlled, nor arises purely from learning. Genetic influences can shape what type of learning will take place, even though environmental influences determine whether a specific thing is learned or not. Gradually, it became apparent that animal behaviour ranges along a continuum, from genetically determined behaviour to behaviour which is entirely learned.

In this section, we will explore the basic mechanisms of behavioural control which have been identified and discussed by comparative psychologists. We will look first at genetically determined behaviour, and then go on to examine the learning mechanisms which animals have been shown to use. Finally, we will go on to examine how the concepts of critical and sensitive periods in development may provide us with a link between these two extremes.

Genetically controlled behaviour

There has been a considerable amount of research into the idea that some forms of behaviour may be controlled directly by the actions of genes. But the problem has always been identifying which forms of behaviour are directly inherited, and which have been learned by the individual animal. Lorenz and Tinbergen (1938) developed a set of four criteria for identifying inherited behaviour, which are listed in Table 22.2.

Maturation

Following these criteria, some early research into inherited behaviour focused on the phenomenon of maturation. The argument here is that if behaviour is genetically determined, then it must have been set at the time that the animal was first conceived. So this should mean that animals will show the relevant behaviour when they get old enough, without needing any opportunity to learn it from other members of their species. If a behaviour appears with maturation, but no external learning, this indicates that the behaviour has been inherited.

The idea that genetically controlled behaviour would emerge without learning led to a number of studies in which animals were raised with restricted opportunities to learn the behaviour from others, or to practise its components. For example, Carmichael (1956) raised tadpoles in a

solution of an anaesthetic drug which prevented them from contracting their muscles. They were moved to clean water when the control group began swimming freely, and the experimental tadpoles also began to swim. Similarly, Grohmann (1939) raised pigeons in tubes so that they could not practise flapping their wings, and found that this made very little difference: they were released at the point where the control birds had begun to fly, and began flying almost immediately.

There was other evidence that some forms of behaviour arose directly from genetic influence. Eibl-Eiblesfeldt (1970) described how squirrels reared in the laboratory on liquid foods still attempted to bury nuts when they were given some, even though they had not had the opportunity to learn this from other animals. Nice (1943) described how newly hatched song sparrows would crouch down in the nest in response to their parent's alarm call even from the very first occasion that they heard it.

Fixed action patterns

If behaviour is genetically determined, then it follows that the animal which is showing that behaviour will not be able to vary what it does. Because the actions have been pre-set, as it were, it would not be possible to change them, and learn new ones. This is known as **stereotypy**: the behaviour will be stereotyped, or always the same each time it is performed. So, as Lorenz and Tinbergen pointed out, another indicator that allows us to distinguish between learned and genetically determined behaviour is whether the behaviour varies – not between individuals, because each member of a species is always slightly different from the next, genetically speaking – but within each individual.

Lorenz (1958) discussed how several animals showed behavioural patterns which were highly stereotyped. By carefully recording the bobbing and diving of ducks in the course of courtship displays, he showed that the actions in which they engaged formed a rhythmic sequence which did not vary at all when it was repeated (Figure 22.2 overleaf). This stereotypy, Lorenz argued, showed that the behaviour had been inherited, and was genetically determined – learned behaviour would have shown far more variation. The fixed, repetitive sequences of behaviour described by Lorenz became known as **fixed action patterns**, or **FAPs**.

Table 22.2 Criteria for identifying inherited behaviour

1 The behaviour will be stereotyped, always appearing in the same form.

2 The behaviour will be species-specific.

3 The behaviour will appear in animals which have been isolated from others of their kind, and therefore have had no chance to learn it.

4 The behaviour will appear fully developed in animals which have been prevented from practising it.

Source: Adapted from Lorenz and Tinbergen, 1938

Figure 22.2 Stereotyped behaviour in ducks

Figure 22.3 Sign stimuli and IRMs

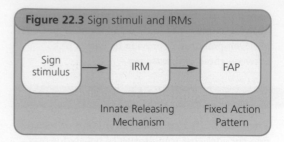

Sign stimuli and releasing mechanisms

Fixed action patterns, it emerged, are triggered off by a relatively simple external stimulus, following the same sequence each time. Tinbergen (1951) investigated the stimuli which would trigger these off. He proposed that the process involves an internal **innate releasing mechanism (IRM)**, which reacts to an external sign stimulus. In Tinbergen's view, the IRM 'releases' the fixed action pattern, which is already energised and ready to come out as soon as the time is right. The external stimulus – the **sign stimulus** – is the indicator that this is the right time (Figure 22.3).

The type of sign stimulus which sets off the IRM is minimal in form, and very specific. For example, Lack (1943) investigated the territorial aggression shown by European robins, and found that this behaviour was triggered off by the red breast of the intruding robin, and not by any other characteristic of the bird. Similarly, Tinbergen found that male sticklebacks reacted to the red bellies of other male sticklebacks. Using models, he showed that this aggressive response could be set off by other red objects. The story goes that he first noticed this response when a stickleback in a tank near the window of his study became frantically agitated each time a red post office van went past!

Tinbergen conducted a series of studies to investigate sign stimuli and how they worked. One of the things that he and his colleagues discovered was that a particularly exaggerated sign stimulus could trigger off an equally exaggerated response. So, for example, he found that ringed plovers would incubate a large, 'supernormal' egg in preference to their own. One explanation that has been put forward to explain why small birds will feed a cuckoo chick which has hatched in their nest is the idea that the young cuckoo's very large gaping mouth acts as a kind of super-stimulus to the parent birds, causing them to neglect their own chick and concentrate on the intruder.

Tinbergen found that movement was also involved in the operation of innate releasing mechanisms. In one experiment Lorenz and Tinbergen constructed an ambiguous model, of a bird shape with outstretched wings, and a short protuberance at one end and a long one at the other (Figure 22.4). If it was pulled in one

Figure 22.4 The 'hawk-goose' shape

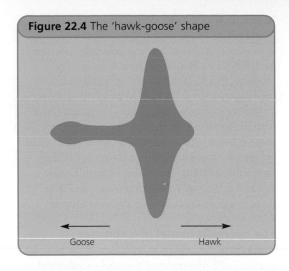

Goose ⟵   ⟶ Hawk

Table 22.3 Characteristics of fixed action patterns

1	*Sterotypy*	The behaviour should always occur in the same form.
2	*Universality*	The behaviour occurs in all members of a species.
3	*Independence of experience*	The behaviour should appear regardless of the individual's past history.
4	*Ballisticness*	The behaviour is fixed and inflexible once it has been triggered off: it does not change while the animal is performing it, regardless of circumstances.
5	*Singleness of purpose*	The action is only shown in the one context, and is not applied to other circumstances, even if it might be useful.
6	*Triggering stimuli*	The behaviour will be reliably triggered by a known stimulus or set of stimuli.

Source: Adapted from Lea, 1984

direction, it resembled a flying goose, with its neck stretched out; but if it was moved the other way it resembled a hawk, with a short neck and long tail. Tinbergen found that when this was moved over young birds, they would crouch low and 'freeze' if the short 'head' was leading and it resembled a hawk, but not if it was moving the other way. So the sign stimulus in this case was not just the shape: it was the shape plus the appropriate movement.

Some psychologists criticised this conclusion, arguing that it was possible that the young birds were not actually responding to the shape itself, but to the sudden onset of the stimulus. Because of the short neck of the 'hawk' shape, the young birds would have experienced the dark patch more suddenly. When it was moved in the 'goose' direction, the long neck meant that there was a more gradual change in the stimulus, which might have been less alarming. But this criticism does not actually affect the idea that the young geese had an innate response triggered off by a stimulus: it is only to do with precisely how that stimulus is specified in the young bird's neural structures.

The original set of criteria drawn up by Lorenz and Tinbergen in 1938 for identifying inherited behaviour did not include the existence of sign stimuli. In the intervening years, however, comparative psychologists have come to consider this to be an important feature of inherited behaviour. Lea (1984) listed six characteristics which fixed action patterns should possess, and which are commonly taken to indicate that the behaviour concerned has been inherited. These are given in Table 22.3. Although some of these

criteria are identical to those of Lorenz and Tinbergen, the existence of sign stimuli which will trigger off the behaviour is now included as one of the identifying criteria of instinctive behaviour.

Ritualisation

Huxley (1914) observed the behaviour of great crested grebes during the mating season. He noticed that their behaviour seemed to involve an elaborate set of rituals before the act of mating. These rituals – which he described as **courtship displays** – always followed the same sequence of actions. Many of the actions were similar to those which might occur in everyday living, but not quite the same. For example, one part of the ritual involved the male presenting weed to the female, as if it were food, and the female accepting it and making motions as if she were eating. Closer observation, however, showed that the 'food' was not actually eaten – the actions were occurring in a stylised, ritual fashion rather than as they would take place in normal everyday living.

Lorenz (1966) performed a number of observational studies of ritualised aggressive encounters between animals, and found that in many species, territorial disputes or other such events seemed to involve ritual **threat displays**, which did not actually culminate in attack. Such displays, Lorenz argued, were valuable to the species, because they prevented the animals from damaging each other and so becoming vulnerable to outside predators.

The displays of ritual aggression which Lorenz described typically involved displays of the species' **natural weaponry**, such as the baring of teeth in the dog, for example, or a cat's extending of its claws. They might also be accompanied by the animal adopting a posture which would make it look more fearsome, such as a cat arching its back and leaning forward, spitting. In mammals, the displays were frequently accompanied by the pilomotor response, in which the animal's hair would stand on end, which served to make it look larger.

The reason why these ritual aggressive displays did not often result in attack, Lorenz argued, was the effect that they had on the other animal. If the other animal was feeling equally aggressive – such as might occur at the borders of a territory – then a ritual 'dance', forming a complex sequence of aggressive actions, would result. This would allow each animal to display its weaponry and to discover whether the other was likely to be stronger. After a while, the ritual would end in one animal giving in.

When an animal stopped the aggressive encounter, it would do so by showing an **appeasement gesture**. Lorenz described appeasement gestures as ritualised acts which were designed to render the individual animal helpless. For example, a young dog rolls over on its back when faced with an aggressive older dog. The action exposes the vulnerable underside of the animal, and puts it in a position where the aggressor could easily kill it. In this way, the animal places itself at the mercy of the other. Lorenz believed that such an action triggered off an automatic, instinctive reaction which inhibited further aggression on the part of the winner. The young dog signals its submission by rolling over, and so halts the attack from the other.

Unfortunately, Lorenz then went on to extrapolate in quite an extreme fashion from his observations, arguing that laboratory rats and human beings were the only two species which did not have such innate appeasement gestures, and that this was what enabled rats to kill one another in the laboratory and human beings to

have wars which involved fighting to the death. This type of extrapolation has not been uncommon in comparative psychology (see Box 22.1 opposite). But, as we have seen in other chapters, there are numerous other explanations for human aggression even in psychological terms, as well as economic and political explanations for wars. In terms of comparative psychology, too, there is some recent research which indicates that appeasement gestures do not always act as the instinctive 'braking' mechanism which Lorenz described. We will be looking more closely at these views of aggression in the next chapter.

The hydraulic model of instinctive behaviour

Lorenz (1950) formulated a model of inherited behaviour and ritualisation. This centred on the idea that, for any given 'instinct', an animal has a basic drive which needs to be consummated by the performance of fixed action patterns. Lorenz proposed that the animal builds up **action-specific energy**, which can be released only by that particular activity. Each different fixed action pattern has its own 'reservoir' of action-specific energy. When the appropriate sign stimulus occurs, IRMs release this energy, and the animal shows the behaviour (Figure 22.5, page 718).

Building on this idea, Tinbergen (1951) proposed that each form of instinctive behaviour works on a hierarchical principle. At the top of the hierarchy is the main drive centre, which builds up action-specific energy through the influence of hormones and other factors. This idea was necessary because it is important to explain why so many fixed action patterns are only released at certain times, like during the mating season. The action-specific energy then flows to the next level down the hierarchy, in the form of motivational impulses which produce **appetitive behaviour**. Appetitive behaviour is behaviour from the animal which makes the release of fixed action patterns more likely, for example the way that the male stickleback patrols the boundaries of his territory, rather than staying in the centre where he is unlikely to meet any potential rivals.

If an appropriate sign stimulus occurs in the environment, the action-specific energy then passes down to the next level in the hierarchy, which is that of **consummatory behaviour** (the fixed action pattern itself). The animal performs the fixed action pattern, and through this, the

Box 22.1 Political undercurrents in 'pop' biology

Research into animal social organisation has led to a number of speculative extrapolations to human society, which often receive exaggerated media attention. For example, in 1967, Desmond Morris published a paperback proposing that human beings were really nothing more than 'naked apes' – that all people were really doing in society was expressing the animal side of their natures, but in a disguised form. Morris rested this argument on parallels which he drew between accounts of animal behaviour and human social practices. He compared the erecting of fences around gardens, for instance, to the territorial behaviour of sticklebacks; the ventures of artists and musicians as manifestations of a 'biological' drive to explore; and religion as an expression of a 'biological' urge to submit to a dominant animal.

There were two themes which permeated the naked ape theory: aggression and sex. Drawing heavily on Lorenz's ideas, Morris argued that human beings were innately aggressive, and that since this was an inevitable part of our biology it was pointless to try to stop it. Wars were inevitable, and could only be minimised by channelling human aggression into 'safe' outlets, like competitive sports. In addition, human beings were the most sexually active of all the animals, and the sexual characteristics of the female body had evolved in order to attract the male, including rounded breasts, bodily hairlessness, and subcutaneous fat.

Morgan (1972) produced a detailed critique of Morris's theory and showed that many of his ideas rested on shaky foundations, to say the least. We have examined some of these elsewhere in these chapters. Like Lorenz, Morris had based his arguments on a very limited range of species, and drawn heavily on the Washburn and DeVore studies of baboon behaviour while largely ignoring other research on more closely related primates. Morgan also suggested that one major weakness of the theory was the way that it had failed to consider the other sex as involved in the process of natural selection or social life. Morris had not considered, for instance, any evolutionary demands which might result from

the needs of child-rearing. Once the survival of women (not just that of men) was taken into account, an entirely different evolutionary picture emerged. For example, several of the physical characteristics which Morris had attributed to 'sexual attraction' made functional sense once the requirements of nurturing the young were considered. Morgan related this one-sided view to the assumptions resulting from the use of the pronoun 'he' to refer to all human beings. (See Chapter 4.)

The 'selfish gene' theory
Another popularisation of evolutionary theory which received considerable publicity, yet rested on very little evidence, was put forward in 1976, by Richard Dawkins, in a book called *The Selfish Gene*. This model drew on Wilson's account of sociobiology, and presented human beings as 'just' survival machines for their genes. The wildly speculative account by Dawkins described such actions as xenophobia, lying, selfishness and hostility to stepchildren as 'inevitable' parts of our biological heritage. More positive aspects of human behaviour, like co-operation, friendship, and helpfulness were ignored, or discussed as if they somehow conflicted with some biological principle. Although Dawkins' arguments were strikingly lacking in supporting evidence, they nonetheless received considerable publicity. Some of the weaknesses in the argument were identified by Hayes (1995) including the problems produced by biological determinism, the use of selected examples only, and the use of 'gene' as a magical concept which did not have much connection with the concept of 'gene' as used by geneticists.

Given the dubious scientific evidence for these theories, why did they become so popular? One answer, according to Rose, Kamin and Lewontin (1984) is because they serve an **ideological** function in society, legitimising existing social practice and drawing attention away from potentially embarrassing social questions. If inner-city riots happen because people are 'naturally' aggressive and selfish, then society can simply blame those people for not having their 'instincts' under control, and leave it at that. If they are

● ● ● ➤

Box 22.1 continued

not, then inner-city riots raise all sorts of uncomfortable questions about social deprivation, unfair economic policies, and racism.

Alternatives and social choices
There are always a multiplicity of theories being put forward, but only some receive attention. For example, Morgan also explored a different view of evolution: the **aquatic ape theory**. This was the idea that human beings, at some time in their evolutionary past, had spent an extended period of time by lake or sea shores, both in and out of the water. Morgan pointed to a number of features of the human body which might be appropriately explained in this way, and which human beings appear to have in common with other mammals which spent long periods of time in water. These included relative hairlessness, and the

'streamlined' angle of human hair distribution on the body; the layer of subcutaneous fat, which land mammals do not usually have, but which provides valuable insulation in water; the slight webbing which human beings have between their fingers and toes, and which other primates do not have; and so on.

As Morgan pointed out, there is at least as much scientific evidence for this approach as there is for the naked ape, yet it was Morris's theory which received the publicity and became well-known, while the aquatic ape theory was pretty well ignored. According to Rose, Kamin and Lewontin, there is a strong political undercurrent to reductionist evolutionary theories like these, and the publicity they receive is a consequence of their implicit political message, not their scientific validity.

action-specific energy is used up (or 'drained away', following the principle of the hydraulic model – Figure 22.6).

Tinbergen used this model to explain a number of different characteristics of inherited behaviour. One of them was the way that such behaviour often seems to become exhausted: a stickleback

which had just engaged in a display of aggression was less likely to react to another stimulus, or if it did, it reacted less energetically. The hydraulic model explained this in terms of the 'reservoir' of action-specific energy having become exhausted, and needing time before it would fill up again. The model was also used to explain how a super-

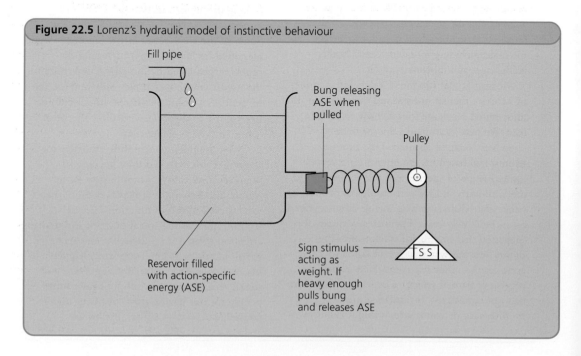

Figure 22.5 Lorenz's hydraulic model of instinctive behaviour

Fill pipe

Bung releasing ASE when pulled

Pulley

Reservoir filled with action-specific energy (ASE)

Sign stimulus acting as weight. If heavy enough pulls bung and releases ASE

S S

Figure 22.6 Tinbergen's hydraulic model

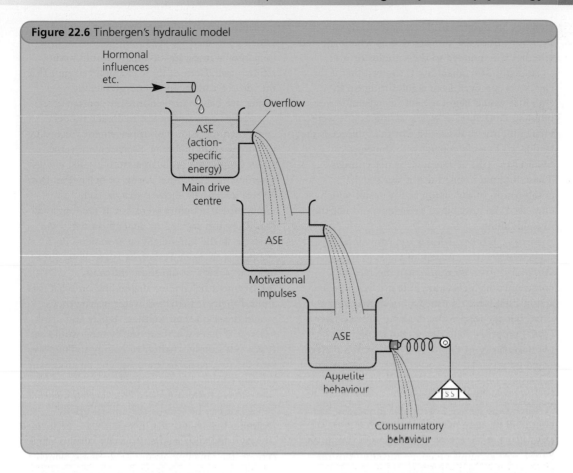

stimulus might work, representing it as putting particularly strong pressure on the innate releasing mechanism. This would mean that more action-specific energy was released, so that the consummatory behaviour which resulted would be more powerfully energised.

Another phenomenon which Tinbergen's model was used to explain was that of **displacement**. Many researchers had observed that animals engaged in a sequence of ritual aggression, for example, would sometimes break off suddenly and do something which seemed completely irrelevant, like preening themselves, or drinking. Tinbergen explained this as being what happens when the animal finds itself caught between two equally powerful, but incompatible, responses. In this example, it would be the drive to continue acting aggressively and the drive to flee. At such times, Tinbergen believed, the action-specific energy would 'overflow' into another instinctive system, producing a different kind of consummatory act.

Criticisms of the hydraulic model

One problem which emerged as researchers began to investigate the hydraulic model more deeply was the effect of feedback. Lorenz and Tinbergen had argued that the performance of the fixed action pattern – the consummatory act – used up the action-specific energy. But in a series of studies, von Holst (1954) showed that the consequences of the action could in themselves provide a further stimulus, resulting in the animal continuing to perform the action.

One of these studies concerned the way that a fly will move to the left if it is faced with a series of vertical bars which are also moving to the left. When the feedback was reversed, by rotating the fly's head such that moving to the left caused the vertical bars to appear to move even more, the fly would continue to turn. But it would not produce this reaction in response to the stimulus alone, because when the fly itself turned to the right (producing a retinal pattern of vertical bars moving to the left), the animal would not continue its movement. There was clearly some **feedback** from the animal's actions which affected whether it responded to the stimulus or not.

Similarly, Moynihan (1953) showed that if the eggs were removed from a gull sitting on its clutch, it would begin to show exaggerated nest-building behaviour, as well as acting as if it were incubating them. It seemed that the gull needs the feedback of tactile contact with the eggs themselves – the action alone is not enough. These findings implied that it was the combination of the action and its result which energised the next bit of behaviour, and not the stimulus alone.

In 1953, Bastock, Morris and Moynihan suggested that the concept of **consummatory stimulation** was more use than the idea of consummatory behaviour, in that it was not the action itself which satisfied (consummated) the drive, but the result of performing the act. Beer (1962) proposed that, rather than being consummatory in themselves, fixed action patterns could be regarded as another form of appetitive behaviour, directing the animal towards the goal of consummatory stimulation.

Some time earlier, Lorenz and Tinbergen had identified the way that a goose will roll eggs towards a nest as a fixed action pattern, produced by the sign stimulus of an egg missing from the nest. But Beer showed that the bird would continue egg-rolling behaviour if it did not result in replacement of the egg. The action itself was not consummatory – it would stop only when the consummatory stimulus (of the egg in the nest) had been achieved. Although this may seem a relatively trivial point, it actually called into question the whole idea of action-specific energies building up and being released by the relevant actions, by suggesting that even instinctive behaviour may be responsive to its environment.

Other problems with the hydraulic model also emerged. For example, several researchers found that even after fixed action patterns had been exhausted by repeated stimulation, they could still be elicited by a slightly different stimulus. Prechtl (1953) found that young chaffinches would still gape in response to vibration of their nest, even after the gaping response had been exhausted in response to sounds. Clearly, the energy which the action involved was still available to the birds. Conversely, Hinde (1954) showed that chaffinches which were repeatedly exposed to the same

predator showed a decline in their alarm calls which continued for very long periods of time – long after a 'reservoir' of energy would have refilled itself. Both of these examples suggest that the idea of a reservoir of energy fuelling instinctive behaviour is not really appropriate.

Another criticism of the hydraulic model concerned the nature of displacement. According to Lorenz and Tinbergen, displacement came about simply as a result of action-specific energy 'overflowing' into other forms of behaviour. But several researchers showed that, in fact, displacement activities were not as random as all that. They too seemed to depend on what was available in the immediate environment. For example, a study by Räber, in 1948, showed that fighting turkeys would show different displacement behaviours depending on what was around them. If there was water nearby, they would break off their fighting display and drink, whereas if there was food nearby they would eat. It was not simply a matter of energy spilling over into the first available response. The environment influenced the response as well.

Andrew (1956) suggested that displacement behaviour can be seen as the animal briefly resuming behaviours that it would have performed anyway. Most displacement activity consists of actions like preening, eating or drinking, which would be interrupted if there is occasion for more urgent behaviour. Andrews suggested that when the animal is faced with conflicting demands (like the urge to fight or flee), each one inhibits the other, and so frees the animal to engage in its normal, low-priority behaviour. This is known as the **disinhibition hypothesis**, because the idea is that the animal's normal routine behaviour has been inhibited by the situation, but the conflicting demands of the aggressive encounter have removed that inhibition.

Overall, then, it is clear that some patterns of behaviour arise from genetic influences. But the mechanisms by which they emerge are not so clear, and it is apparent that some input from the environment is involved. Hailman (1969) showed that even behaviours which once appeared to be entirely innate show some effect of learning. Young gulls peck instinctively at a red spot on the parent's beak when it returns to the nest. This stimulates the parent to regurgitate food. But using models, Hailman showed that the young gulls become increasingly accurate over the first three or four days. The instinct is at least partly learned, with practice. So to see instinctive behaviour as purely mechanistic, released by some single form of energy or drive, does not give us the whole picture.

Animal learning

Where the study of instinctive behaviour developed largely within the European ethological tradition, the study of animal learning developed on the other side of the Atlantic, within the American behaviourist tradition. The assumptions which it was based on were very different and reflected the differing philosophical traditions within the two cultures. Where the work of the ethologist could be traced back to the idea that there were innate or instinctive patterns of behaviour, which in turn could be traced back to the theory of René Descartes, the work of the behaviourists had its origins in the philosophical theory of John Locke, with its view of the infant as a 'blank slate', or *tabula rasa*, waiting for life's experience to inscribe its mark. Although both of these philosophers were writing about human beings, their influence affected comparative psychology, as researchers looked for what they considered to be the roots of human behaviour in that of animals.

Research into animal learning fell firmly into the experimental tradition in psychology: indeed, many psychologists regarded it as the core of that tradition. It is possible to group theories of animal learning into three broad bands, which also represent different periods within the century. During the early part, research into learning tended to focus on what became known as **classical conditioning**: the idea of learning through association. The 1940s and thereabouts saw a new emphasis emerge, with the model that became known as **operant conditioning**. But in the later part of the century, a new framework of more generalised forms of learning began to emerge, drawing together earlier research on learning sets and insight learning and linking this with newer concepts such as learned helplessness.

We looked at all of these forms of learning in Chapter 18, so there is little point in going into them in detail here. Table 22.4 summarises the main forms of animal learning, as identified by the behaviourist researchers and their successors. We can see from the table that the forms of learning have been ordered roughly according to Lloyd

Morgan's canon, with classical conditioning as the most basic form of learning, and insight learning, imitation and cognitive mapping as those requiring more complex activity, in the form of the development of internal representations of the problem, the environment, or the activity of others.

Animal learning, then, involves much more than the original mechanistic associations between stimulus and response envisaged by the early behaviourists. There is still much that we do not know about animal learning – for instance, there has been relatively little investigation of the role of **imitation** in learning, although there has been some. But recent trends towards accepting the importance of cognitive elements in learning have opened the door for more investigations.

Linking instinctive and learned behaviour

So far, we have looked at some of the basic mechanisms which are involved in controlling behaviour: inherited behaviour patterns and animal learning processes. But instances of purely instinctive behaviour that have no learned element at all are quite rare in real life. As we saw earlier, Hailman showed that even an instinctive behaviour such as the young gull's pecking at its parent's beak shows improvement with practice. Similarly, Seligman's work on 'preparedness' in

Table 22.4 Forms of animal learning

Classical conditioning	Learning through the repeated association of stimulus with response (the Law of Exercise).
Operant conditioning	Learning through the pleasant or unpleasant consequences of actions (the Law of Effect).
Learning sets	Learning through the generalisation of trial and error learning.
Insight learning	Learning as a result of cognitive restructuring of the elements of the problem.
Imitation	Learning through the formation of mental representations of the activity, obtained through observation of others.
Cognitive maps	Learning through the formation of mental representations of the environment obtained through experience.

learning, which we looked at in Chapter 18, shows us that 'pure' learning, which has no reference to the animal's needs or innate behavioural tendencies, is also uncommon. In most cases, instinctive and learned mechanisms operate together to produce animal behaviour.

Even fixed action patterns show a component of the behaviour which is sensitive to the environment, and can be modified. Lorenz (1958) showed that the egg-rolling behaviour of a greylag goose that was incubating a nest of eggs consists of two components. One of these is fixed and does not vary, and the other is variable, guided by information from the sensory receptors.

In egg-rolling, the goose rolls the egg back towards the nest by stretching out its neck, putting the underside of its beak in contact with the far side of the egg, and pulling the egg towards the nest. This is a fixed component, and happens regardless of sensory stimuli. But the bird will also make sideways motions of its beak if the egg seems to be slipping out of line, and these movements are guided by the tactile information which it is receiving from the contact between the beak and the egg. So even what appears to be a completely genetically determined behaviour contains a component which is modified by the environment.

Behaviour and environment

In order to understand the links between instinctive and learned behaviour, we need to look in general terms at what behaviour is for. Essentially, behaviour enables an animal to operate on its environment – to perform actions which have some kind of a consequence. In the same way, the environment provides the possibilities for that animal to act effectively. There is what is known as a **dialectical relationship** between a living organism and its environment: each one affects the other.

This is an important point in understanding animal behaviour. Rose, Kamin and Lewontin (1984) point out that the idea that the environment is in some way independent of the animals within it is a myth. All species are continually changing their environment simply through engaging in their routine life-processes. Even an amoeba changes the nature of the water that it swims in, as it removes food particles from it and excretes waste products into it. If we are to understand behaviour, we need to look at behaviour in this context.

If we bear this point in mind, it is easy to see that behaviour patterns which are fixed and unvarying are most suited to a relatively fixed and unvarying environment. Through the process of natural selection, these behaviours would have developed because they gave some kind of evolutionary advantages to the animals which possessed them. In order for this to have happened, the environmental demands on the animal must have been consistent and continuous enough for the trait to become widespread within that species. Such a development tends to take a great many generations.

This does not mean, of course, that all inherited behaviour that we see now has an immediate survival advantage. If the environment changes, it may be that some behaviour patterns will become redundant, but they would still be present in the gene pool. As long as they were not actually disadvantageous for the animal – making it less likely to survive – there is no reason why they would die out. In 1961, Eibl-Eiblesfeldt described how the ground-nesting dove of the Galapagos Islands produces a distraction display when anything approaches its nest, even though there are no natural predators which it might need to distract. Eibl-Eiblesfeldt concluded that this behaviour had evolved in the ancestors of the dove (when it was presumably needed), and had remained within the species even after the islands had been cut off from the main continent.

This example, though, shows us how fixed inherited behavioural mechanisms can be. Natural selection is a slow process: individuals do not change within their lifetimes, and the species as a whole only changes gradually, through genetic transmission, mutation and environmental pressure. This is fine, as long as the environment remains reasonably consistent, or at least only changes very slowly too. But if a species is to survive in a more rapidly changing environment, then it is necessary for it to develop more rapid ways of adapting its behaviour to what is needed. Some species do this by reproducing very fast. Many insects, for example, show evolutionary changes very quickly, because their generations are much shorter. But other species, particularly those with longer life spans, need to develop other mechanisms of adaptation.

The function of learning

Mechanisms of learning provide a way of changing behaviour quickly. If it is capable of learning – in other words, of modifying its behaviour – an individual can develop more adaptive behaviour patterns in response to environmental demands within its own lifetime. So if it lives in an environment which is liable to change quickly, then it makes evolutionary sense if it can adapt its behaviour to the variable circumstances in which it is likely to find itself. The same thing applies to members of a species which is likely to colonise very different environments. What is useful surviva behaviour in the tropics may be suicidal in the northern tundra, so fixed inherited behaviour patterns could become a serious liability.

In such circumstances, the development of effective learning mechanisms becomes a survival trait, because it makes an animal more likely to survive. It also makes an animal more likely to be able to take advantage of survival opportunities as they arise. As we saw in Chapter 10, Hubel (1979) showed how cortical development was particularly evident among carnivores and primates. These are highly opportunistic species, which can adapt their behaviour to suit a wide range of environments. Their increased cortical development is not a coincidence, since forming new associations and processing sensory information is precisely what this part of the brain is used for.

Intermediate processes

Going from instinctive behaviour to learned behaviour, though, is a huge jump, and evolution does not proceed like this. Even though, as Gould and Eldredge (1977) showed, a species may show periods of relatively rapid change followed by periods of stability – a concept known as **punctuated equilibrium** – the evolutionary process itself is an accumulation of small changes. If we see evolution as proceeding by means of small changes, each of which needs to be advantageous to survival, then we need to look for intermediate stages between the two.

One such intermediate stage is the way that not all inherited behaviour is triggered by sign stimuli. Curio, Ernst and Veith (1978) investigated the mobbing response of blackbirds. Mobbing is an innate behaviour which birds show to potential predators while they are nesting. Curio et al. kept European blackbirds in separate cages, but facing one another. Between the birds was a rotatable

box. Each bird could see only the part of the box facing its own cage, and not the part facing the box opposite.

Curio et al. began by showing the birds a stuffed Australian honey creeper, which is not a predatory bird. The birds ignored it. Then one bird was shown the honey creeper while the other was shown a stuffed owl. Immediately, the bird that could see the owl began a mobbing response. The bird in the facing cage watched it for a moment, and then also began the mobbing behaviour. When both birds were shown honey creepers again, the bird in the facing cage showed mobbing behaviour and the other one imitated it. From then on, both birds both showed mobbing behaviour whenever they saw the stuffed Australian honey creeper. They had learned a new target for their inherited behaviour by **imitating** one another. The implication is that it is not sign stimuli which trigger this inherited behaviour, but imitating older members of the species. The behaviour pattern is inherited, but the occasions when it should be shown, are learned.

Critical periods

Perhaps the most important intermediate condition between inherited and learned behaviour is in the case of the critical or sensitive period. A **critical period** is a genetically determined period of time during which the animal is in a state of readiness to learn a particular form of behaviour. If it is exposed to the right kind of environmental stimulus during this period, it will learn very quickly. But if it does not have that kind of environmental stimulus during the period, it will never learn the behaviour, even if later on it is exposed to the stimulus. The genes have 'switched off' the animal's readiness to learn.

There seem to be a number of instances of critical periods in animal development. In 1964, Marler and Tamura investigated the song of the American white-crowned sparrow. These birds have a distinctive song, shared by all members of the species. But they also have a regional 'dialect', which varies from one part of America to another. Young birds which were reared entirely in isolation would sing the basic song, but without any of the additional trills or warbles which formed the dialect.

However, Marler and Tamura found that there was a period when very little exposure to the song of an adult bird was enough to allow a young bird to produce the dialect when it was old enough to sing. Clearly, at that time, they were ready to learn the dialect. But this was only the case if the bird was very young – less than four months old. If it was more than four months old when it was first exposed to a regional dialect it would not learn, even though these birds do not actually begin singing until they are adult. So this implies that there is a critical period, before the bird is four months old, when it is very ready to learn a regional dialect for its song. (We might note too that it forms an example of **latent learning**, since the bird shows no evidence of this learning in its behaviour for some considerable time.)

Sensitive periods

The idea of critical periods may be a bit rigid. There is some evidence which suggests that there are variations on this mechanism: in some cases, a particular time is optimal for learning, but not entirely critical. The idea of the **sensitive period** is a similar concept to that of the critical period, but it contains the idea that it is not the only possible time for learning. Under very extreme conditions, the animal might be able to learn the behaviour outside the relevant period. But it learns the behaviour much more easily, and more quickly, during this time.

Critical or sensitive periods have been suggested as the underlying mechanisms for a number of important aspects of development. Scott (1958) suggested that puppies will become fully tame only if they have some contact with human beings in their first three to four weeks of life – otherwise they will always remain slightly timid. And as we saw in Chapter 4, Lenneberg (1967) suggested that human children had a critical period for language acquisition, although the evidence suggests that it is more likely to be a sensitive period.

It is clear that critical and sensitive periods have a survival value for the animal. Later in this chapter, we will see how a critical (or sensitive) period is involved in the way that some young animals form attachments to their caretakers, in a process known as imprinting. The animals which learn in this way tend to be those which are active soon after birth. The imprinting mechanism means that they learn very quickly to stay close to their parent, which helps them to survive.

In this case, the genetic influence is not determining behaviour directly, as it does in the case of fixed action patterns. That would not particularly help the young animals to survive. Instead, the genes have taken one step backwards. Rather than directly controlling behaviour, they make a certain kind of learning very likely to occur, and it is this learning which then helps the animal to survive. The animal is neither trapped into fixed patterns of behaviour which might be inappropriate, nor is it forced to learn everything from scratch, by trial and error. Instead, it follows its parent around, learns by imitation, and its chances of survival are maximised.

Learning by instinct

There are other examples of **genetic preparedness** in learning. Genetic influences can shape what kinds of things an animal is prepared to learn. Gould and Marler (1987) discussed how animals are much more prepared, genetically, to respond to certain kinds of stimuli as opposed to others. We touched on this concept when we were looking at Seligman's idea of preparedness in **one-trial learning** – animals are much more ready to learn associations between a stimulus and response which has a survival value than ones which do not. So they (and we) learn to avoid food which makes them sick almost instantly, but they take longer to learn associations between a bell ringing and the presence of food.

Gould and Marler (1987) showed that this type of genetic preparedness for learning does not just apply to one-trial learning. In various experiments involving training bees to feed from particular kinds of flowers, Gould showed that bees find it very easy to learn to distinguish flowers by their scents, are less good at learning to distinguish them by their colour, even less good at learning to distinguish them by shape, and find it almost impossible to distinguish flowers by other criteria. They have an inherited predisposition which shapes what type of thing they will learn and how easily they will learn it, and this is directly related to the nature of their environment.

This preparedness to learn extends to other kinds of learning as well. In Chapter 20, we saw how powerfully the human infant is predisposed to respond to other people. It inherits perceptual organisation which makes it more likely to respond to a human face, it learns timing and transactions very quickly and it develops a sophisticated awareness of other people at a very early age indeed, by comparison with other cognitive skills. The implication is that human beings are genetically prepared to respond to social stimuli more than other kinds: we are, after all, social animals. And such a preparedness would help a young human being to survive in almost any kind of environment.

It is possible, then, to see preparedness to learn as being nature's insurance. Although environmental and evolutionary demands have meant that the animal needs to learn its behaviour rather than inherit it, the mechanisms of genetic preparedness to learn mean that the learning which results is that which is most likely to aid the animal's survival.

Imprinting, attachment, and parenting

One of the best ways of seeing how genetic and environmental factors interact in animal behaviour is by looking at the area of imprinting and attachment. Research into how young animals develop attachments to their caretakers is a major area in comparative psychology, which began with ethological observations by Lorenz into the behaviour of ducks and geese. From his boyhood on a farm, Lorenz had observed how young goslings and ducklings follow their mother around while they are young, learning from her and being kept out of danger. He had also observed how members of one species would sometimes 'adopt' young birds from another species, if they were given the eggs to hatch. A hen might rear a brood of ducklings, who would follow her around as if she were their mother.

Imprinting as a special form of learning

Lorenz conducted a number of informal investigations into the attachment process. From these he found that if he was the first creature that a set of young goslings had contact with from hatching they would 'adopt' him as their parent, rather than another bird. From then on, they would follow him around wherever he went – so determinedly that he even found that he had to go swimming in order to get his young goslings to go in the water themselves!

Lorenz noticed that the young birds would make every effort to keep him in view, and would become very distressed if he was not visible. It was obvious that this was not a completely inherited

behaviour, because if it had been, the young goslings would not have been able to 'adopt' a human being as caretaker. But at the same time, it was not the ordinary sort of trial-and-error learning either. Lorenz coined the term **imprinting** to describe the process, because it seemed to him that the animals had received a deep impression, firmly stamped into the brain, of their caretaker.

As researchers investigated imprinting, it became clear that it was a special form of learning, which had two stages. The first was an initial response of 'following', during which the young animal would follow a large moving object around. Once the small animal had followed the same object for a period of about ten minutes, an attachment would develop. From then on, it would avoid all other large moving objects, and make strenuous efforts to keep its 'mother' in sight all the time.

The learning involved in imprinting is particularly interesting, because it provides an example of the type of halfway point between behaviour which is genetically controlled and behaviour which is entirely learned, which we discussed earlier. The young goslings or ducklings were genetically pre-programmed to respond to the first large moving object that they saw, by following it around. Then, after ten minutes, they would learn to distinguish this object from any others, and follow it from that time on. So in imprinting we can see a form of behaviour in which learning is important, but this learning is tightly structured in order to maximise the young animal's chances of survival.

As a survival mechanism too it seems reasonable to assume that if young ducklings can follow the same moving object around for ten minutes, and it does not turn round and eat them, then the odds are that it will be a caretaker of some kind. Anything else would be likely to have wandered off before the ten minutes was up. So the ten-minute period provides a good 'insurance' for the young animal, by maximising its chances of attachment to an appropriate caretaker.

But there are other mechanisms which help to ensure that imprinting occurs in the right context. In 1972, Hess discovered that young ducklings seem to be pre-prepared to imprint on their mother, because they hear her **vocalising** through the shell. When they hatch, they follow whatever moving object is making a sound that is familiar to them. In fact, by rigging up microphones in nesting boxes, Hess found that mother ducks produce a special rate of clucking when hatching is near, which seems to aid this process.

The Law of Effort

Later research confirmed the importance of the visual stimulus in imprinting. Bateson (1966) found that, as the young birds followed their parent around, they tended to keep a fixed distance away from her. Moreover, young birds who were imprinted on human beings stayed further away from their 'parent' than those who were imprinted on geese or ducks. Bateson proposed that these birds had inherited an optimal size for the **retinal image**. If the retinal image of the parent was the wrong size – particularly if it was too small – then the young bird would become anxious. The anxiety could be reduced only by getting the image to the optimal size again. So if a young bird fell too far behind its parent (so that the retinal image became too small), it would become anxious and hurry to catch up.

The anxiety is not necessarily a bad thing. In 1958, Hess showed experimentally that the amount of effort which the young animal has to put into following affects the strength of the imprinted bond. By placing obstacles in the paths of young ducklings as they followed a model duck round a

track, Hess found that the more effort the ducklings had to put in to following, the stronger the attachment which they developed. This became known as the **Law of Effort** (Figure 22.7).

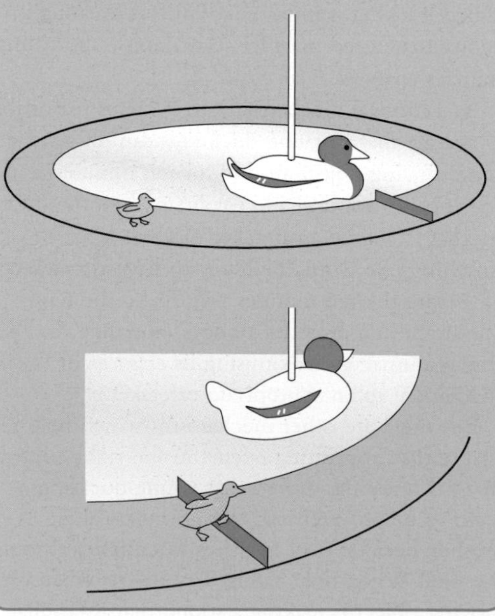

Critical and sensitive periods in imprinting

Some researchers investigated how rigid the genetically determined component of imprinting was. It appeared at first as though there was a strict, genetically determined period of time – a critical period – during which imprinting had to take place. The main evidence for this was the idea that if young ducklings were kept without the opportunity to imprint on a large object, after a while they would not do so at all, and would avoid any suitable large moving objects. The precise timing of this period varies from one species to another, but Ramsey and Hess (1954) discovered that the critical period for mallard ducklings lasts between 5 and 24 hours after hatching. Within that time, imprinting is most likely to happen between the thirteenth and the sixteenth hour after hatching (Figure 22.8).

There has been some controversy, though, as to whether it actually is a critical period, totally determined by the genes, or whether instead it is a sensitive period and can be affected by environmental circumstances. A number of studies found that the period of imprintability could be extended quite considerably if environmental circumstances were modified. For example,

Figure 22.7 Effect in imprinting

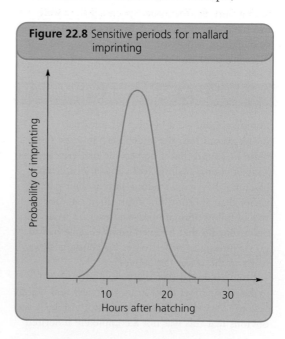

Figure 22.8 Sensitive periods for mallard imprinting

Sluckin and Salzen (1961) showed that if young ducklings were kept in isolation, they could imprint well beyond the critical period. Early experiments had housed the ducklings together, which meant that they could have imprinted on one another. Guiton (1959) showed that the period could be extended if the birds' environment was extremely unstimulating, and Moltz (1960) found that it would extend if ducklings were fitted with translucent hoods so that they were unable to perceive patterns.

As a result of all this, Sluckin (1964) proposed that the period should be described as a sensitive period, rather than as a critical one. It was certainly the best and most likely period for imprinting, but it was not the only possible time when imprinting could occur. This suggested that the timing was not automatically determined by the genes – they did not just 'switch off' imprintability regardless of external circumstances, as the term critical period implied. Instead, they responded to environmental stimuli.

Although this may seem like an academic distinction, it is really all about how rigid the genetic control of behaviour is. In imprinting we see a situation in which the genes induce a 'state of readiness' to engage in this kind of learning; but even here it can be modified by circumstances if those circumstances are unusual enough. However, as far as the average young bird is concerned, it might as well be a critical period, because such extreme circumstances would be very unlikely to happen in nature.

Imprinting as determining adult behaviour

One corollary of the notion of the critical period was the idea that imprinting did not just determine the immediate attachment, but also determined the animal's adult behaviour as well. Lorenz proposed that the parent animal acted as a 'role model' for the young animal, so that when it grew up it would show behaviours appropriate for the species on which it had imprinted. This particularly applied to sexual preference: Lorenz argued that an animal which had imprinted on a member of another species would, when adult, attempt to mate with members of the adoptive species and not those of its own.

Previous researchers had shown that, given the right circumstances, young birds could be induced to imprint on other objects, including in one study a large rubber ball, and in another the yellow rubber gloves worn by the assistant who put food into their cages. Guiton (1966) investigated the long-term effects of this, and showed that, as long as the young animals had subsequent contact with members of their own species, the effects of imprinting could be reversed: such animals would grow up with normal sexual preferences. It was only if they remained separate from members of their own species as they grew up that the disturbances showed.

Imprinting as a species-specific behaviour

The discovery of imprinting caused considerable excitement among researchers, not least because it appeared to present a mechanism which showed how attachments between young animals and their caretakers could form. At first, all attachments were thought of as occurring through imprinting, and studies with mammals, in particular horses and sheep, showed that they, too, seemed to show imprinting. This was taken as evidence that imprinting was a universal mechanism of attachment.

But horses and sheep, like chickens, ducks and geese, are **precocial animals** – their young can move around independently very soon after birth. For a precocial animal, having a mechanism which permits a rapid attachment between the young animal and its parent is a definite survival mechanism, or even a necessity. An animal which is mobile and can wander around on its own within an hour or so of being born or hatched is very vulnerable to predators and other dangers. But other species, including humans, have different conditions for their young, and do not need to develop such rapid attachments. Instead, their attachments can happen more gradually, through a different kind of learning.

Other forms of attachment

Before the discovery of imprinting, the behaviourist school of psychology had argued that an infant develops an attachment to its mother simply because she provides food and warmth. This remained a dominant assumption for some considerable time in America, for two main reasons. One of them was the extremely powerful influence of behaviourist thinking on psychology generally, and the other was to do with the influence of **Lloyd Morgan's canon**, which we looked at earlier in this chapter. Lloyd Morgan's canon was the widely held view that behaviour should wherever possible be explained using the lowest possible mechanism on a scale of psychological complexity. Forming an association between feelings of comfort and the presence of the mother could be seen simply as secondary reinforcement, if it came from feeding.

But in 1959, Harlow challenged this idea, by providing evidence that attachment, at least in primates, can develop as a result of other factors. Harlow performed a series of studies of attachment in infant monkeys. In these, young monkeys were brought up in isolation from their own kind, but with models in their cages from which they were fed. Some of the models (which Harlow referred to as surrogate mothers) were made of bare wire, and some were covered in soft cloth (Figure 22.9).

Harlow showed that the young monkeys found tactile comfort to be far more important than the comfort derived from feeding. They much preferred the cloth-covered models to the wire ones, even when they were fed from the latter. Moreover, they showed every sign of becoming attached to the cloth models. When they were alarmed, for instance by a wind-up teddy bear which marched along beating a drum, young monkeys would cling to the cloth model. The same applied when they were given an **open-field**

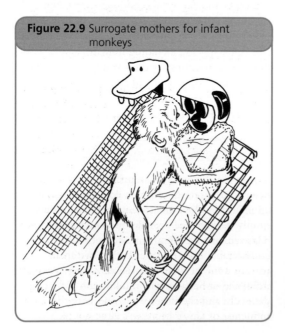

Figure 22.9 Surrogate mothers for infant monkeys

test – that is, placed in an empty space in a strange room. At first they would cling to the cloth model, but then they would gradually peep out, and timidly begin to explore the room. But they would not cling to the wire one, even if the cloth-covered model was not present, and even though they had been fed from it.

It was clear, then, that attachment involved more than just feeding and physical caretaking. From Harlow's research, it appeared initially that the presence of a comforting mother-surrogate model was all that the young monkey infant needed for healthy development. However, as the research progressed, Harlow and his colleagues found that this was not the case. Young monkeys brought up with such models, but in isolation from other members of their species, developed atypically, and showed severe social and behavioural disturbances.

Outcomes of inadequate attachment

Although the young monkeys brought up in isolation showed some degree of attachment to their surrogate mother figures, in 1962 Harlow and Harlow published a paper which showed that they had suffered considerable emotional and social impairment. By comparison with another group of monkeys of the same age, which had been separated from their mothers but had lived with others of the same species (four of them of the same age brought up together), Harlow and Harlow showed that the isolated monkeys continued to show lasting emotional problems.

This impairment included an inability to relate well to other monkeys. They were easily bullied and often found themselves social outcasts. The previously isolated monkeys also engaged in some extremely disturbed behaviour, such as self-mutilation, and when they came into season some of them failed to show appropriate sexual behaviour. Their disturbance was slightly alleviated for some of the monkeys by a treatment in which they were placed together with an adult, well-adjusted monkey, on a sort of 'monkey island' in a zoo.

The disturbance seemed to be quite long-lasting, and this raises ethical issues, some of which are discussed in Box 22.2. For example, in 1976, Ruppenthal *et al.* reported on the long-term effects that the original study had on those monkeys' maternal behaviour. Ruppenthal *et al.* showed how those monkeys who had been unable

Box 22.2 Ethical issues in animal studies

Many of the studies which have been conducted to inform researchers about the nature of attachment have rather questionable ethical implications. For example, a considerable amount of research has centred on the effect of separation from the mother in young monkeys, partly because some researchers consider that it is more ethically acceptable to do such research with monkeys, whereas of course it would not be possible with human beings. More recently, researchers have been questioning whether it is ethically acceptable to conduct such studies with animals either.

Harlow's work on attachment in infant monkeys involved young rhesus monkeys being brought up in isolation, with only a wire or cloth-covered model for company. More recent findings on the nature of social life in the rhesus monkey indicate that even bringing these monkeys up as mother-infant groups constitutes serious social deprivation, as they are such highly social animals (de Waal, 1989). Not surprisingly, bringing them up in such extreme isolation produced severely disturbed behaviour.

In another study (Suomi, Collins and Harlow, 1973), young rhesus monkeys were permanently separated from their mothers, at varying ages. One group was separated after 60 days, one after 90, and one after 120 days. These time periods were selected because what is known as the fear response — the evidence of distress at being separated from the mother — appears to mature at around 70 to 80 days. Perhaps not surprisingly, the most severe reaction to the separation was shown by those infants which were 90 days old. One male and one female from each of these groups was housed singly: the others were housed in pairs. Again, not surprisingly, these monkeys showed greatly increased distress and subsequent disturbance.

In part, these studies need to be interpreted in the context of their times — in particular, the dominance of the manipulative methodology of behaviourism, and a social climate which viewed science as independent of social responsibility. Nowadays, it is open to question whether such studies would be permitted, given the much stricter regulations and guidelines governing animal research and the much greater awareness of social responsibility and ethical issues. Any researcher wanting to conduct research of this nature would need to produce an extremely strong justification of the method, showing how it addressed a question of crucial significance and showing also how psychological pain and distress were to be minimised. But that changes too: at the time that these studies were conducted, it appeared that they were providing us with important information about human attachment. Nowadays, though, their relevance is not quite so obvious.

to form attachments to others as infants had also shown themselves unlikely to be competent in the care of their first offspring — although they sometimes learned from that experience, and were able to look after a second one. We will look at this study in more detail in the next section.

Animal parenting

Animal parenting is often referred to as maternal behaviour, but that is an extremely misleading term for how animals look after their young. In this area, as with others, the principle of **behavioural diversity** is very apparent. There are innumerable different ways of looking after young animals. Ostriches, for example, care for their young in large crèches, containing anything up to 200 small birds. These crèches are cared for by a few adults, who are just as likely to be male as female. Infant sea-horses develop in a pouch in the father's body, and are looked after by him when they become big enough to swim independently, going back into the pouch when danger threatens. And mongooses live in large colonies in which the infants are reared by a group of adoptive 'aunts', who may bear no blood relationship to the young at all.

The topic is often described as 'maternal behaviour' for two reasons. First, the title arose by default in the first half of this century, reflecting the social assumptions of the time. Since, in most human societies (though not in all human families), it is usually the mother who looks after the young, those studying animal behaviour have tended to assume that this will be the case with all other animals. By the kind of selective perception which we looked at in Chapter 2, these expectations led researchers to ignore or disregard the many examples of animal behaviour which have been different from this idea, and only notice the ones which fit with it. And this leads to the second reason, which is that because researchers have tended to ignore other species as 'not typical', we are most well-informed about the behaviour of animals in which the mother does look after the young.

Laboratory rats

The animal that we know most about, of course, is the laboratory rat. Gray (1971) discussed how many generations of breeding in captivity, and unconscious selection for traits such as calmness and being less likely to bite researchers, had resulted in a number of physiological differences which made laboratory rats quite different from wild ones. But even laboratory rats retain a certain amount of instinctive behaviour, particularly when it comes to caring for their young.

Rosenblatt and Lehrmann (1963) described how, before giving birth, a female rat will build a nest by gathering suitable bits of material together into a corner or other secluded area. Immediately before the birth she begins to lick herself, and as the young are born she licks them and the surrounding area as well. In the first week, her maternal behaviour mainly consists of nest-building, suckling the young, licking them and retrieving them if they stray from the nest.

Much of this behaviour appears to be innate. Riess (1950) showed how even female rats which have been brought up in isolation from birth seem to show it. But rats which had never had any experience with holding things would not show the behaviour, which seemed to indicate that even here there could be some environmental influence. However, this study involved going to some rather extreme lengths to ensure lack of practice, including amputating the rats' tails, and it is rather doubtful whether bringing animals up in such an extreme manner can really tell us anything at all about their natural behaviour. Perhaps more acceptably, Kinder (1927) showed that the environment did exert some influence on early maternal behaviour, in that rats built flimsier

nests at higher temperatures than they did when it was cold.

In their second week, the rat pups become more active, and the female enlarges the nest by adding more material to its edges. The pups crawl out of the nest frequently, and will sometimes avoid attempts by the mother to bring or direct them back. They may also attempt to suckle from the mother while still at a distance from the nest, with varying degrees of success. All this means that the mother is called on to show increasingly complex forms of behaviour in dealing with the pups, so simple automatic retrieving responses become less frequent.

By the third week, the pups are beginning to eat other kinds of food. Although they may occasionally be permitted to suckle for a short while, the mother will rarely lie down to nurse them, and turns away more and more often. Retrieving behaviour does not happen any more: the young are left to find their own way back to the nest. She has also ceased nest-building or maintenance behaviour altogether by this time, so the nest material often becomes spread out across the floor. The young by now are quite active, and able to survive independently.

Rabbits

Unlike many other species, the rabbit makes little preparation until just before the birth actually begins. Then the doe rapidly digs a burrow, gathers some hay or straw, plucks hair from her coat (which has become loosened as a result of the hormonal changes at this time) and builds a nest into which the young are born. When they are born, they are suckled for just a few minutes a day. Although maternal care varies somewhat from one breed of rabbit to another, they tend to care for their offspring in the nest for a period of about two to three weeks, after which time the young are active and can fend for themselves.

Much of the rabbit's maternal care seems to centre on the building of a warm nest and suckling the young. Unlike other animals, mother rabbits do not retrieve their offspring if they are found outside the nest. Ross et al. (1963) reported an experiment in which infant rabbits were placed just outside the nest box, in an alleyway. The mother rabbits in the study varied in their reactions: some licked the young rabbits, one tried to suckle them, but others just sniffed at them and one mother even stood on hers, despite their loud protests. None of the mothers made any attempt to replace their offspring in the nest. But again, this study had created a situation which would not have happened in the wild, since young rabbits do not move out of their nest. Parental behaviour and the behaviour of the young seem always to be intimately linked.

Cats

In the last few weeks of pregnancy, the female cat looks for a dry, dark and undisturbed place with something soft on the floor, where the young can be born. The degree of seclusion varies: wild or untamed cats will hide their young securely, whereas domestic cats are often more tolerant. As the young are born, the mother licks them clean and orients them towards her. Schneirla, Rosenblatt and Tobach (1963) see this initial inter-action with the kittens as providing the cat with the basis for developing more complex relation-ships with them later. The young become familiar with the feel of their mother's tongue, and her smell, which will encourage the development of recognition.

After birth, the mother cat will lie encircling the kittens for as long as twelve hours. After this, although she continues with this behaviour most of the time, she will get up and leave the kittens for a brief period at roughly two hourly intervals. When she returns to them, she stands over the kittens and arouses them by licking them vigorously, then lies down and the kittens begin to suckle. Schneirla *et al.* found that the mother cat's encircling of the kittens at this time has a definite quietening effect on them, as does her smell.

Shortly after birth, the mother cat will respond to the vocalisations made by the young, and will retrieve them and bring them back to the nest if she hears them calling. Interestingly, though, Leyhausen (1956) found that the auditory cue is necessary: mother cats will ignore their young at this time if they can see them but not hear them, even if the kittens are out of the nest.

For the first three weeks, the mother cat feeds her kittens regularly, and for quite long periods at a time. This is usually initiated by the mother's returning to the nest and lying down. But from about the fourth week, the kittens are more active and begin to approach the mother for food, even outside the nest. At first, the mother is responsive to these advances, but as time progresses the mother avoids the young more and more, often

evading the kittens by going to a location which they cannot reach. At this time too the young are beginning to show an interest in other kinds of food. This behaviour is seen as an important precursor to weaning, which takes place round about the sixth week.

As the kittens grow older, they accompany their mother while she is within reach, and imitate many of her actions. Kuo (1938) showed that kittens which had been brought up with mothers who often killed rats or mice were much more likely to do so themselves when they grew up. They would also begin hunting-type behaviour at an earlier age than kittens which had not had such a parent. Wilson and Weston (1947) argued that the mother cat does not actually teach the young to hunt directly but, since they are accompanying her, they become aroused and excited at the event of the kill, and so find hunting a rewarding experience later in life. This is almost an exact counterpart to the stimulus-seeking theory of children's play, which we looked at in Chapter 20.

Sheep

One of the questions researchers have investigated is how mother and infant can discriminate between the various members of a herd of sheep, and interact only with one another. Lambs are **precocial**, and learn to recognise the mother quite rapidly. However, they do not follow her around, as young foals do. After feeding, the lamb often falls asleep and the mother moves away to graze, but often the lamb will awaken and wander off, which appears to be distressing for the ewe. Lambs begin to graze with their mothers within a few weeks of birth but tend to wander further away as they grow older, although they will often run back to her and attempt to suckle when they are frightened.

When the mother observes that the lamb is missing, she begins to wander around and bleat loudly. Murie (1944) observed that lambs appear to recognise the calls of their own mothers, although mothers sometimes respond to the bleats of lambs which are not theirs if it sounds similar. Interestingly, vision, at least for older lambs, is important in recognising the mother, as well as sound. Hersher, Richmond and Moore (1963a) observed that if a ewe has just been sheared her lamb will run to her bleat, but then will run straight past her without recognising her. The only exceptions to this which were observed by the research team in studies at their animal behaviour farm were a lamb whose mother had brown legs, and so was easily recognisable, and a goat kid which had been reared by a sheep.

While nursing cats can often be persuaded to adopt another kitten which is not their own, sheep tend to be very resistant to this. Lamond (1949) found that they could usually be persuaded to accept a strange lamb on the first day after giving birth, if the lamb was first sprayed with the mother's milk, which suggests that smell is an important factor. Other techniques, though, like draping the dead lamb's skin on the adoptee, were less successful, despite claims of farmers that the technique had worked in the past.

Hersher, Richmond and Moore (1963b) suggested that there is a sensitive period in which the mother comes to recognise the young, in a process rather similar to that of imprinting. Immediately after birth, the ewe will mother any young animal, but after a few hours she will mother only her own, and reject any others. The researchers suggested that vision was an important factor here, in that mothers will spend much more time sniffing at a strange lamb before butting it away if it looks similar to their own. They are also more likely to accept another lamb for adoption if it looks similar to the one that they have lost.

Hersher also found that, even after the sensitive period was over, it was still just about possible to induce a mother to accept another lamb, but only if the two were kept in close proximity for 24 hours or more, and the mother was prevented from butting the young one away. As with so many other such studies, of course, these are conditions that are unlikely to arise in nature.

Between three and six months of age the lambs are weaned, and the mother gradually loses interest in them. Her calling and suckling behaviours become less and less frequent. At this time, too, the young lambs spend increasing amounts of their time in 'schools' – large groups of others of the same age. By the time they are eight months old, there is little sign of the relationship in the mother's behaviour. The lamb will still occasionally approach her, although this behaviour becomes less and less frequent.

Rhesus monkeys

As we have already seen, Harlow's research teams performed a number of studies of attachment in rhesus monkeys. These studies led, quite naturally, to a number of detailed observations of maternal behaviour, as they tried to identify what the necessary features of infant-rearing were, in order to achieve positive social integration of the young monkey. Harlow, Harlow and Hansen (1963) reported that maternal behaviour towards the young could best be described in terms of three stages, which are listed in Table 22.5.

In 1976, Ruppenthal et al. reported an investigation into whether the lack of attachments in infancy would affect maternal behaviour. There were 50 female rhesus monkeys involved in Ruppenthal's study – the same ones who had been the subjects of Harlow's earlier research into attachment. Altogether, by this time, 25 young monkeys had been reared with wire-mesh surrogate mothers, in isolation in bare wire cages. Through the cages, they could see and hear other monkeys but they were not able to interact with them. A further seventeen monkeys had been reared with cloth surrogate mothers, also in isolation but able to see and hear other monkeys. Eight more monkeys had been reared in two groups of four, with this contact with others of the same age beginning when the monkeys were between two weeks and three months old and lasting for at least four months.

Each of these monkeys became pregnant – some by artificial insemination, some by natural means – and their maternal behaviour was observed. Ruppenthal et al. found that the type of upbringing which the monkey had experienced directly affected its maternal behaviour. While undertaking the observation, the researchers classified behaviour into three types: 'adequate', 'indifferent' and 'abusive' (see Table 22.6), and found that those monkeys reared with either wire surrogate mothers or cloth surrogate mothers tended not to become adequate mothers – they were either indifferent or abusive, most often abusive. Those monkeys which had been brought up with wire surrogate mothers tended to be more abusive towards their infants than those brought up with the cloth surrogates, but none of them achieved standards of mothering described as adequate. Some of the cloth surrogate group were indifferent while most of the wire surrogate group were abusive.

However, those monkeys which had been reared in the presence of their peers did manage to look after their infants. Ruppenthal et al. found that the earlier the age at which the young

Table 22.5 Three stages of maternal behaviour

Protection	This stage lasts for roughly the first month after birth. During this time, the mother keeps close physical contact with the infant, spending most of her time cradling, nursing, grooming, and retrieving the infant when it tries to crawl away. On its part, the infant spends much of its time clinging to its mother's fur and watching events in the neighbourhood, or suckling.
Ambivalence	This stage lasts roughly from two months old (although it begins later with some animals) until the young one is about fifteen months old (again, this is variable, depending on the individuals concerned). During this time, the mother shows both affectionate, high body-contact behaviour and punitive, rejecting behaviour towards the infant. It may be that to refer to it as a stage is rather misleading, in that there are distinct changes throughout this period: at first, the mother shows far more affectionate behaviour than she does punishment, but the amount increases as time progresses, until by the end, the ratio of punishment to attention is very much higher. Towards the end of this stage, mothers sometimes produce apparently unprovoked punishment, often including physically rejecting the youngster by shaking it away or holding it off with an arm.
Rejection	During the third stage, the mother will actively reject the infant, refusing to allow it to approach and make physical contact, and often chasing it away aggressively. However, Harlow *et al.* observed that the youngsters were often seen in close proximity to the mother at this time, even though they did not actually make physical contact themselves; and they emphasised also that individual animals differ in the degree of rejection or affection that they display.

Source: Adapted from Harlow et al., *1963*

Table 22.6 Categories of maternal behaviour

Adequate	Maternal behaviour in which the young infant was fully cared for by the mother, and no intervention by laboratory staff was needed.
Indifferent	Maternal behaviour in which the mother consistently failed to nurse the child, and showed very little interest in it, at least for the first few days. In these cases the laboratory staff would feed the infant, and the mothers typically did not show any reaction when the infants were removed from their presence. This category was maintained for the first few days, but there was evidence that some monkeys appeared to develop an attachment to their infant later on, after having had contact with it for a while.
Abusive	Some monkey mothers showed a violent rejection of the infant, and might even attack and kill it. In these cases, staff intervention was necessary both to feed the infant and to protect it: it proved too dangerous to leave the infant with the mother.

Source: Adapted from Ruppenthal et al., *1976*

monkey was introduced to the others, the more likely it was to become an adequate mother later. It also emerged that those monkeys which had experienced a period of their adolescence on a 'monkey island' in a zoo with a 'normal' male monkey (a study which had seemed to show that the effects of their upbringing were irreversible) were also more likely to produce adequate mothering eventually.

This study appeared to show that although the effects of early experience were not necessarily unchangeable, they might become so for a few individuals. Interestingly, though, even some of the monkey mothers who were indifferent or slightly abusive towards their first infant managed to care for a second infant adequately. Ruppenthal *et al.* found that mothers which had managed 48 hours or more of contact with their first infant almost always exhibited adequate care of the second one, so clearly there was a learning experience going on here. But those whose infants either died or had to be taken away from them before the 48 hours did not learn. In a few extreme cases, some monkeys reacted so violently to their young infants that they killed them very quickly, and therefore never learnt the ability to handle them.

These findings imply that social contact and learning are essential factors in developing adequate mothering techniques, at least in primates. As we have seen, those monkeys which experienced social contact with others when they were young were more able to care for their infants; and the earlier that social contact began, the better. But it did not have to be contact with adults – they were simply having social contact with others of their own age. Similarly, those mothers who had experienced contact with their infants for 48 hours or more were also more likely to become adequate mothers. Ruppenthal *et al.* commented that it was striking how little time was required for monkeys to learn adequate mothering.

Mothering behaviour in general

The study of maternal behaviour in different mammals shows us that there is a considerable amount of variation in how different species bring up their young. And when we look specifically at primates, we see an increased dependence on learning, and quite often the capacity to adapt behaviour in adulthood even in the face of quite serious deprivation or privation in infancy. Given the tendency to generalise from animal studies to human beings, that is an important point to bear in mind.

Another important factor in the study of maternal behaviour generally is the **interaction** between the infant and the mother. It is often difficult to disentangle the interaction between the two – if we wish to study how the mother behaves, we also need to take into account how the infant acts. So, for example, Harlow *et al.* found that although a rhesus monkey would willingly adopt and cuddle a kitten, it would not maintain that behaviour because the kitten itself could not cling to her fur, and would drop away if she did not hold it. Although the mother retrieved the kitten for several days, eventually she gave up and abandoned it. The behaviour of nursing needs to be seen also in the context of the infant clinging to the mother: the one is intimately linked with the other.

We have seen, then, how animal behaviour can be seen as an interaction of genetic, environmental, and social elements. Animals, and human beings too, have evolved a number of different mechanisms which enable them to operate effectively within the constraints of their environments. In the next chapter, we will look at some of the areas of animal behaviour which have particularly attracted the interest of comparative psychologists: at courtship and mating, at social organisation, and at how animals manifest territoriality; and at how research into these areas has informed debates about evolution and evolutionary mechanisms.

Key terms

action-specific energy Energy which is only concerned with one particular type of behaviour, such as eating or drinking, and which is thought to represent an inner drive.

animism Perceiving and responding to inanimate objects (rocks, computers, cars, etc.) as if they were alive and conscious.

anthropomorphism Projecting human qualities, thoughts and feelings onto animals.

appeasement gesture An inherited action supposed to inhibit aggressive behaviour from other members of the species.

appetitive behaviour Behaviour which increases the likelihood of satisfying a need (e.g. seeking water when thirsty).

biodiversity The evolutionary principle that forms of life, behaviour and environmental interaction are as widely varied as possible, in order to exploit as many avenues of potential survival as possible.

chromosomes Long strands of DNA in the cell nucleus, organised in matching pairs.

consummatory behaviour Behaviour which directly satisfies an inner need state, such as drinking when thirsty.

consummatory stimulation Stimulation which directly satisfies an inner need state, e.g. the presence of the egg in the nest for a brooding hen.

courtship displays Sequences of behaviour, distinctive to its species, which a particular animal performs in order to attract a mate.

critical period A genetically-determined time during development when a particular form of learning must take place if it is ever to be learned at all.

evolution The process of species development through small genetic changes leading to adaptive fitness for the individual.

fixed action patterns Inherited sequences of behaviour, performed in response to a sign stimulus.

gene A unit of heredity, represented biologically by a specific DNA sequence.

gene pool The complete range of possible inherited traits available within the gene of a given population of animals or plants.

innate releasing mechanism (IRM) A hypothetical 'trigger' which activates fixed action patterns when the appropriate environmental stimulus is present.

Law of Effort The principle in imprinting that the more of a struggle the young animal has to follow its parent, the stronger its imprinted bond will become.

maturation The process of growing older biologically, and so experiencing genetically-determined age-related changes.

open-field test A test to identify levels of anxiety or attachment, in which the animal or human is placed in a wide open space and its response is observed.

phylogenetic scale An ordering of species hierarchically, usually organised in such a way that human beings are at the highest point and other animal species are 'ranked' according to their degree of similarity to the human being.

phylogeny The sequence of evolution through which a particular species has passed.

punctuated equilibrium An approach to understanding evolution which suggests that evolutionary change occurs in rapid bursts followed by periods of relative stability, in response to environmental changes.

sensitive period A time when an animal is genetically prepared to respond to particular environmental stimuli.

sign stimulus A signal which initiates innate releasing mechanisms for inherited behaviour.

teleological explanation Explanation which emphasises the functions of a phenomenon such as why it occurred or developed.

threat displays Patterns of inherited behaviour which are designed to intimidate others of the same species, and may sometimes preface physical attack.

Summary

1 Comparative psychology is concerned with animal behaviour. Fundamental concepts in comparative psychology include Lloyd Morgan's canon, which states that the lowest possible level of explanation should be used.

2 The theory of evolution is basic to comparative psychology. It includes the principles of biodiversity and behavioural diversity, genetic transmission and, with caution, the idea of the phylogenetic scale.

3 Genetically controlled behaviour takes the form of fixed action patterns, which appear as a result of maturation. They are shown when a sign stimulus triggers an innate releasing mechanism.

4 The hydraulic model of instinctive behaviour suggests that there is a reservoir of action-specific energy which is released in the form of fixed action patterns. This idea was challenged by later researchers.

5 It is possible to see a number of intermediate stages in the control of behaviour between genetically determined behaviour and learned behaviour. These intermediate stages include forms of preparedness in learning, and critical and sensitive periods.

6 Imprinting is a special form of learning in which a young precocial animal identifies a parent figure during a sensitive period, and subsequently follows it around. Research into imprinting has produced the Law of Effort, and some debate about the lasting nature of its effects.

7 Studies of attachment in rhesus monkeys showed that the most important factor for normal social development was contact with other members of the species.

8 Studies of parental behaviour in mammals show that it is generally a combination of inherited and learned components, and becomes more variable as we move higher up the phylogenetic scale.

Self-assessment questions

1 Outline the distinctive features of instinctive behaviour.

2 Describe the main principles of imprinting.

3 What do you understand by the principle of bio-diversity? Give examples of its application to animal behaviour.

Practice essay questions

1 Giving examples, describe the basic mechanisms by which different species evolve.

2 Critically evaluate the hydraulic model of instinctive behaviour.

3 'All learning is genetic in origin'. Using comparative evidence, explain and evaluate this statement.

Test your knowledge of this chapter with our online quizzes and games at: http://www.psych.co.uk

Explore comparative psychology at:

General

http://jieyin.spedia.net/ – Links to sites on evolutionary theory, history, bibliographies and relevant links to both human and animal behaviour.

http://nua-tech.com/paddy/ethology.shtml – Detailed but conversational guide to animal intelligence and behaviour with links to selected sites.

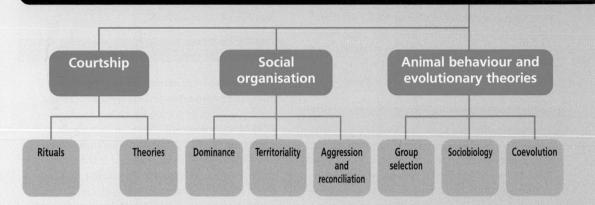

Animal behaviour

Courtship

Social organisation

Animal behaviour and evolutionary theories

Rituals | Theories | Dominance | Territoriality | Aggression and reconciliation | Group selection | Sociobiology | Coevolution

Learning objectives

23.1. Courtship
a identify mechanisms involved in courtship rituals
b describe theories of courtship
c apply theories of courtship to specific examples

23.2. Dominance hierarchies
a descibe features of hierarchical social organisation
b evaluate the concept of linear pecking orders
c descibe a study of hierarchical social organisation in animals

23.3. Social organisation
a outline factors which may influence dominance-based social organisation
b describe a study of environmental influence on animal social organisation
c identify sources of error in animal obervation

23.4. Types of territoriality
a define terms relating to territoriality
b identify different forms of animal territoriality
c describe a study of territorial behaviour in animals

23.5. Theories of territoriality
a describe basic concepts relating to territoriality
b outline theories of territoriality
c evaluate theories of territorial behaviour

23.6. Aggression and reconciliation
a outline Lorenz's model of ritualised aggression
b evaluate explanations of aggressive behaviour in animals
c evaluate the concept of reconciliation

23.7. Evolutionary processes
a define terms relating to evolutionary processes
b evaluate the sociobiological perspective
c outline the principals of coevolution

23.8. Evolutionary theories
a describe different evolutionary theories
b evaluate different theories of evolution
c apply the concept of levels of explanation to animal behaviour

In the last chapter, we looked at some of the basic mechanisms which are operative in animal behaviour: the mechanisms of instinctive behaviour, of learning, and of critical and sensitive periods. In this chapter, we will go on to look at some more instances of animal behaviour, seeing how those mechanisms may be involved in producing courtship and mating rituals, and how they have been used to explain findings concerning social organisation and territoriality; before going on to examine some of the explanations which have been put forward to explain what animals do.

Courtship

Ethologists studying animal behaviour have often been interested in the way that some behaviour patterns seem to occur only in some species and do not occur in others, even if they are closely related. Many courtship rituals come into this category, as does, for instance, the egg-rolling behaviour which Lorenz studied in the greylag goose (see Chapter 22). Animals act in very different ways, and in this section we will look at some examples of the diversity which occurs between species.

The fact that animal behaviour is often specific to a particular species, though, does not mean that we are unable to categorise it. Ethologists have often found it useful to categorise animal behaviour in terms of the functions that it serves. So, for instance, it is useful to compare different types of courtship and mating behaviour, or to look at how animals care for their young, as we did in the last chapter. We will begin by looking at some of the studies which have been concerned with courtship and mating. From there, we will go on to look at some of the wider issues of social organisation, including aspects of territoriality and dominance.

A word of warning: the important thing to remember when we are looking at any category of animal behaviour is how much it varies. As we saw in the last chapter, biodiversity is an important principle of evolution, and so is **behavioural diversity**. Some of the theories which have been put forward to explain animal behaviour have drawn from a very limited range of evidence, and have assumed that all other animals will behave in the same way. But the more we study how animals behave, the more we find that diversity is the rule,

not homogeneity. There are millions of different species of animals in the world, and between them we find almost every possible combination of behaviours. So it is important to be wary of theories which make sweeping generalisations about animal behaviour, because often they can only do so by ignoring the behaviour of a large number of other animals.

Courtship rituals

Ever since the first systematic observations of animal behaviour, researchers have shown that mating is often preceded by elaborate sequences of ritualised behaviour. These are known as courtship rituals. There have been many studies of courtship rituals in animals and it is not possible to cover them all here, so we will just look at some typical examples. In some species, courtship rituals involve highly complex displays, demanding a considerable expenditure of energy. In other species, courtship may be far briefer, or almost non-existent. The study of courtship has provided very fruitful material for ethologists in their study of behaviour in its natural environment.

The courtship of the stickleback
One of the classic studies of courtship was reported by Tinbergen, in 1951. Tinbergen described the results of a series of investigations of the courtship behaviour of male sticklebacks. In this species, the male first selects a piece of territory and builds a nest (rather like a short tunnel) in the centre. He then patrols the outer limits of the territory, chasing away any other males of his species. The male stickleback at this time of year has a bright red belly, and by using models Tinbergen showed that it was the red belly of the male which triggered this aggressive attack.

When a female (who does not have a red belly) approaches the territory, the male begins to swim in an odd, zig-zag fashion. She responds to this by lifting her head and tail, and swimming with her abdomen protruding. At this time, her abdomen is swollen with eggs, and this odd way of swimming displays that. Tinbergen interpreted this part of the ritual as a demonstration that the courtship ritual would be worthwhile, since if the female had recently mated and had no eggs left, there would be little point in continuing with the ritual.

The male then swims to the nest with the female following, and orients the tip of his head towards the entrance. She enters the nest, and the male prods her rear with his head. This seems to stimulate her to lay her eggs. Once she has laid them, she leaves the nest and the male enters it and fertilises the eggs (Figure 23.1). He then chases the female away from the area, and repeats the whole performance with the next female who arrives in the vicinity. As the eggs develop in the nest, the male guards the entrance, fanning water through with his fins, which appears to be a method of ensuring that the eggs are surrounded with properly oxygenated water; and chasing away other fish who might be potential predators on the eggs.

Fixed action patterns

Tinbergen argued that this complex ritual involves a chain of fixed action patterns, which acts as a sign stimulus to release the next behaviour. So the male's zig-zag dance acts as the sign stimulus for the female to show her abdomen, and this in turn acts as a sign stimulus for the male to 'lead' the female to the nest, and so on.

The chain of responses to sign stimuli can be triggered for as long as the male remains in the reproductive state. This state includes the development of the red colouring on the belly, and a high level of gonadal hormone. When the level of gonadal hormone drops, the male ceases to engage in this activity. Most courtship behaviour is seasonal like this, and depends on the complex interplay of internal hormonal levels and external stimuli.

Partly, too, the external stimuli needed may be provided by other members of the species: most female mammals, for instance, come into **oestrus** during the mating season, at which time they release pheromones which help to trigger mating behaviour. Other external factors may include changes in daylength or external temperature. But the study of courtship behaviour is not just a matter of looking for 'triggers' for fixed behaviour patterns.

Theories of courtship

A number of different theories have been forward to explain animal courtship in evolutionary terms. These include the idea that courtship rituals are all about making sure that the animal mates with the right species, and not with some other, similar animal; courtship as a strategy allowing the individual to survive; courtship as a display of fitness; courtship as a means of improving the species; and courtship as strengthening pair-bonding. As with so many explanations in comparative psychology, different explanations seem appropriate to the behaviour of different species, so it is worth bearing all of them in mind.

Courtship as ensuring appropriate pairing

One possible explanation for the high degree of ritualisation in many courtship displays is the idea that having an elaborate and complex ritual is a good way of ensuring that mating takes place only with members of the right species, and not with others. Since some species are closely related, cross-breeding between them might not be impossible, but it would not necessarily be an advantage – given that there was an evolutionary reason for the two species diversifying in the first place.

An elaborate courtship ritual makes sure that if an animal has not inherited the right characteristics it will not perform the proper sequence of actions in the mating ritual, and so will not manage to breed. For example, the ten-spined stickleback has a courtship display which involves similar behaviour patterns to those of the three-spined stickleback. However, the visual stimuli which act as the 'triggers' for courtship behaviour are different, in that ten-spined males are com-

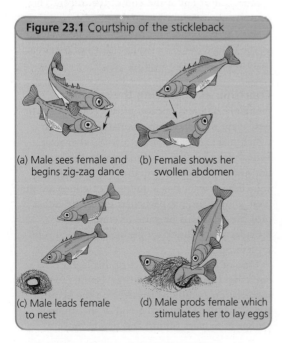

Figure 23.1 Courtship of the stickleback

(a) Male sees female and begins zig-zag dance

(b) Female shows her swollen abdomen

(c) Male leads female to nest

(d) Male prods female which stimulates her to lay eggs

pletely black, while three-spined males have red bellies. As we have seen, it is the redness to which male three-spined sticklebacks respond. Female sticklebacks, too, respond to the visual stimulus which is appropriate for their species. In this way, they do not 'accidentally' pair with the wrong fish.

It is not clear how much evidence is available to test this theory thoroughly. In order to do so, we would need to gather evidence about those animals which have highly ritualised displays and those which do not. We would need to look at the probability of such mis-mating taking place, and at how that might have provided an evolutionary incentive in the past for the species to develop such distinctions. Since habitats and species are continually changing, such a study would be quite difficult to achieve, particularly when we remember that some rituals may have survived because they were helpful in the past, but have no such function now, like the distraction display of the Galapagos dove which was mentioned in Chapter 22. And, of course, there are many species whose behaviour has still never been studied.

Courtship as permitting survival

Courtship inevitably involves the close approach of two members of the same species. If the members of that species happen to be solitary and pugnacious, such an approach may prove very dangerous for a mate. So a courtship ritual may be a useful way of allowing one animal to approach its potential mate in a non-aggressive, reassuring manner, minimising the risk to itself. Spiders are particularly good examples of this type of courtship, because female spiders tend to be larger and stronger than the males, and are also extremely aggressive. A male spider stands an extremely good chance of being eaten should the female catch him.

In some species this happens automatically: the female eats her mate as soon as copulation has finished. Some species of spider, though, have evolved rituals to avoid this fate. For example, the male ground-nesting spider *Pisaura mirabilis* begins his courtship by catching a fly. He then wraps it up in silk before approaching a female and presenting it to her. Then he copulates with her quickly while she is eating the fly, and makes his escape before she has finished. The ritual allows the individual male to survive to mate again on another occasion.

Courtship as display of fitness

Another theory which has been put forward to explain ritualisation in courtship is that such rituals allow the animal to display its physical characteristics to the best advantage. Many (though not all) of the highly ritualised displays which have been studied involve males displaying to females (rather than the other way round). It is thought that these displays may provide an opportunity for the animal to demonstrate its size, strength or stamina. The idea here is that the female will select an animal which produces a good display and indicates its suitability as a mate. So this is an evolutionary mechanism which means that the fittest, strongest animals will become more likely to reproduce, while the weaker ones are less likely to do so.

There are a number of species which engage in this kind of behaviour. Durrell (1966) described watching a male Australian lyre-bird displaying to attract a potential mate. The bird used a large circular area within the forest, which had been cleared of vegetation. Its display involved a loud and elaborate song, containing many trills and other sounds, which attracted females from some distance away. This was accompanied by a 'dance', which included the bird stamping the ground, waving its tail feathers, and even at times swinging upside-down from branches. The female watched the male as he performed, and then either approached or left at the end of the display. The complexity and duration of this display meant that it was a good indicator of fitness and good health, so the female could be assured that her potential mate was strong and healthy.

Courtship as improving the species

A slightly different version of the 'courtship as fitness' view is provided by courtship displays in which male animals compete with other male animals for the chance of mating. In this case, it is not just a question of whether the individual animal itself is fit: it is a question of which are the 'best' animals in that particular group. In such a case, the continual pressure of competition provides an evolutionary pressure for the species to develop.

One of the best examples of this is the courtship behaviour of red deer. Lewin (1978) reported on a study of red deer on the Scottish Isle of Rhum. Towards the end of the summer, groups of females (hinds) and young move to traditional rich pastures, known as rutting grounds. They stay in loosely related groups, and different groups of hinds have claims on different pastures, which vary in their richness. Male stags then come to join these groups of hinds; but only one stag will be tolerated in any one group.

Consequently, at this season, the animals engage in a great deal of ritualised – but extremely fierce – fighting. It begins with a roaring contest: a male will approach a group of hinds, and challenge the incumbent male (one who is already interacting with the group of hinds) by roaring. The other roars back, and if its roaring is more powerful, the challenger will move away. Clutton-Brock, Guinness and Albon (1982) found that the rate of roaring correlates closely with how strong the animal is, so it would make sense for a weaker animal to withdraw at this point.

If the roaring of the two animals is reasonably similar, they will then approach each other and walk shoulder to shoulder, separated by a distance of three to fifteen yards. Sometimes a challenger will withdraw at this point in the ritual too, although an incumbent male is unlikely to do so. If the challenger still wishes to compete, he lowers his head and a fight begins. These deer fight by running at each other and wrestling with their antlers. At times, individuals can be severely injured in the process, so it is difficult to see how Lorenz's ideas of ritualised aggression avoiding intra-species damage (see Chapter 21) would fit in here.

The winner of the contest then becomes the incumbent of the group of hinds, and is able to mate with them as they come into season – always assuming, of course, that he can continue to protect his territory, chase away intruders (it is not unknown for younger males to seize the opportunity to mate while the older one is fighting a challenger) and take on any competitors.

It is easy to see how a competitive ritual of this kind would have the effect of strengthening the species through natural selection. Since only the strongest would usually find the opportunity to mate, the species would be continually developing. Since the natural predators of red deer in the past were hunting animals such as wolves and human beings, breeding for size and strength would have been an evolutionary advantage for the animal. The rut provides an evolutionary mechanism by which such selective breeding takes place.

Courtship as strengthening pair-bonding

Another explanation for courtship rituals is the idea that they strengthen **pair-bonding** between two individuals of the same species. Some species mate for life, yet the pairs still perform courtship rituals each season. This obviously cannot have anything to do with attracting a mate, but ethologists believe that it serves the purpose of strengthening the bond between the two animals. Some rituals involve the male displaying, with the female taking a more passive role as observer, while other rituals involve the mutual involvement of both sexes. Many ethologists see the time and energy which the animals invest in carrying out these rituals as confirming and cementing the attachment between the pair.

One of the first detailed descriptions of this type of courtship ritual was performed by Julian Huxley, in 1914. He observed how a pair of great crested grebes would perform what looked rather like a stately 'dance', with a number of distinct elements. The birds would begin the ritual in January, and carry it on right through the first half of the year – their eggs would be laid between April and August. Huxley noticed that the birds seemed to engage in the ritual particularly intensely if they had been separated for some time, and theorised that performing the ritual strengthened the pair-bonding between the two.

These rituals often involved actions which are usually used for other purposes. One of the most common elements in the ritual of the great crested grebe was the 'head-shaking ceremony', in which the two birds would face each other while swimming in the water, first staying still with their crests and neck frills raised, and then suddenly lowering their beaks and shaking their heads together from side to side. Huxley saw this part of the display as being an example of ritualised aggression and appeasement gestures, built into the courtship ritual.

Another feature of their courtship which happened quite often was the 'penguin dance', in which both birds would submerge, and reappear from the water breast to breast, in an upright position. They would each have water weed in their bills, which they would present to each other. There were other elements in this ritual too, such as the 'cat position', in which the bird would crouch low in the water with its wings partially extended, and the 'ghost position', in which the bird would rear up out of the water, making itself as tall and thin as possible (Figure 23.2). Each of these, Huxley believed, derived from some other behaviour which the bird would show in the normal course of everyday living, but which had been converted into a ritualised form.

If we were to investigate this theory of courtship, there are a number of questions we would need to ask. Such an explanation assumes that pair-bonding is very important to the survival of this particular species. So we would need to ask such questions as: do these animals invest a great deal of energy together, in bringing up their young? And do those animals which do not engage in such rituals (and do not use other methods to strengthen pair-bonding) invest less?

As you can see, it is not really possible to decide between all these different theories of courtship, and to say 'this is the right explanation'. For some species, one explanation seems to be appropriate, while with others a different one applies. A species competition argument makes evolutionary sense in the case of red deer, which have evolved to survive against large predators like wolves. A pair-bonding argument makes evolutionary sense for great crested grebes, which do not have that kind of predator, but which lay very few eggs and both share in the care of the young. It depends not only on the species concerned, but also on the environmental demands on that species.

We also need to bear in mind that the type of fixed, elaborate courtship ritual discussed here does not by any means take place in every species: the prelude to mating behaviour varies a great deal. Although there is usually something (not many animals would immediately begin mating the instant they encountered a suitable partner), it may not take the form of an innate sequence of ritual behaviour. As with human behaviour, animal behaviour is complex, and can be affected by a number of different factors simultaneously.

Social organisation

Some species are solitary; some live in pairs comprising one of each sex. Some species live in family groups; some live in larger groups containing more than one family; and some live in colonies, with anything from a couple of hundred to half a million individuals. Of those which live in pairs, some species mate for life, others choose a new partner each year and some mate with several individuals in one season. Of those which live in large groups, some rear only their own young, some rear young related to them and some rear young which are not biologically related to them at all.

We have already discussed some examples of

Figure 23.2 Courtship of the great crested grebe

these species. Most types of spider, for instance, tend to live solitary lives, and so do orang-utans. Robins, swans and gibbons pair-bond, and stay with the same mate for life. Lions live in large family groups known as prides, with several lionesses to one lion. Jacañas live in similar groups, but with several male jacañas to one female. Gorillas live in groups with several adult males and females, but usually only one or two of the very powerful silverback males. Chimpanzees, baboons and langurs live in large groups containing several different kinship lines. And penguins, seals and herring gulls live in colonies of varying sizes up to half a million individuals, or even more.

The message here is that social organisation among animals is extremely diverse. We can find an example in the animal world of just about any social structure we could possibly imagine – and many more that we would not even think of. There are many species which have never been fully researched, and many more for which research shows hitherto unsuspected patterns of social behaviour. We are not aware of the full diversity of social organisation across the animal kingdom, but from what we do know, the message of behavioural diversity is inescapable.

Expectations and assumptions about animal behaviour

One of the problems which has always beset the study of social behaviour has been that of expectation. As we saw in Chapter 2, what we perceive is often influenced by our expectations and assumptions. When we are studying animals, particularly those animals which are closest to us on an evolutionary scale, it is very easy for people to see what they expect to find, rather than what is actually there. So, for instance, in the explorer Livingstone's diaries, written towards the end of the nineteenth century, he recorded that chimpanzees lived in social groups of about 20 or 30 individuals, organised in monogamous pairs. Moreover, he stated authoritatively that any 'infidelity' between individuals led to the male being punished by the whole group, by being beaten and having his ears boxed.

It has been known for some time that chimpanzees, far from living in monogamous pairs, or even mating only with one dominant individual, engage in sexual behaviour quite freely and 'promiscuously' – although that word too carries

moralistic overtones which are another example of projection. From a modern standpoint, it is easy to see how Livingstone's observations reflected his own Victorian times and moral code. Rather than observing what actually occurred, Livingstone was recording the type of behaviour he expected to find in an animal so close to human beings, and would have noticed only the chimpanzee behaviour which fitted with this.

Similarly, the American psychologist Yerkes, in the first half of the twentieth century, argued that chimpanzees lived in large, loosely structured groups which were led by a leader who was chosen for his qualities of 'initiative, daring, courage and responsibility' (Yerkes, 1939). Again, we can see here how it was his own ideas about human beings which were emerging in his observations, not a factual description of the way that the chimpanzees actually acted. These remarks were reflections of the ideals of American society, and again Yerkes would have noticed those examples of chimpanzee behaviour which fitted with those expectations, and ignored those which did not. There are many more such examples.

The use of metaphor

It is easy to assume that modern students of animal behaviour do not make such mistakes. But in fact this type of error is not uncommon. Partly it occurs because of the way that we use **metaphors** to describe animal behaviour. For instance, we describe the group of hinds who mate with a stag as the stag's 'harem'. This raises images of a human harem, with connotations of power and ownership, and this image can seriously mislead our observations. For example, although ethologists have been studying the rutting behaviour of deer for many years, it is only relatively recently that they discovered that it is the hinds – not the stags – who 'own', or maintain access to, the rich pasture grounds of the rut (Clutton-Brock, Guinness and Albon 1982). The use of the human metaphor misled a number of scientists into assuming that the male controlled everything.

Another reason why such errors occur is because they reflect assumptions that we make about the nature of human society. Unconsciously, we expect animal behaviour to match what we see as inevitable in human society. But, as we have seen, animal behaviour contains so much diversity that it can reflect almost any type of social organisation. Moreover, as we have seen throughout the rest of this book, and particularly in Chapters 7 and 14, ideas about human nature vary widely too. We shall be looking at this issue more deeply later on, but it is important to mention it here because it has had a great effect on the study of dominance in animal social organisation.

Dominance

In 1922, Schjelderuppe-Ebbe reported an ethological study of the behaviour of farmyard fowl. Schjelderuppe-Ebbe observed that these animals showed a definite and regular pattern of precedence when they were given limited opportunities to feed. The same bird would feed first, and be followed by the next bird, and so on. Feeding always took place in the same sequence – each bird had its 'place' and waited for its turn.

Schjelderuppe-Ebbe also observed that this sequence was reflected in antagonistic encounters between the birds. These are encounters which involve aggressive behaviour from one animal towards another. The bird which had fed first would peck at any of the others. That which had fed second would peck at any of the others except the first. The third would peck at any of the others except the first and second, and so on. These farmyard fowl were showing a clear, linear dominance hierarchy – quite literally, a 'pecking order' (this is where the term comes from). Each individual within the flock had its position in the hierarchy, and showed dominance behaviour towards those in a lower position.

Schjelderuppe-Ebbe's findings became widely known among ethologists, and it was suggested that the dominance hierarchy formed the basic pattern of social organisation for all social animals. A number of studies of other species reported the existence of dominance hierarchies. For example, in 1961, Washburn and DeVore reported that baboons also have dominance hierarchies. According to their observations, high-ranking males, which they referred to as alpha males, would act extremely aggressively towards low-ranking ones (beta males), and also towards the females in the group. This was an extremely influential study because its findings were taken up by several biologists, such as Lorenz and Morris, who took it as evidence of the inevitability of the dominance hierarchy in primates, including (and especially) human beings.

If we are to look at this issue scientifically, how-ever, we need to ask about the evidence which was being used to indicate dominance, as well as the species in which such behaviour has been observed. We have already seen how cultural assumptions coloured early observations about chimpanzees. The behavioural signals which are taken by comparative psychologists as indicators of dominance are given in Table 23.1.

Environmental influences on dominance

In 1972, Rowell conducted a systematic investigation of **dominance behaviour** in baboon troops. Rowell found that dominance behaviour in baboon troops varied considerably, according to the type of environment in which the animals were living. Rowell studied three colonies of the same species of baboon as were studied by Washburn and DeVore, but with each colony living in very different conditions. One group lived in a colony in a zoo, which was based around a large open rock where visitors could see the animals freely, and – more importantly – the group could always see one another. Another group lived on the open grasslands of the African savannah, and the third group lived in the forest.

In the zoo colony, the animals showed a rigid hierarchy, with a clear 'pecking order'. Each

Table 23.1 Behaviours assumed to indicate dominance

Priority of feeding	The dominant animal has the pick of available food before other animals are allowed to approach it.
Precedence	Lower-ranking animals step aside to make way for a dominant one.
Eye-contact	Dominant animals will stare freely at others. Lower-ranking animals avert their gaze and may scatter if they are stared at by a dominant one.
Presenting	A lower-ranking animal presents its anal or genital region to a more dominant individual in a mating posture. This can occur regardless of the gender of the two animals concerned.
Grooming	Although all members of a group will engage in grooming, it is sometimes observed that dominant animals are more likely to be groomed by lower-ranking ones than the other way round.

individual had its own place in the hierarchy and would act aggressively towards those below it, while acting submissively to those higher up in the social ranking system. Among the baboons which lived in the open savannah, there was a more flexible social structure. Although it was clear that there was a group of alpha males who were generally dominant over the others, and that similarly some females were dominant over other females, this was not an individual pecking order. Rather, the system seemed to operate in terms of fairly loose groups, and there was far more flexibility in terms of the dominance behaviour shown by the animals. Although those within the alpha male or alpha female groups were generally dominant over those in the beta groups, they did not show clearly ranked hierarchies within their groups.

The third baboon colony, which lived in the forest, showed even more flexibility in its social organisation. Although instances of dominant or submissive behaviour did appear from time to time, there was little or no consistency between animals when it was taken as a whole. Animals which were normally submissive might on occasions appear to adopt a more dominant role; those who were normally dominant might sometimes act appeasingly or submissively towards another. There was no sign of a linear pecking order, or of a systematic group dominance system.

Rowell explained this in terms of the resolution of **antagonistic encounters**: what happens between two individuals who find themselves in conflict. In the forest, if a dispute arose over food or something similar, the individuals concerned would have their aggressive encounter, but then would go off and engage in other concerns. When they did so, they would be out of sight of one another, shielded by trees and vegetation. In the zoo, on the other hand, the individuals concerned each remained within the other's sight, and close by at all times. In addition, the zoo environment was bare, offering little stimulation to the animals, whereas both the savannah and the forest provided a far richer environment which gave plenty of scope for distraction.

This meant that, in the forest, antagonistic encounters would quickly be forgotten as the animals concerned were distracted into different pastimes. But in the zoo there were no such distractions: by remaining within each other's sight, the conflict between the two individuals was intensified rather than being resolved. This meant that eventually the pair would fight it out, and this in turn led to the development of the rigid dominance hierarchy which had been observed. The savannah baboons had a habitat which was somewhere in between: they did not go totally out of each other's sight, but they did have a great deal of open space and many opportunities for distraction, so their antagonistic encounters tended to be over more quickly than those of the caged animals. Rowell argued that the relative looseness of their dominance structure reflected this difference in habitat.

In a similar vein, Jay (1963) observed that arboreal monkeys (those which spend their lives in the trees, like langurs), tend to have a form of social organisation in which dominance is relatively unimportant in daily life. Jay contrasted this with ground-living monkeys, like rhesus monkeys or vervets, which tend to have a social structure in which dominance is much more important. These ideas about the importance of distraction and environment raise questions about the importance of **reconciliation** in social organisation, which we will be coming back to later in this chapter.

Dominance in chimpanzee colonies

Chimpanzees, of course, are the human being's nearest evolutionary relative, and so the question of dominance has been a significant one. We have already seen how the early studies tended to assume forms of social organisation which reflected their preconceptions. In this, it is noteworthy that later researchers who described the existence of dominance hierarchies in chimpanzee behaviour tended to have their primary interest in other fields. This sometimes meant that their existence in chimpanzees was taken for granted, rather than examined explicitly.

For example, Goodall (1974) referred to the chimpanzees at the Gombe Stream reserve as if they had an explicit hierarchy, and even talked of an individual chimpanzee 'moving up a place'. While it is true that individuals sometimes showed behaviour which was clearly oriented towards dominating other animals, this is not the same as the existence of a linear dominance hierarchy in a colony. But the main focus of interest in the study was on maternal behaviour, not dominance.

It may be that this is a misjudgement, of course. Chimpanzees are notoriously adaptable animals, and it could be that the behaviour of the animals at the Gombe Stream reserve really did show a strict dominance hierarchy. An animal as capable of learning as a chimpanzee may well show different types of dominance structures in different troops. And there were differences too between the Gombe Stream animals and other chimpanzee troops, because they were regularly fed on bananas from the research station in order to keep them in one place and stop them from moving on. So their 'natural' nomadic behaviour was changed by the researchers. We will be looking at this later, when we look at territoriality.

Observing dominance behaviour

There are other reasons for doubt as to the existence of the dominance hierarchy, though. Goodall (1968) reported that, in six years of study, something over 600 instances of dominance behaviour had been observed – which does not seem to be very many, given such a very long period of time. It is certainly far fewer instances than, for example, can be seen in the behaviour of farmyard fowl, and it raises questions about whether such relatively infrequent behaviour can really be taken as indicating an underlying hierarchy.

A systematic observation of dominance behaviour is necessary to draw these types of conclusions. In a ten-week study of captive chimpanzees conducted by Hayes (1975), the observed dominance interactions (stepping aside, presenting, etc.) were shown to cancel each other out over time. Although chimpanzee A might step aside for chimpanzee B on one day, on another day chimpanzee B might equally well step aside for chimpanzee A. Someone observing this behaviour and assuming that there was a linear dominance hierarchy could easily notice those behaviours which coincided with their assumptions, and not the ones which did not.

It is important to remember that these criticisms relate to social organisation – whether there is a systematic dominance hierarchy within a group. They are not about whether one single individual acts in a certain way. Individuals always differ, and some are more aggressive and assertive than others. There is clear evidence from Goodall's observations that some chimpanzees were more assertive than others within the group, and were deferred to by others. But that is quite different from having a systematic social structure based on dominance. Without a rigorous examination of

the evidence for dominance, it is easy to assume that such structures exist when in fact they might not.

When researchers have set out to look for evidence of dominance hierarchies among wild chimpanzee troops, they have found a rather different picture. Reynolds, in 1963, conducted an extended study of wild chimpanzees, looking particularly for evidence of dominance. However, there was no sign of any such social organisation in the troops which he studied, even though there were numerous occasions when such behaviour might have appeared. However, Reynolds's study of wild chimpanzees was distinctive, in that, as a trained comparative psychologist, he had taken care not to assume the existence of the behaviour in question, but to observe whether or not the animals showed it, using strict behavioural criteria.

Challenging the pecking order

In 1985, Appleby discussed how the existence of pecking orders in animal societies has been taken for granted by human observers almost throughout the whole of the twentieth century. It is a plausible social construct, because it seems to reflect our own social organisation, and to imply that hierarchy in social structure is inevitable. But more and more evidence suggests that linear dominance hierarchies are less common than they first appeared. Appleby showed that if the data from many ethological studies are examined carefully, linear dominance hierarchies actually turn out to be quite rare. It may be that the behaviour of farmyard fowl, rather than being typical of other species as was at first assumed, is actually quite unusual.

That does not mean, of course, that dominance encounters do not happen. Appleby discussed how, for example, it is not all that uncommon to find a 'triangular' system, whereby animal A may dominate animal B in one encounter, animal B then dominates animal C in another encounter and animal C then dominates animal A. And, of course, there is often continual change within such systems. Animal groups are composed of individuals, and they do not act simply as automata: they learn from experience and adapt their behaviour according to the demands of the situation. The important point, though, is that the idea of the ubiquitous dominance hierarchy, found in all animal societies, does not appear to have much in the way of supporting evidence, despite its superficial plausibility.

Territoriality

The concept of **territoriality** has often been applied to human behaviour, although not always in a particularly scientific manner. For example, Ardrey (1966) used the concept of territoriality put forward by Lorenz to 'explain' wars and other social conflicts in human society. However, there are distinct problems in making such generalisations. We have already identified some of those problems, and will come back to these issues later in this chapter. For the moment, though, one important point to make is that this type of theory often uses a very limited definition of territoriality, as if such behaviour was the same in all animals. But when we look closely at territorial behaviour, we find a rather different picture.

Territory and range

Perhaps one of the most important distinctions which ethologists make is between **territory** and **home range**. Although this was sometimes confused by earlier ethologists, it is now well established that a home range is the area that an animal, or a group of animals, uses – the area in which it finds its food and lives. This is not the same as territory, because in many species their home range will overlap with that of many other members of the same species. Territory can be loosely defined as an area which an animal, or a linked group of animals, will defend against other members of its species.

The traditional view of territoriality is that in which the home range and the territory are pretty much the same and continue all the year round. For the most part, though, this type of territoriality is far less common than is seasonal territoriality and forms of territoriality which are distinct from the home range. As with other aspects of animal behaviour, it is diversity rather than homogeneity which seems to be the rule.

Seasonal territoriality

Full-scale, formal territoriality, in which an animal will defend the same area with equal ferocity all year round, actually seems to be quite uncommon in the animal world. But many birds, fish and mammals will defend a territory at a certain time in the year. This is linked with the breeding season: such animals seek out a territory in which to mate and rear young; and in doing so they will defend that area against any other member of their species – making exceptions only for potential mates. This is the type of territory, for instance, which the male three-spined stickleback maintains. Patrolling its boundaries and chasing off other males is as important a part of its seasonal behaviour as is the courtship ritual which we looked at earlier in this chapter (Tinbergen, 1951).

This type of seasonal behaviour produces relatively simple territories, in which a single animal, or a breeding pair of animals, will defend an area against others of the species. Such behaviour seems to be intimately linked with the social structures which the animals maintain. Many highly territorial species of birds, for instance, form pair-bonds which last throughout the year, and sometimes for life. And the male three-spined stickleback rears his young himself, without the aid of any other member of the species. In these circumstances, it may be that the maintenance and defence of an individual, fixed territory provides the animal with an optimal chance of rearing its young successfully.

Nested territories

Some species, however, with different social structures, have different kinds of territory. One example of this is the **nested territory**, in which several smaller territories are located inside one larger one. Leuze (1980) found that water voles have 'nested' territories. The male water vole defends a large area against other males, but not against other females. Inside the area defended by the males, two or three females will establish a territory and defend it against other females (though not against the male).

Of course, it is not always the male which holds the larger area. Jenni (1974) showed how the female American jacaña maintains a large territory and defends it against other females. Within her territory, several males will establish smaller territories and defend them against each other. The males build the nests and the female lays her eggs in them, which the males then hatch out and rear.

Territory within colonies

In the previous two examples, territory and range have been virtually identical: the animals concerned, once occupying an area, have also tended to use it to forage for food and to bring up their young. But some forms of territoriality are nothing like this. For example, herring gulls have a wide range, sometimes flying for as much as several miles to gather food. But they make their nests in large colonies, sometimes with several thousand pairs of birds in a relatively small area. In this case, the bird's territory consists of the nest itself and the relatively small area immediately around it, and they will defend this against other birds in the colony.

Tinbergen (1951) observed how this behaviour involves a great deal of ritualised aggression in which the birds display to one another but do not resort to actual fighting all that often. The ritual gestures include one bird walking stiffly towards the intruder, stretching upwards with its bill pointing towards the sky, pulling up pieces of grass and lowering its beak across its breast. These actions were interpreted by Lorenz as being a display of the bird's natural weaponry, and would often be countered by the intruding bird showing appeasement gestures and withdrawing from the area.

Ritualised aggression

As Tinbergen's observations of sticklebacks and gulls show, territorial defence can take a number of forms, which depends very much on the species concerned. In some animals, territory is defended by ritual displays of aggression, which are more a matter of mutual threat than anything else – although conflicts will result if an intruder comes too close.

Lack (1943) studied territoriality in robins and found that these birds are fiercely territorial, not permitting any intruders to enter their area. Both members of the pair will defend the area, and in order to do so they will sing and make themselves very conspicuous. Should another robin enter the territory, the resident bird will fly at it with a high-pitched call. Usually, this means that the intruder will depart. If it does not , then the resident will perch on a nearby branch and display its red breast, turning slowly from side to side, holding its head and tail up and flicking its wing feathers. The bird angles itself in such a way as to show as much of its red breast as possible to the intruder, and the whole display could be interpreted as a show of strength. Should the intruder not respond to the display, the two birds will fight; but things do not usually get that far.

As we have seen, Lorenz (1966) argued that an important feature of such displays is their exhibition of **natural weaponry,** like the baring of the teeth when a dog snarls at a rival. In some species,

this natural weaponry has become exaggerated. Male fiddler crabs, for instance, have an extremely enlarged claw, which they wave at one another to signal defence of their territory – a small area of mud which they will defend against neighbours and other intruders. They also use these claws as weapons in battles with other crabs. The claws have become so enlarged that they are now useless for any other purpose – the crab must use its other claw, which is much smaller, for feeding.

There are similar examples of extremely enlarged natural weapons in some other species. Quite why this type of development occurs is not fully known, although a popular explanation, following Lorenz's model, is that the display of natural weaponry is linked with success in courtship. If this is the case, then the animals which show the largest and most intimidating natural weapons will be the ones which pass on their genes to the new generation. In such a case, the natural weapons will evolve to become ever-larger over generations, which can continue until the limb or organ itself has become quite useless for any other function. Gould (1977a) suggested that the extremely enlarged antlers of the now extinct Irish elk, which could achieve a span of up to twelve feet, fell into this category.

Maintaining a territory

Maintaining a territory is not always an easy task, since other members of the species are often ready to compete with a resident territory-holder. Krebs (1976) studied the territories of great tits within an area of woodland, and found that if a pair of birds was removed from that area, a new pair would arrive and take over the territory within just a couple of hours – suggesting that some pairs must have been monitoring the area regularly and were just waiting for a chance to move in if an opportunity arose.

So how do great tits go about defending their territory? Krebs went on to investigate the importance of the birds' song in defending territory. He removed each of the eight resident pairs of birds in a particular area of woodland. Then he 'occupied' three of the territories with continuous recordings of the songs of the former residents. The other territories acted as controls: three were left quiet, and the other two had other recorded sounds. Krebs found that the control areas were invaded very quickly – within a day. But the areas with recorded bird-song were not occupied for about two and a half days, suggesting that the song acts as an important 'keep out' signal.

One possible explanation for why the recorded song did not keep invaders away for any longer than two and a half days may be the fact that it was fixed, and did not change at all in response to the song of the other bird. Krebs noticed that when a recorded song was played at an intruder, the intruder responded with a song which matched the first one. In a contest between two real birds, the territory-owner would then go on to sing another song, including elements from the intruding bird's song. So it is possible that, after a couple of days, it became apparent to the other birds that the song was not being modified appropriately, and so they felt able to move in and occupy the territory.

In seasonal territoriality, territorial displays often go hand-in-hand with courtship. Many bird-songs, for example, are not simply used for defending territories against intruders; they are also used to attract a mate. Catchpole (1981) investigated how reed warblers use songs for dual purposes. By recording reed warbler songs and replaying them to other individuals, Catchpole found that the song was not only an important agent in defending territory, but that it also acted as a courtship ritual, attracting females to the area. Since the reed warbler is a small bird and lives among dense vegetation, an auditory signal like a song would reach further and be more likely to attract a mate than a visual display.

Territory and reproductive fitness

In evolutionary terms, the argument for linking territoriality and sexual selection is that of **reproductive fitness**. A bird which has acquired and is defending a territory is also likely to be fitter, quicker or stronger than other birds, and it already can provide a safe area for nesting and a ready food supply to hand. This makes it likely to be a good prospect as a mate, both in terms of possible advantageous genetic qualities and in terms of care of the offspring. Wynne-Edwards (1962) observed that sizes of territories vary depending on the food supplies available: in years when food is abundant, territories are smaller, but in lean years they are larger. This suggests that the size of the territory may be directly related to providing adequate food for the care of the young.

Of course, things are not as simple as that – they very rarely are, when we attempt to derive general 'rules' of animal behaviour, because species act so differently. The blackbird, for instance, is fiercely territorial (which is why it sings so beautifully) and will not allow competing males in its area at mating time. However, Lea (1984) reports that if the other bird is simply feeding and not competing to attract a mate or to nest, it is allowed to wander within the territory as it pleases. If the territory was just about food provision, this would not be particularly likely.

Game theory approaches to territoriality

Maynard Smith (1972) developed a new method of understanding territoriality in animals, based on the mathematical approach known as **game theory.** In this approach, the researcher uses mathematical models to develop idealised versions of environmental situations and then looks at which type of animal behaviour might 'pay off' best in these situations. The idea is that producing a mathematical model of this type may help to show why it is that some types of behaviour may have an evolutionary advantage, even though on the surface they might not appear advantageous.

An important concept for the game theory approach is the idea of the **evolutionary stable strategy (ESS)**. This is the strategy which allows an animal to maximise its chances of reproducing – in other words, it is the 'best' option for the animal to choose, in evolutionary terms. In Maynard Smith's original example, this involved choosing whether it was better to fight over territory or to withdraw if the territorial display was challenged by another individual. The 'hawk' strategy is always to fight, whereas the 'dove' strategy is to withdraw. Although on the surface it may seem as though the 'hawks' would always benefit in a situation like this, Maynard Smith showed that in fact either strategy was equally likely to maximise the animal's chances of survival.

In game theory, numerical values are given to the possible costs and benefits of each approach. In this type of conflict, there are two costs: the cost of a serious injury (C) and the energy drain of a dispute which takes a long time (T). But there is also the added increase in 'evolutionary fitness' for the winner (V). Maynard Smith set V at 50 units, C at 100 units and T at 10 units. Table 23.2 overleaf shows how conflicts based on this idea, in a population which contained equal numbers of hawks and doves, would work out in practice.

Table 23.2 Game theory approaches to territoriality

	Hawk	Dove
Hawk	0.5 (V – C)	V
Dove	0	0.5 (V – T)

	Hawk	Dove
Hawk	–25	+50
Dove	0	+20

When a dove meets a hawk, there is no dispute: the dove backs down and the hawk gains 50 points. But if a hawk meets another hawk there will be a protracted fight, and the chances of the animal being seriously injured are high. The total number of points available is V – C or 50 – 100, since the cost of a serious injury is 100 and the benefit of winning is 50. So winning a long fight while gaining a serious injury leaves the animal with –50. Since either of the hawks might win, the pay-off for an individual animal in this situation is –25.

On the other hand, if a dove meets a dove, then either may back down, although their territorial displays will take a little time. This means that the total number of points available is V–T or 50–10 (the 10 is for the time which they spend display-ing to one another). Since victory could go to either animal, the amount is halved and the pay-off for an individual dove in this situation is 20. As can be seen from the table, what this actually means is that either type of strategy – hawk or dove – is equally likely to be advantageous to the animal.

Maynard Smith (1972) argued that the balance between hawks and doves is evolutionarily stable, since neither strategy has an advantage over the other. Over time, a population consisting of animals adopting these two strategies will always revert to a 50/50 balance, since a population with more hawks in it would result in more chances of serious injury, while a population with fewer hawks would mean that the hawks were less likely to become seriously injured, and so their popula-tion would gradually increase.

Alternative strategies

A number of researchers have developed this approach, identifying alternative strategies which an animal could adopt. Caryl (1981) described the 'prudent hawk' strategy: the animal fights for a time, but withdraws if it looks as though the fight will go on too long. In this way, it limits the chance of serious injury, and the costs of hawk-like behaviour become less. Another possibility is that the rewards for winning could be higher: an increase of the value of V in this model, means that the balance between hawk and dove strategy becomes very different. A third option is the 'bourgeois' strategy described by Maynard Smith (1974), in which the animal which is already in possession of a territory will fight harder than one which is intruding.

It is possible to identify real-life parallels for each of these strategies in different animal species. Clutton-Brock, Guinness and Albon (1982) showed that red deer are particularly fertile during the first two weeks of October, so it is very advantageous to mate at that time. This would be an example of increasing the value of V in the game theory model. Davies (1978) showed that speckled wood butterflies adopt the 'bourgeois' pattern of territoriality in their temporary mating territories. The first male butterfly to settle in an area becomes the 'owner'. If another male enters the territory, they have a brief, highly ritualised conflict, and then the intruder withdraws. But Davies showed that if both butterflies 'believed' that they had been there first, the battle became very prolonged, and could easily result in injury.

The problem with this type of approach, how-ever, is that it is only *describing* patterns of behaviour. It does not really bring us any nearer to *understanding* the diversity of species behaviour. As we have seen, animals act in many different ways. Some animals, for instance, resolve disputes by teaming up with allies: Packer (1977) showed how male baboons form temporary alliances to help each other when fighting a rival, and de Waal (1984) described similar alliances between chim-panzees. Although it is possible to produce mathe-matical models which would describe this too, it is not at all clear how developing a mathematical model and then finding a species to fit it helps us to understand why animal behaviour should be so diverse in the first place.

As game theory has developed, the models have become more complex. It is possible to develop a game theory model to account for almost any type of behaviour. But the question is really whether, by doing so, we have managed to explain anything. Some theorists argue that all we have really done is develop more elaborate ways of describing animal behaviour, without actually adding to our understanding at all. These theorists see developing ever more complex mathematical models to cope with ever more diverse examples of animal behaviour as a rather pointless task. As Gould (1981) remarked in a slightly different context, it would be better to look for the generating rules and principles underlying the diversity of behaviour.

Another criticism of game theory approaches is that they take the behaviour out of context. By focusing only on the supposed reproductive advantage of a particular type of behaviour, they ignore other environmental pressures on that animal. There is an implicit assumption that the behaviour is only going to depend on a limited range of other factors, and most particularly the other animal's behaviour. But animal behaviour is rarely as mechanistic as that. As we saw in Chapter 22, environmental factors shape what an animal is prepared to learn and how, and, as we saw earlier in this chapter, they can influence social organisation and other forms of behaviour as well. We need to look at the animal's behaviour in its total environmental context if we are to understand how it may have evolved.

Communicating resource-holding power

In real life, of course, it is not just a matter of two equal animals meeting in a potential conflict. Some animals are bigger and stronger than others. Parker (1974) argued that there are **correlated asymmetries** – inequalities – between animals, which, in most conflicts, mean that one animal is more likely to win than the other. The one which is more likely to win is said to have the higher **resource-holding power,** or **RHP.** Resource-holding power is thought to have three dimensions, which are described in Table 23.3.

Parker observed that territorial displays can be seen as ways by which one animal communicates its resource-holding power to another animal. It is to the animal's advantage to weigh up its opponent's resource-holding power, because in this way it can gauge whether it is worth getting into a serious contest or not. In this model, then, ritual and threat displays are seen as a form of communication, rather than simply as ritualised action patterns. They are ways of communicating the resource-holding power of the animal to its opponent. So instead of the relatively simplistic

response strategy presented by game theory, the animal's behaviour is seen as a message which is tailored to the specific evolutionary demands of the situation.

Territoriality in primates

Studies of territoriality in animals, as mentioned earlier, have frequently been used as the basis for arguments about territoriality in humans. If this is the case, then it follows that we should pay particular attention to studies of territoriality in those species which are closest to us – although it is worth noting that those writers who have speculated on human territoriality in this way seem to have concentrated much more on the behaviour of birds and fish than on that of mammals, let alone primates.

As with so many other forms of behaviour, territoriality within the primate family is very varied indeed. Rowell (1972) described strictly territorial behaviour as being rare among primates, in that not many primate species will actually defend a piece of ground against others. Of the few that will, such as gibbons, the territorial contests which take place happen in a kind of neutral territory between the borders of two territories. Typically, the animals will jump up and down, chase each other and show general excitement, before then retiring to their own areas and feeding peacefully (Elefson, 1968). Rather than being a territorial conflict, it seems to be more of a display stating ownership and reaffirming boundaries.

Table 23.3 Dimensions of resource-holding power

1 *Size*
   Bigger animals are more likely to win the fight, and conversely, if the two animals are of equal size, the fights will tend to last longer. This prediction has been supported in Clutton-Brock's observations of conflicts between red deer (Clutton-Brock, Guinness and Albon, 1982).

2 *Weaponry*
   Geist (1966) showed that Stone's sheep with larger horns were more likely to win contests than those with smaller horns.

3 *Information about past experience*
   Thouless and Guinness (1986) reported that female deer may resolve a conflict between two stags on the basis of their previous experience with those particular individuals.

Rowell's own observations of baboons did not show any evidence of territoriality, in the sense of defending a specific area against others. Rather, the baboons would spend a short period in one area, and then move on to another part of the range. This type of nomadic existence appears to be common in a number of species of monkey, particularly forest-living and savannah monkeys.

In the apes closest to human beings, chimpanzees and gorillas, there again seems to be relatively little evidence of territoriality, except among those groups which are living in unnatural conditions of some kind. In the normal run of things, both chimpanzees (Reynolds, 1963) and gorillas (Schaller, 1963) live a nomadic life within a large home range. The troop will move to a source of food, such as a group of fruiting trees, stay there for perhaps two or three days and then move on to another food source. Over the course of a year, they will circle around, covering a very large area.

Although they build temporary sleeping nests in the trees, chimpanzees do not seem to regard these as territory in the sense of defending them against others. Reynolds observed that frequently other groups of chimpanzees will occupy the same home range, and may even approach quite close to another troop. As a general rule there is little aggression between them, but if one group becomes aware of the other, there will sometimes be a chorus of hoots and calls, as each group signals its presence to the other.

Environmental factors in territoriality

There are, of course, exceptions to this; but always these can be related to abnormal conditions which have arisen in some way. For example, van Lawick-Goodall (1974) observed one group of chimpanzees make 'war' on another troop, attacking them and driving them away from the area. However, these were chimpanzees which had been feeding at the Gombe Stream primate study centre, and as we have already seen, their experiences were different from those of most chimpanzees. The centre maintained a group of chimpanzees for study by providing a regular daily supply of bananas. This created a situation which is extremely unusual for a wild chimpanzee group, in that the chimpanzees stayed in the same area throughout the whole year, rather than moving on. Given the chimpanzee's capacity for learning, it may be that this had generated a concept of

territoriality which is not possessed by chimpanzees in a less artificial situation.

Similarly, Fossey (1980) observed a large amount of inter-group rivalry between neighbouring gorilla tribes. Again, however, there were artificial constraints at work. Fossey's observations took place in an area where the natural range of the animals had become seriously depleted by the destruction of the rainforest. The gorillas themselves were also frequently attacked by human hunters. All this meant that the gorillas which were observed were under far more stress than is normal for them, and also had far less space in which to move about. Both of these factors are likely to have been significant in their aggression.

The third group of great apes, orang-utans, are solitary animals which spend most of their time alone. McKinnon (1974) studied Sumatran orang-utans and found that each individual had a definite home range, which would overlap with those of several others. At times, several orang-utans living in the same area would meet at a particularly good feeding site, but these meetings usually tended to be peaceful. The only exception to this was when two of the large males met, at which time there would be conflict between them, resulting in one of them leaving the region.

When looking at the ranges of individual animals, McKinnon speculated that big older males may have some kind of territory, covering an extremely large range; and that the other orang-utans may live within these. However, since these animals may be miles apart from each other, and since they are also relatively shy of strangers, it is difficult to get any conclusive evidence of this. What is certain, though, is that there is nothing in orang-utan behaviour resembling the kind of territoriality shown by the robin or the herring gull.

We can see, then, that territorial behaviour is very variable; and that by no means all animals will acquire and defend a patch of territory. When we are talking about territoriality in animals, it is very important to be clear about exactly what we mean, if we are not to be led into some extremely misleading assumptions.

Aggression and reconciliation

Perhaps the most famous and influential of all of the various theories in comparative psychology was the theory of aggression put forward by Konrad Lorenz (1966). We have already come across several aspects of this theory, like his emphasis on aggressive and appeasement gestures, and the idea that displays of aggression involve exhibiting the natural weaponry of the species. In some respects, as we have seen, this model has proved useful. For instance, the idea of the threat display may have helped us to understand some aspects of territorial and courtship behaviour. But there are aspects of Lorenz's theory which are rather different.

One of these was his highly contentious argument that only laboratory rats and humans would kill other members of their species. These two species, Lorenz argued, lacked the inbuilt inhibiting response to appeasement gestures which could 'switch off' aggressive behaviour on the part of an attacker. As a result, an attack, once started, could continue until the other was dead or dying. In other species, Lorenz claimed (although there is now some evidence to the contrary), an attack would be stopped automatically by an appeasement gesture.

In addition, Lorenz considered that aggression was an instinctive behaviour shown by all species and therefore inevitable. Rather than trying to limit it, it was necessary for society to develop ways of channelling people's aggression. He applied the hydraulic model of action-specific energy which we looked at in Chapter 22, seeing aggressive energies as continually building up within the individual, and needing to have some kind of vent – if necessary through organised competition and team games – because otherwise it would emerge in the forms of social unrest and wars.

In relation to this, Lorenz saw both territoriality and dominance hierarchies as being inevitable features of the natural aggression of all animals, including human beings. Unlike later writers who drew on his theory, he did not distinguish between the sexes, considering both men and women to have equal levels of innate aggression.

We have already seen that there are other explanations for aggression, and that innate behaviours do not seem to be anything like as automatic as he claimed. However, Lorenz's ideas were enormously influential, and are still current today in some quarters. For example, Morris (1981) drew on this theory in discussing the behaviour of football supporters. The perception of people as instinctively aggressive and needing to be tightly controlled is the model which underlies the thinking of many advocates of tight policing and severe penalties in modern society, and relates closely to the theories of crowd behaviour which we looked at in Chapter 17.

Criticisms of Lorenz's theory

The idea that aggression is an innate quality, building up in the individual, has been strongly challenged. It has long been shown that aggressive behaviour can be produced by frustrating or stressful social circumstances: Calhoun (1962) showed how rats in confined spaces with limited resources not only became more territorial but also engaged in increasingly aggressive behaviour, including eventually infanticide and cannibalism. Given this, together with the diversity of behaviour that exists, particularly in those species closest to human beings, the evidence in support of Lorenz's theory becomes very shaky.

One of the weakest points of the theory was that Lorenz drew his illustrative examples from a relatively limited range of species, very few of which were primates. There are many different forms of animal social organisation. Territorial behaviour is not inevitable, nor is the formation of rigid dominance hierarchies: they vary from one species to another. Within the primate group, Lorenz rested almost all of his case on the Washburn and DeVore (1961) study, although, as we have seen, it is unlikely that their account represented a full picture of the behavioural choices of that species. But, as we can see in Box 23.1 overleaf, the reason why his theory became so popular was not because of its scientific basis, but because it reflected influential social opinions which were current at the time.

The importance of reconciliation

The dominance of Lorenz's work within the ethological field also had another outcome, which was to focus attention on antagonistic encounters between one animal and another. But this gives us only half the story. If an animal is living in a social group, it is not just aggressive behaviour which needs to be studied. We also need to look at the process of **reconciliation**: how two animals which have had an aggressive encounter will restore the balance and manage to continue living amicably – or at least peaceably – in the same group.

De Waal (1989) examined how different groups of primates resolved antagonistic encounters, and argued that we can learn a great deal about social

Box 23.1 Comparative theories and the Zeitgeist

Popular theories of animal behaviour have always tended to mirror the 'spirit of the times' – the 'Zeitgeist', and have often taken on political roles by being used as justifications for human social practices. During the latter part of the Victorian period, a popularised version of evolutionary theory was current, in the form of Spencer's Social Darwinism. This portrayed natural life as a vicious battle for the survival of the fittest: and the idea of 'nature red in tooth and claw' was used as a justification of the survival of the fittest in economic terms.

Lorenz's theory of innate aggression was developed during the period immediately surrounding WWII, in which theories of genetic determinism were widely held, particularly in Germany and Austria. Such models, and the idea of the 'naturally' competitive/aggressive character of human beings, formed the foundation of a number of social practices in Germany at the time – to say nothing of the role that theories of genetic determinism in general played in the murder of six million Jews and numerous others.

The 'group survival' theories of Wynne Edwards, which gained popularity during the 1960s, may be matched to the expanding economy and growing social awareness of the time; and Morris's popularised views on sexual selection might also be related to the increased levels of sexual freedom which were so widely discussed at the time.

In the same way, the sociobiological emphasis on kin selection – each looking after their own – made by the sociobiologists may be related to the harsher economic climate of the 1980s, in both Britain and America. Of course, it may be just coincidence, but that seems a little unlikely – remember, we are not looking at why Wilson developed the theory of sociobiology, but at why sociobiological explanations became so popular. A theory that accords with the mood of the times is a theory that people are ready to accept, perhaps far less critically than they might otherwise have done.

As we move into different political times with increasing social debate about ethics, responsibility and accountability, and a growing ecological awareness, sociobiology faces an increasing number of challenges. Researchers are beginning to identify examples of altruistic behaviour with non-related individuals, and to stress the importance of the environment in understanding an animal's behaviour. Modern science, too, reflects its Zeitgeist.

organisation from studying reconciliation. The primates which he studied were: chimpanzees, rhesus monkeys, stump-tailed monkeys and bonobos (which used to be known as pygmy chimpanzees, but are now recognised as a separate species). In each of these species, de Waal identified mechanisms which not only allowed the animals concerned to interact positively together once again, but which also served a broader purpose of promoting social cohesion within the group as a whole.

The kind of reconciliation mechanism identified by de Waal includes the 'collective lie' used by some chimpanzees. In an example of this, one of the older male chimpanzees, after a particularly aggressive encounter with another male, suddenly began examining a piece of ground and hooting loudly, as if he had discovered something of interest. The rest of the group, including the other male, rushed over to have a look. However, the others soon became bored and drifted away, leaving the two males both apparently absorbed, side by side, in examining the ground. De Waal was left in no doubt that this was a reconciliation strategy, supported by the rest of the group. If there really had been something interesting to see, some of the others would have remained around too.

This is only one of several examples of reconciliation behaviour identified by de Waal. Other primate species use different methods for achieving reconcilation, including the use of sexual contact, which occurred strikingly frequently on the part of the bonobo groups. De Waal also discussed human reconciliation strategies, but pointed out that there has been remarkably little research into these. The emphasis on aggression and aggressive behaviour has meant that we have tended to look at only one side of the question – in our own species, as well as in others.

Animal behaviour and evolutionary theories

As we saw in the last chapter, one of the most important questions of comparative psychology concerns how behaviour can be seen in an evolutionary context. Studies of animal behaviour have produced some very different approaches to the understanding of evolution and the way in which natural selection operates.

Group selection

In 1962, Wynne-Edwards proposed that natural selection operates on the species' group as a whole, particularly when it comes to herd animals. Wynne-Edwards observed that the density of a population generally reflects the survival opportunities available for them. In abundant years, territorial animals tend to have relatively small territories, whereas in years when not much food is available, the area which they occupy tends to be larger. Overall, this means that the numbers of members of that species in a food-abundant year tend to be higher than at other times.

Wynne-Edwards saw this as representing an adjustment mechanism which operates in order to maximise the **survival of the group.** The reproductive rate of the animals varies in order to achieve this end, because a group of animals which lowers its reproductive rate in a lean year will have more food available per animal, and therefore will be more likely to survive with few casualties. If a species does not lower its reproductive rate in a lean year, then the group as a whole will become weakened by starvation, and so its survival will be threatened.

Although it might at first seem rather different, Lorenz's theory of ritualised aggression was another manifestation of this type of species survival argument. Lorenz, as we have seen, proposed that animals were inhibited from causing death or serious injury to other members of their species through the existence of appeasement gestures, which acted as automatic brakes on aggressive behaviour. This is linked with Wynne-Edwards's argument that natural selection operates to maximise the survival of the group, rather than the individual: the appeasement mechanisms, according to Lorenz, developed because in this way members of the group did not turn on one another, and could co-operate in order to survive.

Problems with group selection theory

One of the problems of this approach to natural selection, however, is the whole idea that natural selection can act on groups just as well as it can on individuals. It is difficult to see any mechanisms by which this could take place. We can understand how the pressures of natural selection will work on individuals, through the inheritance of characteristics which help that individual animal to survive. It is also possible to see how natural selection might result in a lower overall reproductive rate. For example, Lack (1943) showed how a bird which lays more eggs than others in a lean year may actually end up rearing fewer chicks than those birds which do not lay so many. Because of the shortage of the food supply, the parents may be unable to provide for their brood, and having to distribute inadequate food between them may mean that they all grow up to be less strong than others.

But this is an individual argument, not a group one, even though it would have effects on the total population of the species. Natural selection operates on individuals, not on groups. It means that the individual bird which raises fewer eggs in lean circumstances is more likely to be successful at rearing them. Although this can have its effect in terms of the number of members of that species around in any given year, it is a mechanism which has operated on the individual animals in that species rather than on the group as a whole.

Sociobiology

An alternative approach, which was first put forward by Wilson in 1975, is that of **sociobiology**. Sociobiology became a dominating perspective within current biology and comparative psychology during the 1980s, although there were always a number of biologists and comparative psychologists who did not entirely agree with it. Essentially, sociobiology presents a view of natural selection which argues that even the survival of the individual is not particularly important, as long as the individual's genes survive. Behaviour which does not benefit the individual animal but does benefit its relatives may contribute to the overall fitness of that kinship line, even though it does not contribute to the survival of the animal as an individual.

Wilson developed his theory on the basis of studies of ants and other insect societies. In these, it is not unknown for individual animals to sacrifice themselves in defence of the colony. If natural selection was based on the survival of the individual, Wilson asked, how could this be possible? The reason, he suggested, was that, although the individual itself died, its genes survived in other members of the colony, because all were related. In fact, such self-sacrificial behaviour actually made it more likely for those genes to survive, and this was how the behaviour was maintained and passed on. Rather than the survival of the individual, Wilson suggested that it was the likely survival of those carrying the same genes which was important.

Sociobiology argues that animal behaviour may be explained by looking at its evolutionary function. Central to this is the idea of **inclusive fitness** – the survival of the fittest being the survival of those carrying the fittest genes, rather than the survival of the fittest individuals. This idea was used to explain instances of animal behaviour which at first sight appear to be puzzling in evolutionary terms, at least to those who hold a view of evolution as being continual competition. The occurrence of **altruistic behaviour,** in which one animal will place itself in danger in order to save its kin, was inexplicable in those terms. There are, however, other ways of looking at evolution.

As we saw in Box 23.1 on page 754, Wilson's ideas of kin selection were popularised by Dawkins (1976), who went on to argue that all animals, including human beings, were simply carriers of their 'selfish genes', and therefore constrained to act in ways that would maximise the gene's survival. So, for example, it made sense for relatives to protect their kin and to distrust others, because this would mean that the genes which they shared with those kin would be more likely to be perpetuated. Dawkins went on to argue that such traits as xenophobia (hostility towards strangers), child abuse by step-parents and using language to deceive were only to be expected, and virtually inevitable, since they were part of the biological heritage of human beings.

Criticisms of sociobiology

There have been numerous criticisms of the sociobiological approach. A comprehensive discussion of these was put forward by Rose, Kamin and Lewontin in 1984, who argued that socio-biology as a theory is simply another manifestation of genetic determinism applied to human behaviour, with the new twist of kin selection to make it even more extreme. They argued that, like the other genetically determinist theories put forward by Lorenz, Morris and Ardrey, sociobiology's **reductionist** stance means that it ignores the other levels of explanation – social, cultural, cognitive, and so on – which are equally important in affecting how people behave.

Hayes (1995) discussed how the 'gene' described by sociobiologists, particularly Dawkins, bears very little relationship to the 'genes' studied by geneticists. Sociobiologists use the term 'gene' to mean 'a unit of natural selection' (Dawkins, 1976), but they do not attempt to explain how this connects with a piece of chromosomal material which initiates protein synthesis in the cell. Hayes argued that the sociobiologist's use of the word in this way is inherently misleading and circular. Sociobiologists start from the premise that behaviour must be caused by genes, and then try to explain any form of behaviour as a result of a gene's action. This means that the idea of the gene is used as a magical concept, which does not really explain anything.

Gould (1981) criticised the sociobiologists' methodology and in particular their emphasis on finding individual evolutionary accounts to explain specific instances of animal behaviour. Rather than trying to develop (speculative) individual histories for each kind of behaviour, Gould argued, it is more important to discover the general underlying principles and mechanisms which can explain the whole range of behaviours shown by animals and by human beings. Explaining individual items of behaviour in genetic terms does not explain how alternative behaviours come to be possible.

As with other such theories, sociobiology attempts to portray animal behaviour as conforming to definite, logical and apparently simple rules. In order to do so it works almost entirely on confirmatory instances: it takes examples of animal behaviour which support the idea and ignores those which do not. But, as we have seen, animal behaviour is varied and complex. There are many instances of animal behaviour which do seem to conform to sociobiological principles – such as Wilson's ant societies – and in that respect some of the insights of sociobiological theory have been helpful.

But there are also a number of instances of animal behaviour which do not fit the theory. For example, Packer and Pusey (1982) showed how Tanzanian lions often form coalitions which include a large number of non-relatives who co-operate together in hunting behaviour. Faaborg and Patterson (1981) described how unrelated groups of male Galapagos hawks share a mate, and each bird mates equally often. There are also many examples of non-related individuals helping to care for young, such as happens for instance in mongoose colonies with ostriches, and in some cases of baboon 'aunts' (see, for example, Rowell, 1972).

These examples cannot be explained purely within the sociobiological framework. Sociobiologists tend to dismiss these examples as 'exceptions', but this is not really adequate. If they have evolved at all, they cannot be exceptions to how evolution works. We are as yet very far from charting the social organisation of all species, but already we are aware that animal behaviour is far more complex than the sociobiological framework permits. A theory which cannot take into account the alternative forms of animal behaviour which have been observed cannot be regarded as sufficient in itself to constitute an explanation of even our knowledge of animal behaviour at the present time.

Coevolution

Sociobiology is not the only way of understanding evolution. The sociobiological argument is that it is largely self-contained, ignoring the influence of the social context and environment of the animal. But, as we have seen, the environment can make all the difference to social behaviours such as dominance interactions. There is increasing evidence that animals interact with and shape their environment, as well as simply adapting to it. Trevor (1992) recorded how the elephants in Tsavo national park, in Kenya, acted on and modified their environment over a 30-year time span, in ways that were entirely unanticipated by the managers of the park. Increasingly, researchers are finding examples of **coevolution** – different species evolving together to each other's mutual benefit. An explanation of the evolutionary forces producing animal behaviour needs to take account of this type of interaction with the environment, as well as more conventional adaptation.

Hinde (1987) proposed that it might be fruitful for ethologists to analyse animal behaviour in terms of relationships, rather than as specific instances of behavioural interaction. His discussion shows how some well-documented accounts of animal behaviour, such as courtship rituals, can usefully be seen as **negotiation,** rather than as the mechanistic 'stimulus-with-response-becoming-stimulus' process that has been common. Bateson (1973) discussed how the communicative behaviour of both wolves and cetaceans made more sense when they were considered as manifestations of their underlying relationships, rather than as simple interactions in themselves.

The brain and behavioural adaptation

Another way of understanding how evolution and behaviour interact is to look at the role of learning. In Chapter 22, we saw how, rather than being fixed and unmodifiable, genetic influences can produce a preparedness to respond to certain types of stimulus and to engage in certain types of learning. We also saw how an animal which can learn is in a position to adapt to changes of environment or circumstance within its own lifetime. The implication of this for our understanding of human behaviour is very great.

The really distinctive feature of the human being is the enlarged cerebral cortex. As we saw in Chapter 10, this is the part of the brain which is concerned with learning, association and the interpretation of sensory data. The human being's capacity to learn is that which allows us to adapt to different environments, so that human beings can live in an extremely wide variety of habitats. There may be biological predispositions in this – for example, most human beings seem to respond positively to contact with natural environments and growing things – but this type of preparedness is a long way from a fixed inherited behaviour pattern. As with the predispositions of the human infant, which we looked at in Chapter 20, they are modified and developed through contact with society and culture.

Hubel (1979) suggested that it is possible to see an evolutionary progression in learning capacity, reflected in the increased cerebral development of monkeys and apes, including humans. The ability to learn new forms of behaviour would give a species the capacity to survive in different environments, or to change its behaviour should the environment change suddenly. In such a model, genetically determined behaviour would be less likely in species with high learning capacity, but might be more expected in other species, which were 'lower' on such a 'phylogenetic scale' (Hayes, 1995).

According to this model, then, for the most part we would not expect human beings to display fixed action patterns, unless it was for very basic survival, such as pain avoidance. But our preparedness to learn from other humans, to respond to social demands, to conform to expectations, to make sense of the social world, and so on could easily be examples of the ways in which human behaviour has been shaped by evolutionary adaptive pressures. Such an explanation would go a long way towards explaining the vast diversity of human behaviour – and also the diversity in the behaviour and social organisation of other primates.

Levels of explanation

As we can see, there are many problems inherent in applying comparative perspectives to the understanding of human behaviour. Hinde (1987) identified four issues which can present difficulties for those trying to generalise from ethological observations to human social behaviour. They are listed in Table 23.4. As we have seen throughout this book, human behaviour can be explained on a number of levels, ranging from cultural, through social, individual and personal, to physiological and biological. To take any one **level of explanation** as providing the only explanation is to ignore a great wealth of evidence from other sources. Rose (1983) argued that if we are to understand human behaviour we need to look at a number of levels, not fall into the reductionist trap of focusing on one to the exclusion of all else.

Hinde (1987) argued that, while it is important to include a biological perspective (as one of several) in attempting to explain human behav-

iour, it is equally important to be very cautious in extrapolating from animal behaviour to apparent human parallels. Analogy is not homology – just because two behaviours appear to be similar on the surface does not mean that they actually represent the same thing.

If we carry the concept of **adaptation** to circumstances to its logical conclusion, it is also possible to say that, since human beings modify their environment to suit themselves, there is no longer any mechanism by which natural selection operates on them – even weaker members of the human species are able to survive in the modern world, and the rapid rate of social and environmental change means that pressures for mate selection do not remain consistent over enough generations for systematic changes to take place. As long as we bear in mind the pressures of diversity, the potential for learning and the capacity for relationships inherent in animal species, as well as the importance of interaction with the environment, we will be looking for evolutionary explanations which may eventually be able to come to terms with the full richness of both animal and human behaviour.

Table 23.4 Problems of generalising from animals to humans
There are four main problems in generalising from ethological observations of animals to human behaviour:
1 Differences in cognitive ability between animals and human beings.
2 The human capacity for language and culture.
3 The diversity of both animal species and human behaviour.
4 The problem of taking appropriate levels of analysis in drawing comparisons.
Source: Adapted from Hinde, 1987

Key terms

alpha males Male members of a baboon troop who appear 'dominant' and have higher social status than other males.

beta males Males in a baboon troop who are low-ranking and appear to be 'subordinate' to other males.

correlated asymmetries Features of an animal and its behaviour which are linked, and together indicate how successful that animal might be in a fight – e.g.

the roaring of a stag and its muscular strength and size.

courtship rituals Joint patterns of behaviour performed by two or more animals prior to mating.

dominance hierarchy A form of social organisation in which each animal is ranked, and will act aggressively towards those below it and submissively towards those with higher ranking.

home range The area within which an animal will usually forage for food.

inclusive fitness The sociobiological principle that an act may be genetically beneficial even if it results in an individual's death, as long as that death ensures survival of relatives carrying the same genes.

nested territories Small territories located within larger ones.

reproductive fitness A form of evolutionary adaptation which makes a given individual more likely to mate and reproduce its kind.

resource holding power (RHP) The ability of an animal to undertake whatever is required to retain necessary evolutionary resources, such as territory or access to mates.

sociobiology A reductionist approach to explaining animal behaviour, sometimes applied to humans, which argues that all behaviour is driven by units of survival referred to as 'genes' (not the same as the biological concept), and that individuals and species are simply mechanisms by which these 'genes' can perpetuate themselves.

territoriality The name given to a set of behaviours which involve establishing and maintaining access to a particular area while refusing the same to potential competitors of one's own species.

Summary

1 Explanations for courtship rituals include courtship as ensuring appropriate pairing, as permitting survival of individuals, as displays of individual fitness as improving the species and as strengthening pair-bonding. Examples of animal courtship fitting each of these explanations can be found.

2 Dominance hierarchies, or pecking orders, were originally thought to be the blueprint for the social organisation of all group-based animals. More recent research suggests that linear pecking orders may be much less common than was once supposed.

3 Studies of social organisation in primates suggest that dominance behaviour may be intimately linked with environmental demands. Metaphors and social assumptions have influenced, and sometimes distorted, research into social organisation and territoriality.

4 There are a number of different types of territoriality, including nested territories and territories within larger colonies. Most species seem to show seasonal territoriality. Territorial displays are linked with courtship, and may involve the ritualised display of natural weaponry.

5 Research into territoriality includes the idea of territory as linked with natural resources, and game theory models of territorial behaviour. Another possibility is to see territoriality as a display of resource-holding power on the part of the animal.

6 Lorenz construed animal aggression as a manifestation of an innate drive, channelled into a ritualised display. This may have led people to overlook the importance of reconciliation in social cohesion, both in animals and among human beings.

7 Theories of evolutionary processes include the ideas that: natural selection operates on the group as well as individuals; sociobiology emphasises the gene as the unit of natural selection; and co-evolution emphasises the interaction of different species with one another and their environment.

8 Recent approaches to evolutionary theory emphasise the integration of genes, learning and environment in producing behavioural diversity. Models which look at animal behaviour in terms of levels of explanation appear more productive than reductionist ones.

Self-assessment questions

1 Describe different types of dominance behaviour among primates.

2 Outline the major forms of territoriality.

3 What are the basic mechanisms of sociobiology?

Practice essay questions

1 What do studies of reconciliation tell us about animal psychology?

2 Describe, giving specific examples, the major theories of courtship.

3 How adequate are evolutionary concepts for explaining the behaviour of both animals and human beings?

Test your knowledge of this chapter with our online quizzes and games at:
http://www.psych.co.uk

Explore animal behaviour further at:

General
http://users.erols.com/mandtj/behavior/behavior.html – A wealth of links to sites on all areas of animal behaviour.

Primates
http://www.primate.wisc.edu:80/pin/behavior.html – Links to pages covering all topics regarding primate behaviour.

Animal communication

```
Defining communication
├── Definitions
└── Modes

Forms of communication
├── Specific examples
│   ├── Bees
│   ├── Bats
│   ├── Birds
│   └── Cetaceans
├── Animal 'words'
└── Chimpanzee communication

Animals and human language
├── Chimpanzees
├── Other species
└── Definitions of language
```

Learning objectives

24.1. Forms of communication
a outline key features of communication
b describe different forms of communication
c compare different forms of communication

24.2. Honey-bee communication
a outline the process of bee communication
b describe a study of bee communication
c identify aspects of the bee's communication code

24.3. Frogs and bats
a describe a study of communication in frogs or bats
b identify processes of communication/prey location in frogs or bats
c outline adaptive and maladaptive features of frogs and bat behaviour

24.4. Birdsong
a outline the major functions of birdsong
b describe features of birdsong and its development
c list parallels between birdsong and language

24.5. Whales and dolphins
a describe whale and dolphin vocalisations
b identify apparent functions of whale and dolphin sounds
c describe a study of whale or dolphin communication

24.6. Natural 'words'
a describe a study of animal 'words'
b outline Marler's theory of natural categories
c list different types of chimpanzee communication

24.7. Animal language studies
a outline different methods of teaching language to animals
b describe a study involving teaching animals language
c list major findings of animal language studies

24.8. Teaching animals language
a outline major arguments in the debate on animal language
b apply Hockett's design features to findings from animal language studies
c evaluate animal language studies

What do we mean by animal communication? Some aspects of communication are obvious: one animal does something – say, makes a noise – and the other responds. But sometimes, it is not that clear. We can communicate unintentionally, and so can other animals. A bird singing, for instance, may be communicating its whereabouts to a predator. Even though this would not be the function of the bird's song, the message would be being communicated nonetheless.

Defining communication

There is more than one view about communication, and therefore more than one way of defining it. Slater (1983) defined communication as: *'The transmission of a signal from one animal to another, such that the sender benefits, on average, from the response of the recipient.'* (Slater, 1983: 10). Notice the term 'on average' in this definition. In evolutionary terms, Slater's definition presents the communication as having developed because it confers some **benefit** on the sender. At the same time, however, the definition acknowledges that there may be some occasions, as with the example of bird-song above, when this is not the case.

Krebs and Davies (1978) argued that the reason why communication benefits the sender in the first place is because it allows the sender to **manipulate** the receiver's behaviour. This sociobiological perspective suggests that the reason why communication has evolved is because, by allowing such manipulation, it confers an evolutionary advantage on the sender. So the baby's cry, for instance, is primarily of value because it causes the parents to take action.

Some sociobiologists (though not all) go on from there to emphasise the potential that communication offers for **deception**. Dawkins and Krebs (1978) suggested that any mode of communication offers the opportunities for deception, and went on to argue that therefore, since deception could offer an immediate advantage to an animal by allowing it to manipulate the behaviour of other animals, it was more or less inevitable in animal communication.

Yet a third perspective on communication was suggested by Marler (1984). Marler argued that both sender and receiver benefit to some extent from an act of communication. According to this view, the key element of communication is

mutuality – both sender and receiver are concerned in what is going on. If a bird makes a sound which no other organism hears, then clearly this is not communicating. The essence of communication is that both animals are involved in the process.

Where some sociobiologists emphasise how communication offers the potential for deception and lying, Marler argues that this is not likely to be the whole story. If communication mechanisms were inevitably exploited because they offer the possibility to deceive, as these sociobiologists appear to expect, then they would cease to have any functional advantage in the first place. As a result, they would be unlikely to evolve further. Marler pointed out that by necessity, deceit involves breaking rules – but this very fact implies that most communication must actually follow those rules. If it did not, then the rules would not exist in the first place. So deception, by its very nature and because of the nature of evolutionary mechanisms, must be exceptional.

Modes of communication

At its minimum, then, communication involves the transmission of information from a sender to a receiver. But there are a number of different ways in which information may be transmitted, and this can involve a number of different sensory modes. In Chapter 12, we explored some of the main sensory modes used by human beings. Animals use these modes too, but in addition they have other types of senses, which, as far as we are aware, do not exist in human beings.

Visual communication

Like human beings, animals can communicate using **visual signals**. In Chapter 15, we saw how we communicate non-verbally using visual signals, and at how some of these signals, such as facial expressions indicating strong emotion, have a direct link with our evolutionary past. Some animal communication also involves visual signals passing between one animal and the next. The courtship displays which we looked at in Chapter 23 are a good example of visual communication, as are the displays of aggression involving one animal making itself look as fearsome as possible to an intruder or a rival. Colour can be communication, as we saw with the red belly of the stickleback, and so can the shape of an animal.

Olfactory communication

Communication may also be **olfactory** – in other words, animals can communicate by using smell. Many mammals engage in scent-marking, either to signal their territory boundaries, as cats do, or to indicate that they have been present in a particular area. Dogs, for example, seem more inclined to scent-mark through urination when they are outside their own territory than within it. This is a message that the dog has been in this area, which acts as a signal to other dogs. As we saw in Chapter 22, olfaction is also an important mechanism by which sheep come to recognise their young in the first few hours after birth. In that sense (although this may be stretching the concept of communication somewhat), the lamb could be said to be communicating its presence to the ewe by means of its scent.

Pheromones

In 1959, Karlson and Lüscher identified the existence of volatile substances which were produced by animals and which conveyed information to other animals of the same species. The type of information conveyed by these substances, which they called **pheromones**, appeared to be physiological, from the way that the pheromones particularly affected the hormone system of the animal which received them. They also seemed to be received through, and intimately linked with, the olfactory receptors.

Wilson and Bossert (1963) identified two kinds of pheromones: **primer pheromones**, which produce long-term responses, such as accelerating puberty in the receiving animal; and **releaser pheromones** (sometimes called signalling pheromones), which produce immediate changes in behaviour in the receiving animal. These changes are often concerned with sexual behaviour: Melrose, Reed and Patterson (1971) showed that if a sow in season is exposed to a particular releaser pheromone, she will immediately stand immobile with her back arched, ready for mating. The artificial insemination of farm animals involves the extensive use of pheromones of this kind.

Since their discovery, pheromones have been shown to occur widely within the animal world. They can have quite literally far-reaching effects. One species of moth, for instance, produces a pheromone when it is time to mate which can be detected by other moths from a distance of several miles. Van Toller and Dodd (1988) discussed the evidence that human beings are affected by pheromones as well. As you might imagine, this is quite a controversial issue, particularly in view of the use of attractant pheromones by perfume manufacturers.

Tactile communication

Communication can also be **tactile** – depending on the sense of touch. In one species of spider, for instance, the male approaches the female spider from behind, and gently strokes her. This communicates to the female spider that mating, rather than dinner, is the order of the day. Another species of garden spider shakes the female's web rhythmically before approaching her to mate. This, again, communicates a message about mating to the female, so that she becomes sexually receptive and tolerates the male's approach without eating him. Afterwards, though, is another matter! Male spiders of these species need to make a quick getaway if they are not to form part of the female's next meal.

Auditory communication

Bright (1984) argued that most animal communication actually takes place by means of **sound**. The reason for this is that sound offers a number of advantages over other systems of communication. A message transmitted by sound can change as quickly as a visual signal does, and the signal does not stay around once it has been released, as smells do. Unlike visual signals, sound messages can travel around corners or through thick vegetation. Sound can be used to communicate at night. And it can also reach across a large area of territory, so that an animal can assert its presence without having to visit each part separately.

Morton (1975) performed a comparative study of different habitats, in terms of the way in which they transmit different kinds of sounds. By comparing forest, forest-edge and grassland environments, Morton found that they had very different acoustic properties. Moreover, when the calls from animals living in those habitats were tape-recorded, it was apparent that their communication was 'tailored' to the acoustical properties of the environment – animals in different habitats produced different kinds of sounds.

Only a relatively narrow range of sounds travel well in dense forest environments – sounds between 1585 and 2500 Hz – and these travel only if they are produced from at least five feet above the forest floor. Sounds made on the forest floor itself are quickly lost. Morton found that birds which live within the forest itself (as opposed to high up in the tree canopy) tend to produce calls with an average frequency of 2200 Hz – in other words, calls which spread well through the habitat. They also use changes of tone within the optimum range, which help their calls to spread out over long distances.

In the grasslands, sound transmission is different. For one thing, unlike the forest, how well sound carries is strongly affected by wind and temperature. One similarity with the forest, though, is that sounds which occur near the ground are quickly absorbed: if a sound is to carry any distance, it needs to be made from at least ten feet into the air. Like other researchers, Morton noticed that many (though not all) grassland birds sing while they are flying. This is different from forest birds, which tend to sing while they are perched on branches. Interestingly, in Morton's study, species of birds which lived on the forest edge were equally divided between those whose songs fitted the forest environment and those which fitted the grassland.

The implication, then, is that communication and habitat are intimately linked. As with the other aspects of animal behaviour which we have looked at in the previous two chapters, there is wide diversity between different species in terms of how they communicate. But this diversity is not random. To make sense of it, we need to look at the behaviour in the context of the characteristics and demands of the animal's environment.

Forms of animal communication

Being able to receive and send information using a particular sensory mode is one part of the study of communication. But it is also worthwhile looking at the study of communication in specific animal species. Some of the studies which have been undertaken by ethologists and comparative psychologists have shown how animal communication systems can be both complex and unexpected.

Communication in honey-bees

Honey-bees live in colonies consisting of three castes of bee: queens, worker bees and drones. The majority of the bees in any one hive are worker bees. These are sterile females, who undertake the routine activities of the colony. Each colony also has a single queen, who remains within the centre of the hive and lays eggs. Male bees, known as drones, are hatched within the hive but leave it to follow a newly hatched queen on her mating flight, which takes place almost as soon as she is hatched. After this, the new queen returns to the original hive to collect enough workers to form a new colony, and then the swarm leaves to find a new location and establish a new hive.

While they are maintaining the hive, worker bees collect nectar from flowers, and bring it back to be converted into honey. The workers forage across long distances, and, should they find a rich source of food, will return to the hive to recruit further bees to collect it. In order to do so, they need to communicate the location of the food source to their fellow bees. They do so using a visual code based on movement. When a bee returns from a food source, it carries out a dance, within the hive, which informs its fellow workers where the food is located.

The bee dance

In 1950, von Frisch published a book which described a series of studies decoding the language which the bees used. Von Frisch and his colleagues analysed over 6000 bee dances, correlating them with the location of different sources of food. They found that different elements within this dance carry different items of information. For example, if the food is less than 100 m away, the returning bee simply moves round in a circle, reversing direction periodically. This does not give any specific location, but the workers who see this dance leave the hive and fly around the surrounding area until they have found the source.

If the food is more than 100 m away, the returning bee performs a 'wagging dance', instead of a smooth circling one. One element in this dance is that the bee moves in a figure-of-eight, wagging her abdomen about three to fifteen times a second during a central straight run. The angle of the central run informs the other bees about the direction in which the food is to be found (Figure 24.1).

Figure 24.1 The bee dance

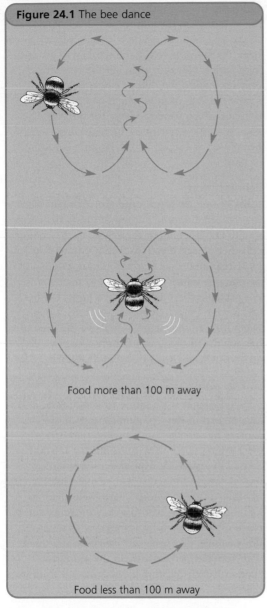

Food more than 100 m away

Food less than 100 m away

on a vertical surface, the line is at an angle from the vertical, and this represents the angle between the sun, the nest and the food. It makes no difference whether the sky is overcast or clear – bees can detect the location of the sun regardless of the condition of the sky.

Frisch performed a number of experiments, investigating how accurate the bees were in communicating this information. In one study, bees were fed on lavender-scented sugar water 750 m away from the hive. Then the food was removed, and a series of lavender-scented boards were placed at varying distances from the hive, along the same route. An observer at each board counted the number of bees which landed there. Most of the bees – over 60% of the total observed – went to one of the two boards on either side of the original feeding place: either the one at 700 m or the one at 800 m. In other words, they had gone as close as possible to the source indicated by the original bees' dances.

It is possible that the bees use more than the dance itself to communicate information. In 1964, Wenner observed that dancing bees also make sounds during the straight run part of the dance, and this might be communication too. In another study, Esch (1967) found that silent dances did not seem to have any effect on the other bees, in that they would not go on from observing the dance to investigating new food sources. So other communicative modes may be involved, as well as the visual. The bee dance represents a complex and impressive form of communication which, as we saw in Chapter 18, may link with the bee's **cognitive map** of an area to maximise the chances of foraging productively.

Frogs and bats

Frogs, as anyone who has lived near a frog-pond knows, can be highly vocal animals. During the mating season, both frogs and toads croak to attract mates. Some species, such as natterjack toads, can be heard as much as 2 km away. Narins and Capranica (1980) found that frogs seem to have highly specialised auditory equipment. Their auditory system is precisely tuned to receive the sounds made by other members of their species at mating time.

In one species of Puerto Rican tree frog, the male makes a two-note call, sounding like 'ko-kee'. They begin calling at dusk and continue

The dancer informs other bees about the distance from the hive at which the food source is to be found using speed. The slower the speed at which the bee performs the figure-of-eight, the further away the food is. So, for instance, if the food is 500 m away, the bee will make six complete dance circuits in fifteen seconds, but if it is 10,000 m away, the bee will make only two figure-of-eight circuits in the same time.

The dance can be performed on a horizontal surface, or on a vertical one. Frisch showed that if it is on a horizontal surface, then the central run points directly towards the food source. But if it is until the early morning. Narins and Capranica noticed that the call seems to change as the night progresses: at first, the frogs call 'ko', but later on, they add the second note and call 'ko-kee'. By playing back to the frogs calls which had been recorded, the researchers found that the first part, the 'ko' call, serves as a territorial warning to other males in the district. The second part, the 'kee' call, is the part which attracts female frogs.

During the early part of the night, then, the male frogs were establishing their territory. Only later would they begin calling to attract the females. When they examined the physiology of the frog's auditory system, Narins and Capranica found that the male frogs were selectively tuned to respond to calls at the same frequency of the 'ko' call, whereas female frogs did not respond to those, but responded to calls of the same frequency as the 'kee' note.

Broadcasting to predators

There are a number of advantages to a species in communicating by sound, as mentioned earlier. But there are disadvantages too. The main one is the fact that sounds are broadcast, so they can be picked up just as easily by predators, looking for a handy meal, as they can be by other members of the same species. In this context, Tuttle and Ryan (1981) observed the behaviour of the mud-puddle rain forest frog. Calling frogs would fall silent if a bat flew across their pond. But if the night was cloudy, so they could not see the bats flying, they would call as usual, and at these times they would often be caught by the bats.

The mud-puddle rain forest frog has a two-part call, which consists of an initial sound rather like 'aow', followed by several short 'chuck-chuck' calls. At times, the male frog will make the full call, but at other times it will limit itself to the 'aow' sound. Research using recorded playbacks showed that, given a choice, female mud-puddle frogs would prefer a male which made the full call, although they would also mate with those making the shorter call if necessary. Tuttle and Ryan wondered whether the reason for leaving out the 'chuck-chuck' part of the call was because of the danger from predators. The 'aow' sound was difficult to locate, but the 'chuck-chuck' sound gave a very clear indicator of where the sender was. It would not just have helped the female to find the frog: it would also have helped the bat.

By playing frog calls through a speaker, Tuttle and Ryan showed that bats did make straight for the sound when they heard the 'chuck-chuck' call of the frog. Sometimes, they would even try to rip open the fabric covering the speaker, to get at the 'frog' inside. Not only that, but the bats would only respond to the calls of edible frogs, and ignore the calls of frogs which had poisonous skins, or which were too large for the bats. The communication system of the frogs, then, was being used as a signal by the hunting bat to find its prey.

Echolocation

It has been known for some time that bats navigate by echolocation: putting out high-frequency sounds and listening to the echoes as they bounce off other objects. Pye (1980) showed that bats have more than one type of echolocation system and use the one which is best suited to their needs. For example, the small European pipistrelle bat uses a wide-range, 'Doppler'-style radar system when it is cruising at 5–10 m above the ground, because this allows it to examine a large volume of air. But when it has detected a target, it switches to a sharp, narrow-band signal which gives it much greater accuracy.

Echolocation is a hunting tool and, as far as is known, bats mostly communicate with one another by audible squeaks when they arrive at the roosting site. But in 1983, Barclay and Fenton carried out playback experiments with little brown bats, and found that they often use the calls of others of their own species to help them to locate food. This meant that they could extend the range of their search by as much as 25 times. In this example, then, one bat was communicating with another inadvertently, in the sense that another bat was picking up information from its calls.

Bird songs

As we saw in Chapter 23, birds use song both in courtship and to define areas of territory. Both of these are communicative purposes: the bird is passing specific messages to other members of its species. Birds communicate for other reasons as well: a blackbird, for instance, will make a sharp 'pink-pink' sound when there is a cat nearby, which warns other birds in the neighbourhood of the danger.

Thorpe (1961) studied the behaviour of gannets

in a colony containing many thousands of birds. Thorpe found that when a bird was returning to its nest it would drift on an updraft of air from the bottom of the cliff upwards, calling as it went. When the bird on the nest heard its mate calling it would call in reply, showing that each bird's call could act as an individual identification signal. Thorpe also calculated that a bird might have as many as fifteen or sixteen different kinds of calls, each serving a different function.

Krebs (1976) investigated how birds seem to sing more intensively in the early morning – the 'dawn chorus'. By investigating what the birds actually did during each day, and how much time they spent on each activity, Krebs found that the dawn chorus serves a largely territorial function. The early morning is not a particularly good time for gathering food, because it is dark, so visibility is lower, and it is also cold, so many insects are still inactive. On the other hand, at this time many birds move around looking for living space, so establishing and defending a territory is necessary.

Bird-song is not just territorial, of course. As we saw in Chapter 23, Catchpole (1981) showed how a bird's song can serve a dual purpose: it can be used to defend a territory and, by indicating to a prospective mate that the singer has a territory to defend, can also attract a female bird. Marler (1984) suggested that the function of song in different bird species might be ranged along a continuum, with those for whom song serves a territorial function at one end, those for whom it serves a mate-attraction function at the other, and with most species falling in between these two extremes – in other words, using song for both purposes.

Learning in bird-song

Slater (1981) suggested that bird calls and bird-song are partly learned from other birds. He found that chaffinches which had been hand-reared, and had not heard other wild birds, made an entirely different kind of 'chink' call from that of wild birds. In one case, Slater observed a laboratory chaffinch in a duet with a wild sparrow, outside the window of the laboratory. The chaffinch imitated the sparrow's 'cheep' whenever the sparrow produced it. Slater concluded that learning through copying is an important part of the way in which birds acquire their songs. And there seems to be a strong genetic predisposition for such learning to take place.

Bird calls can carry a number of different messages (see Table 24.1 overleaf, which lists the calls of the chaffinch). But in addition to their calls, Slater also found that individual chaffinches can have up to five different types of song. Some of these are personal, sung by that bird alone. Others are shared by several birds. In some cases too, Slater observed chaffinches singing songs which were almost identical to those sung by others, but with just a note or two different – possibly because the bird had made an error in copying the song from another.

Slater studied a population of 40 chaffinches on the Orkney Islands and found that between them they had seventeen different song types. So it was not a matter of each bird having its own individual songs – there was a considerable amount of sharing. Slater found that this sharing related to geographical distribution, but that the boundaries were not distinct enough for it to be accurately described as a 'dialect'. Instead, there was considerable overlap between the songs sung in one area and those sung in an adjoining one, but gradually the overlap would become less, until birds a long distance away from one another would be singing entirely different songs.

Parallels between bird-song and speech

In 1970, Marler proposed that bird-song and speech were directly comparable in certain key respects, and that the study of bird-song might provide psychologists with some useful indicators as to the nature and development of speech in human beings. One of the parallels which Marler identified was the way that both humans and birds show a strong genetic predisposition to pick up and imitate certain sounds rather than others. Marler showed that young birds will learn the songs of their own species if they are played to them when young, but they will ignore songs of birds from other species. Similarly, young human beings are surrounded by all kinds of sounds and noises, but it is the human voice to which they listen most closely, and human speech which they imitate.

There were other parallels that Marler pointed out. One of them was that both children and young birds are able to imitate the sounds that they hear so well that dialects can be passed from one generation to the next. Also, each of them will learn much better when they are young. Although there has been considerable debate as to

Table 24.1 The calls of the chaffinch

flight	'Tsupe' or 'Tupe'	Flight/preparation for flight.
social	'Chink' or 'Spink'	Helps separated birds to meet again.
escape	'Cheenk'	Also used during courtship in new pairs.
aggression	'Zzzzzz' or Zh-zh-zh	Used during attack and 'fighting in captive males'.
alarm 1	'Tew'	Most frequent of the three alarms. Common in young birds, but also used by adults of both sexes.
alarm 2	'Seee'	Extreme alarm in breeding male. Note rises and falls and is difficult for predator to locate.
alarm 3	'Huit' or 'Whit'	Moderate danger, used by males in spring.
injury	'Tseee'	Given by birds hurt during fighting.
courtship 1	'Kseep' 'Tsit' 'Tzit' 'Chwit'	Used by males during early pair-formation phase of courtship season.
courtship 2	'Tchirp' or 'Chirri'	Used by males later in courtship season.
courtship 3	'Seeep'	Used by females during breeding season.
begging 1	'Cheep'	Soft note of nestlings.
begging 2	'Chirrup'	Loud, penetrating call of fledgelings.
intermediates	'Huit/Seee', 'Huit/Chink'	Occasional intermediates between alarm and social calls of mature birds.
sub-song	'Chrrp' or various groups of low-pitched rattles	Used by birds in first phase of summer.
song	'Tchip-tchip-tchip-Cherry-erry-erry-Tchip-Tcheweeoo'	Main song, lasting two to three seconds, sung through first half of year and in early autumn.

Source: Adapted from Bright, 1984

whether there is actually a critical period for language learning in humans as there is for bird-song in birds (see Chapter 4), it is still reasonably well established that children learn language better when they are young, and most psychologists believe that there is at least a sensitive period for this type of learning.

Nottebohm (1970) showed that chaffinches have a dominant side of the brain, which processes bird-song. This was another parallel which Marler pointed out: human beings too have a dominant hemisphere for language; and as with birds, although it is possible for such abilities to transfer if there is damage to one hemisphere in childhood, this is less likely to happen as the person grows older.

The idea, then, is that there may be some evolutionary tendencies towards certain kinds of behaviour, which in human beings takes the form of language. This type of tendency is manifest in birds as well. Marler was not suggesting that bird-song is actually a form of language – rather, that

the study of bird-song can shed some light on the evolutionary origins of language. We will return to this issue when we look at the question of warning calls in monkeys, as Marler suggests that there may be parallels there as well.

Whales and dolphins

Cetaceans – the marine mammals known as whales and dolphins – communicate with one another using a number of signals. Most of their communication is through sound, because this is the mode which can travel for the longest distances through water. A number of biologists and comparative psychologists have investigated communication in these animals.

Whale songs
In the late 1960s, a recording of the songs of the humpback whales became a surprise best-seller. The record was a by-product of research into the songs of humpback whales off Bermuda. Using

hydrophones suspended in the water from the outriggers of a small sailboat, Payne and McVay (1971) collected many hours of tapes of whale noises throughout the late 1960s and the 1970s. As the noises were analysed, it became apparent that what was being recorded was a series of sound patterns which were systematically constructed to produce highly complex songs.

Humpback whales, as a general rule, sing only during their breeding season, although it has occasionally been known for one to sing while the whales are migrating from the breeding grounds to their Arctic or Antarctic feeding areas. In one singing session, a whale may sing the complete song several times over, breathing during the natural intervals which occur between phrases of the song. A session can last for quite a long time. One whale was once recorded singing non-stop for more than 22 hours, but after that time the researchers had to give up and go home, so it is not known how much longer the animal carried on.

The sound of the song itself is melodic, consisting of long-drawn-out sequences of notes repeated in regular patterns. The song can be subdivided into a series of **themes**. A theme consists of a group of similar phrases, each of which consists of a series of notes, known as units. The number of themes in a song can vary, from just four or five to as many as eight or ten. All the humpback whales in a particular area at the same time will sing the same song, but the song gradually changes through the season. Some phrases are dropped and new ones are added. These changes are slight, but occur relatively rapidly, with each component changing about once in every two months. So although the song at the beginning of each year is recognisably linked to that which the whales sang the previous year, it is not quite the same.

Although humpback whales do not sing when they are in their polar feeding grounds, they do make social calling sounds. These calls tend to be produced when the whales meet as a group, or when a group is splitting up, but it is not clear whether they are greetings or some other kind of message. They also make social sounds when they are engaging in co-operative fishing, using the 'bubble-net' technique of herding fish together within a ring of bubbles and then rising up within the ring to catch the fish in their jaws.

Singing and courtship

Tyack (1981) found that the humpback whale's singing appears to be linked with something which looks like courtship behaviour – although it is difficult to tell for sure, because it is hard to get close enough to the whale as it swims. Typically, a singing whale will be swimming alone, several hundred metres away from other whales and avoiding other singing whales. In a few cases, though, Tyack observed non-singing whales approaching singers. When this happened, the whale would stop singing, the two would swim together for a short distance, and then the previous singer would swim away and the newcomer would begin singing instead.

Sometimes a singing whale would approach a cow whale with a young calf. If the cow was not sexually receptive (which seemed to be linked with the age of the calf – humpback whales do not begin to ovulate until the previous calf is weaned), she would swim away rapidly. But if the cow and calf continued on the same course, the singer would swim after them and try to join them. If this was successful, the singer would stop singing and swim along with them. Occasionally, the cow and the escort whale would leave the calf at the surface for ten or fifteen minutes and dive deeply. Tyack speculated that mating might be taking place at this time, but, as you might imagine, it is rather difficult to confirm such a speculation.

Occasionally, a threesome of this kind (cow, calf and escort) would swim into the vicinity of another singing whale, who would then begin to approach them. The trio would speed up and swim away. Sometimes, though, the singer would approach and begin a singing contest with the other escort whale, as if to displace him and join the cow. Such contests often attracted other whales, who would all become very excited and act aggressively, slapping each other with their flukes or ramming into one another.

During these episodes, the whales would make a range of **social calls**. Sometimes these would be fragments of songs, taken out of context; but sometimes they would take the form of high-pitched trumpetings and low grunts. Tyack (1983) tried playing these noises back to a group of singing whales, and found that the results were dramatic. When they heard the sounds, the singing whales would instantly stop singing and home in on the loudspeaker, often charging towards the boat at very high speeds. When they reached the boat, they would submerge and circle around as if they were looking for the group that made the sounds. Tyack found, though, that if he played songs instead, singing whales would stop their singing and move away.

It is apparent, then, that the range of vocalisations of whales is very complex, and conveys some definite meanings to other whales. It is difficult for us to place exact interpretations on these, partly because of the difficulties of close observation and partly because we would only be guessing, based on our ideas about the meanings of social behaviour in other animals – and this is often more conjectural than we like to admit. It is possible too that the meaning of the whale-song may lie in some kind of meta-communication of an art form, in the same way that we ourselves enjoy music, and not as specific signals with specific meanings. We can only hope that further research will help us to understand some of these issues.

Dolphins

In 1965, Bastian performed an experiment involving two dolphins in adjacent tanks. The dolphins could hear, but could not see, one another. One of the dolphins was taught to press a paddle in order to receive a reward. The other was not taught anything, but when it was provided with a set of paddles it too pressed the correct one. Bastian argued that the only way that the dolphin could have known what to do was through hearing and understanding the many whistles, squeaks and clicks that the other dolphin maintained throughout the training period.

Dolphins produce a range of sounds, including whistles, squeaks and groans, clicks, rattles and chirps. Roughly speaking, these can be divided into **pulsed sounds**, like the clicks and rattles which are produced as rapidly repeated noise, and **unpulsed sounds**. Pulsed sounds mostly seem to be used for echolocation and navigation rather than as communication between one dolphin and another. There are, however, a few exceptions to this, such as a dolphin producing a pulsed squeak or yelp as an alarm call.

Whistling was one of the first of the dolphin sounds to be investigated, perhaps because it is one of the easiest for human beings to hear – many of the other sounds which dolphins make are in the ultrasonic range, and we need special equipment to detect them. Not all species of dolphins whistle, but it is thought that those which do, use it for communication at times. Dolphins whistle when feeding or when investigating something unusual. In some dolphin groups, each dolphin has a special whistle, which only they make. It is thought that this is used as an identifying call, which helps to keep the whole group together during communal activities like hunting.

Dolphins also whistle when they are in distress, such as when they have become stranded or harpooned. In one study described by Bright (1984), a male dolphin was captured and the whistles it made were recorded. When these were played back to his own school, the animals all turned and fled. But when they were played back to an unfamiliar school, the dolphins reacted with curiosity. There are numerous possible explanations for this, but it does imply that each school may have its own calls and, some believe, even its own 'language' of meaning for whistles.

Norris and Dohl (1980) observed Hawaiian spinner dolphins, and found that they show special bursts of communicative activity at a particular time of day. Most of the time, these animals swim gently around, playing and resting. But in the late afternoon, the group's level of activity increases and they begin to gather together, whistling frequently and engaging in vigorous play, such as leaping out of the water and spinning. The level of excitement within the group mounts, and as it does so the amount and range of vocal activity grows, until eventually all the dolphins are joining in the chorus. When this happens, the group moves out of the bay and begins its evening hunting.

One suggestion is that the vocalisation which is observed in the group at this time is an important agent in co-ordinating and motivating the group, ensuring that each dolphin is alert, active and ready to set off. Typically, during this time, one dolphin will begin calling and the others will join in. Some researchers have suggested that the unanimous nature of the call indicates whether all the dolphins in the group are ready to set off. If some dolphins do not join in, there is a brief lull and then the chorus begins again.

Dolphins, then, are thought to use sound for social co-ordination, as well as for specific signalling about emotional state and possibly danger. A dolphin's brain is very large (see Figure

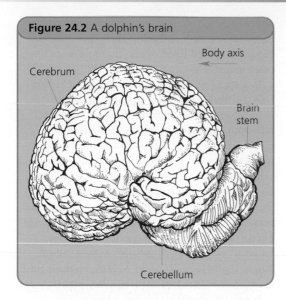

Figure 24.2 A dolphin's brain

Cerebrum

Body axis

Brain stem

Cerebellum

24.2), although the cortex itself is thinner than that of the human brain; so it does seem possible that a sophisticated communicative system might be one of the uses to which that brain is put.

Do animals use 'words'?

One of the major questions about animal communication systems is whether they have 'words' – signals which stand for a specific concept and are used to discriminate between examples of that concept and others. Until relatively recently, most researchers tended to assume that natural animal vocalisations only convey information about basic motivational or emotional states. But some recent studies have suggested that there may be cases where specific conceptual signals are used in animal communication. In order to explore this idea, we need to look very specifically at the features of distinctive animal alarm calls.

In 1980, Robinson found that Belding's ground squirrels can discriminate between birds which are predators of squirrels, like hawks, falcons, and so on, and those which are harmless to them, like white pelicans and turkey vultures. The squirrels give alarm calls when they see the dangerous birds, and run for cover, but they simply chirp and remain where they are if a non-dangerous bird flies over. If a squirrel spots a ground-based predator, it gives an alarm call, and adopts 'posting behaviour' – standing upright on the hind legs – before escaping.

Seyfarth and Cheyney (1980) studied African vervet monkeys. These monkeys have three main predators: martial eagles, leopards and pythons. Each of these represents a different type of threat to the monkey, and so each requires different avoidance behaviour. When an adult vervet monkey gives the 'eagle' alarm call, other members of the troop will look into the sky and run for cover. If the 'leopard' alarm is given, the troop climb into nearby trees, where they will be safer. And if the 'snake' alarm is given, the monkeys look down at the ground around the troop, and run away if they spot a python.

Seyfarth and Cheyney found that vervet monkeys also discriminate between predators, giving quite different alarm calls when they see the three different species which prey on their kind. By playing back recordings of the alarm calls to wild monkeys, Seyfarth and Cheyney were able to show that other monkeys heard and also responded appropriately to these calls.

Learning to give the alarm

What was particularly interesting about their observations was the way that the young vervets learned the alarm calls. While adults almost always gave the correct signals, Seyfarth and Cheyney found that young monkeys often made mistakes. But these mistakes were not random. The young monkeys tended to overgeneralise their responses, giving the 'eagle' alarm when they saw other kinds of birds, or even sometimes a falling leaf; giving the 'leopard' alarm when they saw any other mammals, like warthogs; or giving the 'snake' alarm to small, non-predator snakes or to a stick lying on the ground.

There are two features of this behaviour which are particularly noteworthy. The first is the way that the young monkeys learn to be more precise in their alarm calling. Seyfarth and Cheyney found that when a young monkey hears an alarm from another, it tends to look towards other adults, particularly its mother, before it takes any action. When an infant gives an alarm, other members of the troop will look in the direction that the infant is looking in. If the threat is genuine, they will also give alarms and act appropriately. The young monkey then imitates the behaviour of the adults. If a young monkey gives an alarm inappropriately, the adults will check and then continue with what they are doing. In this way, the young monkey learns that the particular stimulus which it has identified does not need to be accompanied by the avoidance reaction. So observational learning is an important part of learning these signals.

Natural categories

The second aspect of the behaviour which is of interest is the way that the monkey gives the three distinct calls. Although they may sometimes make inappropriate behavioural responses, the young monkeys do not make the wrong call signs for the different types of threat. They would not give the 'snake' call to a bird or the 'leopard' call to a snake. Instead, they seem to use what Marler (1982) described as **natural categories**: they respond differently to things which fly in the air, things which resemble mammals and things which slide along the ground. Seyfarth and Cheyney (1982) suggested that the infants inherit a genetic response to the broad category, which is then refined through the infants' experience.

Marler (1982) proposed that the way in which innate tendencies are refined through experience illustrates a fundamental mechanism of perceptual development. He proposed that generalised innate release mechanisms establish the direction in which the behaviour will develop: in the young monkey's case, the type of stimulus to which the alarm should be given; in the white-crowned sparrow (see Chapter 22), the basic form of the song. These responses are then developed and made more specific through the interaction of the young animal with other members of its species. The young monkey learns to give calls only in response to martial eagles and to ignore other birds; the white-crowned sparrow acquires its regional dialect.

Species-specific calls

The readiness to learn specific natural categories, then, is an example of the kind of **genetic preparedness** – the readiness to learn certain kinds of things – which we discussed in Chapter 22. In view of this, Marler went on to argue that the development of distinctive vocal signals in response to these natural categories would be specific to that particular species, since each species experiences its own environmental demands and has responded to different evolutionary pressures. So animals which were prepared to identify calls for natural categories would also be prepared to recognise the type of 'words' – calls which indicate broad natural categories – which are produced by members of their own species, but less prepared to recognise those produced by other animals.

In a study of vocal sound recognition, Marler (1983) demonstrated that Japanese macaques found it easy to learn to discriminate between calls with the timing of peaks of frequency coming at different points. For example, they could tell the difference between a call with an early peak, and a call of the same length but with the peak occurring towards the end. But they found it far more difficult to learn to discriminate between two calls with similar peaks, but different pitches. By contrast, other species of macaque found it easier to discriminate between calls of different pitches, and harder to learn to distinguish between the timing of the frequency peaks.

It was not that the monkeys were unable to learn. Given enough training, all the monkeys were able to learn all the discrimination tasks. But what was noticeable was the ease with which they mastered some, but not others. This preparedness to learn certain discriminations in preference to others is striking. The evidence reinforces Gould and Marler's (1987) idea that there is an evolutionary background to the types of responses which an organism will learn, which represents a genetic predisposition to respond to certain types of stimulus rather than others.

Marler went on to suggest that the predisposition to respond to natural categories represents a more complex stage in communication than the simple alarm call of an agitated or frightened animal. He suggested that if we are looking for an evolutionary progression between simple signalling and human language, then the type of vocal behaviour shown by young vervet monkeys and the vocal preferences shown by Japanese macaques may provide an intermediate link.

Chimpanzee communication

Another place where we might look for intermediate links between human and animal behaviour is among our closest relatives. As we have seen, chimpanzees live in what seem to be well-ordered social groups, seem to be highly intelligent animals and also seem to be able to communicate with others within their group and engage in co-ordinated action. But they do not use language – or not, at any rate, any form of language which can be detected by human beings. So how should we go about studying their capacity for information-processing and social communication?

Menzel (1984) suggested that there are three different ways of tackling this question. One possibility is to observe chimpanzee interactions within their social groups as closely as possible, taking note of every sound and movement, and to try to use the data to put together a 'dictionary' of what these communication signals mean. A second option is to look at the chimpanzee group as a whole and what is going on within it. From there, the researcher can identify what chimpanzees might be communicating about, and then use that information to see how they go about doing it. And the third is to try to teach a captive chimpanzee to use a human language. Researchers into chimpanzee communication have used all three of these techniques, and we will look at each of them in turn.

Chimpanzee sounds

Chimpanzees communicate with each other using a number of visual and auditory signals. Although some of these involve the whole body – like the threat display, in which the animal jumps up and down, hair standing on end and uttering a series of increasingly loud hoots ending in a scream – most day-to-day communication involves sounds and facial expressions.

One of the most common noises which chimpanzees make is the **grunt**, which is not normally accompanied by any change in facial expression. Chimpanzees may utter soft grunts of contentment when feeding or grooming, or grunts may be exchanged between members of a group during a quiet time. A series of grunts connected by audible intakes of breath, with the mouth slightly open, are sometimes given when one chimpanzee approaches another. These pant-grunts can change into squeaking or screaming, with the animal showing the facial expression known as the 'fear-grin', if the other responds aggressively.

Another common sound made by the chimpanzee is known as the **pant-hoot**. Goodall (1974) described pant-hoots as a series of 'hooo' sounds, connected by audible intakes of breath, gradually increasing in volume, eventually ending in loud 'waaa' sounds. These pant-hoots are accompanied by distinctive facial expressions, and are used on a number of occasions. Typically, they happen at times of mild excitement, such as when the chimpanzees are arriving at a new food source, or when one chimpanzee group joins another.

There is also some slight evidence that pant-hoots may be used to signal where a group is located. Goodall observed that, on occasions, such a call would be given by chimpanzees feeding peacefully in a tree, and would elicit a similar response from another troop some distance away. Marler and Hobbett (1975) identified individual differences in the pant-hoot vocalisation of chimpanzees, which suggested that chimpanzees are able to recognise each other by their distinctive voices.

Other sounds which chimpanzees make include squeaking or whimpering – most common in younger animals – and barking and screaming at times of extreme excitement. Goodall describes the contact call between a mother and her infant as being a soft, single-syllable 'hoo-whimper', accompanied by a pouting expression. This sound is also made by adults, when begging food from another chimpanzee or soliciting grooming. In such cases, the hoo-whimper may turn into a series of louder normal whimpers, if the animal is ignored by the others.

Chimpanzees may **bark** when they are excited, especially when arriving at a favourite food place. A soft version of the bark, sounding a bit like a quiet cough, is also made when one animal is mildly threatening another, but if the threat is more serious the chimpanzee produces a loud 'waa-bark'. A chimpanzee scream or alarm signal – a bit like a 'wraaaa' sound – can be very loud indeed, and reverberate through the forest for some distance, as can the higher-pitched chimpanzee screams.

Facial expressions

Most vocal signals are accompanied by distinctive facial expressions. One of these is the **fear-grin**, in which the animal opens its mouth widely, peeling its lips right back from the teeth. If the chimpanzee is less agitated, the top lip may cover the top row of teeth, but the bottom row remains exposed. In the **play-face**, by contrast, although the mouth is also open, the lips cover both rows of teeth, and the individual usually accompanies this expression by softly panting (see Figure 24.3).

Figure 24.3 Facial expression in chimpanzees

A chimpanzee who is nervous, or slightly but not extremely frightened, often shows a **closed grin**, in which both rows of teeth are exposed, but the jaws are closed. These grins are often accompanied by high-pitched squeaking sounds, which can easily change to screams or whimpers if circumstances change and the chimpanzee feels more threatened.

We can see, then, that chimpanzee communication can convey a wide range of emotions. Many of the expressions are not dissimilar to those adopted by human beings in similar contexts. Goodall described the closed grin of the chimpanzee as the nearest equivalent to the human nervous or social smile. Chimpanzees also appear to pick up a large amount of information from the posture and muscle tension shown by others in the troop, but as yet we do not have a full understanding of these signals.

Chimpanzee communication in its social context

Although it is useful to know something about the 'vocabulary' which chimpanzees use in order to communicate with one another, in effect we can only perceive these signals in their immediate context. So when we are interpreting such signals we can only make sense of those which relate directly to the immediate situation, like the animal's current emotional state or its reaction to a specific stimulus. It is very difficult to use this method of study to find out about more general or abstract messages which an individual might wish to communicate to others of its group.

Menzel (1984) suggested that one way of studying the ability of chimpanzees to communicate with one another is to look at more complex forms of communication which occur spontaneously. One thing which chimpanzees do quite a lot of, in the wild, is foraging for food. So Menzel argued that it might be useful to see how, or if, chimpanzees communicate with one another about food.

Menzel and Halperin (1975) studied this form of communication in a small group of six to eight young chimpanzees. The chimpanzees had been together for over a year, and had come to form a stable social unit. They were put together in a small cage on the edge of a large enclosure, in such a way that they could not see out into the wider area. Menzel and Halperin then performed a series of studies in which one chimpanzee would be taken out from the cage, and carried (usually via a winding route) to a place where food had been hidden. The chimpanzee was shown the food and then returned to the cage. Then the whole group would be released, and their behaviour observed.

Typically, when the group was released the informed animal (referred to as the 'leader') would take the others to the food. But this did not always mean that the leader walked straight there and the others followed. Often, the other chimpanzees would run on several metres ahead, stopping and looking back from time to time, and searching any places which seemed likely to conceal food. It seemed as though they were already aware of what they were looking for.

On some occasions, Menzel and Halperin would hide, not food but a small snake. Again, the animals behaved as though they were aware of what had been hidden. For example, sometimes the leader would stop about 10 m from the place where it had been shown a hidden snake. Then one of the others would pick up a stick, go to the spot at which the leader was staring and club around the area with the stick. This was quite different from their behaviour if food had been hidden, when they would search the hiding place freely with no sign of caution. If the experimenters had removed the snake, the animals would climb the trees or walk along the fence scanning the ground.

Menzel and Halperin were in no doubt that the chimpanzees were aware of what they were looking for, even though only the leader had seen the snake directly. Somehow, it appeared, the leader had managed to communicate the object of their search to the other chimpanzees in the group. During these trials, if the leader had been released but the others did not follow, it would typically take a couple of steps and stop and wait for them, glancing back from one animal to another. If the others still did not follow, the leader would approach them and try to pull them along, at first gently and then more vigorously.

If attempts to 'persuade' the others still had no effect, the lead animal would roll around on the ground, screaming and tearing its hair, whereupon the others would gather round and start to groom it. After such a display, Menzel and Halperin observed, the leader would usually give up and make no more efforts to take the group to the food. But if one of the other animals got up and headed in that direction, the leader would follow, staying behind them as long as they were on the right course. If they began to go the wrong way, the leader would make faces and glance between them and the correct goal, or run to one animal, put a hand on its shoulder and steer it back on course.

During some of the trials, the leader would set out and then appear to give up – perhaps by becoming distracted by something else – but the followers would carry on searching in the same direction for as much as 50 m. Attempts to assess what this behaviour meant were unsuccessful, because if Menzel and Halperin tried keeping the leader back, locked in, the rest of the group would not search at all. Instead, they would whimper and try to open the cage door to release the leader.

It seems, then, as though chimpanzees are able to communicate the approximate location of food sources to one another, and also what is actually there – food, a toy or something dangerous, like a snake. However, this communication may be something to do with the nature of the social group. Menzel and Halperin found that 'stranger' chimpanzees were ignored if they were shown food in the same way and then returned to the group.

Teaching animals to use human language

In many ways, it makes sense that a foraging animal should be able to communicate with others about the locations of objects of interest, especially food. After all, if bees can do it, why not chimpanzees? But this raises the question of the animal's potential for language-like communication, and the amount of flexibility that it has in learning it. The third method of research into chimpanzee language capacity concerns attempts to teach chimpanzees, and also animals of other species, how to use versions of human languages.

Chimpanzee research

Some of the earliest experiments in teaching animals to use human language consisted of attempts to teach chimpanzee infants to speak English. These tended to be unsuccessful because chimpanzees do not have the physical equipment to vocalise as we do. For example, a young chimpanzee, Gua, was brought up alongside their own baby of the same age by Kellogg and Kellogg (1933). Although she was as quick as the human infant, and sometimes quicker, in learning to solve practical problems, Gua learned only about three words in total. In a similar study, during the six years that the young chimpanzee Vicki lived with the Hayes family, she learned only four words: 'papa', 'mama', 'up' and 'cup', although she did use these in appropriate contexts (Hayes, 1950).

Washoe

In 1969, Gardner and Gardner reported on a new approach which they had adopted for teaching human language to chimpanzees. They had observed how important visual signals were to chimpanzees in the wild, and reasoned that perhaps a chimpanzee would find visual signals more compatible with its natural inclinations. Accordingly, they raised a young chimpanzee, Washoe, by teaching her Ameslan – the American sign language for the deaf.

Washoe learned signs much more quickly and more successfully than Gua or Vicki had learned words. She was taught mainly using modelling – she would be shown the sign and then praised if she copied it. But the Gardners also 'moulded' her hands into the right shapes when they were teaching her new signs, if she did not seem to pick them up entirely by imitation. After about ten months of training, when Washoe was twenty months old, she formed her first two-word sentences. By the time she left the Gardners' house, at the age of four, she was able to sign 132 different words, including nouns, pronouns, adjectives and verbs. She could also make over 30 two- and three-word combinations (Gardner and Gardner, 1971). This is not very impressive by comparison with a human four-year-old's 3000 or so words, but it is still far more than many people had previously considered to be possible.

The Gardners devised a double-blind test, to rule out the possibility that Washoe's performance was simply a matter of her trainers seeing what they wanted to see in her behaviour. In this test, one observer was positioned in such as way as to be able to see the picture that Washoe was being shown. The other observer was placed in such a way as to be able to see Washoe, and the sign that she was making, but not the stimulus picture. Washoe was asked to make the sign for each picture, and the observer had to write down what she signed. The procedure was also videotaped. Gardner and Gardner found that, under these circumstances, Washoe achieved accurate signing on 72% of the trials. In addition, when she did make mistakes, she would often give the sign for something related to the picture, like giving the sign for a cat when she was shown a picture of a dog.

There were a number of indications that Washoe might actually be learning to use language, rather than simply responding to the demands of the trainers. One of them was the fact that she was able to coin new words: the first time she saw a swan, her trainer asked her 'What's that?' and she responded with 'water-bird'. Terrace *et al.* (1979) argued that this could simply result from the juxtaposition of the two signs for water and bird, with no semantic link between them, but other researchers (for example Lieberman, 1984) argued that this was unlikely. There were other instances of novel utterances produced by Washoe too. For example, on one occasion, when a small doll was placed in her cup, Washoe signed 'Baby in my drink'.

Washoe would often sign spontaneously, initiating sign-language 'conversations' with her trainers. She also, quite spontaneously, developed 'swear words' – words which she added on to her other utterance to indicate displeasure. For example, she would sign 'dirty' before someone's name if they had displeased her. The implication, then, is that she was using the words she had learned to fulfil communicative intentions: she was actually using language, rather than just producing stimulus-response behaviour.

The Oklahoma colony

Although Washoe achieved a considerable degree of proficiency in using signs to communicate, the Gardners felt that there were several aspects of the study which could have been improved. One of them was the fact that Washoe was on her own, rather than with other young chimpanzees. So any communication which she had using the sign language had to be with her human trainers. In addition, the Gardners and their assistants had needed to learn sign language especially for the experiment, and so they felt that they might have not been using it as fluently as a proficient speaker of Ameslan would. As a result of this, a new study was initiated. This involved a small group of infant chimpanzees being taught to sign by people who had been using Ameslan from childhood. This colony became known as the **Oklahoma colony**, under the leadership of Roger Fouts (Fouts, 1972).

Among other possibilities, this arrangement allowed Fouts to investigate whether signing chimpanzees would communicate with one another. When Washoe herself adopted a young chimpanzee, Loulis, she was observed to be teaching him sign language. And films of the Oklahoma group taken when there were no human beings in the vicinity showed that they seemed to be signing to each other, and to be responding to the messages which were being exchanged.

Fouts also performed a series of experiments similar to those of Menzel, in which one of the chimpanzees was shown where something was hidden and then returned to the rest of the group. After a period of time, the others, but not the original animal, would be let out to search. The results of these tests were generally positive: the other chimpanzees usually searched in the right place. This implied that chimpanzees could use sign language to inform each other of where things were hidden – although, of course, Menzel's studies imply that such communication need not have actually involved signing. It might be that the apes were already able to communicate such concepts in other ways.

Like Washoe, several of the Oklahoma chimpanzees coined new phrases, using Ameslan to describe things that they did not know the signs for. Lucy, one of these chimps, described a radish as 'hurt-cry-fruit'. In addition, Lucy would sometimes use her own sign combinations in preference to the learned ones. Although she knew the sign for watermelon, she would sometimes refer to it as 'fruit-drink' or 'candy-drink'. The implication again is of an active involvement in the use of language and some awareness of language as a tool for communication.

Nim Chimpsky

Terrace (1979) also trained a chimpanzee in Ameslan sign language, in much the same way as Washoe and the other Oklahoma chimps had been trained. After five years of training, Nim had achieved a large number of signs. However, Terrace argued that this did not indicate that the chimpanzee had acquired language. All the skills shown by Nim, he believed, could be explained in terms of stimulus-response learning. As an intelligent animal, Terrace argued, Nim had simply learned finer and finer discrimination, by trial and error – he was not really using language as a tool for communication at all. Terrace *et al*. (1979) were also highly critical of the other chimpanzee language studies, arguing that these too simply represented stimulus-response learning rather than

a fluent use of language. We will be looking at these criticisms in more detail later on.

Terrace (1979) regarded grammatical structure as essential to the definition of language. If there were no such structure, he argued, then Nim could not be considered to be using language. Over an eighteen-month period, Nim signed over 19,000 multi-word utterances, of over 5000 different kinds. But when Terrace conducted an analysis on the data, there was little sign that these utterances were structured according to any set of rules, at least to the criteria which Terrace was setting.

Terrace also argued that further evidence that Nim had not mastered the rules of grammar was provided by his **mean length of utterance (mlu)**. Nim remained consistently at an average 1.5 word mlu – in other words, his utterances were usually just one or two words at a time, and his mlu did not increase as he learned more. Terrace argued that if Nim had really grasped the rules of grammar this would have produced increasingly long sentences. Where Nim did produce longer sentences, they tended to involve repetition, such as 'give banana me banana eat'. This was completely unlike that of a young human child's multi-word sentences, and therefore, according to Terrace, could not be considered to be language, in any formal sense.

There is some doubt, though, as to how far Terrace's own beliefs were influencing the way he interpreted the data. For example, Nim always placed 'more' in the first position in two word sentences. But Terrace disregarded this as an example of understanding the words concerned, and argued that the chimpanzee did not know any other words to express recurrence, so it could have been just a habit rather than an understanding of the relationship. Terrace argued that where Nim did seem to have hit on grammatical structures, this could have come about simply by copying the trainer, which Terrace regarded as 'cheating'. One wonders, at times, how a small human child's performance would have stood up under such rigorous scrutiny!

Sarah

A different approach to teaching chimpanzees language was taken by Premack and Premack (1972). They taught a chimpanzee named Sarah to communicate using plastic symbols which stuck to a magnetic board. The symbols represented concepts such as 'like', 'banana', 'eat', and so on. In the first phase of the research, Sarah would be rewarded for using the appropriate symbol. Although the reward was sometimes physical, like a piece of fruit, most of the time a verbal reinforcement was enough – such as being told 'That's very good, Sarah' by her trainer. When she had learned to associate symbols with concepts, Sarah then had to learn to put them together in two- and later three-word sentences. Eventually, her vocabulary was extended to include not just nouns, but also verbs, adjectives, general class items (like 'colour of') and interrogatives.

As she mastered the system, Sarah showed herself to be capable of some complex problem-solving, including the use of conditional relationships like 'If … then' and comparisons between different objects, such as identifying whether two items were the 'same' or 'different'. She also learned to respond accurately to a symbol which meant 'Give the name of', which implied that she was able to think abstractly about the communication system that she was using. In a double-blind test with a trainer who did not know what the signals meant (so that she could not pick up social cues), Sarah still performed well above average, although not as well as she did with her own familiar trainers (Premack, 1983).

There were limitations on how she used this system, though. One of them was that she did not seem to grasp the idea of word order, or syntax, which can be very important in using human language, or at least English. Word order is unimportant in some human languages, like Finnish, though, so this may not be a valid criticism. Perhaps more important is the criticism that Sarah never used the system spontaneously, to start up a conversation, although she would respond readily enough when asked something by her trainer. The lack of spontaneous use does seem to imply that there was a difference between the way that Sarah used the symbols and the way that a human being uses language.

Lana

Rumbaugh, in 1977, reported on a chimpanzee language experiment at the Yerkes Primate Center in Atlanta. Lana was taught to use a large computer keyboard, which showed symbols, referred to as lexigrams, on a screen. As with Sarah, the lexigrams were linked with different concepts. In Lana's case, though, there was a far wider range of symbols to choose from. In order to achieve a goal, Lana did not just have to use the correct symbols. She also had to express her sentences following the correct word order, according to a set of grammatical rules known as 'Yerkish'. She was rewarded for producing accurate requests by being provided with films, pictures, music, food and liquids.

Rumbaugh reported that, using this system, Lana had been able to learn semantic differences brought about by word order alone – such as the difference between 'Tim give Lana apple', and 'Lana give Tim apple'. On a number of occasions, she corrected herself as she 'wrote'. She also combined words to create names for items that she did not know. For example, when she first saw a ring, she labelled it a 'finger-bracelet'.

However, there was some doubt as to whether Lana had actually learned language, or simply learned to associate a stimulus with a response. Savage-Rumbaugh et al. (1983) showed how Lana's training had allowed for the possibility of either kind of learning, and she did not seem to do very well on specifically conceptual tests. During her training, for example, she would be shown a piece of fruit and asked to name it. If she replied with the name of the fruit she would be given a free choice of rewards, including the fruit itself if she wanted it. This method of training could be interpreted either way. When she named the fruit correctly, it might mean that she had learned its name. Alternatively, it might simply mean that she had learned to produce that response when she saw that stimulus.

The Yerkes chimps

As a result of the work with Lana, and the uncertainties which the training method had produced, Savage-Rumbaugh et al. (1978) went on to train two other chimpanzees, Austin and Sherman. Although they were trained in a similar way to Lana, there were some key differences between them in the training procedure. One was that if they were shown a piece of fruit and named it accurately, their only reward would be the fruit, rather than a free choice of reward.

The new approach to training seemed to be more successful than Lana's had been. In 1980, Savage-Rumbaugh et al. reported a complex test of conceptualisation which the chimpanzees were given. The first stage involved sorting out a mixed collection of foods and tools on to two trays, according to these two categories. Then the chimpanzees were asked to identify object categories: the trainer would hold up an object and the chimpanzee had to respond by pressing the category key which fitted it. In the third stage, the chimpanzees would be required to categorise photographs of the objects, rather than the objects themselves, and in the fourth stage, they would be required to classify the lexigram corresponding to the objects.

This test, therefore, allowed the researchers not simply to assess whether the chimpanzees had a conceptual grasp of categories (in itself an important question), but also the level of abstraction at which they could operate and whether they really did see the symbols of 'Yerkish' as corresponding to objects. Lana had been unable to get beyond the first stage, but Austin and Sherman responded with a high level of accuracy throughout the whole of this test.

In another test, the two chimpanzees were required to communicate about objects which were not physically present. The chimpanzee was first allowed to examine a table of different food items. Then he had to go round a partition to a keyboard and request one of the items. The food was out of sight at the time that the request was made. Once the chimpanzee had been given permission from the trainer, he then went back to the table to collect the item which had been named and took it to the trainer for sharing. Austin and Sherman were also able to undertake this task successfully.

Studies with other species

It is not just chimpanzees who have been trained using this type of method. Researchers have used a number of other species, in order to see if it is possible to train animals to use language. Some of these have been only very limited in their achievements, but others have been more impressive.

Orang-utans
Laidler (1980) attempted to teach Cody, a young orang-utan, to vocalise. During eight months of training, Cody learned only four words, but he was able to use these to discriminate between food and drink, and being brushed or being picked up. Moreover, in the comparable chimpanzee experiment Vicki took six years to learn an

equivalent four words. Laidler felt confident that, had the research continued, Cody would have been able to learn a more extensive vocabulary, but from the relatively short nature of the study, it is not possible to judge whether this was really the case or not.

Gorillas
Patterson (1978) reported a study in which a young gorilla, Koko, was trained in Ameslan. After a year or so, another young gorilla, Michael, was added to the project. Patterson found that both apes appeared to learn to use signs relatively easily, and communicated readily using them. During the seven-year training period, for instance, Koko learned some 400 signs. They would initiate 'conversations' with one another and with Patterson, as well as responding to direct requests and commands. Patterson reported that Koko had developed twenty of her own sign combinations for words that she did not know.

The gorillas also appeared to use the signs which they had been taught to communicate with one another. Patterson reported one occasion in which the younger gorilla, Michael, wished to enter the caravan to join Patterson and Koko. Patterson refused to allow Michael in until he made the correct sign to enter. Through the window, Koko made the sign to Michael, who copied it and was allowed in. On Michael's entering the caravan, Koko signed 'Good sign, Michael'.

There are a number of other instances which implied that the gorillas were learning to use sign language rather than simply producing responses to stimuli learned through conditioning. One of them was the generalisation of words: Patterson reported that, like Washoe, Koko had developed 'swear words'. She would use the words 'dirty' and 'toilet' when she was displeased by someone. Even though she was aware of the literal meaning of these signs and would use them appropriately in other contexts, she also used them as terms of offence.

Another indicator that Koko might have developed some real language ability was the development of prevarication (in this context, another word for lying, or at least saying things which are not meant to be interpreted literally). Patterson reported a number of instances in which Koko used language inappropriately, as part of a game. For example, when asked to 'Tell me something you think is funny', Koko signed 'That red', pointing to a green toy frog.

Dolphins

In 1965, Lilly reported on a series of studies with dolphins which indicated that they could learn to mimic human speech. Lilly began by rewarding the dolphin for matching its own sounds to the number of nonsense syllables uttered by a trainer. Gradually, this was refined until the dolphin matched each sound syllable by syllable. The dolphins learned to do this very quickly, needing far less training and reinforcement than most other animals would have done. After this training, Lilly found that the dolphins were able to count up to ten, and say some simple English words. But mimicry is not the same as linguistic competence, and although a subsequent project is investigating the possibilities of developing a mutual speech system between dolphins and human beings, so far little progress seems to have been reported.

Herman, Richards and Wolz (1984) trained two dolphins to respond to a special language, in which the dolphins showed their comprehension by responding appropriately to requests – they were not expected to produce language themselves. The 'language' included syntactical elements, such as rules for word order (for example, 'object always comes before action'), as well as a wide vocabulary. The two dolphins involved in the project were each trained using a different form of the language. In the version taught to the dolphin Akeakamai, 'words' were signalled by special postures or actions adopted by somebody standing at the side of the pool. The other dolphin, Phoenix, learned a version in which the signals were short noises generated by a computer.

The two dolphins learned quickly, and became able to respond appropriately to a large number of words and phrases (see Table 24.2). In one test, Akeakamai was given 193 completely new sentences and responded accurately to all of them. During the test, all the objects with which she was familiar were in the pool with her, so it was not possible for the dolphin to be unconsciously 'cued' by the equipment provided.

It also seemed as though the dolphins learned to use a type of grammar, in the sense that when they were suddenly provided with four-word sentences, where previously they had only had experience with two- and three-word ones, they would respond appropriately. If they had not been grammatically competent to some degree, they would have found this test more difficult, since word order was very important in understanding the meaning of the sentence. The dolphins also showed that they could find objects that were not immediately present, either because they were hidden and the dolphin had to swim and fetch them (spatial displacement) or because they had not yet been placed in the water (temporal displacement). They also learned to signal, by pressing a paddle, when an object that was required to complete a task was missing.

Herman *et al.* considered their study to show that dolphins were able to comprehend some form of language, in that their behaviour showed comprehension at the level of syntax rather than simply in terms of stimulus-response. The problem, though, is that the dolphins were not producing language themselves, and this may be an important requirement if true language use is to be accepted. Box 24.1 discusses some of the other issues which might be involved in communicating with dolphins and whales.

Table 24.2 Words and phrases learned by the dolphin Akeakamai

Agent
Akeakamai

Objects

window	net	basket
person	speaker	ball
pipe	frisbee	water
hoop	fish	surfboard
phoenix		

Actions

touch with tail	touch with pectoral fin
go through	go over
go under	throw named object
squirt water from mouth at another object	put one object in or on
grasp with mouth	take one object to another

Other words

yes	no	erase	left	right

Source: Adapted from Herman et al., 1984

Box 24.1 Comprehending dolphins and whales

Ever since Lilly's pioneering studies in the early 1960s (e.g. Lilly, 1965), researchers have been seeking to find ways of communicating with dolphins. There are obvious technical problems with such an endeavour, but there may also be problems which are more than just technical. It is open to question how far such a communication would be possible in the first place. Sceptics say that human beings have enough trouble communicating with one another – compare, for instance, the almost total lack of comprehension of each other's lifestyles shown by white north Americans and Native Australians. There are differences in each group's attitude towards their own experience which are so fundamental that some see the two as having almost no points of contact: differences which span beliefs about self and identity, the nature of human interaction with the natural world, the existence or otherwise of non-material dimensions of being, and so on. Yet human beings have at least the advantage that they are operating within the same physiological constraints.

How much more different, then, will the experience of the dolphin or whale be, with such very different physical capacities and knowledge on which to build? Researchers are in little doubt that these animals are highly intelligent, and this is supported by their physiological brain development, as well as the readiness with which they adapt to the demands placed on them by experimenters. But what is the nature of that intelligence? And is it one which we could possibly understand?

Human beings develop their understanding of the world through acting on their environments. They **manipulate** things, and learn from the consequences of that manipulation. They are well equipped, physiologically, to do this, having mobile hands with opposable thumbs, which can remain free while the human being is walking around. They are therefore highly sensitised to this form of learning: developmental psychologists have found that infants respond most strongly to social transactions, and to environmental changes which are contingent on the infant's

activity. To us, manipulating and changing our world is fundamental.

A dolphin, however, is equipped very differently. The nature of its interaction with its world is probably no less complex, but it is fundamentally **experiential** rather than manipulative. The dolphin is excellently equipped to swim, to hunt, and to play; and observations of the way that dolphins explore their environments indicate that they put their intelligence to good use. But this is a very different way of interacting with the environment than that adopted in Western human society. Studies of dolphin intelligence which begin, for example, by seeing how well dolphins can learn to manipulate objects or symbols may simply be starting off on the wrong track – a bit like a society of intelligent bees trying to assess human intelligence by seeing how good we are at interpreting polarised light in finding food sources or building wax combs.

Some researchers, however, feel that there is at least a starting point. Bateson (1973) argued that the communication of social animals, and in particular dolphins and whales, is most likely to be about **relationships**, than anything else. An attempt to establish grounds for communication using that as a starting point would, Bateson felt, be much more likely to be productive than superficial approaches based entirely on Western manipulative frameworks.

Another optimistic sign, too, may be that the dolphins themselves do seem to be trying to help. New dolphins in research centres often spend several days repeating a relatively simple 'signature whistle' to the human beings with whom they are interacting, although they use far more complex signals when they are communicating with other dolphins (Richards, 1986). The action is reminiscent of the ways that human explorers used to try to establish communication with unfamiliar peoples by repeating simple phrases over and over again, beginning by giving their own names. Maybe an attempt to communicate with dolphins should begin from a different starting point, that of allowing the dolphin to teach us its language, in its own way.

But is it really language?

So how successful were these experiments? Did the chimpanzees, gorillas and dolphins really learn to use language? Or did they just achieve a complex form of stimulus-response learning? It is a contentious issue, for a number of reasons. One is that, nowadays, language is regarded as the main discriminator between human beings and animals. The reason for the emphasis on language has partly come about because of the failure of earlier definitions, as animals have been discovered to use and make tools, and so on. So the claim that an animal can be taught to use language hits on a raw nerve for those who like to see people as qualitatively different from animals. Others are sceptical about whether the researchers are simply managing to convince themselves, without rigorous evidence.

One of the main critics of the idea that apes can learn to use language was Noam Chomsky (1972), who, as we saw in Chapter 4, regarded language in human beings as dependent on innate, biological structures, which were not possessed by animals. Chomsky regarded language as unique to human beings, and impossible for animals to achieve. The criticisms of the chimpanzee Ameslan studies produced by Terrace *et al.* (1979) followed Chomsky's theoretical approach, largely centring on the importance of syntax – and particularly word order – in a true language.

Methodological disputes

Terrace *et al.* made a number of methodological criticisms too, some of which were highly contentious. For example, Terrace claimed that, viewing the films of Washoe's 'double-blind' test, it was possible to see the Gardners engaging in unconscious **cueing**. He also claimed that Washoe did not sign spontaneously, and that the lack of linguistic competence shown by Nim Chimpsky demonstrated that chimpanzees were not, in fact, capable of language. Not everybody, however, agrees with Terrace. Several other researchers, notably Lieberman (1984), disputed these claims, arguing that the films did *not* show signs of unconscious cueing, and that there was considerable later evidence for spontaneous signing. In addition, Lieberman pointed out that Nim Chimpsky, unlike the other signing chimpanzees, had been brought up by a succession of trainers, which meant that he had continually been form-ing and breaking close personal attachments. It is possible that this disturbance could have resulted in limited learning on the chimpanzee's part.

Terrace's criticisms did not apply to Patterson's work with gorillas or to the Yerkes chimpanzees, and the evidence from these studies appears to counteract many of the criticisms which Terrace put forward. Many supporters of 'chimpanzee language' argue that, since the first Ameslan experiments, a complicated game of 'moving the goalposts' has been going on. Initially, critics argued that chimpanzees were incapable of developing more than a very limited vocabulary, as had been achieved with the vocalisation experiments. But, as we saw, when researchers began to use visual languages which were more suited to the animals' own abilities, they began to acquire quite extensive vocabularies.

When this happened, the goalposts were moved, and the critics then argued that it could not be language because the chimpanzees did not use it generatively – they did not produce novel utterances. But when both chimpanzees and gorillas began to combine words to produce such novel utterances, the critics changed their criteria yet again, arguing that if it did not fit syntactical criteria like word order, then it could not be regarded as truly language. Yet, as we have seen, some human languages, notably Finnish, do not involve word order. The stringent criteria which are now applied to ape language do not match up to all human languages either.

The real problem, of course, is that this is not simply an academic discussion. The question is all about whether there is a qualitative difference between animals and human beings, or whether any differences are simply quantitative. And, as such, it is a debate which is unlikely ever to be resolved. Some people have always looked for ways to draw lines between human beings and animals, while others have looked for the similarities between them. It is unlikely that the two sides will ever come to an agreement.

Hockett's design features of language

So, if we are to evaluate this topic at all, we need to be clear about what we consider language to be. And in order to do that it makes sense to utilise criteria for language use which were established before this debate became so heated. In 1959, Hockett produced a series of criteria for spoken language, which became known as

Hockett's design features. These criteria are listed in Table 24.3. The first two, obviously, do not apply to language as it has been taught to animals, but then, they do not apply to human sign languages either. But all the languages taught to apes fit the third and fourth criteria, of rapid fading and total feedback. The languages taught to apes are all interchangeable as well, though this does not apply to Herman's dolphin studies.

The sixth criterion was whether the language was specialised, and this applied to both ape and dolphin studies. With regard to the seventh criterion, of semanticity, the evidence does suggest quite strongly that both apes and dolphins could understand the meanings of the words they were using. Gardner and Gardner (1969) demonstrated Washoe's understanding, using double blind tests, which were much more rigorous than those Terrace criticised, and these tests showed that Washoe signed correctly in 72% of the trials. When she did make mistakes, these were not random, but connected in some way, like signing 'cat' in response to a picture of a dog. The dolphins, too, seemed to have a good grasp of the meanings of the words, and rigorous tests prevented them from being unconsciously 'cued'.

Not all chimpanzees established semanticity beyond doubt. Savage-Rumbaugh *et al.* (1983) argued that Lana might simply have learned by stimulus-response association; and Sarah, too, might only have done so. But that was much less likely for Austin and Sherman. Terrace (1979) asserted that the other Ameslan chimpanzees were also only demonstrating stimulus-response learning, but, as we have seen, many researchers in the field disagreed profoundly with his conclusions.

The eighth criterion, arbitrariness, applied to all of the languages which were used in the animal studies. There was also some evidence of the ninth, traditional transmission, since video films of the Oklahoma group of chimpanzees taken when

Table 24.3 Hockett's design features for human language

1	*Vocal / auditory*	It is carried by sound, made vocally by one person and received auditorily by another.
2	*Broadcast / directional*	The sound is broadcast, but the receiver can tell the direction that it is coming from
3	*Rapid fading*	The signal fades quickly.
4	*Total feedback*	The speaker can hear what she is saying.
5	*Interchangeability*	The same person can both send and receive information
6	*Specialisation*	Speech functioning is purely for communication, and not a by-product of some other behaviour.
7	*Semanticity*	Language has meaning.
8	*Arbitrariness*	Language does not resemble its meaning.
9	*Traditional transmission*	Language can be passed on from one generation to the next.
10	*Learnability*	New forms of language can be learned.
11	*Discreteness*	Language is organised into discrete, separate units, and information is coded by the way in which these are combined.
12	*Duality of patterning*	Language patterns operate on more than one level: at the level of the organisation of phonemes into words, and at the level of the organisation of words into sentences.
13	*Displacement*	Language enables a speaker to refer to things which are not immediately present in space and time.
14	*Openness/productivity*	Language can be used to generate novel utterances, which have new meanings.
15	*Prevarication*	Language allows the speaker to talk about things which have not happened, or which are impossible. In short, to lie.
16	*Reflexiveness*	Language can be used to talk about itself, as is happening here.

Source: Adapted from Hockett, 1959

they were alone showed them signing to one another, and also responding to each other's messages (Fouts, 1972). As we have seen, too, Washoe herself taught at least one young chimpanzee to sign.

Learnability

The criterion of learnability has not really be investigated explicitly. But there are certainly hints that the animals can explore new combinations in the elements of their languages. Herman, Richards and Wolz (1984) presented 193 completely new sentences to the dolphin Akeakamai. She dealt with each one accurately. Since the sentences included word order as well, the outcome implied that she had managed to understand and learn some new uses of language. Some of the chimpanzees showed flexibility in their language, too: Fouts (1972) described how Lucy, a chimpanzee in the Oklahoma colony, would call a watermelon a 'fruit-drink' or 'candy-drink', even though she knew the proper name for the fruit.

Discreteness

The languages taught to these animals in these studies have all consisted of discrete, separate units, and almost all of the animals showed that they could combine signs to create meanings: Washoe formed her first two-word sentences at twenty months old, and even Sarah and Lana were able to create simple two- and three-word sentences composed of separate units. Although this is nothing like the competence of a human infant, we do need to bear in mind that language is a species-specific behaviour for humans, not for apes or dolphins.

Duality of patterning

The criterion of duality of patterning is all about grammar. Chomsky (1959) argued that human beings have an innate sense of grammar, which makes human language special and unique. Chomsky argued that this occurred through word-order. Terrace, following Chomsky's model, asserted that the chimpanzees could not be using real language because they did not use word order. Despite Nim Chimpsky's several thousand 'utterances', Terrace argued, there was no indication of any awareness of word order, and there was no such evidence in any of the other studies either. But other researchers disagreed. Rumbaugh (1977) showed that Lana understood the differ-

ence between 'Tim give Lana apple', and 'Lana give Tim apple', and that she would sometimes correct her word order as she typed in her statements or responses. And the dolphins trained by Herman, Richards and Wolz (1984) caught onto the idea of syntax quite quickly.

Displacement

Savage-Rumbaugh et al. (1983) showed that Austin and Sherman had demonstrated displacement by communicating about objects which were not actually there while they were doing so. The chimpanzees were shown a table covered with different food items, but they had to go out of sight of the table if they wanted to ask for any of the items. Fouts (1972) conducted some studies which involved taking one chimpanzee away from the group, showing it something hidden, and then putting it back with the others. Then another chimpanzee would be allowed out, to see if it found the hidden food. It generally did, and video recordings indicated that the chimpanzees were using signs to communicate where the food was hidden. Studies with the dolphins showed that they, too, could understand references to things which were not present at the time.

Openness/productivity

Many of the animals which were taught human languages showed openness or productivity in their use of them. The first time Lana saw a ring, she called it a 'finger-bracelet'. Washoe called a swan a 'water-bird', and Lucy described a radish as a 'hurt-cry fruit'. Sometimes, too, they initiated conversations, and produced novel utterances. When Washoe saw a plane flying overhead, she turned to her trainer and signed 'you, me ride plane'.

Prevarication and reflexiveness

Patterson (1979) reported that the gorillas Koko, and to a lesser extent Michael, had shown prevarication. They seemed to have a sense of humour, and sometimes 'teased' Patterson by deliberately using the signs inappropriately. It was obvious that their language mis-use was deliberate, and not accidental. For example, as we saw earlier, Koko reponded to the question 'tell me something you think is funny', by pointing to a green toy frog, and signing 'that red'. Also, both Koko and Washoe began to use the sign 'dirty' as a kind of swear-word, when they were indicating displeasure. They could use the word properly in its normal context, but seemed to have connected it with disgust, and also used it that way. Hockett's final criterion, of reflexiveness, was also revealed in some of these studies, notably the occasion when the gorilla Michael was shut out of the caravan. Patterson reports that Koko then signed 'good sign, Michael' – using language to talk about language.

We can see, then, that the balance of evidence does indicate that animals can show a remarkable degree of linguistic skill, even if it is not anything like as complex as human language ability. Seuren (1976) argued that the whole 'is it or is not it?' debate over whether these animals are really using language is a futile one, because the study of linguistics is based on how human beings use language, and therefore the discipline is simply not equipped to evaluate language as used by animals. Also, much of the debate is based on an assumption of the Chomskyan model of innate structural linguistic decoding abilities, and ignores the more recent work on the social contexts of human language acquisition which we looked at in Chapter 4.

Whether or not one considers these animals to be using 'language', according to some abstract linguistic definition, it is certainly clear that they are communicating, and using symbols to do so. Moreover, they seem to be communicating with a level of sophistication that would have been inconceivable 40 years ago. Perhaps a more fruitful direction of research might be to explore the possibilities which such communication opens up, rather than becoming bogged down in debates over linguistic structure.

Key terms

Ameslan American sign language for the deaf.

double-blind control A form of experimental control which aims to avoid self-fulfilling prophecies by ensuring that neither the research participants nor the experimenter who carries out the study are aware of the experimental hypothesis.

pheromones Chemicals released into the air which, when received by another animal, exert a direct influence on its hormonal system and sometimes its behaviour.

primer pheromones Pheromones which trigger off a particular form of behaviour, such as mating behaviour.

pulsed sounds Sounds which occur as regular beats on the same frequency.

releaser pheromones Pheromones which trigger off certain forms of behaviour in animals.

Summary

1 Animal communication can take place using a number of sensory modes, including the visual, olfactory, tactile and auditory modes. Olfactory communication can include the use of pheromones. Bright argued that sound is the most flexible form of animal communication.

2 Honey-bees communicate the location of food sources by dancing when they return to the hive. Features of the dance inform other bees about the direction and distance of the food source.

3 Male frog calls have to strike a balance between attracting females and not informing predators as to their location. Bats can use echolocation as a form of communication as well as a hunting tool.

4 Bird-song can serve both territorial and courtship functions. It is often partly learned and partly inherited. Marler identified a number of parallels between bird-song and speech, which may suggest an evolutionary link.

5 Humpback whales sing a distinctive and complicated song, which changes gradually during the course of the year and may be associated with courtship. Dolphins use a variety of sounds, which appear to aid social co-ordination as well as communicating specific messages.

6 Vervet monkeys and ground squirrels use different sounds to identify specific types of predator. Marler suggested that these reflected inbuilt natural categories, which might provide evolutionary links to human cognition and language use. Chimpanzees use both sounds and visual signals to communicate in the wild.

7 There have been some attempts to teach chimpanzees, gorillas and dolphins human languages. The methods used involve teaching sign language or special artificial languages. Some of the animals involved have invented new words and appear to see language as a communicative tool.

8 There is debate about how far attempts to teach animals human languages have been successful. The debate appears to be more concerned with the uniqueness of the human being than about the capacity of the animals concerned.

Self-assessment questions

1 Describe different types of animal sensory reception.

2 What do we know about honey-bee communication?

3 Outline the main features of cetacean communication.

Practice essay questions

1 Discuss the nature and functions of birdsong. How similar is birdsong to human language?

2 Do animals have 'words'? Evaluate this question, drawing on forms of animal communication which have not been specifically taught by human beings.

3 Is it possible to teach non-human animals to use language?

Test your knowledge of this chapter with our online quizzes and games at: http://www.psych.co.uk

Explore animal communication further at:

Animal communication

http://galliform.bhs.mq.edu.au – Online details of experiments into animal communication and behaviour.
http://gears.tucson.ars.ag.gov/ic/dance/dance.html – Detailed information on one type of communication; the bee waggle dance.

Language

http://www.math.uwaterloo.ca/~dmswitze/apelang.html – In depth tutorial and bibliography on the language of apes and how much we should teach them.

Methods and ethics in psychology

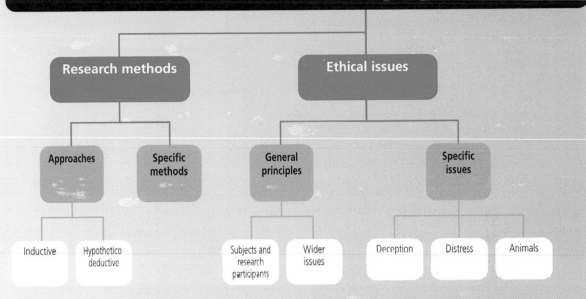

Research methods

Ethical issues

Approaches

Specific methods

General principles

Specific issues

Inductive

Hypothetico-deductive

Subjects and research participants

Wider issues

Deception

Distress

Animals

Learning objectives

25.1. Criteria for psychological evidence
a define terms relating to criteria for evidence
b identify issues of validity, reliability and generalisability
c apply the concept of levels of explanation to psychological research

25.2. Research methods
a define terms relating to methods of research
b describe the major research methods
c identify examples of methods of study in psychological research

25.3. Qualitative analysis
a list different types of interviews
b describe different techniques of qualitative analysis
c identify examples of qualitative methods in psychological research

25.4. Ethical issues
a identify factors leading to concern about ethical issues
b list ethical guidelines for psychologists
c apply criteria for ethical decisions to psychological research

25.5. Deception
a give examples of deception in psychological research
b list criteria for evaluating research incorporating deception
c outline the implications of non-deceptive research for psychologists

25.6. Avoiding personal distress
a outline relevant ethical criteria for psychological research
b describe specific examples of ethically significant past research
c evaluate psychological research in terms of ethical principles

25.7. Animal studies
a identify different types of research into animal behaviour
b list ethical guidelines for animal research
c evaluate past research in terms of ethical issues

25.8. Social responsibilites
a describe the principals of social responsibility of science
b outline applications of cultural awareness in psychological research
c evaluate past psychological work in term sof social responsibility of science

In this book, we have looked at many different aspects of psychology. Psychology, as you have seen, spans a wide range of human experience, and involves awareness of many different levels of explanation. We can look for influences on how human beings act at many levels, some of which are listed in Table 25.1. None of these levels can be taken alone, as sufficient explanation for why people are as they are, but if we take them all together, they can tell us quite a lot.

Psychology is not the only way of explaining human behaviour, of course. Art, literature, history, philosophy and many other areas of human activity are also engaged in exploring and explaining what it is to be human. They go about it in very different ways. What makes psychology special is its claim to be the scientific study of human behaviour and experience. As psychologists, we argue that it is the systematic collection of reliable evidence, and the piecing together of that evidence into theories and explanations, which makes psychology different from those other ways of exploring human nature. But this still is not really an adequate definition, because psychology is not the only discipline which pieces together evidence to build theories – history too does the same thing. The real distinction between psychology and other fields of knowledge about human beings lies in the nature of the evidence which we collect, and the way that we go about collecting it.

Table 25.1 Levels of explanation in psychology

Level	Examples
socio-cultural	Cross-cultural and multi-cultural perspectives, social responsibility of science, ethical questions.
social	Social conformity, obedience, bystander intervention, social roles.
socio-cognitive	Social identifications, social representations, attributions, attitudes, scripts.
interpersonal	Non-verbal communication, language, attraction, relationships.
personal	Personal constructs, motivation, personality, emotion, intelligence.
cognitive	Perception, memory, thinking, representation.
habitual	Classical and operant conditioning, stimulus-response behaviour.
biological	Genetic influences on learning and development, innate tendencies towards sociability and group cohesion.
physiological	Arousal, physiological aspects of emotional experience, sleep, dreaming, physiological aspects of consciousness.

Validity, reliability and generalisability

Traditionally, psychologists have attempted to collect evidence about human beings which fits three criteria. First, it needs to fit the criterion of **reliability**. That is to say, we need to be reasonably sure that, given the same situation, the same behaviour or outcome would happen. Second, it needs to fit the criterion of **validity**. This means that we need to be reasonably sure that what we are measuring or looking at really is what we intended to look at, and think we are looking at. And third, it needs to fit the criterion of **generalisability**. That is, we are interested in finding out about human beings in general. Although this may sometimes mean just investigating one distinctive person, we do so because it might tell us something about other human beings as well.

Sometimes, of course, these criteria can contradict one another. In recent years, for example, many psychologists have come to think that the belief that all psychological data must always be reliable went rather too far at one point. As a result, it led to an emphasis on tightly controlled laboratory-style experiments, which may have been reliable, but were not actually valid representations of what human beings do. Reliability was achieved at the expense of validity. More recent forms of research sometimes concentrate on validity, and recognise that by doing so they may sometimes sacrifice reliability. Overall, though, we need both types of research, and we need to strike a balance between these different methods of finding out about human beings. For this reason, and as you will have seen throughout this book, psychologists employ a wide variety of methods in studying human behaviour. In this chapter, we will look briefly at some of those methods, and then go on to look at some of the ethical and social implications of psychological methodology.

Research methods in psychology

There are a number of different methods of study – ways of finding out about people – which have been used in psychology. In this section, we will look first at the more traditional methods of investigation, beginning with the experimental method as it has been used with people (we will be looking at animal studies later in this chapter). Then we will go on to look at observational studies, case studies, and at survey and questionnaire studies. From there, we will go on to look at some of the methods of study which have become more popular in recent years, even though some of them have been around for a long time. These will include meta-analysis, interview studies including studies of accounts and discourse, action research and other types of qualitative analysis.

Inductive and hypothetico-deductive research

Whatever type of research is conducted, it needs to be a scientific investigation, which is appropriately rigorous. The researcher will use one of two kinds of approach to scientific enquiry: either a hypothetico-deductive approach, or an inductive approach. The **hypothetico-deductive** approach begins with a theory which the psychologist then investigates, by generating hypotheses and testing them. The **inductive** approach involves the psychologists looking at data which has been collected, and using that data to draw out general principles or ideas.

Both types of approach are used widely in science as a whole: a chemist investigating a new compound, for example, might proceed using a hypothetico-deductive approach; while a palaeontologist looking at fossil strata would be likely to adopt an inductive approach. Psychology itself uses both of these approaches. The introspectionists tended to use inductive methods a great deal, and so do many modern researchers such as clinical neuropsychologists. But the behaviourists believed that the inductive approach was unscientific, despite its use in 'hard' science, and so the middle of the twentieth century saw an emphasis on experimental psychology, which utilised the hypothetico-deductive approach.

The hypothetico-deductive approach, as has been said, begins with a theory. That theory will be based on previous observations – either informal ones, drawn from daily experience, or, more likely, theories derived from previous research by other psychologists. The theory is used to generate predictions – statements about what is likely to happen if the theory holds true. These predictions are called **hypotheses.** The researcher then sets up a study which will allow the hypotheses to be tested out, to see if their predictions are confirmed. The outcome of the research provides data which will either support the overall prediction, or disconfirm it. That, in turn, is taken as evidence which either supports the theory, or suggests that some other theory is required to explain the observations (Figure 25.1).

The inductive approach begins with the collection of data, rather than with a theory, and uses that data to identify regularities or **themes,** or to suggest theories (Figure 25.2 overleaf). Sometimes,

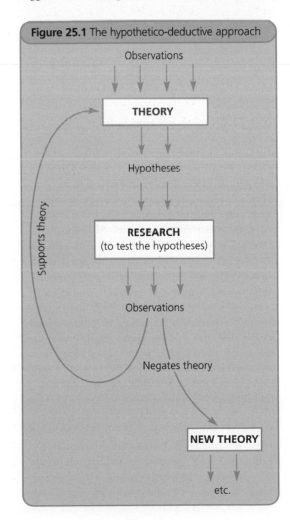

Figure 25.1 The hypothetico-deductive approach

Observations

THEORY

Hypotheses

RESEARCH
(to test the hypotheses)

Observations

Supports theory

Negates theory

NEW THEORY

etc.

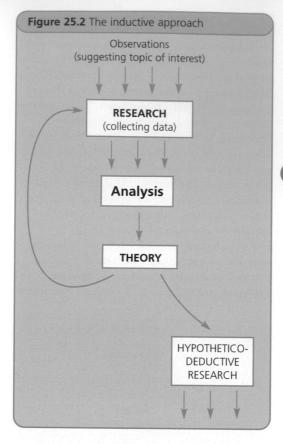

Figure 25.2 The inductive approach

Observations
(suggesting topic of interest)

RESEARCH
(collecting data)

Analysis

THEORY

HYPOTHETICO-
DEDUCTIVE
RESEARCH

an initial mapping out of the area using inductive techniques, and then a rigorous investigation using experimental methods. The study of imprinting, which we looked at in Chapter 22, is a good example of that. Psychologists have always used inductive approaches, even though these have often been under-recognised in methods texts; but modern psychology is much clearer about how the different types of science can fit together.

Experiments

Strictly speaking, an experiment is a method of investigation in which the researcher manipulates the situation in order to bring about a change in the research participant's behaviour. Many psychological experiments, particularly in the physiological and cognitive areas, have involved people responding to such experimental manipulations, under very tightly controlled conditions. For example, many of the studies of selective and sustained attention (Chapter 2) involve asking the research participant to perform a task, and then varying one single aspect of that task – the meaning of a word, which ear it was presented to, the amount of background noise, and so on.

Physiological influences on behaviour have also been studied using the experimental method. Ax's study of the difference between fear and anger, which we looked at in Chapter 13, was a clear example of this: Ax's research participants all experienced the same conditions, except for those aspects designed to induce either fear or anger. The result was a difference in their physiological state, which appeared to have been directly caused by which experimental condition they had experienced. It was important, though, that all the other conditions should be the same, because otherwise they could create differences which did not come from the conditions. Making sure that only the appropriate factors can influence the result is known as **experimental control.** In a formal experiment, we try to control all other possible influences, so that we can be sure that the result really is caused by the conditions we are looking at. But, as we can see from Box 25.1, we can never be completely certain.

The difference between the conditions of the experiment is referred to as the **independent variable** – it is the thing which varies as a result of the researcher's manipulation. In the Smith and Lloyd study on how people act with babies, which

this data collection is reasonably straightforward, such as Penfield's investigations of the various areas of the cerebral cortex, in which it was a matter of stimulating various areas and seeing what outcome they produced. On other occasions, the observations are collected in more complex ways – for example, social psychologists may use interview data or reports to learn about human experiences; or ethologists may collect observations of animal behaviour. Once it has been collected, the data is rigorously analysed. Inductive research is often used to explore a completely new area – for example, Smith (1997) used this approach to look at how women's experiences of pregnancy changed during the period of pregnancy as the pregnancy wore on. By collecting data in the form of interviews, repertory grids and so on, the researcher could look at changes in perceived identity, and also develop themes which might be used as the basis of future research.

Inductive and hypothetico-deductive research strategies are complementary, rather than opposing. Each is used for a different type of purpose; and often research into an area will involve both:

Box 25.1 The concept of statistical significance

In formal experiments, we try to control all the various factors which might influence how our research participants behave. But really, any attempt to control everything completely is doomed to failure. No two things in nature are identical, and no two examples of human behaviour are identical either. We change all the time – we have different thoughts, different moods, are affected by the time of day, month and year, and so on. And any of these may affect how we act in an experiment.

One way of trying to overcome this is to use group data – in other words, to conduct nomothetic studies, in which individual idiosyncracies are balanced out, because the scores from lots of people are all combined together. In this type of study, the psychologist selects a sample of research participants, from the population which is being studied – if it is a study of student behaviour, for example, the population would be students, but the sample would be a group of students who seemed to be typical of that population.

Sampling is necessary, for practical purposes, but it does have some disadvantages. One of them is that we cannot be certain whether the sample really is typical of the population as a whole. There is always the possibility of **sampling error** – the idea that we may have chosen a set of people who are actually quite different from most. And since we can never rule out this possibility completely, there is always the chance that the results we get from our study have simply arisen from chance. No matter how convincing an investigation looks, there is always the possibility that our results have come from sampling error, and not from the thing that we are investigating.

This is where the concept of statistical significance comes in. We cannot rule out the possibility of sampling error completely, but we can say that it is very, very unlikely – and we can put a figure on just how unlikely it is. These figures are known as **confidence levels**, or as expressions of statistical significance. Not every form of psychological research, of course, involves statistical significance – the kind of inductive approach used in many case studies and qualitative research can give us valuable information without needing a statement of significance. But most experiments and other forms of quantitative research do.

Psychologists express statistical significance by using a term known as 'p', which stands for 'the probability that our results have simply happened because of sampling error'. The value of p is given in decimal figures, and these are always less than one. For example: if we said $p < .05$ ('p is less than point zero five'), we would be saying that the value of p is the same as the value of .05, which is five-hundredths, or one-twentieth. In other words, we would be saying that the probability of our results coming from a sampling error is less than one in twenty. A significance level of $p < .01$ would mean that the probability was less than one in a hundred, and so on.

Scientists in all disciplines use probabilities in this way, and they perform statistical tests on their data to calculate what the probabilities are. It is particularly important in psychology, because human beings are so much more changeable than lumps of metal or chemicals – although not even those give identical results every time.

Interestingly, the way that scientists have to take account of remote possibilities, like this, has some social implications. It is often the cause of major misunderstandings between journalists and scientists. Because they are aware that there is always the possibility of sampling error, scientists are very reluctant to make definite statements – they prefer to use language such as 'this might be a possible cause', or 'one possibility is...'. But journalists use much more definite forms of language, and they often misunderstand what they are being told, because they think it means that the findings are much more chancy than they really are, or that the scientist is not sure of them. There is no such thing as absolute proof in science, but society in general often interprets the natural cautions of scientific language as implying a lack of knowledge – which is not at all the same thing.

we looked at in Chapter 19, the independent variable was the apparent gender of the infant – whether it was dressed as a boy or as a girl. This then produced a change in the behaviour of the research participants – they acted differently as a result. Since the difference in their behaviour depended on the independent variable, their behaviour (the thing which the researchers observed or measured) is known as the **dependent variable.** In formal terms, an experiment can be described as a controlled situation in which an experimenter manipulates an independent variable in order to bring about a change in the dependent variable.

Sometimes, the fact that an independent variable does not actually produce a change in a dependent variable can tell us as much as when it does. For example, in Orne's 1962 study of hypnosis (Chapter 11), he found that it was impossible to tell the difference between research participants who were 'really' hypnotised and research participants who were just faking. That, in itself, was a useful piece of information. And it also led Orne to investigate the **demand characteristics** of psychological experiments themselves. When he compared the behaviour of people who knew they were taking part in a psychological experiment with the behaviour of people who did not hold such beliefs, he found that the behaviours were completely different. It was this finding, among others, which led many psychologists to question whether conducting rigorously controlled laboratory experiments was really worthwhile.

Some researchers responded to this by attempting to set up more realistic experimental conditions, such as the student computer dance which was set up to study attraction, by Walster *et al.* (1966), or the way that Newcomb studied the effect of proximity on long-term friendships by arranging free college accommodation for people who participated in the study (Chapter 14). The bystander intervention studies conducted by Latané and others (Chapter 16) were also rather more realistic, even though they still used formal experimental approaches. The whole question of **ecological validity** – how true to real life an experiment is – is an important one, as was shown by the study of memory in football supporters conducted by Morris *et al.* (1981), which we looked at in Chapter 3. In a real-life situation, which mattered to them, people remembered far

more information than when the information was learned only for the experiment.

Researchers are sometimes able to capitalise on **natural experiments,** because they happen to be around at the time and can observe their effects carefully. The study of cognitive dissonance in a religious cult conducted by Festinger et al. (Chapter 17) is a good example of this, as are Sperry's studies of people with the corpus callosum severed, or Holmes's studies of the effects of shrapnel injuries to the cerebrum resulting from WWI (Chapter 10).

Many psychologists also conduct experiments in real-life settings. Baddeley's study of postal workers learning to type postcodes, which we looked at in Chapters 3 and 18, is a good example. The training was being undertaken by the Post Office anyway, so the psychologists concerned were able to organise different training sessions and monitor the result. Crutchfield's study of conformity on a management training course is another example, as was the study of Hofling *et al.* on obedience in nurses (Chapter 16), or Yarnell and Lynch's study of the effects of concussion on memory in American football players (Chapter 3).

In the case of children, for the most part, researchers have only recently become aware of how much the child's own understanding may influence the outcome of a formal experiment, and this too is all about ecological validity. As we saw in Chapter 19, the highly standardised methods which Piaget and other researchers used to investigate the child's cognition seem in themselves to have influenced the results which they found. When McGarrigle and others used more realistic situations, which the children were more familiar with, they found that children were more intellectually capable than they had first appeared. And almost all of our examination of developmental psychology shows how more recent investigations have involved making sure that the task which the child was being asked to perform was one which it could relate to.

Observations

Another important method for finding out about human behaviour is by conducting **observational studies.** These too range from the physiological level of explanation to the social and socio-cultural studies in psychology. For example, Dement and Kleitman's identification of the different levels of sleep came about as a result of observations of changes in EEG patterns as people slept (Chapter 11). This is an example of direct observation, but on a physiological level.

As you might imagine, undertaking experimental investigations of child development is fraught with all sorts of ethical problems. What would happen if we caused damage to a child as a result of experimental manipulation? For this reason, the study of major aspects of child development, like play or attachment, has been largely undertaken using observational methods. Stern's video-recordings of parent-child interaction, or Parke and Sawin's observations of mothers and fathers feeding infants (Chapter 20) were direct observations, in which the participants were well aware that they were being observed. This was true too of Bronfenbrenner's observational studies of child-rearing practices in Russia and America (Chapter 18).

In this type of observational study there is always the problem that people may respond differently because they know that they are being observed. For the most part, researchers conducting this kind of study attempt to acclimatise the research participants to their presence. Observers of children at playgroup or nursery schools, such as in Main and George's study of how abused children interact with others (Chapter 19), tend to spend some time sitting quietly watching the children, until, with luck, the children no longer notice their presence. It is open to question, however, how far they really would act in the same way if the researcher were not present.

In some cases, psychologists have adopted **covert observation** of one sort or another – observation in which the research participants did not know they were being observed. The studies of non-verbal communication in conversation conducted by Kendon and others (Chapter 15) were examples of this type of research, as was the study of how lonely people interact with other people, conducted by Jones *et al.* (1982), which we looked at in Chapter 14. The Ainsworth 'strange situation' studies of attachment (Chapter 20) were also of this type.

The problem with covert observation, however, is that it generally has to be conducted in special locations, where there is equipment such as rooms with two-way mirrors which allow researchers to observe without being seen themselves. And taking people into these artificial settings may in itself affect their behaviour. Consequently, other studies, such as the studies of family teasing and quarrelling conducted by Dunn and her colleagues, or the cross-cultural studies of personal space in Middle Eastern and American cultures (Chapter 14), have adopted an ethological approach.

Ethology

Ethology is a special form of observation. It is the study of behaviour in the natural environment, and, as we saw in Chapter 22, it has been particularly important in the study of animal behaviour. But ever since Schaffer and Emerson used the ethological approach in their pioneering study of infant attachment (Chapter 20), it has been recognised as a valuable way of studying human behaviour too. As Cohen (1987) pointed out, children behave differently when they are at home with their families from how they do when they are being observed in a playgroup. Observing them at home with their families is therefore a better way of going about studying some forms of child behaviour, even if it does mean getting the child used to the presence of the observer.

As we have seen, developmental psychologists have frequently used direct observation. Cognitive psychologists, for the most part, have tended to use experimental methods, but recently some have taken to using observational methods as well. In such cases, they have often used the **diary method,** which is a kind of indirect observation of people's behaviour. In this method, research participants are asked to keep a diary, noting down particular events of interest to the psychologist. For example, Reason used this method very successfully when investigating everyday errors and slips, and Bower also used it as the basis for his investigation of mood and memory (Chapter 3).

Participant observation

Another type of observation which has been used from time to time by psychologists is known as **participant observation.** In this approach, the person observes an event by joining in it and taking part in the same way as anyone else. The Benewick and Holton study of the behaviour of peaceful crowds, or Waddington et al.'s study of the public rallies in support of the miners, which we looked at in Chapter 17, are good examples of participant observation. In both cases, the researchers participated as members of the crowds, in order to understand the social processes involved a bit better.

Indirect observations can also be informative at times, such as Segal's study of the personal friendships among police recruits, or Festinger et al.'s study of friendship patterns in a block of university flats for married couples (Chapter 15). In these, the situations already existed, and the psychologists could learn quite a lot from looking at the friendships which had resulted. In many ways, they were quite similar to a natural experiment, and there is a point where it becomes quite difficult to distinguish clearly between the two. Sometimes a form of behaviour can be identified by looking at the physical traces which it has left behind. As we saw in Chapter 11, Horne was able to identify occasions when drivers had fallen asleep at the wheel by the lack of skid marks left from the accidents. This made it possible to go on to collect statistics, which then showed how these accidents correlated with human biological rhythms.

Clinical observations, too, have been a valuable source of data for psychologists. The theories of personality which we looked at in Chapter 7, and the models of psychological therapy in Chapter 9, were developed by clinical psychologists on the basis of the work they did with their patients. Although these were not single, controlled studies, they were the outcome of many years of systematic professional work, which led to the observation of regularities in the types of problems which clients had, and how they could be helped. From these, the psychologists concerned were able to develop theories about the nature of human personality.

Case studies

Another important way of finding out about people is to look at single cases in depth. A case study may be a study of just one person, or of a single group of people, like a family or an organisation. By concentrating attention on the single case study, it is often possible for a psychologist to explore questions in far more detail than would be possible if they were looking at large numbers of people. The case of John Dean's memory, for example (Chapter 3), provided Neisser with a real-life opportunity to explore in detail the difference between what was generally perceived as an accurate memory, and a tape-recording of the same events.

Case studies have been particularly popular in physiological psychology, since it is often from accidents and surgical interventions that we can learn most about how the human brain functions. The case study described by Sacks about the woman who lost proprioception and Melzack's studies of phantom limbs (Chapter 12) have both been useful in giving us insights into how the brain and the body interact. Broca's original case study of language functions being impaired by localised damage opened up a new area of understanding of human language (Chapter 10). And perhaps the most extensively investigated individual in the whole of psychology is H.M., the man who became amnesiac as a result of surgical damage to the hippocampus (Chapter 3). Psychologists have studied the effects of this lesion ever since it happened, and it has told us a great deal about some of the more obscure aspects of remembering.

Case study methods, then, often allow psychologists to investigate naturally occurring events which could never be studied deliberately. For example, the study of severely deprived children such as the Koluchova twins (Chapter 20) or Genie (Chapter 4) involved looking at these individual children and how they recovered, and this allowed psychologists to gain insight into the psychological effects of severe deprivation which could not have been studied in any other ethically acceptable way.

One of the problems of case studies is that we have no way of knowing how typical those individuals may be of other people. But if we are investigating processes, like physiological functioning or the effects of deprivation, this is less of a problem than if we are investigating more general social circumstances. Even in social psychology, case studies can give us a great deal of insight. For example, in Milgram's studies of obedience (Chapter 16), it was precisely because Gretchen Brandt and Jan Rensaleer acted differently from most other people that they became of interest. Looking at what was distinctive about the past experiences of those two people helped to give some insight into how and why some people will act with principle, according to their own conscience, no matter what situation they are in, while others are more likely to obey authority and not confront them with disobedience.

Questionnaires and surveys

Another important way of finding out about people is to look, not at single people in detail as we do with case studies, but at large numbers of people. Of course, this means that we cannot penetrate very deeply into ideas and motives, but it can still be very useful in letting us know about general trends. Questionnaire studies allow a psychologist to collect information from people who may be widely dispersed.

The fact that questionnaire studies can involve such large numbers of people also makes them suitable for large-scale **longitudinal studies** of particular kinds of human behaviour. The Friedman and Rosenman (1974) study of Type A and Type B behaviour, which we looked at in Chapter 13, involved over 3500 research participants – a number which would be unmanageable using most other research methods.

Some psychologists have treated questionnaire data as informative in its own right. For example, Dion's study of attractiveness in children (Chapter 14) was conducted almost entirely using questionnaires with photographs of the children, as was the Gerbner and Gross study which showed how heavy viewers of television tend to be more paranoid than those who watch television less. As we saw in Chapter 3, Broadbent et al. (1982) showed that questionnaires could be a useful and accurate method for measuring some forms of behaviour, such as everyday errors.

Questionnaire studies are often useful for opening up new areas of investigation. For example, Argyle's questionnaire study of the psychological experience of marriage revealed a number of interesting findings, any one of which could form the basis for future, more detailed research. Often, a psychologist will use a questionnaire as the first part of a study, and then go on to use other methods later. For example, Bem's study of androgyny (Chapter 20) began in this way, and the use of the Sex-Role Inventory questionnaire allowed Bem to identify not just people who fitted typical models of sex-role behaviour, but also those who were more androgynous in their approach, with characteristics of both genders.

Surveys usually, though not always, involve face-to-face methods, but still involve large numbers of people. A survey may simply consist of a questionnaire which is read out to research participants, or it may comprise a highly structured interview, in which each question is pre-scripted and the kinds of replies which people give are carefully coded. For example, the Brown and Harris study of depression in London housewives (Chapter 8) consisted of a survey of 539 women, using a highly structured interview technique. This type of interview is quite different from the rapport-style qualitative interview which we will be looking at later.

Meta-analysis

In recent years, another form of investigation has become popular in the academic literature. As you have probably noticed throughout this book, studies often produce conflicting results: one study may show one thing, while another appears to show the opposite. Sometimes, if we want to find out what the general pattern is, it is useful to look at all (or at any rate, a large number of) the studies which have been undertaken on a particular topic, and to see what the general trends of their findings are. This technique is known as **meta-analysis**.

Meta-analysis has been used in a number of areas within psychology. For example, the meta-analysis of studies of memory retrieval of semantic information conducted by Ball et al. (Chapter 3) comes from the cognitive area, whereas the Rosenberg et al. meta-analysis of studies of implicit personality theory (Chapter 15) is from social psychology, as was the meta-analysis of studies of attitudes and behaviour conducted by Ajzen and Fishbein (Chapter 17). An early meta-analysis was conducted by Naylor, in 1962, into the effectiveness of whole and part learning for skill development (Chapter 18). And, of course, meta-analysis has been particularly valuable in parapsychological research (Chapter 12), since data regarding parapsychological phenomena are, almost by definition, elusive and hard to maintain systematically.

Meta-analyses in themselves do not always agree. As we saw in Chapter 20, the two different meta-analyses conducted by Hall (1978) and by Eisenberg and Lennon (1983) produced different results: Hall found strong gender differences in people's abilities to decode non-verbal signals, whereas Eisenberg and Lennon found much less extreme ones. In part, this difference arises from the different criteria which the researchers take as the deciding factor as to whether these gender differences actually happened. As we saw in Box 25.1, the findings from any one study are always likely to be tentative, and to need some interpretation. And, particularly with topics like gender differences, whether the researchers allow for the possibility of overlap or not, depends on how they themselves perceive the topic, and whether they believe that such overlap is likely. As with every other form of research, the theoretical orientation which the researchers hold will determine which questions they ask, and how they go about asking them.

Qualitative analysis

Recent years have shown a growing emphasis on the use of **qualitative methods** in psychology. The word 'qualitative' is used as a contrast to the use of **quantitative methods,** which involve data collected in the form of numbers, and analysed statistically – although there is not really a hard and fast dividing line between qualitative and quantitative data (Hayes, 1997b). Experiments, coded observations, questionnaires and surveys, and meta-analyses generally use quantitative methods, since they tend to emphasise numerical data and statistical analysis. But sometimes they also yield qualitative information – some aspects of human behaviour simply are not amenable to quantitative analysis, and if we try to reduce the information down to numbers, we can end up losing most of its meaning.

There are many different ways of undertaking qualitative analysis. Sometimes this involves the analysis of interview data and of the accounts which people give about their experience, and we will be looking at this separately. But there are other ways in which psychologists have used qualitative analysis. For example, Saarinen's study of cognitive maps (Chapter 5) involved asking college students to draw maps of their university campuses and looking at their drawings. Janis's study of American foreign policy decisions, which revealed the factors involved in groupthink (Chapter 5), was also a form of qualitative analysis.

In the child development field, qualitative analysis has been useful for studying general orientations, such as achievement motivation. As we saw in Chapter 18, Winterbottom investigated this by asking children to complete a story and looking at the themes which they included, whereas Rosen and d'Andrade asked children to build a tower of building blocks with their parents looking on. Argyle and Crossland also used quali-

tative analysis in their study of positive emotions (Chapter 13). By asking research participants to think about different pleasant experiences and describe them, they were able to identify several dimensions of positive emotions, which formed the basis for further, quantitative research.

Interviews

Interviews have always been an important method in psychological research. There are many different types of interviews, ranging from the tightly scripted formal survey-type interviews to more free-ranging discussions between interviewer and interviewee. Massarik (1981) listed six different types of interview, which are listed in Table 25.2. Survey-type interviews are similar to verbally administered questionnaires, and tend to involve quantitative analysis. But many researchers also use more open, rapport-style interviews, which involve qualitative analysis.

Interviews can be helpful in identifying a number of different aspects of psychological functioning. For example, Lynch's interviews about cognitive maps (Chapter 5) were useful in showing how people saw their own towns. They have their limitations too: as we saw in Chapter 5, Nisbett and Wilson found that people cannot always verbalise accurately about how they go about doing things – instead, they are more likely to produce explanations or justifications. But those explanations in themselves can be of interest, as we saw in Guimond and Palmer's investigations of how student social representations changed as they proceeded through their courses, or Gilbert and Mulkay's investigation of how scientists explained their own and rival theories (Chapter 15).

This technique has also been particularly useful in identifying features of human experience which are traditionally private and personal. For example, as we saw in Chapter 14, interviews have been important in mapping out the processes underlying the development and breakdown of long-term relationships. Kadushin used interviews when looking at adoptive parents and whether their adoptions had been successful (Chapter 20). And they have allowed investigation of several areas of lifespan developmental psychology: studies of the family life-cycle and stages of marriage have tended to be based on interview data, because other methods would be unworkable.

Interviews are often used together with other

Table 25.2 Types of interview

1 *The hostile interview*, in which the interviewer and interviewee have different goals. In a police interrogation, for instance, the interviewee may be seeking to withhold information rather than to provide it to the interviewer; in a confrontational interview between, say, a bored council official and a member of the public there may also be little intention of co-operation.

2 *The limited survey*, like the kind of public market research survey in which you are stopped in the street and asked, say, about your favourite type of yoghurt. These interviews are characterised by very little personal involvement and therefore relative indifference on the part of the interviewer; and aquiescence on a fairly minimal level on the part of the interviewee.

3 *The rapport interview*, which may be clearly defined and have firm boundaries, but which also involves a high degree of positive interaction, casual byplay, and human contact. Sometimes there will be a loose interview schedule, which is used to define the general area of the interview, but not to constrain what is discussed. This type of interview tends to produce high levels of co-operation between interviewer and interviewee.

4 *The asymmetrical-trust interview*, in which one participant (usually the interviewee) is more trustful than the other; such as might be found in a typical doctor–patient interview.

5 *The depth interview*, in which rapport and trust are deliberately built up, with the intention of exploring the views and motivations of the interviewee. This type of interview is increasingly common in psychological research, and is also used in marketing and in anthropological and clinical research.

6 *The phenomenological interview*, in which there is a maximum amount of trust and caring between the interviewer and interviewee. This interview can become an open-ended discussion – there are very few boundaries or limitations placed on the content of the interview.

Source: Adapted from Massarik, 1981

methods of investigation. For example, they have been used to supplement ethological studies of family interactions, such as in the study by Dunn *et al.* on how children comfort their siblings in the home (Chapter 19). Sometimes, too, interview studies have revealed areas of experience that

would not otherwise have become apparent, such as the study of children's playground culture conducted by Iona and Peter Opie (Chapter 4), in which the researchers interviewed children all over the country, inviting them to talk about their games.

Ethogenics

In 1979, Rom Harré argued that the ways in which psychologists had traditionally studied social interaction were often pretty meaningless – because they were so very restricted and took such small units of social behaviour as the basis for their analysis. As an alternative, Harré proposed that the study of social behaviour should adopt the **ethogenic** approach. This involves two very distinctive features which are different from traditional psychological methodology. First, it involves taking the **episode** as the appropriate unit of analysis rather than the act or action – people experience life as a series of episodes, a bit like scenes in a play, and if we really want to get at social experience it is more appropriate to look at whole episodes than to concentrate on simple acts or actions.

Accounts and discourse

The second facet of the ethogenic approach is its emphasis on **account analysis**. Harré argued that people's own accounts of their experience are important and meaningful social data, since they tell us how people understand what has happened to them. And, as we saw in Chapter 7 and elsewhere, it is mostly how people understand what is happening to them which determines how they go on to interact with other people.

Accounts have been used in almost all areas of psychology. Even in physiological studies, reports of patients' experiences have been important – for example, in the open-brain studies of sensation and perception by Penfield and Rasmussen (Chapter 12), or of motivation by Quaade (Chapter 13), what the patients described was necessary data in identifying which parts of the brain were involved in producing conscious experience. In that respect, Harré was not proposing something entirely new: what he was proposing was that account analysis should be recognised as a valid way of finding things out, rather than simply used when there was no alternative.

As we saw in Marsh et al.'s study of football fans (Chapter 17), the ethogenic approach has provided insights into aspects of social behaviour which might have remained elusive using more conventional methods. Many other psychologists have also used account analysis: for example, Ayres's study of relationship maintenance strategies (Chapter 14) was based entirely on accounts collected from couples about how they kept their relationships together. And the accounts of crowd members' experiences collected by Benewick and Holton during the Pope's visit were useful in showing the positive affirming experience of being part of a large peaceful crowd (Chapter 17).

Some aspects of account analysis have focused on how people go about saying things – on the nature of discourse. Potter and Wetherall (Chapter 4) identified **discourse analysis** as an important method for revealing underlying social assumptions. Looking at the way that people say things can reveal a great deal. For example, Lutz's anthropological study of different words for anger in the Ifaluk language showed how very different concepts are often encapsulated in the one English word 'anger' (Chapter 15). In a similar vein, the studies by Spender and others which we looked at in Chapter 4 showed how the use of sexist language can be influential in reflecting social assumptions and also in shaping thought.

Other forms of account analysis have also been useful for psychologists. Stratton and Swaffer showed how analysing underlying attributions could be useful in directing family therapy for parents of abused children (Chapter 15). In this study, it was the nature of the explanations which were being offered by the parents which was of particular note. These explanations showed how beliefs about controllability, or the lack of it, lay at the heart of the problem.

Ethical issues in psychology

Recent years have seen a heightened concern about **ethical issues** on the part of psychologists all around the world. In part, this reflects a growing concern with accountability in all the professions, as society adjusts itself to the implications of consumer capitalism and its emphasis on the individual; in part also, it emerges as a reaction against the old mechanistic schools of thought, as psychology no longer feels a need to defend itself

against claims of being 'unscientific', and begins to explore alternative ways of studying the human being. There are other factors too. But whatever the reasons, the outcome is a very significant shift in emphasis, away from the notion of 'value-free' science, and towards the principle of ethical responsibility for psychologists.

This has a number of implications for the study of psychology. Psychology as a discipline has changed considerably over the years and, as it has changed, so has psychological methodology. Earlier in this chapter, for example, we looked at the newer qualitative methods of investigation in psychology, and at how they are different from the traditional quantitative methods because of their emphasis on social meaning and on the validity of people's own experience. What these methods also encapsulate is an increased respect for the people who are the participants in psychological research.

As you can tell from looking at many of the earlier studies, psychology in the first 60 years of the twentieth century adopted a largely manipulative stance towards its subject matter. The people who took part in psychological research were treated as, and called, 'subjects', and it was assumed that they were essentially passive and would simply respond to the situations which were manipulated by the experimenter. Psychology was not alone in taking this stance, of course. Medicine took a similar approach, as did many other institutions in Western society.

The active 'subject'
During the 1960s and later, however, a number of psychologists began to take the view that perhaps their research participants were not as passive as all that. Rosenthal's work on the self-fulfilling prophecy (Chapter 16), and Orne's work on how the demand characteristics of experiments affect how people behave (Chapter 11), were part of a wide body of research which showed that people are not passive in a psychological experiment: they do not just wait and respond to what happens to them. Instead, they actively try to make sense out of what is going on, and they respond to what they understand to be happening.

In 1977, Silverman showed how many of the supposedly 'classic' demonstrations in psychology, such as conditioning experiments in which people could apparently be trained, unconsciously, to use plural nouns or adjectives by being reinforced when they did so, only 'worked' if the people concerned realised what was happening. Far from being passive 'subjects' in the experiment, they worked out what they were supposed to do and then co-operated with the experimenter to produce the result. From interviews with people who had participated in psychological experiments, Silverman showed that working out what the experimenter was up to was a crucial aspect of being a research participant.

This would not matter, of course, if psychological research had operated on the basis that it was dealing with real, active people. But a great deal of psychological methodology in the first half of the twentieth century had been modelled on the physical sciences: the idea was that the experimenter manipulated, while the subject matter remained inert. To the behaviourists and other experimental psychologists who were influenced by them, the only difference between a human being and a sample of metal was that more care was needed in controlling the conditions when experimenting with human beings.

Research participants

Recent approaches to psychological investigation, as we have seen, work on a very different set of assumptions about research participants. For one thing, they are called **research participants**, and not 'subjects', and this is more than just a change of wording. It reflects a recognition that the person is actively involved and co-operating with the researcher, and that they may in themselves have something valid to offer. In addition, qualitative approaches recognise the value of studying people's own experiences, and of collecting their own accounts of that experience. It reflects a greatly increased respect for the participant in psychological research.

This increased respect means that we also need to re-think many of the practices which were common in psychological methodology in the past. Many past studies in psychology showed a total lack of respect for other people who were involved. For example, the library study of Felipe and Sommer, which we looked at in Chapter 13, involved researchers going into libraries and deliberately invading the personal space of library users, by sitting extremely close to them and timing how long it took before they packed up their books and moved away. While this was not a directly harmful thing to do – nobody was damaged, although they were understandably

irritated – it illustrates very clearly the lack of respect for research participants in the old experimental paradigm. The library users were people carrying on with their own lives, who had a right to get on with their work in peace. But this was not considered: the experimenters took it for granted that they had the right to disrupt others for research purposes.

Deception

Another example of lack of respect concerns the use of **deception** in psychological studies. It was previously thought to be not only useful but desirable and even necessary to deceive research participants about the purpose of the research, because otherwise their awareness might 'contaminate' the findings. But nowadays we take a different attitude to deception. Part of respecting research participants means acknowledging that people have the right to know what is going on. So deception, as a general rule, is not regarded as ethically acceptable in studying people.

In some cases, of course, it is necessary for some deception to take place. But as can be seen from the ethical guidelines listed in Table 25.3 overleaf, such deception must be avoided whenever possible and must only ever be temporary. Psychology research departments now have ethical committees, which assess prospective research and will evaluate, beforehand, whether a study which appears to require deception is really justified. If it is not, or if there seem to be other ways of doing the research, then the researcher will not be permitted to carry out the study.

Permission to deceive

This has sometimes produced very imaginative ways of going about research. For example, in the Gamson et al. study of group rebellion which we looked at in Chapter 15, it was necessary that the participants should not know what the study was about – if they had known, it could not possibly have worked. So rather than act unethically, the researchers produced an inventive technique for getting permission from the research participants to deceive them. People who had volunteered to participate in the research were contacted by telephone and asked if they would be prepared to participate in the following types of research:

Table 25.3 Ethical guidelines for research with human beings

1 Investigators must always consider ethical implications and psychological consequences for research participants.

2 Investigators should inform participants of the objectives of the research and gain their informed consent.

3 Withholding information or misleading participants is unacceptable. Intentional deception should be avoided.

4 Participants must be fully debriefed, so they can complete their understanding of the nature of the research.

5 Investigators must emphasise the subject's right to withdraw from the experiment at any time.

6 All data obtained must be treated as confidential unless otherwise agreed in advance.

7 Investigators must protect participants from physical and mental harm during or arising from investigations.

8 Studies based on observation must respect the privacy and psychological well-being of the people studied.

9 Investigators must exercise care in giving advice on psychological problems.

10 Investigators share responsibility for ethical treatment, and should encourage others to rethink their ideas if necessary.

Source: Adapted from British Psychological Society, 1990

Table 25.4 Criteria for evaluating ethical issues

1 *Utilitarian, cost-benefit criteria*
Do we learn more from the research than we could do from research carried out differently, and if we do, is it worth it?

2 *The effects on the participants*
What will the outcome of our research be for the participants involved? Clearly, if covert observation has no effect whatsoever, this is different from research in which the covert intervention produces change.

3 *Issues of individual integrity*
Have we had to engage in personal dishonesty and manipulation, and if so to what extent may this be offset by humanitarian considerations?

Source: Adapted from Reynolds, 1982

'*a* Research on brand recognition of commercial products.
b Research on product safety.
c Research in which you will be misled about the purpose until afterward.
d Research involving group standards.'

Only those who agreed to the third item were selected for the research (in practice, though, this was virtually everyone). So in this case, although the researchers did deceive their research participants, they only deceived those who had agreed to be deceived in the first place.

Not all deception is unacceptable, though. As we saw earlier in this chapter, in participant research the researcher becomes involved in a social group as a participant rather than as an observer. Clearly, in this case if they were to announce from the start that they were psychologists conducting an investigation, the other people would not be acting as they normally would, and the research would be pointless. The study by Festinger *et al.* of the beliefs of a 'Judgement Day' cult when their prophecy was disconfirmed (Chapter 17) would have been impossible without some degree of deception on the part of the researchers. So too would Rosenhan's study of labelling in psychiatric diagnosis, which we looked at in Chapter 8. Yet this study highlighted a number of socially important issues and was directly responsible for some necessary reforms in the process of psychiatric diagnosis.

Evaluating ethical issues

It is apparent, then, that ethical issues in psychological research involve weighing up the different factors which are involved – there are no simple, black-and-white rules which can always be followed. Reynolds (1982) argued that we should examine ethical issues in social research in the light of three criteria, which are listed in Table 25.4. As we can see from the table, these include not just the social implications of the research, but also the effect on the participants and the integrity of the researcher. There is always an element of judgement involved in ethical decisions, and it is for this reason that psychology departments maintain ethical committees. Judging whether a proposed programme of research is ethically acceptable or not, requires the involvement of several people – it is too important to be left to a single individual researcher.

Applying Reynolds's criteria to Rosenhan's study, we could argue that the information which was gathered could not have been obtained in any other way, and that functionally it was valuable in alerting the professional world to important areas of doubt in psychiatric diagnosis. It is also possible to argue that any ill-effects of the study would have accrued to the researchers alone: it was they who were diagnosed as mentally ill, and thereby entered into a powerless relationship with the medical establishment. On the third criterion, inevitably there was untruthfulness – professions were concealed as well as the false symptom reports – but the use that was made of the knowledge was careful, individuals were not identified and information which could be embarrassing to specific people was not revealed.

Justified deception

There are other studies which show clearly that covert research is sometimes the only option for researchers. Perhaps the most extreme example of this was a paper by Bruno Bettelheim (1943) on social identity within a concentration camp. Bettelheim had spent two years in Dachau before managing to escape, and had therefore had first hand experience of how people managed to maintain, or how they lost, their individual identities in such horrifying conditions. He himself found that he needed to cling on to his identity as a social psychologist very tightly, and during his time in the camp he adopted rigorous mental strategies – including formal memorising techniques, as there were no opportunities for him to take notes – in studying the social processes that were taking place. His research provided valuable insights as to the social processes that were going on between the guards and inmates as well as within the inmates themselves. Hiding what he was doing was essential – if he had not, he could not have survived. But there is no question that his research was ethical in nature.

Not all deception, then, is inevitably unethical. But the cavalier attitude to deception which was adopted by many psychologists in the past is not acceptable either. For the most part, modern psychologists are taking approaches to research which do not need to involve deception – they regard the people they are studying as active participants in the research rather than as subject matter to be manipulated and deceived.

Causing psychological distress

In the case of the Gamson *et al.* study, which we looked at before and in Chapter 16, the research was very carefully monitored throughout. In the end the researchers investigated only 33 groups instead of the planned 80, because the procedure appeared to be too distressing to the research participants. This reflected another prime ethical concern of modern researchers – the need to avoid causing psychological distress to participants.

Little Albert and the students

Avoiding personal distress was not always something which psychologists thought about. The famous 'little Albert' study conducted by Watson and Rayner involved systematically terrifying a nine-month-old child whenever he played with a pet white rat, until he eventually acquired a phobia. Little Albert was selected for the study because he was a phlegmatic child, who had never been known to get upset over anything. But by the end of the study, he was nervous and easily upset. Watson and Rayner never actually did recondition little Albert, as he was removed from the hospital by his mother before they had the chance. In their report of the study, this is treated simply as an inconvenience – there is no awareness at all that causing such distress might be ethically unacceptable. The researchers assumed, automatically, that as scientists they had the right to treat their 'subjects' as they pleased.

Watson and Rayner's study was reported in 1920. By the 1960s, the situation had improved slightly, in that researchers were no longer able to get away with terrifying children in the name of science. But there were still a number of studies being carried out which left much to be desired. In one study of attraction, female students were given personality tests and later asked to wait outside an office for their result (Walster, 1965). While they were waiting, each student was approached by a good-looking young man, who chatted with them and eventually asked for a date. The young man was a confederate of the experimenters.

When the young women entered the office for the results of their personality test, they were given one of two (fake) outcomes: either one which presented them in a positive light, designed to boost their self-esteem, or one which presented their personality in a negative light, designed to lower their self-esteem. They were then asked to assess the attractiveness of a set of people, including the young man they had just met. Walster found that those in the 'low self-esteem' condition rated the young man more highly than those in the high self-esteem. The idea was that they felt more attracted to him because he had given a 'psychological boost' to their confidence at a time when they felt they needed it.

This was a fairly standard kind of study for its time. But its ethical implications are extremely undesirable. The young women participating in the study were not only lied to, but the lies which they were told were deliberately designed to lower their self-esteem. There has been a considerable amount of psychological research which shows how self-esteem is important for psychologically healthy functioning – see Chapters 7 and 14, for instance. So this study, like Watson and Rayner's although less dramatically, involved a blatant disregard for the individual's well-being. Although it passed without comment at the time, it would not be permitted by a modern ethics committee.

Potentially damaging outcomes

In fact, some of the studies which did generate comment often seem to have been conducted much more carefully. Milgram, for example, was very careful to keep in touch with all the participants in his obedience experiments (Chapter 16), and 99% of the participants reported that they were glad to have taken part, even though it had been stressful for them at the time. But his studies were nonetheless criticised by Baumrind (1964), on the grounds that this outcome could not have been predicted. Even if it all worked out for the best, taking risks with people's well-being was not ethically acceptable practice. It was largely the debate resulting from Baumrind's criticisms of Milgram's studies which brought ethical issues so firmly on to the psychological agenda.

But there are, again, costs to be calculated. Milgram found things out about the power of obedience which were entirely unpredictable – those who were consulted beforehand about the likely outcomes of such an experiment wildly underestimated the tendency of people to obey authority. These studies transformed our understanding of the social side of human nature. So we can still learn from Milgram's work even while we recognise that a modern study of obedience would need to involve a rather different approach.

Animal studies

As we have seen throughout this book, psychology includes the study of animal behaviour as well as the behaviour of human beings. We saw in Chapter 22 that there are two reasons for this. One of them – possibly the more important – is that animal behaviour is a source of interest in its own right. The second is that by studying animals we can find things out about human beings too. Animal studies in psychology have ranged from physiological investigations of brain functioning, to behavioural experiments in which animals learn to press levers or perform other tasks in return for rewards, to the ethological observations of animals in their natural habitat. As we can see, not all of these are equally ethically debatable. Few people, for instance, would argue that it is ethically unacceptable to study animals in their natural habitat, and most of the animal studies which we looked at in Chapter 23 were doing just that.

The studies at the other extreme, though, are more debatable. If we look at the ways in which psychologists have investigated the brain and other forms of physiological functioning, we find that these studies often involved vivisection: studies in which parts of an animal's brain or body were removed or severed, in order to observe the effects which then occurred. As with all other ethical issues, there are no simple black-and-white rules to follow here – although individual people, of course, have their own views.

Acceptable research topics

There is an argument that medical research on animals is acceptable whereas commercial research, for example for cosmetics, is not. According to this argument, much physiological research on animals is acceptable since it tends to be concerned with gaining a better understanding of neurological functioning, and does not usually have direct commercial applications. Many people, however, see the early perception studies (Chapter 3) or some of the physiological studies (for example, those on sleep, in Chapter 11) as being needlessly cruel. As animal rights campaigns gained momentum, the value of animal studies was increasingly called into question, and legal restrictions and professional guidelines regarding the use of animals in research became more stringent.

Everyone has their own opinion as to whether

medical research on animals is justified, and it is for you to make up your own mind about this. But there are certainly arguments – and champions – for both sides. For example, Gray (1985) showed how animal experimentation led physiologists directly to a better understanding of how anti-anxiety drugs work, which meant that they could be developed and used far more safely. And Blakemore's work with kittens in restricted visual environments (Chapter 2) increased our understanding of astigmatism in human vision. The argument of these researchers is that, while animal experiments should be restricted and controlled to avoid needless suffering, to prevent all of them would be to throw the baby out with the bathwater.

Those opposed to animal research, on the other hand, counter that animal physiology is different from that of humans, and just because we find a mechanism which looks similar this does not mean that it is the same thing at all. So studies of, for instance, brain structure or functioning in experimental rats will not necessarily tell us anything at all about human beings. Ironically, perhaps, the strongest evidence for this comes from precisely one of these types of animal experiments. As we saw in Chapter 12, Fisher (1964) found that injections of the same neurotransmitter into the same part of the brain of cats and rats produced entirely different responses.

Research guidelines

Ethical guidelines on animal research are now strongly enforced and backed up by the law. Researchers are strictly adjured not to cause animals pain or distress. They are also instructed to ensure that the research is worthwhile. For example, clause 2 of the British Psychological Society's Guidelines for the Use of Animals in Research states:

'*If the animals are confined, constrained, harmed or stressed in any way the investigator must consider whether the knowledge to be gained justifies the procedure. Some knowledge is trivial, and experiments must not be done simply because it is possible to do them. Alternatives to animal experiments should also be considered.*'

(British Psychological Society, 1985: 12)

Defining pain and distress is not all that easy, though. Harlow's monkeys, for instance, suffered

lifelong induced neurosis through being brought up in isolation (Chapter 22). And Jane van Lawick-Goodall gave an account of a chimpanzee, Lucy, who was brought up with human beings and taught sign language, like the chimpanzees which we looked at in Chapter 24. When she grew too large, Lucy was put in with a colony of wild chimpanzees. When a visitor whom she recognised came to visit the chimpanzee colony, Lucy signed desperately: 'Please help. Out.' The long-term perspectives in studies with chimpanzees and gorillas, which are almost always performed with these animals while they are young, seem sometimes to be neglected. Yet one of the most important criteria which we apply to experiments with children is that anything which might cause lasting damage is out of the question.

It is up to each individual person to evaluate how far they consider animal studies to be acceptable, although, as with ethical considerations in studies involving human beings, it is not left entirely up to an individual researcher's judgement. Table 25.5 overleaf gives the ethical guidelines within which all psychologists using animals must now work: they are part of the British Psychological Society's Code of Conduct for professional psychologists. And, as with studies with human beings, proposals for animal research have to be scrutinised for acceptability by specialist committees. As a natural consequence of this, laboratory-based psychological research with animals has become far less commonplace than it was in, say, the 1960s, and it is now much more common to conduct ethological studies rather than experimental ones.

Ethical issues in student practical work

So what does this emphasis on ethical responsibility imply for the conduct of student practical work? Introductory courses in psychology all tend to expect students to undertake a certain amount of practical work, which has to be performed within ethical guidelines. In America, these guidelines are produced by the American Psychological Association; in Britain, by the British Psychological Society and also, for pre-degree psychology, by the Association for the Teaching of Psychology. Taking ethical issues seriously has a number of practical implications for how students need to go about their work.

First, and above all else, there is the question of

Table 25.5 Ethical guidelines for animal research

1 *The law*
Researchers are obliged to abide by the laws protecting animals, as outlined in the Universities Federation for Animal Welfare handbook.

2 *Ethical considerations*
If the animals are confined, constrained, harmed or stressed in any way the investigator must consider whether the knowledge to be gained justifies the procedure ... experiments must not be done simply because it is possible to do them. Alternatives to animal experiments should also be considered.

3 *Species*
Wherever research involves confining animals or the use of procedures likely to cause pain or discomfort the researchers should bear in mind that members of some species may suffer less than others, and should choose the species accordingly.

4 *Number of animals*
Laboratory studies should use the smallest number of animals necessary. This can often be greatly reduced by good experimental design and the use of appropriate statistical tests.

5 *Endangered species*
Members of endangered species should not be collected or manipulated in the wild except as part of a serious attempt at conservation.

6 *Animal suppliers*
Animals should be obtained only from reputable suppliers and full records kept of their provenance and laboratory history.

7 *Caging and social environment*
Caging conditions should take into account the social behaviour of the species: an acceptable density of animals of one species may constitute overcrowding for a different species, while in social animals caging in isolation may have undesirable effects.

8 *Fieldwork*
Fieldworkers should disturb the animals they study as little as possible, since even simple observations on wild animals can have marked effects on their breeding and survival.

9 *Aggression and predation including infanticide*
The fact that pain and injury may come to animals in the world is not a defence for allowing it to occur in the laboratory. Wherever possible, field studies of natural encounters should be used in preference to staged encounters, and if the latter are thought to be necessary, the use of models or animals behind glass should be considered.

10 *Motivation*
When arranging schedules of deprivation the experimenter should consider the animal's normal eating and drinking habits and its metabolic requirements. Also, differences between species must be borne in mind: a short period of deprivation for one species may be unacceptably long for another.

11 *Aversive stimulation and stressful procedures*
Procedures that cause pain or distress to animals are illegal in the UK unless the experimenter holds a Home Office licence and the relevant certificates. The experimenter should be satisfied that there are no alternative ways of conducting the experiment without the use of aversive stimulation. If alternatives are not available, the investigator has the responsibility of ensuring that any suffering is kept to a minimum.

12 *Surgical and pharmacological procedures*
Such procedures should only be performed by experienced staff, and it is a particular responsibility of senior staff to train and supervise others. Experimenters must be familiar with the technical aspects of anaesthesia, and appropriate steps should be taken to prevent post-operative infection in chronic experiments. In pharmacological procedures experimenters must be familiar with the literature on the behavioural effects and toxicity of the drugs being used.

13 *Anaesthesia, analgesia and euthanasia*
The experimenter must ensure that animals receive adequate post-operative care, and that, if there is any possibility of post-operative suffering, this is minimised by suitable nursing and the use of local anaesthetics where appropriate. Regular monitoring of the animal's condition is essential, and if at any time an animal is found to be suffering severe and enduring pain it must be killed (also a requirement of a Home Office licence). Established procedures must be strictly followed for euthanasia, since methods vary from species to species.

14 *Independent advice*
If an experimenter is ever in any doubt about the condition of an animal, a second opinion should be obtained, preferably from a qualified veterinarian, and always from someone not directly involved in the experiments concerned.

15 *Further enquires*
Any researcher uncertain about any aspect of their research with animals should direct enquiries to the appropriate professional bodies.

Source: The Brisith Psychological Society Code of Conduct and Ethical Principles for Psychologists

respect for research participants. This encompasses several things. It involves respecting confidentiality – it should not be possible to identify any of the individual research participants from a report of a practical study. In group studies, of course, there is not much of a problem, but more in-depth case studies can often end up dealing with quite personal issues, and it is important that the confidentiality of those people should be maintained.

Respecting research participants also means that it is necessary to make sure that a study does not involve anything which they might find intrusive, offensive or insulting, if they knew the full extent of what the study was about. I have already discussed how the Felipe and Sommer study was offensive in its lack of respect for research participants. The significant question which needs to be asked is: does this study involve manipulating the participants; or are they co-operating in a joint venture? In assessing this, it is important to consult with other people, even if it is only a group of other psychology students. Other people's opinions are important in this type of question.

Deception, now, is seen as largely unnecessary. More direct ways of finding things out are becoming increasingly common in psychological research. They, in turn, carry their own implications about research skills. It is remarkably difficult, for instance, to design a good questionnaire, but it is a skill which is worth learning. Psychological methods involve, as we have seen, case studies, observations, interviews and questionnaires as well as experiments, so there is plenty of scope for adopting different techniques.

The new atmosphere also led to the emergence of alternative methodologies, like the ethogenic approach outlined by Rom Harré. Such methodologies often include a much greater emphasis on qualitative analysis. Looking at what people say, and how they see things, is increasingly recognised as a valid part of psychology, and qualitative approaches are often the best way of tackling this. They are certainly a lot more direct than the old, manipulative methods which tried to trick people into revealing their ideas, and they generally tell us more about people.

Wider ethical issues

In addition to the ethical issues which are concerned with how psychological research has been carried out, there are the wider ethical issues that

are raised as psychological theory impinges on society as a whole. This is closely linked with the whole question of the **social responsibility of science.** A number of psychological theories have had very powerful social effects – which have not always been to the good of humankind. As we saw in Chapter 6, IQ theory was used from the outset as an instrument of racial discrimination; and in Britain, belief in inherited intelligence is still a powerful factor in the education system, acting as much through self-fulfilling prophecies as anything else. Maternal deprivation theory too (Chapter 20) has left its social traces in Britain. The principle of social responsibility in science is that scientists do not just act in a value-free universe: they must take responsibility for the socio-political implications of their theorising as well as for how they go about their research.

Social responsibility does not just mean identifying ideas or theories which have had negative social effects and bringing to the fore other research which may be more positive. The other side of the coin is what is left out of psychology. As a discipline, psychology has tended in the past to be remarkably ethnocentric, focusing on middle-class white culture. But the pluralism of modern society means that this is no longer adequate. In a modern world, respect for other cultures is an essential ethical principle. The demands of cultural awareness and **multi-culturalism** mean that psychology needs to reflect a wider variety of cultural values, and to incorporate such values into its everyday practices, as is discussed in Box 25.2 overleaf. This is an ethical issue, since it is directly concerned with the implicit devaluing, or ignoring the validity, of people's lives.

Of necessity, this has been only a brief overview of some of the issues raised by ethical considerations in psychology. As we have seen, a full realisation of ethical issues also requires a higher-order appraisal of psychological knowledge and research, to locate it fully within its social context. As students are introduced to psychology, they are also gaining impressions of what psychology is all about. If we judge from its history, psychology is at least partly about manipulation and ethically questionable research practices. But psychology is changing, and new methods, theories and approaches are replacing the old, manipulative techniques.

Psychology is a broad and varied discipline, spanning a range of levels of explanation and

Box 25.2 Equal opportunities and ethical issues

In 1991, the British Psychological Society Working Party Report on the Future of A level Psychology stated:

It is important to consider how changing social contexts have affected our awareness of psychology and the way it is presented to students. The Working Party felt that the issues of equal opportunities and ethics were of prime importance in this regard.

Equal Opportunities

In contemporary Britain people experience discrimination because of their ethnic origin, gender, religion, class, sexual orientation, age or disability. It is important to acknowledge this in any educational setting, but especially in psychology. The principal concern of psychology is the experience and behaviour of people, and therefore it must acknowledge that people have different experiences of the world, and that the world treats people differently according to their personal attributes and qualities.

Psychology often tends to describe a world from a narrow viewpoint, and that viewpoint is largely white, male, middle class and transatlantic. Generalisations are made about 'people', when, in fact, the sample does not include many of the groups that make up our society and the world community. Issues of class, ethnicity and gender are largely ignored in the general work of psychology.

Some examples of this which are found in psychology courses at both A and degree levels are included here, in order to clarify how these issues manifest themselves in psychology curricula. They are examples only, and should not be taken as definitive or even as the single most important instances of their kind:

Sampling   *The view of personal relationships presented in most general texts describes the behaviour of a narrow group of people. Child care, family structure and the norms of everyday living show considerable cultural variation. This is rarely acknowledged in psychology books which tend to portray a particular style of 'family life', as normal, desirable and stereotyped. The psychological study of attraction is largely based on the dating behaviour of heterosexual American college students. The diversity of human relationships is not emphasised within contemporary psychology.*

Concepts   *Some psychological concepts are framed from a narrow viewpoint. An example of this is the notion of 'self-concept'. This emphasises individuality which is a theme of Western philosophy. African and Eastern philosophies, however, emphasise collective identity over individual identity. Attempts to view the experience of Black people within the framework of Western philosophical tradition leads to problems of interpretation.*

Applications   *Applications may reflect the unconscious ethnocentricity of a discipline. One example of the problems created by a narrow view of people in psychology is provided by the question of psychiatric diagnosis. Numerous studies have drawn attention to the different ways that people from different cultural groups are diagnosed and treated by psychiatric practitioners. This is directly affected by the way that we judge the behaviour of people from a different group to ourselves.*

Recommendation 8

a   *That educationalists, psychologists and psychology teachers should maintain and promote a commitment to human dignity, equality and social justice. It is appropriate to use the teaching of Psychology to promote these values, and explicit acknowledgement of this should be made in appropriate contexts.*

b   *All students should be able to feel included within the content of Psychology. Society is pluralist, and it is therefore important to acknowledge that some groups of people have life experiences that should be explicitly recognised as part of the content of mainstream Psychology. This will require special emphasis to be put on cultural, social and individual diversity.*

c   *Language is not neutral: it conveys value systems. Psychology courses at all levels should avoid the use of sexist or racist language, or any term that devalues the experience of some people.*

d   *It is possible to illustrate most psychological concepts with a number of different studies. In drawing up syllabuses and in teaching Psychology, care should be taken, wherever possible, to use examples that are relevant to the widest possible range of people.*

Source: From Hayes *et al.*, 1991

many different approaches to understanding the human being. Understanding people is not an easy task: if it were, there would be no need for psychologists. There are no simple answers. But if we look at problems in as many different ways as we can, and if we try to make sure that we are doing so in a systematic manner, psychological knowledge can get us quite a long way.

Key terms

covert observation Observation in which those being observed are unaware of the fact that they are being studied.

dependent variable The thing which is measured in an experiment, and which changes, depending on the independent variable.

ethical To do with rights and wrongs.

hypothetico-deductive research Research which is conducted on the basis of using theory to generate hypotheses, and then carrying out the research in order to see if the hypotheses appear to hold up. The alternative is inductive research.

independent variable The conditions which an experimenter sets up, to cause an effect in an experiment. These vary systematically, so that the experimenter can draw conclusions about changes.

longitudinal study A study which monitors changes occurring over a period of time.

natural experiments Events in which variables change as a result of natural, political, social or economic circumstances, such that the outcome of these changes can then be studied.

observational study A study which involves simply watching what happens, rather than intervening and causing changes.

qualitative analysis Ways of analysing data which are concerned with describing meaning, rather than with drawing statistical inferences from frequency counts.

quantitative analysis Ways of analysing data which focus on numbers and frequencies rather than on meaning or experience.

statistically significant The term used to refer to a result of statistical analysis which is unlikely to have happened by chance alone. In a research paper, the term would be accompanied by a number (the level of significance) which states just how unlikely it is.

Summary

1 Psychologists use many different methods of studying people. There are three criteria which are important in collecting psychological evidence: validity, reliability, and generalisability.

2 Traditional quantitative approaches to collecting psychological evidence have included the use of experiments, observations, questionnaires and surveys, and meta-analysis. But all of these methods may also give qualitative data.

3 There are many different forms of qualitative analysis, which include looking at how people perform tasks or tell stories, and particularly the use of interviews and discourse analysis. Ethogenic research emphasises the understanding of social experience in the form of episodes and accounts.

4 Ethical issues in psychology have become very important in recent years. They are based on respect for the participant in the research programme, and have also meant that non-manipulative research methods, such as the ethogenic approach, have become more popular.

5 The use of deception or other forms of manipulation in psychological research is not usually considered acceptable. Criteria for evaluating whether deception is acceptable include questions about the value of the knowledge obtained, and about how far the researcher's personal integrity is compromised.

6 Psychologists are required to avoid causing personal distress or discomfort to their research participants. This means that much research conducted in the past would no longer be seen as ethically acceptable.

7 Animal studies in psychology may be ranged along a continuum from strictly confined laboratory investigations to free-ranging ethological studies. Studies involving vivisection are no longer considered to be acceptable except in very special cases.

8 Consideration of ethical issues also includes wider social questions, such as the social responsibility of science, and questions of multi-culturalism and social respect for all human beings.

Self-assessment questions

1 Briefly describe, giving examples, the four main types of validity.

2 Describe three different ways of undertaking qualitative analysis.

3 What are the central concepts in ethical issues with regard to research with animals?

Practice essay questions

1 How far is the experimental method an appropriate technique for studying human behaviour?

2 Are animal studies any use to psychologists?

3 'Taking ethical issues seriously requires a complete re-think of psychological methodology'. Discuss.

Test your knowledge of this chapter with our online quizzes and games at: http://www.psych.co.uk

Explore methods and ethics in psychology further at:

Methods

http://gateway1.gmcc.ab.ca/~digdonn/psych104/think.htm#top – Critical thinking page which analyses testable questions and has a useful bibliography.

http://www.execpc.com/~helberg/statistics.html – Comprehensive page for statistics on the web; articles, resources, links to organisations and discussion groups.

Conduct/ethics of research

http://www.nap.edu/readingroom/books/obas/ – Online book on responsible conduct in scientific research.

http://www.psych.bangor.ac.uk/deptpsych/Ethics/HumanResearch.html – Ethical conduct in research links page.

ability tests Psychometric tests which are designed to measure what someone is already able to do, as opposed to what they might be able to learn in the future.

ablation The removal or destruction of part or parts of the brain by means of surgical techniques, usually involving cutting or burning away the tissue concerned.

absolute refractory period The period of a few milliseconds immediately after the firing of a neurone, when the neurone will not produce another electrical impulse, no matter how much stimulation it may receive.

abstract thought Thought which concerns concepts which do not have an immediate material correspondence, such as 'justice' or 'freedom'.

accent A distinctive pattern of pronunciation in a given language, shared by a regional or socio-economic group.

accommodation The process by which a schema adjusts to new information by extending or changing its form, or even by subdividing into two or more.

accounts People's own verbal descriptions or explanations of events or phenomena, usually given in interviews or conversation.

acetylcholine A neurotransmitter which is particularly found at the motor end plate.

acoustic store An element in Baddeley's working memory model, which stores mental representations of sounds.

acquired dyslexia Dyslexia which occurs as a result of head injury or similar specific cause.

ACTH See adrenocorticotrophic hormone.

action pattern A sequence of behaviour produced by an organism, which is usually considered to be of a fixed nature, and probably inherited as a complete unit.

action potential The electrical impulse produced by a neurone when its stimulation crosses the threshold, and causes it to fire.

action research A method of undertaking social research which acknowledges that the researcher's presence is likely to influence people's behaviour, and so incorporates the researcher's involvement as a direct and deliberate part of the research, with the researcher consciously acting as change agent.

action-specific energy Energy which is only concerned with one particular type of behaviour, such as eating or drinking, and which is thought to represent an inner drive.

adaptation The process of becoming successfully adjusted to environmental demands.

adrenocorticotrophic hormone A hormone produced by the pituitary gland, which stimulates the release of adrenaline into the bloodstream.

affect display A set of actions which is used to indicate an emotional state.

affectionless psychopathy A syndrome outlined by Bowlby, characterised by a lack of social relationships and also of social conscience.

affective To do with feelings or emotions, such as the component of an attitude concerned with feelings.

affective dimension The aspect of an attitude which is concerned with feelings and emotions which are directed towards the attitude's target.

afferent neurone A neurone which carries information from the sensory receptors towards the brain and spinal cord.

affiliation motives Motives which direct behaviour towards making sure that the affiliative needs (for family, friendship or 'belonging') can be satisfied.

affiliative needs Needs which relate to having continuing contact with other human beings; which are concerned with 'belonging' to a set of people in some way, such as through families, social groups, or friendships.

affordances In Gibson's theory of perception, the possibilities for action which are offered by an object (e.g. a tree affords possibilities for climbing, or hiding behind).

after-image A visual image which remains in the visual field after the original stimulation has ceased.

agentic state A mental condition proposed by Milgram in which, he suggested, independence and autonomy and, most importantly, conscience, are suppressed as the individual acts as an agent for someone else.

aggression A term used in several ways, but generally to describe negative or hostile behaviour or feelings towards others.

agoraphobia An excessive fear of open spaces.

AH group tests A series of pencil-and-paper intelligence tests developed by Alice Heim (AH), and designed such that they can be administered to a large group of people at the same time, rather than just to one person at a time. There are different AH tests for different ranges of intelligence.

Aha! experience A sudden experience of enlightenment, in which the solution to a problem is perceived very rapidly.

AI See artificial intelligence.

alarm reaction   A term used to describe the series of physiological responses brought about by the activation of the sympathetic division of the autonomic nervous system.

alcoholic   A person addicted to the drug alcohol.

alexia   Word-blindness, or the inability to identify written words as words, even though the person has no problem with spoken language.

algorithm   A problem-solving operation which, if repeated often enough, will eventually lead to a solution.

all-or-none principle   The principle that a neurone either fires or it does not, with no change in the strength of the electrical impulse.

allele   The name given to one of a pair of matching genes, with one of each pair found on each of a matched pair of chromosomes.

alpha females   Female members of a baboon troop who appear 'dominant' and have higher social status than other females.

alpha males   Male members of a baboon troop who appear 'dominant' and have higher social status than other males.

alpha rhythms   Patterns of electrical activity of the brain which appear in an electro-encephalogram (EEG) when the subject is in a relaxed state, and/or daydreaming.

alternate-forms method   A system for judging how reliable a psychometric test is, which involves comparing the results produced by two different versions of the same test, if they are given to the same subjects.

altruism   Acting in the interests of other people and not of oneself.

ambiguous   Having more than one possible meaning.

Ameslan   American sign language for the deaf.

amnesia   The loss of memory, usually through physical causes.

amphetamines   Drugs commonly used for losing weight, or to provide additional short-term energy in demanding situations.

anal-expulsive   The Freudian idea of an adult character trait produced by children enjoying the act of defecation too much, and so becoming overly generous and giving.

anal-retentive   The Freudian idea of an adult character trait produced by children experiencing over-strict potty training, resulting in their developing mean or miserly characters.

anal stage   The second of Freud's psychosexual stages, in which libido focuses on the anus.

anchoring   A feature of human problem-solving in which people use one item of information as a comparison for further judgements.

anencephalic   Lacking a cerebral cortex.

angular gyrus   That part of the cortex which decodes visual stimuli for reading.

animism   Perceiving and responding to inanimate objects (rocks, computers, cars, etc.) as if they were alive and conscious.

ANS   An abbreviated term for the autonomic nervous system.

anterograde amnesia   The loss of memory for events taking place after the damage producing the amnesia.

anthropologist   A person who studies human cultures.

anthropometric   Concerned with measuring the human being ('metric' = measurement; 'anthropo' = to do with human beings).

anthropomorphism   Projecting human qualities, thoughts and feelings onto animals.

anti-locution   Talk or speech which is directed towards channelling social hostility towards a particular social group – for example, racist talk.

anticipatory schemata   Sets of ideas about what is likely to happen, which in turn direct how we respond to things that do happen.

aphasia   A specific disorder to do with being unable to form words in producing speech.

appeasement gesture   An inherited action supposed to inhibit aggressive behaviour from other members of the species.

appetitive behaviour   Behaviour which increases the likelihood of satisfying a need (e.g. seeking water when thirsty).

approach-avoidance conflict   When a goal is attractive but also has some drawbacks, it often seems more attractive while it is a long way in the future, but less so the nearer it comes. A person may become torn between wanting to achieve the goal and wishing to avoid it.

archetypes   Symbolic figures or objects which, according to Jung, resonate in the collective unconscious and produce powerful mystical responses in the human being.

arousal   A general physiological state in which the sympathetic division of the autonomic nervous system is activated.

articulatory loop   A feature of Baddeley's working memory model to do with how information may be retained in working memory through constant rehearsal.

artificial intelligence (AI)   Computer systems which are able to 'learn' and to produce the same kinds of outcomes as are produced by human thinking.

assimilation   The process of incorporating new information without changing the original character of that which is doing the assimilating. For example, incorporating new information into a schema without changing that schema; or incorporating new cultural groups or ideas into a society without that society changing its character at all.

association cortex The general name given to those parts of the cerebral cortex which do not seem to have a specific, localised function.

attention A state of specific alertness or readiness to react to particular sensory input.

attenuation The weakening of a signal, usually one which is being processed in terms of selective attention.

attitude A relatively stable, learned disposition to act in a certain kind of way towards a target.

attribution The process of giving reasons for why things happen.

attribution theory The explanation of social perception by examining how others allocate intention or meaning to the behaviour of others.

attributional style The distinctive pattern of attributions which an individual makes, in terms of whether events are usually perceived as external, stable, controllable, etc.

audience effects The way that people will often act differently when there are others present or observing, than they would if they were alone and unobserved.

auditory cortex That part of the cerebral cortex involved in hearing.

authoritarian leaders Leaders who act in an autocratic fashion, giving commands and directing action without showing interest in the views of their subordinates, unlike democratic leaders.

authoritarian personality A collection of characteristics found by Adorno to occur together, producing a rigid approach to moral and social issues.

authoritarianism A personality state which involves very rigid approaches to discipline, extreme hostility to social deviants, and a very intolerant, 'black and white' view of right and wrong.

authority figure A person who represents power or status in some way.

autistic children Severely disturbed children who withdraw from reality and contact with others.

autoganzfeld studies Ganzfeld studies of ESP which involve a computer-controlled automated procedure to prevent sensory leakage or unconscious experimenter bias.

autohypnosis Self-hypnosis

autokinetic effect A visual illusion in which a stationary dot of light in a dark room is perceived to be moving.

autonomic To do with the actions of the autonomic nervous system; sometimes used vaguely as a general term for unconscious, automatic neural functioning.

autonomic nervous system (ANS) A network of unmyelinated nerve fibres running from the brain stem and spinal cord, which can activate the body for action, or set it into a quiescent state.

autonomous morality The third of Kohlberg's stages of moral development, in which the individual is making independent moral judgements.

autonomous state A mental condition proposed by Milgram, in which the person is acting and thinking as an autonomous, independent individual, and in which individual conscience is fully active. In this condition, the individual will not do things which go against their conscience; in the agentic state, they will.

autoshaping The way that an animal may develop 'superstitious learning', performing an irrelevant behaviour before or with the desired one in an operant conditioning task.

availability heuristic A problem-solving strategy in which judgements are based on the most current or immediate information.

aversion therapy A technique of behaviour therapy which involves associating unpleasant stimuli with things that are to be avoided.

basic level concept In Rosch's categorisation, concepts which relate directly to action, and seem to link with natural categories.

behaviour shaping A process whereby novel behaviour can be produced through operant conditioning, by selecting naturally-occurring variations of learned responses.

behaviour therapy The process of treating abnormal behaviour by looking only at the symptoms, and using conditioning techniques to modify them.

behavioural Taking an approach to the understanding of human beings which focuses on the behaviour which they are actually showing, while not actually denying other dimensions of human experience.

behavioural dimension See conative dimension.

behavioural psychotherapy Psychotherapy which aims to teach people new ways of coping with problems by learning new ways of acting, e.g. through imitation and modelling.

behaviourism A reductionist school of thought which holds that the observation and description of overt behaviour is all that is needed to comprehend the human being, and that manipulation of stimulus-response contingencies is all that is needed to change human behaviour. Behaviourism denies the relevance or importance of cognitive, personal or other dimensions of human experience.

Berlin-Kay hypothesis The idea that the basic colour terms of a language form natural categories, intrinsic to all human thought, which do not vary from one culture to another except in number.

beta females   Females in a baboon troop who are low-ranking and appear to be 'subordinate' to other females.

beta males   Males in a baboon troop who are low-ranking and appear to be 'subordinate' to other males.

between-group variance   The general variation which is apparent between different samples of scores, such as the difference in height between, say, Pygmies and Europeans.

bilateral ECT   Electro-convulsive therapy which is administered to both cerebral hemispheres simultaneously.

binocular disparity   The difference in the retinal image received by the two eyes – used as a cue for judging distance.

biodiversity   The evolutionary principle that forms of life, behaviour and environmental interaction are as widely varied as possible, in order to exploit as many avenues of potential survival as possible.

biofeedback   The use of electronic signals as indicators, in order to learn voluntary control of autonomic responses.

biological determinism   A reductionist school of thought which holds that all significant human action and thought is caused by, and can be fully explained in terms of, biological factors. Such explanations may encompass genetic or pseudo-genetic factors, other physiological factors such as hormones (adrenaline, oestrogen), or organic brain damage.

bipolar   Having two opposite ends, or poles, with a continuum running between them. For example, the bipolar personal construct of 'kind-cruel' has the two ends represented by the words used to describe it; but some individuals may fit somewhere in between the two extremes – e.g. being mostly kind but not always.

bipolar depression   A disorder in which the person swings from a 'manic' state to a depressed one. Previously known as manic-depressive psychosis.

black box theories   Theories which are concerned purely with stimulus input and behavioural output.

bodily-kinaesthetic intelligence   One of Gardner's seven independent types of intelligence.

bottom-up theory   A theory which begins from the lowest level of observable data and shows how this may combine into higher-order forms.

Broca's area   A specific area in the left frontal lobe, in which damage produces aphasia.

burnout   A problem incurred by voluntary workers, social workers and others in which consistent and frustrating hard work over years produces a sense of emotional numbness, lethargy, and a lack of motivation.

bystander intervention   The issue of when and under what circumstances passers-by or other uninvolved persons are likely to offer help to those who look as though they need it.

Cannon-Bard theory of emotion   The idea that physiological responses and emotional experience are entirely separate.

Cartesian dualism   The idea that the mind and body are entirely separate, distinct entities, with neither influencing the other except in voluntary action.

castration threat anxiety   Freud's idea that the young boy is secretly afraid that his father will castrate him.

CAT scanning   See computed axial tomography.

catastrophe theory   A mathematical model used to illustrate how gradual increases in the intensity of a stimulus can produce sudden and dramatic discontinuities.

catatonic fugue   A psychotic state in which the individual's body becomes rigid and they become unable to undertake voluntary movement.

catecholinergic   A term used to describe nerve fibres which use the neurotransmitters dopamine, noradrenaline or adrenaline.

categorisation   The first stage in the process of social identification, which involves grouping other people into social categories or sets. Research shows that such categorisation, even if based on minimal criteria, may lead to a strong bias in favour of the in-group.

catharsis   The idea that aggressive or other energies can be safely discharged through harmless channels (e.g. highly competitive spectator sports). Although it has been a popular idea, dating from Plato, most research into catharsis implies that cathartic events may actually generate increased aggressive or other energies rather than reducing them.

causal attributions   The reasons which people give for why things happen.

central nervous system   The brain and spinal cord.

central route processing   The direct approach to attitude change, in which the person's attention is directly focused on the ultimate goal; e.g. being directly told to buy a particular product.

centration   In Piagetian theory, this is the child's focusing on one central characteristic of a problem, which can lead to lack of conservation, among other things.

cerebral cortex   The outer covering of the cerebral hemispheres, consisting of six layers of nerve cells, in which information is processed.

cerebral hemispheres   The name given to the two halves of the cerebrum.

cerebrum   The part of the brain responsible for cognition, the co-ordinating of information and the initiation of voluntary action.

charismatic authority   Authority which someone has acquired because of their distinctive personality or abilities.

chemotherapy   Treatment for physical or psychiatric disorders which involves the use of drugs.

chromosomes Long strands of DNA in the cell nucleus, organised in matching pairs.

chunking Combining items of information into meaningful or semi-meaningful larger items, so permitting an extension of the amount which can be held in short-term memory.

circadian rhythms Biological rhythms based on a 24-hour cycle or near equivalent.

clairvoyance Gaining information about objects or the environment without using recognised sensory channels.

classical concepts Concepts in which each example of the concept possesses all of the distinguishing features.

classical conditioning A form of learning which involves direct links between stimulus and response, learned through association.

client-centred therapy An approach to psychotherapy developed by Carl Rogers, in which the client is regarded as the best person to understand and resolve their own psychological problems, and the therapist's role is to provide a supportive environment to enable that to happen.

clinical depression Depression which is so severe that it is considered to be a psychiatric disorder as opposed to merely an unpleasant mood.

clinical interview A technique used by Piaget in studying children, based on asking them questions in an informal setting.

clinical neuropsychology The branch of psychology concerned with investigating how the brain works by studying the effects of brain damage, disease or injury.

cloning The process of creating genetically identical animals artificially, by causing the cells of parent animals to reproduce and develop into whole animals based on genetic information in the cell nucleus.

closure The Gestalt principle of perceptual organisation, which describes how we tend to complete fragmented images mentally, so that they form whole shapes.

cocktail party phenomenon The phenomenon in selective attention in which someone may be attending only to an immediate conversation yet may nonetheless catch their own name if it is mentioned elsewhere.

coding Converting information into a form in which it can be represented in the brain.

coercive power Power which is based on the fact that the person is in a position to force others to obey them, through threat of punishment of some kind.

cognition Mental processes. Cognition includes the processes of perception, memory, thinking, reasoning, language, and some types of learning.

cognitive balance The idea that people prefer their different beliefs to be congruent, and not to contradict one another. Imbalance is thought to lead to attitude change.

cognitive dimension The aspect of an attitude which is to do with thoughts, opinions and beliefs held in relation to the target of the attitude.

cognitive dissonance The tension produced by cognitive imbalance – holding beliefs which directly contradict one another. The reduction of cognitive dissonance has been shown to be a factor in some forms of attitude change.

cognitive maps Mental images about where things are. People develop cognitive maps as they get to know a town or an institution; rats develop one as they explore experiential mazes.

cognitive processes Mental operations, such as thinking, remembering, forming concepts, perceiving, or using language.

cognitive science A multidisciplinary approach to studying artificial intelligence and similar phenomena, bringing together psychologists, linguists, information scientists and others.

cognitive style A distinctive pattern of thinking or problem-solving.

cognitive therapy A form of psychotherapy which is based on changing people's beliefs, attitudes and attributions about their worlds, and so helping them to act more positively and to change things for the better.

companionate love A form of love which is based on mutual friendship and affection, which generally develops over a long period of time.

comparative psychology The study of animal behaviour in such a way as to explore the mechanisms and principles underlying it.

complementary needs hypothesis The idea that some couples are attracted to one another because they are opposite personalities, and therefore each can fulfil the other's personal needs – e.g. one is talkative while the other likes to listen.

complex cells Nerve cells found in the thalamus which fire in response to lines at a particular orientation, anywhere in the visual field.

compliance The process of going along with other people – i.e. conforming – but without accepting their views on a personal level.

componential intelligence The part of Sternberg's triarchic model of intelligence which is concerned with, and consists of, mental process and skills.

Computed Axial Tomography A method of detecting brain abnormality by examining a series of X-ray 'photos' taken successively through the brain.

computer metaphor The idea that the human brain works like a computer in the way that it processes information.

computer simulation   The attempt to develop computer programmes which will replicate human processes such as skill learning or problem-solving.

conative dimension   Also known as the behavioural dimension, this is the dimension of an attitude which is concerned with the tendency to act – how likely it is that the person will take action in accordance with their expressed attitudes.

concrete operational stage   The third of Piaget's four stages of cognitive development, characterised by a need to relate problems to real circumstances or events.

concurrent validity   A method for assessing whether a psychometric test is valid (i.e. really measures what it is supposed to) by comparing it with some other measure which has been taken at the same time – i.e. which is occurring concurrently.

conditioned response   A learned response which is produced to a conditioned stimulus.

conditioned stimulus   A stimulus which only brings about a response because it has been associated with an unconditioned stimulus.

conditions of worth   Internalised ideas about what personal qualities or achievements will make someone a valuable or worthwhile person, which are developed as a result of experiences with other people. According to Carl Rogers, the realism of the individual's conditions of worth are a main factor in the maintenance of self-esteem, or lack of it.

cone cells   Cells in the retina which respond to different wavelengths of light, and therefore indicate colour.

confabulation   Remembering events or information inaccurately as a result of applying pre-existing knowledge.

conformity   The process of going along with other people – i.e. acting in the same way that they do.

confounding variable   A variable which causes a change in the dependent variable, but which is not the independent variable of the study.

connector neurone   A nerve cell found in the central nervous system which links together other nerve cells.

consensus   A factor in the covariance approach to attribution, which is to do with whether other people also act in the same sort of way.

conservation   The ability to recognise that volume, number or mass do not change when presentation changes.

consistency   A factor in the covariance approach to attribution, which is to do with whether the person always, or usually, acts in that way.

construct validity   A method for assessing whether a psychometric test is valid (i.e. really measures what it is supposed to) by seeing how it matches up with theoretical ideas about what it is supposed to be measuring.

constructive alternativism   The principle that each person's psychological reality is constructed on a personal basis, from their own distinctively individual experience.

consummatory behaviour   Behaviour which directly satisfies an inner need state, such as drinking when thirsty.

consummatory stimulation   Stimulation which directly satisfies an inner need state, e.g. the presence of the egg in the nest for a brooding hen.

contact hypothesis   The idea that prejudice can be effectively reduced simply as a result of two groups having frequent contact with one another. In practice, however, there are other conditions which also need to be met (such as that the two groups would have equal status), for the effective reduction of prejudice.

contextual intelligence   The part of Sternberg's triarchic model of intelligence which emphasises that intelligent acts always take place in a context – something which is an intelligent thing to do in one context may be stupid in another. Contexts range from being very specific, like an immediate circumstance or situation, to being very broad, like an entire culture or society.

control group   A group which is used for comparison with an experimental group.

controllable attributions   Judgements about why things happened which contain the idea that they could potentially be directed or controlled – generally by the person who is making the attribution.

conventional morality   The second of Kohlberg's stages of moral development.

convergent thinking   Thinking which is directed towards getting a single 'right' answer to a problem, concentrating on strict logic, and ruling out creative or intuitive thinking.

corpus callosum   The mass of nerve fibres which join the two cerebral hemispheres.

correlated asymmetries   Features of an animal and its behaviour which are linked, and together indicate how successful that animal might be in a fight – e.g. the roaring of a stag and its muscular strength and size.

correlation   When two variables vary together. The variation may be either positive (in the same direction) or negative (in the opposite direction).

correlation coefficient   A number between −1 and +1 which expresses how strong a correlation is. If this number is close to 0, there is no real connection between the two; if it is close to +1 there is a positive correlation – in other words, if one variable is large the other will also tend to be large; and if it is close to −1, there is a negative correlation – in other words, if one variable is large, the other will tend to be small.

correspondent inference theory   A variant of attribution theory which looks at how people infer that an act came from dispositional or situational causes, by drawing on things like whether its consequences affected them personally or not.

courtship displays Sequences of behaviour, distinctive to its species, which a particular animal performs in order to attract a mate.

courtship rituals Joint patterns of behaviour performed by two or more animals prior to mating.

covariance theory A variant of attribution theory which looks at how people judge whether an act was deliberate or not by looking at three aspects of the situation: consensus (whether other people do it too); consistency (whether that person always does it); and distinctiveness (whether they act that way in similar circumstances or not).

covert observation Observation in which those being observed are unaware of the fact that they are being studied.

criterion validity A method for assessing whether a psychometric test is valid (i.e. really measures what it is supposed to) by comparing it with some other measure. If the other measure is assessed at roughly the same time as the original one, then the type of criterion validity being applied is concurrent validity; if it is taken much later, it is predictive validity.

critical period A genetically-determined time during development when a particular form of learning must take place if it is ever to be learned at all.

cross-cueing Using one sensory mode to provide information which makes sense of stimuli being received through another mode. In split-brain patients, cross-cueing refers to clues given by one cerebral hemisphere to the other using slight movements of the body.

curare A nerve poison which works by blocking the reception of acetylcholine at the model end plate, so causing paralysis.

decentre To take another person's point of view.

decision frames The set of assumptions within which a particular decision is made.

deep dyslexia Dyslexia in which people find it particularly hard to comprehend words which cannot be concretely visualised.

deep structure The underlying organisation of a language, concerned with meanings and what the words of that language represent.

defence mechanisms Protective strategies that the mind uses to defend itself against unwelcome or disturbing information.

deindividuation The idea that riots and other types of crowd behaviour can be explained in terms of a kind of 'mob psychology' in which the anonymity produced by the lack of individual identifiers causes people to abandon such aspects of individuality as conscience, consideration, etc.

delta rhythm Patterns of electrical activity of the brain which appear in an electro-encephalogram (EEG) when the person is concentrating very hard.

demand characteristics Those aspects of a psychological study (or other artificial situation) which exert an implicit pressure on people to act in ways that are expected of them.

democratic leaders Leaders who make decisions only after consulting with subordinates and discussing issues with them.

dendrites Branches at the endings of the axons of nerve cells, which allow the cell to make connections with several other neurones.

dependent variable The thing which is measured in an experiment, and which changes, depending on the independent variable.

depressive attributional style A distinctive pattern of making attributions which is often shown by those who are chronically depressed, and which helps to perpetuate the depression.

depth cue Something which gives an indication of how far away an object is.

determinism A style of thinking in which all human action or experience is assumed to be directly caused.

developmental dyslexia A form of dyslexia which does not seem to have any specific organic origin.

dialect A distinctive pattern of language use shared by a regional or socio-economic group, which has its own vocabulary and grammatical forms.

dialectical An interrelationship in which two apparently opposite or opposing entities or ideas combine to form an entirely new synthesis. Each influences the other and is influenced by it, such that together the relationship produces something new.

diary method A way of studying what human beings do in everyday life by asking them to note down specific items of information at regular intervals, or on appropriate occasions.

dice-tossing studies Studies of psychokinesis in which the person aims to influence the fall of a dice.

dichotic listening task A way of studying selective attention by presenting different messages simultaneously to each ear, and asking people to report what they hear.

dictionary unit A word-recognition unit, or logogen, used in models of cognitive processing.

diffusion of impact The observation that bystanders are less likely to intervene to help someone if there are several others present who would be equally likely to be able to help.

diffusion of responsibility The idea that people are less likely to intervene to help someone who seems to need it if there are others present (see diffusion of impact) because they perceive responsibility as being shared between all present, and therefore see themselves as being less personally responsible.

digit memory span   The number of items that a person can repeat accurately, from a list of digits (letters or numbers) which is read out to them only once. Most people can remember about seven, but it is normal for digit memory span to be anywhere between five and nine. Digit memory span correlates with measured intelligence. Since digit span tests often form a component of intelligence tests this may not be very surprising.

diglossia   The ability to speak in more than one form of language, e.g. 'posh' English and colloquial English, as the situation demands.

direct perception   The idea that our nervous system is designed to allow us to pick up relevant information straight from the optic array, without the need for complex cognitive interpretation.

discourse analysis   A method of studying human experience by analysing the things people say to one another, and how they express them, both symbolically and behaviourally.

discrimination   The skill of distinguishing one stimulus from another, usually learned through selective conditioning.

disembedded thought   Thinking which is not applied in any meaningful context, but is just treated as a separate, distinct task with no relevance to the real world.

disorganised schizophrenia   A form of schizophrenia in which the person's thoughts and speech become apparently irrational.

dispositional attribution   When the cause of a particular behaviour is thought to have resulted from the person's own personality or characteristics, rather than from the demands of circumstances.

distinctiveness   A factor in the covariance approach to attribution which is to do with whether the person acts in the same way in similar situations to the one being considered, or not.

diurnal rhythms   Biological rhythms, based on the day/night cycle, and shown by animals which are generally awake during the day.

divergent thinking   Thinking which is intuitive or creative, often involving non-logical 'leaps' or sudden ideas.

DMILS   An abbreviation for 'direct mental interaction with living systems', which is the term used in parapsychology to refer to psi phenomena such as telepathy or healing.

DNA   Deoxyribonucleic acid – the complex molecule chain which occurs in the cell nucleus, and 'codes' genetic information.

dogmatism   A rigid personality trait similar to authoritarianism, but one which can be left-wing too (authori-

tarianism is always right-wing). Like authoritarianism, it includes intolerance of those who differ from the established view, a rigid 'black-and-white' approach to issues, and an extreme and personal categorising of 'us and them'.

dominance hierarchy   A form of social organisation in which each animal is ranked, and will act aggressively towards those below it and submissively towards those with higher ranking.

dopamine   A major neurotransmitter found in the central nervous system.

double-bind   A disturbed pattern of social interaction in which a person becomes trapped by two conflicting and equally unpleasant injunctions, with a third implicit injunction preventing them from escaping from the situation altogether.

double-blind control   A form of experimental control which aims to avoid self-fulfilling prophecies by ensuring that neither the research participants nor the experimenter who carries out the study are aware of the experimental hypothesis.

down-through technique   A method of testing for clairvoyance, in which the participant has to call out the sequence of a pack of Zener cards, before anyone has looked at it. The idea was that this method could distinguish between clairvoyance and telepathy.

dreamwork   The process of using hidden symbolism in dreams to express inner conflicts and unconscious desires.

drive theories   Theories of human motivation which explain why we do things, using the idea that our behaviour is directed towards reducing some inner need. The need then sets up an internal tension, and the desire to reduce this tension forms a pressure to act (the drive) which is only reduced when the need becomes satisfied.

DSM-IV   A system for classifying mental disorders.

dyadic phase   The stage in the breakdown in a relationship where both members of a couple become involved – in other words, where the decision of one partner to end the relationship is communicated to the other.

dynamic equilibrium   A balance between two opposing pressures which is achieved by constant movement and adjustment between them.

dyslexia   A term given to disorders in the processing and interpretation of visual word information.

ecological   Pertaining to 'real-life', or everyday situations, as opposed to artificially constructed laboratory simulation.

ecological validity   A way of assessing how valid a measure or test is (i.e. whether it really measures what it is supposed to measure) which is concerned with whether the measure or test is really like its counterpart in the real, everyday world. In other words, whether it is truly realistic or not.

ECT   See electro-convulsive therapy.

EEG   See electro-encephalogram.

efferent neurone   A neurone which carries information away from the brain and spinal cord.

ego   According to Freud, that part of the mind which is in touch with reality, and balancing its demands with those of the id and superego.

ego-state   Modes of interacting with other people, described by Berne as falling into three types: Parent, Adult and Child.

egocentricity   The assumption that the entire world centres about the self, and that nothing exists except that which impinges directly on the person.

eidetic memory   'Photographic' memory – visual or acoustic memory which is so accurate as to be almost like a factual record.

Einstellung   A form of mental set in which the person becomes unable to solve problems because they are trying to do so within self-imposed constraints.

elaborated language codes   Ways of using language characterised by extensive vocabulary, complex grammatical structure, and an attempt to make meaning verbally explicit.

Electra conflict   A Freudian attempt to explain female gender-role identification by means of a supposed penis envy on the part of the young girl, and rivalry with the mother.

electrical potential   The burst of electricity produced by a nerve cell when firing.

electrical stimulation of the brain (ESB)   Direct positive reinforcement delivered to the brain by means of electrodes implanted in the hypothalamus.

electro-convulsive therapy (ECT)   A psychiatric treatment which involves passing an electric current through the brain, producing an epileptic fit. Believed by some to lift endogenous depression.

electro-encephalogram (EEG)   A record of the brain's electrical activity obtained by attaching electrodes to the scalp.

empathy   Sharing in someone else's feelings; being able to feel with them even though not undergoing the same experience.

empiricism   An approach to knowledge which assumes that all knowledge of the world is learned through the input of information from the five external senses.

enactive representation   Representing information in the mind by means of impressions of actions – 'muscle memories'.

encounter groups   Self-help groups originated by Carl Rogers, designed to generate unconditional positive regard between their members in order to facilitate personal growth.

endocrine system   A network of glands and ducts which release hormones into the bloodstream, and so induce or maintain physiological states of the body.

endogenous depression   A form of depression which appears to occur without any obvious precipitating factors.

engram   The name given to a theoretical 'memory trace' in the brain.

entrapment   The way that people, committees, etc. can become unable to withdraw from unwinnable situations because they feel that they have already invested too much in them to give up.

environmental psychology   The branch of psychology which is particularly concerned with how people's behaviour and experience is influenced by the physical and social environments that they find themselves in.

episodes   Units of social action which are complete and meaningful in themselves while still forming part of an ongoing sequence – much like a scene in a play. Harré proposed that the study of episodes, rather than acts or actions, should form the basic unit of social analysis.

episodic memory   A store of personal experiences and events, tied to specific contexts – memory for things which have happened.

epistemology   The way that a particular type of knowledge works: what counts as valid reasoning or evidence in different areas of expertise or knowledge.

equilibration   The process by which schemata are developed, to take account of new information.

equipotentiality   The idea that learning and memory are distributed throughout the association cortex, and that it is the overall amount of cortex, not specific areas, which determine these abilities.

equity theory   The idea that social conventions and norms are based around a principle of fair, though not necessarily strictly equal, exchange.

ESB   See electrical stimulation of the brain.

ESP   See extra-sensory perception.

ethical   To do with rights and wrongs.

ethnocentricity   Being unable to conceptualise or imagine ideas, social beliefs, or the world from any viewpoint other than that of one's own particular culture or social group.

ethnolinguistics   The study of variation in language as manifest in particular cultural, ethnic or subcultural groups.

ethogenics   An approach to studying social experience developed by Harré, which emphasises the importance of complete episodes and verbal accounts.

ethology   The study of behaviour in the natural environment.

eugenics   The political idea that the human race could be improved by eliminating 'undesirables' from the breeding stock, so that they cannot pass on their supposedly inferior genes. Some eugenicists advocate compulsory sterilisation, while others seem to prefer mass murder or genocide.

evoked potential   A characteristic pattern of electrical activity in the brain which shows up on EEGs (electro-encephalograms), and is produced in response to a particular stimulus.

evolution   The process of species development through small genetic changes leading to adaptive fitness for the individual.

excitatory synapse   A synapse which, when activated, makes the receptor neurone more likely to fire.

existentialist therapy   Therapy which is based on the idea that each individual is ultimately responsible for their existence in the world and the life-choices which they make.

exogenous depression   Depression which is believed to have occurred as a result of external precipitating factors, such as bereavement.

experiential intelligence   The part of Sternberg's triarchic theory of intelligence which is concerned with what the individual has learned from their own personal experience.

experiment   A form of research in which variables are manipulated in order to discover cause and effect.

experimental rigour   The carefulness with which an experiment is conducted; the care taken when conducting an experiment to make sure that all procedures and controls are implemented effectively.

experimenter effects   Unwanted influences in a psychological study which are produced, consciously or unconsciously, by the person carrying out the study.

expert power   Power which is based on the fact that the person has special skills or expertise in a relevant area.

expert systems   Artificial intelligence systems designed to provide human experts with an extended information source, to aid them in making decisions.

external locus of control   The feeling or belief that events are caused by situations or by others, and cannot be influenced by oneself.

extinction   The dying-out of a response through lack of reinforcement.

extra-sensory perception   Acquiring information from a target in the environment, without using normal sensory channels.

extroversion   A general tendency towards outgoing, social behaviour.

eye contact   Mutual gaze, or when two people are each looking at the other's eyes at the same time.

face recognition unit   A hypothetical information-processing unit in the mind which is involved in identifying known people by their faces.

face validity   Whether a test or measure looks on the surface as though it probably measures what it is supposed to.

facilitator   One who acts to encourage positive inter-personal processes to take place, e.g. in an encounter group.

factor analysis   A method of statistical analysis which examines intercorrelations between data in order to identify major clusters or groupings which might be caused by a single common factor.

family therapy   An approach to psychotherapy in which individual dysfunction is seen as a family problem, rather than a personal one, and in which communication patterns and alliances within the family are explored and sometimes challenged.

Faraday cage   An enclosure of metal bars or wires, which blocks electrical and radio transmission. Faraday cages were used in remote viewing studies, because it was believed that psi abilities might occur as a result of the transmission of mental 'electricity' from the sender.

fatigue effect   An experimental effect brought about by the subject's becoming tired or bored.

feature list theories   Theories of concept formation which assume that an item is judged to belong in a category if it possesses the key features of that category.

feedback   Knowledge about the effectiveness of one's performance on a task or set of tasks. Feedback appears to be essential in most forms of learning, and is more effective if it is immediate.

fight or flight response   A physiological reaction produced by the sympathetic division of the ANS in response to threat or anger, which results in the body being activated for energy.

figure-ground organisation   The structuring of visual experience into shapes (figures) against backgrounds.

file-drawer problem   The problem of selective reporting in psychological research, in that only studies with positive findings tend to be reported in journals, while unsuccessful studies tend to remain in the experimenter's filing cabinet and are not sent off for publication.

filter theory   Theories of selective attention which see unwanted information as being excluded, as opposed to wanted information being actively sought.

five robust factors   The recurrent finding that personality questionnaires produce results which, when factor analysed, fall into five groups, thought to represent basic personality traits.

fixation   In Freudian terms, the process of becoming 'stuck' in an early phase of psychological development.

fixed action patterns   Inherited sequences of behaviour, performed in response to a sign stimulus.

fixed role therapy   A form of psychotherapy in which people act out roles different from those which they would normally adopt.

flashbulb memories   Fully complete contextual memories associated with dramatic happenings or events.

forced-choice test A way of conducting research in which the possible responses from the participant are restricted to a limited number of options; in contrast with free-response tests.

formal operational stage The fourth of Piaget's four stages of cognitive development, emphasising abstract thinking and logical reasoning.

fovea The central part of the retina, where the visual image is most clearly focused.

free-response test A way of collecting information from research participants in which they are allowed freedom to say or choose what they like, in contrast with forced-choice tests.

frontal lobe The front part of the cerebrum of the brain.

frontal lobotomy The removal of the front part of the cerebrum, once thought to reduce aggression and now known to damage planning and decision-making abilities.

frustration-aggression hypothesis The idea that frustrating circumstances or events, in which someone is prevented from reaching or achieving a desired goal, can produce aggression. Goals in this context do not need to be specific: for example, oppressive or impoverished social circumstances may frustrate a goal of leading a secure and comfortable life.

functional fixedness The state of being unable to think of any other use for an object except the one that it is normally used for.

fundamental attribution error The way that people tend to apply different standards in attributing reasons for other people's actions than they do with their own. Specifically, people tend to assess their own actions as resulting from situational demands, but other people's as resulting from dispositional causes.

g The abbreviation for 'general intelligence': a kind of intelligence which is supposed to underpin all different types of mental operations, as opposed to more specific types of talents or aptitudes.

galvanic skin resistance (GSR) The electrical conductivity of the skin, which varies with degrees of stress and is therefore used in lie-detector tests and other methods of arousal.

ganzfeld An entirely featureless perceptual field. Ganzfelds were used by the Gestalt psychologists in early research into the nature of perception, and are currently used by parapsychological researchers, as the technique is thought to facilitate ESP.

GAS See general adaptation syndrome.

Gaussian distribution A statistical distribution illustrated by a bell-shaped curve. Also known as the normal distribution.

gene A unit of heredity, represented biologically by a specific DNA sequence.

gene pool The complete range of possible inherited traits available within the gene of a given population of animals or plants.

general adaptation syndrome The process of physiological adaptation to long-term stress, resulting in lowered resistance to illness and other negative outcomes.

general mental ability tests Another term for intelligence tests, which is preferred in occupational testing circles.

General Problem Solver An early computer simulation programme which used means-end analysis to solve simple problems.

generalisation A process by which a learned response will occur in more situations than those in which it was first learned.

genetic determinism A reductionist school of thought which holds that human behaviour, capabilities, etc. are entirely determined (caused) by inherited mechanisms, and therefore not particularly susceptible to environmental influences, except to a very minor degree. Such theories are generally closely associated with right-wing political thinking, and reach their ultimate political expression in the theory of eugenics.

genetic engineering The process of altering genetic characteristics through microscopic intervention.

genetic reductionism The idea that all, or almost all, psychology can be explained simply as a product of genetic influences.

genetic transmission The passing on of inherited characteristics from parent to offspring.

genital stage In Freudian theory, a stage of psychological development around puberty in which libido becomes focused on the genitals and the individual develops an interest in the other sex.

genotype The total set of potential inherited characteristics present in an individual's chromosomes.

geometric illusions Visual illusions which utilise geometric lines and figures to have their effect.

Gestalt psychology A school of psychology which opposed the S-R reductionism of the behaviourists and instead emphasised a human tendency towards wholeness of experience and cognition.

Gestalt therapy A form of psychotherapy which emphasised the importance of complete sensory experience.

GPS See general problem solver.

gradient of colour A monocular cue to depth which concerns how colours appear to fade with distance.

gradient of texture A monocular cue to depth which concerns how textures and fine details of the surfaces of objects appear smoother with distance.

grapheme A basic unit of written language.

grave-dressing phase   The stage in relationship break-down where the couple concentrate on recovering from the break-up, and elaborating their own version of what has occurred.

group polarisation   The observation that people will often make more extreme decisions when they are working in a group than the members of such a group would make as individuals. Such decisions may be more extreme in either direction: they may be more risky or more conservative.

group selection theories   Models of evolution based on the idea that a trait might evolve because it helped the species as a whole to survive rather than the individual.

group therapy   A form of psychotherapy in which several patients interact with one another and the therapist, as opposed to the one-to-one situation of individual therapy.

groupthink   The way that a committee, members of a club, or other group of people may become divorced from reality as a result of their own social consensus. Groupthink means that they may make decisions which are dangerous or stupid because the group fails to question their own assumptions or to take into account unwelcome aspects of reality which may have a bearing on the situation.

GSR   See galvanic skin resistance.

habituation   Becoming accustomed to a stimulus, such that it is no longer registered by sensory neurones.

hallucinogens   Drugs which can cause people to have hallucinations – to see or experience things which are not actually there.

hedonic relevance   The tendency that people have to be more likely to make a dispositional attribution about the cause of something if that something has either pleasant or unpleasant consequences for them. Acts which have neutral consequences are more readily judged to have occurred as a result of the situation.

hemispherectomy   The surgical removal of a complete cerebral hemisphere.

hereditarian   Emphasising inherited mechanisms (e.g. in intelligence) to the exclusion, or minimisation, of other factors.

heritability   A numerical value assigned to intelligence on the misleading assumption that it is possible to separate and quantify inherited and learned components.

hermeneutic   Concerned with the nature of social meaning and interpretation.

heteronomous   Subject to the laws of others.

heuristics   Strategies for solving problems which involve taking the step which looks most likely to lead towards a solution, even if this is uncertain.

hidden observer   A phenomenon observed in hypnosis, in which part of the mind remains detached and observes dispassionately.

high drive state   A condition in which a particular drive is thought to be very strong – in other words, a drive-theory explanation for when an individual is strongly motivated to do something.

hindsight bias   The tendency to perceive a solution as obvious in retrospect, while it was nothing of the sort at the time.

hippocampus   One of the sub-cortical areas of the brain.

home range   The area within which an animal will usually forage for food.

homeostasis   A state of physiological balance or equilibrium in the body.

homophones   Words which sound the same as one another.

homunculus   A distorted image of the body or body-shape, e.g. as represented on the motor and somatosensory cortical areas.

hypercomplex cells   Cells in the thalamus which fire in response to simple shapes or sets of lines.

hypnosis   A condition of extreme suggestibility, in which a person voluntarily co-operates with suggestions made by a hypnotist. It is questionable whether hypnosis is a 'special state', or merely a normal extension of human sociability.

hypnotherapist   One who uses hypnosis to help people to deal with psychological problems, usually through autohypnosis.

hypothetico-deductive research   Research which is conducted on the basis of using theory to generate hypotheses, and then carrying out the research in order to see if the hypotheses appear to hold up. The alternative is inductive research.

iconic representation   Coding information in the mind by means of sensory images, usually, though not always, visual ones.

id   The primitive part of the unconscious personality, according to Freud.

identification   The process of social learning which involves feeling oneself to be the same as, or very similar to, another person and basing one's styles of interaction on that comparison.

ideology   A set of overriding political or philosophical beliefs which govern the assumptions of a particular culture or society.

idiographic   Describing ('graphic') the individual ('idio'). The term idiographic is particularly used to describe those personality tests which are concerned with looking in detail at the characteristics of the single person, and not with comparing that person with other members of the population.

idiolect   The personal or idiosyncratic form of language used by a single individual.

idiosyncratic   Specific to that particular person or group, and not typical of others.

idiots savants   People who appear mentally retarded with respect to general intellectual abilities, yet show outstanding mental ability in one narrow area – like being able to add up extremely rapidly and accurately, or calculate the days of the week of any specific date in the past few thousand years.

illusory correlation   The impression that two events or facts are related because they occur together, even though there may really be no connection between them.

imagery   Forms of mental representation which are based on, and seem to take the form of, physical sensations (e.g. mental pictures).

imitation   Copying someone else's behaviour and specific actions.

implicit personality theory   The intuitive ideas about which character traits normally fit together, which form the basis of everyday predictions about other people and what they are likely to be like.

implosion therapy   A form of behaviour therapy based on 'overkill', in which the person is continually faced with the feared stimulus until their fear dies down.

impression formation   How we develop ideas about what people are like, when we first encounter them.

imprinting   A very rapid form of learning, shown by precocial animals soon after birth, resulting in a rapid and powerful attachment to a parent.

inclusive fitness   The sociobiological principle that an act may be genetically beneficial even if it results in an individual's death, as long as that death ensures survival of relatives carrying the same genes.

independent-measures design   When a study involves comparing the scores from two or more separate groups of people.

independent variable   The conditions which an experimenter sets up, to cause an effect in an experiment. These vary systematically, so that the experimenter can draw conclusions about changes.

inductive research   Research in which investigation and observation are conducted first, and theory is developed on the basis of the outcome. This forms an alternative to the hypothetico-deductive approach of scientific enquiry, and one which is increasingly used in psychology, for example in analysing accounts.

informational power   Power which is based on the fact that the person has particular knowledge which is pertinent to the situation or people involved.

infrasound   Sound which is too low to be detected by human ears.

inhibitory synapse   A synapse which, when activated, makes the receptor neurone less likely to fire.

innate   Literally meaning inborn, this is generally used to mean inherited; passed on through genetic transmission, and therefore not a result of any environmental influences.

innate releasing mechanism (IRM)   A hypothetical 'trigger' which activates fixed action patterns when the appropriate environmental stimulus is present.

insight learning   Learning which takes place as a result of making a sudden mental connection, and seeing the solution all at once; as opposed to more gradual forms of learning in which the solution is arrived at a little bit at a time, like trial and error learning.

instinct theories   The name given to the old-fashioned ideas that the reasons why people do things or act in certain ways is because they are driven by some kind of inborn pressure, or 'instinct'.

insulin shock therapy   An antiquated form of psychiatric treatment in which the patient was subjected to a coma through an overdose of insulin.

intelligence quotient (IQ)   A numerical figure, believed by some to indicate the level of a person's intelligence, which indicates how well that person performs on intelligence tests.

interactionism   The approach to understanding human and animal behaviour which emphasises links between different levels of explanation, and is therefore the opposite of reductionism.

interactive programmes   Computer programmes which are designed to vary their responses depending on the input which they receive from the people using them.

interference   The distortion or disruption of memory which happens as a result of other information being learned or already stored in memory.

intergroup rivalry   Competition between different social groups, which can often lead to powerful hostility.

internal attribution   The judgement that a behaviour or act is caused by sources within the person – i.e. their character, personality or intentions. This is also known as dispositional attribution.

internal locus of control   The belief that important life events are largely caused by one's own efforts, abilities, etc. as opposed to being caused by external circumstances.

interpersonal   Literally 'between persons', this term is used to describe actions or occurrences which involve at least two people affecting one another in some way.

intra-psychic phase   The first stage in relationship breakdown in which one person acknowledges to themselves that their increasing dissatisfaction with the relationship has got beyond the point where things can be salvaged, and makes the decision to end the relationship.

introspection   Looking 'inwards' to analyse or explore one's own mental state, beliefs or ideas.

introversion   A general tendency towards solitary, withdrawn behaviour.

ipsative tests   Tests which are used to show the balance of different characteristics within one individual, but not to compare people with one another.

ipsilateral   Occurring on the same side.

IQ   See intelligence quotient.

IRM   See innate releasing mechanism.

James-Lange theory of emotion   A theory which states that our experience of emotion derives from our perceptions of physiological changes in the body.

jet lag   Disruption of the circadian rhythms of the body caused by the need to adjust rapidly to different time zones.

job aptitude tests   Psychometric tests which assess whether someone is likely to be good at a particular job – in other words, whether they have the right type of mental skills or talents so that they should be able to learn the job quickly and easily.

juvenile delinquent   A young person who breaks the law.

kin selection   A sociobiological concept based on the observation that animals (and humans) will sometimes commit altruistic acts, if necessary sacrificing themselves, in order to allow their close relatives to survive. This is interpreted in sociobiological theory as being an evolutionary mechanism by which the 'genes' (defined as units of heredity, although not the same as the biological concept) which the individual and its relatives have in common, will survive.

kinaesthetic senses   The bodily senses which inform us about the position and state of the muscles, skeletal system and internal organs.

knowledge frame   The context and criteria of relevance within which a given problem is set.

Korsakoff's syndrome   A condition of severe memory loss and anterograde amnesia brought about by long-term alcohol abuse.

labelling theory   The approach to understanding social behaviour which is based on the idea of the self-fulfilling prophecy – that expectations can become self-confirming, because the people concerned act as if they were already true.

latency period   In Freudian theory, a period of childhood during which the libido becomes diffused throughout the body and the child is supposed to become sexually passive.

latent content   The Freudian term for the hidden content of dreams – the meanings which are concealed by the dreamwork.

latent learning   Learning which takes place without producing an immediate change in behaviour.

lateral geniculate nuclei   An area of the thalamus where the cells forming the optic nerve synapse with those leading to the visual cortex.

lateral hypothalamus (LH)   A specific region of the hypothalamus thought to be involved in regulating hunger.

lateral thinking   An approach to problem-solving which deliberately steps outside conventional assumptions and frameworks in seeking solutions.

Law of Effect   The learning principle that actions which have a pleasant effect on the organism are likely to be repeated.

Law of Effort   The principle in imprinting that the more of a struggle the young animal has to follow its parent, the stronger its imprinted bond will become.

Law of Equipotentiality   The principle that all of the association cortex (those parts of the cerebral cortex without specifically localised function) are equally important in learning and memory.

Law of Exercise   The principle that if a stimulus and action occur together regularly, they will come to form a learned association.

Law of Mass Action   The principle that it is the amount of cerebral cortex available which determines effective learning and memory, not the location of that cortex.

Laws of Prägnanz   A set of perceptual principles identified by the Gestalt psychologists, through which visual information is given shape and form.

lay epistemology   The study of how everyday beliefs and social representations are adopted, transmitted and changed, and of what counts as valid knowledge in socially accepted belief systems.

learned helplessness   The way that the experience of being forced into the role of passive victim in one situation can generalise to other situations, such that the person or animal makes no effort to help themselves in unpleasant situations even if such effort would be effective.

learning curve   A distinctive graph pattern produced when mapping the time taken to learn a new behaviour.

learning sets   A preparedness to undertake certain familiar types of learning.

legitimate power   Power which is based on the fact that the person has achieved a relevant position, or as a result of other socially-accepted criteria.

lesion   Some form of damage to an area of the brain or body. Lesions may be accidental or surgically induced.

leucotomy   The cutting of the fibres leading from the frontal lobes of the cerebrum to the rest of the brain.

levels of processing theory   The idea that what determines whether information is remembered, and for how long, is how deeply it is processed – i.e. thought about and linked with other information.

lexical representation of a language The image of the world contained implicitly in the words of that language.

LH See lateral hypothalamus.

libido The sexual and life-affirming energy which Freud initially saw as the energising factor for all human behaviour. In later work, he added the idea of a destructive energy: thanatos.

limerence The term used for a powerful infatuation, to distinguish it from long-term love.

limited capacity model An approach to understanding selective attention based on the idea that the brain can only cope with a relatively small amount of information at a time.

linguistic determinism The idea that thinking is entirely shaped by language.

linguistic relativity hypothesis The idea that thinking depends on language, and so people who speak different languages also inhabit different conceptual worlds.

Lloyd Morgan's canon The principle that animal behaviour should always be explained using the lowest possible level of explanation.

lobotomy The surgical removal of the frontal lobes of the cerebrum.

localisation of function The way that some psychological functions such as language seem to be mediated by very specific areas of the cerebral cortex.

locus of control Where control of what happens is perceived to come from. An internal locus of control means that the person sees it as coming from within themselves – so they are largely in control of what happens to them, or at least in a position to influence it. An external locus of control means that it is perceived as coming from sources outside of the person, and so is not something which the individual can influence.

logogen A hypothetical 'word-recognition unit' used in cognitive models of how verbal information is processed by the brain.

longitudinal study A study which monitors changes occurring over a period of time.

LTM The common abbreviation for long-term memory.

lucid dreaming Dreaming in which the person is aware that they are asleep and dreaming.

macro-PK Psychokinesis in which the parapsychological influence on the target is visible by the naked eye.

Magnetic Resonancy Imaging Scanning the working brain by passing a series of electro-magnetic waves through it, causing neural activity which is then recorded.

mania A form of psychosis in which the person experiences an elated mood and a high level of energy, and often makes wild plans and proposals.

manic-depressive psychosis See bipolar depression.

manifest content The Freudian term for what actually happens in a dream, as opposed to its latent content.

matching Making sure that two sets of experimental materials or subjects are the same in all important respects.

matching hypothesis The idea that members of couples mostly match one another in degrees of physical attractiveness.

maternal deprivation A phrase used to describe a condition of being separated from the mother in the early years of life.

maturation The process of growing older biologically, and so experiencing genetically-determined age-related changes.

mean A measure of central tendency calculated by adding up all the scores in a set and dividing them by the number of scores in that set. Also known as the arithmetic average.

means-end analysis Solving problems by identifying strategies which look likely to bring the solver closer to the ultimate goal.

median A measure of central tendency which is calculated by ranking all the scores in a set in order, from lowest to highest, and choosing the middlemost one.

medical model The approach to understanding abnormal behaviour adopted by members of the medical profession, e.g. psychiatrists.

medulla The part of the brain just above the spinal cord, concerned with autonomic bodily functions.

mental imagery See imagery.

mental representation A theoretical model of how we hold information in the brain.

mental set A state of readiness to learn, think or perceive in certain ways.

mesmerism An old term for hypnotism.

message variables Factors affecting attitude change in advertising, which are directly to do with the information which is being given to people, not just in terms of its content, but also in terms of the forms that it takes.

meta-analysis A research method which analyses the outcomes of several studies investigating the same issues.

metamemory Awareness of how one's own memory works.

metaphorical frame The set of ideas invoked by the use of a particular metaphor, which then sets the context for further discussion.

method of loci The mnemonic strategy which involves organising items to be remembered by visualising them in particular places.

micro-electrode recording   The method of studying the brain by inserting microscopic electrodes to particular sites, and recording the activity of individual nerve cells.

micro-PK   Psychokinesis in which the outcome of the psi influence is too small to be detected by the naked eye, and usually needs to be identified electronically.

minimal group paradigm   An approach to the study of social identification which involves creating artificial groups in the social psychology laboratory on the basics of spurious or minimal characteristics (e.g. tossing a coin), and then studying the in-group/out-group effects which result.

mnemonics   Strategies for helping people to remember information, usually involving cues such as rhyme or imagery.

mob psychology   The idea that a crowd is likely to behave in an irrational and unpredictable, even violent, manner as a result of the people in it descending into a conscienceless and impulsive state. The most recent formulation of mob psychology is the theory of deindividuation. Theories of mob psychology have played a strong political role for over a hundred years, as ways of diverting attention from the possibility that people in riots may actually have genuine grievances which need to be addressed.

mode   A measure of central tendency which is calculated by choosing the score in a set which occurs most often.

modelling   Providing an example which a child can imitate in order to learn styles of behaviour.

molar actions   Movements involving the whole body, e.g. standing up, walking.

molecular actions   Movements involving particular parts of the body only, such as shrugging the shoulders.

monocular depth cue   An indication of how distant something is, which can be detected just as well with only one eye as it can with two.

monotropy   A theory put forward by Bowlby, that infants form only one very strong attachment to their mothers, different from their attachments with other people.

monozygotic twins   Twins which have developed as a result of the splitting of a single egg, and who are therefore genetically identical.

moral therapy   One of the earliest successful forms of treatment for mental patients, developed by Pinel after the French Revolution and based around treating such people with respect.

morpheme   The smallest meaningful units of language.

motion parallax   The way that the visual field changes with movement, such that objects further away appear to change position at a different rate than objects close up, when the viewer is in motion.

motivated forgetting   Forgetting which indicates an unconscious desire to forget, e.g. forgetting an unpleasant event, or an unwelcome appointment.

motivation   That which drives, or energises, a human being or animal's actions – that which makes it be active rather than quiescent.

motor aphasia   A speech disorder which comes about because the person is unable to move their lips and tongue in the necessary way.

motor cortex   The area of the cerebrum which mediates physical movement of the different parts of the body.

motor end plate   The part of the muscle fibre which receives messages from motor neurones, telling the muscle when to contract.

motor neurone   A nerve cell which carries instructions from the brain or spinal cord to the muscle fibres, so producing movement.

MRI   See magnetic resonancy imaging.

multiple personality   A personality disorder in which the person seems to have more than one distinct 'self', each with its own memories and abilities. Brought about by severe childhood trauma.

mutation   A spontaneous change, usually used to refer to genetic changes which produce new heritable traits.

myelin sheath   A fatty coating around sensory and motor neurones which help the neural impulse to travel faster.

nAch   See need for achievement.

nativism   An approach which assumes that knowledge or abilities are innate, and do not need to be learned.

natural categories   Concepts which seem to occur automatically, through inherited influences, as a fundamental part of the animal or human's adaptation to their world.

natural experiments   Events in which variables change as a result of natural, political, social or economic circumstances, such that the outcome of these changes can then be studied.

natural selection   The process by which members of a species which possess adaptive survival traits survive and reproduce, while those which do not, fail to reproduce and die out.

nature-nurture debates   Fairly pointless theoretical debates, popular in the 1950s, concerning whether a given psychological ability was inherited or whether it was learned through experience.

need for achievement   An internal motivation to succeed in life, or in attaining particular goals.

need for affiliation   An internal motivation to belong to a group or family, or at least to be accepted by others.

need for positive regard   An internal motivation to be loved, approved of, or respected by other people.

need for self-actualisation   An internal motivation to develop one's own talents and abilities to the full.

negative after-images   The visual experience of 'seeing' the opposite form of colour or action after prolonged exposure to a single stimulus colour or movement.

negative-psi   The idea that some research participants may exert psychic influence in the opposite direction from that which is being studied. The idea was proposed to explain research findings which were even more unsuccessful than could reasonably be expected by chance. Also known as the psi-missing effect.

negative reinforcement   Encouraging a certain kind of behaviour by the removal or avoidance of an unpleasant stimulus.

neo-Freudian   A psychoanalytic theorist since Freud, who accepts his basic ideas but has developed them further.

nested territories   Small territories located within larger ones.

neural plasticity   The ability of nerve cells and brain tissue to re-grow or to acquire alternative functions in response to damage.

neurotransmitter   A chemical which is released by one nerve cell and picked up by a neighbouring one, making the latter either more or less likely to fire.

nocturnal   Active and alert at night, sleeping or resting during the day.

nodes of Ranvier   Gaps in the myelin sheath of a sensory or motor neurone, which allow ionic transfer across the cell membrane and so produce the electrical potential which forms the nerve impulse.

nomothetic   A term which is used to describe those psychometric tests which are designed to assess how normal or typical someone is, by comparing their scores with what would normally be expected of members of that population.

non-directive   Acting in such a way as to allow interaction with another person to continue without actually indicating how the other person should act, or hinting, implicitly or explicitly, at what they ought to be saying.

non-invasive techniques   Methods of studying the brain or body from the outside, such as the use of brain or body scans.

non-verbal communication   Communication which does not involve language, or words of any form.

non-verbal cues   Acts or signs which communicate information to other people, deliberately or unconsciously, but which do not involve the use of words.

noradrenaline   A neurotransmitter active in the brain, particularly known to be concerned with states of arousal.

noradrenergic receptor   A receptor site on a nerve cell which responds particularly to noradrenaline.

normal distribution curve   A pattern of scores, distributed on a graph, which appears on that graph as a bell-shaped curve. Also known as the Gaussian distribution, this has mathematical properties which mean that the probability, or likelihood, of a given score can be calculated, simply by knowing the value of the mean and the standard deviation.

normative   Representing the norm; typical.

nurturant-receptive relationships   Relationships in which one partner is particularly giving and caring, while the other accepts or receives the care.

OBE   Out of body experience: the experience that some people have of being apparently able to leave their physical bodies, either when sleeping or awake, and allow their consciousness to travel to other physical locations.

object concept   The idea that objects continue to exist even when you are not paying attention to them.

observational study   A study which involves simply watching what happens, rather than intervening and causing changes.

Occam's razor   A principle which states that, faced with two equally possible explanations, the scientific option is to choose the least complex one.

occupational psychologists   Psychologists who deal with people at work. Some occupational psychologists are concerned with recruitment or selection: fitting people to jobs. Others are concerned with human interactions at work: how organisations and departments are managed.

ocular dominance columns   Columns of nerve cells found in the visual cortex in which the cells at each level respond to the same stimulus, received by the same eye.

Oedipal conflict   In Freudian theory, the idea that the young male child wishes to possess his mother sexually, and therefore perceives himself as the direct rival of the larger, more powerful father.

olfactory epithelium   The layer of cells in the nose which responds to direct chemical stimulation, and so forms the receptor for the sense of smell.

one-trial learning   A rapid form of learning, which only takes one event to be learned, such as avoiding a food which has made you sick.

one-way mirror   A special mirror used for observations which allows an observer to see without being seen.

ontological insecurity   A form of insecurity which is to do with one's own personal development and sense of identity.

open-field test   A test to identify levels of anxiety or attachment, in which the animal or human is placed in a wide open space and its response is observed.

operant conditioning   The process of learning identified by B. F. Skinner, in which learning occurs as a result of positive or negative reinforcement of an animal or human being's action.

optic array   The entire pattern of visual information falling on the retina of the eye.

optic chiasma   The part of the brain where the optic nerve from each eye meets, and half of their fibres cross over.

oral stage   In Freudian theory, the period in infancy in which the infant derives pleasure solely from the mouth.

order effect   An experimental effect which arises as a result of the order, or sequence, in which two tasks are presented.

otoliths   Small pieces of calcium carbonate floating in the fluid of the semicircular canals of the inner ear, and involved in the sense of balance.

pandemonium model   A 'bottom-up' theory of pattern recognition in which units responding to distinctive features are organised hierarchically.

paradigm   The framework of ideas, theories and assumptions which is implicitly adopted by an academic community or group of people.

paradoxical sleep   Sleep in which the EEG indicates light sleep but the person is difficult to wake up, and is often dreaming. Also known as REM sleep.

paralanguage   Non-verbal cues contained in how people say things, such as in tones of voice, pauses, or 'um' and 'er' noises.

parallel distributed processing (PDP)   A form of computer simulation in which several different logic pathways are at work simultaneously, with interconnections between them.

parametric test   A statistical test which is used on the assumption that the data would, if a large enough sample were obtained, produce a normal distribution.

paramnesia   A clinical condition in which memories become distorted, rather than lost altogether.

parapsychology   The scientific study of anomalous means of communication or of transmission of information. Parapsychologists conduct research into extra-sensory perception, telekinesis, and DMILS.

participant observation   A method of study in which the investigator joins in the social process being observed, and others involved are unaware that the study is taking place.

particularistic meanings   Meanings of statements or utterances which only apply to their own specific contexts.

pattern recognition   The perceptual structuring of visual information into meaningful shapes and textures.

PDP   See parallel distributed processing.

peer group   A group of people who are considered to be the equals of, or like, the person concerned.

perceived fallibility   A factor in attraction deriving from the observation that people, especially high-achievers, are often liked more if they are seen to make mistakes from time to time.

perceptual constancy   The process of perceiving an object or scene as consistent and unchanging despite variation in the physical light information reaching the eye.

perceptual defence   A process whereby objects or events which are threatening or unconsciously unwelcome, are less easily perceived than more innocuous stimuli.

perceptual set   A state of readiness to perceive certain kinds of stimuli rather than others.

performance decrement   The decline in accuracy which occurs over time as an individual performs a task requiring sustained attention.

peripheral nervous system   The part of the nervous system which links the rest of the body with the brain and the spinal cord.

peripheral route processing   The indirect approach to attitude change, in which attention is not focused directly on the information being transmitted, but is elsewhere.

person schema   The set of memories, knowledge and intentions which someone holds about a particular person.

personal constructs   Individual ways of making sense of the world, which have been developed on the basis of experience. Personal construct theorists argue that getting to understand the personal constructs which someone uses to make sense of their experience is essential for effective psychotherapy, as well as for effective interaction in day-to-day living.

personal space   The physical distance which people like to maintain between themselves and others. This varies according to their relationship with, and attitude to other people, and according to norms and contexts.

personalism   The tendency that people have to be more likely to make a dispositional attribution about the cause of something if that something affects them personally. Acts which do not affect them personally are more likely to be judged as being caused by the situation.

PET scans   See positron emission tomography.

phallic stage   In Freudian theory, a stage in which pleasure for the young child supposedly becomes focused on the genitals, and the child's sexual attention is drawn to the other-sexed parent.

phantom limbs   The name given to the phenomenon experienced by amputees, of still feeling the limb as present and alive even though it has been surgically removed.

phenomenological   Concerned with the person's own perceived world and the phenomena which they experience, rather than with objective reality.

phenotype   The physical characteristics which an individual develops, as evidence of the interaction between their genetic structure and the environment in which they have developed.

pheromones   Chemicals released into the air which, when received by another animal, exert a direct influence on its hormonal system and sometimes its behaviour.

phi phenomenon   The perceptual phenomenon in which discrete stimuli presented in rapid sequence are perceived as linked together.

phoneme   The basic unit of sound in spoken language.

phonology   The rules in a language which are concerned with the links between words and phrases, and the sounds which are used by speakers of that language.

photo-receptor cells   Special cells in the retina (rods and cones cells) which respond to light by altering their chemical structure and so producing an electrical impulse.

phrenology   A nineteenth-century belief that character and other qualities were revealed by systematic irregularities on the skull.

phylogenetic scale   An ordering of species hierarchically, usually organised in such a way that human beings are at the highest point and other animal species are 'ranked' according to their degree of similarity to the human being.

phylogenetic tree   A diagrammatic representation of how different species relate to one another in terms of their evolutionary origins.

phylogeny   The sequence of evolution through which a particular species has passed.

physiological determinism   The approach which states that human and other behaviour occurs as a straightforward consequence of physiological systems.

physiological drives   Motives which are concerned with satisfying physiological needs, such as hunger, etc.

physiological reductionism   The approach to exploring human behaviour which sees only physiological mechanisms (e.g. nerve cells or hormones) as important.

pilomotor response   The part of the fight or flight response which involves the hair standing on end, presumably to make an animal look larger and more fearsome.

pineal gland   A hormonal gland in the brain, thought to be particularly involved in biological rhythms.

PK   The usual abbreviation for psychokinesis.

pleasure centre   The part of the limbic system which, when stimulated electronically, appears to provide feelings of intense pleasure.

pleasure principle   In Freudian terms, the way that the id operates by demanding instant gratification of its impulses, regardless of social convention.

pluralistic ignorance   The way that a group of people will tend to define a situation in such a way that they all appear to be unaware that some emergency or other event which requires attention, is going on.

polygraph   A machine often used to measure stress or anxiety – sometimes known as a 'lie-detector' – which works by measuring many ('poly') different physical indicators that the person is under stress, such as blood pressure, pulse rate, heart rate, and GSR.

pons   The part of the brain situated above the medulla and thought to be involved in sleep and dreaming.

population norms   A set of scores for a particular population (e.g. females aged 18–24) which establishes the normal range of scores for that population, on a particular psychometric test or measure. Tables of population norms are used to judge whether an individual's test result is typical for their population group or not.

positive regard   Liking, affection, love or respect for someone else.

positive reinforcement   In operant conditioning, strengthening learned behaviour by direct reward when it occurs.

positron emission tomography   Scanning the brain by monitoring the uptake of blood by active neurones. Blood distribution is identified by the radioactive labelling of glucose molecules in the bloodstream.

post-hypnotic amnesia   When a person has come out of a hypnotised state but nonetheless continues to forget information because they were instructed to do so while hypnotised.

post-traumatic amnesia   Forgetting which occurs as a direct result of a brain injury or accident.

postural echo   The way that people who are in intense conversation or rapport will often unconsciously mimic one another's stance or posture.

practice effect   An experimental effect which happens as a result of the subject having had practice in the task being studied.

pre-moral stage   The first of Kohlberg's three stages of moral development.

pre-operational stage   The second of Piaget's four stages of cognitive development, characterised by an ability to focus on only one attribute of an object at a time, and an inability to 'decentre'.

precocial animals   Animals which can move about as soon as they are born or hatched.

precognition   Knowledge of events which will happen in the future, which appears to have been obtained without using normal sensory channels.

predictive validity   A method of assessing whether a psychometric test is valid (i.e. really measures what it is supposed to) by seeing how well it correlates with some other measure, which is assessed later, after the test has been taken.

prejudice   A fixed, pre-set attitude, usually negative and hostile, and usually applied to members of a particular social category.

prevarication Lying. Saying things are true when they are not.

primacy effect The way that the first things you encounter make more of an impression than later ones do. So, for example, we are more likely to remember the first items in a list, or the first impression which someone made on us.

primary drive A motive which is concerned with satisfying a basic human need, such as hunger, thirst, or possibly affiliation.

primary reinforcement A reinforcer which satisfies a basic need or drive in the organism, like hunger or thirst.

primer pheromones Pheromones which trigger off a particular form of behaviour, such as mating behaviour.

proactive amnesia A memory disorder in which the person becomes unable to store new information.

proactive interference A problem with memory storage in which information which has been learned interferes with the ability to learn new information.

probabilistic concepts Concepts in which each item is likely to possess the important attributes, but may not necessarily (e.g. that birds can fly).

problem distance The term used in means-end analysis to describe the difference between the immediate situation and the desired goal, or end-state.

programmed learning A technique for applying operant conditioning to the schooling process.

projective tests Psychometric tests which involve providing the person with ambiguous stimuli, and seeing what meanings they read into them. The idea is that this will illustrate the concerns of the unconscious mind.

proprioceptors Nerve cells which receive information from the muscles and skeleton.

prosocial Altruistic, helpful, friendly, or otherwise acting in ways that are beneficial to others.

prospective memory Memory for things which are yet to come, such as remembering an appointment.

protocol analysis The method of study which consists of analysing the steps or protocols involved in solving a problem. This might also include, for example, recording what people say they are doing as they undertake a creative process.

prototypes Typical examples of a concept, containing all the relevant features.

pseudomutuality A process found in some disturbed families, in which family members insist that no conflict exists and maintain a veneer of affection which masks serious underlying hostilities and aggression.

pseudopsi hypothesis The idea that all evidence for parapsychological influence comes from deception or misinterpretation.

psi A general term used by parapsychologists to describe forms of communication which have occurred without the use of ordinary sensory channels.

psi-conducive experimenters Experimenters who generate high success rates from research participants, without using fraud, but with the same research participants being unable to repeat their success with other experimenters.

psi-conducive procedures Ways of conducting experiments which will facilitate the demonstration of psychic abilities among research participants.

psi hypothesis The idea that human beings are able to use new, apparently impossible means of communication under certain circumstances.

psi-inhibitory experimenters Experimenters who seem to inhibit the demonstration of psychic abilities among their research participants.

psi-missing effect See negative psi.

psi-permissive experimenters Experimenters who seem to facilitate the demonstration of psychic abilities among their research participants.

psychoanalysis A form of psychotherapy in which the aim is to analyse the unconscious mind with a view to identifying hidden meanings and motives.

psychokinesis A psychic ability in which the person exerts an influence on a target, across barriers which would normally prevent any such influence.

psycholinguistics The study of language and language structure, particularly in terms of its interaction with thinking.

psychology The scientific study of experience and behaviour. Psychology draws together systematic studies of experience and behaviour using a wide range of methods, and focusing on many different angles and levels of experience.

psychometric tests Instruments which have been developed for measuring mental characteristics. Psychological tests have been developed to measure a wide range of things, including creativity, job attitudes and skills, brain damage, and, of course, 'intelligence'.

psychosocial stages The term given to Erikson's eight life-stages.

psychosomatic disorders Physical problems which have their origin in psychological stresses or other psychological sources.

psychoticism A form of mental illness which involves the individual losing touch with reality.

pulsed sounds Sounds which occur as regular beats on the same frequency.

punctuated equilibrium An approach to understanding evolution which suggests that evolutionary change occurs in rapid bursts followed by periods of relative stability, in response to environmental changes.

pupil dilation The way that the pupils of the eye become larger under certain circumstances, e.g. when it is dark, or when the person is looking at something or someone they find attractive.

qualitative analysis Ways of analysing data which are concerned with describing meaning, rather than with drawing statistical inferences from frequency counts.

qualitative difference A difference in kind, not simply in amount.

quantitative analysis Ways of analysing data which focus on numbers and frequencies rather than on meaning or experience.

random number generator studies Parapsychological research into micro-PK, in which a research participant attempts to influence a random set of numbers generated by a computer.

RAS See reticular activating system.

rational authority Authority which someone has acquired because they are logically the best person to be in charge, owing to their possession of appropriate knowledge or other specific aptitudes.

Rational Emotive Behaviour Therapy (REBT) A form of psychotherapy which mixes rational argument with behaviour therapy techniques.

raw primal sketch A first stage in the processing of visual information, according to Marr's computational theory.

re-learning savings The term given to the way that it takes less time to re-learn information which has been learned previously and then forgotten.

reaction formation A defence mechanism in which a repressed impulse turns into its opposite, e.g. repressed homosexuality turning into aggressive homophobia.

reactive depression Depression which occurs in response to specifically identifiable events.

reality principle The name given by Freud to the way that the ego attempts to balance the demands of the id and superego with the practical demands of reality.

REBT See Rational Emotive Behaviour Therapy.

recall Remembering information by retrieving it from memory.

recency effects The way that the last item of information on a list is usually remembered more clearly than earlier ones.

receptor site A location on the dendrite of the neurone or muscle fibre which is particularly sensitive to specific neurotransmitters, and therefore receives signals from other neurones.

reciprocity The idea that some relationships work because each member of a couple provides the other with the same qualities.

recognition A form of memory in which the person can identify previously learned information when it is presented, although they cannot recall it spontaneously.

reconstruction A form of remembering in which the person can put a previously-learned set of memories in the same order as it was originally learned, even though no conscious memory remains.

redintegration The reconstructing of memories from relevant cues until an apparently complete record is achieved.

reductionism An approach to understanding behaviour which focuses on one single level of explanation and ignores others. The opposite of interactionism.

reference group A group of people to whom an individual will refer – e.g. by modelling their own behaviour on that shown by members of the group.

reference power Power which is based on the fact that the person has the backing and support of other, more powerful agencies.

reflex A response which occurs automatically, and is not mediated by the brain.

reflex arc The minimal set of neurones involved in a reflex action: a sensory neurone, a connector neurone, and a motor neurone.

regression A defence mechanism which involves reverting to adaptive behaviour learned during an earlier period of development.

rehearsal Practice, e.g. the continuous repeating of information to be memorised.

reification The process of treating an adverb as if it were a noun – e.g. seeing 'acting intelligently' as if it were a manifestation of some kind of entity called 'intelligence'.

reinforcement The strengthening of learning in some way. The term is usually used of learned associations, acquired through operant or classical conditioning, but it may also be applied to other forms of learning.

reinforcement contingencies The conditions under which positive or negative reinforcement are given.

relationship-oriented leaders Leaders who make it their prime responsibility to ensure that all the team get on well together and communicate effectively, in the belief that if this is running right, then the necessary tasks will be done. This contrasts with task-oriented leaders.

releaser pheromones Pheromones which trigger off certain forms of behaviour in animals.

reliability problem A problem in both parapsychology and psychotherapy, in which an initial research phase yields highly positive results, but these taper off with repeated studies, or treatments, until eventually, outcomes are little more than chance.

REM sleep   Sleep which involves rapid eye movements, and usually dreaming.

remote viewing studies   Parapsychological studies in which the research participants describe scenes or physical objects located at considerable distances from them, and not perceivable by conventional means. .

repertory grid technique   A system for eliciting personal constructs and showing how individuals use them to interpret their experience.

replication   The repeating of a study by other researchers, in order to ensure that the findings are reliable, and not just an artefact of one particular experimental situation.

reproductive fitness   A form of evolutionary adaptation which makes a given individual more likely to mate and reproduce its kind.

resource holding power (RHP)   The ability of an animal to undertake whatever is required to retain necessary evolutionary resources, such as territory or access to mates.

response bias   A tendency to answer questions or act in a way that is socially desirable.

restricted language codes   Ways of using language characterised by limited vocabulary, simple grammatical structures, and a heavy reliance on shared implicit meaning and paralinguistic cues.

reticular activating system   The part of the brain which mediates sleep, wakefulness and alertness.

retinal image   The pattern of light which falls on the retina of the eye as an image of the external world.

retroactive interference   The memory loss which occurs when new information displaces information which was learned previously.

retrocognition   A counterpart to precognition, in which the person appears to have knowledge of events that have happened in the past, without having had access to that information through normal sensory channels.

retrograde amnesia   A form of memory disorder in which the person becomes unable to recall events or information stored before the disorder occurred.

retrospective study   A study which involves collecting data about events which happened in the past.

reward power   Power which is based on the fact that the person is in a position to distribute rewards or positive benefits to people.

RHP   See resource holding power.

risky-shift phenomenon   A form of group polarisation which involves the observation that some people will tend to make riskier decisions when acting as members of a group or committee than they would when they are acting as individuals.

ritualised aggression   Behaviour which appears to threaten another member of the same species, but which occurs in a set pattern and will cease if the other animal shows appropriate responses.

RNA   Ribonucleic acid – an essential chemical in the physiological expression of genetic information.

RNGS   See random number generator studies.

rod cells   Cells in the retina which respond to minute changes in light intensity, but not to colour.

role   A social part that one plays in society.

role-schema   The total set of memories, actions and intentions associated with a particular social role: the understanding of that role.

S-R learning   See stimulus-response learning.

saccades   Minute, involuntary movements of the eyeball.

sample   The group of subjects used in a study: the selection of people, animals, plants or objects drawn from a population for the purposes of studying that population.

Sapir-Whorf hypothesis   See linguistic relativity hypothesis.

satiation   The experience of having eaten sufficiently to quell hunger.

scapegoating   The process of putting the blame for difficult economic circumstances or other sources of frustration onto some disliked but 'inferior' social group, and so increasing prejudice and intergroup hostility.

scattergram   A diagram used to illustrate correlations.

sceptics   People who are dubious about a theory or idea, and require convincing evidence before they are prepared to accept it.

schema   A mental framework or structure which encompasses memories, ideas, concepts and programmes for action which are pertinent to a particular topic.

schismatic   Liable to cause a schism, or rift, between two parties.

schizophrenia   A mental disorder in which the person experiences a separation or split from reality.

schizophrenogenic families   Families which appear to encourage the development of schizophrenia in certain members through disturbed interactions such as pseudomutuality.

script   A well-known pattern of social action and interaction which has been socially established and accepted, and is implicitly and automatically followed by people in the relevant situation.

search for coherence   The way that members of an in-group look for ways to justify or rationalise their beliefs about the positive attributes of the in-group and the negative attributes of the out-group.

seasonal territory   The most common form of territoriality, in which an animal maintains and defends a territory only at a particular season, e.g. when mating and rearing young.

secondary drives   Motives which do not relate to biological needs, but instead are concerned with acquired or learned preferences.

secondary reinforcement   Something which reinforces learned behaviour because it has previously been associated with a primary reinforcer.

selective attention   The phenomenon by which people select what information they will pay attention to and what they will ignore.

self-actualisation   The making real of one's abilities and talents: using them to the full.

self-concept   The idea or internal image that people have of what they themselves are like, including both evaluative and descriptive dimensions.

self-efficacy beliefs   The belief that one is capable of doing something effectively. Self-efficacy beliefs are closely connected with self esteem, in that having a sense of being capable and potentially in control tends to increase confidence. But the concept is often thought to be more useful than the generalised concept of self-esteem, since people may often be confident about some abilities, or in some areas of their lives, but not in others.

self-esteem   The evaluative dimension of the self-concept, which is to do with how worthwhile and/or confident people feel about themselves.

self-fulfilling prophecy   The idea that expectations about a person or group can become true simply because they have been stated.

self-image   The factual or descriptive picture which people hold of themselves, without the evaluative component implicit in the concept of self-esteem.

self-perception theory   The idea that we develop an impression of our own personality by inferring what we are like from the way that we act.

self-schema   The total set of memories, representations, ideas and intentions which one holds about oneself.

self-serving bias   The idea that we judge our own behaviour more favourably than we judge other people's, mainly because of the fundamental attribution error.

semantic   To do with meaning.

semantic coding   Representing information in the brain by using the meaning of that information to determine how it should be stored.

semantic differential   A form of attitude measurement which involves asking people to evaluate a concept by weighing it up according to several different verbal dimensions.

semantic memory   General world knowledge which does not particularly depend on individual experience.

semantics   Rules determining the assignment of meaning to sentences.

semicircular canals   Structures in the inner ear which are involved in the sense of balance.

sender   A person in a parapsychological study who attempts to 'transmit' information to a receiver, using only thoughts or mental energies.

senile dementia   A form of mental illness which particularly affects old people, in which they become very confused as to where they are and what is happening, and may appear to be irrational. This is also sometimes known as Alzheimer's syndrome.

sensitive period   A time when an animal is genetically prepared to respond to particular environmental stimuli.

sensorimotor stage   The first of Piaget's four stages of cognitive devlopment, characterised by receptiveness to sensory information and the development of the very first schemata through explorations of movement in the environment.

sensory deprivation   The cutting out of all incoming sensory information, or at least as much of it as possible.

sensory leakage   When a flaw in a parapsychological study allows the research participant to gain relevant information through normal sensory channels.

sensory mode   The route by which information comes to the brain, e.g. through vision, hearing, smell, etc.

sensory neurone   A nerve cell which receives information from sense receptors and passes it to the nerve cells of the central nervous system.

sensory projection areas   Areas on the cerebral cortex which receive information from particular senses.

serial reproduction   A method of examining the accuracy of memory by asking people to reproduce what they recall of a story, on several successive occasions.

serotonin   A neurotransmitter particularly found in the brain.

set weight   The phenomenon detected by physiological studies of obesity, that the body appears to have an internal established ideal weight, and that eating or fasting behaviour will happen to maintain that weight.

sheep-goat hypothesis   The distinction between those who believe in psi, and those who do not, which correlates with evidence that the former are more likely to report previous psi experiences, and also to obtain positive results in parapsychological studies.

sign stimulus   A signal which initiates innate releasing mechanisms for inherited behaviour.

signal detection tasks Procedures used in studies of sustained attention in which the person is required to notice, or detect, a small signal whenever it occurs.

simple cells Cells in the thalamus which respond to basic units of visual information, such as a dot or line in a particular place on the retinal image.

situational attribution A reason for an act or behaviour which implies that it occurred as a result of the situation or circumstances that the person was in at the time.

sleeper effect An effect or result from some particular circumstance or event which does not show up immediately, but takes some time to manifest itself.

social cognition The way that we think about and interpret social information and social experience. In developmental psychology, the term refers to a theory of cognitive development which states that social interaction is the most important factor in a young child's cognitive development.

social comparison The process of comparing one's own social group with others, in terms of their relative social status and prestige. Social comparison is important, in that people will tend to distance themselves from membership of a group which does not reflect positively on their self-esteem.

social determinism The belief that human behaviour and experience are entirely produced by social and cultural factors.

social exchange theory An approach to the understanding of social behaviour which sees social interaction as a 'trade', in which the person acts in certain ways in return for some social reward or approval.

social facilitation The observation that the presence of other people can influence how well they perform on a task, often improving their performance.

social identification theory A theory which emphasises how membership of social groups forms a significant part of the self-concept, and can determine reactions to other people and events, such that people respond primarily as group members and not as individuals.

social impact theory A reductionist approach to understanding social phenomena in terms of cumulative factors, such as the number of people present, the immediacy or otherwise of their presence, and the importance of those people to the individual concerned.

social learning The approach to understanding social behaviour which emphasises how people imitate action and model their behaviour on that of others.

social learning theory An approach to child development which states that children develop through learning from the other people around them.

social loafing The observed tendency in some situations for individuals to devote less effort to a group task than they would give to the same task if they were doing it on their own.

social norms Socially or culturally accepted standards of behaviour, which have become accepted as representing how people 'ought' to act and what is 'normal' (i.e. appropriate) for a given situation.

social phase The stage in relationship breakdown where the couple acknowledge publicly that their relationship has ended or is ending.

social representation theory A theory which looks at how shared beliefs develop and are transmitted in social groups and in society as a whole. Such shared beliefs serve an important function in explaining reality, and in justifying social action.

sociobiology A reductionist approach to explaining animal behaviour, sometimes applied to humans, which argues that all behaviour is driven by units of survival referred to as 'genes' (not the same as the biological concept), and that individuals and species are simply mechanisms by which these 'genes' can perpetuate themselves.

sociolinguistics The study of language as it relates to social and cultural phenomena.

sociometry An approach to examining attitudes and social groupings by charting relationships within a group, and who refers to whom in terms of influence.

somatic therapies Forms of treatment which are based entirely around the body, e.g. using drugs to suppress disturbed behaviour rather than attempting to deal with the disturbance using psychotherapy.

somatosensory cortex The area of the cerebral cortex which receives information from sense receptors in the skin.

somatotypes Types of body shape, once thought to indicate personality.

source variables Variables affecting the persuasiveness of a piece of information which are concerned with the origins or purported origins of that information.

speech act An utterance or set of utterances which serves a single social purpose.

speech register The form of language deemed appropriate for a particular social occasion. There are different speech registers to suit different types of occasions, and also to suit different relationships between people – for example, friends would use an intimate speech register, while a patient consulting a doctor would use a formal one.

split-brain studies Studies of brain function in people who have had the corpus callosum severed to control epilepsy, thus separating the two halves of the cerebrum.

split-half method A system for judging how reliable a psychometric test is, which involves splitting the test into two, administering each half of the test to the same people, then comparing the results.

split-span task   A method of assessing selective attention in which the person is presented with two sets of stimuli simultaneously, one to each ear, and must divide their attention between them.

spontaneous recovery   The sudden reappearance of a learned response after it has been apparently extinguished.

standard deviation   A statistical measure which describes how the scores in a normal distribution are spread out on either side of the mean. It expresses the typical amount of diversity which can be expected for that variable.

standardisation   (a) The process of making sure that the conditions of a psychological study or psychometric test are always identical; (b) the process of establishing how the results of a psychometric test will usually come out in a given population, by drawing up sets of population norms; (c) the process of comparing a new psychometric test with older, more established measures of the same thing.

state-dependent memory   A form of remembering which is dependent on its physiological context, e.g. the influence of drugs or emotion.

statistically significant   The term used to refer to a result of statistical analysis which is unlikely to have happened by chance alone. In a research paper, the term would be accompanied by a number (the level of significance) which states just how unlikely it is.

stereotyping   Classifying members of a social group as if they were all the same, and treating individuals belonging to that group as if no other characteristics were salient.

stimulus   An external environmental event to which an organism responds.

stimulus generalisation   The phenomenon whereby an animal which has learned to respond to a particular stimulus will tend to extend its response to similar stimuli.

stimulus-response learning   The name given to the behaviourist approach to learning, which viewed it as a simple association between an external stimulus and the behavioural response, denying any cognitive or mental processing.

STM   The abbreviation used for short-term memory, or memory which lasts for only a few seconds.

Stroop effect   A phenomenon demonstrating automaticity of information-processing, in which the identification of colour is interfered with by the name of a colour given in the stimulus material.

sub-cortical structures   All of the structures of the brain, with the exception of the cerebrum.

sub-vocal speech   Speech which is not actually spoken out loud, but still involves movements of the throat and larynx.

successive approximation   See behaviour shaping

summation   The neurological principle in which the strength of a stimulus is signalled by the total number of neurones firing in response to it.

super-stimulus   A particularly powerful form of sign stimulus, which triggers off a particularly strong response.

superego   In Freudian theory, the part of the unconscious mind which acts as an internalised, strict parent, incorporating ideas of duty, obligation and conscience.

superposition   A monocular depth cue in which images of objects which seem to obscure other images are perceived as being closer.

superstitious learning   See autoshaping.

surface dyslexia   A form of reading disorder in which the person has difficulty with the forms of words and letters, but not with their meanings.

surface structure   The superficial characteristics of a language: its rules of formal grammar and habitual use of words.

survey   A technique of collecting opinions from large numbers of people, generally involving the use of questionnaires.

sustained attention   The process of concentrating consistently on one set of stimuli for a prolonged period of time.

symbolic interactionism   The approach to social understanding which looks at how people perceive and respond to one another as social symbols, such as roles, rather than as individuals.

symbolic representation   The coding of information in the brain by means of symbols as opposed to sensory images.

sympathetic division   The part of the autonomic nervous system which produces a state of arousal when activated.

synaesthesia   A condition in which sensory input becomes distorted and confused, such that sounds may be experienced as touch, etc.

synapse   The junction between nerve cells which is bridged by neurotransmitter chemicals.

synaptic button   See synaptic knob.

synaptic cleft   The small gap between the neurones at the synapse.

synaptic knob   The structure at the end of each neuronal dendrite, which contains vesicles that release neurotransmitters into the synaptic cleft.

synaptic vesicle   Small pockets or reservoirs found on the synaptic button which contain the neurotransmitter chemicals before they are released.

synchronicity   In Jung's analytic psychology, the idea that some events reverberate with more than everyday meaning because they tap into deeper meanings in the collective unconscious.

syntax   Rules governing which combinations of words and word-orders are acceptable within a specific language.

TA   See transactional analysis.

tabula rasa   The idea that a child is born with no prior mental structures, but instead is a 'blank slate', to be written on by experience.

task-oriented leaders   Leaders who focus explicitly on the tasks which have to be done by the team, and who show little or no interest in interpersonal concerns within it, unlike relationship-oriented leaders.

teleological explanation   Explanation which emphasises the functions of a phenomenon such as why it occurred or developed.

telepathy   The transmission of information from one person to another without using normal sensory channels.

temperament   The term used to describe basic differences between infants and people, in terms of their tendencies to respond differently to stimuli, and thought to be a precursor to personality.

template theory   The idea that patterns are identified by matching them up to a stored 'ideal type' or template.

temporal contiguity   Juxtaposition in space and time – in other words, occurring together, or in rapid sequence.

territoriality   The name given to a set of behaviours which involve establishing and maintaining access to a particular area while refusing the same to potential competitors of one's own species.

test-retest method   A system for judging how reliable a psychometric test or measure is, which involves administering the same test to the same people on two different occasions, and comparing the results.

thalamus   The sub-cortical structure in the brain which receives sensory information and relays it to the cerebral cortex.

thanatos   The negative, destructive energy proposed by Freud as a counterpart to the positive sexual energy known as libido, and invoked in order to explain the destruction and carnage of WWI in psychoanalytic terms.

threat displays   Patterns of inherited behaviour which are designed to intimidate others of the same species, and may sometimes preface physical attack.

threshold of response   The point at which a stimulus becomes strong enough to trigger a response only 50% of the time.

token economy   A system involving the use of tokens as secondary reinforcers in the rehabilitation of long-term psychiatric patients.

top-down theory   A theory which explains some aspect of cognition primarily in terms of the overall context and meaning of the information rather than in terms of its stimulus properties.

TOTE unit   A cyclic sequence of behaviour involving the stages Test-Operate-Test-Exit, and proposed as a more appropriate basic unit of behaviour than the simplistic S-R link.

traditional authority   Authority which someone has acquired because of their position in a relevant hierarchy, or because of their social status, irrespective of their personal qualities.

trait   A specific facet of personality.

transaction   A form of behavioural exchange or interchange between two individuals.

transactional analysis   A method of analysing social behaviour which looks at the patterns of behavioural exchange in terms of the ego-states which they reveal.

transduction   The process of converting information from one form to another in physiological terms, e.g. converting the pressure waves which comprise sound into electrical impulses which can be passed to the brain.

triarchic theory of intelligence   A theory of intelligence developed by Sternberg (1985) which argues that intelligence needs to be understood from three distinct viewpoints: (a) the cultural and social context in which an intelligent act occurs; (b) how the person's own previous experience has shaped their responses; and (c) the mental skills and abilities involved in solving problems.

trigrams   meaningless three-letter nonsense syllables, comprising a consonant, vowel and consonant (CVC) sequence.

two-point threshold   A measure of skin sensitivity which is concerned with how far apart two pinpricks must be to be identified as separate stimuli.

two-process theory of memory   The idea that short-term and long-term memory are actually two entirely differen systems, as opposed to different levels of processing.

type A and B personality   Personality syndromes in which A is characterised by impatience, intolerance and a high level of stress, while B involves a relaxed, tolerant approach and noticeably lower personal stress.

ultrasound   Sound which is too high-pitched to be detected by human hearing.

unconditional positive regard   Love, affection or respect which does not depend on the person's having to act in particular ways.

unconditioned response   A response which occurs automatically to a particular stimulus, and does not have to be learned.

unconditioned stimulus   A stimulus which automatically, or reflexively, produces a response.

unilateral ECT   Electro-convulsive therapy applied to one side of the brain only.

unipolar depression   Depression which does not have any manic phase.

universalistic meanings Meanings of statements or utterances which apply generally in broad contexts, and to more than the immediate situation.

validity The question of whether a psychometric test or psychological measure is really measuring what it is supposed to.

vasoconstriction The constriction of blood vessels which occurs as a response to cold.

verbal deprivation hypothesis The idea that children who do not experience extended forms of language may suffer cognitive deficits as a consequence.

vicarious learning Learning through observation of what happens to others.

visual cortex The area of the cerebral cortex which processes visual information.

visual illusion A visual image which tricks the perceptual system, so that it is perceived as something other than it is.

VMH The common abbreviation for the ventro-medial hypothalamus – an area of the hypothalamus particularly involved in hunger regulation.

vocational guidance tests Psychometric tests which are designed to help people to find out what kind of jobs they are suited for.

voice stress analyser A method of analysis which identifies the slightly flattened tones of an individual under stress, by analysing the sound of the voice using a spectrograph.

vulnerability model The idea that some people are particularly vulnerable to disorders such as schizophrenia, but will not develop them if they live in relatively stress-free conditions.

waterfall effect A negative after-effect in which consistent visual experience of movement in one direction produces an after-image of movement in the opposite direction.

Wernicke's area An area of the cerebral cortex which, when damaged, produces problems in comprehending verbal information.

within-group variance Individual differences in behaviour, physique or abilities which occur among members of a given social group or category; e.g. the natural variation in height among members of the same group of pygmies.

working memory Immediate memory, in use at a given time to perform a particular task.

Yerkes-Dodson Law of arousal The principle that performance of any given task can be improved if the person is aroused; but that if the arousal increases beyond an optimal point, performance then declines.

Yerkish A special language invented for chimpanzee studies, involving symbols and a formal grammar.

zeitgebers External signals of daily time-changes, such as daybreak and dusk, which influence human diurnal rhythms.

Zener cards A set of 25 cards bearing distinctive and memorable symbols, used in early parapsychological research.

zone of proximal development Vygotsky's concept of the extent to which the child can learn and develop skills, if aided and taught by others, preferably adults.

ZPD See zone of proximal development.

Bibliography

AARONSON, B. & OSMOND, H. (eds) (1970) *Psychedelics: The Uses and Implications of Hallucinogenic Drugs* New York: Doubleday

ABELSON, R. P. (1976) Script processing in attitude formation and decision making In: J. S. Carroll & J. W. Payne (eds) *Cognition and Social Behaviour* Hillsdale, N. J.: Erlbaum

ABELSON, R. P. & CARROLL, J. (1965) Computer simulation of individual belief systems *American Behavioural Science* **8** 24–30

ABERNATHY, E. M. (1940) The effect of changed environmental conditions upon the results of college examinations *Journal of Psychology* **10** 293–301

ABRAHAM, C. (1997) *Social Psychology: an Applied Socio-Cognitive Approach* Paper delivered at the British Psychological Society Social Psychology Conference, Sussex, September 1997

ABRAMS, R., TAYLOR, M., FABER, R., TS'O, T. WILLIAMS, R. & ALMY, G. (1983) Bilateral vs unilateral electroconvulsive therapy efficacy and melancholia *American Journal of Psychiatry* **140** 463–5

ABRAMSON, L. Y., SELIGMAN, M. E. P. & TEASDALE, J. D. (1978) Learned helplessness in humans: critique and reformulation *Journal of Abnormal Psychology* **87** 49–74

ADAMS, J. A. & REYNOLDS, B. (1954) Effect of shift in distribution of practice conditions following interpolated rest *Journal of Experimental Psychology* **47** 32–6

ADORNO, T. W., FRENKEL-BRUNSWIK, G., LEVINSON, D. J. & SANFORD, R. N. (1950) *The Authoritarian Personality* New York: Harper

AGRAS, W. S., BARLOW, T. H., CHARIN, H. N., ABEL, G. G. & LEITENBERG, H. (1974) Behaviour modification of anorexia nervosa *Archives of General Psychiatry* **30** 343–52

AHRENS, S. R. (1954) Beiträge zur Entwicklung des Physiognomie und Mimikerkenntnisse (Contributions on the development of physiognomy and mimicry recognition) *Zeitschrift für Experimentelle und Angewandte Psychologie* **2** 412–54

AIELLO, J. R., NICOSIA, G. & THOMPSON, D. E. (1979) Physiological, social and behavioural consequences of crowding on children and adolescents *Child Development* **50** 195–202

AINSCOE, M. & HARDY, L. (1987) Cognitive warm up in a cyclical gymnastic skill *International Journal of Sport Psychology* **18** 269–75

AINSWORTH, M. D. S. (1979) Attachment as related to mother-infant interaction *Advances in the Study of Behaviour* **9** 2–52

AINSWORTH, M. D. S., BLEHAR, M. C., WATERS, E. & WALL, S. (1978) *Patterns of Attachment* Hillsdale, N. J.: Erlbaum

AJZEN, I (1988) *Attitudes, Personality and Behaviour* Milton Keynes: Open University Press

AJZEN, I. & FISHBEIN, M. (1977) Attitude-behaviour relationships: a theoretical analysis and review of empirical research *Psychological Bulletin* **84** 888–918

AJZEN, I. & FISHBEIN, M. (1980) *Understanding Attitudes and Predicting Social Behaviour* Englewood Cliffs, N.J.: Prentice Hall

AJZEN, I., TIMKO, C. & WHITE, J. B. (1982) Self-monitoring and the attitude-behaviour relation *Journal of Personality and Social Psychology* **42** 426–35

AKERSTEDT, T. (1985) Adjustment of physiological circadian rhythms and the sleep–wake cycle to shiftwork In: S. Folkard & T. H. Monk (eds) *Hours of Work* Chichester: Wiley

AKISKAL, H. S. & MCKINNEY, W. T. (1973) Depressive disorders: toward a unified hypothesis *Science* **182** 20–9

ALBA, J. W. & HASHER, L. (1987) Is memory schematic? *Psychological Bulletin* **93** 203–31

ALLEN, V. L. & LEVINE, J. M. (1968) Social support, dissent and conformity *Sociometry* **31** 138–49

ALLEN, V. L. & LEVINE, J. M. (1971) Social pressures and personal influence *Journal of Experimental Social Psychology* **7** 122–4

ALLMANN, L. R. & JAFFE, D. T. (1976) *Readings in Abnormal Psychology: Contemporary Perspectives* New York: Harper and Row

ALLOTT, R. (1997) *Image and Action* Paper delivered at the European Society for the Study of Cognitive Systems Workshop, Freiburg im Breisgau, June 1997

ALLPORT, D. A. (1980) Patterns and actions: cognitive mechanisms are content specific In: G. Claxton (ed.) *Cognitive Psychology: New Directions* London: Routledge & Kegan Paul

ALLPORT, D. A., ANTONIS, B. & REYNOLDS, P. (1972) On the division of attention: a disproof of the single channel hypothesis *Quarterly Journal of Experimental Psychology* **24** 225–35

ALLPORT, F. H. (1920) The influences of the group upon association and thought *Journal of Experimental Psychology* **3** 159–82

ALLPORT, F. H. (1924) *Social Psychology* Boston: Houghton Mifflin

ALLPORT, G. W. (1935) Attitudes In: C. M. Murchison (ed.) *Handbook of Social Psychology* Worcester, Mass.: Clark University Press

ALLPORT, G. W. (1954) *The Nature of Prejudice* Wokingham: Addison-Wesley

ALLPORT, G. W. & POSTMAN, L. (1947) *The Psychology of Rumour* New York: Holt

AMERICAN PSYCHIATRIC ASSOCIATION (1980) *Diagnostic and Statistical Manual of Mental Disorders* (3rd ed.) Washington, DC: APA

AMERICAN PSYCHIATRIC ASSOCIATION (1994) *Diagnostic and Statistical Manual of Mental Disorders* (4th ed.) Washington, DC: APA

ANAND, B. K. & BROBECK, J. R. (1951) Hypothalamic control of food intake in rats and cats *Yale Journal of Biological Medicine* **24** 132–40

ANDERSON, C. A., HOROWITZ, L. M. & FRENCH, R DE S. (1983) Attributional style of lonely and depressed people *Journal of Personality and Social Psychology* **45** 127–36

ANDREW, R. J. (1956) Some remarks on behaviour in conflict situations, with special reference to Emberiza spp *British Journal of Animal Behaviour* **4** 41–5

ANNETT, J. (1989) Skills In: A. M. Colman & J. G. Beaumont (eds) *Psychology Survey* **87** London: BPS/Routledge

ANNIS, R. C. & FROST, B. (1973) Human visual ecology and orientation antistropies in acuity *Science* **182** 729–31

ANTAKI, C. & FIELDING, G. (1981) Research on ordinary explanations In: C. Antaki (ed.) *The Psychology of Ordinary Explanations of Social Behaviour* London: Academic Press

APPLE, W., STREETER, L. A. & KRAUSS, R. M. (1979) Effects of pitch and speech rate on personal attributions *Journal of Personality and Social Psychology* **37** 715–27

APPLEBY, M. (1985) Hawks, doves … and chickens *New Scientist* 10th January 1985 16–18

ARDREY, R. (1966) *The Territorial Imperative* New York: Dell

AREES, E. A. & MAYER, J. (1967) Anatomical connections between medial and lateral regions of the hypothalamus concerned with food intake *Science* **157** 1574–5

ARENDT, H. (1963) *Eichmann in Jerusalem: A Report on Banality of Evil* New York: Viking Press

ARGYLE, M. (1981) The contribution of social interaction research to social skills training In: D. Wine & M. D. Smye (eds) *Social Competence* New York: Guildford Press

ARGYLE, M. (1984) *Bodily Communication* (2nd ed.) London: Methuen

ARGYLE, M. (1990) *Relationships* Lecture delivered at Psychology Teachers' Updating Workshop, Oxford 1990

ARGYLE, M. & CROSSLAND, J. (1987) The dimensions of positive emotions *British Journal of Social Psychology* **26** 127–37

ARGYLE, M. & HENDERSON, M. (1984) The rules of friendship *Journal of Social and Personal Relationships* **1** 211–37

ARGYLE, M., ALKEMA, F. & GILMOUR, R. (1971) The communication of friendly and hostile attitudes by verbal and non-verbal signals *European Journal of Social Psychology* **1** 385–402

ARGYLE, M., LALLJEE, M. & COOK, M. (1968) The effects of visibility on interaction in a dyad *Human Relations* **21** 3–17

ARKIN, A. M., TOTH, M. F., BAKER, J. & HASTEY, J. M. (1970) The frequency of sleep talking in the laboratory among chronic sleep talkers and good dream recallers *Journal of Nervous and Mental Disease* **151** 369–74

ARONSON, E. (1976) *The Social Animal* San Francisco: W. H. Freeman & Co

ARONSON, E. & LINDER, D. (1965) Gain and loss of esteem as determinants of interpersonal attractiveness *Journal of Experimental Social Psychology* **1** 156–71

ARONSON, E. & OSHEROW, N. (1980) Co-operation, prosocial behaviour, and academic performance: experiments in the desegregated classroom In: L. Bickerman (ed.) *Applied Social Psychology Annual* Beverley Hills, Calif.: Sage

ARONSON, E., WILLERMAN, B. & FLOYD, J. (1966) The effect of a pratfall on increasing interpersonal attractiveness *Psychonomic Science* **4** 227–8

ASCH, S. E. (1946) Forming impressions of personality *Journal of Abnormal and Social Psychology* **41** 258–90

ASCH, S. E. (1948) The doctrine of suggestion, prestige and imitation in social psychology *Psychological Review* **55** 250–76

ASCHOFF, J. (1965) Circadian rhythm of a Russian vocabulary *Journal of Experimental Psychology: Human Learning and Memory* **104** 126–33

ATCHLEY, R. C. (1976) Selected social and psychological differences between men and women in later life *Journal of Gerontology* **31** 204–11

ATKINSON, J. W. (1964) *An Introduction to Motivation* **2** Princeton, N.J.: Van Nostrand

ATKINSON, R. C. & SHIFFRIN, R. M. (1968) Human memory: a proposed system and its control processes In: K. W. Spence & J. T. Spence (eds) *The Psychology of Learning and Motivation* **2** London: Academic Press

AUSUBEL, D. P. (1961) Personality disorder is disease *American Psychologist* **16** 69–74

AVERILL, J. R. (1980) A constructivist view of emotion In: R. Plutchik and H. Kellerman (ed) *Emotion: Theory, Research and Experience* **1** New York: Academic Press

AX, A. F. (1953) Physiological differentiation of emotional states *Psychosomatic Medicine* **15** 433–42

AXLINE, V. (1971) Dibs: *In Search of Self* Harmondsworth: Penguin

AYRES, J. (1983) Strategies to maintain relationships: their identification and perceived usage *Communication Quarterly* **31** 207–25

BADDELEY, A. D. (1978) The trouble with levels: an examination of Craik and Lockhart's framework for memory research *Psychological Review* **89** 708–29

BADDELEY, A. D. (1983) *Your Memory: a User's Guide* Harmondsworth: Penguin

BADDELEY, A. D. (1986) *Working Memory* Oxford: Oxford University Press

BADDELEY, A. D. (1990) *Human Memory: Theory and Practice* Hove: Lawrence Erlbaum Associates

BADDELEY, A. D. & HITCH, G. (1974) Working memory In: G. H. Bower (ed.) *The Psychology of Learning and Motivation* **8** 47–90

BADDELEY, A. D. & LEWIS, V. J. (1981) Inner active processes in reading: the inner voice, the inner ear, and the inner eye In: A. M. Lesgold & C. A. Perfetti (eds) *Interactive Processes in Reading* Hillsdale, N. J.: Lawrence Erlbaum Associates

BADDELEY, A. D. & LIEBERMAN, K. (1980) Spatial working memory In: R. Nickerson (ed.) *Attention and Performance VI* London: Academic Press

BADDELEY, A. D. & LONGMAN, D. J. A. (1978) The influence of length and frequency on training sessions on the rate of learning to type *Ergonomics* **21** 627–35

BADDELEY, A. D., THOMSON, N. & BUCHANAN, M. (1975) Word length and the structure of short-term memory *Journal of Verbal Learning and Verbal Behaviour* **14** 575–89

BADDELEY, A. D., ELLIS, N. C., MILES, T. R. & LEWIN, V. J. (1982) Developmental and acquired dyslexia: a comparison *Cognition* **11** 185–99

BADDELEY, A. D., GRANT, S., WIGHT, E. & THOMSON, N. (1975) Imagery and visual working memory In: P. M. A. Rabbitt & S. Dornic (eds) *Attention and Performance V* London: Academic Press

BAGLEY, C. & VERMA, G. K. (1979) *Racial Prejudice: The Individual and Society* Farnborough: Saxon House

BAGLEY, C., VERMA, G. K., MALLICK, K. & YOUNG, L. (1979) *Personality, Self-esteem and Prejudice* Farnborough: Saxon House

BALES, R. F. (1950) Interaction Process Analysis Cambridge, Mass : Addison-Wesley

BALES, R. F. (1970) *Personality and Interpersonal Behaviour* New York: Holt, Rinehart & Winston

BALES, R. F. & SLATER, P. E. (1955) Role differentiation in small decision-making groups In: T. Parsons *et al.* (eds) *Family Socialisation and Interaction Process* New York: Free Press

BALL, F., WOOD, C. & SMITH, E. E. (1975) When are semantic targets detected faster than visual or acoustic ones? *Perception and Psychophysics* **17** 1–8

BALL, W. & TRONICK, E. (1971) Infant responses to impending collision: optical and real *Science* **171** 818–20

BALLARD, R. (1983) Personal communication

BANDURA, A. (1969) *Principles of Behaviour Modification* New York: Rinehart & Winston

BANDURA, A. (1972) The stormy decade: fact or fiction? In: D. Rogers (ed.) *Issues in Adolescent Psychology* (2nd ed.) New York: Appleton CenturyCrofts

BANDURA, A. (1977a) *Social Learning Theory* Englewood Cliffs, N. J.: Prentice Hall

BANDURA, A. (1977b) Self-efficacy: toward a unifying theory of behavioural change *Psychological Review* **84** 191–215

BANDURA, A. (1978) The self-esteem in reciprocal determination *American Psychologist* **33** 344–58

BANDURA, A. (1986) *Social Foundations of Thought and Action: a Social Cognitive Theory* Englewood Cliffs, N. J.: Prentice Hall

BANDURA, A. (1988) Perceived self-efficacy: exercise of control through self-belief In: J. P. Dauwalder, M. Perrez & V. Hobi (eds) *Annual Series of European Research in Behaviour Therapy* **2** 27–59

BANDURA, A. (1989) Perceived self-efficacy in the exercise of personal agency *The Psychologist* **2** 411–24

BANDURA, A. & WALTERS, R. H. (1963) *Social Learning and Personality Development* New York: Holt Rinehart & Winston

BANDURA, A., ROSS, D. & ROSS, S. (1963) Imitation of film mediated aggressive models *Journal of Abnormal and Social Psychology* **66** 3–11

BANKS, M. S. & GINSBURG, A. P. (1985) Infant visual preferences: a review and new theoretical treatment *Advances in Child Development and Behaviour* **19** 207–46

BANNISTER, D. (1968) The logical requirements of research into schizophrenia *British Journal of Psychiatry* **114** 181–8

BANNISTER, D. & FRANSELLA, F. (1980) *Inquiring Man: the Psychology of Personal Constructs* (2nd ed.) Harmondsworth: Penguin

BANYARD, P. (1989) Hillsborough *Psychology News* **2**(7) 4–9

BARCLAY, R. & FENTON, B. (1983) Communication through ecolocation in little brown bats *Behavioural Ecology* **10** 271–75

BARD, B. & SACHS, J. (1977) *Language Acquisition Patterns in Two Normal Children of Deaf Patterns* Paper presented to the 2nd Annual Boston University Conference on Language Acquisition October 1977 cited in J. G. de Villiers. & P. A. de Villiers (1978) *Early Language* London: Fontana

BARON, R. A. & BYRNE, D. (1984) *Social Psychology: Understanding Human Interaction* (4th ed.) Boston: Allyn & Bacon

BARON, R. A. & BELL, P. A. (1975) Aggression and heat: mediating effects of prior provocation and exposure to an aggressive model *Journal of Personality and Social Psychology* **31** 825–32

BARON, R. S. (1986) Distraction – conflict theory: progress and problems In: L. Berkowitz (ed.) *Advances in Experimental Social Psychology* (Vol 19) New York: Academic Press

BARON-COHEN, S., LESLIE, A. M. & FRITH, U. (1986) Mechanical, behavioural and intentional understanding of picture stories in autistic children *British Journal of Developmental Psychology* 4 113–25

BARROW, R. (1976) *Common Sense and the Curriculum* London: Allen & Unwin

BARTLETT, F. C. (1932) *Remembering* London: Cambridge University Press

BASS, C. & WADE, C. (1982) Type A behaviour: not specifically pathogenic *The Lancet* 20th November 1982 1147–50

BASTIAN, P. (1965) Dolphin experiment Reported in F. G. Wood (1973) *Marine Mammals and Man: the Navy's Porpoises and Sea Lions* Washington DC: R. B. Luce

BASTOCK, M., MORRIS, D. & MOYNIHAN, M. (1953) Some comments on conflict and thwarting in animals *Behaviour* 6 66–84

BATESON, G. (1955) A theory of play and fantasy *Psychiatric Research Reports* 2 39–51

BATESON, G. (1973) *Steps to an Ecology of Mind: Collected Essays in Anthroplogy, Psychiatry, Evolution and Epistemology* London: Paladin

BATESON, G., JACKSON, D., HALEY, J. & WEAKLAND, J. (1956) Towards a theory of schizophrenia *Behavioural Science* 1(4) 251–64

BATESON, P. P. (1966) The characteristics of content of imprinting *Biological Review* 41 177–211

BAUMRIND, D. (1964) Some thoughts on the ethics of research: after reading Milgram's 'Behavioural study of obedience' *American Psychologist* 19 421–3

BAXTER, L. A. (1986) Gender differences in the heterosexual relationships rules embedded in break-up accounts *Journal of Social and Personal Relationships* 3 289–306

BEATTIE, G. (1984) *The Threads of Discourse and the Web of Interpersonal Involvement* Spearman Medal Address, British Psychological Society London Conference, December 1984

BEATTIE, G. & SPEAKMAN, L. (1983) A load of old rope *The Guardian* 7th March 1983

BEAUMONT, J. G. (1988) *Understanding Neuropsychology* Oxford: Basil Blackwell

BECK, A. T. (1967) *Depression: Clinical, Experimental and Theoretical Aspects* New York: Hoeber

BECK, A. T. (1976) *Cognitive Therapy and the Emotional Disorders* New York: International Universities Press

BECK, A. T., EMERY, G. & GREENBERG, R. (1985) Anxiety Disorders and Phobias: A Cognitive Perspective New York: Basic.

BECK, A. T., WARD, C. H., MENDELSON, M., MOCK, J. E. & ERBAUGH, J. K. (1962) Reliability of psychiatric diagnoses II: a study of consistency of clinical judgements and ratings *American Journal of Psychiatry* 119 351–7

BEER, C. G. (1962) Incubation and nestbuilding behaviour of black-headed gulls: IV. Nestbuilding in the laying and incubation periods *Behaviour* 21 155–76

BEGBIE, G. H. (1959) Accuracy in aiming in linear hand movements *Quarterly Journal of Experimental Psychology* 11 65–75

BEKERIAN, D. A. & BADDELEY, A. D. (1980) Saturation advertising and the repetition effect *Journal of Verbal Learning and Verbal Behaviour* 19 17–25

BELBIN, E. (1958) Methods of training older workers *Ergonomics* 1 207–21

BELBIN, R. M. (1981) *Management Teams* London: Heinemann

BELL, R. A. & DALY, J. A. (1984) The affinity-seeking function of communication *Communication Monographs* 51 91–115

BELOFF, J. (1993) *Parapsychology: a Concise History* London: Athlone Press

BEM, D. J. (1967) Self-perception: an alternative interpretation of cognitive dissonance phenomena *Psychological Review* 74 183–200

BEM, D. J. (1994) Response to Hyman *Psychological Bulletin* 115 25–7

BEM, D. J. & HONORTON, C. (1994) Does psi exist? Replicable evidence for an anomalous process of information transfer *Psychological Bulletin* 115 4–18

BEM, S. L. (1975) Sex role adaptability: one consequence of psychological androgeny *Journal of Personality and Social Psychology* 31 634–43

BENEWICK, R. & HOLTON, R. (1987) The peaceful crowd: crowd solidarity and the pope's visit to Britain In: G. Gaskell & R. Benewick (eds) *The Crowd in Contemporary Britain* London: Sage

BENGTSON, V. L. & TROLL, L. E. (1978) Youth and their parents: feedback and intergeneration In: R. M. Lerner & G. B. Spanier (eds) *Child Influences on Marital and Family Interaction: a Life Span Perspective* New York: Academic Press

BENNE, K. D. AND SHEATS. P. (1948) Functional group members *Journal of Social Issues* 4 41–9

BENTLER, P. M. & NEWCOMB, M. D. (1978) Longitudinal study of marital success and failure *Journal of Consulting and Clinical Psychology* 46 1053–70

BERGER, H. (1929) Über das Elektrenkephalogram des Menschen *Archiv für Psychiatrie und Nervenkrankheiten* 87 527–70

BERKOWITZ, L. (1978) Whatever happened to the aggression frustration hypothesis? *American Behavioural Scientist* 32 691–708

BERLIN, B. & KAY, P. (1969) *Basic Colour Terms: their Universality and Evolution* Berkeley & Los Angeles: University of California Press

BERNE, E. (1973) *Games People Play* Harmondsworth: Penguin

BERNSTEIN, B. (1973) Social Class, Language and Socialisation In: V. Lee (ed.) (1979) *Language Development* London: Croom Helm/Open University

BERRY, D. (1989) *Artifical Intelligence: a Review* Paper delivered at the 'Psychology Teachers Updating Workshop', Oxford 1989

BERSCHEID, E. (1985) Interpersonal attraction In: G. Lindzey & E. Aronson (eds) *The Handbook of Social Psychology* (3rd ed.) New York: Random House

BESTERMAN, T. (1932) The psychology of testimony in relation to parapsychological phenomena: report of an experiment *Proceedings of the Society for Psychical Research* **40** 363–87

BETHLEHEM, D. W. (1985) *A Social Psychology of Prejudice* London: Croom Helm

BETHLEHEM, D. W. & KINGSLEY, P. R. (1976) Zambian student attitudes toward others, based on tribe, class, and rural-urban dwelling *Journal of Social Psychology* **100** 189–98

BETTELHEIM, B. (1943) Individual and mass behaviour in extreme situations *Journal of Abnormal and Social Psychology* **38** 417–52

BEVER, T. G. & CHIARELLO, R. J. (1974) Cerebral dominance in musicians and non-musicians *Science* **185** 137–9

BHARATI, A. (1985) The self in Hindu thought and action In: A.J. Marsell *et al.* (1985) *Culture and Self: Asian and Western Perspectives* London: Tavistock Publications

BILLIG, M. (1990) Collective memory, ideology and the British Royal family In: D. Middleton and D. Edwards (eds) *Collective remembering* London: Sage

BILLIG, M. & TAJFEL, H. (1973) Social categorisation and similarity in intergroup behaviour *European Journal of Social Psychology* **3** 27–52

BILODEAU, I. M. D. & BILODEAU, E. A. (1958) Variable frequency of knowledge of results and the learning of a simple skill *Journal of Experimental Psychology* **55** 379–83

BINET, A. (1913) *Les Idées Modernes sur les Infants* Paris: Flammarian

BINET, A. & SIMON, T. (1905) Méthodes nouvelles pour le diagnostic du niveau intellectuel des anormaux *L'Année Psychologique* **11** 245–336

BINET, A. & SIMON, T. (1911) A *Method of Measuring the Development of the Intelligence of Young Children* Lincoln, Ill.: Courier Co.

BITTERMAN, M. E. & KNIFFIN, C. W. (1953) Manifest anxiety and perceptual defense *Journal of Abnormal and Social Psychology* **48** 248

BLACKMORE, S. J. (1996) *In Search of the Light: Adventures of a Parapsychologist* New York: Prometheus Books

BLAKEMORE, C. (1984) *The Sensory Worlds of Animals and Man* Address given to the Annual Meeting of the Association for the Teaching of Psychology AGM London, November 1984

BLAKEMORE, C. & COOPER, G. F. (1970) Development of the brain depends on the visual environment *Nature* **228** 477–8

BLANCHARD, R. J., KELLEY, M. J. & BLANCHARD, C. (1974) Defensive reactions and exploratory behaviour in rats *Journal of Comparative and Physiological Psychology* **87** 1129–33

BLISS, E. L. (1980) Multiple personalities: report of fourteen cases with implications for schizophrenia and hysteria *Archives of General Psychiatry* **37** 1388–97

BLOS, P. (1967) The second individuation process of adolescence *Psychoanalytic Study of the Child* **22** 162–86

BLUNDELL, J. E. (1975) *Physiological Psychology* London: Methuen

BOAS, F. (1911) *Handbook of American Indian Languages* Washington DC: Smithsonian Inst.

BODEN, M. (1979) *Piaget* London: Fontana

BOGDONOFF, M. D., KLEIN, E. J., SHAW, D. M. & BECK, K. W. (1961) The modifying effect of conforming behaviour upon lipid responses accompanying CNS arousal *Clinical Research* **9** 135

BOLK, L. (1926) *Das Problem der Menschwertung* Jena: Gustav Fischer

BOND, C. F. (1982) Social facilitation: a self-presentational view *Journal of Personality and Social Psychology* **42** 1042–50

BOND, M. H. & VENUS, C. K. (1991) Resistance to group or personal insults in an ingroup or outgroup context *International Journal of Psychology* **26** 83–94

BONO, E. DE (1969) *The Mechanism of Mind* Harmondsworth: Penguin

BONO, E. DE (1977) *Lateral Thinking* Harmondsworth: Penguin

BOURNE, L. E., DOMINOWSKY, R. L. & LOFTUS, E. F. (1979) *Cognitive Processes* Englewood Cliffs, N.J.: Prentice Hall

BOWEN, M. (1960) A family concept of schizophrenia In: D. D. Jackson (ed.) *The Etiology of Schizophrenia* New York: Basic Books

BOWEN, M. (1966) The use of family therapy in clinical practice *Comprehensive Psychiatry* **7** 345–74

BOWER, G. H. (1969) Chunks as interference units in free recall *Journal of Verbal Learning and Verbal Behaviour* **8** 610–13

BOWER, G. H. (1972) Mental imagery and associative learning In: L. Gregg (ed.) *Cognition in Learning and Memory* New York: Wiley

BOWER, G. H. (1981) Mood and memory *American Psychologist* **36** 129–48

BOWER, G. H. & KARLIN, M. B. (1974) Depth of processing pictures of faces and recognition memory *Journal of Experimental Psychology* **103** 751–7

BOWER, G. H. & TRABASSO, T. (1964) Presolution reversal and dimensional shifts in concept identification *Journal of Experimental Psychology* **67** 398–9

BOWER, G. H., MINTEIRO, K. P. & GILLIGAN, S. G. (1978) Emotional mood as context for learning and recall *Journal of Verbal Learning and Verbal Behaviour* **17** 573–85

BOWER, T. G. R. (1966) The visual world of infants *Scientific American* **215**(6) 80–92

BOWER, T. G. R. (1972) Object perception in infancy *Perception* **1** 15–30

BOWER, T. G. R. & WISHART, J. G. (1972) The effects of motor skill on object permanence *Cognition* **1** 165–72

BOWER, T. G. R., BROUGHTON, J. M. & MOORE, M. K. (1970) Infant responses to approaching objects: an indicator of response to distal variables *Perception and Psychophysics* **9** 193–6

BOWLBY, J. (1951) *Child Care and the Growth of Love* Harmondsworth: Penguin

BOWLBY, J. (1956) The effects of mother-child separation: a follow-up study *British Journal of Medical Psychology* **29** 211–47

BOWLBY, J. (1973) *Attachment and Loss Vol II: Separation, Anxiety and Anger* London: Hogarth

BOWLBY, J. (1980) *Attachment and Loss Vol III: Loss, Sadness and Depression* London: Hogarth

BRADLEY, L. & BRYANT, P. E. (1983) Categorising sounds and learning to read: a causal connexion *Nature* **301** 419–21

BRADY, J. V. (1958) Ulcers in 'executive' monkeys *Scientific American* **199**(4) 95–100

BRAINE, M. D. S., REISER, B. J. & RUMAIN, B. (1964) Some empirical justification for a theory of natural propositional logic In: G. H. Bower (ed.) *The Psychology of Learning and Motivation* **18** New York: Academic Press

BRANSFORD, J. D. & JOHNSON, M. K. (1972) Contextual prerequisites for understanding: some investigations of comprehension and recall *Journal of Verbal Learning and Verbal Behaviour* **11** 717–26

BRANSFORD, J. D., BARCLAY, J. R. & FRANKS, J. J. (1972) Sentence memory: a constructive versus interpretative approach *Cognitive Psychology* **3** 193–209

BREGER, L. & MCGAUGH, J. (1965) Critique and reformulation of 'learning theory' approaches to psychotherapy and neurosis *Psychological Bulletin* **63** 338–58

BRELAND, K. & BRELAND, M. (1966) *Animal Behaviour* New York: Macmillan

BREMNER, J. G. (1988) *Infancy* Oxford: Basil Blackwell

BRENNAN, W. M., AMES, E. W. & MOORE, R.W. (1966) Age differences in infants' attention to patterns of differential complexity *Science* **151** 354–6

BREUER, J. & FREUD, S. (1895) Studies on hysteria *The Standard Edition of the Complete Psychological Works of Sigmund Freud* **2** London: Hogarth 1955

BRIGGS, R. (1971) Urban cognitive distances Unpublished doctoral dissertation, Ohio State University, cited in M. Matlin (1983) *Cognition* New York: Holt, Rinehart & Winston

BRIGHAM, J. C. (1971) Ethnic stereotypes *Psychological Bulletin* **76** 15–38

BRIGHT, M. (1984) *Animal Language* London: BBC Publications

BRIM, O. G. (1965) Adolescent personality as self-other systems *Journal of Marriage and the Family* **27** 156–62

BRIM, O. G. (1976) Theories of the male mid-life crisis *The Counselling Psychologist* **6** 2–9

BRITISH PSYCHOLOGICAL SOCIETY (1991) *Code of Conduct Ethical Principles and Guidelines* Leicester: British Psychological Society

BROADBENT, D. E. (1958) *Perception and Communication* Oxford: Pergamon

BROADBENT, D. E., COOPER, P. F., FITZGERALD, P. & PARKES, K. R. (1982) The cognitive failures questionnaire (CFQ) and its correlates *British Journal of Clinical Psychology* **21** 1–18

BROCA, P. (1861) Remarques sur la siège de la faculté de langage articulé suivées d'une observation d'aphemie *Bulletin de la Société Anatomique (Paris)* **6** 330–57

BROMLEY, D. B. (1966) *The Psychology of Human Ageing* Harmondsworth: Penguin

BRONFENBRENNER, U. (1973) *The Two Worlds of Childhood: USA & USSR* New York: Pocket Books

BRONFENBRENNER, U. (1974) The origins of alienation *Scientific American* **231** 53–61

BROOKS, V. B. (1986) *The Neural Basis of Motor Control* Oxford: Oxford University Press

BROOKS-GUNN, J. & PETERSEN, A. (eds) (1983) *Girls at Puberty: Biological and Psycho-social Perspectives* New York: Plenum Press

BROOKS-GUNN, J. & WARREN, M. (1985) The effects of delayed menarche in different contexts: dance and non-dance students *Journal of Youth and Adolescence* **11** 121–33

BROWN, G. W. & HARRIS, T. (1978) *Social Origins of Depression: a Study in Psychiatric Disorder in Women* London: Tavistock

BROWN, H. (1985) *People, Groups and Society* Milton Keynes: Open University Press

BROWN, J. A. (1958) Some tests of the decay theory of immediate memory *Quarterly Journal of Experimental Psychology* **10** 12–21

BROWN, N. R., RIPS, L.J. & SHEVELL, S.K. (1985) The subjective dates of neural events in very long term memory *Cognitive Psychology* **17** 139–77

BROWN, P. L. & JENKINS, H. M. (1968) Autoshaping of the pigeon's keypeck *Journal of the Experimental Analysis of Behaviour* **11** 1–8

BROWN, R. & KULIK, J. (1977) Flashbulb memories *Cognition* **5** 73–99

BRUCE, V. (1988) Perceiving In: G. Claxton (ed.) *Growth Points in Cognition* London: Routledge

BRUCE, V. & VALENTINE, T. (1985) Identity priming in the recognition of familiar and unfamiliar faces *British Journal of Psychology* **76** 373–83

BRUCE, V. & YOUNG, A. W. (1986) Understanding face recognition *British Journal of Psychology* **77** 305–27

BRUCH, H. (1979) *The Golden Cage* New York: Vintage

BRUNER, J. S. (1964) The course of cognitive growth *American Psychologist* **19** 1–15

BRUNER, J. S. (1972) The nature and uses of immaturity *American Psychologist* **27** 687–708

BRUNER, J. S. (1973) The organisation of early skilled action *Child Development* **44** 1–11

BRUNER, J. S. & MINTURN, A. L. (1955) Perceptual identification and perceptual organisation *Journal of General Psychology* **53** 21–8

BRUNER, J. S., GOODNOW, J. J. & AUSTIN, G. A. (1956) *A Study of Thinking* New York: Wiley

BRUNVAND, H. (1983) *The Vanishing Hitchhiker* London: Picador

BRUYER, R., LATERRE, C., SERON, X., FEYEREISEN, P., STRYPSTEIN, E., PIERRARD, E. & RECTEM, D. (1983) A case of prosopagnosia with some preserved covert remembrance of familiar faces *Brain and Cognition* **2** 257–84

BUCHANAN, W. (1951) Stereotypes and tensions as revealed by the UNESCO international poll *International Social Sciences Bulletin* **3** 515–28

BUGELSKI, B. R. & ALAMPAY, D. A. (1961) The role of frequency in developing perceptual sets *Canadian Journal of Psychology* **15** 205–11

BURKS, B. S. (1928) The relative influence of nature and nurture upon mental development: a comparative study of foster-parent foster-child resemblance and true-parent true-child resemblance *27th Yearbook of the National Society for the Study of Education* 219–316 Bloomington, Ill: Public School Publishing Co.

BURNS, R. B. (1966) Age and mental ability *British Journal of Educational Psychology* **36** 116

BURT, C. (1912) The inheritance of mental characters *Eugenics Review* **4** 168–200

BURT, C. (1955) The evidence for the concept of intelligence *British Journal of Educational Psychology* **25** 158–77

BURT, C. (1959) The examination at eleven plus *British Journal of Educational Studies* **7** 99–117

BURT, C. (1966) The genetic determination of differences in intelligence: a study of monozygotic twins reared together and apart *British Journal of Psychology* **57** 137–53

BURT, C. (1972) The inheritance of general intelligence *American Psychologist* **27** 175–90

BUSS, A. R. (1966) Instrumentality of aggression, feedback and frustration as determinants of physical aggression *Journal of Personality and Social Psychology* **3** 153–62

BUTTERWORTH, G. & HARRIS, M. (1994) *Principles of Developmental Psychology* Hove: Psychology Press

BUTTERWORTH, G. JARRETT, N. & HICKS, L. (1982) Spatio-temporal identity in infancy: perceptual competence or conceptual deficit? *Developmental Psychology* **18** 435–49

BYRNE, D. (1961) Interpersonal attraction and attitude similarity *Journal of Abnormal and Social Psychology* **62** 713–15

BYRNE, D. (1971) *The Attraction Paradigm* New York: Academic Press

BYRNE, D. & NELSON, D. (1965) Attraction as a linear function of proportion of positive reinforcements *Journal of Personality and Social Psychology* **1** 659–63

CALHOUN, J. B. (1962) Population density and social pathology *Scientific American* **206**(3) 139–48

CAMPBELL, H. J. (1973) *The Pleasure Areas* London: Eyre Methuen

CAMPBELL, R. (ed.) (1992) *Mental Lives: Case Studies in Cognition* Oxford: Blackwell

CAMPOS, J., LANGER, A. & KROWITZ, A. (1970) Cardiac responses on the visual cliff in prelocomotor human infants *Science* **170** 195–6

CANNON, W. B. (1929) *Bodily Changes in Pain, Hunger, Fear and Rage* New York: Appleton

CANTER, D. & TAGG, S. (1975) Distance estimation in cities *Environment and Behaviour* **7** 59–80

CAPOZZA, D. & VOLPATO, C. (1990) Categorical differentiation and intergroup relationships *British Journal of Social Psychology* **29** 93–5

CARMICHAEL, L. (1956) The development of behaviour in vertebrates experimentally removed from the influence of external stimulation *Psychological Review* **33** 51–8

CARMICHAEL, L., HOGAN, H. P. & WALTER, A. A. (1932) An experimental study of the effect of language on visually perceived forms *Journal of Experimental Psychology* **15** 73–86

CARPENTER, B., WIENER, M. & CARPENTER, J. T. (1956) Predictability of perceptual defense behaviour *Journal of Abnormal & Social Psychology* **52** 380

CARUGATI, F. F. (1990) Everyday ideas, theoretical models and social representations: the case of intelligence and its development In: G. R. Semin and K. J. Gergen *Everyday Understanding: Social and Scientific Implications* London: Sage

CARYL, P. G. (1981) Escalated fighting and the war of nerves: games theory and animal combat In: P. G. Bateson & P. Klopfer (eds) *Perspectives in Ethology 4* London: Plenum

CATCHPOLE, C. (1981) Song is a serenade for the warblers In: G. Ferry (ed.) *The Understanding of Animals* (1984) Oxford: Basil Blackwell

CATTELL, R. B. (1946) *Description and Measurement of Personality* New York: World Book Company

CATTELL, R. B. (1950) *Personality: a Systematic, Theoretical and Factual Study* New York: McGraw–Hill

CATTELL, R. B. (1956) Personality and motivation theory based on structural measurements In: J. L. McCary (ed.) *Psychology of Personality* New York: Grove Press

CATTELL, R. B. (1971) *Abilities: their Structure, Growth and Action* Boston: Houghton Mifflin

CAZDEN, C. (1970) The neglected situation in child language research and education *Journal of Social Issues* **25** 35–60

CHAMPNESS, B. G. (1980) Deumblification: the unkindest cut of all *Bulletin of the British Psychological Society* **33** 117–20

CHAPMAN, L. J. & CHAPMAN, J. P. (1969) Illusory correlations as an obstacle to the use of valid psychodiagnostic signs *Journal of Abnormal Psychology* **72** 193–204

CHASE, W. G. & SIMON, H. A. (1973) The mind's eye in chess In: W. G. Chase (ed.) *Visual Information Processing* New York: Academic Press

CHENG, P. W. (1985) Restructuring versus automaticity: alternative accounts of skill acquisition *Psychological Review* **92** 414–23

CHERRY, E. C. (1953) Some experiments on the recognition of speech, with one and with two ears *Journal of the Acoustical Society of America* **23** 915–19

CHILD, I. L. (1985) Psychology and anomalous observations: the question of ESP in dreams *American Psychologist* **40** 1219–30

CHOMSKY, N. (1959) Review of Skinner's 'Verbal Behaviour' *Language* **35** 26–58

CHOMSKY, N. (1970) Phonology and reading In: H. Levin & J. P. Williams (eds) *Basic Studies on Reading* New York: Basic Books

CHOMSKY, N. (1972) *Language and mind (enlarged Edition)* New York: Harcourt, Brace, Jovanovitch

CLARE, A. (1980) *Psychiatry in Dissent* London: Tavistock

CLARIDGE, G. (1988) *Temperament, Personality and Individual Differences* Lecture given at Psychology Teachers Workshop Oxford University March 1988

CLARK, E. V. & ANDERSON, E. A. (1979) Spontaneous repairs: awareness in the process of acquiring language *Papers and Reports on Child Language Development, Stanford University* **16** 1–12

CLARK, K. B. & CLARK, M. P. (1968) Racial identification and preference in negro children In: E. E. Maccoby, T. M. Newcomb & E. L. Hartley (eds) *Readings in Social Psychology* (3rd ed.) London: Methuen

CLARK, R. E. (1948) The relationship of schizophrenia to occupational income and occupational prestige *American Sociological Review* **13** 325–30

CLARKE, A. M. & CLARKE, A. D. B. (1976) *Early Experience: Myth and Evidence* London: Open Books

CLARKE, A. M. & CLARKE, A. D. B. (1977) Sir Cyril Burt *Bulletin of the British Psychological Society* **30** 83–4

CLARKE, A. M. & CLARKE, A. D. B. (1980) Comments on Professor Hearnshaw's 'Balance Sheet on Burt' In: H. Beloff (ed.) *A Balance Sheet on Burt: Supplement to the Bulletin of the British Psychological Society* **33** 17–19

CLAUSEN, J. A. & KOHN, M. L. (1959) Relation of schizophrenia to the social structure of a small city In: B. Pasamanick (ed.) *Epidemiology of Mental Disorder* Washington, DC: American Association for the Advancement of Science

CLORE, G. & BYRNE, D. (1974) A reinforcement-affect model of attraction In: T. L. Huston (ed.) *Foundations of Interpersonal Attraction* New York: Academic Press

CLORE, G. L., WIGGINS, N. H. & ITKIN, S. (1975) Gain and loss in attraction: attributions from non-verbal behaviour *Journal of Personality and Social Psychology* **31** 706–12

CLUTTON-BROCK, T. H., GUINNESS, F. E. & ALBON, S. D. (1982) *Red Deer: Behaviour and Ecology of Two Sexes* Edinburgh: University of Edinburgh Press

COHEN, D. (1987) *The Development of Play* London: Croom Helm

COHEN, D. (1988) *Forgotten Millions* London: Paladin

COHEN, D. B. (1979) *Sleep and Dreaming: Origins, Nature and Functions* Oxford: Pergamon

COHEN, S. (1973) *Folk Devils and Moral Panics* London: Paladin

COLE, P. M. (1986) Children's spontaneous control of facial expression *Child Development* **57** 1309–21

COLEMAN, J. C. (1974) *Relationships in Adolescence* London: Routledge & Kegan Paul

COLEMAN, J. C. & HENDRY, L. (1990) *The nature of adolescence* (2nd ed.) London: Routledge

COLLINS, A. M. & QUILLIAN, M. R. (1972) Experiments on semantic memory and language comprehension In: L. W.

Gregg (ed.) *Cognition in Learning and Memory* New York: Wiley

COLLINS, B. E. & HOYT, M. F. (1972) Personal responsibility – for – consequences: an integration and extension of the 'forced compliance' literature *Journal of Experimental Social Psychology* **8** 558–93

COLLINS, J. L. (1982) Self-efficacy and ability in achievement behavior Cited in A. Bandura: Perceived self-agency in the exercise of personal agency *The Psychologist* **2**(10) 411–24

COLTHEART, M., MASTERSON, J., BYNG, S., PRIOR, M. & RIDDOCH, J. (1983) Surface dyslexia *Quarterly Journal of Experimental Psychology* **35** 469–95

COMADENA, M. (1982) Accuracy in detecting deception: intimate and friendship relationships In: M. Burgoon (ed.) *Communication Yearbook 6* Beverley Hills, Ca.: Sage

CONRAD, R. (1964) Acoustic confusions in immediate memory *British Journal of Psychology* **55** 75–84

CONRAD, R. (1977) The reading ability of deaf school-leavers *British Journal of Psychology* **55** 75–84

CONWAY, M. A. & BEKERIAN, D. A. (1987) Organisation in autobiographical memory *Memory and Cognition* **15** 119–32

CONWAY, M. A. & RUBIN, D. C. (1993) The structure of autobiographical memory In: A. F. Collins *et al Theories of Memory* Hove: Lawrence Erlbaum Associates

CONWAY, M. A., ANDERSON, S. J., LARSEN, S. F., DONNELLY, C. M., MCDANIEL, M. A., MCCLELLAND, A. G. R. & RAWLES, R. E. (1994) The formation of flashbulb memories *Memory and Cognition* **22** 326–43

COOLEY, C. H. (1902) *Human Nature and the Social Order* New York: Scribners

COOPER, J. & WORCHEL, S. (1970) The role of undesired consequences in arousing cognitive dissonance *Journal of Personality and Social Psychology* **29** 441–5

COOPERSMITH, S. (1968) Studies in self-esteem *Scientific American* **218** 96–106

CORNELIUS, R. R. (1996) *The Science of Emotion: Research and Tradition in the Psychology of Emotion* N. J.: Prentice Hall

CORTEEN, R. S. & WOOD, B. (1972) Autonomic responses to shock associated words in an unattended channel *Journal of Experimental Psychology* **94** 308–13

COSTA, P. T. & MCCRAE, R. R. (1976) Age differences in personality structure: a cluster analytic approach *Journal of Gerontology* **31** 564–70

COTTERELL, N. B., WACK, D. L., SEKERAK, G. J. & RITTLE, R. H. (1968) Social facilitation of dominant responses by the presence of an audience and the mere presence of others *Journal of Personality and Social Psychology* **9** 245–50

CRAIK, I. F. M. & LOCKHART, R. S. (1972) Levels of processing: a framework for memory research *Journal of Verbal Learning and Verbal Behaviour* **11** 671–84

CRANDALL, J. E. (1985) Effects of favourable and unfavourable conditions on the psi-missing displacement effect *Journal of the American Society for Psychical Research* **79** 27–38

CRICK, F. & MITCHISON, G. (1983) The function of dream sleep *Nature* **304** 111–14

CRITCHLEY, M. (1970) *The Dyslexic Child* London: Heinemann

CROSSMAN, E. R. F. W. (1959) A theory of the acquisition of speed–skill *Ergonomics* **2** 153–66

CROW, T. J. (1973) Catecholamine-containing neurones and electrical self-stimulation 2: A theoretical interpretation and some psychiatric implications *Psychological Medicine* **3** 66–73

CRUTCHFIELD, R. S. (1955) Conformity and character *American Psychologist* **10** 191–8

CUBER, J. F. & HARROFF, P. B. (1965) *The Significant Americans: a Study of Sexual Behaviour among the Affluent* New York: Appleton, Century, Croft

CUMMINGS, E. & HENRY, W. E. (1961) *Growing Old* New York: Basic Books

CURIO, E., ERNST, V. & VEITH, W. (1978) Cultural transmission of enemy recognition *Science* **202** 899–901

CURTISS, S. (1977) *Genie: A Psycholinguistic Study of a Modern-Day 'Wild Child'* New York: Academic Press.

CUTRONA, C. E. (1982) Transition to college: loneliness and the process of social adjustment In: L. A. Peplau & D. Perlman (eds) *Loneliness: A Sourcebook of Current Theory, Research and Therapy* New York: Wiley

CZEISLER, C. A., MOORE-EDE, M. C. & COLEMAN, R. M. (1982) Rotating shift work schedules that disrupt sleep are improved by applying circadian principles *Science* **217** 460–63

CZEISLER, C. A., WEITZMAN, E. D., MOORE-EDE, M. C., ZIMMERMAN, J. C. & KNAUER, R. S. (1980) Human sleep: its duration and organisation depend on its circadian phase *Science* **210** 1264–7

DALENOORT, G. J. (1995) The representation of tasks in active cognitive networks *Cognitive Systems* **1** 253–72

DALENOORT, G. J. (1997) On the analysis of tasks for autonomous systems *Cognitive Systems* **4** 261–73

DALTON, K. (1997) Exploring the links: creativity and psi in the ganzfeld *Proceedings of the 40th Annual Convention of the Parapsychological Association* Hatfield, UK: University of Hertfordshire Press

DARLEY, J. M. & LATANÉ, B. (1968) Bystander intervention in emergencies: diffusion of responsibility *Journal of Personality and Social Psychology* **8** 377–83

DARLEY, J. M. & LATANÉ, B. (1970) Norms and normative behaviour: field studies of social interdependence In: J. Macauley & L. Berkowitz (eds) *Altruism and Helping Behaviour* New York: Academic Press

DARWIN, C. (1859) *The Origin of Species* London: John Murray

DARWIN, C. (1872) *The Expression of the Emotions in Man and the Animals* London: John Murray

DASHIELL, J. F. (1930) An experimental analysis of some group effects *Journal of Abnormal and Social Psychology* **25** 190–9

DATAN, N. (1980) Midas and other midlife crises In: W. H. Norman & T. J. Scaramella (eds) *Midlife: Developmental and Clinical Issues* New York: Brunner/Mazel

DAVIDSON, P., TURIEL, E. & BLACK, A. (1983) The effects of stimulus familiarity on the use of criteria and justifications in children's social reasoning *British Journal of Developmental Psychology* **1** 49–65

DAVIES, N. B. (1978) Territorial defence in the speckled wood butterfly (pararge aegeria): the resident always wins *Animal Behaviour* **26** 138–47

DAVIS, K. (1947) Final note on a case of extreme isolation *American Journal of Sociology* **52** 432–7

DAVITZ, J. & DAVITZ, L. (1959) Correlates of accuracy in the communication of feelings *Journal of Communication* **9** 110–17

DAWES, G. S. (1973) Revolutions and cyclical rhythms in prenatal life fetal respiratory movements *Pediatrics* 51 965–71

DAWKINS, R. (1976) *The Selfish Gene* Oxford: Oxford University Press

DAWKINS, R. & KREBS, J. R. (1978) Animal signals: information or manipulation? In: Krebs, J. R. & Davies, N. B. (eds) *Behavioural Ecology: an Evolutionary Approach* Oxford: Blackwell Scientific Publications

DAY, R. H. & MCKENZIE, B. E. (1981) Infant perception of the invariant size of approaching and receding objects *Developmental Psychology* **17** 670–7

DE VALOIS, R. L., ABRAMOV, I. & JACOBS, G. H. (1966) Analysis of response patterns in LGN cells *Journal of the Optical Society of America* **56** 966–67

DE VELLIS, R. F. (1978) cited in de Vellis, R. F. & Callahan, L. F. (1993) A brief measure of helplessness in rheumatic disease *Journal of Rheumatology* **20** 866

DE VRIES, P. H. & VAN SLOCHTEREN, K. R. (1997) Text-processing tasks in autonomous networks *Cognitive Systems* **4** 275–87

DE VILLIERS, J. G. & DE VILLIERS, P. A. (1973) A cross-sectional study in the development of grammatical morphemes in child speech *Journal of Psycholinguistic Research* **2** 267–78

DE VILLIERS, J. G. & DE VILLIERS, P. A. (1978) *Early Language* London: Fontana

DE VOS. G. (1985) Dimensions of the self in Japanese culture In: A.J. Marsell *et al.* (1985) *Culture and Self: Asian and Western Perspectives* London: Tavistock Publications

DE WAAL, F. B. M. (1984) Sex differences in the formation of coalitions among chimpanzees *Ethology and Sociobiology* **5** 239–55

DE WAAL, F. B. M. (1989) *Peacemaking among primates* Cambridge, Mass: Harvard University Press

DEMENT, W. C. & KLEITMAN, N. (1957) The relation of eye movements during sleep to dream activity: an objective method for the study of dreaming *Journal of Experimental Psychology* **53** 339–46

DEMENT, W. C. & WOLPERT, E. (1958) The relation of eye movements, bodily movements and external stimuli to dream content *Journal of Experimental Psychology* **55** 543–53

DEREGOWSKI, J. (1972) Pictorial perception and culture *Scientific American* **227** 82–8

DEUTSCH, J. A. & DEUTSCH, D. (1963) Attention: some theoretical considerations *Psychological Review* **70** 80–90

DI GIACOMO, J. P. (1980) Intergroup alliances and rejections within a protest movement (analysis of the social representations) *European Journal of Social Psychology* **10** 329–44

DIENER, E. (1979) Deindividuation, self-awareness and disinhibition *Journal of Personality and Social Psychology* **37** 1160–71

DIGMAN, J. M. & INOUYE, J. (1986) Further specifications of the five robust factors of personality *Journal of Personality and Social Psychology* **50** 116–23

DINDIA, K. & BAXTER, L. A. (1987) Maintenance and repair strategies in marital relationships *Journal of Social and Personal Relationships* **4** 143–58

DINGWALL, E. J. (1965) The need for responsibility in parapsychology: my sixty years in psychical research In: P. Kurtz (ed.) *A Skeptics Handbook of Parapsychology* New York: Prometheus Books

DION, K. K. (1972) Physical attractiveness and evaluation of children's transgressions *Journal of Personality and Social Psychology* **24** 207–13

DIXON, R. M. W. (1980) *The Languages of Australia* Cambridge: Cambridge University Press

DODD, G. H. (1989) *Aromacology* Paper delivered at the British Psychological Society London Conference December 1989

DOHRENWEND, B. S. & DOHRENWEND, B. P. (eds) (1974) *Stressful Life Events: Their Nature and Effects* New York: Wiley

DOISE, W. (1978) *Groups and Individuals: Explanations in Social Psychology* Cambridge: Cambridge University Press

DOISE, W. (1984) Social representations, inter-group experiments and levels of analysis In: R. M. Farr & S. Moscovici *Social Representations* Cambridge: Cambridge University Press

DOLLARD, J. & MILLER, N. E. (1950) *Personality and Psychotherapy: an Analysis in Terms of Learning, Thinking and Culture* New York: McGraw-Hill

DOLLARD, J., DOOB, L. W., MILLER, N. E., MOWRER, O. H. & SEARS, R. R. (1939) Frustration and Aggression New Haven: Yale University Press

DOMS, M. & AVERMAET, E. VAN (1981) The conformity effect: a timeless phenomenon? *Bulletin of the British Psychological Society* **34** 383–5

DONALDSON, M. (1978) *Children's Minds* London: Fontana/Collins

DONNERSTEIN, E. & WILSON, D. W. (1979) Effects of noise and perceived control on ongoing and subsequent aggressive behaviour *Journal of Personality and Social Psychology* **36** 180–8

DOVIDIO, J. F. & ELLYSON, S. L. (1982) Decoding visual dominance: attributions of power based on relative percentages of looking while speaking and looking while listening *Social Psychology Quarterly* **45** 106–13

DOWD, J. J. (1975) Ageing as exchange: a preface to theory *Journal of Gerontology* **30** 584–94

DUCK, S. W. (1977) *The Study of Acquaintance* Farnborough: Gower

DUCK, S. W. (1980) Personal relationships in the 1980s: toward an understanding of complex human sociality *Western Journal of Speech Communication* **44** 114–19

DUCK, S. W. (1988) *Relating to Others* Milton Keynes: Open University Press

DUCK, S. W. & MIELL, D. E. (1986) Charting the development of personal relationships In: R. Gilmour & S. W. Duck (eds) *The Emerging Field of Personal Relationships* Hillsdale, N. J.: Lawrence Erlbaum

DUCK, S. W. & SANTS, H. K. A. (1983) On the origin of the specious: are personal relationships really interpersonal states? *Journal of Social and Clinical Psychology* **1** 27–41

DUNN, J. (1988) *The Beginnings of Social Understanding* Oxford: Blackwell

DUNN, J. & KENDRICK, C. (1979) Interaction between young siblings in the context of family relationships In: M. Lewis & L. A. Rosenblum (eds) *The Child and its Family* New York: Plenum Press

DUNN, J. & KENDRICK, C. (1982) *Siblings: Love, Envy and Understanding* Cambridge, Mass.: Harvard University Press

DUNN, J. & MUNN, P. (1985) Becoming a family member: family conflict and the development of social understanding in the first year *Child Development* **50** 306–18

DUNN, J. & MUNN, P. (1987) Development of justifications in disputes with mother and children *Developmental Psychology* **23** 791–8

DUNN, J., KENDRICK, C., & MACNAMEE, R. (1981) The reaction of first–born children to the birth of a sibling: mother's reports *Journal of Child Psychology and Psychiatry* **22** 1–18

DURKHEIM, E. (1898) Représentations individuelles et représentations collectives *Revue de Metaphysique et de Morale* **6** 273–302

DURRELL, G. (1966) *Two in the Bush* London: Fontana/Collins

DUVALL, E.M. (1971) *Family Development* Philadelphia: Lippincott

DWECK, C. S. & ELLIOTT, E. S. (1983) Achievement motivation In: P. H. Mussen (ed.) *Handbook of Child Psychology* (4th ed.) IV New York: Wiley

DYER, F. H. (1973) The Stroop phenomenon and its use in the study of perceptual, cognitive and response processes *Memory and Cognition* **1** 106–20

DYSON, J. (1980) Sociopolitical influences on retirement research *Bulletin of the British Psychological Society* **33** 128–30

EAKINS, B. & EAKINS, G. (1978) *Sex Differences in Human Communication* Boston: Houghton Mifflin

EBBINGHAUS, H. (1885) *Memory: a Contribution to Experimental Psychology* Refurbished 1964 New York: Dover

ECHABE, A. E. & PAEZ-ROVIRA, D. (1989) Social representations and memory: The case of AIDS *European Journal of Social Psychology* **19** 543–51

EDWARDS, D. (1997) *Discourse and Cognition* London: Sage

EDWARDS, J. R. (1979) *Language and Disadvantage* London: Edward Arnold

EGETH, H. E., BLECKER, D. L. & KAMLET, A. S. (1969) Verbal interference in a perceptual comparison task *Perception and Psychophysics* **6** 355–6

EHRENREICH, B. & ENGLISH, D. (1973) *For Her Own Good: 150 Years of Experts' Advice to Women* New York: Basic Books

EIBL-EIBLESFELDT, I. (1961) *Galapagos* New York: Doubleday

EIBL-EIBLESFELDT, I. (1970) *Ethology: the Biology of Behaviour* New York: Holt, Rinehart & Winston

EIBL-EIBLESFELDT, I. (1972) Similarities and differences between cultures in expressive movements In: R. A. Hinde (ed.) *Nonverbal Communication* Cambridge: Cambridge University Press

EISENBERG, N. & LENNON, R. (1983) Sex differences in empathy and related capacities *Psychological Bulletin* **94** 100–31

EISER, J. R. (1971) Enhancement of contrast in the absolute judgement of attitude statements *Journal of Personality and Social Psychology* **17** 1–10

EISER, J. R. (1979) Attitudes In: K. Connolly (ed.) *Psychology Survey No 2* London: Allen & Unwin

EISER, J. R. (1983) From attributions to behaviour In: M. Hewstone (ed.) *Attribution Theory: Social and Functional Extensions* Oxford: Basil Blackwell

EISER, J. R. & ROSS, M. (1977) Partisan language, immediacy and attitude change *European Journal of Social Psychology* **7** 477–89

EKMAN, P. & FRIESEN, W. V. (1969) The repertoire of non-verbal behaviour: categories, origins, usage and coding *Semiotica* **1** 49–98

EKMAN, P., SORENSON, R. W. & FRIESON, W. V. (1983) Autonomic nervous system activity distinguishes among emotions *Science* **221** 1208–10

EKMAN, P., FRIESEN, W. V., O'SULLIVAN, M., CHAN, A., DIACOYANNI-TARLATZIS, I., HEIDER, K., KRAUSE, R., LECOMPTE, W. A., PITCAIRN, T., RICCI-BITTI, P. E., SCHERER, K. R., TOMITA, M. & TZAVARAS, A. (1987) Universals and cultural differences in the judgements of facial expressions of emotion *Journal of Personality and Social Psychology* **53**(4) 712–7

ELDER, G. H. (1968) Adolescent socialisation and development *Handbook of Personality Theory and Research* Chicago: University of Chicago Press

ELEFSON, J. O. (1968) Territorial behaviour in the common white–handed gibbon In: P. Jay (ed.) *Primates* New York: Holt, Rinehart & Winston

ELLEMERS, N., VAN KNIPPENBERG, A., DE VRIES, N., & WILKE, H. (1988) Social identification and permeability of group boundaries *European Journal of Social Psychology* **18** 497–513

ELLIS, A. (1977) The basic clinical theory of rational–emotive therapy In: A. Ellis & R. Grieger (eds) *Handbook of Rational-emotive Therapy* New York: Springer

ELLIS, A. & BEATTIE, G. (1986) *The Psychology of Language and Communication* London: Weidenfeld & Nicholson

ELLIS, H. D., SHEPHERD, J. W. & DAVIES, G. M. (1979) Identification of familiar and unfamiliar faces from internal and external features: some implications for theories of face recognition *Perception* **8** 431–9

ELLIS, M. J. (1973) *Why People Play* Englewood Cliffs, N. J.: Prentice–Hall

ELLSWORTH, P. C. & LANGER, E. J. (1976) Staring and approach: an interpretation of the stare as a nonspecific activator *Journal of Personality and Social Psychology* **33** 117–22

EMERSON, J. (1969) Negotiating the serious import of humour *Sociometry* **XXXII** 169–81

EPSTEIN, R., KIRSCHNITT, C. E., LANZA, R. P. & RUBIN, L. C. (1984) 'Insight' in the pigeon: antecedents and determinants of an intelligent performance *Nature* **308** 61–2

ERICSSON, K. A. & SIMON, H. A. (1980) Verbal reports as data *Psychological Review* **87** 215–51

ERIKSON, B. E., LIND, A., JONSON, B. C. & O'BARR, W. M. (1978) Speech style and impression formation in a court setting: the effects of 'powerful' and 'powerless' speech. *Journal of Experimental Social Psychology* **14** 266–79

ERIKSON E. (1968) *Identity: Youth and Crisis* New York: Norton

ERNST, G. W. & NEWELL, A. (1969) GPS: *A Case Study in Generality and Problem Solving* London: Academic Press

ERON, L. D., HUESMANN, L. R., LEFKOWITZ, M.M. & WALDER, L. O. (1972) Does television violence cause aggression? *American Psychologist* **27** 253–62

ESCH, H. (1967) The evolution of bee language *Scientific American* **216** 97–104

ESTES, W. K. (1982) Learning, memory and intelligence In: R. J. Sternberg (ed.) *Handbook of Human Intelligence* Cambridge: Cambridge University Press

EVANS, C. (1984) *Landscapes of the Night: How and Why We Dream* New York: Viking

EYSENCK, H. J. (1947) *Dimensions of Personality* London: Routledge

EYSENCK, H. J. (1952) The effects of psychotherapy: an evaluation *Journal of Consulting Psychology* **16** 319–24

EYSENCK, H. J. (1965) The effects of psychotherapy *International Journal of Psychiatry* **1** 99–142

EYSENCK, H. J. (1985) *The Decline and Fall of the Freudian Empire* Harmondsworth: Penguin

EYSENCK, H. J. & EYSENCK, S. B. G. (1976) *Psychoticism as a Dimension of Personality* London: Hodder & Stoughton

EYSENCK, H. J., BARRETT, P. & EYSENCK, S. B. (1985) Indices of factor comparison for homologous and non-homologous personality scales in 24 different countries *Personality and Individual Differences* **6** 503–4

EYSENCK, M. W. (1979) Depth elaboration and distinctiveness In: L. S. Cermak and F. I. M. Craik (eds) *Levels of Processing in Human Memory* Hillsdale, N.J.: Erlbaum

EYSENCK, M. W. (1984) *A Handbook of Cognitive Psychology* London: Lawrence Erlbaum Associates

EYSENCK, M. W. (1986) Working memory In: G. Cohen, M. W. Eysenck & M. E. Le Voi (eds) *Memory: a Cognitive Approach* Milton Keynes: Open University Press

EYSENCK, M. W. & KEANE, M. T. (1995) *Cognitive Psychology: a Student's Handbook* Hove: Erlbaum UK

EYSENCK, M. W. & KEANE, M. T. (1995) *Cognitive Psychology: A Student's Handbook (3rd ed.)* Hove: Lawrence Erlbaum Associates

FAABORG, J. & PATTERSON, C. B. (1981) The characteristics and occurrence of co-operative polyandry *Ibis* **123** 477–84

FANTZ, R. L. (1961) The origins of form perception *Scientific American* **204** 66–72

FANTZ, R. L. & MIRANDA, S. B. (1975) Newborn infant attention to form of contour *Child Development* **46** 224–8

FARB, P. (1974) *Word Play: What Happens When People Talk* New York: Bantam Books

FARNHAM-DIGGORY, S. (1978) *Learning Disabilities* London: Fontana

FARNHAM-DIGGORY, S. & GREGG, L. W. (1975) Short-term memory function in young readers *Journal of Experimental Child Psychology* **19** 279–98

FARR, R. M. (1996) *The Roots of Modern Social Psychology* Oxford: Blackwell

FELDMAN, D. C. (1984) The development and enforcement of group norms *Academy of Management Review* January 47–53

FELDMAN, J. M. & HINTERMAN, R. J. (1975) Stereotype attribution revisited: the role of stimulus characteristics, racial attitude and cognitive differentiation *Journal of Personality and Social Psychology* **31** 1177–88

FELIPE, N. J. & SOMMER, R. (1966) Invasion of personal space *Social Problems* **14** 206–14

FESTINGER, L. (1954) A theory of social comparison processes *Human Relations* **7** 117–40

FESTINGER, L. (1957) *A Theory of Cognitive Dissonance* Evanston, Ill.: Row, Peterson

FESTINGER, L. & CARLSMITH, L. M. (1959) Cognitive consequences of forced compliance *Journal of Abnormal and Social Psychology* **58** 203–10

FESTINGER, L., SCHACHTER, S. & BACK, K. (1950) *Social Pressures in Informal Groups* New York: Harper & Row

FESTINGER, L., RIECKEN, H. W. & SCHACHTER, S. (1956) *When Prophecy Fails* Minneapolis: University of Minneapolis Press

FIEDLER, F. E. (1978) The contingency model and the dynamics of the leadership process In: L. Berkowitz (ed.) *Advances in Experimental Social Psychology Vol II* New York: Academic Press

FIELD, J. (1976) Adjustment of reaching behaviour to object distance in early infancy *Child Development* **47** 304–8

FIRESTONE, I. J., LICHTMAN, C. M. & COLAMOSCA, J. V. (1975) Leader effectiveness and leadership conferral as determinants of helping in a medical emergency *Journal of Personality and Social Psychology* **31** 343–8

FISCHER, K. W. (1980) A theory of cognitive development: the control and construction of hierarchies of skills *Psychological Review* **87** 477–531

FISCHLER, C. (1980) Food habits, social change and the nature/culture dilemma. *Social Science Information* **19**(6) 937–53

FISHBEIN, M. (1963) An investigation of the relationship between beliefs about an object and the attitude towards that object *Human Relations* **16** 65–116

FISHER, A. E. (1964) Chemical stimulation of the brain *Scientific American* **210**(6) 60–8

FISKE, S. T. & LINVILLE, P. W. (1980) What does the schema concept buy us? *Personality and Social Psychology Bulletin* **6** 543–57

FISKE, S. T. & TAYLOR, S. E. (1983) *Social Cognition* Reading, Mass.: Addison-Wesley

FITTS, P. M. (1954) The information capacity of the human motor system in controlling the amplitude of movement *Journal of Experimental Psychology* **47** 381–91

FITTS, P. M. (1964) Perceptual motor skill learning In: A. W. Melton (ed.) *Categories of Human Learning* New York: Academic Press

FLAMENT, C. (1989) Structure et dynamique des représentations sociales In: D. Jodelet (ed.) *Les Représentations Sociales* Paris: Presses Universitaires de France.

FLAVELL, J. (1979) Metacognitive development and cognitive monitoring: a new area of cognitive development inquiry *American Psychologist* **34** 906–11

FLETCHER, R. (1991) *Science, Ideology and the Media: the Cyril Burt Scandal* London: Transaction publishers

FODOR, J. A. (1983) *The Modularity of Mind* London: Bradford Books

FOLKARD, S. (1983) Circadian rhythms and hours of work In: P. Warr (ed.) *Psychology at Work* Harmondsworth: Penguin

FOSSEY, D. (1980) *Gorillas in the Mist* Basingstoke: Macmillan

FOUTS, R. S. (1972) The use of guidance in teaching sign language to a chimpanzee *Journal of Comparative Physiological Psychology* **80** 515–22

FOWLER, W. (1983) *Potentials of Childhood I: a Historical View of Early Experience* Lexington, Mass.: Heath

FREEMAN, D. (1984) *Margaret Mead and Samoa: the Making and Unmaking of an Anthropological Myth* Harmondsworth: Penguin

FREEMAN, F. N., HOLZINGER, K. J. & MITCHELL, B. C. (1928) The influence of environment on the intelligence, school achievement and conduct of foster children *27th Yearbook of the National Society for the Study of Education* Bloomington, Ill: Public School Publishing Co.

FRENCH, J.D. (1957) The reticular formation *Scientific American* **196**(6) 54–60

FRENCH, J. D., VERZEANO, M. & MAGOUN, H.W. (1953) A neural basis for the anaesthetic state *Archives of Neurology and Psychiatry* **69** 519–29

FRIEDMAN, H. & FRIEDMAN, L. (1979) Endorser effectiveness by product type *Journal of Advertising Research* **19**(5) 63–71

FRIEDMAN, H. S., DIMATTEO, M. R. & MERTZ, T. I. (1980) Nonverbal communication on television news: the facial expression of broadcasters during coverage of a presidential election campaign *Personality and Social Psychology Bulletin* **6** 427–35

FRIEDMAN, M. & ROSENMAN, R. H. (1959) Association of specific overt behaviour pattern with blood and cardio-vascular findings *Journal of the American Medical Association* **169** 1286–96

FRIEDMAN, M. & ROSENMAN, R. H. (1974) *Type A behaviour* New York: Knopf

FREUD, A. (1968) Adolescence In: A. E. Winder & D. L. Angus (eds) *Adolescence: Contemporary Studies* New York: American Books

FREUD, S. (1901) The Psychopathology of everyday life Republished 1953 In: J. Strachey (ed.) *The Standard Edition of the Complete Psychological Works of Sigmund Freud 6* London: Hogarth

FREUD, S. (1909) Little Hans In: J. Strachey (ed.) (1953) *The Standard Edition of the Complete Psychological Works of Sigmund Freud 10* London: Hogarth

FREUD, S. (1920) *Beyond the Pleasure Principle* (1975 ed.) New York: Norton

FROMKIN, S., KRASHEN, S., CURTISS, S., RIGLER, D. & RIGLER, M. (1974) The development of language in Genie: a case of language acquisition beyond the 'Critical Period' *Brain and Language* **1** 81–107

FROMM, E. (1941) *Escape from Freedom* New York: Rinehart

FROMM, E. (1955) *The Sane Society* New York: Rinehart

FROMM, E. (1968) *The Revolution of Hope* New York: Harper & Row

FROMMER, E. & O'SHEA, G. (1973) The importance of childhood experience in relation to problems of marriage and family-building *British Journal of Psychiatry* **123** 157–60

GAHAGAN, J. (1984) *Social Interaction and its Management* London: Methuen

GALE, A. (1981) EEG studies of extraversion–introversion: what's the next step? In: R. Lynn (ed.) *Dimensions of Personality: Essays in Honour of H. J. Eysenck* Oxford: Pergamon

GALINSKY, E. (1981) *Between Generations: the Six Stages of Parenthood* New York: Berkeley

GALLI, I. & NIGRO, G. (1987) The social representation of radioactivity among Italian children. *Social Science Information* **26** 535–49

GALLISTEL, C. R. (1973) Self-stimulation: the neuro-physiology of reward and motivation In: J. A. Deutsch (ed.) *The Physiological Basis of Memory* New York: Academic Press

GALTON, F. (1869) Classification of men according to their natural gifts In: J. J. Jenkins & D. G. Paterson *Studies in Individual Differences* 1961 New York: Appleton Century Crofts

GALTON, F. (1884) *Hereditary Genius* New York: Appleton

GALTON, F. (1888) Co-relations and their measurement, chiefly from anthropometric data In: J. J. Jenkins & D. G.

Paterson *Studies in Individual Differences* 1961 New York: Appleton Century Crofts

GAMSON, W. B., FIREMAN, B. & RYTINA, S. (1982) *Encounters with Unjust Authority* Homewood, Ill.: Dorsey Press

GARCIA, J. & KOELLING, R. A. (1966) The relation of cue to consequence in avoidance learning *Psychonomic Science* **4** 123–4

GARDNER, B. T. & GARDNER, R. A. (1971) Two-way communication with an infant chimpanzee In: A. M. Schrier & F. Stollnitz (eds) *Behaviour of Nonhuman Primates* **4** 117–84 New York: Academic Press

GARDNER, H. (1985) *Frames of Mind: the Theory of Multiple Intelligences* London: Paladin

GARDNER, R. A. & GARDNER, B. T. (1969) Teaching sign language to a chimpanzee *Science* **165** 664–72

GARVEY, C. (1977) *Play* Cambridge, Mass.: Harvard University Press

GARWOOD S. G., COX, L., KAPLAN, V., WASSERMAN, N. & SULZER, J. L. (1980) Beauty is only 'name' deep: the effect of first name in ratings of physical attraction *Journal of Applied Social Psychology* **10** 431–5

GAZZANIGA, M. S. & SPERRY, R. W. (1967) Language after section of the cerebral commissures *Brain* **90** 131–48

GEIST, V. (1966) The evolution of horn-like organs *Behaviour* **27** 175–214

GELFAND, D. M., JENSEN, W.R. & DREW, C.J. (1982) *Understanding Child Behaviour Disorders* New York: Holt, Rinehard & Winston

GERBNER, G. & GROSS, L. (1976) The scary world of TV's heavy viewer *Psychology Today* **9** 41–5

GERVAIS, M.-C. & JOVCHELOVITCH, S. (1997) Health and Identity: the case of the Chinese community in Britain Paper delivered at the British Psychological Society Social Psychology Section Conference, Falmer, September 1997

GESELL, A. (1929) Maturation and infant behaviour patterns *Psychological Review* **36** 307–19

GESELL, A. & THOMPSON, H. (1929) Learning and growth in identical infant twins: an experimental study by the method of co-twin control *Genetic Psychology Monographs* **6** 1–124

GHISELIN, B. (1952) *The Creative Process* Berkeley: University of California Press

GIBSON, E. J. (1969) *Principles of Perceptual Learning and Development* New York: Appleton-Century-Crofts

GIBSON, E. J. & WALK, R. D. (1960) The visual cliff *Scientific American* **202** 64–71

GIBSON, H. B. (1982) The use of hypnosis in police investigations *Bulletin of the British Psychological Society* **35** 138–42

GIBSON, J. J. (1950) *The Perception of the Visual World* Boston: Houghton Mifflin

GIBSON, J. J. (1979) *The Ecological Approach to Visual Perception* Boston: Houghton Mifflin.

GICK, M. L. & HOLYOAK, K.J. (1980) Analogical problem solving *Cognitive Psychology* **12** 306–55

GILBERT, G. N. & MULKAY, M. (1984) *Opening Pandora's Box: a Sociological Analysis of Scientists' Discourse* Cambridge: Cambridge University Press

GILCHRIST, J. C. & NESBERG, L. S. (1952) Need and perceptual change in need-related objects *Journal of Experimental Psychology* **44** 369–76

GILES, H. (1973) Accent mobility: a model and some data *Anthropological Linguistics* **15** 87–105

GILHOOLY, K. J. (1995) *Thinking: Directed, Undirected and Creative* London: Academic Press

GILLIE, O. (1976) Crucial data was faked by eminent psychologist *Sunday Times* 24th October 1976

GILLIE, O. (1980) Burt: the scandal and the cover-up In: H. Beloff (ed.) *A Balance Sheet on Burt: Supplement to the Bulletin of the British Psychological Society* **33** 17–19

GILLIN, J. C., BUCHSBAUM, M. S. & JACOBS, L. S. (1974) Partial REM sleep deprivation, schizophrenia and field articulation *Archives of General Psychiatry* **30** 653–62

GLANZER, M & CUNITZ, A. R. (1966) Two storage mechanisms in free recall *Journal of Verbal Learning and Verbal Behaviour* **5** 351–60

GLASER, R., RICE, J., SHERIDAN, J., POST, A., FERTEL, R., STOUT, J., SPEICHER, C. E. KOTUR, M. & KIECOLT-GLASER, J. A. (1987) Stress-related immune suppression: health implications *Brain, Behaviour and Immunity* **1** 7–20

GLASS, D. C. (1977) *Behaviour Pattern Stress in Coronary Disease* Hillsdale, N J: Erlbaum

GLENBERG, SMITH, S. M. & GREEN, C. (1977) Type I rehearsal: maintenance and more *Journal of Verbal Learning and Verbal Behaviour* **16** 339–52

GLUCKSBERG, S. (1962) The influence of strength of drive on functional fixedness and perceptual recognition *Journal of Experimental Psychology* **63** 36–41

GODDARD, H. H. (1912) *The Kallikak Family: a Study in the Heredity of Feeble-mindedness* New York: Macmillan

GODDARD, H. H. (1913) The Binet tests in relation to immigration *Journal of Psycho-Asthenics* **18** 105–7

GODDARD, H. H. (1928) Feeble-mindedness: a question of definition *Journal of Psycho-Asthenics* **33** 219–27

GODDEN, D. R. & BADDELEY, A. D. (1975) Context-dependent memory in two natural environments: on land and underwater *British Journal of Psychology* **66** 325–31

GOFFMAN, E. (1959) *The Presentation of Self in Everyday Life* New York: Anchor

GOLD, R. M. (1973) Hypothalamic obesity: the myth of the ventromedial nucleus *Science* **182** 488–90

GOLDFARB, W. (1943) Infant rearing and problem behaviour *American Journal of Orthopsychiatry* **13** 249–65

GOLDSPINK, G. (1992) The brain behind the brawn *New Scientist* 1st August 1992

GOLOMBOK, S., SPENCER, A. & RUTTER, M. (1983) Children in lesbian and single-parent households: psycho-sexual and psychiatric appraisal *Journal of Child Psychology and Psychiatry* **24** 551–72

GOOCH, S. (1980) Right brain, left brain *New Scientist* 11th September 790–2

GOODALL, J. VAN LAWICK (1968) The behaviour of free-living chimpanzees in the Gombe stream reserve *Animal Behaviour Monographs* **1** 161–311

GOODALL, J. VAN LAWICK (1974) *In the Shadow of Man* London: Collins

GOODWIN, D. W., POWELL, B., BREMER, B., HOINE, H. & STERN, J. (1969) Alcohol and recall: state dependent effects in man *Science* **163** 1358–60

GOREN, C. C., SARTY, M. & WU, R. W. K. (1975) Visual following and pattern discrimination of face-like stimuli by new-born infants *Paediatrics* **56** 544–9

GORN, G. J. (1982) The effects of music in advertising on choice behaviour: a classical conditioning approach *Journal of Marketing* **46** 94–101

GOULD, J. L. (1986) The locale map of honey bees: do insects have a cognitive map? *Science* **232** 861–3

GOULD, J. L. & MARLER, P. J. (1987) Learning by instinct *Scientific American* **256**(1) 62–74

GOULD, R. L. (1978) *Transformations: Growth and Change in Adult Life* New York: Simon & Schuster

GOULD, S. J. (1977a) *Ever since Darwin: Reflections in Natural History* Harmondsworth: Penguin

GOULD, S. J. (1977b) *Ontogeny and Phylogeny* Cambridge, Mass.: Harvard University Press

GOULD, S. J. (1981) *The Mismeasure of Man* New York: Norton

GOULD, S. J. (1997) *The Mismeasure of Man: revised edition* New York: Norton

GOULD, S. J. & ELDREDGE, N. (1977) Punctuated equilibria: the tempo and mode of evolution reconsidered *Paleobiology* **3** 115–51

GOVIER, E. (1980) Attention In: J. Radford & E. Govier *A Textbook of Psychology* London: Sheldon

GRABB, E. G. (1979) Working-class authoritarianism and tolerance of outgroups: a reassessment *Public Opinion Quarterly* **43** 36–47

GRAY, J. & WEDDERBURN, A. (1960) Grouping strategies with simultaneous stimuli *Quarterly Journal of Experimental Psychology* **12** 180–4

GRAY, J. A. (1971) *The Psychology of Fear and Stress* London: Weidenfeld and Nicholson

GRAY, J. A. (1985) A whole and its parts: behaviour, the brain, cognition and emotion *Bulletin of the British Psychological Society* **38** 99–112

GRECO, P. (1962) Quantité et quotité In: P. Greco & A. Morf (eds) *Structures Génétiques Numériques Élémentaires 13* Paris: Presses Universitaires de France

GREEN, A.J.K. & GILHOOLY, K. J. (1992) Empirical advantages in expertise research In: M. T. Keane & K. J. Gilhooly (eds) *Advances in the Psychology of Thinking* London: Harvester Wheatsheaf

GREEN, C. & MCCREERY, C. (1994) *Lucid Dreaming: the Paradox of Consciousness during Sleep* London: Routledge

GREEN, S. (1987) *Physiological Psychology: an Introduction* London: Routledge & Kegan Paul

GREEN, S. G. & NEBEKER, D. M. (1977) The effects of situational factors and leadership style on leader behaviour *Organisational Behaviour and Human Performance* **19** 368–77

GREENE, J. (1975) *Thinking and Language* London: Methuen

GREGORY, R. L. (1963) Distortion of visual space as inappropriate constancy scaling *Nature* 119 678

GREGORY, R. L. (1968) Visual illusions *Scientific American* November **219**(5) 7

GREGORY, R. L. (1973) The confounded eye In: R. L. Gregory & E. H. Gombrich (eds) *Illusion in Nature and Art* London: Duckworth

GRICE, H. P. (1975) Logic and Communication In: P. Cole & J. L. Morgan (eds) *Syntax and Semantics 3* New York: Academic Press

GRIFFIN, D. (1997) *Social Psychology: an Experimental Approach* Paper delivered at the British Psychological Society Social Psychology Conference, Sussex, September 1997.

GRIFFITH, W. & VEITCH, R. (1971) Hot and crowded: influences of population density and temperature on interpersonal affective behaviour *Journal of Personality and Social Psychology* **17** 92–8

GRIGGS, R. A. & COX, J. R. (1982) The elusive thematic materials effect in Wason's selection task *British Journal of Psychology* **73** 407–20

GROHMANN, J. (1939) Modifikation oder Functionsreifung? Ein Beitrag zur Klärung der wechselzeitigen Beziehungen zwischen Instinckthandlung und Erfahrung *Zeitschrift für Tierpsychologie* **2** 132–44

GROOS, K. (1901) *The Play of Man* New York: Appleton

GROSSMAN, S. P. (1967) *A Textbook of Physiological Psychology* New York: Wiley

GUILFORD, J. P. (1967) *The Nature of Human Intelligence* New York: McGraw-Hill

GUILFORD, J. P. (1982) Cognitive psychology's ambiguities: some suggested remedies *Psychological Review* **89** 48–59

GUIMOND, S. & PALMER, D. L. (1990) Types of academic training and causal attributions for social problems *European Journal of Social Psychology* **20**(1) 61–75

GUIMOND, S., BÉGIN, G. & PALMER, D. L. (1989) Education and causal attributions: the development of 'person-blame' and 'system-blame' ideology *Social Psychology Quarterly* **52** 126–40

GUITON, P. (1959) Socialisation and imprinting in Brown Leghorn chicks *Animal Behaviour* **7** 26–34

GUITON, P. (1966) Early experience and sexual object choice in the Brown Leghorn *Animal Behaviour* **14** 534–8

GUNTER, B. (1983) Do aggressive people prefer violent television? *Bulletin of the British Psychological Society* **36** 166–70

HABER, R. N. (1969) Eidetic images *Scientific American* **220** 36–55

HAGE, D. (1972) There's glory for you, Aphra *The Feminist Literary Magazine* **3** 2–14

HAGESTAD, G. O. & SMYER, M. (1982) Dissolving long-term relationships: patterns of divorcing in middle age In: S. W. Duck (ed.) *Personal Relationships 4: Dissolving Personal Relationships* London and New York: Academic Press

HAIG, N.D. (1984) The effect of feature displacement on face recognition *Perception* **13** 505–12

HAILMAN, J. P. (1969) How an instinct is learned *Scientific American* **221**(6) 98–106

HAITH, M. M. (1980) *Rules that Babies Look By* Hillsdale, N. J.: Lawrence Erlbaum

HALL, E. T. (1968) Proxemics *Current Anthropology* **9** 83–108

HALL, G. S. (1904) *Adolescence* New York: Appleton

HALL, G. S. (1920) *Youth* New York: Appleton

HALL, J. A. (1978) Gender effects in decoding nonverbal cues *Psychological Bulletin* **85** 845–58

HAMILTON, D. L. (1981) *Cognitive Processes in Stereotyping and Intergroup Behaviour* Hillsdale, N. J.: Erlbaum

HANEY, C., BANKS, W. C. & ZIMBARDO, P. G. (1973) Interpersonal dynamics in a simulated prison *Internation Journal of Criminology and Penology* **1** 69–79

HANSEL, C. E. M. (1985) The search for a demonstration of ESP In: P. Kurtz (ed.) *A Skeptics Handbook of Parapsychology* New York: Prometheus Books

HARARI, H. & MCDAVID, J. W. (1973) Name stereotypes and teacher's expectations *Journal of Educational Psychology* **65** 222–5

HARDY, L. (1988) *The Inverted-U hypothesis: A Catastrophe for Sport Psychology* Paper delivered at the British Psychological Society Annual Conference, Leeds, April 1988

HARDYCK, C. & PETRINOVITCH, L. F. (1977) Left handedness *Psychological Bulletin* **84** 385–404

HARKINS, S. & GREEN, R. G. (1975) Discriminability and criterion differences between extraverts and introverts during vigilance *Journal of Research in Personality* **9** 335–40

HARLOW, H.F. (1949) The formation of learning sets *Psychological Review* **56** 51–65

HARLOW, H. F. (1959) Love in infant monkeys *Scientific American* **200**(6) 64–74

HARLOW, H. F., & HARLOW, M. K. (1962) Social deprivation in monkeys *Scientific American* **207**(5) 136–46

HARLOW, H. F., HARLOW, M. K. & HANSEN, E. W. (1963) The maternal affectional system of rhesus monkeys In: H. L. Rheingold (ed.) *Maternal Behaviour in Mammals* New York: Wiley

HARRÉ, R. (1979) *Social Being* Oxford: Blackwell

HARRIS, J. E. & SUNDERLAND, A. (1981) *Effects of Age and Instructions on an Everyday Memory Questionnaire* Paper presented to the British Psychological Society, Cognitive Psychology Section Conference on Memory, Plymouth 1981

HARRIS, P. L. (1983) Infant cognition In: P. H. Mussen (ed.) *Handbook of Child Psychology* **II** (4th ed.) New York: Wiley

HARRIS, P. L. (1988) *Children and Emotion: the Development of Psychological Understanding* Oxford: Blackwell

HARRIS, P. L. & MUNCER, A. (1988) *Autistic Children's Understanding of Beliefs and Desires* Paper Presented at the British Psychological Society Developmental Section Conference, Coleg Harlech, Wales

HARRIS, P. L., DONNELLY, K., GUZ, G. R. & PITT-WATSON, R. (1986) Children's understanding of the distinction between real and apparent emotion *Child Development* **57** 895–909

HASTORF, A. H. & CANTRIL, H. (1954) They saw a game: a case study *Journal of Abnormal and Social Psychology* **49** 129–34

HARTMANN, E. (1984) *The Nightmare* New York: Basic Books

HATFIELD, E. & WALSTER, E. (1978) *A New Look at Love* Reading, Mass.: Addison-Wesley

HAUGEN, E. (1966) Dialect, Language, Nation *American Anthropologist* **68** 922–35

HAVIGHURST, R. J. (1964) Flexibility and the social roles of the retired *American Journal of Sociology* **59** 309–11

HAVIGHURST, R. J., MUNNICHS, J. M.A., NEUGARTEN, B. & THOMAE, HANS (1969) *Adjustment to Retirement: a Cross-national Study* Assen, the Netherlands: Van Gorcum

HAYES, D. S., BOLIN, L.J. & CHEMELSKI, B. E. (1981) Preschoolers' understanding of physical and emotional states as memory-relevant variables cited in: H. Gardner *Developmental Psychology (2nd ed.)* Boston: Little Brown & Co.

HAYES, K. J. (1950) Vocalisation and speech in chimpanzees *American Psychologist* **5** 275–6

HAYES, N. J. (1975) *Dominance Relationships in an Captive Chimpanzee Colony* (unpublished: University of Leeds)

HAYES, N. J. (1977) (ed.) *Doing Qualitative Analysis in Psychology* Hove: Psychology Press

HAYES, N. J. (1983) *African Religion and Western Science: some Barriers to Effective Science Teaching* M. Ed. Thesis, University of Leeds (unpublished)

HAYES, N. J. (1991) *Social Identity, Social Representations and Organisational Culture* PhD thesis CNAA/Huddersfield

HAYES, N. J. (1995) *Psychology in Perspective* Basingstoke: Macmillan

HAYES, N. J. (1997a) *Successful Team Management* London: ITBP

HAYES, N. J. (1997b) Qualitative research and research in psychology In: N. J. Hayes (ed.) *Doing Qualitative Analysis in Psychology* Hove: Psychology Press

HAYES, N.J. (1998) Organisational cultures as social representations I: myths and metaphors *Human Systems* **9**(1)

HAYES, N. J., BANYARD, P., BRADBURY, R., HIRSCHLER, S., HUMPHREYS, P., SLOBODA, J. & SYLVA, K. (1991) *The Future of A Level Psychology* Leicester: British Psychological Society

HAYNES, H., WHITE, B. L. & HELD, R. (1965) Visual accommodation in human infants *Science* **148** 528–30

HEARNE, K. M. T. (1981a) A 'light-switch' phenomenon in lucid dreams *Journal of Mental Imagery* **5** 97–100

HEARNE, K. M. T. (1981b) Control your own dreams *New Scientist* 24th September 1981

HEARNSHAW, L. S. (1979) *Cyril Burt: Psychologist* London: Hodder & Stoughton

HEARNSHAW, L. S. (1980) A Balance Sheet on Burt In: H. Beloff (ed.) *A Balance Sheet on Burt: Supplement to the Bulletin of the British Psychological Society* **33** 17–19

HEARNSHAW, L. S. (1992) Burt Redivivus *The Psychologist* **5** 168–70

HEATH, R. G. (1963) Electrical self-stimulation of the brain in man *American Journal of Psychiatry* **120** 571–77

HEBB, D. O. (1949) *The Organisation of Behaviour* New York: Wiley

HEBB, D. O. (1955) Drives and the conceptual nervous system *Psychological Review* **62** 243–54

HEIDER, F. (1944) Social perception and phenomenal causality *Psychological Review* **51** 358–74

HEIDER, F. (1958) *The Psychology of Interpersonal Relations* New York: Wiley

HEIM, A. (1970) *Intelligence and Personality* Harmondsworth: Penguin

HELD, R. & HEIN, A. (1963) Movement produced stimulation in the development of visually guided behaviour Journal of *Comparative and Physiological Psychology* **56** 872–6

HELLER, N. (1956) An application of psychological theory to advertising *Journal of Marketing* **20** 248–54

HELMREICH, R., ARONSON, E. & LEFAN, J. (1970) To err is humanising – sometimes! Effects of self-esteem, competence and a pratfall on interpersonal attraction *Journal of Personality and Social Psychology* **16** 259–64

HENDRICK, C. & HENDRICK, S. S. (1988) Lovers wear rose-coloured glasses *Journal of Social and Personal Relationships* **5** 161–83

HENLE, M. (1962) On the relation beween logic and thinking *Psychological Review* **69** 366–78

HENLEY, N. (1977) *Body Politics: Power, Sex and Nonverbal Communication* Englewood Cliffs, N. J.: Prentice Hall

HEPBURN, C. & LOCKSLEY, A. (1983) Subjective awareness of stereotyping: do we know when our judgements are prejudices? *Social Psychology Quarterly* **46** 311–18

HERING, E. (1878) *Outlines of a Theory of the Light Sense* Cambridge, Mass.: Harvard University Press

HERMAN, L. M., RICHARDS, D. G. & WOLZ, J. P. (1984) Comprehension of sentences by bottlenosed dolphins *Cognition* **16** 129–219

HERRNSTEIN, R. J. & MURRAY, C. (1994) *The Bell Curve: Intelligence and Class Structure in American Life* New York: Simon & Schuster

HERSHER, L., RICHMOND, J. B. & MOORE, A. U. (1963a) Maternal behaviour in sheep and goats In: H. L. Rheingold (ed.) *Maternal Behaviour in Mammals* New York: Wiley

HERSHER, L., RICHMOND, J. B. & MOORE, A. U. (1963b) Modifiability of the critical period for the development of maternal behaviour in sheep and goats *Behaviour* **20** 311–20

HERZLICH, C. (1973) *Health and Illness: a Social-Psychological Analysis* London: Academic Press

HESS, E. (1965) Attitude and pupil size *Scientific American* **212**(4) 46–54

HESS, E. H. (1958) 'Imprinting' in animals *Scientific American* **198**(3) 81–90

HESS, E. H. (1972) 'Imprinting' in a natural laboratory *Scientific American* **227**(2) 24–31

HETHERINGTON, A. W. & RANSON, S.W. (1942) The relation of various hypothalamic lesions to adiposity in the rat *Journal of Comparative Neurology* **76** 475–99

HEWSTONE, M. (1989) *Causal Attribution: From Cognitive Processes to Collective Beliefs* Oxford: Blackwell

HILGARD, E. R. (1965) *Hypnotic Susceptibility* New York: Harcourt Brace Jovanovitch

HILGARD, E. R. (1977) *Divided Consciousness: Multiple Controls in Human Thought and Action* New York: Wiley

HILGARD, E. R., WEITZENHOFFER, A. M., LANDES, J. & MOORE, R. K. (1961) The distribution of susceptibility to hypnosis in a student population: a study using the Stomford Hypnotic Susceptibility Scale *Psychological Monographs* **75** No 512

HIMMELFARB, S. & EAGLEY, A. (eds) (1974) *Readings in Attitude Change* New York: Wiley

HINDE, R. A. (1954) Factors governing the changes in strength of a partially inborn response, as shown by the mobbing behaviour of the chaffinch *Proceedings of the Royal Society of London Series Series B* **142** 306–58

HINDE, R. A. (1970) *Animal Behaviour: a Synthesis of Ethology and Compative Psychology* (2nd ed.) New York: McGraw-Hill

HINDE, R. A. (1983) Ethology and child development In: P. H. Musson (ed.) *Handbook of Child Psychology II (4th ed.)* New York: Wiley

HINDE, R. A. (1987) *Individuals, Relationships and Culture: Links between Ethology and the Social Sciences* Cambridge: Cambridge University Press

HINTON, J. (1967) *Dying* Harmondsworth: Penguin

HITCH, G. J. (1980) Developing the concept of working memory In: G. Claxton (ed.) *Cognitive Psychology: New Directions* London: Routledge & Kegan Paul

HOBSON, R. P. (1986) The autistic child's appraisal of expressions of emotion Journal of *Child Psychology and Psychiatry* **27** 321–42

HOCHBERG, J. (1970) Components of literacy: speculation and exploratory research In: H. Levin & J. P. Williams (eds) *Basic Studies in Reading* New York: Basic Books

HOCKETT, C. F. (1959) Animal 'languages' and human language *Human Biology* **31** 32–9

HODOS, W. & CAMPBELL, C. B. G. (1969) Scala naturae: why there is no theory in comparative psychology *Psychological Review* **76** 337–50

HOFLING, K. C., BROTZMAN, E., DALRYMPLE, S., GRAVES, N. & PIERCE, C. M. (1966) An experimental study in the nurse–physician relationship *Journal of Nervous and Mental Disorders* **143** 171–80

HOGG, M. A. & VAUGHAN, G.M. (1995) *Social Psychology: An Introduction* London: Prentice Hall/Harvester Wheatsheaf

HOLDING, D. H. (1985) *The Psychology of Chess Skill* Hillsdale, N. J.: Lawrence Erlbaum

HOLDING, D. H. & REYNOLDS, R. I. (1982) Recall or evaluation of chess problems as determinants of chess skill *Memory and Cognition* **10** 237–42

HOLLAND, A. J., HALL, D. J., MURREY, R., RUSSELL, G. F. M. & CRISP, A. H. (1984) Anorexia Nervosa: a study of 34 twin pairs and one set of triplets *British Journal of Psychiatry* **145** 414–18

HOLLAND, J. L. (1966) *The Psychology of Vocational Choice: a Theory of Personality Types and Model Environments* Waltham, Mass.: Blaisdell

HOLMES, D. S. (1974) Investigation of repressions: differential recall of material experimentally or naturally associated with ego threat *Psychological Bulletin* **81** 632–53

HOLMES, G. (1919) Disturbances of vision by cerebral lesions *British Journal of Opthalmics* **1**

HOLMES, T. H. & RAHE, R. H. (1967) The social readjustment rating scale *Journal of Psychosomatic Research* **11** 213–18

HOLST, E. VON (1954) Relations between the central nervous system and the peripheral organs *British Journal of Animal Behaviour* **2** 89–94

HOMANS, G. (1961) *Social Behaviour: its Elementary Forms* New York: Harcourt Brace Jovanovitch

HOMANS, G. (1974) *Social Behaviour: its Elementary Forms* (2nd ed.) New York: Harcourt Brace Jovanovitch

HOMME, L. E. DE BACA, P. C., DEVINE, J. V. STEINHORST, R. & RICKERT, E. J. (1963) Use of the Premack principle in controlling the behaviour of nursery school children *Journal of the Experimental Analysis of Behaviour* **6** 544

HONORTON, C. (1985) Meta-analysis of psi ganzfeld research: a response to Hyman *Journal of Parapsychology* **49** 51–91

HONORTON, C. (1992) The ganzfeld novice: four predictors of inial psi performance *Proceedings of the 35th Annual Convention of the Parapsychological Association*

HONORTON, C., BERGER, R. E., VARVOGLIS, M. P., QUANT, M., DERR, P., SCHECHTER, E. I. & FERRARI, D. C. (1990) Psi communication in the ganzfeld: experiments with an automated testing system and a comparison with a meta–analysis of earlier studies *Journal of Parapsychology* **54** 99–139

HOOKER, D. (1952) *The Prenatal Origins of Behaviour* Lawrence: University of Kansas Press

HORNE, J. A. (1988) *Why We Sleep* Oxford: Oxford University Press

HORNE, J. (1992) Stay awake, stay alive *New Scientist* 4th January 1992

HORNE, J. A. & MINARD, A. (1985) Sleep and sleepiness following a behaviourally 'active' day *Ergonomics* **28** 567–75

HOROWITZ, E. L. (1936) Development of attitude to the word 'Negro' *Archives of Psychology* **194**

HOROWITZ, L. M., FRENCH, R. DE S. & ANDERSON, C. A. (1982) The prototype of a lonely person In: L. A. Peplan & D. Polman (eds) *Loneliness: a Source-book of Current Theory, Research and Therapy* New York: Wiley

HORSFORD, B. (1990) *Cultural Issues and Psychiatric Diagnosis* Paper delivered at Abnormal Psychology Study Day, Nottingham University, December 18th 1990

HORTON, R. (1967) African traditional thought and Western science In: M. F. D. Young (ed.) (1971) *Knowledge and Control* Cambridge, Mass.: Addison-Wesley

HOUSE, R. J. (1971) A path-goal theory of leadership effectiveness *Administrative Science Quarterly* **16** 321–38

HOVLAND, C. I. & SEARS, R. (1940) Minor studies in aggression IV: Correlation of lynchings with economic indices *Journal of Psychology* **9** 301–10

HOVLAND, C. I., LUMSDAINE, A. A. & SHEFFIELD, R. D. (1949) *Experiments in Mass Communication* Princeton: Princeton University Press

HOWE, M. A. (1989) The strange achievements of idiots savants In: A. M. Colman & J. G. Beaumont (eds) *Psychology Survey* 7 Leicester: British Psychological Society

HOWE, M. A. (1990) Does intelligence exist? *The Psychologist* **3** 490–3

HOWE, M. A. (1998) *Principles of Abilities and Human Learning* Hove: Psychology Press

HRABA, J. & GRANT, G. (1970) Black is beautiful: re-examination of racial preference and identification *Journal of Personality and Social Psychology* **16** 398–402

HUBEL, D. H. (1979) The brain *Scientific American* **214**(3) 44–53

HUBEL, D. H. & WIESEL, T. N. (1968) Receptive fields and functional architecture of monkey striate cortex *Journal of Physiology* **195** 215–43

HUBEL, D. H. & WIESEL, T. N. (1977) Functional architecture of macaque monkey visual cortex *Proceedings of the Royal Society of London Series B* **198** 1–59

HUBEL, D. H. & WIESEL, T. N. (1979) Brain mechanisms of vision *Scientific American* **241**(3) 150–62

HUDSON, L. (1966) *Contrary Imaginations: a Psychological Study of the English Schoolboy* Harmondsworth: Penguin

HUDSON, R. A. (1980) *Sociolinguistics* Cambridge: Cambridge University Press.

HUGHES, M. (1975) Egocentricity in children Unpublished PhD thesis, Edinburgh University, cited in M. Donaldson *Children's Minds* London: Fontana

HULL, C. L. (1920) Quantitative aspects of the evolution of concepts *Psychological Monographs* **123**

HULL, C. L. (1943) *Principles of behaviour* New York: Appleton Century Crofts

HUMPHREY, G. (1951) *Thinking: an Introduction to its Experimental Psychology* New York: Wiley

HUMPHREY, T. (1969) Reflex activity in the oral and facial area of human fetuses In: J. F. Bosma (ed.) *Oral Sensation and Perception* Springfield, Ill.: Thomas

HUNTER, I. M. L. (1964) *Memory* Harmondsworth: Penguin

HUSTON, T. L. (1973) Ambiguity of acceptance, social desirability and dating choice *Journal of Experimental Psychology* **9** 32–42

HUSTON, T. L. & LEVINGER, G. (1978) Interpersonal attraction and relationships In: M. R. Rosenzweig & L. W. Porter (eds) *Annual Review of Psychology* **29** Palo Alto, CA.: Annual Reviews

HUTT, C. (1970) Specific and diverse exploration In: H. Reese & L. Lipsett (eds) *Advances in Child Development and Behaviour* New York: Academic Press

HUXLEY, J. S. (1914) *The Courtship of the Great Crested Grebe* Proceedings of the Zoological Society of London **35**

HYMAN, R. (1994) Anomaly or artefact? Comments on Bem and Honorton *Psychological Bulletin* **115** 19–24

HYMAN, R. & HONORTON, C. (1986) A joint communiqué: the psi ganzfeld controversy *Journal of Parapsychology* **50** 351–64

IANNIRUBERTO, A. (1985) Prenatal onset of motor patterns Paper presented to the Conference on Motor Skill Acquisition, NATO Advanced Study Institute, Maastricht, Netherlands, cited in G. Bremner *Infancy* Oxford: Blackwell

IRWIN, M., DANIELS, M., RISCH, S. C., BLOOM, E. & WEINER, H. (1988) Plasma cortisol and natural killer cell activity during bereavement *Biological Psychiatry* **24** 173–8

ISTOMINA, Z. M. (1975) The development of voluntary memory in children of preschool age Reprinted in: U. Neisser (1982) *Memory Observed: Remembering in Natural Contexts* San Francisco: W.H.Freeman & Co.

IVERSON, S. D. & IVERSON, L. L. (1975) *Behavioural Pharmacology* New York: Oxford University Press

JACKSON, J. M. & LATANÉ. B. (1981) All alone in front of all those people: stage fright as a function of number and type of co-performers and audience *Journal of Personality and Social Psychology* **40** 73–85

JACOBS, P. A., BRUNTON, M. & MELVILLE, M. M. (1965) Aggressive behaviour, mental abnormality and the XXY male *Nature* **208** 1351–2

JACOBSON, A. & KALES, A. (1967) Somnambulism: All-night EEG and related studies In: Kety, S. S., Evarts, E.V. & Williams, H. L. (eds) *Sleep and Altered States of Consciousness* Baltimore: Williams & Wilkins

JAFFE, D. T. & KANTER, R. M. (1979) Couple strains in communal households: a four-factor model of the separation process In: G. Levinger & O. Moles (eds) *Divorce and Separation* New York: Basic Books

JAFFE, P.G. & KATZ, A. N. (1975) Attenuating anterograde amnesia in Korsakoff's Psychosis *Journal of Abnormal Psychology* **84** 559–62

JAHODA, M. (1958) *Current Concepts of Positive Mental Health* New York: Basic Books

JAMES, W. (1890) *Principles of Psychology* New York: Holt

JANIS, I. L. (1972) *Victims of Groupthink* Boston: Houghton Mifflin

JANIS, I. L. (1983) *Groupthink* (2nd ed. revised) Boston: Houghton Mifflin

JANIS, I. L. & FESHBACH, S. (1963) Effects of fear arousing communications *Journal of Abnormal and Social Psychology* **48** 78–92

JAY, P. (1963) Mother-infant relations in langurs In: H. L. Rheingold (ed.) *Maternal Behaviour in Mammals* New York: Wiley

JELLISON, J. M. & DAVIS, D. (1973) Relationships between preceived ability and attitude similarity *Journal of Personality and Social Psychology* **27** 430–6

JENKINS, C. D., ZYZANSKI, S. J. & ROSENMAN, R. H. (1978) Coronary prone behaviour: one pattern or several? *Psychosomatic Medicine* (**40**) 25–43

JENNI, D. A. (1974) The evolution of polyandry in birds *American Zoologist* **14** 129–44

JENSEN, A.R. (1969) How much can we boost IQ and scholastic achievement? *Harvard Educational Review* **33** 1–123

JENSEN, A. R. (1970) IQs of identical twins reared apart *Behaviour Genetics* **2** 136

JODELET, D. (1991) *Madness and Social Representations* London: Harvester Wheatsheaf

JOHNSON, C. E., WOOD, R. & BLINKHORN, S. F. (1988) Spriouser and spriouser: the use of ipsative personality tests *Journal of Occupational Psychology* **61** 153–62

JOHNSON, P. (1984) The acquisition of skill In: M. M. Smyth & A. M. Wing (eds) *The Psychology of Movement* London: Academic Press

JOHNSON, R. D. & DOWNING, L. E. (1979) Deindividuation and valence of cues: effects on prosocial and antisocial behaviour *Journal of Personality and Social Psychology* **37** 1532–8

JOHNSON-LAIRD, P. N. (1983) Ninth Bartlett Memorial Lecture: thinking as a skill *Quarterly Journal of Experimental Psychology* **34** 1–29

JONES, E. E. & BERGLAS, S. (1978) Control of attributions about the self through self-handicapping strategies: the appeal of alcohol and the role of under-achievement *Personality and Social Psychological Bulletin* **4** 200–6

JONES, E. E. & DAVIS, K. E. (1965) From acts to dispositions: the attribution process in person perception In: L. Berkowitz (ed.) *Advances in Experimental Social Psychology* vol 2 New York: Academic Press

JONES, E. E. & HARRIS, V. A. (1967) The attribution of attitudes *Journal of Experimental Social Psychology* **3** 1–24

JONES, E. E. & MCGILLIS, D. (1976) Correspondent inferences and the attribution cube: a comparative reappraisal In:

J.H. Harvey *et al.* (eds) *New Directions in Attribution Research* **1** Hillsdale, N. J.: Erlbaum

JONES, M. C. & BAYLEY, N. (1950) Physical maturing among boys as related to behaviour *Journal of Educational Psychology* **41** 129–48

JONES, W. H. (1981) Loneliness and social contact *Journal of Social Psychology* **113** 295–6

JONES, W. H. & RUSSELL, D. (1980) The selective processing of belief disconfirming information *European Journal of Social Psychology* **10** 309–12

JONES, W. H., HOBBS, S. A. & HOCKENBURY, D. (1982) Loneliness and social skills deficits *Journal of Personality and Social Psychology* **49** 27–48

JOURARD, S. M. (1966) An exploratory study of body accessibility *British Journal of Social and Clinical Psychology* **5** 221–31

JOUVET, M. (1967) The sleeping brain *Scientifican American Offprints* San Francisco: W. H. Freeman & Co.

JOUVET, M. (1972) The role of monamines and acetylcholine-containing neurons in the regulation of the sleep-waking cycle *Ergebnisse der Psychologie* **64** 166–307

JOYNSON, R. B. (1989) *The Burt Affair* London: Routledge

JUEL-NIELSEN, N. (1965) Individual and environment: a psychiatric-psychological investigation of monozygotic twins reared apart *Acta Psychiatrica et Neurologica Scandinavica* Monograph supplement 183

JUNG, C. G. (1953–1978) H. Read, M. Fordham & G. Alder (eds) *The Collected Works of C. G. Jung* Princeton: Princeton University Press

JUNG, C. G. (1964) *Man and his Symbols* New York: Doubleday

KADUSHIN, A. (1976) Adopting older children: summary and implications In: A. M. Clarke & A. D. B. Clarke (eds) *Early Experience: Myth and Evidence* London: Open Books

KAËS, R. (1984) Representation and mentalisation: from the represented group to the group process In: R. M. Farr & S. Moscovici *Social Representations* Cambridge: Cambridge University Press

KAGAN, J. (1970) The determinants of attention in the infant *American Scientist* **58** 298–306

KAHN, W. A. (1989) Towards a sense of organisational humor: implications for organisational diagnosis and change *Journal of Applied Behavioural Science* **25** 45–63

KAHNEMAN, D. (1973) *Attention and Effort* Englewood Cliffs, N.J.: Prentice Hall

KAHNEMANN, D. & TVERSKY, A. (1972) Subjective probability: a judgement of representativeness *Cognitive Psychology* **3** 430–54

KAHNEMANN, D. & TVERSKY, A. (1973) On the psychology of prediction *Psychological Review* **80** 237–51

KAHNEMANN, D. & TVERSKY, A. (1984) Choices, values and frames *American Psychologist* **39** 341–50

KALES. A. & KALES, J. D. (1984) *Evaluation and Treament of Insomnia* Oxford: Oxford University Press

KALLMANN, F. J. (1938) *The Genetics of Schizophrenia* New York: J. J. Augustin

KALLMANN, F. J. (1946) The genetic theory of schizophrenia *American Journal of Psychiatry* **103** 309–22

KALLMANN, F. J. (1952) Genetic aspects of psychoses In: *The Biology of Mental Health and Disease* New York: Hoeber

KAMIN, L. (1974) *The Science and Politics of* IQ Harmondsworth: Penguin

KAMIN, L. J. (1969) Selective association and conditioning In: N. J. Mackintosh & W. K. Honig (eds) *Fundamental Issues in Associative Learning* Halifax: Dalhousie University Press

KAMIN, L. J. (1979) Interview *The Guardian* 5th November 1979

KANNER, L. (1943) Autistic disturbance of affective contact *The Nervous Child* **2** 217–50

KARLINS, M., COFFMAN, T. L. & WALTERS, G. (1969) On the fading of social stereotypes: studies in three generations of college students *Journal of Personality and Social Psychology* **13** 1–16

KARLSON, P. & LÜSCHER, M. (1959) Pheremones: a new term for a class of biologically active substances *Nature* **183** 55–6

KASL, S. V. & MAHL, G. F. (1965) The relationship of disturbances and hesitations in spontaneous speech to anxiety *Journal of Personality and Social Psychology* **1** 425–33

KASTENBAUM, R. (1979) Exit and existence: society's unwritten script for old age and death In: D. D. van Tassel (ed.) *Ageing, Death and the Completion of Being* Philadelphia: University of Pennsylvania Press

KATZ, D. (1960) The functional approach to the study of attitudes *Public Opinion Quarterly* **24** 163–204

KAY, H. (1955) Learning and retaining verbal material *British Journal of Psychology* **46** 81–100

KAYE, K. (1982) *The Mental and Social Life of Babies* London: Methuen

KELLEY, H. H. (1950) The warm-cold variable in first impressions of persons *Journal of Personality and Social Psychology* **18** 431–9

KELLEY, H. H. (1967) Attribution theory in social psychology In: D. L. Vine (ed.) *Nebraska Symposium on Motivation* Lincoln, Neb. University of Nebraska Press

KELLEY, H. H. (1973) The process of causal attribution *American Psychologist* **28** 107–28

KELLOGG, W. N. & KELLOGG, L. A. (1933) *The Ape and the Child* New York: Whiltlesey House

KELLY, G. (1955) *The Theory of Personal Constructs* New York: Norton

KELMAN, H. C. (1958) Compliance, identification and internalisation: three processes of attitude change *Journal of Conflict Resolution* **2** 51–60

KELMAN H. C. & HOVLAND, C. I. (1953) Reinstatement of the communication in delayed measurement of attitude change *Journal of Abnormal Social Psychology* **48** 327–35

KENDON, A. (1967) Some functions of gaze direction in social interaction *Acta Psychologica* **26** 22–63

KENNEDY, A. (1984) *The Psychology of Reading* London: Methuen

KERCHOFF, A. C. & DAVIS, K. I. (1962) Value consensus and need complementarchy in mate selection *American Sociology Review* **27** 295–303

KERTESZ, A. (1979) *Aphasia and Associated Disorders: Taxonomy, Localisation and Recovery* New York: Grune & Stratton

KIESLER, C. A. (1971) *The Psychology of Commitment: Experiments Linking Behaviour to Belief* New York: Academic Press

KILHAM, W. & MANN, L. (1974) Level of destructive obedience as a function of transmitter and executant roles in the Milgram obedience paradigm *Journal of Personality and Social Psychology* **29** 696–702

KIMBLE, G. A. (1949) Performance and reminiscence in motor learning as a function of the degree of distribution of practice *Journal of Experimental Psychology* **39** 500–10

KINDER, E. F. (1927) A study of the nest-building activity of the albino rat *Journal of Experimental Zoology* **47** 117–61

KLEIN, M. (1932) *The Psycho-analysis of Children* London: Hogarth

KLINE, P. (1984) *Psychology and Freudian Theory: an Introduction* London: Methuen

KNAPP, M. L. (1984) *Interpersonal Communication and Human Relationships* Boston, Mass.; Allyn & Bacon

KNAPP, M. L., HART, R. P. & DENNIS, H. S. (1974) An exploration of deception as a communication construct *Human Communication Research* **1** 15–29

KOGAN, N. & WALLACH, M. A. (1967) Risk-taking as a function of the situation, the person and the group In: G. Mandler *et al.* (eds) *New Directions in Psychology II* New York: Holt, Rinehart & Winston

KOHLBERG, L. (1969) *Stages in the Development of Moral Thought and Action* New York: Holt Rinehart & Winston

KÖHLER, W. (1925) *The Mentality of Apes* New York: Harcourt Brace

KOHN, M. L. (1973) Social class and schizophrenia: a critical review and a reformulation *Schizophrenia Bulletin* **7** 60–79.

KOLB, D.A. (1985) *Experiential Learning: Experiences as the Source of Learning and Development* New York: Prentice Hall

KOLUCHOVA, J. (1976a) Severe deprivation in twins: a case study In: A. M. Clarke & A. D. B. Clarke (eds) *Early Experience: Myth and Evidence* London: Open Books

KOLUCHOVA, J. (1976b) A report on the further development of twins after severe and prolonged deprivation In: A. M. Clarke & A. D. B. Clarke (eds) *Early Experience: Myth and Evidence* London: Open Books

KOWET, D. (1983) *The Jet Lag Book* New York: Crown

KOZLOWSKI, A. T. & BRYANT, K. J. (1977) Sense of direction, spatial orientation and cognitive maps *Journal of Experimental Psychology: Human Perception and Performance* **3** 590–8

KRAEPELIN, E. (1913) *Psychiatry (8th ed.)* Leipzig: Thieme

KRAL, V. A. (1978) Benign senile forgetfulness. In: R. Katzman (ed.) *Alzheimer's Disease: Senile Dementia and Relating Disorder* New York: Raven Press

KREBS, J. (1976) The song of the great tit says 'Keep Out' In: G. Ferry (ed.) *The Understanding of Animals* Oxford: Basil Blackwell

KREBS, J. R. & DAVIES, N. B. (eds) (1978) *Behavioural Ecology: an Evolutionary Approach* Oxford: Blackwell

KRECH, D., CRUTCHFIELD, R. S. & BALLACHEY, E. L. (1962) *Individual in Society* New York: McGraw-Hill

KRETSCHMER, E. (1925) *Physique and Character* New York: Harcourt Brace

KREUTZER, M. A., LEONARD, SISTER C. & FLAVELL, J. H. (1975) Prospective remembering in children In: Neisser, U. (1982) *Memory Observed: Remembering in Natural Contexts* San Francisco: W.H.Freeman & Co.

KRUGLANSKI, A. W. (1980) Lay epistemo-logic, process and contents: another look at attribution theory *Psychological Review* **87** 70–87

KRUGLANSKI, A. W., BALDWIN, M. W. & TOWSON, M. J. (1983) The lay epistemic process in attribution making In: M. Hewstone (ed.) *Attribution Theory: Social and Functional Extensions* Oxford: Blackwell

KUHLMAN, C. (1960) Visual imagery in children Unpublished doctoral dissertation, Harvard University, cited in J. S. Bruner *et al. Studies in Cognitive Growth* New York: Wiley

KUO, Z. Y. (1938) Further study of the behaviour of the cat towards the rat *Journal of Comparative Psychology* **25** 1–8

KURTH, S. B. (1970) Friendship and friendly relations In: G. J. McCall *et al.* (eds) *Social Relationships* Chicago, Ill.: Aldine

KURTZ, P. (1985) Spritualists, mediums and psychics: some evidence of fraud In: P. Kurtz (ed.) *A Skeptic's Handbook of Parapsychology* Buffalo, NY: Prometheus Books

LABOV, W. (1972) The logic of nonstandard English in V. Lee, (ed.) (1979) *Language Development* London: Croom Helm/Open University

LACK, D. (1943) *The Life of the Robin* London: Penguin

LAIDLER, K. (1980) *The Talking Ape* London: Collins

LAING, R. D. (1956) Mystification, confusion and conflict In: I. Boszormeny-Nagy & J. L. Framo (eds) *Intensive Family Therapy* New York: Harper & Row

LAING, R. D. (1961) *Self and Others* Harmondsworth: Penguin

LAING, R. D. (1965) *The Divided Self* Middlesex: Penguin

LAING, R. D. (1967) *The Politics of Experience* Harmondsworth: Penguin

LAING, R. D. & ESTERSON, G. W. (1968) *Sanity, Madness and the Family* Harmondsworth: Penguin

LAKOFF, G. (1975) *Language and Woman's Place* New York: Harper & Row

LAKOFF, G. & JOHNSON, M. (1980) *Metaphors We Live By* Chicago: Chicago University Press.

LALLJEE, M. (1981) Attribution theory and the analysis of explanations In: C. Antaki (ed.) *The Psychology of Ordinary Explanations of Social Behaviour* London: Academic Press

LALLJEE, M. (1991) Personal Communication

LALLJEE, M. & WIDDICOMBE, S. (1989) Discourse Analysis In: A.M. Colman & G. Beaumont (eds) *Psychology Survey 7* Leicester: BPS Books

LAMB, M. E. (1977) The development of mother-infant and father-infant attachments in the second year of life *Developmental Psychology* 13 637–48

LAMM, H. & MYERS, D. G. (1978) Group-induced polarisation of attitudes and behaviour In: L. Berkowitz (ed.) *Advances in Experimental Social Psychology* 11 145–95 New York: Academic Press

LAMOND, H. G. (1949) Mothering a lamb *Sheep and Goat Raising* 29 (9) 36–8

LAPIÈRE, R. T. (1934) Attitudes vs actions *Social Forces* 13 230–7

LARSEN, S.F. & LASZLO, J. (1990) Cultural-historical knowledge and personal experience in appreciation of literature *European Journal of Social Psychology* 20 (5) 425–40

LASHLEY, K. S. (1929) *Brain Mechanisms and Intelligence* Chicago: University of Chicago Press

LATANÉ, B. (1981) The psychology of social impact *American Psychologist* 36 343–56

LATANÉ, B. & DARLEY, J. M. (1968) Group inhibition of bystander intervention in emergencies *Journal of Personality and Social Psychology* 10 215–21

LATANÉ, B. & HARKINS, S. G. (1976) Crossmodality matches suggest anticipated stage fright, a multiplicature power function of audience size and status *Perception and Psychophysics* 20 482–8

LATANÉ, B. & RODIN, J. (1969) A lady in distress: inhibiting effects of friends and strangers on bystander intervention *Journal of Experimental Social Psychology* 5 189–202

LATANÉ, B., WILLIAMS, K. & HARKINS, S. (1979) Many hands make light work: the causes and consequences of social loafing *Journal of Personality and Social Psychology* 37 822–32

LAWRENCE, T. (1993) Bringing in the sheep: a meta-analysis of sheep/goat experiments In: M. J. Schlitz (ed.) *Proceedings of the 36th Annual Convention of the Parapsychological Association*

LAZARUS, R. S. & MCCLEARY, R. A. (1951) Autonomic discrimination without awareness: a study of subception *Psychological Review* 58 113–22

LE MAGNEN, J. (1972) Regulation of food intake *Advances in Psychosomatic Medicine* 7 73–90

LEA, S. E. G. (1984) *Instinct, Environment and Behaviour* London: Methuen

LEAHY, A. M. (1935) Nature-nurture and intelligence *Genetic Psychology Monographs* 17 235–308

LEARY, T. (1965) *The Politics of Ecstasy* London: Paladin

LEARY, T., ALPERT, R. & METZNER, R. (1965) Rationale of the Mexican psychedelic training centre In: R. Blum (ed.) *Utopiates: the Use and Users of LSD – 25* London: Tavistock

LE BON, G. (1895) *The Crowd: A Study of the Popular Mind* New York: Viking Press

LEE, J. A. (1976) *The Colours of Love* New York: Bantam

LEFF, J. (1992) Over the edge: stress and schizophrenia *New Scientist* 4th January 1992

LEFF, M.J., ROATCH, J. F. & BUNNEY, W. E. (1970) Environmental factors preceding the onset of severe depression *Psychiatry* 33 293–311

LEIBOWITZ, S. F. (1970) Hypothalamic b-adrenergic 'satiety' system antagonises an a-adrenergic 'hunger' system in the rat *Nature* 226 963–4

LENNEBERG, G. H. (1967) *Biological Foundations of Language* New York: Wiley

LERNER, M. J. & LICHTMAN, R. R. (1968) Effects of perceived norms on attitudes and altruistic behaviour towards a dependent other *Journal of Personality and Social Psychology* 9 226–32

LERNER, R. M. (1985) Adolescent maturational changes and psychosocial development: a dynamic interactional perspective *Journal of Youth and Adolescence* 14 355–72

LERNER, R. M. & KARABENICK, S. (1974) Physical attractiveness, body attitudes and self-concept in late adolescents *Journal of Youth and Adolescence* 3 7–16

LESGOLD, A. M. (1984) Human skill in a computerised society: complex skills and their acquisition *Behaviour Research Methods, Instruments and Computers* **16**(2) 79–87

LESLIE, A. M. (1987) Pretense and representation: the origins of 'theory of mind' *Psychological Review* **94** 412–26

LESLIE, A. M. & FRITH, U. (1988) Autistic children's understanding of seeing, knowing and believing *British Journal of Developmental Psychology* **6** 315–24

LEUZE, C. C. K. (1980) The application of radio tracking and its effect on the behavioural ecology of the water vole In: C. J. Armlaner & D. W. Macdonald (eds) A *Handbook of Biotelemetry and Radio Tracking* Oxford: Permagon

LEVENKRON, J. C., COHEN, J. D., MUELLER, H. S. & FISHER, E. V. (1983) Modifying the Type A coronary-prone behaviour pattern *Journal of Consulting and Clnical Psychology* **51** 192–204

LEVENSON, R. W., EKMAN, P. & FRIESEN, W. V. (1990) Voluntary facial action generates emotion–specific autonomic nervous system activity *Psychophysiology* **27** 363–84

LEVIN, H. & WILLIAMS, J. P. (1970) *Basic Studies on Reading* New York: Basic Books

LEVINSON, D. J. (1978) *The Seasons of a Man's Life* New York: Knopf

LEVY, B. A. (1971) Role of articulation in auditory and visual short-term memory *Journal of Verbal Learning and Verbal Behaviour* **10** 123–32

LEWIN, K., LIPPITT, R. & WHITE R. K. (1939) Patterns of aggressive behaviour in artificially created social climates *Journal of Social Psychology* **10** 271–99

LEWIN, R. (1978) Rutting on rhum In: G. Ferry (ed.) *The Understanding of Animals* Oxford: Basil Blackwell

LEYHAUSEN, P. (1956) Das Verhalten der Katzen *(Felidae) Handbook of Zoology, Berlin* **10**(21) 1–34

LIDZ, T. (1975) *The Origin and Treatment of Schizophrenic Disorders* London: Hutchinson

LIEBERMAN, P. (1984) *The Biology and Evolution of Language* Cambridge, Mass.: Harvard University Press

LIEBMAN, R., MINUCHIN, S. & BAKER, L. (1974) The use of structural family therapy in the treatment of interactable asthma *American Journal of Psychiatry* **131** 535–40

LILLY, J. C. (1965) Vocal mimicry in tursiops: ability to match numbers and durations of human vocal bursts *Science* **147** 300–1

LINTON, M. (1975) Memory for real-world events In: D. A. Norman & D. E. Rumelhart (eds) *Explorations in Cognition* San Francisco: Freeman

LIVINGSTON, R. E. (1967) Brain circuitry relating to complex behaviour In: G.C. Quarto, T. Melnechuck & F. O. Schmitt (eds) *The Neurosciences: a Study Program* New York: Rockefeller University Press

LOCKE, J. (1700) *An Essay Concerning Human Understanding* (4th ed.) Republished New York: Dover (1959)

LOEW, C. A. (1967) Acquisition of a hostile attitude and its relationship to aggressive behaviour *Journal of Personality and Social Psychology* **5** 335–41

LOFTUS, G. R. & LOFTUS, E. F. (1975) *Human Memory: the Processing of Information* New York: Halsted Press

LOGAN, G. D. (1988) Towards an instance theory of automisation *Psychological Review* **95** 492–527

LORANT, J. & DECONCHY, J.-P. (1986) Entrainement physique, categorisation intergroupe et representations sociales / Sports training, inter-group categorization and social representations *Cahiers de Psychologie Cognitive* **6**(4) 419–44

LORENZ, K. (1950) The comparative method in studying innate behaviour patterns *Symposium of the Society of Experimental Biology* **4** 221–68

LORENZ, K. (1958) The evolution of behaviour *Scientific American* **199**(6) 67–78

LORENZ, K. (1966) *On Aggression* New York: Harcourt, Brace & World

LORENZ, K. & TINBERGEN, N. (1938) Taxis und Instinkthandlung in der Eirollbewegung der Graugans *Zeitschrift für Tierpsychologie* **2** 1–29

LORZETTA, J. T. (1955) Group behaviour under stress *Human Relations* **8** 29–52

LOTT, A. & LOTT, B (1968) A learning theory approach to interpersonal attitudes In: A. Greenwold, T. Brock & T. Ostrom (eds) *Psychological Foundations of Attitudes* New York: Academic Press

LUCHINS, A. S. (1942) Mechanisation in problem-solving: the effects of Einstellung *Psychological Monographs* **54** (Whole No. 248)

LUCHINS, A. S. (1959) Primacy – recency in impression formation In: C. I. Hovland (ed.) *The Order of Presentation in Persuasion* New Haven, Corn: Yale University Press

LUTZ, C. A. (1990) Morality, domination and understandings of 'justifiable anger' among the Ifaluk In: G. R. Semin and K. J. Gergen (eds) *Everyday Understanding: Social and Scientific Implications* London: Sage

LYNCH, K. (1960) *The Image of the City* Cambridge, Mass.: MIT Press

LYONS, J. (1981) *Language and Linguistics: an Introduction* Cambridge University Press

MAASS, A & CLARK, R. D., III (1983) Internalisation versus compliance: differential processes underlying minority influence and conformity *European Journal of Social Psychology* **13** 197–215

MAAS, H. (1963) The young adult adjustment of twenty wartime residential nursery children *Child Welfare* **42** 57–72

MACHIAVELLI, N. (1513) *The Prince* (1977 translation: R. M. Adams) New York: Norton

MACKAY, D. G. & FULKERSON, D. (1979) On the comprehension and pronounciation of pronouns *Journal of Verbal Learning and Verbal Behaviour* **18** 661–73

MACKWORTH, N. H. (1950) Researches on the measurement of human performance *Medical Research Council Special Report* **268** London HMSO

MACLACHLAN, J. (1983) Making a message memorable and persuasive *Journal of Advertising Research* **23**(6) 51–9

MACMILLAN, M. (1996) Phineas Gage: a case for all reasons In: C. Code et al. (eds) *Classic Cases in Neuropsychology* Hove: Psychology Press

MACNICHOL, E. F. (1964) Three-pigment color vision *Scientific American* December 1964

MAIER, N. R. F. (1955) *Psychology in Industry* New York: McGraw Hill

MAIER, S. F. & SELIGMAN, M. E. P. (1976) Learned helplessness: theory and evidence *Journal of Experimental Psychology* **105** 3–46

MAIN, M. & GEORGE, C. (1985) Responses of abused and disadvantaged toddlers to distress in agemates: a study in the day care setting *Developmental Psychology* **21** 407–12

MAIN, M. & WESTON, D. (1981) The quality of the toddler's relationship to mother and father: related to conflict behaviour and readiness to establish new relationships *Child Development* **52** 932–40

MAIN, M., TOMASINI, L. & TOLAN, W. (1979) Differences among mothers of infants judged to differ in security *Developmental Psychology* **15** 472–3

MALINOWSKI, B. (1927) *Sex and Repression in Savage Society* New York: Harcourt Brace Jovanovitch

MALONE, D. R., MORRIS, H. H., KAY, M. C. & LEVIN, H. S. (1982) Prosopagnosia: a double dissociation between the recognition of familiar and unfamiliar faces *Journal of Neurology, Neurosurgery and Psychiatry* **45** 820–2

MANIS, M., DOVALINA, I., AVIS, N. E. & CADOZE, S. (1980) Base rates can affect individual predictions *Journal of Personality and Social Psychology* **38** 231–48

MARAGONI, C. & ICKES, W. (1989) Loneliness: a theoretical review with implications for measurement *Journal of Social and Personal Relationships* **6** 93–128

MARAIS, E. (1969) *The Soul of the Ape* New York: Atheneum

MARAÑON G. (1924) Contribution à l'étude de l'action émotive de l'adrénaline *Revue Française d'Endocrinologie* **2** 301–25

MARCIA J. E. (1966) Development and validation of ego-identity status *Journal of Personality and Social Psychology* **3** 551–8

MARKMAN, E. (1977) Realising that you don't understand: a preliminary investigation *Child Development* **48** 986–92

MARKS, D. (1981) Sensory cues invalidate remote viewing experiments (letter) *Nature* **292** 177

MARKS, D. & KAMMANN, R. (1978) Information transmission in remote viewing experiments (letter) *Nature* **274** 680–1

MARLER, P. R. (1970) A comparative approach to vocal learning: song development in white-crowned sparrows *Journal of Comparative and Physiological Psychology* **71** 1–25

MARLER, P. R. (1982) Avian and primate communication: the problem of natural categories *Neuroscience and Biobehavioural Reviews* **6** 87–94

MARLER, P. R. (1983) Monkey calls: how are they perceived, what do they mean? In: J. F. Eisenberg & D. G. Kleiman (eds) *Advances in the Study of Mammalian Behaviour: Special Publication of the American Society of Mammalogists* **7**

MARLER, P. R. (1984) Defining communication Cited in: M. Bright (ed.) *Animal Language* London: BBC Publications

MARLER, P. R. & HOBBETT, L. (1975) Individuality in the long range vocalisations of wild chimpanzees *Zeitschrift für Tierpsychologie* **38** 97–109

MARLER, P .R. & TAMURA, M. (1964) Culturally transmitted patterns of vocal behaviour in sparrows *Science* **146** 1483–6

MARQUES, J. M. & YZERBYT, V. Y. (1988) The black sheep effect: judgemental extremity towards ingroup members in inter and intra group situations *European Journal of Social Psychology* **18** 287–92

MARR, D. (1976) Early processing of visual information *Philosophical Transactions of the Royal Society of London Series B* **275** 483–524

MARR, D. (1982) *Vision: a Computational Investigation into the Human Representation and Processing of Visual Information* San Francisco: W.H. Freeman & Co.

MARR, D. & NISIHARA, H. K. (1978) Representation and recognition of the spatial organisation of three-dimensional shapes *Proceedings of the Royal Society of London Series B* **200** 269–94

MARSELLA, A. J. DEVOS, G. & HSU, F. L. K. (1985) *Culture and Self: Asian and Western Perspectives* London: Tavistock Publications

MARSH, P., ROSSER, E. & HARRÉ, R. (1978) *The Rules of Disorder* London: Routledge

MARSHALL, J. C. & NEWCOMBE, F. (1973) Patterns of paralexia: a psycholinguistic approach *Journal of Psycholinguistic Research* **2** 175–99

MARSHALL, J. R. (1984) The genetics of schizophrenia revisited *Bulletin of the British Psychological Society* **37** 177–81

MARTIN, M. & JONES, G.V. (1983) Distribution of attention in cognitive failure *Human Learning* **2** 221–6

MARTYNA, W. (1978) What does 'he' mean? *Journal of Communication* **238** 131–8

MARTYNA, W. (1980) The psychology of generic masculine In S. McConnell-Ginet, R. Borker & N. Furman (eds) *Women and Language in Literature and Society* New York: Praeger

MASLOW, C., YOSELSON, K. & LONDON, M. (1971) Persuasiveness of confidence expressed via language and body language *British Journal of Social and Clinical Psychology* **10** 234–40

MASLOW, A. H. (1954, 2nd ed. 1970) *Motivation and Personality* New York: Harper & Row

MASSARIK, F. (1981) The interviewing process re-examined In: P. Reason & J. Rowan (eds) *Human Inquiry: a Source Book of New Paradigm Research* Chichester: Wiley

MATTESON, D. R. (1977) Exploration and commitment: sex differences and methodological problems in the use of identity status categories *Journal of Youth and Adolescence* **6** 353–74

MAYNARD SMITH, J. (1972) *On Evolution* Edinburgh: Edinburgh University Press

MAYNARD SMITH, J. (1974) The theory of games and the evolution of animal conflicts *Journal of Theoretical Biology* **47** 209–21

MAYO, E. (1933) *The Human Problems of an Industrial Civilisation* London: Macmillan

MBITI, J. S. (1970) *African Religions and Philosophy* New York: Doubleday

MCARTHUR, L. A. (1972) The how and what of why: some determinants and consquences of causal attribution *Journal of Personality and Social Psychology* **22** 171–93

MCCLELLAND, D. C. (1961) *The Achieving Society* Princeton, N.J.: Van Nostrand

MCCRAE, R. R. & COSTA, P. T. JR. (1985) Updating Norman's 'adequate taxonomy': intelligence and personality dimensions in natural language and in questionnaires *Journal of Personality and Social Psychology* **49** 710–21

MCDOUGALL, W. (1932) *The Energies of Men* London: Methuen

MCFARLAND, C. & ROSS, M. (1982) The impact of causal attributions on affective reactions to success and failure *Journal of Personality and Social Psychology* **43** 937–46

MCGARRIGLE, J. & DONALDSON, M. (1974) Conservation accidents *Cognition* **3** 341–50

MCGEOCH, J. A. (1942) *The Psychology of Human Learning: an Introduction* New York: Longman

MCGINLEY, H., LEFEVRE, R. & MCGINLEY, P. (1975) The influence of a communicator's body position on opinion change in others *Journal of Personality and Social Psychology* **31** 686–90

MCGREGOR, D. (1960) *The Human Side of Enterprise* New York: McGraw-Hill

MCGUIRE, W. J. (1968) Personality and susceptibility to social influence In: E. F. Borgatta & W. W. Lambert (eds)

Handbook of Personality Theory and Research Chicago: Rand McNally

MCKENZIE, B. E. & DAY, R. H. (1976) Infants' attention to stationery and moving objects at different distances *Australian Journal of Psychology* **28** 45–51

MCKINNON, J. (1974) *In Search of the Red Ape* London: Collins

MCNEMAR, Q. (1938) Newman, Freeman and Holzinger's twins: a study of heredity and environment *Psychological Bulletin* **35** 247–8

MEACHAM, J. A. & LEIMAN, B. (1982) Remembering to perform future actions In: U. Neisser (ed.) *Memory Observed: Remembering in Natural Contexts* San Francisco: W.H. Freeman & Co.

MEAD, G. H. (1934) *Mind, Self and Society* Chicago: University of Chicago Press

MEAD, M. (1928) *Coming of Age in Samoa* published 1970 Harmondsworth: Penguin

MEAD, M. (1972) *Culture and Commitment* St Albans: Panther

MEDDIS, R. (1977) *The Sleep Instinct* London: Routledge & Kegan Paul

MEDDIS, R. (1979) The evolution and function of sleep In: D. A. Oakley and H. C. Plotkin (eds) *Brain, Behaviour and Evolution* London: Methuen

MELNICK, M. J. (1971) Effects of overlearning on the retention of a gross motor skill *Research Quarterly* **42** 60–9

MELROSE, D. R., REED, H. C. B. & PATTERSON, R. L. S. (1971) Androgen steroids associated with boar odour as an aid to the detection of oestrus in pig artificial insemination *British Veterinary Journal* **127** 497–501

MELZACK, R. (1973) *The Puzzle of Pain* New York: Basic Books

MELZACK, R. (1992) Phantom limbs *Scientific American* April 1992 90–6

MELZACK, R. & WALL, P. (1982) *The Challenge of Pain* Harmondsworth: Penguin

MENDEL, G. (1866) Experiments in plant hybridisation Trans. in J. A. Peters (ed.) *Classical Papers in Genetics* Englewood Cliffs, N. J.: Prentice Hall

MENZEL, E. W. & HALPERIN, S. (1975) Purposive behaviour as a basis for objective communication between chimpanzees *Science* **189** 652–4

MENZEL, G. W. (1984) Human language – who needs it? In: G. Ferry (ed.) *The Understanding of Animals* Oxford: Blackwell

MENZIES, R. (1937) Conditioned vasomotor responses in human subjects *Journal of Psychology* **4** 75–120

MESTEL, R. (1993) Cannabis: the brain's other supplier *New Scientist* 31st July 1993

MIDDLETON, R. (1976) Regional differences in prejudice *American Sociological Review* **41** 94–117

MIELL, D. E. & DUCK, S. W. (1986) Strategies in developing friendship In: V. J. Derlega & B. A. Winstead (eds) *Friendship and Social Interaction* New York: Springer-Verlag

MIKULINCER, M. (1986) Motivational involvement and learned helplessness: the behavioral effects of the importance of uncontrollable events *Journal of Social and Clinical Psychology* **4** 402–22

MIKULINCER, M. (1988) The relation between stable/unstable attribution and learned helplessness *British Journal of Social Psychology* **27** 221–30

MILES, L. E., RAYNAL, D. M. & WILSON, M.A. (1977) Blind man living in normal society has circadian rhythm of 24.9 hours *Science* **198** 421–3

MILES, T. R. (ed.) (1978) *Understanding Dyslexia* London: Hodder & Stoughton

MILES, T. R. & MILES, E. (1975) *More Help for Dyslexic Children* London: Methuen

MILGRAM, S. (1963) Behavioural study of obedience *Journal of Abnormal Psychology* **67** 371–8

MILGRAM, S. (1970) The experience of living in cities *Science* **167** 1461–8

MILGRAM, S. (1973) *Obedience to Authority* London: Tavistock

MILLER, N. & DICARA, L. (1967) Instrumental learning of heart rate changes in curarised rats: shaping and specificity to discriminative stimulus *Journal of Comparative and Physiological Psychology* **63** 12–19

MILLER, C. & SWIFT, K. (1976) *Words and Women: New Language in New Times* New York: Doubleday

MILLER, D. T. & ROSS, M. (1975) Self-serving biases in the attribution of causality: fact or fiction? *Psychological Bulletin* **82** 213–25

MILLER, G. (1997) *Social Psychology: an Evolutionary Approach* Paper delivered at the British Psychological Society Social Psychology Conference, Sussex, September 1997

MILLER, G. A. (1956) The magical number seven, plus or minus two: some limits on our capacity for processing information *Psychological Review* **63** 81–97

MILLER G. A., GALANTER, E. & PRIBRAM, K. H. (1960) *Plans and the Structure of Behavior* New York: Holt, Reinhart & Winston

MILLER, G. R., MOGEAU, P. A. & SLEIGHT, C. (1986) Fudging with friends and lying to lovers: deceptive communication in interpersonal relationships *Journal of Social and Personal Relationships* **3** 495–512

MILLER, J. G. (1984) Culture and the development of everyday social explanation *Journal of Personality and Social Psychology* **46** 961–78

MILLER, N. & DICARA, L. (1967) Instrumental learning of heart rate changes in curarised rats: shaping and specificity to discriminative stimulus *Journal of Comparative and Physiological Psychology* **63** 12–19

MILLER, N. E., BAILEY, C. J. & STEVENSON, J. A. F. (1950) Decreased 'hunger' but increased food intake resulting from hypothalamic lesions *Science* **112** 256–9

MILLER, S. (1968) *The Psychology of Play* Baltimore: Penguin

MILNER, B. R. (1966) Amnesia following operation on temporal lobes In: C. W. N. Whitty & O. L. Zurgwill (eds) *Amnesia* London: Butterworth

MILNER, D. (1973) Racial misidentification and preference in 'black' British children *European Journal of Social Psychology* **3** 281–95

MILTON, J. & WISEMAN, R. (1997) Ganzfeld at the crossroads: a meta-analysis of the new generation of studies In: *Proceedings of the 40th Annual Convention of the Parapsychological Association* Hatfield, UK: University of Hertfordshire Press

MINSKY, M (1975) A framework for representing knowledge In: P. H. Winston (ed.) *The Psychology of Computer Vision* New York: McGraw Hill

MINUCHIN, S. (1974) *Families and Family Therapy* Cambridge, Mass: Harvard University Press

MISCHEL, W. (1968) *Personality and Assessment* New York: Wiley

MISCHEL, W. (1973) Towards a cognitive social learning reconceptualisation of personality *Psychological Review* **80** 252–83

MITCHELL, J. C. (1952) Some aspects of tribal social distance In: A. A. Dubb (ed.) *The Multi-tribal Society* Lusaka, Zambia: Rhodes-Livingstone Institute

MOGENSON, G.J. & PHILLIPS, A. G. (1976) Motivation: a physiological construct in search of a physiological substrate In: J. M. Sprague and A. N. Epstein (eds) *Progress in Psychology and Physiological Psychology* **6** New York: Academic Press

MOLTZ, H. (1960) Imprinting: empirical basis and theoretical significance *Psychological Bulletin* **57** 291–314

MONEY, J. & EHRHARDT, A. A. (1972) *Man and Woman, Boy and Girl* Baltimore: The Johns Hopkins University Press

MONIZ, E. (1936) *Tentatives Opératoires dans le Traitement de Certaines Psychoses* Paris: Masson

MONK, T. H. & FOLKARD, S. (1985) Shiftwork and performance In: S. Folkard and T. H. Monk (eds) *Hours of Work* Chichester: Wiley

MOORHEAD, G. FERENCE, R. & NECK, C. P. (1991) Group decision fiascoes continue: space shuttle Challenger and a revised groupthink framework *Human Relations* **44**(6) 539–50

MORAY, N. (1959) Attention in dichotic listening: affective cues and the influence of instructions *Quarterly Journal of Experimental Psychology* **11** 56–60

MORAY, N. (1969) *Listening and Attention* Harmondsworth: Penguin

MORGAN, C. L. (1894) *Introduction to Comparative Psychology* New York: Scribner's

MORGAN, C. T. (1943) *Physiological Psychology* New York: McGraw-Hill

MORGAN, D. L. (1986) Personal relationships as an interface between social networks and social cognitions *Journal of Social and Personal Relationships* London: Academic Press

MORGAN, E. (1972) *The Descent of Woman* London: Open Books

MORRIS, D. (1967) *The Naked Ape* New York: McGraw-Hill

MORRIS, D. (1981) *The Soccer Tribe* London: Cape

MORRIS, P. E. (1982) Research on memory in everyday life In: P. Sanders, N. Hayes, R. Brody & L. Jones (eds) *A Handbook for GCE Psychology Students* Leicester: ATP Publications

MORRIS, P. E., GRUNEBERG, M. M., SYKES, R. N. & MERRICK, A. (1981) Football knowledge and the acquisition of new results *British Journal of Psychology* **72** 479–83

MORRIS, R. L. (1986) What psi is not: the necessity for experiments In: H. L. Edge, R. L. Morris, J. Palmer & J. H. Rush *Foundations of Parapsychology: Exploring the Boundaries of Human Capability* London: Routledge & Kegan Paul

MORRIS, R. L. (1991) *Taking the Para out of Parapsychology: how Psychology can help in evaluating Psychic Claims* Paper delivered at the British Psychological Society Annual Conference April 1991

MORRIS, R. L., CUNNINGHAM, S., MCALPINE, S. & TAYLOR, R. (1993) Toward replication and extension of autoganzfeld results *Proceedings of the 36th Annual Convention of the Parapsychological Association* Toronto, Canada

MORRIS, R. L., DALTON, K., DELANOY, D., & WATT, C. (1995) Comparison of the sender / no sender condition in the Ganzfeld *Proceedings of the 38th Annual Convention of the Parapsychological Association* held in Durham, N. Carolina, August 1995

MORRIS, W. N. & MILLER, R. S. (1975) The effects of consensus-breaking and consensus-preempting partners or reduction of conformity *Journal of Experimental Social Psychology* **11** 215–23

MORTON, E. S. (1975) Ecological sources of selection on avian sounds *American Naturalist* **109** 17–34

MORTON, J. (1979) Facilitation in word recognition: experiments causing change in the logogen model In: P. A. Kolers *et al.* (eds) *Processing of Visible Language* **1** New York: Plenum

MORUZZI, G. & MAGOUN, H. W. (1949) Brain stem reticular formation and activation of the EEG *Electro-encephalography and Clinical Neurophysiology* **1** 455–73

MOSCOVICI, S. (1961) *La Psychoanalyse: son Image et son Public* Paris: Presses Universitaires de France

MOSCOVICI, S. (1976) *Social Influence and Social Change* London: Academic Press

MOSCOVICI, S. (1980) Towards a theory of conversion behaviour In: L. Berkowitz (ed.) *Advances in Experimental Social Psychology (Vol 13)* 209–39 New York: Academic Press

MOSCOVICI, S. (1984) The phenomenon of social representations In: R.M. Farr & S. Moscovici (eds) *Social Representations* Cambridge: Cambridge University Press

MOSCOVICI, S. & FAUCHEUX, C. (1972) Social influence, conformity bias and the study of active minorities In: L. Berkowitz (ed.) *Advances in Experimental Social Psychology (Vol 6)* 149–202 New York: Academic Press

MOSCOVICI, S. & HEWSTONE, M. (1983) Social representations and social expectations: from the 'naïve' to the 'amateur' scientist In: M. Hewstone (ed.) *Attribution Theory: Social and Functional Extensions* Oxford: Blackwell

MOSCOVICI, S. & PERSONNAZ, B. (1980) Studies in social influence V: minority influence and conversion behaviour in a perceptual task *Journal of Experimental Social Psychology* **16** 270–82

MOSCOVICI, S. & PERSONNAZ, B. (1986) Studies on latent influence by the spectrometer method I: the impact of psychologisation in the case of conversion by a minority or a majority. *European Journal of Social Psychology* **16** 345–60

MOSCOVICI, S. & ZAVALLONI, M. (1969) The group as a polariser of attitude *Journal of Personality and Social Psychology* **12** 125–35

MOSCOVICI, S., LAGE, E. & NAFFRECHOUX, M. (1969) Influence of a consistent minority on the responses of a majority in a colour perception task *Sociometry* **32** 365–80

MOWER-WHITE, C. J. (1977) A limitation of balance theory: the effects of identification with a member of the triad *European Journal of Social Psychology* **7** 111–16

MOYNIHAN, M. (1953) Some displacement activities of black-headed gulls *Behaviour* **5** 58–80

MUGNY, G. (1982) *The Power of Minorities* London: Academic Press

MUMMENDEY, A. & SCHREIBER, H. J. (1984) Social comparison, similarity and ingroup favouritism: A replication *European Journal of Social Psychology* **14** 231–3

MUNDY-CASTLE, A. C. (1966) Pictorial depth perception in Ghanaian children *International Journal of Psychology* **1** 290–300

MURDOCK, B. B. (1962) The serial position effect of free recall *Journal of Experimental Psychology* **64** 482–8

MURIE, A. (1944) The wolves of Mount McKinley *US Department Interior Fauna Series* **5** Washington: US Government Printing Office

MURPHY, J. H., CUNNINGHAM, I. & WILCOX, G. (1979) The impact of program environment on recall of humorous TV commercials *Journal of Advertising* **8** (Spring) 17–21

MURRAY, D. J., MASTRONARDI, J. & DUNCAN, S. (1972) Selective attention to 'physical' vs. 'verbal' aspects of colored words *Psychonomic Science* **26**(6) 305–7

MURSTEIN, B. I. (1971) A theory of marital choice and its applicability to marriage adjustment In: B. I. Murstein (ed.) *Theories of Attraction and Love* New York: Springer

MUSGROVE, F. (1963) Inter-generation attitudes *British Journal of Social and Clinical Psychology* **2** 209–23

MYERS, D. G. & KAPLAN, M. F. (1976) Group-induced polarisation in simulated juries *Personality and Social Psychology Bulletin* (2) 63–6

NARINS, P. M. & CAPRANICA, R. R. (1980) Neural adaptations for processing the 2-note call of the Puerto-Rican tree frog, *elentherodactylus-coqui Brain and Behaviour* **17** 48–66

NASH, J. (1978) *Developmental Psychology* (2nd ed.) N. J.: Prentice Hall

NAYLOR, J. C. (1962) *Parameters Affecting the Relative Effectiveness of Part and Whole Training Methods: a Review of the Literature* New York: US Naval Training Devices Centre Report UD.950 1

NELSON, R. D. & RADIN, D. I. (1987) When immovable objects meet irresistible evidence *Behavioural and Brain Sciences* **10** 600–1

NEISSER, U. (1976) *Cognition and Reality: Principles and Implications of Cognitive Psychology* San Francisco: W.H.Freeman & Co.

NEISSER, U. (1981) John Dean's Memory: a Case Study *Cognition* **9** 1–22

NEISSER, U. (1982) *Memory Observed: Remembering in Natural Contexts* San Francisco: W. H. Freeman

NEMETH, C. & BRILMAYER, A. G. (1987) Negotiation versus influence *European Journal of Social Psychology* **17** 45–56

NEMETH, C., SWEDLUND, M. & KANKI, B. (1974) Patterning of the minority's responses and their influence on the majority *European Journal of Social Psychology* **4** 53–64

NEUMANN, P. G. (1974) An attribute frequency model for the abstraction of prototypes *Memory and Cognition* **2** 241–8

NEWCOMB, T. M. (1961) *The Acquaintanceship Process* New York: Holt, Rinehart & Winston

NEWCOMB, T. M. (1968) Interpersonal balance In: R. P. Abelson *et al.* (eds) *Theories of Cognitive Consistency: A Source Book* Chicago: Rand McNally

NEWELL, A. & SIMON, H. A. (1972) *Human Problem Solving* Englewood-cliffs, N. J.: Prentice Hall

NEWMAN, H. H., FREEMAN, F. N. & HOLZINGER, K. J. (1937) *Twins: a Study of Heredity and Environment* Chicago: University of Chicago Press

NEWSON, J. (1974) Towards a theory of infant understanding *Bulletin of the British Psychological Society* **27** 251–7

NICE, M. M. (1943) Studies in the life-history of the song sparrow II *Transactions of the Linnaean Society of New York* **6** 90–146

NICOLSON, N., COLE, S. G. & ROCKLON, T. (1985) Conformity in the Asch situation: a comparison between contemporary British and American university students *British Journal of Social Psychology* **24** 91–8

NIEMEYER, R. K. (1959) Part versus whole methods and massed versus distributed practice in the learning of selected large muscle activities *62nd Proceedings of the College of Physical Educational Associations for Men* Washington: AAHPER 127–5

NILSEN, A. P. (1973) *Grammatical Gender and its Relationship to the Equal Treatment of Males and Females in Children's Books* Unpublished PhD Thesis: University of Iowa

NISBETT, R. E. (1972) Hunger, obesity and the ventromedial hypothalamus *Psychological Review* **79** 433–53

NISBETT, R. E. & ROSS, L. (1980) *Human Inference: Strategies and Shortcomings of Social Judgement* Englewood Cliffs, N.J.: Prentice Hall

NISBETT, R. E. & WILSON, T. D. (1977) Telling more than we can know: verbal reports on mental processes *Psychological Review* **84** 231–59

NISBETT, R. E., CAPUTO, C., LEGANT, P. & MARCEK, J. (1973) Behaviour as seen by the actor and as seen by the observer *Journal of Personality and Social Psychology* **27** 157–64

NOBLES, W. W. (1976) Extended self: rethinking the so-called negro self-concept In: R. L. Jones (ed.) *Black Psychology* New York: Harper & Row

NOGRADY, H., MCCONKEY, K. M., LAURENCE, J. R. & PERRY, C. (1983) Dissociation, duality and demand characteristics in hypnosis *Journal of Abnormal and Social Psychology* **92** 223–35

NOLLER, P. (1985) Negative communications in marriage *Journal of Social and Personal Relationships* **2** 289–301

NOLLER, P., LAW, H. & COMREY, A. L. (1987) Cattel, Comrey and Eysenck personality factors compared: more evidence for the five robust factors? *Journal of Personality and Social Psychology* **53** 775–82

NORMAN, D. A. (1976) *Memory and Attention* (2nd ed.) Chichester: Wiley

NORMAN, D. A. & BOBROW, D. G. (1975) On data-limited and resource-limited processes *Cognitive Psychology* **7** 44–64

NORMAN, D. A. & SHALLICE, T. (1980) *Attention to Action: Willed and Automatic Control of Behaviour (CHIP Report 99)* San Diego, Calif.: University of California

NORMAN, W. T. (1963) Toward an adequate taxonomy of personality attributes: replicated factor structure in peer nomination personality ratings *Journal of Abnormal and Social Psychology* **66** 574–83

NORRIS, K. S. & DOHL, T. P. (1980) Behaviour of the Hawaian Spinner dolphin, *stenella longirostris Fish Bulletin* **77**(4) 821–49

NORTHCRAFT, G. B. & NEALE, M. A. (1987) Experts, amateurs and real estate: an anchoring-and-adjustment perspective on property pricing decisions *Organisational Behaviour and Human Decision Processes* **39** 84–97

NOTMAN, M. (1980) Adult life cycles: changing roles and changing hormones In: J. G. Parsons (ed.) *The Psychobiology of Sex Differences and Sex Roles* New York: McGraw-Hill

NOTTEBOHM, F. (1970) Ontogeny of bird song *Science* **176** 950–6

OFFER, D. (1969) *The Psychological World of the Teenager* New York: Basic Books

O'KEEFE, J. & NADEL, L. (1978) *The Hippocampus as a Cognitive Map* Oxford: Clarendon Press

OLDS, J. & MILNER, P. (1954) Positive reinforcement produced by electrical stimulation of septal area and other regions of rat brain *Journal of Comparative and Physiological Psychology* **47** 419–27

OLSON, D. (1977) From utterance to text: the bias of language in speech and writing *Harvard Educational Review* **47** 257–82

OLTON, D. S. (1979) Mazes, maps and memory *American Psychologist* **34** 583–96

OPIE, I., & OPIE, P. (1959) *The Lore and Language of Schoolchildren* Oxford: Oxford University Press

ORNE, M. T. (1962) On the social psychology of the psychological experiment: with particular reference to demand characteristics and their implications *American Psychologist* **17** 276–783

ORNE, M. T. (1979) On the simulating subject as quasi-control group in hypnosis research: what, why & how? In. G. From & R. E. Shor (eds) *Hypnosis: Research Development and Perspectives* (2nd ed.) New York: Aldine

ORNSTEIN, R. E. (1986) *The Psychology of Consciousness* (2nd ed.) New York: W. H. Freeeman & Co

OSGOOD, C. E. (1966) Dimensionality of the semantic space for communication via facial expression *Scandinavian Journal of Psychology* **7** 1–30

OSWALD, I. (1970) *Sleep* Harmondsworth: Penguin

OVERTON, D. A. (1972) State dependent learning produced by alcohol and its relevance to alcoholism In: B. Kissin & H. Begleiter (eds) *The Biology of Alcoholism 2: Physiology and Behaviour* New York: Plenum Press

OWENS, R. G. & NAYLOR, F. (1989) *Living While Dying* Wellingborough: Thorsons

PACKER, C. (1977) Reciprocal altruism in *Papio anubis Nature* **265** 441–3

PACKER, C. & PUSEY, A. (1982) Co-operation and competition within coalitions of male lions: kin selection or game theory? *Nature* **296** 740

PAILLARD, J., MICHEL, F. & STELMACH, G. (1983) Localisation without content: a tactile analogue of 'blind sight' *Archives of Neurology* **40** 548–51

PARKE, R. D. & O'LEARY, S. (1976) Father-mother-infant interaction in the newborn period: some findings, some observations and some unresolved issues In: K. Riegel & J. Meacham (eds) *The Developing Individual in a Changing World* **2** *Social and Environmental Issues* The Hague: Mouton

PARKE, R. D. & SAWIN, D. B. (1980) The family in early infancy: social interactional and attitudinal analyses In: F. A. Pederson (ed.) *The Father–Infant Relationship: Observational Studies in a Family Context* New York: Praeger

PARKER, G. A. (1974) Assessment strategy and the evolution of fighting behaviour *Journal of Theoretical Biology* **47** 223–43

PARKER, I. (1997) *Social Psychology: A Critical Approach* Paper delivered at the British Psychological Society Social Psychology Conference, Sussex, September 1997

PARKES, C. M. (1964) The effects of bereavement on physical and mental health: a study of the case records of widows *British Medical Journal* **2** 274

PARKES, C. M. (1972) *Bereavement: Studies of Grief in Adult Life* Harmondsworth: Penguin

PARKES, C. M. & WEISS, R. S. (1983) *Recovery from Bereavement* New York: Basic Books

PARKES, C. M,. BENJAMIN, B. & FITZGERALD, R. G. (1969) Broken heart: a statistical study of increased mortality among widowers *British Medical Journal* **1** 740

PARKIN, A. J. (1996) H.M.: the medial temporal lobes and memory In: C. Code et al. (eds) *Classic Cases in Neuropsychology* Hove: Psychology Press

PARTEN, M. (1932) Social participation among pre–school children *Journal of Abnormal and Social Psychology* **27** 243–69

PASAHOW, R. J. (1980) The relationship between an attributional dimension and learned helplessness *Journal of Abnormal Psychology* **89** 358–67

PATRICK, G. T. W. (1916) *The Psychology of Relaxation* Boston: Houghton-Mifflin

PATTERSON, F. G. (1978) The gestures of a gorilla: language acquisition in another pongid *Brain and Language* **5** 72–97

PATTERSON, F. G. (1979) Conversations with a gorilla *National Geographic* **154**(4) 438–65

PATTON, R. G. & GARDNER, L. I. (1963) *Growth Failure in Maternal Deprivation* London: C. C. Thomas

PAULUS, P. B. & MURDOCK, P. (1971) Anticipated evaluation and audience presence in the enhancement of dominant responses *Journal of Experimental Social Psychology* **7** 280–91

PAVLOV, I. P. (1927) *Conditioned Reflexes: an Investigation of the Physiological Activity of the Cerebral Cortex* New York: Dover

PAYNE, R. S. & MCVAY, S. (1971) Songs of humpback whales *Science* **173** 585–97

PEARCE, J. M. (1987) *An Introduction to Animal Cognition* Hove: Lawrence Erlbaum Associates

PEDERSEN, F. A., CAIN, R. & ZASLOW, M. (1982) Variation in infant experience associated with alternative family roles In: L. Laosa & I. Sigel (eds) *The Family as a Learning Environment* New York: Plenum

PENFIELD, W. (1959) The interpretive cortex *Science* **129** 1719–25

PENFIELD, W. & RASMUSSEN, T. (1950) *The Cerebral Cortex of Man: a Clinical Study of Localisation* Boston: Little, Brown & Co.

PENNINGTON, D. C. (1982) Witnesses and their testimony: the effects of ordering on juror verdicts *Journal of Applied Social Psychology* **12** 318–33

PEPLAU, L. A. & PERLMAN, D. (1982) *Loneliness: a Sourcebook of Current Theory, Research and Therapy* New York: Wiley

PERLS, F. HEFFERLINE, R. F. & GOODMAN, P. (1951) *Gestalt Therapy* Harmondsworth: Penguin

PERNER, J. (1988) Higher-order beliefs and intentions in children's understanding of social interaction In: J. W. Astington, P. L. Harris & D. R. Olson (eds) *Developing Theories of Mind* New York: Cambridge University Press

PERNER, J. & WIMMER, H. (1985) 'John thinks that Mary thinks that...': attribution of second-order beliefs by 5 to 10-year old children *Journal of Experimental Child Psychology* **39** 437–71

PERNER, J., LEEKAM, S. & WIMMER, H. (1987) Three year olds' difficulty in understanding false belief: cognitive limitation, lack of knowledge or pragmatic misunderstanding? *British Journal of Developmental Psychology* **5** 125–37

PERRIN, S. & SPENCER, C. (1980) The Asch effect: a child of its time? *Bulletin of the British Psychological Society* **32** 405–406

PESKIN, H. (1973) Influence of the developmental schedule of puberty on learning and ego-functioning *Journal of Youth and Adolescence* **4** 273–90

PETERSEN, A. C. & CROCKETT, L. (1985) Pubertal timing and grade effects on adjustment *Journal of Youth and Adolescence* **14** 191–206

PETERSON, L. R. & PETERSON, M. J. (1959) Short–term retention of individual items *Journal of Experimental Psychology* **58** 193–8

PIAGET, J. (1932) *The Moral Judgement of the Child* London: Routledge & Kegan Paul

PIAGET, J. (1952) *The Origins of Intelligence in Children* New York: International Universities Press

PIAGET, J. (1959) *The Language and Thought of the Child* London: Routledge and Kegan Paul

PIAGET, J. (1962) *Play, Dreams and Imitation in Childhood* London: Routledge

PICHERT, J. W. & ANDERSON, R. C. (1977) Taking different perspectives on a story *Journal of Educational Psychology* **69** 309–15

PILIAVIN, I. M., RODIN, J. & PILIAVIN, J. A. (1969) Good Samaritanism: an underground phenomenon? *Journal of Personality and Social Psychology* **13** 289–99

PILLEMER, D. B. (1984) Flashbulb memories of the assassination attempt on President Reagan *Cognition* **16** 63–80

PLATOW, M. J., MCCLINTOCK, C. G. & LIEBRAND, W. B. (1990) Predicting intergroup fairness and ingroup bias in the minimal group paradigm *European Journal of Social Psychology* **20** 221–39

PÖPPEL, E., HELD, R. & FROST, D. (1973) Residual function after brain wounds involving the central visual pathways in man *Nature* **243** 295–6

POPPER, K. (1959) *The Logic of Scientific Discoveries* London: Hutchinson

PORTER, H. (1939) Studies in the psychology of stuttering: Part 14 – Stuttering phenomena in relation to size and personnel of audience *Journal of Speech Disorders* **4** 323–33

PORTER, J. D. R. (1971) *Black Child, White Child* Cambridge, Mass.: Harvard University Press

POSNER, M. L., PETERSEN, S. E., FOX, P. T. & RAICHLE, M. E. (1988) Localisation of cognitive operations in the human brain *Science* **240** 1627–31

POSTMAN, L., BRUNER, J. S. & MCGINNIES, E. (1948) Personal values as selective factors in perception *Journal of Abnormal and Social Psychology* **43** 142–54

POTTER, J. (1997) *Social Psychology: a Discursive Approach* Paper delivered at the British Psychological Society Social Psychology Conference, Sussex, September 1997

POTTER, J. & REICHER, S. (1987) Discourses of community and conflict: the organisation of social categories in accounts of a 'riot' *British Journal of Social Psychology* **26**

POTTER, J. & WETHERELL, M. (1987) *Discourse and Social Psychology: Beyond Attitudes and Behaviour* London: Sage

POWER, M. J., ASCH, P. M., SCHOENBERG, E. & SOREY, E. (1974) Delinquency and the family *British Journal of Social Work* **4** 13–38

POWLEY, T. L. (1977) The ventromedial hypothalamic syndrome, satiety and a cephalic phase hypothesis *Psychological Review* **84** 89–126

PRECHTL, H. F. R. (1953) Zur Physiologie der angeborenen auslosenden Mechanismen I: Quantitative Untersuchungen über die Sperrbewegung junger Singvögel *Behaviour* **1** 32–50

PRECHTL, H. F. R. (1984) Continuity and change in early neural development In: H. F. R. Prechtl (ed.) *Continuity of Neural Function From Prenatal to Postnatal Life* Oxford: Blackwell

PREMACK, A. J. & PREMACK, D. B. (1972) Teaching language to an ape *Scientific American* **227** 92–9

PREMACK, D. B. (1959) Toward empirical behaviour laws: Part 1 positive reinforcement *Psychological Review* **66** 219–33

PREMACK, D. B. (1962) Reversibility of the reinforcement relation *Science* **136** 255–7

PREMACK, D. B. (1983) Animal Cognition *Annual Review of Psychology* **34** 351–62

PRENTICE-DUNN, S. & ROGERS, R. W. (1982) Effects of public and private self-awareness on deindividuation and aggression *Journal of Personality and Social Psychology* **43** 503–13

PRESTON, M. S. & LAMBERT, W. E. (1969) Interlingual interference in a bilingual version of the Stroop color-word task *Journal of Verbal Learning and Verbal Behaviour* **8** 295–301

PRITCHARD, R. M. (1961) Stabilised images on the retina *Scientific American* **204**(6) 72–8

PRITCHATT, D. (1968) An investigation into some underlying associative verbal processes of the Stroop colour effect *Quarterly Journal of Experimental Psychology* **20** 351–9

PULLUM, G. K. (1989) The great Eskimo vocabulary hoax *Natural Language and Linguistic Theory* **7** 275–81

PUSHKIN, L. & VENESS, T. (1973) The development of racial awareness and prejudice in children In: P. Watson (ed.) *Psychology and Race* Harmondsworth: Penguin

PUTHOFF, H. E. & TARG, R. (1981) Rebuttal of criticisms of remote viewing experiments *Nature* **292** 388

PYE, D. (1980) Adaptiveness of echolocation signals in bats: flexibility in behaviour and in evolution *Trends in Neurology* **3** 232–5

QUAADE, F. (1971) Sponatanprognosen ved adipositas; den intestinale-shunt-operations rationale og indikation *Nordic Medicine* **85** 733 Cited in Blundell, J. (1975) *Physiological Psychology* London: Methuen

QUATTRONE, G. A. & JONES, E. E. (1980) The perception of variability within in-groups and out-groups: implications for the law of small numbers *Journal of Personality and Social Psychology* **38** 141–52

RABBIE, J. M. & HORWITZ, M. (1988) Categories versus groups as explanatory concepts in intergroup relations *European Journal of Social Psychology* **18** 117–23

RÄBER, H. (1948) Analyse des Balzverhaltens eines domestizierten Truthahns *Behaviour* **1** 237–66

RADIN, D. I. (1997) *The Conscious Universe: the Scientific Truth of Psychic Phenomena* New York: HarperEdge

RADIN, D. I. & FERRARI, D. C. (1991) Effects of consciousness on the fall of dice: a meta-analysis *Journal of Scientific Exploration* **5** 61–84

RAMM, P. (1979) The locus coeruleus, catecholamines and REM sleep: a critical review *Behavioural and Neural Biology* **25** 415–18

RAMSEY, A. O. & HESS, E. (1954) A laboratory approach to the study of imprinting *Wilson Bulletin* **66** 196–206

RAMSAY, R. W. (1977) Behavioural approaches to bereavement *Behavioural Research and Therapy* **15** 131–5

RANDI, J. (1982) *Flim-flam: Psychics, ESP, Unicorns and other Delusions* New York: Prometheus Books

RASMUSSEN, T. & MILNER, B. (1977) The role of early left–brain injury in determining lateralisation of cerebral speech functions *Annals of the New York Academy of Sciences* **299** 355–69

RAUGH, M. R. & ATKINSON, R. C. (1975) A mnemonic method for learning a second language vocabulary *Journal of Educational Psychology* **67** 1–16

RAWLINSON, G. E. (1975) How do we recognise words? *New Behaviour* **2** 336–8

REASON, J. T. (1979) Actions not as planned: the price of automatisation In: . Underwood & R. Stevens (eds) *Aspects of Consciousness I* London: Academic Press

REASON, J. T. (1984) Absentmindedness and cognitive control In: J. E. Harris and P. E. Morris *Everyday Memory, Actions and Absentmindedness* London: Academic Press

RECHTSCHAFFEN, A., GILLILAND, M. A., BERGMAN, B. M. & WINTER, J. B. (1983) Physiological correlates of prolonged sleep-deprivation in rats *Science* **221** 182–4

REES, W. D. & LUTKINS, S. G. (1967) Mortality of bereavement *British Medical Journal* **4** 13

REEVES, A. G. & PLUM, F. (1969) Hyperphagia, rage and dementia accompanying a ventro-medial hypothalamic neoplasm *Archives of Neurology* **20** 616–24

REHM, J., LILLI, W. & VAN EIMEREN, B. (1988) Reduced intergroup differentiation as a result of self categorization in overlapping categories: a quasi experiment *European Journal of Social Psychology* **18** 375–9

REICH, B. & ADCOCK, C. (1976) *Values, Attitudes and Behaviour Change* London: Methuen

REICHER, S. D. (1984) The St. Pauls' riot: An explanation of the limits of crowd action in terms of a social identity model *European Journal of Social Psychology* **14** 1–21

REITMAN, J. S. (1974) Without surreptitious rehearsal: information in short-term memory decays *Journal of Verbal Learning and Verbal Behaviour* **13** 365–77

RESCORLA, R. A. (1968) Probability of shock in the presence and absence of the CS in fear conditioning *Journal of Comparative and Physiological Psychology* **66** 1–5

RESCORLA, R. A. (1972) Informational variables in Pavlovian conditioning In: G. H. Bower (ed.) *Psychology of Learning and Motivation* **6** New York: Academic Press

RESCORLA, R. A. & SOLOMON, R. L. (1967) Two-process learning theory: relations between Pavlovian conditioning and instrumental learning *Psychological Review* **74** 151–82

REYNOLDS, P. D. (1982) Moral judgements: strategies for analysis with application to covert participant observation In: M. Bulmer (ed.) *Social Research Ethics* London: Macmillan

REYNOLDS, V. (1963) Behaviour and social organisation of forest chimpanzees *Folia Primatologica* **1** 95–102

RHINE, J. B. (1937) *New Frontiers of the Mind* New York: Farrar & Rhinehart

RHINE, L. E. & RHINE, J. B. (1943) The psychokinetic effect: the first experiment *Journal of Parapsychology* **7** 20–43

RICHARDS, D. G. (1986) Dolphin vocal mimicry and vocal object labelling In: R. T. J. Schusterman, J. A. Thomas & F. G. Wood (eds) *Dolphin Cognition and Behaviour: A Comparative Approach* Hillsdale, N.J.: Lawrence Erlbaum

RICHARDSON, J. T. E. (1984) Developing the theory of working memory *Memory and Cognition* **12** 71–83

RICHARDSON, J. T. L. (1989) Knowledge representation In A. M. Colman & J. G. Beaumont (eds) *Psychology Survey* 7 London: BPS/Routledge

RIESS, B. F. (1950) The isolation of factors of learning and native behaviour in field and laboratory studies *Annals of the New York Academy of Science* **51** 1093–102

ROBINSON, S. R. (1980) Anti-predator behaviour and predator recognition in Beldings ground squirrels *Animal Behaviour* **28** 840–952

ROE, A. (1945) The adult adjustment of children of alcoholic parents raised in foster homes *Quarterly Journal of Studies on Alcohol* **5** 12–15

ROETHLISBERGER, F. J. & DICKSON, W. G. (1939) *Management and the Worker* Cambridge, Mass.: Harvard University Press

ROGERS, C. A. & FRANTZ, C. (1962) *Racial Themes in Southern Rhodesia* New Haven: Yale University Press

ROGERS, C. R. (1951) *Client-centred Therapy* London: Constable

ROGERS, C. R. (1957) The necessary and sufficient conditions of therapeutic personality change *Journal of Consulting Psychology* **21** 95

ROGERS, C. R. (1961) *On Becoming a Person: a Therapists View of Psychotherapy* London: Constable

ROGERS, C. R. (1970) *Carl Rogers on Encounter Groups* New York: Harper and Row

ROKEACH, M. (1948) Generalised mental rigidity as a factor in ethnocentrism *Journal of Abnormal and Social Psychology* **43** 254–78

ROKEACH, M. (1960) *The Open and Closed Mind* New York: Basic Books

ROKEACH, M. (1973) *The Nature of Human Values* New York: Free Press

ROSCH, E. H. (1973) Natural categories *Cognitive Psychology* **4** 328–50

ROSCH, E. H. (1974) Linguistic relativity In: F. Silverstein (ed.) *Human Communication: Theoretical Perspectives* Hillsdale N. J.: Erlbaum

ROSCH, E. H. (1975) Cognitive reference points *Cognitive Psychology* **7** 532–47

ROSCH, E. H., MERVIS, C. B., GRAY, W. D., JOHNSON, D. M. & BOYES BRAEM, P. (1976) Basic objects in natural categories *Cognitive Psychology* **8** 382–439

ROSE, S. (1983) *Biology, Ideology and Human Nature* Address delivered to the Annual General Meeting of the Association of the Teaching of Psychology, London 1983

ROSE, S. & SERAFICA, F. C. (1986) Keeping and ending casual, close and best friendships *Journal of Social and Personal Relationships* **3** 275–88

ROSE, S., KAMIN, L. J. & LEWONTIN, R. C. (1984) *Not in our Genes: Biology, Ideology and Human Nature* Harmondsworth: Penguin

ROSE, S. A. & BLANK, M. (1974) The potency of context in children's cognition: an illustration through conservation *Child Development* **45** 499–502

ROSEN, B. C. & D'ANDRADE, R. (1959) The psychosocial origins of achievement motivation *Sociometry* **22** 185–218

ROSENBERG, M. J. & HOVLAND, C. I. (1960) Cognitive, affective and behavioural components of attitudes In: C. I. Hovland & M. J. Rosenberg (eds) *Attitude Organisation and Change* New Haven, CT: Yale University Press

ROSENBERG, M. J., NELSON, C. & VIVEKANATHAN, P. S. (1968) A multidimensional approach to the structure of personality impression *Journal of Personality and Social Psychology* **9** 283–94

ROSENBLATT, J. S. & LEHRMAN, D. S. (1963) Maternal behaviour of the laboratory rat In: H. L. Rheingold (ed.) *Maternal Behaviour in Mammals* New York: Wiley

ROSENHAN, D. L. (1973) On being sane in insane places *Science* **179** 250–8

ROSENHAN, D. L. (1975) The contextual nature of psychiatric diagnosis *Journal of Abnormal Psychology* **84** 462–74

ROSENHAN, D. L. & SELIGMAN, M. E. (1984) *Abnormal Psychology* New York: W. W. Norton & Co.

ROSENMAN, R. H., BRAND, R. J., JENKINS, C. D., FRIEDMAN, M., STRAUS, R. & WURM, M. (1975) Coronary heart disease in the Western collaborative group study: final follow-up experience at $8\frac{1}{2}$ years *Journal of the American Medical Association* **233** 872–7

ROSENTHAL, R. & FODE, K.L. (1963) The effect of experimenter bias on the performance of the albino rat *Behavioural Science* **8** 183–9

ROSENTHAL, R. & JACOBSEN, L. (1968) *Pygmalian in the Classroom: Teacher Expectations and Pupil Intellectual Development* New York: Holt, Rinehart & Winston

ROSENZWEIG, S. (1954) A transvaluation of psychotherapy: a reply to Hans Eysenck *Journal of Abnormal and Social Psychology* **49** 298–304

ROSNOW, R. L. (1968) One-sided vs two-sided communication under indirect awareness of persuasive content *Public Opinion Quarterly* **1968** 95–101

ROSS, H. S. & KILLEY, J. C. (1977) The effect of questioning on retention *Child Development* **48** 312–14

ROSS, L., AMABILE, T. & STEINMETZ, J. (1977) Social rules, social control, and biases in social perception processes *Journal of Personality and Social Psychology* 35 485–94

ROSS, L., LEPPER, M. & HUBBARD, M. (1975) Perseverence in self-perception and social perception: biased attributional processes in the debriefing paradigm *Journal of Personality and Social Psychology* **32** 880–92

ROSS, S., SAWIN, P. B., ZARROW, M. X. & DENENBERG, V. H. (1963) Maternal behaviour in the rabbit In: H. L. Rheingold (ed.) *Maternal Behaviour in Mammals* New York: Wiley

ROTTER, J. B. (1966) Generalised expectancies for internal vs external control of reinforcement *Psychological Monographs* **80**(1)

ROWELL, T. (1972) *The Social Behaviour of Monkeys* Harmondsworth: Penguin

RUBIN, K. H., FEIN, G. G. & VANDENBERG, B. (1983) Play In: E, M, Hetherington (ed.) *Handbook of Child Psychology IV: Socialisation, Personality and Social Development* New York: Wiley

RUBIN, Z. (1973) *Liking and Loving: an Invitation to Social Psychology* New York: Holt, Rinehart & Winston

RUMBAUGH, D. M. (1977) *Language Learning by a Chimpanzee: the Lana Project* New York: Academic Press

RUMELHART, D. E. (1980) Schemata: the building blocks of cognition In: R. J. Spiro *et al.* (eds) *Theoretical Issues in Reading Comprehension* Hillsdale, N. J.: Erlbaum

RUMELHART, D. E. & NORMAN, D. A. (1982) Simulating a skilled typist: a study of skilled cognitive-motor performance *Cognitive Science* **6** 1–36

RUMELHART, D. E. & NORMAN, D. A. (1983) Representation in memory *Center for Human Information Processsing Technical Report No. 116* La Jolla, Calif.: University of California

RUPPENTHAL, G. C., ARLING, G. L., HARLOW, H. F., SACKETT, G. P. & SUOMI, S. J. (1976) A 10-year perspective of mother-less monkey behaviour *Journal of Abnormal Psychology* **85** 341–9

RUSBULT, C. E. (1987) Responses to dissatisfaction in close relationships: the Exit-Voice-Loyalty-Neglect model In: D. Perlman & S. Duck (eds) *Intimate Relationships: Development, Dynamics and Deterioration* Beverley Hills, Ca.: Sage

RUTTER, M. (1979) Maternal deprivation 1972–1978: new findings, new concepts, new approaches *Child Development* **50** 283–305

RUTTER, M. (1981) *Maternal Deprivation Reassessed* (2nd ed.) Harmondsworth: Penguin

SAARINEN, T. F. (1973) The use of projective techniques in geographic research In: W. H. Ittelson (ed.) *Environment and Cognition* New York: Seminar Press

SACHDEV, I. & BOURHIS, R. Y. (1987) Status differentials and intergroup behaviour *European Journal of Social Psychology* **17** 277–93

SACKS, O. (1985) *The Man who mistook his Wife for a Hat* London: Picador

SAEGERT, S., SWAP, W. & ZAJONC, R. B. (1973) Exposure, contact and interpersonal attraction *Journal of Personality and Social Psychology* **25** 234–42

SAGAR, H. A. & SCHOFIELD, J. W. (1980) Racial and behavioural cues in black and white children's perceptions of ambiguously aggressive acts *Journal of Personality and Social Psychology* **39** 590–8

SANDFORD, R. N. (1936) The effects of abstinence from food on imaginal processes *Journal of Psychology* **2** 129–36

SAPIR, E. (1947) *Selected Writings in Language, Culture and Personality* Los Angeles: University of California Press

SARBIN, T. R. (1967) On the futility of the proposition that some people be labelled 'mentally ill' *Journal of Consulting Psychology* **31** 447–53

SARBIN, T. R. & SLAGLE, R. W. (1972) Hypnosis and psychophysiological outcomes In: E. Fromm & R. E. Shor (eds) *Hypnosis: Research, Developments and Perspectives* Chicago: Aldine-Atherton

SAVAGE–RUMBAUGH, E. S., RUMBAUGH, D. M., & BOYSEN, S. L. (1978) Symbolic communication between two chimpanzees (*Pan troglodytes*) *Science* **201** 641–4

SAVAGE–RUMBAUGH, E. S., RUMBAUGH, D. M., SMITH, S. T. & LAWSON, J. (1980) Reference: the linguistic essential *Science* **210** 922–5

SAVAGE–RUMBAUGH, E. S., PATE, J. L., LAWSON, J., SMITH, T. & ROSENBAUM, S. (1983) Can a chimpanzee make a statement? *Journal of Experimental Psychology: General* **112** 457–92

SCARBOROUGH, E. & FURUMOTO, L. (1987) *Untold Lives: the First Generation of American Women Psychologists* New York: Columbia University Press

SCHACHTER, S. (1964) The interaction of cognitive and physiological determinants of emotional state In: Advances in *Experimental Social Psychology vol 1* New York: Academic Press

SCHACHTER, S. (1971) Some extraordinary facts about obese humans and rats *American Psychologist* **26** 129–44

SCHACHTER, S. & SINGER, J. E. (1962) Cognitive, social and physiological determinants of emotional states *Psychological Review* **69** 379–99

SCHAFFER, H. R. & EMERSON, P. E. (1964) The development of social attachments in infancy *Monographs of Social Research in Child Development* **29** no. 94

SCHALLER, G. B. (1963) *The Mountain Gorilla* Chicago: University of Chicago Press

SCHANK, R. & ABELSON, R. (1977) *Scripts, Plans, Goals and Understanding: an Enquiry into Human Knowledge* Hillsdale, N. J.: Erlbaum

SCHANK, R. C. (1975) The role of memory in language processing In C. N. Cofer (ed.) *The Structure of Human Memory* San Francisco: Freeman

SCHATZMAN, M. (1992) Freud: who seduced whom? *New Scientist* 21st March 1992

SCHATZMANN, M., WORSLEY, A. & FENWICK, P. (1988) Correspondence during lucid dreams between dreamed and actual events In: J. L. Gackenbach and S. LaBerge (eds) *Conscious Mind, Sleeping Brain: Perspectives on Lucid Dreaming* New York: Plenum

SCHECHTER, E. I. (1984) Hypnotic induction vs. control conditions: illustrating an approach to the evaluation of replicability in parapsychology *Journal of the American Society for Psychical Research* **78** 1–27

SCHEIBE, K. E., SHAVER, P. R. & CARRIER, S. C. (1967) Color association values and response interference on variants of the Stroop test *Acta Psychologica* **26** 286–95

SCHJELDERUPPE-EBBE, T. (1922) Beiträge zur Sozialpsychologie des Haushuhns *Zeitschrift für Psychologie* **88** 225–52

SCHLECHTER, E. I. (1984) Hypnotic induction vs control conditions: illustrating an approach to the evaluation of replicability in parapsychology *Journal of the American Society for Psychical Research* **78** 1–27

SCHLITZ, M. J. & HONORTON, C. (1992) Ganzfeld psi performance within an artistically gifted population *Journal of the American Society for Psychical Research* **86** 83–98

SCHMIDT, H. O. & FONDA, C. (1956) The reliability of psychiatric diagnosis *Journal of Abnormal and Social Psychology* **52** 262–7

SCHMEIDLER, G. R. (1943) Predicting good and bad scores in a clairvoyance experiment: a preliminary report *Journal of the American Society for Psychical Research* **37** 103–10

SCHMEIDLER, G. R. (1945) Separating the sheep from the goats *Journal of the American Society for Psychical Research* **39** 47–50

SCHMEIDLER, G. R. (1997) Psi-conducive experimenters and psi-permissive ones *European Journal of Parapsychology* **13** 83–94

SCHNEIDER, J. W. & HACKER, S. L. (1973) Sex role imagery and use of the generic 'man' in introductory texts: a case in the sociology of sociology *American Sociologist* **8** 12–18

SCHNEIRLA, T. C., ROSENBLATT, J. S. & TOBACH, E. (1963) Maternal behaviour in the cat In: H. L. Rheingold (ed.) *Maternal Behaviour in Mammals* New York: Wiley

SCHULTZ, M. (1975) The semantic derogation of woman in B. Thorne & N. Henley (eds) *Language and Sex: Difference and Dominance* Rowley, Mass.: Newbury House

SCHWARTZ, A. CAMPOS, J. & BAISEL, E. (1973) The visual cliff: cardiac and behavioural correlates on the deep and shallow sides at five and nine months of age *Journal of Experimental Child Psychology* **15** 86–99

SCHWARTZ, B. & GAMZU, E. (1977) Pavlovian control of operant behaviour In: W. K. Honig & J. E. R. Staddon (eds) *Handbook of Operant Behaviour* Englewood Cliffs, N. J.: Prentice Hall

SCLAFANI, A. & SPRINGER, D. (1976) Dietary obesity in adult rats: similarities to hypothalamic and human obesity syndromes *Physiology and Behaviour* **17** 461–71

SCOTT, J. P. (1958) Critical periods in the development of social behaviour in puppies *Psychosomatic Medicine* **20** 42–54

SEARS, R. R., MACCOBY, E. E. & LEVIN, H. (1957) *Patterns of Child Rearing* Evanston, Ill.: Row, Peterson

SEGAL, M. W. (1974) Alphabet and attraction: an unobtrusive measure of the effect of propinquity in a field setting *Journal of Personality and Social Psychology* **33** 517–20

SELFRIDGE, O. G. (1959) Pandemonium: a paradigm for learning In: *The Mechanisation of Thought Processes 1* London: HMSO

SELIGMAN, M. E. P. (1970) On the generality of the laws of learning *Psychological Review* **77** 406–18

SELIGMAN, M. E. P. (1971) Phobias and preparedness *Behaviour Therapy* **2** 307–20

SELIGMAN, M. E. P. (1975) *Helplessness: on Depression, Development and Death* San Francisco: Freeman

SELIGMAN, M. E. P. & MAIER, S. F. (1967) Failure to escape traumatic shock *Journal of Experimental Psychology* **74** 1–9

SELLTIZ, C., EDRICH, H. & COOK, S. W. (1965) Ratings of favourableness about a social group as an indication of attitudes towards the group *Journal of Personality and Social Psychology* **2** 408–415

SELMAN, R. L. (1980) *The Growth of Interpersonal Understanding: Developmental and Clinical Analyses* New York: Academic Press

SELYE, H. (1956) *The Stress of Life* New York: McGraw-Hill

SEUREN, P. (1976) Paper delivered at the VI Congress of the International Primatological Society, Cambridge, UK, 1976, reported in 'Monitor', in: G. Ferry (ed.) *The Understanding of Animals* Oxford: Basil Blackwell

SEYFARTH, D. M. & CHEYNEY, D. L. (1980) The ontogeny of vervet monkey alarm calling behaviour: a preliminary report *Zeitschrift für Tierpsychologie* **54** 37–56

SEYFARTH, D. M. & CHEYNEY, D. L. (1982) How monkeys see the world: a review of recent research on East African vervet monkeys In: C. T. Snowdon, G. H. Brown & M. R. Petersen (eds) *Primate Communication* London: Cambridge University Press

SHAFFER, L. H. (1975) Multiple attention in continuous verbal tasks In: P. M. A. Rabbitt & S. Dormi (eds) *Attention and Performance 5* London: Academic Press

SHALLICE. T. & WARRINGTON, E. K. (1970) Independent functioning of verbal memory stores: a neuropsychological study *Quarterly Journal of Experimental Psychology* **22** 261–73

SHALLICE, T. & WARRINGTON, E. K. (1980) Single and multiple component central dyslexic syndromes In: Coltheart *et al.* (ed.) *Deep Dyslexia* London: Routledge & Kegan Paul

SHANAB, M. E. & YAHYA, K. A. (1977) A behavioural study of obedience in children *Journal of Personality and Social Psychology* **35** 530–36

SHANON, B. (1980) Lateralisation effects in musical decision tasks *Neuropsychologia* **18** 21–31

SHAPIRO, K. L., JACOBS, W. J. & LOLORDO, V. M. (1980) Stimulus-reinforcer interactions in Pavlovian conditioning of pigeons: implications for selective associations *Animal Learning and Behaviour* **8** 586–94

SHATZ, M. (1978) Conceptualisation and awareness in Piaget's theory and its relevance to the child's conception of language In: A. Sinclair, R. J. Jarvella and W. J. M. Levett (eds) *The Child's Conception of Language* Berlin: Springer

SHAVER, P. & HAZAN, C. (1985) Incompatibility, loneliness and 'limerence' In: W. Ickes (ed.) *Compatible and Incompatible Relationships* New York: Springer Verlag

SHAVER, P., FURMAN, W. & BURMESTER, D. (1985) Aspects of a life transition: network changes, social skills and loneliness In: S. Duck & D. Perlman (eds) *Understanding Personal Relationships Research: an Interdisciplinary Approach* London: Sage

SHAYER, M. & ADEY, P. (1981) *Towards a Science of Science Teaching* London: Heinemann

SHEA, B. C. & PEARSON, J. C. (1986) The effects of relationship type, partner intent and gender on the selection of relationship maintenance strategies *Communication Monographs* **53** 352–64

SHEEHY, G. (1976) *Passages: Predictable Crises of Adult Life* New York: Dutton

SHELDON, W. (1942) *The Varieties of Temperament: a Psychology of Consititutional Differences* New York: Harper

SHELDON, W. H. (1954) *Atlas of Men: a Guide for Somatotyping the Human Male at all Ages* New York: Harper & Row

SHERIDAN, C. L. & KING, K. G. (1972) Obedience to authority with an authentic victim *Proceeedings of the 80th Annual Convention of the American Psychological Association* **7** 165–6

SHERIF, M. (1935) A study of some social factors in perception *Archives of Psychology* **27** no. 187

SHERIF, M. (1936) *The Psychology of Social Norms* New York: Harper and Row

SHERIF, M. & HOVLAND, C. I. (1961) *Social Judgement: Assimilation and Contrast in Communication and Attitude Change* New Haven: Yale University Press

SHERIF, M., HARVEY, O. J., WHITE, B. J., HOOD, W. R. & SHERIF, C. W. (1961) *Intergroup Conflict and Co-operation: The Robbers Cave Experiment* Norman, Ok.: University of Oklahoma Press

SHERRARD, C. (1997) Repertoires in discourse: social identification and aesthetic taste In: N. J. Hayes (ed.) *Doing Qualitative Analysis in Psychology* Hove: Psychology Press

SHIELDS, J. (1962) *Monozygotic Twins Brought Up Apart and Brought Together* London: Oxford University Press

SHIFFRIN, R. M. & SCHNEIDER, W. (1977) Controlled and automatic human information processing II: perceptual learning, automatic attending and a general theory *Psychological Review* **84** 127–90

SHOBEN, E. J. WESCOURT, K. T. & SMITH, E. E. (1978) Sentence verification, sentence recognition, and the semantic/episodic distinction *Journal of Experimental Psychology: Human Learning and Memory* **4** 304–17

SHUTTLEWORTH, E. C. JR., SYRING, V. & ALLEN, N. (1982) Further observations on the nature of prosopagnosia *Brain and Cognition* **1** 307–22

SIDDIQUE, C. M. & D'ARCY, C. (1984) Adolescence, stress and psychological well-being *Journal of Youth and Adolescence* **13** 459–74

SIEGEL, M. & STOREY, R. M. (1985) Daycare and children's conceptions of moral and social rules *Child Development* **56** 1001–8

SIGALL, H. (1970) The effects of competence and consensual validation on a communicator's liking for the audience *Journal of Personality and Social Psychology* **16** 251–8

SIGALL, H. & OSTROVE, N. (1975) Beautiful but dangerous: effects of offender attractiveness and nature of the crime on juridic judgement *Journal of Personality and Social Psychology* **31** 410–14

SIGAUD, O. (1997) *From Reflexes to Intentionality: the Role of Anticipation* Paper delivered at the meeting of the European Society for the Study of Cognitive Systems, June 1997, Freiburg-im-Breisgau

SIGMAN, M., MUNDY, P. SHERMAN, T. & UNGERER, J. A. (1986) Social interaction of autistic, mentally retarded and normal children and their caregivers *Journal of Child Psychology and Psychiatry* **27** 647–55

SILVERMAN, I. (1977) *The Human Subject in the Psychological Laboratory* New York: Pergamon

SILVERMAN, I. & SHULMAN, A. D. (1970) A conceptual model of artifact in attitude change studies *Sociometry* **33** 97–107

SIMON, B. & BROWN, R. (1987) Perceived intragroup homogeneity in minority majority contexts *Journal of Personality and Social Psychology* **53** 703–11

SKINNER, B. F. (1938) *The Behaviour of Organisms* New York: Appleton-Century Crofts

SKINNER, B. F. (1953) *Science and Human Behaviour* New York: Macmillan

SKINNER, B. F. (1957) *Verbal Behaviour* New York: Appleton-Century-Crofts

SKINNER, B. F. (1969) *Contingencies of Reinforcement* New York: Appleton-Century-Crofts

SKINNER, B. F. (1972) *Beyond Freedom and Dignity* Harmondsworth: Penguin

SKODAK, M. & SKEELS, H. M. (1945) A follow-up study of children in adoptive homes *Journal of Genetic Psychology* **66** 21–58

SKODAK, M. & SKEELS, H. M. (1949) A final follow-up study of one hundred adopted children *Journal of Genetic Psychology* **75** 85–125

SLATER, A., ROSE, D. & MORISON, V. (1984) New-born infants' perception of similarities and differences between two- and three-dimensional stimuli *British Journal of Developmental Psychology* **2** 287 94

SLATER, E. & SHIELDS, J. (1969) Genetic aspects of anxiety *British Journal of Psychiatry* **3** 62–71

SLATER, P. J. B. (1981) Chaffinch song repertoires: observations, experiments and a discussion of their significance *Zeitschrift für Tierpsychologie* **56** 1 24

SLATER, P. J. B. (1983) The study of communication In: T. R. Halliday & P. J. B. Slater (eds) *Communication* Oxford: Blackwell

SLOVIC, P. & FISCHOFF, B. (1977) On the psychology of experimental surprises *Journal of Experimental Psychology: Human Perception and Performance* **3** 544–51

SLUCKIN, W. (1964) *Imprinting and Early Learning* London: Methuen

SLUCKIN, W. & SALZEN, E. A. (1961) Imprinting and perceptual learning *Quarterly Journal of Experimental Psychology* **13** 65–77

SMELSER, N. J. (1962) *Theory of Collective Behaviour* New York: Free Press

SMETANA, J. G. (1981) Preschool children's conception of moral and social rules *Child Development* **52** 1333–6

SMETANA, J. G. (1984) Toddlers' social interactions regarding moral and conventional transgressions *Child Development* **55** 1767–76

SMETANA, J. G., KELLY, M. & TWENTYMAN, C. T. (1984) Abused, neglected and nonmaltreated children's conceptions of moral and socio-conventional transgressions *Child Development* **55** 277–87

SMITH, C. & LLOYD, B. (1978) Maternal behaviour and perceived sex of infant revisited *Child Development* **49** 1263–5

SMITH, C. A. & LAZARUS, R. S. (1993) Appraisal components, core relational themes, and the emotions *Cognition and Emotion* **7** 233–69

SMITH, F. (1973) *Psycholinguistics and Reading* New York: Holt, Rinehart & Winston

SMITH, J. A. (1997) Developing theory from case studies: self-reconstruction and the transition to motherhood In: N. J. Hayes (ed.) *Doing Qualitative Analysis in Psychology* Hove: Psychology Press

SMITH, M. B., BRUNER, J. S. & WHITE, R. W. (1956) *Opinions and Personality* New York: Wiley

SMITH, M. B., BROWN, H. O., TOMAN. J. E. P. & GOODMAN, L. S. (1947) The lack of cerebral effects of d-turbocurarine *Anaethesiology* **8** 1–14

SMITH, P. B. (1983) Social influence processes in groups In: J. Nicholson and B. Foss (eds) *Psychology Survey* 4 Leicester: British Psychological Society

SMITH, P. B. & PETERSON, M. F. (1988) *Leaderships, Organisations and Culture* London: Sage

SMITH, P. M. (1985) *Language, the Sexes and Society* Oxford: Blackwell

SMITH, S. D., KIMBERLEY, W. J., PENNINGTON, B. F. & LUBS, H. A. (1983) Specific reading disability: identification of an inherited form through linkage analysis *Science* **219** 1345–7

SNOW, C. (1979) The development of conversation between mothers and babies In: V. Lee (ed.) *Language Development* Milton Keynes: Open University Press

SNYDER, M., TANKE, E. D. & BERSCHEID, E. (1977) Social perception and interpersonal behaviour: on the self-fulfilling nature of personal stereotypes *Journal of Personality and Social Psychology* **35** 656–66

SNYGG, D. (1938) The relation between the intelligence of mothers and of their children living in foster homes *Journal of Genetic Psychology* **52** 401–6

SOLLEY, C. M. & HAIGH, G. (1958) A Note to Santa Claus *TPR The Menninger Foundation* **18**(3) 4–5

SOLOMON, G. F. (1969) Emotions, stress, the CNS and immunity *Annals of the New York Academy of Sciences* **164** 335–43

SOMMERHOFF, G. (1996) Consciousness as an internal integrating system *Journal of Consciousness Studies* **3**(2) 139–57

SONG, M.-J., SMETANA, J. G. & KIM, S. Y. (1987) Korean children's conceptions of moral and conventional transgressions *Developmental Psychology* **23** 577–82

SORENSON, R. C. (1973) *Adolescent Sexuality in Contemporary America: Personal Values and Social Behaviour, Ages Thirteen to Nineteen* New York: World

SPANOS, N. P. (1982) A social psychological approach to hypnotic behaviour In: G. Weary & H. L. Mirels (eds) *Integrations of Clinical and Social Psychology* New York: Oxford University Press

SPANOS, N. P. & HEWITT, E. C. (1980) The hidden observer in hypnotic analgesia: discovery or experimental creation? *Journal of Personality and Social Psychology* **39** 1201–14

SPEARMAN, C. (1904) General intelligence objectively determined and measured *American Journal of Psychology* **15** 201–93

SPEARMAN, C. (1923) *The Nature of 'Intelligence' and the Principles of Cognition* London: Macmillan

SPEARS, R. & MANSTEAD, A. S. (1989) The social context of stereotyping and differentiation *European Journal of Social Psychology* **19** 101–21

SPELKE, E., HIRST W. & NEISSER, U. (1976) Skills of divided attention *Cognition* **4** 215–30

SPENCER, H. (1873) *Principles of Psychology* New York: Appleton

SPENDER, D. (1980) *Man Made Language* London: Routledge & Kegan Paul

SPERRY, R. W. (1961) Cerebral organisation and behaviour *Science* **133** 1749–57

SPIEGEL, D., BLOOM, J.R., KRAEMER, H. C. & GOTTHEIL, E. (1989) Effects of psychosocial treatment on survival of patients with metastatic breast cancer *Lancet* 1989: **2** 888–91

SPIES, G. (1965) Food versus intracranial self-stimulation reinforcement in food-deprived rats *Journal of Comparative and Physiological Psychology* **60** 153–7

SPITZ, R. A. (1945) Hospitalism: an inquiry into the genesis of psychiatric conditions in easly childhood *Psychoanalytic Studies of Childhood* **1** 53–74

SPRECHER, S. (1987) The effects of self disclosure given and received on affection for an intimate partner and stability of the relationship *Journal of Social and Personal Relationships* **4** 115–28

SQUIRE, L. R. (1992) Declarative and nondeclarative memory: multiple brain systems supporting learning and memory *Journal of Cognitive Neuroscience* **4** 232–43

SROLE, L., LANGER, T. S., MICHAEL, S. T., OPLER, M. K. & RENNIE. T. A. (1962) *Mental Health in the Metropolis: the Midtown Manhattan Study* New York: McGraw-Hill

STANG, D. J. (1973) Effects of interaction rate on ratings of leadership and liking *Journal of Personality and Social Psychology* **27** 405–408

STANLEY, J. (1973) Paradigmatic woman: the prostitute Paper presented to Linguistic Society of America

Conference, 1973, cited in D. Spender *Man Made Language* London: Routledge & Kegan Paul

STERN, D. (1977) *The First Relationship: Infant and Mother* London: Fontana

STERN, E., PARMELEE, A. H. & HARRIS, M. A. (1973) Sleep state periodicity in prematures and young infants *Developmental Psychobiology* **6** 357–65

STERN, W. C. & MORGANE, P. J. (1974) Theoretical view of REM sleep function: maintenance of catecholamine systems in the central nervous system *Behavioural Biology* **11** 1–32

STERNBERG, R. J. (1977) *Intelligence, Information-processing and Analogical Reasoning: the Componential Analysis of Human Abilities* Hillsdale, N.J.: Lawrence Erlbaum

STERNBERG, R.J. (1985) *Beyond IQ: a Triarchic Theory of Human Intelligence* Cambridge: Cambridge University Press

STERNBERG, R. J. (1987) *The Triangle of Love* New York: Basic Books

STERNBERG, S. (1966) High speed scanning in human memory *Science* **153** 652–4

STODGILL, R. M. & COONS, A. E. (eds) (1957) *Leader Behaviour: its Description and Measurement* Columbus, Oh.: Ohio State University

STONER, J. A. F. (1961) *A Comparison of Individual and Group Decisions involving Risk* Masters thesis, MIT School of Industrial Management (unpub.)

STORMS, M. D. (1973) Videotape and the attribution process: reversing actors' and observers' points of view *Journal of Personality and Social Psychology* **27** 165–75

STRACK, F., SCHWARTZ, N. & GSCHNEIDINGER, E. (1985) Happiness and reminiscing: the role of time perspective, affect, and mode of thinking *Journal of Personality and Social Psychology* **49** 1460–9

STRACK, F., SCHWARTZ, N. CHASSEIN, B., KERN, D. & WAGNER, D. (1990) Salience of comparison standards and the activation of social norms: Consequences for judgements of happiness and their communication *British Journal of Social Psychology* **54** 303–14

STRATTON, P. M. (1983) Biological preprogramming of infant behaviour *Journal of Child Psychology and Psychiatry* **24**(2) 301–9

STRATTON, P. M. (1997) Attributional coding of interview data: meeting the needs of long-haul passengers In: N. J. Hayes (ed.) *Doing Qualitative Analysis in Psychology* Hove: Psychology Press

STRATTON, P. M. & SWAFFER, R. (1988) Maternal causal beliefs for abused and handicapped children *Journal of Reproductive and Infant Psychology* **6** 201–16

STRATTON, P. M., HEARD, D., HANKS, H., MUNTON, A., BREWIN, C. R. & DAVIDSON, C. R. (1986) Coding causal beliefs in natural discourse *British Journal of Social Psychology* **25** 299–313

STRATTON, P. M., MUNTON, A. G., HANKS, H., HEARD, D., BREWIN, C. & DAVIDSON, C. (1988) *The Leeds Attributional Coding System Manual* Leeds: LFTRC

STRAUSS, J. & CARPENTER, W. (1981) *Schizophrenia* New York: Plenum Press

STROH, C. M. (1971) *Vigilance: the Problem of Sustained Attention* Oxford: Pergamon

STROOP, J. R. (1935) Studies of interference in serial verbal reactions *Journal of Experimental Psychology* **18** 643–62

SUGARMAN, L. (1986) *Life-span Development: Concepts, Theories and Interventions* London: Methuen

SULLIVAN, L. (1976) Selective attention and secondary message analysis: a reconsideration of Broadbent's filter model of selective attention *Quarterly Journal of Experimental Psychology* **28** 167–78

SUOMI, S. J., COLLINS, M. L. & HARLOW, H. F. (1973) Effects of permanent separation from mother on infant monkeys *Developmental Psychology* **9** 376–84

SUPER, C. (1976) Environmental effects on motor development: the case of 'African infant precocity' *Developmental Medicine and Child Neurology* **18** 561–7

SWENSON, C. H., ESKEW, R. W. & KOLHEFF, K. A. (1981) Stages of family life cycle, ego development and the marriage relationship *Journal of Marriage and the Family* **43** 841–53

SZASZ, T. S. (1961) *The Myth of Mental Illness* New York: Dell

TADDONIO, J. L. (1976) The relationship of experimenter expectancy to performance on ESP tasks *Journal of Parapsychology* **40** 107–14

TAJFEL, H. (1969) Cognitive aspects of prejudice *Journal of Social Issues* **25** 79–97

TAJFEL, H. (1972) Some developments in European Social Psychology *European Journal of Social Psychology* **2** 307–22

TAJFEL, H. (1981) *Human Groups and Social Categories: Studies in Social Psychology* Cambridge: Cambridge University Press

TAJFEL, H. & JAHODA, G. (1966) Development in children of concepts and attitudes about their own and other countries: a cross-national study *Proceedings of the XVIII International Congress of Psychology* Moscow Symposium **36** 17–33

TAJFEL, H. & TURNER, J. C. (1979) An Integrative Theory of Intergroup Conflict In: W.G. Austin & S. Worchel (eds) *The Social Psychology of Intergroup Relations* Monterey, Cal.: Brooks/Cole

TAJFEL, H. & WILKES, A. L. (1963) Classification and quantitative judgement *British Journal of Psychology* **54** 101–14

TAJFEL, H., BILLIG, M.G., BUNDY, R.P. & FLAMENT, C. (1971) Social categorization and intergroup behaviour *European Journal of Social Psychology* **1** 149–78

TALLAND, G. A. (1968) *Disorders of Memory and Learning* Harmondsworth: Penguin

TARG, R. & KATRA, J. (1997) Psi-Conducive Protocols *European Journal of Parapsychology* **13** 95

TARG, R. & PUTHOFF, H. E. (1974) Information transmission under conditions of sensory shielding *Nature* **251** 602–7

TART, C. T., PUTHOFF, H. E. & TARG, R. (1980) Information transmission in remote viewing experiments (letter) *Nature* **284** 191

TAYLOR, S. E., FISKE, S. T., ETCOFF, N. L. & RUDERMAN, A. J. (1978) The categorical and contextual bases of personal memory and stereotyping *Journal of Personality and Social Psychology* **36** 778–93

TEGER, A. I. (1979) *Too Much Invested to Quit. The Psychology of the Escalation of Conflict* New York: Pergamon

TENNOV, D. (1979) *Love and Limerence: the Experience of being in Love* Lanham, MD: Madison Books

TERMAN, L. M. (1916) *The Measurement of Intelligence* Boston: Houghton Mifflin

TERMAN, L. M. & MERRILL, M. (1937) *Measuring Intelligence: a Guide to the Administration of the New Revised Stanford Binet Tests of Intelligence* Boston: Houghton-Mifflin

TERRACE, H. S. (1979) *Nim* New York: Knopf

TERRACE, H. S., PETITTO, L. A., SANDERS, D. L. & BEVER, T. G. (1979) Can an ape create a sentence? *Science* **206** 891–902

THIBAUT, J.W. & KELLEY, H. H. (1959) *The Social Psychology of Groups* New York: Wiley

THOMAS, M. H., HORTON, R. W., LIPPINCOTT, E. C. & DRABMAN, R. S. (1977) Desensitisation of portrayals of real-life aggression as a function of exposure to television violence *Journal of Personality and Social Psychology* **35** 450–8

THOMPSON, C. P. & COWAN, T. (1986) Flashbulb memories: a nicer interpretation of a Neisser recollection *Cognition* **22** 199–200

THORNDIKE, E. L. (1911) *Animal Intelligence: Experimental Studies* New York: Macmillan

THORPE, W. H. (1961) *Bird-song* London: Cambridge University Press

THOULESS, C. R. & GUINNESS, F. E. (1986) Conflict between red deer hids: the winner always wins *Animal Behaviour* **34** 1166–71

THOULESS, R. H. (1974) *Straight and Crooked Thinking* (3rd ed.) London: Pan paperbacks

THURSTONE, L. L. (1928) Attitudes can be measured *American Journal of Sociology* **33** 529–54

THURSTONE, L. L. (1938) *Primary Mental Abilities* Chicago, Ill.: The University of Chicago Press

TIMBERLAKE, W. & ALLISON, J. (1974) Response deprivation: an empirical approach to instrumental performance *Psychological Review* **81** 146–64

TINBERGEN, N. (1951) *The Study of Instinct* Oxford: Oxford University Press

TINBERGEN, N. (1963) On the aims and methods of ethology *Zeitschrift für Tierpsychologie* **20** 410–33

TIZARD, B. & HODGES, J. (1978) The effect of early institutional rearing on the development of eight-year-old children *Journal of Child Psychology and Psychiatry* **19** 99–118

TODER, N. L. & MARCIA, J. E. (1973) Ego-identity status and response to conformity pressure in college women *Journal of Personality and Social Psychology* **26** 287–94

TOLMAN, E. C. (1932) *Purposive Behaviour in Animals and Man* New York: Century

TOLMAN, E. C. (1948) Cognitive maps in rats and men *Psychological Review* **55** 189–208

TREVARTHEN, C. (1969) Communication and co-operation in early infancy: a description of primary intersubjectivity In: M. Bullowa (ed.) *Before Speech: the Beginnings of Interpersonal Communication* Cambridge: Cambridge University Press

TREVOR, S. (1992) *Survival Special: Keepers at the Kingdom* Anglia Productions, first broadcast ITV (UK) 21/8/92

TRIESMAN, A. (1960) Contextual cues in selective listening *Quarterly Journal of Experimental Psychology* **12** 242–8

TRIESMAN, A. (1964) Verbal cues, language and meaning in attention *American Journal of Psychology* **77** 206–14

TRIPLETT, N. (1898) Dynamogenic factors in pacemaking and competition *American Journal of Psychology* **9** 507–33

TROWBRIDGE, M. H. & CASON, H. (1932) An experimental study of Thorndike's theory of learning *Journal of General Psychology* **7** 245–60

TULVING, E. (1972) Episodic and semantic memory In: E. Tulving and W. Donaldson (eds) *Organisation of Memory* New York: Academic Press

TULVING, E. (1983) *Elements of Episodic Memory* New York: Oxford University Press

TULVING, E. (1985) How many memory systems are there? *American Psychologist* **40** 385–98

TULVING, E. & PEARLSTONE, Z. (1966) Availability versus accessibility of information in memory for words *Journal of Verbal Learning and Verbal Behaviour* **5** 381–91

TULVING, E., MANDLER, G. & BAUMAL, R. (1964) Interaction of two sources of information in tachistoscopic word recognition *Canadian Journal of Psychology* **18** 62–71

TURNER, J. C. (1991) *Social Influence* Milton Keynes: Open University Press

TUTTLE, M. D. & RYAN, M. J. (1981) Bat predation and the evolution of frog vocalisations in the neotropics *Science* **214** 677–8

TVERSKY, A. & KAHNEMANN, D. (1973) Availability: a heuristic for judging frequency and probability *Cognitive Psychology* **5** 207–32

TVERSKY, A. & KAHNEMANN, D. (1974) Judgement under uncertainty: heuristics and biases *Science* **185** 1124–31

TVERSKY, A. & KAHNEMANN, D. (1981) The framing of decisions and the psychology of choice *Science* **211** 453–8

TWINING, W. E. (1949) Mental practice and physical practice in learning a motor skill *Research Quarterly* **20** 432–5

TYACK, P. (1981) Interactions between singing hawaiian humpback whales and conspecifics nearby *Behavioural Ecology* **8**(2) 105–16

TYACK, P. (1983) Differential response of humpback whales *Megaptera novaengliae* to playback of song or social sounds *Behavioural Ecology* **13**(1) 49–55

TYERMAN, A. & SPENCER, C. (1983) A critical test of the Sherifs' robbers cave experiments: intergroup competition and cooperation between groups of well-acquainted individuals *Small Group Behaviour* **14** 515–31

TYLER, L. E. (1965) *The Psychology of Human Differences* New York: Appleton Century Crofts

ULLMAN, M., KNIPPER, S. & VAUGHAN, A. (1973) *Dream Telepathy* New York: Macmillan

UNDERWOOD, B.J., BORUCH, R. F. & MALMI, R. A. (1978) Composition of episodic memory *Journal of Experimental Psychology: General* **107** 393–419

UTTS, J. (1991) Replication and meta-analysis in parapsychology *Statistical Science* **6** 363–403

UTTS, J. (1996) An assessment of the evidence for psychic functioning *Journal of Scientific Exploration* **10** 3–30

VAILLANT, G. E. (1977) *Adaptation to Life* Boston: Little, Brown

VALENSTEIN, E. S. (1967) Selection of nutritive and non-nutritive solutions under different conditions of need *Journal of Comparative and Physiological Psychology* **63** 429–33

VALINS, S. & RAY, A. A. (1967) Effects of cognitive desensitisation on avoidance behaviour *Journal of Personality and Social Psychology* **7** 345–50

VAN DIJK, T. A. (1987) *Communicating Racism: Ethnic Prejudice in Thought and Action* Newbury Park, Ca: Sage

VAN TOLLER, S. & DODD, G. H. (1988) *Perfumery: the Psychology and Biology of Fragrance* London: Chapman & Hall

VELLUTINO, F. (1979) *Dyslexia: Theory and Research* Boston Mass.: MIT Press

VERNON, M. D. (1962) *The Psychology of Perception* Harmondsworth: Penguin

VERNON, P. E. (1971) *The Structure of Human Abilities* London: Methuen

VOGEL, G. W. (1975) A review of REM sleep deprivation *Archives of General Psychiatry* **32** 749–61

VOLKOVA, V. D. (1953) On certain characteristics of conditioned reflexes to speech stimuli in children *Fiziologicheskii Zhurnal SSSR* **39** 540–8

VON BEKESEY, G. (1960) *Experiments in Hearing* New York: McGraw-Hill

VON FRISCH, K. (1950) *Bees: their Chemical Senses, Vision and Language* Ithaca, NY: Cornell University Press

VROOM, V. H. (1984) Leadership and decision-making In: *Symposium on Democratisation and Leadership in Industrial Organisations* Osaka, Japan: Osaka University

VROOM. V. H. & JAGO, A. G. (1978) On the validity of the Vroom–Yetton Model *Journal of Applied Psychology* **63** 151–62

VROOM, V. H. & YETTON, P. W. (1978) *Leadership and Decision-making* Pittsburgh: University of Pittsburgh Press

VYGOTSKY, L. S. (1962) *Thought and Language* Cambridge, Mass.: MIT Press

VYGOTSKY, L. S. (1967) Play and its role in the mental development of the child *Soviet Psychology* **12** 62–76

WADDEN, T. & ANDERTON, C. H. (1982) The clinical use of hypnosis *Psychological Bulletin* **91** 215–43

WADDINGTON, D., JONES, K. & CRITCHER, C. (1987) Flashpoints of public disorder In: G. Gaskell, & R. Benewick (eds) *The Crowd in Contemporary Britain* London: Sage

WAGNER, W. ELEJABARRIETA, F. & LAHNSTEINER, I. (1995) How the sperm dominates the ovum – objectification by metaphor in the social representation of conception *European Journal of Social Psychology* **25** 671–88

WAGSTAFF, G. F. (1981) *Hypnosis, Compliance and Belief* Brighton: Harvester

WAGSTAFF, G. F. (1987) Hypnosis In: H. Beloff & A. Coleman (eds) *Psychology Survey 6* Leicester: BPS Books

WALLACE, P. (1977) Individual discrimination of humans by odor *Physiology and behaviour* **19** 577–9

WALLACH, M. A., KOGAN, N. & BEM, D. J. (1962) Group influence on individual risk-taking *Journal of Abnormal and Social Psychology* **65** 75–86

WALLESCH, C. W., HENRIKSEN, L., KORNHUBER, H.-H. & PAULSON, O. B. (1983) Observations on regional cerebral blood flow in cortical and subcortical during language production in normal man *Brain and Language* **25** 224–33

WALSTER, E. (1965) The effects of self–esteem on romantic liking *Journal of Experimental Social Psychology* **1** 184–97

WALSTER, E. & FESTINGER, L. (1962) The effectiveness of 'overheard' persuasive communications *Journal of Abnormal and Social Psychology* **65** 395–402

WALSTER, E. & WALSTER, G.W. (1969) The matching hypothesis *Journal of Personality and Social Psychology* **6** 248–53

WALSTER, E., ARONSON, V. & ABRAHAMS, D. (1966) On increasing the persuasiveness of a low prestige communicator *Journal of Experimental Social Psychology* **2** 325–42

WALSTER, E., WALSTER, G. W. & BERSCHEID, E. (1978) *Equity: Theory and Research* Boston: Allyn & Bacon

WALSTER, E., ARONSON, V., ABRAHAMS, D. & ROTTMAN, L. (1966) Importance of physical attractiveness in dating behaviour *Journal of Personality and Social Psychology* **4** 508–16

WARRINGTON, E. K. & WEISKRANTZ, L. (1973) An analysis of short term and long term memory defects in man In: J. A. Deutsch (ed.) *The Psychological Basis of Memory* New York: Academic Press

WARRINGTON, E. K. & WEISKRANTZ, L. (1982) Amnesia: a disconnection syndrome *Neuropsychologia* **20** 233–48

WASHBURN, S. L. & DEVORE, I. (1961) The social life of baboons *Scientific American* **224**(6) 62–71

WASON, P. & SHAPIRO, D. (1971) Natural and contrived experience in a reasoning problem *Quarterly Journal of Experimental Psychology* **23** 63–71

WASON, P. C. (1966) Reasoning In: B. Foss (ed.) *New Horizons in Psychology* Harmondsworth: Penguin

WASON, P. C. (1968) Reasoning about a rule *The Quarterly Journal of Experimental Psychology* **20** 273–81

WASON, P. C. & JOHNSON-LAIRD, P. N. (1972) *The Psychology of Reasoning: Structure and Content* Cambridge, Mass.: Harvard University Press

WATSON, D. & PENNEBAKER, J. W. (1989) Health complaints, stress and distress: exploring the central role of negative affectivity *Psychological Review* **96** 234–54

WATSON, J. B. (1903) *Animal Education* Chicago: University of Chicago Press

WATSON, J. B. (1913) Psychology from the standpoint of a behaviorist *Psychological Review* **20** 158–77

WATSON, J. B. & RAYNER, R. (1920) Conditioned emotional reactions *Journal of Experimental Psychology* **3** 1–14

WATSON, J. B. & WATSON, R. R. (1928) *Psychological Care of Infant and Child* New York: Norton

WATSON, J. S. & RAMEY, C. T. (1972) Reactions to response-contingent stimulation in early infancy *Merrill-Palmer Quarterly* **18** 220–7

WATSON, O. N. & GRAVES, T. D. (1966) Quantitative research in proxemic behaviour *American Anthropologist* **68** 971–85

WAUGH, N. C. & NORMAN, D. A. (1965) Primary memory *Psychological Review* **72** 84–104

WEBB, W. B. (1974) Sleep as an adaptive response *Perceptual and Motor Skills* **38** 1023–7

WEBB, W. B. (1975) *Sleep the Gentle Tyrant* Englewood Cliffs N.J.: Prentice Hall

WEBER, M. (1921, trs. 1947) *The Theory of Economic and Social Organisation* New York: Free Press

WEIMA, J. (1964) The relationship of personality and non-personality factors to prejudice *Journal of Social Psychology* **63** 129–37

WEINBERG, R. S. GOULD, D. & JACKSON, A. (1979) Expectations and performance: an empirical test of Bandura's self-efficacy theory *Journal of Sport Psychology* **1** 320–31

WEINER, B. (1979) A theory of motivation for some classroom experiences *Journal of Educational Psychology* **71** 3–25

WEINER, B. (1985) An attributional theory of achievement motivation and emotion *Psychological Review* **92** 548–73

WEINER, B., NIERENBERG, R. & GOLDSTEIN, M. (1976) Social learning (locus of control) versus attributional (causal stability) interpretations of expectancy of success *Journal of Personality* **44** 52–68

WEINGARTEN, H. P. (1982) Diet palatability modulates sham feeding in VMH-lesion and normal rats: implications for finickiness and evaluation of sham-feeding data *Journal of Comparative and Physiological Psychology* **96** 223–33

WEISKRANTZ, L. (1980) Varieties of residual experience *Quarterly Journal of Experimental Psychology* **32** 365–86

WEISKRANTZ, L. (1986) *Blindsight: a Case Study and Implications* Oxford: Oxford University Press

WEISKRANTZ, L. (1988) Some contributions of neurophysiological aspects of vision and memory to the problem of consciousness In: A. J. Marcel & E. Bisiach *Consciousness in Contemporary Science* Oxford: Clarendon Press

WEISS, J. M. (1972) Psychological factors in stress and disease *Scientific American* **226**(6) 104–13

WELFORD, A. T. (1958) *Ageing and Human Skill* Oxford: Oxford University Press

WELFORD, A. T. (1976) *Skilled Performance: Perceptual and Motor Skills* Glenview, Ill.: Scott. Foresman & Co.

WELKER, W. I. (1959) Escape, exploratory and food-seeking responses of rats in a novel situation *Journal of Comparative and Physiological Psychology* **52** 106–11

WELLMAN, B. (1985) Domestic work, paid work and network In: S. W. Duck & D. Perlman (eds) *Understanding Personal Relationships Research: an Interdisciplinary Approach* London: Sage

WELLS, G. (1979) Variation in child language In: V. Lee (ed.) *Language Development* London: Croom Helm/Open University

WENNER, A. M. (1964) Sound communication in honeybees *Scientific American* **210** 116–24

WERNICKE, C. (1874) *Der aphasische Symptomenkomplex* Breslau: Cohn und Weigart

WETHERELL, M. & POTTER, J. (1988) Discourse analysis and the identification of interpretative repertoires In: C. Antaki (ed.) *Analysing Everyday Explanation: a Casebook of Methods* London: Sage

WHEELER, R. H. & CUTSFORTH, T. D. (1925) Synaesthesia in the development of the concept *Journal of Experimental Psychology* **8** 149–52

WHITTAKER, E. M. (1982) Dyslexia and the flat earth *Bulletin of the British Psychological Society* **35** 97–9

WHITTY, C. W. M. & ZANGWILL, O. L. (1966) *Amnesia* London: Butterworth

WHORF, B. L. (1956) *Language, Thought and Reality* New York: M.I.T. Press

WICKELGREN, W. A. (1974) *Speed-accuracy Tradeoff and Information Processing Dynamics* Paper presented at the Annual Convention of the Psychonomics Society, 1974

WIESENTHAL, D. L., ENDLER, N. S., COWARD, T.R. & EDWARDS, J. (1976) Reversability of relative competence as a determinant of conformity across different perceptual tasks *Representative Research in Social Psychology* **7** 35–43

WIGDOR, R. N., NELSON, J. & HICKERSON, E. (1977) The behavioural comparison of a real vs a much nursing home Paper presented at the Annual Meeting of the Gerontological Society. Cited in: L. H. Bower (1982) *Humanising Institutions for the Aged* Lexington, Mass.: Lexington Books

WILDER, D. A. (1984) Intergroup contact: the typical member and the exception to the role *Journal of Experimental Social Psychology* **20** 177–94

WILLIAMS, J. G. & SOLANO, C. H. (1983) The social reality of feeling lonely: friendship and reciprocation *Personality and Social Psychology Bulletin* **9** 237–42

WILLIAMS, K., HARKINS, S. & LATANÉ, B. (1981) Identifiability as a deterrent to social loafing: two cheering experiments *Journal of Personality and Social Psychology* **40** 303–11

WILLIAMS, M. (1968) The measurement of memory in clinical practice *British Journal of Social and Clinical Psychology* **7** 19–34

WILLIAMS, M. (1969) Traumatic retrograde amnesia and normal forgetting In: G. A. Talland and N. C. Waught (eds) *The Pathology of Memory* New York: Academic Press

WILLIAMS, M. D. & HOLLAN, J. D. (1981) The process of retrieval from very long-term memory *Cognitive Science* **5** 87–119

WILLIAMS, W. M. & CECI, S. (1997) Are Americans becoming more or less alike? Trends in race, class and ability differences in intelligence *American Psychologist* **52** 1226–35

WILSON, C. & WESTON, E. (1947) *The Cats of Wildcat Hill* New York: Duell, Sloan and Pearce

WILSON, E. O. (1975) *Sociobiology: the New Synthesis* Cambridge, Mass.: Harvard University Press

WILSON, E. O. & BOSSERT, W. H. (1963) Chemical communication among animals *Records of Progress in Hormone Research* **19** 673–716

WILSON, S. C. & BARBER, T. X. (1983) The fantasy-prone personality: implications for understanding imagery, hypnosis and parapsychological phenomena In: A. Sheikh (ed.) *Imagery: Current Theory, Research and Application* New York: Wiley

WIMMER, H., GRUBER, S. & PERNER, J. (1984) Young children's conception of lying: conceptual realism – moral subjectivism *Journal of Experimental Child Psychology* **37** 1–30

WINCH, R.F. (1958) *Mate-selection: a Study of Complementary Needs* New York: Harper & Row

WINNER, E., ROSENSTEIL, A. K. & GARDNER, H. (1976) The development of metaphoric understanding *Developmental Psychology* **12** 289–97

WINNICK, W. A. & DANIEL, S. A. (1970) Two kinds of response priming in tachistoscope recognition *Journal of Experimental Psychology* **84** 74–81

WINSLOW, C. N. (1937) A study of the extent of agreement between friends' opinions and their ability to estimate the opinions of each other *Journal of Social Psychology* **8** 433–42

WINTERBOTTOM, M. (1953) The sources of achievement motivation in mothers' attitudes towards independence training In: D. McClelland *et al.* (eds) *The Achievement Motive* New York: Appleton-Century-Crofts

WISEMAN, R. & MORRIS, R. L. (1995) Recalling pseudo-psychic demonstrations *British Journal of Psychology* **86** 113–25

WISEMAN, R., SMITH, M. & KORNBROT, D. (1996) Exploring possible sender-to-experimenter acoustic leakage in the PRL autoganzfeld experiments *Journal of Parapsychology* **60** 97–128

WITKIN, H. A. (1959) The perception of the upright *Scientific American* **200**(2) 50–6

WITKIN, H. A., DYK, R. B., FATERSON, H.F., GOODENOUGH, D. R. & KARP, S. A. (1962) *Psychological Differentiation* Chichester: Wiley

WITKIN, H. A., MEDNICK, S.A., SCHULSINGER, F., BAKKESTROM, E., CHRISTANSEN, K. O., GOODENOUGH, D. R., HIRSCHHORN, K., LUNDSTEEN, C., OWEN, D. R., PHILIPS, J., RUBIN, D. B. & STOCKING, M. (1976) Criminality in XYY and XXY men: the elevated crime rate of XYY males is not related to aggression *Science* **193**, 547–55

WITTENBORN, J. (1951) Symptom patterns in a group of mental hospital patients *Journal of Consulting Psychology* **15** 290–302

WOLFF, P. (1969) The natural history of crying and other vocalisations in early infancy In: B. M. Foss (ed.) *Determinants of Infant Behaviour IV* London: Methuen

WOLPE, J. (1958) *Psychotherapy by Reciprocal Inhibition* Stanford: Stanford University Press

WOOD, D. J. (1981) Problem-solving and creativity In: C. I. Howarth & W. E. C. Gillham *The Structure of Psychology: an Introductory Text* London: George Allen & Unwin

WOOD, F., TAYLOR, B., PENNY, R. & STUMP, D. (1980) Regional cerebral blood flow response to recognition memory versus semantic classification tasks *Brain and Language* **9** 113–22

WOODWORTH, R. S. (1899) The accuracy of voluntary movement *Psychological Monographs* **3** no.3

WORD, C. O., ZANNA, M.P. & COOPER, J. (1974) The non-verbal mediation of self-fulfilling prophecies in interracial interaction *Journal of Experimental Social Psychology* **10** 109–20

WORTHINGTON, A. G. (1969) Paired comparison scaling of brightness judgements: a method for the measurement of perceptual defence *British Journal of Psychology* **60**(3) 363–8

WUNDT, W. (1862) *Beiträge zur Theorie der Sinneswahrnehmung* Leipzig: C. F. Winter

WUNDT, W. (1905) *Grundriss der Psychologie* Leipzig: Engelmann

WUNDT, W. (1900–1920) *Volkerpsychologie: eine Untersuchung der Entwicklungsgesetze von Sprache, Mythus und Sitte* 10 vols. Leipzig: Engelmann

WYNNE, L. C., RYCKOFF, I. M., DAY, J. & HIRSCH, S. I. (1958) Pseudomutuality in the family relations of schizophrenics *Psychiatry* **21** 205–20

WYNNE-EDWARDS, V. C. (1962) *Animal Dispersion in Relation to Social Behaviour* New York: Hafner

YARNELL, P. R. & LYNCH, S. (1973) The ding: amnestic states in football trauma *Neurology* **23** 196–7

YERKES, R. M. (ed.) (1921) Psychological examining in the United States army *Memoirs of the National Academy of Science* **15**

YERKES, R. M. (1939) Social dominance and sexual status in the chimpanzee *Quarterly Review of Biology* **14** 115–36

YOGMAN, M. W., DIXON, D., TRONICK, E. Z., ALS, A., ADAMSON, A., LESTER, B. M. & BRAZELTON, T. B. (1977) Father-infant and mother-infant interaction in the first year of life *Child Development* **48** 167–81

YOUNISS, J. (1980) *Parents and Peers in Social Development* Chicago: University of Chicago Press

ZADNY, J. & GERARD, H. B. (1974) Attributed intentions and informational selectivity *Journal of Experimental Social Psychology* **10** 34–52

ZAHN-WAXLER, C. & RADKE-YARROW, M. (1982) The development of altruism: alternative research strategies In: N. Eisenberg (ed.) *The Development of Prosocial Behaviour* New York: Academic Press

ZAHN-WAXLER, C., RADKE-YARROW, M. & KING, R. A. (1979) Child rearing and children's prosocial dispositions towards victims of distress *Child Development* **50** 319–30

ZAJONC, R. B. (1965) Social facilitation *Science* **149** 269–74

ZAJONC, R. B. (1968) Attitudinal effects of mere exposure *Journal of Personality and Social Psychology* **9** 1–27

ZAJONC, R. B. & BURNSTEIN, E. (1965) The learning of balanced and unbalanced social structures *Journal of Personality* **33** 153–63

ZELAZO, P. R. (1976) From reflexive to instrumental behaviour In: L. P. Lipsitt (ed) *Developmental Psychobiology: the Significance of Infancy* Hillsdale, N. J.: Erlbaum

ZIMBARDO, P. G. (1969) The human choice: individuation, reason and order versus deindividuation, impulse and chaos In: W. J. Arnold & D. Levine (eds) *Nebraska Symposium on Motivation 17* Lincoln: University of Nebraska Press

ZUCKERMAN, M., KUHLMAN, D. & CAMAC, C. (1988) What lies beyond E and N? Factor analysis of scales believed to measure basic dimensions of personality *Journal of Personality and Social Psychology* **54** 96–107

Index

Bold numbers indicate a substantial entry.